The Book of

IRISH FAMILIES

Great & Small

Volume I

Second Edition

- by -

Michael C. O'Laughlin

CONTENTS

Origins, History, Arms. 1
Family history from the Archives of the Irish Genealogical Foundation.

Location Index 268
18,000 family locations extracted from the 'Master Book of Irish Surnames'.

Surname Index 297
Master Index to the set (to date).

Province Map .... (ii)
Key .... (iii)
Ancient Map .... (iv)
Source List .... (vi)
Family Research .... (viii)
Barony Map 364
Ireland Map 368

ISBN: 0-940134-15-2

Box 7575, Kansas City, MO. 64116 U.S.A.
www.Irishroots.com

Hardbound Works By the Same Author:
Complete Book For Tracing Your Irish Ancestors. $26. (0-940134-02-0)
The Complete Book of Irish Family Names. 1987. $15. (0-940134-41-1)
The Irish Book of Arms. 1988. $75. (0-940134-07-1)
Irish Settlers on the American Frontier. $34.50. 1985. (0940134-43-8)
The Book of Irish Families Great and Small. 1992. $28. (0-940134-08-X)
Master Book of Irish Surnames. $26. 1993. (0-940134-32-2)
Master (Atlas) & Book of Irish Placenames. $24. 1994. (0-940134-33-0)
Families of Co. Kerry, Ireland. 1994. ($32) (0-940134-36-5)
Families of Co. Clare, Ireland. 1996. ($32) (0-940134-37-3)
Families of Co. Cork, Ireland. 1996. (0-940134-35 -7)
Families of Co. Limerick, Ireland 1997. (in process)
Families of Co. Galway, Ireland . (in process)
Families of Co. Waterford, Ireland. (in process)
Families of Co. Tipperary, Ireland. (in process)
Beginners Guide to Irish Family Research. ($15) 1990.
Journal of Irish Families. 1986 - present. monthly. (ISSN 1056-0378)
Irish Families e-mail bulletin. (monthly via the world wide web.)

Rare Book Reprints Published by the I.G.F.:
Keatings' 'History of Ireland' 3 volume set. $125. (0-940134-44-0)
The Poetry and Song of Ireland. O'Reilly. (1865). $45 (0-940-134-43-8)
Irish Names and Surnames. Rev. Patrick Woulfe $39.95 (0-940134-40-3)
Tribes/Customs of Hy-Many. O'Donovan. (orig.1873) $104. (0-940134-39-X)
Tribes/Customs of Hy-Fiachrach. O'Donovan. (1874) $129. (0-940134-38-1)
Gaelic Titles & Forms of Address. Duhallow. 2nd edition. (0-940134-27-6)
A Social History of Ancient Ireland. 2 volume set. P. Joyce. (0-940134-24-1)
King James Irish Army List, 1689. D'Alton (1855). (0 940134 23 3)
Ortelius Map of Ireland 1572. ($20) (ancient map)

Published on behalf of the members of the Irish Genealogical Foundation. Updates, corrections and comments on this book will appear in, and should be directed to:

OLochlainns Journal of
Irish Families
Box 7575
Kansas City, Missouri, 64116 U.S.A.

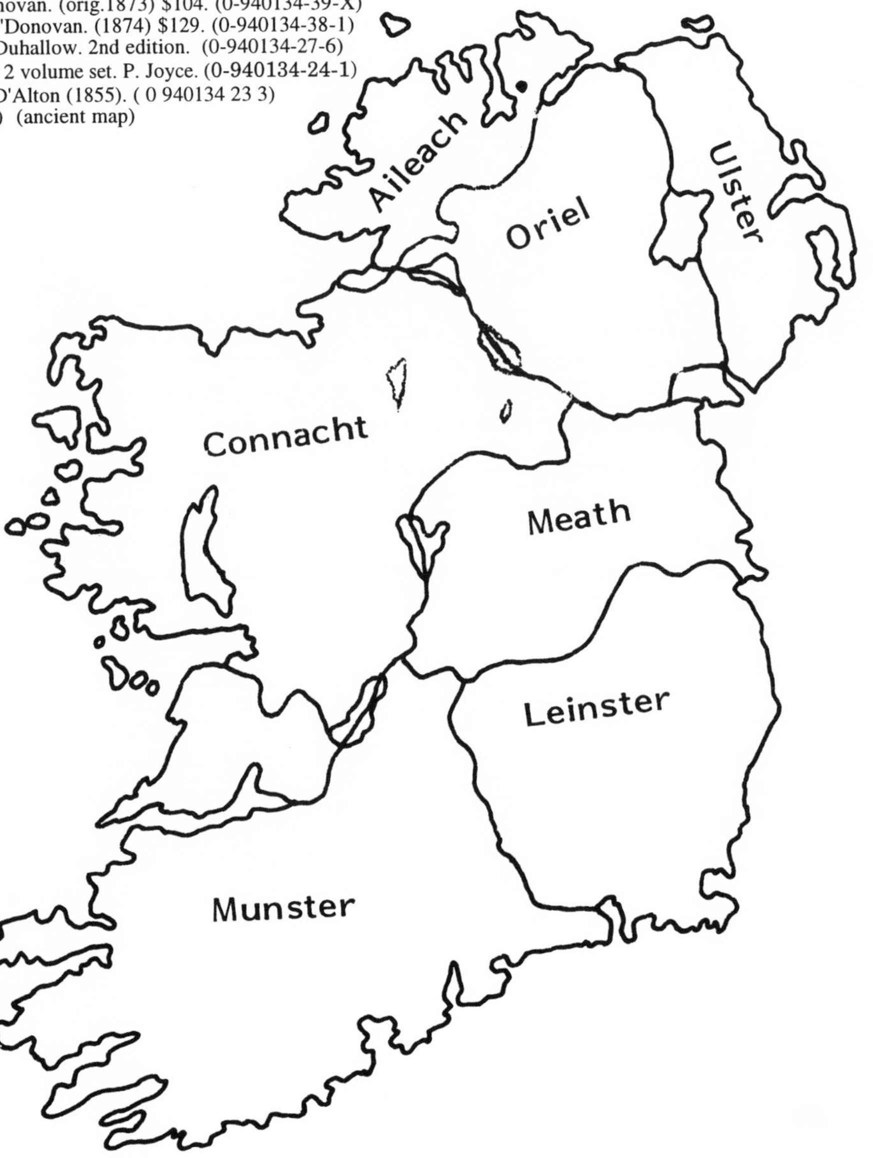

Key to Terms and Abbreviations

<u>1659</u> (C) - refers to Pettys' census of 1659.

<u>Principal Name</u> (PN) - refers to names so given in the 1659 'census'.

<u>1890</u> (B) - refers to Mathesons work on Irish families, notably the 1890 Birth Index of Ireland.

<u>Keatings</u> (K) - refers to Keatings History of Ireland, as published by the I. G. F.

<u>Woulfe</u> - refers to the works of Fr. Patrick Woulfe, notably *Irish Names and Surnames*.

<u>O'Hart</u> - refers to the works of John O'Hart, notably *Irish Pedigrees*.

<u>Irish Book of Arms</u> - refers to the book of that title, as published in 1988. Plate # refers to specific page of that work. Arms not illustrated in the work you are now reading, are given there.

<u>Settler Family</u> - a family known to have settled in Ireland from another country. Most often used for those arriving in the 17th century from Scotland.

<u>Variant spelling</u> (V) - other ways to spell the name, or spellings sometimes confused with each other. Check listings for all spellings given.

<u>Sept</u> - a word used instead of Clan by modern writers. The word 'clan' is acceptable. Remember that the Irish and the Scottish Clan are different.

<u>Galloglass</u> - also galloglas etc.. a term used to describe heavily armed fighting men, often found in the service of Irish chieftains in Ulster. Given to have arrived here from Scotland.

<u>Co.</u> - abbreviation used for county.

<u>PMO</u> - Poll Money Ordinance.

<u>Ulster</u> - province of Ireland.see map

<u>Munster</u> - "

<u>Leinster</u> - "

<u>Connaught</u> - "

<u>Irish Families</u> - families living in Ireland, of all nationalities and religions. Naturally including all families that have settled in Ireland.

<u>*</u> 35 etc..- denotes specific location for the name as given in the *Complete Book of Irish Family Names*.

Introduction To Irish Families

Entire volumes have been written on any given Irish Family. Here we cover thousands of families, and are necessarily limited. We do provide a starting point and an overview however, to help the reader discover his Irish Family heritage. I have relied on basic research tools in completing this first edition work.

Mathesons' 1890 birth index of Ireland gives us the probable location of your family at that time. Pettys' 'census' of 1659 takes us back centuries, and provides us with older spellings of Irish names, a point well taken.

Keatings classic *History of Ireland*, which I was fortunate to publish some years ago, figures heavily in this work as well. Our edition of that work includes the topographical poems on the families of Ireland. References from the same are found often in this text.

The *Complete Book of Irish Family Names*, and the *Irish Book of Arms*, two previous works, also figure in this work. Our location index is extracted from the former, and the arms displayed are from the latter. More information is found in both original works.

Contributions from friends and members over the previous decades have been invaluable. Many members of the *Irish Family Journal* have written complete books on their individual families. With due judgment, this has pointed me in the right direction.

Some errors will undoubtably occur in this first edition, and many entries appear in unedited form. Over 200 pages of updated material awaits future publication. Your assistance is welcome in correcting any shortcomings.

Michael C. O'Laughlin

Introduction

An entire volume can be devoted to any given Irish family found within these pages. Covering thousands of families here, we are necessarily limited in space. We do provide a starting point, however, to help you discover your Irish family heritage. Subsequent volumes in this series uncover more information on the families in this, the first volume in the set.

I have relied upon basic research tools in completing this edition. Mathesons' 1890 birth index of Ireland gives us the probable location of the family in 1850 and in 1890 (with some notable exceptions). Pettys' 'census' of 1659 goes back two centuries, providing some locations and spelling variations for Irish family names. The spelling of Irish names is fluid and artistic - and apt to change slightly at any moment for family members on the hunt for ancestors.

Keatings *History of Ireland*, the first rare book the IGF published, is another important source. That work included the topographical poems on the families of Ireland. References from the same are often found in this text.

The Master Book of Irish Surnames and the *Irish Book of Arms* also figure in this series (IGF editions). The former holds 80,000 surname/location references, in index form. The latter focuses on heraldic lineage of specific families when possible. More information is found in both of these original works.

Contributions from friends and researchers over previous decades have been invaluable. We have also borrowed freely from the 'Journal of Irish Families', and from the archives of the Irish Genealogical Foundation. Many readers of the first edition have written books on their individual families now. With due judgment this has pointed us in the right direction in compiling subsequent volumes for *'Families of Co. Kerry'*, *'Families of Co. Clare'''* *'Families of Co. Cork'*, and *'Families of Co. Limerick'*. In those volumes we strive to become more specific for each family name given.

Cautions

The illustrated arms displayed within these pages need to be understood by the reader. While these arms do bear a relationship to the name they appear above, they do not necessarily link your family name to a coat of arms. Strictly interpreted, arms belong only to the family they were granted to. (Historically the Irish seem to have a looser interpretation of this rule.) In any event, Irish names may have more than one origin, and families with the same name may not be related at all! Many arms, particularly those with no official 'documentation' in our offices, appear only in our Irish Book of Arms, and are not displayed here.

The location index found at the end of this work is a partial extract from the *Master Book of Irish Surnames*. More data is found in that work.

We often speak here of just one branch of one Irish family. Your family may be unrelated, or may be a branch of a family found elsewhere. These entries serve as a starting point for the serious researcher.

Spelling

Do not attach too much importance to the exact spelling of your name. Spelling changes are common. The same family can be found using 5 different spellings of their name, at the same time in history. The tendency is widespread, particularly in earlier centuries.

"Mc, Mac, and O" have been added to and dropped from Irish surnames at will. Be aware that your family may have dropped or added these prefixes from your name. As a result, our index lists your name alphabetically - ignoring these prefixes. In other words, names are sorted by the first letter after the "Mc, Mac, or O" prefix. Hence, O'Sullivan appears as if it were spelled simply as Sullivan in our index.

Format

Entries on family names are arranged in the following order:

(1) When available, the coat of arms linked to the name appears above the name which is in bold type. All arms shown in this volume were actually used by families in Ireland, acknowledged by recognized authorities.

(2) Beneath the name is the source from which the arms are taken.

(3) Occasionally we list a Gaelic or more ancient form of the name on the next line in regular type. (note we have not punctuated these). We suggest those interested in the gaelic consult *Irish Names and Surnames* by the Rev. P. Woulfe. The IGF edition of that work contains a new surname index, which proves most helpful to researchers.

(4) The next line, in italics, gives variant spellings of the name as available.

(5) The history associated with the name

The amount of information found will vary with each name. Please consult all possible spellings of the name. More information may appear in other volumes to this Irish Families set. Names not covered here will appear in other volumes of our *Irish Families, great & small* series.

The surname index to this first volume , (and to volumes 2, 3, 4, and 5), is found in part III of this book. The researcher should consult that index as well as the location index found in part II of this book.

The location index (see part II) represents extracts taken from larger, more detailed listings found in the *Master Book of Irish Surnames*. Space limitations do not allow reprinting all the index listings found in that book. In fact, there are over 50,000 listings from that book which we did not have room for at all! We have included as many surnames as possible to give hope to Irish family researchers. These listings may prove particularly helpful for those with less common names. The student of Irish family names would do well to consult that work independently.

Some errors will occur within these pages, and some entries appear in unedited form. The budget and scope of this project dictate these human limitations. Your assistance in making future volumes more complete is indeed appreciated.

Regular updates on the series are published in the journal of Irish Families, and your comments and additions are welcome. In keeping with the times, our 'email' address is: Irelande@compuserve.com

- Michael C. O'Laughlin
editor 1/21/97

Useful Terms and Abbreviations

1659 or (C) - refers to the 'census' of 1659.
Principal Name (PN) - refers to names given as such in the 1659 census.
1890 (B) - Refers the the 1890 Birth Index of Ireland by Matheson.
Keatings (K) - Keatings *History of Ireland*'
Woulfe (w)- Fr. Patrick Woulfe, author of *Irish Names and Surnames.*
O'Hart - refers to the work of John O'Hart, notably *Irish Pedigrees*.
Irish Book of Arms - refers to the book of that title, as published in 1988 by the IGF. Arms not listed in *Irish Families, great & small* are given in the *Irish Book of Arms.*
Settler Family - A family known to have settled in Ireland from another country. Most often used for those arriving in the 17th century from Scotland.
Variant spelling (V) - Other ways to spell the name, or spellings sometimes confused with each other. Check listings for all spellings given.
Sept - A word used instead of clan by some modern writers. The word 'clan' is acceptable. Remember that the Irish and the Scottish clan are different.
Gallowglass - also spelled as galloglas, etc.. a term used to describe heavily armed fighting men, often found in the service of the Irish chieftains in Ulster. Given to have arrived here from Scotland.
Co. - abbreviation for County.
PMO - Poll Money Ordinance
Ulster - Province of Ireland
Munster - Province of Ireland
Leinster - Province of Ireland
Connaught - Province of Ireland
Irish Families - Families living in Ireland, of all nationalities and religions, naturally including families that have settled in Ireland over time.
* 35 - An asterisk, followed by a number denotes a specific numbered location for the name as found in the *Master Book of Irish Surnames.*

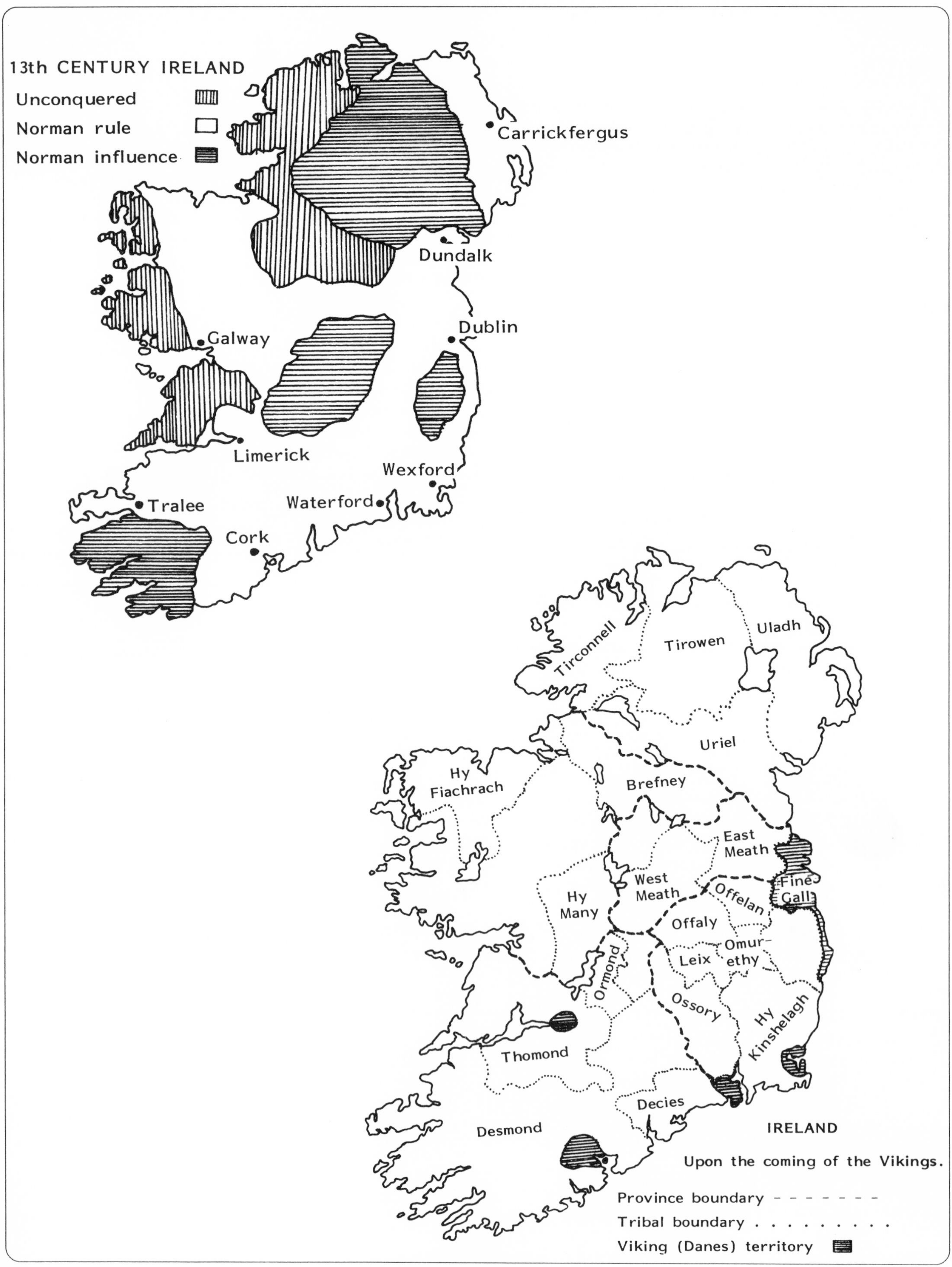
13th CENTURY IRELAND
Unconquered
Norman rule
Norman influence
Carrickfergus
Dundalk
Dublin
Galway
Limerick
Wexford
Waterford
Tralee
Cork
Tirconnell
Tirowen
Uladh
Uriel
Hy
Fiachrach
Brefney
East
Meath
West
Meath
Fine
Gall
Hy
Many
Offelan
Offaly
Omur-
ethy
Leix
Ormond
Ossory
Hy
Kinshelagh
Thomond
Decies
Desmond
IRELAND
Upon the coming of the Vikings.
Province boundary
Tribal boundary
Viking (Danes) territory

Families Settling in Ireland

English

Many English families have settled in Ireland from the 12th century. Often, the native Irish were forced to "translate" their names into an English sounding one. Therefore, English names may belong to settlers from England, or from old Irish families who adopted an English surname. The 50 most numerous names of England in 1853, all found in Ireland, are given:

Smith	Walker	James
Jones	Hughes	King
Williams	Edwards	Morgan
Taylor	Lewis	Allen
Davies	White	Moore
Brown	Turner	Parker
Thomas	Jackson	Clarke
Evans	Hill	Cook
Roberts	Harris	Price
Johnson	Clark	Phillips
Wilson	Cooper	Shaw
Robinson	Harrison	Bennett
Wright	Ward	Lee
Wood	Martin	Watson
Thompson	Davis	Griffiths
Hall	Baker	Carter
Green	Morris	

Scottish

Due to the close proximity of the north of Ireland and Scotland, migrations between these two countries have been constant. The great settlement of Scottish families took place in the 17th century during the plantation of Ulster by the British Crown. Later, these "planter" families came to America, becoming known as the Scotch-Irish. The 50 most numerous names of Scotland, all found in Ireland:

Smith	Clark	Hunter
McDonald	Paterson	Hamilton
Brown	Young	Kerr
Thomson	Fraser	Grant
Robertson	McLean	McIntosh
Stewart	Henderson	Graham
Campbell	Mitchell	White
Wilson	Morrison	Allan
Anderson	Cameron	Simpson
Scott	Watson	McGregor
Miller	Walker	Munro
McKenzie	Taylor	Sinclair
Reid	McLeod	Bell
Ross	Ferguson	Martin
McKay	Duncan	Russell
Johnston	Gray	Gordon
Murray	Davidson	

Welsh

The name "Walsh", (in Irish, Brannagh or Breathnach), meaning a Briton or Welshman, is found early in Cork, Dublin, Kerry, Kilkenny, Tipperary, Wexford, Waterford & Galway. The name remained numerous in Cork, Mayo, Waterford, Galway, Dublin and Wexford in 1890. Some Welsh families given in Ireland:

Howell	Merrick	Rossiter
Lawless	Hore	Sinnott
Lillis	Cod	Stephen
Lynagh	Stafford	Quiney
Lynott	Whitty	Walsh

Anglo-Norman

The Anglo-Norman invasions of the 12th century brought many new families to Ireland. Some took on Irish names. Anglo-Norman families in Ireland:

Barry	FitzEustace	Marshall
Bellew	Fitzgerald	Montmorncy
Bermingham	Fitzhenry	Mortimer
Burke	Fitzmaurice	Nangle
Carew	Fitzsimons	Nugent
Clare	Fitzstephen	Petit
Cogan	Gernon	Prendergast
Dalton	Grace	Purcell
Darcy	Hussey	Roche
De Courcy	Keating	Staunton
Delamere	Lacy	Taaffe
Dillon	Le Poer	Talbot
Tyrell	Verdon	Tuite
		Vesey

German Palatinate

Families came to Ireland in the 18th century from the Palatinate of the Rhine, in Germany. In 1709 some 7,000 of these refugees arrived in England. Thousand were sent to North America, settling in Pennsylvania and North Carolina. In Ireland they are found centered in Co. Limerick, but many moved on to America after settling in Ireland. Names given:

Baker	Latchford	Reynard
Bovanizer	Ligier	Ruttle
Bowen	Millar	Shire
Doube	Lodwig	Stark
Delmege	Modlar	Switzer
Gilliard	Pyper	Teskey
Smyth	Heavenor	Neazor

Cornish

Cornish, or Briton families are found in Ireland, under names like Jagoe, Lanyon, Pascoe, Pender, Pendred, Penrose, Vivian, Tredennick, Tresilian, and Trevelyan.

Danish (Viking)

The Danes (Lochlainders, Ostmen, Vikings) had colonies in Ireland for over 3 centuries. Centered in Dublin and Meath (in Fingall), and in Wexford, Waterford, Cork and Limerick, they settled on the coasts of Ireland, (see map), from the 8th century. Some old settler names given:

Betagh	Gould	Skiddy
Coppinger	Harold	Sweetman
Dowdall	Palmer	Trant
Drumgoole	Plunket	Ost

Jewish

Found resident in Dublin and other large cities earlier, many Russian and Polish Jews settled on the south side of Dublin city from 1881-1890. Family names of:

Coplan	Matufsky	Wachman
Fridberg	Rabinovitch	Wedeclefsky
Greenberg	Rossin	Weiner
Hesselberg	Statzumsky	Winstock
Maisell	Stuppel	

Huguenot

French and Fleming Huguenot families settled in the latter 17th century at Dublin, Kilkenny, Waterford, Cork, Portarlington, and Lisburn. Noted for making linen, cloth and lace etc.. Some families given:

Barre	Crommelin	Guerin
Blacquiere	Delacherois	Hazard
Boileau	Drelincourt	Hassard
Chaigneau	Dubourdieu	La Touche
Du Bedat	Du Cros	Le Fevre
Champion	Fleury	Lefroy
Chenevix	Gaussen	Lefanu
Corcellis	Logier	Maturin
Trench	Saurin	Perrin
De'Vignoles		

Source List

The Irish Family Series

(v1)***The Book of Irish Families, great & small.** Master volume to the IGF set of Family histories. Arms, origins, locations as available. Subsequent volumes research families by specific counties, and in more detail. Each volume contains over 1,000 surnames. Volumes completed to date include:

(v2) ***The Families of County Kerry, Ireland.** 272 p., ISBN: 0-940134-36-5

(v3) ***The Families of County Clare, Ireland** 178 p., ISBN: 0-940134-37-3

(v4) ***The Families of County Cork, Ireland** 220 p., ISBN: 0-940134-35-7

(v5) ***The Families of County Limerick, Ire.** 200 p., ISBN 0-940134-31-4

***Sloinnte Gaedeal is Gall**
by the Rev. Patrick Woulfe. ISBN 0 940134 40 3 'Irish Names and Surnames'. The original, dictionary of Irish surnames by Woulfe, (1923) with notes on Gaelic origins. IGF edition includes valuable new index.

***The Master Book of Irish Surnames**.
The Master INDEX of Family names, Locations, Origins, Spelling Groups and Sources. Includes the index to all IGF works, the birth index, the 1659 census etc.. 80,000 entries. The Largest collection in print. 320 p. ISBN 0 940134 32 2

****Annals of the Kingdom of Ireland**
by the Four Masters. 1851. (*ed*. John O'Donovan.)

***Tribes & Customs of Hy Many.**
John O'Donovan. ISBN 0940134 39 X. This classic work by the noted antiquarian covers Roscommon /Galway Families and history of the area. 212 p.

***Tribes & Customs of Hy Fiachrach**
by John O'Donovan. ISBN 0 940134 38 1. This classic work by the noted antiquarian covers Co. Mayo and Sligo Families and history of the area. 500 + pages.

***Keatings History of Ireland**.
Complete 3v. set. IGF index with genealogies. O'Mahoney translation. Footnotes, folk history and legend. ISBN 0 940134 46 2.

***Irish Settlers on the American Frontier**
by O'Laughlin. The #1 work on the Irish settling in Missouri westward 1770-1900. ISBN 0940134 25 X.

Placenames

***The Master Atlas & Book of Irish Placenames**
Placename Locator for all of Ireland. Maps clearly indexed to find your placename . 17th & 19th century names. Spellings. Appendix. 40,000 listings. 60 Maps. 250 p. ISBN 0 940134 33 0.

***King James's Irish Army List** 1689
D'Alton. 1,000 pages. (1855). The family history of the Wild Geese in Ireland and abroad. New index captures hundreds of families missed in previous edition. A Primary archival source. hardbound. ISBN 0 940134 23 3

***A Social History of Ancient Ireland**..
P. W. Joyce. 2 vol. set, 350 illus., maps, customs, law, art, heroic sagas and domestic life of the Irish. 1318 pages. hardbound. ISBN 0 940134 24 1

***The Irish Book of Arms**
The largest Illustrated collection of Irish Coats-of-Arms in print, with specific individuals granted arms. Includes old Irish and settler families. Over 1,000 arms. ISBN 0 940134 07 1

***Gaelic Titles and Forms of Address.**
Second edition, modern day updates on chiefs, clans & associations. softcover.120 pages. A rare treatise. ISBN 0 940134 27-6

***The Poetry and Song of Ireland.**
by John Boyle O'Reilly, with footnotes & illus. ISBN 0 940134 43 8

****An Atlas of Irish History**
by Ruth Dudley Edwards. New York. 1981. An excellent beginning overview of Irish History.

****The Great Hunger**
by Cecil Woodham Smith. London. 1962.

****The Famine Immigrants, 1846-1851**
(Lists from the port of New York). 7 Volume set. Baltimore. 1983.

***Beginners Guide to Irish Family Research.**
The very direct and simple guide. Address lists and phone numbers to call. ISBN 0 940134 03 9

***Ortelius Map of Ireland.**
Originally published in 1572 a.d., location of Families,Old English/Latin.

****The Complete Book For Tracing Your Irish Ancestors.** ISBN 0 940134 02 0.

****Irish Books in Print**. Cleary. Wicklow 1984.

****Irish Pedigrees**
by John O'Hart. 2 volume set. Dublin. 1892.

***Journal of Irish Families**. Monthly Periodical.

****1659 Census of Ireland.**

****Journal. American-Irish Historical Society**
1898-1941. Annual publication. N.Y. and Boston.

*Published by the Irish Genealogical Foundation.
**On hand at the IGF Library.

Finding Your Irish Family

Beginning the Search

Finding your family in Ireland is not at all impossible. The main requirement is that you invest time and common sense. That is the basic truth of the matter. If you are ready to do that, with a sense of patience, you will discover much about your Irish family.

Three basic tools at your disposal can be used right now, and they will produce results. They are; your phone, your mailbox, and your library. First draw a little chart showing your family as far back as you know. Then the fun begins.

Phone other members of the family and ask for help on the chart. Call families with the same last name as yours in Ireland and America. Call a library and ask them if any genealogical groups, or researchers are around to help. You get the idea now.

Combine your attack by sending letters to the same type of folks given above. Go to your library and find a few books that will give you background information. The library can supply you with much more, including books from other libraries, obituary columns from newspapers, and names of local researchers. (Call a library in the area of the country where you want the research done - then ask for the name of a possible researcher.

We also recommend the "Beginners Guide for Tracing Your Irish Ancestors" to start quickly and inexpensively on your search. Information on this page is taken from that source. (available from: Irish Family Journal, Box 7575, Kansas City, MO. 64116. $9.95 + $2 post.)

After completing the above you will want to move on to census research. Names of centers are given here.

10 Concrete Steps

1. Make a simple family tree chart

2. Search Family Records.
   The old family bible, old letters, photograph albums, etc..

3. Talk to all family members.

4. Check the obituary column written on your ancestor in the local newspaper where he lived.

5. Go to the local library. Consult books there that will help.

6. Use the phone to contact local and out of state sources.

7. Use your mailbox to emphasize your point, write clean, simple letters for help.

8. Contact organizations that can help you.

9. Consult the 1890 birth index of Ireland, by Matheson. Look for your family, and other ways to spell your name.

10. Consult the census records in America to help determine your families origins.

Helpful Addresses

The Irish Family Journal
Box 7575
Kansas City, MO. 64116

Genealogical Helper
Box 368
Logan, Utah 84321

L.D.S. Genealogical Library
35 NW Temple Street
Salt Lake City, Utah 84150

Federal Archives Branches

For each of the following, when writing, address inquiries to:
Chief, Archives Branch
Federal Archives and Records Center

Locations of Federal Archives:

380 Trapelo Road
Waltham, MA. 02154

Building 22-MOT Bayonne
Bayonne, N.J. 07002

5000 Wissahickon Ave.
Philadelphia, PA. 19144

1557 St. Joseph Ave.
East Point, GA. 30344

7358 South Pulaski Rd.
Chicago, IL. 60629

2306 E. Bannister Rd.
Kansas City, MO. 64131

4900 Hemphill Street
P. O. Box 6216
Fort Worth, TX. 76115

Building 48, Denver Fed. Center
Denver, CO. 80225

1000 Commodore Dr.
San Bruno, CA. 94066

24000 Avila Rd.
Laguna Niguel, CA. 92677

6125 San Point Way, NE
Seattle, WA. 98115

Let The Reader Understand:

The illustrated arms displayed here bear some connotation only to the name found directly below it. These arms may have no relationship to your family whatsoever. Please consult the *Irish Book of Arms* for better understanding. Arms not displayed here-in are found in the Irish Book of Arms.

The location index found at the end of this work is a partial extract from the *Complete Book of Irish Family Names.* More data is found in that work. The names in the location index are not included in our regular index. Consult both indexes at the end of this book.

We often speak here of just one branch of one Irish Family. Your family may be unrelated, or may be a branch of the family found elsewhere. These entries serve as a starting point for the serious researcher.

Do not attach too much importance to the exact spelling of your name. Spelling changes are common. The same family can be found using 5 different spellings at the same time in history. This tendency is common, even in the last century.

Mac and Mc have been used interchangeably, and today we can not say there is a difference between the two ways of spelling the prefix.

"Mc, Mac, and O" have been added to and dropped from names at will. Be aware that your family may have added or dropped these prefixes from your name. Our index lists your name alphabetically, ignoring these prefixes. Therefore, when looking for O'Sullivan, look for Sullivan in the index.

As this is the first edition of *Irish Families great and small,* some errors and omissions will appear here until corrected in the next printing.

Your personal research may shed new light on the history contained within this volume.

Sample Format

Irish Surname Here

1. Where family arms were found.
2. Old or gaelic spelling.
3. Variant spellings of the name.

Background information appears here. The Arms given in each case relate historically to the family name given. The arms, when available, are shown directly above the family name. Arms not shown in this work may be found in the Irish Book of Arms. All arms shown in the book you are now reading were used by families in Ireland, granted by either the Irish or English authorities.

Amount of information varies with each name. Please consult all spellings of the name given above to understand your Irish Family name.

Space limitations do not permit giving all available information on a given family name at this time.
Consult location index for further listings not given in the body of this book. Several thousand additional family names are found in that section. Information there is necessarily sparse, but it may provide clues as to locations and spellings of your family name.

For more information, consult the Complete Book of Irish Family Names, from which these location listings were taken.

Adair

Irish Book of Arms plate 266

Adaire, Adayre, Adare

The family name of Adair is primarily given to Scottish settler families who arrived in Ulster beginning with the 17th century plantations of that area. Many of the name are found with considerable land holdings in Ireland, including lands in Donegal and Leix (Queens Co.).

Spelled as Adaire in the 17th century we find the family given in counties Longford and Antrim. The family name is often found in Antrim, Down and Londonderry, and one family of the name is cited in Offaly. We find the spelling of Adayre and Adare in the Poll Money Ordinance records of 1660-61.

Abberton

Aberton

The Abberton family is of English origins when found in Ireland, found in our records in Co. Galway, and said to have arrived there coming from Ulster in the 1700's.

Abbott

Abbot, Abott, Abot

Abbot is a common English name which is often found in Dublin, and most families of this line are said to be of Anglo-Norman origins. There were 11 births of the name in the 1890 birth index, in scattered locations.

Abercrumber

This family name is found in the 17th century in Co. Leitrim, and belonged to a settler family in Ireland at that time.

Actery

This family name is found in Co. Westmeath in the 17th century.

Mac Adam

Irish Book of Arms plate 82

Adams, Adam, McAdams

According to "Keatings History" the name is given as an Irish name which was also adopted by Anglo-Norman or English families in lieu of their original surnames.

The Barrys of Cork changed their name to MacAdam. (see McAdams).

The MacAdam family of Blackwater House, Co. Clare descend from one of the name who purchased the estates of Blackwater, Co. Clare in 1684.

Mac Abraham

Abrehan, MacAbram, Abraham, Judge,

We find the name of Abraham most often linked to Co. Cork in our records, and some of the name are found in Co. Armagh as well. We find the name on record in Cork for several centuries spelled as Abraham. Another variant spelling of the name found in Ireland is Abram. Although some of the name are of likely settler origins in Ireland, most are believed to be of true Irish stock. Abraham, then, is a "translation" of an earlier Gaelic name.

Absom

This family name is found in Limerick in the 17th century.

Ackland

This family name is found in Co. Kilkenny in the 17th century.

Adderly

A family name of Co. Cork in the 17th century.

Adderton

A family name of Co. Kilkenny in the 17th century.

Mc Adams

Irish Book of Arms plate 78

Mac Adaim etc..

Adams, Mac Adam, Adamson, Adam

The surnames of Adam, Adams, Mc Adams, etc.. stem from more than one source. In the large cities such as Dublin and Belfast, the name is more often of Scottish origins.

Several place names can be found commemorating families of the name in Ireland. The place name Ballymacadam can be found in Counties Mayo, Tipperary and Kerry. Ballymacadam can be found near Tralee in Kerry, and near Clogheen. Castlemacadam is found near Rathdrum.

In County Cavan McAdam is used for Mac Caw. In Armagh for Macadden. In County Cork the name was taken on by some of the Norman family of Barry. In more modern times the name is found in Monaghan as well.

The final 's' found in the name of MacAdams may help you in your search at first. The further back you search, the more variable spellings you will have to consider, for names like Adam and Adams are often interchanged.

Adams is of course, a common name in England and some of the name have settled in Ireland over the centuries. It is as well of Irish origins. Adams is used as a synonym of Aidy and Eadie in Co. Down. In 1659 the name was found in Cork, Kilkenny and Londonderry. In the 1890 birth index it is found in Antrim and Londonderry, and 23 of 25 births were recorded in the province of Ulster, in the north of Ireland.

Arms for various families of the name, are found in the 'Irish Book of Arms', published by the Irish Genealogical Foundation. Plate 78 of that work gives the arms for 'Adams of the Northlands.'

'A Genealogical History of Adams of Cavan', by P. W. Adams was published in London, in 1903.

Adamson

Irish Book of Arms plate 46

The Adamson family is found centered in counties Armagh and Down in the latter half of the 19th century. The Adamson family of Glenfarne Hall, Co. Leitrim, originally of England, are found in the Irish Book of Arms.

Addis

A family name most often linked in our records with counties Westmeath and Cork.

Mac Adory

Mac Adorey

A name seldom found in our records, but several families of the name are found in Co. Antrim

Adrian

Adryan, Adrien, Adrain, Drain, Drean,

Some of the name of Adrian etc...may actually be of the old Irish family of O'Drean. Subsequently the name may be found as Drean and Drain. This Irish family was found anciently in Roscommon, where they served as chiefs of Calry. Note the place name of Ballydrain near Tullynakill.

Additionally, the name spelled as "Adryan" in the 17th century is found in Co. Dublin. This family name is traditionally linked to the province of Ulster in Ireland.

Aggas

This family name is found in Co. Westmeath in the 17th century.

O'Aherne

Irish Book of Arms plate 145..

Oh Eachtighearna, etc

Aghearn, Ahern, Ahearn, Aherin, Aheron,

Anciently the name of O'Aherne was translated from the original Gaelic as O'Hagherin. The original Gaelic is said to have been taken from 'each' meaning a horse, and 'tighearna', meaning a lord. Legend has said that the family was of the Eoganacht tribe settling originally in Waterford, Cork and Clare.

Anciently the Aherne family hailed from Clare. There, not far from Limerick, in the barony of Bunratty Lower, 'Six Mile Bridge' marks their ancient lands up until the 14th century.

O'Ahern is given as a chief of Ui Cearnaidh in Keatings History, and was said to rule 'as far as the hospitable port of Shannon, in County Clare.'

By the year 1659 the family had been forced to the south, and is found numerous in Cork and Waterford. In modern times Counties Cork and Limerick are the centers for the name. The spellings of Hearn and Hearne are found yet in Waterford today.

Two other origins for the name exist. 'Hearn' may be of English origins in Ireland. It may also come from the Irish family of 'OhUidrin' in County Offaly, where this name is used as a variant spelling on occasion.

This name, like many others, is found serving in the Irish Brigades in France and Spain in earlier times.

When of foreign origins, Aherne is said to mean "at the corner", denoting the location of the family in the past.

Other spellings associated with the name, O'Heffron, Hagherin, O'Heerin, and Haverian are given as variant spellings in use over 100 years ago.

The 1890 birth index finds the name in Cork and Limerick.

Alcock

Irish Book of Arms plate 50

Alcocke

One tradition gives the family arriving with Henry II from Surrey in England and settling in Downpatrick. Three branches of the family were found in the province of Munster. One at Ballynoe, Co. Carlow, another at Wilton Castle, Co. Wexford, and another at Dunmore in Co. Waterford. The Alcock family name is traditionally linked to counties Cork and Waterford.

One Waterford family descends from the Very Rev. Alexander Alcock, Dean of Lismore. The Alcock family of Wilton, Co. Wexford, descends from John Alcock of Downpatrick, found there in the late 17th century.

Aghwell

A family found in the city of Dublin in the 17th century.

Aghmooty

Aughmuty, Auchmuty, Achmuty, Amooty,

Families of the name of Aghmooty and its various spellings are found centered in Co. Longford in the 17th century, and particularly in the barony of Longford there. One Scottish family of the name is found in Co. Cavan near Tullyhunco, and they came to hold sizable estates there.

Agharne

Agherns, Aherne

The name of a family of Co. Cork in the 17th century, also found spelled as O'Agherns.

Aldwarth

Irish Book of Arms plate 95

Aldworth

The name of a family found in Cork city in the 17th century. The Aldworth family of Newmarket, Co. Cork, descend from Richard Aldworth who obtained grants of land from the Earl of Desmonds forfeited estates near Short Castle, Mallow in Cork, during the reign of Elizabeth.

Agnew

Gnive, Gnew

Agnew families are found numerous in the baronies of Glencarn and Belfast, Co. Antrim in the 17th century and in counties Antrim, Armagh and Down in the latter half of the 19th century.

In records preceding the above, the name is found spelled as Gnive or O'Gnive etc.., and has been said by some to have belonged to a Scottish family who settled in Ireland.

Older records also give us another source for the name of Agnew today. de Agneaux, or D'Agneau is also found as the name of a family arriving at the time of the Norman invasions of Ireland in the 12th century.

In America we find one family of the name in the 18th century settling in the state of Pennsylvania, said to have originally been of Ulster heritage.

Aiken

Ekin, Aikens, Aikins, Aicken, Aitken,

Families of the name are found centered in Co. Antrim in the 19th century. Most of the name found in Ireland are of Scottish and English descent, originating in many cases from the English name of Aitken. These families are centered in the province of Ulster, although several of the name are found in Dublin. The spelling of Eakin is found often in Donegal.

Alexander

Irish Book of Arms plate 96, 139

Mac Alsandair

Alexandar, Alex., Elshinder,

The family of Alexander is assumed to have arrived here from Scotland. Old records show evidence of the name in Antrim and Down in the 1600's, coming from Scotland and arriving in Ulster.

Some of the name descend from the Rev. Andrew Alexander, a Presbyterian who arrived in Ulster, coming from Scotland in the early 1600's.

While the name is assumed to be of the province of Ulster when found in Ireland, in the 17th century it is documented as well in Dublin City.

Alexander is also an English name, with many variants found in older records, such as Elshinder, Mac Calshender and Kalshander.

O'Hart gives one family of the name as settling in Tyrone, since the reign of James I, and cites them as 'Alexander', barons of Caledon. The name is further found here as being of the 'Clan Colla', from which many noble families here are found in Connaught, Meath, and Scotland and Ulster. The name is further given as one of the principal families of Ireland in the 1600's.

The family name is also given among the 'adventurers for land' in the 1640's. The former gives the family of Alexander of Forkill House, Co. Armagh, and they descend from one of the name who was born in Co. Donegal.

In America, 'Alexander' ranks as the 98th most popular name in the country, making American family research on this family somewhat time consuming in the absence of a proven family tree.

The name in the United States of course, can stem from several countries of origin, not the least of which is Ireland herself!

Mac Allen

Irish Book of Arms plate 11

O'hAillin

Mac Allan, Hallinan, Alleyn, Allyn, Alin,

We find the name of 'Allen' in Ireland most often as being of Scots or English origins. Allen ranks among the top 50 most numerous names in England and Ireland, and many of the name are of English heritage originally.

One English origin of the name comes from a Welsh saint. The Scottish families of the name (Mac Ailin), may come from the Campbells, who came to the province of Ulster in Ireland, at the invitation of the O'Donnells.

In Donegal and Derry the use of the name as a synonym of 'Mac Callion' has also been given.

In County Tipperary the name may have sprung originally from the name of Hallinan. In the same county and in Offaly the name is said to have come originally from O' hAillin at times.

As would be expected, numerous 'Allen' listings are found in the index of standard genealogical reference books. Numerous listings are found in the works of O'Hart and Burke.

In the census of 1659 we find McAllen as a principal name of Dublin City, and "Alin" in Tipperary. In the 1890 birth index the spelling of McAllen is given centered in Co. Antrim, and "Allen" was given in Antrim, Armagh and Dublin at that time.

One John Allen (1476 - 1534) was Archbishop of Dublin and Lord Chancellor of Ireland. He was assassinated by the followers of Lord Thomas Fitzgerald.

In the Irish Book of Arms we find one Joshua of the name who was a viscount, seated at Palmerstown, Co. Dublin. We also find one John Allen (living in 1618), of Rathlumney in O'Harts work.

4

Mac Andrew

Irish Book of Arms plate 67 (Andrews)

Andrew, Andrews, Fitzandrew

One family of the name hails in olden times from Co. Mayo, where they are said to descend from a branch of the Norman family of Barrett. In modern times the name is found centered only in Mayo, as evidenced by the 1890 birth index. Earlier records however also find the name in Co. Kerry, where you will note the place name of Ballymacandrew.

The normally separate name of "Andrew" is found in Meath in the 17th century and the name of Andrewes, a common spelling of the name in that time, is found fairly widespread. By the time of the 1890 birth index, the name of Andrews is found centered in Antrim and Down.

The Andrews family of Rathenny, Kings Co., were granted those estates in the 17th century. The Andrews family of Ardara, Co. Down are given in the Irish Book of Arms.

Aildwood

A principal name of Co. Kilkenny in the 17th century.

Airey

Airy

A family name traditionally linked with the province of Ulster in Ireland.

Albonagh

A principal name of Co. Sligo in the 17th century.

Armstrong

Irish Book of Arms plates 68, 33, 117

Armestrong, Lowery, Trinlavery, Lavery,

Armstrong is one more example of a common English name found in Ireland. It is of course an English name when found here, particularly in the province of Ulster in northern Ireland.

Due to the translations of the old Irish family names into English, it may be of older Irish origins as well.

Lavery and Traynor are two names which have been translated from their original gaelic into the English name of Armstrong.

In the 17th century we find Armstrong as a principal name of the county of Fermanagh; also in Leitrim and Sligo. We find the spelling of Armstronge at that time located in Tipperary.

In the 1890 birth index we find the name given in Antrim, Fermanagh, Cavan and Tyrone with a total of 140 births.

Mention has also been made that the name may be of Welsh origins as well.

In America Armstrong ranks among the top 200 most numerous names in the country.

In O'Hart several of the name are mentioned among the '1649 officers' including 'John, Robert, Capt. Thomas, Sir Thomas, and Quartermaster ' Armstrong.

Arms for several families of the name are found in the Irish Book of Arms. Three of the name given there are: 1) Henry Bruce Wright Armstrong of Killylea, Co. Armagh, who served as high sheriff, 2) Armstrong of Farney Castle and Mount Heaton, and 3) Heaton-Armstrong of Roscrea, Kings County (Offaly).

Arthur

Irish Book of Arms plates 61, 241

Mac Aurthur, Arthurs, Arthure, Aurthur,

Those of the Arthur family name in Ireland may spring from the Scottish name of MacArthur.

The name is found in Ireland prior to the Norman invasions of the 12th century. Here, the family is found as being quite prominent in Limerick, serving as Mayors and Bishops etc.. from that time onwards. In this case, the family may be of Norse or Viking heritage.

Keating lists the name as 'MacAurthur' in Limerick, being centered in the barony of Pubblebrien.

The census of 1659 gives Arthur as a principal name of Co. Clare, as well as being found in Limerick city, Dublin, Kings, and Wexford. Well over 20 individuals of the name served as mayors for the town of Limerick.

In the 19th century birth index there were more of the name of Arthurs than of Arthur. The most numerous location for the name at that time was in counties Antrim and Tyrone.

Some of the name from Ireland are also found in France in the 18th century.

Today the surname ranks near the top 1,000 most numerous names in America.

Arms for the families of the name of Arthur are given in the Irish Book of Arms.

The Arthur family of Glanomera, Co. Clare is given to spring originally from the name of "Artureighs". They held lands in Limerick which were lost in the Cromwellian wars, and they then moved to Glanomera, Co. Clare. This family claims Irish descent, and it was certainly the pro-Irish actions of the family which caused them to lose their lands.

Ashe, Ash

Irish Book of Arms plate 46

Ash, Nashe, Nash, Ashebrook

The Ashe family is found several centuries ago in Kildare, Cavan, and Meath, where they achieved some prominence. They are listed as found in Kildare at least by the 15th century.

The family can be found in later records in the Limerick and Kerry areas of Ireland. All families of the name in Ireland have been assumed to be of Anglo-Irish stock. Some of the name were adventurers for land, and arrived at the time of the Cromwellian settlement.

Sir Thomas Ashe, Knight, and John Ashe gentleman, are given in the precinct of Tullagharvy, Co. Cavan as servitors.

O'Hart gives the pedigree of one John Ash (d.1636), of St. John's, near Trim, Co. Meath, who was buried in St. Patricks of Trim; his son was Thomas. One Rev. Weldon Ashe was Prebendary of Tuam and incumbent of Annaghdown, who died in 1874.

The 1890 birth index finds the name of "Ashe" centered in counties Kerry and Antrim. The census of 1659 finds the name in Limerick City, Londonderry, Kildare, Kilkenny and Clare.

The arms of one Beresford-Ash of Ashbrook, Co. Londonderry are given in the Irish Book of Arms.

Alcorn

The name of a settler family in Ireland found in counties Donegal and Londonderry in the 19th century.

Alderdice

Alderdise

The name of a family found centered in counties Antrim and Armagh in the 19th century.

Athy

Irish Book of Arms plate 26

de Athy

de Athy, deathy, d'Aethy, Aethy

The place name of 'Athy' in Co. Kildare marks one family of the name in Ireland. The family, of Norman origins, settled here fairly early. Several of the name are found in the 14th century in this county, as given in the Red Book of Ormond.

Most notably the Athy family was a leading one in Galway city. Indeed, they are given as one of the '14 tribes of Galway'. While not the most prominent of the tribes, they did achieve position in that city, and one William de Athy, was treasurer of Connaught in 1388.

In Keatings History, we find the 'Athys' listed among several English and Welsh families settling in Galway town in the 12th and 13th centuries. As a whole however, the name has always been relatively rare in Ireland, making family research somewhat easier for this family than for Kelly or Murphy.

O'Hart also shows a spelling of D'Aeth, which became 'Death' in Ireland. As such, D'athy could have become Dathy or Deathy.

The arms shown above are those of Athy of Renville, Co. Galway, who served as High Sheriff for Co. Galway. They descend from Edmond Athy, of Galway, who was married to Margaret, daughter of Stephen Lynch of Galway.

The name is not very numerous in America either, for it does not appear on the list of the 2,000 most common names in the U. S. A..

Aldersee

A family name of Co. Westmeath in the 17th century.

Atkinson

Irish Book of Arms plate 51

Atkins

O'Hart finds one family of the name who emigrated to America (to the state of Virginia) from Cumberland, England in 1750. The Atkinson family of Glenwilliam Castle, Ballingarry Co. Limerick and Skea House, Co. Fermanagh is found in the Irish Book of Arms. The Atkinsons of Cangort, Kings Co. are given to descend from Anthony Atkinson, of the Island of Kiltobrett, Kings Co., in the early 17th century.

The 1890 birth index finds the family most numerous in Antrim, Armagh and Down. The name of Atkins is found in Co. Cork at that time.

Aldin

McAldin

A family name traditionally linked with counties Monaghan and Down in Ireland.

Alding

The name of a family found in the city of Dublin in the 17th century.

Aldrich

The name of a family found in Co. Monaghan in the 17th century.

Aldwood

Oldwood

The name of a family found in Co. Kilkenny in the 17th century.

6

Mac Auley

Irish Book of Arms plates 142, 145, 227

Mac Amhalghaidh, etc..

Cauley, MacAulay, MacAwley, Macauley,

Mac Auley, Mac Awley etc.. is recorded in Keatings History as chief of Calraidhean-Chala. Here he tells us: 'The fair Mac Auley rules over the entire of the ports of Calry'.

This includes the parish of Ballyloughloe, barony of Clanlonan in Westmeath, and ports along the Shannon River. According to Mac Geoghegan, they held part of the barony of Kilcoursey in Kings County.

The Irish sept of the name above were known as 'Lords of McGawleys Country' and are again found in the Four Masters works as 'Chiefs of Calry. Anciently descended from Niall of the Nine Hostages they took their name from Auley, a descendant of Niall. Specific pedigrees on this great family may be found in the genealogical office in Dublin.

Another completely separate family was a branch of the MacGuires of Co. Fermanagh, where we find the barony of Clanawley named in their honor. Most anciently this family was 'Mac Amhlaoibh'.

Another possibility is descent from the Scottish settlers here, particularly in the north of Ireland near Belfast.

In the 17th century Mc Aully was a principal name of Antrim, and Mac awly was a principal name of Fermanagh, while McAwly was found in Sligo at that time.

A century ago the name was given as most prominent in Antrim and Donegal, where the name still remained one of Ulster.

Arms for families of the name are found in the Irish Book of Arms. One motto for Macaulay found there was 'Dulce Periculum'

Mac Auliffe

Irish Book of Arms plates 145, 217

Mac Amhlaoibh

McAulife, Aulife, McAuliffe, Awlif

This great family is cited by the noted poet O'Heerin thusly:

'Far beyond the beautiful river Ella, to the west of Glen Salcain of tall trees, a fair land of affluence undenied: The territory belongs to the noble Mac Auliffe'

Some of the name descend from the MacCarthy family originally, where they became centered at Castle MacAuliffe, located near Newmarket.

O'Heerin gave them as chiefs of Cork as mentioned above. Their territory was in the barony of Duhallow in Cork, running to the border of Limerick. It is reported that the last chief of the name of this family served as a colonel of a regiment in Spain, who died in 1720.

This Cork family was the most numerous and prominent of the name, with branches in surrounding territories.

In the 17th century McAulife is found as a principal name in Co. Cork, as was the spelling of the name as 'Aulife'.

The name has remained one primarily of Co. Cork into modern times, with Cork being given in the 1890 index as the location for this family.

This family name is also of note as a tribe of the Hy Fiachrach, found near the banks of the River Moy in Killanley, in the parish of Castleconnor, in County Sligo, in more ancient times. Today however, it is difficult to trace back to that area. In County Waterford the family name is mentioned along with O'Bric, O'Foley and O'Keane as a family of the Decies, and can be found there in the 12th century.

Aylmer

Irish Book of Arms plates 18, 53, 56

Aighlmear

Ailmer, Aylemer, d'Aylmer

The Aylmer family in Ireland is given to be of Anglo-Saxon origins. The family name is found in Ireland in the wake of the Anglo-Norman invasions of the 12th century. At that time it is located in Co. Kildare.

In the 17th century Aylmer is a principal name of Kildare, also being found in Clare, Limerick and Meath at that time.

Keatings History gives the family as a principal one of the city and county of Dublin.

The Irish Book of Arms gives Aylmer of Courtown, Kilcock, Co. Kildare, who were descended from Richard Aylmer, of Lyons, Co. Kildare. Also given are the Hendrick-Aylmer arms of Kerdiffstown, Co. Kildare.

"The Aylmers of Ireland" by F. J. Aylmer, was published in London in 1931. Mention of the family is also made in the Kildare Archaeological Society.

Ale

The name of a family found in Co. Waterford in the 17th century.

Mac Aleary

The name of a family traditionally linked to counties Sligo and Antrim in our records.

Mac Aleavey

The name of a family found centered in Down and Armagh in the 19th century.

Aylward

Irish Book of Arms plate 76

Aighleart

Ayleward, Aileward, Elward

The family of Aylward is found in Ireland as an old and respectable family of Anglo-Norman origins. It is on record here from the time of the 12th century Norman invasions onward.

The family is often associated with Co. Waterford, and has been there from the 14th century at least. Many of the name are found in Kilkenny, as well. Note the townland of Aylwardstown in the barony of Ida, Co. Kilkenny. The variant spelling of Elward is found in Carrrick-on-Suir.

After the Aylwards settled in Ireland they became 'more Irish than the Irish themselves', so the old saying goes. They became a part of the Irish way of life.

Spelled as both Aylward and Ayleward, this family name is given as a principal one in Co. Waterford in the 17th century.

The family name is found in the Irish Book of Arms on plate 76. This family was given as Toler-Aylward of Shankhill Castle, Co. Kilkenny, and of Bloomfield, Co. Roscommon. They are cited as an old family in Ireland, descended from Richard Ayleward of Faithlegg, Co. Waterford. This line of the family possessed Glensillan, which subsequently became known as "Aylewardstown" in Co. Kilkenny.

Mac Aleenon

Mac Aleenen

A family traditionally linked to Co. Fermanagh in our records, not known to be related to the family of Mac Alindon which is a surname of Ulster.

Bagnall

Irish Book of Arms plate 33

Bagenal

According to "Keatings History" the name is given among the chief Anglo-Norman and English settlers in Ulidia, under DeCourcey and his successors.

Bagnalstown can be found in the barony of Idrone East, Co. Carlow. Some of the name descend from Sir Nicholas Bagenal of Staffordshire, England, who settled in Ireland during the reign of Elizabeth I.

The Bagenal family of Benekerry, Co. Carlow is given in the Irish Book of Arms.

The 1890 birth index finds the family most numerous in Kings Co. at that time.

Mc Aleer

A name found centered in Co. Tyrone in the 1890 birth index, with 13 of 17 births being recorded there at that time.

Mc Aleese

The name of a family traditionally linked to the province of Ulster in Ireland, where most of the name were found in Antrim and Londonderry in the 19th century.

Mc Alinden

MacAlenden

The name of an old Irish family found anciently in the territory of Oriel, and centered in Co. Armagh.

Alley

Ally

A name found more anciently in Co. Kildare, and of possible Norse origins, but in modern times we have no record of the name to date.

7

Bagot

The Irish Book of Arms plate 91

Bagott

The Bagot family of Aughrane Castle and of Ballymoe, Co. Galway, descend from Edward Bagot of Harristown, King's Co., and of Walterstown, Co. Kildare.

Allison

Alison, Ellison, Alleson, Allisson

In earlier days the name of Allison is often found in County Donegal, but today it is considered a name most numerous in County Antrim.

Scottish immigrants of the name account for many 'Allison' families in the north of Ireland today. The Scottish name of Ellison has often been used interchangeably with Allison.

In the 1890 birth index the name is found in Antrim, with traditional locations for the family in Milford Union, Co. Donegal and Newry Union in Counties Armagh and Down.

We also find mention of the name in Dublin and Limerick in the 16th century.

Mc Allister

McAlester, Lester, MacCallister,

Of the many forms of this name, McAlester is found in 1659 as a principal name of Antrim, and McAllester is found as a principal name of Londonderry at that time. In the 19th century McAlister was found most often in Co. Antrim and McAllister was a spelling found centered in Antrim as well.

The family is generally given as a family who arrived from Scotland in the military service of the MacDonnells of Ulster (as galloglas), and subsequently settling permanently in Ireland.

Ball

Irish Book of Arms plate 128

One noted family of the name originates in Dublin from Major Robert Ball (d.1637). The main locations for the family in the 19th century were Antrim, Meath and Dublin.

Allman

Allmen, Alman

Note the place name of Almondstown, previously Almanston for the location of at least one family of the name in Co. Louth. The family is said to have settled in Ireland in the wake of the Norman invasions. We also find the name in Co. Kerry in the 19th century.

Altimas

Altmas

A Palatine family of Co. Wexford found settled there for at least 2 centuries.

Anderson

Andersen

Anderson is a family name found commonly in Scotland, and rather numerous in the north of Ireland, but can be found throughout the country. The most common locations for the name in the 19th century were in Antrim, Down, Dublin and Derry. Some 175 births of the name were recorded in 1890.

Mc Aneny

Irish Book of Arms plate 258 (McAnany)

Mac Anany, Mc Aneney

Under this spelling of the name, this family is found centered in Co. Tyrone in Ireland.

O Bannion

Irish Book of Arms plates 45, 259

O Banain

O'Bannon, Banane, Banion, Banin,

The O'Bannion families, with all the various spellings they have taken, come from several completely separate origins in Ireland.

The most prominent O'Bannion family came from Co. Fermanagh, in Lower Ormonde. It is found in Fermanagh in our ancient pedigrees as well. 'O'Banan' was given as a principal name in this county in the 17th century. 'The Book of Lecan' contains information on this family as well.

Note the place name of Ballybannon by Lough Mask, in County Mayo. One old O'Bannion stronghold was at Leap Castle, in the barony of Clonlisk, where the family was found in the 17th century as well.

The name is found in Tipperary in the Hearth Money Rolls, and in that county the name 'Banan' was a principal one in the 17th century. It is also found there as 'Bannon' a century ago, when 21 births were recorded of the name.

It should also be noted that under the spelling of 'Banan', it was a principal name of Kings County (Offaly), in the census of 1659.

Keatings History cites the name as a family of Co. Mayo, and of northern Tipperary, and gives O'Bannan, of the Ui Dechi, as chief over "The extensive land of fair fortresses'. O'Heerin cited the "fruitful country which they inherit, is the estate of the tribe of O'Bannon." This land is given in the north of Co. Tipperary, and many of the name resided there at the time of the above writings.

Both Banon and Bannon are given in the Irish Book of Arms, including the family of Banon, of Broughall Castle in Kings Co. (Offaly).

8

Barcroft

Irish Book of Arms plate 28

One noted English family of the name is found in the Glen, Newry, Co. Down, and the Irish Book of Arms finds the family founded here by Ambrose Barcroft, of the Haigh, near Foulridge.

Anesley

The name of a family found centered in Co. Kildare in the 17th century.

Anger

Angier, Aungier

The spelling of the name as "Anger" is found in Dublin city in the census of 1659.

Anglin

Anglin, Angland, Anglind

The name of a family traditionally linked to Co. Cork in our records, going back for several centuries.

Angus

A family name found centered in counties Down and Antrim in the 19th century.

Ankettill

Ankettle

The family name of Ankettill is found in Co. Monaghan in the 17th century, and it is here where the name is most often traditionally linked. The name of Ankettle, a likely variant spelling of the above name, was found in Co. Tipperary in the 17th century. One John Anketell (d.1638) is found in Newmarket, Co. Cork.

de Barnwall

Irish Book of Arms plate 10 (Barnewall)

Barnewall, Barnwell

According to "Keatings History" the name is of Anglo-Norman origins and they were styled Lords of Bearhaven with large possessions in that area. They were subsequently expelled by the O'Sullivans and settled in Dublin and Meath, and founded the families of Barnwall who became Barons of Trimblestown and Turvey, and viscounts Kingsland.

They are given among the principal Norman families of Co. Cork.

According to "Keatings History" the name spelled simply as Barnwall, was that of a principal family of Dublin city or county, and of Anglo-Norman descent.

Today, of course, the name is found largely only as "Barnwall", with the "de" prefix removed.

Nicholas Barnewall, Lord Kingsland, served as an officer in Lord Limerick's Dragoons. This family is found settled at Turvey in Co. Dublin for some time.

Anthony

According to "Keatings History" the name is among the chief families of English descent settling in Waterford and Tipperary. These English families primarily possessed the territory called Gal-tir, signifying the country of the foreigners," now the barony of Gaultiere." We further find the name in Co. Waterford in the 17th century.

Mac Any

One noted family of the name is found in Carragh, Queens Co., in Ireland, and subsequently in Ballyneskeagh, Co. Meath.

Barrett

Irish Book of Arms plates 75, 145, 266

Baroid, Baireid

Barett, Barret, Barnett, Barrat, Bartnett,

Barrett families spring from more than one source. Some of the name arrived in Ireland from England.

Several of the name arrived in Ireland a with the 12th century Anglo-Norman invasions. They have been said to be Welsh by some, Normans by others, and Anglo-Saxon by others. The main areas of early settlement were in Co. Cork, and the Galway-Mayo areas of Ireland.

In Cork we find the Barratt family, whom Woulfe says was of Norman origins. 'Barretts Country' as their lands became known, would have been in the barony of Barrets in Co. Cork. The name is found in the 17th century in Cork city, spelled with one or two 't's' at the end of the name. It was found in Dublin at that time as well.

The Barrett families of northern Co. Mayo became known as 'Lords of Tirawley'. The chief of the name was at times referred to as 'MacWattin' and is given in the works of the Four Masters as MacVaittin, according to O'Donovan. The spelling of 'MacPadine' has also been given as an alias for the chief of the name in Co. Mayo. These Mayo families held considerable lands until the end of the 1600's, when they suffered confiscations.

In the 17th century the name is also given in Clare and Kerry, etc.., giving testimony to the growing numbers of the name in Ireland at that time. A century ago the name was fairly widespread, with Dublin and Cork heading the list of counties most populated with Barrett families.

The Irish Book of Arms gives one family of the name as Barrett-Hamilton of Kilmanock House, Co. Wexford.

Barrington

Irish Book of Arms plates 11, 67

OBearain

Barington

Barrington has been found in Ireland as a place name since Medieval times, and stands here as a tribute to those of the name in this country. A name of English origins, several families are found in the Irish annals.

One captain Barrington took over the lands of O'Moore in Leix (Queens) in Elizabethan times. Needless to say, this gave rise to some dispute between the two parties involved. Given as a chief English family there, they are cited as one of the "7 tribes" of that area.

The same county produced notable men of the name by the end of the 16th century and one served as M. P. for Maryborough in 1613.

In Limerick a Barrington family settled in the aftermath of the Cromwellian upheavals at the end of the 17th century. At the same time, families of the name have been said to have settled in Cork and centered at Glenstal in Limerick. Barringtons Hospital is of note in more modern times in Limerick City.

For a more complete look at the name in the 17th century we find Barrington families in Wexford, Antrim, Queens, and Londonderry in the census of 1659.

Several of the name are found in the Irish House of Commons and the House of Lords in 1797. Sir Thomas Barrington of Hatfield, Broadoaks, Essex, England, is given to be the ancestor of one Irish family of the name.

Sir Jonah Barrington, author of Barringtons "Historic Memoirs of Ireland" , was a lively writer of his time.

A century ago 7 scattered births of the name were recorded.

The old Irish family name of O'Bearain has also been said to have been changed the name to Barrington.

Barry

Irish Book of Arms plates 61, 75, 79, 105..

de Barri, O'Beargha, de Barra

Barre, Barri, Barrie, Berry, Barr, Barrye,

Barry is an old and respected family, of Irish and Norman origins. Linked with Cork, the name is found there after the 12th century Norman invasions. Some say the name came from Wales.

One Phillip de Barri received lands in the baronies of Barrymore, Orrery and Kinlea in Co. Cork. Tradition has it that he was influential due to his mother's connections with the Anglo-Norman conquerors of the land.

Phillip was, on his mother's side, of Welsh nobility, and his father was a Norman noble. He and his brother, Robert were among the early Norman invaders of Ireland. He also founded an Augustinian Abbey.

The family motto 'Boutez en avent' (to strike forward), gave rise to the name of 'Buttevant', a family center in Cork.

The Barry family developed several branches. Note the baronies of Barrymore and Barryroe, two centers for the name. Other branches of the family included Barry Mor, Barry Og, Barry Maol, and Barry Laidir. The Barry family of Firville, Co. Cork are earlier found in Elm Park, Farran, Co. Cork, as given in the Book of Arms.

Another Barry family in Cork, took the name of McAdam, from Adam Barry, found near Rathcormac, in Cork.

The Irish family of O'Beargha, (also called Barry), were chiefs in the barony of Kenry, Co. Limerick.

The Barry family of Sandville, Co. Limerick is given in the Irish Book of Arms. In the 17th century we find the name in Clare and Cork, and a century ago in Cork, Limerick and Waterford. The Harold-Barry family of Ballyvonare, Co. Cork, assumed the Barry name upon taking possession of nearby lands.

Barton

Irish Book of Arms plate 41

de Bartun

Bartun, de Bartun, Bartun

The Barton family is said to have taken their name from an English place name, and are given to have been in Ireland from the 13th century onwards.

Early records show the name as 'de Bartun'. One family of the name is found in Co. Kildare, near Straffan, at the beginning of the 17th century.

Other locations for the name include Kilcullen, in Co. Kildare and Kilkenny city. Thomas Barton, of Barton Hall, Lancashire, arrived in Ireland with Essex and obtained lands in Co. Fermanagh. This line is found in Clonelly, Co, Fermanagh, Rochestown in Tipperary and at Straffan in Kildare in more modern times.

One family entered the wine trade in France and later returned to Ireland, at Grove, in Co. Waterford.

Several of the name are assumed to have arrived in Ireland with the Cromwellian settlements.

The name is also found early in the barony of Eliogarty, Co. Tipperary.

Arms for one family of Barton, of Grove, Co. Tipperary, are shown above.

Archdale

Archdall

A name found centered in Co. Fermanagh in the 17th century.

Ardagh

Ardough, Ardogh

A rare name in Ireland, records of the family are found in Co. Louth, and in Co. Waterford as landowners. The spelling of the name of Ardough is found in Dublin city in the 17th century and may represent the same family.

Bateman

Irish Book of Arms plate 12

Batemen

Families of the name of Bateman are found in counties Kerry and Down in Ireland in the 17th century. Some two-hundred years later the name is found centered in Cork and Dublin. The name is most often found associated with Co. Cork in our records for the last several centuries.

Several of the name have arrived from foreign shores here, beginning with the 12th century Norman invasions of Ireland.

Archdeacon

Archdeakin, Archdekin, Cody, Codd.

The name of Archdeacon is found less often today than in earlier times in Ireland. This is due in part to the fact that some of the name changed to 'Cody'.

The name of Cody was assumed by the Archdeacons of Kilkenny, who date back to the 13th century in Ireland.

Nicholas Archdeacon was Bishop of Kilmacduagh and Kilfenora from 1800 - 1824.

In the 17th century Archdeacon is found in County Cork, 'Archdeakin' is found as a principal name in Tipperary, and 'Archdekin' as a principal name of Kilkenny at that time.

In the 19th century birth index the name is given in County Kilkenny, and in the Union of Kanturk, Boherboy district.

Ardenton

Ardonton

The name of a family found in Louth/Drogheda in the 17th century.

11

Batt

The Irish Book of Arms plate 57

Bat

The Batt family of Rathmullan, Co. Donegal, settled here coming from Cornwall, and they obtained considerable lands in Co. Wexford around the year 1650.

Archer

Airseir

le Archer, Larcher

The family of Archer in Ireland was one of the noted 'Tribes of Kilkenny' in more ancient works. The name arrived in Ireland with the coming of the Norman invasions of the 12th century, and they were originally an Anglo-Norman family.

In the 12th century we have found one 'Ralph Larcher' from le Archer, as a burgess in Dublin city.

In the County of Westmeath, note the place name of Archerstown around the time of the invasions. Archersgrove, Archersleas, and Archersrath can all be found on maps of Ireland from earlier times.

Keatings History gives the Archer family as a principal one of Anglo-Norman descent.

In the 17th century the name is found in Armagh and Kilkenny. By the time of the 1890 index the name is given in Counties Armagh, Dublin and Antrim as most numerous.

There are a surprising number of families of the name in America today. Here the name of Archer ranks among the top 900 most numerous surnames in the country.

Ardglasse

The name of a family found in Co. Down in the 17th century.

Battersby

The Irish Book of Arms plate 99

The Battersby family of Loughbawn, Co. Westmeath descend from William Battersby of Smithstown, Co. Meath and are given in the Irish Book of Arms. The 1890 birth index finds the family most numerous in Co. Dublin, with 5 recorded births of the name at that time.

Ardiff

Ardif

We find record of one of the name in Co. Kildare in times past.

Ardill

Ardell, Ardhill

This family name is most often linked with the northern parts of Co. Tipperary in Ireland.

Mc Ardle

MacCardle, Mc Ardill

An old Irish family of the territory of Oriel in Ireland, found centered subsequently in Louth, Antrim and Monaghan. The family is said to have been a branch of the McMahons there.

It is not known if any relationship exists between McArdle and the name of Ardill, but likely they represented entirely different families. Knowing the changing forms of Irish names however, it would not be surprising to find a few McArdles who had changed the name to McArdill.

Bayly, Bayley

Irish Book of Arms plate 24

One branch of the Bayly family arrived from Yorkshire and settled in Ireland under Cromwell's regime. They are found early in the parish of St. Bride, Dublin in the 17th century; and one of the family is found in Fisherstown, Queens Co. subsequently. Another family of the name settled in Canada, coming from Dublin around 1836, settling in the township of Oro originally.

The family of Bayly of Ballyarthur, Co. Wicklow, was founded in the early 19th century, and they are found in the Irish Book of Arms.

Mac Aree

Garry, MacIlharry,

Families of the name of "MacAree" are found centered in counties Antrim and Monaghan in the 19th century. The family is most often traditionally linked to Co. Monaghan in historical records. In the works of Matheson, we find the names of MacIlharry and Garry given as synonyms of MacAree. On the surface it appears that this name may have been taken from the gaelic "Mac an Riagh" meaning son of the King.

Argue

Families of the name of "Argue" are found centered in Co. Cavan in our records. The name spelled as such is not found in ancient records of Ireland, and is of either recent introduction or the "translated" form of an older Irish name.

Beamish

Irish Book of Arms plate 33, 105

Beemish

The surname of Beamish is found in Co. Cork since the 17th century. One family of the name is found settling in Co. Kerry, coming originally from England. Several families of the name are found in Cork as landholders and one branch of the name is found seated in Kerry in the works of Burke. Both the 17th century "census" and the 1890 birth index find the name centered in Co. Cork.

The Beamish family of Comphull, Co. Sligo is found in the Irish Book of Arms, as is the Beamish family of Ashbourne, Co. Cork.

Arkins

Arkens, Harkins

A family found in Co. Clare in our records, and perhaps some of this name stem from the similar sounding name of Harkins, although we have no evidence of this. According to Woulfe the name comes from the gaelic "orc" meaning pig. Harkins is a name found in Donegal, far to the north of Arkin homeland

Arland

Arlan, Arlend

The name of an English family found settled earlier in Co. Waterford.

Arundell

Paul Arundell of Chediock, had a son named Paul (d. 1636), who was of Main, Co. Limerick

O'Beirne

Irish Book of Arms plates 145, 260

Burns, Byrnes, Burn, Bierne

The family of O'Beirne is one of longstanding in Ireland, and has been confused with several other similar names. It can be found today spelled as any of the above.

Originally O'Beirne was a family of the Province of Connaught. They were centered in Roscommon and Mayo, and branched out later into Leitrim. Under the main spelling of the name as shown above, the family was concentrated in Roscommon and Leitrim a century ago. At this time the family was centered around Strokestown Union, in the Roosky district, and in the Roscommon Union, in the district of Roscommon.

In early times the name is found near Ballinrobe, in Co. Mayo, and in the 13th century they are said to have overthrown the O'Monaghans of Co. Roscommon.

Arms for families of this name are found in the Irish Book of Arms. (see Burns, Byrnes etc..in this work)

Mac Atasney

MacAtarsny, Tarsney, MacEntasny

A fairly rare name in Irish records, the MacAtasney etc..families are found centered in counties Tyrone and Armagh no later than the 16th century.

Mac Atavy

Mac Atavey, Tavey

We find the name sometimes in Co. Monaghan.

Bellew

Irish Book of Arms plate18

According to "Keatings History" the name is given as among the "great families, either of English or Norman descent, settled in Meath in early times. The Bellews achieved the title of barons of Duleek, Co. Louth.

In 1445 Philip Bellew is found as Bailiff of Dublin, and later generations produced a mayor of that city and other notables. A branch of the family is found in Castlebar and in Ballinrobe, Co. Mayo circa 1829.

The main location for the Bellew family in the 19th century was in Co. Louth.

Mc Ateer

MacIntyre

The family is found early in Co. Antrim, and subsequently in Co. Donegal and nearby Sligo. The name on occasion has been interchanged with the name of MacIntyre there.

Attridge

Atteridge

A name found in Co. Cork in our records from the 19th century, and assumed to be of English origins.

Audley

According to "Keatings History" the name is given among the chief Anglo-Norman and English settlers in Ulidia, under DeCourcey and his successors.

Beresford

Irish Book of Arms plates 4, 42, 46

Bearsford

As the name suggests, members of the Beresford family arrived in Ireland with the plantation of Ulster. One of the name is found in charge of the London Company there. The family is later found holding great power in Co. Waterford, where they were connected to the de la Poers'. (Sir Marcus Beresford married the lady Catherine Le Poer, thereby becoming the earls of Tyrone, marquises of Waterford, and barons of Decies.)

Several of the name are found in official records of the past, including Rt. Hon. J. Beresford, John Claud Beresford and Marcus Beresford, who all served in the "Irish" House of Commons in 1797. One of the name was Archbishop of Tuam at that date as well. Lady Araminta Monck, nee Beresford has been given as well.

The name is also given as a principal family name in the County and City of Dublin , at some time from the 12th to the 18th centuries.

Families found in the Irish Book of Arms include those of Pack-Beresford of Fenagh, Co. Carlow, and those of Beresford-Ash of Ashbrook, Co. Londonderry.

Aungier

Angier, d' Aungiers

In at least one instance given to be a Huguenot family settled in Ireland of longstanding in Dublin. We also find at least one family of the name in Co. Longford.

Babe

We find some of the name in Co. Louth.

Berridge

The Irish Book of Arms plate 77

Beridge, Burridge

The Berridge family of Ballynahinch Castle, Connemara, Co. Galway is given in the Irish Book of Arms.

Austin

Oistin, Mac Aibhistin

Austen, Austine, Auston, Austan

The Austin family name is found scattered throughout Ireland. It is considered to be, for the most part, of English origins here. The name has been in Ireland since the 12th century, the time of the Norman invasions.

The birth index of the last century gives Antrim and Dublin as principal locations for the family.

The spelling of Austine is found in the census of 1659 and it is given as a name of County Down at that time.

In America the name is rather popular today, ranking among the top 225 names in that country.

Mac Aveeley

McAvealy, Mac Aveely

According to "Keatings History" the name is given as an Irish name which was also adopted by Anglo-Norman or English families in lieu of their original surnames.

The Staunton families of Co. Mayo are said to have changed their name into Mac Aveeley.(meaning the "son of the Knight".

Backas

Backus

A name found in Co. Waterford in the 17th and 18th centuries in our records.

Bingham

The Irish Book of Arms plate 81

The Bingham family of Bingham Castle, Co. Mayo descend from George Bingham, military Governor of Sligo in 1596. The 1890 birth index finds the family most numerous in Down and Antrim.

O'Baiskind

O'Baiskinn

According to "Keatings History" the name is that of a family of chiefs of Triocha Cead Corca Baiskind, which is now the barony of Moyarta, in Co. Clare.

O'Heerin speaks of them thusly;

"Another chief of this land of music,
Noble is the origin of his descent,
Was O'Baiskinn's stately tree,
A tribe that marched with force."

Balbirnie

Balburnie, Balburney, Burney, Birnie

See " An Historical Account of the Family of Balbirnie" by William Balbirnie, (then of Cork County), published in 1854.

The names Mac Burney and Birnie are also found in Ireland, and several families of those names arrived here from Scotland.

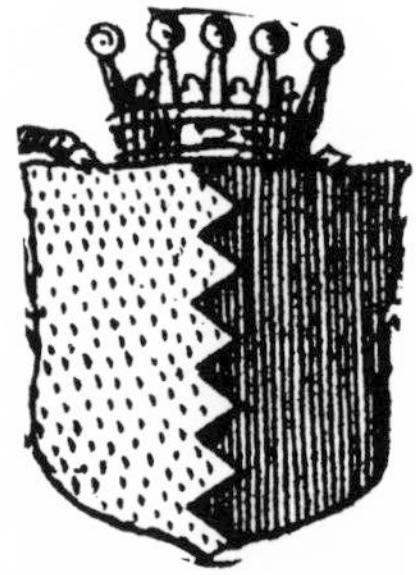

Birmingham

Irish Book of Arms plate 6

Mac Fheorais, de Bermingham

Bermingham, Berminghan, Bremigan,

'Berminghams Country' referred to in the annals of Irish history, is to be found in the barony of Dunmore in Co. Galway. In Co. Kildare, Castle Carbury served as their stronghold. This family is well noted in historical works from the time of the 12th century Norman invasions.

Of Anglo-Norman descent, the first of record to arrive here was Robert de Bermingham, of Castle Bermingham in Warwickshire. He arrived with Strongbow at the time of the invasions.

The family name is found more often in Leinster and Munster in Irish records, but they are found as well as Lords of Athenry in Connaught. The census of 1659 records the name as a principal one of Kildare, and also in Kings Co., spelled as Bermingham. (Virtually no distinction between different spellings of the name can be made today.)

Of the noted families of the name are the "Lord Barons of Athenry", those of Rahinely, Co. Kildare, those of the Grange, Co. Kildare, and those of Mylestown, Co. Tipperary. The names of these families are found spelled as Bermingam in older records.

A century ago 23 births were recorded under the spelling of Bermingham, and 17 bore the name of Birmingham. At that time the principal locations for the name were Dublin, Kings (Offaly), and Cork counties.

Arms for members of this family are found in the Irish Book of Arms.

Piers de Bermingham adopted the name of Mac Fheorais, which was later changed to Corish, a name subsequently found in counties Galway and Kildare.

Black

Irish Book of Arms plates 46, 119, 145

Blake, Blacker...

Black is a family name most often found in the province of Ulster. It may be of either Scottish or English origins, outside of a few of the name who translated their names into Black from an original gaelic name. The name was found as a principal one of Co. Antrim, and also found in Co. Londonderry in the 15th century. (see index)

Several other names have likely been shortened into Black on occasion. Names like Blackand of Dublin, Blackbourne, Blacken, Blackender, Blackham, Blacker, Blacknell etc.., can all be of foreign origins when found in Ireland.

In the 1890 birth index the name of "Black" is given in counties Antrim, Armagh, Tyrone, and Down.

In the Irish Book of Arms several families of the name of Blake, and Blacker are given. Including those of Blake of Renvyle, Co. Galway, originally of "Caddell" origins, in the barony of Dunkillon, Co. Galway. (see Blake).

"Blacker" of Carrick Blacker, Co. Armagh, and of Woodbrook, Co. Wexford, is also given in the Irish Book of Arms.

Baldrick

Balrick, Boldrick

The name of an English family found in Co. Donegal, said to have arrived in Ireland during the time of Cromwell.

14

Blacker

The Irish Book of Arms plate 66

Black, Blaker

The Blacker family of Carrickblacker and Woodbrook, Co. Wexford, and Carrickblacker, Co. Armagh is found in the Irish Book of Arms.

Baker

English occupational name.

le Bakere, le Baker

The all too common name of Baker is found in all four provinces of Ireland. An English name taken from the obvious occupation, it is found early in Ireland, at least back unto the 1200's.

The census of 1659 gives the name in Kilkenny, Leitrim and Cork. The Birth index shows Dublin and Antrim as locations for the name in the 1800's. Interestingly enough, Rooney finds the name coming from Scotland in 1642 and settling in Dublin, Cork and Tipperary.

From O'Hart: Thos. Baker, alive in May 1652. Sir James (Enrollments 1821-1825) . George (Connaught Certificates- transplanters 1653-54). Benjamin & Capt. John of the 1649 officers. Peter (1702-03) listed as Forfeiting Proprietor.

Edward of Cork and Kerry, Henry of Kilkenny, William of Kilkenny, Thomas of Meath are all given as soldiers of the commonwealth.

Blake

Irish Book of Arms plates 46, 119, 145

le Blaca, de Blaca

Caddell, Blacagh, Blakes, Bleach, Blouk,

The Blake family is one of the 'Tribes of Galway', descended from Richard Caddell, sheriff of Connacht in 1303. They became extensive landowners in Galway, including lands in the barony of Dunkellon. Originally their family name was Caddell. 'Blake' was an epithet meaning 'the Black'. Hence you will find the name written, Caddell, alias Blake, le Blaca or Niger.

Blake is an English name, but this family is said to have come from Wales. They held lands at Ballimacroe in Galway for centuries, and it is here where they are traditionally located. A branch of the family settled in Kildare, where you will find at least three townlands by the name of 'Blakestown'. In Galway they held lands into the last century. Areas connected to the name were; Renvyle, Menlo, Ardfry, Balgunin and Kiltullagh to name a few.

In Co. Mayo at Kilnock the O'Brien-ffrench-Blakes are of record, and in Wicklow the name is found at Kiltegan.

Some Blakes are of Irish origins coming from O'Blachmhaich, which became O'Blowick and Blake in the western parts of the country.

The church of St. Nicholas in Galway City was of special interest to the Blake family, who were long time supporters of its upkeep.

The book entitled 'Blake Family Records 1600-1700' by Martin J. Blake will be of interest to family researchers.

In the 17th century we find the name in Cork, Kings (Offaly), and Clare counties. A century ago it was most numerous in Cork, Galway and Clare, with some of the name in Co. Antrim in Ulster. Blake ranks around the 400th most popular name in the U.S.A.
(see Black entry for more info).

Blakeney

Irish Book of Arms plate 40

Blakney

The Blakeney family of Castle Blakeney, Co. Galway are found with one early branch of the name in Thomastown, Co. Limerick.

Balfe, Balffe

Balf, Balfour

This Anglo-Norman family is found settled early in Co. Meath, where they became prominent by the 15th century. William Balfe was a burgess of Athboy in 1409. Michael W. Balfe (d. 1870), wrote "The Bohemian Girl", one of his operas of note.

Several are given of the name in our records. John Balfe, of Crige, Co. Middlesex, England, is found on the Fleming pedigree. Michael Balfe, of So. Park, Co. Roscommon is given, and the spelling of Balffe is given as prominent in the 16th century, while the spelling of Balfe was given in the 15th century.

O'Hart gives "Balbh" as the root word of Balfe, as cited in the O'Beirne genealogy, but of this I have no knowledge.

Only 7 births of the name are given in the 1890 birth index of Ireland. The name of Balfour, presumably a completely separate name, could have been shorted to Balf by some.

Bland

Irish Book of Arms plate 24, 50

Blend

Several of the name are found in Killarney as 18th century Vicars. This family was of English extraction. One Mr. John Bland of this family settled in Virginia, (U.S.A.), and was buried in London. The Bland family of Blandsfort, Queens Co., was founded by one Col. John Bland who purchased lands there in 1699, according to the Irish Book of Arms.

The Bland family of Derriquin Castle, Co. Kerry, is traced back to Rev. James Bland, Archdeacon of Limerick. The family originally came from York, before settling in Ireland.

Baldwin

Baudwin

One family of the name is found in Mount Pleasant, Kinalmeaky, Co. Cork in Ireland. The name is said to come from either Thomas Balbhan Fitzmaurice, son of Patrick, seventh lord of Kerry, or from Baudwin or Baldwin, Earl of Flanders.

County Waterford was the main location for the name in the 19th century.

Ballagh

Ballough

Families of this name in times past came from several different origins in Ireland and is thought to have been more like a nickname or an epithet given to a person to help identify him from others of his family.

In modern times the name is quite rare, but can be found in Co. Monaghan.

16

Blaney

Irish Book of Arms plate 11 (Blayney)

Blany, Blayney

Families of the name of Blaney are found in the 17th century centered in Co. Monaghan, where one family of the name is found with large holdings of property, and in the 19th century the name is found centered in Co. Antrim. Traditionally linked to Co. Monaghan in the past, the name was often found there spelled as Blayney.

Ballenger

Ballinger

A name found in reference works on Co. Clare, and the family is assumed to have arrived here from England in the past.

Ballester

Ballesty, Baliste

Another of the rare names found in Ireland, and is likely of settler origin when found here. The name is found in England, and has been said to come from the translation of "balestier" or the "man with the cross-bow." One family of the name is found in Co. Westmeath.

Bambrick

Families of the name of Bambrick are found centered in Queens Co. in the 17th century, and subsequently in nearby Kilkenny. Several of the name are found in the military in that century in Ireland. We have no record as to the origin of the name at this date, but it has been said that the family is of Scottish or English extraction.

Bambury

Bamberry

A family we sometimes find in Co. Kerry, and at least two of the name are found serving as Mayors of Limerick.

Blennerhassett

Irish Book of Arms plate 74

Hassett, Blenerhaset, etc..

The name is often associated with the area of Tralee, in Co. Kerry, and it is in Kerry where the name is also found in the 17th century, of English settler origins. Reference to the name under a variant spelling I believe has been found in counties Limerick and Fermanagh, in the 17th century.

In the Irish Book of Arms Blennerhassett of Ballyseedy, Co. Kerry, is given. Of English origins in this case, they were said to settle in Ireland around 1580 a.d... The first of this line was Thomas of Flimby, Co. Cumberland, England, who obtained grants of land in Co. Kerry.

Bane

Bayne, Baynes, White

In the 17th century we find the name of Bane fairly widespread in Ireland; in Counties Cork, Limerick, Tipperary, Carlow, Kildare, etc... In more modern times the name is a rare one, perhaps due to the fact that "Bane" was used as an alias or as a identifying nickname of sorts. Hence, it may have been used for only one generation in many instances.

Families of the name were also found common in older records in the Clare/Galway region of Ireland.

Some of the name may descend from "Bayne" or "Baynes" families from Scotland and England.

The name of Bane may also have been translated into the English surname of "White", for in gaelic ban means white.

Banigan

Bannegan

A name found most often in northwest Ireland in our records.

Bligh

The Irish Book of Arms plate 60

The Bligh family of Brittas, Nobber, Co. Meath descend from John Bligh of Rathmore, Co. Meath around the year 1660 or earlier.

Banks

Some of the name of Banks found in Ireland are of English extraction. Others descend from old Irish families by means of "translating" their name into English as Banks. The 1890 birth index finds eight births of the name recorded in Ireland. The census of 1659 finds the family centered in Dublin.

Barber, Barbour

Barbador, le Barbour, Barbier

The census of 1659 finds families of the name of Barber centered in Tipperary, and at the end of the 19th century the family is found centered in Co. Antrim. Note also the place name of Barberstown in Co. Dublin, where the name has been on record for some time in Dublin City.

Most of the name can be found centered today near the cities of Dublin and Belfast. Some of the name are of Scottish heritage having settled centuries ago in Ulster.

Older records find some families of the name spelled as le Barbour .

Bardane

A name found sometimes in Co. Waterford in our records, and likely related to the spellings of Bardon, Bardan etc.. found in Longford and Westmeath in the 17th century.

17

Blood

Irish Book of Arms plate 105, 106

Bloud

The family name of Blood has traditionally been linked to Co. Clare in Ireland from the 17th century onward. One of those to settle in Clare, had a branch which settled in Westmeath for some time as well. The above family was of foreign extraction, settling here most likely from England. Several other individuals of the name are found settling here from England,but the Co. Clare family of the name is of some note.

The Blood family of Cranagher, Co. Clare is given in the Irish Book of Arms, as is the Blood family of Ballykilty, Co. Clare.

The latter descend from Matthew Blood of Cragaunboy, Co. Clare.

Barron

Baron

There are several origins for the Barron name in Ireland. In the province of Ulster a branch of the O'Neills are said to have adopted the name. In the counties of Waterford and Wexford the name stems from the Fitzgerald family who served as barons of Burnchurch in Kilkenny.

Some of the name were originally of Scottish heritage before settling in Ireland.

The main locations for families of the name in the 19th century were in Antrim, Donegal, Wexford and Waterford.

Barter

The name of an English family found settled in Co. Cork.

O Boland

Irish Book of Arms plate 54

O Beollain

Bolan, Bowland, Bullion, Beolan, Beolane

O'Beollain was the more ancient spelling of the name of O'Boland or Bolan in Ireland. It is seldom found with the 'O' prefix and is found both as Bolan and Boland.

There appears to be at least two separate origins of the name. In Co. Sligo they are found centered at Doonalton, in the barony of Tireragh. The family is also found at Drumcliff, in the barony of Carbury in Sligo in connection with St. Columbans church.

In Thomand, a Dalcassion family of the name descends from Mahon, the brother of Brian Boru. They are found near the shores of Lough Derg, in the barony of Clonderlaw, in Co. Clare. "Baile ui Beolain" meaning Ballybolan, was formerly found in the town presently named Mountshannon in Clare.

In the 17th century the family is found in Co. Offaly. The census of 1659 finds the old spelling of 'Beolan' in Offaly and Sligo, 'Beolane' was a principal name in Clare at that time as well as in Offaly. Note that the 'd' on the end of the name was not present in these instances, but has been added on in more modern times.

O'Hart gives the arms of the Bolands of Ulster as : Sa. three fleurs-de-lis ar., and the crest as: A church and spire ppr.

Basnett

A name found in Dublin in older records.

Basquill

We find an isolated mention of the name in Co. Mayo.

Bolton

Irish Book of Arms plate 33

Bolten

The name of Bolton was fairly widespread in Ireland by the time of the census of 1659. It is found then in counties Down, Dublin, Queens, Louth and Waterford.

Primarily considered a name of the province of Ulster, the family can often be found in Co. Antrim, Co. Derry, and as would be expected in Dublin city. Many can be found as landowners in the 19th century and previously, outside the areas of Ulster.

Bolton itself is a name of English origins, and it is generally given to be a name of English extraction when found in Ireland. The Bolton family of Castle Ring, Co. Louth is given in the Irish Book of Arms.

Bastable

Barnstaple, Barnstable

For several centuries families of the name are found in counties Cork and Kerry.

One member reports the name to have originated from the name of a town in England which was Barnstaple or Barnstable.

Bastick

Bostock, Bostick

The name of an English family, often found in Co. Offaly. Bostock may be an earlier form of the name, found before the time of Cromwell in Ireland.

de Bath

According to "Keatings History" the name is one of a family of note in Meath. The de Bathes were a noted family of Athcarn.

Bomford

The Irish Book of Arms plate 58

The Bomford family of Gallow and Ferrans, Co. Meath are found in the Irish Book of Arms.

Battle

Battell, Batell, Bataille

The 1890 birth index of Ireland finds only 6 recorded births of the name of Battle, which was centered at that time in Co. Sligo. The name is also found in England, but the Co. Sligo family is said to be of old Irish origins.

Baxter

MacBaxter, Bacstar, Bagster

The census of 1659 finds the family of Baxter centered in Donegal and Dublin. Fairly common in Irish records, the name is traditionally linked to the province of Ulster, where many of the name stem from the Scottish family of MacBaxter. By the end of the 19th century the name is found centered in Co. Antrim there.

Bayne

Ban, Bain, Baine, Bane

Those of the Bayne name in Ireland may be of Scottish or English extraction.

Beakey

Bakey, Beaky

A family of Clare and Wicklow, given by Woulfe to have taken the name from the gaelic "Beice" meaning to cry or weep.

O'Bean

White

According to "Keatings History" the name is cited as that of a clan of Mayo and/or Sligo, and the same family also took on the name of White.

Bonynge

The Irish Book of Arms plate 58

The Bonynge family is found given in the Irish Book of Arms.

Beard

One family of the name is found in Colstown in Kings County, (Offaly), and in Smithstown, Co. Meath.

Beasley

Beasly

The name of an English family found settled in Ireland from no later than the 17th century.

Beasty

A name found in Co. Mayo in our records.

Beatty

Beattie, Beaty, Betagh, Batey

Beatty families are traditionally found in the province of Ulster. They are assumed to be of Scottish heritage there. A fairly common name, some are said to have originally been of the "Batey" family of Scotland. Others may stem from the older family name of Betagh.

Spelled as Beattie, the name is centered in Antrim and Down. Spelled as Beatty the name is found in Dublin, Armagh and Tyrone in the 1890 birth index.

O'Beci

Beck

According to "Keatings History":

"O'Beci, chief of the fair land, Rules over Bantry of delightful bloom; Heroes, whose noble actions I certify. They are of the race of Fergus of Ulster."

Families of the name of Beck are found in the Antrim and Down in the 1800's.

18

Bowen

Irish Book of Arms plate 35

The Bowen families of Hollymount, Co. Mayo and of Bown's Court Co. Cork are found in the Irish Book of Arms. The main location for the family in the 19th century was in Co. Cork.

Beecher

Becher

The name of an English family found settled in Co. Cork for some time.

Begg

Beg, Beggs, Bigg, Bigge, Begge, Big,

Families of the name of Begg are found in Roscommon and Antrim, those of the spelling of Begge are found in Co. Westmeath, and those of the name of Beggs are found in Co. Antrim in the census of 1659 in Ireland. No doubt these names have been interchanged with each other over time.

In Ulster some of the name descend from English families of the name, often spelled as Bigge in England. Others are thought to be of old Irish extraction, where the name may have sprung from the old gaelic word of "beg" meaning small.

Similar sounding names may at times serve as shortened forms of the names given above. For example "Big" of counties Tipperary and Clare, and Biggins of Mayo may have at times been used interchangeably with Begg, Beggs etc..

In the 19th century the spelling of Beggan was found mainly in Monaghan, and the name of Begg was most numerous in Antrim and Dublin.

Boyd

Irish Book of Arms plate 71

Boid

A name most often found in the province of Ulster in Ireland, and assumed to be of Scottish origins when found there. Both "Boyd" and "O'Boyd" were given as principal names of Co. Antrim in the census of 1659. Boyd was found as well in Monaghan and Dublin City at that time.

The spelling of "Boyde" (it is common in earlier days to find an "e" on the end of many names), was given as a principal name of Co. Down in 1659. In more modern times the name is found as given above and in Antrim, Donegal and Londonderry.

The Irish Book of Arms gives the family of Boyd-Rochfort of Middleton Park, Co. Westmeath.

O Begley

Irish Book of Arms plate 253

O Beaglaoich

Bagley, Bigly, O Begley

One family of this distinguished name in Ireland is given anciently in Co. Donegal, in the north of Ireland. In the barony of Kilmacrennan one can find the parish of Tulloghobegley there, as testimony to their early occupation.

The name is also found in Counties Cork and Kerry. In Kerry they are said to have arrived as gallowglass in the 15th century, coming from a branch of the Donegal family.

The name appears to have been centered in Co. Kerry and Donegal a century ago, at which time 'Begley' was the preferred spelling of the name

Arms for families of the name are found in the Irish Book of Arms.

Behan

The name is traditionally linked to counties Dublin, Kildare and Kerry.

Boylan

Irish Book of Arms plate 145

O Baoigheallain

Boyland, Boreland, Bullion

The ancient territory of Oriel marks the Boylan territory in Ireland. The families center of power is to be found in the barony of Dartry, in Co. Monaghan.

Of the same descent as the O'Flanagans of Fermanagh, the are found in O'Dugans 14th century poems as "the Bold Kings of Dartry". This same work gives the family skillful horsemanship and blue eyes.

This family spread from Monaghan into Fermanagh and Armagh, and were found in Louth, Cavan and Meath too.

Their reign of power was broken by the MacMahons, but the family held sway in the barony of Dartry, in Monaghan, their old center.

As with the name of Boland, Boylan is found in modern times without the 'O' prefix, and this may result in some confusion between the two names.

In the 17th century the Boylan name is found in Dublin, Kildare, Louth and Drogheda and Meath in the census of 1659. When spelled as O'Boylan, the name was a principal one of Monaghan.

Belfore, Belfour

Balfour, Balf, Belfour

Found as a principal name of Co. Fermanagh in the census of 1659, under both the spellings of Belfore, and Belfour. The spelling of Balfore is found in Co. Antrim, where the name was most numerous in the 19th century.

Bellingham

de Bellingham

One noted English family of the name was of Castle Ballingham in Co. Louth.

O Boyle

Irish Book of Arms plate 36, 122, 146

O Baoighill

Boal, Boil, Boyl, Bole, Bog

Boyle accounts for one of the 50 most popular surnames of Ireland. Three separate families of the name exist, Irish, English and Scots.

First, a native gaelic family was centered in Co. Donegal. This O'Boyle family was centered in Cloghineely, and was noted for a ruddy complexion. They have always been associated with that part of Ireland. There was also note of a Boyle family near Dysart, in Co. Armagh, who are said to have originally come from the barony of Boylagh in Donegal. They are also found in Derry.

Scottish settlers arrived with the 17th century plantation of Ulster in Ireland and settled in and around Limavady, in Co. Derry. They are said to have come from Renfrewshire in Scotland.

The families dealt with above are in the old province of Ulster, in the north of Ireland. In the south, Richard Boyle, arrived from England in 1588. He became the Earl of Cork and obtained lands in Cork and Waterford, including the properties of Sir Walter Raleigh. He is said to have became the first colonial millionaire. He was involved with the city of Bandon, and ousted the Mahonys and Donovans etc.. from their positions of power in that area.

While most dropped the 'O' from the name a century ago, O'Boyle was still the most prominent spelling in County Mayo at that time. (5 O'Boyles were born in Antrim at that time too.) 'Boyle' was then centered in Donegal, Antrim and Mayo.

About two centuries earlier, O'Boyle was found in Antrim, Donegal and Monaghan etc..and Boyle in Monaghan, Tipperary and the capital...

One family of the name is found in estate papers in the National Library.

Boyne

Irish Book of Arms plate 11

Boyn

In the 19th century birth index we find the Boyne family centered in Co. Dublin in Ireland. The family name can be found in several locations in Ireland. We find the family of O'Boynes in Co. Armagh in the 17th century, and at that time McBoyheen is found in Leitrim and O'Boyhan is found in Co. Westmeath. These no doubt represent more than one original family.

Bell

Bell is a family most often found in the province of Ulster, and of likely Scottish origins there, as the name is one of the 50 most numerous in Scotland itself. "Bell" was given as a principal name of Co. Antrim in 1659, and subsequently found in Antrim, Down, Tyrone, Armagh and Dublin.

Belton

de Weldon

Weldon, de Weldon, Weldun

'de Weldon' was the original spelling of this name for many in. This name was of Anglo-Norman origins. The name is as well, a name of English settlers in Ireland.

A century ago, 12 births of the name are found, mainly in counties Longford and Louth.

Bennett

Irish Book of Arms plate 266

One noted family of the name was from Banffshire, Scotland, one member of which went on to found the "New York Herald" Newspaper in America.

In 1890 the family is found in Cork, Dublin, Antrim, Armagh and Down.

Brabazon

Irish Book of Arms plate 2

According to "Keatings History" the name is that of a principal family of Dublin city or county, and of Anglo-Norman descent.

One noted family of the name is found in Ballinasloe, Co. Roscommon in the early 17th century.

O'Berga

According to "Keatings History" the name is that of a family who served as chiefs of Tuath Rossa, in Co. Limerick. It was said that "O'Berga of fair country held, The districts of Ui Rossa, a rich portion."

O'Bergin

Bergen, Bergin

Older references to this family are found in Leix (Queens Co.), and Tipperary, and the family is subsequently found centered in the barony of Geeshill, Co. Offaly. The census of 1659 finds the name a principal one of Co. Kilkenny, spelled at that time as Bergin, and found at that time in Queens Co. as well.

20

Mac Brady

Irish Book of Arms plate 67, 146, 226

Mac Bradaigh

Briody, Bradey, Mac Bradey

The powerful and respected Brady family is traditionally linked with the old territory of Breffni in Ireland. Here they were centered near the town of Cavan, in Co. Cavan. This is in the barony of Loughter Upper. Many are documented in the Annals of the Four Masters. In older works we find that some have said this family stemmed from a branch of the O'Carrolls of Calry, in Co. Leitrim.

In Co. Clare, some by the name of Grady have changed their names to Brady. This was done centuries ago. The main branch of this family was in Kiballyowen, in Co. Limerick, where the name was changed to Brady as well, but later it was changed back to Grady for the most part in Limerick. Local residents have told us that the name was changed to Brady by those who sided with the British cause of the day.

In the 17th century it is interesting to note that in the census of 1659 Brady was a principal name of Longford, and that O'Brady is found in Fermanagh at this time. Mac Brady, of course, would be the more proper spelling, but often the wrong prefix was added back onto an Irish name, after having been abandoned of its 'correct' prefix earlier. The Brady name was also given in Louth, Meath, Westmeath and Leitrim at that time.

Brady ranks among the top 100 most numerous surnames in all of Ireland. With over 200 births shown in the 1890 index, Co. Cavan leads the list for the name, with Dublin, Antrim, Meath and Longford also given as locations with many of the name.

Arms for members of the Brady family can be found on plates 67, 146, and 226 of the Irish Book of Arms.

Brasier

Irish Book of Arms plate 26

Brazier, Brazer

The Brasier family of Ballyellis, Co. Cork, is earlier found in Co. Londonderry when the family obtained extensive grants of land. The same family is also found in Co. Donegal at the earlier date.

Best

Bestwill

Families of the name of Best are found to have arrived in Ireland, coming from England, no later than the 17th century. Families of the name are found at that time in Dublin, Kilkenny and Cork in Ireland. Several of the name are found as landowners in Kilkenny and Carlow. Curiously the family name is not often found in or near the province of Ulster, where, by the end of the 19th century, the name is found most numerous in counties Antrim and Tyrone.

Note the name also of "Bestwill" found in Co. Westmeath in the 17th century. It could also survive in the form of Best in today's families.

Beston

Best

The name of an English family found settled in Co. Limerick from at least the 16th century.

Betagh

According to "Keatings History" the name is one of a family of note in Meath. They are found to be of Norman descent here, and centered in the area of Moynalty.

Bethel

Bethel is given to be a Palatine family found settled in Co. Limerick. In Ulster and elsewhere we find the name to be of Welsh extraction.

O Brennan

Irish Book of Arms plate 146, 224

O'Braonain, MacBranain

Brennan, Brannan, Briane, Brenon,

Brennon families represent one of the 30 most numerous families in all of Ireland in modern times. The name may stem from either MacBrennon or O'Brennon, and since the 'O' and 'Mac' prefix has generally been discarded it is difficult to determine which origin is correct without some research. To further complicate matters, several unrelated families of O'Brennan existed in more ancient times.

Perhaps the best known of the name hails from the old geographical division of Ossory, in modern Kilkenny. Here they were known as chiefs of Ui Duach (Idough), in the north of the county, roughly within the old barony of Fassadinin and Idough in earlier times.

Other families are found of the name of O'Brennan. In the 17th century we find O'Brenane as a principal name in Co. Kerry, and O'Brenan as a principal name of Co. Carlow.

Mac Branain, or Mac Brennon, of Co. Roscommon, served as chief of Corcachlann, and in this county we find as well the spelling of O'Brenan in the Roscommon and Athlone district. The name of 'Brennan' was a principal one of County Roscommon in 1659 also. It is thought that the O and Mac prefix before the name has been interchanged here, and that most of the name of this family are more properly 'Mac Brennon.'

Of variant spellings it should also be mentioned that 'Brenane' was found in Tipperary and Brenon was a principal name of Kilkenny in 1659.

One century ago the name was fairly widespread as one might expect, with Kilkenny, Dublin, Sligo and Mayo heading the list of counties with most of the name.

21

O Brien

Irish Book of Arms plates 29, 30, 146

O'Briain, Mac Ui Bhrian

O'Bryan, O'Brian, O'Brein,

One of the most outstanding of all the great families of Ireland, most O'Briens can trace their descent back to the 10th century when the great high king, Brian Boru, came to prominence. It is he from whom the name is taken.

During this time, the family maintained a fierce struggle for their independence with the Anglo-Norman invaders. They succeeded in holding their freedom as chiefs of the Thomand and Limerick territory until the year 1543, when they accepted the English title of 'Earl of Thomand.', rejecting their gaelic titles. (Thus investing their title with the English crown.)

This Thomand name can be found in several branches subsequently. O'Briain, or O'Brien held extensive territory along the Cummeragh mountains, including the lands between Dungarvan and the river Suir. Another family of the name were the Mac I Briens, a branch of the O'Briens of Thomand, who had large possessions in the barony of Owney and Arra, in Tipperary and in the barony of Coonagh in Co. Limerick. They were styled Mac-I-Briens, lords of Arra and Coonagh, and several of them are given in older records.

In Co. Limerick, the barony of Pubblebrien stands in their honor.

One of the most popular names in all of Ireland, it is to be found widespread throughout the entire country today. A century ago most of the 'O'Briens' were found in Cavan and Galway, and the 'Briens' in Cork, Tipperary, Wexford and Waterford. This is of course, aside from the natural numerous counts of the name in the nations capitol of Dublin.

The name remains strong in and near its original territories in Co. Clare.

Brinkley

The Irish Book of Arms plate 79

Brinkly

The Brinkley family of Fortland, Co. Sligo, is given in the Book of Arms.

Biggar

Bigger, Bickerstaff, Biger

Most of the name of Biggar etc.. in Ireland are of Scottish origins, settling in Ulster no later than the 16th century. The name, under various spellings is found in Armagh quite often. The birth index of 1890 finds the "Bigger" family in Kilkenny. The sometimes related name of Bickerstaff is found in Down and Antrim at that time. In 1659 we find the family name centered in Co. Antrim and Londonderry as Bickerstaff.

The family is also centered in Down in early records, where the name serves as a synonym for the Irish MacGivern.

O Biggins

O Biggane, O Beagain, O Bigin

Beggane, Biggins

The name of O'Biggins, which was also translated as Beggane in Ulster and Biggins in Mayo, is believed to have come from the word 'beag', meaning small or little. Therefore the name can be found translated as Little and Littleton as well, and it is found as such in the province of Munster.

A century ago 'Biggins' was found in Co. Mayo with 6 births total, and Beggane, is given in Monaghan, with a total of 7 births of the name in all.

De Bigods

"Keatings History" gives the name as that of an ancient titled family in Co. Carlow, found alongside the Mowbrays, Howards and Butlers etc..

O Broder(ick)

Irish Book of Arms plates 146, 201,..

O Broder, Mac Bruadair

Brodders, Brooder, Brothers, Bradner,

The old and respected name of (O) Broder in Ireland has several separate and distinct origins here. In Co. Cork the O'Broders are found in the barony of Barrymore. A presumably separate family of the name is located in Co. Galway. Here note the place names of Ballybroder commemorating the family name, in the parishes of Kilmeen and Loughrea.

A century ago the name was most often found in the counties of Kerry and Limerick, some of whom doubtlessly came from Co. Cork.

Although the name of 'Bruadar' is also a Scandinavian one, and many claim Norse origins for the name, it has been on record in Ireland centuries before the Anglo-Norman invasions.

Many Broders are also found using the name of Broderick in formal situations, and reverting to the name of Broder among family and friends. Broderick is of course, a common English name and hence was translated from the Irish name of Broder, as a convenience.

The Brodericks may have Welsh origins as well, coming from the name of 'Ap-Roderick'. One was of definite English extraction though. Sir Alan Broderick, the Surveyor General of Ireland in the 17th century.

Arms for families of the name can be found in the Irish Book of Arms plates 201 and 146.

Binchy

Binchey, Benchy

The name of an English family found settled in Co. Cork in the 17th century.

22

Browne

Irish Book of Arms plates 52, 112, 137...

Brunach, le Brun

Broune, Brown

Brown(e) families comprise one of the 10 most numerous names in Scotland and England, and one of the 50 most numerous names in Ireland. Often a name of English or Scottish origins when found in Ireland, the final 'e' in the name appears common in Ireland.

One of the noted 'Tribes of Galway', this family was of Anglo-Norman descent, coming from the name of le Brun. They are still of note to this day.

In the north of Ireland, in the province of Ulster, many Brownes are of Scottish settler origin. They were among the Ulster Scots settlers in the 17th century.

The Brownes of 'Killarney' who settled in Co. Kerry under Elizabeth the First, are of English heritage and have remained on or near their territory into modern times. We also find the name early in Co. Limerick, near Camus.

In Co. Mayo we find the name centered near Breaghwy, and in the barony of Kilmaine, in this county the first High Sheriff was John Browne, from his line descend Barons and Earls of the name.

In the 17th century we find 'Browne' more often in the north of Ireland and 'Brown' in Co. Cork, in the census of 1659. Roughly the same pattern can be found a century ago. 'Brown' was found at that time mostly in Cork, Mayo, Wexford and Dublin and 'Browne' mostly in Ulster and the capital.

Estate papers in the National Library in Dublin, relate to Browne families.

Several families of the name are found in the Irish Book of Arms. These include the Brownes of Riverstown, Co. Cork, Of Breaghwy, Co. Mayo, of Brownestown, Co. Mayo, and of New Grove, Co. Clare. The pedigrees of several of the name in Wexford, London, Ireland, and Galway are given by O'Hart.

Bruce

The Irish Book of Arms plate 106

De Bruys

The Bruce family of Benburb, Co. Tyrone, descend from Thomas De Bruys of Clackmannan ss given in the Irish Book of Arms.

O'Billry

Bill, Billery

According to "Keatings History" the name is that of a chief in Ui Conaill Gabhra, now the baronies of Upper and Lower Connello, in Co. Limerick. O'Heerin spoke of them thusly;

"O'Billry, bestower of cattle,
Was chief of fertile Conall Gaura,
Bounteous men of the fair plains,
Rich lands of teeming crops"

The name of Bill, which could serve as a shortened form of the name, is found mainly in Co. Anrim, where 4 births of the name are found in 1890.

Bindon

Note the place name of Bindon Street in Ennis Co. Clare. Traditionally linked with Clare and Limerick in older records, the family is also found early in Tipperary. Individuals of the name served as Mayor of Limerick and Sheriff of Clare. One family of the name came to possess Clooney, in Co. Clare for several generations.

Birrell

Birel, Berrill

The name of an old family of Co. Louth, assumed to be of English extraction.

Bissett

According to "Keatings History" the name is given among the chief Anglo-Norman and English settlers in Ulidia, under DeCourcey and his successors.

Bryan

Irish Book of Arms plate 103

The Bryan family is most often associated with Co. Kilkenny in Ireland. Much confusion exists as to the spelling, for it is easily confused with Brien, O'Brian etc...

The census of 1659 gives the spellings of McBryan, O'Bryan and MacBryan. The name, under these spellings and without the prefix was quite widespread at that time. Several unrelated families are represented in that "census" under these spellings.

Spelled simply as Bryan, the name was a principal name of Antrim at that time. Spelled as O'Bryan the name was a principal one of Fermanagh, and as MacBryan a principal name of Longford.

Although these spellings may serve some purpose when searching older records, they are often of little use today, for the name has been changed and distorted so much. (see O'Brian).

By the time of the 1890 birth index of Ireland the name was dispersed in several counties, with Dublin and Kilkenny heading the list. Under the spelling of "Bryans" the name was found in Antrim and Down at that time.

The Bryan family of Upton and Borrmount Manor, Co. Wexford are given in the Irish Book of Arms.

Blackhall

Blackall

The name of a settler family, who likely arrived here from England, found in Limerick in the 17th century and in Dublin and Clare subsequently. At least one family of the name is found in Ulster at the above date as well.

Buckley

Irish Book of Arms, plate 9 (Bulkeley)

O'Buachalla

O'Buhilly, Boughla, Bohelly, Buckeley,

Buckley is one of the top 100 most numerous names in all of Ireland. It is as well a common English name, from which some of the name in Ireland have sprung. O'Hart gives the name as arriving with the 12th century Norman invasions.

As for the Irish of the name, O'Buachalla was a name of County Offaly (Kings) under several different spellings. One center for the name has been given as near Lemanaghan in that county.

In the 17th century we find the family name in Queens Co. (Leix) as Buckly, in Dublin as Buckley, and in Louth and Drogheda as Bulkely. One century ago the name was most often found in Cork and Kerry, being followed by Dublin and Tipperary as well.

O'Hart gives the Buckleys as viscounts of Cashel, and as among the modern nobility (19th century) of Tipperary and Waterford.

'Buckely' ranks as one of the more numerous names in America, being among the top 700 names in that country.

Arms for the family of Bulkeley are found in the Irish Book of Arms plate 9. One noted Bulkeley family in France is said to be of English origins. (see Bulkeley).

Blackney

Blakeney, Blakney

According to "Keatings History of Ireland" the name is that of one of the chief old English families which settled in Co. Carlow.

24

Bulkeley

Irish Book of Arms plate 9

Buckley

One family of the Bulkeley name can be traced back to William Bulkeley, Archdeacon of Dublin.

Blackwell

Families of the name of Blackwell are found in counties Clare, Dublin, Cork, and in Dublin city in the census of 1659. The family is on record in Co. Clare for several centuries and the name is also found in Co. Tipperary at an early date. In Tipperary, several of the name are found as landowners in the barony of Ikerron during the Cromwellian settlement.

Blackwood

According to "Keatings History" the name is given as of the family who became barons of Dufferin, and they were among the chief families of Ulidia at an early date. The main location for the name in the 19th century was in Co. Antrim.

Blair

Blare, Blaire

Blair is a family name most often found in the province of Ulster, and centered in Co. Antrim where it was a principal name in the 17th century. In more modern times the name is also found in Londonderry and Tyrone.

Blanchfield

de Blancheville, Blanchvill, Blanch

de Blancheville, is given as a variant spelling of Blanchfield in Co. Kilkenny. Subsequently found in Kilkenny in 1659, listed as Blanchvill, it is also found in Co. Tipperary then. This name could be shortened simply to Blanch, a spelling is found in Co. Waterford then.

Bunbury

Irish Book of Arms plate 40

Bunberry

The Bunbury family of Cranavonane, Co. Carlow is found in the Irish Book of Arms. They were from Stanney, Co. Chester, and so of foreign origins.

Bleahan

Bleehan

Bleeheen, Bleheen, Blehein, Bleheine

Spelled as Bleheine and as Blehein this family is found in Co. Galway, where the names of Melvin and Melville have been used in place of Bleahan etc...

Bluett

Bluet

Bluet, Blewitt

The name of a family we find in counties Cork and Limerick for several centuries. The name is likely of original French extraction.

Blundel

Blundell

According to "Keatings History" the name is given as among the principal English and Welsh families settling in the town of Galway and other parts of the country in the twelfth and thirteenth centuries.

Blunden

Blundon

A family we find mention of in Co. Kilkenny, settled there no later than the 17th century, and of foreign extraction.

Bollard

Bullard

The name of a family, often found in Dublin, of whom several were noted as merchants. In Ireland no later than the 17th century.

Burdett

The Irish Book of Arms plate 53

The Burdett family of Ballymany, Co. Kildare, and of Coolfin in Kings Co., are of the same line and are given in the Irish Book of Arms.

Boale

Boal, Bole, Boyle, Bowles, Boles

The family has traditionally been associated with the province of Ulster in Ireland and may stem from several different sources. Some of the name may actually be more properly named Boyle or O'Boyle, and their name has been badly translated as Boale, Boal, Bole, etc.. Others of the name descend from English settlers of the name of Bowle or Bole etc..

Those of the name spelled as Boal in the 19th century are found centered in Antrim and Down. "Boale" was given as a principal name of Co. Antrim in the 17th century. The spelling of Boles, had only 7 recorded scattered births in 1890. The spelling of Bowles however, we find in Co. Cork in the 17th century "census".

Today, of course, these names have been used interchangeably, particularly so for those who settled abroad in the centuries past.

Bogan

Boggan, Boggin, Bogan, Boghan,

In the census of 1659 Boghan was given as a principal name of Co. Kildare in Ireland, which may bear some reference to the families below. In the 19th century birth index Bogan families are found centered in Co. Wexford. The family name has been traditionally linked to Co. Donegal and with Co. Wexford in the past.

The use of the name of O'Bogan has been officially reported in the last century.

Burgess

Irish Book of Arms plate 49

Burges

The Burges family of Parkanaur, Co. Tyrone is found in Co. Dublin in the late 17th century. The 1890 birth index finds the family most numerous in Co. Dublin, under the spelling of Burgess.

Boden, Bowden

O'Boden, Boden, Bowden, Boudon,

The names of Boden, O'Boden and Bowden etc.. are found early in counties Kilkenny and Kildare in Ireland. This family name, without the "O" prefix of course, is generally assumed to be the name of families settling in Ireland from England.

The most popular spelling of the name in our records is as Bowden, and eight births of the name were recorded in the 1890 index, in scattered locations. Of the various spellings of the name, "Bothwell" and "Baldwin" have been officially reported as a synonym of Boden.

Note the place name of Bodenstown in Co. Kildare, and Ballyboden which are two of several place names linked to the family in older records.

Some of the name may actually be from "O'Buadain" or O'Boden, more anciently from Co. Kilkenny.

Two names could have been shortened to Boden as well, those of Boding and Bodington, both of which are found in Co. Louth in the census of 1659.

Burke

Irish Book of Arms plates136, 139...

de Burgo

Burgh, de Burgh, Bourke, Burk

One of the 20 most numerous names in Ireland, Burke was one of the most common names arriving in Ireland as a result of the 12th century invasions.

The earliest and most noted of the Burke/Bourke families in Ireland descend from William de Burgo who took the place of Strongbow as chief governor of Ireland. He is often referred to as 'William the Conqueror' by writers.

By the year 1179 large portions of land were granted the 'de Burgos' or Burkes in the province of Connacht. They became 'more Irish than the Irish themselves' adopting the Irish way of life. They had chiefs styled in the Irish fashion and observed the ways of Brehon law.

The original spelling of de Burgo was replaced by Burgh, Burke, Bourke etc.. but the older form of de Burgo remained for several centuries in Irish records. In the 17th century 'Burk' was a principal name of Kings Co., 'Burke' was found in Galway, Cork and Dublin, the spelling of 'Bourk' was a principal name in Limerick, and Bourke was such in Clare at the time of the 1659 census.

The Burkes and the O'Flaherties were said to be two of the families most feared by the tribes of Galway city. Great troubles existed between the two families however. Grace O'Malley (Grania, the pirate queen), was the widow of O'Flaherty, and then married Richard Burke. The son of that union later fought with the English at the battle of Kinsale. In the 16th century Richard de Burgo drove the O'Flaherties from their lands in Connacht as a result of the confiscations of the day.

Galway, Cork and Dublin were centers for the name for centuries. A century ago the spelling of 'Bourke' was centered in Tipperary, Limerick and Mayo.

25

Burns, Beirne

Irish Book of Arms plate 147 O'Byrne

O'Broin, Birrane

Byrnes, O'Byrne, Burns, O'Beirnes,

The names of Burn(s), Byrne(s), Beirne, etc.. represent several different families. Many of the same family will spell their names differently, so it is difficult to depend on spelling for assistance. Due to similarity in sound and spelling these names have been used interchangeably from time to time.

Burns, a common Scottish name, arrived in Ireland with the plantations of Ulster centuries ago. When found outside of Ulster, it may be of separate origins entirely, regardless of spelling. In the province of Connaught the name may be a translation of MacConboirne.

The spellings of "Byrne" and O'Byrne account for one of the top 10 names in Ireland. Originally of Co. Kildare, they were forced into Wicklow, being centered in Ballinacor. Today the name is numerous there, and in Dublin. The original "O" before the name was generally dropped. This family held lands within the pale in Ireland, and fought constantly against the "invaders".

The name of "Beirne" or Biernes, represents a separate family. They are of the province of Connaught, early of Roscommon and Mayo, and later in Leitrim. Roscommon and Leitrim held most of this name in 1890. They are found seated near Ballinrobe in Co. Mayo, and are on record as subduing the the Monaghans of Co. Roscommon.

The following are locations for spellings of the name documented in the last century. Burns and Byrnes were found in Banbridge Union, Loughbrickland district. Burn, in Ballymahon Union, Ballylesson District. Beirne, in Strokestown Union, Roosky District. Bierne, in Roscommon Union, Roscommon Dist..(see O'Byrne)

26

Burrowes

The Irish Book of Arms plate 97

Borrowes, Burrows, Borowes

The Burrowes family of Stradone House, Co. Cavan descend from Robert Borowes who settled in Ireland at Dumlane, Co. Cavan at the time of the settlement of Ulster by King James I. The 1890 birth index finds the family most numerous in Co. Down.

Bodkin

Irish Book of Arms plate 266

Bodken, Budkin, Baudkin, Boudakyn,

The family of Bodkin is found in Ireland descending from Maurice Fitzgerald, from whom also sprang the Earls of Desmond and Kildare. Thomas Fitzgerald, gr. grandson of Maurice, is accredited with the origination of the name of Bodkin here. It is said that his use of the spear or 'baudekin' in battle led him to victory, and hence the name came into being.

For others of the name its origin has been given to mean 'little baud', a form of Baldwin said to mean 'bold friend'.

According to "Keatings History" the name is given as among the principal English and Welsh families settling in the town of Galway and other parts of the country in the twelfth and thirteenth centuries.

One of the renowned 14 tribes of Galway, they received large portions of land there in 1242. They are found prominent in the area, furnishing Bishops, army officers and doctors.

O'Hart gives Thomas Bodkin, M.D. of Tuam, Co. Galway.

In the census of 1659 the family is found in Co. Clare.

Burtchaell

Irish Book of Arms plate 25

Burtchael

The Burtchaell family of Brandondale, Co. Kilkenny, was founded by Michael Burtchaell of Burgagemore, Co. Wicklow in the 17th century, and that family is found in the Irish Book of Arms.

Bonar

Boner, Bonnaire, Bonner, Crampsey,

Bonar, Boner, etc. is often found in the Province of Ulster in the north of Ireland, particularly in Donegal. Bonner is another spelling of the name there.

In the 1890's the name is given in Inishowen Union, in Co. Donegal, spelled as Boner. This name has also been used as a synonym for Crampsey.

Another origin for the name is in Co. Limerick. Here the name is said to be of Palatine origins, coming originally from the word 'bonnaire', French for polite or courteous.

Bolger

Irish Book of Arms plate 253

O'Bolger

The Bolger family name is found as a principal one of Co. Carlow and also found in Kildare, Kilkenny and Wexford in the census of 1659. The 1890 birth index find the name in the same area, i.e. Wexford, Kildare etc..

It is often found centered along the Carlow, Kilkenny and Wexford borders in Ireland. At least two sources cite the name as O'Bolger most anciently.

Bogue

Bogue, Bogues, Buoige, O'Buoige

The family name of Bogue is found in the 19th century birth index centered in Co. Fermanagh. In earlier days the name is found mainly in Co. Cork in our records, including the 1659 census.

Burton

The Irish Book of Arms plate 72

The Burton family of Burton Hall, Co. Carlow, descend from Sir Edward Burton, Knt. of Longner who served under King Edward IV. The 1890 birth index finds the family most numerous in Dublin and Antrim.

Bonass

Bonas

The name of an English family found sometimes in Ireland.

Bolster

The name of an English family found settled in Co. Cork.

Bonfield

Bonnfield, Bonefield, de Bonneville

The name of a family we find in counties Clare and Limerick, whose name may be taken from the older form of de Bonneville. Given to be an Anglo-Norman family.

Bor

One family of the name is found in Co. Wicklow in the early 17th century, said by O'Hart to have originally come from Utrecht, Holland.

Bourchier

Boucher

One noted English family of the name of Bourchier is found in Baggotstown and Kilcullane in Co. Limerick in the 17th century.

The name of Boucher is found with only 9 recorded births in 1890.

Bury

Irish Book of Arms plate 79

Burye, de Bury, Beery, Beary

Families of the name of Bury and Burye are found in the census of 1659 in Co. Kildare. One family of the name is found in Limerick near that time. Other reports find the name in Co. Cork at an early date as well.

In more modern times the family name is found in counties Antrim, Mayo and Offaly. Most of the name are believed to have been descended from Norman settlers of the name, sometimes found as de Bury, etc... Due to similarity in sound, some of the name are also said to have used the names of Barry and Berry interchangeably with Bury.

The Bury family of Charleville Forest, Kings county, is given in the Irish Book of Arms. The Bury family of Little Island, Co. Cork, and of Curraghbridge, Co. Limerick descend from one John Bury of Shannon Grove, Co. Limerick.

Bohane

Bohan

The census of 1659 finds the name of Bohane as a principal one of Co.Leitrim, while that spelling was found concentrated only in Co. Cork in the 1890 birth index.

The spelling of "Bohan" is most often found to indicate the location of the name in counties Leitrim and Galway.

Bowler

Boler

The Bowler family name traditionally is linked with Co. Kerry in Ireland. Note the townlands of Ballybowler North and South in the barony of Corkaguiney in that county. Bowler was a principal name of Co. Kerry in the census of 1659, and in 1890.

Bushe

Irish Book of Arms plate 37

A Huguenot family of Ireland as given by some sources. The Bushe family of Glencairn Abbey, Co. Waterford is found in the Irish Book of Arms.

Bowdran

Bowdern, Bowdren, Bowdran, Budran,

The family name of Bowdran or Bowdern etc.. was a principal one of the county of Waterford in the 17th century. The spelling of the name in that record was as Bowdran.

The family name is found in Co. Waterford and parts of Co. Cork for several centuries. The spelling of Boudron or Boudran is a much older one, predating the above Bowdran families by several centuries. It likely represents an originally separate name entirely.

Bowe, Bowes

Bowe, Boe, Buo, O'Bowe, O'Bough, Bowes

The Bowe family is found early in Co. Kilkenny, and subsequently in Co. Waterford, where the name has been said to come from the gaelic name of O'Buadhaigh.

Both "Bowe" and "O'Bowe" are found as principal names of Queens Co. (Leix) in the census of 1659. In more modern times the name was more often found in Kilkenny, in the 1890 birth index.

Spelled as O'Boe we find the name as a principal one of Kilkenny and in Wexford in the 17th century. The spelling of Boe is found as a principal name of Tipperary, as well as being found in Kilkenny.

The sometimes unrelated name of Bowes is found located mainly in Co. Dublin in the 19th century.

27

Butler

Irish Book of Arms plates 109......

le Botiler, Fitzwalter

Buttler

One Butler family descends from 'Theobald Fitzwalter' who arrived in Ireland in 1177 with Henry the II. He was appointed Chief Butler of Ireland in 1177. His younger brother, Thomas, came with Prince John of England to Waterford in 1185. This family is referred to as the 'Ormond Butler' family.

Theobald's son, Theobald, assumed the name of le Botiler. His descendants then took the name of Butler.

This family built many castles and Abbeys. They are found in the baronies of Ormond Upper and Lower in Tipperary, and at Kilkenny Castle in Co. Kilkenny. In 1391 the center for these Ormond Butlers had moved from Gowran to Kilkenny Castle, which remained a center into the 20th century.

The noted 'Ormond Manuscripts' were given to the National Library of Dublin, and they contain much family data.

The Ormond Butlers and the Geraldines (the Fitzgeralds), held power over the country for some time. Great feuds existed between these two families.

MacRichard was the name which a branch of the family used, and from which descend the Earls of Ormond.

"The Butlers of Co. Clare" by Sir H. Butler Blackall, is a source on the family in Co. Clare. In modern times the 'Butler' society in Kilkenny, brings members of the family together worldwide.

A century ago the name was most common in Dublin, Kilkenny, Tipperary and Waterford in Ireland.

The Butler family of Priestown, Co. Meath, and of Altameenagh, Laghey, Co. Donegal are given to be of the same line. They descend from a Prebendary of Killanully, Co. Cork, in 1672, and subsequently a Rector in Co. Kerry.

28

O'Byrne, Byrnes

Irish Book of Arms plate 147

O'BROIN

O'BYRNE, BURN, BIERNE, BYRON,

A name prominent throughout Irish history, the family is traditionally associated with the province of Leinster in Ireland. As the 7th most common name in all of Ireland, it can be difficult to trace the history of any one family. Several completely unrelated families now use the name in both Ireland and America.

Byrne is found listed in the census of 1659 as a principal name of Co. Carlow, as well as in counties Louth, Meath, Queens and Wexford.

O'Byrne is also found as a principal name of Co. Carlow in 1659. Both the spellings of "McByrne" and "O'Byrne" were used as late as in the last century, and of course, most of those families eventually simply shortened the name to "Byrne".

Originally found in Co. Kildare, the family was forced into Co. Wicklow and centered in Ballinacor there.

It is most likely that the name of Byrnes stems from the original name of Byrne or O'Byrne, as those are the most popular forms of the name. Byrnes is a unique spelling, in that it has the "s" at the end of the root name.

In the works of Matheson, "Byrnes" is given as a variant of Burns and Byrne. The specific location given for Byrnes, was in the registrars district of Loughbrickland, Bandbridge Union, in the 1890's. (see Burns)

Published materials:

"The O'Byrnes and their Descendants" published in Dublin in 1879.

"History of the Clan O'Byrne and other...septs", by Rev. P. L. O'Toole. published in Dublin in 1890.

Mac Cabe

Irish Book of Arms plates 147, 253

McCaba

Macabe, Mac Cabe, Mac Caba

The Mac Cabes came to Ireland as captains of the galloglass who served the O'Reillys and O'Rourkes. They came from the Hebrides islands off the coast of Scotland to Ireland in the 14th century. These galloglass were proud fighting men in Ireland, serving the needs of the Irish chieftains. As such, they served in Breffni ORourke and Breffni O'Reilly, referring to the early name applied to the lands of these chiefs.

McCabe was given the title of 'Constable of the two Breffnys', and it is in these areas where they are most plentiful today. By the time of the 17th century, Cavan , Monaghan and Fermanagh were homelands for the name.

The great fall of the family came in 1691 when their lands were confiscated as a result of the Battle of Augrim. Indeed, the whole order of the country had been reversed in that century.

In the 18th century 'Cahir McCabe' is listed as among the most eminent of bards, harpers and musical composers of Ireland.

Mac Cabe also ranks among the top 900 most common names in America. It has also been proposed by some that these MacCabes were actually a branch of the Scottish Mac Leods most anciently.

The American Protestant bishop who became known as 'Chaplain MacCabe' is of note in the civil war in America. This line hailed from Co. Tyrone.

A century ago the name was most common in Cavan, Monaghan and Dublin. Two centuries prior, it is found in Fermanagh, Monaghan and Louth.

O Cahill

Irish Book of Arms plates 147, 216, ...

O'Cathail, Mac Cathail

McCahil, McCall, Cahil, Cahill

Families of the O'Cahill name in Ireland spring from several origins, and have almost always dropped the 'O' prefix from the name.

Traditionally the name one of Galway and Clare. In ancient times one family was centered in Galway, near the Clare border, where the head of the family was 'Chief of Kinlea'. In the 17th century Cahill and O'Cahill are found as principal names in Clare, but this does not seem to be the case later. Cahill was also found in Tipperary and Longford in the 17th century.

In Keatings History one family of the name is found in Cork and Kerry, descending from the same line as the O'Connors of Kerry. The name is given as one of the chiefs of Finn-coradh, along with O'Flattery in Thomand (Clare ..). O'Heerin also makes note of a family of the name on the borders of Tipperary and Kilkenny who held sizable lands in Carlow and Wexford.

There is also the possibility that some of the name stem from MacCahill. This name has been noted in the north of Ireland, particularly in Donegal and Cavan.

Mention of another family is found in Co. Kerry, in the barony of Magunihy, by Lough Leane.

One need only to look at the place names of Ireland to imagine the influence of the family. Two Ballycahills are found in Tipperary. Ballycahill is also found alongside Galway Bay in the barony of the burren, in Co. Clare, and in Co. Galway in the barony of Longford.

At the turn of the century the name was most popular in Cork, Kerry, Dublin and Kilkenny.

29

O' Bracken

Braken

Both the names of Brackane and Bracken were found as principal names of Kings Co. (Offaly) in the census of 1659. The name is given in that county and in Dublin in subsequent records. The name stems from O'Breacain when of possible old Irish origins, and is found centered in Tullamore, Co. Offaly in more modern times as well. The family is found as well in Kildare, near the Offaly border.

Bradshaw

Bradshaw is assumed to be a name of English origins when found in Ireland, and is found settled here from the 17th century. The name is found in Dublin city and Fermanagh in the census of 1659, and in Antrim, Tipperary and Dublin in the 1890 birth index.

Arms not Pictured

Arms given as on plates 200 and above in the Irish Book of Arms are not shown here. They are considered to be of unproven or false origins. For those interested, please consult the Irish Book of Arms for full illustration of those arms.

Furthermore, in the interest of enlightened education on the subject, some commercial operations are more than willing to sell you "illegitimate" items of any sort. Please do not accept items as being connected with your family name without some research.

Bradley

Irish Book of Arms plate 232

O Brallaghan

Bradly, O'Bradly, O'Brolchain, O'Bolchan

Bradley of course, a well known name of English origins, is found both of English and of native Irish extraction in Ireland. MacLysaght even claimed that the name was most often Irish when found here.

Of Irish origins, members of the O'Brallaghan family are said to have assumed the Bradley name at times. In counties Cork and Derry this is taken to be the case.

We quote from Keatings classic history, "The O'Brolchains, or O'Brolchans, a name sometimes changed to Bradly. These were a numerous clan near Derry, but originally of the Kinel Feradaigh, in the south of Tyrone, and were a branch of the Kinel Owen" They were located near Derry, and came originally from the south of Co. Tyrone.

It has been stated as well that County Cork is full of Irish Bradleys. The name is given a century ago as being most numerous there, and in Londonderry, Antrim, Tyrone and Donegal. Of course many are to be found in Dublin at that time too.

Some two centuries earlier we find Bradly in Roscommon and Athlone Burrough, in the census of 1659.

The Brologhans of the western highlands in Scotland, are of the same line as the Irish Brologhans of Co. Derry. Thus some of the name may have arrived from Scotland.

Adding some confusion for family researchers abroad, Bradley ranks among the top 200 most numerous names in America.

In O'Hart one 'Thomas Bradley,"M.D. is given as of Kellysgrange, in Co. Kilkenny.

Caldwell

Irish Book of Arms plate 85

Coldwell, Calwell, Colavin, Cawldwell,

A well known name of foreign origins in Ireland, some native Irish families have adopted the name as well. Of foreign origins the name may have come from Scotland or England.

In the 17th century the family is found in Co. Fermanagh, while only one century ago the name was found most often in Antrim, Londonderry and Tyrone.

Of the possible Irish origins of the name, 'Horish' and 'Hourisky' of Co. Tyrone have been changed to Caldwell on occasion, and in Cavan, Coolavan and Cullivan have reportedly done so as well.

The Irish Book of Arms gives Caldwell of New Grange, Co. Meath, and this family was of original Scottish heritage, and earlier settled in Dublin.

Mac Cadden

no arms found

Mac Cadain

MacCaddan, Cadden, Mac Adam, Macaddon

The name of Mac Cadden stems from a family of County Armagh, where the name has also been given as a synonym of McAdam on occasion.

The variant form of 'Cadden' formed by dropping off the Mac prefix, was found with only 6 scattered births a century ago.

The family has also been said to have Scottish origins settling in Donegal by some, but of this I know not.

In Keatings History of Ireland one 'O'Machoiden' is given as the chief of Mughdorn, or Mourne. This is as well in the north of Ireland, in the province of Ulster. Some have translated this name into MacCadden according to records.

30

Bray

O'Breaghda

O'Bree, de Bri, Di Bre, Bree

The Bray family is found in the wake of the Norman invasions, in Clonmel, with several prominent persons of the name there. This family name may have several origins in Ireland, however.

It may have been taken from O Breaghdha, an Irish family in the province of Munster, who are found in O'Heerins work. Still others may have come from 'de Bre', meaning 'of the place called Bre'. The 'de' prefix denotes the obvious foreign origins.

In the seventeenth century we find the name in Louth and Drogheda, and in Co. Leitrim in the 1659 census. One century ago the name is given in Counties Cavan and Dublin. The name is as well, on record in the Co. Tipperary Hearth Money Rolls, and in various records it is found in Cork also.

Keatings History cites the name as O'Bree, as the chief of the free Moy Sedna, of Irish origins.

Bowyer

Bowyr

The name of an English family most often found in the city of Dublin, and also in Co. Longford for several centuries.

O'Bregan

O'Breghain

According to Keatings History the family is given as chiefs in the barony of Imokilly, in Co. Cork. They were thus mentioned by O'Heerin:

"A valiant clan, warlike in pursuit, Ruled Imokilly of the hospitable banquets; Two tribes possessed the smooth plains, O'Bregan and the fair O'Glasin"

O Brazzil

O Breasail, MacBrassill

Brazil, Brassil, Brazel, Brassell, O'Bressyl

Now it should be known that the family name of O'Brazzil, etc.., has been traditionally associated with the counties of Waterford and Offaly (Kings) in Ireland. Spelled as Brassell the name is found as a principal one of Co. Waterford in the 17th century in the barony of Upperthird. It is as well found in Kings Co. at that time.

In more modern times 'Brazil' is found as being of Dublin and Wexford at the turn of the century. It has many apparent variant spellings of which are included MacBrassill, which hailed from Galway in more ancient times.

Mac Brearty

MacBrairty

Families of the name of Mac Breary are found centered in counties Tyrone and Donegal in the 19th century birth index and it is found most often in Co. Donegal in our records.

O'Bric

Irish Book of Arms plate 214

Brick, Brickley

According to "Keatings History" the name is given as the other head of the Decies, and of the same descent as O'Felan. The O'Brics were styled as Lords of South Desi, in the south of Co. Waterford, but in earlier times they were expelled from that land by the Eugenians of Desmond. They are spoken of thusly;

"O'Bric the exactor of tributes,
With him the wise and fair O'Felan....
In the south of woody Inis Fail,
O'Bric's fair lot along the waves,
From Lee Logha to Liathdrum".

The name of Brick belongs to a family of Co. Kerry, the main location for the name in the 19th century. The name of Brickley is found centered in Co. Cork at that time.

Breen

Irish Book of Arms plate 225

O Braoin, MacBraoin

Brien, Briene, OBraein, Brawne, Bruen

The 'Breen' family of Ireland is an old and respected one. The name may come originally from O'Breen or Mac Breen. MacBreen was anciently centered in the barony of Knocktopher, in Co. Kilkenny, within the more ancient territory of Ossory. In the wake of the 12th century Norman invasions the power of this family was broken by the Walsh family, hence they settled in Wexford, where the name was most popular a century ago.

Keatings History gives the family thusly: "Mac Breen, of the land of the fortress, Rules over the clans whom I remember". O'Hart gave Mac Breen as a chief in Kilkenny, and as present in Tyrone as well.

The O'Breens were centered in the barony of Brawney in Westmeath, where they were known as Lords of Brawney (Breaghmani) in earlier days. O'Hart gives the arms of this family as 'Or, a dexter hand couped at the wrist gu, on a chief of the last a mullett betw. two crescents or." He also gives Breen and Brawne as variant spellings of the original 'O'Braoin'. This family also held land in Offaly.

In the 17th century 'Breen' is found as a principal name of Queens County (Leix), and O'Breene is found as a principal name of Kerry, as well as being found in Wexford at that time.

A century ago the name was found most popular in Wexford, Dublin and Kerry

Mc Breheny

Breheney, Brehaney, McBrehuny, Brehony

Breheny is found in Roscommon and Sligo in the 1890 birth index and McBrehuny is found as a principal name of Co. Sligo in the census of 1659. The name, or likely variants of the same are found in Co. Galway on occasion as well.

31

Brereton

Brerton, Breerton

The census of 1659 finds families of the name of Brereton in Cork and in Queens Co. (Leix). In 19th century records we find the name centered in Dublin and in Kings Co. (Offaly).

Under the spelling of Breerton, we also find families of the name living in Co. Antrim. The name can be found numerous in the earlier mentioned counties in the 16th and 17th centuries, when many of the name settled here coming from England.

O Breslin

Irish Book of Arms plate 213

O'Breaslain

Breslawn, Breslaun, Breslane, Bresland,

Now it should be known that the O'Breslins were a noble family in the north of Ireland. Here they served as distinguished 'brehons', coming from the county of Donegal. The family remained most numerous in that county one century ago.

The name is often found in that area of Ireland, O'Breislen is found in the barony of Kilmacrenan on the banks of Lough Swilly, and they are given as chiefs here in the works of the Four Masters. The MacSweeneys apparently overtook them in the wake of the Norman invasions there. The are also found in Fermanagh, serving as brehons, and erenaghs of Derryvullen.

In Keatings History we find the family of O'Breslen settled near the Shannon River, and it was said that these lands were 'obtained by the force of battle, Its fierce chief and brave in conflict, Is O'Breslen of the well proportioned limb'.

Arms for the family of this name are found in the Irish Book of Arms plate 213.

Brett

According to "Keatings History" the name is that of a principal family of Dublin city or county, and of Anglo-Norman descent.

One noted family of the name was seated at Coltrummer, Co. Meath in Ireland, no later than the early 17th century. The main location for the name in the 19th century was in Co. Sligo, and in Co. Dublin.

Mac Bride

Mac Giolla Brighde

Kilbride, McGilbride, Mulbride, Bride

The Mac Bride family name is traditionally associated with the old province of Ulster, comprising the north of Ireland. As one would expect, some of the name in this area will be of Scottish origins as well as Irish.

They are found most early in the County of Donegal, where they served as erenaghs of Raymunterdoney. The name is later found in County Down, in the 1659 census as a principal one of that county.

O'Mulbride - Mac Bride, coming from the Irish O'Maoilbrighde, is also found as a chief in the barony of Athlone in Co. Roscommon, east of the River Suck. Mulbride has been given as a variant of McBride in Keatings History, and no doubt there has been some interchanging of the name early in history.

Kilbride (MacKilBride) is the form of the name in the province of Connaught. and the name is also found as Gilbride at times in Ireland. In both cases the original Mac before the name was dropped. Kilbride has only 7 recorded births a century ago, all in the province of Leinster and Connaught. Mac Bride at that time, was still found in Antrim, Donegal, and Down most commonly, remaining a name of the north of the country.

Several of the name are cited in O'Hart's work were of Co. Donegal heritage and migrated to Montreal, Canada.

Boyce

O'Buadhaigh

Boys, Boy, Boyse, de Boys, Boice, Bwee,

The 19th century birth index finds Boyce families centered in the province of Ulster, in counties Donegal, Down and Westmeath. Most of the name are assumed to be of English origins when found in Ireland, and the same are found settling here early in the 17th century. One of the name is found with considerable holdings in Co. Tipperary.

Note the place name of Boystown in Co. Meath, a county where early settlement is also noted by those of the name.

Of those arriving from England the name is said to have originally been taken from "bois" meaning "the wood". Of those of the name in Co. Donegal and surrounding areas of Ulster, they are said to be of old Irish heritage springing from the family of O'Buadhaigh.

Britton

Britain, Brittaine, Brittan, Briton,

Families of the name of Britton are found in Co. Westmeath in the 17th century in Ireland. Related spellings include those of Britain, Briton, and Brittaine. Even with these variant spellings the name is relatively rare in Ireland.

The name is said to have been taken from Brittany in France, and some early records show the spelling of le Briton. Families of the name are found in several areas, including those of Co. Tipperary in the 17th century.

The spelling of McBritany, given as a principal name of Antrim in the census of 1659, could perhaps be shortened to Britan, etc... but most of that name are more properly of the McBratney name.

32

O'Briody, Brody

Irish Book of Arms plate 201

Brady, Brody, MacBrody

The "O" before the name has been longed dropped off for the family of O'Briody. The family is found early in Longford and Cavan, and subsequently in Westmeath.

At the turn of the last century counties Longford and Cavan still served as the main centers for the name.

O'Hart gives the name of MacBrody as an ancient clan of Munster and as hereditary historians to the families of the old territory of Thomand. In the 16th century this family is found centered in Ibrackan in Co. Clare, and subsequently in the barony of Inchiquin, Co. Clare.

One Maolin MacBrody is given as helping to translate the New Testament into Irish, as published by Ussher, in Dublin in 1602. The "Contention of the Bards" was also said to have been under the direction of Tiege MacBrody of Clare along with O'Clery of Donegal.

Arms noted at the head of this column are those of "Brody", a common modern day spelling of the name by some.

The 1890 birth index finds the family most numerous in Co. Clare, under the spelling of Brody.

Briscoe

Briscoe is a name of settler origins when found in Ireland and it is most often linked with Dublin in our records. It is here where we find the name in the 17th century as well. Occasional references to the name are found in Tipperary and Cork in our records.

Brocas

Brokas, Brocas

One of the rarer names found in Ireland, the family is traditionally linked to Dublin, where several of the name are found as noted artists. Families of the name here are of English descent, but the name is as well found among the Huguenots who settled in Great Britain.

Brooks, Brooke

Settler origins

Brook, Brooke, Brookes, Brooks

The name of Brooks is found under several spellings, used interchangeably on occasion. Brooks, is the favored spelling today.

The census of 1659 finds Brook and Brooke in Donegal. Brooks is found in Cork and the spelling of Brookes is found in Tipperary, Cork, Dublin City, Londonderry, Kildare and Kilkenny then.

Brooks is found in Cork and Dublin in the 1890 birth index. Noted that these spellings have changed over time. 'Brooks' today could stem originally from Brookes, etc..

One source gives Brooke as settling in Dublin in 1690 and of English origins. Many of the name of Brooks settled in Ireland in Cromwellian times.

One family descends from Basil Brooke, an official of the Elizabethan regime in Ireland, and the family is found at Rantavan, Co. Fermanagh as early as 1685. Sir Basil Brook served as prime minister of Northern Ireland (Lord Brookesborough). This family has been connected with collecting Irish poetry.

Some of the name could stem from Irish origins, the name being changed into the English word 'Brook' or Brooks.

Charlotte Brooke (1745-1793) was an enthusiast of Gaelic poetry , from Rantavan, Co. Fermanagh. Henry Brooke (d.1783) was an Irish poet and father of the above mentioned Charlotte.

Two Brooke pedigrees are found, those of Leicestershire, England, and those of Navan, Co. Meath, who were originally from Chesire, England. Arms for the English family are given by O'Hart.

One family of the name claims descent from Sir Thomas Brooke of Cheshire, England, and they are found settled in Navan, Co. Meath no later than the early 16th century.

Broe

O'Brugha

Brew, Broo, Broghe, de Berewa, de Bruth

Families of the name of Broe are found in Kildare and Dublin in the 1890 index for Ireland. Several centuries ago we find the name in counties Leix and Kilkenny. While many of the name are of old Irish origins coming from the name of O'Brugha, others likely stem from the Norman name of de Berewa and de Bruth, found in Ireland with the coming of the 12th century Norman invasions.

O'Brogan

Irish Book of Arms plate 253

The name, spelled as "Brogan" is found as a principal one of Westmeath in the census of 1659 and subsequently most prominent in Mayo and Donegal under that spelling.

When found spelled as Broghane in 1659, the name was a principal one of Kings Co. (Offaly). The latter spelling has died out, and we do not know if these two families are of completely separate origins or not.

Brownlee

Brownlow

One family of the name is said to be a branch of the Brownlow family of the Tyrconnell area, who settled in Ireland from Co. Lincoln, England, centered in Derrylard, Portadown, Co. Armagh, on the estate of Lord Charlemont.

Brownlee is found centered in Co. Antrim and Co. Armagh in the 19th century.

Burnett

Burnet

One family of the Burnett name can be traced back to Ballygriffan, Co. Monaghan. They held many lands there which were lost under the Cromwellian regime, and the name becomes scarce thereafter. One Patrick Burnet is found head of a line settled in Enniscrone, Co. Sligo and in Newry Co. Down.

33

Mac Burney

MacBurnie

The name of a Scottish family settling in Ulster, often found around the city of Belfast.

Boyton

de Boyton

The Boyton family is found in Roscommon and Athlone Burrough in the 1659 census of Ireland. According to the works of Woulfe one family of the name is found in Tipperary dating back to the 13th century, and here the name comes from that of an English town. The name is further found in some records as de Boyton, and this family is found many centuries earlier than the previous one mentioned. Of the latter line, they are traditionally linked to Cashel and Co. Cork. Note the name of Boytonstown in that area in the early 14th century.

Brophy

The Brophy name is said to have come from O'Broithe, originally of Co. Leix (Queens County). The name is found most often in Dublin, Kilkenny, Queens and Tipperary in the 1890 birth index. The family name is found in Co. Carlow in comparatively recent times as well.

Brosnan

Irish Book of Arms plate 249

Brosnahan, Bresnahan, Brosnane

Brosnan is a family name most often found in Co. Kerry and Co. Limerick in Ireland. Under the spelling of Bresnahan the name is most often found in Cork in older records. The 1890 birth index finds the family most numerous in Co. Kerry, under the spelling of Brosnan.

Mac Broudin

According to "Keatings History" the name is given in the barony of Inchiquin, in Co. Clare.

Boycott

Boycot

One Capt. Charles Boycott (d.1897) gave rise to the term of "boycott" in modern day parlance. He was of an English family, and is on record in Tipperary, Fermanagh and Co. Mayo in Ireland. Some of the name are found resident in Doneraile in Co. Cork in our records.

Broughall

Brothel, Brohel, Broughill, Brohale,

The family name of Broughall is often traditionally linked to Co. Kildare in Ireland. The census of 1659 finds the family in Dublin.

Broy

de Broy, O'Broy

Families of the name of Broy may descend from "de Broy" or "O'Broy" as found in older records. The former spelling would denote a Norman ancestry, the latter Irish. The traditional location for the Irish family of the name has been cited as in Co. Kilkenny.

O'Bruen

Families of the name of Bruen etc.. are traditionally linked with Co. Roscommon in Ireland. The 1890 birth index confirms that location for the family. One English family of the name of Bruen is also found settling in Roscommon in the 16th century, and subsequently found in Co. Carlow with great holdings of land.

Brunnocks

According to "Keatings History" the name is among the chief families of English descent settling in Waterford and Tipperary. These English families primarily possessed the territory called Gal-tir, signifying the country of the foreigners," now the barony of Gaultiere."

Bunworth

Bunworthe

The name of an English family traditionally linked with Co. Cork in Ireland, given to have settled there in the 17th century.

Bryson

Briceson

Families of the name of Bryson are found centered in Co. Londonderry in the 19th century. These likely represent families who had settled there from England several centuries earlier. It is also found that some of the name in Ulster are said to be of old Irish origins

Bugler

Buggler

Bugler is found to be an English settler name found in Co. Clare, centered in the barony of Tulla.

Buggle

Bugle

The name of an English family found in Dublin and Kildare in our records.

O'Buggy

Bugy

The Buggy or O'Buggy name has been found in counties Wexford, Queens and Kilkenny in our research, where the name is most numerous in the 19th century.

Bulfin

Bullfin

Records of the last century in Ireland find the name of Bulfin in Co. Offaly .

Burnside

One Robert Burnside of Scotland is found settling during the plantation of Ulster originally at Raphoe in 1608, and subsequently in Corcreevy, Co. Tyrone. The main locations for the name in the 19th century were in counties Londonderry and Antrim.

Bunting

Buntin, Buntine, Bunton

A family name traditionally linked with counties Armagh and Tyrone and the province of Ulster in Ireland. The 19th century birth index places the family mainly in counties Antrim and Armagh.

34

Busher

The name of a settler family found in the wake of the Norman invasions in Co. Wexford.

Busteed

Busted, Bustead

The Busteed family is traditionally linked to the county and city of Cork for several centuries. Most of the name appear during the Cromwellian settlements. In the 17th century we find the name often spelled as Bustead.

Buttimer

Buttamore, Buttamore

The Buttimer family is found settling in Ireland no later than the 17th century in our records. The family is traditionally linked to Co. Cork in older, and in the more modern records.

Butterly

Butterley

The name of an English family found settled in Co. Louth for several centuries.

Byron

O'Broin

O'Byrne, Burn, Beirne, Byron, MacBrinn,

The Byron family name is considered to be most often a name of English origins when found in Ireland. It could also be a variant spelling of other Irish names such as O'Beirne, Byrne, etc..

As spelled 'Byron' the name is given a century ago as centered in Dublin and Antrim. In the census of 1659 we find the spelling of Byrine in County Carlow.

Brakey

Braky, Breaky, Breakey

The name of a family traditionally associated with Co. Monaghan in Ireland.

Bramston

A branch of the family originally from Essex in England is found settling in Munley, Clones, Co. Monaghan, and they are said to have been one of the first families of the name to settle in Ireland.

Brannelly

Branley, Branly

A rare name in Ireland, it has been linked to the east of Co. Galway in our records

O'Brannigan

Irish Book of Arms plate 253

Branigan, Brannigin

The Brannigan name is said to have been taken from O'Brannagain most anciently, and the family is found in Armagh and Monaghan in the 1890 birth index. Spelled as Branagan the name is given in Dublin at that time. In more modern times the name is found centered near Drogheda, Co. Louth, and some of the name are found in Kilkenny as well.

Most references to the name find it in the province of Ulster in our records.

De Burgh

The Irish Book of Arms plate 81

The De Burgh family of Oldtown, Co. Kildare is given in the Irish Book of Arms.

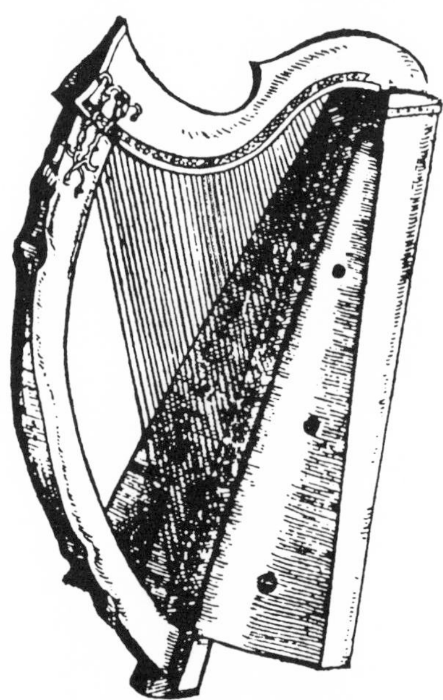

Ulster Plantation

One or more of the following families are given as among the Scottish and English Undertakers of the Plantation of Ulster in Ireland.

ENGLISH:	SCOTTISH:
Rolleston	Douglasse
Sacheverell	Acheson
Brownlowe	Craig
Matchett	Lawder
Powell	Hamilton
Dillon	Stewart
Brownlowe	Hepburne
Stanhowe	Crayford
Heron	/Crawford
Cope	Lindsey
Ridgewaie	Clapen
Leigh	/Claphame
Edney	Boyd
Ridgeway	Dromond
Parsons	/Drummond
Turvin	Haig
Glegge	McAula
Tuchet	Cuningham
Audley	Cunyngham
Blunte	Maclellan
Davys	Murraye
Clare	Mackee
Willson	McCullock
Russell	Dunbar
Barnes	Vans
Mansfield	Coningham
Cornewall	Balfoure
Remyngton	/Balfour
Barkeley	Wishart
Coach	/Wiseheart
Wirrall	Monepeny
Bogas	/Moneypeny
Calvert	Trayle
Sedborough	Smelhome
Flowerdewe	/Smailholme
Blenerhassett	Home/Hume
Archdale	Gibb
Warde	Lindsey
Barton	Fowler
Honynge (or	Dunbarr
Hennings.)	Achmootie
Waldron	/Achmouty
Fishe	Browne
Butler	Stuart
Lusher	Baillie
Wyrall	Raleston
Tailor	Downbarr

O Callaghan

Irish Book of Arms plates 65, 131...

O'Ceallachain

Callahan, Callihan, Calahan, Calaghan,

The great ancestor of the O'Callaghan, sept was Ceallachan, King of Munster (d. 952). They are originally found in the barony of Kinlea in Cork, from whence they were forced to the north, near Mallow, following the Anglo-Norman invasions. With the coming of Cromwell the power of the family was broken, and the main family branch was transplanted to Co. Clare.

In Clare you will find 'O'Callaghans Mills' named in their honor, where descendants remain to this day. Most are in their traditional Cork homelands.

One of the 50 most numerous names in all of Ireland, the 'O' prefix before the name had largely been dropped by the time of the great immigrations to America. Today in Ireland the 'O' prefix is being assumed once again.

An entirely separate family, that of O'Ceileachain, is found in the ancient territory of Oriel (Armagh, Louth and Monaghan). They are found using the family names of Callaghan and Kelaghan. The Kelaghan spelling of the name is mostly found in Westmeath.

In the 17th century the name was found in Clare, as well as being a principal name of Donegal. In 1890 the name was most numerous in Cork, Kerry and Dublin.

Several families of the name became armigerous. Arms found in the Irish Book of Arms include those of O'Callaghan of Maryfort and Fort Anne in Co. Clare, and O'Callaghan = Westropp of Maryfort of Clare.

Found widespread throughout the world many are listed in the Irish Brigades in France, and in Spanish and American records of earlier times. The chief of the name into modern times was also given as being a citizen of Spain.

Mac Calmont

Irish Book of Arms plate 89

The name of a Scottish settler family traditionally linked with Co. Antrim in Ireland. In Scotland the family name is that of a branch of the Clan Buchanan. The census of 1659 finds the name a principal one of Co. Antrim, centered in the barony of Belfast.

The McCalmont family of Abbeylands, Co. Antrim are given in the Irish Book of Arms.

Cadigan, Cadogan

One family of the name of Cadogan in Ireland was of Welsh origins, and others of the name descend from O'Ceadagain. The family has been traditionally associated with Co. Cork, and the Skibbereen area in that county. The name remained mainly in that area until the turn of the last century.

Cagney

Cagny

The name of an Irish family traditionally given in Co. Cork.

Cahalane

Cahalan, Cahillane

A name of Cork and Kerry in Ireland, according to the 1890 birth index, and the name is also found in Co. Tipperary on occasion.

O'Caheny

According to "Keatings History" the name was originally found in the barony of Erris in Co. Mayo where the family served as chiefs. Few of the family name were found at the time of that writing. The spelling of the name was anciently O'Caithnaidh.

35

Mac Cann

Irish Book of Arms plates 147 and 246.

Mac Annadh

MacAnna, Canny, MacCanna

The McCann family became known as 'Lords of Clanbrasill' in Co. Armagh by the shores of Lough Neagh. One Donnell MacCanna ruled as a chief of Clanbrassil into the late 16th century. The name remains here and in Co. Clare into modern times. It is further stated that in Clare, Mayo and Limerick the family name has been changed to 'Canny', which may have originated as a nickname for the McCanns.

The family name is also found in Co. Louth, dating back several centuries, in the Union of Ardee.

O'Hart in his Irish Pedigrees states that the McCans descend from the MacMahons of Co. Monaghan. The name is most properly taken from 'Mac Anna' (Annadh), but the 'c' in Mac has become part of the root surname. Mac Canna is formed by adding another 'c'. The final letter 'a' in the older spelling has largely been dropped.

'Canny' is another form of the name which was found in Clare and Mayo in the 1890 birth index. The more common McCann was centered in the north of Ireland and in Dublin at that time. In the 17th century 'McCan' was a principal name in Dublin and Londonderry, McCanna was found in Fermanagh and McCann in Armagh at that time.

Arms for one family of the name are found in the Irish Book of Arms on plates 147 and 246.

For more information the book entitled 'Origins of the McCanns' by A. Mathews, (1978) Ireland, will be of service.

36

Carberry

Irish book of Arms plates 18, 235

Carbry

At least two families of the name, apparently unrelated, account for the name in Ireland today. O'Cairbre, of the barony of Clonlonan in Co. Westmeath was the ancestor of one branch that became erenaghs of Galloon, in the barony of Coole, Co. Fermanagh.

Others of the name descend from MacCairbre, of the barony of Glenahiry, in Co. Waterford. Note the place name of Ballymacarbry there.

In the census of 1659 Carbery was a principal name of Waterford, O'Carbry a principal name of Armagh, and the name was also in Kildare, Dublin and Meath at that time.

Mac Caherty

Caugherty, Cagherty, McCafferky

This is the name of a family traditionally linked to Co. Monaghan in Ireland. The name is also given by some as a variant spelling of McCafferky of Co. Mayo.

Mc Cahon

Cahan

The name of a family traditionally linked to Co. Antrim in Ireland. See Mc Cahon.

Cairns

Kearns

The name of Cairns is found most often in the province of Ulster in Ireland. It is generally accepted as a settler name arriving from Scotland. The family has been given in Antrim, Down, Armagh, Sligo and Donegal at various times. In Ireland no later than the 17th century, and given in the 1890 birth index as most popular in counties Antrim, Down, and Armagh.

Carden

The Irish Book of Arms plate 107

The family of Carden of Barnane, Co. Tipperary are found to descend from John Carden of Templemore, Co. Tipperary, settled there around 1650, this family is given in the Irish Book of Arms.

Callan

Irish Book of Arms plate 239

Callen, Calan, Callin

The name of O'Callan was a principal one of Monaghan, Callan a principal name of Dublin, and McCallan a principal name of Fermanagh in the census of 1659. Mainly a name of Louth and Monaghan in modern times, the name of McCallan was given in Antrim in the 1890's birth index.

Mac Callery

The MacCallery family name is traditionally linked to Co. Sligo in Ireland. It is as well found in Dublin city records.

Mc Callion

McAllion, McCallon

A family of Scottish extraction who arrived in Ireland in the service of the O'Donnells. They served as "galloglas", or heavily armed fighting men.

Calderwood

Catherwood

A name of the province of Ulster, it is generally accepted to be of Scottish origins when there. Found centered in Co. Antrim in the 1890 index.

Calthorpe

Calthrop

Sir Charles Calthrop, (or Calthorpe), was attorney General for Ireland. This line descends from Sir Wm. Calthrop.

Mac Caffrey

McCafferty plate 203 Irish Book of Arms.

Mac Gafraidh

Mac Cafferky, Mac Goffrey, Caffreys, Mac

Members of the MacCaffrey family in Ireland are said originally to descend from the Maguire family of Co. Fermanagh. Note the place name of Ballymacaffry, in the barony of Magherastephana in Co. Fermanagh, near the Tyrone border, marking a center for the name in earlier days.

One hundred years ago the name remained most populous in the two counties mentioned above. Two centuries earlier MacCaffrey had remained a principal name of Co. Fermanagh. The name here, on its traditional lands has retained the Mac prefix for the most part. The name is found as Caffrey however, in Dublin, Meath and Cavan in the 1890 index.

Several are found among the fighting men of Corcorans Irish Legion and Meaghers Irish Brigade of civil war fame in the U. S. A..

The name is said to come from MacGafraidh originally, from which some took the name of MacGoffrey instead of MacCaffrey.

This family name is often confused with Mac Cafferty and Mac Cafferky of Co. Mayo, but there is no known relationship between the two.

Mac Cafferty, from the old spelling of Mac Eachmharcaigh, has also kept its 'Mac' prefix, except in Co. Cavan where Cafferty is numerous. Mac Cafferky, another spelling of the same name is found in Mayo and Roscommon spelled as Cafferky in the 1890 birth index.

McCafferty itself is most numerous in Donegal, Londonderry and Antrim in that index.

Even though there is no relationship between the two families, MacCafferty/ MacCafferky and MacCaffrey are often confused and sometimes interchanged .

37

O Cahan

Irish Book of Arms plates 227, 260...

O'Cathain

Keane, O'Kane, Kane, Kean, Cahane

Modern day members of the O'Cahan family most often spring from the old Irish family of O'Cathain. The name is found both as O'Cahan and Mac Cahan in Irish records and variant spellings are most numerous.

In the north of Ireland 'Kane' is often found as the spelling of this family name, and Keane is found in the south and west of the country.

In Clare the MacCahan family, as it has been often written, were connected with the church of St. Senan, and are found more often as 'Cahane' in that area today. Some say that this family is a branch of the O'Cahan families from the north of Ireland, in the old province of Ulster.

In Ulster, one family of the name served as inaugurators of the great ruling family of the O'Neills. They held sway in Derry quite early and were centered in Keenaght and Coleraine until the downfall of the gaelic order in that area.

O'Heerin gives the family in Co. Waterford as a distinct and separate group, descending from 'O'Cein'

In the 17th century it is interesting to note the different spellings of the name. Cahan was a principal name of Waterford, McCahan of Antrim, O'Cahan of Londonderry and Roscommon, Cahane of Clare, and O'Cahane was a principal name in County Cork.

Moving into more modern times, when Kane and Keane have been substituted for the above spellings we find 'Kane' in Antrim, Londonderry and Dublin. Keane was in Galway, Clare, Kerry and Mayo at that time.

Origins may be difficult to trace due to the interchanging of these names.

O Callinan

Irish Book of Arms plate 260. Callanan

O'Callanain

Callenen, Cullenen, Callanan, Calnan,

We learn from Keatings History that the " O'Cullenans, or Mac Callenans, were hereditary physicians, and many of them very learned men in Ormond." This work further states that "The O'Callanans and O'Canavans" were mentioned by O'Flaherty as hereditary physicians in Galway.

Indeed this family had developed a tradition in the medical arts serving under the ruling MacCarthy family in Carbery, Co. Cork with distinction.

Several are found in King James II army, including at least one physician. The name is found centered in Clare in both 1659 and 1890 as Callinan and Callinane respectively. Callanan is found in Galway and Cork.

The family was said to have originated in Galway, and they were anciently co-arbs of Kilcahill. This is one name where the 'O' prefix had been largely dropped by the last century, and it has remained so to this day.

O'Hart gives the O'Callanans of Desmond as of separate origins from the O'Callanans of Connaught. The principal members of the family and locations for each are given there, along with poetry by an O'Callanan, that was published in Cork in 1861. There-in it was said that that Their ruined castles stood "in mournful silence, to the east of Clonakilty". Their lands being held then by people "alien in language and race".

In 1659 Callinane was a principal name of Clare, and in 1890 the spelling of Callanan was most prominent there. Galway and Cork were also primary locations for the name at the latter date. "Callinan" was a spelling of the name centered in Clare at that time.

O Carey

Irish Book of Arms plate 107

O'Ciardha

Cary, Carie, Keary, Kary, McCarey

Ruling as 'Lords of Carbury' in Co. Kildare until the Norman invasions, the name is more properly spelled as O'Keary. O'Ciardha, or O'Carey was of the southern Ui Neill tribe most anciently. Other Irish families have changed their name into Carey as well.

In Tyrone and Galway Carey is used for Kerin, and in Galway it is used for the older name of O'Carra. The name is most often found in the province of Munster in Ireland, and some of the name are likely of settler origin, as well as native Irish.

In the 17th century we find 'Carey' and Carie in Co. Londonderry, and McCarey as a principal name of Westmeath. Both names, McCarey and O'Carey have been shortened into Carey.

Keatings history cites the family as numerous in Mayo and Sligo and further speaks thusly:

'O'Carey rules over Carbery of Bards,
He is of the tribe of Niall of the 9 Hostages,
There are none but themselves there,
of the clans of Niall over Leinster."

O'Hart gives the 'Keary' family (MacCeachraigh) of Galway as distinct from 'Carey'. He states that 4 generations ago one of the family migrated to Woodford, and that they still lived near Loughrea, Craughwell and Portnumna in his day.

The arms of Cary-Cadell of Harbourstown, Co. Cork, are found in the Irish Book of Arms, with some information.

Carey is a numerous name outside of Ireland as well. Many can be found in fighting brigades in Europe and the name is one of the top 500 in America.

The 1800's birth index finds Carey centered in Cork, Dublin, Tipperary, Mayo and Kerry.

Carleton

Irish Book of Arms plate 47

Carlton

The Carleton name is a settler family name in Ireland, as well as being of old Irish origins. Some of the name of O'Carolan were said to have adopted the name of Carleton or Carlton.

The birth index of 1890 finds the name centered in Co. Antrim. The Irish Book of Arms gives the family of Carleton of Clare and Tipperary, where one of that line served as High Sheriff. This family originally settled in Cork from abroad.

Mac Cambridge

Cambridge

Cambridge and MacCambridge families are of settler origins in Ireland. When the original name was Cambridge, it is of English extraction, taken from the name of that town in England. As MacCambridge the family is found mainly in Ulster, where the family was originally from Scotland.

In both the 17th and 19th century the family is found centered in Co. Cork under the spelling of Cambridge. That spelling was as well found in Antrim in the more modern index, where it is likely just the shortened form of McCambridge. "McCambridge" was found in Antrim and Donegal in the 19th century birth index.

Canavan

Irish Book of Arms plate 253

Canavon, Canaven

Only 22 births of the Canavan name are recorded in the 1890 birth index. While the family was dispersed throughout the country then, the name is traditionally connected to Galway and the province of Connaught. They are on record as serving as hereditary physicians to O'Flaherty in several sources.

The variant spelling of "Canovane" is given in Co. Clare in the 17th century.

O Carroll

Irish Book of Arms plates 29, 140, 147

Cearbhal

Carrol, Caroll, Carol, Mac Carroll,

One of the top 25 surnames of Ireland, several families use the name. Two of these families remain distinct now.

O'Carroll of Oriel sprang from Monaghan and Louth, where the family remains today. The most famous of the name were the O'Carrolls of Ely. Centered in north Tipperary and western Offaly, they ruled over several chiefs and held the baronies of Clonlesk, Ikerrin and Eliogarty, to name three.

These O'Carrolls held a castle at Birr, in Kings and O'Heerin gives them as: 'Lords to whom great men submit, are the O'Carrolls of the plain of Birr.'

Rising to the peak of their power before the Norman invasions, they were in Kilkenny. Among their strongholds were (Mc)Cadamstown, Leap, and the town of Callen in Kilkenny.

The Ely O'Carrolls took their name from 'Cearbhal', Lord of Ely, who was among the Irish chiefs at the great battle of Clontarf, which broke the power of the Vikings in Ireland.

With the decline of the power of the family they continued to remain centered near Birr, in Co. Offaly.

In Leitrim and Sligo O'Carroll was chief of Calraighe, near Dartry in the barony of Dromahaire in Leitrim, and in the parish of Calry in Sligo.

The O'Carrolls of Ossory in Co. Kilkenny are mentioned by O'Heerin as "O'Carroll of the Reddened Spears", and likely were centered in the baronies of Gowran and Slogh Liag.

O'Carroll, the prince of Loch Lein in Co. Kerry was cited by O'Heerin in the 11th and 12th centuries. There is also the family of 'MacCarroll' in Ulster.

The Carroll family of Ashford, Co. Wicklow, are earliest found in Co. Dublin in the 18th century.

Mac Cartan

Irish Book of Arms plates 147, 254

MacArtain

MacArtan, Mac Carton, Cartan

The lands anciently referred to as 'McCartans' country are found in Co. Down, where the family served as chiefs of Kinelarty. More properly the name should be Mac Artan, but the 'c' in Mac has been added to the name to form Mac Cartan or Carton.

As a rule they were allied to the ruling Mac Cennis family, and in the 14th century they are recorded as lords of Iveagh, which was Magennisis country.

The 1800's birth index finds the name in Down and Armagh, spelled as MacCartan. In the 17th century however, 'Cartan', is given as a principal name of Kildare, and it is also found in Louth at that time.

The Mac Cartan family is cited in the works of Carew, and notably so through the 16th century. Keatings History also cites the name thusly: 'Mac Artain or Mac Cartan, chief of Kinel Fagartaigh, now the barony of Kinelearty and Dufferin.'

A McCartan genealogy given in O'Hart, (Co. Down), gives the family motto as 'Buallim se" meaning 'I strike him.' Separate arms and crests are given to the older 'MacArten' family in his work.

Mac Candless

MacAndless, MacAnliss, McCandlish

Families of the name are found primarily in the province of Ulster, centered there in county Down. The family is often given to be of Scottish extraction by some. Only 5 births of the name were recorded in the 1890 birth index of Ireland.

Carter

Irish Book of Arms plate 46

possible variant of MacArthur

MacArthur

Carter is a name which is fairly common in England. The English Carters certainly account for many of the name in Ireland. The name, found as 'le Carter' as early as the 1300's in Ireland, has also been adopted in some cases as a form of spelling 'MacArthur'.

Carter is found in Limerick city, Kildare and Londonderry in the census of 1659, and is as well found in the Poll Money Ordinance survey. In the more modern birth index, Dublin and Galway are listed as principal counties of residence.

'McCarter' is another form of the name. In 1659 we find McCarter as a principal name in Donegal, and in more modern times McCarter is listed as from Antrim and Londonderry.

The Irish Book of Arms give the family of Carter of Shaen Manor, Co. Mayo.

Canning

Those of the name may be of Irish or English extraction in Ireland. The Cannon family of Donegal and Leitrim has been said to have adopted "Canning" as a surname on occasion. Others were settler families arriving from England during Cromwellian times.

The name seems to be centered in Co. Londonderry in our records.

Cantrell

The name of Cantrell can also be found in England, and most of the name are assumed to be of that extraction. One family of the name is given in Co. Leix, as Quakers in the 17th century.

Mac Carthy

Irish Book of Arms plate 147

Mac Carthaigh

Carthy, Mc Arthy, McCarthy, Macarthy,

Mac Carthy is the #1 Mac name in all of Ireland, and one of the top 12 names in the country. An ancient and powerful sept, the family name is the third most numerous in Cork Cork overall.

McCarthy castles and monuments are well known. The Muckross estates in Kerry, Blarney Castle in Cork, and Cormacs Chapel on the Rock of Cashel attest to the past of this great family.

Of the many branches of the name, the 'McCarthy Mor' thrived in Kerry, seated at Muckross by Killarney. The barony of Muskerry branch was seated at Blarney Castle in Cork. The 'MacCarthy Reagh' hailed from Carbery in Co. Cork and a branch of the same is found in Spring House and as Counts of Toulouse in France.

McCarthy Glas is given in Dunmanway, McCarthy Duna or Dooney is given in Ballyneadig and Lyradane, and O'Hart gives the pedigree of a MacCarthy of Minnesota, U.S.A..

Continuously tied to the province of Munster and Desmond, the family descends from Eoghan, through Cartach, lord of the Eugenians, who died at the hands of a Lonergan in 1045 according to the 4 Masters. The Annals of Innisfallen record much family history.

The title of 'MacCarthy Mor' was also used by a branch of the family in France for some time.

In 1659 Carthy was a principal name in Clare, and McCarthy was a principal name of Clare, Cork..., and McCarthey a principal name of Cork City. O'Carthy is even found in Cork dating back several centuries. The 'Mac' prefix however has generally been retained.

39

Mc Cartney

Irish Book of Arms plate 34

McArtney, McCartny

The name of a Scottish family settling in Ireland no later than the 17th century, found centered in Co. Antrim. This family was of the Clan McIntosh of Scotland.

The McCartney family of Lissanoure, Co. Antrim, of Scottish origins, is found in the Irish Book of Arms.

Campbell

Irish Book of Arms plate 209

Cambell, Cample, Camp, Kemp

Campbell ranks among the top 10 most numerous names in Scotland, and among the 50 most popular in Ireland. Not surprisingly, most of the name were found in the province of Ulster in Ireland. Some of the name came to Ireland as galloglass in centuries past, and all are given to be of Scottish origins when found in Ireland.

Both McCampbell and Campbell are given as principle names in Co. Antrim in the census of 1659. Variant spellings include that of Cample.

In the 1890 birth index of Ireland some 349 births of the name were recorded. The vast majority (279) were in the province of Ulster, and the least were in the province of Munster (8), to the south.

While the Campbells of Donegal are given to be of Scottish heritage originally, and they have settled in neighboring counties in Ulster, some members assert that the Campbells of Tyrone were originally an entirely separate family, of Irish origins.

Casement

Irish Book of Arms plate 33

MacCasmonde, Casmond

Families of the name of Casement are found centered with considerable holdings in Co. Antrim, Ireland. The family is found most anciently on the Isle of Man, and is of Manx origins, found often at Peel there. The believed earlier form of the name was as MacCasmonde or Casmond. Some of the name are found for a time in counties Dublin and Limerick early.

The Casement family of Magherintemple, Co. Antrim is given in the Irish book of Arms. They were said to have come from Ramsey, Isle of Man in the early 18th century, and were originally of French extraction.

Campion

of French origins

Champion, Campyon, Campian

The Campion family name is often found in older Irish records. The name itself is said to have come from foreign origins, meaning "a champion" or one engaged in battle. In the census of 1659 "Campian" is found as a principal name in Queens county (Leix), in the barony of Ossory. "Campion" is given as a name of Co. Cork in the same record.

In more modern times the name is found in Queens ,(Leix), and Kilkenny counties in the 1890 birth index of Ireland. In Griffiths Survey, from the middle of the last century, the name is numerous in counties Leix and Kilkenny.

Edmund Campion (1569), was a Jesuit historian, of English connections. William Campyon (1578) was a soldier listed as receiving pardon. William Campion (1590) was the dean and Archdeacon of Ferns. Thomas Campion is found in Co. Cork in 1659.

Cassan

The Irish Book of Arms plate 86

The Cassan family of Sheffield House, Queens county finds origins in Montpelier, whence they removed to Holland, and then settled in Ireland.

O Cannon

O'Canain

Cannan, Gannon, Kennon, MacCannon

Irish families bearing the Cannon name may spring from one of at least two distinct Irish clans. One family springs from O'Canain of the south of Galway in Ui Maine, where the name is no longer prominent. Another family descends from O'Canannain or O'Canann of the territory of Tirconnel. This family became known as the 'Kings of Cinel Conaill'.

The O'Donnells broke the power of this family in the 13th century, although the name has remained in its original territory into modern times. Traditionally the name is often identified with the county of Donegal, where, along with Leitrim and Mayo it was found numerous in the 1890 index.

Mac Cannan and Mac Cannon families are still found in the ancient territory of Oriel, and the name is found in Dublin city and Meath in our records. One of the name was the Sheriff of Monaghan in the 17th century.

Ancient records show the family name centered near Clones, moving into Monaghan, and later into Louth.

The census of 1659 finds O'Cannon as a principal name of Leitrim, and Cannon in Antrim, Donegal, etc..

One O'Cannon castle was to be found near Letterkenny in Ireland.

One Col. Alexander Cannon, in the service of James II in 1691, left France to settle in Scotland. One 'Thomas Cannon" was among the jury members who condemned Robert Emmet to death.

40

O Cassidy

Irish Book of Arms plates 148 & 255

O'Caiside

Casaday, Casidy, Casley, Cassedy,

O'Cassidy country is anciently found in Co. Fermanagh where family members can be found yet today. This family served as hereditary physicians and ollavs to the ruling Maguires.

Keating cites 'Mac Cassidy' along with MacArdell and Duffey etc.. as one of the chiefs clans of Monaghan as well. Roderick Mac Cassidy was an archdeacon of Clogher who 'partly compiled the Annals of Ulster'.

The 1890 index finds the family in Donegal, Dublin, Antrim and Fermanagh. Spellings of the day in the 17th century included Cassadie in Kings Co., Cassedy in Louth, and O'Cassady of Donegal and Fermanagh. O'Cassidy was also a principal name of Fermanagh.

O'Hart gives several Cassidy listings. Patrick Cassidy, M.D. of Tyrone, Ireland and Rhode Island, U.S.A., and Cormack O'Cassida (Cassidy) is given in the barony of Glenawley in Fermanagh with 100 acres under the plantation of Ulster.

Cassidy was also cited as 'Chief of Coole' and another of the name served in 1745 in the Irish Brigades of France as quartermaster in FitzJames Horse Regt..

In the first census of the United States we find the name of Casaty, which may be an Americanization of the name.

Arms for some families of the name appear on plates 148 and 255 in the Irish Book of Arms.

Caufield

Irish Book of Arms plate 25, 253

(Mac Cathmhaoi)

Cawfield, Caulfield, M'Caulfield,

It is certain that Caufield is a variant of Caulfield, which in turn, often comes from the Irish name of MacCawell in Ireland. (see Caulfield)

Passenger Lists for Caufield:

Thomas Caufield. age 21 male, laborer, aboard 'Stephen-Whitney', April 6, 1846, Liverpool to New York.

Cathne. Caufield. age 17, female, seamstress. aboard 'Perseverance', May 18, 1846. Dublin to New York.

H. Caufield. age 24, male, Farmer. aboard 'Lord Ashburton', June 1, 1847, Liverpool to New York.

Cantwell

The name of Cantwell is found as a principal name of Tipperary, and is found as well in Kilkenny in the census of 1659. Subsequently, Tipperary and Dublin have become the main locations for the name. Some of the name are of Anglo-Norman origins, coming originally from the name of de Kentwell.

Carlin

possible form of Carolan around Tyrone.

O'Carlin, Carlan(d), Carolan

While Carlin is most likely of foreign origin when found in Ireland, it has also been shown to be of Irish stock. For example, the name of Carolan in county Tyrone, is said to have been forsaken for the use of Carlin.

The birth index of the last century finds Carlin to be a name of Tyrone and Londonderry, with specific locations given as follows: Ballynacargy in Mullingar Union, Ballynahinch in Downpatrick Union, Belfast #9 Belfast Union, Castlefin in Strabane Union, and Keady in Armagh Union.

Caulfield

Irish book of Arms plate 25

Mac Cathmhaoil

McCall, Caffrey, Gaffney, Calfhill,

Caulfield is the name of an English family that settled in Ulster, and of other origins as well. 'Castlecaulfield' which was earlier called Alconecarry, in Tyrone, served as the seat of the settler family of Sir Toby Caulfield. The name of Calfhill is also used with this family.

In Keatings History (v-3), a powerful clan in Tyrone, Clan Cathmaoil, changed its name to Caulfield. These are actually thought to be the MacCawells, found in the barony of Clogher, in Tyrone. The many variant spellings of the name may lead to confusion among researchers. It appears that the name began to adopt many other spellings several hundred years ago.

The census of 1659 finds the name in Dublin city, and in the Poll Money Ordinance Survey. In the 1890 birth index the name was located in Mayo, Antrim and Monaghan. Milesian families gives the name of the Irish family as a member of the Hy Nial Tribe, settling in Leitrim, Armagh and Tyrone.

The name is also that of a prominent English settler family mentioned above, in the province of Ulster. Sir Toby Caulfield was granted Abbey lands in Armagh and Derry, in 1607. O'Hart documents the above individual as obtaining lands in Tyrone, and also lists him under 'Grantees of Estates'. The Earl of Charlemont (Caulfield), was also cited as one of the 'Lords of Parliament'.

The Caulfield family of Donamon Castle, Co. Roscommon, are of the arms shown. Possible further references:

'A short biographical notice of....the Caulfield family." by Bernard Connor. Dublin. 1808.

'The MacCathmhaoils of Clogher" by S. O Dufaigh. Clogher. II, 1957

Mc Causland

Irish Book of Arms plate 40

McAusland, McAuslan

The name of a Scottish family which settled in Ulster no later than the 17th century, found centered in Co. Antrim.

Carew

Irish Book of Arms plate 228

The Carew name stems from a settler family in Ireland, of Anglo-Norman origins. Found earliest in the Waterford/Cork region of Ireland, the name is subsequently given in Co. Tipperary.

In the 17th century the main locations given for the name are in Cork, Limerick and Waterford. By the end of the last century the name was most common in Tipperary.

O'Hart gives the pedigree of Carew, those descended from Richard Carew, son of Otho Fitzgerald, who was surnamed "De Curio", hence according to that source, the name of Carew came about.

Carmody

Irish Book of Arms plate 262

Carmedy

The name of Carmody has been traditionally associated with the counties of Clare, Kerry and Limerick in Ireland. The census of 1659 gives Carmody as a principal name of Co. Clare, and the birth index of 1890 gives the name in Clare, Kerry, and Limerick.

42

Chambers

Irish Book of Arms plates 55, 127

Chambres

The name of Chambers or Chambres is generally accepted as a settler name in Ireland, coming originally from England. Most of the name are cited in the province of Ulster.

In the 17th century we find the name in Dublin City, Armagh, Cork and Kerry. By the end of the last century, the name was centered mainly in Ulster.

The Irish Book of Arms gives Chambers of Fosterstown, Trim, Co. Meath, as descended from Joseph, of Taylorstown, Co. Wexford. They held lands in and near the baronies of Shelburne, Bargy and Bantry. In the barony of Shelburne they resided in the Taylorstown Castle at one time.

One pedigree for the name is found in O'Hart. The Chambre family of Dungannon House, Co. Tyrone is given in the Irish Book of Arms.

Carson

The name of Carson is found in the province of Ulster. It is given to be a settler name arriving from Scotland centuries ago. The traditional location for the name was in Antrim, Down and Tyrone in the 1890 birth index. Other sources find the name in Limerick and Dublin in the 16th century.

Cashin

Irish Book of Arms plate 213

Cashen, Cashine

The Cashin family has traditionally been associated with Queens Co. (Leix). It was a principal name of that county in the census of 1659. O'Cashin and McCashine are two spellings that may have given rise to the name.

Some even give one family of German origins of the Cashin name in Ireland.

Chamney

The Irish Book of Arms plate 107

The family of Chamney of Schomberg, Co. Wicklow, descend from John Chamney, b. 1650, of Shillelagh Forge and Bullard Co. Wicklow, and of Ballynellot, Co. Wexford.

O Carolan

Irish Book of Arms plate 249

O'Caireallain, O'Cearbhallain

Carrolan, Carrollan, Kerlin, Carleton

The O'Carolan family in Ireland has at least two distinct origins. The first comes from O'Caireallain, chief of Clan Diarmada, an old geographic territory which contains Clondermot, in the barony of Tikeeran, Co. Derry.

Another distinct origin is found in O'Cearbhallain of the Cavan-Monaghan area. This family also spread into Meath. This is the birthplace of the famous harper and bard Turlough O'Carolan (1678-1738). He was born at Newton, Co. Meath, and died at Alderford, Co. Roscommon. He was buried at the old church of Kilronan.

Several of the name are found among the clergy in Co. Derry.

The 'O' prefix before the name has generally been dropped. Moving into modern times the name is found in Mayo and Cavan in the 1890 index, with representatives as would be expected in Dublin.

Keatings cites the name as follows: "O'Carolan, a name sometimes Anglicized to Carleton,...now the parish of Clandermod or Glendermod in Derry".

O'Hart gives O'Carolan as a chief in Londonderry, and as present in Meath. He further gives 'Kerlin' as a variant spelling of the name.

Arms for the name are found in the Irish Book of Arms plate 249.

Charley

The Irish Book of Arms plate 101

Charlie, Charly

The Charley family of Seymour Hill, Co. Antrim, descends from the family of Chorley or Charley, who came from the north of England to settle in Belfast in the 17th century. They are subsequently also found in Finaghy, Co. Antrim.

We also find the spellings of Charlie etc.. as given to Huguenot families who were naturalized in Great Britain.

Carr

Irish Book of Arms plate 269

several possibilities

O'Carr, MacElhar, Kerrane, Kerr, Mulcair,

The origins of the Carr family in Ireland can be difficult to trace. First of all, it may be of English extraction when found in Ireland. Then, of course, it may be taken from the Scottish name of Kerr. This leaves several Irish names which have also changed to Carr, such as Carey, Kerrane, Mulcair, and Mac Elhar.

In the census of 1659 Carr is found as a principal name of county Down, and also in Meath. The birth index shows the name to be of Donegal, Galway and Dublin at the turn of the 19th century. To further complicate matters, Milesian families gives the name as coming from Scotland in 1602, and settling in Cork and Limerick. (For which I have no substantiation).

O'Carr is listed as a principal name of Armagh and Down in the census of 1659 as well. This would certainly seem to point to an older Irish heritage, considering they used the 'O' prefix.

The problem of too many Carrs is made no easier in America. Today Carr ranks as the 203rd most popular name in America with an estimated count of 110,700 individuals.

Chevers

Irish Book of Arms plate 37

Cheevers

The Chevers of Killyan House, Co. Galway have furnished High Sheriffs to the town of Galway, and are so given in the Irish Book of Arms.

Carragher

Mac Fhearchar

Caraher, Carraher, MacCarraher,

The Carragher family name can be tied to 'Oriel' which was a more ancient geographical division of Ireland. The traditional area for the name is said to be on the Monaghan and Armagh border. The birth index from the last century gives Newtownhamilton in Castleblaney Union as a traditional location as well.

In the works of Woulfe, the name is also said to have come from the Scottish 'Farquhar'. We also have mention of the family of Carragher moving to Scotland in Medieval times, the name was commonly spelled there as 'Caraher'.

'MacCarehir' is found in Dysart, Co. Louth in 1616, and in 1663 MacCarraher is found in the Hearth Money Rolls for county Monaghan, in the barony of Dartree. The name is also found numerous times among the will records of County Louth.

According to "Keatings History" the name is given as belonging to a chief clan who possessed parts of Louth in ancient times.

Cashman

The name of Cashman has been traditionally linked with Co. Cork in Ireland, and it remained so at the end of the last century, where most of the name were still found.

Chichester

Irish Book of Arms plate 2

One Lord Chichester is found as Baron of Belfast in 1612, and of this line was Sir John Chichester, Governor of Carrickfergus, who was beheaded in 1597 as a result of an expedition against the MacDonnels.

Carty

Irish Book of Arms plate 201

O Carthaigh

O'Carty, McCarty, Carthy, M'Carty,

Although the name of Carty may be spelled as Carthy on occasion, it is not a common variant of McCarthy. Most of the name appear to have come from the Province of Connaught.

Going back to the census of 1659, we find both Carty and McCarty listed therein. Carty is given as a principal name of Limerick here, and is also found in Waterford. McCarty, on the other hand is given as a principal name of County Cork on this census.

In the more modern birth index the name had moved to Roscommon, Wexford, Galway and Longford in the 1890's. Traditional locations around this time were given as Achill district in Westport Union, in County Mayo, and in the Rathvilly district of Baltinglass Union, which covers parts of Carlow, Kildare and Wicklow.

Waterford Union was given as another traditional location.

Mac Clancy

Irish Book of Arms plates 148 and 253

Mac Fhlannchaidh

Glanchy, Clanchy, Glancy, Clansy

There are at least two Mac Clancy septs of Ireland. The more well known of the two hails from County Clare. Here in the north of Clare they held their seat of power at Cahermaclanchy in the barony of Corcomroe. This family may also be referred to as the 'Thomand' Clancys, an older geographic division marking their territory.

'Clanchy' is a variant spelling of Clancy, and is found in Clare in the census of 1659 as a principal name.

The family spoken of above is said to be a branch of the McNamara family of County Clare. They likely moved away from the center of MacNamara country and settled in the north of Clare. Here they became hereditary brehons to the noted O'Briens of Clare.

The second Irish sept or clan of the name is found in Co. Leitrim near Dartry in the barony of Rosclogher. The leader of the family was known as the 'Chief of Dartry'. One seat of power for the family was said to be a castle built on Lough Melvin.

In 1659 Clancy was a principal name of Limerick and Clansy was found in Waterford. Although the name is generally found as Clancy, it is more properly spelled as MacClancy.

One John Clancy was a sergeant in Corcorans Irish Legion of American Civil War fame, and several are found in the military ranks of the Spanish Netherlands.

The 1800's birth index finds the name most often in Clare, Leitrim, Galway and Tipperary.

Arms for the family name are found in the Irish Book of Arms on plates 148 and 253.

de Clare

Irish Book of Arms plate 9 (titled)

Clare

According to "Keatings History" the name is given as one of the early settler families in counties Clare and Limerick, arriving after the 12th century Norman invasions. The main location for the name of Clare in the 19th century was in Co. Dublin.

O Casey

Irish Book of Arms plate

O'Cathasaigh

Casey, MacCasey, O'Cahassy, Kasey

Several completely separate families bear the name of Casey in Ireland today. By some counts 6 or 7 completely separate septs or clans have existed. In Co. Dublin the family is found as 'Lords of Suaithni' and they were centered there in the barony of Balrothy west.

In Co. Fermanagh individuals of the name served as erenaghs of Devenish. A Dalcassion family of the name was centered near Liscannon, near Bruff in Co. Limerick.

The name is as well found centered in or near Tirawley in Mayo, Mitchelstown in Cork, and in the barony of Athlone in Roscommon in more ancient times.

Note the ancient remains of 'Casey's Lios' at Ballygunnermore in Co. Waterford.

The 1800's birth index shows some 254 Casey births, with Cork, Kerry and Dublin heading the list as the most numerous counties of the name.

Casserly

Casserley

The Casserly name is traditionally associated with county Roscommon in Ireland, and it is in that county where the name is found in the 1890 birth index.

Clarke

Irish Book of Arms plates 94 and 219

Clarke, O'Clery

Clarke, Clairke, Clarkins, Cleary, Clerke,

In Ireland the name of Clark(e) may be of Irish or English origins. The old Irish families of the name likely stem from the original spelling of O'Clery. 'Clarke' is also a name noted in the Woodford area of Galway, in connection with mining operations in the 18th century, (of the Ulstermen). (see Cleary)

A common name, it is most commonly found in the province of Ulster at the time of the 1800's birth index. The name is however found throughout the country. The counties with the largest numbers of the name at that time were Antrim, Dublin, Mayo, Cavan and Louth.

In Co. Cavan, Clark families are believed to be of the older Irish stock of O'Clery, and Keatings work gives them in the baronies of Clankee and Tullygarvey in Cavan. They were said to be a branch of the more ancient family from Connaught and Donegal.

Keatings also gives the family as 'chiefs of Ui Fiachra Finn' and tells us that they were the bards and historians to the O'Donnells, and the authors of the Annals of the Four Masters.

Clarke was a numerous name by the 17th century and it was found as a principal name in Dublin city and elsewhere by that time.

Clark(e) ranks among the 40 most numerous surnames in both Scotland and England, as well as in Ireland. It may be assumed that many arrived in Ireland from those places.

Both spellings are common in America today as well. Clark ranks among the top 20 names and Clarke ranks among the 420 most common names.

The arms for Clark of Largantogher, Co. Londonderry, who settled there in 1690, are given in the Book of Arms.

44

Clement(s)

Irish Book of Arms plate 54, 62, 129..

Mac Clement, Clements, MacLemont,

A Huguenot family of Ireland as given by some under the name of Clement. The Clements family of Killadoon, Co. Kildare, and of Lough Rynn, Co. Leitrim are of the same line, as given in the Irish Book of Arms.

Many families of the name of Clements are of English settler extraction, settling in Ireland no later than the 17th century. Of this line was the Earl of Leitrim. The 1659 census finds the family centered in Antrim and the city of Cork and the 1890 birth index gives the family in Antrim as well, all under the spelling of Clements.

The Irish family of the name of MacLamond is also on record as having changed their name to MacClement and likely subsequently to Clements.

The Scottish name of Lamont is also a somewhat similar surname which, as with the above, is found mainly in the province of Ulster.

Mac Caughey

Mac Eachaidh

Cahey, Mac Aghy, Mac Caghey, Mac

The (Mac)Caughey name appears to be a name associated with the province of Ulster for several hundred years. 'Caughey' is found in Counties Down and Antrim in the 1890 index, and McCaughey is given in Antrim and Tyrone in the same record of births in Ireland. At the time the traditional location given for the name was the Glasslough district in Monaghan Union, County Monaghan.

The Hearth Money Rolls for County Tyrone list 'Mac Cahee' as a surname some 300 years ago.

O Clery

Irish Book of Arms plate 57, 219

O'Cleirigh

Cleary, Mac Cleary, Clerken, Cleery,

The O'Clearys were a leading family in the diocese of Kilmacdugh in Galway, until the 13th century, when many moved elsewhere.

County Donegal boasts the most famous of the name. Many settled in Cavan too, where it is believed the name was changed to Clark(e). The name is also centered in Kilkenny where it remains today. The family is also found in Tipperary and Waterford.

At least two other names have been changed into Cleary. In Co. Limerick, in the barony of Coshma, Clerkin has been shortened Clerk and Cleary. Mac Aleary or MacClery of Co. Antrim has also been changed to Clery .

In the 17th century Cleary was a principal name of Tipperary and found in Waterford, Kilkenny and Louth. The variant spelling of Cleere was a principal name of Kilkenny and found in Queens and Tipperary. O'Cleery was a variant spelling which was a principal name of Donegal at that time. These spellings are now interchangeable.

The interchangeability of Clark(e) and O'Cleary has often been recorded. The general registrar of births noted this trend specifically in Tuam Union in Co. Galway, and in Enniskillen Union, Co. Fermanagh. Keatings also cites "O'Clery, a name sometimes Anglicized to Clarke". That source gives the family as of the Ui Fiachra race, being chiefs of Ui Fiachra Finn.

One of the first to use a formal family name, they take the name from Cleirach, chief in the 10th century. Many of the name are distinguished in literature.

In Donegal they became bards and historians to the O'Donnells, and they were authors of the Annals of the Four Masters. Others settled in Breffny.

Cliffe

Irish Book of Arms plate 40

Cliff

One noted family of the name is found in Mulvan, Co. Wexford. The Cliffe family of Bellevue, Co. Wexford were originally of Westminster, settling in Ireland under the command of Cromwell in 1649. The family then obtained lands in Wexford and Meath.

Caskin

variant of Askin or Gaskin

Gaskin, Askin, (Gascoigne)

A very rare name in Irish records, several possibilities exist to explain the 'Caskin' origin in Ireland. Unlikely, although possible, 'Askin' is an English name found in Ireland, which is said to be a variant of Heskin.

A more likely answer is that the Caskin name is a variant spelling of Gaskin. This spelling has been found in Ireland from the 1200's onward, and is considered a name of the province of Leinster. Note the place name of Gaskinstown, County Meath.

In the census of 1659 Gaskin is found in County Louth, and in the 1890 birth index in Dublin. The original form of the name is said to be Gascoigne i.e. originating in Gascony.

Chamberlain

Chamberlayne

According to "Keatings History" the name is given among the chief Anglo-Norman and English settlers in Ulidia, under DeCourcey and his successors. Among noted families of the name in our files are Chamberlayne of Kilrisk and Kilmacree Co. Dublin, and Chamberlayne of Athboy, Co. Meath

45

Mc Clintock

Irish Book of Arms plate 24

The name of a Scottish family who first settled in Ulster no later than the 16th century, found centered in Co. Donegal.

McClintock families of Rathvinden, Co. Carlow and those of Dunmore, Co. Donegal are given in the Irish Book of Arms.

Canny

MacCanny, O'Canny, Canny,

Families of the name of Canny are found centered in counties Clare and Mayo in 19th century Ireland. Two completely separate families are thought to bear the name today. Those of O'Canny, a family anciently of Co. Mayo, and those of MacCanny often found in the Limerick/Clare area of Ireland. One family of the latter is found centered at the Castle of Drumbanny in the latter 16th century.

Cantillon

Cantlin, Cantlon

Families of the name of Cantillon, Cantlin and Cantlon are of Norman extraction when found in Ireland, settling here with the coming of the Norman invasions of the 12th century. They become most prominent at Co. Kerry in short time, and are found centered there at Ballyheigue. The family is also found in several centuries in Co. Limerick. The name is earlier found as de Cantelupo and as de Cauntelo, called so after a place name in France.

46

Close

Irish Book of Arms plate 102

Many of the name of Close are descended from English settler families in Ireland, on record in Monaghan and Antrim in Ireland since the 17th century. Older Irish families of the name here adopted the name in place of their own O'Clusaigh, according to several sources.

Both the census of 1659 and the 1890 birth index find the name mainly in Antrim.

The Irish Book of Arms finds the family of "Close of Drumbanagher" of Co. Armagh. This family descended originally from Richard Close of Yorkshire, England, and eventually settled in Co. Monaghan, and later in Lisburn, Co. Antrim, Ireland.

Canty

Cantey, County

Families of the name of Canty are traditionally associated with Co. Cork in Ireland. Canty was a principal name of the barony of Kinalmeaky in Co. Cork in the 17th century and was found in Cork and Limerick in the 19th century birth index. Several noted poets of the name are found in older records.

Capplis

Caplise, Caplice, Capels, Capples

The name of an English family found settled in Tipperary and Cork.

Cardwell

Families of the name of Cardwell may spring from one of several different origins. First, some of the name settled here from England. Second, the name has been interchanged with Caldwell and Carroll on occasion. By the time of the 1890 index, the name of Cardwell was found centered in Co. Antrim in Ireland.

Cobbe

Irish Book of Arms plate 50

Cobb

The Cobbe family of Newbridge House, Co. Dublin settled there, coming from Southampton originally.

Mc Carney

Carney, Karney, Carny, Kearney

The works of Woulfe place the McCarney family centered in Ballymaccarney in Co. Meath more anciently. In modern times we find the name dispersed and often found in the province of Ulster, including Co. Monaghan. The name of "Carney" is found centered in Mayo in the 19th century. (see Kearney)

Mc Carrig

Carrick

Families of the name of MacCarrig or Carrig are traditionally linked to Co. Clare in Ireland, where it is assumed to be the name of an old Irish family. Some of the name descend also from de Carraig or de Carrick, a family of settler origins in Ireland.

The similar name of McCarrick or Carricke, is found in Co. Kerry and Dublin City in the census of 1659. In modern records this name is often found in the province of Ulster, in the north of Ireland, which may represent later settlers of the name in Ireland.

Mc Carron

MacCaron, McCarren

The McCarron family name is traditionally linked to the Donegal and Derry area of Ireland.

Mac Catigan

Cattigan

The name of a family found in Co. Mayo.

Coddington

The Irish Book of Arms plate 88

The Coddington family of Oldbridge, Co. Meath are given in the Irish Book of Arms.

Mc Carroll

Carroll, Carrol, Caroll

Families of the name of McCarroll are found centered in Queens county in the 17th century, where McCarroll was found to be a principal name at that time. Several centuries later, the 19th century birth index finds the name of McCarroll centered in Co. Londonderry. Note also that the family name of McCarroly, was found as a principle name of Roscommon in the 17th century, and some of the name are likely to be found as McCarroll or Carroll today. That name is also found in Co. Westmeath.

There are believed to have been at least two separate families using the name of McCarroll. One branch of the name are believed to be a branch of the MacCarville family of Ulster. In that instance, the name of McCarroll was simply often used instead of McCarville by way of "translation" of the name.

Some of the name of Carroll in Ireland are McCarrolls, others are O'Carrolls. It takes some amount of research to determine which family is which.

Mc Caughan

The name of a family traditionally linked to Co. Antrim in Ireland.

O Coffey

Irish Book of Arms plates 148 and 259

O'Cobhthaigh

Coffee, Cowhey, Cowhig, Cofee

There are several families that go by the name of Coffey etc.. in Ireland. They can be found in western Co. Cork, Galway, Roscommon and a family of bards by the name hail from Westmeath.

Keatings gives the family in an ancient genealogy which traces the family to the son of Ith. The O'Cowhys, (O'Coffeys), are cited as anciently powerful, with 7 castles on the coast in the barony of Ibane and Barryroe. They were found as 'Lords of the country of Triocha Meona, of the white-stoned shore, valiant foes in sea fights'.

They are as well given as a clan of note in Westmeath, and as a branch of the O'Kellys, the princes of Ui Mani, in the barony of Clonmocnoon, Galway. (Tuam Cathraigh).

In Cork the Coffeys are of the same early stock as the O'Driscolls, and the name is often found as Cowhig and Cowhey. Note the place name of Dunocowhey there. These are likely the most numerous family of the name.

In Westmeath, where the O'Coffeys have attained some fame as bards and poets anciently, the name has been less prominent in modern times.

Roscommon bears the location of yet another family center. Here the family is actually a branch of the O'Maddens of Ui Maine.

In the 17th century 'Coffey' is found in Westmeath and 'Coffy' is a principal name there too, as well as being found in Roscommon. In more modern times the 1800's index finds the name Coffey in Kerry, Tipperary, Dublin, Cork and Roscommon.

The variant spelling of Coffie is given in 1659 as a principal name of Roscommon. Note the place name of Rathcoffey, in Kildare and Leix.

Cole

Irish Book of Arms plate 20

Coal

One noted Cole family is found in Newland, Co. Dublin. The main locations for the name in the 19th century were in counties Dublin, Londonderry, Armagh, Down and Kings.

Carruthers

Carrothers, Caruth

The name of Caruthers is given to be a settler name in Ireland, the name itself coming from a place name in Scotland. As may be expected, the family is found centered in the province of Ulster, although it has also been found in Dublin City and in Waterford at a fairly early date. Seven scattered births of the name are found in the 1890 index.

The name of Caruth, may simply be a shortened form of Caruthers, but we have no evidence of this at present.

Cartmill

Kertmel, de Kertmel, Cartmell

The name of a family traditionally linked to Co. Armagh in Ireland. A settler family in Ireland, some members believe that the name came from the place name of "Cartmell" in England. Five births of the name were recorded in 1890, all in Co. Antrim.

Mac Cavana

MacCavina, Caveny

The name of a family found in modern times in Co. Antrim and surrounds.

Chaffee

Chafe, Chaffy, Chafy

One of the name has been traced back to Richard Chamberlain or Chamberlen etc.. who lived in the 14th century. This family is found settled in Kilrisk and Kilmacree in Co. Dublin

Mac Colgan

Irish Book of Arms plates 148 and 237.

Mac Colgan, O'Colgan

Colgen, Colgun, Coligan, Colligan,

Originally there were at least two families, Mac Colgan and O'Colgan. O'Colgan appears to have been discarded as a surname and the more numerous Mac Colgan was adopted by members of both families.

The O'Colgans hailed from the barony of Tirkeeran in Co. Derry, and they are also noted settled in the Inishowen peninsula of Co. Donegal, and as ancient chiefs, one of whom later settled in Kildare (Keatings). O'Dugan stated that O'Colgan was a chief in Tirkeeran in the 14th century, and it was these who served as erenaghs of Donaghmore at Inishowen.

The Colgan family is also found centered in the in the barony of Garrycastle in Co. Offaly (Kings Co.). Note the place names of Kilcolgan Beg and Kilcogan Mor in the barony bordering on Westmeath.

O'Hart, in his work, found Colgan in Co. Louth down to the 15th century and gave them as chiefs in Kildare, with families in Down and Armagh.

In the 1800's birth index 'McColgan' is found as the preferred spelling of the name in Donegal and Londonderry. 'Colgan' (without the 'mac') was found more often in Dublin, Kings (Offaly) and Antrim.

Cherry

Sherry

The Cherry family is traditionally associated with Co. Down when found in Ireland. Most of the name are accepted as being originally of English heritage. The 1890 birth index gives the name in Co. Down as well. Some undocumented sources find the family settling in Limerick and Tipperary in the 17th century.

48

Colhoun

The Irish Book of Arms plate 97

Calhoune, Calhoun, Colquhoun

The Colhoun family of Carrickbaldoey. Co. Donegal are likely descended from Alexander Colquhoun, who was granted 1,000 acres of land in Donegal upon the plantation of Ulster. This is a settler family. The birth index of 1890 finds the family centered in counties Londonderry and Tyrone.

Causgrove

Irish Book of Arms plate 264

O'Coscraigh

Cosgrove, Cosgroove, Cosgrave,

The Cosgrove or Causgrove name most likely stems from O'Coscraigh, found in the provinces of both Ulster and Connaught. In Connaught the name may be found near the shores of Galway Bay, and in Ulster the name has been used for several more ancient ones. One O'Cosgrave chief was given in the barony of Bantry, in Co. Wexford, and the family was said to be 'a noble tribe with hawk like sparkling eyes'.

Another similar sounding name, MacCosgrave, is found in Monaghan and Wicklow, is a separate family altogether. The name may come from this source as well.

Spelled as 'Cosgove' the name was found in Mayo and Galway, as well as Ulster, in the 1890 birth index.

The Cosgraves of Wicklow and Queens Counties changed their name to Lestrange (per Keatings).

Cheasty

The name of a family most often linked to Co. Waterford in our records.

Collier

Irish Book of Arms plates 259

Coileir

le Collier, Colyer

The Collier name is usually of English origin when found in Ireland, although the name has been on record here since the 14 century. The census of 1659 finds the name as a principal one of County Meath, and also in Dublin city. The birth index shows the name in Wexford, at the turn of the last century.

le Collier was the older Anglo-Norman spelling of the name.

Cheevers

According to "Keatings History" the name is one of a noted family in Meath. Some of this line held the title of " Baron of Mount Leinster". Nicholas Cheevers of Ballyhally, Co. Wexford gave rise to families of the name in Macetown, Co. Meath who controlled lands in the barony of Killyan in Co. Galway. Another family of the same line is found in Mountaine, Co. Dublin in the 17th century.

Cheney

Chainey, Cheyney, Chesney

Families of the name of Cheney are found settling in Ireland in the early 17th century. One family of note obtained sizable lands in Co. Fermanagh. Subsequently the family is found in Cork and Kildare. Similar appear names are found in our records, i.e.. Cheyne and McCheyne, the latter of which was recorded in the 19th century works of Matheson.

Collins

Irish Book of Arms plates 59 and 229

O'Coileain

Collen, Culhane, Cullane, Cullen,

One of the most numerous names in all of Ireland, Collins ranks among the top 30 names in the country. Although this is a recognized English name, it is also of Irish origins.

Anciently the family is recorded as chiefs of the barony of Connello, Co. Limerick by O'Heerin. He also cites the name O'Cuillein (O'Cullen, or Collins), as chief of Eoganacht Arodh, in Tipperary, as follows:

"O'Cullen who has gained good fame,
Rules over the hospitable Eoganacht
of Ara."

O'Cuilean was another Irish sept of the Corca Laoidhe, which Anglicized its spelling to Collins. In Ulster the name comes from the older MacCoileain which has been changed to Collins.

The Irish name of Cullane, a variant of Collins, comes from Co. Limerick.

Counties Cork and Limerick are the most highly populated with the name in modern times, with Dublin, Galway, Antrim, Kerry and Clare also being given in the 1890 birth index for the name.

Arms for some families of the name are found on plates 59 and 229 in the Irish Book of Arms.

Individuals of the name:

(C) Charles Collins of Wexford.

Faustian Collins, Poll Money Ordinance of 1661.

John Collins, Limerick City, Tipperary, Kilkenny and Poll Money Ord. of 1661.

Willim Collins, Kilkenny.

Collis

Irish Book of Arms plate 62, 77

Families of the name in Ireland are found most prominently in Co. Kerry, where they held substantial lands and influence, with several of the name being found as sheriff etc... . The family can also be found among the merchants of Dublin through two centuries at least. The census of 1659 finds the family in both counties Sligo and Kerry. Several are found receiving lands in Cromwellian times.

Mc Chesney

from French Chesnaye (chesnai) meaning

Chesney, Quesnay, Chesnaye, Cheney.

Chesney is a name which can be found in Ireland at the time of the plantation of Ulster. It is found here with the 'Mac' prefix on several occasions. It as well can be found at earlier dates in Ireland. The name may come from the French 'Chesnai' meaning oak grove. Of the McChesneys of County Down, several are found in the 'Dictionary of National Biography' (Ireland).

Milesian families gives the name in Donegal, arriving from Scotland in 1702.

Francis Rawdon Chesney (1789 - 1872) of note concerning the Suez Canal.

Chifley

Schifley, Shifley, Chifly

Chifley was the name of one family found at Thurles, and of that line came one who became prime minister of Australia.

Christie

Christy

The name of Christie is traditionally associated with Co. Antrim in Ireland. The birth index of 1890 finds the name there as both Christy and Christie.

O Concannon

Irish Book of Arms plates 148 and 260

Cuceannan, O'Concheanainn

O'Connanen, O'Concanain, Concanon

O'Dugan spoke more anciently of the Concannon family thusly:
'The Ui Diarmada of protecting men,
Their heroes are Kinsmen to Kings.
Governor of the territory is
O'Concanain, its undisputed chief.' The Ui Diarmada spoken of here refers to a district bordering Roscommon and Galway in the baronies of Roscommon and Ballymoe.

And so it has always historically been so, with the Concannon family found in and around Co. Galway. MacLysaght states that the family is of the sept of the Ui Maine, descending from one 'Cuceannan' (d. 991). Fr. John Ryan and Rooney state that they are of the Ui Briuin tribe.

In any event they are cited as chieftains of the lands of the Ui Diarmada through the 15th century, and held one center of power at Kilkerrin in Co. Galway in the barony of Tiaquin

The Composition Book of Connaught in the 16th century gives the center of the name at Kultullagh, in the parish of Kilkerrin. Family members note the Abbey at Knockmoy which honors one 'Maurice O'Concannon'.

The birth index of 1890 finds the family in Galway, as well as in Mayo and Roscommon.

The crest found in the Book of Arms is unique in that it depicts an elephant.

Claffey

Claffy

Only 7 births of the name are recorded in the 1890, in scattered locations. Families of the name are also found in Co. Roscommon.

Condon

Irish Book of Arms plate 148

Condun

de Caunteton, Condron, Condan

The barony of Condons found in the northeast of Co. Cork was named in honor of the Condon family there. Here they were centered at the castle of Cloghleagh near Kilworth.

The Condon family is not an ancient Irish one. They arrived in Ireland with the coming of the Norman invasions here. As with many other settlers, they eventually became thoroughly Irish.

The 17th century brought many troubles to the family as it did for so many others. Several are found on the wrong side of the 'law' during this period of time.

The Irish family of O'Condubhain is also said to have corrupted their name into Condon. They were of the north of Ireland in Ulster. The spelling of 'O'Condon' is to be found in Keatings History.

In the census of 1659 the name was a principal one of County Cork, and found in Limerick, Tipperary and Kerry as well. In the 1890 index 'Condon' births were recorded in Counties Cork, Tipperary and Kerry. Some sources give Cork and Tipperary as the original counties of settlement for the family in Ireland.

Arms for one family of the name are found in the Irish Book of Arms, plate 148.

Christopher

Christopher was a principal name of Waterford in the census of 1659, and it is in that county where we have most often found the name. They are found in that county in the barony of Decies and elsewhere. Subsequently we find the name in Leitrim and Cork.

50

O'Connell

Irish Book of Arms plates 36, 112,...

O'Conghail

Connell, Connel, Conel, Conall,

Many separate families of this name exist, and it is the O'Connells of Kerry who are most noted. Anciently they ruled as chiefs of Magunihy in Kerry. By the 11th century the O'Donaghues forced the O'Connells towards the west coast. Here, protected by the McCarthy Mor, they served in hereditary positions at Ballycarbery.

With the coming of Cromwell the chief of the name was forced into Clare, where the family can be found in modern times. (Note Maurice O'Connell who lived near Lisdoonvarna)

The most famous of the modern period was Daniel O'Connell (1775-1847), a brave representative of the Catholic cause. He was of the Kerry family, born at Carhen. His genealogy has been traced in ' O'Connell Family Tracts' (1947) which is in print today.

Other O'Connell families have faded into history. In Ulster the O'Connaills of Derry are found more anciently. In Galway the O'Connaills of Galway held sway in earlier times.

The 'O' prefix before the name had largely been dropped in previous centuries, leaving the name simply as Connell. Today the reverse is true, with many families once again using the full name of O'Connell.

In the topographical poems of O'Dugan the O'Connells of Oriel and Ui Maine are cited, but they vanished from prominent records centuries ago.

McConnell is a separate and distinct family from the north of Ireland and was found in Limerick and Tipperary.

The 1659 census finds McConnell as a principal name of Antrim, and in Donegal, Down, Derry and Longford.

O'Connell represents one of the top 25 names of Ireland.

O Connellan

Irish Book of Arms plates 45, 240.

O'Conallain, O'Coinghiollain

Connalan, Connellan, O'Connellane,

Although the Connellans are often found as Conlan or Conlon today, in earlier times the form of Connellan was more prominent. Several family names have shortened themselves into Conlan over time in Ireland.

Two main families of Connellan are given here. The first came from the Roscommon/Galway area of Ireland from Conallain and the second was centered in Co. Sligo (O'Coinghiollain)

In the 17th century the following spellings and locations were found concerning the family. O'Connellane was a principal name of Armagh; Connellan a principal name of Louth; and Connalan a principal name of Westmeath. In the 1890 birth index only 8 births were recorded of the Connellan name. Some had changed the name to Conlan and Conlon by then.

Keatings History cites 'O'Kendellan or O'Connellan prince of Ui Laeghari or Ive-Leary", an extensive territory in the counties of Meath and Westmeath, descended from Laegari, monarch of Ireland at the time of St. Patrick.

The parish of Castletown Kendellan in Westmeath gives one location for the name, as does the townland known as Kendellans town by Navan.

O'Dugan further finds the name of O'Connellan as "chief of Crioch Tullach" in Co. Tyrone. and says the name has been changed by some to Connolly.

The O'Connellans of the barony of Gallen and Kilmain in Co. Mayo were said to have been a branch of the Meath family but they were 'long settled in Mayo, Sligo and Roscommon" according to Keatings.

The arms of Connellan of Coolmore, Co. Kilkenny are given above.

O Connolly

Irish Book of Arms plates 92 and 149.

O'Conghaile, O'Congheallaigh

Conneely, Connolly, Conoly, Connoly,

The O'Connolly name is one of the top 30 names in all of Ireland. Several unrelated families are on record here. This family name is also often confused and interchanged with similar sounding names such as Coneely and Conly.

The most famous family of the name was that of O'Conghaile of Co. Monaghan in Ulster. They were of the southern Ui Neill, one of the Four Tribes of Tara and Princes of Bregia in more ancient times. They were subsequently driven into Monaghan with the coming of the Norman invasions.

The O'Connollys of western Co. Cork in the province of Munster are more anciently of note in the old territory of O'Donovan there.

The O'Connollys of Ui Maine, in the province of Connaught, are associated with county Galway today where the preferred spelling is Conneely.

The 1800's birth index finds Conneely in Galway and Connolly in Cork, Monaghan, Galway, Antrim and Dublin. In the 17th century 'O'Connoly' was a principal name of Monaghan; Connoly a principal name of Louth; and Connolay a principal name of Waterford.

The arms of Conolly of Castletown, Co. Kildare are given in the Irish Book of Arms. They descend from the same line as William Conolly, 18th century speaker of the House of Commons in Ireland.

J. G. Connolly was a Lt. in the 2nd Regt. of Corcorans Irish Legion of Civil War fame in America. The name is found in Meaghers Irish Brigade of the day, as well as in the Spanish army in Europe.

O'Connor Kerry

O'Connor Don

O Connor

Irish Book of Arms plates 70, 87 and 111

Conchobhar

O'Conor, Coner, Conier, Conner, Conyer

One of the most numerous names in Ireland, several unrelated families account for the popularity of this name.

The most noted of the name are from the old province of Connaught, descended from Conchobhar, King of Connaught who died in the year 971.

The main branches of this family were: The (1) O'Conor Don, from whom we have one of the last High Kings of Ireland. The O'Conor Don also had two branches of its family, (2) The O'Connor Roe, and (3) The O'Connor Sligo family. Arms also exist for the (4) O'Connor Faly and the (5) the O'Connor Corcomroe families.

The O'Connors of Kerry, who held sizable estates in the north of that county, were forced north with the coming of the Norman invasions, but still held sway in the barony of Iraghticonnor. One center of power for the family in this region was at Carrigafoyle Castle. This family accounts for a great many of the name.

The O'Connors of Clare (Corcumroe) hail from the barony of Corcumroe, and are descended from the same ancestor as the O'Loughlins of the Burren. The Offaly O'Connors descend from Cathaoir Mor, the Irish King of the 2nd century. They met with decline in the 16th century after much turmoil and warfare.

The Co. Derry family of the name (in the region of Keenaght) declined with the rise of the O'Kanes of that area around the time of the 12th century Norman invasions of Ireland. Some of the name remain there to this day.

Although some live and die by the spelling of the name, i.e. O'Connor or O'Conner, no distinction can be made in the spelling of the name today. These spellings have been interchanged at will.

O Conroy, Conry

Irish Book of Arms plates 149 and 249

O'Maolconaire, Mac Conraoi, Conrai

O'Mulconry, Conery, Conary, Conrahy,

The names of Conry and Conroy have been so often taken on by other families and mistranslated by others that it is often difficult to determine their origins.

At the turn of the last century official records show Conroy families using the names and spellings of: Conary, Conrahy, Conree, Cunree, Cory, Mulconry and King. The same shows that Conry was less distorted with Connery, Mulconry and Conroy being used interchangeably with that name.

More properly the name stems from O'Conrai of the eastern Galway/ Roscommon areas, and from Mac Conraoi of the barony of Moycullen in the west of Galway.

The most noted are of O'Maolconaire. They were centered in the parish of Clooncraff near Strokestown in Roscommon and commonly spelled the name as Conry. They served as poets to the chieftains of the area and are easily found in the records there.

Keatings work cites Mac Conroy thusly: ' Mac Conroy possesses in peace, Gno Mor of the numerous harbors.' Mac Conroy was chief of Gno Mor which lay upon the western banks of Lough Corrib, between that lake and Galway Bay, in the barony of Moycullen, Co. Galway.

O'Hart gives the O'Maolconrys as ancient chiefs in Teffia or Westmeath, when they crossed the Shannon River in the 10th century and received lands from the O'Connors, Kings of Connaught. They are given here in the barony of Roscommon, Co. Roscommon, as hereditary historians and bards. In 1846 the head of that family was then living in Berkshire, England, under the name of Sir John Conroy.

51

Mac Considine

Irish Book of Arms plate 149

Mac Consaidin

Mac Considin, Consadine, McConsidn,

The Considine family name is traditionally associated with Co. Clare in Ireland. Their line of descent can be traced back to Domhall Mor O'Brien, a King of Munster (d. 1194). The family is not often cited in the historical records we normally review, and the name actually came into being later than most other Irish surnames.

In 1659 the name is found in Clare as Considin, McConsidin, McConsidn, and Mac Considan, and was a principal name of Clare at that time.

The family has remained in this area for generations, with Counties Clare and Limerick remaining Considine country into modern times.

Keatings History places the family in the barony of Ibracken in Co. Clare. The Histories of Clare by Frost and White are good places to start family historical research here.

'Mac Considin' is given as among the most important families in Ireland at the beginning of the 17th century as found on the 'Ortelius Improved...map of Ireland. They are again given in Clare.

Arms for the family name are found on plate 149 in the Irish Book of Arms.

Church

Families of the name of Church are on record as settling in Ireland from the 17th century onward. The 1659 census places the name in Co. Londonderry. Several families of the name are found early settled in Co. Derry, and subsequently in the Cork and Kerry areas of Ireland. We do not know if they represent completely separate families of the name or not, at this time.

52

Conway

Irish Book of Arms plates 18 and 210

Connmhaigh, Conmhachain...

Conaway, McConway, O'Conway,

The family name of Conway is traditionally associated with Co. Clare. It is found in that county as both O'Conway and MacConway. These are often referred to as the Thomand Conways.

In Co. Tyrone the Conway name can stem from the Irish 'MacConmidhe, in Co. Mayo from O'Conmhachain, and in Sligo from O'Conbhuidhe.

One family of the name in Co. Kerry was actually of Welsh heritage, being settled there in the 16th century. They held lands at Killorglin in Kerry and in Co. Dublin. This family also donated sons to King James' Irish army.

There were also the Conway Barons, of Anglo-Irish extraction, who settled early in Ireland as well.

In the 17th century McConway is found as a principal name of Kings Co. (Offaly). Conway is also found in Co. Kilkenny at this time.

In Keatings History MacConmedha (MacConway) is cited as a principal chief of Tefia, in the territory of Muintir Laodagain. Teffia formed a great portion of the ancient kingdom of Meath.

The 1800's birth index gives the name primarily in Mayo, Tyrone and Dublin at that time.

Variant spellings of the name such as Convey and Conboy have been reported, but these are relatively scarce names in any event.

One of the Conway arms illustrated in the Irish Book of Arms gives the motto "Fide-et-amore".

In America today the surname of Conway ranks among the 700 most numerous names in the country.

Conyngham

Irish Book of Arms plate 12

Cunningham

Of one family of Co. Donegal of the line of Alexander Conyngham, we find him mentioned as a scion of the House of Glencairn, Scotland, settling in Ireland in 1600. He resided in Rossgul, Co. Donegal.

Chinnery

One family of the name is found settled in Mallow, Co. Cork in the 17th century, and others of the name are often mentioned in Co. Limerick in our records. Further information can be found in the Estate Papers at the National Library in Dublin.

Clavin

Claveen

A family name traditionally linked to Co. Kildare in our records.

Clayton

Branches of the family are found in Doneraile and Moyallow in Co. Cork. Robert Clayton was Bishop of Clogher and was born in Dublin in 1695. Only 12 births of the name were recorded in the 1890 index.

Mc Clean

McLean, McCleen

The name of a Scottish family who arrived in Ireland as a "galloglas" family. The galloglas or gallowglas were heavily armed fighting men often found in the service of Irish chieftains.

Clerian

A name of Co. Monaghan.

Cooke

Irish Book of Arms plate 77 (Cooke)

Cooke, Cook

Cook or Cooke families may be of English heritage when found in Ireland, for this is one of the top 50 names in that country. Found prominent at times in Cork and Tipperary, the seat of power for the name is found at Kiltinan Castle, Castle Cook, and Cordangan.

One English family of the name is said to have been brought here by John Cook who settled in Co. Carlow during Cromwellian times. The family lands were lost however as a result of supporting the cause of King James. The family is later found centered in Kilturra, Ballymote, Co. Sligo. This family is noted to have been of different extraction than others of the name.

MacHugo has been said to have been interchanged with this surname at times.

Catelyn

Irish Book of Arms plate 207 Catlin

Catelline, Catlin

Sir Nathaniel Catelyn, served as speaker for the Irish House of Commons in 1634 and died in 1637, being buried at St. Nicholas's in Dublin.

Mac Clifferty

A name of Co. Tyrone.

Clinton

According to "Keatings History" the name is given among the chief Anglo-Norman or British families settling in Louth quite early. The main location for the name in the 19th century was in Co. Dublin and in Co. Louth.

53

Cooper

Irish Book of Arms plate 27, 67

The Cooper family of Cooper Hill, Co. Limerick, is given in the Irish Book of Arms as a branch of the Tuthill line.

The Cooper family of Markree Castle, Co. Sligo was founded by a Cornet in Colooney's regiment of Dragoons. The birth index of 1890 finds the family centered in Antrim and Dublin counties.

Cleborne

Claiborne, Clairborne, Cliborne, Clibborn

Families of the name of Cleborne are found in St. John's Manor, Co. Wexford and in Ballyculitan-Castle Co. Tipperary, and they are said to be of the same line.

Spellings for the name are numerous, and in O'Hart we fine Claiborne of Romancock of Virginia (USA), Claiborne of Dinwiddie and Windsor, Virginia (USA), Claiborne of Halifax County Virginia, Claiborne of Missouri, Mississippi and Louisiana, (USA).

Clibborn, said to have come from the same family name, is found at Moate Castle, Co. Westmeath, and "Clibborn" is found of Bath, England and of Dublin, Ireland

Mac Clelland

Irish Book of Arms plate 226

Mac Lellan, Cleland, Mc Clelland..

The (Mac) Clelland name in Ireland is usually of a Scottish heritage. As expected, the name is concentrated in Northern Ireland. 'McClelland' is found in Milesian Families as a Scottish family who settled in Antrim in 1572, in the census of 1659 the name is given in Donegal, and in the 1890 index it was a name in Antrim, Down, Armagh, Londonderry and Monaghan. Milesian families also gives the name a separate origin in Londonderry, as being a tribe of the Hy Fiachra.

Coote

The Irish Book of Arms plate 105

Coot

The Coote family of Mt. Coote, Co. Limerick is given in the Irish Book of Arms. The birth index of 1890 finds the family centered in Co. Dublin.

Clifford

Cliff

The name of Clifford in Ireland may be either of English or older Irish origins when found here. The Irish of the name are most often found in Co. Kerry in modern times, and the name is as well given in Sligo in the census of 1659.

Clinch

Clench, Clenche, Clinchey, Clinchy

Families of the name of Clinch are found in Dublin in the census of 1659. Often spelled as Clench in earlier records, the name is thought to be of English origins, and is most often found in Dublin and the surrounding area of the pale.

Clisham

A name traditionally linked to Co. Galway.

Cloherty

The name of Cloherty is traditionally linked to Co. Galway in Ireland, where all of the name were found in the 1890 birth index of that country.

Clune

The Clune family name is traditionally associated with Co. Clare in Ireland, and with Ballymacloon in that same county. The name of McClune is also found. The 1890 birth index finds the family in Co. Clare as well.

Cope

Irish Book of Arms plate 92, 96

Copeland

We find reference to one Richard Cope of Rathamane, Co. Carlow in the early 17th century. The Cope family of Drummilly, Co. Armagh have been in that area for over 300 years. The Cope family of Loughgall Manor, Co. Armagh descend from Anthony Cope of Portadown, Co. Armagh and they are given in the Irish Book of Arms.

Cloonan

The Cloonan name is traditionally linked with Co. Galway in Ireland, the same location as given for the name in the 1890 birth index. The name of O'Clonine, which may account for some of the name of Cloonan today, was given as a principal name of Longford in the census of 1659.

Mac Clory

McClorey

The MacClory family has been traditionally linked to Co. Down in Ireland. The 19th century birth index confirms that location for the name. Some reference to the name is also given in Co. Antrim, and one source gives the family as being originally from Scotland.

Clossick

A rare name to find in Ireland, the origins of this family are unclear. Most of the family are found in Co. Mayo in our records, and many of the name are found in and near Swinford in that county. Most give the family to be an old Irish one, and not of foreign extraction.

54

Cornock

The Irish Book of Arms plate 95

The Cornock family of Cromwellsfort, Co. Wexford, descend from a military man of the name who obtained a grant of lands in that county and they are given in the Irish Book of Arms.

O'Clohessy

O Clochasaigh

O'Clossey, O'Clohessy, O'Cloghessy,

The family name of (O)Clohessy etc.. is traditionally tied to counties Clare and Limerick, and is rarely found outside of this geographic area. Some of the name have been found in northern Co. Tipperary, thus the claim that the name is of the older geographic region of 'Thomand'. The birth index of 1890 finds the name in Clare and Limerick, continuing to support this fact. The family seems to have been centered in Ballynaglearach, parish of Ogonellow, in County Clare. This family is said to have later located in the townland of Ballycloghessy, (barony of Islands) which is aptly named.

Surprisingly few of the name are found in the History of Clare by Frost, but among them are one 'Thomas Cloghessy', who died in 1582, and who was owner of Ballynagleragh. His son Art exchanged these lands with Turlogh MacMahon for those of Lissanair, parish of Kilmihil. Also one 'Donald Crom (the stooped) Cloghessy conveyed lands at the end of the 16th century to David Cloughessy. These were also lands of Ballinaglearagh.

'Thomas Cloghessy' is listed as a Catholic priest of Clare in 1704, of Clondagad and Kilchreest parish. Listed under sureties in this roster was one Turlogh O'Brien of Bealacorick.

Cornwell

Irish Book of Arms plate 67

of foreign origins

Cornwall, Cornewell

Cornwell is not an ancient family name of Ireland. It is of likely English or Scottish origin. This is supported by the fact that the name is found only in Londonderry in the census of 1659.

Mc Clure

McLure

The name of a Scottish family who arrived in the province of Ulster no later than the 17th century. Some Irish families are also said to have adopted the name of McClure.

Mc Cloud

One family of the name is found on the Isle of Skye, and are said by O'Hart to have originally been of the Scottish name of MacLeod. One John McCloud, who was a fisherman at Rush in Co. Dublin is found in the mid 19th century. He moved to America, landing in New York and settling in Norwich, Connecticut.

Clyne

Cline, Clin, Clyn, Kilclyne, Clynes

The Clyne family is found centered in Leitrim and Longford in the 1890 birth index of Ireland. The old Irish families of the name descend from Kilclyne or more properly Mac Gilclyne (Mac Giolla Chlaoin). This was anciently a family of Co. Roscommon, where we find the place name of Ballykilcline marking their territory. Norman families of the name are also found in Ireland, often spelling their name as Cline, Clin, or Clynes. The spelling of McCline is also found in our records.

O Corrigan

Irish Book of Arms plates 149 and 218.

OCorragain

Carrigan, Corigan, Corrican, Corregan,

Most Corrigan families today may trace their origins to Fermanagh, where they are of the same descent as the Maguires of that county. The name has become rather widespread, but not too numerous in modern times.

Most references to the name are found in Fermanagh historically, but several sources find the family in the barony of Owney and Arra, near Nenagh in Co. Tipperary.

In 1659 both O'Corrican and O'Corrigan were principal names of Fermanagh. 'Corrigan' was a principal name of Longford at that time. All three spellings have generally become the same in modern times. For the most part the 'O' prefix before the name had been dropped before the start of the 1900's.

O'Hart finds the family in Westmeath as well as in Fermanagh in his works.

The 1890 birth index shows 74 births for the name in Dublin, Mayo, Fermanagh, Monaghan and Louth.

Arms for the name are found in the Irish Book of Arms plates 149 and 218.

Coakley

Colkly, Colclough, Coakeley

Coakley is a variant spelling of the English name of Colclough or Colkly, which has been found in Co. Wexford in or near Tintern. Some of the name of Kehilly, an older Irish family, have adopted the name as well, most of whom are found in Co. Cork.

In modern times, the family name is given centered in Co. Cork in the 1890 birth index. The name of Colclough was still centered in the province of Leinster at that time.

55

Cosby

Irish Book of Arms plate 49

One family of the name is found settled in Stradbally, Queens Co. (Co. Leix) in the early 17th century. The Cosby family of Stradbally Hally, Queens Co., is given in the Irish Book of Arms.

Mc Cluskey

Irish Book of Arms plate 262

Mac Bhloscaidh

McCluskey, McClosky, McLoskey

The Mc Cluskey or McCloskey family is traditionally associated with Co. Derry in Ireland, and the same remains true today. They descend from Mac Bhloscaidh, and are a branch of the O'Cahans. One Blosky 'O'Cahan is given in the year 1196 as the ancestor of this family of Derry. His son, Donnough is mentioned in the Annals as well.

One traditional location for the family in Derry has been Benady Glen. The McCloskeys were of note in O'Cahans country, and often feuded with the neighboring O'Mullans. In the parish of Dungiven, McLoskey was a leading family.

In the 1890 index McCloskey is found mainly in Londonderry (Derry) and McCluskey in Antrim and Dublin. In the 1659 census the name was a principal one of Londonderry as well.

Arms for the name are found on plate 262 in the Irish Book of Arms.

Coghill

The name of an English family traditionally linked to Co. Kilkenny.

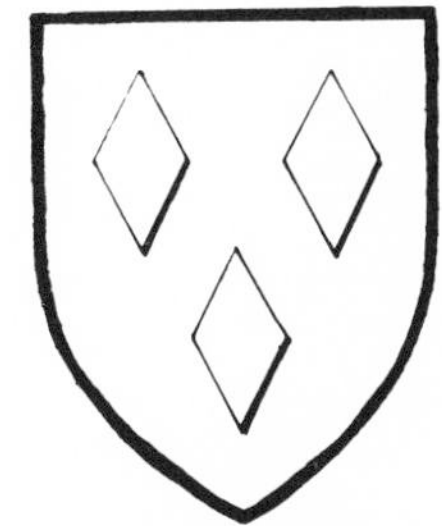

Mac Costello

Irish Book of Arms plates 210 and 149

de Nangle

Costolloe, Costelo, Costellow, Costillo,

Costello families are most often of early Norman descent when found in Ireland. Most will trace themselves back to Gilbert de Nangle in the 12th century.

According to "Keatings History" the name is given as an Irish name which was also adopted by Anglo-Norman or English families in lieu of their original surnames.

The de Angulos, or Nangles, of Meath and Mayo, changed their names to Mac Costello.

With the addition of 'Mac' before the name in some early records, this may be the first Norman name to do so. Rightly so in that the Costellos became 'more Irish than the Irish themselves' according to some. They also developed a feud with the native MacDermott family of the area however.

Having settled in the province of Connaught early, their lands in the barony of Costello in eastern Co. Mayo were held until the 16th century. During that century the chief of the name was centered in Ballaghadereen,in present day Co. Roscommon.

Costello is also found as a principal name of Tipperary in the 17th century. In more recent times Costello was most popular in Mayo, Dublin and Galway, while Costelloe was found in Limerick, Galway and Clare.

Several other names on occasion have been changed to Costelloe. Cushely, Costly and Casserly are examples.

Keatings records 'Gilbert de Angulo, or Nangle, obtained Magherigallen, now the barony of Morgallion in Meath. Jocelin, son of Gilbert Nangle obtained Navan and Ardbraccan. The Nangles were afterwards barons of Navan.'

Mac Cotter

Irish Book of Arms plate 150

Mac Oitir, MacCoiter

O'Cotter, Cotter, Cottor, Kotter,

The traditional homeland for the Cotter family has always been in County Cork. Here you can find several place names using 'cotter' , including the townland of Ballymacotter in the barony of Imokilly.

The name is more properly spelled as Mac Oitir, or Mac Otter, but as is often the case, the 'c' in Mac has been borrowed to form Cotter. Oitir was a common Norse personal name, thus Mac Oitir meant son of Oitir. The family is however still assumed to be of native gaelic origins.

Mac Cotter appears to have been popular centuries ago, but at some point before the 1800's most families had dropped the 'Mac' prefix.

We have one early reference to Mac Oitir in the 12th century, of the Hebrides, who ruled in Dublin, but do not know of any connection between him and the Co. Cork families.

Several works have been done on the Cotter families of Rockforest, Mallow, Co. Cork, for those wishing to pursue research further.

O'Cotter is found as a principal name in Cork in 1659. This is thought to be a mistaken use of the 'O' prefix.

Sir James Laur. Cotter served in the Irish House of Commons in 1797. Family members have served in the Spanish armies, and 'James Cotter's Dragoons are noted in 1690 in Ireland.

O'Hart gives O'Cotter of Rockforest, Mallow, Co. Cork and gives Kotter, Mac Cottyr and McCottir as variant spellings. Gibsons 'History of Cork', gives Cotter as of Danish origin, but we have no confirmation in this matter.

William Cotter of Coppingerstown Castle, Co. Cork, forfeited estates as a result of the troubles of 1641.

56

Cottingham

The Irish Book of Arms plate 67

The Cottingham family is given in the Irish Book of Arms.

Coates

origins likely outside Ireland

Cotes, Coats

The name of Coates is generally found in the province of Ulster, and particularly in Tyrone, Antrim and Fermanagh. In modern times the name is found in Dublin and Ulster. The census of 1659 finds the name in counties Fermanagh and Antrim.

Burke gives the seat of the name as being in Rathmore, Co. Antrim. This 'Coates of Rathmore' family is also found in Glentoran, Co. Down.

Codd

Cod

The Codd name is given to be a settler family name of English extraction when found in Ireland. The family is most often found in the county of Wexford here, and the name spelled as Codde, was as well cited in Waterford. Keatings History gives the name as that of an old English settler family in Wexford.

The census of 1659 also finds the name centered in Co. Wexford in Ireland.

Cody

Coady, Coddy

The Archdeacon family of English origins accounts for some of the Cody family in Ireland. That family arrived after the Anglo-Norman invasions.

Cody was given in 1659 as a principal name of Tipperary, and it was found in Kilkenny and Queens Co. as well then. In 1890 the name is given in Co. Galway. "Coddy" a likely related spelling was found as a principal name of Tipperary in the 17th century.

Mac Coughlan

Irish Book of Arms plates 150, 264.

Mac Cochlain, O'Cochlain

Coughlan, Coghlan, Coghlane, Cohalan,

Those of the Coughlan name today may properly be of either Mac Coughlan or O'Coughlan origins. O'Coughlan hails from the baronies of Carberry and Ballymore in Cork, where the family remains to this day.

In the 17th century 'Coghlane' was the primary spelling of this surname in Cork, where it was a principal name in the census of 1659. Coughlan and Coghlan were primary spellings of the name by the time of the 1890 index of Ireland. The 'O' prefix before the name has been generally dropped for centuries.

Mac Coughlan hailed from the barony of Gerrycastle in Offaly. This family was the better known of the two, and they are well documented in history. The chief of the name was cited as 'chief of Delvin MacCoughlan.

MacCoughlan was noted for possessing many castles, and they are cited as such by the Four Masters. They held power longer than most Irish families. In the 1600's they still held vast tracts of land in Co. Offaly. They remained as landlords into the 19th century near Banagher. In 1659 'Coghlan' was a principal name in Co. Offaly, and it was apparently the preferred spelling in that area.

Keatings cites the O'Coghlans as an old and respected family of County Waterford. They are further cited as 'Lords of Ahra', which comprised the present barony of Garrycastle in Kings County. They are also twice cited as being of Dalcassion descent.

In the 1890 index the most common spelling of the name was as Coughlan, with Coghlan running a fairly close second. Both were most common in Cork at that time, but the later is found in Dublin at that time in some numbers.

Cramer

The Irish Book of Arms plate 89

Kramer

The Cramer family of Ballindinisk House, Co. Cork, descend from Tobias Von Cramer or Kramer, of Lower Germany, who settled in Ireland in the early 17th century.

Coen

Cohen

The name of Coen or Cohen may come from several origins when found in Ireland. Cohen, is of course a well known Jewish surname which could have been changed to Coen. In the Galway and Roscommon areas of the country the name may come from O'Cadhain, of old Irish origins. In Co. Down, some of the name of Cowan may have taken on the spelling of Coen, due to obvious similarities.

The birth index of 1890 finds the name listed in Galway and Roscommon as Coen.

Cogan

Coogan

The name of Cogan may spring from two separate origins. First, there was the Anglo-Norman family of De Cogan, in Cork. Second, the "Coogan" family has used Cogan as a spelling. Cogan is given in Cork and Kildare in 1890, "Cogane" is given as a principal name of Cork in 1659.

Colbert

The 1890 birth index finds the Colbert name centered in Cork and Waterford. Prior to that, we find the name most numerous in Co. Waterford. Some families of the name here arrived from England, and some may have arrived directly from France.

57

Crampsy

Irish Book of Arms plate 91

Crampsie, Bonar, Crampsey, Cramsie

The Crampsy family can be traced back to Co. Donegal in Ireland. Here, the family also uses the name of Bonar as a synonym of Crampsy in Inishowen Union.

The Cramsie family of O'Harabrook, Co. Antrim descend from a settler family who settled at Ballymoney in that county around 1709.

The birth index of 1890 finds the family centered in Co. Donegal.

O Colahan

O'Culachain, MacUallachain

O'Collaghane, Collagan, Cuolaghan,

There are at least two separate origins for this family name, which may be spelled in several different ways. O'Culachain was the name of a sept of the Ui Fiachrach in County Mayo, close to Carra. Here they may be found centered in the parish of Lusmagh, barony of Garrycastle, Co. Offaly. They are also mentioned as the 'Lords of Sil Anmchadha' of that area in Co. Galway.

MacUallachain (from 'proud') was the sept in the barony of Garrycastle in Offaly.

The census of 1659 gives 'O'Collaghane' as a principal name in County Kerry, and at that time the spelling of Collagan was also in use. The MacColleghans held lands in Galway and Offally into the 17th century .

Colfer

Calfer

Families of the name of Colfer are traditionally linked to Co. Wexford in Ireland.

Crawford

Irish Book of Arms plate 80

Crawford is a name traditionally linked to the north of Ireland, in the province of Ulster. Assumed to be of Scottish origins in most cases, several place names stand in honor of this family in Ulster, notably Crawford's Hill, Crawfordsburn and Crawfordsland.

One family of the name, of Millwood, Co. Fermanagh, is also found settled in Snowhill, Co. Fermanagh. Of this line one Henry Crawford (b. 1713) came to America.

The Crawford family of Stonewold, Co. Donegal and the Crawford family of Dunmucrum, near Ballyshannon, Co. Donegal are given in the Irish Book of Arms.

The birth index of 1890 finds the family centered in Antrim, Londonderry, Down and Tyrone.

Coll

Cole

The names of Coll and McColl are found in Co. Donegal in Ireland. A few of the name are found in Limerick as well. Those of Donegal are said to descend from a galloglass family from Scotland by the name of MacColla, who came to Ireland in the service of Irish chieftains.

The name may also serve as a shortened form of Colley, and has also been found spelled as Cole. (see Colley)

Mac Colleghan

Cuolahan, O'Cuolahan, Coolican,

This family is traditionally linked to Co. Galway in Ireland when of MacCuolaghan heritage. When of O'Cuolaghan heritage the family is found centered in Co. Mayo in our records.

Creagh

Irish Book of Arms plates 90, 98

Craobhach

Craig, Craige, McCragh, Cragh, McCreagh

The Creagh family is a branch of the O'Neills of Co. Clare. The name is often connected with Clare, Limerick and Cork. A leading family in Clare, they are found both as 'wild geese' fighting in the service of France and Spain on the continent and in the service of the British army as well. Several families of the name became Protestant in Co. Clare. Others were transplanted there during the time of Cromwell, into Clare and Limerick.

The name itself may come from 'craobh' meaning branch. Legend has it that they carried branches with them into battle against the Vikings at the battle of Limerick. Hence note the importance of the branches in the Creagh arms.

The name may also be of Scottish origins when found in Ulster, the name stemming from 'crag'.

When spelled as Craig, the name is more often of Scottish origins when found in Ulster, but the two spellings, Creagh and Craig have been used interchangeably on occasion.

Craig is found in Antrim, Tyrone and Londonderry in 1890. In the census of 1659 it is also in Londonderry. When spelled as Craige, the name is a principal one of County Antrim in 1659 and is also found in Londonderry and on the Poll Money Ordinance.

Creagh is a principal name of Clare in 1659, and is also in Limerick at that time. There were 17 births under that spelling in 1890. Cragh is a principal name of Waterford in 1659, and McCragh is found in Cork, Limerick City and Waterford at that time.

The name is also found in Cork for several centuries. The arms for Creag of Bally Andrew and for Butler-Creagh of Clare are in the Irish Book of Arms.

58

O Crean

Irish Book of Arms plates 150 and 228

OCroidheain, O'Croidheagain

Crehan, Cregan, Creegan, Mac Crean,

Keatings History cites 'O'Crean' as being numerous in Mayo and Sligo, and these Creans descended from the O'Croidheain family of Donegal who subsequently spread into Sligo and then Mayo. The 'O' prefix before the name had been generally dropped centuries ago, and it is also found as McCrean on occasion.

The O'Creans were a relatively quiet sept of the Cinel Eoghan of Donegal who migrated to Sligo rather early. They are noted as prospering merchants as early as the 16th century. At that time the center for the name was at Ballynegare, headed by one John O'Crean. ' O'Crean of Annagh' was also a noted family in Sligo.

O'Crean and O'Cregan are said to stem from the same origins, and the names have been used interchangeably. The Crehan spelling is often found in Galway and sometimes in Clare.

The Irish family names of Curran and Cureen may also be changed into Crean, particularly in the Cork/Kerry area of Ireland.

The census of 1659 finds O'Crean in Donegal, as would be expected, with the 'O' prefix.

Moving into the 1800's we find Crean most common in Kerry, Cork and Wexford. Crehan was most numerous in Galway at that time.

Arms for the name are found on plates 150 and 228 of the Irish Book of Arms.

Collopy

Callopy

A family of Co. Limerick.

Crofton

Irish Book of Arms plate 23

The name of a family found most often in counties Roscommon and Sligo in our records. The family is given to be of English extraction originally. In the 17th century we find the name in Roscommon, Leitrim, and the city of Dublin as well. One family of the name is found centered in Lisdurn, Co. Roscommon in the early 17th century. The Crofton family of Lakefield, Co. Leitrim is given in the Irish Book of Arms, said to have originally been of Co. Meath in the 18th century, according to that source.

Colley, Cooley

Cooly, MacColly, Collie, Coley, Cowley,

Most of the Colley name in Ireland are of Anglo-Norman extraction, although some of the name may actually be of the Irish family of "Mac Cuille".

In the 1659 census, the spelling of Colly is given as a principal name of Roscommon in the barony of Ballintubber. This family is usually found with a "Mac" before the name in older records

Richard Colley, Marquis of Wellesley, was the eldest son of Garrett, the first earl of Mornington. He was Lord Lt. of Ireland and he married in 1825. The first Lord Mornington assumed the surname and arms of Wesley or Wellesley. Another family of the name is found in Balcarrick, and is given by O'Hart as well. Of that line was John Colley, who was Seneschal of Wexford.

"Robert Cowley or Colley" was bailiff of Dublin in the year 1515, and was likely of English descent. There is a discussion of this by O'Hart.

Croker

Irish Book of Arms plate 53

Croker, Kroker, Groker

The Croker family has been long associated with Co. Limerick (for several centuries in our records) and Co. Waterford. Several families are found subsequently in Co. Cork as well. Richard Croker (d.1922) was of Tammany Hall fame and power.

One family of the name is said to have arrived with the Cromwellian settlement of the 17th century.

The Irish Book of Arms gives the family of Croker of Ballynagarde and Blackwater, Co. Limerick. This family was said in this work to be originally of Devon (England).

Columby

A family of Co. Westmeath, apparently of settler origins. The name may have originally been taken from the English surname of Columbine.

Mc Comb

The name of a Scottish family found settled in Ulster, originally of the Clan McIntosh in Scotland.

O' Conan

Coonan

Families of the name of O'Conan are found centered in Co. Leitrim in the census of 1659.

Conaty

Irish Book of Arms plate 203 Conaghty

Conaghty

A name we find linked to the county of Cavan in our records. The main location for the name in the 19th century was in Co. Cavan.

Crosby, Crosbie

Irish Book of Arms plate 65

Crosbie

One family of the name is found in Co. Kerry in the 17th century in the area of Ardfert and Aghadoe. The Crosbie family of Ballyheigue Castle, Co. Kerry, are given to be a branch of the Crosbies of Ardfert, a family with ties in Queens Co. as well as Co. Kerry.

The birth index of 1890 finds the family centered in Dublin.

Comerford

Commerford

According to "Keatings History" the name is among the chief families of English descent settling in Waterford and Tipperary. These English families primarily possessed the territory called Gal-tir, signifying the country of the foreigners," now the barony of Gaultiere."

The same source finds an old English family of the name in Wexford as well. We find the family most numerous in Kilkenny and Dublin in the 19th century.

Mac Comisky

Comiskey, Comesky, Commiskey,

Families of the name of Comiskey and McCommiskey, etc.. are found in Ireland with many variant spellings of the name here. In the works of Woulfe we find the family centered in counties Westmeath, Longford and Cavan. In Mathesons works we find the name of Comerford being used by MacComisky families as well.

59

O Crowley

Irish Book of Arms plates 150 and 212

O'Cruadhlaoich

Krowley, Crowly, Croly, Crole, Crolly

The Crowley families today may trace their line back to 'Cruadhloach'. The family actually began as a branch of the MacDermots of Moylurg in Co. Roscommon.

The name has all but vanished from its original homeland however. A branch of the Roscommon family moved into Cork near Dunmanaway, establishing an independent seat for itself. Their seat of power lay Kilshallow, just west of Bandon. Many are found in the service of the ruling Mac carthys.

By 1659 both Crowly and O'Crowley were principal names of Co. Cork, and O'Crowle was found in Clare at that time. The 'O' prefix before the name was subsequently discarded.

By the close of the 1600's the power of this family was broken. Many of their lands were taken over by Richard Boyle, the Earl of Cork.

O'Hart also gives the name as changed into Campion, Hardy, Lake, Locke and Poole, for which we have no substantiation.

Rev. George Croly, was a poet, author and novelist born in Dublin in 1780, and he was a 'staunch Tory'.

Peter O'Neill Crowley was born in 1832 at Ballymacoda in Cork. In 1867 he and a few others took refuge in the Kilcloney wood in Cork, 'where these Fenians were defeated on March 31, resulting in his death.'

For beginning research purposes the name may be considered one of Co. Cork, and it is so listed in the 1890 birth index.

Arms for the name are found in the Irish Book of Arms, plates 150 and 212.

O Cullane

Irish Book of Arms plate 150

O'Coileain, O'Cuilleain

Collins, Culhane, Cullane, Culane

The O'Cullane family can be a very difficult one to trace in Ireland due to the fact that it has been changed into several other surnames. It is as well a surname which can be found in England.

Keatings History cites the name of "O'Cuillein, now Cullane and Collins", as a chief in the barony of Connello, Co. Limerick. This family were known as 'Lords of Connello' until the settled in Cork in the 13th century. "O'Cuillein, O'Cullen, or Collins" is also cited as chief of Eoganacht Aradh, which was most likely in the barony of Owney and Arra in Tipperary.

In the 17th century O'Cullane is found as a principal name of Donegal, and also in Cork and Limerick. Cullane was at that time a principal name of Cork, and found in Limerick as well. Culane was a principal name of Clare at that time. The spelling of Culhane can be found often in Limerick, the homeland of the family.

Many of the original name of Cullane are believed to have changed into 'Collins' over the years. Collins is one of the top 30 names in Ireland, and has absorbed several different names due to their similar sounds.

Arms for the name can be found on plate 150 of the Irish Book of Arms.

Conboy

A name found linked to counties Galway, Roscommon, Sligo and Mayo in our records. The main location for the name in the 19th century was in Co. Roscommon, and in Co. Sligo.

60

O Cullen

Irish Book of Arms plates 9, 142, 150.

O'Cuilinn, O'Cuileamhain

O'Cullen, Cullin, McCullin, Culloon,

Among the 90 most numerous names in Ireland, several families have assumed 'Cullen, or Cullin' as the spelling of their names. Cullen comes from both O'Cullen, and Mac Cullen, and research is necessary to determine origins.

The most populous family is that of O'Cuilinn of Glencullen by the Dublin and Wicklow border. Note the barony of Kilcullen on the Wicklow and Kildare border. Other place names are found commemorating the family name. In Wexford note two townlands by the name of 'Cullenstown' in the barony of Bargy and Shelmalier West, likely a branch of the family to the north there.

Many spellings are related to 'Cullen'. Culloon, McCullin, Culhoun and Cullinan (of Donegal), have all been used interchangeably with Cullen.

In 1659 Cullin was a principal name of Donegal; O'Cullen was so in Armagh; McCullin was so in Monaghan; Cullen was so in Carlow.

The counties of Dublin and Wexford have held most of the name in 1890, with some in Kildare and Wicklow then.

The Irish Book of Arms lists several Cullen arms, including Cullen of Corry, Leitrim, whose motto was 'Carpe diem".

Condron

Condran, Conran

Linked earlier to Offaly in Ireland, in modern times we also find the family in County Wexford. The main location for the name in 1890 was in Carlow, and in Cos. Dublin, Kildare and Kings.

O Cullinan

Irish Book of Arms plate 150

O'Cuileannain

Culenain, Cullinane, O'Cullenane,

Cullinan(e) has been traditionally found as a name of the counties of Cork, Clare and Waterford. Spelled as Cullinane, the majority of the name hailed form Cork and Waterford in 1890. The spelling of Cullinan was favored in Clare, and the Quillinan spelling of the name is found, though less frequently, in Tipperary at that time.

Similarly in the 17th century I find Cullinane in Cork and Waterford, and O'Cullenane as a principal name of Cork.

The family can be traced back to the barony of Barryroe in Co. Cork, where they can be found into modern times centered around Clonakilty. In Cork they are recorded as chiefs, alongside the Donegans, in the barony of Orrery. They were hereditary physicians in the province of Munster, and cited as very learned men of Ormond.

Co. Donegal bears another presumably unrelated family of the name. Here they are found centered near Mullinashee more anciently, but in modern times the name has faded away, perhaps in favor of spelling the name as Collins or Cullens.

Arms for the name can be found in the Irish Book of Arms plate 150.

Mac Conley

MacConnla

MacConly

Families of the original Irish name of MacConley or MacConly are found in the old geographic territory of Offaly in Ireland. Some of the name of Conly and Conley are of this family, not of the family of O'Connolly.

Cunningham

Irish Book of Arms plate 10

O'Connagain, MacCuinneagain

Counihan, Cunningham, Conyngham,

Cunningham is one of the top 75 most numerous names in all of Ireland. The name may be of Irish, English or Scottish origins.

Cunningham is actually an English name into which some Irish have changed their name. When found in Ulster one may assume it likely of Scots origin. Several are on record as having settled their in the 17th century. Also in Ulster, some of the native Irish Mac Donegans of Co. Down have changed their names to Cunegan, often Anglicized to Cunningham.

When 'Cunningham' is of Irish origins it stems from either 'O'Connagain or Mac Cuinneagain'. The name here would mean 'descendant of Conn'. One family was of Co. Sligo heritage, the other of the Galway/Roscommon area.

Several other families have changed their names to Cunningham. Counihan and Connihan of Co. Kerry for one, and Conaghan of Donegal for another.

To make matters more complicated, there are over 20 variant spellings of the name of Cunningham on record. Although Cunigan is now rare, Counihan is found in Kerry in 1890. Cunigane is found in Leitrim and O'Cunigane was a principal name of Clare in the 17th century.

O'Hart also gives one Rodger O'Cunnivane (b. 1680), whose descendant was living in Dublin in 1887 as John Cunningham. This family was also connected to Co. Clare.

Arms for the name are found on plate 107 of the Irish Book of Arms.

Mac Curtin

Irish Book of Arms plates 150, 233

MacCurtain

MacCruitin, MacCuirtin, Curtaine,Curtin

The MacCurtain family is found early in Co. Clare, in the barony of Corcomroe, along with the O'Connors and O'Loughlins, near Ennistymon. Here they served as ollaves to the O'Briens of Thomand. Noted poets, scholars and bards, one Hugh MacCurtin of Clare, a lexicographer , was author of several odes and elegies of the day.

Counties Limerick, Cork and Kerry are also associated with the name in modern times, and these counties are given along with Co. Clare as locations for the name in the 1890 index.

O'Curtaine was a principal name of Co. Cork, as well as being found in Kerry and Limerick in the census of 1659. McCurtain was a principal name of Kerry, and McCurtane a principal name of Limerick at that time as well.

Some of the name are found in the ranks of the Spanish army as found in O'Hart.

Mac Conefrey

Confrey, Confree

A name we find linked to Co. Leitrim in our records. The main location for the name in the 19th century was in Co. Leitrim as well.

Conley

O'Conghaile

Conly, Connolly, Connell, Kinnealy,

This name is a variant spelling of several more common names. The most obvious choices are the names of Connolly and Conneely. O'Connoly was a principal name of Monaghan in 1659 and found in Cork, Monaghan, Galway and Antrim in 1890.

We do find the name of ' Conly ' in the census of 1659 listed as coming from the city of Dublin. (see spellings given)

Cusack

Irish Book of Arms plate 76, 151

de Cussac

Cusacke, Cusake, Cussack, Cussacke

Families of Cusack in Ireland have taken the name from the older 'de Cussac' etc.. The earliest of the name in our records arrived in Ireland with King John in the early 1400's. Andreand Geoffrey 'de Cusack' obtained considerable lands and power until well into the 1600's.

Holding some sway in Clare, Kildare, Roscommon and Meath, their power was broken in 1691 as supporters of the Catholic cause. Many are found in the military from here on. One Thomas Cusack is found as mayor of Dublin in 1409.

In Meath the Cusacks' were barons of Clonmullen. In Mayo, a branch of the former Cusacks' (of Killeen, Meath), settled relatively early. Families of the name are also found in the barony of Tirawley in Mayo, as verified by the 'Composition Book of Connacht'.

In the last century the name was most common in Limerick, Cavan and Clare. In the census of 1659 it is found as a principal name of Meath, Kings, and Clare.

In the older records the name is quite common in Kings County (Offaly). Here the name is most often found as Cussack in 1659, with plenty of the spellings of 'Cussacke and Cusake' as well.

The 'Irish Book of Arms' gives the arms of Cusack of Gerardstown, (of Abbeyville House, Co. Dublin)

Connery

Irish Book of Arms plate 249

Conry, Conery, Conroy

A name we find in Co. Limerick.

Mc Caskey

Irish Book of Arms plate 253

Mac Ascaidh (of Norse origin)

Casky, Caskey, Mac Askie, M' Caskie

McCaskey is said to have originated from a personal name, of Norse origin. Most common to the province of Ulster, Counties Tyrone and Derry are most often associated with the name today.

In the 1890 birth index the name is given as one of County Antrim in Ulster, when the 'Mc' prefix is dropped to form simply 'Caskey'. From Milesian families we have a reference that McCaskey is a of the Hy Nial tribe, centered in County Tyrone (?). As a name in America 'McCaskey' does not rank among the top 2,000 in number.

The Caskey families of Carnaboy, and of Gorticloughan are cited in the book: "Families of Ballyrashane a district in Northern Ireland" by T. H. Mullin. In 1759 one 'Samuel Caskey' was listed concerning the lands of Gorticloughan land deeds. Among others found, one David Caskey married Jean Wylie and raised a family of eight. Matilda McCaskey of Carnaboy (parish of Ballyrashane), married John McCurdy of Croaghmore. First child born in 1819.

Passengers from Ireland:
James McCaskey, aboard Ship Rising Star, from Newry to Philadelphia arriving June 17, 1812.
George and Martha, aboard Brig Pallas, from Lough Swilly to Philadelphia, July 2, 1812.
Ellen and John, aboard Brig Nancy, from Newry to Philadelphia. May 4, 1816.

Other:
John McCaskey, from a list of Jurymen of Tyrell County, (U.S.A.), in 1740.

O Coleman

Irish Book of Arms plate 248

O'Colmain, Mac Colmain, O Clumhain

Colman, Coalman, Clovan, Cloven,

Families by the name of Coleman in Ireland may stem from one of at least three separate origins. Some of the name are doubtlessly of original English heritage who settled in Ireland over time.

Of the Irish of the name, some stem from the older spelling of O'Clumhain which became Coleman and Clifford in Co. Cork.

Mac Colman, another independent family of the name, is found as a chief clan of Co. Louth more anciently. MacColman is also cited as a variant spelling of MacCalmont, found in Co. Antrim in the 17th century. This name is said to be of Scottish origin, coming from the Buchanan clan.

One family of the name is found centered in the barony of Tireragh, Co. Sligo, cited as being of the Ui Fiachrach tribes.

In 1659 the name is listed as a principal one of Waterford, Dublin and Meath. Also given are Humphrey Coleman of Limerick, John Coleman of Cork City and Ralph Coleman of Dublin City.

In the 1890 birth index some 128 births are recorded primarily in Cork, Roscommon, Dublin and Waterford, mainly in the province of Munster. The family name remains most numerous in Co. Cork to this day.

Arms for the name are found in the Irish Book of Arms plate 248.

Eliphalet - marriage record, 1805 A. D. Chester, Mass.

John- 1735 A. D., Overwharton Parish, Stafford Co., Virginia.

John - 1760 A. D., Fort Pitt, Pittsburgh, PA.

Michael - 1768 A. D., Passenger Lists, arriving at Boston?

Patrick - 1777 A. D., Private in the Delaware Regiment in the revolutionary war.(USA)

Robert and Thomas - "Irish Pioneers in the south.

William - Connecticut Irish in the revolutionary war.

Collum

MAC COLUIM

COLUM,COLLOM,COLUMB,

There are at least two separate areas of origin in Ireland for the name of Collum. When found originally spelled with a "Mac" prefix it is usually found in the province of Ulster, in the north of Ireland. When found without the prefix in earlier times the location for the name seems to be in Co. Longford. Most anciently however, the "Mac" preceded the name in both these areas.

We do not know if the two families are related, or if they spring from two completely separate ancestors.

In Co. Longford the name of Culme is also found. Collum has been used as a variant spelling of that family name, even though the two are not related.

Individuals of the name:

Padraig Colum - (b. 1882) The famous poet of Longford origins.

Lieut. Philip Collum, given as one of the "Forty-Nine" officers in O'Hart.

The name is not found under the exact spelling of Collum in the 1659 census, in our preliminary searches.

Passengers From Ireland:

John Collum, age 18, aboard "Thaetus", Nov. 18, 1847.

William Collum, age 20, aboard "Eliza-Keith", April 29, 1848.

Thomas, Betsy, and infant, of the name of Collum listed aboard "Ashland", June 5, 1849.

O'Connaughton

O'Conachtain

Connorton, Connington, Naughton,

In our current edition of Keatings History 'O'Conachtain, or O'Conaghty' of Cabrach, in Tireragh is cited in the Mayo/Sligo area. Of some historical note, they are said to have originally come from the north of Sligo, settling into Roscommon as well. In more modern times, the name is found in the 1890 birth index in Galway and Roscommon.

Traditionally this family served as guards at the inauguration of the King of the Province of Connaught.

Colvin

USUALLY OF ANGLO-SAXON ORIGIN.

COLVAN, COLVIL, COLVILLE, COLVEN.

The Colvin name is given by some undocumented sources as anciently located in Waterford, Cork and Limerick. The same sources give that the family arrived here with the coming of the 12th century Norman invasions of Ireland, and that the family is of Norman descent.

In the 1890 birth index there are 6 recorded births of the name, listed in scattered locations. Some of the name may actually be of the "Colavin" family, who used "Colvin" as a variant spelling of the name. They represent two separate families however. When the Colvin family name is found in the province of Ulster, or in the city of Dublin, the likelihood of being of foreign origins increases.

Individuals of the name:

FROM THE DUFFY FAMILY PEDIGREE, OF COUNTY MONAGHAN. 'MARY DUFFY WHO MARRIED A MR. COLVIN, OF DUBLIN'.

Passengers from Ireland:

'John and James Colvin'. ABOARD SHIP HARMONY. FROM LONDONDERRY ARRIVING IN PHILADELPHIA ON OCTOBER 31, 1811.

'

Conlon

Conlan, Conlen

We find the name used as a variant spelling of Connellan in our records. The main location for the name in the 19th century was in Co. Roscommon, and in counties Mayo and Sligo, but it is found throughout the country in smaller numbers.

63

Mc Caskey

Irish Book of Arms plate 253

Mac Ascaidh (of Norse origin)

Casky, Caskey, Mac Askie, M' Caskie

McCaskey is said to have originated from a personal name, of Norse origin. Most common to the province of Ulster, Counties Tyrone and Derry are most often associated with the name today.

In the 1890 birth index the name is given as one of County Antrim in Ulster, when the 'Mc' prefix is dropped to form simply 'Caskey'. From Milesian families we have a reference that McCaskey is a of the Hy Nial tribe, centered in County Tyrone (?). As a name in America 'McCaskey' does not rank among the top 2,000 in number.

The Caskey families of Carnaboy, and of Gorticloughan are cited in the book: "Families of Ballyrashane a district in Northern Ireland" by T. H. Mullin. In 1759 one 'Samuel Caskey' was listed concerning the lands of Gorticloughan land deeds. Among others found, one David Caskey married Jean Wylie and raised a family of eight. Matilda McCaskey of Carnaboy (parish of Ballyrashane), married John McCurdy of Croaghmore. First child born in 1819.

Passengers from Ireland:
James McCaskey, aboard Ship Rising Star, from Newry to Philadelphia arriving June 17, 1812.
George and Martha, aboard Brig Pallas, from Lough Swilly to Philadelphia, July 2, 1812.
Ellen and John, aboard Brig Nancy, from Newry to Philadelphia. May 4, 1816.

Other:
John McCaskey, from a list of Jurymen of Tyrell County, (U.S.A.), in 1740.

Curphy

A name found in the province of Ulster, said to be the Manx spelling of the name of Murphy.

Mac Cawley

Irish Book of Arms as McAuley

MacAmhalghaidh (son of Auley), &

MacAwley, Cauley, Magawley, MacAuley,

There is more than one point of origin for the 'Cawley' name in Ireland. The noted family of Westmeath and Offaly held lands known as 'McGawley's Country', and were seated in Ballyloughnoe in Co. Westmeath. The Four Masters cite the family as 'Chiefs of Calry'. The pedigree of one family in Ireland, descended from Niall of the Nine Hostages, is recorded in some detail in Dublin Castle. The chief of the name in the 1800's was one Count Magawley Cerati.

Another origin of the name is found in Munster, where the gaelic form was originally MacAmhlaoibh, and translated into its present form.

The name, taken from similar gaelic roots, has also been one of the surnames of Scottish settlers in Ulster.

Keating cites the name as 'O'Cawley ...O'Cadhla, or O'Cawley, chief of Conmachi Mara, now the barony of Ballynahinch, in the county of Galway'.

In the census of 1659 'McCawly' is cited as a principal name of Fermanagh. Milesian Families cites the O'Cawley name as of the Hy Nial Tribe, settling in Galway, Leix, and Westmeath. The 1890 birth index shows McCawley as traditionally located in Letterkenny Union, County Donegal. Cawley is then found in Mayo and Sligo, with a traditional location cited in Killala, County Mayo. The name is not among the 2,000 most common in the U. S. A. today.

William Cawley. under 1661 act of settlement. (Regicides of Charles I, per O'Hart)

Curragh

Curraugh

Individuals of the name of Curragh are found in the city of Dublin in the 16th century in our records. We also have record of a family of the name in Co. Down.

Cochrane

From a Scottish Toponymic.

Cochran, Corcoran, Cuggeran, Cockrane,

The name of Cochrane is said to have its origins in Scotland. The name is most common in Northern Ireland, a common feature of originally Scottish names in Ireland.

Spelled as Cochrane the name is found in Antrim, Londonderry, Down and Tyrone in the 1890's birth index. Two particular locations for the name were given as : Balrothery Union, in Dublin County and in Newry Union of Counties Armagh and Down.

The Cochranes of Ballyclough and Revellagh, of Gorticloughan, and of Liswatty, are found in the publication: 'Families of Ballyrashane, a district in Northern Ireland.' by T. H. Mullin.

Passengers from Ireland:
John Cochran, aboard Ship Harmony, from Londonderry to Philadelphia, Oct. 31, 1811.
Mr. Cochran, aboard Ship Westpoint, from Londonderry to New York, arriving before Nov. 23, 1811.
A. Cochran, aboard Ship Protection, departed Belfast Feb. 24, 1812, to New York before April 11, 1812.
Richard, Mary Ann, Jane, Agnes, Issac. of Grange. aboard Ship James Bailey, Belfast to N.Y., Oct. 26, 1815.
Samuel Cochran, aboard Ship Foster, from Londonderry to N. Y. arrived June 4, 1816.
Robert Cochran, of Londonderry, aboard Brig Mount-Bay, Londonderry to N.Y., arriving Aug. 12, 1816.
Moses, Anne, Thom., William, Samuel, Joseph. All of Dromore. Aboard Brig Ann, from Belfast to N.Y. May 13, 1817.

Sinclair, St. Clair

One Scottish family of the name is found settled sometimes in Holyhill, Co. Tyrone. The 1890 birth index finds the family most numerous in Armagh and Londonderry.

64

Corcoran

Irish Book of Arms plate 202

Corcrain

MacCorcoran, O'Corcaran, Corckron,

Corcoran families of Irish descent may descend from either Mac Corcoran or O'Corcoran. O'Corcrain origins are to be found near Lough Erne in Co. Fermanagh. Mac Corcrain hails from Offaly (Kings). In Mayo and Sligo the family is likely of O'Corcoran descent. In Offaly and Tipperary, more likely of Mac Corcoran heritage.

'Corcoran' is cited as a clan of Ormond and Desi, where Mac Corcoran was said to be chief of Clan Ruainni according to O'Heerin. Those of the name in Kerry may actually descend from another source, that of O'Corca.

In America note the famous 'Corcorans Irish Legion' of Civil War fame.

In the 17th century the spelling of Corckron is given as a principal name of Kilkenny; Corkerin was so in Waterford; and O'Corkerane was so in Cork. In modern times the name hailed from Mayo, Cork, Tipperary, Dublin and Kerry, according to the 1890 index.

O'Hart gives the variant spelling of Coghrane. He gives them as descending from the O'Carroll Ely pedigree, where they were chiefs in north Tipperary, in the barony of Slieveardagh, parish of Killenaule, and near Cleenish in the barony of Clanawly in Fermanagh.

He gives the family as falling from power at the time of the 12th century Norman invasions, then settling in Cork, Kilkenny and Waterford.

In Kilkenny the family obtained lands from the Fitzwalters or Butlers who held their ancient patrimony. A senior branch of this line was represented by the Corcorans of Enniscorthy, Wexford.

The Co. Cork branch of the family settled in Carbery, and were represented in 1887 by Jeremiah (Dan) O'Corcoran, of Bengowne, parish of Murragh.

Mac Cormack

Irish Book of Arms plates 238 and 264

O'Cormacan, Mac Cormaic

McCormick, McCormac

MacCormack is a numerous name in Ireland. The name may come originally from O'Cormac, Mac Cormack, or may have Scottish origins when found in Ulster as well.

The 1890 index shows McCormick as the preferred spelling in the Ulster counties of Antrim and Down. McCormack is favored in Dublin, Mayo, Roscommon and Limerick. The shortened form of Cormack is found in Kilkenny and Tipperary in much smaller numbers.

In 1659 Cormac was a principal name of Kildare, O'Cormack a principal name of Cork and also found in Limerick, while McCormack was a principal name in Down also found in Cork, Kerry, Limerick and Roscommon.

McCormick at that time was found as a principal name of Antrim and in other Ulster counties. Origins for the name are unsure, and it probably was taken on by several unrelated families at the same time. (i.e. McCormack simply means 'son of Cormac').

Counties Fermanagh and Longford show the name early as well, and a McCormack family of Cork (Muskerry) was of some note, also.

O'Cormacan is an example of another name which may have been changed into McCormack or Cormac. Cormican is found in Galway in the birth index as well, adding some confusion for these two names.

The name comes into prominence later than many others, and it is therefore thought that the name was taken on by families at a later date than most others.

Note the famous Irish tenor, John McCormack in America.

Arms for the name are found on plates 238 and 264 in the Irish Book of Arms.

(O)Counihan

O'Cuanachain

Coonihan, Counahan

Counihan has always been traditionally linked to the county of Kerry in Ireland.

Mc Coy

Mac Ahodha (son of Hugh), Mac *Coy, Mac Cooey, MaKay, Coonahan,*

The name of McCoy is taken from MacAodha, meaning son of Hugh. As such it is more properly spelled as MacKay. Woulfe, in his work on Irish names said the name was localized in Limerick, but it can be found in Ulster as well. One family of the name came from Scotland as gallowglass (fighting men) , in Ireland. They may have originated in the south of Scotland.

Numerous in Ireland, it is considered a name of the north, concentrated in the counties of Armagh and Monaghan. The name usually comes from Scotland.

Some inferences have been made between McCoy and MacHugh or O'Hugh. I have no documentation on this. However since McCoy is taken to mean "son of Hugh" (Mac Ahodha), the name of O'Hugh is of possible relationship. MacHugh can be found in Co. Cavan, and O'Hugh in Co. Down.

Some give the name settled in Co. Tyrone, coming from Scotland in 1710. The 1890's index records births in Counties Antrim, Armagh and Monaghan under the spelling of McCoy. When spelled as 'Coy', only 5 births were recorded, in scattered locations.

The name of MacCooey has been interchanged with McCoy, coming originally from the Irish spelling of Mac Cobhthaigh. When the name is found as 'Coy', without the prefix it is presumably from McCoy, the prefix of Mc or Mac having been dropped at some time. As the birth index indicates most of the name have retained the Mac. 'Coy' is not found in the census of 1659.

Rev. Edward Mac Coy (1839 - 1872) was a noted writer.

Sir Frederick MacCoy (1823 -1899) born in Dublin and noted Australian.

'Kid' MacCoy' the noted boxer.

65

Coyne

O'Cadhain

Coyn, Coin, Kine, Barnacle, Coen,

Coyne is considered to be a name from County Mayo, found centered near Partry, in Ireland. It is one of several variant spellings of the gaelic ' OCadhain', which appears early in Mayo, near Partry.

The name of Kilcoyne is found in Mayo and Sligo as well. If the 'Kil' prefix were dropped from the name you would have simply 'Coyne'. There is a certain amount of relationship between these two names, perhaps more than just a variant spelling.

The 1890 birth index records 54 births of this spelling at that time. 27 births were recorded in Galway and 8 births in Mayo. The majority of the family was recorded in the province of Connaught at that time.

Families of the names of Cohen and Coen, are traditionally given to be of Irish extraction when found in Ireland, despite the similarity of the Jewish name of Cohen etc.. The names of Coyne, Kyne and Coen are all given in counties Galway and Mayo in the 1890 birth index of Ireland.

At least one of the name is given as a descendant of one of the wild geese in France, with the rank of Capitaine. Joseph Sterling Coyne, (1803-1868) was a noted playwright and one of the founders of 'Punch.'

Individuals of the name in our files:
EDMUND. LISTED UNDER THE 'FORTY-NINE' OFFICERS.
JOHN. NAMES OF PERSONS IN THE GRANTS.
JOHN. NAMES OF PURCHASERS OF ESTATES '1702-3'.
A.A.
CAPITAINE,L.H..DESCENDANTS OF THE WILD GEESE OF FRANCE.
OTHER
JOSEPH STERLING COYNE. 1803-1868.PLAYWRIGHT AND ONE OF THE FOUNDERS OF 'PUNCH'.
REV. JOSEPH COYNE,P.P.. 1839-1891. AUTHOR.

Cummins

Irish Book of Arms plate 203

O'Coimin

Comyn, Commons, Cummings, Cumming,

The 'Cummins' family name in its various forms may be of old Irish origin, or may have come from settlers in Ireland of English or Norman origins. The English spelling of the name more often includes the 'g' at the end of the name, as Cummings, or Cumming. That spelling was most popular in Antrim, Dublin, Cork and Tipperary in 1890.

Commins was a spelling found in Mayo and Waterford, and Commons a spelling of Galway and Mayo at that time.

The old Irish families of the name likely stem from O'Coimin, though the 'O' prefix before the name has been dropped. Found earlier in the province of Connaught, they were erenaghs to the church of St. Cuimin, in the barony of Tirawley, in Co. Mayo. Note also Kilcummin parishes in the barony of Magunihy in Co. Kerry and in Limerick.

In the north of Ireland records show the name of Mac Coimin in Armagh as landholders.

Comyn is the spelling of an Norman family of the name found in Ireland. Note that one John Comyn was Archbishop of Dublin in the 12th century.

Keatings History cites the 'O'Commins' as a family in Roscommon as well.

O'Hart, speaking of O'Cummins gives them as paramount in Mayo and Sligo before the 12th century Norman invasions. They subsequently settled in Cork and Waterford according to his account. Some of the family lived in and to the south of Bandon, Co. Cork, at the time of his writings.

Arms for the name can be found in the Irish Book of Arms plate 203.

OCurry, Corry

Irish Book of Arms plate 216

O'Comhraidhe

Corry, Cory, Corra, Currie, Corrie

The O'Currys' of Clan Torna, are anciently found as chiefs in the barony of Kerricurrehy in Co. Cork, according to O'Heerin.

The O'Corrys (O'Currys) are also cited in the barony of Tuyllygarvey in Cavan, near Cootehill. It should be remembered that Currie and Corrie are also names used by Scottish settlers in the North of Ireland. Currie is also the name of the Clan MacDonald in Scotland.

The name of Corry may be of Ulster Scots origin when found in the north of Ireland in older records. Around Co. Clare, and in the old territory of Thomand, Corry has been used instead of Curry, which presumably is an unrelated name.

In the 1890's index both Curry and Corry are found in Antrim, with Corry being found in Clare as well. McCurry, several centuries earlier is found as a principal name of Antrim as well. Many believe that this 'Mc' prefix was added to the name by mistake at that time. We have no conclusive evidence of the same at this time.

In Co. Westmeath we find a family of the name who served as chiefs of Moygoish. Another noted O'Curry family is found hailing from the territory of 'Thomand', in County Clare, as early as the 14th century.

John Curry M.D., was a distinguished Catholic physician and writer born in the early 18th century. He was descended from the O'Corra family of Cavan, who lost their estates in 1641-1691. Two of his sons were officers in the Austrian service.

Currid

Early records give the family in Co. Sligo, and subsequently the name is found in Dublin as well. In the 1890 birth index 5 of the name are found in Sligo and 1 in Wexford.

66

O Cooney

Irish Book of Arms plate 253

O'Cuana, O'Cuanaich

Coony, Coonahan, Coonan, Cooihan,

The O'Cooney family is found earliest in the north of Ireland in Co. Tyrone. O'Dugan cites O'Cuanaich or O'Cooney as a clan of Tir Eogan (Tir Owen) in the 12th century. O'Hart gave O'Cooney, along with O'Bailey as a chief of Clan Fergus, among the Irish clans of Tir Owen.

The family is next found relocated in the province of Connaught, in the townland of Ballycooney, Loughrea barony, in Co. Galway. From here they spread into Co. Clare and the name is found widespread in Ireland today.

Other family names have been changed into Cooney as well, accounting for some of its popularity. Both Coonihan and Coumey, the latter mainly of Co. Cork, have been changed into Cooney.

The name can be found in the diocese of Elphin, for here Dearmid O'Cuana is found as the 'great priest of Elphin'.

In the census of 1659 Cooney is found as a principal name of Clare, and by 1890 it is found centered in Mayo and Dublin.

Family members note the place name of Ballycooney in Galway.

Arms for the name can be found in the Irish Book of Arms plate 253.

Cooley

Cooly

Families of the name of Cooley etc.. in Ireland are found centered in Galway and Antrim in the 19th century birth index. In the Galway region they may descend from the family of Kilcooley, with Cooley serving as a shortened form of the longer name. For families in the province of Ulster Cooley may have been a name taken on by several different families, including those of Colley, Cowley and Coole.

Cooling

A name we find in Co. Wicklow.

Corr, Corry

O'Corra

Curr, Corra, Corry, Curry, Corrie

Families of the name of Corr are found numerous in county Meath and the name is also found in Co. Tipperary in the census of 1659. With the "O" prefix, as O'Corr the name is found as a principal one of Armagh, and also in Londenderry at that time. The 19th century records show the name centered in Dublin and Tyrone however.

Much confusion can come about for some of the name, for Corr can serve as a shortened form of O'Corry, Curry, and MacCorry. Further complicating matters, some of the name of Corry, are in fact from Scotland originally, subsequently settling in Ireland.

In the census of 1659 Corry is found in Co. Fermanagh, and McCorry is a principal name of Fermanagh.

The name of Corr is said to have been taken from the more ancient name of O'Corra in the province of Ulster. We also find record of the name in Dublin, Kilkenny and Louth. In Co. Cork the name of Corr may have actually been interchanged with Curry at times.

Cornyn

Irish Book of Arms plate 206

O Cuirine

Curneen, O'Curreen, Currin, Curreen,

O'Cornyn is listed in Milesian families as an ancient family of Ireland of the Dairine Tribe, located in County Donegal. When spelled as Curreen the name is associated with Co. Waterford.

Corner

The name of a family most often found in Co. Armagh in our records.

Cormican

O'Cormacain

Cormacan, Cormacin

The name is found in counties Galway, Clare and Roscommon in our records, the first of which seems to be the center for the name in more modern times, as evidenced by the 1890 birth index.

O'Cosgry

O'Cosgraidh

Cosgrave

According to "Keatings History" the name is given as coming from O'Cosgraidh, being translated into both Cosgry and Cosgrave. This family is mentioned by O'Dugan and O'Heerin thusly;

"O'Cosgrave of the numerous clan, Rules over saffron-clad conquering . warriors....The subduer of foreigners . . . resides here, I mean O'Cosgrave on the . . plain of Cualan."

The family of O'Cosgrave is again cited by O'Heerin in "Keatings History" thusly; "From the Barrow eastward to the Slaney,

Is the country possessed by the Clan Cosgrave, The host of Bantry of ringleted hair, A noble tribe with hawk like sparkling eyes." The territory possessed by Cosgrave was in the barony of Bantry, in Co. Wexford.

Given again as an ancient family of Wicklow or Queens, the "Mac Coscrys or Cosgraves...changed their names to Lestrange.

Mac Coskley

According to "Keatings History" the name is given as among the numerous and powerful clans, with large possessions in the counties of Carlow and Wexford.

Mac Costigan

Mac Oistigin

Costigin

In older records the Costigan family is found in the territory of Ossory, and moving into more modern records the name is found often in Co. Tipperary. The name of Costigan is centered in Dublin, Kilkenny and Queens in the 19th century.

Cottle

Cottel

Note the place name of Cottlestown, in Co. Sligo likely marking one center for the name. This name is of likely Norse origins.

67

O'Cosgrave

Irish Book of Arms plate 264 Cosgrove

O'Cosgraidh

Cosgrove

According to "Keatings History" the name is given as coming from O'Cosgraidh, being translated into both Cosgry and Cosgrave. This family is mentioned by O'Dugan and O'Heerin thusly;

"O'Cosgrave of the numerous clan, Rules over saffron-clad conquering . warriors....The subduer of foreigners . . . resides here, I mean O'Cosgrave on the . . plain of Cualan."

The family of O'Cosgrave is again cited by O'Heerin in "Keatings History" thusly; "From the Barrow eastward to the Slaney,

Is the country possessed by the Clan Cosgrave, The host of Bantry of ringleted hair, A noble tribe with hawk like sparkling eyes."

The territory possessed by Cosgrave was in the barony of Bantry, in Co. Wexford. Spelled as Cosgrave, the name is found most often in Dublin and Wexford in the 19th century. The spelling of Cosgrove is mainly found in counties Mayo and Galway.

Corscadden

A family name extremely rare in our records, in which we find a few of the name in Co. Dublin, in relatively recent times.

Corrodan

Corridan, Cordan

The family name of Corrodan, Corridan, etc..is traditionally linked to Co. Kerry, where the variant spelling of Cordan is also found. Most anciently the family is found in Co. Clare as well.

Coulter

O'Coltarain

According to "Keatings History" the name is given as the Anglicized version of O'Coltarain, who served as chiefs in the barony of Castlereagh.

The birth index of 1890 finds the family centered in counties Antrim, Down and Fermanagh.

Cox, Mac Quilly

Mac an Choiligh

Cocks, Quill, Koch

Cox is, of course, found as an English name, but it is also of Irish origins. Of the families in Ireland of the name, they may come from either source.

The Irish families of the name of Cox are thought to descend from the gaelic family of Mac an Choiligh, which means 'son of the cock".

Traditionally linked with Co. Roscommon, it is here and in Dublin where the name is most often found in modern times. The old spelling of MacQuilly has fallen by the wayside in modern times. In older days the family served as Co-arbs of St. Barry of Kilbarry in Co. Roscommon.

Other explanations exist for the name. The French name of Koch could become Cox, in Ireland. According to MacLysaght the Irish name of Mac Conchoille, has also been changed to Cox.

In the 17th century "census" of 1659 Cox was given in Dublin city, Louth and Limerick.

Walter or "Watty" Cox was the son of a Westmeath blacksmith and was born around 1770. In 1797 he established the "Union Star" publication, and after visiting America he founded the "Irish Monthly Magazine", which held many biographies. He died in 1837. He, at one time, tried to cut off the head of King Williams statue in Dublin, but retired from his task upon finding his tools unsuitable for the purpose, according to O'Hart.

Cowman

MacCowman is given as a principal name in Co. Wexford in the 17th century, and here the name is considered to be of Irish origins. In Dublin, a Quaker family of the name of separate origins is found, and in Co. Wexford Cowman has been substituted for the name of Cummins.

Mc Cracken

MAC REACHTAIN

MAC CRACKEN, MC CRACKIN

McCracken is given to be a variant of Mac Naughten in the north of Ireland. This family traces itself back to the noted Stuarts of Scotland, and the Milesians of ancient Ireland. Some sources give the name as settling in Co. Fermanagh in 1642.

John Stuart McCracken, who was born in Co. Down, Ireland, in 1816, arrived in America at the tender age of 7 years. He and his four brothers learned the printing trade in Cincinnati. In 1838 he reportedly brought the first printing press to (Shawneetown), Illinois. He also published the only newspaper in Jefferson City, Missouri, and owned land there. (From "Irish Settlers on the American Frontier" I.G.F.).

One Mrs. McCracken was responsible for making the first American Flag to be carried into Mexico City as a result of the Mexican American wars. With no red coloring available for the American flag, it waved proudly as the pink, white, and blue colors waived in the wind.

In the 1890 birth index 33 recorded births of the name are found centered in counties Antrim and Down.

Craddock

A family named traditionally linked with counties Kerry and Kildare from the 14th century. Note the place name of Craddockstown in both Kilkenny and Meath. One of the name served as High Sheriff in Co. Wicklow in the 17th century.

Crangle

The name of a family often found in Co. Down, given by Woulfe as of the same descent as Cronnelly which is found outside of that area as a rule

Craughwell

The name of a Galway family, in which county we find the town of Craughwell.

68

Creamer

Creemer, Cramer, Creamor, Kramer

Several families of the name are found with lands in Co. Kilkenny in Ireland, where the family was of some note. The family name is also found in the city of Dublin in the 17th century as "Creamer". Some confusion may arise as to the origins of the name, for, when spelled as "Cramer" it represents some families which are unrelated. The name of Creamer is also the name of an English family, that might have settled in Ireland over time.

In Co. Cork we find the name of Cramer as well, but here one family of the name descends from "Von Kramer" according to the works of Burke.

Mc Creary

Mac Ruidhri (as varient of MacRory)

M'Arory, McCreery, MacGrory, M'Roary,

Some 5 births of the name of McCreary were recorded in the 1890 birth index, just enough to be listed on that survey. The location of the name however, was not centered in any one place. In the census of 1659 McCreery is found as a principal name of County Antrim in Ulster. The same name, MacCreery, is a variant spelling of Mac Rory in County Tyrone, which is in Ulster as well. Tyrone is considered to be a traditional location for the name.

MaCrory, and Mac Grory are also spellings found in Ulster.

The name of McCreary is not among the top 2,000 surnames in the U. S. today. (see McCrory)

O'Credan

O'Criodain

Creedon, Creaton

According to "Keatings History" the name is given to a chief of the parish of Magheramisk, in the barony of Massareene, in the province of Ulster.

The name of Creedon is found centered in Co. Cork a century ago, and the separate name of Creaton is found at that time with 8 scattered births

O'Creehan

O'Criochan

Crehan, Creegan

According to "Keatings History" the name is given as a numerous one in Fermanagh, and many of the name had changed their name to Creighton by translation.

In the 19th century the spelling of Cregan is found in Limerick and Meath, as Creegan in Limerick and Sligo, and as Crehan in Galway.

Mac Creesh

Families of the name of MacCreesh are traditionally linked to Co. Down in Ireland, and the 19th century birth index finds the family centered nearby in Co. Monaghan.

Cremin

Cremen, Crimeen, Creman

The family of Cremin is most often found in counties Cork and Kerry in Ireland, where the name is taken from the older spelling of O'Cruimin. On occasion the name of McCarthy has been used interchangeably with Cremin.

Crifferty

The name of a Co. Fermanagh family sometimes changed to Clifford.

Crilly

MacRaghallaigh

Ancient records find the family of the name as a family of the old territory of Oriel. Counties Derry and Monaghan are sometimes linked with the name, but the main location for the family in the 19th century is found in Antrim, Londonderry and Louth.

Croffy

Craffy

A fairly rare name in Ireland, it has been sparingly found in the counties of Galway and Offaly.

Mac Croghan

Mac Criomhthainn

Crohan, McCrohon, Crehan.

There are several locations for this family name in Ireland. The name itself is said to have come from the gaelic for 'fox'. In the Dingle peninsula / Blasket Island area the family is a branch of the O'Sullivan clan. One center of power was at the castle of Letter near Cahirciveen. Several of the name are of note in the 'rebel' ranks during times of war, and the name is also found in Spain.

Other centers of the name can be found in 1) Mayo and Galway and in 2) Sligo and Donegal.

'McCrohon' has been given as a Scottish name arriving in 1603 and settling in Antrim. In the census of 1659 we find the name as a principal one of County Roscommon when spelled as Croghan. As Croghen the name is given in County Clare at the same time. In the more modern 1890 birth index the name is given as one of Co. Kerry, and indeed that is considered to be the traditional homeland of the family.

Croke

Crok, Croc, Crooke

A name not uncommon in older records, the Croke family is found in Kilkenny at an early date. Note the name of Croke Park in Ireland, named for Rev. T. William Croke (d.1902), a great supporter of athletics in Ireland.

The Rev. Dr. Croke was archbishop of Cashel, and James Croke, Esq.., was a Commander in the Royal Navy. Also in the military service, Don Edmundo Croke was given as serving in the Spanish Netherlands in 1653.

Families of the name of Croke are found most numerous in Tipperary and Waterford in the 19th century.

It is as well found that the Huguenot family name of Le Blount, has been Anglicized as Croke on occasion in earlier times.

69

Cromie

Crommie, Crommy, O'Cromy, Cromie,

Families of the name of Cromie and Crommie are given in the 19th century birth index as centered in counties Armagh and Down. The name of O'Cromy is found in the census of 1659 as a principal name of Co. Armagh as well.

Some of these families descend from the Scottish families of Abercrombie and Cromie, names well known in that country.

The family is traditionally considered to be one of Co. Down and its surrounds in Ireland.

Cromwell

Gromwell, Grummell, Cromewell

Families of the name of Cromwell, or Gromwell are found in Ireland from the 15th century onward. Several of the name are noted as officials in Co. Limerick at an early date. The surname of Grummell has also been reported as a variant spelling of Cromwell, specifically in Co. Kerry.

In the 17th century census of 1659 we find the name of Cromewell centered in Co. Down

Cronekan

Crone

The name of a Co. Cork family found centered near Youghall.

Cussen

The name of Cussen is given to be one of an Anglo-Norman family found settled in Cork and Limerick at least as early as the 14th century. One of the line is found centered at Newcastle West in Limerick.

In the 1890 birth index 3 of the name are given in Cork and 2 in Limerick.

O Cronin

O Croinin

Cronyn, Cronen, O'Croneene, O'Cronine.

The (O) Cronin name is taken from O Croinin family of Corca Laoidhe in ancient days, they were a noted family that served as erenaghs of Gougane Barra. The name is seldom found with the 'O' prefix in modern times. Today the descendants of this family are common in Counties Cork and Kerry. In the birth index for the turn of this century, some 260 householders were given in County Kerry. Note the place name of BallyCroneen in East Cork.

According to some modern estimates, the name is near the top 100 names of Ireland in number today, although it was not so in the past.

OCroneene is found in the census of 1659 as a principal name of Kerry, in the barony of Magunihy, and in Limerick in the barony of Connello. O'Cronine is found in that same work as a principal name of County Cork. Any of the spellings appear as Cronin today.

The 1890 index records the name in Cork, Kerry and Limerick.

From O'Harts work:

Individuals of the name:

Philip Cronin, Irish American Brigades, Corcorans Irish Legion. died of wounds, 6 Oct. 1864.

Research sources:

'County Kerry, Past and Present' by Jeremiah King.

'The Kenmare Manuscripts.'

Histories of Co. Kerry in general.

Crossan

Mac an Chrosain

Crossen

The 1890 birth index find the Crossan family centered in Co. Derry, but the name is as well found in other counties in the north of Ireland, notably in Donegal, Tyrone and Leitrim.

O'Crottie, Crotty

According to "Keatings History" the name is found as descending from a branch of the O'Brien family who were princes of Thomand. They held lands around Lismore, and many families of the name remained in Waterford at the time of that writing.

Most families of the name of Crotty were found in Clare, Waterford and Cork in the 19th century.

Mac Crowne

Crown, Crowane, Croghane

It is often said that the Crowne or MacCrowne families of Ireland are actually a branch of the Croghan family of Co. Roscommon.

Cruise, Cruys

Cruys

According to "Keatings History" the name is one of a noted family in Meath. Of this line we find the Cruises of Cruisetown and of Cruise-Rath.

The noted family of Rathmore, Co. Meath are said to have possessed the castles and estates of Cruisetown and Moydorragh, near each other in the barony of Moydorragh. The name is often spelled earlier as Cruys, and subsequently as Cruise, in the same family.

Most families of the name of Cruise are found in Co. Dublin in the 19th century.

Mac Crystal

Christal

Families of the name of Crystal are generally agreed to be of Scottish origins when found in Ireland. As such, it is a name of the province of Ulster, often found in counties Armagh and Tyrone, although Woulfe finds the family originally in Co. Down.

70

Cudahy

O' Cuidighthigh (from "helper")

Cuddihy, Cudihy, Cudahey, Cuddahy,

Cudahy (Cuddihy) is a name traditionally associated with Co. Kilkenny in Ireland. The name remains distinct in that area today, as well as in the capital city of Dublin. Anciently the name is found associated with Co. Cork, and around 1214 A.D. it is found with the prefix 'Mac'. Earlier spellings also included O'Codihie, O'Kuddyhy and is found in the 16th century fiants. There were 22 Cuddihy householders in the Tipperary Hearth Money Rolls, (Kilkenny not available), and the name was numerous in the Ormond area in Ireland. 'Cuddihy' is found in the 1890's birth index in Co. Kilkenny as well. The many forms of spelling the name in Ireland have begun to disappear, with 'Cuddihy' being adopted by most families as the preferred form of the name. The name is now relatively rare.

When researching the name, you should be aware of the different spellings used in the past, as well as the common spelling used today.

Cudmore

Families of the name of Cudmore are given to be originally of English extraction, found centered in Co. Cork from the 17th century.

Cuggeran

The name of a family found in Co. Clare.

Culleton

Colletan, Cullaton, Culliton, Cullington

Families of the name of Culleton are found centered in Co. Wexford in the 19th century. The variant spelling of Colleton is found more often in Kilkenny and Carlow.

Culligan

O'Cuileagain

Quilligan, Culigan

A name traditionally linked with counties Clare and Limerick in Ireland. The name is found centered mainly in Co. Clare in the 19th century.

Mc Cutcheon

Irish Book of Arms plate 201

Mac Uistin (Irish), Mac Uisdin (Scots)

Mac Question, Mac Whiston, Houston,

The name of McCutcheon is taken from a branch of the Scottish clan MacDonald. In Ulster the name is mainly of Tyrone and Antrim. The older Scottish spelling is taken from Mac Uisdin, and the Irish from Mac Uistin. The name may have been taken from the Scottish Christian name of Hucheon, and is also related to the spelling of Hutchinson. The spellings of Kitchen and Kitson are also used.

The name appears in the Hearth Money rolls of 1663 for Donegal and in Derry wills back to 1864. The birth index gives Tyrone, Armagh, and Down as locations for the name in 1890. Milesian families gives the family name as one of the Eogonacht Tribe, settled in Tipperary and Armagh.

Mc Cusker

Mac Oscar, Cusker, Cosker

Keatings history of Ireland (v-3) gives McCusker as one of the chief clans of Monaghan, citing them as 'MacCuskers or Mac Oscars' sometimes changed to Cosgraves, who possessed a district in Monaghan, near Carrickmacross, adjacent to the county of Louth. Additionally they are cited as a branch of the Mac Guires in Fermanagh, seated at Ballymacosker. McCusker is used as a synonym of Cosgrave in Oriel and Cusker and Cosker are found in Wexford.

The birth index of 1890 lists the name as located in county Tyrone. In Milesian families the name is given as one of Scottish heritage, settling in Antrim in 1660.

Mac Connick

The name of a family traditionally linked to Co. Wexford, and found as such in the census of 1659. Woulfe gives this family as descended from the O'Farrell family of Co. Longford.

O'Conole

Connole, Conoyle

Families of the name are traditionally linked to Co. Clare in Ireland. A relatively scarce family name today, many of the family likely now appear as Connolly and some perhaps Connell.

O'Conran

Irish Book of Arms plate 253 Conran

O'Conarain

Condron, Condran, Coneran

Families of the name of Conran are traditionally linked to counties Leix and Offaly in Ireland, and are found there in the 1659 census. Undocumented sources also give the name in Co. Waterford at an early date. Note the place name of Ballyconran in Co. Wexford

O'Convally

According to "Keatings History" the name is that of one of the principal chiefs of Teffia, as found in the works of O'Dugan. They are found alongside the Quinns, O'Kearneys and O'Loughnans in Teffia.

Convery

Canvery

A name we find linked to Co. Derry in the north of Ireland, around the district of Magherafelt.

Mc Conville

MacConmhaoil

McConvile

An old Irish family anciently of the territory of Oriel, subsequently found most numerous in Armagh and Antrim.

Conyers

Conyer

Families of the name of Conyer and Conyers are found in the 17th century in Co. Kerry in Ireland. Some of the family may actually be "Connors" under a variant spelling. The name however is most prominently found in Kerry where an English family of the name is found settled.

71

Mac Cooey

The name of a family traditionally linked to Co. Armagh, in Ireland, and they are separate and distinct from the families of MacCoy found in Ireland. (Although some may have mistakenly taken on the latter name.).

Coogan

Cogan, Cogane

A name found early in Co. Galway, it is subsequently found in Monaghan, Carlow and Kilkenny in our records.

Coolaghan

According to "Keatings History" the name is cited as that of a clan of Mayo and/or Sligo.

Copeland

According to "Keatings History" the name is given among the chief Anglo-Norman and English settlers in Ulidia, under DeCourcey and his successors. The main location for the name in the 19th century was in Co. Armagh, and in Co. Antrim.

Coppinger

Copinger, Coppenger

Coppinger is a name linked to Co. Cork in Ireland, and in Cork city several are found as important city officials. The family appears to have remained centered in Cork over the centuries, and the family name is originally said to be of Norse origins.

Two well know families of the name hail from Ballyvolane and Barryscourt in Co. Cork. The Right Rev. William Coppinger, Bishop of Cloyne, was of the Barryscourt family.

Lieut. Don Joseph Coppinger in 1788 served in the Hibernia regiment in the service of Spain.

Corballis

One family of the name is found in the County of Dublin and the barony of Balrothery. The family lost their lands during Cromwellian times and came to settle in Dublin, where one became a Timber Merchant.

Corbally

According to "Keatings History" the name is one of a noted family of Meath.

Corbett

O'Corbain

Corban, Corbane

Families of the name of Corbett in Ireland may be either of old Irish or English extraction. Family members will note the place names of Corbetstown in Co. Offaly and Co. Westmeath.

Several Irish families have changed their names to the more common name of Corbett, making early family history sometimes difficult to trace.

In the 17th century we find the name given in Carlow, Dublin, Westmeath and Cork, some two centuries later the name is mainly found in Cork, Tipperary and Galway.

Mc Cord

Cord

The name of a family traditionally tied to Co. Antrim, and recorded as such in the 19th century birth index. Some sources give the names of both Cord, and McCord, as settler families in Ulster.

Cordue

Cordew?

An extremely rare name in our records, found in Co. Clare.

Corduff

The name of a family we find centered in Co. Donegal, and sometimes in Co. Mayo.

Corkery

Corkerry, Corcoran, Corkry

A name often found in counties Cork, Limerick and Kerry in our records, it is as well found as a variant of the name of Corcoran. The name is most numerous in Co. Cork in the 19th century.

(O)Cournane

O'Curnain

Our records find the name in Co. Kerry, where it also serves as a variant spelling of Courtney.

Mc Court

Mac Court

The name of an Irish family found in the old territory of Oriel, subsequently given to counties Louth and Armagh.

Courtney

Irish Book of Arms plate 266

O'Curnain

The Irish of the name are traced into Co. Kerry, where the name is found interchanged with the original Irish name of Cournane.

Others of the name of Courtney were originally of English extraction, settling in Ireland in the 16th century on at least one occasion, where they took control of Desmond lands in counties Limerick and Kerry.

In the 19th century the family is mainly found in Kerry, Antrim and Dublin.

Cowan

Cowen

The family name of both Cowan and McCowan are given as principal names in the 17th century in Co. Antrim. Our 19th century records find the family centered in counties Antrim, Down, and Armagh.

Some of the name have used the separate names of McKeown and McCone etc.. in place of Cowan.

Cowell

One noted family of the name is found as being of Logadowden, in Co. Dublin, in the 18th century. At that same time period Thomas Cowell of Ballymore Eustace and Harristown is given.

The family is also found in Tynan, Co. Armagh in the early 17th century, of a line which also held lands in Co. Monaghan. Families of the name are also found in Enniscrone, Co. Sligo in the 19th century.

Coyle

Irish Book of Arms plate 207

Cool, McCool

Coyle is a family name which has been traced back to Ulster in earlier times, and is also found as McCool there.

The family is found in some numbers in Donegal, Cavan, Londonderry, Dublin, Tyrone and Cavan.

Cullivan

Colivan, Colavan, Colovin, Colavin

The name of Cullivan is relatively scarce in Ireland, but is was officially recorded in the works of Matheson in the 19th century. Related spellings are given to be those of Colovin, Calwell, Cauldwell, Caldwell, Colavin, Coldwell, Collwell, Conwell, Colwell, Horish and Kilwell. That is, these names have been used interchangeably at times with one another.

It is apparent that the name is used by several unrelated families according to the above report.

The spelling of "Cullivan" is given in the district of Ballyhaise, in the union of Cavan, in Co. Cavan. The family is considered to have been one of the province of Connaught anciently, and is subsequently found centered in Co. Cavan.

Culloty

Culoty

A name linked in our records to Co. Kerry. The name is often cited in the areas near Glenflesk, Killarney, and Tralee in that county.

Mc Cullough

McCulloch

McCullogh, McCullagh

Most of the name of McCullough etc.., are of Scots origin, being found mainly in the province of Ulster in Ireland. Some Irish families of the name of Mac Cu Uladh, are also said to have adopted the name.

Mac Cullow

MacCullough, McCullow

Families of the name of Cullow and MacCullow are traditionally linked to Co. Tyrone, centered near Gortin in that county.

Cully

O'Colla, Mac Colla

McCully, Cullen

The family name of McCully or Cully is found in the province of Ulster in northern Ireland. In more modern times (1890 a.d.), the name of Cullen was reported as interchangeable with Cullen in Meath.

Mac Cumiskey

Comisky, Comasky, Comeskey...

Families of the name are found early in Co. Monaghan, and in the works related to the 1890 birth index, Comerford was given as a synonym to Comiskey in Co. Longford. The name is found under various variant spellings in Cavan, Louth, Westmeath, Monaghan and Longford.

O'Cuning

According to "Keatings History" the name was often changed to Gunning from the original name of O'Conuing, who was chief in the barony of Small county, in Limerick. They are thus mentioned by O'Heerin;

"Aes Grei of the finest plains,

Was owned by O'Cuning of Crioch Saingil, He cheerfully held the beauteous Grian, From the noble race of Eogan."

Mac Cunneen

O'Coinin, O'Cuineain

Rabbitt, Kenyon, Kenning, Quinan,

Several independent families of Ireland have used this surname. Cunneen has been translated into 'Rabbitt' in some areas. Furthermore, families of this line may spring from either Mac Cunneen or O'Cunneen originally.

Mac Coinin can be found centered earlier around Erris, Co. Mayo, and O'Coinin is found in Offaly (Kings Co.) in ancient days as well.

Kinnane, also found in interrelated spellings with the above, is found centered in the territory of Thomand in Co. Tipperary. Here we find the spelling of 'Kinane' in the 1890's birth index in modern times.

One other note regarding the name, is that both the 'O' and 'Mac' prefix were dropped in earlier days and are seldom found in modern day descendants.

Mac Curdy

The Curdy or MacCurdy family is traditionally linked with Co. Antrim in Ireland, and is found as a principal name there in the 17th century. At the end of the last century the name remained there, as well as in Co. Londonderry.

Mac Curley

The Irish Book of Arms plate 212

Mac Thoirdealbaigh

Turley, Kerley, Curling, Turly, Terry

Families of the Curley name are found in olden days in Counties Galway and Roscommon, coming from the older spelling of Mac Thoirdealbaigh (son of Turlough). Turley , Turly and possibly Terry, are obvious forms of this name as well.

Family members will be pleased to find both Ballymacurley, and Curleys Island in the barony of Ballymoe in Co. Roscommon.

As to earlier spellings of the name, both MacTurlogh and Mac Turlagh are found in the census of 1659 as principal names in Co. Limerick. In the same century 'Curley' is found in Co. Cork, while in the 1890's index Curley is found in Roscommon, Galway and Dublin

73

Dalton

Irish Book of Arms plates 151, 267

de Alton, d'Alton

Alton, Daltin

Another of the distinguished families to settle in Ireland after the coming of the Norman invasions. 'Daltons Country' was a name given to their holdings in Westmeath, where the chief of the name was known as 'Lord of Rathconrath." Here they are found centered at Mount Dalton.

The name comes from the older form of de Alton or D'Alton (meaning' of Alton'), a place name of England. It is said that one Walter Dalton was the first to arrive in Ireland. He married the French King's daughter, and fled to England en route to Ireland.

The Daltons settled early in Teffia, Co. Meath, where they built many castles, as they did in Westmeath. In the 14th century the name is found in Tipperary and Cork, and several hundred years later a branch of the family settled in Co. Clare. O'Hart also gives the family as a chief one of Kilkenny and Waterford since the English invasions.

Having become one with the Irish cause, they were broken with the coming of Cromwell, as were so many other families of Ireland.

In the 1890's index Dalton is found in Westmeath, but more often in Dublin, Waterford, Limerick and Kilkenny. In the census of 1659 Dalton is found as a principal name of Tipperary, and in Kilkenny and Westmeath as well.

In America the notorious 'Dalton' gang hailed from more violent times in that country. D'Altons 'History of Dublin' may be of special interest to those of the name.

O'Daly

Irish Book of Arms plates 72, 151

O'Dalaigh

Daily, Dawley, Dawly, Dayley, Dealy,

The surname 'Daly' ranks as the 24th most popular name in Ireland. The family was anciently centered in the barony of Magherademon in Westmeath, which today includes part of the barony of Moyashel as well.

The Dalys' are a family of poetic and literary note, for they are found prominent in these fields in places where they have settled. A number of poets of the name are found in Clare, near Galway Bay. In the barony of Carbery in Cork, O'Daly was the official poet to the Mac Carthys. In Cavan, the O'Dalys and O'Mulligans served the leading family of Breffny, the O'Reillys.

In Galway they held power into the last century as 'Barons of Dunsandle'.

The 1890's birth index finds Daly in Cork, Dublin, Kerry, Galway and Kings Counties. O'Daly was rare by then. Keatings History finds the family serving as 'hereditary poets and antiquaries' to the Mac Carthys. They are found in the barony of West Carberry in Cork, as bards to the Carews, O'Mahoneys and others. Further, we find 'The O'Dalys' in the barony of the Burren in Clare. Given as chiefs of Teffia, their territory is given in the barony of Clonlonan in Westmeath.

Of the O'Dalys in Galway and Roscommon anciently, Keatings History says they are a branch of the O'Donnells of Donegal, princes of Tirconnell, whose tribe name was Clan Dalaigh. The family settled in Connaught as early as the 12th century becoming noted poets and scholars.

The Daly families of Castle Daly, Co. Galway are found in the Book of Arms.

'The O'Dalys of Muintuavara: a story of a bardic family", by Dominic Daly was published in Dublin in 1821.

Daniel

Irish Book of Arms plate 47 (Daniell)

Daniell

A Huguenot family of Great Britain, according to several sources. The Daniell family of New Forest, Co. Westmeath, descend from Bridges Daniell of Dublin in the 18th century.

Most of the name are found in Dublin, Limerick and Waterford in the 19th century.

Mc Dade

Mac Daibheid

McDaid, Mac Davitt, Mac Devitt.

McDade, McDaid etc... is said to have come from MacDaibheid, meaning son of David. It is essentially considered a name of Ulster in counties Donegal and Derry. The name can also be found as MacDavitt, MacDevitt and Davison. According to one account the McDade family can be traced back to David O'Doherty (d. 1208), chief of Cinel Eoghain.

Milesian families gives the name in Limerick and Galway in 1171, and of Norman origin spelled as McDade. Spelled as McDaid the same source gives the family in Limerick, Galway and Donegal, with the same origins.

The birth index show the family in Donegal, Londonderry and Tyrone in more modern times.

Daffy

A name mostly found in Co. Clare and surrounds in our records.

74

Darby

Irish Book of Arms plate 77

Mac Darby, Mac Derby

Families of the name of Darby may have taken this surname from Diarmuid, from which the names of Darby and Dermot are said to have been taken. Our records find the name of Darby most often in Kings Co. (Offaly) in earlier times. As Derby, the name is found most numerous in Tipperary in the 17th century. At least some of the name are found arriving from England.

When found to the north, in the province of Ulster, the family likely springs from separate origins.

The Darbu family of Leap Castle, Kings county, is given in the Irish Book of Arms.

Dagg

Dag

Families of the name of Dagg are given in the 19th century in the provinces of Leinster and Munster, with a total of 7 births recorded in 1890 a.d.. Families of the name are found in both counties Wicklow and Wexford, as well as a good amount of the name in Dublin.

Dahill

Dayhill

Families of the name of Dahill, or O'Dathaill more anciently are given by Woulfe as centered at Silmurray in Co. Roscommon and subsequently in Co. Tipperary. Our records also show the name in Co. Cork. The 1890 birth index found the name centered in Tipperary as well.

Darcy

Irish Book of Arms plates 39,45

D'Arcy

de Arcy, de Arci, O'Darcey, Mac Darcy

Families of the Darcy name may spring from either Irish or Norman origins. We cannot determine origins based upon the spelling of the name, for some Irish families assumed the Norman (D') prefix found as D'Arcy.

The Norman D'Arcy families are found in Co. Meath in the 1300's. Around this time, Sir John D'Arcy was chief Justice of Ireland. The D'Arcy family of Platten, Meath, and of Hyde Park in Westmeath are both said to be of Norman heritage.

Of the old Irish of this name, some descend from the Irish 'clan' of O'Dorchaidhe. One such family hailed from Galway and used the name of Dorcey as well. Another is found in Co. Mayo by Partry near Lough Mask. O'Donovan points out that the Darcys, known as one of the 'twelve tribes of Galway', were of native Irish origins, stemming from the Dorceys' of Mayo.

According to "Keatings History" the name is given among the principal English and Welsh families in the town of Galway by the 13th century.

'MacDarcy' is found early in Leitrim. O'Donovan gives them in Oughteragh in the year 1310, and the 'Annals of Loch Ce' find MacDarcy serving as a chieftain in Leitrim in the latter half of the 14th century. In more modern times, the 1890's birth index finds Darcy in Dublin and Tipperary most often.

The Irish Book of Arms shows the arms for D'Arcy of Co. Westmeath, D'Arcy of Corbetstown, D'Arcy of Co. Galway, Co. Mayo, and Co. Clare.

The book entitled 'Complete Pedigree of the English and Irish Branches of the D'Arcy Family' was published in London in 1901.

Daunt

Irish Book of Arms plates 58, 60

Duant, Dount

The Daunt family is found in Co. Cork as early as the 16th century, near the towns of Cork and Kinsale.

Various families of the name descend from Daunt of Owlpen Manor of Co. Gloucester in England, whereupon some of the name settled in Ireland.

They are found first settled in the reign of Elizabeth when Thomas Daunt became lessee of Tracton Abbey near Kinsale. James Daunt of Tracton Abbey was High Sheriff of Cork in 1627, as were several others of the name up to 1749.

Other branches of the family name are Daunt of Fahalea, Carrigaline, Co. Cork, and Daunt of Kilcascan Castle, Ballyneen, of whom William Joseph O'Neill-Daunt was a representative. He was said to have a first cousin living in San Paulo, Brazil. Also found given in the records is one Richard Daunt, Esq.., of Knocknamana, Co. Cork.

Dallaher

Dollaher, Dollagher

Families of the name of Dallaher, Dollagher, etc.. are traditionally linked to the county of Limerick in Ireland

Dancey

The name of an English family found settled in Co. Cavan no later than the 19th century.

O'Davoren

Irish Book of Arms plates 151, 222

O'Duibhdabhoireann

Davoran, Davorin, Davern

Davoren is a respected name in Co. Clare and it is here you will find 'O'Davorens Town', (Cahermacnaghten), which was the cite of their 'legal' school in medieval Ireland. They were a noted brehon family in the area and are found near Lisdoonvarna in Co. Clare. O'Davoren is found as the chief Brehon of Corcomroe (1364) in the works of the Four Masters.

As to different spellings of the name, Davoren is now relatively scarce, compared to the more popular modern day spelling of Davern. Clare and Tipperary remain homelands for the family today.

In the 17th century O'Davorin was a principal name of Co. Tipperary, and O'Davoren a principal name of Co. Clare. The 1890 index shows 'Davern' in Tipperary in more modern times.

Speaking of the ancient territory of Thomand and Co. Clare, Keatings History cites "O'Dobharchon' or O'Davoran, chief of Muintir Lidheagha, or the O'Liddys, the tribe name of this clan : 'The O'Davorans of wise and learned men,
Chiefs of O'Liddy of whom I treat
They belonged to the clans of Sinnell, and are the maintainers of nobility. "

Dane

The family of Dane is found centered in the Roscommon/Mayo areas of Ireland. Dane was a principal name in Co. Roscommon as well as being found in Fermanagh in the 17th century.

Some unconfirmed reports say that the name may be of Scots origins when found settling in Tipperary. Most are assumed to be of English or Irish origins when found in Ireland.

Dawson

Irish Book of Arms plate 60

D'Ossone, Daweson

Members of the Dawson family were granted lands under the acts of settlement in the 17th century. Of this line is found one Capt. John Dawson, of Drummany, Co. Monaghan. His son, James, is found settled in Co. Cork. Another of the line is found at Kilmore in Co. Monaghan in the 17th century.

Some reports also give this name as coming from the earlier foreign spelling of D'Ossone.

Dannaher

O'Duinechair

Danaher

According to "Keatings History" the name is taken from O'Duinechair, and Anglicized as Dinnahane, O'Dinan and Dannaher. The family is given as hereditary chiefs of Eoganacht Uaithne Agamar.

The family name is found anciently in Co. Tipperary and subsequently in Co. Limerick. The 1890 birth index gives 6 births in Limerick and 2 in Dublin at that date.

Darditz

Dardis

One noted family of the name is found in Johnstown, Co. Westmeath in the early 17th century. According to Keatings History the "Dardis" family name was a noted one of Co. Meath as well. Six births of the Dardis name are recorded in the 1890 birth index in the province of Leinster.

O'Day, O'Dea

Irish Book of Arms plate 102,151

O'Deaghaidh

O'Dee, O'Dea, Daw, Day, O'Dayly

The most common spelling of the name is O'Dea, commonly found in Co. Clare in modern times. As such, O'Dea is a principal name of Limerick in the census of 1659. Anciently it was stated that O'Dea was of the Dal Cais, and found in Kerry, Limerick and Clare. In the birth index of the last century the family was still in Clare and Limerick.

Spelled simply as 'Day' the name is found in the census of 1659 in Co. Tipperary. There were 13 recorded births of the 'Day' name in 1890, but none of them in the province of Connaught.

A leading family of Co. Clare, and chiefs of the barony of Inchiquinn, several O'Dea castles are recorded there.

The battle of Dysart O'Dea, and the cross of Dysart O'Dea are of historic interest. Family members please note the place names of Dysart O'Dea and Tally O'Dea commemorating the clan.

Of the Clare family, Aryan stated that ' O'Dea is the inheritor of the country, of the brown, nut producing plain."

Of the family in Tipperary it was mentioned that ' 'Slav Audi of the fair lands, O'Dea inherits as his estate, a band of that tribe from the head of the plain." (the barony of Slieveardagh).

The "Day" family and arms are given in the Irish Book of Arms as well.

In isolated instances the name of O'Day may simply be a shortened form of O'Daily, but I have no proof of this.

O'Dee has been found more as a name of Tipperary and Waterford. 'Daw' may well be of English origins as well as a form of O'Dea.

The pedigree of O'Dea of Connally Fermaic in found in volume 3 of Keatings History and 'The History and Topography of the County of Clare', by James Frost should prove interesting.

 76

De Burgh

The Irish Book of Arms plate 81

The De Burgh family of Oldtown, Co. Kildare is given in the Irish Book of Arms.

Dargan

Irish Book of Arms plate 263

Deargain

Dorgan

Dorgan is a spelling of the family name found more often in Co. Cork, and it is there where you will find the place name of Ballydorgan. The Dargan spelling is most often found in the province of Leinster.

The birth index at the end of the last century shows the name of Dargan in Dublin.

Darly

Darley

Families of the name of Darly are found in the 17th century centered in Kings Co. (Offaly), and spelled as Darley they are found in Co. Cork. For modern purposes, one cannot distinguish origins based on the slight spelling change found here.

The name is often traditionally linked with the city of Dublin, and most of these families are considered to be of English extraction having taken their name from a place in England.

De la Touche

La Touche, Touche

A Huguenot family of Ireland by some accounts. The La Touche family of Bellevue, Co. Wicklow and of Drumhearney, Co. Leitrim are given in the Irish Book of Arms.

De La Cherois

The Irish Book of Arms plate 76

The De La Cherois family of Donaghadee, Co. Down, were originally from France, from the town of Cheroy or Cherois, a small town near Sens, in the province of Champagne. It is said that the name is derived from the town mentioned above.

Mac Darrah, Darragh

Mac Dubhdara

Darra, Darrach, Darren, Darragh, Mac

The (Mc) Darrah family has been traditionally located in County Antrim, in Northern Ireland. McDarragh is found as a principal name of Antrim in the census of 1659, where the family name was concentrated in the barony of Glencarne. Likewise, in the 1890 birth index the name is given as Darragh, found primarily in Antrim again.

Some students of Irish Families believe the name to be of Scots heritage in Ireland (notably Mac Giolla Domhnaigh in ' Some Anglicized Surnames in Ireland'.) It is also interesting to note that O'Darrah, or O'Dubhdara to be precise, is found in Keatings History of Ireland as a chief of Oirghialla. This territory is roughly that of the county of Fermanagh, and it is stated that this family was probably related to the Maguires.

Due to the translation of the gaelic 'dair' which means oak, the name has sometimes been found changed to Oakes.

Deegan

Irish Book of Arms plate 263 (Deagan)

Deagan, Dugan, Degane

This family is found in early records in the barony of Clandonagh, in Co. Leix. The name is found most numerous in Dublin, Kings and Queens counties in the 19th century.

Deane

Irish Book of Arms plate 54

According to "Keatings History" the name is given as among the principal English and Welsh families settling in the town of Galway and other parts of the country in the twelfth and thirteenth centuries.

The Deane family of Glendaragh, Co. Wicklow are given as coming originally from Gloucester before settling in Ireland.

The birth index of 1890 finds the family centered in Mayo, Cork and Down.

Davis

Davies, MacDavid

A not uncommon name in Ireland from the 16th century forward, most of the name arrived from foreign shores from that time onwards.

Some families of the name of MacDavid in Ireland have also taken on the name of Davis in Co. Wexford.

Several references are found in the older records of Ireland, and the name was often spelled as Davies then. Davis is given as a branch of the Burke family in one instance, and the Davis family of Gwin Taney in Flintshire was also of note.

Sir John Davys or Davis, Knight, was given as a servitor in the barony of Glenawley in Co. Fermanagh. Another John Davis is found serving in Corcorans Irish Legion in the American civil war, and he was killed by a guard while being held prisoner. The line of Sir John Davis is given as settling in Co. Tyrone, in the north of Ireland. Thomas Davis is found in Co. Donegal, in the north of the country as well.

There are over 20 listings for the name in O'Harts work.

The name is found most numerous in the province of Ulster, in the county of Antrim.

Deasy, Dease

Irish Book of Arms plate 105

Deasey, Deece, Dease

While in modern times the name of Deasy is linked with Cork, anciently the name is also said to stem from Mac an Deisigh, where modern day descendants are found in counties Sligo, Mayo. Claim is also made that the name was taken from 'Deiseach', found anciently in the baronies of the Decies in Co. Waterford, later settling in Co. Cork.

The Dease family of Turbotson, Co. Westmeath, claim descent from an old family there. This family is found to have held property there from the 13th century, down into modern times. They are given in the Irish Book of Arms.

The birth index of 1890 finds the family centered in Cork with 24 births, and in Mayo with 9 births at that time.

Davock

MacCavock

Note the place name of Ballydavock in Co. Mayo likely marking one homeland for the Davock family in Ireland. We have found a few of the name in Co. Galway as well, where the family is said to descend from the noted Burke (de Burgo) family. The name of MacCavock denotes the same family as Davock, under a different spelling adopted some time ago.

Deely

Deeley, Devily, Deelie

The family of Deely is traditionally linked to the county of Galway in Ireland.

Deeny

Deeney, Peoples

The names of Deeny, Deeney, and Peoples were used interchangeably in the past, and the name is found earliest in the Donegal/Derry area of Ireland.

O'Delaney

Irish Book of Arms plates 120, 137

O'Dubhshlaine

Dulany, Delane, Dillane, Dellany,

O'Delaney country is found in co. Leix (Queens Co.), in the barony of Upperwoods. The name in some cases has been shortened to 'DeLane', as is the case in Co. Mayo. In the 17th century the family is found in Leix and Kilkenny. Spelled as Dellany it was a principal name of Kings County (Offaly) at that time.

In the 1890's birth index the spelling of Delaney was preferred over that of Delany by a 93 to 65 margin. The name is seldom found with its 'O' prefix as O'Delaney. The primary locations for the name at that time were in Dublin, Queens, Tipperary and Kilkenny.

Keatings History cites the Delaneys as a clan of note in the barony of Upper Ossory in Queens County and also in Kilkenny. O'Delany, chief of Tuath-an-Toraidh, was thus mentioned by O'Heerin:

"High chief of the productive territory,
From the delightful Coill Oughteragh,
Is O'Delany, the man of hospitality,
From the mountain of the most
delightful bay."

The Irish Book of Arms gives Delany of Bagnalstown, Co. Carlow, whose motto was "Depressus tamen extollor." The arms of Dr. William Delany of the same location, are shown in this work as well.

O'Deighan

According to "Keatings History" the name is given as that of the chiefs of the twelve Ballys, or Townlands, of O'Duibhghind, a district near Loughrea, Co. Galway.

77

O Dell

Irish Book of Arms plate 98

Odle, Wodell

The name of Odell or O'Dell is found to have settled in Co. Limerick as early as the 16th century, where the family is said to be of English extraction. Another form of the name was Odle. This is not an Irish "O" name in the classic sense. It is a settler name, and never had this old Irish prefix attached. It is a settler name which happened to begin with an "O". Some of the name today treat the spelling as if the name were spelled O'Dell, which is not the case. Odell or Odle would be more correct.

The name is also said to stem from the original spelling of Wodell.

The Odell family of Kilcleagh Park, Co. Westmeath descend from John Odell of Ballingarry, Co. Limerick, a Major in the army and they are given in the Irish Book of Arms.

DeCourcy

DeCourcey, Courcy, Courcie, Curcy

Sir John De Courcy was one of the most noted of the Anglo-Norman invaders of Ireland in the 12th century. His chief castle was found at Downpatrick. Through some intrigue, DeCourcy was later banished from Ireland, and he subsequently died in France.

Deery

The Deery family name is given to be one of counties Monaghan and Tyrone, in the north of Ireland.

78

O'Dempsey

Irish Book of Arms plates 151, 245

O'Diomasaigh

Demsey, Demsy, Demcy, Dempsy,

O'Dempsey is found as 'Lord of Clanmaliere', whose possessions included parts of Philliptown and Geashill in Kings, part of Portnahinch in Queens and part of Offaly in Kildare, including Monastervan. Of the same descent as the O'Connors Faly, they were Lords of Offaley and Clanmaliere.

O'Dempsey commanded the Irish clans who fought to defend Kildare and Offaley from the incursions of Strongbow in 1173. He refused to surrender and great battles took place. Dempsey was one of the few to actually defeat Strongbow and the English in battles in Ireland.

The main castle of the clan was at Geashill, in Kings County. They held many other castles including those in the barony of Offaley in Kildare, and one at Ballybrittas in the barony of Portnehinch, in Queens County.

The end of power for the Irish family came during the Elizabethan wars. From this point on, some of the name can be found on the English side in conflicts, until the coming of the 17th century when many of the family rose again in the cause for independence.

St. Evin was the patron saint of the O'Dempsey family. The name is seldom found with the 'O' prefix at the end of the last century, with 'Dempsey' being the preferred spelling of the name.

In the 17th century Dempsey was a principal name of Kildare, and found in Kings County as well. 'Dempsy' was a principal name of Queens Co., and found in Westmeath and Waterford.

Spelled as O'Demsie, the name is found as a principal one of Londonderry.

Dermot O'Dempsey was the man responsible for constructing the Cistercian Abbey at Monasterevan.

A name of the Leinster in 1890.

Denny

Irish Book of Arms plate 84

Dennehy

The name of Denny, on at least one occasion, was that of an English settler family in Co. Kerry. The Irish Book of Arms gives the Denny family of Moorstown, Co. Tipperary and of Drumlone, Co. Fermanagh.

de Lap

O Lapain

Lappin, O'Lappin, DeLappe, Dowlapp,

The name of Delap is used as a modern day form of O Lapain, or Lappin, an Irish family of Armagh and surrounding areas (including parts of Tyrone and Antrim). A noted family of Donegal, the chief of the name was styled 'Lord of Cenel Enda', prior to the 12th century. Record of the name there has become scarce since.

DeLapp is found in the census of 1659 in county Donegal, O'Lappin and DeLappe in the Hearth Money Rolls of Co. Derry of 1665. That same century Dowlapp, Dulapp, and Dunlapp are found in Antrim Inquisitions for 1635. One of the first hereditary surnames, it is cited by the Four Masters in the tenth century where one of the name served as Bishop of Raphoe, others as erenaghs, in Derry.

The name is used for Dunlop in Counties Derry and Fermanagh, and has been found in County Mayo and the Connemara area, with the Christian name of Penelope, Penny or Nappy being prominent. In Milesian families the name is given as a Scottish one, settling in Donegal in 1600.

Mac Dermot

Irish Book of Arms plates 25, 41,..

MacDiarmada

Dermott, Dermitt, Dermody, McDermitt

One of the 100 most numerous names in Ireland, MacDermot is also the 2nd most popular name in Roscommon.

MacDiarmada, meaning 'son of Dermott', of Sligo, centered near Coolavan, are the most noted of the name. Princes of Moylurg, with vast estates in Roscommon, their lands included the baronies of Boyle in Roscommon and Tirerrill in Sligo, and lands by Castlebar in Mayo.

Known as hereditary marshals of Connaught, their main stronghold and castle is found on the Rock of Lough Key on an island by Boyle in Roscommon. With the coming of Cromwell the family declined, yet the McDermott remained as prince of Coolavin with some holding in Sligo.

The MacDermot Roe sept is found in Roscommon, seated at Kilronan. They were known as sponsors to the famous bard O'Carolan. He was laid to rest at Kilronan with others of the family.

O'Dermott or MacDermott is cited as a chief of Bredach in the barony of Inisowen, on the west of Lough Foyle.

The 1890 index finds 'Dermott' with 6 births (Leitrim), and Mc Dermott had 189 births in Roscommon, Dublin, Donegal, Galway and Tyrone.

In 1659 the name is found in Dublin, Kildare, Fermanagh, Leitrim, Louth, Clare, Limerick, Roscommon and Sligo under various spellings.

The MacDermott family of Alderford, Co. Roscommon, is also found referred to as the "MacDermott Roe" branch of the name in the Irish Book of Arms.

Hereditary marshals of Connaught, centers for the name include the barony of Inisowen on the banks of Lough Foyle, the barony of Tirerrill in Sligo, and Castlebar in Co. Mayo.

79

Desmond

Irish Book of Arms plate 2 (titled)

Esmond

Given to be a family of the western parts of Co. Cork in our records. In the 1890 index 32 of 34 recorded births were given in Co. Cork.

de Long

of Norman origin

Long

De Long is a Norman name found in Ireland, and is cited in Keatings History as such. The census of 1659 shows the family in Roscommon, Dublin, Clare and Kilkenny. The 1890 birth index shows Cork and Dublin to be the counties of residence at that time. In Milesian families the name is given in Donegal and Derry, coming originally from England in 1640.

The name is often found simply as 'Long' without the Norman prefix. In that case the name could be from the Norman de Long, the Irish O'Longain, or the English 'Long'. In county Donegal, any of these origins may apply. In Co. Cork, where the name was most numerous at the turn of the century as 'Long', it is the name of an Irish erenagh family in the parish of Moviddy and Canavoy (O Longaigh)

Deering

Deering, Dearing

Families of the Deering name are generally given as settling in Ireland, coming originally from England. Several are found among the rolls of landowners in Ireland from the 17th century onward. The 19th century birth index finds the name centered in Co. Monaghan, but we find several of the name in earlier days in Dublin, Kings (Offaly), Carlow and Kildare.

Devereux

Irish Book of Arms plate 72

Deveraux, Devery, Deverell, d'Evrvex

A name of Norman extraction, the Devereux family is found in Wexford in the 12th century. The spelling of Deverell is given in Leix and Offaly.

The Devereux family of Ballyrankin House, Co. Wexford are found earliest settled in Kilrush in that county, being descendants of Nicholas Devereux who settled there in the reign of King John.

In 1890 the name is given in Co. Wexford.

Delafield

de la Field

One family of the name is found in Knockbuy and Derrynachally in Co. Monaghan in the early 17th century.

Delahoyde

Delahoid, Delahyde

"Keatings History" gives the name as that of a principal family of Dublin, and of Anglo-Norman descent. This work also gives the family of Delahoid, as one of note in Co. Meath.

Delahunty

Delahunt, Dullanty, Delanty

Given to be a name of Offaly in our records, the 1890 birth index finds the family of "Delahunt" centered in Co. Kildare in the 19th century.

Delamere

According to "Keatings History" the name is one of a family who obtained large possessions of land in Westmeath and Annaly, along with the Daltons'.

Den

One family of the name is found in Grenane, Co. Kilkenny, early in the 17th century.

Dick

The Irish Book of Arms plate 95

The Dick family of Co. Wicklow are given in the Irish Book of Arms.

Delargy

Families of the name of Delargy are given to be an old Irish family, and not of Norman origin as the "De" before the name might suggest. The name traditionally linked to counties Antrim and Mayo.

Delmore

De Lamere, Delamere, De Lamare

According to some accounts, one of the name of De Lamere came to Ireland with the 12th century Norman invasions. This Herbert De Lamare controlled parts of Westmeath and held many possessions in that area.

One John de Lamare is credited by some with building the Castle of Street, in Maghbreacry, Co. Longford, where he was seated at the end of the 13th century.

Dennehy

Irish Book of Arms plate 247 (Denehy)

Denehy, Dennehey

Traditionally given to be a name of the Cork/Kerry area in Ireland, 26 births were recorded in Cork, and 9 in Kerry, in the 1890 birth index of Ireland.

80

Dickson

Irish Book of Arms plate 69

Dixon, Dick

While some of the name may be of obscure Irish origins, at least 99% of the family is of English or Scottish heritage. Many of the name settled in Ulster in the 17th century, and the name remains there to this day.

Of those of the name in Co. Mayo, it has been said that they were originally of a family found in Co. Donegal, settling subsequently in Mayo.

Of the Dickson family of Donegal and Leitrim, John Dickson is found in Ballyshannon, Donegal and his son is found in Woodville, Co. Leitrim in the middle of the 18th century.

The Dickson family of Kildimo House, Co. Limerick is found in the Irish Book of Arms.

The birth index of 1890 finds the family name centered in Antrim and Down, spelled as Dick. Spelled as Dickey we find families of the name most numerous in Co. Antrim. Dixon is found centered in Dublin and Mayo, and Dickson is found most numerous in Down and Antrim in that index.

Denvir

Denver

The name of a family said to have settled in Ireland no later than the 17th century, the name is most often found in Antrim and Down.

Derenzy

According to "Keatings History" the name is given as that of an old English family who settled in Wexford.

Dillon, Dillion

Irish Book of Arms plates 119, 138..

de Leon

Dillon, Dillion, Dillane, Dologhan,

Considered to be thoroughly Irish, 'de Leon', otherwise known as Dillon, arrived in Ireland with the coming of the Norman invasions. Sir Henry de Leon of Brittany received lands in Westmeath as a result of the invasions.

' Dillons country' came to refer to nearly all of the county of Westmeath, which was populated by the family.

The family also became barons in Kilkenny West, and another branch was centered in co. Mayo. Keatings History cites the name as a principal one of Galway and Dublin cities. This work also speaks of a Dillon who traveled to France in the 7th century and became Duke of Aquitane. His descendants returned to Ireland as 'de Leon' (?).

Burke's Peerage gives several pages to members of the Dillon family. Sir James Dillon of Proudstown is found here as "ancestor of the Dillons...Earls of Roscommon..Lords of Clonbrock...of Proudstown and Skrine."

The Dillons were created Counts as early as 1171 and have held high office since then, in Ireland and France. The family name can be found in France yet today, and it is still considered to be an Irish name.

O'Dillane (O'Duilleain) is a name of Limerick and northern Kerry, sometimes found as Dillon.

Remaining powerful into modern times the name is centered in Co. Meath and the west of Ireland today. One prominent center of power can be found at Portlick Castle, just north of Athlone, near Lough Rea.

In 1659 Dillan is found in Carlow, O'Dillene and O'Dillane in Limerick, O'Dillon in Roscommon and Dillone in Kings County.

O'Dinneen

Irish Book of Arms plates 119, 138..

O'Duinnin

Dinan, Downing, Dinane, Dynan, Dineen

The Dinneen surname is seldom found with the 'O' prefix. It is a name of Co. Cork in Ireland. The Dineens descend from the O'Duinnin sept of that county, and are anciently of the corca Laoidhe.

The family served as poets and antiquarians to the McCarthy Mor and the Sullivans. Dinan and Dynan are variant spellings in Co. Cork. Some of the clan adopted the English surname of Downing, a name of Cork and Kerry.

O'Hart gives 'O'Dinan' or Downing as chiefs of Uaithne, now the barony of Owneybeg in Limerick.

At the turn of the last century Dineen and Dinneen were the two preferred spellings of the name, both of which were centered in Co. Cork. Earlier, in the census of 1659, Dinane was a principal name of County Cork.

Dervan

Dirvan, Derwin, Derivin

Families of the name are rare in our records but do appear in the Galway and Roscommon areas of Ireland.

Devane

O'Dubhain

Duane, Dwane

The name is most often found in Kerry and Galway, and has also been interchanged with names such as Dwane and Duane. The Devane family is found most numerous in Co. Kerry in the 19th century.

Devey

Deevy, Deevey

The name of Devey, etc.. is found early in Co. Leix, and subsequently is found more widespread in adjoining areas; e.g., Kilkenny.

Dobbin

Irish Book of Arms plate 97

Dobyn, Dobbyn

There are several variant spellings of the name found in older records, and the family is found early at Carrickfergus, Co. Antrim, and subsequently in counties Armagh and Waterford.

The name is assumed to be of English origins, and some of the name settled in Ireland in the 17th century.

The Dobbin family of Armagh, of Drummula House, Co. Louth, descend from two brothers of the name who came from Carrickfergus to Armagh in 1690.

The birth index of 1890 finds the family centered in Antrim.

Dermody

Irish Book of Arms plate 253

O'Diarmada, Mac Diarmada

MacDermot, Darmody, Dermoody

Dermody families are found dispersed throughout the counties of Cavan, Westmeath, Kilkenny and Galway. The origins of the name have proved difficult to trace.

Dermod, itself, is sometimes given as a variant spelling of Dermott. Hence, the possible original spelling of the name may spring from the same source as McDermott or O'Dermott.

O'Dugan cites O'Duibhdiorma as both (O) and (Mac) Dermott, in the barony of Inishowen, and he further states that this family was distinct from the MacDermotts of Moylurg in Co. Roscommon.

MacDermotts are also cited as chiefs of the barony of Tirerill, in Co. Sligo.

Not a common name, 9 births under the name of Dermody were recorded in the 1890's index.

O'Doherty

Irish Book of Arms plates 262, 152...

O'Dochartaigh

Dogherty, Doghertye, Dohorty, Dorrity,

The O'Doherty name has always been one of Co. Donegal, and so it remains today. The family can be traced back to its origins in the barony of Raphoe, Co. Donegal. They descend from the same line as the O'Donnells.

One of the top 20 names in all of Ireland, spelled as Dogherty it is found most often in Donegal, Londonderry and Mayo. As 'Doherty' it is found most often in Londonderry, Mayo and Donegal in the 1890 index (in order of predominance).

Extending their territory from Raphoe, they became Lords of Inishowen peninsula. They remained as chiefs of Inishowen down to the reign of James I, when Sir Cahir O'Dogherty was killed in a battle with the English.

The McDevitts of the same areas are an offshoot of this family, descending from David O'Doherty, a chief of the name in the 13th century.

Here is another name which had dropped the 'O' prefix by the time of the coming of the last century. (In the 1890 index only 7 O'Doherty births were recorded.) Modern day residents continue to reverse this trend by adding the 'O' back onto the name.

In the 17th century I find O'Doghertye as a principal name of Donegal, and also in Londonderry. Dogherty was a principal name of Sligo, and O'Dogherty was of Donegal and Fermanagh.

Another, rare form of O'Doherty may spring from the old spelling of O'Dubhartaigh as does the name of Doorty in the Co. Clare area.

Dolling

Irish Book of Arms plate 34

One family of the name in Ireland was said to be of ancient French descent. Around the year 1580 one member of the noted family embraced the Huguenot persuasion and was forced to flee to England. Henceforth some of the family settled in Ireland. These are the Dollings of Magheralin, Co. Down, as found in the Irish Book of Arms.

Devaney

ODUIBHEANNAIGH

DEVENNEY, DUVANY, DOVANY,

Families of the name of Devaney and its variant spellings are found in several locations in Ireland. The name is most often traditionally linked with Co. Donegal in the north of Ireland. In the same province of Ulster, many of the name are found in Co. Armagh, and it is not know if they represent two completely separate and unrelated families or not.

In the census of 1659 we find the name in their old territory near Inishowen, which also bears out the following quote from v-3 of Keatings History:

"Mac Duvan(e)y, Chiefs of Kinel Nenna, or Kinel Enda. This District lays in Inishowen."

The family is further cited in Co. Down in the same work:

"O'Duvan(e)y Chief of Kinel Amalgaidh or Ambalgaidh Ui Morna or Ui Mughroin, now Clanawley, in the County of Down."

By the time of the 1890 birth index the name was mainly in Mayo, Galway and Leitrim.

Individuals of the name:

CONOR O'DEVANY- BISHOP OF DOWN AND CONNOR FROM 1582-1612 (FOUND IN THE FOUR MASTERS).

82

Dolmage

The Irish Book of Arms plate 98

Delmege

The Delmege or Dolmage family of Rathkeale, Co. Limerick, are said to be of Alsatian origins, settling in Co. Limerick at the time of Louis XIV. It is also said that the family came to Ireland under religious persecution in their homeland.

Devere

Irish Book of Arms plate 252

Mac Dever, Diver, Devereux, Dever

From our limited records the name of Devere may have come from several origins and appears to be a variant spelling. It is possible that the name stems from Devereux, a name earlier of Co. Wexford. This would account for the final 'e' at the end of the name.

The location of the name when traced back to Ireland may play a most important part in determining its origins. Dever, a name of Mayo in the birth index, and Diver a name of Donegal, may also be related to the name, being a variant spelling. O'Dever is cited in Milesian families as of ancient Irish heritage, being a Eugenian tribe in Mayo and Donegal. In the same source, the name is cited as well as a Norman name, arriving in 1171 in Wexford.

In O'Harts work we find an emotional poem written by De Vere, entitled 'Wail of Thomand', which decries the loss of the old order and loyalties of the Irish chieftain of the area.

Devilly

Devilley, Devally, Diffly, Deffely

The families of the name of Devilly and its variant spellings are most often linked to counties Galway and Roscommon in Ireland.

Domville

Irish Book of Arms plate 22

Domvile

We find the Domvile family of Loughlinstown, Co. Dublin, given in the Irish Book of Arms.

O'Devine

Irish Book of Arms plate 229

O'Daimhin

Devin, Davine, Devane, Divine

The O'Devine' family ruled as 'Lords of Tirkennedy' in Fermanagh. The Four Masters cite a Devine as a co-arb of Derry , along with other chiefs of Tirkennedy down into the 15th century.

In the 17th century 'Devane' is found as a principal name of Tipperary, and the same spelling is found in Co. Kerry in the 1890 birth index. Devine ranks as the most popular spelling of the name in 1890 and was found in Tyrone, Dublin and Roscommon. Devany, was found in Mayo, Galway and Leitrim.

In Co. Louth 'Devin' appears to be the more accepted form of the name today. Families of the name of Devin are usually originally of the Devine or O'Devine family, and this spelling is often found in Co. Louth. Devin is also used for "Davin" in Co. Tipperary.

Jenkin O'Devin is given in O'Hart in the precinct of Dungannon, Co. Tyrone, as a grantee during the Ulster plantation.

The Maguires supplanted the O'Devines in Fermanagh around 1264, according to O'Hart. Elsewhere he gives O'Devine as a chief in Tirkennedy until 1427 A. D.. Fiacha O'Daimhin was the last Lord of the same, before the Maguires took hold. From that county emigrated James Devine in 1713, who settled near Kilkee in Co. Clare. Female members of this line are found in Davenport, Iowa, in the U. S. A. in the 1880s

Mac Donagh

Irish Book of Arms plates 152, 211

Mac Donnchada

MacDonough, MacDonagh, MacDonogh,

The MacDonogh family in Ireland may be traced to several different origins, the most noted of which is descended from the McDermott family. The McDermotts were a powerful family in Roscommon and Sligo. In Sligo MacDonough chiefs became Lords of Tireril or Lords of Corran in the barony of Corran. One branch of this family is said to have settled in Thomand (in or near Co. Clare).

Another, separate family of the name hails from Co. Cork. The chiefs of the name were known as princes of Duhallow at one point. Their chief residence was at Kanturk Castle. This family descends from the MacCarthy family of note in the area. Earlier a name of some mention, MacDonogh has faded from prominence in the area today.

In 1659 Donogh was a principal name in Tipperary, as was McDonnough. 'Donogh Oge' denoting a specific branch of the name, was a principal name of Co. Cork at that time.

Keatings History makes mention of the MacDonoughs as of the Ui Briuin race, being descended from Brian, King of Connaught in the 4th century. (ui Briuin centered anciently in Cavan and Leitrim.)

The 1890 index shows McDonagh in Galway, Roscommon and Mayo - in much greater numbers than the 'Donaghy' spelling found in Antrim, Londonderry and Tyrone. McDonogh in the 17th century was fairly widespread, being a principal name in Clare, Cork, and found in numerous other counties including Kerry and Limerick.

83

Mac Donlevy

Irish Book of Arms plate 152

Mac Duinnshleibhe

Dunleavy, Leavy, Donleavy, Dunlavy

In the more ancient records this family name is recorded in the north of Ireland. Here it is found in the 1100's in Co. Down and in Cos. Antrim and Donegal.

The Mac Donlevys were a chief family of Down and southern Co. Antrim until they met defeat in 1177 with the coming of the Norman invasions. They then moved into Donegal and served as hereditary physicians to the ruling O'Donnells.

This surname is cited anciently as O'Dunnslebi, or Mac Dunnslebi, as being the King of Uladh. Moving into modern times the name is found in Mayo and Sligo, the only two counties given in the 1890 birth index.

O'Hart gives a pedigree of some sorts for one family of the name. This is of one 'Don Levi' of the princes of Ulidia (Uladh) in Ulster. This family apparently had connections with the continent.

'A Genealogical History of the Dunlevy Family', by G. D. Kelley published in Columbus, Ohio in 1901, may be of interest to family members.

O'Devoy

Deevoy, Deevey, Deevy, Divey

Families of the name are most often associated with Queens Co. (Leix), in Ireland. It is found in that county as a principal name in the 17th century. The Devoy family was one of the 7 septs of Leix, the chief families of which were transplanted to Co. Kerry in 1607. We do not find the family firmly established in Co. Kerry in our records to date.

Mac Donnell

Irish Book of Arms plates 106, 152

MacDomhnaill

McDaniell, McDonald, Donnell, Donel

One of the 100 most numerous names in Ireland, McDonnell may be traced to one of several origins.

Some of the name descend from the McDonnells of Argyllshire, Scotland. They came from Scotland in the 13th century settling in Antrim (Ulster). The leading line of this name were known as 'Lord of the Isles'. They came to Ireland as 'gallowglass' (fighting men), in the service of the leading Irish families in Ulster. Eventually they took the lands of the McQuillans of Antrim, including their castle at Dunseverick, and in the Glens of Antrim.

Randal MacSorley MacDonnell was Earl of Antrim in 1620. Curtis says that this family was in the service of the Burkes, in Co. Mayo, in 1399.

The Mac Donnell name may also have sprung from older Irish families. First, MacDomhnaill, or McDonnell of Fermanagh, and secondly, the McDonnells of Thomand and Co. Clare who served as bards to the O'Briens. They descend from Domhnall (Donal), son of King Murtagh Mor O'Brien. The name here is also spelled as McDaniell.

Some of the name of MacDonald, may have changed their name to MacDonnell, simply due to the similarity in sound.

In the 17th century McDonell was a principal name of Antrim, as well as being found in Armagh, Fermanagh, Cork, Limerick, Dublin and Kings Counties etc...The name was numerous in the 1890 index, in Dublin, Mayo, Antrim, Galway and Cork at that time.

The Irish Book of Arms includes the McDonnell family of New Hall and Kilkee, Co. Clare. They claim descent through Daniel McDonnell, of Kilkee, who held the estates of Kilbreckan, and lands in Galway and Limerick city.

O'Donnell

Irish Book of Arms plates 152, 201

ODomhnaill

O'Donell, Donnal, Donal, Donel, Donnell

One of the 50 most numerous names in Ireland, the O'Donnells are a notable family of Ireland. The main family of the name descends from Niall of the Nine Hostages, a high-king of 4th century Ireland. Their lands, anciently known as Tir Conaill (Tyrconnell - Connells lands), are found in Donegal.

The inauguration site of the O'Donnells was at Carraig Dun, (The Rock of Doon), at Kilmacrenan, near Letterkenny. Linked with the great O'Neills of Ulster, they intermittently formed alliances with the same, against the English, and vice-versa. Rising into prominence in the 13th century, they are recorded earliest around Kilmacrenan, before coming to power.

The name of O'Donnell is taken from 'Donal' (d.901), a descendant of Niall of the Nine Hostages. Perhaps the most famous of the name was Red Hugh (b.1572) or Hugh Roe O'Donnell who served as chief of the name. He escaped from Dublin castle as a youth, and thereafter led his forces against the British at the Battle of Kinsale in 1601. He was then forced to Spain in exile and defeat, to be poisoned there by a man named Blake at the direction of the British Crown.

Two other O'Donnell families are of note here. Those of Corcabaskin in Co. Clare and those of the Ui Maine (Hy Many) in Co. Galway.

In the 17th century O'Donell was a principal name of Donegal and also found in Fermanagh, Londonderry and Kilkenny. O'Donnell (with two n's), was a principal name of Antrim at the time. The 1890 birth index gives O'Donnell in Donegal, Mayo and Galway.

84

O'Donnellan

Irish Book of Arms plates 86, 152, 118

O'Domhnallain

Donlan, Donlon, Donelan, Donnellen

The origins of the Ui Maine (Hy Many) family of the name of O'Donnellan have been traced to the south-eastern part of Co. Galway. The center of power for the family appears to be in the barony of Kilconnell, at Ballydonellan. Their castle at Ballydonellan was built in 936, and has been rebuilt at least once due to fire damage.

The O'Donnellan family is of some repute as ollavs and poets, and they are recorded as such in the Annals of Irish history. Keatings History cites the family as "Domhnallain, or O'Donnellans, chiefs of Clan Breasail, a district in the barony of Letrim, county of Galway." These Donnellans are cited by O'Dugan as:

"Noble the blood and achievements
Of the O'Donnellans of handsome figure
Rushing to the battle like a torrent,
Such are the yellow-haired Clan Breasail

This family is said to have descended from Domhallan, the Lord of clan Breasail. In the 1890 birth index 'Donnellan' was found in Clare and Mayo. Spelled as Donelan it was given at this time in Galway, and as Donlon it is found in Co. Longford.

In the census of 1659 Donellan is found in Dublin.

The Donelan family of Sylanmore, Tuam, Co. Galway descends from the ancient Irish family of O'Donnellan.

O Donnelly

Irish Book of Arms plates 152, 208

O'Donnghaile

Dannelly, Donaldson, Donelly, Donely,

The O'Donnelly family is primarily from the province of Ulster in the north of Ireland. One can trace the family back to Neill the Great through Donnghaile O'Neill, a descendant of the same. Most anciently the O'Donnellys were of the Cinel Eoghan tribes and they are found earliest in Co. Donegal.

As the family grew in power they moved east towards Ballydonnelly, in Dungannan Middle Barony, Co. Tyrone. Ballydonnelly castle here marks the seat of power for the clan. The castle was obtained later by Lord Caulfield, and hence was renamed Castle Caulfield. Continuing to grow, the family became numerous in Co. Antrim as well.

Note two place names called 'Ballydonnelly' in Antrim, marking the further settlement of the family. Co. Antrim remained the county with the most of the name in the 1890 index.

In ancient times the chief of the name served as hereditary marshal for O'Neills army, and many achieved distinction.

One of the 100 most numerous names in Ireland, there is at least one other origin of the name. One O'Donnelly sept descends from O'Donnghalaigh, of Co. Tipperary in lower Ormond. The history there remains unclear to us.

In the 1659 census 'O'Donelly' was a principal name in Armagh and also found in Leitrim, and 'Donelee' was given as a principal name of Longford.

The name has remains one of Ulster today, with Tyrone, Antrim and Armagh being centers for the name. The name is found often in Dublin as well. Keating gives the family several times citing them as "of Ormond of the Smooth Plain", as chiefs at Ballydonnelly, Tyrone, and as a chief in Inishowen.

O'Donoghue

Irish Book of Arms plates 65, 152

Donnchadh

Donaghue, Donahue, Donahoe, Donojo,

The name of O'Donoghue springs from the gaelic personal name of Donnchadh. Several unrelated individuals named Donnchadh (Strong Warrior?), became founders of the name. The Donoghues are one of the largest families of Ireland.

The O'Donoghues of Co. Kerry were the most powerful family of the name. They descend from Oilioll Olium (234 a.d.), and the Eugenien line, taking their name from Donnchadh in 1063. Their ancient clan names were Cinel Laoghaire and Clan tSealbach.

Originally of the Desmond area of Cork, they were driven into Kerry by the MacCarthys and O'Mahoneys. There they became Lords of the area surrounding Killarney, founding the O'Donoghue Mor (of Lough Lein) line (extinct in 1582) and the O'Donoghues of the Glen, seated at Killaha Castle; at Glenflesk. A local descendant tells of the imported marble which once decorated the Killaha castle.

The lands of the O'Donoghues were the last to be taken by Cromwells invasion, and the O'Donoghues of the Glen resisted, retained their title as such.

The ancient burial place for both of these families can be found near the ruins of Ross Castle and Aghadoe Hill.

Several legends remain concerning the O'Donoghues. Once a year the O'Donoghue rises from the depths of the lakes riding a white steed.....and the legend of the crooked knife etc...

Other O'Donoghue septs are found in Cavan, Galway, Ossory and Tipperary. 'The O'Donoghue Book' is available from the Irish Family Journal, and may be of interest to family members. An extensive entry on the family is found in *Families of Co. Kerry, Ireland*, v.2 of the Irish Families series.

O'Donovan

Irish Book of Arms plates 64, 111

O'Donnabhain

Donovane, Donavan, Dingavan

The O'Donovan name is considered to be a family of Cork today, but the beginnings of this family are found in Limerick. They were centered in their chief castle at Bruree in the barony of Kenry, near the River Maigue. In fact, 11 of the name O'Donovan were born in Cork and Limerick in 1890. The spelling of the name with the 'O', was rare, as 211 of the name 'Donovan' were found in Cork.

The family takes their name from one 'Donovan', a chief in 977, one of his descendants, Crom O'Donovan was seated at Crom Castle by the river Maigue in Limerick.

Keatings History finds them as chiefs of Clan Cathail and their chief residence was known as Castle Donovan, in Co. Cork, earlier in history.

With the coming of the Norman invasions the family moved into the West of Cork. Here they were centered in the baronies of East and West Carbery. They subsequently settled in Kilkenny and Wexford as well.

The chief of the name was recognized into modern times, and as late as 1560 the chief was inaugurated by the MacCarthy Reagh.

The noted Dr. John O'Donovan has left much information concerning the name.

Donovane, McDonovane and O'Donovane were all registered as principal names of Co. Cork in the 17th century. It is assumed that the Mc Donovane spelling was used in error.

John H. Donovan is found as a captain in the 69th N.Y. Volunteers (1861-1865) in America. Edward Donovan is found mentioned as a "mariner" in the Pennsylvania Gazette in 1772 in the U.S.. There are estate papers in the National Library on this family.

O'Doran

Irish Book of Arms plate 153

O'Deorain

Dorian, Doran, Doren, Dorane

In Keatings History the O'Dorans are found to have "held the office of hereditary brehons of Leinster, and had extensive possessions under the ancient Kings". When the Mac Murroghs were inaugurated as Kings of Leinster at Cnoc-an-Bogha, "O'Doran, the chief brehon of Leinster" was in attendance.

O'Doran reigned anciently as one of the seven septs of Leix, along with O'Devoy, McEvoy, O'Dowling, O'Kelly, O'Lalor and O'Moore. Scattered from their territory in Leix they are said to have settled in the barony of Bantry in Co. Wexford and in Co. Kerry.

They arrived in Kerry due to the fact that leading families of the name were transplanted there in 1609. In the 16th century they were centered at Chappell in Wexford and became a leading family of the day. Note the place name of Doransland in Co. Wexford in tribute to the family.

The family name is also found in Ulster, descended from O'Deoradhain. Here they were centered in counties Down and Armagh.

O'Doran was a principal name of Down, and Dorane a principal name of Wexford and Louth in 1659. Doran in found in Kildare, Meath and Wexford at that time.

By the time of the 1890 birth index Doran is found in Dublin, Wexford, Down and Armagh.

Dirrane

Dirane, Derane, Derrane

A name traditionally linked with Co. Galway in Ireland.

Douglas

Irish Book of Arms Douglass plate 66

Dubhghlas

Douglass, Dougles

The Douglas family in Ireland may be considered a family of Ulster. They are of the noted Scottish clan of the name, and are found primarily in Antrim and Londonderry in modern times. More anciently Douglass was given as a name of Scotland, settling in Co. Down in 1640.

The arms of one Blacker-Douglass family of Grace Hall, Co. Down, are given in the Irish Book of Arms

Mc Devitt

Mac Daibheid (son of David)

Mac Davitt, Davison, Mac Daid, Devitt,

The McDevitt sept in Ireland was founded by one David O'Doherty (d. 1208), who was a chief of Cenel Eoghain. The name has been numerous in Donegal, and in adjoining areas of Tyrone and Derry in Northern Ireland. It is significant to note that the name remained localized in this area alone, and is not widespread elsewhere in Ireland. To this day McDevitt remains a name of Donegal, with the name being found here in the 1890 index, as well as in Tyrone and Londonderry.

Note the townland name of Ballydevitt in the barony of Banogh, Co. Donegal, and another of the same name in Derry. Without the 'Mc' prefix, spelled as Devitt, the name was found in Clare and Dublin in the 1890 index. These locations are distinct from those found with the Mc prefix. In Milesian families the name is also listed as a Norman one, arriving in 1171 and settling in Cork, Limerick and Galway. Dr. James MacDevitt, (1832 - 1897), who was the Bishop of Raphoe and author of "The Donegal Highlands".

86

O'Dowd

Irish Book of Arms plates 153, 259

O'Dubhda

Doody, Duddy, Dodd, Doud, Dowds

The O'Dowds were inaugurated princes of the Ui Fiachrach at Carn Amalgaidh, near Killala. The family has been noted to have produced strong and large sized men in earlier days.

The O'Dowds are spoken of as 'chiefs' of more ancient times in Ireland. One branch of the name settled in Co. Kerry, becoming known as 'Doody' instead of O'Dowd.

Another ancient family of O'Dubhda settled in Co. Derry, where it is thought the name became 'Duddy'. In the 1890 birth index, the family is found most often in County Sligo.

The family anciently controlled lands in Mayo and Sligo, including the baronies of Erris and Tirawley in Mayo and the barony of Tireragh in Sligo.

The power of the clan was reduced by the Norman invasions early on in Irish history, and their estates were later confiscated during the Cromwellian wars.

Spelled simply as 'Dowd', without the 'O' prefix, the birth index lists the family as found in Roscommon, Dublin, Kerry and Galway. In modern times the 'O' has been added back onto this name in many instances.

For interesting and more detailed accounts see : 'The Tribes and Customs of the Hy Fiachrach".

(O) Individuals:

DAVID O'DOWD, TEIGE MACPHELIM O'DOWD, DONOGH MACCOSNY O'DOWD, DAVID MACJAMES O'DOWD, TEIGE REAGH O'DOWD. CONFISCATIONS IN THE COUNTY OF SLIGO, BARONY OF TIRERAGH.

LISTED AS INTERMARRIED WITH THE 'MILMO' FAMILY, OF MEXICO, UNITED STATES.

Dowdall

Irish Book of Arms plate 53

According to "Keatings History" the name is that of a principal family of Dublin city or county, and of Anglo-Norman descent. From the same source we find that the name was of a noted family in Meath, where they were centered in Athlumney.

The Dowdall family of Mountown, descends from Walter Dovedale of Palmerson in Co. Meath in Ireland.

The birth index of 1890 finds the family centered in Dublin and Louth.

Diamond

O'Diamain

A name found earliest in Co. Derry and subsequently in Donegal and Mayo, always traditionally linked to the province of Ulster in Ireland. The family is found most numerous in Londonderry and Antrim in the 19th century.

Diggin

Digin

The name of a family traditionally found in Co. Kerry in Ireland, and this is where they remained centered in the 19th century. Note that the name of Digan, is also found in the 19th century in Kings Co., and this is believed to be a variant spelling of another name entirely.

O'Dinerty

Irish Book of Arms plate 247

Dinnerty

According to "Keatings History" the name is given by O'Heerin apparently on the borders of Tipperary and Kilkenny, alongside O'Hamery.

O'Dowling

Irish Book of Arms plate 153, 231

Dunlaing

Doolen, Doolin, Dooling, Dooly, Dowlan,

The O'Dowlings were one of the noted' 7 septs of Leix.' Their territory was marked here in the west of Queens County (Leix) by the path of the River Barrow. This land became known as O'Dowlings country. They subsequently spread into Kilkenny, Carlow and Wicklow near Rathdrum. Note the place name of Ballydowling in these areas.

O'Heerin gives O'Dowling (O'Dunlaing) as a chief of Siol Elaigh and the Lagan anciently, and stated that O'Dowling "was the warrior of the Lagan". This territory was the barony of Shilelagh, in the south of Wicklow.

Leading families of the 7 Septs notes above were transplanted to Co. Kerry in 1609, hence several references to the name are found in County Kerry.

Many of the name settled in Dublin City relatively early in time. Hence, we find Dowling more numerous in Dublin in 1890, than in either Kilkenny or Queens (Leix).

Most agree that the majority of the name in Ireland are of native Irish origins, and not of English extraction, for the name is an English one as well.

According to O'Hart the O'Dowlings were driven from the barony of Fertullagh, Co. Westmeath, by O'Melaghlin, settling then in Ely O'Carroll territory. The O'Dowling (or O'Dulaing) portion of the family were chiefs in Co. Wicklow and Queens Co..

Several Dowlings are found in the Irish Brigades in the service of France in the 18th century.

Doyle

Irish Book of Arms plate 153

O'Dubhghaill

Doil, Dooal, Dyle, McDoyle, O'Doyle

It is held by many that the Doyles are of old Norse origins in Ireland. This is based upon several points. First, the name may be taken from the Irish 'dubh-ghall', meaning foreigner or dark stranger. This term was used in describing the Norse (Vikings) when settling in Ireland. Secondly, the name is found mainly on the coast, where the Norse likely settled, in Carlow, Wexford and Wicklow. Thirdly, one cannot find the name in any of the old Irish genealogies, as other Irish families have been. The name appears rather late on the scene, it would seem.

But due to the great popularity of the name, Doyle is among the top 20 names in all of Ireland, there are surely other Irish origins as well.

In the province of Ulster, Doyle has been used for MacDowell, a gallowglass family of the Hebrides. MacDugall is a Scots family in Co. Roscommon, and it stems from the same old Irish spelling as does Doyle.

Keatings History mentions Doyle as among the clans that had large possessions in Carlow and Wexford.

Principal locations for the name in the last century were in Dublin, Wexford, Wicklow, Carlow, Kerry and Cork. It is interesting to note that McDoyle was found as a principal name in Westmeath, and that O'Doyle a principal name of Carlow and Wexford in the 17th century.

The 'O' before the name (or the Mac?), fell largely out of use after that date.

John Doyle was a member of the Irish House of Commons in 1797. A Doyle of the same name was a member of the 3rd Regt. of Corcorans Irish Legion. Arthur Conan Doyle of course, was the creator of Sherlock Holmes.

Doynes, Doyne

Irish Book of Arms plate 55

According to "Keatings History" the name of "Doynes" is that of one of the chief old English families to settle in Co. Carlow.

The family of "Doyne" is found centered in Kilkaran, Queens Co., in the early 17th century as well. The Doyne family of Wells, Co. Wexford is given in the Irish Book of Arms.

O Dillane

The name of a family traditionally found in the counties of Kerry and Limerick, and distinct from the families of Dillon in Ireland, although some may have in fact adopted the Dillon spelling of the name.

Both the names of O'Dillane and O'Dillene are found as principal name of Co. Limerick in the 17th century. Families spelling the name as Dillane are given in Limerick, Galway and Kerry in the 19th century birth index.

O'Dilleen

Dillon, Dillane

Much confusion can result between the separate families of Dillon, Dillane and Dilleen. No doubt several families of the Dilleen name now bear the name of Dillon. The name, though scarce, is most often found in the Galway/Clare area of Ireland.

Note that the spelling as O'Dillene is given in Co. Limerick as a principal name in the 17th century. This is considered to be a separate family, often found as Dillane, and Limerick is a traditional homeland.

Drake

Irish Book of Arms plate 97

According to "Keatings History" the name is one of a noted family in Meath. Notably the Drake family is found centered in Drak-rath.

The Drake family of Stokestown, Co. Wexford descend from Roger Drake, an agent for the Victuallers of the Navy, who received a grant of Stokestown and other lands in Co. Wexford.

The birth index of 1890 finds the family centered in Down and Monaghan.

O'Dinan

According to "Keatings History" the name is taken from O'Duinechair, and Anglicized as Dinnahane, O'Dinan and Dannaher. The family is given as hereditary chiefs of Eoganacht Uaithne Agamar.

In the 1890 index 7 births of the name of Dinan are recorded in Co. Cork.

Dinnahane

Irish Book of Arms plate 253 (Dinehan)

Dinahan, Dinehan,Dinaghane, Deenihan,

According to "Keatings History" the name of Dinnahane is taken from O'Duinechair, and Anglicized as Dinnahane, O'Dinan and Dannaher. The family is given as hereditary chiefs of Eoganacht Uaithne Agamar.

Dinaghan, Dinaghan, Deenihan, Deynihan, etc.. families are most generally associated with Co. Kerry when found in Ireland. Several sources give the ancient location of the family in Co. Limerick.

O'Driscoll

Irish Book of Arms plates 153, 230

O'Drisceoil

Driskol, Driscall, Driskol, Driskill

The O'Driscolls are traditionally associated with Co. Cork, Ireland, but originally sprang from Kerry. The Sullivans forced them into Cork, where they became centered around Baltimore.

The family may trace its descent back to Eidersceoil in the year 910 A.D.. He was of the Corca Laoidhe clan in the diocese of Ross. Like other families, the fortunes of the Driscolls fell with the coming of Cromwell to Ireland.

Family researchers may note that the 'O' prefix had been generally dropped in the last century. The 1890 birth index shows 121 of the name Driscoll and only 13 as O'Driscoll, all centered in Co. Cork. A quick check of todays Irish phone book will show that this trend has reversed itself, with the 'O' being added back to the name.

In 1659 Driscoll and O'Driscoll are found in Cork as principal names, with O'Driscoll also found in Co. Clare.

In Keatings History O'Driscoll is found with castles at Dunashad and Dunalong, near Baltimore, as well as the castle of Dunamore on Capeclear Island.

O'Driscoll was cited thusly:

'O'Driscoll, head chief of the land
of Corcaluighe, I now treat of
He seized upon the coasts of Cleri,
A headland meet for princely lord.'

In 1460 The O'Driscoll built a monastery near their Cork homeland. Many fought with James II in the 17th century, and suffered the results.

Cornelius O'Driscoll was a colonel in the Irish Brigade in 1707.

O'Donovan gives us a more detailed account of this family (1849), in the Miscellany of the Celtic Society.

Driscoll is estimated to be among the top 1100 names in America today.

Drought

Irish Book of Arms plate 42

The Drought family of Lettybrook in Kings Co. is found in the Irish Book of Arms. Around the year 1600 a numerous family of the name is said to have settled in Co. Carlow, from whence they spread into Kildare, Kings and Queens counties.

O'Devlin

Irish Book of Arms plate 247

O'Doibhilin

Develin, Divelin

The family of O'Devlin is traditionally linked with counties Sligo and Tyrone in Ireland. The main family of the name hailed from Dungannon barony in Co. Tyrone, near Lough Neagh (by the borders of Derry and Tyrone). Here the family served as 'Lords of Munterdevlin'.

According to "Keatings History" the name is given as "O'Dobhalen, or O'Devlin,.. another chief in Corran", of the Ui Fiachrach. (The territory of the Ui Fiachrach comprised the counties of Mayo and Sligo).

The name has always been considered one of the province of Ulster. Another family of the name is found in Co. Sligo, in the barony of Corran, and is so cited in both Keatings History and O'Hart. Once of note, they have faded into the pages of history as a distinct and separate O'Devlin family. Some say that the name in this case was changed to Dolan, accounting for its disappearance.

The name remains a name of Co. Tyrone and of Ulster to this day. Families are found in Antrim, Tyrone, Armagh, Dublin, and Londonderry in the 1890 birth index.

The existing 1659 census does not cover Co. Tyrone, but we do find 'Divelin' listed in Co. Antrim at that time.

Drury, Drew

Irish Book of Arms plate 25 (Drew)

Mac an Druaidh

Drewery, Drew, Drewry, Druery.

The name of Drury is cited in the census of 1659 as being of Dublin City, and appears as well in the Poll Money Ordinance survey. In the birth index of 1890 it is found only in Roscommon. When spelled as Druery, which may represent the spelling of Drury today, the name is found in Roscommon in the 1659 census as well.

The name is also an English name, said to be taken from the French, meaning sweetheart. The spelling of the name has taken on some localized forms in the past. Drew was common in Louth and Monaghan, while Drury was a favorite in Roscommon, and Drew(e)ry was found in Cavan. It is interesting to note that druadh, the root of the gaelic name, means Druid in the original language.

The Drew family of Drewscourt, Co. Cork is given in the Irish Book of Arms.

Diskin

Disken

A name traditionally linked to Co. Galway, some say that the family settled there from Co. Sligo originally.

Diver

Dever, Divers

A family name often found in Co. Donegal, the family appears to have subsequently branched out into Mayo, where variant spellings such as Divers and Devers appear. The family is found centered in Co. Donegal in the 19th century under the spelling of Diver.

O'Duff

Irish Book of Arms plate 6 (Earl of Fife)

O'Duibh

Gilduff, Kilduff

According to "Keatings History" the name is found to be that of a chief of Ui Crimthain, and they were given by O'Heerin as "O'Duff rules over Ui Crimthain, Chief of the country of great produce, A land which yields the finest fruits."

Their lands were said to contain most of the baronies of Maryboro, in Queens County. Presumably many of the name have dropped the "O" prefix becoming known simply as "Duff". This may lead to some confusion with the name of Kilduff or Gilduff, which are also found simply as "Duff". (see also Gilduff)

Dobbs

The family name of Dobbs is assumed to be of English origins when found in Ireland, and several families of the name are found in Co. Antrim. Some of the name are found to the southeast of Ulster as well.

Dockery

Dockry, Dockory

A name linked to Co. Roscommon in our records.

Doheny

Duheny

This family is found early in Co. Cork and subsequently in Tipperary/Kilkenny and surrounds.

O'Duggan

Irish Book of Arms plates 238, 153

O'Dubhagain

O'Duggan, Dugan, Doogan, Duggen,

Prominent in Co. Tipperary for centuries, the O'Dugans are cited as ancient chiefs of Fermoy in Co. Cork, by the noted O'Heerin:

'Chief of Fermoy of well fenced forts,
Is O'Dugan of Dunmannan-
A tribe of Gaels of precious jewels'.

O'Heerin also mentions a sept of O'Duibhgan as chiefs in the barony of Shelburne, in Co. Wexford. O'Duigin is also found in the barony of Tulla, in Co. Clare.

The main families of the name are found in the ancient provinces of Munster and Connaught. The pronunciation of the name in the west of Ireland is as 'Doogan' and is often spelled as such in Co. Donegal. When spelled as Dougan, the name is most often found in the northeast of Ireland (Ulster). Spelled as Duggan in the 1890 index, it was most popular then in Cork, Dublin, Tipperary and Waterford. As Dugan the name is found in Antrim, Down and Londonderry at that time.

In 1659 the name of Dugan was a principal one of Co. Waterford, while Dugen was found as a principal name of Kings County (Offaly). McDugan is even cited in Milesian families as a Eugenian tribe, found anciently in Cork and Galway. O'Dugan was cited as a Eugenian tribe of Wexford and Cork by the same source. The prefix has been often dropped on both names, thus they become simply Dugan in most cases.

Note the place name of Ballyduggan by Loughrea, probably in memory of the separate family of Dugan of Ui Maine (Hy Many).

89

O'Dunne

Irish Book of Arms plates 86, 153

O'Duinn, O'Doinn

Dunne, O'Doyne, Dun, Dunn

The chiefs of the O'Dunn(e) family in Ireland were known as Lords of Ui Regan in Co. Leix (Queens County), where the family originates. They were centered in the barony of Tinnahinch, in Leix, with Brittas as a major stronghold.

The name has also been found in the kingdom of Meath as a chief in the district of Tara.

The 27th most common surname of Ireland, the name seems to have lost its 'O' prefix some time ago, and it remains so to this day in the majority of cases. The two main spellings of the name are found as Dunn and Dunne. The latter is the most common form. In the 1890 birth index 51 births were recorded as 'Dunn' and 313 births as Dunne. 'Dunn', a common spelling in Ulster is found in Antrim, Down, Tyrone and Londonderry. Dunne was found in several locations, including Dublin, Queens, Kilkenny, Kings, Kildare, Cork, Tipperary and Cavan.

In earlier times O'Doyne was a common way to spell the name.

In 1659 'Dunn' was found as a principal name in Dublin, and in Kildare and Kings Counties, while McDunn was found as a principal name of Fermanagh. 'Dun' was also a principal name of Kings and Queens counties at that time.

The noted O'Heerin speaks of the O'Dunn family thusly:

'Over Ui Riagain of the mighty victories are active warriors who conquer in battle, O'Dunn is the chief of the conquering troops, The mainstay of the battling spears.'

The Irish Book of Arms gives 'Dunne of Brittas', the chief of Ui Regan, who built Castlebrack in Queens Co.. This line is traced back to the year 1427.

90

O'Dwyer

Irish Book of Arms plates 153, 225

O'Duibhir

Dwire, Dwyre, Dwyar, Dwier

The O'Dwyers were anciently a noted clan in Co. Tipperary. Here, in the baronies of Kilnamanagh Upper and Lower their seat of power is to be found. This ancient territory can be found on the map between Thurles and the border of Co. Limerick. The 'O' prefix previously dropped from the name, has been added once again in modern times.

At the end of the last century only 25 births were recorded under the O'Dwyer spelling, found in Tipperary, Limerick and Clare. Spelled as Dwyer 155 births were recorded, found in Tipperary, Cork, Dublin, Kerry, Limerick etc...

In 1659 O'Dwier and Dwier are variant spellings of the name found in Limerick, Dwire in Kings Co., and O'Dwyre in Tipperary. Both Dwyer and O'Dwyre are found in Clare and Tipperary at this time. Most of the name in Ireland had adopted the form of Dwyer by 1890 however.

O'Dwyer is given by O'Heerin as chief of Ui Amhrith and he spoke thusly of the family:

"Ui Aimrit, the land of hospitality,
is inherited by the tribe O'Dwyer
Above all others they own the country,
They are the pillars each battle ford."

Keatings History says the O'Dwyers were chiefs of note in ancient times. Some of the O'Dwyers were commanders in the Irish brigade in the service of France. General O'Dwyer is mentioned by Mac Geoghegan as governor of Belgrade, and there was an admiral O'Dwyer in the Russian service.

William O'Dwyer (b. 1890), of Co. Mayo heritage became the mayor of New York, U.S.A..

'The O'Dwyers of Kilnamanagh' by Sir M. O'Dwyer was published in London in 1933.

Echlin, Echline

Irish Book of Arms plate 76

Echling, Ecclen, Ecclin, Aglin

This name is said to be found as Echlin in Ireland and Echline in Scotland in older records. Readers will find "the Genealogical Memoirs of the Echlin Family" by Rev. J. Echlin very interesting. The author served as J.P. for Co. Down in the middle of the 19th century.

The Echlin family of Ardquin, Co. Down, settled in Ireland coming from earlier origins in the co. of Fife. The first of the name is found in Ireland around the year 1613.

Disney

Disny

Families of the name of Disney are found in counties Westmeath and Louth in 17th century Ireland. Several families of the name are found in scattered areas of Ireland during that century, and some of the name arrived during the Cromwellian settlement here. In more modern records the name is of diminished numbers in Ireland.

The surname of Disney is believed to be taken from a French place name.

Dolphin

The name of a family found in Ireland from the time of the 12th century Norman invasions. They are said to have been of English origins. Several branches are found in Co. Galway, where the family became quite prominent by the 17th century. They are often found among the rolls of landowners in that county.

Doorley

Doorly

A name found in connection with Co. Offaly in our records.

Edge

The Irish Book of Arms plate 51

The Edge family of Clonbrock, Queens Co., is given in the Irish Book of Arms.

Dolan

Irish Book of Arms plate 208

O Dubhlain, O Dobhailen

O'Dolan, Dolane, O'Doelan, Doolan

One family of the Dolan name has traditionally been found in the barony of Clanmacnowen in Co. Galway, and in the barony of Athlone in Co. Roscommon. Keatings History gives the family as numerous in Cavan as well.

The Dolan name ranks among the top 1,000 most numerous names in America today, with an estimated 30,000+ family members.

A further study of the locations of the family discloses that Dolan is a principal name of Leitrim in 1659, as well as being found in Roscommon at that time. Moving up to the 1890 birth index, it is quite common in Fermanagh, Roscommon and Cavan, to name but a few modern day locations for the family.

The unique spelling of 'Dolane' was found as a principal name of Roscommon in the 17th century. O'Dolan is found as a principal name of Fermanagh at that time as well. As most of the time the name is found without its 'O' prefix today, this clue may prove useless.

O'Doohan

Doughan, Dooghan

The family name spelled as Doohan and O'Doohan is traditionally found in Co. Clare. Doohan is also found numerous in Co. Donegal in the 19th century birth index, and this is assumed to be of completely separate origins.

 91

Mc Donald

Irish Book of Arms plate

OF SCOTTISH ORIGIN

MACK, MAC, MCDANIEL, MCDONNELL,

In the census of 1659 we find the McDonald name as a principal one in Antrim. According to some sources, one family of the name is said to have come to Ireland from Scotland in 1506, and settling here in Donegal and Derry.

In the 1890 index the family name is found in Dublin, Antrim, Cavan, Wexford and Carlow.

The family name is given in Keatings History (v-3), and the foundation publication "Irish Settlers on the American Frontier".

The McDonald name can be considered a name of the province of Ulster as a rule. It has been used interchangeably with several other surnames, most notably that of McDonnell.

Documented Passengers from Ireland:
WILLIAM M'DONALD- ABOARD THE 'BELISARIUS'-DUBLIN TO NEW YORK. BEFORE JULY 5, 1811.
ROBERT M'DONALD - OF PORTAFERRY. ABOARD SHIP PROTECTION. BELFAST TO NEW YORK. BEFORE SEPT. 20, 1811.
THOS. MCDONALD- ABOARD BRIG MARGARET. FROM SLIGO TO NEW YORK. AUGUST 8, 1816.

Individuals of the name:
M'DONALD-GRAND CHANCELLOR OF LEGION OF HONOR, FRANCE. (ETIENNE JACQUES JOSEPH ALEXANDRE M'DONALD.
MILES MCDONALD - LIEUTENANT, 69TH NEW YORK VOLUNTEERS. THE IRISH AMERICAN BRIGADES.
OVER 20 LISTINGS FOUND IN 'IRISH SETTLERS IN AMERICA' VOLUME 1. BY O'BRIEN.

Possible sources for further information:
'THE MACDONALDS OF MAYO' BY G.A. HAYES-MCCOY. JOURNAL OF GALWAY HISTORICAL SOCIETY.

Donegan

Irish Book of Arms plate 236

O Donnagain

Dunnigan, Dunigan, Donnegan, Dungan,

The surname of Donegan was adapted by no less than four independent septs in earlier days in Ireland. The census of 1659 find the name as a principal one of County Westmeath. The name has been connected to the barony of Rathconrath in that county, along with the barony of Athlone. The name is as well found in Co. Sligo in early records for that county.

O'Donegan's country lies in Co. Cork, in the baronies of Orrery and Duhallow. Early on the territory was wrested from them by the Norman Barry family. In Westmeath you will find Dunegan Castle, near the town of Athlone. In the same county, the Donegan of Westmeath also controlled the manor of Kildrought, Co. Kildare, and were as well found in counties Leix and Offaly

The name is listed in Keatings History (v-3) at least 3 times, including the following:

"O'Donnagain or Donnegan, chiefs of ..Muscry of the three plains, now the half barony of Orrery....The country of O'Donnegan is certified, The great Muskery of the Three Plains, it belongs to the host of polished steel"....The O'Donnegans ...according to the Annals of Inisfallen were princes...in Tipperary....According to O'Dugan the Donegans were chiefs in baronies in the county of Derry as well.

Dr. Edmund Dunnegan, Bishop of Connor and Down, died imprisoned in 1629.

Thomas Donegan, Dongan Earl of Limerick (of the famous Dongan Charter of 1686.)

O'Dooley

Irish Book of Arms plate 232

O'Dubhlaich

Dooly, Dowly

The O'Dooley family served as 'Lords of Furtullagh' in the 11th and 12th centuries, as recorded by the Four Masters. This territory is located in the south of Co. Westmeath. The family was subsequently forced into Co. Offaly (Kings Co.) and settled there in the barony of Ballybritt.

Their new territory was in the hands of the Ely O'Carrolls, and soon the families were strongly allied, with the chief of the O'Dooleys becoming the official inaugurator of Ely O'Carroll.

Offaly is now considered the center of Dooley country due to the traditional presence of the name there from ancient times. The family has spread as well into Counties Tipperary and Leix.

The 1890's birth index shows the name in Dublin and Offaly. In the 17th century 'Dooley' was a principal name in Tipperary and 'Dooly' a principal name of Kilkenny.

The 'O' prefix before the name had generally been dropped long before that index was compiled.

Keatings History records O'Dooley here as a chief of Fertullach, in the barony of Fertullagh in Westmeath.

O'Doorie

According to "Keatings History" the name is that of a family of Doon Branni and Tuath Congali, and it was given that they "are chiefs of the country of Ui Congalei; Their fortresses lie round the beauteous Boruma, A tribe remarkable for their golden tresses."

92

O'Dooyiorma

O'Duibhdiorma

According to "Keatings History" the name as given above was sometimes changed incorrectly to McDermott or O'Dermott, but they bear no relationship with the McDermott family of Moylurg in the province of Connaught.

The family of subject here is found as "chiefs of Bredach", a territory which lay along the western banks of Lough Foyle, comprising the parishes of Upper and Lower Moville in the barony of "Inisowen". The name of that district was still preserved at the time of the old writings on this family, in the small river named Bredag, which fell into Lough Derg.

Dorrance

The name of Dorrance is a rare one in Ireland, and it is rare to find printed material on the same. We do have in our files however, an article on the Dorrance family from Ireland. They made an early settlement in Rhode Island, in what became the town of Foster.

About 1715 one George Dorrance (b. 1675, d. 1754) and his two sons, George and James, came from Ireland. They bought land which became known as the Dorrance purchase. For some 65 years Connecticut and Rhode Island disputed jurisdiction over this land. Dorrance Mills soon arose, with a sawmill and grist mill, on a local stream on their estate.

The family continued to be a prominent one of Rhode Island into the next century. The Dorrance name was still found in Rhode Island in this century and is likely still there today. At one time, Dorrance Street was a leading thoroughfare in Providence; if it still remains to this day I have no idea.

Passengers from Ireland:
Alex., Catherine, and Mary Ann (infant), listed as farmers from Belfast, aboard 'Korea', July 23, 1849, to New York.

O'Downey

O'Dunadhaigh

MacEldowney, Muldowney, Gildowney,

The most numerous of the Downey name today are of the Luachair sept, springing from the contiguous areas of Cork, Kerry and Limerick. Luachair was the name of an old geographical division comprising that modern day area. Here the O'Downeys ruled as chiefs. Some have changed the name to Dowling in this area, which is a popular name in Co. Kerry.

A separate family of O'Downey hails from Co. Galway, and they were known in ancient times as 'Lords of Sil Anmchadha'. They are of the same descent as the O'Maddens.

'Mac Downey' or more precisely MacEldowney, a name of Co. Derry, is an Ulster name of separate origins. It is sometimes found simply as 'Downey', stemming from Mac Giolla Domhnaigh.

Muldowney is also found in Co. Down. Of other related names, Gildowney and Downey were synonyms in Newry Union, County Down at the close of the last century.

O'Molony and O'Muldowney have also been used interchangeably on occasion and of course those who were originally Muldowney, Gildowney etc,.. have at times shortened the name to Downey. Muldowney has been found often in Co. Kilkenny.

In Co. Cork Downey and Dawney are sometimes used for the more popular name of Doheny.

In the 1890 birth index Downey was found most often in Cork, Kerry, Antrim, Galway and Limerick.

Downs

O'Dubhain

Downes

The Downs or Downes surname is said to have been taken from O'Dubhain in counties Clare and Limerick. The most common spelling according to the 1890 index was 'Downes', which was given in Clare, Limerick and Dublin at that time. Milesian Families gives the name as an English one, settling in Limerick and Tipperary in 1172.

O'Drennan

Drinan

According to "Keatings History" the name is O'Drennan or Drinan, chief of Slieve Eise Finn and of Kinel Sedna, a district on the borders of Clare and Galway. They were thus mentioned;

"The lands about the fair Slieve Eise,
Are possessed by the Clan Sedna of melodious bards, A tribe who firmly support their clans; Chief of their territory is O'Drennan."

The Drennan family is found most numerous in counties Antrim and Tipperary in the 1890 birth index.

Duckett

According to "Keatings History" the name is among the chief families of English descent settling in Waterford and Tipperary. These English families primarily possessed the territory called Gal-tir, signifying the country of the foreigners," now the barony of Gaultiere."

Duffin

O Duibhinn

Duff, Duffyne, ODoghwyn

In the Census of 1659 the name of Duffin is found as a principal name in the county of Louth. By the time of the 1890 birth index, the name was found primarily in Antrim and Waterford. Waterford is considered to be a traditional location for the name as well. It has mainly been found a name of Eastern Ulster and of County Louth in particular.

The name is found in the Hearth Money Rolls in Monaghan and Armagh in 1664, and the name was in Ballymena, Co. Antrim in the late 18th century. The name bears a Bishop of Kildare as early as 1148. The spelling of O'Duffyne is found in Cork more anciently, and ODoghwyn is another old spelling found in Waterford.

93

O'Duffy

Irish Book of Arms plate 243

O'Dubthaigh

Duhig, Doohey, Dowey, Duffey, Duffie,

Duffy is taken from the gaelic 'O'Dughthaigh' or O'Duffy. The root word is 'dubh', meaning black or dark. The name ranks as one of the top 50 surnames in Ireland, and among the 700 most populous families in America.

There are at least two noted families of the name. Both appear to originate in the province of Leinster. Noted locations for the family include: the parish of Lower Templecrone, diocese of Raphoe, Co. Donegal. Also in Donegal in the barony of Boylagh on the west coast. Note the location of Lissyduffy in Roscommon barony by Strokestown. The family is also found in Monaghan, and in Mayo the name of O'Diff has become Duffy.

When found in the province of Leinster the name is cited as a chief family of Co. Monaghan in ancient times, of the same descent as the MacMurroughs. Around the turn of the century the family was most popular in Mayo, Monaghan and Donegal.

The Cross of Cong in the Dublin Museum was made by an O'Duffy (1123 a.d.). Also mentioned as a family of note in Galway and Roscommon, several of the name are found as Archbishops of Tuam and of Elphin.

In modern times Duffys' Circus has traveled through Ireland bringing pleasure to one and all.

Of variant spellings, O'Duffie was a principal name of Monaghan, Duffie a was so in Louth and also in Westmeath, and Duffy was found in Longford and Westmeath in 1659. Today most spell the name simply as Duffy.

Sir Charles Gavan Duffy (b. 1816), a journalist in Dublin, became the Prime Minister of Victoria, Australia in 1835.

O'Dullaghan

O'Dalachain

According to "Keatings History" the name is given as a family among the chiefs and clans of Tir Conaill in the twelfth century. This family served as chiefs of the Tuath Bladhadh.

The 1890 birth index finds the Dullaghan family most numerous in Co. Louth.

O'Dunady

Irish Book of Arms plate 239

Dunnady

According to "Keatings History" the name is given as chief of Slieve Luachra, that is the district about the mountains of Slievelogher, on the borders of Limerick and Kerry, they are thus cited by O'Heerin;

"The plain of Luachra, a productive country, Belongs to the liberal O'Dunady, A tribe of hard fighting battles, A district of fair well-watered lands."

Durkan

Irish Book of Arms plate 234

DUARCAN (DHUARCAIN = PESSIMIST)

DURCAN,DORCAN,MACDURKAN,

The Durkin family has always been traditionally linked to the province of Connaught in Ireland. More specifically, the counties of Mayo and Sligo are where the family calls home.

The name is overwhelmingly found spelled as "Durkan" in Ireland. That exact spelling is found some 48 times in the 1890 birth index, while "Durkin" a less used form of the name, was found with 14 births recorded under that spelling.

Part of the O'Hara family in Co. Sligo also changed their names to Durkin. In this area you can find the name in the barony of Gallen, at a fairly early date. We also find a "MacDorkain", another early spelling of the name, in Co. Mayo in the 17th century.

Individuals of the name:

THE MOST REV. PATRICK DURCAN WAS THE BISHOP OF ATHENRY FROM 1852-1875.

ANTHONY DURKIN, ABOARD 'NAOMI', JAN. 25, 1849. FROM LIVERPOOL.

MARTIN DURKIN, ABOARD 'ST. PATRICK', JAN. 25,1849. FROM LIVERPOOL.

PATT. DURKIN, ABOARD 'ENTERPRISE', JULY 31,1848, FROM LIVERPOOL

MARY AND PHOEBE DURKIN ARE ALSO FOUND IN 'THE FAMINE IMMIGRANTS' V-3.

Arms not Pictured

Arms given as on plates 200 and above in the Irish Book of Arms are not shown here. They are considered to be of unproven or false origins. For those interested, please consult the Irish Book of Arms for full illustration of those arms.

Furthermore, in the interest of enlightened education on the subject, some commercial operations are more than willing to sell you "illegitimate" items of any sort. Please do not accept items as being connected with your family name without some research.

94

Durnan

O'Duirnin

Durnin, Durnian, Durnion, Durnane,

There are several spellings of this name, which may have sprung from separate origins. In more modern times the name of 'Durnin' was given in Louth in the 1890 index, alongside Durnian and Durnion. O'Durnane is also found in Co. Louth and is considered to be a form of Durnin. 'Durnion' has been found in Tyrone, Fermanagh and Donegal. Note the place name of 'Ballydurnian' in Co. Antrim. Dornan is also found in Antrim and Down in modern times.

Durning is more likely a separate name of English origin from the 1500's in Ireland.

Farrell and Ennis O'Durnyne. Landowners in the barony of Tirawley, Co. Mayo. (1635 Straffords Inquisition)

Mac Duvany

Mac Dubhain, O'Duibhenaigh

According to "Keatings History" the MacDuvany name is that of a family who served as chiefs of Kinel Enda, or Kinel Nenna. This district was to be found in Inisowen.

From the same source it is given that O'Duvaney was a chief of Clanawley, in Co. Down.

Doonan

Doonane

A family name linked early to Co. Fermanagh, and subsequently to counties Roscommon and Leitrim.

Draughan,

Droughan, Draughan, Droughon, Drohan,

The names of Drohan, Droughan and Draughon are traditionally linked with counties Waterford and Tipperary.

Drumm

Drum, Drummond, Drummy

The name of Drumm can be taken from the Irish name of "O'Droma", and it was this family mentioned as erenaghs anciently, found centered in Tullyhaw, Co. Cavan and near Knockninny in Fermanagh. They are often found mentioned in the old territory of Kinawley which overlaps the areas mentioned above..

"Drummy" is a name found in Co. Cork, and some of that name may have shortened the spelling simply to "Drumm" or conversely, Drummy may have been a form of the original Drumm.

The family name of Drummond, which is a separate Scottish name, has also been used for Drumm, at times.

The 1890 birth index gives the name of Drum centered in Fermanagh, Drummond centered in Antrim, and Drummy centered in Cork and Sligo.

Duignan

Irish Book of Arms plate 221

Duigenan, Dignam, Dignan

A name of the midland and western areas of Ireland, most often associated with the province of Connaught. The name is found most numerous in Leitrim and Roscommon in the 19th century.

Dunphy

Originally cited in the old geographical territory of Ossory, the family is found centered in Co. Kilkenny early, and subsequently in Co. Waterford.

The Dunphy family is found most numerous in Waterford and Dublin in the 19th century.

Mc Dowell

Irish Book of Arms plate 211

MacDugall, McDowll

The name of a Scottish family who settled in Ireland prior to the 17th century. They are a noted galloglas family. The galloglas were heavily armed fighting men often found in the service of Irish chieftains. In Scotland the name is found earlier as MacDugall.

Dormer

One noted family of the name is found in Co. Wexford, traced back to Denis Dormer, said to be the first of the name to settle in Ireland. Those of the name here are often found to be of English extraction. It is in Wexford that the name is most often found, although some of the name we have found in Kilkenny as well.

Some of the name may be of Irish extraction, with Dormer serving as a variant spelling of Diarmod or Dermott.

Dracot

One family of the name came from Peasly in England and settled in Mornantown, Co. Meath. Henry Dracot of that family served as Master of the Rolls.

Mac Donough

Dennis, Denny, Donough, Donaugh

Several families of the name are found in Ireland. Those of MacDonough, the lords of Duhallow, of Munster, are considered to be a separate family from those given below.

Many families of the name of MacDonough are found in Co. Sligo, where the name may be found centered at Tirerill anciently. Said to be a branch of this family are the MacDonoughs of Wilmont House, Parish of Portumna, Co. Galway. Several here are given as Catholics, and found among the ranks of country gentlemen and Justices of the Peace in Galway.

Durrian

Dawson

Families of the name in Co. Donegal are found to have also used the name of Dawson as a synonym. Durrian is generally assumed to be a variant spelling of Doran. Several landed families of Dawson of course, are of English extraction.

95

Dorney

Dorny

Families of the name of O'Dorney are found with a principal family name of Co. Cork in the 17th century, and the family is given as centered there, and in Co. Tipperary in the 19th century birth index of Ireland.

O'Dorohy

Dorohey

Families of the name of O'Dorohy and Dorohey, etc.. are traditionally linked to Co. Kerry in Ireland, often found centered near Kenmare.

Dudican

Dudicane, O'Dowdican

The name of Dudican, and its variant spellings are traditionally linked to families in counties Sligo and Donegal in Ireland.

Dowse

Dousse

Families of the name of Dowse are found in Ireland quite early. Many of the name are found in the city of Dublin, and some arrived during the Cromwellian settlement of Ireland. It is not however, considered primarily a name of Ulster, it is more often found in Dublin and surrounding counties, though never in large numbers in our records.

Draddy

The name of a family in Ireland strongly linked with Co. Cork, and found centered there for several centuries. The name is not found to have been numerous.

O'Drea

Drew

The family name of O'Drea was given to be a principal one of Co. Kilkenny in the 17th century. The name of Drea is also found in Co. Kerry in several instances in our records.

Some of the O'Drea name may have become "Drew" over time, even though the Drew family is generally considered to be an English one in Ireland.

Drumgoole

Drumgool, Dromgoole, Drumgoold,

A family of Ireland traditionally identified with Co. Louth. The spelling of Drumgold is found in the 17th century in the city of Dublin.

O'Ducey

Ducy, Ducie, Doocey, Doocy

The name of a family of Ireland traditionally found in counties Tipperary and Waterford.

Dunlea

Dullea, Dunleavy, Donlea, Delea

Families of the name of Dunlea are found centered in Co. Cork in the 19th century birth index. They are also found occasionally in our records to the north of Cork, but the name does not appear to have settled in the province of Ulster. Some give the name of Dunlea, as a shortened form of Dunleavy. Others give names such as Dullea as synonyms, but of the latter we have no proof in our records.

The Dunleavy family is found most often in counties Mayo and Sligo in the 19th century.

Dunseath

Dunsheath, Dunseith, Dunseeth, Dunshee

The name of a family found settling in Ireland in the 17th century, most often located in the province of Ulster in our records.

Durack

The name of a family traditionally noted in connection with Co. Clare in Ireland and of some note when found settling in Australia as well.

Mac Dyer

MacDyre

In the 17th century we find the family name spelled as O'Dyer, where it was a principal name of Co. Limerick. Other records find the name as Dyer in Cork, Roscommon and Sligo and Donegal.

Dow

The name of Scottish families found settled in Ulster, and Dow has been given as a branch of Clan Buchanan as such.

Dring

Dreng

The name of a Co. Cork family, presumably of English origins.

Drislane

A fairly rare name in Ireland, we find mention of some of the name in Co. Cork.

Dunning

Those of the Dunning name in Ireland may be of Scottish or English extraction. Some of the name are found centered near Athlone, in Co. Roscommon.

Edgeworth

Irish Book of Arms plates 54, 122, 126

Edgworth, Edgewurth

The Edgeworth family, traditionally associated with Co. Longford in Ireland, was originally of Anglo-Norman origins in Ireland. One story states that about the year 1563 two brothers came to Ireland, probably under the patronage of "Essex & Cecil", as those first names have been used continuously in that family. Note the place name of Edgeworths town.

Two of the same line of descent that we have found are Col. Henry Edgeworth of Lizard, near Edgeworthstown, Co. Longford, and Rev. Essex Edgeworth of Templemichael, Longford.

The Irish Book of Arms gives the family of Edgeworth of Kilshrewly, Co. Longford, and Edgeworth of Edgeworts town.

Eager

Eager, Egar, Eagers, Eagar

Families of the name of Eager /Egar etc.., are found in several areas of Ireland. In Co. Kerry several of the name are found from the 17th century, and they were of some influence at that time there. This line is found earlier in Queens county. Not a particularly numerous family, they are however found far to the north in the province of Ulster, as well as in Kerry.

Mac Elderry

Mac Ilderry

Our records find the family of MacElderry in the county of Antrim in Ireland.

Mac Egan

Irish Book of Arms plates 208, 154

Mac Aod hagain

Keegan, Egan, Hegan, Eagan, Hegan,

Perhaps more properly spelled as Mac Egan, the name is most often found as Egan or Keegan today. Found most anciently in Galway, the family has served as brehons to the Ui Maine, and Mac Egan was brehon to the O'Connor Faly. As well, the Mac Egans and the O'Connells are found as marshals to the forces of the O'Kellys of the Ui Maine.

The family also settled in Tipperary, Kilkenny and Offaly .

The Mac Egans were chiefs of Clan Diarmada in the barony of Leitrim in Co. Galway. Their castle was to be found on DunDoighre, (Duniry), and O'Dugan spoke thusly of the Mac Egan clan:

'Precedence for his valor and fame
Be given to Mac Egan the noble
Record him for the activity of his warriors,
of his prosperity and great renown.'

Keegan was formed as a variant spelling by dropping the 'Mac' prefix, and adding the hard 'c' from Mac back onto the name. In other words, the Ma was dropped, forming cEgan. (Keegan).

In the 17th century Eagan, Egane and McEgane were all principal names of Tipperary. 'Egan' was a principal name of Kings, and McEgan of Roscommon. By the time of the 1890 index the name was usually spelled simply as Egan.

Keating cites the MacEgans as hereditary brehons to the McCarthy Mor, and they served as brehons in Cork and Kerry, as well as being hereditary brehons in the barony of Arra, Ormond.

MacEgan was cited as chief of Clan Fear a Muighe in Breffney. This is thought to be the same as Mac Cagadhain, chiefs of the barony of Dromahaire, Co. Leitrim.(see Tribes and Customs of the Hy Many.')

96

Ellison

Irish Book of Arms plate 35

Elison, Ellis

Those of the name of Ellison in Ireland are given largely to be families of English descent. The works of Woulfe may differ from this, but we have no records to indicate otherwise. The family is found here from the 17th century onward. The 19th century birth index places the family in counties Antrim and Down. Several families of the name can be found in and around Belfast in modern times and we find mention of the name in Kilkenny as well.

The name Ellis is found centered in Dublin and Antrim in the 19th century.

Earl, Errill

The family of Errill, found subsequently written as Earl, is found centered in Carbery, Co. Kildare in the 18th century. Earlier the family name is found in the 15th century in Westmeath, up until the time of the Cromwellian settlement. Father Edward Earl (d.1846), was said to be the first of the family to spell the name as "Earl", and he was found buried in Carbury chapel in which a tablet was inscribed in his honor.

The name is found centered in the province of Leinster in the 19th century.

Ebrill

Abrill, Ebril

The family name of Ebrill is found in the county of Limerick in Ireland, and it is also believed to be the same name as that which is spelled as Abrill by some. The name of Abril or Abrill is of likely French origins when found in Ireland.

Mac Enroe, Crowe

Irish Book of Arms plates 154, 86

MacConchradha

Mac Crowe, Mac Enchroe, Crow, Crough

Most of the name of MacEnchroe or MacEnroe now use the name of Crowe in Ireland. Crowe, is of course, a well known English name found in the north of Ireland.

Crowe is also used for the Irish family of Mac Conchradha (MacEnchroe), who hailed from the old territory of Thomand, seated in the barony of Inchiquin. Today, these families are found mainly in Clare and Tipperary.

Although many 'Crowes' are found in Co. Antrim, they are assumed to be of English settler extraction.

Of the Irish family of the name, note the place name of Skaghvicencrowe in Co. Clare. The name is said to literally mean MacEncroes thornbush. It is connected to the family, for the thornbush is used on some arms of the family. The motto below the arms of this Clare family actually reads 'Skeagh Mac En Chroe".

The 1890's birth index finds 'Crowe' in Antrim, Tipperary and Clare. By this time, 'McEnroe' is given only in Co. Cavan.

In the census of 1659 'Mc Encroe' is found as a principal name of Co. Clare. It is obvious that the 'Mac' prefix was dropped subsequently, and the name shortened simply to Crowe.

The Irish Book of Arms gives Crowe of Dromore House, Co. Clare.
From O'Hart:
William Crowe, Inrolments, (1821-25)

Edmundson

Sir James Edmundston of Strivelin in Scotland was the founder of the line which settled on Braiden Island, Co. Antrim early in the 17th century, in the person of Archibald Edmundson

Estrange

Irish Book of Arms plate 33

L'Estrange

A Huguenot family of Ireland as given by some families. The L'Estrange family formerly of Clonsheever and of Norfolk is found in the Irish Book of Arms.

Mac Elligott

Irish Book of Arms plate 237

Eligot, McElliot

According to "Keatings History" the family is given as an ancient one in Co. Kerry, from whom the parish of Ballymacelligott, in the barony of Trughenachmy, got its name. Note also the older place name of Ballyelegot in Co. Waterford.

The family is given further of Galey,parish of Coolceragh, Co. Kerry. In 1653 Edmund McElligott of the same area was transplanted and the family is found subsequently in Co. Limerick in Ireland. In that same year Maurice MacElligott forfeited the O'Brennan Castle and was transplanted. Earlier, in 1590, in the barony of Trughanacmy, parish of Ballymacelligott, the Ballymacelligott castle was lost, along with 3 others in that parish.

Many of the family are found transplanted or "resettled" by the powers that then existed, but most of the name will eventually find early family roots in Co. Kerry. One of the name is found in the Irish Brigades of France, as a colonel.

Mac Elheron

MacElheran

It should be noted that MacElheran is a name which comes from the Scottish Clan of MacDonald, so some of the name may stem from that source. The name is one of Ulster, and Woulfe gave them as of the midlands of Ireland.

97

Eustace

Irish Book of Arms plates 34, 82

IU STAS (LATIN/GREEK ROOT WORD)

EUSTACE, USTACE, EUSTICE, Eustis,

Eustace belongs to an anglo-norman family in Ireland centered near the pale, (the area near Dublin.). The family has been noted often as being influential. Often found in alliance with the native Irish of the land, this led to the fall of the families' power, at least in part. Note the place name of "Ballymore Eustace" on the Kildare and Wicklow borders. The family is found several times in Kildare in the 17th century.

The family is found in official positions in the aftermath of the 12th century Norman invasions. One is in the company of James II on his arrival in Ireland. Several can be found in local records as sheriffs etc..

Sir Richard Fitz Eustace was Baron of Castle Martin around the year 1200 a.d.. Early individuals of the name include those of Robertstown, Co. Kildare and Ballydoyle, Co. Cork. Sir Maurice Eustace held many lands in Dublin and Kildare, but they were confiscated as a result of his strong support for King James, whose troops he commanded.

Numerous earlier, the 1890 index finds only 9 births of the name, which may have come from "Eustacius", meaning "fruitful". Over 30 listings of the name are given in O'Harts' work. The Eustace families of Kilcock, Co. Kildare and of Newstown, Co. Carlow are given in the Irish Book of Arms.

Individuals of the name:
Sir Richard Eustace -'Lord Chancellor'
Sir Edward Fitz-Eustace, (1454) 'Lord Deputy'. Of this line was the Baron of Portlester- his son. Founded the Monastery of New Abbey in Co. Kildare. Another founded the Dominican Priory at Naas in the 14th century.
James Eustace-' 3rd Visc. Baltinglass'.

Evans

Irish Book of Arms plate 42

One noted family of the name is said to have come from Wales, settling in Ireland as a result of services rendered in the Cromwellian wars. As the story goes, he fell in love with one Miss Mahoney, THE O'Mahoneys daughter, whose father he had helped defeat. He resigned his commission and married the girl. The family is subsequently found in Shanagolden, Co. Limerick, and later in Carrass Court, Co. Cork.

The Evans family of Gortmerron House, Co. Tyrone was founded by a Captain in the English army during the time of Charles I. He obtained estates in Kilkenny and in Queens county, where he served as alderman and mayor of the former mentioned town of Kilkenny.

The birth index of 1890 finds the family centered in Dublin, Londonderry and Antrim.

Early

Earley, Erley, d' Erley

Families of the Early name in Ireland are found in the city of Dublin in the 17th century, and subsequently they are found centered in Leitrim in the 19th century. The above family was of old Irish descent, but those of the name in Co. Kilkenny who spelled the name as d' Erley, Erley, Erly, etc.. are given to be of Norman descent, settling in Ireland not too long after the 12th century Norman invasions.

Enright

Enrite, Enraught, Enraght

A name found commonly in Cork, Kerry and Clare, the 1890 birth index gives the family most numerous in Co. Limerick at that date.

Mac Evoy

Irish Book of Arms plates 154, 219

Mac Fhiodhbhuidhe

MacVeagh, Mac Elwee, MacGilloway,

The Mac Evoy family is another of the noted '7 Septs of Leix' (Queens County). They were centered there in Mountrath and Raheen parish. Although traditionally thought of as a family of that area, the McEvoys were in part transplanted to Co. Kerry along with the other of the 7 Septs of Leix. In 1609 leading families of the name from Leix were so settled in Co. Kerry.

The MacEvoys of Queens Co. are cited by O'Heerin:

'The ancient county of Fighbuigh, of the fair lands, Is a good Lordship for a chieftain The Clan MacEvoy are its inheritors, The Yellow haired host of hospitality.'

Their territory is cited in the barony of Stradbelly in Queens Co.. They were of the Clan Colla of Ulster and also possessed a territory in Teffia called Ui Mac Uas, now the barony of Moygosh in Westmeath. Some of them have now changed the name to Mac Veagh.

The family was early known as chiefs in the barony of Moyish in Co. Westmeath.

The names of other families have been converted to Mac Evoy as well. In the ancient territory of Oriel the MacVeagh name has on occasion been interchanged with Mac Evoy. In Donegal and Derry, MacElwee and Mac Gilloway have also been changed to Mac Evoy.

In the 1890 birth index McEvoy is found concentrated in Dublin, Louth, Armagh and Queens counties. McElwee is found in Donegal and Londonderry, and McVeigh is found in Antrim and Down at that time.

Eyre

Irish Book of Arms plate 68

Ayre, Ayres, Eyres

We find the family of Eyre centered for several centuries in Eyreville, in Co. Galway. The Eyrecourt castle and town are said to have been built by one Col. John Eyre, who had received grants of land in return for services rendered concerning the settlement of Ireland. The name was originally of foreign origins, found settling during Cromwellian times in Ireland. It is given in the lineage of this family that Giles Eyre, of Brickworth, Wilts, Sheriff 1640, sat with three of his sons, in the Council of Oliver Cromwell.

Additionally, the name of Eyres is found in the census of 1659 in Co. Waterford.

Elliott

Irish Book of Arms plate 237

Elliot, Eliott

Elliott is a well known English name, and can be found in Medieval records in Ireland. Most of the name arrived with the plantation of Ulster, settling in northern Ireland. The traditional location for the name in the past has always been counties Cavan and Fermanagh, but the name is also found in Leitrim in the last century.

The census of 1659 finds the name in Antrim and Fermanagh, and in 1890, when spelled as Elliot the name is given to be of Fermanagh, Antrim, Dublin and Donegal.

Mac Elvogue

The name of a family found in Co. Tyrone.

99

Mac Elroy

Irish Book of Arms plate 253
Mac Giolla Rua
MacGilroy, Kilroy, Gilroy, MacGilleroy, Elroi

MacElroy, Kilroy, Gilroy etc.. can all stem from the same older gaelic spelling of the name 'Mac Giolla Rua'. Note the place names of Ballymacilroy and Ballymackilroy in Ulster. One is found in the barony of Magherastephana in Co. Fermanagh, the other in the barony of Clogher, Co. Tyrone. Yet another is found in the barony of Upper Toome, Co. Antrim.

The preferred spelling of the name in Ulster is with the 'mac' prefix as McIlroy, and McElroy. Moving down to the province of Connaught, Kilroy and Gilroy are preferred. In Roscommon you may even find the spelling recorded as Kilroe.

Most anciently, reference to the name is found in Co. Fermanagh, east of Lough Erne. Often mentioned in the Annals of Irish history, McIlroy and McElroy were the most common forms of the name in 1890, concentrated in Antrim, Down, Fermanagh and Londonderry.

Gilroy was found in Leitrim and Mayo, Kilroy in Mayo, Roscommon and Sligo at that time. In 1659 McIlroy was a principal name of Antrim, Armagh and Down. McGilroy and McKilroy were principal names of Fermanagh then.

In the works of O'Hart, Kilroy is noted as chief of Clonderlaw, Co. Clare. Further, in 1653, the son of the last Kilroy chief, settled in Keenagh, in the barony of Tyrawley, Co. Mayo. Of his line one 'Michael Kilroy' came to America in 1847, living in Deerpark, Maryland.

The name is often said to have meant 'son of the red haired (youth?)' in gaelic.

Emmet

Emet

Families of the surname of Emmet have been found in Tipperary, Waterford and Cork. The name is given to be originally of Anglo-Norman extraction.

The name is found prominent in some Irish affairs, notably Robert Emmet (d.1803), who met his end as a result of the troubles of 1798.

O'Hart gives a family of the name in both Ireland and America. John Emmet was one of the 1649 officers. William Emmett was an officer in the Cromwellian army, whose will was executed in the diocese of Cashel. He was of the same line as Robert Emmet above, of a family who resided in Cork. Also of this line was Robert Temple, who settled in Boston and married the daughter of the Massachusetts governor. The family name is given as well in the State of Virginia, U.S.A..

English

Aingleis
L'Englys, L'Angleys, Lenglas, Englonde, England, Inglis, Mac Gallogly

The name of English, in its many forms has been on record in Ireland since the 12th century. In counties Limerick and Tipperary, the name is considered completely Irish, even though it may have been originally of foreign origins. Several of the name are on record as property owners in Dublin and Louth.

The census of 1659 finds English as a principal name of Tipperary, and also in Dublin. The birth index of 1890 shows the name in Tipperary, Antrim and Dublin. Milesian families shows the name as an English one, settling in Derry in 1642. The Irish variant of 'Mac Gallogly' is also associated with the name.

Among noted individuals in Tipperary in 1600, the Carew Calender gives 'English' of Cloghemenecode and Rahine as respected families.

Esmonde

Esmond, Estmound, D'Ezmondiis

The family of Esmonde has been traditionally linked with Co. Wexford, since the time of the 12th century Norman invasions. The family is given to be of Norse origins most anciently.

Several of the name are found in rebellion against the powers that were in times past. One Dr. John Esmonde was hanged as a result of the troubles in 1798. Robert Esmonde of Johnstown is found in Co. Limerick, and Lawrence Esmond served in the French Irish legion at the beginning of the 1800's.

"Sir William Estmound, D'Ezmondiis, or Esmonde", was Knight of Johnstown Castle, barony of Forth, Co. Wexford. (The ancestor to Lord Esmonde of Lymbrick and Sir Thomas Henry Grattan Esmonde, Bart., M.P..)

Everard

Everhard

According to "Keatings History" the name is among the chief families of English descent settling in Waterford and Tipperary. These English families possessed the territory called Gal-tir, signifying the country of the foreigners," now the barony of Gaultiere." The same work finds the family as a noted family of Meath.

Of one of the oldest families of the name, we find them centered in Fethard, Co. Tipperary. Of this line, some later are found of note in Waterford, in Randalstown, Co. Meath and in Ardfinane, Co. Tipperary. They are said to descend from the Everhard or Everard who arrived in England with William the Conqueror in the 11th century.

Sir John Everard was said to have possessed the town of Fethard and several castles and lands in the area, including holdings in Waterford.

100

O'Erc, Ercke

O'Heirc

Ercke, Erck

According to "Keatings History" the name is given to a family who served as chiefs in the barony of Massareene, in the province of Ulster. The name of Ercke is found most often in Co. Tyrone in our records.

Erskine

Erskin

One noted family of the name can be found in Dublin, descended from John Erskin, who served as Earl of Mar, in the early 17th century.

The family is found most numerous in Co. Antrim in the 19th century.

Euleston

One family of the name, of the House of Euleston in Lancashire settled in Ireland and provided us with Tristram Euleston, of Drumshallum, Co. Louth, who also served as Constable of Dublin Castle in the early part of the 17th century.

Mac Elmeel

Mac Michael, MacMeel

The 1890 birth index of Ireland finds the family of MacElmeel centered in Ulster, with Co. Monaghan holding many of the name there. The McElmoyle family has not been found to be related to the Mac Elmeel family, but some confusing is bound to have arisen between these two similar sounding names. Woulfe in fact, gives these two names as being one in the same, and it is possible that they represent branches of the same ancient line.

Ennis

Ennes, Enniss, Ennoss, Enos

The 17th century finds the name of Ennis as a principal one of Dublin, and it is also found in Kings County at that time. The possible variant spelling of Ennos was also a principal name of Dublin at that time. The name of Enos and Enose, are both principal names of Co. Kildare in the census of 1659 as well.

Co. Kildare and adjacent counties hold most of the name in older records, and one should be aware that the Scots name of Innes, bears no relationship to Ennis.

The Ennis family is found most numerous in Dublin and Kildare in the 19th century.

Mac Entaggert

Teggarty, Tiger, Teggart, MacEtegart, Taggert, Tagert

A family name of the province of Ulster, in modern times we find the family centered in Co. Antrim. Note the place name of Ballymactaggart in Co. Fermanagh, found in the barony of Lurg, an ancient location for the family.

Mac Entee

MacEtye, MacEntee, MacAtee

The name of a family traditionally linked with the province of Ulster in Ireland. In the 17th century the name of MacEntee was a principal one of Co. Monaghan and remained so into modern times, with many of the name settling in Cavan by the time of the 1890 birth index.

Mac Erlean

MacErlen, MacErlyn, McErlain, McErleen

Both the names of MacErlean and McErlain are given in Antrim and Derry in the 1890 birth index. Undocumented sources give some of the name as of Scottish origins.

Ewing

Ewings, Ewin, Ewen

Families of the Ewing name are traditionally linked to the province of Ulster in Ireland. Some prominent members of this family name are also found in Dublin, and they may be of Ulster origins ultimately.

The census of 1659 finds the name in Donegal, and several centuries later the name is centered in Londonderry, Tyrone and Antrim in Ulster as well.

Ensor

An English family name found in Co. Armagh.

Our Thanks to the members of The Irish Family Journal For Supporting this Research

101

Fagan

Irish Book of Arms plate 108, 154

(Norman origins) O'Faodhagain

Fegan, Hagan, Feehan, Fagin, Feagan,

The families of Fegan etc...are traditionally linked with Dublin and nearby areas into modern times. Some dispute remains as to their origins.

The name may, in fact, stem from Norman origins, and in some cases may be a form of the Irish O'Hagan, or from O'Faodhagain of County Louth. Woulfe a mentions possible origins as a branch of O'Hagan, while others disagree. Others believe Fagan to be a completely separate Irish family of the ancient territory of Oriel.

The first of the name we have found is one 'William Fagan' who in 1200 a.d., held property in Dublin. He may be of the family seated near Feltrim, Co. Dublin in that era. This family developed branches in both Kerry and Cork counties. The Kerry branch held some notoriety in France in the 1700's.

Keatings History mentions the O'Fagans as a numerous clan in Meath and Westmeath, in which there were many respectable families of the name, the head of which had the title of Baron of Feltrim in Fingal (Dublin).

Keatings also says that Fagan 'some of whom have been called O'Fagan and Mac Fagan, are considered by some to be of Irish origin, but according to others they were English or Danish in descent, and the name is still numerous in the counties of Meath, Westmeath and Dublin. No doubt, both origins may hold true, adding to the confusion.

In 1659 Fagan was a principal name of Meath and found in Westmeath as well. The 1890 birth index finds the name mainly in Dublin and Leitrim.

The Fagan family of Feltrim descends from Thomas Fagan of Dublin, who married Amy Nangle in the year of 1524.

O'Fahy

Irish Book of Arms plates 154, 248

O'Fathaigh

Fahey, Faghy, Vahey, Foy, Fay, Fahie

Fahy country has always been found in Co. Galway, in the barony of Loughrea. The name is numerous in the area of Tipperary in the 17th - 19th centuries.

The 1890 birth index finds the family in Galway, Tipperary and Mayo, with Fahy as the preferred spelling, with some 72 births. Fahey had 47 births in scattered locations at that time.

O'Fahy was also cited as a principal name in Sligo in the census of 1659.

Note the place name of Fahysvillage in Galway. The O'Fays or O'Fays' are in Keatings History as a clan of Ui Maine in Galway, with the O'Horans, O'Lanes, Larkins and O'Gevennys.

The Fahy Institute in Argentina was named for Fr. Anthony Fahy (1805-1871) an Irish priest in that country.

Both the Fahy and Fahie spellings are found among the ranks of the 69th Regt. of Corcorans Irish Legion.

O'Faherty

O'Fathartaigh

Flaherty

The Faherty family hails from Co. Galway, centered in the barony of Clare near Lough Corrib. Due to similarity in sound and spelling, some family members are found as Flaherty today.

Fant

L'enfaunt, La Font, La Fant

Note the name of Fantstown in Co. Limerick. Early settler families of the name are said to have spelled the name with an L' or "La" prefix as L'Fant or La Font etc..

Falkiner

The Irish Book of Arms plate 106

Folkiner, Fowlkiner

The Falkiner family of Mt. Falcon, Co. Tipperary is given in the Irish Book of Arms.

Mc Fadden

Mac Phaidin

Faddin, Fadian, Fadyen, etc..

The name of McFadden is a name of northern Ireland, and an Ulster name of both Irish and Scottish heritage. Mac Phaidin, from which the name is originally taken, stands for son of Patrick. Without the 'Mac' prefix the name was more common in Mayo than elsewhere.

Donegal is said to be the homeland of the Irish of the name, at least where it is possible to distinguish between the two. The census of 1659 gives McFaden as a principal name of Donegal in that century. The 1890 index shows the name in Donegal, Antrim and Londonderry, and Milesian families gives the name as a Scottish one, arriving in 1660 and settling in Antrim.

Falls

O' Maelfabhail

McFalls, MacFall, M'Falls

This name, when found simply as 'Falls' with no Mac prefix is assumed to be an English name which settled in Ulster. Here the name was often found in CO. Tyrone from the 1600's onward.

McFall is found in Antrim and Londonderry in the 1890 index, and is given as settling in Antrim in 1650 from Scotland in Milesian Families. Mac Phail is another spelling found used in the past. Arms for the name are found in Burkes General Armory.

102

O'Fallon

Irish Book of Arms plates 80, 154

O'Fallamhain

Fallin, Fallen, Fallan, Fallon, Falloon,

The ruins of a Fallon stronghold are found in the townland of Milltown, Dysart parish, in the barony of Athlone, Co. Roscommon. They are recorded as chiefs in the area. The head of this family ruled an area which included the above Dysart parish, along with the neighboring parish of Camma in Roscommon.

Individuals of the name have resided in the area into modern times, and the chief of the name remained in Dysart parish in the 16th century. This was the family of Ui Maine, and references to them appear in the Annals of Irish history.

One branch of this family held lands in Ballinasloe, and held claim to the former family's heritage. Early records also show this family name in Co. Meath, but it disappears with the arrival of the Norman invasions.

The variant spelling of Falloon is found commonly in Armagh.

In Keatings History, O'Fallon is found as 'Lord of Crioch na-g-Cedach', named from Olill Cedach, son of Cathair Mor, King of Leinster in the 2nd century. O'Fallons country was found near Athlone in Co. Westmeath, but they were later driven to the other side of the Shannon river, into Co. Roscommon.

O'Dugan speaks of the family thusly: 'The O'Fallons who marched with force Were chiefs of Clan Uadach of wine banquets, Men who let not their spears decay. Of those are the freeborn clans.'

In 1659 Fallon was a principal name of Roscommon, and Fallan is given there as well. Falloon is in Armagh in the 1890's birth index, and Falloone is found in Clare in the 17th century.

The Fallons of Netterville Lodge, Co. Galway descend from a chief whose son settled in Runnimead, Co. Roscommon.

O'Farrell

Irish Book of Arms plates 63, 154

O'Fearghaill

Farral, Farel, Ferrall,

O'Farrell. the Lord of Annaly in Co. Longford, was seated at his fortress, 'Longphuirt Ui Fhearghaill'. Hence came the name of the town and County of Longford in all probability. The family is often cited in the Annals of the Four Masters and other ancient Irish texts. Of this family two branches are well known, O'Farrell Boy (buidhe - yellow), and O'Farrell Bane (Ban - meaning white or fair).

One of the top 40 names in all of Ireland, most are found near their original territory in and near Co. Longford. Of the O'Farrells of Annaly, one Ceadagh O'Ferrall perished in the battle of the Boyne in 1691, and three of his sons served in the Irish Brigades of France, where some of the name settled in Picardy.

One Roger O'Ferrall compiled the noted genealogical work, 'Linea Antiqua' in 1709, which of late can be found in the hands of the genealogical office in Dublin.

At the end of the 1800's only 19 births were recorded under the spelling of O'Ferrell, and 311 were spelled as Farrell primarily in Dublin, Meath, Longford, Louth and Westmeath.

In 1659 Farrall was a principal name in Dublin, also found in Roscommon. Farrell, at that time, was a principal name in various counties.

As a rule the 'O' before the name has been lost for many generations up until the turn of the century.

Also of note, Mac Rannall or Reynolds, of the race of Ir, or Clanna Rory, were of the same stock as the O'Ferralls of Annaly.

O'Farrelly

Irish Book of Arms plates 242,

O'Faircheallaigh

Farely, Farelly, Ferrely, Ferly, Farley

O'Farrelly is a name which has been changed into several different forms, including the English name of Farley. In Keatings History the O'Farrellys were cited as a numerous clan, particularly in the parish of Mullagh, in Co. Cavan.

This family is found seated in the Loughter Lower barony, in Co. Cavan. Here they served as erenaghs of Drumlane Abbey, which later became an Augustine Abbey. They were also Co-arbs of St. Mogue.

There was also a family of the name centered near Knockainy in Limerick, which was found in O'Heerins topographical poems, but of this family there is little information in our files.

Traditionally considered a family of Cavan and Meath,(a Breffny clan), the name has remained most popular in those counties, as well as in Dublin, into modern times.

Of possible variant spellings, 'Farely' was in Cork in 1659 and Fairley in Down at that time. Ferrally remained as a principal name in Limerick then, and Ferily was found in Clare.

The 1890 birth index records some 69 births of the Farrelly name, mainly in Cavan, Meath and Dublin.

The "y" at the end of the name can also be dropped, thus forming the name of Farrell for some.

The Irish Book of Arms gives families of the name as "O'Farrell of Dalyston, Co. Galway", one of whom served as high sheriff, descended from the O'Ferrals of Mornin and Bawn, Co. Longford. They were resident in the Castle of Mornin in 1688. One burial place for the family was at the churchyard of Moydow, in Co. Longford.

103

Farren

Irish Book of Arms plate 142

Farren, Fearon, Farron

Most of the name of Farren are found early in counties Donegal and Derry in the north of Ireland. Some interchanging of the name may have occurred with surnames such as Fearon, Fearen etc.. The name remained most numerous in Donegal and Londonderry in the the 19th century.

O'Falvey

Irish Book of Arms plate 203

O FAILBHE

FEALY (NORTH KERRY), FALLAHER

The Falvey name is considered to be a name of County Kerry from the earliest times down to modern day records. The name is also found in counties Cork and Clare. Individuals of the name are recorded as chiefs of Corcaguiney from the 1100's until the collapse of the Gaelic order. They were powerful chiefs and hereditary admirals of Desmond. The name was also cited as a rebellious one in the 17th century in Ireland. The family managed to maintain lands into modern times around Cahirciveen.

In 1690 four 'Falveys' served as officers in King James Army. Quoting from Keatings 'History of Ireland' :
'O'Falvey the warrior'....
'From Mang westward is the estate possessed by O'Falvey as far as Ventry.. without dispute an extensive land, was obtained by O'Shea, Chief of Iveragh'.

Some 16 births of the name are recorded in 1890, found mainly in Cork, Clare and Kerry.

Individuals of the name:

(P1) Dennis Falvey. Age 25. Aboard John-Garrow. June 2, 1846. Ireland to New York.

Fr. Donough O'Falvey, who was hanged in Cork, during the Elizabethan persecutions.

Fay

Irish Book of Arms plate 93

du Fay, Faye, Fey, Fee, Foy, de Fae, de la

A name of Anglo-Norman origins in Ireland, found settled early in Co. Westmeath, and in modern times in Dublin. The Fay name is also used by the Irish family of O'Fay (O'Fiaich) of the province of Ulster.

The census of 1659 finds O'Fee in Co. Fermanagh.

O'Hart gives a branch of the name springing from "Fief or Fay", in the parish of St. Honorine-Du-Fay, in Normandy, which was held by a family of the name.

Nicholas Fay of Ballinure, Co. Kildare was confidant to the Earl of Kildare. The family is also found centered at Trumroe, Co. Westmeath. George Fay of Jamestown, Queen Co. and George Fay of Castlepollard are found as well.

"Fays Ford" on the River Boyne was so called in honor of one Captain Fay who was said to be the last man to stand in the way of the Williamite army there. Note the older place name of Faybrook in Co. Cavan as well.

Sir Richard De Fay is the earliest of the name on one pedigree, he was a knight of De Lacy, Lord of Meath, who in 1219 was sent on a mission to the King.

Thomas Fay of Annsbrook and Mayo House, Co. Meath, settled in Cavan in 1780 and was ancestor of Fay of Faybrook and of Moyne Hall in Co. Cavan.

The Irish Book of Arms gives Fay of Faybrook, Co. Cavan. Other sources tell that the name of Fay has been found in records of the Pale from the time of King John. Many of the name are found in the Book of Lecan, including those seated at Dernegara Castle, in Westmeath, from whom descends Fay of Faybrook.

O'Finnegan

Irish Book of Arms plates 154, 257

O'Fionnagain

Finegan, Finegane, Finigan, Finnigan,

The O'Finnegan families are fairly widely distributed throughout Ireland. Two separate origins are thought to exist for those bearing the name today. Anciently O'Fionnagain is found in the barony of Ballymore, Co. Roscommon and in the nearby baronies of Ballmoe in Co. Galway, marking one location for the name. Note the place name of Ballyfinnegan in the baronies of Ballymoe and Castlereagh here.

The other location for the family name is found near the borders of Cavan, Meath and Monaghan, which more anciently comprised a part of Breffni.

In Keatings History the Finnegans were given along with other clans as resident in Mayo and Sligo in the 12th century. It is also given that 'MacGilla Finnagain' or O'Finnegans, a name sometimes rendered Finnucane,' along with O'Kenny, was a chief of Clan Laithemhain, also called Muintir Cionaith, a district in the barony of Moycarnon, Co. Roscommon. They are thus mentioned by O'Dugan:

'Mac Gilla-Finnegan the mild,
and the valiant Clan Kenny,
Two tribes who are fair to be seen
Rule over the brave Clan Flahavan.'

Finegan is found as a principal name of Louth , and O'Finegane as a principal name of Sligo in the 17th century.

The 1890 birth index finds 'Finegan' as the preferred spelling of the name, with some 52 births in Monaghan, Galway and Louth. 'Finnegan' had 39 recorded births mainly in Armagh and Cavan at that time.

104

Finny

Irish Book of Arms plate 25

Finney

The Finny family of Leixlip, Co. Kildare, is given to have come earlier from Westminster, subsequently settling in Ireland, as given in the Irish Book of Arms.

Fanning

Fannin, Fannon, Faning

The Fanning families are found in Ireland in the wake of the 12th century Norman invasions, centered in the barony of Slievardagh in Co. Tipperary. Note the place name of Fanningstown in Co. Kilkenny, and similar names in Limerick, marking the family earlier in history. They were also a noted family of Ballingarry. Several of the name served as Mayors of Limerick city.

The family is found most numerous in counties Wexford, Tipperary and Waterford in the 19th century.

Fannon

OFionnain

Fannin, Fanning, Fanin, Fanan,

Although we have not accumulated much information on the name of Fannon to date, the name is found in the 1890 birth index. Here it is found in the counties of Wexford, Tipperary and Waterford. When found in Roscommon and Galway, it is believed to have come from the original spelling of Fanning.

One Don Ricardo Fanan (Fanning) is listed in 1663 as a Capitan of the Irish who served in the Spanish Netherlands.

The name or variant is found in Keatings History. O'Hart gives Fanning of Ballingarry and Fanningstown, Co. Limerick, and several of this line were mayors of Limerick.

Fitzgerald

Irish Book of Arms plates 42,44, 81, 83,..

MacGearailt

Fitzerald, Fitzgerrald, Fitzgerold,

A popular name in Ireland, Fitzgerald means 'son of Gerald, hence the Irish translation as 'Mac Gearailt'. Most descend from Maurice, son of Gerald, constable of Pembroke and of a Royal heritage in Wales. He accompanied Strongbow to Ireland during the Norman invasions, and received lands as a result.

In the province of Leinster the family head became the Earl of Kildare and then the Duke of Leinster. The Kildare family was powerful, with castles at Maynooth and Kilkea. Some are referred to here as 'Knights of Glin.' The families war cry was 'Crom Abu.'

In Munster they served as Earls of Desmond, being known as knights of Kerry, centered at Dingle. Their war cry was 'Shanid Abu' and they are estimated to have held 1 million acres of land. They became barons of Decies, holding castles in the baronies of Coshmore and Coshbride in Waterford. Some of this line settled in England.

The Fitzgerald family of Moyvane, Co. Kerry descend from Garrett Fitzjohn Fitzgibbon, of Coolcam Castle, in the barony of Clangibbon, Co. Cork. This was a branch of the Fitzgibbons known as the white knights.

Some settled in the parish of Mayo, Co. Mayo, known as 'Clanmorris' and their chief was called MacMorris. (The Fitzgeralds of Kilkenny were transplanted here in the 17th century.).

In Waterford some descend from the baron of Burnchurch, Co. Kilkenny. (Others took the name of Baron). The family also held lands in Limerick, Cork and Kerry, seated near Askeaton in Co. Limerick and in Newcastle West.

The ape depicted in the family arms above, saved the infant son of Maurice Fitzgerald in the 13th century.

FitzGibbon(s)

Irish Book of Arms plates 39, 155

Mac Giobuin, Mac Giobain

Mac Gibbon, Gibbons, Fitzgibbon

The Fitzgibbon and Gibbons families in Ireland may in some cases be of English extraction, as Gibbons is a name often found there. The more Irish of the name may spring from Fitzgibbons who arrived early with the Norman invasions (@1170). Others of the name stem from the noted Burke family of Co. Mayo, who were at one time referred to as 'MacGibbon' Burke (of Norman origins).

Fitzgibbon is traditionally associated with Co. Limerick, and has remained primarily a Limerick name today. The head of this family was known as 'The White Knight' of Desmond. Their lands, known as Clangibbon, are found in the baronies of Condons and Clangibbon in
Co. Cork, near the border of Co. Limerick.

The Mayo Fitzgibbons, of Norman origins, may be marked by the place name of Ballymacgibbon in Co. Mayo.

Our records show one Maurice Fitzgibbon of Crohana House in Kilkenny in the 19th century.

Keatings History cites the Fitzgibbons as a branch of the Fitzgeralds, as among the early Norman settlers in Limerick and Clare.

The Irish Book of Arms gives Fitzgibbon of Crohana, Co. Kilkenny. David Fitzgibbon, alias 'Mac an tShen Ridire' or the son of the old knight was of this line. He had two sons, Gerald and Maurice, of Ballynahinch, Co. Limerick. Gerald, the elder son, possessed Knocklong, Hamonstown and Ballyscadden, Co. Limerick. He died in the last half of the 16th century.

Fitzgibbon was a principal name of Limerick in the 17th century and remained so in the 1890 birth index.

105

Fitzherbert

Irish Book of Arms plate 99

Fitz, Fitzhubert

One family of Fitzherbert is on record as settling in Co. Cavan at least by the 17th century. The family cited was of English extraction, with roots in Staffordshire, England.

The Fitzherbert family of Black Castle Co. Meath and of Shantonagh, Co. Monaghan are given to be of the same line, descended from William Fitzherbert, of Shercock, Co. Cavan.

Mc Farland

McFarlan, Farlan, McPartland

The name of a Scottish family found settled in Ulster no later that the 17th century in Ireland. The name is sometimes confused with the separate name of McPartland.

Farragher

The Farragher family is traditionally linked with counties Galway and Mayo in the west of Ireland.

Farrissey

Farrissy

A name linked to Counties Mayo and Leitrim in our records.

O'Faughnan

Families of the name of Faughnan are found centered in Co. Leitrim in the 19th century.

FitzMaurice

Irish Book of Arms plate 3, pge. 40

originally descended from Raymond le

Fitzmorice, Fitzmorish, Morrish, Morrice,

The district surrounding 'Lixnaw' in County Kerry marks some territories held by 'Maurice', the son of Raymond le Gros. It is from this Maurice that the current-day name originates, along with all of its many spellings. This Maurice built Malahuffe Castle according to O'Hart, and of this line was Thomas, of Liscahan and Kilfenora. Piers FitzMaurice of Ballymacquin is also cited. The family was originally in league with Dermott MacCarthy, and were Earls of Kerry.

Of the many spellings of the name, "Fitzmaurice" is found in County Kerry quite early in Ireland. Fitzmorrice is also given as a principal name of Kerry in 1659. Fitzmorrish is found in Kerry and Clare at the same date. Fitzmorish however, is given as a principal name of Waterford at that time. (see Morris)

Farrington

de Faryngton, de Feringdon, de Farindon

Farrington is a name which has not been very numerous in Ireland. The birth index of 1890 recorded the minimum of 5 births for the name, scattered throughout the country. 'Farrington' an English toponymic, has been on record in Ireland for several centuries however, dating back to at least the 1300's.

As rare today as it has always been, the name is of some note in county Cork, where one family of the name settled, coming from Lancashire in the middle of the last century..

Fitzpatrick

Irish Book of Arms plates 5, 155, 231..

MacGiolla Phadraig

MacGilpatrick, Fitz, Patrick, Fitch,

Fitzpatrick is the exception to the rule. It is the only 'Fitz' name of ancient Irish origins, and not of Norman heritage. The name was originally Mac Giolla Phadraig, known as 'Lord of Upper Ossory'. The chief of the name ruled over parts of Leix and all of Kilkenny. Later confined to the barony of Upper Ossory, in Leix, The family was driven into Cavan and Leitrim early by the English. The name was taken from a chief in the the 10th century.

O'Heerin speaks of 'MacGilpatrick: 'To MacFilpatrick of the fine fortress, the land of Ossory is by law ordained, From Gladhma, southward to the sea; Brave are his battalions in the battles.'

In Keatings History, 'the Fitzpatricks, a numerous clan' in Cavan, found in the baronies of Tullyhunco and Loughtee. A branch of the Ossory family, they settled in Cavan early. The name is found in Fermanagh, and is associated there with the MaGuires.

The family declined in power with the coming of the Ormond brothers. They surrendered to Henry III, but lost a great deal as supporters of William III.

'Fitzpatrick' may have been taken as a name by others since it could simply mean 'son of Patrick'. In 1659 Fitzpatrick is found in Leix, Kilkenny, Tipperary and Meath. In the 1890 birth index this name is found in Dublin, Queens, Cork, Tipperary and Cavan.

Of variant spellings of the name, Kilpatrick is formed from 'gilpatrick' or Giolla Phadraig, referring to the oldest spelling of the name. Kilpatrick is found mainly in Co. Antrim in 1890.

One of the top 100 names in Ireland, several sources for family origins are sure to exist. (See 'History of the Diocese of Ossory', by Corrigan)

Fitzwilliam

Irish Book of Arms plate 3 (titled)

One family of the name of Fitzwilliam is found by O'Hart as of Merrion, Co. Dublin. This was the line of Sir Richard Fitzwilliam (d.1595). Of the same line it is said that Richard Fitzwilliam became governor of the Bahama Islands in the early 18th century.

Feddis

A scarce name in Ireland, traditionally linked to Co. Fermanagh there.

O'Fedegan

The Fedegan name was given as a principle one of Co. Louth in the 17th century. Early records find the family in Co. Monaghan as well.

Fee

Irish Book of Arms plate 219 (McFee)

O'Fiaich

McFee, Fay, O'Fay, O'Fee

A name of the north of Ireland, in the province of Ulster. The family is most numerous in Antrim, Cavan and Fermanagh in the 19th century.

Feehan

Feaghan, Feighan

The Feehan name is often traced back to Co. Tipperary and it may have been confused with names such as Fegan in Louth. The Feehan name is found most often in Co. Louth in the 19th century.

Furlong

According to "Keatings History" the name is of an old English family settled in Wexford. Wexford held most of the name in the 19th century as well.

O'Flaherty

Irish Book of Arms plates 155, 242

O'Flaithbhearthaig

Flagherty, Faherty, Laverty, Lafferty

'From the ferocious O'Flahertys - God defend us,' was the motto displayed in Galway by the enemies of the O'Flaherty clan. O'Flahertys Castle at Aughnanure near Galway stood as their stronghold, and its' remains stand today.

Until the coming of the Norman invasions, they were found on the eastern shores of Lough Corrib. At this time they were forced to the opposite side of the Lough. O'Flaherty was known as Lord of Moycullen and Iar Connacht, with lands from Galway Bay to Killary Harbor and the Aran Islands.

In the north, the spellings of Laverty and Laherty are found, due to a different pronunciation of the same Irish name. In Donegal the head of the family was known as the 'Lord of Aileach', and was said to be the 'Tanist' of Tyrone, by the Four Masters. This family was likely of separate origins from the above.

Flaherty has been a name of Galway. The 1890 index shows 88 births in Galway and Kerry spelled as Flaherty. Other spellings found were Laverty in Antrim, and Lafferty in Donegal, Londonderry and Tyrone.

In Keatings History we find the following words: 'Clan Murcadha of the fortress of hospitality was governed by the Clan Flaherty of swords, Who from the shout of battle would not flee; To them belongs the regulation of the fair ports. 'Found as chiefs in the barony of Clare, Co. Galway by O'Dugan, they had the main sea force around Lough Corrib, on the islands of which they had castles. Their name, according to Keatings meant 'a chief of noble deeds'

Constant feuding took place between O'Connor, Burke and O'Flaherty in Galway. The Joyces, formed alliances with the powerful O'Flaherties.

106

O'Flanagan

Irish Book of Arms plates 155, 259

O'Flannagain

Flanagan, Flang, Flanigan, Flannagan,

The 69th most popular name in all of Ireland, several unrelated families of this surname are found. The most well known are those of the barony of Frenchpark, in Roscommon. They spring from the same line as the O'Connors, serving as hereditary stewards to the Kings of Connaught. Their traditional lands are found near Mantua and Elphin.

Families of the name are found in Offaly in the barony of Ballybritt, and in Toora, Co. Fermanagh

A chief of the name is found in Eli O'Carroll country in Kings Co.. Another is in the baronies of Iffa and Offa by the Tipperary and Waterford border according to O'Heerin.

O'Flanagan is also given as a chief of the barony of Maherboy in Co. Fermanagh. In 1659 we find O'Flanigane and Flanigane as principal names in Clare. Flanigan was in Roscommon and O'Flannagan in Fermanagh at that time. By 1890 principal locations for the family were in Roscommon, Dublin, Mayo, Clare, Galway and Fermanagh.

In O'Hart we read of O'Flanagan, chief of Tuath Ratha, or the district of the Fortress, a territory which extended from Belmore to Belleek, and from Lough Melvin to Lough Erne, comprising the present barony of Magheraboy.

He gives 5 families of the name, those of Ely O'Carroll territory, those of Connaught, of Fermanagh, of the ancient territory of Oriel, and of Uactar Tire, now the barony of Upperthird in northwest Waterford. These last were broken shortly after the 12th century English invasions, being usurped by the family of Le Poer (Power), who retained many of those lands in modern times.

 107

Fleming

Irish Book of Arms plate 155

Pleamonn (Flemish)

Flemon, Flemming, Flemmyng, Flemyng,

Families of the name of Fleming in Ireland were originally from Flanders. They have arrived in Ireland at different times, and may descend from several families of the name in Flanders.

The Fleming name is more often associated with Scotland, where many settled, as they did in Wales. They arrived in Ireland near the time of the Norman invasions, as well as during the time of the Plantation of Ulster.

In Co. Meath a prominent family of the name was established around the 12th century. As Lords of Slane, they held Slane Castle into the 1600's.

Many of the Fleming family can be found in Ulster, where they arrived from Scotland at the time of the plantation of Ireland. Those of the name in Co. Cork may have arrived at the same time.

Keatings History cites the family as a principal Norman one of Co. Cork. Richard and Thomas Fleming held Crandon and other districts in Meath. They were the barons of Slane, a branch of which became viscounts of Langford. Also of note in Meath were the 'Flemings of Staholmock'. They are also cited as a principal family of Norman descent in the city and county of Dublin. The De Flemmings, barons of Slane, are also cited here as a chief Anglo-Norman family settled in Louth.

In the 17th century Fleming was a principal name of Cork City and also found in Kilkenny. 'Flemming' was a principal name of Limerick, and in Waterford and Dublin city. 'Flemminge' was in Kildare; Flemyne was a principal name of Tipperary; and Flemyng was so in Waterford.

At the end of the last century the name was most populous in Antrim, Dublin, Galway, Londonderry, Cork and Mayo.

Flood

Irish Book of Arms plate 42

Mac Maoltuile or O'Maoltuile.

Floyd, MacTully, MacAtilla

The name of Flood is found in Keatings History as one of the 'many respectable' families of Kilkenny. In Irish the name is taken from Maoltuile. The root word 'tuile' means flood. Hence the translation from the old gaelic into the modern name of Flood. Some of the name in Ireland are English. In the north of Ireland 'Flood' has also been used for the Welsh surname 'Floyd'.

In the birth index the name is found primarily in Dublin in 1890, but was given in Wexford and Longford in the 1659 census in Ireland. Others find the name in Kilkenny in 1646, of Welsh origin.The Irish Book of Arms gives Solly-Flood of Ballynaslaney House.

Feely

Feeley, Feehily, Feheely

The name of Feely can be found in the area of Roscommon, Mayo and Leitrim, as well as in Co. Cork. In the 19th century we find the name of Feely most numerous in Donegal and Roscommon.

Feerick

Ferick

A name found early in Co. Mayo and subsequently in Co. Galway.

Fenton

Fenaghty

The name of Fenton is that of a settler family from England, several Irish families likely "adopted" the name. The family is found most numerous in Kerry and Antrim in the 19th century,

O'Flynn

Irish Book of Arms plates 155, 200

O'Floin

Flyng, Flinn, Fleens, O'Lynn, O'Flynne,

One of the 50 most popular names in Ireland, O'Flynn families are of different origins. Most have long ago dropped the 'O' prefix from the name.

In Cork two apparently unrelated septs gave rise to the name, accounting for the great numbers of the family in this county. One was seated at Ardagh Castle, in West Cork, in the barony of West Carbery, as part of the Corca Laoidhe. The O'Flynns of Muskerry were in the barony of East Muskerry and served as Lords of Muskerrylinn.

The O'Flynns of Roscommon were centered in the barony of Castlereagh, seated at Kiltullagh and Kilkeevin.

In the province of Ulster, another O'Flynn family is found in southern Armagh near Lough Neagh. They trace their line to a King of Ireland in the 4th century. Due to the local pronunciation of the name here, the 'F' in Flynn has sometimes been lost, forming O'Lynn.

Keatings History states that O'Flynn was chief of Arda and Ui Baghmna, according to O'Heerin, a territory in the barony of Carbery. The Muskerry family held territory from the River Dripsey to Ballyvoorney. We quote: 'O'Flynn Arda of the blooming woods, A tribe of the purest pedigree; Heir to the lordship is each man, They are the clan of Ui Baghamna.' Ui Baghamna was then the barony of Ibane and Barryroe, which adjoined Carbery.)

In Ulster O'Flynn ruled with O'Donnellan as chief of Lough Neagh over the baronies of Toome and Antrim, Co. Antrim (northern Clanaboy.)

The name is found under several spellings in the 1659. Flyne in Waterford, O'Flyne and Flyng in Cork, Flyn in Louth, O'Flynne in Cork City, and Flynne in King's County and Cork.

O'Fogarty

Irish book of Arms plates 155, 207

O'Fogartaigh

Fogerty, Gogarty

The O'Fogarty family is anciently found in Co. Tipperary, Ireland and is considered to be an ancient Irish family. The family is still to be found in in Co. Tipperary, including the area near Thurles, and their former seat of power, 'Castle Fogarty'.

Eliogarty is the name of the barony in Tipperary named after this family. In 1072 the Annals of Ulster describe the O'Fogarty chief as 'O'Fogarty, King of Ely'. They ruled over southern Ely, and O'Carroll ruled over northern Ely (Ely O'Carroll).

The name in Gaelic was spelled O'Fogartaigh, and has been said to mean exiled, outlawed or expelled.

The location of Castle Fogarty can be found on the full page map of Tipperary in the' Complete Book For Tracing Your Irish Ancestors', indexed under 'C' for castle. One William Fogarty was an adjutant in the Irish American brigades, who resigned in 1863.

The Fogarty name is well documented in Irish history, and is found in Keatings History. O'Heerin gives Fogarty as chief of the southern Ely:

'South Ely of well established tributes- Its clans are of the race of Eocaidh Balderg- A country of affluence, abounding in Hazel Woods, It is the land which O'Fogarty obtained.'.

Most of the name have dropped the 'O' prefix long ago, and 61 births of the name were recorded in the 1890 birth index, primarily located in Tipperary and Dublin.

The name of Gogarty, is presumably of completely separate origins, stemming from the old family of MagFhogartaigh.

Foot

The Irish Book of Arms plate 53

The Foot family, of The Rower, Co. Kilkenny came to Ireland in the 17th century and the earliest of the name is found in Lord Drogheda's regiment.

O'Feeney

O'Fidhne, O'Finannaidhe

Feeney, Feeny, Finny, Finney

Feeney families will find that their name is traditionally associated with the province of Connaught, particularly in the counties of Sligo, Mayo, Galway and Roscommon. Note the place names of Ballyfeeney (Feeneys' town) in the baronies of Roscommon and Ballintober North in County Roscommon.

There were two families of Connaught which assumed the name of (O)Feeney. One was O'Fiannaidhe of Mayo and Sligo and the other was O'Fidhne of Galway and Roscommon counties. Whether these two families stem from the same common ancestor I am unable to determine.

Feeney was the most popular spelling of the name in the 1890 index, with some 46 births recorded in Sligo, Mayo and Galway. 'Feeny' had 26 births in the counties of Galway and Roscommon.

In the census of 1659 O'Feeny was a principal name of Londonderry, and also in Sligo.

O'Feenaghty

O'Finnachta

According to "Keatings History" the name is that of the chiefs in the two half baronies of Ballymoe, in the counties of Roscommon and Galway. Two distinct chiefs of the name are given; that of Clan Murrogh, and that of Clan Conway. O'Feenaghty, chiefs of Clan Conway had their castle at Dunamon, near the River Suck, in Co. Roscommon.

Forbes

Irish Book of Ams plates 3, 253

Forbs

The Forbes in Ireland are usually of Scottish origins. Note the place name of Castle Forbes in Co. Longford, where the name has been since the 17th century. This family is found in the Irish Book of Arms.

The Forbes of the Earls of Granard descend from the Scottish House of Forbes, and Sir Arthur Forbes was sent from Scotland to Ireland in 1620, he was buried at Newtown Forbes, Longford, which was a center for the name.

The pedigree of Forbes of Clann Ferbisigh, of supposed Irish origins are given by O'Hart as representing the "Irish" Forbes. This family was also known as MacFirbis. The birth index of 1890 finds the family centered in Antrim and Tyrone.

Fegan

Feghan, Fagan

The Fegan name is linked with counties Dublin, Armagh and Louth, and sometimes confused with O'Hagan.

Finglas

According to "Keatings History" the name is that of a principal family of Dublin , and of Anglo-Norman descent.

Frame

A rare surname in Ireland, our records show scattered locations for the name including Ulster, Cork and Dublin.

Fyan

Fyans

Family members note the placename of Fyanstown in Co. Meath. The name is also in the city of Dublin, where several are found as officials quite early.

109

Fortescue

Irish Book of Arms plate 39

The Fortescue family of Stephenstown, Co. Louth is found in the Irish Book of Arms.

Fenelon

Irish Book of Arms plate 216 (Fenelon)

Finnellan, Fenlon, Fenlon

Many families of the name today are likely of Huguenot descent, have settled in Ireland some generations ago. Others are of an old Irish family by the name of O'Fionnalain, who served as lords of Delvin in Westmeath. The coming of the 12th century Norman invasions dispersed these Irish families of the name, found today as Fenlon and Fenelon.

Families of the name of Fenlon are found centered in Carlow, Dublin and Wexford in the 19th century.

Fennell

Fennelly, Fyenell, Fenell

English settler families of the name of Fennell are found in Tipperary and Cork around the 16th century, and some of them were Quakers. The Irish families of the name may also descend from the old gaelic family of O'Fionnghaill, found early in Carlow and Waterford.

Accordingly, families of the name may be of Irish or English extraction when found in Ireland. The census of 1659 finds the family in Dublin, Kilkenny, Queens and Cork counties. The 19th century birth index gives them centered in Clare and Dublin. Those of the Fennell name may as well represent a shortened form of the separate and unrelated name of Fennelly. The Fennelly family is found centered in Co. Kilkenny in the 19th century.

Fowler

The Irish Book of Arms plate 62

The Fowler family of Rahinston and Rathmolyon, Co. Meath is found in the Irish Book of Arms. The birth index of 1890 finds the family centered in the province of Ulster, with 10 of 17 recorded births there.

Fennessy

O'Fionnghusa

Fenessy, Fennessey

The name of Fennessy is linked with counties Tipperary and Waterford in Ireland. This is particularly true along the Tipperary/Waterford border. According to some, one family of the name served as chiefs of a district near Cashel, in Tipperary.

We find Richard Fennessy (d.1747) with a farm at Ballynattin, near Clerihan just south of Cashel in Tipperary, and in the townland of Shanbally. This family also had branches of the name in Limerick and Waterford. Several of the name are found given as "Nurserymen" in those areas. Other family members are subsequently found in the north of Ireland and in Fulton County, Illinois in America.

The Fennessy family is found most numerous in Co. Waterford in the 19th century.

Mac Feorais, Peorais

According to "Keatings History" the name is given as Irish, and also adopted by Anglo-Norman or English families in lieu of their original surnames.

The de Berminghams of Connaught and other places took on the name of MacFeorais or Peorais, signifying the "son of Pierce", one of their chiefs.

Fox

Irish Book of Arms plates 71, 104,124

Sionnach

Shinnock, MacAshinah, Shanahy,

When found in Ireland, families of the Fox surname may be of several origins. The name may come from settlers from England. One family, of Mountfox, near Kilmallock in Co. Limerick is an example of that. Most are assumed to be of Irish origins however.

In most instances, the name of 'Fox' arose as a nick-name. In Westmeath, Keatings History finds the name coming from O'Catharnaigh, the head prince of Teffia. The name was later rendered as Kearney. The Sinnach O'Catharnaighs were the chief branch of the name, & Sinnach was translated into Fox in English. Hence the family name became Fox, and the chief of the name was designated as 'an Sinnach' or 'the Fox'. Their territory contained parts of the baronies of Rathconlan and Clonlonan in Westmeath and the barony of Kilcourcy in Kings Co. (Offaly).

Many other families have taken on the name of Fox, but it appears that this happens in isolated instances throughout the country. These names have been recorded by the registrar-general as being interchanged with Fox; Shonogh in Galway, Shinnock in Kilkenny, Shunny in Louth, Shanahy in Westmeath, Shinogh in Mayo, Mac Shanaghy in in Louth, and Mac Ashinah in Tyrone.

In 1659 Fox was a principal name of Clare and found in Westmeath and Kings. In 1890 the name was mainly in Dublin, Longford, Tyrone and Leitrim.

The Irish book of Arms finds Fox of Kilcoursey, the Irish family who possessed the barony of Kilcoursey in Kings County, losing their lands circa 1641. Also given was Fox, of Fox Hall, Longford, of the same Irish line who repurchased the castle of Rathreogh from the O'Farrells prior to 1560.

110

Francis, Frank

Irish Book of Arms plate 42

Francis, Frances, Frank, Franks, Franck,

Families of the name of Francis, Frances, etc.. in Ireland are given to be of Norman heritage, and are not an old gaelic family. The name carries with it the obvious meaning of "the frenchman". The 1659 census finds the name in the city of Dublin, and the 19th century index finds 13 births of the name recorded in 1890 as Francis in scattered locations. Unconfirmed sources also find the name as settling in Co. Wexford.

The name of Franks, Franke,or Frank is as well taken to mean "the Frenchman". Spelled as Franke this family is found in Co. Wexford in the 17th century, and mention of families of the name are found in counties Limerick, Leix and Offaly. Note the earlier placename of Frankford, assumed to have been connected with these families. This place has subsequently been renamed as Kilcormac.

The Franks family of Westfield, Queens Co., and of Garrettstown and Dromrahane, Co. Cork, are given in the Irish Book of Arms.

Mc Ferran

McFerrin, McFerron, Ferren

In the 19th century families of the name McFerron are centered in Antrim and Down, and the spelling as "Ferran" is found in the 1890 birth index as well.

O'Finneran

Fineran

A family name of Ireland traditionally linked with counties Roscommon and Galway in Ireland, and found centered in the latter in the 19th century.

French

The Irish Book of Arms plates 74,77,156

de Freynes

Ffrench

In Keatings History we find that in the 12th and 13th centuries several English and Welsh families etc... settled in the town of Galway and other parts of the country. The Ffrenches are given as one of the principal families who did so, and eventually they became one of the 14 tribes of Galway.

The line of the most noted family of the name arrived first in England, coming from France with William the Conqueror.

(Theophilus de French is given to be the founder of this family)

This line subsequently settled in Co. Wexford with branches later in Galway (early 15th century), and Roscommon, where they became known as the 'Ffrenches of Ffrench Park'. They are on record in Roscommon from the early 1600's.

In 1659 French was a principal name of Wexford and found in Roscommon and Cork as well. By the time of the 1890 birth index the center for the name was given in Co. Antrim, with a total of 24 births recorded in all of Ireland.

The Irish Book of Arms includes 'French of Cloonyquin, Co. Roscommon, Ffrench of Monivea Castle Co. Galway, in the barony of Tiaquin, and Ffrench of Marino, Co. Cork.

Walter French was the Sovereign of Galway in 1444.

O'Freely

O'Frighile

O'Friel, Freel, Freily, Friely...

(O) Freely is a name commonly associated with County Mayo, and is traditionally considered to be the center of the name. (see O'Friel)

O'Friel

Irish Book of Arms plates 156, 232

O'Firghil

Freal, Freel, O'Friell, Freil, Frehill,

The Friel name may stem from the same root as the Farrell surname in Ireland. The family is said to descend from Eoghan, brother of St. Columbkille, and they were hereditary co-arbs of Kilmacrenan in County Donegal.

These Friels also held the distinguished honor of inaugurating 'The O'Donnell' as the Lord of Tirconnell. The diocese of Raphoe shows many Friels and O'Friels among the ranks of the clergy there.

Found primarily in the province of Ulster in the north of Ireland, Donegal, Tyrone and Londonderry held most families of the name in the 1890's birth index. No births are recorded in the provinces of Leinster and Munster, but 5 births were found in Connaught and 38 in Ulster.

The name of O'Frehill or Frehill is given to be a variant spelling of Friel or O'Friel, traditionally found in Co. Mayo.

Spelled as 'Friel', without the 'O' prefix, the name is not found in the census of 1659 often, but O'Friell is listed in 1659 as being a principal name of Donegal. This trend has continued into modern times, for the 'O' is most often found before the name in the 1890 index as well.

O'Dugan gives O'Firghal, or O'Freel, as a clan of Tir Eogain in the 12th century, as found in our volumes of Keatings History.

One John Friel is found on a petition for land in New York State in September of 1772. Several of the name are on record sailing from Liverpool and Londonderry to New York (U.S.A.).

111

Fuller

Irish Book of Arms plate 37

The Fuller family of Glashnacree, Co. Kerry possessed lands in Dingle, Ballybunion and other areas in Kerry, before the noted plantation settlers arrived in that county. The birth index of 1890 finds the family centered in Cork.

O'Ferrigan

Feregan, Ferrigan

A name linked to Co. Down in Ireland in our records.

Furnell

An English family name found in Cork and in Limerick several generations ago.

Ferriter

Feritter, Ferreter

A name given to be of Dublin and Kerry quite early in Irish History, and originally this family was of Anglo-Norman origins. They are as well found prominent on the Blasket Islands subsequently. Note the place name of Ballyferriter in the area of the Dingle Peninsula. The family is found centered in the barony of Corkaguiny there.

Ferry

Our records find the Ferry family linked to Co. Donegal, in the north of Ireland.

Finan

A name often linked to the province of Connaught in Ireland, i.e. Roscommon, Mayo, Sligo etc.. We find the family most numerous in Roscommon and Sligo in the 19th century.

Fullerton

Irish Book of Arms plate 37

Fullarton, Fuller

The Fullerton family is traditionally found in the province of Ulster. In the 19th century they remained centered in Antrim and Down. The family is assumed to be of Scottish origins, and the first of that line is said to have arrived from Scotland during the time of James I. Note the placename of Fullarton in Scotland.

The presumably separate name of Fuller is found in Cork and Kings Co. in the 17th century, and in the 19th century we find the name of Fuller centered in Cork. Fuller, could serve as a shortened form of Fullerton for some.

The Fullerton family of Ballintoy, Co. Antrim, is found in the Irish Book of Arms.

Mc Fetridge

Mac Pheadruis (Son of Petrus?)

Fettridge, Fetrick, Fetrish.

In the 1890 birth index the name is found in Antrim and Londonderry. In the census of 1659 the name is found in Antrim presumably spelled as MacPhetrish. It remains a name of the in Antrim and Derry today.

Fewer

The name of families in Kilkenny and Waterford. Fewer has also been given as a variant spelling of Feore.

Furey

Fury

Some have traced the Furey family back to Co. Westmeath anciently, but the name is traditionally found in Co. Galway, where the name was most numerous in the 19th century.

Fulton

The Irish Book of Arms plate 69

The Fulton family of Braidujle, Co. Antrim is given in the Irish Book of Arms. The birth index of 1890 finds the family centered in Antrim, with all of the name located in the province of Ulster.

Fians

Fyans, Fyan, Feighan, Foynes

The 'Fians' family name is most likely taken as a variant spelling of the name Fyans, which has been found in Dublin since the 1400's. Some of the name served as mayors of Dublin. The name has also been changed to Faghan.

On record as landowners in Co. Meath, note the place name of Fyanstown. Molshir Fyan, from Inrolments of the Decrees of Innocents, from O'Hart. Alderman Fyan, Cassandra Fyan, Melcher Fyan, from the '49 Officers, (1649), per O'Hart.

Flinter

The name of a family found sometimes in Co. Kildare and Co. Wicklow.

Figgis

Seemingly a very rare name found only in recent times in the city of Dublin in our records.

Filgate

The name of one family found in Co. Louth, settled there from the 17th century.

Finnerrell

The name of a family found sometimes in Co. Clare.

Field

Arms given by O'Hart

Feild, Delafield, Delafeld

The family name of Field is traditionally linked to Dublin, and they were originally a settler family of Anglo-Norman extraction. The family name is as well cited as being a main settler family in Co. Cork.

Several families of the name are cited in older works including, the Delafields of Fieldstown, Co. Meath, and De La Feid (sometimes Field), of Derrynashally, Co. Monaghan. Robert De La Field of Knockbuy, Co. Monaghan is given as well.

In the census of 1659 Field was a principal name of Co. Cork, as well as being found in Waterford and Louth. Spelled as "Feild" the name was given in Co. Limerick at that time. In more modern times the 1890 birth index finds the family centered in Dublin and Cork.

According to "Keatings History" the name of O'Fihelly was Anglicized to Field, and they were given by O'Brien as chiefs in west Barryroe.

Mac Finneen

According to "Keatings History" this name was given to a branch of the MacCarthys, or according to others a branch of the O'Sullivans. They were a clan of note in Co. Kerry.

Finnevar

Mac Fionbhair

According to "Keatings History" the name is given to the chiefs of Muintir Greadain, a district in the southern part of Leitrim. The original spelling is given as Mac Fionbhair.

Frewen

Frew

The name of a family found in Co. Cork.

O'Finn

Fionn

MacFinn, MacFhinn, Maginn, MagPhinn

The Finn family is found throughout Ireland, although less appear in the province of Ulster than elsewhere.

Three separate origins of the name have been said to exist, and are generally believed as being correct: 1) O'Finn of Connacht, found in the barony of Dunkellin in Galway, who were erenaghs of Kilcogan, 2) of the southern portion of the old territory of Oriel, which comprised Louth and parts of Ulster. This family has yet to be well uncovered in our research to date,

3) O'Finn of Sligo, where the family served as chiefs of Calry near Lough Gill, in the barony of Carbury. Note the barony of Coolavin, possibly named in their honor from 'Cuil O ghFinn', said to mean 'hiding place of O'Finn'.

MacFinn is also found in ancient records and has variant spellings such as MacFhinn, MagFhinn, and Maginn.

In Keatings History O'Finn and O'Carroll were given as chiefs of Calraighe (Calry),'a district adjoining Dartry, in the present barony of Dromahaire, Leitrim, and which appears to have comprehended an adjoining portion of Sligo,' (near the present parish of Calry in Sligo). 'This district comprised the parishes of Drumlease and Killargy in Leitrim, with part of the parish of Calry in Sligo.'

Surprisingly, Finn is most common in Co. Cork in modern times, and in Mayo, Dublin and Roscommon in the 1890 birth index. In the 17th century both O'Finn and McFinne are found as principal names in Co. Cork as well. The reason for the numerous families of the name here remains unclear. Perhaps a branch of one of the above families settled here, or an entirely independent family of the name exists here.

Fitzharris

Fitzharry, Fitzhenry

Recorded in some instances as an Anglo-Norman family settling early in county Wexford, the name is also found as Fitzhenry there. Subsequently we find the family in Carlow and Dublin, and the name of Fitzhenry is also found in and around the area of Killeen, Co. Meath.

We find one Mathew Fitzharris, of Maghmain, Co. Wexford as chief of the name, and of his line was Sir Edward Fitzharris of Kilfenan, Co. Limerick, who left 7 sons upon his demise.

Fitzhenry

According to Keatings "History " the name is given as that of an old English family which settled in Wexford.

FitzSimmons

Irish Book of Arms plate 269

of Norman origin

Fitzsimon, Fitzsimmon, Fitz, Fitzsymon,

Fitzsimmons is perhaps the only 'Fitz' name found more often in England than in Ireland. It does however date back to the Norman invasions in Ireland. The 'Fitz' prefix is of Norman origin.

John DeCourcy, in 1177 brought some of the name to Co. Down. In the 1200's some of the name followed the Predergasts' to Mayo, where they remained strong into the late 1500's owning several castles, including Castlereagh.

In the 14th century the name arrived from Cornwall, England and settled in Dublin. Today it is common in Dublin, Cavan and Down.

Fitzsimons seems to be the most common spelling in the 1800's, although many variants exist such as Fitzsimon, Fits, Fitz, Symons etc..

Fitzsimmons is given in Dublin, Down and Cavan in the 1890 birth index of Ireland.

113

Ferguson

Irish Book of Arms plate 237

Fergesun, Fergusen

The name of a Scottish settler family in Ulster. In Scotland the name ranks among the top 40 most numerous surnames, and as expected, several families have settled in the north of Ireland over time.

The Ferguson family is found most numerous in Antrim, Down, and Londonderry in the 19th century. The name of Fergus is found centered in Co. Mayo at that time.

Finnerty

Irish Book of Arms plate 203

Fenaghty, Finerty

A name often found linked to Co. Galway in Ireland, it is found most numerous in the province of Munster in the 19th century.

O'Flannery

Irish Book of Arms plate 203

O'Flannabhra

Flanury, Flanory, Flanery

Families of O'Flannery descent in Ireland may spring from one of two accepted origins. The 'O' prefix before the name had been largely dropped in the last century, and so it remains today.

O'Flannery of the Ui Fiachrach is found centered near Killala, in Co. Mayo. The other O'Flannery was of the Ui Fidhgheinte, being centered within the baronies of Upper and Lower Connello in Co. Limerick. This Limerick family of the name is found most often in Limerick today, near Nenagh. The Mayo family still remains near its old homeland.

In Keatings History O'Flannery is cited as a chief of Dal Carbri, a territory in the barony of Kenry in Co. Limerick. They are also cited as 'Princes of Cashel of white standards'.

The main locations for the name at the close of the 19th century were in Mayo, Tipperary, Galway and Clare. When speaking of variant spellings of the name in the 17th century, 'Flanory' is found in Tipperary and Flanury was a principal name of Tipperary at that time.

Freeman

(Mac an Saoir)

The name of Freeman is common outside of Ireland and is of likely English origin when found in Ireland. This of course will not always be the case, due to the fact that so many Irish names have been changed into English sounding ones. In one instance at least the name of Freeman has been used in place of the Irish Mac an Saoir.

The census of 1659 finds the name in Londonderry, Tipperary, Carlow and Dublin. In more modern times some 20 scattered births were recorded in the 1890 index. Milesian families gives the name as a Saxon one, settling in Limerick in 1646.

FLING

O'FLOINN

FLYNG, FLYNE, FLYNN, FLINN, FLEENS

The Irish family name of "Fling" is given to be a variant spelling of the name of Flynn. This is confirmed in the work of Matteson, where the names of Flinn, Fleens, and Fling were given to be different spellings of the Flynn name. The family has been found traditionally located in counties Cork and Roscommon in Ireland. The census of 1659 however, lists families of the "Fling" spelling primarily in Waterford and Tipperary.

In the year 1659, we find the following: Offling- was a principal name of Co. Waterford. OFling- was a principal name of Co. Waterford. OFlinge- was a principal name of Tipperary. Fling- was a principal name of Waterford. Flinge- was a principal name of Tipperary.

Passengers from Ireland:

JOHN AND RICHARD , ABOARD WATERLOO, APRIL 8,1850.

DAN'L. , ABOARD 'ADA-ALICE' , NOV. 17 1848.

GEO. F., ABOARD 'JAMESTOWN' OCT. 28 1848.

ANN AND JOSEPH, ABOARD 'BOREAS' MAY 9, 1849.

BRIAN, ABOARD 'SARAH AND LOUISA' APR. 6, 1849.

JOHN, ABOARD 'CORNELIA', JUNE 11, 1849.

THOMAS, ABOARD 'INFANTA' MAY 5, 1849.

O'Foley

Irish Book of Arms plate 235

O'Foghladha

Fowloo, Foli, Fooley, Fooluiah, Fowly,

One of the 100 most numerous names in Ireland, the Foleys descend from the O'Foghladha sept of Waterford., in one case.

The name has remained of Waterford into modern times and spread into Cork and Kerry. 'Foly' appears as a principal name of Carlow in 1659, and O'Fowly was a principal name of Wexford . O'Fowlowe and Fowlue were both principal names of Cork, and O'Fowlue was of Kerry, with Fouly found as a principal name of Wexford. Of the many spellings of the name, Foley is the main spelling in modern times.

The 'O' prefix before the name has been dropped as a rule, making it difficult to be sure of which Foleys may be of English heritage, for Foley is a name of families in England as well.

Considering how many families of the name there are in Ireland, several origins of the name surely exist. Some sources give the name as of Norman origin as well as Irish.

James Foley was found in the Regts. of Corcorans Irish Legion, and John Foley was found in Meaghers Irish Brigade according to O'Hart. His work finds both Foley and O'Foley in the service of the Spanish army.

In modern times the name was found most often in Kerry, Cork, Waterford and Dublin in the 1890's birth index.

Most commonly found in the province of Munster, MacSharry (MacSearraigh) is a completely separate name which has been translated into Foley. This is likely due to the translation of 'searraigh' into the English 'foal'.

Over 15 of the name are found in the book entitled "Irish Marriages 1771-1812" by Henry Farrar.

John Henry Foley, (b.1818) was a famous Irish sculptor.

114

Foran

Irish Book of Arms plate 203

O Fuarain

O'Forhane, O'Foran, Forhan, Forane

The name of Foran shows up earliest in the county of Waterford, and is today considered a name of Waterford and Limerick. As the 1890 birth index shows, the name is still of these two counties today, in addition to Dublin. Foran is found in the census of 1659 as a principal name of Waterford, and also in Kings, Queens, and Kildare. Spelled as Forane in the same census, the name remains a principal one in county Waterford. Milesian families gives the name as an ancient Irish one, being of the Hy Brune tribe, in County Galway.

Lawrence Foran, an Irish scribe in the 1700's from Waterford, put together the Book of Port Law, in 1780. The name has also been connected with the name of Ford, as a variant.

Foy

O Fiaich

Fee, Fey, Fye, Fay, Hunt, Foye

The Foy name has been changed to several similar sounding forms as listed above, including being translated into Hunt in earlier days. It is considered a name of county Cavan and the northern parts of the province of Connaught.

In the census of 1659 the name of Foy is found in Dublin, as is the variant spelling of Foye. The more recent 1890 index places the name in Mayo, Cavan and Dublin.

Forde

Irish Book of Arms plate 252

Foran, MacKinnawe, Foorde, Foord, Foard

When found in Ireland, Ford families may descend from any of several unrelated families. Many Fords here are of English extraction, arriving as settlers and merchants at various times in history.

One noted English family which settled in Meath, came from Devonshire in England, in the 14th century.

Several old Irish origins exist as well. Irish families have mistranslated their name into Ford in more than one instance. In Co. Cork many of the name Foran (O'Fuarthain) adopted the name of Forde. In the southern parts of Connemara members of the MacAneave (MacGiollarnath) family adopted Forde as their surname, as did the family of MacCosnamha (Mac Kinnawe), also of the province of Connaught.

In Keatings History it was stated that those from Mac Consnamha, the chiefs of Clan Kenny, originated near Lough Allen, in the parish of Innismagrath, in Co. Leitrim. (Keatings says the district was then known as the Muintir Mountains.). The name was given to have already been largely anglicised to Ford at the time of that writing, and the family as such was numerous at that time there.

'Forde' rather than 'Ford' was the most common spelling of the name in 1890, when the name came primarily from Galway, Cork, Mayo and Dublin. There were 154 births of 'Forde' at that time, and only 39 births of 'Ford'.

In 1659 Ford was found in Dublin City in the census.

Mac Finnucane

Finucane

A name found most anciently in our records in Co. Clare, and subsequently in counties Limerick and Kerry.

Flahaven

Flavin, Flaven

Our records find the name centered near Youghal in Co. Cork, and in parts of Co. Waterford.

Flatley, Flattelly

Flattelly, Flatly

A name said to have its early origins in Co. Sligo, but found in modern times in Co. Mayo, especially in the area around Knock, Co. Mayo. According to "Keatings History" the name of Flattelly, from which those of the shorter spelling originate presumably, is cited as that of a clan of Mayo and/or Sligo.

The Flatley family is found most numerous in Co. Mayo in the 1890 birth index of Ireland.

Flattery

Irish Book of Arms plate 258

Flatery

A name linked in earlier times to the barony of Kilcoursey in Offaly and to the barony of Moyfenragh in Co. Meath. The family is found most numerous in Kings Co. in the 19th century.

Fortune

Farshin

The Fortune name is traditionally linked to Co. Wexford in Ireland, and although it certainly appears to be of foreign introduction, we have no evidence of the same to date. The spelling of "Farshin" has also been recorded as a synonym of Fortune.

Fraser

Frazer, Frazier

Fraser ranks among the top 20 most numerous names in all of Scotland, and so it is not surprising to find the name in the province of Ulster in Ireland. The name is also found spelled as Frazer, notably in Co. Antrim.

Fraser families are found most numerous in counties Dublin, Antrim and Down in the 19th century.

Frawley

A name most often found in Co. Clare and in nearby parts of Co. Limerick.

115

Forster

One family of the name is found given in Co. Galway and as chief of Clooneene, in that area in the early 17th century. Major James Forster of that line served as High Sheriff of Galway. Mention is made of Forster-street, Galway.

Fitzelle

Fizzell

A name found in more ancient times in the province of Ulster in Ireland, "Fitzelle" and Fizzell are given as synonyms in 19th century records of Co. Kerry. Here, the name is more properly Fizzell.

O'Flannelly

Irish Book of Arms plate 256

O'Flannell, Flaneley, Flanly, Flannelley

An Irish family name traditionally linked with Co. Mayo in Ireland.

Floyd

Flood

A fairly scarce name of Ireland, sometimes found in the province of Ulster. Our records find the family name in Kerry, Westmeath, Dublin, and Kilkenny in the 17th century. Flood has also been officially reported as a synonym of Floyd.

Folan

The name of an old Irish family traditionally linked to Co. Galway in Ireland, where 90% of the family can be found down into modern times. A few of the name were also found nearby in Co. Mayo.

Forrestall

Forestall, Foristel, Forrestal, Forstall,

"Forestall" is given in the census of 1659 as a principal name of Queens Co.. Our records find the family most prominent in earlier days in Co. Kilkenny and Wexford. Spelled also as Forstall, the name is given as a principal one of Kilkenny, as well as being found in Wexford and Clare in the 17th century.

Note the old placename of Forrestallstown in Co. Kilkenny where one branch of the family was found centered. The family is considered to be of English origins when found in Ireland.

The name of Forrest, a sometimes shortened form of Forrestall, is found most numerous in Co. Cork in the 19th century.

Foyle

Foyll

Families of the Foyle name are found rather sparingly in Ireland. We find the name from time to time in Dublin, and in Queens Co. in Ireland.

Fraher

Farragher, Farraher

Families of the Fraher name are found centered in Co. Waterford and Limerick in the 19th century. It is believed by many that Fraher is simple a shortened form of the name of Farraher, a popular name in Mayo and Galway.

Frahill

O'Freathail

Frehill

Frahill families in Ireland are said to actually have been of the "Farrell" name in earlier days. Frahill is given as a variant spelling, and is sometimes confused with the name of Frehill, said to be of different origins altogether.

Frain

Freyn, Freyne, Frane, Frein, de Freyne

Families of the name of Frain are found centered in the counties of Mayo and Roscommon in the 1890 birth index of Ireland. Spelled as Frayne we find families of the name in Co. Westmeath in the 17th century.

Note the family of the Barons de Freyne, of Co. Roscommon in Frenchpark, who are of French extraction originally. The similar sounding name of Freeney, Freny or Frainy is sometimes given as a variant spelling of Frain, and can sometimes be found in Dublin.

Fullam, Fulham

de Fullam, Fulham

The family of Fullam is tradtionally linked to Swords in Co. Dublin, where they are on record for several centuries. In the 17th century the name is a principal one of the city of Dublin, as well as being found in Meath at that time.

The name of Fulham was also a principal name of Dublin and found in Dublin city in the 17th century. Two centuries later Fulham is found centered in Dublin and Kings Co. (Offaly). Some interchanging between these two names is reported.

Furphy

A scarce family in Ireland, the family is most often linked to Co. Armagh in the province of Ulster. One noted family of the name is found in Australia.

Fivey

Quig, Quigley

The name of a family found in Co. Down.

Frizell

Fresel, Freisel, Frizil, Frizzle, Frizelle

The family is listed as Frizell in the 1890 birth index with 8 births of the name in Ulster and Connaught only. The spelling of Frizzle is given with several traditional locations in that index. We find the name in Ulster and in Co. Cork in earlier times.

O'Gallagher

Irish Book of Arms plates 156, 251

O'Gallchobhair

Gallougher, Gallagher, Gallaher, Colliher,

Gallagher etc.. is among one of the top 20 most numerous names in all of Ireland. The Gallagher family name has always been associated with Co. Donegal, anciently and into modern times. Here their old territories are marked by the baronies of Tirhugh and Raphoe, in which Ballybeit and Ballynaglack served as seats of their power.

Here in Donegal they are recorded as commanders of O'Donnells cavalry forces. Keatings History finds the O'Gallaghers as descended from the warrior Gallchobhair, in the above named baronies. It further cites their castles at Ballyshannon and Lifford there.

Numerous clergy of the name are found in Raphoe in older records.

In the 17th century Gallaghur was given as a principal name of Leitrim and O'Gallogher as a principal name of Donegal. In the 1890's birth index, 488 births are recorded primarily in Donegal, Mayo, Tyrone, Sligo and Londonderry.

One interesting source for further information on the family is the book 'Irish Chiefs and Leaders' published in Dublin, 1960.

The variant spellings of this families name are numerous, so be aware of possible changes here.

Gale

Gaule, Mac Gale

The name of Gale is found in the census of 1659 as a principal name of Kilkenny, and also in Westmeath and Wexford. The form of MacGale is used as a variant spelling of MacCall in the north of Ireland, particularly in county Tyrone.

Galloway,

Irish Book of Arms Galwey plate 12

DE GALLAIDHE

GALWEY,GALLWEY,GALLWAY,

The name of Galloway in Ireland is believed to have sprung from the same source as "Galwey". In this case the name is found quite early dating back to the 13th century according to some sources. Two areas of Ireland seem to have been associated with this family. They are found in the north of Ireland , in the province of Ulster, and in Cork.

When the family is found in Ulster, it is likely a family of Scottish origins. Those in Cork, settled in that county in the 14th century, may be of foreign or old Irish extraction. O'Hart and Burke say that the Cork family is descended from the Bourke or de Burgo family of Galway, and the territorial name of Galway followed them into Cork. This family is centered in Kinsale, Cork.

In the census of 1659 we find the name spelled as Galway, Galwey,Gallwey and Gallway. One Wm. Galwey is found of Skibberin Town, in Co. Cork then.

In the 1890 birth index the name, spelled as "Galloway" is found with 9 recorded births, mostly in Co. Antrim. Eight of the births were in Ulster.

The name of Galway etc... was said to have been taken on by a branch of the family of John De Burgo (Burke), who was commonly known as John of Galway around the year 1360 a.d..

We find two pedigrees of the name, one of "Galway of Kinsale, Cork", who descend from a branch of the Bourke family, and of the same line but settled in Limerick.

Individuals of the name:

Michl. Golloway, Age 16, male, aboard "Isaac Webb", Oct. 6, 1850. Liverpool to New York.

Charles Galloway, age 20, male, aboard "Infanta", July 29, 1850. Liverpool to New York.

116

Galt

The Irish Book of Arms plate 66

The Galt family of Ballysally, Coleraine, Co. Londonderry is found settled in Londonderry from at least the early 17th century.

O'Galligan

Gilligan, Gilligin

Older records find the name centered in Co. Sligo along with its variant spelling of Gilligan. In modern times the name is centered in areas near Co. Cavan.

Gamble

Gambell, Gamel, Gammel

The Gamble family is given to be one of English extraction when found in Ireland. The census of 1659 finds the family in Londonderry and the city of Cork under that spelling. In the 19th century they are found centered in Antrim, Down and Londonderry.

Gandsey

unknown to us at this time.

? Gansey, Gannessy, Gann...

We do not have the origin of this surname on hand at this time. The origin seems unclear at this point and is subject to speculation. The name is not in the 1890 index, the census of 1659, the 'Famine Immigrant' passenger lists', O'Harts Landed Gentry, Irish Families, or Surnames of Ireland...etc..

The closest name I have found to date is Gansey. James and John Gansey, both listed as mechanics aboard ship Carthage, June 9, 1847, Liverpool to New York. Perhaps future research will yield more results.

117

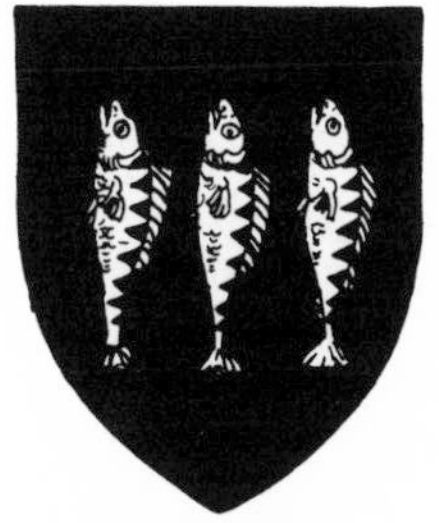

O'Galvin

Irish Book of Arms plate 156

O'Gealbhain

Galvan, Gallivan, Gallivane

The "O" prefix before this family name has generally been dropped, leaving us with the three common spellings of Galvin, Galvan, and Gallivan.

Earliest we find the family in County Clare. They are documented at the Battle of Corcomroe Abbey there in 1317. Branches of the family are later found established in counties Kerry and Roscommon.

The 1890 birth index finds the name of 'Galvin' in Cork, Clare, Kerry and Roscommon, with some 62 births. The spelling of Gallavan however, was centered only in Co. Kerry, with 32 births of that spelling.

In the 17th century "Galvan" is found in the barony of Athlone in County Roscommon where it was a principal name. The name was found in Cork at that time as well. The "Gallivan" spelling was prominent in Co. Kerry, even at that time.

One Chris. Galvin is found in the 2nd Regt. of Corcorans Irish Legion, and in the Spanish Army.

O'Gnives, Gneeves

According to "Keatings History" the name is listed among the chiefs of Moy Ith. This territory comprised parts of the baronies of Raphoe and Tirkeeran in Derry. Their territory in the 12th century is given in Moy Ith, and they served as hereditary bards to the O'Neills. This name has been changed to Agnew by 'mistranslation'.

O'Gara

Irish Book of Arms plates 156, 202

O'Gadhra

Gara, Geary, Guiry, Geary

It is often assumed the names of O'Gara and O'Hara, are of the same lineage. Gadhra, founded the O'Gara's, and he was nephew to Eadhra, founder of the O'Haras.

O'Gara held sway in the south of the barony of Leyny, in Sligo. The O'Haras ruled as chiefs in the north. These two families alternately ruled this territory.

By the 13th century the O'Garas had spread into Mayo in the barony of Costello. They assumed the title of "Lords of Coolavin" subsequently, with their seat of power in Coolavin Barony near "Lough Gara". Here, near the shores of Lough Gara, the "Moygara Castle" of the O'Garas, served as the seat of the name.

According to Keatings History they retained considerable lands in Sligo down to the 17th century, and one of them, Fergal O'Gara, lord of Moy OGara and Coolavin is justly celebrated as a great patron of learned men. Particularly so of the O'Clerys, and other authors of the Annals of the Four Masters.

O'Dugan gives O'Gara as a "Chief of Lieney-Lord of Cuil Obh-Finnm (Coolavin)", and also of Sliabh Lugta, which was part of the barony of Costello in Co. Mayo.

In Limerick and Kerry a branch of the name is said to have settled, where the spellings of Geary and Guiry are also found.

In 1659 both McGara and O'Gara were found as principal names of Sligo. By 1890 however O'Gara was found in Roscommon and Mayo, and "Gara" was in Donegal, Roscommon, Mayo and Down. "Gara" was the most popular form of the name in that index.

Col. Oliver O'Gara commanded a regiment of the Irish Brigades in France.

Garrett

Irish Book of Arms plate 22

The Garrett family of Kilgaran of Co. Carlow is given in the Irish Book of Arms. The birth index of 1890 finds the family centered in Down, Antrim and Dublin.

Ganly

Ganley

The Ganly or Ganley family name is said to be a variant of Shanly or Shanley in some instances. Some 11 births of the name are recorded in 1890, mainly in the province of Connaught.

Mc Gann

Irish Book of Arms plate 243

Magannaidh

Mac Gannon, Mc Cann, Mc Ganna, M'Gan

There is more than one possible origin for this surname. It can serve as a variant spelling of Mc Cann in the province of Connaught, or as a shortened form of Mac Gannon in Co. Mayo, etc... In the census of 1659 McGann is found as a principal name of County Louth, it has also been cited as a family of Galway. A possible related spelling, McGanna, was found as a principal name of County Leitrim in 1659 as well.

Garahan

Garrahan, Garaghan

The Garahan family is anciently linked with Co. Fermanagh in Ireland, and subsequently with adjacent areas.

Garland

Garlan, Gernon, Gartland, McGarland

Families of the name of Garland are found centered in Dublin and Monaghan in the 19th century. The name of Gernon has been used as a synonym.

Garstin

The Irish Book of Arms plate 93

Garstan, Garsten

The Garstin family of Braganstown, Co. Louth are given in the Irish Book of Arms.

O'Gaffney

Irish Book of Arms plate 259

O'Gamhna

Gaughney, Keveny, Caulfield, Gaffey,

The surname of Gaffney is one of the more difficult to trace in Ireland. Numerous Irish family names have been translated into or changed to Gaffney.

In Keatings History MacGaffney is cited as a numerous clan of Co. Cavan. The family has been cited there and in Roscommon as coming from MacCarrghamhna, which has also been translated into the English name of MacCaron.

The 'O'Gamhna' sept of the territory of Ossory has used the name of Gaffney, but it is most often found as Caulfield into modern times.

Similar instances can be found in other areas. In Galway we find the same situation, with Caulfield and Gaffey names etc..being used for the same family.

Keaveny or Geaveney of the province of Connaught has become Gaffney on occasion.

In the 1890's index 68 'Gaffney' births were recorded primarily in Cavan, Dublin and Roscommon. In the 17th century 'Gaffny' was numerous in Longford. Here in the Granard Union of Co. Longford Gaughney was reported as a synonym of Gaffney in the 1800's.

'Gaffey' in the last century was found in Roscommon and Galway..

O'Hart gives MacGamhnaigh, Anglicized to Gafney, MacGafney, and Chamney, as stemming from the Maguire pedigree.

Mac Garvey

Irish Book of Arms plates 156, 228

MacGairbhith, O'Gairbith

Garvan, Garvin, Garvy

Although the family name of Garvey can be found both as MacGarvey and O'Garvey in ancient times, today only Garvey and Mac Garvey survive.

In Keatings History the O'Garvans are found in the pedigrees under Corc, the ancestor of the O'Donaghues of Kerry, the O'Mahoneys and others. The name is known in Cork and Kerry in modern times, and could actually descend from O'Garbhain (Garvan).

Although the "O" has been dropped from the name, the main O'Garvey family is found in the barony of O'Neilland East, in Co. Armagh. Here they held sway until the rise of the McCanns. O'Garvey is also found in the east of Co. Down, and they may be of entirely different origins.

"Mac" Garvey or MacGairbhith is found anciently in Co. Donegal, and is of separate origins as well. Garvey is also numerous in Co. Mayo, but most likely it is taken from Garvin in that county.

In 1659 Garvy was a principal name of Co. Down. In 1890 Garvey is found in Mayo, Galway and Louth. McGarvey is found in Donegal and Londonderry at that time. Garvin had 5 recorded births in the same index.

Gogarty

Mag Fhogartaigh

Fogarty

Gogarty is found as a variant spelling of Fogarty. The 1890 birth index finds the family most numerous in counties Meath and Louth.

Gware

One family of the name is found in Courtstown, Co. Kilkenny in the 17th century.

118

Gentleman

Irish Book of Arms plate 51

The Gentleman family of Ballyhorgan and Mountcoal, Co. Kerry, is found in the Irish Book of Arms.

Mac Gannon

O'Geanain, Mag Fhionnain

Cannon, Cannan, McGann, Gann, Kennon

The Gannon family is traditionally associated with Co. Mayo. In 1890 the most common location of the name was in Co. Mayo, although the family is found in Dublin and Leitrim then.

Some assertions have been made of a "Gannon" family settling in Kildare at the end of the 17th century, coming from France. Of this I have no personal knowledge. In the 17th century the Ganan name is found in Meath.

Of the name in Leitrim, "McGanna" was found in 1659 as a principal name there, which may cause some confusion.

The obvious similarity between the sound and spelling of Gannon and Cannon should also be noted by family researchers. The two may have been interchanged in specific cases.

O'Cannon was also found as a principal name of Leitrim in 1659. Some interchanging between these names has doubtlessly occurred.

From our records of Irish marriages we find Alice Gannon marrying Joseph Brady in 1812, we further find John Gannon, a grocer: Gt. Britain St.= Quartermass, Miss., Oct. 1806.

In America John Gannon of Queens Co., New York is given in 1715 of Capt. Timothy Bagleys light horse company. Joseph Gannon was one of the troops enlisted in Orange Co., N.Y., for the revolutionary war.

One William Gannon is found of Kildare Parish, Kings Co., Ireland, aboard the "Brig John", sailing from Galway to New York on 8/2/1816.

 119

Mac Geoghegan

Irish Book of Arms plates 156, 206

Mag Eochagain

Gegan, Gehegan, Gahagan, Geoghan

The family of Geoghegan hails from the barony of Moycashel in Co. Westmeath, Ireland. Castle Geoghegan, near Kilbeggen, was the seat of the families power.

In Keatings History the Mac Geoghegans were one of the principal branches of the southern Ui Neill, and were called Kinel Fiacha, descended from Fiacaidh, a son of Niall of the Nine Hostages. They held sway in Moycashel, as mentioned above, and in parts of Rathconrath and Fertullagh as well.

Spoken of many times in the Annals of the 4 Masters as chiefs of Kinalea (Kinel Fiacha), the power of the family fell with the coming of Cromwell to Ireland. Castletown , Co. Westmeath marks a center for one family of the name.

In the 17th century Geoghegan is found as a principal name of Kings County (Offaly), and in Westmeath, but the 1890's index gives the family mainly in Dublin and Galway.

Gately

O'Gately, MacGatteley, O'Cattely

The Gately family is traditionally linked with Co. Roscommon, and in particular with the barony of Athlone in that county. The original name is generally found given as O'Gately, (with the O' prefix), but the census of 1659 puts a "Mc" before the name as McGattely, listing that as a principle name of Roscommon.

Mac Geraghty

Irish Book of Arms plate 157, 213

Mag Oireachtaigh

Gerty, Jerety, Gerity

Mac Oiraghty was the more ancient form of the name of Mac Geraghty or Geraghty. They descend from the same stock as the O'Connors, Kings of Connaught.

Keatings History records that:

"Mac Oiraghty of the steeds was the
ruling chief of Muintir Roduiv of right -
ful laws- A fearless warrior as he ranged the woods."

Also chief of Clan Tomaltaigh, their lands were situated in the barony of Roscommon, Co. Roscommon. After losing some of their lands, some of the clan settled in Mayo and Sligo, " and are to this day the chief possessors of the island of Inis Murray", off the coast of Sligo. It is said that they named the island, as they were former head chiefs of Siol Murray.

Those of the name at Croagh Patrick in Co. Mayo, kept an antique bell traditionally said to have been one of those used by St. Patrick in ancient times.

The Galway Geraghtys are doubtless of the same origins as those mentioned above. By the 1890's the name was centered in Galway, Mayo and Dublin.

In the 17th century "Geraghty" was a principal name of Co. Sligo.

Gaynor

Gainor, Gayner

A name traditionally linked to Co. Westmeath and surrounds. The family is found most numerous in counties Dublin, Westmeath and Cavan in the 19th century.

Gernon

Irish Book of Arms plate 51

Gernan, Garnon, Garland

The Gernon family name is given as a principle one of Co. Louth in the 17th century, as well as being found in Cork and Roscommon at that time. The Gernon family of Athcarne Castle, Co. Meath is found in the Irish Book of Arms.

Mac Garry

Irish Book of Arms plate 242

Mag Fhearadhaigh

Garrie, Garrihy, Garry, Garrey

The more ancient form of the Mac Garry family name is Mag Fhearadhaigh. With the "Mag" prefix being changed to "Mac", both Garry and MacGarry are forms of this surname.

The chief of the name is given in the Composition Book of Connaucht in the 16th century, in Moygarry, Co. Sligo. In the 17th century MacGarry was a principal name of Leitrim. By 1890 there were some 14 reported births scattered throughout Ireland of the name of Garry.

With the "Mac" prefix Antrim, Dublin, Roscommon and Leitrim were centers for the name in the 1890 birth index.

Garrie, by the way, was the name of a Huguenot family naturalized in Great Britain/Ireland between 1681 - 1701.

Gibney

Givney, Gibny

The 1890 birth index of Ireland finds the name centered in Dublin and Cavan at that time.

120

Gibbings

The Irish Book of Arms plate 99

The Gibbings family of Gibbings Grove, Co. Cork settled in Ireland at Shanagolden, Co. Limerick during the reign of Elizabeth.

The family is on record in Ireland from the early 17th century.

O Garvan

Irish Book of Arms plate 238

O'Garbhain

Garven, Garvane, Garvey, Garvin

Garvan is a well known name in Counties Kerry and Cork in Ireland. The name comes from O'Garbhain meaning rough (Garbh). Essentially considered a family of the province of Munster, they are of the same heritage as the Moriaritys of Kerry, sometimes spelled as Garvey today. (Note that the Garveys of Co. Mayo are said to have originally been of the Garvin family.)

In the census of 1659 'Garvane' is given as a name of Co. Clare. Other sources find the name as an ancient Irish one in counties Mayo and Tipperary. They are considered to be an Eugenian tribe.

Geaney

Geany, MacGeaney, O'Geaney, Geane,

The name of O'Geaney is seldom found today with the 'O' prefix. Many of the name of MacGeaney however are on record in modern times.

The former family was found centered in Cork and Kerry, and both the spellings of Geaney and Geany were found in use in Co. Cork in the 19th century birth index.

The MacGeaney family though not numerous, are sometimes found in Ulster.

O Gaughan

Irish Book of Arms Gahan plate 243

O'Gaibhtheachain

Gauan, Gahan, Gavaghan, Mac Gahan.

There are several possible homelands for this name, although it is generally considered to be a family of the Ui Fiachrach, in the province of Connaught. In county Mayo O'Gaibhtheachain of Crossmolina was chief of Calry in the barony of Tirawley. Here in Mayo the 'Gaughan' spelling was most common in the last century, particularly in the Bellmullet area. The spelling of 'Gahan' on the other hand was found in Leinster.

Of other note, O'Gaoithin (Geehan, Gahan) is of County Roscommon and Gahan is also found more anciently on the Wicklow and Wexford border. Note the place name of Ballygahan near Arklow. 'McGahan' is found more commonly in Louth.

Getty

The Getty name is that of a settler family in Ulster, originally coming from Scotland. Found centered in Antrim, the earlier Scottish form of the name was said to be Dalgetty. The family was found most numerous in Antrim and Londonderry in the 19th century.

Gavin

Irish Book of Arms plate 203

Gavan, Gaven

In modern times the Gavin family has been most often found in Mayo and Galway, but the name is found to stem from two different origins. The family of O'Gabhain of the province of Connaught and the family of O'Gaibhin of the province of Munster presumably represent two separate families in earlier times.

Mc Gildea

Irish Book of Arms plate 86

Gilday

The 19th century birth index finds the name of Gildea centered in Donegal and Mayo in the north of Ireland. Unconfirmed sources also give the family in Limerick.

The Gildea family of Clooncormack, Co. Mayo, are found in Co. Mayo from at least the early 18th century and they are given in the Irish Book of Arms.

Mac Gauran

Somers

According to "Keatings History" the name is taken from the gaelic name of Mac Samhradhain, meaning "a bond of strength". The are found centered in the barony of Tullaghagh, in Co. Cavan.

The name was also translated into the surname of "Somers", from the word Samhradh, which means summer.

The MacGaurans were very numerous at the time of that documentation, in the counties of Cavan and Leitrim.

The name of Gaughran is found in the 1890 birth index with 4 births in Meath, and 1 in Louth.

Mac Ginty

Irish Book of Arms plate 249

Ginty, Maginty

Families of the name of MacGinty are anciently found in Co. Donegal and are traditionally linked with that county in Ireland. The name of Ginty is also reported in Co. Mayo in the 19th century.

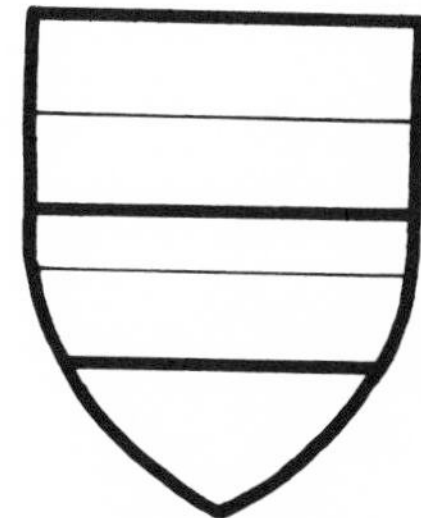

Mac Gilfoyle

Irish book of Arms plates 247, 157

Mac Giolla Phoill

Guilfoyle, Gilfoil, Powell

From Keatings History we find that "Mac Gilla-Phoill" (i.e. follower of St. Paul), or Mac Gilfoyle, chief of Clan Conliagan, is thus mentioned by O'Heerin:

"A chief for whom the nut trees produce fair fruit, Rules over Clan Quinlivan of immense wealth, The scion of Birra of the warlike tribe, Is Mac Gilla-Phoill of fair fortune."

The Mac Gilfoyles appear to have been located on the borders of Tipperary and Kings county. They are also found centered earlier near Shinrone, Co. Offaly, in Ely O'Carroll territory.

In modern times "Guilfoyle" etc.. is not a numerous name. It is given only in Dublin, with a total of 11 births in the 1890 index. The Mac prefix before the name had largely fallen into disuse by that time as well.

In the 17th century McGilfoyle was a principal name of Queens County (Leix).

The name has also been reportedly changed to Powell on occasion.

O'Gelbroin

Gelbroin

According to "Keatings History" the name is found as a chief of Clar Life, and is cited thusly ;

"The plain of Liffey of Black Ships,
A verdant country of the finest produce,
Westward of Tara, the house of Conn,
O'Gelbroin is the chief of the fair land."

These lands mentioned appear to be near the Kildare and Dublin border, on the plains of Liffey.

Mac Gillycuddy

Irish Book of Arms plates 58, 157

Mac Giolla Chuda

Mac Gillicuddy, Mac Gillacuddy

MacGillycuddys' Reeks mark the homeland of the MacGillycuddys in Co. Kerry, where they are the highest mountains in all of Ireland. The family descends from the O'Sullivan Mor line, and were even known as O'Sullivan into the 16th century. Family researchers may find reference to "O'Sullivan, alias MacGillycuddy" in written documents referring to the family in olden days.

The family served as chiefs of a territory in the barony of Dunkerron in Co. Kerry, at the base of the mountains named in their honor, according to Keatings History. They are found as well in the neighboring barony of Magunihy.

The chief of the name in more modern times, "The MacGillycuddy of the Reeks", were centered near Beaufort, Co. Kerry.

A relatively rare name in Ireland, it has always been a name connected with Co. Kerry down to modern times. The 1890's index shows only 6 births of the name "MacGillycuddy", all in Co. Kerry.

The Irish Book of Arms gives notice to MacGillicuddy of the Reeks. This family shows Cornelius or Connor McGillycuddy (b. 1580) who died by shipwreck in 1630, as the founder of the line. They later held sway in Carnbeg Castle, Co. Kerry.

Gilkinson

The name of a family traditionally linked with Co. Tyrone in our records.

Gilman

Irish Book of Arms plate 68

Gillman

Families of the name of Gilman and Gillman are found in Co. Cork in the 17th century. The latter spelling was given in Cork city specifically. The family name is traditionally linked with the baronies of East and West Carbury.

The Gillman family of Clonakilty, Co. Cork are said to have descended from an officer in the army who settled in Ireland around 1690.

The Gilman family is also given as one of the Huguenot families naturalized in Great Britain.

Mc Gettigan

O hEitigen

Getigan, Gettigan, Ettigan, Gattins

The 1890 birth index of Ireland finds all of the family of McGettigan in Donegal. Some earlier records find the name in Co. Tyrone, where the name is thought to have originated. Mac Ettigan is actually closer to the oldest spellings of the name, and some give the family as of old Norse origins in Ireland. The ancient records of the name also show both the "O" prefix and the "Mac" prefix used alternately on the name.

Giblin

Families of the name of Giblin are linked to Co. Roscommon in the past and present. In the 1890 birth index 19 of the name are given in Roscommon, and 6 of the name are given in Mayo.

Gorry

Gorey, Gorrey, Gurry

The Gorry family is traditionally linked with Co. Offaly in our records.

Gledstanes

The Irish Book of Arms plate 66

The family of Gledstanes of Fardross, Co. Tyrone is given in the Irish Book of Arms, and the arms shown above have been extracted from the same.

Gibbons

Irish Book of Arms plate 203 (Gibbon)

MacGibbon, Fitzgibbons, Gibbon

Families of the name of Gibbons may stem from any of several separate origins. Some likely come from the family of Fitzgibbon, having dropped the "Fitz" from the name.

In Mayo the MacGibbon Burkes are found centered in Ballymacgibbon, in the barony of Kilmaine. MacGibbon of course, could be shortened to Gibbon simply by dropping the "Mac" before the name. (Some of the Burke family adopted the name of MacGibbon(s).)

The family is found centered at one time in the barony of Erris, Co. Mayo. These are said to have been a branch of the Fitzgibbon family. In the 1890 birth index, 47 of the name are in Mayo, and 7 of the name are given in Co. Galway.

Gilbey

Gilbee, O'Gilbie, Killby, Gilbey, Gilboy

Most families of the Gilbey name are assumed to be of English extraction when found in Ireland. Note the place names of Gilbey etc.. in England.

The name of O'Gilbie has been interchanged with Killby and Gilbey according to official reports.

The name of O'Gilbie may actually represent the separate family often called Gillboy.

Gouvernet

Gouverney, Governey

The name of a Huguenot family known to have settled in Ireland according to at least one source.

Goff

Irish Book of Arms plate 46

The Goff family of Carrowroe Park, Co. Roscommon descend from early settlers of the name in Co. Dublin.

Gibson

Gibsen, Giblin, Gipsey

The complete book of Irish Family Names lists the following for 'Gibson':

A) anciently of Antrim and Carlow, arriving in 1590 from England.

B) Found in Dublin circa 1659.

C) In the birth index for the last century, the name is found most often in Down and Antrim.

The majority of the Gibson name in Ireland are of Scottish descent. They arrived with the Scottish settlements of the 17th century in the province of Ulster.

When of the above mentioned Scottish origins, they are said to be a branch of Clan Buchanan. The family is often found in the city of Belfast in Northern Ireland.

Gibson is said to be the 109th most popular name in America today.

Individuals of the name:

John Gibson. Inrollment of the decrees of Innocents. (per O'Hart)

George Gibson. Grantee of Estates, 1688.

Seafowle Gibson of Meath and William Gibson of Wexford, listed as soldiers of the commonwealth.

Listed as '49 officers (1649) per O'Hart:

Ens. Daniell Gibson
Major "
Surgeon Nathaniel "
Richard "
Col. Richard "
Col. Seafowle ".

Gore

Irish Book of Arms plates 21, 48, 79

Gor.

In Ireland Gore is considered to be a name of English origin. The name is said to have been taken from gor, meaning a strip of land. Several are found in the 17th century among the Anglo-Irish gentry. Mayo, Sligo and Clare appear to be the most common counties associated with the name.

The census of 1659 finds the name in County Clare and in the 'Complete Book of Irish Family Names' it is found in the Poll Money Ordinance Records. Milesian Families gives the name in Clare and Leitrim, arriving in 1642 as a Norman name.

The arms accompanying this brief history are those of Sir Ralph Gore, found on plate 21 of the Irish Book of Arms. This family was seated at Manor Gore, Co. Donegal. Two other families of the name are given in that work, including Gore of Derrymore, Co. Clare.

Mac Gilchrist

MacIlchrist, Gilchrist, Kilchrist, Gilcrest,

Families of the name of Gilchrist may descend from Scottish extraction when found in the province of Ulster, for several families of the name hail originally from that country. Those tracing back to other areas of Ireland, such as Co. Longford, may find the family to be of old Irish origins.

In the 17th century the spelling of Gilcrest is given in Co. Antrim where the name is of likely Scottish heritage, and 12 births of the name are recorded under Gilchrist in the 1890 birth index.

123

O'Gorman

Irish Book of Arms plates 248, 157

Mac Gormain

Mac Gorman, Bloomer, Gormon

Most Gormans are thought to have originally spelled the name as Mac Gorman, but the Mac prefix has been widely dropped from the name. Many MacGormans who became simply "Gorman", later added an "O" back onto the name instead of the "Mac", thus becoming O'Gorman. The two names may be one in the same!

The family is anciently found in the barony of Slievemargy, near Carlow in Leix (Queens). Forced from their homeland with the coming of the Norman invasions, they moved into Monaghan where the "MacGorman" spelling was often used. They were also in Clare, in the barony of Ibracken, where most O'Gormans are found today.

Keatings History gives the family as chiefs of territory comprising parts of the baronies of Moyarta and Ibracken in Clare. This branch of the family served as hereditary marshals to the O'Briens and held considerable lands in Clare.

The place name of Gormanstown or Gormanston, is common, for it can be found in Meath, Westmeath, Wicklow, Limerick, Tipperary and Dublin.

O'Dugan and O'Heerin give O'Gorman or MacGorman as chiefs in Queens Co. (Leix) and speak thusly of them:
"MacGorman of great valor,
Rules over the fair Ui Barchi...
of the melodious race of Dari Barach,
O'Gorman took possession of the lands,
A chief who actively rushed to battle"

In the 17th century Gorman was a principal name in Clare, and found in Dublin, and O'Gorman was a principal name of Armagh. McGormon was as a principal of Monaghan, and in Louth.

In 1890, "O'Gorman" is found mainly in Clare.

O'Gormley

Irish Book of Arms plate 215, 157

O'Gairmleadhaig

Gormaly, Gormooly, Gorman, Grimes

The O'Gormley family is found most anciently in Co. Donegal in the baronies of North and South Raphoe. O'Dugan gives O'Gormley as a clan of Tir Eogain in the 12th century, where they were chiefs of Kinel Moain or "Moen, now the barony of Raphoe" in Donegal. This district derived its name from Moan, one of the descendants of Eogan.

O'Gormley is further cited as a chief of Partry, and ancient territory in the Partry Mountains of Mayo, along with the Darcy or Dorcey family. "The present parish of Ballyovey, also called the parish of Party" shows the location of this ancient territory.

The O'Gormleys of Donegal cited earlier were driven from their lands there in the 14th century by the O'Donnells. They are subsequently found in the nearby towns of Derry and Strabane, across the River Foyle.

In Co. Roscommon you will find the O'Gormalys of Lough Key, of whom O'Donovan believes to be distinct from those of the name in Co. Tyrone.

Both O'Gormley and McGormley are found in the census of 1659, principal names in Armagh, with the former being found in Londonderry as well. 'Gormley' was already a principal name of Dublin then, as well as being in Roscommon.

By the time of the 1890 index, Gormley had 44 recorded births, given only in Antrim and Tyrone. Grimes was reported at that time as a synonym of Gormley in Co. Tyrone.

Mc Ginn

Irish Book of Arms plate 218

McGin, Maginn, McGing

The name of McGinn belongs to an Ulster family, often found in Co. Mayo.

Gould

Irish Book of Arms plate 56 (Goold)

Gould, Goold, Goule

In at least one instance the name comes from an English settler family in Co. Cork. Others find a family of the name descended from the Danes who landed and settled in Co. Cork. Thomas Gould served as the Mayor of Cork in the early 17th century. Others of the name are found as aldermen there.

Another branch of the above family is also given of Rossbrien, Dromadda and Athea, Co. Limerick.

The 1890 birth index finds the family name spelled as Goold most numerous in county Cork.

Mac Gilduff, Kilduff

Irish Book of Arms plate 201

Kilduff

According to "Keatings History" the name is that of "Mac Gilladuibh, or Mac Gillduff". In the annals cited, one Manus MacGiolladuibh is mentioned as chief of Teallach Gairbheith, "now the barony of Tullygarvey, in Co. Cavan.

MacGilduff is as well found as a chief in Caladh, along with O'Leahy, in the barony of Kilconnell, Co. Galway. The name here is said to have sometimes been changed to Kilduff.

Some of the name have dropped the "Gil" or "Kil" from the name becoming simply "Duff". (see O'Duff)

Mac Gilhooley

Gilhool, Gilhooly

Families of the name of Gilhooly are found centered in Co. Leitrim in the 1890 birth index. Gilhool was also cited as a variant spelling at that time. Some of the name are found in Co. Limerick as well. Anciently the family is found centered in Co. Leitrim as well.

124

Mac Govern

Irish Book of Arms plates 253, 157

Mag Shamhradhain

Magauran, McGoverin, M'Govran,

The families of McGovern and Magauran spring from the same ancestor - each taking on a different English spelling of the old Irish name of Mag Shamhradhain.

Mac Govern is however, the preferred spelling of the name in modern times, with only 10 births recorded as Magauran (in Co. Cavan), and 102 recorded as McGovern (in Fermanagh, Cavan and Leitrim). In earlier times the opposite may have been true. In the 17th century the spelling of "MacGovern" is seldom found.

Keatings History says that the name designated a bond of strength , and they served as chiefs of Eochaidh (today known as Tullyhaw), in Co. Cavan. They are seated in that county near Ballymagauran in the barony of Tullyhaw.

The name was then generally found as Magauran, with some translating the name into 'Somers' instead, from the word Samhradh, which signifies summer.

From the chiefs and clans of Galway and Roscommon we find another reference to O'Gauran or O'Gabrain, chief of Dal Druithne districts about Loughrea. This is a family of entirely separate origins.

Gilleece

Gillice, Gilleese

Spelled as Gilleece this family name is found in the 1890 birth index with 8 total births, in Munster and Ulster. The name is said by some to be a form of MacAleese, found often in Co. Fermanagh.

Gradwell

Irish Book of Arms plate 35

The Gradwell family of Dowth Hall, Co. Meath, and of Carlanstown, Co. Westmeath are given in the Irish Book of Arms.

Gilgunn, Gilgan

Gilgan

Gilgunn is the name of a family found early in Co. Fermanagh. As Mac Giolla Dhuinn, it has subsequently become numerous in Leitrim as well. Note the similarity in spelling with the name of Gilgan.

Gilgan is fairly rare name of Ireland, linked to the Sligo/Leitrim area in earlier times, with Sligo being the center for the name in the 19th century. The name of Gilgunn, also found in Leitrim, has doubtlessly been interchanged with the "Gilgan" spelling.

Gillen

O'Giollain

Gillan, Gillin

A family name found often in Sligo and nearby parts of Ulster, interchanged with the spelling of Gillan. The ancient family of O'Giollain is found originally centered near Tyrone and Donegal.

The spelling of Gillan is centered in Antrim and Sligo, and the spelling of Gillen is centered in Antrim, Donegal and Tyrone in the 19th century.

Mac Gillanders

Glanders

The name of a family traditionally linked with Co. Monaghan.

O'Grady

Irish Book of Arms plates 26, 125

O'Gradaigh

Graddy, Brady, Gready

Most anciently the O'Gradys are found in Co. Clare, but they are traditionally linked with Co. Limerick, where for centuries the chief family of the name has been found at Kilballyowen.

Keatings History gives O'Grada or O'Grady, as chief of Kinel Donghuile, a large territory comprising the present barony of Lower Tullagh in Clare.

The O'Gradys are thus designated by O'Heerin, and several chiefs of the name are mentioned in our annals:

"O'Grada took the entire lands
of the profitable Kinel Dongali,
His swords yellow hafted are keen,
Strong are the blows of his forces in battle. "

In Clare, one family of the name assumed the alias of Brady, and it is said that they were aligned with the English. These were the Bradys of Raheen.

The O'Grady name has been interchanged with Graddy and Gready, which are separate names, of no relation to the O'Gradys. Gready was taken from older form of Mag Riada or O'Greada.

Both Grady and O'Grady were principal names of Clare, and found in Limerick in the 17th century. Grady was found in Tipperary at that time as well. The 1890 birth index gives O'Grady in Clare, Limerick, Dublin and Roscommon. Grady is found in Mayo, Clare, Kerry and Roscommon at that time. McGrady was found in Antrim and Down.

In most ancient times the O'Gradys were a Dalcassion sept of Killana soogla by the river Fergus in Co. Clare. By the 14th century they are found at Tuamgraney, and they held lands in both Galway and Clare at that time.

In Limerick some are found on the Cappercullen estates, known in modern times as the Glental estate.

125

Graham

Irish Book of Arms plate 69

Grahams

The name of Graham is generally assumed to be a Scottish name which settled in Ulster earlier than most. It is among the 50 most numerous names of Scotland, and among the 100 most numerous names of Ireland. It is however also used for Gormely and Grehan as a variant spelling. Traditionally it has been located in Antrim and Fermanagh, as well as in the city of Dublin.

Graham is found as a principal name of Antrim, and also in Fermanagh in the census of 1659. In more recent times the 1890 index finds the name in Antrim, Down and Dublin. Spelled as Grahams it is also given as a principal name of Queens in the 1659 census.

In the Irish Book of Arms the family of Graham of Drumgoon, of Ballinakill, Letterfrack, Co. Galway is given.

One family of the name is noted in Whitechurch, Co. Kildare in 1565. Several were removed with force into Ireland by the King around 1606 according to this account.

Gillespie

Mac Giolla Easpuig

Gillesby, Glaspy, Glashby, Gilespy,

The name is considered to be primarily one of the north of Ireland in the province of Ulster, and many different ways of spelling the name are to be found, including the spelling of Glaspy found in Co. Mayo.

Gillespie is found most numerous in Antrim, Donegal, Armagh and Tyrone in the 19th century.

Mac Grath

Irish Book of Arms plate 157, 249

Mac Raith

Magrath, MacGraw, Magraw, MacGra

Two separate families of the name above are known to exist in Ireland. The first is found around Termon Mac Grath near the Donegal-Fermanagh border. The River Termon is found nearby. The other family of the name is found most anciently in Co. Clare, and spread into Tipperary and Waterford.

O'Dugan gives the Magraths in the 12th century as holding lands at Termon Magrath, where they had a castle in the parish of Templecarne.

The Clare family served as hereditary poets to the ruling O'Briens of the area. In Waterford, where the name has been established for many generations, Magraths Castle can be found in the city of Waterford.

In modern times McGrath, the most popular spelling of the name, is found centered in Tipperary, Cork and Waterford with some 233 birth in the 1890 index. "Magrath", with some 31 births, was found in Waterford, Antrim and Tyrone at that time, and McGraw had only 5 births, all in Ulster.

In the 17th century McGrath was a principal name of Tipperary, as well as being found in Clare.

Miler Magrath, Archbishop of Cashel and Bishop of Emly, was born in Fermanagh around 1522, though originally a Franciscan Friar he became Protestant. Some of his sons were Catholic, yet tried to maintain themselves by appearing otherwise, according to O'Hart. He died at Cashel and was buried in the Cathedral under a monument previously erected by himself, which remained into modern times.

Gray, Grey

Irish Book of Arms plate 63

de Gray, le Gray, MacIlrea, Graye

Families of the name of Gray and Grey in Ireland are generally given to be of foreign extraction when found here. Some arrived from England over the centuries, others originally of the name of le Grey or De Gray are of Norman origins. Others of the name are of Scottish origins when found in Ireland, and some arrived with the Cromwellian settlement of Ireland. One such is listed as a trooper by the name of Gray who was disbanded in Co. Sligo.

The name is also found in Wales, as Lord Powys, where 5 of the name of Grey and Gray are given from 1413 onwards.

The name is mainly of the province of Ulster in modern times.

Sir John Gray, M.P., was born in Claremorris, in Co. Mayo in 1816. A noted supporter of Daniel O'Connell, he was also proprietor of the Freemans Journal, and according to O'Hart he was of the Protestant Religion.

A few of the name may be Irish, for Gray has been listed as a variant of Colreavy in Co. Longford, and as a variant of MacGilrea in other sources.

Gilpin

Most of the name of Gilpin are of English extraction when found in Ireland, at least according to our records to date. The name is of the province of Ulster in Ireland and in 1890 it is found centered in Armagh and Cavan.

Giltrap

Gilthorpe, Gilstrap

A name not found in our older records to date, several families of the name are found in Dublin and surrounds in modern times.

126

Green, Houneen

Irish Book of Arms plates 201, 35, 115, 132

O hUaithnin

Huneen, O'Houneen, Greene, O'Honeen

Families of the name of Green(e) may stem from many origins. This name is one of the most popular of England, and many in Ireland are of English origins.

There are many native Irish families who took on the name of Green. This is due in part to the gaelic form of their names meaning something akin to 'Green'. For example, 'uathne' means green in gaelic, 'glas' can also be translated as green, and 'faithche' likewise can be connected to the color of green. Hence many names like 'O'Houneen' (O hUaithnin), MacGlashan and O'Fathaigh could be translated into the English name of 'Green'.

By the end of the 19th century Green was the preferred spelling of the name with 105 births in Dublin, Antrim and Galway. 'Greene' had 47 births in Tipperary and Clare, and this family is most likely of older Irish origins.

In the 17th century 'Green' was found in Tipperary and Dublin, while 'Greene' was in Cork, Kildare, Kilkenny and Dublin. MacGreene is found as a principal name of Longford. The MacGreenes mentioned above are likely an older Irish family which kept the 'Mac' prefix while translating the root of their name into the English "Greene".

Keatings History also cites the name as "O'Honeenm (in Irish OhUaithnin) who Anglicized the name to Green, were numerous in Tipperary and Clare."

The Irish Book of Arms gives Greene of Greenville Co. Limerick, Greene of Millbrook Co. Kildare, and Greene formerly of Greenville, Co. Kilkenny, whose motto is Nec timeo nec spermo.

"Pedigree of the family of Greene" was published in Dublin in 1899, and "Green Family of Youghal, Co. Cork" was published there in 1902.

Greer

Irish Book of Arms plate 86, 106

Grear, Grier

The name of a settler family from Scotland, found often in Ulster , particularly in Antrim, Down and Armagh. One Henry Greer settled in Ireland in the 1600's, coming originally from Northumberland.

One family of the name is said to descend from the MacGregors and Griersons of the Clan MacAlpin of Scotland. They are found centered in Ireland at Sea Park, Carrickfergus.

The Greer family of Tullylagan, Co. Tyrone are given to descend from Henry Grier, of Rock Hall and of Redford, near Grange, Co. Tyrone. He came to Ireland in 1653. The Greer family of Sea Park, Co. Antrim is given in the Irish Book of Arms.

Gilmore

Irish Book of Arms plate 254

Mac Ilmurray

Gilmour, Gillmore, Gilmer, Killmore

The family name of Gilmore is centered in the province of Ulster, and is often found in Co. Antrim and in the barony of Castlereagh in Co. Down. The Irish of the name are said to have taken the name from Mac Giolla Mhuire or MacIlmurray.

The most popular form of spelling for the name was as "Gilmore" which had 54 births recorded in Co. Antrim in the 1890 index. Gilmour, at that time had 18 births recorded in scattered locations throughout Ireland.

Our edition of Keatings History gives, "The MacGillmores, a warlike clan, who possessed the districts of the great Ards."

Griffin

Irish Book of Arms plates 157, 264

O'Griobhtha

Griffen, Griffins, Griffy, Grifith, O'Griffy,

Among the top 100 surnames in all of Ireland, Griffin was often earlier found as O'Griffy, taken from the Irish O'Griobhtha. Today Griffin is the preferred spelling of the name, as it was in the 1890 birth index, with some 216 births, primarily in Kerry, Clare, Cork, Limerick, Galway and Mayo.

The family may be of several origins, including Irish, British or Welsh. "Griffiths" is a popular name in England, and has been found as Griffin on occasion in Ireland. Settlers of the name arrived in the wake of the Norman invasions from Wales, and no doubt thereafter.

Of the native Irish of the name, they may hail originally from Co. Clare or Kerry. Ballygriffy, in the barony of Inchiquin, Co. Clare, marks the origins of the Thomand family, which spread into adjoining counties. They were seated at Ballygriffey castle, Dysart Parish, close to Ennis in Clare.

Another family of the name was centered in Co. Kerry, at Ballygriffin, in the barony of Glanarought. There is also the place name of Ballygriffin in Coshma barony in Co. Limerick. The Limerick family may stem from either of these two families, we do not know.

In the 17th century O'Griffen was a principal name of Cork and in Kerry. O'Griffin is also found in Cork, and Griffin in Limerick and Westmeath

127

Grogan

Irish Book of Arms plate 117

Grogane, Groggan, Grugane, Grugan,

The name of Grogan was a principle one of Westmeath, and Grogane was a principle name of Kings (Offaly) in the census of 1659. By the time of the 19th century birth index Grogan is found centered in Dublin, Tipperary, Mayo and Clare. Other records find the family in Limerick in the past as well. Note the name of the townland of Ballygrogan in Co. Tipperary.

Mac Gilligan

Irish Book of Arms plate 249

MacGiollagain

Magilligan, Galligan, Gillen

Note the place name of 'Magilligan's Strand' by Lough Foyle in northern Co. Derry. Here in Derry the name has sometimes changed to Gillen, and has been of some importance in Ulster history. 'Mac Gilligans Country' was the name given to the territory they held in the 1500's and 1600's in Derry. Here they ruled along with O'Mullane and Mac Cluskey, under the O'Cahan chieftain. Note also the parish of Tamlaght Ard here which was formerly known as 'Ard Mac Gilligan' in the 16th century.

'Galligan' often used as a variant spelling of Gilligan, also represents a completely separate family from Connaught, located primarily in Co. Cavan for the last several centuries. The 1890 index gives Gilligan a total of 32 births, coming primarily from Dublin. Some 26 of these births were from the provinces of Leinster and Connaught at that time.

Groves

The Irish Book of Arms plate 109

Grove

The Grove family of Castle Grove, Co. Donegal are said to descend from Thomas Grove of Castle Shanahan, Co. Donegal who is found there in the 17th century.

The birth index of 1890 finds families centered in Kerry and Antrim, under the spelling of Groves.

Mc Gill

Gill, MacGill

The name of McGill is most often found in the province of Ulster in Ireland, and represents the shortened form of several different "Gil" names. The name may also stem from the Irish name of Mac an Ghaill.

Some of the name may also be of foreign "settler" introduction to Ireland.

Gill is found most numerous in counties Dublin, Galway, Mayo and Longford in the 19th century.

Mc Gimsey

Mac Dhiomasaigh, from diomasach

Mac Gimpsey, McGimpsey, McGimpsy

The name of McGim(p)sey is not a common one in Ireland. In 1865 only 13 births were recorded, and in 1866 some 10 of the name were found. In the 1890 birth index some 8 births of the name were recorded, all near the traditional location of the name, 7 births in county Down and 1 in Antrim.

The family has traditionally been located in and around Newtownards, Co. Down, and has never strayed to any extent to any other location in Ireland.

Grubb

Irish Book of Arms plate 63

Grub

The Grub families in Ireland are generally accepted as being of original English extraction before settling here. The name is found in Waterford and Tipperary several centuries ago, and some of the name may be of Scots origins, as a variant of the name MacRob.

Some of the name are found settling in Ireland during the Huguenot immigration, during the reign of Louis XIV.

The Irish Book of Arms gives the family of "Grubb of Ardmayle", Co. Tipperary, of Co. Waterford in the year 1656, and subsequently settling in Kilkenny and Tipperary.

Girvan

Girvin, Garvan

Families of the name of Girvan are found centered in Co. Antrim for several centuries. Those of the name may be of Scottish descent, particularly when found in that area of the country. Woulfe suggests that Girvan may serve as an alternate spelling of Garvan, which is a completely separate name.

Girvan is found most numerous in Co. Antrim in the 19th century.

Mac Girr

Mac an Ghirr

MacGerr, MacGhir

McGirr is given as a principle name of Co. Armagh in the census of 1659. The family is further found centered in Co. Tyrone in the 1890 birth index. These two counties are traditionally linked with the name.

128

Gervais

Irish Book of Arms plate 38

A Huguenot family of Ireland as given by some sources. The Gervais family of Cecil Manor, Co. Tyrone, descend from Jean Gervais, of Tournon, Guienne, France.

Mc Ginley

McGinly, McKinley

The name of McGinley is traditionally linked to Co. Donegal in Ireland. The similar sounding name of McKinley has also been found used by this family.

St. George

The Irish Book of Arms plate 103

The St. George family of Wood Park, Co. Armagh are said to descend from Baldwin St. George who arrived as a companion-in-arms with the Conqueror, whose descendants flourished in England for several centuries.

Mc Guinness

Irish Book of Arms plate 110, 249

MagAonghusa

Magennis, Guinness, Mac Genis,

McGuinness is a very well known name in Ireland. The Guiness Brewery is connected to the family of the name in Co. Down. The family is essentially one of the northern portions of Ireland.

In Keatings History we find the pedigree of Magennis of Ui Eath, descended most anciently from Ir. Here, Aengus Og Magennis was given as the 1st of the name. Keatings also gives the "Magennises" as Lords of Iveagh, in Dal Riada (Co. Down). From the 12th century they ruled as Lords of Iveagh.

The chief of the family name was inaugurated in Co. Down on "the footstone of Aonghuis" near Warrenpoint. This stone still exists according to some in the area.

The McGuinness castle and estates at Rostrevor came into the hands of the Trevor family. Rostrevor was first known as Castle Roe (Rory), in honor of Rory Magenniss. Another castle of the name was at Warrenpoint known as Narrow Water Castle. The McGuinness castle at Rathfriland was passed to the Hawkins family by Charles II.

The family is noted in the battles of 17th century, but their great power was destroyed at that time. Many went on to serve in foreign armies on the continent.

In the census of 1659 "McGinis" is given as a name of Co. Down, and "McGinnis" as a principal name of Co. Monaghan. In more modern times "McGuinness" is given in 1890 in the counties of Dublin, Monaghan and Louth. At that time the "McGinnis" spelling was said to be traditionally from Leitrim, in Manorhamilton Union.

Anciently, O'Rooney served as hereditary bards and poets to the McGuinness family.

Mac Guire

Irish Book of Arms plates 158, 202

Maguidhir

Maguire, McGwyer

One of the top 40 names in Ireland, MacGuire or Maguire is associated with Ulster and Fermanagh, where it has been recorded as the most numerous name.

The chief of the name resided at his castle in Enniskillen, near Lough Erne.

In Keatings History it states that from Colla-da-Chrioch were descended from the MacGuires, lords of Fermanagh and barons of Enniskillen. They are of the same descent as the MacMahons, lords of Monaghan, the O'Hanlons and the O'Kellys of Ui Maine.

O'Dugan gives MacGuire thusly:
"MacGuire, the chief of hosts,
Rules the mighty men of Manach,
At home munificent in presents,
The noblest chief in hospitality"

The Maguires were inaugurated as princes of Fermanagh at the top of Caileagh, a mountain near Swanlibar, on the borders of Cavan and Fermanagh, and at Lisnaskea. They possessed all of Fermanagh which was called "MacGuires Country" and maintained their independence as Lords of Fermanagh till the reign of James I, when their lands were confiscated.

Several chiefs of the name are mentioned during the Cromwellian wars, and some were officers in the Irish Brigades in France, as well as in the Austrian service. Several are noted men, such as Charles MacGuire, archdeacon of Clogher, in the 15th century, the author of the "Annals of Ulster".

McGuire is the prominent spelling in Roscommon and Mayo. The most prominent spelling of the name was Maguire in the 1890 index, found mainly in Fermanagh, Dublin, Cavan and Donegal. More on the name can be found in "Irish Chiefs and Leaders", by Rev. Paul Walsh.1960. Dublin.

129

Mac Grory, McCrory

Irish Book of Arms plate 254

Mac Ruaidhri, O'Ruaidhri

Mac Rory, Mac Grory, Rodgers, Rogers,

In Keatings History it was said that "O'Ruaidhri, or O'Rory, now Anglicized to Rogers, was lord of Finn Fochla, in Bregia", (Meath/Dublin area), and was further cited as a prince of Finnfochla, and "an experienced chief".

The ancient Gaelic sept of Mac Rory, (Mac Ruaidhri - son of Rory), was of Tyrone, also settling in nearby Derry. This sept furnished erenaghs for Ballynascreen, in the barony of Loughlinsholin. MacCrory and MacGrory are used as forms of the name in Ulster. To further complicate matters, some Mac Rorys came from Scotland and settled in Ulster as gallowglass in the 1300's'.

The name was fairly common in earlier days, but is today rather rare. One reason for this is that those of the name in the south of Ireland have sometimes changed the name to Rodgers, or Rogers. In other cases, the name was used for one generation only and then altered to a completely different, (perhaps the original) name. Due in part to the fact that the name meant 'son of Rory', to the son only! The name seems to have been treated as a personal nickname at times.

The name is centered in the north of Ireland in the 1890 birth index in the forms of "McGrory" and "McCrory". The former had 12 births recorded in Donegal and Londonderry. The latter had 34 births in Tyrone and Antrim.

In that area the family has old roots, and they are found around Ballynascreen in the barony of Loughinsholin in Co. Derry. The name remains one of Ulster.

Mac Gee, Magee

Irish Book of Arms plate 205

Mag Aodha

Magee, McGhee, Ghee

Mac Gee and Magee are names traditionally associated with the province of Ulster, and so they have remained there into modern times. Several origins of the name exist there, and it is most often spelled as Magee. The old Irish form of the name is Mac Aodha (son of Hugh).

Some of the name are of Scottish origins. They arrived during the plantations of the 17th century. One line of this strain was said earlier to have come from Ireland to Scotland, then migrating back to Ireland at the time of the plantations.

In Co. Antrim you will find Island Magee, marking an early territory of the family on Lough Larne. Anciently we also find a chief of the name in Co. Westmeath, but they disappear from our records near the time of the Norman invasions.

In Keatings History, O'Maolgaothe, was found among the clans of Tir Connaill in the 12th century, as a chief of Muintir Maoilgaoithe, some of whom Anglicized their name to Mac Ghee. The Mac Gees are also cited as a chief clan of Ulster as "The MacGees of Islandmagee". The family name is also cited as anciently in Co. Sligo.

In the 17th century "census" McGee is given in Antrim, Fermanagh and Leitrim. Magee at that time was given in Antrim, Armagh and Down. By the 1890's we find Magee primarily in Antrim, Armagh and Down, and "McGee" in Donegal and Tyrone.

The book " The Magees of Belfast and Dublin" by F. J. Bigger was published in Belfast in 1916.

Martha Magee (1755 - 1846) was the founder of MAGEE University in Derry.

Mc Givney

Mac Dhuibhne

Mac Avinna, Mac Avinue, Mac Evinney

The name of McGivney belongs to the county of Cavan in Ireland. This is confirmed in the 1890 index, with all births of the name belonging to that county. The diocese of Kilmore is the traditional location for the name in Ireland.

Michael Joseph MacGivney (d. 1890), founded the Knights of Columbus in 1882. He was the son of an Irish immigrant to America.

O'Glaisin

According to Keatings History the family is given as chiefs in the barony of Imokilly, in Co. Cork. They were thus mentioned by O'Heerin:

"A valiant clan, warlike in pursuit, Ruled Imokilly of the hospitable banquets; Two tribes possessed the smooth plains, O'Bregan and the fair O'Glasin"

Flemish Names

Brock, Groot, Kettle, Kettel, Raymond, Rochett, Spiller and Stocker are given as Flemish names. Others are found as:
De Grote, changed to Groot.

De la Pryme as Pryme,Prim, Prym.

Goupe, changed to Guppy.

Haestricht, changed to James.

Hoek, changed to Leeke.

Thungut, changed to Dogood & Toogood.

130

O'Gleeson

Irish Book of Arms plate 201

O'Glesain

Gleason, Glissane, O'Glissane, Glyssane,

" O'Glaisin" is given by O'Heerin and others as a chief of Ui Mac Calli, "Now the barony of Imokilly in the county of Cork". They are spoken of thusly:

" A valiant clan, warlike in pursuit,
Ruled Imokilly of the hospitable banquets; Two tribes possessed the smooth plains - O'Bregan and the fair O'Glasin. "

This family is subsequently found in the barony of Owney and Arra in Tipperary. That county was the most popular location for the name in the 1890 index.

The family is also found in Limerick, Dublin, Kilkenny and Cork. They held some lands in Tipperary, descending from the same ancestors as the O'Donegans, but they were subsequently lost with the coming of Cromwell.

In the 17th century O'Glassane and O'Gleasane were principal names of Limerick, and Glysane and Glyssane were principal names of Tipperary.

Glissane was a principal name of Clare and Tipperary, and O'Glissane was a principal name of Limerick and Clare at that time.

Glison was found in Kilkenny, and O'Glissan in Clare, citing only two more spellings of the name.

Mac Gloran, O'Gloran

O'Gloiairn

According to "Keatings History" the name is given as belonging to the family which served as chiefs of Callainn. They are thus given by Aryan;

"O'Gloran, the flourishing scion,
Obtained a territory in a delightful country, A smooth land about charming Callan, He inherits a country without reproach."

The parish of Callen in the barony of Kells, in Co. Kilkenny, stands as a marker of the family lands.

Glynn, Glenn

Mag Fhloinn

McGlynn, O'Glynn, Glenn, Glenny,

While the Welsh name of "de Glin" may be the source for a few of the name in Ireland, other origins of the name surely account for most Glynn families in Ireland. One family of the name probably originates in Athlone, Co. Roscommon, and they are now found in the province of Connaught.

When spelled with a "y" instead of an "e", as in Glynn, the name is most often located on the west coast of Ireland. (In Galway, Mayo, Dublin and Clare). When spelled as Glenn the name has been found in Antrim and Londonderry in the north of Ireland in the 1890 index. Using the spelling of O'Glynn and Glynn, the family is found as a principal one of Westmeath in the 17th century.

McGlynn appears as the second most common spelling of this surname group in the 1890 index, with some 39 births recorded. Today in America of course, the name could have been changed easily into the "other" spelling. Adding to the problem for family researchers is the fact that names like Glennon were shortened into Glenn, on occasion.

The name could have been taken from a' ghleanna', meaning of the glen, or glen. It is also taken from Mag Ghloinn , an older Irish spelling of the name. Origins of the name remain clouded at this time.

Individuals of the name:

Samuel Blen aboard Ship "Mary", from Londonderry to Philadelphia, June 17, 1811.

John Glenn, of Coleraine, aboard ship Mary, Londonderry to Philadelphia, July 8, 1812.

O'Gormog

According to "Keatings History" the name is given as one of a family who served as chiefs of the Ui Fiachrach (which comprised the counties of Mayo and Sligo), centered in Carra.

Goss

O'Gusain

Goslin, Gosnel, Gossan, Gaussen, Gason,

Goss is a very rare name, which when found, is usually associated with the province of Connaught in Ireland. A possible Irish origin of the name would come from O'Gusain, (gus = meaning vigor). Possible related names include Gason, Gossan etc.., as shown above. All of those names could have been shortened to form the name of Goss. The possibility remains that the name could have been brought to Ireland from foreign shores.

Gough

O Cuachain, Mag Eothach,

Goch, Mac Geogh, Goff, Coch

Many of the name of Gough in Ireland are actually of Welsh origin. The name is found in Ireland as early as the 1200's, settled in Waterford and Dublin. Most of these are of Welsh heritage, and are found as merchants and administrators of the day. The name has also been used as a synonym with Mac Geogh.

Two Irish origins exist to explain the name as well. The ancient family of O' Cuachain, originally of Mayo, and now all but extinct, and the family of Mag Eothach (Mac Keough Sept).

Spelled as Gough the name is found in 1659 as a principal name of Waterford, in 1890 it is found in Dublin and Wexford, and Milesian families finds the name to be an English one, settling in Wexford and Roscommon in 1643. As McGough the name is found as a principal one of county Monaghan in 1659, and in the last century in county Mayo. At least two of the name served as mayors of Waterford in the 15th and 17th centuries. The name is also cited as that of a leading family of Youghal.

In the last century several of the name in Ireland, from the province of Munster, are found as British army officers. The name is also tied to the 'rebel' cause, earlier in Irish history.

Sir James Gough - purchased Kilmanahan Castle estate (of Waterford).

Nicholas Gough - Mayor of Waterford in 1435 and 1441.

Sir Edward Gough - Mayor of Waterford in 1660.

Mac Gowan, O'Gowan

Irish Book of Arms plate 247

Mac an Ghabhain

Smith, Magown, Mageown, Magowan

The old Irish form of the name Macgowan is Mac an Ghabhain, meaning son of (the) Smith. Hence many of the name took on the name of Smith, which is as well a common English name.

One of the chief families of Breffny, the MacGowans originated in Co. Cavan near the Co. Leitrim border.

O'Gowan is also the name of an ancient family in Ulster, centered near Ballygowen in Co. Down.

Keatings History gives MacGowan as a powerful clan of the race of IR, or the Clanna Rory, who descend from the warrior Conail Kearnach. They were mostly expelled by the English into Donegalk from which great numbers of them emigrated to the county of Leitrim,where they were still very numerous in Rossinver, as well as in Co. Cavan at the time of the writing of that history.

The MacGobhains or O'Gobhains were very numerous in the parishes of Lavey, Laragh and Killinkere, in Co. Cavan. They were of great strength and bravery, and served as chiefs of the Gallowglasses under the O'Reillys. Originally a clan in Dalaradia, (Co. Down), in early times they produced many ecclesiastics, learned men and poets too numerous to list.

In the 17th century Gowan was a principal name of Monaghan, O'Gowen and McGowen principal names of Fermanagh. "McGowan" was a principal spelling found in Donegal and in Monaghan at that time.

The 1890 index shows McGowan in Donegal, Leitrim and Sligo as the preferred spelling of the name with some 112 births. The Magowan spelling had 28 scattered births, and the spelling as Gowen was in Cork at that time.

Grace

Irish Book of Arms plate 266

Gras, le Gras, le Gros.

The census of 1659 finds the name of Grace as a principal name of Tipperary and Kilkenny. Note the place names of Castle Grace, Grace's Wood, Graceland, Grace's Court, Gracefield, etc...

The prominent family of the name descends from Raymond le Gros or le Gras, a noted figure in the Anglo-Norman invasions. He married the daughter of Strongbow, and was viceroy in 1176. He naturally assumed land after the conflict, and County Kildare was known as Graces County to some.

In 1690 the Grace estate amounted to over 30,000 acres under Robert Grace. His son lost the lands in 1701. Several of the name are found as officers in James II army, and the name is usually identified as a Catholic one in Ireland. Two of the name were abbots of the Monastery of Jerpoint.

We find three pedigrees given of the name.. One as Barons of Courtstown, Co. Kilkenny, another of Courtstown, and another of Mantua, Roscommon. The family is found at Moyelly Castle in Queens County too.

One of the name is noted for defending Athlone, saying "I will defend till I eat my old boots". He died in defense of the area, along with members of his family according to the account, in 1691.

Mention is also made of Gerald Grace of Ballylinch Castle, Co. Kilkenny.

For possible further research:

Memoirs of the family of Grace, by S. Grace. London 1823.

Survey of Tullaroan....history of the family of Grace. Dublin. 1819.

Origin of the Grace family of Courtstown, Co. Kilkenny...Richard Langrishe. RSAI. XXX (1900), XXXII (1902)

Mc Grail

Irish Book of Arms McGreal plate 203

Mag Reill, Mac Neill

McGreal, McGreale

Mc Grail is assumed to be a variant spelling of the more common McGreal. In older gaelic form the name was Mac Neill, changing to Mag Reill in more ancient days. The family is traditionally associated with counties Mayo and Leitrim in Ireland. Here they were of gallowglass heritage, being heavily armed fighting men settled in that area.

As might be expected the 1890 index gives Mayo and Leitrim as locations for the name in more modern times, and Milesian families gives the same location anciently for the name, further stating that they were of the Hy Brune tribe.

Passengers from Ireland:

John McGrail aboard 'Spartan' June 1847 from Liverpool to N.Y., 20 yrs. old, farmer.

Mary McGrail aboard 'Thomas' May 11, 1846, Liverpool to N.Y., 6 yrs. old.

Michael (30 yrs. old, tailor)" "

Patrick (2 yr. old child) "

Ann (21 yr. old spinster) "

Granger

grangier, Le Graunger

Grainger

The Granger or Grainger surname is taken from the French 'grangier' meaning farm steward. It is found most often in Northern Ireland in the county of Antrim from the 1600's onward. Spelled as Le Graunger it has been found in the province of Leinster. In the more modern 1890 birth index 9 births of the name were recorded. Milesian families gives the name as an English one, settling in Waterford in 1640.

132

Grant

According to "Keatings History" the name is among the chief families of English descent settling in Waterford and Tipperary. These English families primarily possessed the territory called Gal-tir, signifying the country of the foreigners," now the barony of Gaultiere." The 1890 birth index finds the family most numerous in counties Antrim and Donegal.

Grattan

Gratan, Gratten, MacGretten

Our records show the name of Grattan in Tipperary, Dublin and Ulster. It is generally accepted as the name of settler origins in Ireland. Henry Grattan (d. 1820) was a noted politician in Ireland, and member of the Irish House of Lords in 1797.

According to "Keatings History" the name is that of a principal family of Dublin city or county, and of Anglo-Norman descent.

It has also been put forward by Woulfe that this name is a form of the Scottish family of MacNaughton.

Gunning

According to "Keatings History" the name is often taken from the original name of O'Conuing, who was chief in the barony of Small county, in Limerick. They are thus mentioned by O'Heerin;

"Aes Grei of the finest plains,

Was owned by O'Cuning of Crioch Saingil, He cheerfully held the beauteous Grian, From the noble race of Eogan."

The 1890 birth index finds the family most numerous in Co. Antrim.

Graven

Gravenor, Craven ?

We have little information as yet on the Graven family, or on what other spellings may exist of the name. Two possible areas for research include the names of Gravenor and Craven.

Gravenor, which could easily have dropped its 'or' ending, might have been the original spelling of the name. In the census of 1659 the name is found in Ireland, in the City of Cork.

'Craven' could as well be another or earlier form of the name. Milesian families gives the name as a Welsh one, settling in Waterford and Kilkenny. It is also found the 1890 birth index with 9 scattered births recorded.

The above is pure speculation however, and the name may have purely independent origins.

Graves

The family of Graves is found earliest in Offaly, Limerick and Dublin in Ireland. The census of 1659 finds the name in Dublin, Meath and Louth. We also have at least one instance of the name in Bandon, Co. Cork. The 1890 birth index finds the family with 5 recorded births, in scattered locations.

O'Harts work gives one of the name as having served in the Austrian military, as well as the Baron Groves separately.

One family of the name is found in more modern times in the Cloghan Castle in Co. Offaly. This line was a noted Protestant family of the name.

Gregory

Gregry, Gregorie

The Gregory name is found early in Dublin, but it is historically most often associated with Co. Kerry. In more modern times the name is found in Galway, and of that line was the famous Lady Gregory (d.1932).

The Gregory name is also found associated with the siege of Derry in 1689. The census of 1659 finds the name in Tipperary, Waterford and Louth.

Mc Guirk

MAG OIRC

MAGUIRKE, MCGURKE,M'QUIRK,GURK

The McGuirk family of Ireland is found early in Co. Tyrone, and subsequently numerous in Co. Antrim as well. The family traces its descent back to Niall Naoighiallach.

Family members take note of the place name of Ballygurk, in Co. Derry, which denotes an early center for the name there.

The McGuirk family is given as one of the "hereditary keepers" of St. Colmcille's Bell. They served as erenaghs of the parish of Termonmahuirkk in the barony of Omagh, Co. Tyrone. Several of the name are noted in the Hearth Money Rolls, notably in counties Armagh and Monaghan.

The troubles of the 17th century brought an end to the power of this family, as is the case with so many other native Irish family of the region.

The 1890 birth index of Ireland gives the spelling of "McGuirk" with 17 recorded births of the name, mainly in Dublin.

Individuals of the name:

FATHER BRIAN MACGURK--(B.1622).

PATRICK MCGUIRK, AGE 20, GROOM, ABOARD 'JAMESTOWN', JULY 3, 1850.

133

Gwynn

Gwyn, Gwinn, Gwinnett

Families of the name of Gwynn in Ireland are assumed to be of foreign origins when found here. Perhaps the most noted family of the name were the "Gwynnes" of Co. Down, found there after the Cromwellian wars.

The name is also found in Tipperary, Longford and Kildare.

The name of Gwinnett, also rarely but sometimes found in Ireland, may have been shortened to Gwynn or Gwin as well.

Gordon

Gorden

The name of Gordon is that of a settler family in Ulster, often of Scottish origins. This is not surprising, for Gordon ranks among the top 50 most numerous names in Scotland. The 1890 birth index finds the family most numerous in counties Antrim, Dublin and Down.

Greaney

Mac Grainne, O'Grainne

A name traditionally linked to counties Kerry, Limerick and Galway. The 1890 birth index finds the family most numerous in counties Kerry and Galway.

Greehy

Greehey

A name found along the area of the Waterford and Cork borders.

Grehan

Irish Book of Arms plate 260

O'Greachain

Greehan

A name which is often found in the west of Ireland in older records, including counties Galway, Westmeath and Sligo.

Mc Glinchey

Mag Loingsigh

McGlinchy

The family of McGlinchey is found early in Donegal, and subsequently in counties Derry and Tyrone.

Mc Goldrick

A relatively rare surname in Ireland , said to have been a branch of the O'Rourkes of Breffni.

Mc Gonigle

Mac Congail

McGonigal, McGonnegal

A family found anciently in Co. Donegal and subsequently in Co. Derry.

Mc Guigan

Maguigan, McGuckin, McGookin,

The majority of the name of McGuigan are found in the province of Ulster in Ireland. Several variant spellings of the name are known to exist, and are often localized to specific areas. McGuigan is common in Co. Derry, McGookin in Co. Antrim, and McGuckian in Leitrim.

Guest, Guist

Guist

A very rare name in our records, we have to date found only one of possible individual of the name, one "Ethel-Guest" in the pedigree of the Nicholson family of New Rochelle, New York. The name of "Guist" is found in Co.Waterford in the 17th century, and these two names may very well be one and the same.

Given

Giveen, MacKevin, MacAvin

Most of the name of Given and Giveen are linked with the province of Ulster in Ireland. Woulfe states that the name of MacGiven comes from the same source as the names of MacKevin and MacAvin.

Mc Givern

Biggar, Montgomery, McGiverin, McGivi

Families of the name of McGivern are found in counties Armagh, Down and Antrim in the 1890 birth index. The names of Biggar and Montgomery have been officially reported as synonyms of McGivern

Mac Gladdery

McGladdery, McGladery, McGlade,

The name of MacGladdery is one of the province of Ulster for several centuries. One finds the use of both O'Gladdery and MacGladdery, and although most consider them to be one in the same, O'Donovan gives them as completely separate surnames. The spelling of MacGlade has been officially reported as a variant spelling of MacGladdery. MacGlade is given in Antrim and Londonderry in the 19th century.

Some give the names of MacGlade and McGladon as names of Scottish origins as well. McGladon is a name found in Antrim as well.

Glascock

Glasscock

Glascock is found as a principal name of Co. Kildare in the 17th century. Most of the name are given to be of English extraction in our records, and some mention of the name is made in Co. Wexford as well.

Glasgow

Glascow is considered to be a name of the province of Ulster in Ireland. It is found centered in counties Tyrone, Antrim and Armagh in the 19th century birth index. Many of the name may in fact derive it from the city of Glascow, not so distant from the shores of Northern Ireland.

Those of the name in Co. Tyrone may have old Irish origins rather than Scottish.

Mc Glory

Glorney, McGloyre, McClory

McGloyre was a principal name of the city of Dublin in the 17th century, and that name is taken to be a likely variant of McGlory.

134

Godfrey

Gohery, Godfry

In the 17th century Godfrey families are found centered in Cork and Londonderry. Records of the 19th century birth index show the family most often in Mayo, Tipperary and Kerry. The name of Gohery is given to have been used as a synonym with Godfrey. The name may have immediately arrived from England or from the Norsemen, and its ancient origins are said to be Norse.

According to "Keatings History" the name is given as one of the "other" principal English families in Co. Kerry, alongside Fitzmaurice, Brown, Stack and Rice, etc..

Going

Goin, Goine, Gowing

In some cases the name of Going is said to be of English extraction, and Woulfe gives the name to stem from the old Irish family of Mac an Ghobhann , which also gave rise to the names of McGowan and Smith. The name is most often associated with Co. Tipperary in our records.

Gold, Golden

Golding, Goulding, Goldrick, Goldsmith

Families of the name of Gold are found centered in Cork in the 17th century, where many families of the name were said to be of original English extraction.

In the 19th century the name of Golden is found centered in Mayo, Sligo, Kerry and Cork. This can be a complicated matter for Goldrick, Gold and Golding are also synonyms of Golden. Hence we have several families, of entirely different origins found using the same name.

Golding is a name found centered in Galway in the 19th century and McGolrick is found in Tyrone, Fermanagh and Sligo at that time. Another "gold" name, that of Goldsmith could have as well been shortened to Gold. Goldsmith is found settling in Ireland no later than the 17th century with some of the name in Co. Longford.

Mac Gourley

Irish Book of Arms plate 203 (Gorley)

Gorley, O'Gorley, Gourley, McGorly

The MacGourley name is traditionally associated with county Antrim in the north of Ireland. The name of O'Gorley is also found is several sources as another possible spelling of the name of Gorley etc...

Mc Greevy

Macreavy, Magreevy, McGreevey, Creevy

Families of the name of McGreevy are found in counties Down and Antrim in the 19th century. The spelling of Crevy is found in the 17th century in Westmeath, and could possibly be a variant spelling of the name.

Grennan

de Grenan, O'Grennan, Greenan

Families of the name of Grennan are found centered in Mayo and Dublin in the 19th century. They are traditionally linked to Co. Mayo and surrounds in our records.

The old Irish family of the name is to be found in Mayo, and those of County Dublin may be of Norman descent. The name of Greenan is found centered in Co. Cavan and is not a known variant of Grennan.

Gribben

Gribbin, Cribben, O'Gribben, MacGribben

Families of the name are traditionally linked with the province of Ulster in Ireland. The 19th century birth index finds the family centered in counties Antrim, Armagh and Down.

The name is found with both the "O" and "Mac" prefix before it.

Gubbins

Families of the name of Gubbins are traditionally linked with county Limerick in Ireland, and are found there no later than the 17th century. Other families of the name are found in the province of Ulster, but they may be of separate origins altogether.

Glendening

Glandenning

A Scottish family name found settled in Ulster in the 17th century.

Gloster

Glouster

An English family name, likely taken from the place name of Gloucester. Found most often in Limerick and Kerry in our records.

Gorevan

Mac Govern

The name of a family traditionally given in counties Sligo and Mayo, and given in Woulfe's work as a variant spelling of MacGovern. Others, notably MacLysaght, give the name as a variant of Garvin.

Gosnell

The name of a family found in fairly modern times in Co. Cork.

Mac Griskin

Grisken

A family name of Co. Leitrim.

Mac Grotty

A family name most often found in Ulster.

135

Hackett

Irish Book of Arms plates 92, 158

Haket

MacHackett, Haket, Hakett

The Hackett family name is one which arrived with the Norman invasions in the latter half of the 12th century in Ireland. A Norman family name, Hackett is taken from "Haket" a common personal name of Norman origins.

The name is soon found in several counties. In Waterford and Tipperary they are cited as a chief family of English descent.

The place names of Hacketstown, Hackettsland, and Ballyhackett are numerous, being found in Carlow, Derry, Dublin, Antrim, Cork and Waterford.

Castle Hackett is to be found in Co. Galway in the barony of Clare near Tuam, and served as a seat of power for the family in earlier days.

In the 17th century Hackett was a principal name of Tipperary and found in Westmeath as well. Despite the widespread areas the name has been found in earlier days, the 1890 birth index shows the name only in Tyrone, Dublin and Kilkenny.

In the Irish Book of Arms is given Hackett of Riverstown, Co. Tipperary, descended from Robert Hackett of English, Kings County (Offaly)

Hadley

of English origin

Hadly

The name of Hadley is of English origin when found in Ireland with few exceptions. In Milesian families the name is listed as English, arriving 1n 1476 and settling in Limerick and Galway.

O'Hagan

Irish Book of Arms plate158, 264

O'hAodhagain

Hegan, Aiken, O'Hagain, O'Hagane, Fagan

A distinguished name traditionally linked with the province of Ulster, O'Hagan served as the inaugurator of O'Neill, the King of Ulster. The family seat of power was to be found near Tullaghoge, in the barony of Dungannon Upper in Co. Tyrone. The stone chair upon which the O'Neill princes were proclaimed was found here. It was destroyed in 1602 by Mountjoy.

O'Donovan states that O'Hagan inaugurated O'Neill by putting on his golden sandal or slipper, and hence the sandal always appears in the armorial bearings of the O'Hagans.

According to O'Dugan, "O'Hagain, or O'Hagan' was chief of Tulachog in the parish of Desertcreight, in the barony of Dungannon in Tyrone.

In recent years one can see the increased number of O'Hagans in Ireland, but Hagan outnumbers O'Hagan by an almost 2 to 1 ratio in the 1890 birth index.

O'Hagan was found in Antrim, Louth and Down. Hagan was given in Antrim, Tyrone and Armagh at that time.

In the 17th century O'Hagane was a principal name in Co. Limerick and O'Hagan a principal name of Armagh, also found in Londonderry.

According to O'Hart, an O'Hagan of Tirowen acquired standing in Meath by marrying into the O'Melaghlins. DeLacy, by charter granted him lands, titles and interests in Meath. Hence he changed his name to Fagan, and became an ardent supporter of his Anglo-Norman friend and protector.

Hall

Irish Book of Arms plate 30, 90

M'Hall, Hull, Mac Caul

A well known English locative name, which is found in Ireland as well. This family name can be found in the province of Munster from the 1300's, and in the province of Ulster since at least the 1600's.

In Milesian Families the name is given in Dublin, Donegal, Galway and Down, arriving in 1570 from England. In the census of 1659 the name is found in Antrim, Kildare and Down.

In more modern times, the name is found in Antrim, in the 1890 birth index. The Irish Book of Arms gives the family of "Hall of Rowantree and Tully House, Co. Monaghan."

Hallissey

Hallisy

A name traditionally linked to counties Cork and Kerry, as confirmed by the 1890 birth index of Ireland.

Halpin

Halfpenny, Halpenny, Halpen

A name often linked to Dublin, Clare and Limerick in the past, said to stem from O' hAilpin anciently. In Ulster the name has been confused with Halpenny and Halfpenny.

The 1890 birth index finds the family name of Halpin most numerous in counties Dublin and Clare. Halfpenny is given in Co. Louth in that index.

O'Hairnin

According to "Keatings History" the name is listed among the chiefs of Moy Ith. This territory comprised parts of the baronies of Raphoe and Tirkeeran in Derry. Their territory in the 12th century is given as in the north of Co. Tyrone.

136

O'Halloran

Irish Book of Arms plates 158, 215

O'hAllmhrain

Halloron, Hallorin, Hallaron, Hallurane

O'Halloran..etc.. families may spring from two separate origins in Ireland. The first was of Co. Galway and they served as chiefs of Clann Fearghaile, a territory near Lough Corrib.

These O'Hallorans are given by O'Flahertys Ogygia, on the east side of the river of Galway, near Lough Corrib. From this line was descended O'Halloran the historian. According to O'Hart, Clan Fergail territory included Galway city anciently, and the family held a castle at Barna, near the sea, 3 miles west of Galway. They held 24 townlands east of the river "Gallimh", including Roscam, about 3 miles S.E. of Galway. In the 13th century, along with the O'Flahertys, they were driven into west Connaught where they built the castle of O'Hery in Gnomore, and according to tradition the castle of Rinvile, in northern Connemara. According to Hardiman, another O'Halloran family, of Munster, was also present in Thomand.

The Thomand family is found fairly close to the above O'Halloran family, in Clare. They served as chiefs of Faith ui-Hallurain, a territory between the baronies of Tulla and Clare, in Co. Clare, near Lough Derg. This family has also branched out into Limerick.

Due to the close proximity of these two separate families, specific origins in bordering areas may be difficult to figure out. Branches of both families are sure to be found in Limerick.

At the end of the last century O'Halloran was centered only in Limerick, and Halloran was found in Clare, Galway and Cork, according to the birth index.

In 1659 Hallurane and O'Hallurane were principal names of Co. Clare.

Hamilton

Irish Book of Arms plates 11, 43, 45, 75..

Hamiltone, Hamill

Hamilton is the name of a well known Scottish family planted in Ireland who became prominent after settlement. Note the place name of Manorhamilton in Co. Leitrim. The Hamiltons of Ballymoney are noted in the book 'Families of Ballyrashane' by Mullin.

In older records Claude Hamilton is listed as a Scottish Undertaker in the barony of the Fewes, Co. Armagh, during the Ulster plantation. Sir George Hamilton is found in the precinct of Strabane, Co. Tyrone, and Robert Hamilton is found in the precinct of Magheriboy, in Co. Fermanagh. Sir Alexander Hamilton, of Endervicke, Scotland , was found in Tuyllyhunco, in Co. Cavan.

Milesian families gives the name in Dublin, Donegal, Down and Cavan arriving in 1640 from Scotland. In the 1890 birth index the name is found in Antrim, Down, Tyrone, and Londonderry. The spelling of Hamiltone was used in the census of 1659 to record the name in County Down. The arms of one James Hamilton, Earl of Clanbrassil, are found in the 'Irish Book of Arms', among 6 listings for the name.

Included in that work are Hamilton-Stubber of Moyne and Castle Fleming of Queens Co., Hamilton of Kellyleagh Castle, Co. Down, Hamilton of Cornacassa, Co. Monaghan, of whom it is said that two brothers came to Ireland together, one settling in Monaghan and the other in Down, and the family of Barret-Hamilton of Kilmanock House, Co. Wexford. The family of Hamilton of Ballymacoll, Co. Meath, are given in the Irish Book of Arms as well.

Handcock

Irish Book of Arms plate 50

Hancock, Hand

The Handcock family of Carantrila Park, Co. Galway descends from William Handcock of Twyford, in Co. Westmeath. This family is given in the Irish Book of Arms.

The birth index of 1890 finds families of the separate name of Hand centered in Co. Dublin.

O'Hamery

According to "Keatings History" the name is given by O'Heerin apparently on the borders of Tipperary and Kilkenny, alongside O'Dinerty.

Hamill

O'hAghmaill

O'Hamill, Hamil, Hamilton, O'Hammoyle

The family name of Hamill may be of Irish or foreign origin when found in Ireland. Associated with Co. Tyrone, the family was anciently of Cenel Eoghain, and settled into Armagh and Monaghan as well. Here, they were also poets to the O'Hanlon, and the spelling of O'Hammoyle is found. The name may also come from the Scottish name of Hamilton and can be found in Co. Derry in earlier days.

In 1659 the name of 'Hamill' is found in Co. Monaghan, and in the 1890 index the name is given in Antrim, Armagh and Louth. In Keatings History O'Hamill is cited among the chiefs and clans of Tir Eoghain in the 12th century.

O'Hanlon

Irish Book of Arms plates 158, 213

O'hAnluain

Hanlan, Hanlin, Handion, Hanlen

Anciently the O'Hanlons were cited as chiefs of Ui Meith Tiri, "now the barony of Orior" in Armagh, who held the office of hereditary standard bearers of Ulster. In today's words, this means that the O'Hanlons were chiefs of Orior in the baronies of Upper and Lower Orior in Armagh. They are also found in the O'Neilland barony.

In modern times the name has spread further. In the 1890 birth index "O'Hanlon" had 22 recorded births in its homeland of Armagh and in Co. Dublin. Hanlon, without the "O", had 95 births in Dublin, Kerry, Louth and Wexford.

In the 1659 census both O'Hanlen and O'Hanlon were principal names of Armagh as might be predicted. Hanlon was as well a principal name of Kildare and found in Louth at that time, too.

Rev. John Canon O'Hanlon (1821-1905), was the author of "Lives of the Irish Saints" among many other published works.

Hammond

Hamond, Hamon

The earliest families of the name of Hammond in Ireland were of Norse origins, although some of the name are recorded as arriving in more recent times. The family can be found in ancient records in the province of Leinster.

Hamon was said to be an ancient Norman family name brought to Ireland by two "Hamon brothers", who settled at Portarlington in Ireland. The name was said by O'Hart to have sometimes been changed to Hammond.

The 1890 birth index finds the family most numerous in Co. Donegal.

O'Hanly

Irish Book of Arms plates 158, 213

O'hAinle

Hanley, Handly, Henley, Hanily, Hanly

O'Hanly is given anciently as "O'Hainlidhe, or O'Hanleys, chiefs of Kinel Dobhtha", which was a large district in the barony of Ballintober in County Roscommon along the Shannon River. Note the place name of Doohyhanly here in Roscommon.

In the 17th century Hanly and O'Hanly were principal names in Co. Roscommon. With the "ey" ending as Hanley, the name was given in Co. Kildare at that time, as well as Hanely being found in Tipperary.

In the 1890 birth index Hanley is given only in Cork with 35 recorded births. 'Hanly' had some 60 births recorded in Roscommon, Galway, Limerick and Tipperary.

Hanahoe

A name linked with Co. Mayo in Ireland according to our records.

Hanna

Hannah

A settler family from Scotland which settled in Ulster, notably in Antrim and Down. The 1890 birth index finds the family most numerous in Antrim, Down and Armagh.

Hourihane

Hurihane, Hourihan

A name traditionally linked to the western portion of Co. Cork, down unto modern times.

137

O'Hannon

Irish Book of Arms plates 158, 201

O'hAnain

Hanneen, Hannen, Hannin, Hannon

Information on the O'Hannon family is relatively rare when compared to other armigerous families of Ireland.

Traditionally identified with Co. Limerick in Ireland, this family is often found given as a Dalcassion sept cited in Limerick and Clare, and several believed variants of the name are found elsewhere. O'Haneen was a principal name of Clare; Hanin a principal name of Roscommon; and Hanon a principal name of Armagh in the 17th century in the census of 1659.

The numerous spellings of the name are now primarily found in two forms, that of Hannon and Hannan in modern times.

A sometimes separately cited family of the name is found as a tribe of the Ui Maine, or Hy Many, descending possibly from a 4th century King of Connaught. They are found alongside the O'Maddens under the ruling O'Kelly clan of the day, and are anciently found in the southeast portion of Co. Galway, not too far from the Dalcassion sept of the name.

In the 1890 birth index Hannan had 32 births in Cork and Sligo, while Hannon had 44 births in Galway, Roscommon and Limerick.

It is doubtlessly true that in isolated instances other names have been changed to O'Hannon, names like Hanahan of Limerick, and Hanneen of Galway.

The 1659 census given above found the barony of Athlone in Co. Roscommon as a center for the name of O'Hannon, and the Haneens were found in the barony of Bunratty, Co. Clare at that time.

Patrick Hannon (d. 1925) was the discoverer of the gold fields of Kalgoorlie in Australia.

138

O'Hanraghty

Irish book of Arms plates 158, 248

O'hAnrachtaigh

Hanratty

The Hanrattys are anciently found as a family of the territory of Oriel, where they possessed parts of Co. Armagh which was contained in that territory. They are further cited as "of Ui Meith Macha". As Lords of Ui Meith they held lands in the north of Co. Louth.

In the wake of the Norman invasions the family moved into Co. Monaghan, settling in the barony of Cremorne there, and near Castleblaney.

In the 1890 index "Hanratty" was the preferred spelling of the name with some 30 births recorded in Louth, Armagh, Monaghan and Dublin.

Hampston

Hampton, O'Hamson, O'Hanson, Hampson

Our records remain sparse concerning this surname. It is probably of origin outside of Ireland, at least in the beginning of the family tree, likely from England. Of similar sounding names, O'Hanson is found in the census of 1659 as a principal name of county Londonderry. Hampton is found as early as the 1300's, and in the 1600's in Co. Down. The English name of Hampson, may also serve as a form of the name on occasion.

Hampton is found as a name of Ulster in the 1890 index, and is given as a family of Armagh arriving in 1590 from England in Milesian families.

The most likely area to search, given no further information, would be the province of Ulster in Northern Ireland. After this, consider the city of Dublin.

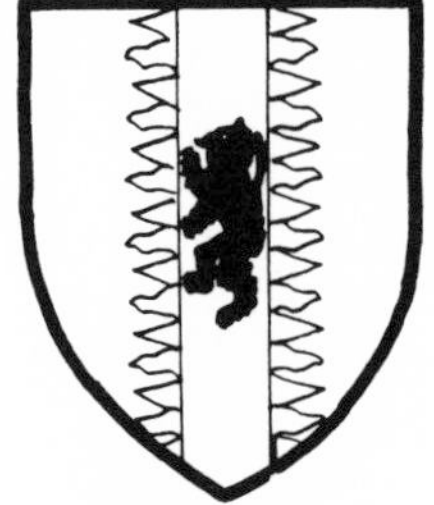

O'Hara

Irish Book of Arms plates 103, 158

O'hEaghra

Harah

O'Hara is one of the few names in Irish history which has consistently kept the "O" before the name. It appears that the O'Haras have outnumbered the Haras at all times in written records, a rare feat considering the pressures that existed to drop the Mac and O from all Irish names. By the time of the 1890 index, 105 O'Haras are found in Sligo, Dublin, and Antrim, and only 5 "Haras", all from Galway.

The family descends from Eaghra, a chief in the barony of Leyney in Sligo. Two branches are found in the 14th century, the "O'Hara Boy" by Colooney, and the "O'Hara Reagh" at Ballyhara.

According to Keatings History: "The O'Haras, a branch of the great family in Sligo, have long been settled in Antrim", and are so to this day.

O'Hara is further cited in more ancient times as: "O'Headra, or O'Hara, chief of Luighni" (Leyney) in Sligo, "but Lieney anciently comprised part of the baronies of Costello and Gallen in Mayo." From the 12th to the 17th century they held their rank as lords of Lieney, and had large possessions to the period of the Cromwellian wars. The O'Haras are thus designated by O'Dugan:

"The Lords of Lieney, of high fame:
The men of Lieney, of warlike swords."

These O'Haras were descended from Olild Olum, King of Munster in the third century. They possessed great lands in Sligo up to the last century. The families of Cooper Hill and Annaghmore held lands and are of note into modern times.

Those in Sligo of English political persuasion are found as "Barons of Tyrawley" in the 18th century.

'The Book of O'Hara' is an ancient work documenting the O'Hara chiefs.

Harkness

Irish Book of Arms plate 22

The Harkness family of Garryfine and Temple Athea, Co. Limerick, who descend from the William Harkness family of Londonderry in the early 18th century, is given in the Irish Book of Arms.

The birth index of 1890 finds the family centered in Antrim.

O'Hanrahan

Irish Book of Arms plate 211

O'hAnrachain

Hourihane, Hourihan, Hanraghane,

The O'Hanraghans are found as a clan of note in Tipperary along with the O'Lanigans and Magraths in more ancient times. They are given as "O'Hindradhain, or O'Hanrahan" chiefs of Corcaraidhe, "now the barony of Corcaree", in the Co. of Westmeath at that time as well.

They have traditionally been considered as a family which originated in Clare and Tipperary, the 2 counties in which they are found in the 1890 birth index, under the spelling of Hanrahan. O'Hart does give them also as chiefs of a district in Co. Tipperary.

Of the variant spellings of the name, Hanrahan is also found as Handrahan in Tipperary. It is further said to spring from the same old Irish name which became Hourahan, and Hanrahan. Hourahan is a name found in Cork.

Spelled as "Hanraghan" the family name is found as a principal one of Sligo in the 17th century. O'Hanraghane was a principal name of Clare, and the without the "O" prefix it was found in Limerick. Spelled as O'Hanrahane it was a principal name of Tipperary at that time.

139

Harman

The Irish Book of Arms plate 84

Harmon

The Harman family of Palace, of Carrigbyrne, Co. Wexford are given in the Irish Book of Arms. The birth index of 1890 finds the family centered in Wicklow, under the spelling of Harmon.

Hargon

Irish Book of Arms plate 245

OhArgain

Hargan, Hourigan, Arragan, O'Hargan,

Hargon is considered a name of county Cork in Ireland. It is also used as a form of Hourigan in Limerick, Arragan in Waterford and Tipperary. The name of Hargan is found in the birth index with 5 births, concentrated in the province of Ulster.

O'Hargan is cited in Milesian families, as an ancient Irish family of Clanna Rory, in County Cork.

Harkins

O hEarcain

Harkin

While Harkin is sometimes found in England, in Ireland the name may stem from the older spelling of OhEarcain. This Irish family served as Erenaghs of Inishowen, and have been associated with the county of Donegal.

In Milesian families the name is given in Dublin and Cork, arriving in 1171 from Wales. The name is also given in the surname index of Keatings History of Ireland. Spelled as Harkin, the name is found in the 1890 index as a family of Donegal and Londonderry, with 32 births in the former, and 8 births in the latter county given.

Harold

Irish Book of Arms plate 61

Harrold, Haroid

Harold families in Ireland may trace their ancestry back to Dublin, where "Harolds Cross" is to be found or back to Co. Limerick where individuals of the name are found in public service. They are a family given to be originally of Norse origins. They are cited several times in both Limerick and Clare in olden times.

In more modern times the name has been found in Cork and Kerry.

An older form of the name is given to be Haroid, and is given as such in O'Harts work.

The Irish Book of Arms gives the family of Harold-Barry of Ballyvonare, Co. Cork. They were originally of Harolds Cross, Dublin and subsequently of Singland and Pennywell in Co. Limerick.

O'Harney

Oh Athairne

Harny, Haherney, O'Harney

The Irish family of Harney is found in Tipperary and Galway in the 1890 birth index. Spelled as Harny the name is found as a principal one of Waterford, and also in Roscommon in 1659. Spelled as O'Harney the name is listed in Keatings History of Ireland.

Haherney is given as an earlier spelling of the name, and the family is said to have been traditionally located in Roscommon and the province of Connaught.

Hallinan

Irish Book of Arms plate 203

O'hAilgheanain

Halinan, Hallinane

A name traditionally linked to counties Cork, Limerick and Tipperary, and the 1890 birth index finds the family most numerous in Co. Clare.

O'Hart

Irish Book of Arms plates 49, 159

O'hAirt

Harte, Hairt, Hart

The O'Hart family is one of the noted "Four Tribes of Tara", along with O'Regan, O'Kelly and O'Connolly. These tribes of Tara are also described as princes of Bregia, and appear to have possessed territories near Tara in Meath, along with areas in Co. Dublin. They were known as "Lords of Teffia".

With the coming of the Norman invasions the family is found settling in the barony of Carbury in Sligo. Here in Sligo they were a family of note with large holdings of land until the coming of Cromwell in the 17th century.

The O'Harts are said to descend from "Art" the son of "Conn of the Hundred Battles". The "O" prefix before the name has long been dropped by most families. The preferred spellings of the name are as "Harte", which had 58 births in Sligo, Leitrim and Roscommon, and "Hart" which had 64 births in Antrim, Dublin and Cork, in the 1890 index.

John O'Hart (1824-1870), wrote "Irish Pedigrees, the origin and stem of the Irish Nation", a tremendous genealogical compilation. He includes much there-in on the O'Harts of Sligo, which may be of interest to family researchers.

The Irish Book of Arms contains several listings, including Hart-Synot of Ballymoyer, Co. Armagh.

The "Family History of Hart of Donegal" was published in 1907 by H. T. Hart.

140

O'Hartigan

Irish Book of Arms plates 159, 217

O'hArtagain

Hartagan, Hartican, Hart

The Hartigan family is primarily found in the counties of Clare and Limerick in older records that we have researched. It is here that the family likely originated, in and about the old territory of Thomand.

This is rather a rare family name in Ireland, with only 16 births of the name recorded in 1890, all of those were in Co. Limerick. In the census of 1659 "O'Hartigan" was given as a principal name of Co. Clare as well.

One early record of the name shows that "Dunlaing O'Hartigan" fought at the battle of Clontarf, led by the last High King of all Ireland, Brian Boru, in his battle against the Danes.

O Hare

Irish Book of Arms plate 245

O hIr, OhEir.

Hare, Haire

The name of Hare, of course, is common in England, but in Ireland the name is said to be most often of Irish origin. It is one of the few names which retained the 'O' prefix when other names temporarily dropped theirs. O'Hare is the Irish family of the name, and was of Oriel and county Armagh. The center of the family was in the barony of Oriel, in County Armagh. The name remains in that area to this day, having spread into Antrim, Down and Louth. The 1890 index shows the name in Antrim, and as O'Hare in Armagh, Louth and Down.

Milesian families lists the name as an ancient Irish one being of the Eoganacht tribe in Clare and Armagh.

O'Hartley

Irish Book of Arms plate 80

O'Hartgoile

Hartley, Hartly

According to "Keatings History" the name is given as belonging to the chief of Crioch na g Cinel, "a delightful district In the land of the fertile soil, A country the fairest under the sun, Its rightful heir is O'Hartley." They are further given as having their lands adjoining those of O'Larkin.

The Hartley family of Beech Park, Co. Dublin, is given in the Irish Book of Arms and may be of foreign origins.

Harford

Hereford, Hertford

We find the name of Harford as a principle one of Dublin in the 17th century, and it is still centered there in the 19th century records at our disposal. Of likely English origins, coming from the place name of Hereford etc.., the family name has been in Ireland for many centuries. Earlier records of the family also show the name in Co. Kilkenny.

The 1890 birth index finds the family most numerous in Co. Dublin.

Hargadon

Hargadenm, Hargedon

A name traditionally associated with Co. Sligo in Ireland. The 1890 birth index finds the family most numerous in Sligo, Leitrim and Roscommon.

Harvey

Irish Book of Arms plate 88, 92

Harvy, Hervey, Hervie, Harvey,

The Harvey family is given as settling in Ireland from England originally. The family is said to have joined Strongbow upon arrival here. They are as well given as one of the 'adventurers for land' in Ireland during the Cromwellian period. They are found at or near Bargy, in Co. Wexford. Several old Irish families may have 'translated' their names into Harvey as well. O'Harrihy is one such example, and O'Hart gives Garvey as another possibility.

In more modern times the name is of the province of Ulster, in the north of Ireland.

One of the name was a Col. in the Irish Legion in the service of France in the year 1814.

The Irish Book of Arms gives the family of Malin Hall of Co. Donegal. Another family of the name, of Mintiaghs, Co. Donegal are also found with their name spelled as Hervey, as well as Harvey.

The Hervey family of Killian are given in the Irish Book of Arms. The birth index of 1890 finds the family centered in Antrim, Dublin, Down and Donegal when spelled as Harvey.

Hollywood

According to "Keatings History" the name is that of a principal family of Dublin city or county, and of Anglo-Norman descent. The 1890 birth index finds the family most numerous in Co. Louth.

Hoyne

The name of Hoyne is traditionally linked with the county of Kilkenny in Ireland, centered near Thomastown in many of our records.

Hatton

The Irish Book of Arms plate 105

The Hatton family of Clonard, Co. Wexford, is first found in 17th century Ireland, coming originally from co. Northampton. The birth index of 1890 finds the family centered in Leinster and Ulster, with 7 scattered births of the name.

Hannigan

Irish Book of Arms plate 201

O hAnnagain

Hennigan, Hannagan

A name fairly widely dispersed in Ireland by the time of the 1890 birth index. The 1890 birth index finds the family most numerous in counties Dublin, Waterford and Tyrone.

Hardy

Harty, Hardiman, Hard

Hardy families are assumed to be of English origins when found in Ireland. Some Irish families may have 'changed' their name into this form however, based upon the gaelic word for "hard". It is possible that the name of Hardiman was shortened to Hardy also. Hardiman is a name of Co. Galway.

We find families of the name in Dublin in 1659, and in Louth, Dublin and Tyrone in the 19th century.

Hahn

Haghen, Haughan

Hahn may be a variant spelling of other names when found in Ireland. Several possibilities exist as to the original spelling. Consider every name that begins with Han or Haugh.

The most likely origin is that of Haughan or Haghen. Haghen is found in the birth index of 1890 and was said to be traditionally located in Cootehill Union (of Monaghan and Cavan).

Hawkins

Irish Book of Arms plate 34

John and Joseph Hawkins appear in the rolls of the military in Ireland in the mid 17th century, and are listed as receiving lands in Ireland for their services.

One family of the name is also found centered in Loughrea, Co. Galway, and members of that family are said to have settled in New Richmond, Wisconsin, USA.

The Hawkins family of St. Fenton's, Co. Dublin are found in the Irish Book of Arms.

The birth index of 1890 finds the family centered in Antrim, Galway and Cork.

Harbison

Harbinson, Harbeson, Harvison, Herbeson

A name generally given to be of Ulster Scots origins found settled mainly in Co. Antrim there. Some of the name may be of English origins as well. In Co. Down we find the name confused with "Herbert".

The 1890 birth index finds the family most numerous in Co. Antrim.

Hardiman

Students of Irish history will note the renowned James Hardiman (d.1855), who was a writer and a lawyer. Among his works are "The History of Galway" (1820), and "Irish Minstrelsy" (1831). He was said to have been a native of Galway, where he spent much of his last years.

The 1890 birth index finds the family most numerous in Co. Galway.

Hayes, Hays

Irish Book of Arms plates 159, 242

O'hAodha

O'Hea, Heys, Hoy, Heas, O'Hugh

There are several unrelated families of the Hayes name found in Ireland. The older Irish name of O'Hea has often been changed to Hayes, and Woulfe gives over 10 families who changed from the older O'hAoda to O'Hea and Hayes. O'Hea itself remained as the main spelling in Co. Cork, but Hayes is also most often found in that county in the 1890 index.

Keatings History finds the O'Heas as chiefs of Pobble O'Hea in the barony of Carberry in Cork. Further, "O'Haodha, O'Hea or Hayes" was found as chief of Musgraidhe Luachra, which lay between Kilmallock and Ardpatrick, in the barony of Coshlee in Co. Limerick.

"O'Haodha, supposed to be Hughes or O'Hea, chief of Olba (probably Odra or Oddor), in the barony of Skrine near Tara" is one family of the name.

In Kildare "O'Hugh or O'Hea" was given as a chief of Ui Mella.

Hayes may come from de la Haye, and Hayes is given as one of the chief Anglo-Norman families in Wexford. This is likely, for Hayes is a common English name, and de la Haye is a Norman name found early in Ireland.

In the 17th century both Hea and O'Hea were principal names in Clare, and found in Cork, Limerick, Kerry, Tipperary and Waterford. Hayes has likely replaced Hea and O'Hea in several of these areas. "Hayes", at the time of the 1659 census was found in Cork, and "Hay" was a principal name of Wexford.

The 1890 birth index shows "Hay" as a name of Ulster, but as "Hayes" the name is more often found in Cork, Limerick, Tipperary, and Dublin, among others.

The name itself, means descendant of Aodh (Hugh) most likely, as does the name of Hughes in Ulster.

Heard

The Irish Book of Arms plate 96

The Heard family of Kinsale and Pallastown, Co. Cork, is said to have been founded in Ireland by a family member who arrived in Cork with Sir Walter Raliegh in 1579 as given in the Irish Book of Arms.

Hanvey

Irish Book of Arms plate 253

O'Ainbith

Hanvy

According to "Keatings History" the name is given as a chief of Ui Eachach Coba, "now the barony of Iveagh", in or near Co. Down. 4 of 5 recorded births of the name are found in Ulster in the 1890 birth index.

Hassan

Hassen

This family is linked to Co. Derry in Ireland, and is often found in the Sperrin Mountain district there.

Hyland

Hylan, Hiland, Hilan

Early records find this family in Waterford, and subsequently in the surrounds of Co. Kilkenny. The 1890 birth index finds the family name spelled as Hyland most numerous in Mayo, Dublin and Queens. When spelled as Hiland the name is given most often in Co. Antrim.

O'Heffernan

Irish Book of Arms plates 159, 211

O'hIfearnain

Hiffernan, O'Heffernain, Heffernane

"O'Ifernan, or O'Heffernain" was chief of Uaithne Cliach, which was a territory in the barony of Owney and Arra in the county of Tipperary most anciently. In Keatings History it is said that they were a branch of the O'Heffernans of Clare.

In Co. Clare, the family is found centered in the barony of Inchiquin, near Corofin, from whence it is believed they settled across the Shannon River into the barony of Owneybeg in Co. Limerick. The Ryan family would later assume dominance in that area as well.

In the "Book of Rights" the O'Heffernans are found cited as one of the four tribes of Owney.

"Heffernan" remained centered at the end of the last century in Tipperary. It is given only in that county in the birth index for that period.

In the 17th century Heffernane was found in Limerick in the 1659 census, and Hiffernane was a principal name in Clare, being found in Limerick and Tipperary as well.

The book "The Heffernans and their times", was published by Patrick Heffernan in London, in 1940.

Hosty

Mac Oiste

Hasty, Mac Costy, Mac Costey, Mac

Hosty families are traditionally linked with counties Mayo and Galway in Ireland. Hasty or Hastie has also been given as a variant spelling of the name, and in some cases that name has become Hastings according to reports.

142

O'Hegarty

Irish Book of Arms plate 159

O'Heigceartaigh

Haggarty, Hegerty, Hagerty, Eagerton,

The O'Hegarty family is associated with areas in Ulster and strangely enough far to the south of Ireland in Co. Cork. Both families are said to descend from the same line of Ulster. Most anciently the family can be found near the Donegal/Derry border.

They are found centered in this area at various times in the baronies of Tirkeenan and Loughinsholin in Derry, and in the barony of Inishowen in Co. Donegal.

In Co. Cork the family is found in the baronies of Carbery West and Barrymore. This branch of the family was found most numerous in the 1890's birth index followed by those of the name in Donegal, Clare, Londonderry and Mayo.

Of the variant spellings of the name in the 17th century, "O'Hegertie" was a principal name of Cork, "O'Hegerty" of Donegal, and "O'Heggertye" of Londonderry. Although popular at that time, the 'O' prefix before the name has largely been dropped moving into modern times.

In O'Hart we find one William Stuart Hagerty of London, b. 1836, whose ancestors settled in England for 200 years, before his daughter returned to Ireland marrying an O'Leary connected with the slate trade in the vale of Avoca. Hence, this Hagerty from England was really Irish.

Harty

A name traditionally found in counties Cork, Kerry and Tipperary in Ireland.

143

Hemphill

Irish Book of Arms plate 42

The Hemphill family of Springhill have been most associated with the city of Dublin in our records. The birth index of 1890 finds the family centered in Londonderry and Tyrone.

Harrington

O'Hungerdell

Harroughten, Harington, Heraghty

The name of Harrington is of both English and Irish origins when found in Ireland. The family is found in Dublin for several centuries now, with the census of 1659 locating the family there at that time. Many of these are said to be of English origin.

Harrington families are also associated with Counties Cork and Kerry, and the name is more likely of Irish origins in that area of the country. In Kerry, the name may come from the old gaelic spelling of O'Hingerdell or O'Hungerdell (OhIongardail). Hungerdell, an early form of Harrington for some families, is found in the census of 1659 as a principal name in the barony of Kinalmeaky in Co. Cork.

Keatings History finds that the "O'Aireachtains" Anglicized their name to Harrington, and they were a clan of the Ui Mani, in Co. Galway. These may have spread into the nearby Mayo areas as well.

In the 1890 birth index Harrington families had some 119 births recorded in their names, mainly in Cork, Kerry and Mayo. The name remains one of Cork to this day.

Also given is one Sir Henry Harrington, who was knighted at Christ Church, Dublin, in 1574.

Henchy

Irish Book of Arms plate 87 (Henchy)

Hennessy

The name of Henchy is said to stem from the name of Hennessy, and is found in Co. Clare most often.

Harris

of likely English origin

Harrihy

Families of the name of Harris are usually of foreign extraction in Ireland. Most were planter families of English heritage. Milesian families gives the name as one of Limerick and Tipperary arriving in 1642 in England. The census of 1659 finds the name in Limerick, Dublin, Antrim and Cork. In more modern times the 1890 index finds the name in Dublin, Cork and Antrim. Harrihy has been given as a related spelling on occasion.

One pedigree of Harris of Devonshire England, shows one of the family who died at Cahirenony, Co. Cork in 1636, and who was buried at Kilcredan, Co. Cork.

Harrison

Harrison, Harisson, Harrisen

One of the top 30 most numerous names in England, most are of English origins when found in Ireland. As would be expected, most of the name are found in Ulster and in Dublin.

The 1890 birth index finds the family most numerous in Antrim, Dublin and Down.

Halligan

Halligham, Hallaghan

A name traditionally linked to Armagh and Louth. Confusion exists between this name and the name of Hallaghan.

The 1890 birth index finds the family most numerous in Roscommon, Dublin, Louth, Armagh and Mayo.

Hendrick

Irish Book of Arms plate 56

Mac Annraic

McHendrick, Henrick

The Hendrick or McHendrick name stems from the older form of Mac Annraic, which is of Norse origin meaning Henry. In County Wexford the name is considered to be part of the Mac Murrough clan. In modern times the name has been found in Dublin.

The Irish Book of Arms gives the family of Hendrick-Aylmer of Kerdiffstown, Co. Kildare.

The birth index of 1890 finds the family centered in Dublin.

O Hartnett

O'hAirtneada

Harknett, Harnett, Hartnetty, Hartnet.

The Hartnett name is traditionally associated with counties Cork and Kerry. Records of landowners in that area will quickly confirm this. They are found centuries ago in the province of Munster, and are considered to have originally come from county Cork. Milesian families gives the name as a Norman one, settling in Kerry in 1171.

The 1890 birth index finds the family most numerous in Limerick and Cork.

Hastings

Hestings, Histon, Hestin, Hestion

Hastings is a well known English family name, though some of the name in Ireland, in Co. Clare and surrounds may well be of Irish origins. Several Irish families are said to have changed their names into Hastings, among them are the families of Histon and Hestin. The 1890 birth index centers the family in Mayo and Clare, while undocumented sources also find the family in Co. Cork in the wake of the Norman invasions.

144

Henn

Irish Book of Arms plate 22

The arms of Francis Blackburne Henn, of Paradise Hill, Co. Clare, Barrister-at-Law, Resident Magistrate, Co. Sligo are given in the Irish Book of Arms. Of relatively recent introduction into Ireland.

Hartray, Hartry

Hart, Harty, O'Hart

Hartray or Hartry is a rare name in Ireland. In more ancient times one can find record of this family in the province of Connaught, and researchers have reported the name in the Waterford and Tipperary areas there.

Some people of the name of "Hart" or Harty, may actually be Hartray in disguise, as a result of shortening the name simply to Hart. That is another family altogether.

A check of the Irish phone book reveals some of the name of "Harty" in Tipperary and Cork in modern times.

O'Haverty

According to "Keatings History" the name is given as that of the chiefs in the barony of Athenry, in Co. Galway.

Hoban

Hobane, Huban, Hubane

The Hoban family is found centered in Mayo and Kilkenny in the 19th century. Undocumented reports also give the name in Limerick in the 17th century, and of German origins in that one instance if true.

O'Hennessy

Irish Book of Arms plates 41, 159

O'hAonghusa

Hensey, Henchy, Henesy, Hennesy,

O'Haengusa, or O'Hennessy was chief of Clan Colgan. The name means descendant of Aonghus or Angus. This family was centered near Kilbeggan next to the hill of Croghan in the north of Offaly. Here they are found along with O'Hamhirgen and spoken of thusly;

"Another chief who is known to us, O'Hennesey who rules over Clan Colgan His lands are fair beyond those of the Fenians of Fal, He closely adjoins the borders of Croghan".

The above Hennessys who were also of the barony of Lower Phillipstown of Offaly, are credited with having spread into Tipperary and Clare as well.

O'Dugan further mentions O'Hennesey, chief of "Galena Beg", now the parish of Gallen, in the barony of Gerrycastle, near the river Liffey on the Meath/Dublin border. This branch apparently declines with the Norman invasions of the 12th century.

In Westmeath, "O'Haengusa, or O'Hennesy, chief of Ui-Mac-Uais, now the barony of Moygosh", ruled the original territory of the MacEvoys (MacVeaghs).

Another O'Hennessy family is found in Co. Cork, by Rosscarbery. Note the place name of Ballyhennessy there.

Of the variant spellings of the name in the 17th century "Henesy" was a principal name of Limerick, "Henessy" a principal name of Clare, and also in Tipperary, Waterford and Kilkenny. "Hennessy" was found in Clare at that time as well. Of their original territory in Kings (Offaly), both Hensie and Hensey are found in that area, and are likely variant spellings of the name.

By the time of the 1890 birth index "Hennessy" is found in Cork, Limerick, Tipperary and Dublin.

Mc Henry, McEniry

Irish Book of Arms plates 154, 233

Mac Inneirghe, O'hInneirghe

MacEninry, Mac Henry, O'Henry,

As most of the above surname have changed the name to 'Henry' by now, it is fitting to study the matter in some detail.

The name of Henry or MacHenry is primarily found in the north of Ireland, although it can be found elsewhere. Henry may be of Scots, Anglo-Norman, or old Irish origins.

(Mac)Henry or Henery can descend from O'hInneirghe, the Irish chieftain of Cullentra in Co. Tyrone, who also held sway in parts of Co. Derry.

In Co. Limerick MacHenry may be used for the older Mac Inneirghe or MacEniry. This family hailed earliest from the barony of Upper Costelloe in Co. Limerick near Castletown MacEnery.

Fitzhenry, also shortened to Henry by dropping the Fitz prefix, arrived in Ireland with the coming of the Anglo-Norman invasions of the 12th century.

Other 'Henrys' may be of more recent arrival in Ireland, arriving with the Scottish and English settlers from the 17th century. They are assumed to be concentrated in Ulster and Dublin.

Mac Eneiry is cited in the Annals of Irish history as chief of the Corca Muikedha, or the barony of Upper Connello as:

'Mac Eneiry, hero of precious gems,
Rules Corca Muikeda of the mounds;
A noble Fenian who doth flourish,
As doth fair bloom on Apple tree.'

In the 1890 index some 132 births of 'Henry' were found primarily in Antrim, Sligo and Tyrone. McHenry had some 14 births in Antrim, Londonderry and Limerick, while McEniry had only 5 births in all.

145

Hepenstal

Irish Book of Arms plate 56

Hempenstal, Hempstall

The name of a family traditionally linked with Co. Wicklow in Ireland, and of English origins. The are found in Wicklow with some possessions no later than the 18th century. One undocumented source also gives a Wicklow family of the name of Hepenstall a German origin, arriving there in the year 1718 a.d., this appears unlikely however.

Hassett

?

O'Hassey, Hasset, Hasett, Haset, Blenner

The Hassett family is found traditionally linked with counties Clare and Tipperary in Ireland. In the census of 1659 we find families of the name of Hassett in Co. Kerry, (and families of Blenner Hassett or Bleuer Hasset in Co. Fermanagh).

Under the name of O'Hassey, they are cited as chiefs of "Kinel Tighearnaigh". We have no proof however that these families were one and the same.

It is also interesting to note that the name is not a numerous one in Britain, leading one to believe that most of the name are of other, or Irish origins.

The 1890 birth index shows 11 born of the name, primarily in Clare and Tipperary, as would be expected.

Hosford

Horsford, Horseford

The Hosford family is traditionally linked to Co. Cork in Ireland. Records of the family name appear in the 17th century, and they are given as English in origin.

Herbert

Irish Book of Arms plate 22, 93

A Huguenot family of Ireland as given in some instances. One Herbert family, those of Muckruss, Co. Kerry, in Ireland from the 17th century, are given in the Irish Book of Arms. The Herbert Family of Cahirnane Co. Kerry is found in that source as well. The birth index of 1890 finds the family centered in Dublin and Limerick.

Haughton

Houghton, Haghan, Hotten

Most of the name of Haughton and Houghton in Ireland are of likely English extraction, although a few of the name will be found to be of old Irish families, due to the 'translation' of the name from gaelic into English.

We find record of some of the name in Dublin and Cork in the 18th century, of English extraction. In the 17th century the family is found centered in Dublin and Wexford. One of the name is found as Mayor of Waterford in the 17th century as well.

Hayden

One family of the name is found in Ballymorren, Co. Tipperary in the early 17th century. The 1890 birth index finds the family most numerous in Dublin, Carlow and Tipperary.

Haughey

Hoy

The name is found centered in the Donegal/Armagh region of Ireland in the 1890 birth index.

Hewitt

Irish Book of Arms plate 58

Hewet, Hewett, Hewetson, Hewison,

Hewitt families are generally assumed to be of English extraction when found in Ireland. In more modern times the family is found centered in the province of Ulster, found primarily in Antrim and Armagh. Early records however, often find the family in Co. Cork in the 17th century, and subsequently in Dublin. The census of 1659 gives the family in Clare and Cork as well.

Of the origins of the name itself, it comes from a form of "Hugh", in England. The name of Hewetson, from which some of the name of Hewitt may come, is found in Co. Kilkenny in the 17th century.

The 1890 birth index finds the family most numerous in Antrim and Armagh.

Hearne

Irish Book of Arms plate 242

Hearn, Ahearn, Ahearne

We find families of the name most often in Co. Waterford in Ireland. The name can be of English origins, or it can be of Irish origins when taken as a shortened form of O'Ahearne.

Hearty

Harty

We find the family centered in Louth and Monaghan. The similarly spelled name of "Harty", found in the province of Munster, far to the south of the Hearty homeland, has caused much confusion. Needless to say, these two names have been interchanged often, and they likely represent two completely unrelated families.

146

O'Hickey

Irish Book of Arms plates 159, 230

O hIcidhe

Hickie, Hicky

The O'Hickey (O hIcidhe) family is found serving as hereditary physicians to the O'Briens of Thomand in more ancient times. The name is likely taken from the gaelic word meaning 'healer'. A Dalcassion sept, historically they are found in Clare, Limerick, Tipperary and in Cork and Dublin in the 1890 birth index.

Spelled as 'Hickey' the name is listed as a principal name of Cork and is also found in Kildare in the census of 1659. Spelled as Hickie the name is listed as a principal one of Co. Clare, also being found in Limerick and Kildare at that time. With the 'O' prefix, as O'Hickie and O'Hicky it is found as a principal name of County Limerick.

Found simply as 'Hicky" the name is given in 1659 as a principal name of Clare, and was also found in Limerick, Tipperary, Waterford, Carlow and Kilkenny. In modern times, the name could have easily changed from one form to the other.

An article entitled 'The O'Hickeys', by J. Hickey can be found in the N. Munster Antiquarian Society Journal, v. VIII no. 1, 1958.

Heaphy

A name found centered in counties Waterford and Cork in the 19th century. The 1890 birth index finds the family most numerous in Co. Cork.

Heaney

O' hEighnigh

Heany

The family is linked to the old Territory of Oriel in Ireland anciently. In modern times the name is often found in Armagh, Louth and Antrim.

Hickman

Irish Book of Arms plate 46

The Hickman family of Fenloe, Co. Clare is found in the Irish Book of Arms as is the Hickman family of Tyredagh Castle and Kilmore, Co. Clare.

O'Hea

Hay, Haye

According to "Keatings History" the name is found in Carberry, where the family served as chiefs of Pobble O'Hea.

The family is found centered in the 17th century in Gleann-a-Rouska, and this was of the Desmond line of the family. The family name is also found in West Barry-Roe, in 1720. In the latter 19th century the family name is found settled in Woodfield and Keelrovane in Lasavaird, Clonakilty. Also in Bullerstown in Bandon.

Heaslip

Hazlip, Heyslip, Heslip, Heslop, Hayslip,

Families of the name of Heaslip, etc.. are most often found in the province of Ulster during the last several centuries.

Hederman

Hedroman, O'Hedroman, Hettroman,

The name of a family given to be of old Irish origins, and traditionally linked with Co Clare.

Heavy

Heavey

Families of the Heavy or Heavey name are given in the 19th century birth index as scattered throughout Ireland, with the exception that the name is not found in the province of Ulster. Both of the above spellings were used then, in about equal numbers. The family is often linked with Athlone, Co. Roscommon.

Hickson

Irish Book of Arms plate 38

The Hickson family of Fermoyle, Co. Kerry, descends from a Co. Cambridge family, in Ireland from the late 16th century.

Heffron

Haverin, Hevron, Havron, Haveron

The name of Heffron, etc.., is most often found in the province of Ulster in Ireland, and the 1890 birth index gives us all of the name in Co. Mayo as well.

Mac Hale

Irish Book of Arms plate 203

Mac Ceile

Hale, MacKeal, Howell, MacCail

The Mac Hales are a well established family of Co. Mayo, a place where nearly all of the name have remained centered up until the end of the 19th century. They served as erenaghs of Killala in Co. Mayo.

O'Hart cites "MacHale" of Tubbernavine, parish of Addergoole, Co. Mayo. Here, one John MacHale archbishop of Tuam, was the first of his family to spell his name so. His grandfather and father spelled it as MacKeal, and older ancestors spelled in as Mac Cail.

"Hale", which may be formed by dropping the "Mac" prefix of MacHale, is also a name of foreign origins in Ireland. Hale is found as a chief family of English descent in counties Waterford and Tipperary. In these counties, as in Ulster, the name of "Hale" may more likely be of foreign origin in most cases.

In the 17th century McHale was found in Limerick and Kilkenny. The index of 1890 however gives McHale exclusively as a Mayo name. "Hale" at this time was found in Cork and Antrim.

147

O'Higgin

Irish Book of Arms plates 159, 250

OHuigin

Higgins, Hagans, Higgens, Higins,

O'Higgins and its variant spellings rank as one of the 100 most numerous names in Ireland. Higgens may be of either Irish or English origins. The Irish likely descend from OhUigin.

The family is traditionally linked with the barony of Tirerril in Co. Sligo. O'Higgins has been cited as a notable clan of Westmeath. Several of the name are found as property owners in the west of Ireland in the 19th century.

In Keatings History, O'Higgins is found as a clan of note in Westmeath. In the 17th century O'Higgan was a principal name of Kings, being found as well in Queens and Roscommon. O'Higgin was a principal name of Roscommon, and found in Sligo in that era. O'Higin, was given as a principal name of Roscommon.

By the close of the last century Higgins is given in Mayo, Galway, Dublin, Roscommon , Cork and Antrim, with half of the estimated population of the name in Connaught.

Higginson, a name of separate origins, can probably be found shortened to Higgins on occasion. In the 1890 index Higginson was given only in Antrim.

In 1677 William Higgin was granted 26 townlands in Galway and Roscommon that had been forfeited in 1641 by the Bermingham family. The lands of Carropadden, Beagh and Keeloge, were in the possession of Thomas Higgins of Tuam, in 1877. According to O'Hart, these lands were originally granted in consideration of the family estates in Westmeath, which had been confiscated by Cromwell.

Bernardo O'Higgins (1780-1846) was known as the 'liberator' of Chile. Several of the name were distinguished poets of Ireland.

Higginson

The Irish Book of Arms plate 89

The Higginson family of Carnalea House, Co. Down, was founded in Ireland by one of the name who accompanied William III to Ireland. The birth index of 1890 finds the family centered in Co. Antrim.

O'Hehir

O hAichir

Hare, O'Hare, Hegher

The family name of O'Hehir, Hare or Hehir, etc.. is traditionally linked with Co. Clare and the old territory of Thomand. O'Heerin cites O'Haitchir or O'Hehir as chief of Hy Flanchadha and Hy Cormac in the barony of Islands in Co. Clare.

The family name remained centered in Co. Clare in the 1890 birth index with 28 births of the name, all given counties Clare and Limerick. The spelling of the name at that time was given as Hehir.

They were thus designated by O'Heerin:

"Of the race of Eogan of Oirir Cliach
Are the Ui Cormaic of the fair plain,
To O'Hehir belongs the fertile country,
A lord from whom great nobles sprung....
Chiefs who are powerful in each house
Are of the noble clans of O'Hehir, They rule over Ui Flancha of hospitable mansions, They are noble and well armed Fenian warriors"

Hendron

Hendry, Henderson

The name of a family traditionally linked with Co. Armagh in Ireland. The use of Henderson has been officially recorded as a synonym of Hendron.

Hingston

The Irish Book of Arms plate 80

Higstone

The Hingston family of Aglish, Co. Cork descends from an officer in the Parliamentary army in the time of Charles I. The family settled in Co. Cork, and came to purchase Aglish, East Muskerry.

O'Heitigein

O'Etigan, Hetigan

According to "Keatings History" the name is listed among the chiefs of Moy Ith. This territory comprised parts of the baronies of Raphoe and Tirkeeran in Derry. Their territory in the 12th century is given as in "three districts called Teallach Caghalain, Teallach Duibhailbe, and Teallach Braenain."

Helm

not of likely gaelic origin

Helme, Hulme

The name of Helm is not of likely Irish origin. The name of Hulme, of similar sound, is found in County Kildare in the census of 1659. O'Brien, in his noted works published by the American Irish Historical Society, found two of the name spelled as Helme. As follows:

Benjamin and Elizabeth Helme, Grantors of Land in 1799 a.d., New York City.

Obadiah Helme and wife, June 18, 1794, Grantors of Land, New York City.

Heraghty

Heraty, Heraughty

Found in Donegal and Mayo in the 1890 birth index of Ireland.

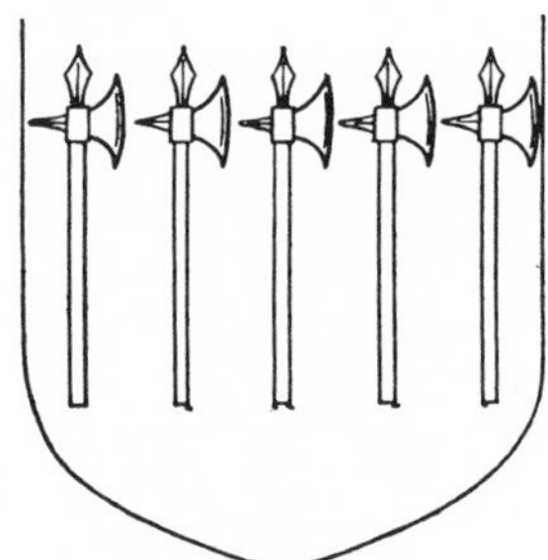

Hodder

The Irish Book of Arms plate 93

The Hodder family of Fountainstown, Co. Cork and of Inveresk, Belfast are given to be of the same family and are given in the Irish Book of Arms.

Hallaghan

Hallahan, Hallagan, Halligan

A name traditionally linked to the counties of Cork and Waterford. Some confusion may exist between this name and the name of Halligan, although Halligan is traditionally found far to the north of the Cork/Waterford area.

The 1890 birth index finds the family most numerous in Co. Cork.

Henebry

Hynebry, Hanebry, Henneberry

The Henebry family name is rare in Ireland in modern times, but researchers have found reference to the family quite early in Dublin, and subsequently in Kilkenny and Waterford.

One original spelling of the name was found to be as de Hynteberge in Co. Dublin.

Some of the name of Henneberry may have shortened the name to Henebry as well. The 1890 birth index finds the family name of Henneberry most numerous in Waterford and Tipperary.

Henehan

Heneghan, Henihan, Henikan

The name of Henehan is linked with Co. Mayo in Ireland, and it is found as a synonym of the name of "Bird" in Tuam Union, Co. Galway, not far from Mayo.

O'Hogan

Irish Book of Arms plates 160, 209

O h Ogain

Ogan, Hogin, Hogen, Hogane, Hogain

The Hogan family is found centered in the territory of Thomand, and they are often cited as a Dalcassion family. The head of the family was seated at Ardcony, in the barony of Lower Ormond in Tipperary, near Nenagh. They held territories in Clare as well. Note the place name of Ballyhogan in the parish of Dysart in Clare.

Several unrelated families of the name are known to exist in Ireland. O'Donovan gives O'Hogan of Co. Cork as an independent family from others.

'O'Haedhagain or O'Hogan, chief of Crioch Cein' was mentioned by O'Heerin thusly:

'O'Hogan of Croich Kian
Rules..Clan Inmanein of the fair land
A district which enriches each field,
With honey-dew on all its blossoms'

The O'Hogans on the map of Ortelius are around Lower Ormond in Tipperary.

O'Dugan finds O'Hogain as a chief of Carrichbrack, in the barony of Inisowen, in the territory of Tir Eogain. (Tirowen).

In the 17th century O'Hogan was found in Limerick City and County, and in Longford. Hogan was a principal name of Clare, among others, and 'Hogane' was a principal name of Clare, and found in Cork, Limerick, Tipperary and Waterford.

"O'Hogan" was also a principal name of Clare, and found in Limerick and Cork cities as well.

By the time of the 1890 index, Hogan was given in Tipperary, Dublin, Limerick, Clare, and Cork. And that spelling had become the accepted form of the name by that time.

In America, Fr. John J. Hogan, played an important role in the settlement of Missouri, and organized the "Irish Wilderness" settlement in that state.

148

Holmes

Irish Book of Arms plate 22

several possibilities i.e...Mac Thomais..

Holme, Homes, Mac Combs, Mac Comish,

The name of Holmes and its various forms, may be of English or Scottish origin. It is usually assumed to be of Scots heritage when found in Ireland. It is a name which is found throughout the country, but is especially common in the north of Ireland. This is confirmed by the 1890 birth index which gives Antrim as the principal location of the name, along with Dublin.

Several distinct origins of the name exist, including the usage of the personal form of the name of Thomas in conjunction with the older 'Mac' prefix. (i. e. Mac Thomais).

The family of Holmes of Moycashel, descends from an officer in the army of William the III, and the Holmes' of St. Davids, Co. Tipperary, from the 17th century are found in the Book of Arms.

In Milesian Families the name is found in Kerry and Limerick arriving from Scotland in 1596. In the census of 1659 the name is found in Limerick, Kildare, Wexford and Cork. In America the name is the 140th most common surname, with an estimated 140,000 members. Individuals of the name:

William Holmes, Esq.,Quebec,daughter Arabella married in 1808.

Jane Holmes of Surock, found in Clibborn pedigree.

Peter and Thomas Holmes, from Inrollments of the decrees of Innocents

Sir Robert Holmes, found in Connaught Certificates.

8 of the name listed as 'Forty-Nine Officers' in O'Harts work.

Capt, Thomas Holmes (Wexford) under 'Soldiers of the Commonwealth'

Peter Holmes listed under 'Purchasers of Estates 1702-1703.

Honan

Irish Book of Arms plate 120

Honeen

The family names of Honan and Honeen are both found sometimes in the areas in and around Co. Clare. Some give these families as of separate origins entirely, but the two spellings are sure to have been used interchangeably on occasion. The name of Honan is rather rare, and is not found in the census of 1659 or in the birth index of 1890.

Herlihy

Hurley, Hurly, O'Herlyhy, Herlihey

One family of the name is found centered in Ballyvourney, Co. Cork in the early 17th century, and O'Herlyhy is given as a principal name of Co. Limerick in the census of 1659. The 1890 birth index finds the family most numerous in counties Cork and Kerry. Herlihy is often confused or changed into Hurley,Herley, etc...

Hernon

Hernan

The name of Hernon is traditionally linked to Co. Galway and the Aran Islands.

Herr

O hAichir (bitter or sharp)

Hehir, Hegher

When of Irish origin in Ireland, this name would likely stem from O hAichir. More modern forms of this name include Hegher and Hehir. The name is numerous in Clare and Limerick, but not outside of those specific areas. The 1890 index gives O'Hehir as found in Clare and Limerick to support this statement.

Hone

Irish Book of Arms plate 10

Howen, O'Hone

This name is given in at least one instance to a family originally from Holland. Others of the name may be of older Irish origins, and the name is found in older records as O'Hone at times. We find O'Hone as a principle name of Co. Fermanagh in the 17th century.

Heslin

Heslen

Our records find the name linked to the area around the barony of Mohill, in Co. Leitirm.

Hession

The name of Hession is found mainly in Galway and sometimes in Mayo at the time of the 1890 birth index of Ireland.

Hester

Hestor

Families of the Hester name are traditionally linked with counties Mayo and Roscommon, and are found centered there in the 19th century birth index.

Hipwell

A family name sometimes associated with Queens Co. (Leix), in Ireland.

Hillery

Hillary, Hill

The Hillery family name is linked to Co. Clare when tracing the roots of Dr. Patrick Hillery, who served as president of Ireland in the latter half of this century. Note also the place name of Mt. Saint Hilary in Co. Cork, another area of the country where the name is found. These families are sometimes found cited as of Norman extraction.

149

O'Horan

Irish Book of Arms plate 160

O hOdhrain

Haughran, Harhan, Haran, Haren,

Families of the name of Horan, etc.. may spring from one of several origins in Ireland.

Keatings History finds O'Horan, a clan of the Ui Mani, in Galway. They were centered in the Galway/Mayo areas, and remain near there to this day.

"Harhan", was another family, found in Co. Clare, and it has been changed into Horan on occasion.

O'Horahan, of Co. Cork, is another name which has become Horan, through the process of shortening the original name. They served anciently as erenaghs of Ross.

The census of 1659 finds the name of Horan as a principle one of Kildare. Spelled as Horane, the name is found as a principle one of Kings County in the same record.

The 1890 index shows 63 births of the name Horan. They were found mainly in Mayo, Kerry, Tipperary and Roscommon at that time.

Hilliard

Hillard, Hillyard, Hilyard

Most families of the name are found in Co. Dublin in more modern times, but official records also give the name in Co. Kerry at the turn of this century.

The 1890 birth index finds the family most numerous in Co. Dublin.

Hingerty

A name on record as being used interchangeably with the name of Harrington. Most agree that the Hingerty name, which is now scarce, was originally the name of an older Irish family.

150

Hore

Irish Book of Arms plate 131

According to "Keatings History" the name is given as that of an old English family which settled in Wexford.

Hill

Hull

Families of the name of Hill in Ireland may often be assumed to be of English extraction, for the surname of "Hill" ranks among the top 30 most numerous names in all of Ireland. As expected the family is often found in Ulster and in Dublin, where so many settler families are found.

Hillsborough, Co. Down, marks one family of the name who arrived in Ulster in the 16th century.

The 1890 birth index finds the family most numerous in Antrim, Dublin and Down.

Hovenden

Hovendon, Ovington, Offington

The Hovenden family is traditionally linked to the province of Ulster in Ireland, and they are said to have arrived as mercenaries from Scotland by some, while others give the family an English origin. In both cases the family seems tied to the activities of the O'Neill family in Ulster. In any event the name is found rather widespread in our records. Co. Armagh and Co. Tyrone are common places for the family name in Ulster, and the name is also found in Cork, Down, Tipperary and Clare in 17th century records.

O'Houlihan

Irish Book of Arms plates 160, 208

O hUallachain

Holian, Holohan, Houlihan, Hulihan,

There were at least two separate families who formed the origins of the Houlihan surname in Ireland. The name is found more anciently spelled as O hUallachain, and the family is found in Counties Offaly (Kings) and Clare, denoting two separate 'clans'.

In Offaly, the Houlihans served as chiefs of Clan Colgan alongside the O'Hennessys.

Keatings History gives "O'Huallachain, or O'Hoolaghan", sometimes Anglicized as O'Coulaghan and Mac Conlaghan, to show a few of the many different spellings of the name. They were given by O'Dugan to be chiefs of Siol Anmachadha.

Branches of these Houlihan families have spread southwards independently, so that many of the name are found in Co. Cork.

In the 17th century both Hologhane and Hologhon were found as principal names of Kilkenny, showing two more variants of the name. Other spellings include Oulihan, Hoolahan, Whoolahan and Holoughan to name but a few.

By the 1890's Houlihan was recorded in Kerry, Limerick, Cork and Clare. "Holohan" was found in Kilkenny at that time.

William Oullahan was a merchant in Dublin, (1781), and from his line, John in 1877 was living in Baltimore, Md.. The firm "Oullahan and Co." miners, in Stockton, California, stems from this line also. Family members were noted in O'Hart as having settled in New York and Washington D. C. as well.

Houston

Irish Book of Arms plate 50

Huston

The Houston family of Orangefield, and of Roddens, Co. Down, are given in the Irish Book of Arms. The birth index of 1890 finds the family centered in Antrim, Londonderry, Armagh and Down.

Hoey

O'Heoghy

According to "Keatings History" the name is found as a family of the areas of Armagh and Down, in the old territory of Craobh Ruadh. The family was said to have sprung from a branch of the Mac Dunslevy family.

The 1890 birth index finds the family most numerous in counties Dublin and Louth.

Holland

Hollande, Holohan, Mulholland

Spelled as Holland, the name is found in the 1659 census in Kerry, and in the Poll Money Ordinance Survey. Spelled as Hollande in this same 'census', it is given as a name of Monaghan. The final 'e' could have been dropped at any time by your ancestors. Moving into more modern times, the 1890 index shows the spelling of Holland found in Cork, Galway and Dublin. The name is also found in the index to Keatings History of Ireland.

To further complicate matters, in Limerick the name of Holland may be a shortened form of Mulholland, and in Clare it may be used as a variant of Holohan.

151

Howth

Irish Book of Arms plate 7, 17

According to our published version of "Keatings History of Ireland" the name of Howth belongs to a principal family of Dublin city or county, and they are given in that source as of Anglo-Norman descent.

Hodnet

According to "Keatings History" the name of Hodnet was often exchanged for the Irish name of "MacSherry". They were found at Court MacSherry, their chief residence.

The 1890 birth index finds the family most numerous in Cork and Tipperary.

Haley

O'hailche, O'haille

O'Halley, O'Haley, O'Hally, Haly

More anciently the family of Haley was found as a principal name in County Tipperary in 1659. At the same time 'O'Haley' was given as a principal name of Limerick. Of the Halley families in Tipperary and Waterford, some claim descent from the Mulhall family originally, but are said to descend from O'hAilche most anciently. In County Clare, near Ennis, another small family is found, said to have come from O'hAille. Note the place name of Ballally, possibly connected to the family. This family has been said to have been of "old standing" in Co. Galway, and the head of the elder branch of the family was Simon Haly, of Ballyhaly in 1730 according to O'Hart.

According to "Keatings History" the name of "O'Hally" is probably taken from O'Alchi or O'Halchi, who was chief of Tuatha Faralt. The lands of that family are given as "A plain of fair fortresses and a numerous tribe, Like the lands of the shallow rivers of Taiti."

Hughes, MacHugh

Irish Book of Arms plates 61,160,251

Mac Aodha (son of Hugh)

Hughe, Hewson, MacKay, MacCoy,

Mac Hugh (MacAodha) means son of or descendant of Hugh. The original gaelic name has become Mackee, MacKay, MacCoy and Hughes in some cases. Hughes, a well know settler name, is more popular than McHugh. This is not surprising since Hughes is among the 20 most common names in Wales and England.

In Keatings History Mac Aodha, Aodha or Mac Hugh are principal chiefs of Teffia, (Muintir Tiamain)."O'Haodha, O'Hugh or O'Hea" is cited as a chief of Ui Degadh by O'Heerin, in Co. Kildare.

Further locations for the family are found in Keatings History. "O'Haedha, or O'Hugh, chief of Esruadh, now Ballyshannon, in the barony of Tir Hugh in Donegal (Tir Connaill). "O'Haedha, or O'Hugh", chief of Fernmoy, Co. Down, on the borders of Antrim and in the barony of Lower Iveagh. Mac Hugh is given among the clans who settled in Cavan and was also found as "Mac Aedha, or Mac Hugh, also called Hughes", chief of Clan Cosgraidh, a district on the eastern side of Lough Corrib in Galway, where they were chiefs of the barony of Clare. O'Hughes was numerous in Mayo and Sligo, and "O'Haodha, Hughes or O'Hea" served as chief near the barony of Skrine, near Tara.

Hughes is one of the top 40 names in Ireland. In 1659 O'Hugh is in Armagh, Monaghan, Carlow and Longford. McHugh was in Fermanagh and Hughes was in Louth then. By 1890 McHugh was mainly in Mayo, Donegal, Fermanagh and Galway. Hughes was in Armagh, Antrim and Dublin.

The Hughes family of Ballycross, of Co. Wexford, came here from Wales.

Hume

The Irish Book of Arms plate 95

Reference to the Hume family is found as "Hume (now Dick) of Co. Wicklow" and they are given in the Irish Book of Arms. This family is given also of Carantrila Park, Co. Galway.

The birth index of 1890 finds the family centered in Co. Antrim.

Hood

MacHood, Hudde, Mahood

"Hood" families are found bearing one of the principle names of Co. Wexford in the 17th century. Two centuries later the family name is found centered in Co. Antrim. The name is often found in the province of Ulster, and there it is believed that some of the name come from "MacHood" or O'Hood originally. Of course, many of the name are originally of English extraction.

Hopkins

Habbagan, Hobb, Hobkine

Hopkins is a well known English name, and some families in Ireland are descended from that line. In that case the name comes from "Hobb", which is akin to the name Robert. Note the place names of Hopkinstown in Co. Meath and Hopkinsrea in Co. Tipperary. In some cases however the name is of Irish origins, particularly when traditionally found in Co. Mayo. Habbagan is also officially given as an alternate spelling of Hopkins, and in that event the family name may well be Irish.

In the 17th century we find families of the name in Dublin, Westmeath and Kilkenny, and two centuries later the family is centered in Mayo and Dublin in the 1890 birth index.

Some sources contend that families of the name settled in Clare and Galway from Wales in the early 18th century.

Humfrey

The Irish Book of Arms plate 78, 104

Humphry, Humphrey, Humphrys,

The Humfrey family of Cavanacor, Co. Donegal, descends from one John Humfrey who came to Ireland in 1655 from Cumberland, settling at Donard in Co. Wicklow.

The Humphrys family of Ballyhaise House, Co. Cavan and the above mentioned family are given in the Irish Book of Arms. The birth index of 1890 finds the family centered in Armagh and Dublin.

O'Holleran

Halloran

The O'Holleran spelling is taken from the name of O'Halloran, and the former is found mainly in counties Mayo and Galway as documented by the 1890 birth index.

Howard

most likely of English origin

O'Hure, O'Hawrde, Hogart.

Milesian families finds the name in Cork, Kerry and Limerick, arriving in 1172 from England. The census of 1659 shows the name in Tipperary, Cork and Dublin. In more modern times the name remains in Dublin and Cork, as evidenced by the 1890 birth index.

In addition to the English origins, the old Irish family name of O hIomhair, in Co. Clare has also been changed into Howard. (O'Hure). In Clare they are found along with the O'Deas, and were located near Mt. Callan, and were a family of note in the early 14th century.

According to Woulfe, the names of Hogart and Howard are synonyms; also found in Keatings History of Ireland. In Keatings History the Howards are cited as a chief English family of Wicklow.

Hungerford

The Irish Book of Arms plate 109

The Hungerford family of Inchodony, (the Island), and of Castle Ventry, Co. Cork, are said to be a cadet branch of the Hungerford family of Somerset, of English origins.

Howlin

Howling, Holden, Huolyn

Families of the name of Howlin, etc.. are traditionally linked with Co. Kilkenny in Ireland. Here they served as Lords of Kilree and held sway in the barony of Kells. By the time of the 17th century the name of Howlin was a principle one of Co. Wexford and remained as the center for the name in the 19th century. Spelled as Howling we find the name as a principle one of Co. Kilkenny in the 17th century.

Of the landed family in Kilkenny, they are said to have descended from a Welsh family by the name of Huolyn in the wake of the Norman invasions in the latter half of the 12th century.

In some cases the name of Howlin has been changed to Holden by certain branches of the family. This may cause some confusion, for Holden is the name of English families which have settled in Ireland from time to time as well.

Hoy

Hay, Haughey, Haughy

Hoy is a name traditionally linked to the province of Ulster in Ireland. It has long been a variant spelling of the more familiar Haughey. The 1890 birth index finds the family most numerous in Antrim and Down.

Hunt

Irish Book of Arms plate 41, 93

Le Hunt, Feeheny, Fey, Hunter, Hunte

Many of the name of Hunt settled in Ireland, coming from England originally. Due to the "translation" of old gaelic names into English forms, many of the name are thought to be of Irish origins as well.

The Hunt family of Cummer More, Kilcommon, Co. Tipperary is given in the Irish Book of Arms.

The census of 1659 finds the family in Limerick, Dublin and Kildare, and the 19th century birth index gives the family as centered in Mayo, Roscommon, Dublin and Waterford.

The separate name of "Hunter" is a name traditionally linked with the province of Ulster in Ireland.

The Le Hunte family of Artramont House, Co. Wexford is given in the Irish Book of Arms as is the Hunt family of Danesfort, Co. Cork, who descend from an old English family of Warwick.

Holly, Holley

Quillan, Holly, Holley

Families of the name of Holly and Holley are found in two distinct areas of Ireland. One location is in the province of Ulster, where the name was centered in Londonderry in the last century. The other location is in the Kerry/Cork region of Ireland. The latter of which was given as a primary location for the name in the 19th century birth index.

Of passing note, the name of Hollyday, also found in Co. Cork in the 17th century, could have been shortened by some into Holly. Quillan has been reported as used interchangeably with Holly.

153

O'Hurley

Irish Book of Arms plates 69,123,160

O hUirthile

Herlihy, Murily, Murhila, Hurly, de Hurle

O'Hurley families are of at least two separate origins in Ireland. The 'O'Herlihys or O'Hurleys' were chiefs of a district in the barony of Muskerry. O'Heerin gives them as wardens of the church of St. Golonait of Ballyvoorny. The most numerous of the name, they are found mainly in Co. Cork. Some claim they also settled in Clare. They are also found centered in Ballynacarriga Castle, in the barony of East Carberry.

Of the O'Herleys of Thomand we find the ancient notation: "O'Toirdhelbhaidh, or, as it is written in the books of Leacon and Ballymote, O'Urthaile, Anglicized to O'Hurley. This was a Dalcassion family: also designated Clann Tail, a term applied to Dalcassians." O'Heerin speaks thusly:

"O'Hurley of the tribe of Tail,
Near dwells Killaloe of St. Flannan:
Delightful are its woods and productive its plains, and from thence westward to the Shannon".

This family is found near Kilmallock in Limerick, where they were centered at Knocklong Castle. Note the place name of Rathurley in the parish of Kilruane in nearby Co. Tipperary.

Of the O'Hurleys of Limerick, Dermod O'Hurley was an Archbishop of Cashel.

The Irish Book of Arms finds Hurly of Glenduff, Tralee, Co. Kerry, of Limerick origins and also Hurly of Bridge House, Co. Kerry, whose motto was "Dextra vinvit cor".

In the 1890 index there were 134 "Hurley" births and 42 Herlihy births recorded. Herlihy was of Cork and Kerry. Hurley was of Cork, Waterford, Dublin and Galway.

"The Family of O'Hurley" was published in 1906 in Cork by Rev. P. Hurley.

Hussey, O'Hosey

Irish Book of Arms plates 83, 133

OhEodhusa

Hussy, de Hose, de Houssaye

Irish families of the name of Hussey or O'Hosey may spring from Irish or Norman origins in Ireland. The Norman name of de Houssaye, de Hose or de Hosey became Hussey after settling in Ireland. They are found in the barony of Lower Deace in Co. Meath.

On record in Ireland at an early date "Hugh de Hose or Hussey" obtained "Dees, or the barony of Deece in Meath". The Husseys were made barons of Galtrim. These lands were granted by Hugh de Lacy, who obtained the whole kingdom of Meath from Henry II in the year 1172. One branch of the name settled in Co. Kerry.

The Husseys are as well cited as a principal family of Anglo-Norman descent in the county and city of Dublin, as found in Keatings History.

Of the Irish of the name, they are said to be found in the province of Connaught, coming from the gaelic O hEodhusa. This family is found earliest in Fermanagh, where they served as bards to the MacGuires.

Husseys are found as property holders in Kerry and Meath into the last century.

In the 17th century Hussey was found in Kildare, Meath and Kerry in the 1659 census. By the time of the 1890 birth index there were only 26 recorded births of the name, in the counties of Kerry, Galway and Roscommon.

The arms of Hussey of Rathkenny, Co. Meath are shown in the Irish Book of Arms. This family was granted lands in Galtrim, barony of Deene, Co. Meath and between Grange Gorman and the Liffey in Dublin, around the year 1200.

Hyde

Irish Book of Arms plates 55, 75

Most often found in Cork and Kilkenny in older records, Douglas Hyde (d.1949) was the first president of Ireland. One noted family of the name was found at Castle Hyde, in Co. Cork. The Hydes were originally a settler family here.

One Edward Hyde was the Earl of Clarendon, and the family name is as well given as a principal one by the close of the 17th century.

The Irish Book of Arms gives the family of Hyde of Lynnbury, Co. Westmeath, and the family of Hyde of Castle Hyde.

The birth index of 1890 finds the family centered in Cork and Antrim.

O'Huada, O'Fuada

According to "Keatings History" the name is cited as that of a clan of Mayo and/or Sligo.

Hudson

of English origin

Hudson is a name of likely English origin when found in Ireland. It has been concentrated in two areas, namely that of Dublin, and in the province of Ulster.

In Milesian Families the name is found in Kerry arriving in 1460 from Scotland, according to this author. In the census of 1659, the family is found in Carlow and Dublin, as well as in the Poll Money Ordinance Survey. The more modern 1890 birth index still found the name in Dublin.

One Abraham Hudson was married Feb. 5, 1782, at the 1st Presbyterian Church in Morristown, N.J.

Hannah Corbit Hudson married March, 1787, Westmoreland County, Virginia.

154

O'Hynes

Irish Book of Arms plate 159

O'hEidhin

Hines, Haynes, Hynes, Heyne

Families of the name of Hynes may be of English or Irish heritage. The O'Eidin family can also be found as O'Heyne. They are found as chiefs in Galway, centered in the barony of Kiltartan. One of their castles can be found near Kinvara, known as Dun Guaire or Dungory Castle in Galway.

These O'Heynes, along with the O'Clerys and O'Shaughnessys held the territory of Ui Fiachra in Galway, (the diocese of Kilmacdugh).

The O'Heynes, along with others were given as "old and respectable families" in the county of Cork in Keatings'.

O'Heidhin, or O'Heyne, anglicized to Hynes, was styled prince of Ui Fiachra Aidhni. His territory included the barony of Kiltartan, and parts of the baronies of Dunkellin and Loughrea in Galway. They descended from Guairi Aidhne, King of Connaught , known for his hospitality and charity. It was common to say "as generous as Guaire", and poets said his right hand grew longer than the left, because he constantly had it extended in giving charity.

The man from who the name was taken was "Eidhin", one of their 10th century chiefs. One of the family, Maolrunanaidh O'Heyne, served as commander under Brian Boru at the battle of Clontarf. It was also noted that Brian Boru was married to the daughter of Flann, the father of Maolrunanaidh.

The family remained as large property holders into the last century. O'Heynes Church or Abbey, marks the territory of the ancient family.

As expected O'Heyne is found in the 17th century in Clare and Limerick. In 1890 we find "Hinds", Hynds, and Hynes as variant spellings (The latter two were in Down and Roscommon).

Harper

le Harpur (When of Norman Origins)

Harpur, Harp, Harpor.

The Norman name of 'le Harpur', (the Harper), is found early in Irish records, dating from the 13th century or earlier in the province of Leinster.

The English families of the name 'Harper' are numerous in the province of Ulster, as may be expected from early settlement schemes in that area.

This does not deny the possibility of ancient Irish heritage in isolated instances, of families with this name. The complete book of Irish Family Names lists several sources including: a) Milesian Families list the location of the name in Antrim, arriving in 1640 A.D. of Norman descent, b) The index from the last century lists Antrim as the principal county for the name.

The Harper family name has a connection with Wexford where you find the name of Harperstown and from the place name index in O'Laughlins 'Irish Ancestors'. 'Harperstown Ho.' is listed in Wexford at the turn of this century.

(O) Thomas Harper. 'Forfeiting Proprietor in Ireland, Bishops Lands'

(0) Patrick Harper. 'Inrollments of the decrees of innocents..marked 1821-1825

From the Journal of the Irish American Historical Society:

John. Militia Company at Brunswick and Topsham, ME. 1723 a.d.

Patrick. Early Immigrants to Virginia. (1623 - 1666)

Robert. Land grant to Settlers in New York. (1763)

" Professor of Kings College, N.Y. (1761 - 1777)

" and wife. Property owners and businessmen of New York. (1791)

Harper was also the name of a ships captain sailing from Philadelphia to Dublin in 1752.

Harper is given as the 205th most popular name in America today.

O'Healy

Irish Book of Arms plates 219

O'hElidhe

O'Hely, O'Haly, O'Healihy, Hally, Heally,

O'Healy families in Ireland may originate from one of two entirely separate lines. The first was centered in the barony of Tirerril in Co. Sligo, near the Curlew mountains on the shores of Lough Arrow. The location of Ballyhely will also help you mark the spot.

The second family is found in Co. Cork and are spoken of as "Chiefs of Pobble O'Healy", a large parish in the barony of Muskerry. The O'Helys are also given as an old and respectable family in Waterford, according to Keatings History.

There are many placenames bearing the Healy name such as Ballyhely, Ballyhealy and Healysland in Ireland.

"Healy" was the preferred spelling of the name in the 1890's index, with some 291 births in Cork, Kerry, Dublin, Galway, Roscommon and Mayo. The name ranks among the top 50 most numerous in all of the country.

In the 1659 census both O'Healy and Healy are found as principal names of Cork, and found as well in Tipperary, Kildare, Kerry, Limerick and Sligo. "O'Hely" was also a principal name of Sligo and "Hely" a principal name of Limerick at that time as well.

The possible variant spelling of Hally is found only in Tipperary in the 1890 index.

The Wallis-Healy family of Dublin is noted in O'Harts work, as well as the O'Healys of Donoughmore and the John Hely-Hutchinson family of Ireland.

It is further noted that the surname of "Kerrisk" is said to have come from one Pierce O'Healy of Co. Kerry, due to its translation as meaning "son of Pierce".

Horgan

Horgen, Horrigan

A name linked to Co. Cork and Co. Kerry in Ireland. The name may actually stem from the longer form of Horrigan or Hourigan. The 1890 birth index finds the family most numerous in Cork with 40 recorded births, and in Kerry, with 21 recorded births at that time.

O'Hora

O'Hara, Horohoe, Horoho, O'Harroghue

O'Hora has been used as a variant spelling of O'Hara, but it may also be a separate name in its own right. By the time of the 1890 birth index families of the name of O'Hora are found centered in Co. Mayo, but we find earlier members of this family name in Co. Antrim as well. In Mayo, the Horohoe family is often found in or near Swineford, and some O'Horas may actually stem from the same line as the Horohoes, simply adopting a shorter spelling of the name.

Horton

not of likely Irish origin

Horten

Little information exists in our records for this surname. It is of likely English origin. In Milesian families the name is found in Dublin and Wexford, arriving in 1666 from England. In the works of O'Brien published by the American Irish Historical Society, two of the name were found to be Irish, as follows.

Elizabeth (1773) and Nancy (1789) Horton, Faquier County and Norfolk County Virginia Marriages.

Levi Horton, married Anna Kenny, March 8, 1758, (Stoughton and Canton, Mass.)

Hubbard

not of Irish origin

Hubberd

While an uncommon name in Ireland, the surname is found in the census of 1659 as principal name of county Waterford.

One 'John Hubbard' is found listed among the 'Forty-Nine Officers' in Ireland, in the works of O'Hart. Additionally one Epaphroditus Hubbard was married on Oct. 20, 1785, in Faquier County, Virginia, U.S.A.

In the works of Mattheson the name is cited traditionally in Macroom, Co. Cork.

Howley

Irish Book of Arms plate 233

Howly, O'Howley, Wholey

Families of the name of Howley are given centered in counties Clare, Mayo and Sligo in the 1890 birth index of Ireland. This appears to be a location of long standing for this family which seems to be an old Irish one. Some of the name may have English roots, particularly in other areas of the country, for Howley is an English surname as well. The name of Whooley or Wholey has also been interchanged with the name of Howley. Whooley is also on record as coming from the O'Driscoll family in Co. Cork, and that of course represents an entirely separate family.

Histon

O'hOistin

Hestin, Hestion, Hastings, Hastie..

Histon is found in Limerick, said to have arrived there from Mayo. The name was Hestin in Mayo, where the family was aligned with the McDermots of Moylurg. The Hestin name is linked Westport Union in County Mayo.

French Names

Reported as anglicised as given below:

French Name:	Changed to:
Batchelier	Bachelor
Baudair	Baudry
Beaufoy	Boffy
Bois	Boys
Bouchier	Butcher, Boxer
Bourgeais	Burgess
Boyer	Bower
Brasseur	Brassy
Breton	Britton
Chapuis	Shoppee
Conde	Cundy
Coquerel	Cockerill
D'Aeth	Death
Dargent	Dargan
Defoix,DeFoy	De Foe, Defoe
DelaTranche	Trench
De Leau	Dillon
De Moulins	Mullins
D'Orleans	Dorling, Darling
De Proux	Diprose
D'Espard	Despard, Dispard
Despard	Despair
De Vere	Weir
Dieudonne	Dudney
Drouet	Drought, Drewitt
Dulau	Waters
Du Quesne	Du Cane
Gebon	Gibbon
Guilbert	Gilbert
Huyghens	Huggins/ Hig'ins
Jolifemme	Pretyman/hans'mbdy
Koch	Cox
Lacroix	Cross
Le Blanc	White
Le Blount	Croke
Le Cog	Laycock
Le Fevre	Smith
Le Jeune	Young
Le Maitre	Masters
Le Maur	Brown
Le Monnier	Miller
Le Noir	Black
Lenoir	Lennard
Le Roy	King
Letellier	Taylour
Levereau	Lever
L'Oiseau	Bird
Mahieu	Mayhew
Merineau	Meryon
Masurier	Measure
Momerie	Mummery
Olier	D'Olier, Oyler
Pain	Payne, Paine
Paul	Paull
Pelletier	Pelter
Petit	Pettitt
Philippot	Philpot
Pigou	Pigot
Planche	Plank
Renalls	Reynolds
Reveil	Revill
Sauvage	Savage, Wild(e)
Saveroy	Savery
Say	Soy
Scardeville	Sharwell
Souverain	Suffren
Taillebois	Talboys
Tonnelier	Cooper
Villebois	Williamis/Wiliams

156

Mc Ilveen

McElveen, McIlvaine, McIlwaine,

The name of McIlveen and its various spellings are said to be found most anciently in Co. Down, and subsequently in Antrim. Of the variant spellings of the name, McIlvaine is actually a spelling assigned to a Scots family also found in Ireland.

Mc Intyre

McIntire, McAteer

The name of a Scottish family settling in Ireland no later than the 17th century, found numerous in Co. Antrim. The name is also said to be a variant spelling of the name of McAteer.

Ireland

Irish

Our records find the name of Ireland in Co. Louth in the 17th century, and subsequently centered in Antrim and Armagh into the 19th century. The name in more modern times might be also found simply as "Irish". We believe that Irishmen going abroad came to be known as "Irish" or "Irishmen" , i.e. de Yrlande, and this name arrived back in Ireland on occasion as a new surname. It is also likely that some of the name adopted it upon arriving in America, Australia etc.., having had a completely different surname in Ireland.

Irvine

Irwin, Erwin, Ervine, McIrvin, Irving,

The names of Irvine and Ervine, are often found equated with the names of Irwin and Erwin. They actually represent two distinct families. Note the place name of Irvinestown in Fermanagh. This marks the former family of the name, who had many holdings there and in Donegal and surrounding areas. Some give the name of Irvine as coming from a Scottish place name, others give Irwin as of English origins. The noted Patrick Woulfe gives both names as of Irish origins, but most of the name in our records appear to be of origins outside of Ireland.

We further find some sources giving Irvin and Irvine as arriving from Scotland in the 17th century. We find Irving given in the census of 1659 in Co.Sligo.

Irwin is found as a principle name of Fermanagh in the census of 1659 and, and is found centered in Armagh, Antrim, Tyrone and Londonderry some two centuries later. The name of Irwing is found as a name of Co. Roscommon in the 17th century as well.

Itchingham

Etchingham

One family of the name is found in Dunbrody, Co. Wexford early in the 17th century. (One Osborne Itchingham).

Mc Ilcreve

McIlcrivy

A principle name of Co. Armagh in the 17th century, both the spellings of McIlcreve and McIlcrivy are given as such in the census of 1659.

Mac Inerney

Irish Book of Arms plate 160

Mac an Airchchinnigh

Nerney, Macanerny, McInnerney,

MacInerney, in Irish means son of the erenagh. Erenaghs were the keepers of church estates, and they often held a hereditary position. Hence, when the use of surnames came about, several of the position assumed the name given above, meaning, son of the Erenagh.

Most often found in connection with counties Limerick and Clare, it is there where we find the name of McInerney in the 1890 birth index. They were centered in the barony of Lower Bunratty, at Ballycally in Co. Clare. They were also associated with the parish of Kiconry there.

Other completely separate families have assumed the name as well. This is noted in Co. Roscommon, where the name has likely been shortened to Nerney.

McInerhny and McInerny are both found as principal names of County Clare in the 17th century. The name remained centered in the barony of Bunratty at that time.

MacInerney is also given as a variant spelling of MacEniry, Lord of Connello in Co. Limerick. This family held considerable lands there up until the Cromwellian settlement.

Mc Ilwaine

Mac Giolla Bhain

Kilbane, McIlvaine, McIlveen, McIlveen

The Irish family of McIlwaine originated in Co. Sligo, and the name is found most often as Kilbane rather than McIlwaine. Much confusion exists between McIlwaine and the Scots name of McIlvaine, for they are found used interchangeably at times.

157

Irwin

Irish Book of Arms plate 85, 88, 104

Erwin, Irvin, Irvine

The Irwin family of Rathmoyle, Co. Roscommon descends from John Irwin of Ballinderry, b. 1618. The Irwin family of Derrygore, Co. Fermanagh descends from George Irwin who died in Derrygore in 1791. The Irwin family of Mount Irwin, Co. Armagh is given in the Irish Book of Arms, as are the other two families cited.

The birth index of 1890 finds the family centered in Armagh, Antrim, Tyrone and Londonderry. Much confusion arises between the names of Irwin and Irvin or Irvine, and they are sometimes used interchangeably. Several of the name are found with large holdings of land in centuries past, with one seat of power in Co. Fermanagh.

Ivers

Ivors, Iver, McIvor, Ievers

Those of the name of Ivers may be either of English or Irish descent. Note the placename of Mountievers in Co. Clare, in the barony of Bunraty Lower, said to have been named for an English family of the name which settled there.

The name of McIvor may have given rise to the name today found in Dublin and Louth. (McIomhair?)

The 1890 birth index finds the family most numerous in Dublin and Louth.

Ivory

The name of Ivory is assumed to be an English settler name when found in Ireland. One such family is found settling in Waterford in the 1600's, and the name is subsequently found in Dublin, as would be expected.

Jackson

Irish Book of Arms plate 37

According to "Keatings History" the name is among the chief families of English descent settling in Waterford and Tipperary. These English families primarily possessed the territory called from them Gal-tir, signifying the country of the foreigners," now the barony of Gaultiere."

The Jackson family of Carramore House, Co. Mayo, are said to descend from a Captain in Cromwell's army, who purchased lands in the barony of Tyrawley, Co. Mayo.

Jackson is one of the top 30 most numerous English surnames, and several of the name have arrived in Ireland over the centuries.

The birth index of 1890 finds the family most numerous in Antrim, Armagh, Dublin, Cork and Mayo.

Jacob

One William Jacob, of Cambridgeshire (d.1532) was founder of the line of the Jacob family of Bromley, England, and of the Jacob families of Co. Wexford, Queens County and Co. Dublin in Ireland.

Here they are found sometimes settled at Sigginstown, Co. Wexford.

The 1890 birth index finds the family most numerous in Co. Dublin.

Joy

The name of a family found in Clare in the 17th century and centered in Waterford in the 19th century.

Jamison

Irish Book of Arms plate 75 (Jameson)

of scottish origin

Jameson, Jamisone, Jamieson

Jamison is a well known Scottish name which settled in Ireland on more than one occasion. The spelling of Jamieson is given in Milesian families as settling in Limerick and Galway in 1656, coming from Scotland. 'Jameson' is listed in the same work as settling in Galway in 1756 from Scotland.

Jamison is found in the 1890 birth index in Antrim and Down, while Jameson is found in Dublin at this date. The Jamieson spelling is also found in Antrim and Down at this time.

The Irish Book of Arms gives the family of Jameson of Windfield, Co. Galway.

Judge

Of the Irish families of the name, "Judge" can be found as a variant spelling of Breheny. The name may as well be of an English (or other) settler family in Ireland. The 1890 birth index finds the family most numerous in Mayo, Dublin and Tyrone.

Justice

The name of a family found in Cork and Kerry in the 17th century.

158

Jennings

Irish Book of Arms plate 72

Mac Sheoinin

Jenings

The two best known origins of the name of Jennings in Ireland, trace the family to foreign origins. Some of the name have arrived from England and settled permanently in Ireland.

In the province of Connaught, the Jennings name stems from the Burke (de Burgo) family tree. The Burkes arrived with the Anglo-Norman invasions of the 12th century in Ireland. A branch of the family assumed an Irish name by becoming 'Mac Sheonin', and subsequently this became translated as Jennings. The founder of this family is said to be one Seoinin (John) Burke. Hence, son of John would become, Mac Seoinin in its Irish form. They held considerable properties in Mayo and Galway in the baronies of Kilmaine and Dunmore respectively.

By the time of the 1890 birth index Jennings is found in Mayo, Galway, Cork and Armagh. There were 63 recorded births of the name at that time.

The Irish Book of Arms gives Jenings of Ironpool, Co. Galway, who was then J. P. for the county and city of Dublin. They claimed descent from de Burgo, and their pedigree is given in O'Ferrals' Line Antiqua', down to 1709.

Several of the name are found in the ranks of the military serving in the Irish Brigades on the continent.

Johnson

Irish Book of Arms plate 108

Johnston, Johnstone

Most of the name of Johnson in Ireland are of English or Scottish extraction. The name is common in both of those countries, and several unrelated families of the name have arrived in Ireland over time from those sources. Perhaps more of the name are of English extraction, for Johnson is one of the top 10 most numerous names in that country.

The name of Johnston, a separate Scottish name, is often interchanged and confused with Johnson.

Of some of the possible Irish of the name, "MacShane" which can be translated as McJohn or son of John, doubtlessly accounts for some of the name of Johnson in Ireland.

The Johnson family of Rockenham, Co. Cork, is given to descend from William Johnston or Johnson, at native of Scotland who settled in Ireland around 1670. This family is given in the Irish Book of Arms.

The birth index of 1890 finds the family centered in Cork, Dublin and Antrim.

Johnston

Irish Book of Arms plate 75

Johnstone

One of the 20 most numerous names of Scotland, it is not surprising to find many of the name in the north of Ireland. Johnston is as well, one of the top 40 most numerous names in all of Ireland. Older records often give the name as Johnstone.

The Johnston family of Kilmore, Co. Armagh and of Blackhall, Co. Dublin are given to be of the same descent. Their common ancestor was William Johnston, an architect sent from Scotland to rebuild the destruction caused during the "rebellion of 1641".

The birth index of 1890 finds the family centered in Cavan and Londonderry when spelled as Johnstone, and in in Antrim, Down, Fermanagh, Armagh and Dublin when spelled as Johnston.

Jolley

Jolley, Joley, July, Joly, Jolliff

Several families of the name can apparently be found in Ireland, and it is assumed that they arrived at different times here. In the works of O'Hart we find one family of the name at least, being given as of Huguenot origins. The name may come from the french "joli" or from other beginnings. More than one family is said to have arrived from England here over time. While the name can certainly be spelled as Jolley, Jolly and Joly, the spelling of July or Jully etc.., may be of different origins, or may represent the same family name.

In the 19th century we find the family centered in Dublin, although records show the name in Offaly, Tipperary and Clare in earlier times. Both Jolly and Jolliff have been reported in Cork, arriving from England in the 17th and 16th centuries respectively.

159

Jones

Irish Book of Arms plate 27, 33, 44

Mac Seoin

The name of Jones has been the most numerous surname in all of Wales, and the 2nd most numerous in all of England. Not surprisingly the name is found in every county in Ireland in our records, and is often found in the city of Dublin.

The name is most often of foreign origins when found in Ireland, but it does not rank among the top 100 names of this country according to the 1890 birth index. In the province of Connaught the name is perhaps found less often than elsewhere.

With a grand total of 152 births being recorded in 1890, over half of the name are found in Dublin at that time. In the 17th century we find the name as a principal one of Co. Louth as well.

The Jones family of Jonesboro, Co. Meath, descend from William Jones of Crossdrum in that county, and this family is found in the Irish Book of Arms. The Jones family of Ardnaree, Co. Mayo, and the Jones family of Moolum, Co. Kilkenny are as well found in that work. The latter family descends from Bryan Jones of Dublin, said to have come from an ancient family in Wales. He received a grant of lands from King James I in 1622.

A publication for possible further research is "The Jones in Ireland", by Robert Leach, published in Yonkers, New York, in 1866.

Mac Jordan

Irish book of arms plate 160

Mac Siurtain

MacJordan, MacSiurtan, MacShurton,

The Jordan family were among the chief Anglo-Norman and English settlers of Ulidia under De Courcey and his successors. Ulidia was an ancient territorial division which included Down and parts of Antrim.

It is further stated in Keatings History that the de Exeters of Mayo changed their name to 'Mac Jordan.' Settling in Ireland following the Norman invasions of the 12th century, this family assumed the name of MacSiurtain or MacJordan.

'MacJordans Country' is found in the barony of Gallen in Co. Mayo. The name when translated means descendant of Jordan, in this case one Jordan d'Exeter.

Those of the name given above became thoroughly Irish in manner and custom, and adopted well to the way of life in Ireland.

In the 17th century Jordan was a principal name of Waterford and Jordane is found in Tipperary. Other spellings of the name include Jordon, Jordin, and Jordane.

By the time of the 1890 birth index 'Jordan' was the main spelling of the name, with births recorded in Dublin, Mayo, Antrim and Galway.

Joynt

le joint (Huguenot name)

Joint

The name of Joynt in Ireland has been found to be a Huguenot name, taken from the French 'le joint', meaning slim or graceful. It is a name which has been traditionally associated with counties Limerick and Mayo in Ireland. The Poll Money Ordinance Survey also lists the name, under the spelling of Joint.

Joyce

Irish Book of Arms plate 160

Seoighe

Shoye, de Jorse

The Joyce, or de Jorse, family came from Wales to Galway in the reign of Edward I. They formed alliances with the O'Flahertys, chiefs of Connaught, and received large grants of land in Connemarra, in the barony of Ross, and near the borders of Mayo a large territory which is still known as Joyces' country. Here they are 'very numerous to the present day', and many of them were remarkable for immense strength of body and gigantic stature.

The earliest of the name in Ireland of which we have record of is one 'Thomas de Jorse'. He arrived from Wales in 1283 and married into the Thomand O'Brien family, thus helping the family no doubt, to rise in power in the area.

Of the same family of Joyces in Ireland are said to be : the Joyces of Joyce Grove, Co. Galway, those of Oxford, near Doonamoona in Mayo, those of Woodquay in Galway town, and those of Merview near the town of Galway.

The family of Joyce is also found centered in Edgesworthstown, in Co. Longford.

One of the noted 14 tribes of Galway, several are found as mayors of that town.

By the time of the 1890 birth index Joyce is found in Galway and Mayo, with some 164 births.

Persons of note of the name, James Joyce (1882 - 1941), author of 'Ulysses' comes first to mind.

160

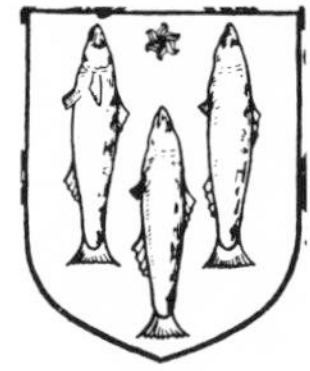

Kane

Irish Book of Arms plates 77, 247

O'Cathain

Kain, Cain, Cahan, Cahane, Kaine,

The name of Kane belongs to a myriad of similar sounding names and spellings. It is easy to see and note the confusion between Cane, and Caine, and Kane etc... The name of Cahan is also used interchangeably in Ireland. An interesting account of the same can be found in 'The Ulster Clans', by Rev. T. H. Mullin and Rev. J. E. Mullan, published in Belfast, 1966.

'Kane' is listed in the 1890 birth index as being a name of Antrim, Londonderry and Dublin. O'Kane is found in the census of 1659 in Antrim, and in 1890 in Londonderry and Antrim. With the O' prefix it is also given as an ancient Irish family of the Hy Nial tribe, in Londonderry and Tyrone.

Mc Kane is also listed in the 1890 index, with some 8 births recorded, over half of which were in Ulster. The Irish Book of Arms gives the family of Kane of Drumreaske, Co. Monaghan.

The Kane family of Drumreaske, Co. Monaghan is found in the Irish Book of Arms.

In America today the name ranks as the 483rd most popular , with some 52,000 family members.

From the works of O'Hart:

Joseph Kane. (Grantees of Estates under the Williamite confiscations)

Joseph Kane. (Names of purchasers of estate)

William J. Kane. Irish American Brigades, resigned May 11, 1863, rank =1st Lt..

James Kane. not mustered. 1st Lt., 2nd Regt. of Corcorans Irish Legion.

T. Kane., Esq., of Whitehall, Co. Clare, M.D., J.P.

Kavanagh

Irish Book of Arms plates 32, 160

Caomhanach

Keevan, Cavanagh, Kavanaugh

The Kavanagh surname is the 53rd most popular name in Ireland. The family descends from the MacMurrough line, the first of the name being Donal Kavanagh, son of Dermot Mac - Murrough. Donals father, King of the Leinster, helped start the Norman invasions of the 12th century. (Through his daughter and Strongbow).

The name stems from Caomhanach, meaning 'follower of St. Caomhan.' Note that the name does not have the common 'O' or 'Mac' prefix . The name was likely used as an epithet, although it has been recorded as O'Kavanagh.

The MacMurroughs were kings of Leinster prior to the Norman invasions, remaining prominent as the Kavanaghs came to the fore. They held the lands of Ui Cavenagh, "now the barony of Idrone East, in Carlow" - according to Keatings History. In Carlow the O'Cavanaghs were barons of Balian, and their original territory was in Carlow and Wexford.

In Wexford, Enniscorthy Castle served as a center for the name and in modern times it has been a museum.

Roscommon, Wexford, Kilkenny, Carlow and Kildare served as centers in the 17th century. Dublin, Wexford and Wicklow did the same - 1890 index.

Keatings History finds the name as "O'Caomhain", a name Anglicized to O'Keevan and O'Cavanagh, as a senior branch of the O'Dowd family, chief of border lands of Sligo and Mayo. This is a separate family and variant spelling.

Art MacMurrough O'Cavanagh, who fought the English in the 14th century, is a noted figure. Donal O'Cavenagh, surnamed Spainagh or 'The Spaniard" was another leader who fought against Queen Elizabeth. Kavanagh is the most common spelling of the name today.

Keane, O'Kane

Irish Book of Arms plates 74, 77, 247

O'Cein

Kane, Cane, Cain, Kain, Cahan, Kean,

Among the 100 most numerous names in Ireland, Keane, Kane, Cahan, etc.. has several separate origins and these names have often been used interchangeably.

Among the chiefs and clans of Tir Eoghain in the 12th century was "O'Cathain, or O'Kane, who was of the race of Eogan, or a branch of the O'Neills and who was chief of Keenaght of Dungiven (Glengiven). This family was also chief of Creeve, now in the barony of Coolerain." Later this powerful clan possessed much of Derry, which was called "O'Kanes Country". Here the O'Kanes served as the inaugurators of the great O'Neill family, holding sway till the Ulster plantation.

O'Cein or O'Kean, chief of Hy Fodhladha, on the borders of Tipperary and Waterford is mentioned by Aryan: "O'Kean from Machuin Meadaidh. His fame shall spread over tribes." In Waterford this family was centered in the barony of Decies without Drum.

The O'Keanes of Thomand are another of the name. Nearby the Cain(e) family of Galway of the Ui Fiachrach is found.

MacKean (Mac Eain) is of Scottish origins in Donegal and Derry. The Mac Cahans of west Clare are separate, and served as co-arbs of St. Senan.

Spelled as 'Kane' the name is found centered in Antrim, Londonderry and Dublin in 1890. 'Keane' was a name of Galway, Clare, Kerry and Mayo; and Cain was a name of Mayo at that time.

The Keanes' of Beech Park, Co. Clare, descend from the family of Co. Derry. One of the name settled at Ballyvoe, near Ennis in the 1600's.

In 1659 'McCane' was a principal name of Armagh, and O'Kane was in Antrim. Keane is the most numerous spelling of all these names today.

161

O'Kearney, Carney

Irish Book of Arms plates 161, 219

O'Catharnaigh, O'Cearnaigh

Carney, Keherney, McCarney,

Several origins exist for this name. Anciently one family can be found as O'Cearnaigh in Mayo near Moynulla, another was found in the Clare/ Tipperary area. The most noted descend from O'Catharnaigh of Kilcoursey (Teffia), Co. Offaly.

Keatings History mentions that the O'Kearneys were a clan near Kinsale, in Cork, where they are placed on the Map of Ortelius, and where they are given by O'Heerin as chiefs of Ui Floinn.

The O'Kearneys of Clare were chiefs of Abhuin Ui Chearnaidh, or O'Kearneys river, a district around Six-Mile-Bridge, in the baronies of Tulla and Bunratty.

O'Dugan gives O'Kearney, as prince of Teffia and says "High princes of Teffia, who obtained renown, is O'Caharey of the battling arms". Their name was rendered O'Kearney and they possessed extensive lands in Teffia, or Westmeath, and many of the name remained there. The chief branch of the name was called Sinnach O'Catharnaigh, and the word Sinnach, which means fox, led to the chief of the name being called 'an Sinnach' or 'The Fox'.

They were of the race of Ui Neill, and their territory comprised extensive districts in Teffia, containing parts of the baronies of Rathconrath and Clonlonan in Westmeath, and parts of the barony of Kilcourcy in Kings Co..

In the 1890 index 'Carney' was only given in Mayo. 'Kearney' was given in Dublin, Cork and Antrim with 3 times the population of 'Carney'.

In 1659 'Kearney' was a principal name of Tipperary and found in Waterford. 'Kearny' was a name of Kilkenny. 'O'Carney and O'Carny' were principal names in Donegal and 'Carney' was a name of Tipperary and Louth.

Keating

Irish Book of Arms plates 161, 213

Cethyn, Ceitinn

O'Keating, MacKeating, Keeting

The Keating name, which is also found in England, arrives in Ireland in the wake of the Norman invasions of the 12th century. They are noted as early settlers in Wexford.

They are found as well among the chief families of Waterford and Tipperary and are given as among the old English families of Wexford in Keatings History. They are noted there-in as serving as barons of Kilmananan. The family is often found noted in opposition to the English, particularly in Co. Carlow.

By the time of the 1890 birth index, 130 births were recorded in Cork, Kerry, Tipperary and Dublin.

In the census of 1659 the spelling of 'Keatinge' is found as a principal name of Tipperary. 'Keating' is found as a principal name of Waterford, and in Kildare and Kilkenny among other locations.

The most noted of the name is Dr. Geoffrey Keating (1570-1644), author of the famous 'History of Ireland' , a rare source of Irish history and legend currently available in reprint from the Irish Genealogical Foundation. Much information from his work is included in this book. Of his line were some Keatings of Tubrid, Co. Tipperary, in the last century.

The name of Keating was in some cases taken from Cethyn, which was a personal Welsh name. Keating has also replaced the separate surname of Keaty of Co. Limerick on occasion.

Individuals of the name;
Luke and Catherine, Queens County, New York, in the 1800's.
Hanna, 1732 a.d. Ulster County, N. Y.
Henry Keating, Charleston , S.C. 1817.

O'Keefe

Irish Book of Arms plates 161, 263

O'Caoimh

O'Keeffe, Keefe, Keife, Kiefe

The O'Keefe family has always been identified with Cork, and they remained there in the 1890 index, with the majority of Keeffe and O'Keeffe hailing from that county. A surprising number of families kept the 'O' prefix before the name at that time, and even more have added the 'O' back in modern times.

The O'Keefes served as marshals of Desmond and princes of Fermoy. They had several castles, the chief of which were those of Dromagh and Dunragil. O'Keeffe is anciently given as a chief of Glanworth in the barony of Fermoy, Co. Cork according to O'Heerin.

Forced from their original land in Cork with the coming of the Norman invasions of the 12th century, the Roche family assumed control of their lands. 'Pobble O'Keeffe' marks the area towards which they moved, to the west of their original lands, in Cork, near Duhallow.

O'Heerin spoke of them as "O'Keeffe of the brown and handsome brows, ...chief of Glen Avon.".

One of the 100 most numerous names in Ireland, the O'Keefes descend from Art Caemh, the son of a King of Munster .

In addition to Cork, 'Keeffe' was also found in Waterford, Kerry and Kilkenny. 'O'Keeffe' was found in Limerick and Dublin in the 1890 index.

In the 17th century Keefe was a principal name of Kilkenny, O'Keefe was so in Cork (and found in Limerick). 'O'Kiefe served as a principal name of Limerick and was also found in Clare.

In the past the most popular form of spelling the name has included the double 'e' and double 'f' as in O'Keeffe.

Father Eoghan O'Keefe (d. 1726) was the president of the Bards of Northern Cork. One of the name served as a general in the Irish Brigades of France.

O'Kelly

Irish Book of Arms plates 29, 119...

Ceallach

Keely, Queally, Keily, Kellye, Kehily,

The surname of O'Kelly springs from the personal name of Ceallach said to infer war or contention.

Descended from Milesius, King of the Celts, Kelly is the 2nd most popular name in Ireland, and among the top 60 names in America. Several unrelated families of O'Kelly are found in Ireland, accounting for its great popularity today.

Most prominent are those of Ui Maine who descend from a chieftain in 874 A.D.. Various branches of this family bear different arms, but all use the green enfield as their crest, and that animal was adopted after the battle of Clontarf in 1014 A.D.. It is said that it rose from the sea saving a fallen comrade.

The O'Kellys were treasurers of Connaught, with castles in Galway and Roscommon. With the coming of the 12th century invasions they fell into decline. The O'Kelly of Gallagh however, retained his title into this century.

Ancient Kelly burial grounds are located at Clonmacnois and Kilconell.

Other O'Kelly septs are found in Breagh (Meath and Dublin), Ulster (Derry, in the barony of Loughinsholin), Leighe (Laois), Gallen (Laois), Magh Druchtain (Laois), Ui Teigh (Wicklow), Og Ceallaigh (Sligo, Templeboy parish), Corca Laoigdhe (Cork), and Clanbrasil MacCoolechan (Down).

Princes of Ui Maine, O'Kelly castles are found at Aughrim, Garbally, Monivea, Maylough, and Castle Kelly is in Galway. Co. Roscommon held castles at Athlone, Athleague, Crobeg, Galy and Shryne of the O'Kellys.

Michael "King Kelly" (b. 1857) was an early baseball star in America. Jack Kelly, Olympic medal winner, was the grandfather of Princess Grace.

Mac Kenna

Irish Book of Arms plates 161, 263

Mac Cionaoith

Kennagh, Kenah, Ginnaw

The MacKenna surname is among the 100 most numerous names in Ireland. In ancient times, as well as today, the Mac Kennas are a family of the province of Ulster, in the north of Ireland.

Most anciently they are found of the Ui Neill in Ulster, but the name is found as far south as Cork and Kerry. They are anciently given as chiefs of Truagh, in the barony of Trough, in Co. Monaghan in modern times. They are found several centuries later in the parish of Maghera, in Co. Down.

O'Dugan gives the name in Truagh as well, but says that the family was originally of Meath.

The MacKenna family has in general kept the 'Mac' prefix before the name. It is noteworthy to recall that only 21 births of the name are given as 'Kenna' in the 1890 index, mainly in Dublin and Tipperary. 'MacKenna' on the other hand had over 200 recorded births, mostly in Ulster, at that time.

Many of the name have been of literary note in the last few centuries. In the 17th century 'census' of 1659, the name of 'Kenna' was found as a principal name of Kildare and in Queens county. McKenna was a principal name of Monaghan at that time.

Shirleys History of Monaghan ties the family to Portinaghy, parish of Donogh, where one of the name was sheriff. In 1640 sixteen McKennas were in the barony of Trough, 3 of whom were Protestants. All had small holdings limited to a townland or two.

In 1659 there were over 90 heads of families of this clan in Monaghan.

Patrick McKenna, in 1591, was granted Ballydavough, Ballymeny, and Ballylattin, and 12 estates besides. Some of this line withdrew to Spain.

O'Kennedy

Irish Book of Arms plates 87, 161

O Cinneide

Quenedy, Kenneday, Kenedie, Kenedy

Kennedy is one of the 20 most numerous surnames in Ireland. The name is taken from Cinneide, nephew of the great high-king Brian Boru. O'Kennedy is given by O'Heerin as a chief of Glen Omra. Of the Dalcassion race, they held the barony of Upper Ormond in Tipperary. This family held its rank from the 12th to the 16th century. O'Heerin spoke thusly:

"O'Kennedy, the reddener of spears, Rules over the smooth and wide Glen Omra, His tribe possesses the brown plains gained by valor; He has obtained his lands without opposition."

Found early at Killaloe in the barony of Tulla Lower in Clare, note the place name of Killokennedy parish.

Forced by O'Briens and MacNamara to other lands, we find the family as 'princes of Ormond' at a very early date.

The family divided into 3 branches as follows. 1) Kennedy Don (Brown), 2) Kennedy Fionn (Fair), and 3) Kennedy Rua (red). They are recorded as settled in Antrim in the 17th century - but the name may be Scottish, for Kennedy is also a Scottish name there.

Note the variant spelling of Quenedy in France, just as Queely has been said to be a variant of Kelly in that country.

In 1659 Kennedy was a principal name of Meath, O'Kennedy and MacKenedy were names of Limerick, Kenedie of Westmeath, O'Kenedy of Londonderry and Mac Kenedy of Limerick.

By the time of the 1890 index we find Kennedy with some 446 births, mainly in Tipperary, Dublin and Antrim. There was also a minor branch of Kennedy of the Ui Maine.

The Kennedy family of Baronrath, Co. Kildare are also found seated at Straffan, and Newcastle Lodge, in that county.

O'Kenny, Kenney

Irish Book of Arms plates 68, 96

O Cionnaoith

Keaney, Keany, Kinney, Kinnie,

O'Kenny families may claim any one of several origins in Ireland. Most of the name are considered to be of true Irish origins coming from OCionnaoith, of either Tyrone or Galway, or from the O Coinne family of Co. Down. Others, in lesser numbers, are doubtlessly of foreign origin, coming from France or England and settling in Ireland.

O'Dugan finds O'Kenny as chief of Moy Ith along with O'Quinn. Moy Ith was in the area of the barony of Raphoe, and in the barony of Tirkeeran in Derry.

The "MacKennys or Keaneys" are also mentioned among the several clans in the county of Leitrim, not mentioned by O'Dugan.

Among the 80 most numerous names in all of Ireland, most originally hailed from Galway, Roscommon (and Dublin city). It remains so to this day. They represent the old Ui Maine Kennys.

A 'Kenny' family of English origins is noted to have settled in Wexford and branched into Galway and Roscommon.

In the census of 1659 'Kenny' is a principal name of Kildare, as well as being found in Kilkenny and Kings etc... O'Kenny was a principal name of Armagh and McKenny a principal name of Fermanagh in that census. Spelled simply as 'Keny' it was a principal name of Kildare and as O'Keny it was a principal name of Armagh. Most of these variant spellings are found simply as Kenny today.

Of the English families of the name one family from Somerset held lands in Galway and Roscommon in Ireland.

In the Irish Book of Arms there is a Fitzgerald-Kenney of Kilclogher, Co. Galway, and Kenney-Herbert of Castle Island, Co. Kerry.

Mac Keogh

Irish Book of Arms plates 255, 161

Mac Eochaidh

Kehoe, Keoghe, Keogh, M'Keo, Keough

The MacKeoghs are found in various locations in Ireland today, and they are fairly numerous family. By the time of the 1890 index three areas are identified with three spellings of the name. McKeough had 13 births in Westmeath, Keogh had 96 births mainly in Dublin, and Kehoe had 51 births in Wexford.

Anciently we find 3 origins of the name. "MacCeoch or MacKeogh" chief of Uaithni Tire is given in Owney, a territory later comprising the baronies of Owney and Arra in Tipperary, and Owneybeg in Limerick.

O'Heerin cites them thusly, "Over Uaithni Tire of rich produce, Rules MacKeogh as his chosen place.". In Tipperary the name of Ballymackeogh in the barony of Owney and Arra is noted.

A second family of the name is found in Athlone barony in Co. Roscommon. They were known as 'Lords of Moy Finn. (Magh Finn). This territory was known as MacKeoghs Country into modern times. The place name of Keoghville in the parish of Taghmaconnell stands in tribute.

The most noted family is found in Leinster. The MacKeoghs as chief bards were present at the inauguration of the MacMurrough as Kings of Leinster. Anciently found along with the O'Byrnes and O'Tooles in Co. Kildare, they subsequently are found in Wicklow and Wexford. The spelling of the name as Kehoe is most numerous in Wexford today.

In the 17th century 'Keoghe' was a principal name of Clare, McKeogh of Limerick, McKeoghe of Carlow, and Kehoe was a name of Kilkenny.

The horse of Capt. Keough, of the famous battle of Little Big Horn,was the only survivor of that battle.

163

Mac Keon

Irish Book of Arms plates 161, 235

MacEoghain

MacKeown, MacKeone, Owens,

The MacKeon name stems from the original Irish Mac Eoghain, which means son of John or Owen. This helps to explain several variant spellings of the name in Ireland. Names such as Mac Owen or Owens, Johnson etc...

MacKeown is often a name of Scots origin when found in Ulster, due to the Scottish settlers who arrived in the Glens of Antrim in the 13th century. It is said that some of these originally went under the name of Bissett. Note the placenames of Keonbrook in Co. Leitrim and Ballymakeown by Belfast.

The Irish families of the name are thought to originate in Co. Sligo anciently, moving into Co. Leitrim in more modern times.

A branch of the name is believed to have settled in Galway, thus accounting for the name there. We find them in the barony of Kiltartan on territory referred to as "Termon Brian MacOwen".

The surname of Owens may spring from MacOwens or O hEoghain. The latter family is often found in Co. Clare.

In the 1890 birth index McKeown was by far the preferred spelling of the name with some 119 births, mainly in Ulster. McKeon had 40 births in Leitrim and Louth, and McKeone had 12 births. Keon is found in Donegal, Down and Fermanagh in that era.

In the census of 1659 'McKeoine' was a principal name of Leitrim, McKeone a principal name of Leitrim, and O'Keoyne a principal name of Sligo.

In Keatings History the MacKeons are given as one of the clans of Roscommon.

164

O'Kieran, Kearns

Irish Book of Arms plate 161

O Ceirin

Kearon, Kerrane, Kearns, Kerin, Keerin,

O'Ceirin or O'Keerin was chief of an ancient territory in the barony of Costello, Co. Mayo, which comprised the parishes of Aghamore, Bekan and Knock. They remained on their original lands but fell in prominence in the area. They remain in Mayo to this day.

It is interesting to note that the Mayo family is said to have branched into Co. Clare. In 1659 O'Kerine is found in Clare, and Kerin in counties Kerry and Clare. O'Kerin was found in Sligo at that time. The most numerous spelling of the name in Clare and Kerry is Kerin.

O'Ciaran is given by O'Heerin, along with O'Brien and O'Halloran, as a chief in the barony of Imokilly in Co. Cork in ancient times, which possibly indicates a completely distinct family of the name. By 1890 the name is scarce in Co. Cork.

"O'Ciarain, or O'Kieran" is also given as a chief of Fearnmuigh by O'Dugan, as a clan of Tir Eogain.

Of the variant spellings of the name, Kearon has been found in Wicklow, Kerrane and Kearns in Mayo, and Kerin in Clare, Cork and Kerry. Perhaps the name in Clare is of Kerry/Cork origins as well as Mayo origins. MacKieran is also found in more ancient times in Donegal.

The 1890 birth index finds the family name of Kearns most numerous in Dublin and Mayo.

Individuals of the name are noted as erenaghs of Killaghtee in the diocese of Raphoe in the 17th century.

Mc Kiernan, Tiernan

Irish Book of Arms plates 170, 251

Mac Thighearnain

Mac Ternan, Tiernan, MacKiernan,

The names of McTiernan and McKiernan are believed to have come from the old gaelic name of "Mac Thighearnain", and the family is most often found in Co. Louth under the spelling of Tiernan. The 1890 birth index records 27 births there under that spelling. McKiernan had 9 births recorded in widespread locations.

Several unrelated families adopted this Irish name in days past. In Co. Cavan we find MacTiernan noted as the "defender of valiant chiefs". They are found in the barony of Tullyhunco. According to Keatings History the name was MacTiernan, alias Mac Kiernan, and Anglicized by some to Masterton. They were noted as numerous in Cavan and Leitrim at the time cited there, and they were said to descend from the famous O'Rourkes of Breffny.

Another family is cited in Keatings as "MacTighernain, or MacTernon, chief of Clan Fearghoile" in Co. Donegal in the province of Ulster. The name has also been cited as numerous in Fermanagh in times past.

Another family of the name is found in Co. Roscommon, and they are believed to be a branch of the O'Connors of the province of Connaught.

McTernan is found as a principal name of Leitrim in 1659. Kiernan was found as a principal name of Roscommon at that time.

Both O'Kernan and Mac Kernan were principal names of Fermanagh in 1659, and the Kernan spelling was prominent in the city of Dublin at that date.

King

Irish Book of Arms plate 23, 71, 73, 230

MacConraoi, O'Conraoi

Conry, Conroy, McAree, Gilroy,

King is one of the top 40 most numerous names of England. It is one of the 100 most popular names found in Ireland. Many of the name are certainly of foreign origins when found here.

Several old Irish families translated their old gaelic names into "King" on occasion. Among the candidates for such actions were the Conroy, Conry, McAree and Gilroy families. Mac an Righ, in gaelic stands for "son of the King", therefore, similar sounding names could be translated into the English name of King.

By the end of the 16th century one center for the name is in Roscommon, although it is not listed as a center for the name in the 1890 index there.

O'Cionga (O'Kinga) was the name of an old Irish family on Inismor Island in Lough Rea, and they were of note in Co. Westmeath as well.

The MacConroy family of Moycullen have been known to use the name of King also. In the last century they are found in Ballymaconry.

In the complete book of "Irish Family Names" the name of King is found as follows: 1) An ancient Irish Dalcassian sept settled in Cork, Limerick and Tipperary, 2) A principal name of Westmeath in the census of 1659 and 3) Found in Dublin, Galway, Antrim, Mayo and Limerick in the 1890 birth index, with 203 births of the name at that time.

Several families of the name are given in the Irish Book of Arms. Some are of note as influential including those who were the Earls of Kingston, Co. Cork, and the line of the Archbishop Wm. King (d.1729), who was a Protestant. Families of the name in that work include the Kings of Ballylin.

165

Kingan

The Irish Book of Arms plate 71

Kinghan

The family of Kingan of Glenganagh, Co. Down, descends from William Kingan, of White Abbey, Co. Antrim. The birth index of 1890 finds the family centered in Down and Mayo under the spelling of Kinghan.

O'Keenan

Irish Book of Arms plate 225

O Cianain

Keon, Kinane, Kennan, MacKeenan,

The ancient territory of Oriel marks the land in which the O'Keenan family is found at an early date. Here they are noted as serving as historians to the Maguires of Fermanagh. They are found spread out into Monaghan, Antrim, Down and Louth as well.

The family is cited by the Four Masters in the 14th century, and one of the name is given as the chief scribe of the "Book of Magauran".

'Keenan' is found in the 1890 birth index in Antrim, Monaghan, Dublin and Down. Among the variant spellings reported at that time was O'Keenan.

In the 17th century 'McKeanan' is found as a principal name in Co. Kerry, and McKenan was a principal name in Leitrim. These 'Mc' families may be separate from other Keenans, and they may indeed be variant spellings of other family names of the day. "O'Kenan" is found as a principal name of Armagh and "O'Kennan" as a principal name of Londonderry in 1659. The 'O' prefix shows up in Ulster on this 1659 census.

A representative of the Keenans, chiefs of Fermanagh, Sir Patrick Joseph Keenan, of Delville, Glasnevin, Dublin, was born in 1826, and was the son of John Keenan, of Phibsborough, Dublin.

Frank Keenan (b. 1859), American actor and the son of an Irish immigrant.

Kingsmill

The Irish Book of Arms plate 68

The Kingsmill family of Hermitage Park, Co. Dublin are given in the Irish Book of Arms.

O'Kelleher

Irish Book of Arms plate 207

O Ceileachair

Kelliher, Keller

The O'Ceileachairs, or O'Kellehers were originally of Co. Clare. Family members may trace their line back to a nephew of the last great high-king Brian Boru. The family name is still found in Clare, but the great majority of the name are found in Counties Cork and Kerry at the end of the last century.

In fact, the majority of the name are found transplanted in Co. Cork in the 14th century.

Spelled as Kelleher (with an 'e') there were 92 recorded births in Cork and Kerry. Spelled as Kelliher (with an 'i') the name is more widely distributed, and 24 births were recorded under that spelling in the 1890 index.

Confusion may exist in the variant spelling of 'Keller', more properly a German surname. None the less, in Ireland, Keller can be a form of Kelleher.

O'Hart says the O'Kellehers held lands from the 12th to the 16th centuries in Munster, but could not locate the family pedigree. "Donogh O'Kelleher, Bishop of Ossory, died in 1048 A.D.", the foregoing seems to be the earliest reference to the name from O'Hart at any rate. Other early references are hard to find, if at all.

From the same source we find that the Rev. Kelleher, of Glanworth, Co. Cork, represented the senior branch of this sept. A younger branch of the family was represented by Alderman Keller, of Cork, during O'Harts time, thus showing the change from Kelleher to Keller at that point in time.

Kingston

Irish Book of Arms plate 13 (titled)

Kingstone

The Kingston family has always been associated with the western parts of Co. Cork, and it has remained so into modern times. The name, as it sounds, is of English extraction. The 1890 birth index finds the family most numerous in Cork with 37 recorded births, and in Dublin, with 3 recorded births.

Mc Kee

McKay, McGee, McKey, McKeye,

Families of the McKee name are traditionally tied to the province of Ulster in Ireland. Here it is fairly widespread, being found as a principle name of Antrim, and in Armagh, Donegal and Down in the census of 1659. Antrim, Down and Armagh were the principle locations for the name two centuries later, as found in the 1890 birth index of Ireland.

Origins of a particular family of the name may be difficult to trace. When found as Keyes, the name may have arrived from England, or may simply be a different form of McKee. The same kind of confusion holds true for name like McKay and Mackey etc..which may be distorted forms of McKee at times.

Keegan

Irish Book of Arms plate 220, 239

Egan, Eagan, Eagen, MacEgan, MacKeegan

The name of Keegan can be linked to the midlands of Ireland most often. The 1890 birth index finds the family most numerous in counties Dublin, Roscommon, Wicklow and Leitrim.

166

O'Kinneally

Irish Book of Arms plate 162

O Cinnfhaelidh

Quinnelly, Kennelly, Kinneally, Kinealy

O'Kinealy is anciently given as a chief of a territory comprising parts of the baronies of Coshma and Small in Co. Limerick, and the family is thus mentioned by O'Heerin:

"The Eoganacht of fertile Grian Gaura,
A land producing sweetest apples,
A crown of female households in fame,
Belongs to (O'Kinealy) of red arms."

The location of the family in more modern times is found in the barony of Connello in Co. Limerick. The family fell from prominence in the wake of the Norman invasions of the 12th century.

Although not the most numerous of surnames, some 10 recorded births are found in the 1890 index under the spelling of Kenneally. That spelling was given in Cork, Waterford and Tipperary. As Kennelly some 9 births were recorded as well.

Quinnelly is sometimes found as a variant spelling of Kinneally around Co. Cork in Ireland, but Quinnelly is actually another name entirely.

One William Kenealy (d.1876) was the Mayor of Kilkenny. Dr. Kenealy OSFC, was the first Archbishop of Simla, India.

Mike (10 yrs.), Cathe. (2), Mary (8), and Cathe. (38), Kennelly are found listed aboard ship "Harmony" on April 16, 1847, (during the time of the great famine in Ireland). The ship sailed originally from Liverpool to New York. One Mary Kennelly (age 28) was found aboard the "Henry Clay", April 26, 1847, arriving at the port of New York.

Mc Kinney, Kenney

Irish Book of Arms plates 68, 96, 256, 259

O'Cionnaoith, MacCoinnigh

Kinnie, Kenney, McKinney, O'Kinney,

The O'Kenny families of Ireland are found documented in our version of Keatings History of Ireland. According to O'Dugan, they were chiefs of Moy Ith. The name is as well, one of the 100 most numerous surnames in all of Ireland.

As might be expected there are several distinct origins for the name. Most often the family hails originally from the Galway/Roscommon area, as a sept of O'Cionnaoith of Hy Maine.

In the north, in the province of Ulster, the name is found more anciently in counties Tyrone and Down, and they may descend from the Irish family of O'Coinne, but this is unproven.

The family name is found as a chief clan of Co. Louth (as MacKenny), and the MacKennys or Keaneys are found mentioned as numerous in Leitrim in more ancient times.

Of the many spellings of the name, Kenney is linked most often with Co. Leitrim.

To complicate matters some, the name is also one of settler families from England. One English family from Somerset was owner of lands in Galway and Roscommon for some time as well as other unrelated Kinneys being in that area.

The birth index of 1890 finds the name of McKinney listed with 42 births in the counties of Antrim and Tyrone.

Kinsella

Irish Book of Arms plates 162, 255

Cinnsealach

Kinsellagh, Kinsela, Kinchella, Kinselow,

Kinsella families descend from the noted Dermot MacMurrough, the 12th century King of Leinster who helped initiate the Anglo-Norman invasions of Ireland. The Kavanaghs who descend from the same line, along with Kinsella, represent two Irish surnames which do not have the 'O' or 'Mac' prefix in front of their names. This is a rare event, inasmuch most Irish family names were preceded by those prefix's early in history.

The family is found centered in the barony of Gorey in Co. Wexford in both ancient and modern days. References are found in many works referring to the name of this territory as "the Kinsellaghs".

In the 17th century Kinselagh etc.. is found as a principal name in Counties Wexford, Carlow and Kildare. "Kingshellogh" was an interesting principal name of Queens Co. (Leix), and is likely a variant spelling.

By the time of the 1890 birth index "Kinsella" is found with 81 births in Dublin, Wexford, Wicklow and Kildare.

Keary

One family of the name is found centered in Durhamstown, Co. Meath (and also in Skreen), in the early 18th century.

The Keary family of Co. Galway is considered to be a completely separate family (MacKeighry). They are found for several centuries settled in Woodford Co. Galway. The family is also found in Portumna, Loughrea and Portumna.

Kirkpatrick of Mohill co. Leitrim.

Arms.—Argent, a saltier and chief azure, the last charged with three cushions or.
Crest.—A hand holding a dagger, in pale, distilling drops of blood.
Motto.—I mak sicker.

167

Kirkpatrick

Irish Book of Arms plate 139

Kirk, Patrick

Families of the name of Kirkpatrick are given to be of Scottish origins, and not surprisingly are found centered in the province of Ulster in Ireland. Some of the name of Kirkpatrick are believed to have become "Kilpatrick" in Ireland. The family of Kirkpatrick is found centered in Co. Antrim in the 19th century.

Kiloughery

Killoughry, Killoury

A scarce name in our records, the family is linked with Co. Clare in Ireland.

Keaveney

Irish Book of Arms plate 234

O Geibheannaigh, Mac Geibheannaigh

Keaveny, Keeveny, Kevney, Guiney,

The Keaveney family is said to be an old family of Ui Maine, and is found to this day in that area. Originally the name could have included a Mac or O prefix. In isolated instances the name has even been interchanged with the name of Kavanaugh. Spelled as Keaveny the name is found in the 1890 index in Galway and Sligo. Listed as O'Keveney, the name is found in Keatings ancient work as follows:

"O'Caibhdeanaich, O'Coveney, or O'Kevenys, chiefs of Magh Airbh and Clar Coill, are thus mentioned by O'Heerin

"Over Moy Arve let us now record
O'Keveney, of the woody plain,
Head of each conference was the fair counselor,
who resides at Coill O'Cathosaigh.

The plain of Magh Airbh comprised the present barony of Cranagh, in Kilkenny".

Kirkwood

The Irish Book of Arms plate 101

The Kirkwood family of Woodbrooke, Co. Roscommon and of Curramabla, Co. Sligo are of the same descent and are given in the Irish Book of Arms. The birth index of 1890 finds the family centered in Antrim with 7 births, and in Limerick with 1 birth of the name at that time.

Kendall

Kindell, Kendal

In the Book of Irish Family names we find but one reference to the exact spelling of Kendall. Here counties Longford and Fermanagh are given as locations for the name, and it was said from one source to have arrived in 1786 from England.

There are obvious similarities to the Irish name of Kindellan, which if shortened would become Kindell. They were centered in Meath and Westmeath in ancient days, but the name has largely become of form of Connellan or other variant spellings today. I have no record of the name actually stemming from Kindellan in any event.

The name is most likely of foreign origins in Ireland, and this should help direct your search more effectively; i.e., start with Ulster and the pale surrounding Dublin, if you have no other clues.

Mc Kendry

McKendree

The name of a family in Ireland traditionally linked to Co. Antrim. Woulfe gives the name of McKendry as a variant spelling of McHenry.

O'Kirwan

Irish Book of Arms plates 54, 162

OCiardubhain

Kerovan, Kyrvan, Kerwan, Kirwin

The Kirwan family was one of the 14 tribes of Galway, and was a prominent force among that group of families. Early documents have cited the name as English or Welsh when it is found in Galway city.
Indeed, most of the so called "tribes" of Galway were of foreign origin, but it is held that Lynch and Kirwan were of old Irish stock, not of foreign introduction.

The separate and distinct family of O'Kerovan, is also found to have used the name of Kirwan as a variant spelling.

The name is recorded earliest in Co. Louth, and it is not found in the city of Galway until after the Norman invasions of the 12th century. This gave some reason for the name being thought to be of foreign introduction there.

By the time of the 1890 birth index of Ireland, 59 births were recorded in Dublin, Wexford and Tipperary. It is strange to note that the name was not found in Galway in that index.

"Kirwan" of Cregg is found in the Irish Book of Arms, traced back to William Kirwan who settled in Galway town in 1488. This work gives Stephen Kirwan of this line as the ancestor of Kirwan of Castle Hackett. Several of the latter served as sheriffs, alderman and Mayors of Galway. Thomas Oge of this line, also had the epithet of "caoch" attached to his name.

O'Hart also gives one Andrew Kirwan, alderman of Galway, who was ancestor of Kirwan of Cregg, who died in 1578.

168

Knox

Book of Arms plate 56, 57

Knox is the name of a settler family from Scotland often found concentrated in Ulster and Dublin. Some early records show the family in Donegal, and subsequently the name is also found in Tipperary and elsewhere.

The family of Knox of Brittas were originally of Prehen. The Knox family of Mount Falcon, Co. Mayo, and the Knox family of Clonleigh, Co. Donegal are given in the Irish Book of Arms.

The birth index of 1890 finds the family centered in Antrim and Londonderry.

Kearns

O'Ciarain

Kerns, Cairns

A name often found linked with Co. Cork in the past. There are several possible Irish origins of the name.

Keady

Keaty, McKeady, McKeedy, McKeedy

The family of Keady is found in the 1890 birth index centered in Co. Galway. Earlier records show the name with both the "O" and "Mac" prefix at times. The family is most often found in Galway and Mayo, and usually without any prefix at all in our records dating from the 17th century, when found with a prefix however, it is usually as "Mc" or "Mac" Keady.

Mc Kibbons

Mac Fhibin (son of Phillip?)

Mc Kibben, McKibbin, O'Kibbon

The spelling of the name as ' McKibbons' does not show up in the 1890 birth index. McKibbin is however listed in Counties Down and Antrim. The more traditional way of spelling the name would be as Mc Kibbin.
O'Kibbon is found in the 1890 index with scattered births.

McKibbin is listed in Milesian Families as arriving in Dublin and Derry in 1586, and of Scottish heritage.
The name appears to essentially be one of the province of Ulster in Northern Ireland.

The name is not among the top 2,000 names in the U.S.A. today.

Kickham

Little information has come to light for us on this surname. They are assumed to be of fairly recent introduction into Ireland, and some of the Kickam family name are found in Dublin City in the census of 1659.

Kidd

Kid

Families of the name of Kidd in Ireland are generally assumed to be of Scottish or English extraction. As would be expected, the name is one of Ulster and the surrounds of Dublin. The 1890 birth index finds the family most numerous in counties Antrim, Armagh and Dublin.

Kiely

O'Cadhla

Keily, Kieley, Keely, Kealey, Kealy,

This family is traditionally linked to the areas around Waterford, Limerick and Cork. Much confusion may result from the similarities between this name and the many "Kelly" surnames and variant spellings. The 1890 birth index finds the family name of Kiely most numerous in counties Cork, Limerick and Waterford. The spelling of Keeley at that time is found in Dublin, Wicklow and Galway.

Kilpatrick

Mac Ciolla Phadraig

Gilpatrick, Fitzpatrick, Kirkpatrick

The old form of the name from which Kilpatrick arises is that of Macgilpatrick. Some of the original name later took on the name of Fitzpatrick as well. Macgilpatrick stood for servant of or follower of St. Patrick. The "gil" in the name stems from giolla, which usually has some special religious significance.

Kilpatrick can also be of Scottish origins in Ireland, and in this case the family is usually found settled in the province of Ulster.

The family name is also found recorded in Leix, (Queens Co.).

The 1890 birth index records the name with some 24 births in County Antrim, under the spelling of Kilpatrick.
need 1659

169

Kilroy

Irish Book of Arms plate 253

Gilroy

One family of the name has been said to stem from the barony of Clonderlaw, Co. Clare. It was further found that near the year 1653, under persecution from the Cromwellian forces, one of the name settled in Keenagh, near Mount Nephin, in the barony of Tyrawley, Co. Mayo. The same famiy was said to have been found in that area in the 19th century.

The 1890 birth index finds the family most numerous in Mayo, Roscommon and Sligo.

Kinahan

Irish Book of Arms plate 225

O'Coinneachain

Kinaghan, Kinegam, Kinnegan, Kinigan

The Kinahan etc.. family can find early roots near the course of the Shannon River. The family name is often found in the surrounds of the Roscommon, Offaly and Westmeath county borders at the point of overlap.

Some confusion with the surname of Cunningham has been reported, and the names have been interchanged on occasion.

Kinane

Kinnane, Ginnane, Guinane

The Kinane family name is traditionally linked to Co. Tipperary in Ireland. Among other spellings for the name are those of Guinan, Guinane, Kinnane, and Ginnane.

Kincade

Kincaide, Kinkaid

The name of a Scottish family found settled in Ireland, particularly in the province of Ulster. One family of the name is found in Co. Sligo, with some holdings of note.

Mac Keag

MacKeague

McKeag and McKeague are both names traditionally linked to the province of Ulster in Ireland. The name is found early centered in Co. Down there, and some sources give the name as Scottish in origin.

Kinch

Kinche, McKinch

The name of a family traditionally linked to counties Wexford and Wicklow in Ireland. We find no evidence of the name of Kenchella (Kinsella), being shortened to Kinch, but it is a possibility.

Mc Kinley

Irish Book of Arms plate 265

McKinly, McGinley

The name of a Scottish family which settled in the province of Ulster, found most numerous in Co. Antrim. Some confusion and interchanging of names has taken place between McKinley and the Irish name of McGinley

O'Keevan

Irish Book of Arms plate 234

O'Caemhain.

Kevan, Keevane

According to "Keatings History" the name is given as to belonging to a chief of Moy Linny, a district in the barony of Antrim.

Kirby

O'Ciarmhaic, also of English origin

O'Kirby, Kerribly, Kerwick

The name of Kirby may be of either English or Irish extraction originally. Milesian families states that the name settled in Roscommon and Cavan in 1760 from England. The 1890 Birth index finds the name in Mayo, Kerry and Limerick. In Mayo the name may come from the original spelling as 'Kerribly'. In Kilkenny the family is found as 'Kerwick', and in Waterford as 'Kervick'.

In Keatings History O'Kirwick (Kirby) is said to be 'the mainstay of the territory" in which they resided. In the same work, a 12th century O'Kirby was 'King' of Aine, in the parish of Knockany, barony of small county, Co. Limerick. The name remains near these areas in modern times.

The 'O' prefix is seldom used with this name.

Kirk

Quirk

Kirk families in Ireland are assumed to be of Scottish extraction originally. As such, it is a name of the province of Ulster, with many records of the name found in Co. Louth as well. Some interchanging of the name with "Quirk" has occured, due to similarity in sound.

The 1890 birth index finds the family most numerous in Armagh and Louth.

O Kirwick

O'Ciarmaic

According to "Keatings History" the name is a form of O'Ciarmaic, which was often changed to Kirwick and Kirby. They served as chiefs of Eoganacht Ani, called by O'Halloran, Ani Cliach, now the parish of Knockaney, in the barony of Small County, Co. Limerick. They were thus cited by O'Heerin;

"O'Kirwick is the mainstay of the territory, A country inhabited by the most noble tribes, They are Ui Enda, Ani, and Auluim"

Kissane

Kisane, Gissane

The Kissane family is traditionally linked to Co. Kerry in Ireland.

Kilcoyne

Caoin

Coyne, Coen, Coin

The name of Kilcoyne, of which Coyne can be a variant of at times, is primarily found in the province of Connaught in Ireland. Most specifically we find the name in Mayo and Sligo.

As to origins of the name, Kilcoyne is thought to spring from 'caoin' meaning gentle, and to have been taken from St. Caoin. The formal meaning of the name 'Kilcoyne' would then be 'follower of St. Caoin'.

The birth index of 1890 finds the name in Mayo and Sligo in Ireland.

Kilcullen

Kilgallen, Kilgallon

The name of a family found centered in the barony of Dromore West in Co. Sligo, and surrounding areas, given as such in the 1890 birth index of Ireland.

170

Kilgallen

Kilgallon

The name of a family traditionally centered in Co. Mayo, and remaining there into the 19th century.

Mc Kernan

Irish Book of Arms Keirnan plate

Mac Thighearnain

Kernahan, Kiernan, Mc Kern

While the Kernan family traces its roots back to the MacTiernan sept, it is also spelled as Keirnan etc.. The main family originated in the area of Breffny, another is in Connaught and is affiliated with the O'Connors, a third branch is found in Fermanagh. It is in Fermanagh that the family spells the name most often as 'Kernan' or 'MacKernan'.

Supporting this claim the name of McKernan is found as a principal name in county Fermanagh on the 1659 census, as is the name of O'Kernan. At this time Kernan was a principal name in Dublin city, also found in Longford and Westmeath. The 1890 birth index records 12 births, all in Ulster.

Under other spellings of the name, counties Cavan and Leitrim rank as the most numerous McKiernan territory.

Kernahan is also another spelling related to the name.

Kilkelly

Irish Book of Arms plate 205

Mac Kilkelly, Killikelly, Kilkelley

The name of Kilkelly is said by many to be a variant spelling of the older form of Killikelly in Co. Galway. Many of the name have simply dropped the "Kil" prefix and become known as "Kelly".

We find the family of Kilkelly centered in the counties of Roscommon and Galway in the 19th century. One center for the name was at Cloghballymore in Galway. The original form of the name was as Mac Giolla Cheallaigh, i.e. Mac Gil Kelly.

Kilkenny

Kilkenny families are found centered in counties Leitrim, Mayo and Roscommon in the 19th century birth index of Ireland. In some cases Kilkenny families have likely shortened the name simply to Kenny, which of course, is a completely unrelated family.

O'Killeen

The name of Killeen is most often linked in older days to Co. Mayo, and the family remains there to this day. Placenames incorporating the name can be found elsewhere however. Note the townland of Ballykilleen in Offaly. The name is also found in Co. Clare in our records. The 1890 birth index finds the family most numerous in Clare, Mayo and Kings.

Killian

Mac Coilin ?

Killen, Killien, Killeen, Killion

The surname of Killian is traditionally found in Counties Roscommon and Westmeath in Ireland. The family has remained centered in these areas into modern times. The 1890 birth index finds 13 births of the name, all given to Roscommon and Westmeath, under the spelling of Killian.

Of variant spellings of the name, Killian and Killien are found in Clare and Galway, while Killion is found mainly in the traditional areas of Westmeath and Roscommon.

Killilea

Gillilea, Mac Kililea, Killelea

Killilea families are traditionally linked with Co. Galway and Co. Roscommon in Ireland, according to our records. The family remained in those two counties at the time of the 1890 birth index of Ireland.

Mc Kay

Mackay, Mackey

The name of a Scottish family settling in Ulster no later than the 17th century in Ireland. They were of the clan McKay in Scotland, and are found often settled in Co. Antrim.

Mc Killip

Mac Philib

Mac Killop, Kellops, Killips.

The McKillip name represents a branch of the Scottish Clan MacDonald. As would be expected the name is concentrated in Northern Ireland, and is found as a principal name (McKillop) of Antrim in 1659. It was also listed as among the 'principal Irish names with some Scotch' in the barony of Glencarn, Co. Antrim, at that time.

Kellops, Killips, and Killop are variant spellings.

Killoran

Gilloran

The name of a family traditionally linked to counties Roscommon and Sligo in our records, as evidenced by the 1890 birth index of Ireland.

Killough

Kelloch, Mac Kelloch, Killogh, Kellough

The name of a family of Northern Ireland given to be a branch of the Scottish clan MacDonald, more properly spelled as MacKelloch. In the census of 1659 we find the name in Co. Louth spelled as Killogh.

Kilmartin

Mac Giolla Mhartain

Gilmartin , Gilmarten

Both the names of Kilmartin and Gilmartin stem from the same old Irish family, that of Mac Giolla Mhartain. In the census of 1659 both spellings are found in Co. Fermanagh. In the 19th century birth index Gilmartin was found centered in Sligo and Leitrim.

Kerr

Car, Carr, Kar

The name of Kerr may generally be assumed to be of Scottish origins when found in Ireland. In Scotland, the name ranks among the top 50 most popular names in all the land. As would be expected, the family has been centered in Ulster, in Co. Antrim.

The 1890 birth index finds the family most numerous in Antrim, and in lesser numbers in Down and Tyrone.

Mc Kelvey

McElwee, McCalvey, McKelvy, McKilvie,

The family of McKelvey is found most anciently in Co. Donegal and subsequently in Co. Derry.

Mc Kissick

Mac Isaac

Mc Kissock, McKissack,,,

The McKissick name in Ireland is of Scottish origin. As expected it is an Ulster name. MacIsaac is a variant spelling used in Scotland as well. The birth index of 1890 shows the name as 'Kissick' being traditionally located in the Doagh district, Antrim Union, County Antrim.

Mac Kitterick

Ketterick, MacKitterick, Ketrick, Kittrick

The family of MacKitterick is traditionally tied to counties Monaghan and Armagh in Ireland. It has been found shorted to forms such as Kittrick and Ketrick. One family of the Ketrick name is tied to Westport in Co. Mayo. Spelled as Kitterick, all births of the name were found in that county in 1890 as well. With the "Mac" prefix the name is found mainly in Ulster at that time.

O'Kivlehan

Kevlihan

The name of a family said by Woulfe to have served as coarbs at Fore in Co. Westmeath. Several others of the name are to be found in Co. Sligo and surrounds in our records.

Knatchbull

One English family of the name is found centered in Co. Kilkenny in Ireland in the early parts of the 17th century.

Kneafsey

Crampsie, Cramsey, Bonar, O'Knawsie,

The Kneafsey family name appear to be an outdated form of an Irish family name traditionally linked to Co. Donegal. While some of the above spelling are still found in Ireland, it was becoming a rare surname by the turn of this century. It is also found spelled as such in Co. Mayo.

Most often it appears that the name is spelled as Boner, Bonar and sometimes Cramsie in Co. Donegal.

Mc Knight

Irish Book of Arms plate 209

McKneight, Mac Aveely, Fitzsimons,

Families of the name of Knight may be of Scots, English or Irish origins. Keatings History gives the name when speaking of the chief races of Norman descent settled in Ossory, Leix and Offaley. As given there, Fitzsimons took on the title of Mac Ridire, which was anglicized as Mac Ruddery, i.e. son of the knight. Mac Knight could also mean "son of (the) Knight". Further given in that work are the Stauntons of Mayo who changed their name to MacAveeley, in Irish Mac-an-Mhilidh, meaning son of the Knight as well.

Scots families of the name of McKnight are actually "MacNeachtain", the earlier form of the name.

The 1890 birth index finds McKnight centered in Antrim and Down, and Knight is found in scattered locations at that time. In the 17th century we find the name in Roscommon, Dublin and Kerry.

Knott

Nott, Knot

"Knot" families are found in the city of Dublin in the 17th century, others of the name are found from time to time in scattered locations in Ireand. Originally the name of Nott was believed to have come from separate origins, and both are believed to have arrived in Ireland after the 12th century Norman invasions.

Knowles

sometimes from O Tnuthghail

Newell, Knowls, Knowels, Knowle,

The name of Knowles is most likely of English extraction when found in Ireland. Spelled as Knowles the name is found in County Cork in the 1659 Census, and in Dublin and Antrim in the more modern 1890 index. The 1659 census shows as well, the spelling of Knowle, also in Co. Cork.

In Ulster, particularly in Down, the name is considered English. There was however an old Irish sept in county Kildare by the name of Newell, which may be corrupted to the above spelling.

One English family of the name is found in Kinsale, Co. Cork, settled in the 17th century.

Kyle

Kyle is the name of a Scottish settler family who settled in Ulster at least by the time of the 17th century settlements. We have most often found the name in Co. Derry. The 1890 birth index finds the family most numerous in Antrim and Londonderry.

Kerrigan

Carrigan

Take note of the placename of Ballykerrigan in the barony of Clanmorris in Co. Mayo, not extremely far from a subsequent location for the family name in Co. Donegal. The 1890 birth index finds the family most numerous in counties Mayo and Donegal.

Kyne

Kine, Coyne

The name of Kyne is traditionally linked to the county of Galway in Ireland. Families of the name may spring originally from the older form of the name "O'Cadhain", which can also be found translated as Coyne. The 1890 birth index finds the family most numerous in Galway, and with 1 birth of the name in Co. Mayo.

172

Kenefick

Kennefick, Kenneficke

The name of a family traditionally linked with Co. Cork and surrounds in Ireland. The family is given as arriving in Ireland in the wake of the Norman invasions, in the 13th century, settling in scattered locations.

Kennelly

Irish Book of Arms plate 225

O'Cinnfhaolaidh

Kenneally, Kineally

The family is found early in Co. Limerick, often around the baronies of Conello, and subsequently in Tipperary, Waterford and Cork. The 1890 birth index finds the family most numerous in counties Cork, Waterford and Tipperary.

Mc Keever

Mac Iomhair

McIver, McIvor

The name of McKeever is traditionally linked with counties Antrim and Derry in Ireland. The possible variant spelling of McIvor is more often found in Tyrone and Derry.

Kenrick

Kendrick, McKenrick, McKendrick

Families of the name of Kenrick are given with only five births in the 1890 index, four of those were in Munster. The family has also been cited as that of an old family of the province of Ulster. Kendrick is another spelling used by the same family. The name of McKendry has no proven connection to that of McKenrick in our records.

Kent

The settler name of Kent is traditionally linked with counties Cork and Meath. Note the name of Kentstown in Co. Meath. Early reference to the name is found near Dublin, where Kent of Daneston was a prominent force.

O'Hart gives the name in Tipperary by the 15th century at least, and we find one Major Kent, in King Williams Army. In the census of 1659 the name of "Kent" remained a principal name of Tipperary as well.

The 1890 birth index finds the family most numerous in Cork.

O Kerins

Irish Book of Arms plate 213

O Ciarain, OCeirin

O'Kerin, Kerin, Mac Kieran

The name of Kerin is found in the birth index as being located in counties Kerry and Clare in comparatively recent times. In the census of 1659 O'Kerin was given as a principal name of county Sligo. The name is considered primarily to be one of the province of Connaught more anciently. Today the name can still be found in Monaghan, Fermanagh, and in lesser numbers in Cork.

The name may also be a variant of MacKieran, as an older Donegal name.

Mc Kerlie

MacCairill, Cairle

A family of Scottish heritage of some note in Galloway for several hundred years. They are found there into modern records, and also in the north of Ireland. The earlier form of the name is said to have been MacCairill, and subsequently Cairle.

Kett

Early pedigrees find the name of Connor Kett, of the Burren, near Ballyvaughan in Co. Clare, who settled in Kilbaha in the west of Clare and was living in 1690. It was said that this Connor had a brother who served in the Spanish fleet. The family is found in the same area, namely that of Farrahy, near Kilkee into the late 19th century.

Kettle

Kettyle

A fairly rare surname of Ireland, some families so called are of English origins, and some of the same may have settled in Ireland over time. Others of the name may descend from MacKettle or MacKettyle.

Kevane

O'Ciabhain

Keevane

Our records show the Kevane family anciently in Co. Cork and subsequently centered in nearby Co. Kerry.

Mc Kevitt

McKevit

The name of a family found centered in Co. Louth in the 19th century, traditionally located in that county and adjacent areas. It is believed that the name stems from the MacDevitt family which was of Co. Donegal origins.

Keys

Keyes, Kee, Kees

The Keys or Keyes family name is most often found in the province of Ulster, often centered in Co. Fermanagh. The name may be either of English extraction or from the Irish McKee, (Mac Aoidh), or in isolated cases from the Irish McGee. (McGee = Gee = Kee or Key).

The 1890 birth index finds the family name of Keys most numerous in Fermanagh and Antrim, and spelled as Keyes most numerous in Tipperary and Wexford.

173

Lacey, de Lacy

Irish Book of Arms plate 162

de Leis, del essse

Lacy, Leash, de Lees, Lacie, O'Lacy, Lacye

Among the chief families of settlers in Limerick, Clare and Louth, may be included the distinguished name of Lacy or de Lacy.

In the year 1172 Henry II granted Hugh de Lacy, in exchange for the service of 50 knights, the whole kingdom of Meath, of which he was made Lord Palatine, with the same powers as the King of Meath.

De Lacy divided Meath among his chiefs who were commonly known as De Lacys' barons. Robert de Lacy received Rathwire in Westmeath, where his descendants became barons.

The de Courcey family was in conflict in no small degree with de Lacy 'clan'. De Lacy prevailed in banishing the former power and the family became Lord of Meath and Earls of Ulster.

Former seats of power for the name can be found at Bruff, Bruree and Ballingarry.

The above families are certainly the most well know of the name and the de Lacys of Limerick, who were of some military note, may be of different origins entirely.

The name can be found earlier spelled as del Esse and de Lees before becoming the now common Lacy or de Lacy. It should be noted that the Irish family of O'Laitheasa of Wexford is also found using the name of Lacy on occasion.

Spelled as Lacie, the census of 1659 finds the name in Limerick, and O'Lacy and Lacye are found as well.

In the 1890 birth index both "Lacy" and "Lacey" are found in Wexford, Dublin and Galway.

"The Roll of the House of Lacy" by E. de Lacy-Bellingarri, was published in Baltimore in 1928.

Lally

Irish Book of Arms plates 162, 224

O Maolalaidh

Mullaly, O'Mullally, Laly

In Ireland, families of the name of Lally were originally called Mullally. They were of the Ui Maine anciently, before the time of the Norman invasions of the 12th century. The family lost power as a result of their conflicts with the Burke clan, but they remain in the province of Connaught into modern times. Looking at the 1890 birth index we find "Lally" as the most common spelling of the name with 34 births is Mayo and Galway. The older form of Mullally was still in use, with 8 births of the name recorded.

They are found centered in the area of Tuam, Co. Galway in earlier times, and in the census of 1659 "Laly" was found in Roscommon.

Lally's Regiment of the Irish Brigades in the service of France can be found in the 18th century.

O'Hart gives Mullally of Moenmoy, Co. Galway, and O'Donovan says the family was then removed to Tuam, in the Castle of Tollendal, 4 miles north of Tuam in Galway. The Lallys and O'Naghtens were chiefs in turn of Moenmoy. Around the time of the Norman invasions they were forced to settle at Tollendal, where they became tributary to the Lord Bermingham.

In 1617 Isaac Laly, head of the family was seated at Tullaghnadaly according to O'Hart, and William Laly was of Ballynabanaby and Daniel Laly was of Lisbally.

The head of this family, after the battle of Aughrim, removed to France, and was the ancestor of Count Lally Tolendal, a colonel in the Irish Regiment in the service of France, who was beheaded in 1766. His son vindicated the outrage perpetrated upon his father and was made a Peer of France. (see Mullaly)

O'Lalor, Lawlor

Irish Book of Arms plates 69, 162

O'Leathlabhair

Lalor, O'Lalor, Lawler, Lawlor

O'Lalor was one of the 7 septs, or families, of Leix, and the O' prefix is generally not found with the name today. The leading members of the 'septs' were transplanted to Co. Kerry in 1609, but most of the family remained near their traditional lands. Records of the family can be found in the estate papers in the National Library of Ireland in Dublin.

Note the name of Lalors mills, where the 7 septs were were officially defeated by the signing of a treaty.

The Lalor families can be found in the same ancient genealogies as the O'Connors of Kerry and the O'Mores, as given in Keatings History (IGF). They are spoken of as follows: "The "O'Lawlors, or Lalors, took their name from Leathlabhor, prince of Dalriada, or Ulidia, now in the county of Down, in the tenth century, who was their ancestor, and they are therefore of the Irian race, or Clanna Rory of Ulster, and of the same descent as the O'Moores, princes of Leix...".

In ancient times they held extensive lands in Leix, in the baronies of East Stradbally and East Maryborough, Queens County. One principal seat of the family name was at Disert, near the rock of Dunamase. From here a branch of the family settled in Tipperary. A branch of this line is found in the Irish Book of Arms.

"Lalor" is found in the 1659 census as a principal name of Kildare, and also in Kilkenny. In more modern times the name is found in Dublin, Leix, Wicklow and Wexford in the 1890 index. In that work "Lawlor" is the preferred spelling of the name with 59 births, followed by Lalor with 42 births, and Lawler with 41 births of record.

174

Lambert

Irish Book of Arms plates 3, 79

not of likely gaelic origin

Lambart, Lamberton

Lambert is considered traditionally to be a name of English extraction when found in Ireland. Milesian families records the name in Galway, arriving in 1630 from England, and in County Mayo arriving in 1642 of Norman origin. The census of 1659 finds the name in Cork City, Louth, Roscommon, Dublin, Kings and Waterford. In the 19th century the name is found centered in Wexford and Dublin.

The name is as well found in the surname index to Keatings History of Ireland.

The Irish Book of Arms gives the family of Lambert of Broohill, Co. Mayo.

Lane

not of likely Irish origin

McLane, Lehane, Lyne, Lyons

The name of Lane is recorded as coming from both Scotland and England before settling in Ireland. Milesian families records the name as settling in Dublin and Wicklow in 1640 and of English extraction. The same source states that McLane settled in Derry in 1686, coming from Scotland.

The census of 1659 finds the name in Cork, Londonderry, Limerick and Tipperary. In more modern times, the name was found in the 1890 index most prominently in counties Cork and Limerick. Other English names with which Lane may be confused include Lehane, Lyne, and Lyons.

Langley

The Irish Book of Arms plate 99

Langly

The Langley family of Brittas Castle, descend from Henry Langley, of Priestown, later called Langley Lodge in Co. Tipperary and are given in the Irish Book of Arms.

Landers

de Londres

Londers

The name of Landers is most often assumed to be an Anglo-Norman one, and is found in several areas of Ireland. The family is most traditionally linked with the southern quarter of Ireland. The 1890 birth index finds the family most numerous in Waterford and Kerry.

O'Lenaghan

Irish Book of Arms plate 244

O Leannachain, O Luingeachan

Lenihan, Lenighan, Linehan,

The Lenaghan family is traditionally linked with county Roscommon in Ireland. The family is found centered in Tuamna, in the barony of Boyle, on several occasions.

The census of 1659 finds the spelling as "Lenaghan" in Co. Sligo. The 1890 birth index finds the name in Antrim, both as Lenaghan, and McLenaghan. County Cork was the most popular location for the name at that time with 50 births recorded there under the spelling of Linehan. The name, spelled as Lenihan in Co. Limerick with 14 births of the name in that index.

Maurice Lenihan (d.1895) was the author of the work entitled "The History of Limerick".

Lawrence

Irish Book of Arms plate 102

St. Lawrence

The name of Lawrence was brought to Ireland by English settlers no later than the 17th century, and the name is often found within the surrounds of the pale in Ireland.

The Lawrence family of Lisreaghan, Co. Galway, arrived in Ireland in 1571 in the retinue of Sir John Perrot, Lord President.

Lawless

arms in O'Hart

Lawles, Outlaw, Outlawe, Laweles, Labhles

Families of the name of Lawless in Ireland are said to have taken their name from the English word of 'laghles' or Outlawe. One noted family of the name is found in Cloncurry, Co. Kildare. They were originally of English extraction.

The name is found several times after the 12th century Norman invasions of Ireland in Dublin, Galway and Mayo.

The census of 1659 finds the family in Kilkenny and Dublin, and it is in Dublin where the name is most prominent today.

Note the name of Mount Lawless in Australia, so named after an Irish family who settled there.

"Honest Jack" Lawless, b. 1772, was a noted politician of the Dublin family of the name. John Lawless was of Shank Hill, Co. Dublin..

The pedigree of Lawless of Co. Kilkenny is given in O'Harts work.

Hon. Edward Lawless, third Lord of Cloncurry (d.1869) was laid to rest at the family mausoleum at Lyones in Co. Kildare.

We have further mention of one Robert Lawless of Abington, Co. Limerick, and of one General William Lawless (d. 1814 Paris), who was promoted to that position by Napolean in 1813 a.d..

175

Leader

Irish Book of Arms plate 32

The Leader family of Stake Hill, Co. Cork is found in the Irish Book of Arms.

Langan

O'Longain

Langen

Families of the name of Langan are traditionally linked with Co. Mayo in Ireland.

Ledwidge

Ledwich, Ledwith

One Ledwidge family settling in Ireland is said to be originally of German heritage, settling in England, and subsequently in Ireland.

Families of the name are generally given as settling in Meath around the time of the 12th century Norman invasions of Ireland.,and subsequently they were prominent in Westmeath in the14th century.

Others of the name are found to be among the leading "citizens" in Co. Kilkenny by the year 1600. In the census of 1659 the spelling of Ledwich is found in Co. Roscommon, and Ledwidge was a principal name of Westmeath at that time.

Note the placename of Ledwichtown in Co. Westmeath, so named in their honor.

Frances Ledwidge (d. 1917), the poet, was one of the Westmeath family. William Ledwidge, lending some strength to the argument for German origins perhaps, was an opera singer born in Dublin who changed his name to Ludwig!

Ledwich is a variant spelling of the name and visitors to Dublin will note the Ledwich Medical School, named after Thomas Ledwich (d.1858).

The 1890 birth index finds the name of Ledwith most numerous in Co. Dublin.

O'Leary

Irish Book of Arms plates 162, 204

O Laoghaire

Lairy, Leery, Oylear, Oiler

O'Leary, along with its variant spellings rank among the top 70 names in Ireland. In the 1890 index "Leary" outnumbered "O'Leary" by a 3 to 1 margin. That trend has begun to reverse itself in modern times, with many adding the "O" back onto the name.

Both of the above spellings are most often found in Cork and Kerry, but Leary is also found in Wexford and O'Leary in Limerick in the same index.

The O'Learys are traditionally tied to Cork throughout history. They served as chiefs of Iveleary, of the Ithian race, and possessed the city of Roscarbery in ancient times. Iveleary, or "O'Learys Country" as it was called, can be found in Muskerry, in Cork, between Macroom and Inchageela. Several of their castles stood here, including those of Carrigafooky, Carrignaneela, Carrignacurra, Dundarierk, and Drumcurragh.

The family is found early in Cork, and they were later forced by the Norman invasions into the lands of MacCarthy of Muskerry, in Cork. Note the two place names of Ballyleary in Cork, testifying to the O'Learys of the past.

In the "census" of 1659 "O'Leary" is given as a principal name of Cork City, and in Kerry. "Leary" is also a principal name of Cork, being found in Kerry, Clare, etc... "Leery" is another variant spelling of the name. A confusing situation is that when the 'mac' prefix is dropped from MacCleary, you can end up with "Leary" as well.

Family members are numerous among the ranks of fighting men on the continent and in Ireland. The name has become "Oyler" and Oiler in France, by moving the 'y' sound to the front of the name instead of leaving it at the end.

O'Lee, Lea

Irish Book of Arms plate 30

Mac an Leagha, O'Laoidhigh....

Lea, MacLee, MacAlea, McLee, O'Lee,

Families of the surname of "Lee" in Ireland may stem from any one of several origins. Lee is a common name in England, and some of the name are originally from there. Lee is also an old Irish family name, stemming from families of O'Lee and MacLee. This helps to account for the widespread location of the name in Ireland.

In Co. Galway the name stems anciently from O'Laidhigh. They produced several medical men of note, and served as hereditary physicians to the O'Flahertys of Connaught.

In Cork and Limerick we find the family stemming from O'Laoidhigh, and in Leix (Queens), we find MacLaoidhigh as an early form of the name. In Ulster there is Mac an Leagh, also known as MacAlee and Lee when shortened.

Research is needed to determine from which line a "Lee" family descends.

In the 1890 index "Lee" is found mainly in Antrim, Dublin, Galway and Limerick with some 120 births given. McLee was still found as a variant spelling, confined to certain areas at that time.

In 1659 "Lee" is found as a principal name of Co. Waterford. The spelling of "Lea" was common at that time however, found in Louth, Queens, Carlow, Dublin and Roscommon.

In the same census Leah and Leagh are found in Co. Cork, and they may serve as variant spellings of Leaghy or other local names, though no doubt some of the name of Leah and Leagh have now become Lee.

Lee, when of English origins, is given by several sources as having been settled in the early 1600's in Co. Tipperary. This accounts for one instance of the Lee family arriving from England.

176

Leech

Irish Book of Arms plate 65, 105

Leach, Mac an Leagha

Families of the name of Leech in Ireland are generally of Scottish origins. One branch of the name is found settled in Co. Mayo, and they were originally from Chesire. The name is also found in Co. Wicklow subsequently. Some of the name may be of Irish extraction, due to translation of Irish surnames into English sounding forms.

The Leech family of Clooncorra is found in the Irish book of Arms as is the Leech family "late of Kippure".

The birth index of 1890 finds the family centered in Dublin.

Larminie

A name traditionally associated with Co. Mayo in Ireland and found settled in the 18th century near Newport, in that county.

Leyne

O Laighin or O Laoghain possible gaelic

Lyne, O'Leyne, Leen, Leane, Lyons,

Several family names become inter-related when studying this name. However, for the closest spelling to Leyne, we find O'Leyne in the census of 1659 as a principal name in County Cork, and also found in Limerick. The Lyne spelling is most often associated with Co. Kerry, where by the way, Lyons is often used as a synonym. The spelling of Leane is also found in Co. Kerry and is said to be a variant spelling of Lyne as well. In county Cork, the family name is associated with the medical professions.

The name is found in the surname index of Keatings History of Ireland, and in the book 'Irish Families'.

In the works of Matheson the name was found to be in the Dingle Union, near the turn of the last century.

Leehey

Irish Book of Arms plate 32, 225

O Laochdha

Leehy, Lahy, O'Leahy, Leahey, Lehy

The Leehy family is found in the census of 1659 as a principal name of the city of Cork. As O'Leahy more anciently the name springs from O'Laochdha, and is numerous in the province of Munster. Counties Cork, Kerry, Limerick and Tipperary have held most of the name into modern times. The Irish Book of Arms gives the family of Leahy of Southill, Co. Kerry.

Mc Larnon

McLernon, Mac Clarnon, Mc Larinon, Mc

The McLarnon family name is traditionally tied to the province of Ulster in Ireland. It is found centered in Co. Antrim in the 1890 birth index of Ireland. Many of the name will be of Scottish origins when found in the north of Ireland, but others are of Irish origin here.

Larrissey

Larissey, Larrissy, Larissy

At least one family of the name of O'Larrissey or O'Learghusa hailed anciently from the barony of Carra in Co. Mayo. Subsequently the name is found in several counties. As Larissy it is found as a principle name of Queens Co. (Leix), in the census of 1659, in the barony of Maryborough. Moving into the modern period, another location for the name is in Co. Kilkenny.

Lamont

The name of a Scottish family settling in Ulster no later than the 17th century. The name is found centered in Co. Antrim there.

Leeson

Irish Book of Arms plate 63

Leason

A fairly rare name in Ireland, some Leeson families had arrived in Ireland in the 17th century, coming originally from England. Others may be more properly of the "Gleason" or "O'Lyshane" families of old Ireland. In modern times the name is often connected to the city of Dublin. Leeson Street in Dublin was named after the Earl of Milltown.

O Laughran

O'Luchrain

O'Lougheran, O'Loughran, Lochrane,

The Laughran family is associated with Co. Armagh in Irish history. Originating there, they spread into the adjoining county of Tyrone. The name can be found in the ancient 'Annals' of history.

A noted ecclesiastical family of Co. Armagh, they are listed as priests, deans, and Franciscans there.

As Loughran, the name is found in Tyrone, Antrim and Armagh in the 1890 index.

Lavelle

La velle, Lavell

The name of Lavelle is traditionally linked with Co. Mayo in Ireland, and is considered to be a name from an established old Irish family. The 1890 birth index finds the family most numerous in Mayo and Galway.

Lamb

We find that most of the name of Lamb are of settler origins, coming from England. Some Irish families may have translated their names into Lamb as well.

177

LeFroy

The Irish Book of Arms plate 96

The family of Lefroy of Carrigglas Manor, Co. Longford are given in the Irish Book of Arms.

Laverty

Irish Book of Arms plate 203

Laferty, Lavarty

The name of Laverty is one of the province of Ulster found early in Co. Tyrone and in Co. Antrim. Some confusion exists between Laverty and Lavery, for the names have been used interchangably on occasion. These two names however, are believed to be of separate origins altogether. The 1890 birth index finds the family most numerous in Antrim.

Lavery

Laverty

Lavery is a name traditionally linked to the province of Ulster in Ireland, often found in Antrim and Armagh among other counties there. The 1890 birth index finds the family most numerous in Armagh, Antrim and Down.

Landy

Landa, Landers, Lawndy, Laundy, de Launde

The Landy family is traditionally linked to counties Kilkenny and Tipperary earliest in Ireland. In more modern times we find the name centered in counties Tipperary and Galway in the 1890 birth index. At the time of the census of 1659 we find the name under various spellings, including that of Laundy, centered in the barony of Balrothy in County Dublin.

Leigh

The Irish Book of Arms plate 70

Leigh, Liegh, Lye, Mac Lye

The Leigh family of Rosegarland, Co. Wexford is said to descend from the family of Francis MacLaoighsigh, MacLysach, MacLye, or Lye. He obtained lands near Geashill, in Kings Co. in 1552.

Laffan

One family of the name is found in Garristown and Lurgo in Co. Tipperary in the 17th century. The 1890 birth index finds the family most numerous in Limerick, Tipperary and Wexford.

Laird

The name of a Scottish family settling in Ulster not later than the 17th century. The 1890 birth index finds the family most numerous in Co. Antrim.

Lanigan

O'Lonagain

Lanagan

Families of the name of Lanigan are traditionally linked with counties Tipperary and Kilkenny in Ireland. The 1890 birth index finds the family most numerous in Co. Kilkenny.

Lappin

Lapin, Lapp

The Lappin family name is one of the province of Ulster in Ireland. We find many older references to the name in Co. Donegal. The 1890 birth index finds the family most numerous in Armagh, Tyrone and Antrim.

Love

The name of both Scottish and English families found in Ireland. The family name is traditionally linked to Co. Derry in Ulster.

Lendrum

The Irish Book of Arms plate 60

The Lendrum family of Magheracross, Co. Fermanagh, where the family has been found to have served as High Sheriffs.

Lardner

le Larndiner

The Lardner family name is sometimes of English origins when found in Ireland. The family is also found in Co. Galway, and here they are said to have been of old Irish origins.

Law

Lawless, Outlawe

The name of Law is largely a settler name in Ireland, arriving here from both Scotland and England over the centuries. Names such as Lawless have likely been shortened simply to Law by some. The 1890 birth index finds the family most numerous in Co. Antrim.

Leonard

Lenard

Most of the name in Ireland are surely of English origins, but a few may come from old Irish families who had thier names 'translated' into English sounding forms.

The 1890 birth index finds the family most numerous in Dublin, Sligo and Cork.

Lernighan

Lernihan, Lerhihan

A family name of Co. Clare according to our records.

Lyness

Lynis, Lynass

Lyness is traditionally linked to the province of Ulster. In 1890 the name is found centered in Antrim and Down, under the spellings of Lynas and Lyness.

178

Lentaigne

The Irish Book of Arms plate 54

The Lentaigne family of Tallaght is given to be of an ancient family in Normandy in the Irish Book of Arms.

Leamy

Leany

The name of a family most often associated with Co. Tipperary in Ireland. The name of Leany is also given in Co. Tipperary at that time, and we do not know if this represents the same family or not.

Leavy

Levy, Levi

The name of Leavy etc.. is considered to belong to an old Irish family found anciently in Longford and subsequently in Westmeath and Monaghan.

O'Lehan

O'Liathan

According to Keatings History the Lehan family (or O'Liathan more anciently), is given by O'Heerin as territory in Co. Cork, known more recently as the barony of Barrymore named after the Anglo-Norman family of Barry, who later became its possessors. This family built Castle Lehan, now Castlelyons. They are thus mentioned by O'Heerin:

"Lord of Ui Liathain, a warrior of fame,
is the hardy leader of the battalions of Munster, Of Ui Anmcadha he is rightful chief, The host of keen arms, of high nobility."

The 1890 birth index finds the family most numerous in Cork.

Leslie

Irish Book of Arms plate 62, 79, 101

Lusty, Losty, Lastly, Lasty, Lesley

The Leslie family is considered to be a family that settled in Ireland, coming from Scotland no later than the 17th century. Branches of the name are found in several areas of Ireland, both in the north and south of the country.

One family is found settled in or near Tarbert, Co. Kerry, another is found in Monaghan, another in Antrim, and yet another in Down. The exact relationship between these families remains clouded, but it is said that they all arrived from Scotland.

The Irish family now bearing the name of Leslie may be originally of the O'Losty, O'Lasty etc.. name. This family is traditionally of Co. Donegal.

The Leslie family of Leslie Hill, Ballymoney, Co. Antrim is found in the Irish Book of Arms.

The Leslie family of Ballibay, Co. Monaghan descend from George, the 4th Earl of Rothes and are given in the Irish Book of Arms.

The birth index of 1890 finds the family centered in Londonderry.

LeMass

Not a common name in our records to date, but Sean Lemass (d. 1971) served as prime minister of Ireland in modern times. This name may likely be a shortned form of another "le" name.

Levallen

One family of the name is found in Co. Cork at Waterstown, descended from an officer in King James II army.

Lewis

Irish Book of Arms plate 99

Families of the name of Lewis are assumed mainly to be of English or Welsh extraction when found in Ireland. This is so because the name ranks among the top 30 most numerous in both England and Wales. The name is found fairly widespread in Ireland.

The Lewis family of Inniskeen, Co. Monaghan and of Seatown, Co. Dublin are of the same descent and are given in the Irish Book of Arms.

The birth index of 1890 finds the family centered in Dublin, Antrim, Cork and Tipperary.

Lestrange

Le Strange, Strange

According to "Keatings History" the name of Lestrange was adopted by families of the name of Coscry and Cosgrave, who are given as ancient clans in Wicklow and Queens County.

Other families are on record as having settled in Ireland coming originally from Norfolk, England, and settling in the Roscommon area.

The 1890 birth index finds the family with 8 births in scattered locations at that date.

Lett

de lette, lete, de Leyte

Not a numerous family of Ireland, one family of the name is found in County Wexford in the 17th century, near Newcastle. This line was granted lands as a result of the Cromwellian conflicts. The origins of the name itself are unclear, it could stem from the Norman "De Lette" etc.. Another possibility exists that in isolated instances it could serve as a shortened form of Letimore, Letsam, Letsome etc.. This is not known to have happened however.

179

Lidwill

Irish Book of Arms plate 23

Ledwill, Ledwell, Lidwell

The family of Lidwill of Co. Tipperary in the 19th century, is found earlier of Shannaghmore, Co. Carlow, with possessions at Castle McDermott in Co. Kildare earlier.

O'Liddy

O'Lideadha

Liddy

Liddy and O'Liddy are traditionally linked with Co. Clare in Ireland. The 1890 birth index finds the family most numerous in Clare with 6 births, and in Antrim, with 3 births, spelled as Liddy.

Lillis

'laghles' (Old English form of Lawless)

Lawless, Lawson, Lill,...

The name of Lillis is said to be a variant of of the name of 'Lawless', in Counties Clare and Limerick. The 'Lillis' spelling is also found in County Cork. This is but another example of local spelling variants within Ireland itself. In the 1890's birth index the name is found in the province of Munster, with 4 out of 5 births being recorded there.

Some of the name are said to have settled in Ireland, coming from Wales, after the English invasion.

A traditional location for the name has been given as 'Cookstown Union, in County Tyrone'. The name appears as well in the surname index of 'Great Families of Ireland' and 'Irish Settlers on the American Frontier', two Foundation publications.

Litton

The Irish Book of Arms plate 104

Litten

The Litton Family of Ardavilling, Co. Cork, descend from Thomas Litton of Dublin, b. 1657, and they are given in the Irish Book of Arms.

Leyden

O Loideain

Lydon, O'Lydon, Liddane

The family name of Leyden is found in the 1890 birth index in counties Sligo and Clare in Ireland. Several distinct spellings and locations exist for the name. When spelled as Leyden it is most often a name of county Clare or surrounding areas in the province of Connaught. The similar sounding name of Liddane is also found in Clare. When found as O'Lydon, the name is said to be of Galway or Mayo extraction.

Lilly

Mac Alily, Lillie, Lilley

The name of Lilley is found to be a name of England, and in some cases families in Ireland today may originate from England. Others are found to be from "MacAlilly", an old Irish name, centered near Enniskillen in Co. Fermanagh. Under both spellings of Lilley and Lilly, the name is centered in counties Antrim and Down in the 1890 birth index. Some find the name of McLilly in Co. Donegal as well, and unsubstantiated listings show that family of Scottish origins in the 17th century.

Lloyd

Irish Book of Arms plates 26, 31, 52, 61

Loyd

The name of a Welsh family found in all four provinces of Ireland. The name has been found centered in the Roscommon and Limerick area and its surrounds, as well as elsewhere in Ireland.

Of those of the name arriving from England are given the Lloyd family of Losset, Co. Cavan.

The Lloyd family of Lossett, Co. Cavan are those found in the Irish Book of Arms, as well as the Lloyd family of Beechmount, Co. Limerick, Lloyd of Croghan House, Co. Roscommon, and Lloyd of Rockville, Co. Roscommon. The latter is said to descend from a High Sheriff of Roscommon in 1719.

The birth index of 1890 finds the family centered in Tipperary.

Limbrick

Limerick

A rather rare name of Ireland, apparently unconnected to the county of that name. The name is most often connected with the province of Ulster in Ireland, and specifically in Co. Down on several occasions in our records.

Lindsay

Lindesay

The name of a settler family from Scotland, settling in the province of Ulster in Ireland no later than the 17th century. The name of one such family is found centered in Co. Tyrone. The 1890 birth index finds the family most numerous in Antrim, where 50% of the family was located.

180

Loftus

Irish Book of Arms plates 6, 41

Loftis, Loughnane

This name has been cited in reference works as Scottish, English and Irish. Milesian families finds the name in Dublin and Clare, settling in 1563 from Scotland. The census of 1659 shows Dublin and Wexford as principal locations, while the more modern birth index shows County Mayo as the traditional homeland for the family name.

When Irish, especially in the province of Connaught, the name is said to have been taken from the original spelling of 'Loughnane'.

The Irish Book of Arms gives the Loftus family of Mount Loftus, Co. Kilkenny.

Little

Lyttle

The Little family, when found in Ireland, may be of either Scottish or English heritage. As would be expected most of the name are found in the province of Ulster, though other families of the name are found elsewhere. The 1890 birth index finds the family most numerous in counties Antrim, Dublin and Fermanagh.

Livingston

Livingstone, Levingston

The name of a family of Scottish heritage found settling in the province of Ulster in Ireland no later than the 17th century. Several of the name are found settled in Dublin as well. The name is said to sometimes be found as Levingston(e). The 1890 birth index finds the family most numerous in Armagh, Antrim and Dublin.

Lombard

Irish Book of Arms plate 52

Lumbard, Lumbarde, Lombarde

The place name of Lombardstown, in Co. Cork marks the traditional area of location for the Lombard family in Ireland. They are noted there as influential in politcal and financial affairs from an early date. They are assumed to have arrived in Ireland after the Ango-Norman invasions of the 12th century.

The name is earlier often spelled as Lumbarde, and they are given as a family in Ireland prior to the 15th century by several sources.

The Irish Book of Arms gives the family of Lombard of South Hill.

The birth index of 1890 finds the family centered in Co. Cork, where all of the name where located.

Lockhart

Lockart, Lockheart

The name of a Scottish family settling in the province of Ulster in Ireland, no later than the 17th century. The name is found most often in our records in counties Armagh and Antrim.

Lodge

One family of the name is found settled in Clonfada, Co. Limerick in the early 17th century.

Losse

One English family of the name is found settled in Dublin in the early 17th century in our records.

O'Lonergan

Irish Book of Arms plate 162

O Longargain

Londrigan, Ladrigan, Lundergan,

The O'Lonergans were ancient chiefs of Cahir, and surrounds in Tipperary. In the 14th century they were overthrown by the Butlers, earls of Ormond. The O'Lonergans were, in ancient times, a powerful family, three of the name are given by Ware, as archbishops of Cashel in the 12th and 13th centuries.

This early territory spoken of was east of Lough Derg in Tipperary. Their new lands appear to have been near Cashel as cited, and Cahir where the chief of the name was seated.

In Galway there is also a family of the name, likely a branch of the above mentioned Thomand sept. Found at Ballynabanaby, in the parish of Kilgerril, they served as harpers to the O'Kellys of Ui Maine.

"Lonergan", the most common spelling of the name is recorded with 49 births in Tipperary and Waterford in the 1890 index. The rarer spelling of Londrigan is found in Tipperary, Waterford, Kilkenny and Cork, with only 5 births in all.

In the 17th century the name was centered in its old home territory as "Lonergan", Lonergane, and Lonnergane, each of which was noted as a principal name of Tipperary.

O'Hart gives a junior branch of the Tipperary family moving to south Connaught, and becoming hereditary harpers to the O'Kellys, as cited above. His work also states that the Castle of Ballinamanaley, in the parish of Fohenagh, barony of Kilconnell, is said to have belonged to this family, and according to tradition, Lowville, the seat of the MacDonaghs, marks another residence of the 'music loving' Lonergons. This name is frequently found in the annals of Irish history.

Longfield

Irish Book of Arms plate 29

The Longfield family of Longueville, Co. Cork, is found in the Irish Book of Arms.

Logan

Irish Book of Arms plate 268

Loghan

According to "Keatings History" the name is given among the chief Anglo-Norman and English settlers in Ulidia, under DeCourcey and his successors.

The name is also given to belong to that of a Scottish family settling in the province of Ulster no later than the 17th century. They are found most numerous in Co. Antrim. Some of the name may also stem from the Irish family of Loghan (O'Leoghain).

Long, Longan

Mac Longachain

MacLongahan

According to "Keatings History" the name is that of a chief of a territory partly in the barony of Owney and Ara in Tipperary and partly in the barony of Coonagh, Co. Limerick. They are found alongside the O'Dwyers in that area.

The 1890 birth index finds the family name of Long most numerous in counties Cork, Dublin, Limerick, Kerry and Donegal.

Lynott

Lynnott

The name of a Norman family found in Ireland from the 13th century onwards.

Mac Loughlin

Irish Book of Arms plates 162, 163

O Maoilsheachlainn

MacLaughlin, MacGloughlin, Melaghlin,

The MacLoughlin family name in Ireland may stem from one of two completely independent septs. When shortened to "Loughlin" or Laughlin, some confusion may exist as to whether the original name was O'Loughlin or MacLoughlin.

One family descends from O Maoilsheachlainn, and they were known as O'Melaghlin into the 18th century. They descend from Malachy II, King of Ireland (d. 1002 a.d.), who fell to the powers of the great Brian Boru. The name is said to mean follower of Seachlainn, i.e. St. Secundinus. The Norman invasions of the 12th century mark the families continued decline from power. The family in more modern times was found as McLoughlin in Meath.

The second family of the name stems from MacLochlainn, (son of Lochlainn), of the northern Ui Neill in Innishowen, Co. Donegal. They are prominent in Co. Derry as well. The spelling of MacGloughlin is also used in Dublin today. They began to decline in power in the middle of the 13th century. A branch of this family settled in Leitrim under the leadership of the O'Rourke clan, and it is so recorded in the Composition Book of Connacht.

McLaughlin was the preferred spelling of the name in 1891, with some 191 births recorded mainly in Antrim, Donegal, Londonderry, Tyrone and Dublin. McLoughlin had 170 births recorded in various locations.

"The MacLaughlins or Clan Owen, was published by T. P. Brown in Boston, in 1879.

181

O'Loughlin

Irish Book of Arms plates 163, 220

O Lochlainn

O'Loghlen, O'Lochalinn, O'Laughlin,

Traditionally known as Lords of the Burren, this name comes from Co. Clare, the county which has always been the center of O'Loughlin country.

Lochlain (A.D. 953) is the man from whom the name is taken. Originally from the same clan as the O'Conners, two brothers split the clan with one forming the O'Loughlins and the other the O'Conners in the 10th century.

Corcomroe was the area inhabited by this family, and they ruled over the area known as the Burren, meaning the "Rocky Place."

O'Loughlin retained all of the Burren until the invasions of Cromwell. The occupiers remarked that the Burren, "had not enough water to drown a man, wood enough to hang him, nor dirt enough to bury him. This statement may have been true then, but the O'Loughlins thrive there to this day none the less.

Early O'Loughlin ancestors may have come from northern Ireland, and may not be an ancient Dalcassion sept. An ancient Dane or Viking heritage is also possible stemming from the possible word origins of "Lochlainn", a word used to describe the same. MacLoughlin is an entirely separate family.

Most powerful on the shores of the Atlantic and Galway Bay in earlier times, the Burren is still the heart of O'Loughlin country today.

Family researchers take note of the "History and Topography of County Clare" by J. Frost, Dublin 1883, and the "O'Loughlin Book", Irish Genealogical Foundation, Kansas City, 1981. The former work contains hundreds of the name not found in its index.

Another family used the name anciently, they were near Dublin, and are cited as Kings of Ireland.

182

Lowe

Irish Book of Arms plate 43

Low

Most of the name are found to be of English extraction, found settled in both the northern and southern ends of Ireland. It has also been said that the Irish family name of McLoy in the old territory of Oriel has been changed to Lowe in some instances.

The family of Low of Sunvale, Co. Limerick is found in the Irish Book of Arms. The Low family of Kilshane, Co. Limerick traces its descent from Simon Low, of Cork and Galbally, Co. Limerick, son of John Low who settled in Co. Tipperary.

The birth index of 1890 finds the family centered in Dublin.

Looby

Luby, Looby, Lubey, Loobey, Lube

Families of the Luby name and its variant spellings are most often linked with Co. Tipperary in Ireland, where families of the name are found settled by the 17th century. We also find some reference to the family name in Co. Kildare at that time. The most common spelling of the name in our records is as "Looby" in Co. Tipperary. Note the placename of Ballylooby. Most families of the name are assumed to have settled in Ireland from abroad.

The 1890 birth index finds the family most numerous in Co. Tipperary.

Lynskey

O'Loinscigh

O'Lynskey, Lynch

The name of Lynskey or Lynsky is believed to be a form of Lynch, found particularly in Mayo and Galway. It is here in Mayo and Galway that the name is found in the 1890 birth index. When spelled as above the name is not found in the 1659 census of Ireland.

O'Lowry

Irish book of Arms plates 85, 92, 130, 137.

O Labhradha

Lowery, Lavery, Loughry

Irish families of the Lowry or Lavery name descend from O Labhradha, a sept of the province of Ulster anciently. In later days they are found in Co. Down, near Moira.

Three branches of the name are of record. That of Trin-Lavery (which has also been translated as Arstrong - from trean - meaning strong), that of Roe-Lavery, from rua meaning red, and from Baun-Lavery, from 'ban' meaning white.

These Irish families above have remained in the province of Ulster into modern times for they are found in counties Armagh, Antrim and Down in the 1890 birth index. Laverty was located mainly in Ulster as well at that time.

The "Lowry" surname is also found in Ulster as a result of 17th century settlers arriving there from Scotland. Scottish families are found here under the spelling of Laurie as well. The Earl Belmore family is recorded as arriving from Scotland at that time and settling in Co. Tyrone, and he was said to be of the Laurie family of Maxwelton.

In 1659 Lowry and O'Lowry are found as principal names of Antrim and Donegal respectively. The name is as well given in Fermanagh and Down among other locations.

Numerous listings in the Irish Book of arms are given, including Lowry of Pomeroy House, Co. Tyrone, Lowry of Rockdale, Co. Tyrone, and those of Robert Swinborne Lowry.

Lucas

Irish Book of Arms plate 62

The name of an English family found settled in Ireland comparatively early. Several of the name are found settling in Ireland from both England and Scotland. The 1890 birth index finds the family most numerous in Tyrone and Cavan.

O'Looney

Irish Book of Arms plate 201

Lunney, Loony

According to "Keatings History" the name is listed among the chiefs of Moy Ith. This territory comprised parts of the baronies of Raphoe and Tirkeeran in Derry. Their territory in the 12th century is given as in a district known as the Monter Loney Mountains in Co. Tyrone.

The 1890 birth index finds the family most numerous in counties Cork, Clare under the spelling of Looney.

Loughnane

Loughnan

While we have little information on this family to date, the census of 1659 found the family in Wexford, and the Loughnan name was a principal one of that county at that time. The 1890 index shows the family had 10 recorded births, in every province except that of Ulster.

In the third volume of Keatings History 'O'Lachnain' or O'Loughnin, is given as a chief of Modbarn Beag, or Little Mourne. The family was cited among the chiefs of the Dalaradia.

Lowther

One English family of the name is found at Skryne Abbey, Co. Meath , Ireland no later that the early 17th century.

183

Ludlow

Irish Book of Arms plate 58

Ludlowe

One English family of the name is said to be found in Ardsalla, Co. Meath.

O Lydon

O Loideain

Leyden, Lyden, Liddane, Lydden

O'Lydon, when spelled as 'Lydon' is a name of Galway and Mayo in Ireland. This is evidenced by the 1890 birth index showing the same. This spelling is a popular form of O Loideain. The name has also been changed to Leyden in County Clare and surrounding counties, and to Liddane in County Clare. (M)

Lynam

Lynagh, Leynagh, Lynan

The birth index of 1890 finds Lynam families centered in Dublin and Kings counties. Many of the name are found in Kings Co. (Offaly) through the centuries in Ireland. Others of the name are found in scattered locations, and Woulfe says that in Co. Offaly the Lynam name is used for several family names in the area.

References to this family are found early in Wexford and Carlow, and subsequently in Dublin.

Lundy

Lunde, de Lunde, Lunn

The name of Lundy is most often found in Ulster in relatively modern times, but earlier the name is found regularly in Kilkenny and Tipperary. The family is most often assumed to be of foreign origins originally, of Norman or English descent.

The 1890 birth index finds the family name of Lunn most numerous in Co. Armagh.

O Logue

O'MAOLMHAODHOG, O'LAOGHOG

LOOGUE, MULVOGUE, LEECH, LEE,

The family name of O'Logue, or Logue, can be of Irish origins when found in Ireland. One such old Irish family which took on the name is anciently found around Athlone and Athenry. A notable family of the day, the name is still to be found in Galway and Clare today.

Members have put forth several possible origins for the Irish of the name. One origin goes back to Ulster, in the areas of Donegal and Derry, where the family is originally found as "O'Maolmhaodhog". Another gives the family of "O'Laoghog", of the province of Connaught.

The 1890 birth index of Ireland gives the name as most common in Londonderry and Donegal, and it is in the Glenties District in Donegal where the name is traditionally found.

In the Journal of the American Irish Historical Society we find reference to one John Logue, of Venango Township in Butler County, PA., as a landowner in 1796. Patrick Logue is given as a private in the 1st Regt. of the Pennsylvania line in the Continental Army. One Thomas Logue was also given in the Pennsylvania Archives.

Cardinal Michael Logue, (d.1924) served as the Archbishop of Armagh.

Passengers From Ireland:

JAMES LOGUE, ABOARD SHIP HARMONY, LONDONDERRY TO PHILADELPHIA, OCT. 31, 1811. FROM SHIP RECORDS OF THE FAMINE IMMIGRANTS: ALEX, ANN, JAS., JNO., THOS., WM..,HUGH, MAGY, MICHAEL. ,ISABELLA , MARY, PAT, ANDREW,
BRIDGET, CATHR., ENNES, JUDY, MARGT., SARAH, THOMAS.

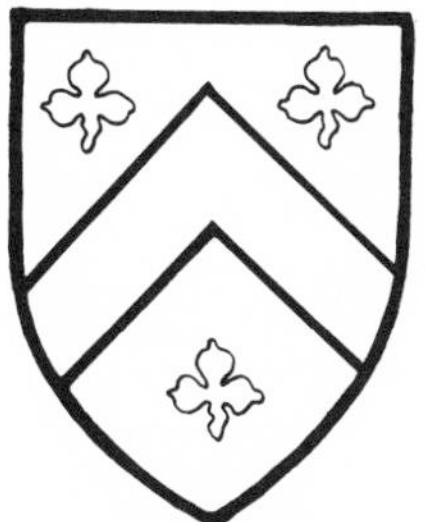

Lynch

Irish Book of Arms plates 88, 89, 163

O Loingshigh, de Lench

Leyns, Lynchy, O'Lynch, MacLychy

The Lynch family may descend from the Norman family of 'de Lynch' or from the old Irish family of O Loingsigh.

Near Limerick we find O Loingsigh with the Danes, cited by O'Heerin: " The O'Lynches, men of lands, dwell in that wood opposite the foreigners."

MacLynchy was given as a chief of Gleann Binne as "MacLoingseachain", a clan of Tir Conaill, in the 12th century.

O'Lynch is given as a chief in Down and parts of Antrim by O'Dugan. The "O'Loingsys or O'Lynches" were said to be numerous in Sigo and Mayo, and separately in Co. Cavan and in Meath.

The Norman families of the name are found settled near Trim in Meath, from whence some settled in Galway in the 15th century. (note the placename of Lynches Knock in Meath). This family was one of the 14 tribes of Galway, and many served as mayors of Galway city.

In 1484 Dominick Lynch received the citys charter under Richard III. Stephen, his son, received the 'Wardenship" of Galway from Pope Innocent VIII. James Lynch, mayor in 1493, hung his own son for the breaking of a law which required the death penalty. The story was commemorated at the gate of the old jail , and put down in writing there. Lynch's Castle, built in 1320, is close by. It is interesting to note that the origins of the term "Lynching and Lynch Law' are also said to have come about from actions of one named Lynch in America. This is attributed to Col. Charles Lynch (d. 1796).

Thomas Lynch (d. 1779) was the youngest signer of the American Declaration of Independence.

The Irish Book of Arms gives Lynch of Partry House, Co. Mayo, and Lynch B. Staunton of Clydaugh, Co. Galway.

Lyons

Irish Book of Arms plates 31, 94, 115

O Liathain, OLaighin

Lyon, Lehane, Lane, Leyne, O'Lyne,

Two families of the name of Lyons or Leyne are found. In Kerry 'O'Laeghain, O'Leyne or Lane, is given as chief of Ui Ferba. The same spellings have been given to a family of Galway, near Kilconnel, where the name is often found as Lyons. O'Donovan says the two familie are separate, giving the Lane family of Trughanacmy, in Co. Kerry as unrelated, of the spelling of O'Laoghain.

"O'Liathan, or O'Lehan", or Lyne and Lyons, is given by O'Heerin as chief of the barony of Barrymore before the Barry family took control. These O'Lehans took their name from a chief in the 11th century, Cuilean O'Liathan, who built Castle Lehan, (Castlelyons, north of Youghal), the chief seat of the family. Thus spoke O'Heerin;

"Lord of Ui Liathain, a warrior of fame, is the hardy leader of the battalions of Munster; Of Ui Anmcadha he is rightful chief- The host of keen arms, of high nobility."

This family likely originated in Limerick, with a branch in Barrymore.

The favored form of the name is "Lyons" in 1890, found in Mayo, Cork, Galway etc... "Lyne" was in Kerry, "Lane" in Cork and Limerick, and "Lehane" of Cork and Kerry then.

In the 17th century O'Lyne was a name of Kerry and Roscommon, Lyne a name of Clare, Lyon a name of Kildare, and Lyons was in Kings and Tipperary.

Some of the name Lyon are Scots.

The Lyons family of Croom, Co. Limerick settled there in the 18th century and the Lyons of Old Park, Co. Antrim descend from David Lyons of Belfast of the 17th century..

The Lyons - Montgomery family of Belhavel, Co. Leitrim descend from a family in Wesmeath. (Book of Arms.)

Mac Lysaght

Irish Book of Arms plates 20, 163

Mac Giolla Iasachta

Lysat, Lysaght, Mac Gyllysaghta

Families of the name of Lysaght or Mac Lysaght will likely be able to trace their origins to the Clare/Limerick area of Ireland. The family has been traditionally linked to these areas throughout history. The "Mac" prefix had generally been dropped, even at the time of the 1890 birth index, which recorded only 13 births of the name in Co. Limerick. Some of the name have added the Mac back onto the name in more recent times.

The family stems from a branch of the O'Briens of Thomand. They are found early in Ennistymon in Co. Clare, and one branch of the family settled in Co. Cork, founded by a 17th century protestant of the name.

In Keatings History we find Mac Gilla Iosachta, as a name Anglicized to Lysaght, and found on the map of Ortelius near Ennistymon in Co. Clare as well.

The surname of Mac Giolla Iasachta which became Mac Aleese, is a separate and distinct surname, despite the similarities of appearance in the original gaelic.

The late Edward MacLysaght, chief Herald of Ireland in the 20th century, is one to whom family researchers and historians owe much. His work "Irish Families" served as a classic reference work for those interested in general Irish family histories.

Loughran

Irish Book of Arms plate 220

O'Luchrain

The name of an old Irish family traditionally linked with the province of Ulster, and found in Antrim, Armagh and Tyrone in the 1890 birth index.

Lyster

The Irish Book of Arms plate 97

Lister, Lester

The Lyster family of Rocksavage and of Derby are given in the Irish Book of Arms.

Lunney

Lunny, Luney

Note the place name of Munterlooney possibly denoting an early location for the family in Ireland. The family name is traditionally linked with counties Fermanagh and Tyrone in the north of Ireland. The 1890 birth index finds the family most numerous in Fermanagh.

Lutrell

According to "Keatings History" the name is that of a principal family of Dublin city or county, and of Anglo-Norman descent.

Note the place name of Luttrellstown, near Lucan, Co. Dublin, where the family is on record from the 17th century.

Lucey

Lucye, Lucy

The name of Lucey is traditionally linked with the county of Cork in Ireland. These are believed to be of old Irish extraction, although some of the name may have arrived from England over time.

One English family of the name is found in Doogary, Co. Fermanagh. The 1890 birth index finds the family most numerous in Cork with 35 births, and in Kerry, with 4 births of the name.

184

185

Larkin, Lorcan

Irish Book of Arms plate 238

O Lorcain

O'Lorcain, O'Lorcan, Lorkan

The Larkin, O'Lorcan, etc... family name springs from the older Irish spelling of O'Lorcain. Four separate origins most likely exist for the name. They are located in counties Tipperary, Galway, Wexford and Armagh.

O'Lorcain, or Larkin, is given as a chief of Fothart, and mentioned by O'Heerin thusly;

"The Fenian heroes of Forth of the Carn, The fair rising ground of strength and beauty, A hero whose deeds are mighty in spears, He is the affluent chief O'Larkin."

The territory of these O'Larkins, was in the barony of Forth, in Co. Wexford, and Carn, where their castle was at Carnsore point. They ruled here prior to the Norman invasions.

In Co. Armagh they possessed lands along with the O'Neills and McCanns in the more ancient territory of Oirghialla. The native chiefs held their independence here down to the reign of Elizabeth, when Armagh was formed into a county in 1586 A.D.. Here they were chiefs of Farney and West Ui Breasail.

The O'Lorcains, or O'Larkins were also cited as a clan of the Ui Mani, in the county of Galway, where they were of the same descent as the O'Maddens.

The name is also found in Tipperary, where the chief family of the name served as erenaghs of Lorrha.

In the 1890 index Larkin is found with 85 births in Dublin, Armagh, Galway and Tipperary. In the 1659 census "Larkin" was found in Kings (Co. Offaly), and "Larkan" was a principal name of Louth among other areas, and that spelling was found in Dublin, too.

The name is said to have been taken from the gaelic word "Lorc" meaning rough or fierce, according to some.

Lavin

O Laimhin, O'Lamhain, O Flaithimhin

Lavins, Levins, Lavan, Laffan, O'Lavin,

The Lavin family has been traditionally found in the province of Connacht centered in Mayo and Roscommon. The 1890 index of Ireland confirms this with 42 recorded births of the name, citing Mayo and Roscommon as the counties of origin. The 1864 index confirms 46 births at that date. As to the estimated strength of the name in each county, Mayo is said to hold twice as many as Roscommon.

The Lavin name has been translated into 'hand' on occasion.

The name ranks prominently as one found among the followers of MacDermot Roe of Roscommon in the 16th century.

MacLavin, another family entirely, is said to be of the Mullavin sept, found in County Westmeath.

From passenger lists:
John Lavin, age 18, male, aboard Underwriter, April 7, 1851, from Liverpool to New York.
Michael Lavin, age 22, male, Laborer, aboard Eudocia, Aug. 7, 1851, Liverpool to New York.
Pat Lavin, age 20, male, Weaver, aboard Java, Sept. 16, 1851, Liverpool to New York.
Martin Lavin, age 24 male, Laborer, aboard Trumbull, Sept 18, 1851, Liverpool to New York.
Mary Lavin, age 21, female, servant, " " "
Ellen Lavin, age 44, female, aboard Hungarian, Oct. 13, 1851, Liverpool to New York.
Eliza Lavin, age 9, female, child, " "
Mick Lavin, age 45 male, laborer, aboard David-Cannon, Nov. 8, 1851, Liverpool to New York.
Bridget Lavin, age 55, female, " "

O'Lennon,

Irish Book of Arms plate 229

O Leannain, O Lionnane

Linnane, O'Lennan

The O'Lennans or O'Lennons are recorded as chiefs of a large territory of land in the barony of Tiaquin, which was made into 6 divisions called the "6 Sodhans" of Galway. O'Lennan was given by O'Dugan along with the MacWards, O'Scurrys, O'Cashins, O'Gillays and Maginns, as the 6 chiefs of this territory after it had been divided. O'Dugan spoke thusly of them:

"The 6 Sodhans let us not shun,
Their chiefs are not to be forgotten;
Brave are their predatory hosts,
To whom belonged the spear armed
. Sodhans."

This family was one of the name in Ireland. The history of the name can be difficult to trace because several families have changed their name to Lennon. This is further complicated by English settlers of the name found in Ireland.

Lennane or Linane is one Irish family that has also been changed into Lennon. They were of the Corca Laoidhe situated near Glandor Harbour. O'Leanain accounts for two more separate families of the name, including the above family of the Sodhans, where the name is sometimes found as Lennon. The other family was of the Hy Fiachra, and they are found in Mayo, where the name is also commonly found as Leonard.

The Four Masters find O'Lennon in Co. Fermanagh, where they served as erenaghs of Lisgoole.

In 1890, 103 births of Lennon were given in Dublin and Armagh. Linane had 10 births and Linnane 5 births, all given in Limerick, Kerry and Clare.

In 1659 O'Lennon was a principal name of Louth, O'Lennane of Cork, and Lennan of Dublin and in Louth.

McLennan is also found arriving from Scotland and settling in Co. Antrim.

186

Maconchy

The Irish Book of Arms plate 55

The family of Maconchy of Rathmore, Co. Longford and of Raheny, Co. Dublin are of the same line. They are given to be descended from the Scottish family of Maconochie, settling in Co. Longford in the 17th century. George Maconchy of Dublin, had his arms registered in Ulsters Office, during the reign of George the II.

O Madigan

Irish Book of Arms plate 241

O Madagain

Maddigan, Madegan, Madigane,

The Madigan Family has been found settled in areas of County Clare and Limerick in Ireland. Fairly numerous, they are said to have been a branch of the Madden family of County Galway. Likewise in Antrim and Derry, the name of Madden has been confused with Madigan.

The family is cited in Keatings History as 'O'Madagans, or O'Maddens' chiefs in the barony of Longford in Co. Galway and in the parish of Lusmagh on the opposite side of the Shannon River, in Kings County.

Spelled more anciently as Madigane, we find the census of 1659 giving the name as a principal one in County Clare. In the same records, O'Madigane is found as a principal name of County Limerick. In more modern times we find 27 'Madigan' births recorded in Counties Limerick and Clare, as documented in the 1890 birth index.

Passengers

Cath. Madigan, age 20, aboard 'La Grange', June 25, 1847. From Newry to New York.

James Madigan, age 21, Aboard 'St. Patrick', March 27, 1846. From Liverpool to New York.

O'Madden

Irish Book of Arms plates 55, 163

O Madain, O Madadhain

Madigan, MacAvaddy, Madagane, Maddin,

The family of O'Madden, of Ui Maine, can be found on the banks of the Shannon River. Their territory included parts of the barony of Longford in Co. Galway, and the barony of Garrycastle in Kings Co. (Co. Offaly).

In Keatings History "O'Madagain or O'Madadhain Anglicized O'Madden" was given in Longford barony and on the other side of the Shannon in the parish of Lusmagh in Kings Co.. They are given as a branch of the Clan Colla, of the same descent as the O'Kellys, princes of the Ui Maine.

They held sway after the 12th century Norman invasions, under the Burke family, who were of Norman descent.

Madigan, likely an older form of the name, comes from the same old gaelic spelling as Madden. It is common to find that a Madigan has shortened his name into Madden.

Madigan is found mainly in Limerick and Clare in the 1890 birth index, with some 27 births given. Madden had some 107 births, in Galway, Cork, Dublin and Antrim. Madden has as well been found in Antrim and Derry. Some believe that they are a branch of the Galway-Limerick family cited above.

It should be noted that there are English families of the name, and Maddentown in Co. Kildare is named for the same.

In 1659 "Maddin" was a principal name of Tipperary, "Madden" was so in Kings, and O'Madagane was so in Limerick. "O'Madigane" was found as a principal name of Clare and Limerick.

The Madden family of Hilton Park, Co. Monaghan, are given in the Irish Book of Arms, (see the "Tribes and Customs of the Hy Many (Ui Maine)" by O'Donovan.

Magan

Irish Book of Arms plate 41

The Magan family of Clonearl, Kings Co., and of Killyan, Co. Meath, are found earliest at Cloney, Co. Westmeath.

This name should not be confused with the names of Maginn or McCann.

Maguire

Irish Book of Arms plate 202

Maguidhir

MacGuire, MacGwyer

The Maguire family is traditionally associated with Co. Fermanagh in Ireland, and it has been prominent there since the 15th century.

As the 39th most popular name in all of Ireland, it was also found in counties Dublin, Cavan and Donegal in the 1890 index.

O'Dugan cites the MacGuires as chiefs of Fermanagh, and according to legend they were officially inaugurated on the borders of Cavan and Fermanagh, on Cuilcagh Mountain near Swanlibar, or at Lisnaskea. Co. Fermanagh itself came to be known as MacGuires Country during thier reign of power.

Many of the name are found among the ranks of the wild geese, fighting in the armies of France and Austria.

A Maguire was baron of Enniskillen and fought with James II against William of Orange. The family remained barons up to 1795 in the court of France. see MacGuire.

Mahaffy

Mahaffy is generally accepted as the name of a Scottish family found settled in Ireland, which is often found in Co. Donegal.

187

Magenis

'he Irish Book of Arms plate 71

Magennis, Gennis

The family of Magenis of Finvoy Lodge , Co. Antrim is found in the Irish Book of Arms.

Mannion

Irish Book of Arms plate 232

O Mainin

Mannin, Manning, O'Mannion, Mainin,

The O'Mainin or O'Mannin, or O'Manning family is found given as chief of Sodhan, a large territory in the barony of Tiaquin, which was made into 6 divisions, called the 'six Sodhans'.

The O'Mannins were centered at the castle of Clogher, in the barony of Tiaquin, in Co. Galway. Later they became centered at Menlough, in the parish of Killascobe, in that same barony.

A prominent family of the Ui Maine territories, it is said that they descend most anciently from the Picts, a people who resided in Ireland before the coming of the Celts or Milesians.

The fate of the family declined at the hands of the O'Kelly clan prior to the time of Cromwell, and grew worse subsequently.

"Manning" has been given early as a variant spelling of the name of this old Irish family. This is also a surname of English origins, and some of the name will likely be of English heritage in Ireland.

Some 91 Mannion births were recorded in the 1890 index, primarily in Galway and Roscommon. Manning, which is also of English origins, had 54 births, in Cork and Dublin.

Maher, Meagher

Irish Book of Arms plates 61, 216, 164

O Meachair

Magher, Maheir, Mara, O'Meachair,

Ranking among the top 90 surnames in Ireland, the most numerous spelling of the name is as "Maher", which had some 176 births recorded in the 1890 index, as opposed to "Meagher" which had only 27 births. The former were located in Tipperary, Dublin and Kilkenny.

Anciently they served as powerful chiefs in the barony of Ikerrin in Co. Tipperary, and they have been found centered near Roscrea. "O'Meachair, or O'Meagher", by some rendered Maher, was chief of Crich-Ui-Cairin, or O'Carins country, and they are spoken of thusly by O'Heerin;

"Powerfully they have peopled their land, The O'Meaghers of the land of Ui Carin, The tribe who dwell at Bearnan Eli, It is right to extol their fame."

Related to the Ely O'Carrolls, they remain on their traditional lands to this day, having been recorded there prior to the 12th century Norman invasion. It is true to note that they did not fall from power at the time of the Norman invasions, as did so many other Irish families.

"Magher" was a principal name of Carlow and Wexford in 1659. Meagher, was a principal name of Clare, and in Tipperary, Queens. "Meaghir", was a principal name of Waterford at that time.

"Historical Notices of the O'Meaghers of Ikerron", published in 1887, by J.C. O'Meagher in London, and is of note.

The 'O' prefix has generally been dropped from the name in Ireland, but in the census of 1659 it is interesting to note that O'Meagher, was still found as a principal name of Tipperary, their original homeland.

Meaghers Irish Brigade was of some fame in the American Civil War.

Mac Mahon

Irish Book of Arms plates 26, 57, 153

MacMathghamha

Mahon, Maghan, Mann, Maughan

Two great families of the MacMahon name are found in Ireland. The first are the MacMahons of Thomand (Clare). The second are the MacMahons of the old territory of Oriel in the 13th century.

Keatings History gives "Mac Mathghamha, or MacMahon", as succeeding to the chieftainship of Corca Baskin,where they were Lords. They ruled the baronies of Moyarta and Clonderlaw in Clare, down to the reign of Elizabeth. They were a branch of the O'Briens, descended from Brian Boru, and not related to the MacMahons of Ulster and Co. Monaghan.

A MacMahon castle was found at Carrigaholt in Co. Clare, and in 1602 the last chief of the name died at the battle of Kinsale accidently at the hands of his own son.

The MacMahons of Ulster are found anciently in Monaghan and Louth, and they increased in power at the expense of the O'Carrolls. As Cromwellian times approached they fell from power. They held sway until the reign of Elizabeth, when Monaghan became a county.

One of the 70 most populous names of Ireland, it is the most popular name of Co. Clare, and the 3rd most numerous name of Monaghan.

When the 'Mac' prefix is dropped the name of "Mahon" appears. Mahon represents another family entirely. In 1659 the name was fairly widespread, being a principal name of Fermanagh, Clare and in Limerick, Louth and Leitrim. "Mahon" was a principal name of Clare and found in Dublin then.

The 1890 birth index shows "Mahon" in Dublin and Galway, with McMahon in Clare, Monaghan, Limerick and Dublin. The name itself is said to come from the Irish word for 'bear'.

188

O'Mahoney

Irish Book of Arms plates 27, 163

O Mathghamhna

Mahoney, Mahowney, McMahoney,

In Keatings History "O'Mathghamhna, (O'Mahowna), or O'Mahoney", is given by O'Heerin as a chief of Ui Eachach, and the barony of Kinelmeaky in Cork. Ui Eachach became Ivaugh, which comprises the whole peninsula in the barony of West Carbery, extending from Ballydehob to the bay of Dunmanus. They also possessed the barony of Kinnalea in Cork. They also held a large territory in Muskerry, south of the river Lee in Cork, and also in the territory called Tiobrad, in Co. Kerry.

The O'Mahoneys had castles at Rosbrian, Ardintenant, Blackcastle, Ballydesmond, Dun Beacon, Dunmanus and Ringmahon, situated on the coast.

Mathghamhna, from whom the name is taken, fell in the battle of Clontarf in 1014 A.D.. His mother was the daughter of the great Brian Boru, last great high king of Ireland. O'Heerin speaks of them thusly:

"Ivahagh, most western part of Banba (Ireland), is the great estate of O'Mahoney A well watered land of fair fortresses-...Of Kinnalmeaky, of pleasant fields.All round Bandon, of fair woods, The Warlike chief, in victory surpreme, Is O'Mahoney of the coast of white foam."

The "O" before the name was largely dropped by the time of the 1890 index with 25 births spelled as O'Mahoney at that time, all in Cork. Mahoney, on the other hand, had 276 births, in Cork, Kerry and Limerick.

In the 17th century (O) or (Mac) Mahowne was a principal name in Cork, Tipperary, Dublin, and found in Kerry as well. "McMahoney" was given as a principal name of Clare and "O"Mahoney was in Cork, Clare, Kerry, Limerick and Tipperary at that time.

O'Malley

Irish Book of Arms plates 163, 241

Maille

Maley, Melia, Malley, Malia, Mailey,

The O'Malley family name has always been associated with Co. Mayo and surrounds in Ireland. Furthermore, many of the name have retained the "O" prefix instead of dropping it, as most other families did during troubled times.

In Keatings History one branch of the family was found in Tuath Luimnighe, or in the district of Limerick.

O'Malley, chief of Umhal, was said by O'Dugan to have lands divided into two territories. The name has been rendered sometimes into Umalia and Ui Mallia. Their territory comprised the present baronies of Murrisk and Burrishoole in Co. Mayo. The O'Malleys are of the Ui Briuin race, descended from Brian, King of Connaught in the 5th century, who was the progenitor of the O'Connors, Kings of Connaught, of the O'Rourkes, O'Reillys, MacDermots and other chiefs. They are thus designated by O'Heerin;

"A good man yet there never was,
of the O'Malleys, who was not a mariner,
of every weather they are prophets,
A tribe of brotherly affection and of friendship."

The family is known for their exploits at sea, as their motto "Terra Marique Potens" (Powerful on land and sea), suggests. Doubtlessly, the most famous sea captain of Ireland was Grace O'Malley, a noted rebel and most accomplished seafarer. Many accounts of this woman are available. The family was also known as "Manannans", denoting them as sea-gods of a sort.

In the 1890 index "Malley" was the preferred spelling of the name with 85 births in Mayo and Galway. O'Malley ranks 2nd with 30 births in their Mayo homeland and "Mailey" is a spelling recorded in Antrim at that time.

O'Malone

Irish book of Arms plates 66, 164

O Maoileoin (of St. John)

Mallone, Malloone

The O'Malones were anciently a powerful family in the province of Connaught. They are often cited with events involving the "Abbey of Clonmacnois" in Co. Offaly in earlier times.

Some have said that they descend from the O'Connors, the kings of Connaught, but this appears doubtful according to many accounts. In Keatings History the O'Malones are given as holding large territories in the barony of Brawney in Westmeath. They as well came to hold the title of barons of Clan Malone and barons Sunderlin of Lake Sunderlin in that county as well.

Those of the name in the Clare area are given as a likely branch of the Clonmacnois family of O'Malone, and those in Wexford are of uncertain origins.

By the time of the 1890 index "Malone", which had dropped its "O" prefix altogether, had 100 births given in the counties of Dublin, Wexford and Clare.

In the census of 1659 "Malone" is found in Dublin, Kildare, and Westmeath. "Mallone" was in Dublin city and in Kings (Offaly) and Queens (Leix) counties. "Malloone", another variant spelling of the name was in Kings Co. at that time, and it was as well a principal name of Co. Clare.

It appears that although the family was numerous in Offaly in the 17th century, by the turn of the last century the line had dwindled there.

The Malone family of Baronston, Co. Westmeath is found in the Irish Book of Arms.

189

O'Maloney

Irish Book of Arms plates 93, 114, 137, 164

O Maoldhomhnaigh (servant of the

Mallowney, Maloughney, Malowny,

The O'Molonys were a Dalcassion sept of Kiltanon, by Tulla, in the eastern part of Co. Clare. They are found in Keatings history and given as follows : "The O'Moloneys were chiefs of Cuiltenan, now the parish of Kiltonanlea in the barony of Tully, County of Clare. They remain in the Clare, Limerick and Tipperary regions.

In the 1890 index we find the name of Maloney in Limerick, Clare and Tipperary with 119 births, and the spelling of Malony had 34 births recorded. The census of 1659 finds the spelling of O'Malowne being used, and as such it is given as a principal name of County Cork .

When found in Tipperary the name is sometimes a variant spelling of Maloughney, a separate sept altogether. Some of the name in the north of Ireland descend from O'Maolfhachtna, also corrupted to Maloughney, and MacLoughney.

The Irish Book of Arms give one "Molony of Cragg, Co. Clare." This line traces itself back to John O'Molony who died in 1610, and whose motto is given as "In Domino et non in arcu meo sperabo." One Alfred Molony of that family is cited.

Aboard Ship Radius, Captain Clark, from Cork, arrived at New York before May 11, 1811:
Margaret,John & Jerry Maloney Agts.
Marriages- Walker's Hibernian Magaz.,
John Maloney, 4th Dragoons to Miss Leggett, daughter of J. Leggett of West Hampnett, Sussex, in London. June, 1809. / Mrs. Malony to Capt. Dominick Dalton. 1786./ Walter Weldon Malowny to Miss Spellissy at Limerick. Jan.

O'Mangan

Irish Book of Arms plate 164

O Mongain

Mongan, Manghan, Mangin, Manion,

"Mangan" is the most popular spelling of this family name today, as it was in the 1890 birth index where it is given 52 births, coming from Dublin, Limerick, Kerry and Mayo. The earlier spelling of "Mongon" held only 6 births at that time, 5 of which were in the province of Connaught.

Both counties Mayo and Cork have been cited as centers for the name in ancient times, and it is assumed that each of these counties accounts for a completely separate and unrelated family.

In Keatings History the "O'Mongans or O'Mangans", chiefs of Breach Magh are given in the district of the parish of Kilmore Moy, in Co. Sligo. (The name is given in Co. Tyrone as well at that time.)

Thought to be of later introduction to Co. Limerick, note the place name of Ballymongane in both that county and in Clare.

Other surnames have been corrupted to Mangan or Mongan, in particular the completely unrelated names of Manahan and Mannion.

In the census of 1659 "O'Mongane" was given as a principal name of Cork, although it does not appear on the 1890 index there.

They are listed as a principal family of Co. Dublin by O'Hart.

Maddock

Maddox, Maddocks

A family name linked to Co. Wexford in the 19th century according to our records. The name is of likely English or Welsh extraction when found in Ireland.

Mansergh

The Irish Book of Arms plate 94

The Mansergh family of Grenane, Co. Tipperary are given in the Irish Book of Arms.

Mackey

McKey, Mac Key, Macky, MacKay,

Several spellings exist relating to the Mackey surname in Ireland and America. In the census of 1659 Mac Key is given as a principal name of Londonderry, also found in Louth. The 1890 birth index of Ireland finds the name of Mac Key in Dublin, Cork, Tipperary and Antrim.

In other sources families of the name of McKey are given as of the Hy Many tribe, in counties Leitrim and Donegal in ancient Ireland.

In Ireland the Ormond sept of 'O'Macdha' was located near Nenagh, note the place name of Ballymackey. Here the name has been mistranslated into Mackey on occasion as well.

The 1890 birth index finds the family name of Mackie most numerous in Co. Armagh.

Mackle

Mackell, MacGill, MacKell

A name linked to the province of Ulster in our records of Ireland.

We find record of the name in Armagh, Tyrone and Down.

190

Mansfield

Irish Book of Arms plate 73

Maunsel, Monsfield

Mansfield is found as a principal name in Co. Waterford in the 17th century. Two centuries later the birth index finds the family centered in counties Cork and Kerry. Note the place name of Mansfieldstown in Co. Louth. Note also the family of the name, centered at Castle Annagh in county Tipperary in Ireland.

The Mansfield family of Morristown Lattin, Co. Kildare is given in the Irish Book of Arms.

Macken

Irish Book of Arms plate 249 (Mackin)

O'Macain, Mac Maicin

Macain, Mackin

The name of Macken may stem from the older family names of O'Macain or Mac Maicin. The former are found in both Cork and Mayo, while the later is found in the old territory of Oriel in Ireland. The 1890 birth index finds the family in Mayo, Louth and Monaghan.

Mackessy

According to "Keatings History" the name is that of a family who served as chiefs in a district of Co. Limerick.

Magner

Magnier, Magnir, Magnor

The Magner family is traditionally linked to Co. Cork in Ireland. In the 17th century Magner was a principal name in that county, and two centuries later it is found centered there and in Co. Limerick in the birth index.

According to "Keatings History" the name is of the family who gave their name to Castle Magner.

Mac Manus

Irish Book of Arms plates 164, 257

Mac Maghnuis

Manis, Manice, Manus

The MacManus families of Ireland may descend from one of at least two independent origins. The name itself may mean "son of Magnus" (The Great), taken from the Latin and adopted by this Irish family, but some also claim it to be of Norse origin.

The MacManus family of Co. Fermanagh are a branch of the MacGuires. They are noted as a "formerly numerous clan", chiefly in Tirkennedy, who had control of the freight on Lough Erne, and they held the office of hereditary supervisors of the fisheries under MacGuire.

Belle Island on Lough Erne was called Ballymacmanus in earlier times, and it is here in Fermanagh that the family remains centered, with 138 recorded births of the namd in the 1890 birth index. It was as well a principal name of Fermanagh in the 17th century.

In Co. Roscommon the Mac Manus family is found in the barony of Boyle, said to have descended from Maghnus, son of Turlough O'Connor, King of Ireland. Their seat of power is cited in the parish of Kilronan.

The name is also cited more anciently as prominent among the families of Co. Cavan and Co. Mayo.

In the 17th century the name is found in Leitrim, Sligo and Roscommon, in the census of 1659.

Magahan

MacGahan

The name of a family traditionally linked to Co. Louth in Ireland.

Marley

Irish Book of Arms plate 31 (Marlay)

Marly, Marlay

The "Marley" family is found centered in Co. Westmeath in the 17th century, and the spelling of O'Marly was a principal name of Co. Armagh at that time. Moving into more modern times the name is most often found in counties Donegal and Mayo. Those of the name may stem from either native Irish or English descent. One family of the latter category is found with holdings in Co. Longford.

The Marlay family of Belvedere, Co. Westmeath is given in the Irish Book of Arms. The first of this line was John Marlay, a merchant of Newcastle on Tyne.

Magoon

uncertain

MAGON, MAGONE, MCGOUNE, ETC....

Families of the name of Magoon are relatively rare in historical records. It seems that this spelling is likely a variant of a more popular Irish name such as Magone or McGoune. Magone is a variant spelling of MacKeown, and McGoune was found as a principal name in Co. Antrim on the census of 1659.

Four of the name are found in our records however. One "Henry Magoon" is listed among the names selected from the Rosters of Colonial Soldiers who fought in King Phillips War, 1675 - 1676. (IAHS).

Three of the name, presumably of the same family are found aboard the "Virginian" on May 15, 1846, which sailed from Liverpool to New York. Bridget Magoon, age 27, wife. John Magoon, infant, male son. Thomas Magoon, age 28, male, weaver by occupation.

191

Marsh

Irish Book of Arms plate 43

The Marsh family of Jerpoint, Co. Kilkenny is found in the Irish Book of Arms. Only 5 births of the name where recorded in the 1890 index.

Major

Majur

Families of the name of Major are found centered in Co. Londonderry in the 17th century and subsequently they are most numerous in counties Antrim and Down into modern times. Considered to be a family found traditionally in the province of Ulster, most of the name are given to be originally of English descent.

O Mallon

Irish Book of Arms plate 221

O'Meallain

Malloone, O'Malowne, O'Mellon

The birth index of 1890 finds the Mallon family in Armagh, Tyrone and Antrim in northern Ireland. This Irish family was a branch of the Cinel Eoghain in County Tyrone more anciently. The lands of the family were known as 'O'Mellons Country'. The family was as well, the hereditary keeper of the Bell of St. Patrick. In Milesian families the family of O'Mallon was said to be of the Hy Brune tribe, settled in Mayo, Sligo and Tyrone in ancient days.

According to Keatings History, the Mallons were listed under the chiefs and clans of Tir Eoghain and territories in the 12th century. Here they are described by O'Dugan as follows: "O'Meallain, chiefs of Siol Aodha-Eanaigh".

Marshall

Irish Book of Arms plate 63

Marshal, Marshell

A family name of accepted English extraction in Ireland, found as early as the 17th century in Co. Kerry. The 1890 birth index finds the family most numerous in Antrim, Londonderry, Down and Dublin.

Mandeville

According to "Keatings History" the name is among the chief families of English descent settling in Waterford and Tipperary. These English families primarily possessed the territory called from them Gal-tir, signifying the country of the foreigners," now the barony of Gaultiere." They are mentioned again as among the chief families settling in Ulidia, under DeCourcey and his successors.

Manley, Monley

Monnelly, Munnelly, Manley, Munley

The origins of the Monley, Manley surname in Ireland remain unclear at present. This is a surname found in Britain, so at least some of the name may originate from that country.

The name of Manley is found in the 1890 birth index with a total of 21 births, all given in Cork and Wicklow. The possibly related surnames of Monnelly and Munnelly were both found in Co. Mayo at that time.

Marmion

Merryman, Marriman

The surname of Marmion has been used for the name of Merryman at times, and it may stem from that name originally, but the clouds of time have covered the origins of the name for us today. It may also well be a name of Norman origin.

Marsham

Irish Book of Arms plate 31

The Marsham family of Headfort House, Co. Leitrim is found in the Irish Book of Arms.

Mannix

O Mainichin

Mannihan, Manahan, Manihan

The homeland of Mannix families in Ireland is to be found in Counties Cork and Kerry, where the name is given with 6 births in the 1890 index.

They are found most concentrated in the southwest portion of Co. Cork, and are believed to have descended from O'Mainichin. They are recorded on their lands around Ross Bay, under the dominance of the ruling O'Hennessy clan.

A rare name in Irish records, the family remains centered near its original homeland to this day.

Manahan and Manihan are two variant spellings of the name. Furthermore, in the province of Ulster, far removed from the Mannix homeland in Cork and Kerry, the name of MacNiece is also said to have been corrupted to Mannix.

Marisco

According to "Keatings History" the name is given as among the chief Anglo-Norman families who arrived in Ireland with Strongbow in the 12th century and received large grants of land in Co. Wexford. The individual of the name cited as such was one "Hervy de Monte Marisco" who shared estates in that county with Fitzstephen and Fitzgerald.

192

Martin,

Irish Book of Arms plate 31, 82, 252,...

O Martain, Mac Giolla Mhartain

Martin, Martyn, Marten, Kilmartin,

Martin is one of the top 50 names in Ireland, Scotland and England. Hence, origins may stem from any of these countries. Several Irish origins for the name exist, including forms of Gilmartin, Kilmartin and O'Martin.

In Co. Tyrone the name may come from O'Martain, MacMartain or Gilmartin, as several families of the name can be traced there. The MacMartins of Tyrone are given to be a branch of the O'Neils. We also find MacGiolla Mhartain, of the barony of Clogher who spread into Fermanagh as well. O'Martin may be found in Tyrone as well, and it is found in Westmeath in the 1500's.

One family was one of the original 14 tribes of Galway, settling there during the Anglo-Norman invasions of the 12th century along with de Burgo (Burke).

From the "Complete Book of Irish Family Names", we find the following:
1) Martin, a principal name in Ulster in 1659, and from Scotland sometimes.
2) Martyn, a Norman family settling in Galway in 1171, and a principal name of Dublin in 1659.
3) Marten, the name of settlers from Holland, in Down and Louth in 1710.
4) McMarten - Principal name in Co. Fermanagh in 1659.
5) Kilmartin - In 1659 in Fermanagh, and in Roscommon in 1890.
6) Gilmartin in Sligo/Leitrim in 1890.
7) Martine, a principal name of Down, and found in Cork and Dublin in 1659.

These names can be found spelled differently today. Irish families may have had a Mac, O, Gil, or Kil, prefix.

The Irish Book of Arms gives Martin of Wiche, Co. Worcester, of foreign origins, and Martyn of Tulira, Co. Galway.

Massy

Irish Book of Arms plate 31

Massey

The Massy family of Kingswell House, and of Grantstown Hall, Co. Tipperary is given in the Irish Book of Arms. The name is as well, given as that of a Huguenot family found in Great Britain.

The birth index of 1890 finds the family centered in Down.

Mathews

Mathewes, Matthews

The name of Mathews is likely originally an English name found in the north of Ireland and in County Louth. Spelled as given it is found in 1659 in Roscommon, Tipperary, Kilkenny and Cork City in 1659. By 1890 it is given in Louth, Dublin, Antrim and Down. When spelled as Mathewes it is found as a principal name of County Louth in 1659. Spelled as Matthews in 1890 it was found in Louth, Dublin and Antrim, and Milesian families gives it of Welsh origin arriving in Cork, Kerry and Limerick in 1172.

In Keatings History, when speaking of the 'McMahon' family, the princes of Monaghan, it is stated that several McMahons changed their names to Mathews in earlier days.

One English family of the name is found settled in Thurles, Co. Tipperary.

Marnell

Mornell

The name of a family found in Clare, Kilkenny and Tipperary in our records. They are most often linked with Co. Kilkenny into modern times.

Maunsel

Irish Book of Arms plate 58, 105

Monsell, Maunsell, Mansill, Mansel

A family name of Norman origins, the family is often associated with Co. Tipperary in Ireland. The Maunsell family of Oakly Park, Co. Kildare and Blackwater, Co. Clare are of the same line. They descend from one John Maunsell of Limerick and Queens county in earlier times.

The Maunsel family of Fanstown, Co. Limerick is given in the Irish Book of Arms.

O'Marky, Markey

O'Marcaigh

According to "Keatings History" the name is given as belonging to a chief clan who possessed parts of Louth in ancient times.

They are found in older works in the old territory of Oriel in Ireland. In more modern times the family is found most numerous in Louth, Monaghan and in the city of Dublin. The 1890 birth index finds the family most numerous in Monaghan and Dublin.

Manning

Irish Book of Arms plate 232

of likely English origin

Mannin, Maning

The family name of Manning is considered to be a name of English origin in Ireland in most instances. The name is most common in Dublin and Cork counties in Ireland, as evidenced by the 1890 birth index. The name may be found as a synonym of Mannin at times. It is interesting to note that in Milesian families, the name of O'Manning was said to be in County Galway, a branch of the Clanna Rory tribe in Ireland. The name is also found in the surname index to Keatings History of Ireland.

193

Maxwell

Irish Book of Arms plate 35

The name of a Scottish family found settled in the province of Ulster in Ireland no later than the 17th century. The Maxwell family of Ballyrolly, Co. Down, of Scottish origins, is found in the Irish Book of Arms.

The birth index of 1890 finds the family centered in Antrim, Down and Dublin.

Masterson

McMaster

According to "Keatings History" the name is given as that of an old English family which settled in Wexford. They are on record in that county from at least the 17th century onward.

The name of McMaster, meaning son of Master, has obvious similarities to the name of Masterson. The two names are said to have been confused with each other in the Longford/Cavan area and surrounds.

The 1890 birth index finds the family most numerous in Dublin, Longford and Cavan.

Marren

O'Mearain

Marran, Marron

The oldest references to this name appear to be in Co. Monaghan, and subsequently in Co. Sligo. The 1890 birth index finds the family most numerous in Monaghan when spelled as Marron, and in Co. Sligo when spelled as Marren.

Maypother

Irish Book of Arms plate 58

Maypowder, Mapother

One family of the name is found in Co. Roscommon centered near Killingboy, and were originally of Dorset, England in the 16th century.

The Mapother family of Kilteevan, Co Roscommon was founded by Richard Maypowder originally of Dorset in England, and coming to settle in Roscommon.

Martell

According to "Keatings History" the name is given among the chief Anglo-Norman and English settlers in Ulidia, under DeCourcey and his successors. Also according to "Keatings History", the name is given as belonging to a principal Norman family in Co. Cork.

Marwards

According to "Keatings History" the name is that of a principal family of Dublin city or county, and of Anglo-Norman descent.

Mc Master

Masterson

The name of a Scottish family settled in Ulster no later than the 17th century in Ireland. Masterson is a variant spelling of the name which is also found used for Mac an Mhaighistir of Co. Longford, which was an Irish family.

Meade

Irish Book of Arms plate 88, 90, 91

Mead, Meed

One family of the name descends from Robert Meade who was born in Ireland, married in the Barbadoes Islands, and died in Philadelphia in 1754. Several of the name are found being transported to the Barbadoes in the 17th century, being considered "rebels" in Ireland.

The Meade family of Ballintober, Co. Cork and the Meade family of Burrenwood Co. Down, are given in the Irish Book of Arms. The Meade family of Ballymartle, Co. Cork is given as one of ancient Irish extraction as found in Burke's Peerage.

The birth index of 1890 finds the Meade family most numerous in county Cork.

Mattimore

Of English origin or variant of the Irish

Individual found in search:
Mick Mattimore, 28 years old, 'sawer', aboard British Queen, June 29, 1848.

Mac Maurace

Maurice, Morris

According to "Keatings History" the name is given as an Irish name which was also adopted by Anglo-Norman or English families in lieu of their original surnames.

The Fitzgeralds changed their name to MacThomas and MacMaurace.

Merna

Mernagh

Families of the name are traditionally found in Co. Wexford and surrounds in our records.

194

Meadows

The Irish Book of Arms plate 55

Meddows

The Meadows family of Thornville, Co. Wexford descend from one William Meddows or Meadows, of the city of Wexford, found there in the early 18th century.

Merrick

O' MEARADHAIGH (ALIAS MERRY ?),

MERRICKE,MEYRICK,MAYRICK

Families of the name of Merrick in Ireland, may reportedly be from any one of three origins. Some of the name will be of English heritage here, for the name is found often in England. Others of the name may claim Welsh origins, arriving early in the province of Connaught.

In Co. Waterford we find that Merrick has been substituted for "Merry" as a family name. It would seem that this could work both ways, for "Merry" could be a simple short form of Merrick on occasion.

In the 1890 birth index of Ireland only 7 births of the name are recorded. This in itself makes it a relatively rare surname. Going back to the census of 1659 we find only one listing of the family name, and that spelled as "Merricke". The individual in question was one Cornett Merricke, of Dublin City.

Passengers From Ireland:

JOHN MERRICK , AGE 26,COLOR MAKER, ABOARD 'DE HA', AUG. 24, 1848,

ANTHONY & BRIDGET MERRICK-ABOARD 'PRINCETON', JAN.31,1849.

MARY MERRICK-AGE 21 FEMALE-SERVANT,ABOARD 'J.Z.' JAN. 10, 1850.

JUDITH,MATILDA,LATRES,OBEL,ROSABELLA, ABOARD 'CANTON' APRIL 2,1849, FROM CORK.

O'Meara, O'Mara

Irish Book of Arms plates 164, 246

O Mearaidhe

Marra, Marah, O'Meera

"O'Meara, a goodly prince, the chief of Ui Fahy, holds wide lands, and Ui Niaill of the race of Eogain the Fair, are all the heroes whom I enumerate". Such are the words written about the O'Meara family by Aryan, as found in Keatings History. The same source finds the family an ancient one, centered in Co. Waterford. Here they held extensive territory in the barony of Upper Ormond around Tipperary.

The name of their stronghold, Tuaim-ui-Meara, is found today in the name (and area) of the town of Toomavara.

They are considered anciently to have been in the north of Co. Tipperary. Several are of note in the military ranks, both in Ireland and abroad, as evidenced by the famous General O'Meara.

Meara and O'Meara are found in about equal numbers in the 1890 birth index. "Meara" was a name of Tipperary and O'Meara of Dublin, Limerick and Tipperary. "Mara", a less common spelling, had 21 births given at that time.

In the "census" of 1659 "Mara" is given as a principal name of Tipperary, along with Meara and O'Meara being in that county.

O'Meehan

Irish Book of Arms plates 164, 206

O Miadhachain

Meighan, Meegan, McMeekin, Mehegan,

The O'Meehan family most anciently hailed from the west of Co. Cork, where they are found to be of the same descent as the MacCarthys. By the time of the Norman invasions they are found centered in Co. Leitrim, in the barony of Rosclogher. (Note the placename of Ballaghmeehin in Rossinever parish in that county.)

They are as well, cited as chiefs in the barony of Connello, Co. Limerick, along with O'Sheehan and O'Cullane. Keatings History gives the name as numerous or prominent in the Mayo/Sligo area, as well as in Co. Leitrim.

They are found as well as a notable sept in Co. Clare, and are numerous there in the census of 1659. They remained in Clare at the turn of the last century, when they are also found in Galway, Sligo, Donegal and Dublin.

Of the variant spellings of the name in the 17th century, "O'Meehan" was a principal name of Fermanagh, "O'Meeghane" a principal name of Clare, and O'Meaghan was a principal name of Tipperary.

The Meegan families found in Co. Monaghan continued to use that spelling of the name in the 1890 birth index of Ireland.

"Meehan" was by far the most popular spelling of the name in the 19th century, by which time the "O" prefix had been removed from the name.

Separate families in Cork and Antrim, i.e. Mehegan in Cork and McMeekin in Ulster, have also on occasion changed their names to Meehan.

195

Miller

Irish Book of Arms plate 36

Millar, Miler

The name of Miller is often found in Co. Antrim and the province of Ulster in Ireland. It is generally assumed to be a name of English or Scottish heritage when found in Ireland. The Miller family of Milford Co. Mayo and Blindwell, Co. Galway descend from one Robert Miller who was among Cromwells men, and settled earlier in Ballycushion, Co. Mayo.

The birth index of 1890 finds the family centered in Antrim with 50% of the name found in that county, and also in Londonderry and Dublin.

May

de May, Mey, Mayo, Mayes, Mayberry,

Families of the name of "May" spring from several separate origins. Some are of English beginnings originally, others stem from ancient Irish families. In the 17th century we find the family in Queens and in Cork County. Two centuries later we find the family name of "May" centered in Co. Sligo. Of course, the name may serve as a shortened form of Mayberry or Mayes. The former is common in Antrim, the latter in Antrim and Armagh.

Meekin

Mc Meekan, McMeeken, Meek, Meeke

Families of the name of Meekin are traditionally found in the province of Ulster in Ireland. Spelled as McMeekin we find the family centered in Co. Antrim in the 1890 birth index. It is interesting to note that the names of "Meeke" and Meek are found centered in Co. Antrim for several centuries, and some of the name may be of the same old family as the Meekins.

Minchin

Irish Book of Arms plate 88

Minch

The family name of Minchin is given to be a name of English settler families in Ireland, and they came to be well established in counties Tipperary and Offaly here. The census of 1659 further finds the family in Tipperary. We do find a curious listing of the name of O'Minchin, centered in Tipperary, but this may be in error.

The Minchin family of Annagh, Co. Tipperary are given in the Irish Book of Arms.

Meenan

Meenhan

Families of the name are found centered in Donegal and Tyrone in the 19th century birth index of Ireland. This family name is separate from the family of Meenaghan found in Co. Mayo, although it sounds and is spelled similarly.

Meere

Mears, de la Mere, Myers, O' Meara

Families bearing this name may have arrived from England, or they may be of older Irish origins here. In Co. Clare we find the name of O'Mere, etc.. in older works, and the family here is assumed to be of Irish heritage. One note of caution is that the name of O'Meara has also been shorted simply to Meer, Mear, etc.., but this is an entirely different family.

Meldon

Irish Book of Arms plate 259

Melden

One family of the name is found in Fore, Co. Westmeath, and subsequently of Casino, Miltown, in Dublin City.

O'Molloy, Mulloy

Irish Book of Arms plates 46, 164, 247

O Maolmhuaidh

Mulloy, Molley, Molloy, Millea, Mullee,

The extensive lands of the O'Mulloy or Molloy clan comprised the 'present' baronies of Eglish or Fearcall, Ballycowan, and Ballyboy in Kings County, (Co. Offaly). They originally formed a part of the ancient kingdom of Meath. The O'Mulloys were of the same race as the southern Ui Niall, or Clan Colman, descended from Niall of the 9 Hostages.

They are thus designated by O'Dugan; "The prince of Fercall of the ancient swords is O'Mulloy of the free born name; Full power had fallen to him, He held his country uncontrolled."

As Lords of Fercal in Co. Offaly, one chief is recorded as being the official hereditary English standard bearer in Ireland. A branch of this family settled in Co. Roscommon as "Green Molloy", and another early form of the name was O'Mulmoy.

In the province of Connaught the name is of separate origins, descended from O'Maoil Aoidh (of St. Aoidh). Here the names of Millea, Mullee, and Miley are found. They too may be corrupted forms of Molloy etc...

"Molloy" was the preferred spelling of the name in the last century as it had 153 births in Dublin, Galway, Mayo, Kings, Donegal, etc...

In the census of 1659(O')Mulloy is a principal name of Leitrim and Donegal, while Molloy was a principal name of Kings and found in Roscommon, etc... "Molley" is also a spelling found as a principal name in Kings Co. at that time, and it is a variant of O'Molloy.

The Mulloy family of Strancally Castle, Co. Waterford is given in the Irish Book of Arms.

Montgomery of Grey Abbey, co. Down.

Motto.—Honneur sans repos.

196

O'Monaghan

Irish Book of Arms plates 93, 114, 137

O Manachain

Monaghan, Monnaughan, Monohan,

The O'Monaghans descend from Manachan, a 9th century warrior. The family is recorded as chiefs of 'Mura O'Mannachain' or Tir Briane of the Shannon, along the Shannon River, in the barony of Ballintober, Roscommon, in the parishes of Kilmore of the Shannon, Cloonaff, Aughrim and Kilumed. (Roscommon and Boyle baronies).

Given by the Four Masters as 'Lords of the Three Tuathas of Co. Roscommon', they were overpowered by the O'Briens, and subsequently by the O'Hanleys, also ancient chiefs in Ballintobber.

The family is anciently found in Co. Rocommon near Elphin and Jamestown, but by the time of the 1890 birth index the family is found most numerous in Galway, Mayo, Dublin and Fermanagh.

Monaghan was the preferred spelling of the name in 1890 by a 2 to 1 margin over Monahan. The name was found in Galway, Mayo, Dublin and Fermanagh at that time. Monihan has been a spelling of Cork and Kerry.

In the 17th century 'Monaghan' was numerous in Donegal, and O'Monaghen in Fermanagh. 'Monegan' is found in Longford then, and McMonaghan has also been found as a variant spelling.

"Monk" has also been used as a variant spelling of the name, coming from the English translation of Manachain.

The Dominican Church of Athenry, Co. Galway holds a Monaghan tomb dating to the 17th century.

Note the pioneer town of Monahans, in Ward County, Texas, U.S.A.. The name is found early in America. William Nonahan (or Monahan) is found in the land records of Virginia in 1654, and James Monahan, from Goffstown, is found petitioning the New Hampshire Legislature in December, 1777.

Montgomery

Irish Book of Arms plate 135, 141

Montgomry

The name of a family from Scotland which settled in the province of Ulster in Ireland in the 17th century. The 1890 birth index finds the family most numerous in Antrim and Down.

Morrissey

Irish Book of Arms plate 203

O Muirgheasa

Morris, Morrison, Moris, Morisey,

Families of the name of Morrisey may spring from any of several separate and unrelated families in Ireland. The native Irish of the name descend from O Muirgheasa, in Carbury and Tireragh baronies, near Sligo bay in Co. Sligo. The name is scarce in that area in modern times. Waterford, Limerick and Cork are the most populated with the name today.

The name is given in Keatings History as one of the Mayo/Sligo area anciently.

As is visually evident, the name easily becomes Morris by dropping the "ey" from the end of the name, and this has been done by some. Others of the name are said to have used similar name of Morrison as a variant spelling.

There is also a Norman family of the name of de Marisco, or de Marecy, and they could easily have adopted Morrisey for their name in Ireland.

It should be noted that there are English families of the Morrissey name in Ireland as well.

In the 17th century Morissey, Morresse, and Morisey are given as principal family names of Tipperary, and "Moressy" as a principal name of Waterford.

de Montmorency

The Irish Book of Arms plate 57

The de Montmorency family of Castle Morres, county Kilkenny, Ireland is found given in the Irish Book of Arms. The arms above are of that family.

O'Morgan

Morgen, Morgin, Morahan, Murrigan

The name of Morgan is quite common in Ireland, with some 132 births in the 1890 index in counties Antrim, Armagh, Down, Dublin and Louth. Morgan is a common English name, and many of the name in Ireland are originally of that stock, descending from settlers who arrived from England. Morgan is also a Welsh name, and that doubtlessly accounts for some of the name in Ireland as well.

In specific instances some Irish families have adopted the name according to several reports, namely the Morahan and Murrigan families who 'translated' those names into Morgan on occasion.

The family is found in the old territory of Oriel, and has been cited as a principal Norman family of Co. Cork, and as an old English family who settled in Co. Wexford.

Morley

Morly, Morrally, Morrelly

Families of the name of Morley are given in Cork City and County in the census of 1659. Two centuries later they are found centered in Co. Mayo. Morley, of course, is an English name, and many families originally came from that country before arriving in Ireland. In other areas, such as in Mayo where the name was numerous, the family is actually most likely of Irish origins, having adopted "Morley" as the English spelling of the name.

O'Mooney

Irish Book of Arms plates 90, 165

O Maonaigh

Meeny, Meany, Mainey, Meaney

The O'Mooney family can be traced back to several origins in Ireland. The O'Mooneys are placed in Queens County on the map of Ortelius anciently. Note the townland of Ballymooney there in modern times. In the nearby county of Offaly there is a townland of the same name, marking a prominent location for the family. Here they are recorded as hereditary caretakers of St. Monahan's shrine in Lemanaghan parish.

In Ulster we find the descendants of Monach, from whom the name Mooney has sprung, in Ardara parish, in the diocese of Raphoe, where they served as erenaghs of Shanaghan.

The spelling of "Mainey" is common in the province of Munster.

"O'Maonaigh, or O'Meeneys, sometimes made O'Mooneys", were also chiefs of Clan Murthuile. This was a district in Ballintober, Co. Roscommon. O'Dugan mentions this family thusly; Chief of Clan Murthuile is O'Mooney".

In neighboring Co. Sligo perhaps the same family is found in the barony of Tireragh. It should be noted that several townlands called Ballymeeny are found there, and the O'Mooney name may also be found as Meany and Meeny.

"Mooney" is the common spelling of the name, with 136 in Dublin, Antrim and Kings in the 1890 index. "Meany" was found in Kilkenny and Clare at that time with 34 births.

In the 17th century "Meany" was a principal name of Waterford. Moony, was so in Offaly and Westmeath, and Mooney was a principal name of Kildare, being found in Kilkenny.

In the Irish Book of Arms "Mooney of the Doon" in Kings Co. is given as the Irish family of the barony of Barrycastle.

O'Moore

Irish Book of Arms plates 49, 50, 70

O'Mordha, de Mora

More, Moor, Moir, Morey, O'More, Muir,

Under various spellings of the name in Ireland, the More or O'Moore family can be traced to English and Irish origins. 'Moore' is an English name, and it is also a form of the Irish "O'Moore".

Being the 20th most popular name in Ireland and among the top 40 names in England, the name is well represented.

English families settled in the province of Munster in the 12th century. Their name is said to stem from the word 'moor', meaning 'strong mountain' etc.. The ancient Irish family of the name descend from O'Mordha (meaning noble?). The ancestor from whence they sprung was one of the Red Branch knights of Irish legend.

The O'Mores were the leading tribe of the "7 Septs of Leix", and as such, some of the clan were transplanted to Kerry. Keatings History gives that St. Fintan was their patron saint.

Burkes Landed Gentry (1912 a. d.), gives over 10 families of the name that claimed Scottish or English roots.

The Moore family is found in the 17th and 19th century in counties Antrim and Dublin. "Moor" is found in 1659 as a principal name of Kings county as well.

McMore has been found in Offaly and Kildare, while O'More is said to have originated in Kerry, Down, and Leix.

"Moore" is the 11th most common name in the U.S.A. today.

The Moores of Moore Hall, Co. Mayo, came from Alicante,Spain, but were originally from England. Moore was also the name of the Earls of Drogheda. The Moores of Barmeath settled in Ireland from at least the 14th century. The Moore family of Barne, Co. Tipperary originally settled in Clonmel, Co. Tipperary around 1635.

O'Moran

Irish Book of Arms plates 165, 250

O Morain, O Moghrain

Moarn, Moeran, Moren, Morin, Mourn,

(O')Moran is one of the 60 most numerous surnames in all of Ireland, and it has been traditionally tied to the province of Connaught. The name is very widespread, being found in every county in the country.

One family of the name springs from O'Morain of Co. Mayo, where they were chiefs near Ballina. O Moghrain or O Mughrain, was the founder of a completely separate family hailing from the Galway/Roscommon area. They served as chiefs of Criffon, in the barony of Killian and part of the barony of Ballymoe in Galway. They were seated near Ballintober in Roscommon.

The family of the name bearing a coat of arms is more properly referred to as Morahan, and they were found in Offaly and Kildare. This family bears a coat of arms under the name of O'Moran.

MacMoran or MacMorrin is a separate family as well, distinct from the above. There was also a noted family of Ballinamoore in Co. Leitrim by the name of Moran.

In the 17th century O'Moran was a principal name of Donegal and also found in Roscommon. Moran was quite numerous at that time, being a principal name of Kildare, as well as being in Kings, Meath, Westmeath, Leitrim, Roscommon and Sligo.

Moren and Morin were both principal names of Kildare at that time. Keatings History mentions the name as numerous or prominent in the Down/Armagh area and the Mayo/Sligo area in Ireland.

Of related spellings, "Morrin" is also a name found in England, and some of the name may stem from this heritage.

198

O'Moriarty

Irish Book of Arms plates 165, 244

O Muircheartaigh

MacMoriarty, Murtagh

The O'Moriartys of Co. Kerry are of the same stock as the O'Donaghues and O'Mahoneys of that region. They were centered in the west of Kerry, in the baronies of Corkaguiney and Trughanacmy, centered in the Castlemaine Harbor area most anciently, even prior to the Norman invasions of the 12th century.

With the coming of that invasion the family fell from power, as the Fitzgeralds rose to power there. They have remained in county Kerry into modern times however.

In Keatings History, O'Moriarty is given in the parish of Templenoe, and some adjoining districts in the barony of Dunkerron. They are spoken of as chiefs of Aes Asdi, and given by O'Heerin thusly;

"Aes Asdi of the plain of Flocks,
Which the chief of the O'Moriarty obtained".

In Co. Meath, near Kells, another family of this old Irish name exists. It is thought that the name was 'translated' into Murtagh here. Murtagh is as well, a name of Scottish origins in Ireland.

Meskell

Miscall, Mescal, Miskelly

Families of the name of Meskell and variant spellings are often found in Co. Clare and surrounding areas. Spelled as Meskell, we find the name in the city of Cork in the 17th century. The name is found in several locations in our records, but not particularly centered in any one county. Variant spellings of the name in the north of Ireland, may actually represent completely unrelated families.

O'Moroney

Irish Book of Arms plates 165, 237

O'Maolruanaigh

Maroney, Marony, Mulroone, Mulrooney

Moroney or Maroney etc.... is considered to be a Clare name, although several independent septs of the name seemed to have existed in ancient times. In the 1890 birth index the name is found in Clare, Limerick and Tipperary. In Milesian Families the name of O'Moroney is given as a Dalcassion Sept, located in County Clare anciently.

In Co. Fermanagh the name remains closer to its original gaelic, being spelled as 'Mulrooney'. Here in Fermanagh the family held great power until the rise of the Maguires in that area. When spelled as Maroney, etc.. the name is traditionally given to Co. Clare, and in older times into County Galway as well.

The name of Morny, presumably a separate name, is given in Keatings History in the territory of Thomand, which includes Co. Clare.

Melody

Melodey, Meledy, Maledy

The name of Melody, which is not a common one in Ireland, had only 5 recorded births in the 19th century birth index, all in Munster and Connaught. In relatively recent times the family is centered in the north of Co. Clare and in adjoining areas of Galway.

Mc Menamin

Mac Meanman

McMenamen, McMenemen

The name of an Irish family traditionally linked to Co. Tyrone and Co. Donegal in Ireland.

Morris, Maurice

Morris arms plate 70, Fitzmaurice 3

O Muirgheasa

Mores, Morrison, Morres, Fits, Fitz,

Most families of the names of Morris, Fitzmaurice and Fitzmorris in Ireland were originally of foreign origins. The name is common in England and Wales, so this accounts for many of the name. "Morises" of Norman origin are given in Ossory, Leix, Galway and Offaly in Keatings History, and the family is found of Welsh heritage settling in the 12th and 13th centuries.

In Kerry the noted family of the name of Fitzmaurice are found early. Often the Fitz prefix is dropped from the name forming "Maurice, Morrice, Murris, Morres", etc... This line is represented by the "Earls of Kerry" who descend from Raymond le Gros. They were in alliance with Dermod MacCarthy, king of Desmond and recieved lands in Kerry around Lixnaw. This was possessed by his son Maurice, and hence became known as Clanmaurice. They later became known as the Fitzmaurices, earls of Kerry, and were of Anglo-Norman origins. In 1890 there were 21 recorded births of the name Fitzmaurice in Kerry. Fitzmaurice has also been used in place of "Morris" in Co. Roscommon.

"Morris" was one of the 14 tribes of Galway. This family was of Norman origin. Originally called "de Marreis", then, Mares, Mareis, Moris, etc...

Morrissey has been shortened to Morris on occasion, notably in Sligo.

Fitzmaurice has remained a name of Co. Kerry. "Morris" was recorded in the 1890 index with some 115 births in Dublin, Mayo, Tyrone and Monaghan.

MacMorrice, considered a variant spelling of Fitzmaurice by some, was a principal name of Kerry in the 17th century, while McMorris was a name of Cork as was Morris. Morrice and Fitzmorish were principal names of Waterford at that time. (see Fitzmaurice)

Morrisson

Irish Book of Arms plate 56

Morrison, Morrisen

Being among the top 30 most numerous name in Scotland, it is not surprising to find most of the name in the province of Ulster in Ireland, centered in counties Antrim and Down. Due to similarity in sound or meaning, some confusion exists between the names of Morrison, Morrisey, MacMaurice, Fitzmaurice etc...

The Morrison family of Coolegegan, Kings county, is found in the Irish Book of Arms.

Moher

Mogher, O' Mohir, Moir

The census of 1659 gives the family as a principal one of Co. Cork at that time. It is here, and in Waterford, where the family has been traditionally located for centuries. The spelling of Mogher, which is given as a variant spelling of Moher, at least at times, was a principal name of Waterford, and found in Kilkenny in the same census.

Molan

Moland, Mulholland, O' Mollane,

The name of Molan is taken to be of older Irish origins, as a shortened form of Mulholland. The name of Moland is more often of English origins. The names of Mollane and Mollan as given in some records likely represent separate families, and O'Mollane was given as such in Co. Clare in the 17th century.

Mc Monagle

McMonigal, Mc Monegal, McMonigle

Families of the name are traditional given as a clan of Co. Donegal in Ireland, and the name is also found in Co. Derry in some numbers in our records.

O'Mullally

Irish Book of Arms plates 162, 224

O'MAOLALAIDH

Lally, Mulally, Mullaly

The Mullaly family is considered to be one of Ui Maine. They were constantly at war with the Burkes after the Norman invasions. Originally they were located just south of the Tuam area in Galway. After the seige of Limerick, many went on to fight in the wars on the continent, as part of the famed Wild Geese of Ireland.

The family is found in Keatings History of Ireland thus: 'O'Maelalaidh or Mulally, sometimes made Lally'. They are listed here under the section entitled families of the Ui Mani and Ui Fiacrach Aidni. Several Bishops and clergy of the name became prominent in the area from the 13th century onwards.

In the 1890 index there are some 14 births under this name, 8 births of the name are recorded under the spelling of Mullally, in scattered locations. Lally, on the other hand, lists 34 births, found mainly in Mayo and Galway. In Milesian families the name of O'Mullally is given as a family of the Hy Brune, in County Galway.

The family is found primarily in the provinces of Leinster and Munster, and the counties of Mayo and Galway have always been a traditional location for the name in Ireland.

Individuals of the name:

William Mulally- Noted in Newington, New Hampshire @ 1755 a.d.)

Passengers From Ireland:

Mary -Aboard "Louisa" From Waterford to New York, arrived June 16, 1846.

Watt- (Male) From Dublin to New York. Aboard "Perseverance", May 18, 1846.

Anna, Michl., Patrick- From Liverpool to N. Y. Aboard "Home" Oct. 31, 1848.

199

Mullan, Mullen

Irish Book of Arms plates 165, 226

O Maolain

Mullin, Mullen, Mullane, Mullins,

The family name(s) of Mullan, Mullen, Mullane, Mullin etc.. rank amoung the top 70 most numerous names in all of Ireland. As might be expected several origins for the name exist. Scottish settlers of the name of MacMullen who arrived in Ulster in the 17th century became Mullen, simply by dropping the Mac prefix to the name.

In Co. Tyrone the Irish family of O'Meallain has also become Mullan and Mellan in official records. In Galway the name of Mullan is said to be taken from "Mullan", who was descended from one of the kings of the province of Connaught, and of the same line as Concannon.

In Ulster a separate family is found in the Tyrone/Derry area, often Anglicized as O'Mullane, in the territory of O'Cahane. Many of the name also descend from O'Maolain in Connaught.

In Keatings History we also find the O'Mullens given as one of the Leinster clans, numerous in Meath, Dublin and Kildare at that time.

In 1890 the most common spelling of the name was Mullan, with 92 recorded births in Tyrone, Londonderry, Galway, and Antrim. This is followed by the "Mullen" spelling with 72 births and the Mullin spelling with 53 births.

In the 17th century (O) and (Mac) Mullan were given in Antrim, Armagh, Down and Londonderry. "Mullane" was a name of Cork then, as well as in 1890. (Mc) Mullen was a principal name in Louth and Antrim, and Mullin a principal name of Antrim at that time.

In the 1890 index Mullins was given in counties Cork and Clare.

O'Mulvihill

Irish Book of Arms plates 165, 220

O Maoil Mhicil

Mulville, Mitchell, Mullvihill

It is anciently written that the O'Mulvihills, also known as "Mulville and Mitchell", were chiefs along with Mac Brennan in Corca Achlann, a large district adjoining Kinel-Dobhtha in the barony of Roscommon. This district formed part of the Tuatha in which was situated the Sleive Baun Mountain.

The family was to be found here on the banks of the Shannon River in Co. Roscommon in the 12th century. With the coming of the Norman invasions however, the prominence of the family declined.

From their lands in Roscommon they spread into Co. Longford where they are found on the in 1659. They are subsequently found in Clare, Kerry and Limerick. In more modern times the name is given in Kerry and Limerick in the 1890 birth index.

Keatings History records Mulville and Mitchell as variant spellings of the name. This is confirmed in the 1890 index, with "Melville" in Kilrush Union of Co. Clare and Mitchell in Glenamaddy Union, Co. Roscommon both being given as variant spellings of Mulvihill.

The armigerous family of the name is found seated at Knockanira, Co. Clare in the 19th century. "Doonmulvihill" (now Doon) near Ennis in Clare marks an early location for the name in that county. The same line is given as being of Killowen in Co. Clare as well.

The name itself is said to have been taken from O Maoil Mhicil, meaning follower of St. Michael. The O'Mulvilles of Killowen, Co. Clare are said to have founded a branch of the family in Listowel, Co. Kerry.

Murphy

Irish Book of Arms plates 29, 166, 227

Murchada

Murchoe, MacMurrough, Murfhy, Morphy,

Murphy is the #1 surname of Ireland, and among the 50 top names in America. Several unrelated families share this name, accounting for its popularity. The name usually stems from the personal name of Murchada.

One family is founded by Murchada, a prince of east Wexford in the 10th century. This most prominent Murphy family is the one of Leinster, being centered in Co. Wexford. The chief of the name was called "The O'Morchoe" and they were seated at Oulartleagh.

Most commonly found in Cork and Kerry, the family is traditionally tied to the barony of Muskerry in Co. Cork.

Other Murphy families were found in the Tyrone/Sligo area, and it is the most numerous of all names in Co. Wexford, Co. Carlow, and Co. Armagh in Ulster.

The ancient 'O' prefix attached to most families of the name has been dropped by most Murphy families. The Augustinian Abbey at Ferns, in Wexford is an ancient burial place of the family.

Place names in Ireland commemorating these families include: Ballymurphy in Carlow, Ballymurchoda in Limerick, and Ballymurphy in Belfast to name a few.

The name is attached to numerous inventions. The "Murphy Bed" was one designed to fold up into the wall when not in use. Early settlements in America were named "Murphysboro" and the like. The "Murphy Wagon" was of great fame in its day, for it replaced the old "Conestoga Wagon" for thousands of Irish immigrants heading into the American Frontier from St. Louis. Its inventor, Joseph Murphy, was an Irish immigrant who arrived in America alone at a tender age, rising to great prominence after finding no one to receive him upon arriving in America.

200

Mac Murrough

Irish Book of Arms plate 166

Mac Murchadha

Murphy, Kavanagh, Kinsella, Davis, Mac

The MacMurroughs, or sept of Mac Murchadha, were ancient kings of Leinster . They maintained held the title of kings of Leinster, with large possessions in Wexford and Carlow, down to the reign of Elizabeth, and waged war with the English for many centuries. Art Mac Murrough O'Cavenagh, famous for his contests with the English forces under King Richard II in the 14th century, was one of the most celebrated chiefs. Donal O'Cavenagh, surnamed Spainagh, or the Spaniard, was a leader in Leinster, in the Elizabethan wars. The ancient kings of Leinster had residences at Dinnrigh, Leighlin, and at the Naas in Kildare. Later they had castles at the old city of Ferns, and at Old Ross in Wexford and at Ballymoon in Carlow.

The Mac Murroughs were inaugurated as kings of Leinster at a place called Cnoc-an-Bogha, attended by O'Nolan, the Kings Marshal, chief of Forth, in Carlow; by O'Doran, the chief Brehon of Leinster and by Mac Keogh, his chief bard. They are given by O'Heerin: ..." A scion from whom no unkindness we'll recieve, With MacMurrogh we will take our abode...The High-King of Naas, the tree of Brogha, The Lord of Leinster is Mac Murrogh."

Keatings finds the O'Cavanaghs as representatives of the Mac Murroghs. They held a territory called Ui Cavenagh, now the "barony of Idrone East, in Co. Carlow".

Dermot Mac Murrough (d. 1171), was the responsible for the coming of the Norman invasions, by seeking the support of the King Henry II.

This name has almost disappeared, found now as Mac Morrow, Kavanagh, Kinsella, Davis and Murphy.

201

Meyer (Myer)

O'Meidhir

Myers, Meyers

Despite the fact that the name of Meyers, Myers, Meyer, etc... is not always thought of as Irish when found abroad, it can be a true Irish family name.

The name is believed to be of the west of Ireland, stemming from O'Meidhir or Meere. Spelled as Myers the name is found in Wexford and Antrim in the 1890 birth index of Ireland.

The name of course, is also found elsewhere, and may be of distinct English, French or German origins.

Mockler

Mauclere

Mackler

According to "Keatings History" the name is among the chief families of English descent settling in Waterford and Tipperary. These English families primarily possessed the territory called from them Gal-tir, signifying the country of the foreigners," now the barony of Gaultiere." The Mockler family arrived here with the coming of the 12th century Norman invasions of Ireland.

Note the place name of Grangemockler in Co. Tipperary, where the family has long been found. The name of Mockler is found in older rccords written as "Maucler" and "Mauclerc" etc..

The 1890 birth index finds the family most numerous in Tipperary.

Moffatt

Moffat, Moffett, Mofitt, Mofett

The above name is given to be that of a Scottish family settling in the province of Ulster no later than the 17th century in Ireland. The 1890 birth index finds the family most numerous in Antrim, Sligo and Tyrone.

Moy

Moye

The family name of Moy is most often cited in Co. Donegal in our records, and it is possible that families of the name are of English, as well as Irish descent. Those of Donegal are assumed to be of old Irish descent.

Moylan

Moylen

The name of an old Irish family traditionally associated with counties Clare, Cork and Tipperary.

Moyles

Moyle

Moyles appears to be the preferred spelling of the name into modern times, but earlier the name was often found simply as Moyle. The family name is given as Moyles in the last century and several of the name were found in Co. Mayo at that time.

Muckian

Muckeyin, MacKean, MucKeen, Muckeen

Sometimes confused with the Scottish family of MacKean, those bearing the Muckian or Muckeyin name are of separate origins. They are most often found in counties Monaghan and Down in Ireland.

Mellon

O'Meallain

Mellen, Mellan

An old Irish family of the province of Ulster, found centered in Co. Tyrone.

O'Mergain

According to "Keatings History" the name is that of a chief of Eoganacht Ros Argid, and they were cited as "To O'Mergain belongs the land Of the fair Eoganacht of Ros Argid, A lord in peace and a vulture in war, Resides near the great Carn Mughani."

Minogue, Minoge

The family name above is traditionally linked to Co. Clare in Ireland, and is that of an old Irish family. The 1890 birth index finds the family most numerous in Clare spelled as Minogue, and spelled as Minnock we find the name centered in Kings Co., with 4 births at that time.

Moorhead

Morehead, Muirhead

The name of a Scottish family found centered in Co. Antrim, in the province of Ulster in Ireland.

O'Morny

According to "Keatings History" the name is found in the barony of Lower Connello, of the ancient territory of Thomand.

Meyler

Maelor, Mailor, Fitzmeiler

One noted family of the name is found centered in the Manor of Duncormack in Co. Wexford, down to Cromwellian times, said to descend from a "Mailor or Maylor" who went out of Pembrokeshire to accompany Strongbow in his conquest of Ireland.

Several are found in early records of the 14th century in official capacities. One Pierce Fitzmeiler is found in 1302.

The 1890 birth index finds the family most numerous in Co. Wexford.

Mulchinock

Mulshinock, Mulshinoge, Mulshenagh

The name of a family traditionally tied to Counties Cork and Kerry in Ireland. Spelled as Mulshenoge the name is found in Co. Cork in the 17th century in the town of Mallow. Arms for the family are officially recorded in the Genealogical Office in Dublin.

O'Mulclohy

According to "Keatings History" the name is given as belonging to a family which served as chiefs of Cairbre, now the barony of Carbury, Co. Sligo. Mulclohy has as well been found to have been 'translated' into the name of Stone for many members of this old Irish family.

O'Muldoon

Irish Book of Arms plate 223

Muldoone

According to "Keatings History" the name is that of a chief in Eoganacht Ani. They are spoken of as "Over Eoganacht Ani in order rules- A numerous tribe from o'er the waves, These armed Fenians from Aughrim."

The 1890 birth index finds the family most numerous in Fermanagh and Galway.

202

Mulgrew

O'Mulgrue, Mulcrew, Grew, Mulcreevy

The name of a family traditionally linked with Co. Tyrone in Ireland. An older form of the name has been said to be that of Mulcreevy, which is now rare. The 1890 birth index finds the family most numerous in Tyrone.

Mulhall

O'Maolchathail

Mulhal

The name of an old Irish family traditionally linked to counties Leix, Carlow and Kilkenny. The 1890 birth index finds the family most numerous in Dublin, Kilkenny, Carlow and Queens.

Mulholland

The name of an old Irish family traditionally linked with the province of Ulster, even into modern times. Several independent, unrelated families of the name have been reported, including the family of the name in Co. Donegal. The 1890 birth index finds the family most numerous in Antrim, Down and Londonderry.

Mulkerrin

Irish Book of Arms plate 204

Mulkerin, Mulkern, O'Mulkerin, O' Mulkerane, Mulherin

The Mulkerin family is traditionally linked with Co. Galway in Ireland. Spelled as O'Mulkerane the name is found as a principal one of Co. Armagh in the 17th century. Mulherin, Mulheren, Mulherrin etc..., are said to be forms of the same name, and they are often found in the province of Ulster in Ireland, of possible separate origins.

O Mullaney

Irish Book of Arms plate 207

O'Maoileanaigh

Mullany, Mulaney, Mulleeny

The census of 1659 finds Mullany families in Kilkenny and finds Mullany as the principal name in Waterford. In the same records, O'Mullany is found as a principal name of County Roscommon, particularly in the barony of Boyle. More anciently, in Milesian Families O'Mullany is cited as a Dalcassion family in Waterford, Sligo and Longford.

Note the place name of Ballymullany near the Roscommon and Sligo border.Patrick F. Mullany (1847 - 1893) who held the pen name of Brother Azarias, in America.

Mullarkey

Mullarkey, Mollarky, Mallarky

In the 17th century members of the Mullarky family bore a principal name of Co. Sligo. Two centuries later the family is found centered in counties Mayo, Galway and Sligo as "Mullarkey". Most anciently the family is found in Co. Donegal, and subsequently to the south as mentioned.

Milford

According to "Keatings History" the name is that of a family who ruled a district extending along the western banks of the Moy, between Ballino and Killala. O'Maolfoghmair and O'Maolbrennuin were the two chieftains there. The former name had been changed to Milford by some, and the latter became Mulrennin.

Mulqueen

The name of a family most often linked with counties Limerick and Clare in our records.

Mullerick

Millerick, Mulderrig

The name of a family often found in Co. Cork. Woulf gives the family of Mulderrig in Mayo as of the same line, but using another spelling of the name.

Morrow

Irish Book of Arms plate 250

MacMorrow, MacMurrough

The name of Morrow may stem from the older family spelling of MacMuireadhaigh, found centered anciently in Co. Leitrim. The name is also found centered early in Roscommon and subsequently in the province of Ulster in Ireland, where some of the name may be of Scottish extraction.

The 1890 birth index finds the family most numerous in Antrim, Donegal, Armagh and Down.

Mowbray

According to "Keatings History" the name is that of an ancient titled family in the county of Carlow, found alongside the Howards, Butlers and Carews, etc..

Moody

Mody, Mudy, Moode, Moodie

Moody is a name primarily given to the province of Ulster in Ireland, and particularly in Antrim and Down in more modern records. Most families of the name here are of English origins

de Montchenseys

According to "Keatings History" the name is given as among the ancient titled families in Wexford, and they are cited as Lords of Wexford.

O'Mulrenan

Irish Book of Arms plate 223

Maolbrennuin

Mulbrennan

According to "Keatings History" the name is that of chiefs in the barony of Roscommon, near Cruachan. We quote from our edition of that work :

"O'Mulbrenan of renown,
Was chief of Clan Conor of the fertile plains, Their men above all others I record, They are of the Clan Cathail."

Also according to "Keatings History" , the name is that of a family who ruled a district extending along the western banks of the Moy, between Ballino and Killala. O'Maolfoghmair and O'Maolbrennuin were the two chieftains there. The former name had been changed to Milford by some, and the latter became Mulrennin.

Mulrooney

O'Maolruanaidh

Rooney, Roony, Mulroony

Two separate Irish families of the name have been found, those of Co. Fermanagh and those of Co. Galway.

O'Mulledy

According to "Keatings History" the O'Mulledy family is given to be a family name of note in former times in Co. Westmeath. The lands of this family appear to have adjoined those of Mac Coghlan, and were probably in the barony of Garrycastle, in Kings County, and in Clonlonan, in Co. Westmeath.

Mulroy

Mulry

The family of Mulroy is traditionally linked with Co. Mayo in Ireland, and the name of Mulry, believed to be of separate origins, is found in Mayo as well.

O'Mulcahy

Irish Book of Arms plate 253

O Maolchathaig

Mulclohy, Muckley, Mulchay, Cahy,

Mulcahy families in Ireland are thought to have originated anciently in the south of Tipperary, near the borders of Cork, Limerick and Waterford, counties which bear the name into modern times. The "O" before the name has largely been dropped by families of the name.

A fairly rare surname in Ireland, Mulcahy had 76 recorded births of the name in Cork, Limerick, Waterford and Tipperay in the 1890 index. Several variant spellings and names have been used for this family. Cahy, MacCahy, and Caughy are reported in Down in earlier times, and O'Mulclohy has even become Mulcahy on occasion.

The O'Mulclohys were chiefs in the barony of Carbury, Sligo. Carbury derived its name from Carbri, son of Niall of the Nine Hostages. This name has also been Anglicized to "Stone", and there were many families of that name there when it was cited in Keatings History (v-3).

In the 17th century Mulcaghy was a principal name of Waterford and O'Mulclahy a principal name of Limerick city.

O'Hart gives Mulcahy of Whitechurch, Waterford of which line was Edmund Moore Mulcahy of Ballymakee, J.P. for the Cos. of Waterford and Tipperary. the first of two to hold that title.

The Mulcahys of Ardpadden, Co. Waterford are sometimes said to be a branch of the above. They in turn formed the branch that settled in "Killkeany, Co. Waterford. Thomas Mulcahy of Ardpadden owned the following townlands in the parish of Kilbrien, Co. Waterford. Namely : Scart, Baracree, and Kilbrien, and he afterward got the townland of Killkeany for his son John.

Mc Millan

Irish Book of Arms plate 212

McMullan, McMullen, McMillen

The name of a Scottish family settled in Ulster no later than the 17th century in Ireland. In Scotland they were said to be of the Clan McMillan. The 1890 birth index finds the family name of Millen most numerous in Co. Antrim.

O'Mulligan

Irish Book of Arms plate 230

O Maolagain

Milligen, Milliken, Mulgan, Mullagen,

O'Mulligan, or "O'Maelagain" is given in Keatings History as chief of Tir Mac Caerthain, a territory included in the baronies of Raphoe and Boylagh in Co. Donegal. With the disturbances of the 17th century this clan was dispossessed of its power there, until today they are primarily located in Mayo, Monaghan and Dublin. O'Dugan also gives O'Mulligan as a clan of Moy Ith in the 12th century, who as well settled in Tyrone at that time. Their name was also noted as being Anglicized to "Molineux" according to Keatings History.

"O'Maolchein, probably O'Milliken or O'Mulligan, some who have changed the name to Molyneaux, chief of Tuath Damhuigh", was also recorded by O'Herrin as being in the territory adjoining O'Hennessy thusly;

"Over Tuath Damhuigh of the fair fortress, Is O'Maolchein of the happy heart.".

In the 17th century Mulligan was found as a principal name of Westmeath alongside with Mullican. With the O prefix, both names were found numerous in Fermanagh at that time. Spelled as Mullegan, the name was found in Antrim and Longford.

The O'Mulligans and O'Daleys are also found in Co. Cavan as hereditary bards to the O'Reillys.

"Mulligans Irish Brigade" was to be found in the American Civil War, serving in several distinguished battles, including the Battle of Lexington.

204

O'Murrigan

O'Muireagain

According to "Keatings History" the name is found to be one of the principal families of Teffia.

Murray

Irish Book of Arms plate 253

O Muireadhaigh, Mac Giolla Mhuire...

Murry, Kilmurray, Murrihy, McMurry, Mac

The name of O'Murray, Murray etc.., ranks among the top 20 names in all of Ireland. Several origins for the name, in Ulster many are descended from Scottish settlers, and the name is among the top 20 surnames of Scotland as well.

The Irish name, O'Muireadhaigh (O'Murry), is found centered in Ballymurry, in the barony of Athlone, Co. Roscommon. In this area Keatings History finds O'Murray as a chief of the barony of Carra, in Mayo, and as chief of the north of the barony of Tyrawley in Mayo, serving as chiefs of the Lagan.

Keatings further gives the name as numerous in Cavan and Leitrim. In Leitrim we find Mac Murry or Mac Morrow, as chiefs in Loghmoyltagh.

In Ulster there is MacIlmurray (Murray), in the barony of Castlereagh, Co. Down, the county where O'Murry is given in O'Connors map of Ortelius.

Murray families are found in Cork, centered near Ballywidden in the barony of Carbery. They are probably descended from O Murrihie, a separate family.

Locations for the name in the 17th century include both"O" and "Mac" Murray as principal names of Donegal, and McMurrey as such in Londonderry, with Murry in Dublin, and in Kildare, Westmeath and Roscommon.

McMurry was a name of Down, Murry a name of Antrim and others. O'Murry was a principal name of Armagh, and in Down, Cork and Longford at that time.

Keatings finds the name in Kildare as "O'Muirthe or O'Muiridhe, probably O'Murray", chief of Kinel Flathemhuin. They were cited as "O'Murray, of great eloquence, chief of fair Kinel Flahaven"

Murray is the most common spelling of the name today, and McMurray is found often in Antrim and Armagh.

Several Murray place names are found.

Mulvaney

O Maoilmheana, O Maolmhaghna

Mulvany, Mulvanny, Mulvenna

When spelled as Mulvany the name had 4 recorded births in the 1890 birth index, none of whom was in Ulster. When spelled as Mulvanny, there were no births in the province of Ulster. In America of course, the name may now be spelled in a variety of ways.

In the works of Woulfe the name of Mulvany is said to come from O Maolmhaghna, in County Donegal more anciently. The name today, however, hails mainly from the province of Leinster.

Mulvenna

A family name traditionally linked to Co. Antrim in Ireland, and it is in that county where the name was found in the 1890 birth index.

Mulvey

Mulvy

The family of Mulvey in Ireland is traditionally linked to Co. Leitrim, and it has remained so into modern times.

Munroe

Monroe, Munrow

A well known Scottish name sometimes found settled in Ireland, it is also on record as being used for the name of Mulroy in Co. Mayo.

O'Murcan, Murcain

According to "Keatings History" the name is found as a chief of Fidhgaibhle and cited as " Over Liffey's plain of the fertile slopes, O'Murcan, chief, rules green Fidhgaibhle".

Murdock

Murdoch

The name of Murdoch is that of a family who settled in Ireland, coming originally from Scotland, and they are found most numerous in Co. Antrim.

Millett

Milet, Millet, Mellot, Milette

The family name of Millett can be found in several areas of Ireland. As Milet and Millette we find the name given in Co. Antrim in the 18th century. Other sources find the name in Kilkenny, Tipperary and Co. Mayo. No doubt several families of the name arrived in Ireland over the centuries, and several different surnames may actually be represented by Millet and variant spellings.

Murnaghan

Murnahan

A scarce name in Ireland, never very numerous, most often tied to the province of Ulster in Ireland.

Murnane

O Murnain

Marnane, Murnan, Murnain, Murney,

In the works of Woulfe we find the name of Murnane, and it variants, as originating in the old geographical territory of Thomand, in Ireland.

The 1891 birth index gives us the counties of Limerick and Cork as locations for the name of Murnane, with some 14 births recorded at that time. This family is traditionally considered to be of Limerick and upper Co. Clare, as this coincides roughly with the old territory of Thomand. In more recent times the name is also cited in county Cork.

In the 16th century we find the name in Limerick, Kerry and Cork which includes several variant spellings of the name. Of the Marrinan family, which is also found spelled as Murnane at times, it should be noted that some members of the family elected to use the name of Warren instead.

Mac Muregain

According to "Keatings History" the name is given as that of a prince of East Liffey, and mentioned in the Irish Annals in battles with the Danes in the 10th century.

Mulry

Mullery, Mulmory

The name of a family connected with counties Mayo, Galway and Roscommon in our records. Mulroy is actually a separate name, most often found in Co. Mayo and given by some in Co. Longford. Mulry was given as a principal name of Roscommon in the 17th century, and found centered in Galway some two centuries later.

Murtagh

O MUIRCHEARTAIGH

Murtaugh, Murta, Murdock, Murdoch,

The name of Murtagh and its variant spellings may be of Scottish or Irish origins. An old Irish family located near Kells, in County Meath is said to be the origin of Irish Murtaghs. The name was anciently spelled the same as O'Moriarty, and may stem from the gaelic word for navigator.

In the census of 1659 Murtagh is found as a principal name of Longford, and in Louth, Westmeath and Roscommon. Mc Murtagh was found as a principal name of Cork, and in Limerick and Wexford at that time.

By the time of the 1890 birth index, the name of Murtaugh was found primarily in Dublin and Sligo counties, with a total of 58 births given for the family name.

When the name is found in the province of Ulster it is likely of Scottish origin, and it is used here for a synonym of Murdoch, the common form of the name in Scotland.

To the south, in the province of Leinster, the name is more likely of ancient Irish origins.

Individuals of the name per O'Hart:

TERENCE MURTAGH. OF NEW YORK CITY IN 1880.

GREGORY MURTAGH OF LACLUNAGH,BARONY OF MOYDOW, COUNTY LONGFORD.

JOHN MURTAGH OF SHRULE BARONY, COUNTY LONGFORD.

(THE LAST TWO NAMES WERE LISTED UNDER CONFISCATIONS)

Milligan

Miligan, Millican, Millikan, Millikin,

The name of Milligan is understandably confused with the name of Mulligan in Ireland. Some interchanging of the two names has doubtlessly taken place over centuries. The name of Milligan, etc.. has been traditionally linked with the province of Ulster in Ireland. The 1890 birth index finds the family most numerous in Co. Antrim with 50% of the name there, and in Down and Londonderry.

Mills

The name of Mills, in Ireland is generally considered to be a name of English extraction. The family name is often found in the province of Ulster as would be expected, as well as in Dublin and elsewhere in the country. The 1890 birth index finds the family most numerous in Antrim.

Minihane

Minihan, Minighane, Munnihane

Considered to be a family separate from the Monaghan family, both occupied the same territory in Ireland, and may well stem from the same source. The birth index of the last century gives the Minihane family centered in Co. Cork, and the spelling of Minighane was a principle name of Co. Clare in the 17th century. Moving into modern times the family is given to be one of Co. Cork.

Mitchell

Mitchel, Michell

Families of the name of Mitchell are given to have settled in Ireland over the centuries, most likely of English origins. Some of the name in Ulster are also cited as being of Scots heritage. The family name is listed among those who were adventurers for land during Cromwellian times in Ireland.

Mitchell ranks among the top 30 most numerous names of England, so it is not surprising to find the name fairly widespread in Ireland.

In Co. Galway it has been officially reported that Mitchell was interchanged with the Irish surname of Mulvihill.

The 1890 birth index finds the family most numerous in Antrim, Galway and Dublin.

In America, the family is found as well in the famed Corcorans Irish Legion, during the American civil war.

Palatine Families

These families are given as settling in Ireland, those with an asterisk (*) are given as tenants on the Adare estate, onto which property they were settled around 1777 a.d..

Baker	Long
*Barkman	*Millar
Barrowbier	Mich
Benner	Modler
Bethel	Neizer
Bowen	*Piper
Bowman	Rhineheart
Bovinger, changed	Rose
to (Bobanizer)	Rodenbucher
Brethower	*Ruckee
Cole	*Switzer
Coach	*Sparling
*Corneil	*Stark
Cronsberry	*St. John
Dobe	St. Ledger
*Dulmage	Straugh
Embury	Sleeper
*Figgle	Shoemaker
Grunse	*Shier
Gruer	Sweltzer
Heek	*Shoultare
Hoffman	Shunewire
*Hifle	Tesley (Tesky)
*Heavener	Tettler
Glozier	Ursburlbaugh
Lawrence	Williams
Lowes	Young
Ledwick	

206

Nagle, Nangle

Irish Book of Arms plate 166

de Angulos

Neagle, Nangle

In the year 1172 Henry II granted lands to Hugh de Lacy including the entire kingdom of Meath. DeLacy divided Meath among his chiefs who became known as De Lacys barons. Gilbert de Angulo, the Norman from whom the name Nangle comes, obtained Magherigallen, "now the barony of Morgallion in Meath". Jocelin, son of Gilbert Nangle, obtained Navan and Ardbraccan. The Nangles later became "barons of Navan".

Many of the Nangles of Meath and Mayo took the name of MacCostello, and from them the barony of Costello in Mayo derived its name.

The Nangles are also cited in Keatings as a principal family of Anglo-Norman descent in the county and city of Dublin.

In Co. Cork Nagle and Neagle are the main spellings of the name, and in the barony of Fermoy here, near Ballyhooly one can find "Nagles" mountains.

In the 17th century "Nangle" was a principal name of Westmeath, and "Nagle" was a principal name of Limerick, and found in Waterford as well.

O'Hart says that Jocelin de Angulo, the first baron of Navans eldest son, was the ancestor of Nangle in Leinster and Nagle in Munster. Sir Richard Nagle was attorney general for Ireland in the reign of King James II. His brother Piers, of Annakissey, was high sheriff of Co. Cork. His descendant, Piers Nagle as well, was living in 1861.

Some 39 births of the name are recorded in Co. Cork in the 1890 birth index.

Mac Nally

Irish Book of Arms plates 166, 227

Mac an Fhailghigh

Mac Anally, McAnelly, Knally, McNelly

From the old gaelic spelling of Mac an Fhailghigh, it is believed that the modern day names of Mac Nally and Mac Anally have sprung.

Woulfe seems to believe that families of the name are of Norman or Welsh origins, and that they settled into Co. Mayo. In that county and in Roscommon the name is often found simply as Nally today.

With the Mac prefix, as either MacNally or MacAnally the name seems to be of the north of Ireland, in counties Armagh and Monaghan, and Antrim, and this is supported by the census of 1659. McAnully however, was reported as a principal name of Kildare at that time as well.

The majority of the above families are to be found in the province of Ulster, and many are found in the two major cities of Dublin and Belfast in Ireland.

O'Hart gives Nealan and Neylan as names which have been changed into Nally and Mac Nally.

In the census of 1659 we find the name as a principal one of County Westmeath in the barony of Rathconrath.

The separate and distinct name of McNelly, can easily have been confused with Mac Nally, and these names are bound to have been confused with each other.

Mc Namee

Mac Conmidhe

The name of McNamee is traditionally linked to Co. Derry, where it is said they served as hereditary poets to the noted O'Neill family of Co. Tyrone.

Mc Namara

Irish Book of Arms plates 166, 241

Mac Conmara,

Mac Conmara, or Mac Namara, according to Keatings History took their name from a 10th century chief named Cumara, a descendant of Conall Echluath, or Conall of the Swift-Steeds, who was king of Munster in the 4th century. The word Cumara, (Conmara), signifies a warrior of the sea.

The Mac Namaras were chiefs of Tricha Ced Ui Caisin, which territory is now the barony of Tullagh, in Co. Clare; it also contained part of the barony of Bunratty. They were sometimes styled chiefs of Clan Cuileain, which was the tribe name of the family. They are spoken of thusly by Aryan; "A princely chief of well fought battles is Mac Namara from Magh Adair, A land of riches in his country, It is the territory of Clan Caisin".

The Mac Namaras held the office of hereditary marshals of Thomand, where they had numerous castles.

McNamara remains a name of Clare to this day, and the branch of the family at Bunratty were seated at Bunratty Castle for a time. The second most common name in Co. Clare, they are noted throughout the history of that county.

They served as lords of Clancullen in eastern Clare, and the Bunratty branch were known as Mac Namara Fyne (Fair), and the branch in Upper and Lower Tulla baronies were known as Mac Namara Reagh (red or swarthy).

Mac Namara was a principal name of Limerick city in 1659. In the 1890 index Clare, Limerick, Mayo, Dublin and Cork held families of the name.

Napper

Irish Book of Arms plate 99 (Naper)

Naper, le Naper, Napier

The name of a settler family in Ireland most often connected with county Meath and also in counties Down and Wexford. On record in Ireland from earlier times, one family of the name obtained lands in Meath in the wake of the Cromwellian invasion.

The Naper family of Loughcrew, Co. Meath are found in that county as early as the late 16th century, where several of the name where of note.

The birth index of 1890 finds the Napier family centered in Antrim and Down.

O'Nedi

According to "Keatings History" the name is found in the plain of Kerry where they ruled along with Clan Conari. They were noted as a clan of the most active pitch in battle.

Mc Neela

McNeely

McNeela is a name traditionally linked to the province of Connaught. It is often confused with McNeely, and many McNeela families are said to have changed the spelling to McNeely.

The spelling of McNeilly is of the province of Ulster, particularly Co. Antrim, and is not thought to be of any relation to the McNeela family of Connaught.

Some trace the name back to more ancient origins in Co. Galway, and one family of the name is found in the Castlebar area of Co. Mayo for at least 3 generations according to one members report.

Nash

Irish Book of Arms plate 56

Ash, Neish, Naish, Nasse, Nashe

One English family of the name held lands in Worcester and is subsequently found in Farrihy, Co. Cork in the 18th century and in Dublin in the 19th century.

The Nash family of Finnstown and Howth, Co. Dublin are of the same line, tracing their descent to Patrick Nash or Naish, of Kanturk, Co. Cork, in the 17th century.

The birth index of 1890 finds the family centered in Kerry and Limerick.

Mc Naul

from Mac Anaul ?

MacNally, McNulty...

Considered to be an Irish family name of the province of Ulster, it may have originally sprung from Mac Con Uladh. This would account for the name coming from the earlier spelling of Mac Anaul. Several other possibilities exist. In Dublin the name may come from MacNally, and you may always find corrupt forms of names such as Naulty, ...which could have been further changed to McNaul.

Navin

Irish Book of Arms McNevin plate 258

Mac Cnaimhin ?

Mac Nevin, Nevin, Knavin

The birth index of 1890 records the name of Navin only in County Mayo in Ireland. It is also documented in Galway, being a tribe or family of the Ui Maine. Here the name was MacNevin or Knavin, coming from Mac Cnaimhin anciently. The family here were considered physicians and poets of the Ui Maine. (Also found spelled as Hy Many etc...)

Naughton,

Irish Book of Arms plates 166, 262

O Neachtain

O'Naghten, Mac Naughton, Nochtin,

O'Naghten is a name centered in Galway, Mayo, Roscommon and Clare. Scottish and English families of the name of McNaghton are found in Ulster.

In Keatings History (v3) we find the name as "O'Neachtain, or O'Naghten, sometimes made Norton." Norton of course, is an English name too.

The best known of the O'Naughton clan in Ireland are given by O'Dugan as chiefs of Moenmoy, along with O'Mulally. O'Dugan cites them as "The chiefs of Moenmoy the champions... Two who defend that district are O'Naghten and O'Mulally..Their warfare is heavy in battles, the land is theirs as far as Ui Fiachra."

Their territory an extensive plain, comprised much of the baronies of Loughrea and Leitrim in Co. Galway. Subsequently, they are found in the barony of Athlone in Roscommon, after the Norman invasions. Here they are found as 'Chief of the Fews', where they have remained into modern times.

Another family is found centered in the barony of Inchiquin in Co. Clare, near Corofin, not far from the origins of the first family given. Due to the close proximity of the two, some ancient relationship may exist. This family is said to descend from the O'Quinns.

In the 17th century 'Naghten' was a principal name of Roscommon, and Naghtenn was found there as well. McNaughten is given as a primary name of Co. Antrim, of likely Scottish heritage, and Naughten was given as a principal name of Westmeath.

In America, Norton ranks among the top 400 names in the country. Those wishing further insights on the family may consult O'Donovans 'The Tribes and Customs of the Hy Many".

O'Neilan

Irish Book of Arms plate 166

O Niallain

Neylan, Nelan, Nilan, Niland, Newland,

The O'Neilan family anciently spelled the name as O'Niallain, and they are found anciently in the old territory of Thomand. In the 1890 birth index Co. Clare was the most popular location for the Neylon name. Clare has been the traditional center for the name, and the name is found here on the census of 1659 as well.

Spelled as Neilan the name is found in Galway, Roscommon and Sligo, with some total of 12 recorded births in 1890. The spelling of Nilan had 7 recorded births at that time. Neylon had 13, given in Co. Clare.

A primary source for history of the family would be the written histories on county Clare by Frost, and by White, but even here there is not as much mention of the name as one might expect.

Note that Ballyally Castle served as a stronghold for the family in earlier days.

The 'O' is generally never found at the beginning of the name anymore.

O'Hart says that some of the name changed it to Mac Nally, or Nally, and he gives a Protestant Bishop of Kildare, one Daniel O'Neylon, as living in 1583. His son William was from Turlogh, in Co. Clare.

The name of course is easily changeable to O'Neil or O'Neill, by the dropping of the 'an' suffix at the end of the surname. This of course is a different family entirely, but some O'Neils today are sure to have O'Neilan heritage.

O'Neill, McNeill

Irish Book of Arms plates 166, 201, 253

Neel, Neil, Niel, Nihill, Neele, Nielson,

One of the top 12 most numerous surnames in all of Ireland, several unrelated families of the name exist in Ireland.

The most celebrated family of the name descends from "Conn of the 100 Battles", and they served as High Kings of Ulster.

Members of this family can be found in Tyrone, Derry, Donegal and surrounding areas most anciently. Tullaghoge, Co. Tyrone, was the ancient inauguration cite for new leaders of the family. Of much note and legend is the "red hand" of Ulster appearing on the arms of this family.

A separate family of the name is found in Co. Clare, in the barony of Bunratty. They were cited in the topographical poems as O'Neill or O'Nihell, chief of Clan Delbuidhe, and 'The land of Clan Dalvy of the poets was ruled by O'Neill, chief of Finnluarach, The forces of Tradree came to his fortress, the descendant of the yellow-haired chiefs".

Another family of the name is found in the barony of Rathvilly, Co. Carlow. Another still is found in the barony of Decies in Co. Waterford, believed to have spread into nearby Tipperary and Cork counties.

The MacNeills, who settled in the province of Ulster, came anciently from Scotland, and one of the name is found as a galloglass. They are found most settled in counties Antrim and Derry.

More people spell the name with the "O" prefix than without it, by a 2 to 1 margin, in the 1890 birth index. This is rather rare for Irish names at the time.

"The O'Neills of Ulster: their history and genealogy" was published by Mathews in Dublin in 1907".

Netterville

Irish Book of Arms plate 8 (titled)

Nutterville, Nettervill

According to "Keatings History" the name is given as among the "great families, either of English or Norman descent, settled in Meath in early times. The Nettervilles achieved the title of barons of Dowth.

Also according to "Keatings History" the name is that of a principal family of Dublin city or county, and of Anglo-Norman descent.

Nelson

Neilson, Nielson

Families of the name of Nelson, etc.. may be of either Scottish or English extraction when found in Ireland. When spelled as Neilson it is in the same form as often found in Scotland. When spelled as Nelson it is in the form found common in England. These spellings have been interchanged at times though, so this is by no means a hard and fast rule in identifying your family heritage. The name is found in Ireland prior to the 17th century, and it is assumed many families of the name have settled here over the centuries.

The 1890 birth index finds the family most numerous in Antrim, Down, Londonderry and Tyrone.

Newell

Newel, Knowles

The name of Newell is traditionally linked to the province of Ulster in Ireland, where it is likely of foreign extraction originally. Some of the name may as well be Irish, but we have no documentation on this.

The 1890 birth index finds the family most numerous in Down and Antrim.

Neville

Irish Book of Arms plate 38

Nevill

One well known family of the name is found settled in Co. Kildare in the 17th century, of the line of Richard Neville, of foreign extraction. The name is as well often found in Cork and Limerick, and its origins there are unknown to us at present.

The Neville family of Ahanure, Co. Kilkenny and of Rockfield, Co. Dublin is found in the Irish Book of Arms.

Newby

The name of Newby is a very rare surname in Ireland. We find reference to the name of Newbigging in O'Hart, but that name does not likely bear any resemblance to Newby (i.e. names like Newby could be shortened versions of names like Newbi(gging). We plan further research on this name in the future and welcome any contributions of research.

Newcomb

Newcomen, O'Nee?

Newcom, Newcome

The name of Newcomb (Newcomen) in Ireland is found in Dublin in the 16th and 17th centuries. Subsequently the name appears in Mayo quite frequently. It is possibly a form of O'Niadh (O'Nee). Newcomen is found in the census of 1659 in Dublin, Kildare and Longford. In Milesian Families Newcomb is listed as being of Saxon origin settling in Dublin in 1630.

Mac Norgan

Minorgan, Norgan

We find families of the name linked to Co. Carlow in the 19th century records of Ireland.

Newman

Irish Book of Arms plate 23

Newmen

The name of Newman is assumed to be of English extraction when found in Ireland, and one Richard Newman is found in Cork in the 17th century. The name is also found in Dublin in our records.

The Newman family of Newberry Manor, Co. Cork, is given in the Irish Book of Arms. The birth index of 1890 finds the family centered in Cork, Meath and Dublin.

O'Neny, O'Nena

Bird

According to "Keatings History" the name is listed among the chiefs of Moy Ith. This territory comprised parts of the baronies of Raphoe and Tirkeeran in Derry. Their territory in the 12th century is given as in Connally Naena, in Tyrone, bordering on Monaghan. Of this family was Count O'Neny, of Brussels. in the Austrian service, under the empress Maria Theresa.

The name has often been changed or 'translated' into "Bird".

Mac Nevin

Irish Book of Arms plate 258

Nevin, Navin, McNeven

According to "Keatings History" the name is given as that of the chiefs in the parish of Tynagh, barony of Leitrim, in Co. Galway.

Mc Nabb

A Scottish family name sometimes found in Ireland.

Newton

The Irish Book of Arms plates 57, 59

The Newton family of Dunleckney Manor, Co. Carlow is found in the Irish Book of Arms. The Newtons of Killymeal, Co. Tyrone, descend from Rycharde Newton, town clerk of Carrickfergus in 1595.

Mc Nelly

MacNellagh

McNeley, MacNeilly, Nelly, Nellie,

The MacNelly family, hopefully in most instances can be traced back to a sept of Clanrickard in Connaught (also the Mac Neilly family). When found simply as Nelly, the name is more often than not found in County Clare.

MacNellagh has been found in Co. Longford, and Woulfe equates it in his work with Connelly, Mac Neilly and Nelly. The confusion as to the original form of your name in Ireland is understandable. Many possibilities exist. McNally can easily become McNelly in America or Ireland. MacNeely is another ill used variant spelling particularly in County Antrim, which is actually a name of Galway (Mac Conghaile).

The MacNeilly (Mac an Fhilidh) family is another example. The MacNeillys are an ancient sept of Antrim, and some McNellys have changed their names to MacNeilly.

Dennis McNely, in Augusta Co. Virginia Land Certificates.

In Tazewell County, Virginia the name of McNeely appears in public records from 1799 - 1819.

Sarah Nelly: listed in Connaught Certificates in O'Harts work.

John MacNeilly aboard ship Hibernia from Belfast to New York, arrived before Nov. 30, 1811.

210

Nicholson

Irish Book of Arms plates 49, 100

Nichols, Nicolsen

Families of the name of Nicholson may originate from Scotland or England when found in Ireland. At the time of the 17th century settlements the name is found in Ulster, as well as being documented specifically in Co. Sligo at that time.

Several lines of the name are to be found. Among the various families of the name are; Nicolson of Portree, Isle of Skye in Scotland, those of Plymouth and London in England, and those of Detroit, in the USA descended from the same lines, as found in O'Hart. Additional lines are found as Nicholson of Philadelphia, Nicholson of San Francisco, Nicolson of Australia, Nicholson of Co. Down and of New York etc..

In so far as Nicholson can be taken to mean "son of Nichol", the name may have been interchanged with MacNicholl which carries the same meaning.

The Nicholson family of Balrath Burry, Co. Meath, settled in Ireland from York. The Nicholson family of Ballow Co. Down, and of Falmore, Co. Donegal are of the same origins, and the first of that family in Ireland arrived in the reign of King James I, settling near Bangor, Co. Down.

Mc Nicholas

McNichols

The McNicholas family is traditionally linked, almost exclusively, to Co. Mayo in Ireland. Here they are found as a branch of the Deburgo (Burke) family.

Noble

Irish Book of Arms plate 43

Nobel

The name of Noble is assumed to be of English extraction in Ireland, and it is found here no later than the 17th century. Many of the name are found in Fermanagh and Antrim, as well as in the city of Dublin, which comes as no surprise.

The Noble family of Glassdrummond, Co. Fermanagh, is on record there from at least the early 18th century. The birth index of 1890 finds the family centered in Antrim and Dublin.

Mc Nulty

Irish Book of Arms plate 253

Mac an Ultaigh

Nulty, MacAnulty, Nolty, Nolte,

The MacNulty family is traditionally given to be a family of Co. Donegal, in the old province of Ulster in ancient Ireland. This is most fitting for the name can be translated as meaning "son of the Ulsterman" in gaelic.

Mac Anulty is another early form of the name when it was earlier translated into English.

McNulty is the preferred spelling of the name in the 1890 index, where some 69 births are documented, mainly in Donegal and Mayo. Nulty, also had some 16 births recorded in that same index, and it was mainly of Co. Meath.

In the 17th century Nulty is given as a name from the city of Dublin as well.

As for variant spellings of note, 'Mac Connulty' of Co. Clare is believed to be a variant of the early spelling of Mac Anulty.

Owen McNulty served in Meaghers Irish Brigade in the 69th New York Volunteers of American Civil War fame.

O'Nolan

Irish Book of Arms plates 93, 166, 201

O Nuallain

O'Nowlan, Knowlan, Knowland, Noland,

One of the top 40 most numerous surnames in all of Ireland, one would expect to find many separate origins of the name. We have on file only two possibilities. One family of the name originates in the western portion of Co. Cork.

The majority of the name descend from the "O'Nuallain, O'Nolan or O'Nowlan" chief of (Forth) Fotharta Fedha, and are cited by Aryan thusly;

"O'Nolan, a faultless hero,
The hospitable chief of Fothart"

Their territory was in the barony of Forth, in Co. Carlow. Several of this line are found spelling the name as Nowlan here in the last century. They served as marshals of Leinster and presided at the inauguration of the Mac Morroughs, kings of Leinster, and remained numerous in Carlow and Wexford, as well as being found in Dublin and Wicklow in the 1890 birth index.

In the census of 1659 Nolan was a principal name of Carlow, Kilkenny and Wexford. Noland was a principal name of Carlow, and Nollane a principal name of Tipperary at that time.

Spelled as Nowlan, it is a principal name of Kildare and in Wexford. As Nowlane, a principal name of Dublin, as Nowland a principal name of Dublin and found in Kildare and Queens. Knowlan and Knowland were in Longford and Westmeath at the time of the 1659 census.

The "O" prefix has generally been dropped from the name for centuries.

The Irish Book of Arms gives Nolan of Ballindarry, Co. Galway, who descend from the Nolans of Ballinrobe Castle, Co. Mayo. He owned Iskerone, and a castle and two manors in Co. Sligo.

211

Nugent

Irish Book of Arms plates 50, 62, 167

de Nogent

Nughent, de Nugent, Nogent

In ancient times the Nugent family name was originally spelled as "de Nugent", denoting the territory in France known as Nogent, which traces their origins to that country.

They arrived in Ireland with the coming of the Norman invasions. In reward for services rendered by the Nugent family, (by Gilbert de Nugent), they were granted Delvin, and Gilbert de Nugents descendants became barons of Delvin by the 15th century, and later Earls of Westmeath. It is said that Hugh, Richard and Gilbert de Nugent were the first to arrive in Ireland. Richard was a cousin of Hugh.

The name spread in Ireland, with one family of the name found at Aghavarten Castle by Carrigaline in Co. Cork.

Traditionally the name has been linked to Meath and Westmeath, on the lands which they were granted. Keatings also gives them as an early Norman family in Waterford and Tipperary.

By the time of the 17th century we find the family in Limerick, Roscommon and Waterford. In 1890, the name is given in Armagh, Dublin, Cork, Tipperary and Tyrone.

Nugent castles are in Westmeath. At Delvin, a seat of power in earlier days, their old castle was found. They also occupied Cloyne Castle, not to far distant from the first. Ballinlough Castle was also a castle occupied by the family. Those interested should consult the "Dictionary of National Biography" (England) for further information on Nugent families of note.

There are as well, estate papers on record at the National Library of Ireland.

The Irish Book of Arms gives Nugent of Portaferry House, Co. Down, and Nugent of Farren Connell, Co. Cavan.

Nary, Neary

Mac Naradhaigh and O Naradhaigh

Menarry, Mac Nary, Mac Neary, McNari,

The McNary families in Ireland hail from the old territory of Oriel. The early forms of 'Mac Naradhaigh' include Mac Nary and Mac Neary. In more modern times the spelling of 'Menarry' has become most common.

One must distinguish between the McNary families as mentioned above, and the O'Neary families of the province of Connaught, which is found as O'Neary and O'Nary. The O prefix is most often dropped, leading to confusion as to which name was originally correct. This family is found as mentioned, particularly in counties Mayo, Louth, and Roscommon and takes its name anciently from O Naradhaigh. The name is also often found in Dublin.

The name of Narey is found in Milesian Families and is given as a Scottish name arriving in 1596 in County Donegal. Strokestown Union in County Roscommon has been given as a more traditional location for the name of Nary in modern times.

Fr. Nicholas O'Naraighe, O.F.M., Provincial dating from 1504 - 1508.

Edmond O'Nary of Clongreagh, Co. Roscommon, from the Composition Book of Connaught in the 1500's.

Rev. Cornelius Nary (1658 - 1738) of Co. Kildare. author-parish priest of St. Michan's in Dublin.

Nihane

Nihan, Nyhan, Neehane, Neenan

A family traditionally associated with Co. Cork in Ireland. Some sources record the use of Neenan as a synonym for the name, but in most cases Neenan represents a completely separate family.

Nixon

The name of Nixon is traditionally linked with counties Fermanagh and Cavan in Ireland. Most of the name are likely of English extraction, with the name found here no later than the 17th century. The 1890 birth index finds the family most numerous in Antrim, Cavan and Fermanagh.

Normile

Normoyle

The name of a family traditionally associated with the Clare/Limerick area of Ireland and the family remained centered there into the 19th century. Woulfe gives the name as meaning "son of the hound of Fermoyle" (MacConfhormaoile).

Norris

le Norrys, Nurse, Nourse, Nowry, Norrice

In Ireland from early times, the family name of Norris is fairly widespread. The name is also found in England. One early form of the name is given as le Norreys, and several notables of the name are found in the province of Munster in the 16th century. The 1659 census finds the name as Norris in Cork and Carlow at that time as well. The spelling of Norrice has also been cited in counties Down and Monaghan, and may represent the same families is specific instances. Some give the name as meaning "the northman", others give the name as arriving from Wales in the 13th century, and others find families of the name arriving from England over time.

212

Mc Naboe

Victory, McNabo, McNabow, Monaboe

The surnames of McNaboe and Victory are often said to be one in the same. They are both traditionally tied to Co. Cavan in Ireland. In some works the name of McNabb is given as a shortened variant spelling of McNaboe, but in most instances that is a completely unrelated family. Earlier spellings were as Mc Anaboy etc..

Nicholl

MacNiocaill

Nicholl, Nicoll, Nicholson

Nicholl is traditionally linked to the province of Ulster in Ireland. The name may well often come from "Nicoll", a name of Scotland. It may as well be of Irish extraction, coming from the old name of Mac Niocaill. Some of the name may have originally been "Nicholson", who simply shortened the name to Nichol(l). The 1890 birth index finds the family most numerous in Antrim and Londonderry.

Oliver

Irish Book of Arms plate 76

One family of the name is found in Drogheda at the beginning of the 17th century. The Oliver family of Castle Oliver, and of Cloghanodfoy, Co. Limerick are found in the Irish Book of Arms, and one of that line served as M.P. for Limerick in 1661.

O'Neligan

O'Niallagain (from the name Niall

Nelligan, Nelligon...

(O) Neligan appears as early as the 1500's in Counties Kerry and Cork, but is not found in some older sources. They appear in Leinster early . One Richard Nelgan, associated with the Kavanaghs, was a translator for Richard II and the Irish chiefs in 1315 A.D..

County Kerry held over 30 families of the name in 1890. In 1865 twelve registrations of the name were made, mostly from Counties Cork and Kerry. It is interesting to note that the name was not recorded in the 1890's birth index however. The name is to be found in Ireland in modern times.

In the 15th century John and Nicholas Neligan are found in Kilkenny.

The place name of Ballynelligan can be found close to Lismore, in Ireland.

Noone

The family is believed to have originated in Co. Sligo as O'Nuadhain, and to have settled in Roscommon, Galway and surrounds. The 1890 birth index finds the family most numerous in Galway, Roscommon and Mayo.

Orpen

Irish Book of Arms plate 30

The Orpen family of Ardtully, Co. Kerry is said to have been found settling in Killorglin in that county in the 17th century. This line is said to have originally settled here from Norfolk in England.

O'Nunan

Irish Book of Arms plate 201

Oh Ionmhaineain, O Nuanain

Noone, Nuane, Noonan, Nunan, Neenan,

The O'Nunan or Noonan family, etc.. has generally dropped the "O" prefix from its name today. The early records find the family in the area of Desmond, centered in Co. Cork.

Keatings History gives O'Nunan as a chief of Tullaleis and Castlelissen, "now the parish of Tullilease", in the barony of Duhallow in Co. Cork. Here they were hereditary wardens of St. Brendons church.

O'Hinmhuinen is also given here as a chief of Tuath Saxon, and that is believed to be an earlier spelling of the name as well. Aryan speaks of them thusly:

"Tuath Saxon of the fair pleasant plain,
To O'Hinmanen I proclaim,
A country of harbors abounding in influence, Belongs to the hardy sept of Clan Conari".

"Neenan", a much rarer name found in Co. Clare, may have become confused with Nunan on occasion. Some Neenans may have become Nunans as a result.

In the 1890 index "Noonan" was the preferred spelling of the name with 83 births recorded in Cork, Clare, Limerick and Tipperary.

In the 17th century Nonane and O'Nonane were both principal names of Co. Limerick.

213

Nyland

Irish Book of Arms plate 231

O'Niallain

Neylan, Neyland, Nilan, Niland

The Nyland name springs from the older form of O'Neilan, and is found mainly in Co. Galway along with the spellings of Nilan and Niland. A fairly rare spelling, and not found too easily in Irish history, the family was centered in older times in County Clare.

The original name is thought to have originated in the older geographical division of Thomand. Indeed Frosts 'History of Clare', the 1659 census and the Composition Book of Connaught (1585) all find the name in County Clare.

Mc Naboola

Benbo, Banbo, McNabola, McNabully

A fairly rare name of Ireland, the spellings of Benbo and Banbo have been officially recorded as synonyms of McNaboola. For this we have no reason to date. Several of the name are found in counties Sligo and Leitrim.

Neeson

Mac Neece, Mac Nee, Nason

The name of a family traditionally linked to the province of Ulster in Ireland, and it is there, particularly in Co. Antrim, where the family remained centered in the 19th century. Various theories exist as to the origin of the name. Some give it as a form of MacNee, others give it as of separate Irish origins. McNeice is also a name of Co. Antrim. The 1890 birth index finds the family most numerous in Antrim, spelled as Neeson.

Ogilby

Irish Book of Arms plate 97

A Huguenot family of Ireland and/or Great Britain according to some sources.

The Ogilby family of Ardnargle and Dungiven, Co. Londonderry, settled in Ireland at the time of the plantation coming from Calhame, in Aberdeenshire, Scotland.

Odlum

Adlum, Adlam, Adlum

The name of a family traditionally linked with Co. Offaly (Kings Co.), and in Ireland from the 17th century.

Orr

The name of a Scottish family settling in the province of Ulster in Ireland no later than the 17th century. It is a relatively numerous name in that area of the country, found often in Antrim, Down, Derry, etc..

Owlsly, Ouseley

Ouseley, Ousley

One family of the name from England settled around 1640 in Ireland, centered around Ballycogley in Co. Wexford.

Orme

The Irish Book of Arms plate 59

The Orme family of Owenmore, Co. Mayo and Enniscrone, Co. Sligo are given in the Irish Book of Arms.

Ormsby

The Irish Book of Arms plate 73

The Ormsby family of Ballinamore, Co. Mayo, descends from the family of Thomas Ormsby of Cummin, Co. Sligo. The Ormsby family of Gortner Abbey, of Co. Louth, of this line one Henry Ormsby settled in Ireland in the reign of Queen Elizabeth.

Owen(s)

Irish Book of Arms Owens plate 87

Often of Welch origin

Owens, McOwen, Owenson

The name of Owen (or Owens) may stem from several sources. It is on record as a Welsh name in Ireland, often confused with Owenson, MacKeown, MacOwen and even Hinds.

When spelled as 'Owen' some show the name in Waterford and Kilkenny, arriving in 1713 from Wales. The census of 1659 gives the name as one of Monaghan, Limerick and Kildare. With the Mc prefix, McOwen is found in the same census as a principal name of County Clare, and also in Cork, Kerry, Limerick, Waterford and Kildare. The 'Owen Oge' was also listed in the same work as a principal name of Cork.

The Irish Book of Arms gives the name as Owens of Holestone, Co. Antrim. In 1890 the family is centered in Dublin, Roscommon and Cork.

214

Pakenham

Irish Book of Arms plates 19, 26

Packenham

The Pakenham family is said to be of English origins when found in Ireland. Note Pakenham Hall in Co. Westmeath (Tullynally). One of the name is found as the Earl of Longford, and several are found in the service of the British army.

The Irish Book of Arms gives the family of Pakenham-Mahon of Strokestown, Co. Roscommon.

Mc Partland

Mac Parthalain?

Partlan, Parlan, Partlin, Pharlon, Bartley,

The McPartland name is generally considered to be one of the Province of Ulster in Ireland. One noted family in the district of Oriel were noted poets and scribes. Of the many spellings of the name, MacFarlane is said not to be a related one, although it is found in Tyrone and Armagh as well.

The obvious connection to Mac 'Parthalain', a mythical Irish hero from distant Greece, has been given with regards to the origin of the name. Of the many variant spellings of the name, perhaps Bartley is the most unrecognizable when compared with the original.

The birth index of 1890 finds McPartlan and McPartlin in County Leitrim. When spelled as M'Partland the specific area of Enniskillen Union was given.

Patten, Patton

Pattin

The name of a family from Scotland which settled in Ireland, in the province of Ulster, as has been most common over the centuries. The 1890 birth index finds the family most numerous in Antrim and Down when spelled as Patton, and in Mayo when spelled as Patten.

Palliser

Irish Book of Arms plate 30

The Palliser family of Annestown is given in the Irish Book of Arms.

Paget

Pagett, Paget, Pagit

A very rare name in Ireland in older records, we find reference to Paget being among the names of foreign refugees who settled and were naturalized in Great Britain and/or Ireland before the reign of Louis XIV of France. They are listed under the Huguenot section in O'Harts work.

In the 17th century we find the name of Paget in Queens Co., (Leix), and as Pagett we find the name in Fermanagh at that time.

Parle

Parl, Pearl, Perrill, Parrell

The name of a family traditionally linked to Co. Wexford in Ireland, where all of the name spelled as Parle are given in the 19th century birth index. The spellings of Perrills and Pearls found in Co. Clare, may be of different origins altogether.

Parnell

Seemingly a rare name in Ireland in more modern times. Charles Stewart Parnell (d.1891), the famous spokesman for the Nationalist Party, was born in Avondale in Co. Wicklow. Of this same line, earlier in history, several were M.P.'s in Queens Co.. Of this same family, the Rev. Thomas Parnell (d. 1717) was Archdeacon of Clogher.

We find no formal entry in the 1890 birth index charts under the name of Parnell, attesting to the scarcity of the name.

Palmer

Irish Book of Arms plate 30

Most of the name are assumed to be of English extraction when found in Ireland. They are found settled in Antrim at the time of the 17th century settlements of Ulster, and earlier still in Co. Kerry.

One family of the name are found as "Barons of Limerick and Viscount Castlemaine". The Palmer family of Rahan, Co. Kildare and of Clonlost, Co. Westmeath are those of the arms given above.

The birth index of 1890 finds the family centered in Antrim.

Parsons

MacParson, Mac Pherson

The Parsons family is found seated at Birr Castle in Co. Offaly (Kings Co.). The place name of Birr, had at one time been changed to Parsonstown.

Sometimes the name is found as MacParson, and this may indicate a separate Irish family who adopted this spelling as their own. In any event, most of the name in Ireland will be of true English extraction most anciently.

In the Pedigree of Parsons of Ireland we find Sir William Parsons who was Lord Justice of Ireland in 1643. Sir Laurence Parsons of Birr and Birr Castle is cited as well, and Lowther Parsons is given as holding St. Johns in Co. Wexford.

Pawlett

The family of Sir Amias Pawlett , of Garrylogh, Co. Wexford is found early in the 17th century there.

215

Parker

Irish Book of Arms plate 34

Park, Parks

Several families of the name of Parker are to be found in Ireland. Most are assumed to be of original English extraction. They are found in the 17th century not only in Ulster, as was common with settler families of the day, but in Limerick and Tipperary as well. Another noted family of the name hails from Co. Cork.

One William Parker of Dublin is of the line of a family which came to settle later in Philadelphia.

The Parker family of Bally Valley, Co. Clare, is earlier found in Co. Limerick in the late 17th century, and can be found in the Irish Book of Arms.

The birth index of 1890 finds the family name of Parker centered in Antrim and Cork. The name of Parks is found in Antrim and Armagh, and the name of Park is most numerous in Antrim and Tyrone at that time.

Patterson

Paterson, Pattersen

The name of a family who came from Scotland and settled in the province of Ulster no later than the 17th century. The name is assumed to be of Scottish heritage when found here, partly due to the fact that Patterson is one of the top 20 most numerous surnames in all of Scotland.

The name is also found to be of possible Irish extraction for members of the Irish "Cussane" family are said to have taken on the Patterson name in Co. Galway.

Patrick

Irish Book of Arms plate 91

O'MAOLPHADRAIG (MULPATRICK)

MACPATRICK, FITZPATRICK,

The family name of Patrick, and related spellings are to be found in Ireland quite early. When found as "Patrick" the family is assumed to be of Scottish origins in Ireland. It should also be noted that Patrick and MacPatrick are of the Scottish Clan of Lamont. The name was found most often, though not numerously in the province of Ulster in relatively modern times.

Old records however, show a family of Co. Longford which is given as Mulpatrick. In addition, remember that any member of the Fitzpatrick name could easily have "dropped the Fitz", to become simply "Patrick".

According to "Keatings History" the name is given as an Irish name which was also adopted by Anglo-Norman or English families in lieu of their original surnames. The de Courcys of Cork changed their name to Mac Patrick.

In the census of 1659 the name of "Patrick" is found in Co. Kilkenny as a principal name of the area. O'Mulpatrick is as well found in that census, and this family was given in Fermanagh and Longford at that time.

The Irish Book of Arms gives the family of Patrick of Dunminning, Co. Antrim, of Scottish heritage in the year 1606.

Prey

Pray, O'Prey

The name of a family traditionally associated with Co. Down in Ireland, and they are likely of old Irish origins.

Peacocke

The Irish Book of Arms plate 57

The Peacocke family of Skevanish, Innishannon, Co. Cork, descend from one George Peacocke of Graige, Co. Limerick, who purchased lands in the barony of Pobble O'Brien in that county. Only nine scattered births of the name are found in the 1890 birth index of Ireland.

Mac Peake

Peak, Peake

The name of a family traditionally tied to Counties Derry and Tyrone in Ireland, earliest spelled as MacPeake. The name of Peake, found in several areas of Ireland, may serve as a shortened form of MacPeake, or may spring from families of that name who arrived from England over time. Some of the name are also given as of Scottish origins in the 17th century in Co. Derry. In the 17th century we find Mc Peake as a principal name in Londonderry, as well as being found in Dublin city and Meath.

Pelly

de la Pelle, le pele, Pelle, Peile

Families of the name of Pelly, Pelle, etc.. in Ireland today likely represent several unrelated families. The family is most often linked to Co. Galway in Ireland, and sometimes in the adjacent counties of Clare and Roscommon from the 17th century onward. The name could stem from earlier spellings such as de la Pelle, or Le Pelle.

Peoples

Peebles, Pebbles, Deeney, Peables, Pebles

The name of a family traditionally linked to the province of Ulster and the county of Donegal in Ireland. Of Irish origins, the name is said to have been taken from the gaelic "daoine", meaning people.

216

Pennefather

Irish Book of Arms plate 30

Pennefeather, Pennyfather, Pennyfeather,

The Pennefather family of Rathsallagh, Co. Wicklow, settled in Ireland from Stafford in the 17th century and obtained grants of land in Co. Tipperary in 1666.

The birth index of 1890 finds the family name of Penny centered in Co. Antrim.

Peppard

Pepper

One family of Peppard, of Drogheda, is said to descend from Peter Peppard who served as Justiciary of Ireland in the latter half of the 12th century. The 1890 birth index finds the family name of Pepper, most numerous in Dublin and Antrim. Pepper has been a known variant spelling of Peppard in the past.

Perkins

Perkens

The Perkins name is generally assumed to have originated outside of Ireland. In Milesian Families the family is said to have come from Wales in 1682 and settled in Dublin and Limerick.

Peterson

Patterson, Peters

Peterson is generally considered to be a name of foreign origin when found in Ireland. Milesian Families lists the family of Welsh origin, arriving in Limerick and Galway in 1646. The census of 1659 finds the name in Limerick City.

The 1890 birth index finds the family name of Peters most numerous in Tipperary.

Pepper

Irish Book of Arms plate 26

Peppard

The Pepper family of Ballygarth Castle, Co. Meath, was founded by Capt. Charles Pepper who obtained grants of land in Meath in 1666, as found in the Irish Book of Arms. The birth index of 1890 finds the family centered in Dublin and Antrim.

Petit

Pettit

One William Le Petito arrived with De Lacy during the Norman invasions of the 12th century, obtaining lands in Westmeath, and were styled as barons of Mullingar. From this man the name of Petit is supposed to have come, in at least one instance.

Phepoes

According to "Keatings History" the name is that of a principal family of Dublin city or county, and of Anglo-Norman descent.

Phibbs

of English origin

Phipps, Phillip

Phip has been used by the English as a pet name for Phillip. In Ireland it is said that Phibbs is a variant of Phipps, believed to have been in usage for several centuries as such. In the 1890 birth index the name of Phibbs is found in County Sligo.

Pollock

A family of Scottish extraction which settled in the province of Ulster in Ireland no later than the 17th century. The 1890 birth index finds the family most numerous in Antrim and Tyrone.

Perceval

The Irish Book of Arms plate 80

The Perceval family of Temple House, Co. Sligo descends from George Pervceval, b. 1635, the youngest son of Sir Philip Perceval, a well known statesman.

Mac Philbin

Mac Phillip, Phillips

The name of a family traditionally linked with Co. Mayo, where the name has been most numerous in the past. In that county, and in Co. Galway the name was found most numerous in the 19th century. The names of McPhillip and Phillips are also believed to have been taken on by members of the MacPhilbin family. Those two names however, are used by completely unrelated families as well.

Mac Pierce

Peirce, Pers, Pearce, Pearse, Piers

The names of Pierce, Pearce etc.. are assumed to have belonged to English settler families in Ireland, and the name is found under several different spellings.

According to "Keatings History" the name is given as an Irish name which was also adopted by Anglo-Norman or English families in lieu of their original surnames.

The Butlers changed their name to MacPierce.

Padraig Pearse (d.1916), was a revolutionary leader of the Irish interests. Sir John B. Piers was given as a baronet in Meath.

The 1890 birth index finds the family most numerous in Dublin and Wexford.

217

Peyton

Irish Book of Arms plate 83

Payton, Patten, Pettane

The Irish families of the name of Peyton etc.., are found in Co. Donegal and subsequently in Co. Mayo. The barony of Raphoe in Co. Donegal held many of the name in earlier times. Spelled as Peyton the family was most numerous in Co. Mayo in the latter half of the 19th century, but that spelling is also given in Co. Westmeath in the 17th century. Some are of English descent, notably one family in Leitrim.

The Peyton family of Laheen, Co. Leitrim is found in Ireland in the early 17th century.

Mc Polin

Mc Polan, Polan, Poland, Polin

Families of the name of McPolin are given as centered in Co. Armagh in the 19th century. The similar sounding name of Poland may not be related, but Woulfe says otherwise in his works.

Powell

The Irish Book of Arms plate 51

Ap Howell

The family of Powell of Bawnlahan, Co. Cork is traced back to the Powells or Ap Howells of Penkelly, as found in the Irish Book of Arms.

Mc Phillip, Phillips

Irish Book of Arms plate 54

Philips, Phillip

Many of the name of foreign extraction are found in Ireland, for Phillips is quite numerous in both England and Wales, ranking among the top 50 most numerous names in both of those countries. While the name is found in many locations, one family of the name is found with holdings in Co. Kilkenny in the 17th century.

According to "Keatings History" the name of Mc Phillip is also given as an Irish name which was also adopted by Anglo-Norman or English families in lieu of their original surnames.

This is a name found to be adopted by the Burkes (or De Burgo) family of Connaught.

The 1890 birth index finds the family most numerous in Mayo, Antrim and Dublin.

Potter

le Poter, Poter

We find record of the Potter family in Co. Kerry and in Dublin City in the 17th century. Families of the name are found often in distant locations however, as several are given in counties Down and Galway as well. The name likely simply means "the maker of pots", and most are given as of English heritage when found in Ireland.

Princely

One family of the name came from the north of Ireland and settled in New Jersey around 1830. Some of the family are found in Massachusetts a decade later.

Piggott

Irish Book of Arms plate 48

Pigott

According to "Keatings History" the name is given to a family found as principal Norman settlers in Co. Cork. The Pigott family of Capard, Queens Co., was granted lands in that county in 1562.

The birth index of 1890 finds the family centered in Cork and Dublin.

Prunty

Pronty, Bronte, Pronte

The name of Prunty is traditionally identified with the province of Ulster, and with Co. Down and Co. Longford, where the family appears to be centered. The 1890 birth index finds the family most numerous in Longford.

Punch

Ponce, Ponz

Families of the name of Punch are of long standing in Co. Cork. Punch was in fact a principal name of Cork City in the 17th century, and Cork and Limerick were the main locations for the family some two centuries later. The family is believed to have been a Norman one, arriving in Ireland in the wake of the Norman invasions of the 12th century.

The 1890 birth index finds the family most numerous in Cork with 4 births of the name and in Co. Limerick with 2 births of the name.

Purtill

Purtle, Purtel, Purthill, Pursell, Purshell

Families of the name of Purtill are found centered in Co. Limerick and in the province of Munster in 19th century Ireland. The name is on record in Co. Clare and Tipperary as well, and it has been recorded there as a synonym of Purcell.

218

Pike

The Irish Book of Arms plate 85

Pyke

The Pike family of Glendarary, Co. Mayo descend from the first of the name in Ireland, one Richard Pike, of Sarsfield Court, Co. Cork. A family of English origin as given.

Pyne

Pine

Pyne families are most often found in records relating to Co. Cork in Ireland. They are found centered there, and in Co. Clare in the 19th century birth index. The name is on record in Ireland from the 17th century onward. Most of the name are assumed to have been originally of English descent.

Quilty

Mac Quilty, O'Quilty, O' Kilte, Kielty

The Quilty name is most often associated with Co. Limerick in Ireland, and it remained most numerous there and in Co. Waterford in the 19th century. Sometimes the name of Quilty has been translated into names like "Wood" and "Small", based upon the likely meaning of the root word of the name in gaelic (Coill or Caol). The Limerick family is assumed to have been O'Quilty, but the name of MacQuilty is to be found in Ulster, and that family is of likely separate origins altogether.

The 1890 birth index finds the family most numerous in Limerick and Waterford.

Qualter

Qualter is known to be a variant spelling of McWalter in the Mayo/Galway region of Ireland.

Plunkett

Irish Book of Arms plates 108, 167

Blanchet ?

Plunket, Plunkitt

In several old sources we find the Plunketts listed among the leading families of foreign origin in Ireland. They are specifically singled out as being of Danish origin among lists of Anglo-Norman families. The name itself is cited by leading authorities as of old French origins, coming from a corruption of the word "blanchet", meaning white. When the name arrived in Ireland is believed to have been at the time of the 12th century invasions.

The "Plunketts" have remained a noted "Irish" family from that time onwards, with considerable influence as a Catholic family in Ireland over time. In 1975, Oliver Plunket was canonized a saint, being the first such from Ireland in over 750 years! He served as archbishop of Armagh and Primate of Ireland before being hanged, drawn and quartered in 1681.

Linked with Meath, Louth, and the north of Dublin, they achieved rank as Lords of Killeen and Earls of Fingall. Sir Christopher Plunkett, lord of Killeen, is of the line of the Barons of Louth and the Earls of Dunsany.

Dunsany castle stands as a Plunkett castle into modern times, and the Plunkett family name is listed as a true Irish name among rolls of Irish families.

The Plunkett family of Portmarnock House, Dublin, descend from Henry Plunkett who was the Mayor of Dublin in 1546.

From Keatings History we find "The Plunketts, a family of Danish descent, became Earls of Fingal, and branches of them barons of Dunsaney, and Earls of Louth", and citing the De Berminghams who were "earls of Louth" it goes on to say "A title afterwards possessed by the Pluketts, a family of Danish descent".

Pooler

The Irish Book of Arms plate 99

The Pooler family of Tyross, Co. Armagh are given in the Irish Book of Arms.

Mc Quaide

Irish Book of Arms McQuaid plate 249

Mac Uaid

McQuaid, McQuade, Mac Quoad

McQuaid, and its variant spellings such as McQuide are considered to be originally of County Monaghan in Ireland. The name is taken from the gaelic 'Mac Uaid' (meaning son of Wat). Without the prefix the name can be found most often in County Limerick.

Spelled as McQuaid the name is found in the 1890 index in counties Monaghan and Fermanagh. When spelled as McQuade it is found as a principal name of Monaghan in 1659, and as a family of Antrim in 1890. Under this spelling the family is also given as a part of Clanna Rory, anciently located in Monaghan, according to Milesian families.

Spelled as MacQuoad etc.., the name is found in Monaghan and Armagh in the Hearth Money Rolls in the 17th century.

Bernard John MacQuaid (1823 - 1909) First Bishop of Rochester, (in the United States)

The name is said to stem from Mac Uaid, which could mean "son of Wat". The "Q" found in the name today likely comes from the "c" in Mac which preceded Uaid.

219

Porter

Irish Book of Arms plate 108

le Porter (English)

le Porter

The name from which Porter can be taken was 'le Porter' and as such it is a well known English name. In modern times it may be considered a name of the province of Ulster. When of English origin it is found in Ireland quite early, with the exception of the province of Connaught, in the west of Ireland. It is a fairly numerous name throughout Ireland today, and is found as both a Catholic and Protestant name.

There is no scarcity of material to research for those of the name of Porter. Note the abundance of place names bearing the Porter name. Portersland and Portersgate are found in Wexford, while Porterstown is found in Meath, Westmeath, Kildare and Dublin.

The census of 1659 finds the name as a principal one of County Donegal, and Milesian Families gives the name as English, arriving in Tyrone in 1640.

The Porter family of Belle Isle, Co. Longford is given in the Irish Book of Arms, as is the Porter family of Clogher Park, Co. Tyrone.

Quilligan

O'Cuileagain

Culligan

The family of Quilligan is said to have originated in Co. Clare most anciently and subsequently spread into Limerick. The spelling of Culligan is most common to the Co. Clare families in our records. The 1890 birth index finds the family most numerous in Limerick and Cork.

Power, Powers

Irish Book of Arms plates 69, 82, 167

Le Poer

de Poher, Powre, Powers, Poor, Poors

One of the 60 most numerous names of Ireland, Power is spelled as Poher, le Poer, and Powre etc.. It is said to have been taken from the French "povre" meaning poverty stricken. The family arrived in England in 1066 with William the Conqueror, arriving in Ireland with the Normans in the 12th century.

In 1177 King Henry II granted the county of Waterford to Robert Le Poer, the Kings marshal. The Le Poers from the 13th to the 16th century held the titles of barons of Donisle and of Carraghmore, Viscounts of Decies, and Earls of Tyrone. Numerous in their original lands in Waterford and Kilkenny, the name became spelled as Power, and they held most of the baronies of Decies and Upperthird. Their lands were called "Powers Country".

In Co. Wicklow Robert Le Poer was granted the lands of Baltinglass and Lismore, and Powerscourt Castle is found in that area today. Powerscourt Gardens are of international repute.

Sir Piers Power, Sheriff of Waterford became Baron le Poer of Curraghmore in Waterford under King Henry VIII. They also held the titles of Count de le Poer Beresford, and Marquess of Waterford.

The "Power, now de la Poer" family of Gurteen Le Poer, Co. Waterford is given in the Irish Book of Arms.

Most numerous in Waterford today, Power was a principal name of Co. Clare and Powre was so in Tipperary in 1659. In the 1890 birth index Power is found in Waterford, Cork and Dublin.

The early spelling of de la Poer or Poer was a principal name of Waterford in 1659, and Poer was still reported in two specific areas in the 1890 birth index.

That index shows the spelling of Poor being used for Power in Co. Kilkenny.

Pratt

Irish Book of Arms plate 45, 53

The Pratt family of Gawsworth, Co. Cork descends from the Rev. James Pratt who was rector of Athnowen, Co. Cork, in the latter half of the 18th century. The Pratt family of Cabra Castle, Co. Mayo is found in the Irish Book of Arms.

Plummer

Irish Book of Arms plate 25

Plumer

The Plummer family of Donoman, Co. Limerick, sometimes found at Castle Quin in that county, is earlier found settled in Co. Cork. The first of the family to settle in Ireland died in 1715, according to the Irish Book of Arms.

220

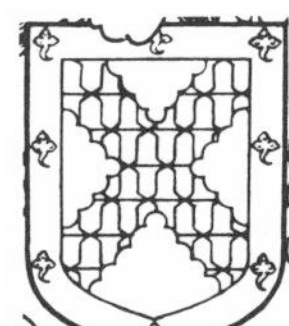

Prendergast

Irish Book of Arms plates 83, 269

de Prendergast

Pendergast, Pendergas, Pender, Pendy,

The Prendergas or Pendergass etc...family may trace their line of descent back to Maurice de Prendergast, who arrived with Strongbow in the Anglo-Norman invasions of the 12th century. He became one of the leading families to obtain large grants of land in Ireland as a result of his service in those invasions.

The most noted location for the family is in Waterford and the south of Co. Mayo, where the family has traditionally been linked. The name is also given as settling early in Cork and Tipperary, according to Keatings History.

In the 17th century "Prendergrass" was a variant spelling of the name which was prominent in Co. Wexford. Prendergast was found in Clare, Tipperary and Kilkenny at that time. Pendergast was found in Tipperary, and Pendergas was a principal name of Carlow at that same time.

Prendergast became the preferred spelling of the name by the time of the 1890 index, when the family was centered in Mayo, Dublin and Waterford.

The name has also been shortened simply to "Prender", and this is noted several times in Co. Wexford. The family name is also spelled as Pendy and Pinders in Offaly, and as Pindy near Dingle in Kerry, according to the 1890 index report.

In Galway one Prendergast family held lands formerly owned by the O'Shaugnessys, as a result of the defeat of James II. These Prendergasts were of English political persuasion.

The Irish Book of Arms gives Prendergast of Ardfinnan Castle, Co. Tipperary, dating from the early 1700's.

Preston

Irish Book of Arms plate 98

de Preston

The name of Preston in Ireland is given to have originally come from England. The name itself is first found in records as de Preston in counties Dublin and Meath.

The family is found as Viscounts of Gormanstown, and are cited as Viscount Preston of Dublin. They are as well given in Meath prior to the 17th century and in Dublin prior to the 15th century in Ireland.

Keatings History finds the name among the great families of English or Norman descent settled in Meath in early times, and as a principal family of Dublin city or county of Anglo-Norman descent.

The Preston family of Swainston, Co. Meath descend from John Preston of Dublin and of Ardsallagh, Co. Meath.

Prior

Mac Prior, MacGilprior, MacInprior

We find record of the Prior family in Queens county in the 17th century and the family is given as centered in Co. Cavan in the 19th century. Early references to the name are scattered, and some of these families may have been of Norman stock, settling here after the 12th century invasions of Ireland. Others of the name are true old Irish families. Several place names are linked to the family such as Priorstown, Priorspark etc.., but they may refer to the position of a "prior", rather than the family name. Simply put, the Irish of the name may come from the gaelic, meaning descendant of, or follower of, the prior.

Price

Irish Book of Arms plate 43

ApRice, Rhys

ApRice, Rhys, Rice

Many of the name of Price in Ireland are of Welsh extraction, where the name is found in earlier forms as ApRice, apRhys, Rhys, etc..

The Price family of Saintfield House, Co. Down, is found in the Irish Book of Arms. The birth index of 1890 finds the family centered in Dublin and Antrim.

Puxley

The Irish Book of Arms plate 94

Puxly, Pucksly

The Puxley family of Dunboy Castle, co. Cork descend from John Puxley of Galway who settled around 1730 at Dunboy in Cork.

Purcell

Irish Book of Arms plates 44, 167

Puirseil

Pursell, Purtill, Purcill, Purshell, Porcel

The Purcell family descends from Norman families of the name and family members are found both in Ireland and England. They arrived in Ireland after the 12th century Norman invasions. Their traditional lands are found in Counties Tipperary and Kilkenny, where they were often allied with the (Ormond) Butlers. Kilkenny and Tipperary were still the main centers for the name in 1890, along with Dublin.

In Tipperary they were found centered in the barony of Eliogarty, at Loughmoe Castle, near Thurles. Here the chief of the name was known as the "Baron of Loughmoe" in the service of the 1st Earl of Ormond. He resided sometimes in the Castle of Loughmoe.

The family became quite Irish and served proudly in the military and religious ranks of the nation. Many are found in the ranks of the wild geese, found in Irish regiments on the continent, and "Purcells Horse Regiment" is of some note there.

In the 17th century the name remained in Tipperary, as well as in Kilkenny, Queens and Westmeath counties. Spelled as Pursell the name was a principal one of Co. Wexford. "Purshell" was used in Roscommon then. The name is said to have been taken from the French word "porcel".

The Irish Book of Arms finds one "Purcell-Fitzgerald of the Little Island, Co. Waterford.". O'Hart gives Purcell as Baron of Loughmoe in Tipperary as does Mac Firbis. Of this line one individual came to Maryland and served as a surgeon and Protestant minister. He also gives Purcell of Esker, Co. Kilkenny, who married into the Dillons of Drumrany and lost lands as a result of that alliance.

Purdon

Irish Book of Arms plate 69

The census of 1659 finds the Purdon family settled in Limerick, Cork and Clare. Some of the name are said to have settled in Co. Louth in the 16th century. The family so named in Co. Clare is said to have descended from the Purdons of Dublin several centuries ago. Several families of the name are found in the aftermath of the Cromwellian invasions of the 17th century.

The Purdon family of Tinerana, Co. Clare was founded by James Purdon of Cumberland, who settled at Lurgan Race in Louth in the time of Henry VIII.

Quane

Quan, Quaine, O' Quane, Mac Quan, Quann

McQuan is given as a name of Co. Leitrim and Monaghan in the 17th century, but the Quane family is more often linked to counties Cork, Waterford and Tipperary in our records. O'Donovan says that anciently the family came from Co. Sligo. Perhaps the McQuan references actually refer to the McQuaid family, for the two names have been used as synonyms.

Mac Queale

Quail, Quayle, Queale

The name of a family of Manx origins according to several sources, where the name is said to have originally meant "son of Paul". Most of the name are found in counties Dublin and Antrim. The pronunciation of the name has been as "Quail" in the past.

Quinlisk

Grimes, Conliss, Cunlis, Quinlish

The name of a family found most often in Tipperary and Offaly in our records.

Purefoy

The Irish Book of Arms plate 69

The Purefoy family of Greenfields, Co. Tipperary descend from one of the name found in that area as the High Sheriff in 1856, of apparent recent introduction into Ireland.

O'Quill

Irish Book of Arms plate 201 (Quill)

O'Cuill

Wood, Woods, Quillan, Quilkin

The family of Quill or O'Quill is traditionally located in counties Cork and Kerry in Ireland. By the time of the 19th century birth index the family was found mainly in Co. Cork, under the spelling of Quill. Some of the name of "Wood" and "Woods" are of the same family as Quill, but their surname was "translated" as Wood, etc.. In isolated instances Quill may serve as a shortened form of Quillan, Quilkin etc..

Quirk

Irish Book of Arms plate 201

O'Cuirc

Quirke

The name of an Irish family traditionally associated with Tipperary and Kerry. We find one William McQuirk born in Co. Meath around 1810, who served as a carpenter at Conyngham Castle, on the Boyne River, near Slane. He married and moved to Norwich, Connecticut around 1845.

Quinlivan

Irish Book of Arms plate 241

Quinlevin, Quin

According to "Keatings History" this family has sometimes changed its name to Quin. They are given as numerous in Tipperary and Limerick. The 1890 birth index finds the family in Co. Clare.

O'Quigley

Irish Book of Arms plate 167

O Coigligh

Twigley, Cogley, O'Quigley, Kegley,

The Quigley name is found today mostly in the province of Ulster, primarily in Donegal and Derry. It is found as well in the province of Connaght, in counties Sligo and Galway. The name is said to have come from a branch of the Northern Fiachra, centered in the barony of Carra in County Mayo. The name is scattered throughout Ireland in modern times. During the troubles of the 17th century some of the name are found settled in County Louth.

In the census of 1659 Quiggly is found as a principal name of Queens (Leix) county, O'Quigley as a principal name of Donegal also found in Londonderry, and Quigley is listed in the birth index from the last century in the following counties: Londonderry, Dublin, Donegal, Galway, Louth and Sligo.

In Wexford the spelling as 'Cogley' is found, and in Meath the spelling of 'Kegley' exists

The name is found in revolutionary war records and is documented in the 1700's in Virginia, New York and New Hampshire:

John Quigley, Nov. 20, 1778, 80 acres, Westmoreland County Virginia. Land Grants.

John, Thomas and William, Francestown, N. H., 1774, (from State Papers)

Thomas, Thomas Jr., and William, Aug. 1775, Petitioners to N. H. Legislature.

John and Ellen, July 16, 1669, of Appamattox, in Co., Westmoreland, VA.

George, Private, 3rd Regt., New York Continental Line, at Saratoga.

Thomas, Master of Privateer in the service of the colony of CT., 1738.

Mac Quillan

Irish Book of Arms plate 167

Mac Ughilin

Quilan, Quill, MacCovelin, Mac Quillians

There is some controversy over the origins of the name MacQuillan. It is generally believed that the family arrived early from outside of Ireland. O'Hart gives the "Mac Quillians" as powerful chiefs in Antrim of Clan Colla and says they were thought to have come from Scotland. In Co. Down, the name is given as "Mac Covelin of the Rout (or Mac Qullan)", a Welshman. Welch descent seems likely.

The first of the line may be one Hugelin de Mandeville, but many protest saying that the name is based on the Irish "son of Llewellyn".

Following the 12th century invasions of Ireland, the family is found settled in the north of Co. Antrim in the province of Ulster. Here they became "Lords of the Route", centered at the Castle of Dunluce. Their territory can be found in the baronies of Dunluce and Kilconway. They also became known as Princes of Dalriada, and served as High Constables of Ulster in the 1300's.

The McDonalds invaded the family territory in Antrim and a great battle ensued. In the end the MacDonalds vanquished the Mac Quillans by the 16th century.

Dubourdieu, who surveyed Antrim, remarked that "a lineal descendant of the chief MacQuillan" lived on the road between Belfast and Carrickfergus, by the silver stream, and said that he likely was far happier as a good farmer than his ancestor was in earlier days.

The family became numerous in Antrim and Armagh, and in the 1890 birth index MacQuillan was most numerous in Antrim and Monaghan.

222

O'Quinlan

Irish Book of Arms plates 241, 167

O Caoindealbain

Kindellan, Quinlevan, Connellan, Conlan,

The Quinlan, Quinlivan and Kindellan families of Ireland can all stem from the same Irish family of O'Caoindealbain, which was subsequently translated into the English forms given above. They are a noted family of the Ui Neill tribes, found anciently centered in Co. Meath. Here the name is found as Kindellan and Connellan at times. (These Kindellans are also found in Spain in the 17th century, and that spelling is found there into modern times).

The family suffered as did most others, with the coming of the 12th century Norman invasions, but they were not immediately dispossessed of all their lands and powers until the time of James II in Ireland.

The variant spelling of "Quinlivan" is most associated with Co. Clare, as evidenced by the 13 births recorded there in the 1890 index. "Quinlin" was given as a principal name of Tipperary in the census of 1659, and Quinlan remained as the favored spelling of the name in 1890 with Tipperary and Kerry being centers for the name at that time. Kindlon is also said to be a variant spelling of the name in Co. Louth.

In Keatings History we find "O'Quinlivans, some of whom have changed their name to Quinlan, are numerous in Tipperary and Limerick".

Several of the name are found in military service, as are James and Francis Quinlan who served in Meaghers Irish Brigade in the New York Volunteers.

223

O'Quinn

Irish Book of Arms plates 167, 168

O Cuinn

Quin, Queen, Quen, O'Cuinn, Quinne.

The Quinn name is one of the top 20 most numerous surnames in Ireland, and it is the most numerous surname of Tyrone. Several unrelated families of the name are known to exist.

In Clare the Quinns were centered around Corofin in the barony of Inchiquin and are given there by Aryan as "O'Quinn of the honest heart...around Corofin of the banquets."

O'Cuinn was also a principal chief of Teffia and their chief stronghold was at their castle in Rathcline, Co. Longford, as found in Keatings History.

O'Quinn is also found as a chief of Moy Lugad, in Keenaught of Glengiven, in Co. Derry.

The O'Quinns are further found in the Glens of Antrim, along with the MacGees and Mac Alisters. The family name is also found in France, and note the street named "Rue O'Quinn" there.

The early form of this name was O'Cuinn, meaning descendant of Conn, and one Niall O'Cuinn met his fate at the battle of Clontarff in 1014 A.D..

In the 17th century Quinn was a principal name of Waterford and (O) Quinn was found in Dublin, Kings, Down and Tipperary. In the 1890 index, Quinn (with 2 n's), was the most numerous spelling of the name, being found in Dublin, Tyrone, Antrim and Roscommon. The spelling of McQuinn was also found in Co. Kerry then.

Much is made as to the spelling of the name with one or two n's. (Such claims are made for many names). No difference can arbitrarily be claimed from the spelling of the name. No doubt some families spelled their names differently to show that they were not related to the 'other'. In isolated cases could denote political differences.

O Rafferty

Irish Book of Arms plate 168

O'Raithbheartaig

Rafter, O'Ragher, O'Raftery, Roarty,

The Rafferty family is found most anciently in Ireland in the Donegal/Sligo area in the north of the country. They are noted as co-arbs of St. Columcille on Tory Island. They, were as well known as one of the "Seven Pillars of Skreen" in Co. Sligo in olden times, and they are now dispersed throughout the country.

In the birth index for Ireland around 1890, some 54 births were recorded under the spelling of Rafferty, coming mainly from Antrim, Tyrone and Louth.

O'Rafferty is sometimes cited as a tribe of the Hy Nial, settled in the Sligo and Donegal areas. Counties Tyrone and Louth appear to be centers for the name in more modern times.

Many spellings and names can be confused with that of Rafferty. The name of "Raftery", represents a separate family which descended from O'Reachtaire in the province of Connaught. Roarty is another name thought to have been confused, or used, for Rafferty.

The spellings of O'Raverty and O'Raaverty are found in Co. Armagh in the census of 1659 and in the Hearth Money Rolls from previous centuries.

The name of Rafter is found in Dublin, Queens and Mayo in the 1890 index, and Raftery is found in Galway and Roscommon at that same time. The locations of these names at that time point to separate origins for each.

Rainey

Irish Book of Arms plate 36

most likely of English origin.

Raney, Reaney, Raine

While the name of Rainey is most likely of English origin when found in Ireland, it may also be a variant spelling of Reaney.

In the 1890 birth index Rainey is found in Counties Antrim and Down in the north of Ireland, where the name is most numerous. The 'possible' variant spelling of Raine is found in the census of 1659 and is given as a principal name of County Waterford.

The Irish Book of Arms gives the name of the family of Rainey-Robinson, originally of Antrim, finding one member of the family who died in 1606 in Ireland.

Racards

Racard, Rackard, Mac Richard, Mac

The name of a family found in Co. Wexford in the early 19th century, and the name is said to be a variant spelling of Mac Richard or MacRickard.

Raleigh

Rally, Ralagh, Rawley, de Ralleye

Families of the name of Raleigh are found centered in Limerick and Tipperary in the 19th century. Under the spelling of Ralagh we find some of the name in Co. Limerick in the 17th century. As Rawley the name was a principle one of Co. Limerick in the census of 1659. Note the placename of Rawleystown in Co. Limerick. Most families of the name are assumed to be of English descent

Ridgway

Ridgeway

One family of the name is found centered in Rossonell, in Co. Kilkenny early in the 17th century.

Ram

Irish Book of Arms plate 43

The family of Ram of Clonattin, Co. Wexford is found in the Irish Book of Arms.

Raftery

O Reachtaire (from reacht meaning decree)

Rafter, O'Raghter, O'Raftery

The Raftery name has been traditionally found in Co. Mayo, and is said to have descended from the O'Reachtaire family of Co. Galway. The name is found as well in Counties Roscommon and Sligo. Raftery has also been cited as a small sept of Kilkenny.

Rafter is one shortened form of the name and is given as a principal name of Queens Co. (Leix) in the census of 1659. In the 1890 index the name of Rafter is given in the counties of Dublin, Queens and Mayo. It is also found as a variant spelling in Mayo.

In the Birth Index of Ireland the 'Raftery' name is cited in Galway and Roscommon in the last century. It was said to have been traditionally associated with Mullingar Union in County Westmeath. Brief mention of the name is made in the works of MacLysaght on Irish Families.

One 'John Raftery' of Athlone, Co. Westmeath, is found on board the Brig 'John', from Galway and arriving in New York on August 2, 1816.

Passengers:

William Raftery, age 22, male, Laborer, aboard 'Western World' June 21, 1851, Liverpool to New York.

Denis Raftery, age 25, male, aboard 'Pessore', Nov. 29, 1850, from Liverpool to New York.

Michl. Raftery, age 21 male, Laborer, aboard 'Irvine', Dec. 27, 1850, Galway to New York.

Rathborne

The Irish Book of Arms plate 84

The Rathborne family of Scripplestown and of Kilcogy, Co. Cavan are given in the Irish Book of Arms.

Ratican

O'Raghtigan

Ratigan, Ractigan, Rhattican.

The name of Ratican is a variant spelling of O'Raghtigan as given above. In gaelic the name is said to be taken from the root word of 'Reacht', meaning decree.

The name can be found with both the Mac and the O prefix in Irish history. It is listed as an 'O' name in the Annals (1488).

The family is associated with the parish of Clooncraff, St. Finnens, in Co. Roscommon. The 1890 index gives Mayo and Roscommon as locations for births.

Real

Reel, Really, O'Really, O'Realy, Realy

In the census of 1659 we find the family name of Realy as a principal one of Dublin, and also in Co. Meath. O'Realy was a principal name of Cork, and O'Really was a principal name of Fermanagh at that time. Several separate families are represented by the above reports. Some are doubtlessly of the O'Riley family, merely using a variant spelling of the name. Others may more properly be of the O'Rahilly family. To further complicate matters we find the name of Mc Real given as a variant spelling in the Complete Book of Irish Family names.

The 1890 birth index finds the family most numerous in Leinster and Ulster, with 5 recorded births of the name under the spelling of Reel.

224

Redmond

Irish Book of Arms plate 168

Raymond (Norman origins)

Redmon, Redmont, Redmun, Radman,

The Redmond family is found to be an Anglo-Norman family in Keatings History. They are found as one of the chief families receiving large grants of land in Co.Wexford after assisting Strongbow in the 12th century invasions of Ireland. These families settled in Wexford and in the census of 1659 they are found as a 'principal name' of Kings County (Offaly), as well as in Wexford. By the time of the 1890 birth index the name was listed in Wexford, Dublin and Wicklow with 79 births. "McRedmond" at that time is found in Kings Co., as it was in 1659, and has been cited in Mayo earlier. That family is of separate Norman origins. It is said that McRedmond was a spelling adopted by a branch of the Burke family in the past.

The first family of the name cited above are found settling in the barony of Forth, and are shown there on the Map of Ortelius. The original name from which Redmond was taken in this family was that of "Raymond", and this, the most noted family of the name descends from the same line as Raymond Le Gros. He was among the chief Anglo-Norman invaders in the 12th century.

It is also said that a branch of the MacMurroughs of Co. Wexford adopted the name of Redmond as well.

Mac Rannall

Irish Book of Arms plate 218

MacRunnell, McRannell

According to "Keatings History" the name of Mac Rannall became "Reynolds". The original family was found mainly in Leitrim and in part of Longford. They had castles at Rinn, Leitrim and Lough Scur.

225

Reeves

The Irish Book of Arms plate 107

The Reeves family of Besborough, Co. Clare, descend from a respectable family in Sussex, and they are found settled in Ireland around the reign of Charles I.

Reap

Reapy, Rape

The name of a family most often linked with Co. Mayo in Ireland. The spelling as Reapy is most often found in Co. Galway however.

O'Reddan

Rodan, Ruddan, Ruddanes, Reddin

The name of a family of Co. Clare in our records, and spelled both as Reddan and Reddin we find the family with a total of 13 births, none of which were in the province of Ulster. Separate families of longstanding in the city of Dublin and Leix are on record, and O'Rodan was a principal name of Co. Donegal in the 17th century. We have no evidence to date linking these families.

Reddy

Ready, Reddington

We find the name of Reddy linked to Co. Kilkenny in Ireland, and as is the case with so many Irish names, the family is found in Dublin as well. The 1890 birth index finds the family most numerous in Dublin and Kilkenny.

O'Regan

Irish Book of Arms plates 168, 227

Riagain

Reagan, Reegan, Ragan, Raygan,

Regan and O'Regan..etc. families rank among the top 100 most numerous names in Ireland. The "O" prefix before the name had been generally dropped by the time of the 1890 index, recording 219 Regans births in Cork, Roscommon and Mayo. O'Regan had 16 births in Cork and Limerick at that time. The families given above represent several, unrelated lines.

O'Regan, along with O'Hart, O'Kelly and O'Connolly is given as one of the four tribes of Tara in ancient days. They held lands around Tara in Meath and into Dublin. They are also noted as "Princes of Bregia". Some of the name today are found in Queens (Leix).

O'Regan is also given as a chief of Ui Riagan, a territory forming the barony of Tinnehinch in Queens County, where the parish of ORegan or Rosenallis marked their lands. Of this old Irish family was Maurice Regan, secretary to MacMurrough the King of Leinster. He wrote on Strongbows 12th century invasions in Ireland, as found published in Harris' Hibernica. Sir Teigue O'Regan was a noted officer in the army of King James II.

In the old territory of Thomand, in Co. Limerick, one O'Regan family descends from Riagan, a nephew of Brian Boru - the last great high king of Ireland who defeated the Vikings at the Battle of Clontarf. Some of the name in Limerick may be from the Regans of Queens Co. as well. O'Regan was listed as a principal name of Limerick and Roscommon in the census of 1659.

Spelled as both Regan and Regane the family name appears often in Co. Cork. It is found as a principal name of Cork, under several spellings in the census of 1659, and Cork remained the main location for the name in 1890.

O'Reilly

Irish Book of Arms plate 29, 64, 139

O'Raghallaigh

Reily, O'Relly, Riley, Reyley, Really,

One of the 12 most numerous names of Ireland, the O'Reillys are a family of the east Breffni, descending from Raghallaigh, in the 10th century. Anciently of the line of Aodh Fionn, king of Connaught in the 7th century, the family was most powerful prior to the Norman invasions in Co. Cavan, with lands in Meath and Wesmeath too.

The word "Breffni or Breffny" in gaelic meant "hilly" lands, a name which suits the area. This area was known as Breffni O'Reilly, and in 1584 they were incorporated into the new county of Cavan. In the town of Cavan, the chief of the name was found on Tullymongan Hill, and Shantemon Hill nearby is the inauguration place of "The O'Reilly".

"O'Reillys Money" was currency used by this family, which was banned in the English pale in the 15th century.

Counties Cavan and Longford remained Reilly country into modern times, and Dublin, Meath and Mayo were prime locations for the name in the 1890. The spelling of O'Reilly was listed only in Dublin then. Reilly had a total of 503 births under that spelling. The patron saint of this family was St. Maedoc.

Several unrelated families of the "Reilly" etc.. name are found in Ireland. Woulfe finds several including those of O'Raithile of Ulster. These independent families have all corrupted the spellings of their names into one of the many Reilly spellings, account for the large amount of families of the name today.

The Irish Book of Arms finds one O'Reilly of Baltrasna, Co. Meath, and O'Reilly of East Breffni.

Several works have been done on the O'Reillys, and many from the 1940's onward can be found yet today.

226

Reynell

Irish Book of Arms plate 37

A Huguenot family of Ireland as given by some sources. The Reynell family of Killynon, Co. Westmeath settled in Ireland in the 17th century coming from Devon.

Renehan

Reneghan, Renehan, Renighan,

Originally spelled with the O' prefix before the name, as Ronaghan the family was listed as a principal one of Co. Armagh, in the barony of Tiranny in the census of 1659. In more modern times some of the name can be found in Co. Cork and in Co. Offaly, the names of Ferns and Feeron are used as synonyms of Renehan on occasion.

Reville

Revell, Revill

Families of the name of Reville and/or Revell are found centered traditionally in Co. Wexford, in or near the barony of Bargy. This is substantiated by both the census of 1659 and the birth index of 1890. The name is also a very common English one, and most families of the name likely originally hailed from that country.

Mac Revy

According to "Keatings History" the name is given as an ancient chief of Moylurg, before the time of the Mac Dermotts. This spelling was said to have been taken from Mac Riabhaigh anciently.

Ringrose

Rose, Ring

The Ringrose family is one originally of England, and several families of the name are found in Co. Clare in Ireland. The name is now a scarce one in Ireland.

Riall

The Irish Book of Arms plate 60

The family of Riall of Old Conna Hill, Co. Dublin, descend from one Charles Riall, of Heywood, Clonmel.

Ring

O'Rinn, Wrenn, Reen, Rynn

The barony of Imokilly in Co. Cork has been the location for this family back into ancient times, and it has remained so into modern times. The similar sounding name of Wrenn or Wren is a name of families settling here from England originally, but some of the O'Rinn or Ring family have changed the name into that spelling over time as well. One such English family of the name of Wrenn is found centered at Ballylongford, Co. Kerry.

The 1890 birth index finds the family name of Ring most numerous in Down and Antrim.

The name of Ringland, common in counties Down and Ulster, bears no known relationship to the name of Ring to our knowledge.

Rowland

Roland, Rolandson, Rowlendson

Rowland families are found centered in counties Mayo and Galway in Ireland in the 19th century. Assumed to have arrived in this country originally from England, some give the family as settling in Meath in the 17th century.

Richardson

Irish Book of Arms plates 75, 94

Richardsen

The families of Richardson in Ireland may be of either Scottish or English extraction originally. The family like many others is found settled in Co. Antrim in the 17th century, but is on record earlier in Ireland. One noted family of the name is found a century earlier with holdings in Monaghan, and in Cavan and Tyrone.

The Richardson family of Lisburn, of Cedarhurst, Co. Down, is given in the Irish Book of Arms. The Richardson family of Rossfad and Rich Hill, Co. Fermanagh are given in the Irish Book of Arms.

The birth index of 1890 finds the family centered in Dublin and Antrim.

Ruxton

Irish Book of Arms plate 39

The Ruxton family of Ardee House, Co. Louth descends from a family settled earlier at Shanhoe, Co. Meath. One of the name obtained considerable lands in Louth under the Acts of Settlement. Some of the name are found serving as High Sheriff in the 17th century.

227

O'Riordan, Reardon

Irish Book of Arms plates 168, 251

O'Riordan

Reardon, Rierdon, Rierdan, Reordon,

Most anciently the O'Riordan, Reardon etc.. family is found recorded in Tipperary, but they soon settled in Co. Cork, with which they have traditionally been identified. Cited as having been distinguished military chiefs in more ancient times, they were known as the O'Riordans of Muskerry there. Note the place name of Ballyreardon, in the barony of Barrymore, in Cork which commemorates the family.

Always the most numerous in Cork, they are also found in Kerry and Limerick in the 1890 birth index with some 159 births.

One family of the name, of Derryroe in Co. Cork, left to reside in France where they became Peers of that nation. Another branch of the family is cited as ancient historians of Eile.

As it is with so many Irish names, the "O" prefix was dropped from its spelling by the time of the 1890 birth index. A look at the telephone directories in modern times will show that that trend is reversing itself. The "O" has been added back onto the name by many.

Of variant spellings of the name in the 17th century, O'Riordane and O'Rierdane were both principal names of Co. Cork, while O'Rierdan was a principal name of Limerick and Rierdan was found in Clare at that time.

Robert(s)

Irish Book of Arms plate 51, 102

Robertson

The name of Robert is sometimes given as that of a Huguenot family found naturalized in Great Britain. The Roberts family of Dormstown Castle, Co. Meath, is found in the Irish Book of Arms.

The Roberts family of Kilmoney Abbey, and of Co. Cork are found in the late 17th century in Cork, around which time they obtained Bridgetown and other property in Cork.

Rodman

The name is a likely variant of Redmond, and as Rodman is found in Co. Wexford as early as the 17th century. One John Rodman is found in 1655 being banished to the Barbadoes in the West Indies. In the late 17th century an apparently separate family of the name is found settling in Coleraine, Co. Londonderry. Some of that family came to America, and those in Ireland were noted as Presbyterians.

Rush

Rushe, Ruish, Ruishe, Rushford

Rush was recorded as most numerous in Co. Mayo in the 1890 birth index of Ireland, and they likely represent the family centered earlier in the barony of Tireragh in Co. Sligo. An apparently separate family of the name is found in the Armagh/Monaghan area of the country. A third possibility exists that the family is of English origins when found in Ireland, for Rush is a well known name in that country.

The name of Rushford, also recorded in the 1890 index, could as well have been simply shortened to Rush on occasion.

Robertson

The Irish Book of Arms plate

Roberts

The Robertson family of Huntington Castle, Co. Carlow are given in the Irish Book of Arms.

Ronayne

Irish Book of Arms plate 222

O'Ronain

Roughneen, Ronan, Ronane

The family of O'Ronayne is found in Keatings history of Ireland as an 'old and respectable family of County Cork.' He also speaks of them as one of the 'ancient Irish Families' in Waterford. When spelled as Ronane, this name is found as a principal one of County Waterford in 1659. In the 1890 index Ronayne is given to be in County Cork with some 13 births. Ronan is found in Cork as well, with some 12 births.

Concerning related variant spellings, Roughneen and Ronan are considered to be the most obvious. Considering the root of the name to come from the older O'Ronain (from gaelic for red), several independent families assumed the same spelling of the name. Many now are considered to be extinct lines. Today the name is considered to be one of eastern County Cork.

Margaret Ronayne married to Thos. Brown. 1778. (From Irish Marriages by Farrar).

Robert Ronayne, College Green, nr. Youghal, married to Catherine Gratricks. Oct. 1805. "

Mary Ronayne aboard ship Alknomac, from Sligo on Oct. 3, 1811, to Newport, R.I., on Dec. 24, 1811.

228

Robinson

Irish Book of Arms plate 36

Robinsen, Robenson

Families of the name of Robinson are found throughout Ireland. They are generally assumed to be of Scottish or English extraction when found here. Many of the name are English settlers, for Robinson is among the top 20 most numerous names in England. The Robinson family is found settled in Ulster in the 17th century, along with the numerous other settler families of the day.

The 1890 birth index finds the family most numerous in Antrim, Down, Dublin, Armagh and Tyrone.

Rossiter

of likely English origin

Rossitor, Rosster, Rositer, Rossetor,

One of the earlier English families to settle in Ireland, the name appears to be centered in County Wexford, in the barony of Forth, and is found there in some number. Believed to have been taken from an English toponymic, the name is also found spelled as Rossitor and Rosster. The 1890 birth index finds the name in Counties Wexford and Wicklow. Spelled as Rossetor, the family is found as a principal one of County Wexford in the census of 1659.

Roche, Roach

Irish Book of Arms plates 168, 267

de la Roche, de Roiste

de Rupe, de la Rupe, Roach, Roch

The "Roche" family name is a fairly common one in Ireland, with the "Roach" spelling being most common in the 1890 index of births. At that time 183 births were recorded in Cork, Wexford, Dublin, Limerick and Mayo.

The name comes from the French "de la Rupe" meaning "of the rock", and the family first arrived here with the coming of the 12th century Norman invasions.

Roches Country, in the barony of Fermoy, in Co. Cork, was formerly held by the O'Keefes'. Keating says that the Roche family became Viscounts of Fermoy and Baron Fermoy was chief of the name in that territory.

Place names incorporating this family name are common. Rochestown can be found over 10 times, and at least half of them are found in Co. Wexford. Rocheshill is in Co. Dublin, and Rochestreet is in Limerick.

In 1659 we find "Roch" as a principal name in Clare, Cork and Kerry among others. Counties Wexford and Cork are the most traditional areas associated with the name.

The names of Roche and de la Roche are given as names of Huguenot families as well.

Roy

A name tied to counties Antrim and Down in the province of Ulster, of likely settler origin there. Of similar names, such as Royall of Limerick city in the 17th century and Roycroft of Co. Cork in the 19th century, the possibility exists that some of those may have shortened the name simply to Roy in those areas.

Rochford

Irish Book of Arms plate 28, 33

Rocheford, Roachforde, Rochfort

One family of the name of Rochford is found of Kilbride, in Co. Meath, and is said to have been there since the early 15th century. In older records the name of Rochfort is found , and it may be an earlier spelling of the name for some families.

The Rochfort family of Rochfort Bridge, Co. Westmeath, are given to descend earlier from the location of Agherry in Co. Wicklow. The Rochfort family of Clogrenane, Co. Carlow are also found in the Irish Book of Arms.

The 1890 birth index finds the family most numerous in Dublin, spelled as Rochford.

Ramsey

Ramsay, Ramseye, Ramseye, Ramsy

The name of a Scottish family who settled in the province of Ulster in Ireland no later than the 17th century. The 1890 birth index finds the family most numerous in Antrim.

Rankin

Ranken

The name of a Scottish family which settled in the province of Ulster in Ireland no later than the 17th century. The family is found centered in Derry and Donegal.

229

Roe

Irish Book of Arms plate 57

O Ruaidh

Rowe, Mac Enroe, etc...

In the census of 1659 the Roe family is given as a principal name of County Cork, also being found in Limerick, Tipperary etc... Milesian families gives the name in Wexford in 1666, coming from England. This brings us to the more modern 1890 birth index, where 21 births were recorded under this name, in scattered locations. This is to be expected, for there are several unrelated origins of the name.

It may be gaelic, coming from the sept of O'Ruaidh in more ancient days. It may be of English extraction being derived often from the English 'Rowe'. Thirdly, it may come from a shortened version of Mac Enroe. Lastly, it may come from the gaelic word for 'red' or ruddy, as has been cited in County Waterford.

The 'Roe' family of Ballyconnell House Co. Cavan, arrived in 1647 with the English forces, and are the arms bearing family of the name cited above.

Reidy

O'Riada

Reddy, Riedy, Reidey, Reedy

The family of Reidy or Riedy etc.. is found early in Tipperary and subsequently into modern times in counties Clare and Kerry. Some confusion results from similar names such as Reddy etc.., and some of the name are of likely foreign introduction as well.

Rolleston

Irish Book of Arms plate 23

Roleston, Roulstone, Roulstone,

The Rolleston family of Ffranckfort Castle, Kings county, is given in the Irish Book of Arms.

Families of the name of Rolston in Ireland are assumed to be of English extraction. As would be expected the name is most numerous in the province of Ulster. An earlier form of the name is sometimes found as Rolleston.

The 1890 birth index finds the family most numerous in counties Tyrone and Antrim spelled as Rolston.

Riddles

Riddell

According to "Keatings History" the name is given among the chief Anglo-Norman and English settlers in Ulidia, under DeCourcey and his successors. The 1890 birth index finds the family most numerous in Co. Antrim under the spelling of Riddell.

Ridge

Ridgeley, Ridgeway

Ridge families are found centered in Co. Galway, (in the Connemara region), in the 1890 birth index, and it is here where the family is traditionally located. Families of the name are assumed to have settled here from England for the most part. Some of the name may have shortened the names of Ridgeway and Ridgeley into Ridge, but they are of distinct families.

Rigney

Rigny, Mac Regnie

The name of a family traditionally associated with Kings County in Ireland, born out by the fact that they appear most numerous there in both the census of 1659 and the 1890 birth index. One center for the name was in the barony of Garrycastle in that county.

Rose

Irish Book of Arms plate 60

A Huguenot family of Ireland according to some older records. The Rose family of Ahabeg, Co. Limerick and Foxhall, Co. Tipperary, are found first settling in Co. Limerick in the 17th century, have come to Ireland from co. Devon.

Rogan

O'Ruadhagain

O'Rogan, O'Rogane.

The O'Rogans were an important family of the territory known as Oriel in earlier days in Ireland. You will also find them in Co. Leitrim. The Oriel sept was of note in the baronies of Armagh and Iveagh in County Down into the 12th century. When spelled as O'Rogan, the census of 1659 gives the name as a principal one of County Down. O'Rogane, however, was given as a principal name of County Cork in the same census. By the time of the 1890 index, 'Rogan' is found in Antrim, Down and Leitrim.

The O'Rogans of Kinelarty, Co. Down are found in a Chancery Roll in 1550. The Annals record the family in Westmeath in 1402, when they were fending off attacks from the English.

Most prominent in the north of Ireland, one of the name is listed as a major supporter of O'Donnell in 1601, and the Hearth Money Rolls in the 17th century also support the location of the family there.

Concerning variant spellings, names such as 'Roghan' are not considered to be the same family as the Rogans, which is found more often in Clare, Tipperary and Cork. Some confusion and interchanging of these two names however, may have come about over the centuries.

Ross

Irish Book of Arms plates 60, 89, 104

Rossiter, Rosswell...

The Ross family is most often considered as a Scottish family when found in Ireland, particularly when in Ulster. Further south, in Dublin and Cork, the name may be of English origin. The census of 1659 finds the name in Down, Louth, and numerous other locations. Milesian families gives the name as a Scottish one, settling in Co. Clare in 1625. The more modern 1890 index finds the name mostly in the north, in Counties Antrim and Londonderry.

George Ross, of Fortfergus, was High Sheriff of County Clare in 1664, and first of the family seat in Co. Clare. Descended from the Rosses of England, their arms were sculptured on the church wall of Clondegad, near the final resting place of the above mentioned. Also given in the Irish Book of Arms is 'Ross of Bladensburg', of Rosstrevor, Co. Down.

Rowan

The Irish Book of Arms plate 73

Roughan

The Rowan family of Mount Davys, Co. Antrim, is of Scottish origins, coming from the parish of Govan, co. Lark.

Rothe

Irish Book of Arms plate 86

Rooth, Roth, Ruthe, Ruth, Rothwell

The Rothe or Ruth family has been traditionally linked with Co. Kilkenny. Here you will find several distinguished individuals of the name dating from the 13th century.

The name is given most often in O'Harts work as "Rooth" and in his work we find John Rooth, Mayor of Kilkenny in 1689, Francis Rooth in the borough of Wexford in the 1689 parliament, and one of the name of Roth as an officer in the 7th Regt. Irlandes.

One family of the name is found in Kilkenny, descended from William Rothe, of Lancashire, England. This family was centered at Ballraughtan and Tullaghmaine in Kilkenny, and a branch of the same family is found at New Ross, in Co. Wexford.

The Rothe family of Mount Rothe, and of Colitrim, Co. Cork, are said to descend from John Rothe, fitz William, in the year 1172 in Ireland.

In 1890 we find the name of Rothwell centered in Wexford and Dublin.

Mac Ruddery

According to "Keatings History" the name is given as an Irish name which was also adopted by Anglo-Norman or English families in lieu of their original surnames.

The Fitzsimons of Kings County took on the name of Mac Ruddery, signifying the son of the Knight.

Ruddy

O Rodaigh (possible)

Roddy, Rudy, Rody

The name spelled as Ruddy is found in the 1890 birth index in counties Mayo, Donegal and Armagh. The name is said to have been taken from O Rodaigh of County Leitrim, but it appears to have separate origins when found in Donegal.

230

O'Rourke

Irish Book of Arms plates 168, 251

O'Ruadraic

Rorke, Roark, Roarke, Rorque, McRourke

The name of O'Rourke and its' variant spellings rank among the top 100 most numerous names in all of Ireland. Known as the Lords of Breffny, they ruled in Ireland before the coming of the 12th century Norman invasions. They held sway in Leitrim, Cavan, Meath and Sligo, and several of the name served as King of Connaught.

One O'Rourke castle is found in the barony of Dromahire, where the family was centered at one time. They held castles at Leitrim, Cloncorick or Carrickallen, and at Castle Car, near Manorhamilton. They were inaugurated as chiefs of Breffni (Breffny), at Croaghan, near Killeshandra.

Constantly at war or alliance with the neighboring O'Reilys of Breffni, the O'Rourke clan saw its decline with the coming of Cromwell to Ireland. The family has spread to the four corners of the world, including Russia, America, Poland and Australia.

In Keatings History we find "MacRourke" in the barony of Rathconrath, Co. Westmeath, near the Hill of Ui sneach. The family name was prominent under many different spellings in the census of 1659. Rorque in Kildare, O'Rorke in Louth, Rorke in Louth and Westmeath, Rourke in Kerry and Waterford, and O'Rourke in Leitrim.

In the 1890 birth index only 31 O'Rourke births were recorded, and 136 births were recorded as Rourke in Dublin, Leitrim, Roscommon and Wexford. The spelling of McRourke has been documented as well.

231

Rowley

Irish Book of Arms plate 53, 98

Rowly, O'Rowley, de Roley

Families of the name of Rowly are found in Londonderry and families of the name of Rowley are found in Armagh, Fermanagh and Londonderry in the census of 1659. By the time of the 1890 birth index the family name is found as most numerous in Co. Mayo.

O'Donovan gives the family of Rowley in the parish of Kilshesnan, in the barony of Gallen in Co. Mayo, and these were of old Irish extraction.

Others of the name are assumed to be of English origins, particularly those in the province of Ulster. The Rowley family of Mount Campbell, Co. Leitrim, and the Rowley family of Marlay Grange, Rathfarnham, Co. Dublin are given in the Irish Book of Arms.

Rogers

Rodgers

Rogers is a fairly numerous English name, and many of the name in Ireland are of English extraction. As expected, most of the name are found in the province of Ulster in Ireland.

Some Irish families of the name of McRory (McCrory), have adopted the name of Rogers. The 1890 birth index finds the family numerous in Antrim, Down, Dublin and Roscommon.

Ruane

O'Ruadhain

Ruayne

This family is said to have its beginnings in Co. Galway in the barony of Clonmacnowen, and is subsequently found in Co. Mayo into modern times.

The 1890 birth index finds the family most numerous in Mayo with 26 births of the name, and in Galway, with 6 births of the name in that index.

Ruttledge

Irish Book of Arms plate 36

Rutledge

The Ruttledge family of Bloomfield, Co. Mayo and of Barbersfort, Co. Galway are found in the Irish Book of Arms. The birth index of 1890 finds the family centered in Tyrone.

Russell

Rusell, Russel

The families of Russell found in Ireland date back to around the time of the 12th century Norman invasions. The most noted of the family name can be found continuously in Downpatrick.

Many other families of the name are given as settling over time in Ireland. O'Hart gives Counties Down and Limerick as early locations for the name here. Edward Russell is given as an English undertaker of Lifford, barony of Raphoe, Co. Donegal. Keatings History gives the name as belonging to that of a principal Norman family settling in Cork, and as among the chief Anglo-Norman and English settlers in Ulidia, under DeCourcey and his successors.

In 1772, at least one family of the name departed from Ulster to America. They settled first in Pennsylvania and then in Virginia and were in the company of one Gilbert Christian, among several other families.

The 1890 birth index finds the family most numerous in Antrim, Dublin and Down.

O'Ryan, Mulryan

Irish Book of Arms plates 169, 222

O Maoilriain, O Riain

O'Mulryan, Royan, Ruan, Rouane,

Ryan families rank as one of the ten most numerous in Ireland. The older forms of O'Ryan and O'Mulryan etc.. have largely been discarded.

It appears that most Ryans today descend anciently from the O'Maoilrian family of Co. Tipperary. This family held Owney in Co. Tipperary and Owneyburg in Co. Limerick. They are found on the Map of Ortelius in that area. These lands were once known as "Owney Mulryan", referring to the older spelling of the name there.

Keatings History also gives the O'Ryans as an ancient family of note in Carlow, Tipperary and Waterford, and as numerous and respectable in Kilkenny.

A family of Ryans unrelated to the first family given above descend from the O'Riains, Lords of Ui Drona, of Co. Carlow. (refer to the barony of Idrone in Co. Carlow for the location of Ui Drona). This family was also of note and remained on their lands after the fall of the gaelic order. They are not however, found as numerous there in the 1890 birth index. This family can be traced back much further than the other, claiming descent from a Leinster King in the 2nd century a.d..

Both Ryan and O'Ryan were principal names of Limerick in 1659 and Tipperary, Waterford, Wexford and Carlow held many of the name as well at that time. Of the now unusual spelling of Mulrian, it was a principal name of Limerick town and county, with several spelling variations there, as well as in Tipperary and Waterford.

Ryan is found most numerous of all names in Limerick and Tipperary. today. O'Mulryan or O'Ryan in also found in Spain.The National Library of Ireland in Dublin, has estate papers on the family.

Rye

The Irish Book of Arms plate 85

The Rye family of Ryecourt, Co. Cork, are given in the Irish Book of Arms.

Ryland

Families of the name of Ryland are found in Dungarvan, Co. Waterford in the 17th century, and also of Youghal in Co. Cork where one of the name was made Mayor in 1716.

Rynn

Rynd, Rinn, O'Rinn, Wrenn, Ring, Reen

Several of the name are to be found in County Clare in our records, and it is uncertain if any relationship exists between this family and the Rinn family of Co. Cork. The name of Rynd is given in Co. Fermanagh in the 17th century, but we know of no certain relationship here.

Rynd

The Irish Book of Arms plate 78

The Rynd family of Ryndville, Co. Meath is found in the Irish Book of Arms. Some undocumented sources find families of the name arriving from Scotland in the 17th century, settling in Meath and Fermanagh.

Rea

Mac Raith, Mag Raith

Raw, Mac Crea, Reagh, Reavy, Wray, Ray,

The name of Rea is often of Scottish origin in Ireland, and is commonly found in Antrim and Down in modern times. Some of the name arrived with the plantation of Ireland, but the name has been in the country before that time as well. Note the place name of Ballymacrea in Co. Antrim (Dunluce barony). Of the plantation 'Rea' families, at least one of the name is found in County Cavan.

In the census of 1659 we find the name of 'Rea' in Kildare, and O'Rea is given as a principal name of Limerick (barony of Owney). This name in Limerick may be taken from O'Riabhaig. In the Fiants from the last half of that century the name may be found as O'Rea, O'Ree and O'Reigh. To further complicate matters Rea may also have come from 'Reagh' meaning swarthy, a 'nickname' which could have been found in any part of Ireland in more ancient times.

At least one family of the name of 'Wray' settled in Ulster prior to plantation coming from Yorkshire. The family can be found in Donegal, Derry and Antrim. In some instances the Wray and Rea spellings are used interchangeably however.

Note also the placename of Rayestown, Co. Meath, where in 1392 John Ray was involved with a real estate transaction.

Of place names in America, note Rheatown, and Rhea County in Tennessee. John Rhea, (1753 - 1832), was an American congressman of Co. Donegal heritage. The above mentioned town and county were named after this Rhea family in America.

Thomas Matthew Ray. (1801 - 1881) born in Dublin. Prominent member of O'Connell's Repeal Association.

Reid

Irish Book of Arms Reed plate 265

Reed, Reede, Mulready, Reade, Mulderrig,

The 81st most common surname of Ireland, the name ranks 13th in Scotland as well. The normal confusion exists when trying to determine its origin, due to the great number of Scottish and British families of the name in Ireland.

Reid is a numerous name in England, and as expected is concentrated in northern Ireland. The Irish name of Mulready has also been abbreviated into forms of Reid. Mulderrig, another Irish name, has also been loosely translated into Reid. Spelled as Reid the name is found in Antrim, Dublin, Down, Tyrone and Armagh in the 1890 index. This confirms the primary location as the province of Ulster in northern Ireland.

Spelled as Reed, Milesian Families give the name as a Welsh one, settling in Clare and Galway in 1170. The census of 1659 finds this spelling in Tipperary and the spelling as Read in Antrim. Also found in Tipperary at this time is the spelling of Reede. These various spellings have been used interchangeably throughout history, so one should be aware of the variant spellings when researching. To further illustrate the spelling problems involved in researching this name, the spelling of Reade is given in the 1659 census as a principal name of Londonderry.

The name of O'Reidy (O'Riada) has been recorded in Co. Tipperary where the chief of the name was titled the 'King of Aradh'. Counties Clare and Kerry still hold descendants of this line.

In America Reid ranks as the 230th most common name, with an estimated 100,000 family members.

Thomas M. Reid, Lt. Col. in the Irish American Brigades (Corcorans Irish Legion) dismissed June 16, 1864.

MAC RANNALL

Reynolds

Irish Book of Arms plate 218

Mac Raghnaill

Mac Rannall, Grannell, McRannall,

Mac Raghnaill, or Mac Rannall , is an Irish name, sometimes Anglicized to Reynolds. They were chiefs of a territory comprising almost all of the "present baronies of Leitrim, Mohill, and Carrygallen in Co. Leitrim with a portion of Co. Longford." The family is said to be of the race of Ir, or Clanna Rory, and of the same stock as the O'Ferrals, princes in Longford.

They were often involved with the O'Rourkes of Breffny. They held some power however, down to the coming of Cromwell, when they lost their standing like so many other families.

Family castles are found at Rinn, Leitrim and Lough Scur earlier. The Lough Scur family received large estates in Leitrim and Roscommon as a result of the 'Restoration and Acts of Settlement". This can be further documented in the "Journal of the Royal Society of Antiquaries" , v-35.

One center for the name was at Moynish in Leitrim. Elizabeth MacRannal of the Lough Scur family was one of the first to change the name to Reynolds, and she was known as the English MacRannall. That family fought for James II in Ireland. Many spellings are found of this name. McGrannal , Magrannel and Grannell to name a few. McReynolds has been used in Antrim. Reynolds is itself also of English origins, so some number of the name are of English descent in Ireland.

The Reynolds name however has remained linked to Co. Leitrim, its original hailing ground, down to the present day. It is also found in Dublin, Antrim and Louth in the 1890 birth index, with a total of 113 births overall.

As would be expected, Reynolds was a principal name in 1659 in Co. Leitrim.

Rice

Rhys (Welsh)

Roice, Rhys

Families of the name of Rice may stem from ancient Welsh origins when found in Ireland. In the province of Munster it is said that the name comes from the Welsh name of Rhys. The family name is found in Limerick, Kerry, Cork and Waterford for several centuries. The census of 1659 finds Rice as a principal name of Limerick City, and at the beginning of that century O'Hart finds Rice in Kildare and Kerry.

The brief pedigrees of the two Rice families presented by O'Hart include "Rice of Carrignifyly, Co. Kerry, and Rice of Dingleicoush, Co. Kerry. Neither is said to be an original Irish family. Pierce Rice was a sheriff of Kerry, and Lord Chief Baron Rice was among the Lords of the treasury in 1689 per that source.

In Keatings History the Rice family is cited in Co. Kerry, and it was noted that they were centered at one time around the town of Dingle there. The are also given as a family of foreign stock settling in Waterford and Tipperary in that same source.

By the time of the 1890 birth index of Ireland we find some 99 births of the name concentrated in Ulster, in the counties of Antrim, Armagh, Louth and Dublin. Why the family name is concentrated only here in modern times is unsure. In O'Donovans works we find that the family of Mulcreevy of Co. Down went by the name of Rice as well. This of course, would represent an entirely distinct family of the name, of ancient Irish, and not Welsh extraction.

There are records relating to the family in the Public Records Office, Four Courts, Dublin, Ireland.

O'Rooney

Irish Book of Arms plate 202

Mulrooney, O'Ruanaidh

Mulrooney, Runey, Roony, Roney,

The Rooney family can be found in Co. Down of long and good standing. Note the place name of Ballyrooney in that county. They are often found associated with the Diocese of Dromore, and with the art of poetry in the above areas. They are as well cited in the barony of Lower Iveagh, in Co. Down.

Note the place name of Rooney's Island in Donegal, another remembrance of the family name. It is also found that in the west of Ulster and just south of there, the name of Rooney is a shortened form of Mulrooney. It is sure that some of the name of Rooney today, were actually Mulrooneys in the past. In counties Mayo and Sligo these names have been recorded for centuries as well.

Mulrooney was given as one of the three chiefs of Crumthan, along with O'Cahill and O'Moran in Keatings History. Their territory included the barony of Killian and some of Ballymoe in Co. Galway.

O'Heignigh and O'Mulrooney are cited as chiefs in Oriel, of Muintir Maolruanaidh and of Maoith Leirg Monach.

In 1659 the spelling of 'Roney' was a principal name of Co. Louth and Co. Sligo. One Patrick Roonye was found in Monaghan at that time as well.

The 1890 birth index indicates that there were some 119 births of 'Rooney' in Dublin, Leitrim, Down, Antrim and Mayo at that time. Only 12 births of Mulrooney were recorded at that time, due in part to the dropping of the 'Mul' prefix to that families name.

Sadleir

The Irish Book of Arms plate 103

Sadler

The Sadleir family of Castletown and arms of the family are given in the Irish Book of Arms. The birth index of 1890 finds the family with 12 births of the name, in scattered locations.

Savadge, Savage

Wild, Wilde, Sage

According to "Keatings History" the name is given among the chief Anglo-Norman and English settlers in Ulidia, under DeCourcey and his successors.

In Co. Down "Savage" is given as one of the principal families in the 17th century, and a branch of that line was said to have settled in Kilkenny. The barony of Ards, in Co. Down marks one early center for the name, and families of the name are found in Ulster from the time of the 12th century invasions of Ireland.

O'Hart also gives the name as that of a Huguenot family in Ireland or England between the years 1681-1712.

Several are found in the Irish parliament including Rowland Savage of the Burrough of Hillsburrough and Francis Savage who is found in the Irish parliament in the year 1797. Arthur Savadge is found as a knight in the 17th century in Ireland, Don Juan Savage was a Lieutenant in 1768 in the Hibernia Regiment with Spain.

The name has been said to have been interchanged with the surnames of Wild, and Sage according to several sources.

The family is often found on the Irish side in conflicts from the 15th century onwards.

It was also reported in early works that some of the name used the surname of "Wilde or Wilde" in place of the original "Savadge".

Sanders,

Irish Book of Arms plater 45

Sanderson

Note the place name of Castle Saunderon in Co. Cavan in the barony of Tullygarvey, Saundersourt in Co. Wexford and Saundersgrove in Wicklow. These are but a few place names attached to the name and its various spellings.

The name is of both English and Scottish extraction when found in Ireland, and many families of the name have settled here over time, in several different areas. Some of the name are found as High Sheriffs in Co. Tyrone in our records.

The Sanders family of Charleville Park, Co. Cork, and they obtained the park mentioned above by deed from the Boyles in 1697.

The birth index of 1890 finds the family name of Saunders centered in Dublin and Antrim.

Sall

Saul, Sale, de la Salle

The family of Sall, or earlier de la Salle is given to be of Norman origins, settling in Ireland in the wake of the 12th century invasions. The census of 1659 finds some of the name in Co. Waterford under the spelling of Sall. The name is rather widespread in older records, including being found in Meath, Dublin and Kilkenny.

Siggins

Sigen, Siggens

The name of a family found often in Wexford and Kildare in Ireland, earlier forms of the name may include Sigen and Sygen, which are of long standing in Ireland, found in records after the 12th century Norman invasions.

Sanderson

The Irish Book of Arms plate 100

Sanders

The Sanderson family of Cloverhill, Co. Cavan are given in the Irish Book of Arms.

Salmon

O' BRADAIN (GAELIC ORIGIN)

SAMMON,SALAMAN,SOLOMAN,SALLM

There are several possible origins for families of the name of "Salmon " in Ireland. While not an extremely common name, it is found fairly widespread throughout the country.

In the 1890 birth index 24 births of the name were recorded. Seven were found in Leinster, 2 in Munster, 6 in Ulster and 9 in Connaught.

An English family of the name is found in counties Leix and Kilkenny from the 16th century onwards, and some of the name likely descend from this settler family.

The Irish name of Bradden or O'Bradain, in the province of Connaught, where most of the name were found in modern times, has been changed into Salmon by some. Note the variant spellings of Sammon, and Samon, found most often in Co. Clare. These two names, understandably have been used as variants of "Salmon".

Individuals of the name:

JAMES SALLMON. ADJUCATIONS OF THE FORTY NINE OFFICERS.
CAPT. ROBERT SALLMON. "
""" "
THOMAS SALMONE. "
"

FROM THE CENSUS OF 1659;
JOHN SALMON. MERCHANT.
FROM THE CITY OF DUBLIN.

OTHER
REV. GEORGE SALMON, D.D..
1819-1904. DUBLIN UNIVERSITY .

235

Sands

Irish Book of Arms plate 78

Sand, Sandes, Sandys

We find the Sands family in scattered locations in our records. In the 17th century families of the name are found in Kildare, Wexford, Kerry and Dublin to name some locations. The birth index of 1890 finds the family centered in Antrim and Armagh. The name is on record in Ireland in the 16th century and earlier, and most are assumed to have descended from English settler families originally. One family of the name of Sandys, in Kerry, settled in the 17th century there, and are said to descend from an officer in Cromwells service. The spelling as Sandes is not uncommon in Co. Kerry as well.

The name of Sandys, in the 17th century is also found in Co. Longford, and there and in Roscommon, several of the name are found in official positions.

The Sandes family of Sallow Glen, Co. Kerry, descend from William Sandes who arrived in Ireland with Cromwell in 1649. He was granted large estates formerly in the possession of the O'Connor family. The Sandes family of Greenville, Co. Kerry descend fro John Sandes, of Moyvane, Co. Kerry, as given in the Irish Book of Arms.

Scurry

Scarry

Keatings History gives O'Sguarra (O'Scurra) or O'Scurry as one of the chiefs of the six sodhans, a large territory in the barony of Tiaquin, in the eastern part of Co. Galway. The other chiefs were MacWard, O'Lennan, O'Cashin, Maginn, and O'Giallain. Some confusion arises between this family and the separate family of O'Scoireadh found in Waterford and Kilkenny.

This is a fairly rare name in our records when spelled as Scurry.

Sankey

The Irish Book of Arms plate 74

The Sankey family of Coolmore, Co. Tipperary. The first of the line in Ireland was a English soldier who commanded a brigade in Ireland, and who became M.P. for Co. Cork, Co. Waterford and for Co. Tipperary.

Sayers

MAC SAOGHAIR, (ANGLO = SAOGHAR)

SEARS. SAY.

Families of the name of Sayers in Ireland are generally taken to be of English settler origins. The name is most often found in the area around Dublin, in Co. Kerry, and in Ulster.

Some of the name are said to have come from the Irish family of Mac Saoghair however.

In the 1890 birth index of Ireland there were only 8 recorded births of the name, in scattered locations. The name remains relatively rare into modern times.

Individuals of the name:

EDW. SAYERS, M.D. MARRIED TO MISS LYSAGHT, AT CASTLE HARRISON, CORK. JUNE 1774.

J. SAYERS, OF ST. HELENS, CO. DUBLIN, MARRIED TO MARGT. TALBOT AT MALAHIDE CASTLE. AUGUST, 1804.

M. SAYERS. MARRIED TO R. TALBOT.1806 A.D.

Scaden

Scadden, Scadan

The name of a family associated with Co. Tipperary in our records, but little has been officially recorded on the origins our activities of the family to our knowledge.

Sarsfield

Irish Book of Arms plates 89, 169

Sairseil, de Sharisfeild

Archfield, Sarsefeld

Keatings History gives us reference to the Sarsfield family in three locations. That is, in Co. Cork, in Counties Limerick and Clare, and in the county and city of Dublin. The census of 1659 also found the family name in Kildare, Limerick and Clare.

The family was granted lands in the 14th century in Co. Cork, and some of this line are subsequently found in and near Lucan, Co. Dublin.

In Co. Limerick the family is found centered at Killmallock.

The Sarsfield family of Doughcloyne, Co. Cork are given in the Irish Book of Arms.

"Sarsfields Rock" at Ballyneety,was so named in honor of Patrick Sarsfield (d. 1693), the famous Irish patriot.

Scahill

Mac Scahill, O'Scahill

The name of a family most often associated with counties Galway and Mayo in modern times. Information on this name is scarce at present.

Scallan

Scallon, Skallan

The Scallan family is strongly linked to the barony of Forth in Co. Wexford in our records, and it was found there as a principal name in the 17th century. The 1890 birth index finds the family most numerous in Wexford, with over 50 per cent of the name located there.

236

O'Scanlon

Irish Book of Arms plates 169, 201

Scannlain

O'Scannell, Scanlan, Scanlane, Skanlane

Families of the name of Scanlon can find their family commemorated in place names such as Ballyscanlon, Ballymacscanlon, Scanlansland and Scanlans Island in Ireland.

Those of the name may find origins from one of several different family lines. Some descend from Mac Scannlain of Louth, others from O'Scannlain of the province of Munster, and others still from O'Scannell of the north of Ireland in counties Sligo and Donegal. These names have been interchanged from time to time, so origins may be difficult to determine without some specific research.

Keatings History gives the family of O'Scanlon in Co. Kerry, and again separately in Co. Limerick in the barony of Pubblebrien, along with the MacArthur family.

In the older territory of Oriel we find "Mac Scannlain" centered at Ballymacscanlan, in the barony of Lower Dundalk barony in Co. Louth. In more modern times the family had faded from view there.

Counties Kerry, Clare and Sligo were all principal locations for the name of Scanlon in the 17th century. Scannell was a principal name of Cork and Kerry at that time, as it was later in the 1890 birth index.

That index shows 54 births of Scanlon and 42 births of Scanlan, concentrated in Kerry, Clare, Sligo, Limerick and Cork.

Both the "O" and the "Mac" prefixes found before the name in earlier days has been dropped for all practical research purposes today.

Scott

Irish Book of Arms plate 100, 124

The family name of Scott is not surprisingly the 10th most common name of Scotland, and among the 90 most numerous names in Ireland as well. It is generally assumed that the name is of Scottish origins when found in Ireland.

Since most of the name are found in the province of Ulster, this is more evidence of Scottish origins, due to the large number of settler families arriving their from Scotland.

County Antrim seems to be the traditional center for the name today, but early records find the name in Fermanagh and Offaly (Kings Co.), as well.

In the 1890 birth index of Ireland 196 births of the name were recorded mainly in Antrim, Down, Londonderry and Dublin.

Of note here is that in more ancient times the Irish were referred to as Scots, i.e. coming from Scotia, an early name used for Ireland.

The Irish Book of Arms gives the family of Scott of Willsboro in Co. Londonderry, and in 1696 they are found purchasing lands in Ireland.

Scally

Skelly, Mac Skally, O'Skelly

We find Scally as a principal name of Co. Longford in the 17th century, and most numerous in counties Roscommon, Westmeath and Dublin in the 19th century. O'Skelly etc.. may serve as a variant spelling for O'Scully, particularly in Co. Cork. m

O'Scully

Irish Book of Arms plates 79, 201

O Scolaidhe

Skully, Scully, Scullion, Scullin, Sculy,

The family name of O'Scully is said to have originally come from the gaelic "O'Scolaidhe", meaning student. Anciently of Co. Westmeath, the Norman invasions forced the family into Co. Tipperary and surrounding areas of the province of Munster. One family of the name settled in Delvin, Co. Westmeath to settle in Lorrha, Tipperary. They are on record as serving as erenaghs of St. Ruans Church there. Note the place name of Ballyscully in that area on the other side of the Shannon river.

The Rock of Cashel in Co. Tipperary served as an older Scully burial place. The family is known to have settled near here in the 17th century, and "Skullys Cross" at Cashel is one famous attraction of the area. In more modern times Scully is recognized as a name of Co. Cork, being found most often there in the 1890 birth index. That spelling was also found in Dublin, Carlow and Kings. Under the spelling of Scally the name is found in Roscommon, Westmeath, Meath and Dublin at that time..

The Scully family of Mantle Hill, Co. Tipperary is found in the Irish Book of Arms.

In the original homeland of the O'Scullys, Co. Westmeath, both Skally and Skelly were found as principal names in 17th century records.

The name of Scullion or Scullin, which represents an originally completely separate family in the province of Connaught, has also been found to use the name of Scully. This family can be found in Ballyscullion, in the diocese of Derry.

One William O'Scully was found in possession of lands in Dublin in 1256.

237

Seagrave

Irish Book of Arms plate 59

Segrave

According to "Keatings History" the name is that of a principal family of Dublin city or county, and of Anglo-Norman descent.

One family of the name descends from Captain John Segrave, of Cabra, Co. Dublin, found there in the late 18th century. Of this line was the Segrave who died at the hands of the great Hugh O'Neill at the battle of Clontibret. This family supported the cause of King James II, until the fall of Limerick.

Semple

Sempill, Simple

The name of a family traditionally linked to Ulster in the 17th century. Settlers of the name here may have arrived from either Scotland or England, for the name is found in both of those places. In more modern times the family name is found centered in Co. Antrim. The census of 1659 also finds the family in Co. Donegal.

Sexton

Irish Book of Arms plate 234

Sexten, Sextan

The name of Sexton may usually be assigned to be of English origins when found in Ireland. Other sources give common Irish origins of the name to the family of O'Seasnain, traditionally of Co. Limerick, notably in the works of MacLysaught. The 1890 birth index finds the family most numerous in Cork, Clare, Limerick and Cavan.

Seymour

The Irish Book of Arms plate 60

The Seymour family of Limerick is found in the Irish Book of Arms, holding positions of Alderman, Sheriff, and Mayor in that county in the 18th century.

O' Sharkey

O'SEARCAIGH (FROM SEARCACH =

O'SHARKEY,O'SERKY,SHARKET,

Families of the name of Sharkey in Ireland are traditionally linked with Co. Tyrone, in the province of Ulster. The name has spread as well into surrounding areas, most notably Co. Louth.

In the 1890 birth index of Ireland, 57 births of the name were recorded as "Sharkey", and most of the family was found in Roscommon, Donegal, Tyrone, Dublin and Louth.

The "O" prefix before the name has been generally dropped by family members for the last several centuries.

Individuals of the name:
SEAMUS O'SHARKEY--GAELIC POET AROUND 1720 A.D.

Passengers From Ireland:

EDWD. SHARKEY-AGE 30-ABOARD 'CAMBRIDGE'JAN. 9, 1850.

JNO. SHARKEY- AGE 21, ABOARD 'DROMAHAIR', OCT. 3, 1849. FROM SLIGO.

JOHN SHARKEY-AGE 20,ABOARD 'SARDINIA' OCT. 31, 1849.

THOS. SHARKEY-AGE 36, ABOARD PHILADELPHIA, APRIL 23, 1850.

MICHAEL SHARKEY-AGE 35, STONE MASON, ABOARD 'DEWITT-CLINTON' MAY 26, 1850.

Shackleton

Irish Book of Arms plate 114

Shakleton, Shackletone

The name of a noted Quaker family in Ireland, who arrived here coming from Yorkshire in the 18th century. This line is found centered in Co. Kildare, where they are connected to the well known school in Ballintore.

Mac Shane

Irish Book of Arms plate 224

Mac Seain

McShane

According to "Keatings History" the name is listed among the chiefs of Moy Ith. This territory comprised parts of the baronies of Raphoe and Tirkeeran in Derry. Their territory in the 12th century is given as in Co. Tyrone. The name was also changed to "Johnson" by translation.

Traditionally given as a family of Ulster, one branch of the name has been said to be descended from the O'Neills of Ulster.

Mc Sharry

Mac Searraigh

MacSherry, Foley, Feley

McSharry is found in Leitrim, Donegal and Sligo with 29 births in 1890. McSherry, had 10 births are recorded in Armagh at that time.

One spelling of the name in gaelic, "Searrach", helped form the root of the name, meaning foal in English. Therefore some use the name of Foley. Historically one family is found in the area of the old territory of Breffny, centered in Co. Leitrim.

In Ulster, as given in Armagh above, the family is believed to be of entirely different origins. The two main spellings given in the birth index have been used interchangeably at times

Mac Shanley

Irish Book of Arms plates 169, 210

MacSeanlaoich ?

Shanly, Shanley

The MacShanly or O'Shanley family is found historically in Co. Leitrim (often near Fernaught in that county). The chief of the name was known as "MacShanly of Dromod" here. Of that line, some of the name settled in Meath for a time, but subsequently returned home to Dromod. This family was granted lands in Roscommon as a result of the restoration in the 17th century. The MacRannells, longtime neighbors of the Shanley clan, destroyed the power of the MacShanleys in the 15th century.

The name is often found with the O' prefix before it, instead of the Mac. We have no knowledge of the reason for this, or if it denotes a separate family.

O'Shaughlin

Mac Giolla-Seachloinn

According to "Keatings History" the name is found in the parish of Dysart in Co. Westmeath, where the family was of some note.

Shaw

Shawe

The name of Shaw, when found in Ireland is most generally assumed to be of Scottish origins. The most noted family of the name hailed from Dublin, but others are found throughout the country, including those of Galway and Ulster. The 1890 birth index finds the family most numerous in Antrim, Down and Dublin.

O'Shannon,Shanahan

Irish Book of Arms plate 5

O Seanachain, MacGiolla t-Seanain

Shanahan, Gilshenan, Shannen,

Irish families of the name of Shannon may stem from one of at least three separate origin there. They may descend from O'Shanaghan , O'Seanain, or from MacGiolla Seanain. No research we have uncovered has connected this name to the River Shannon however.

The O'Seanin family was anciently found in counties Carlow and Wexford, but it is not found numerous there in either 1659 a.d. or 1891 a.d. records. Spelled as Shannon the name was most often found in Antrim, Clare and Roscommon in the 1890 index.

In 1659 Shannon was found in Cork, and Shannahan under various spellings was a principal name of Limerick, Waterford and Tipperary.

Mac Giolla Seanain and Shannahan are found in Co. Clare, and both names are said to have been changed into Shannon in that area.

According to Keatings History Shannahan was Anglicized mistakenly into "Fox" and "Shannon". These O'Shanaghans were chiefs of a territory known as the "woods of Ui Rongali" near Eibhline or Slav Felim, near Feakle. Their power was laid to ruin in the early 14th century by the MacNamaras. Subsequently they spread into Cork, Kerry, Tipperary, Limerick and Waterford, the main locations for the Shanahan name in the 1890 birth index.

17th century records also show that O'Seanan was a principal name of Enniskillan, Co. Fermanagh.

238

O'Shaughnessy

Irish Book of Arms plates 169, 244

O Seachnasaigh

O'Shanassy, Shoughnessy, Shanessy,

O'Shaughnessy country is found in Galway, in the barony of Kiltartan, and in nearby areas of Limerick and Galway. Most of the family is found here today.

O'Shaughnessy was of the same descent as O'Heyne, and was chief of Connally Hugh of Echty, a mountainous area near the borders of Galway and Clare. Keatings History cites Connally Hugh as a large district in the barony of Kiltartan. They took command of the area over the Cahills and O'Clerys, and these lands became known as "O'Shaughnessys country".

They served as chiefs before the 12th century Norman invasions, and were anciently of the southern Ui Fiachrach, descending from King Daithi, the last pagan King of Ireland. Their lands included the diocese of Kilmacduagh.

A branch of this family is found in Limerick in the 1600's. Spelled as Sheaghnisy and Shaughinisy the name is a principal one of Limerick in 1659.

The "O" prefix is often found on the name. In 1890, 30 O'Shaughnessy births are found in Limerick and 41 are found as Shaughnessy in Galway.

St. Colmans holy crozier was said to have the power to make one return a stolen item. It was held by the family for centuries, and is now found in the National Museum of Ireland.

O'Hart relates that in 1843 a barber in Galway represented this "once noble family". For more information see: "Tribes and Customs of Hy-Fiachra".

Several are found in the Irish Brigades of France. Robuck O'Shaughnessy, chief of the name (d.1754) strove unluckily to recover the families property, and his son Joseph converted to the Established Church for the same purpose.

239

O'Shea

Irish Book of Arms plates 94, 169

O Seaghdha

O'Shee, Shee, Shea, Shay, McShea, Shey

O'Seaghda, O'Seadha, or O'Shey was given as a chief of Iveragh in ancient times. O'Shea, Falvey and O'Connell were three chiefs who possessed the lands of that area according to Aryan. O'Shea lands were in the west of Kerry, in the barony of Iveragh. O'Shea is given to be the strengthening bond of the eastern parts of the territories of the three chiefs. They are cited as numerous in former times in Kilkenny and Waterford, according to Keatings.

The O'Shees of Kilkenny, perhaps a line of the family of Co. Kerry, served as one of the noted tribes of Kilkenny. Robert Shee was Sovereign of Kilkenny city in the 15th century. In Tipperary another family is found noted in the place name "Sheesland", from the 14th century. By 1890 "Shea" was five times more popular than "O'Shea". Both were found mainly in Cork and Kerry.

O'Shea,.. ranks among the 50 most numerous surnames in all of Ireland.

O'Shee was a principal name of Kilkenny and of Queens county (Leix) in the 17th century. Kilkenny seems to be associated with the spelling of O'Shee. In the census of 1659 "Shea" was a principal name of Clare, and McShea was found in Kilkenny.

The family was powerful in Kerry prior to the Norman invasions, but later lost prominence, although the family remains numerous there to this day.

Other than Cork and Kerry, Co. Limerick also served as a center for the name of O'Shea. Kilkenny, Tipperary and Waterford held many of the name of Shea in the 1890 birth index.

The O'Shee family of Gardenmorris, Co. Waterford, and of Sheestown, Co. Kilkenny are of the same line as given in the Irish Book of Arms.

O'Sheehan

Irish Book of Arms plates 169, 259

O Siodhachain

Sheahan, Shane, Sheean, Sheen,

O'Sheehan, O'Meehan and O'Cullen all served as chiefs in the barony of Conello in Co. Limerick. Anciently the chief of the O'Sheehans is found in the barony of Lower Connello in Limerick.

Over time the family has spread into Cork and Kerry. Those two counties, and Co. Limerick were the main locations for the name in 1890. The "O" prefix before the name had been dropped by that time, but the 1659 census shows the name with the "O" quite often.

O'Sheaghane was a principal name of Limerick, O'Sheehane of Cork city, and O'Sheghane of Clare at that time. In that same record "Shehane and Sheghane" were both principal name of Cork, without the "O" prefix.

One of the top 80 most numerous names in all of Ireland, the name is highly concentrated in the Cork, Kerry, Limerick region.

O'Sheehans are also found in the territory of the Ui Maine, holding hereditary positions (trumpeters) to the O'Kellys, not too far from the Limerick O'Sheehans. It is not known from whence they came, or if they were a branch of the families cited here.

The rather rare spelling of McSheaghan was found as late as the 1890 birth index. This may represent an entirely different family, i.e. stemming from a name like Mac Sheehy, or may simply be a variation of the spelling of O'Sheehan.

The original meaning of the name in the old gaelic has long been said to mean peaceful, coming from the word "siodhach". This is disputed by some.

Mac Sheehy

Irish Book of Arms plates 169, 258

Mac Sithigh

Sheehy, Sheahy, Mac Shee, Joy

The Sheehy and MacSheehy families in Ireland are noted as gallowglass who came from Scotland. The gallowglass were heavily armed mercenaries who most often arrived in the service of Irish chieftains. Eventually they settled in Ireland permanently.

In Scotland these families were of the Clan MacDonnell, and they are given in Ireland in the 14th century. MacSheehy and O'Hallinan are given as chiefs of Ballyhallinan, in the barony of Pubblebrien, Co. Limerick, according to O'Hart. This 'warlike' clan was brought from Connaught in the 15th century by the Fitzgeralds, earls of Desmond, who appointed them as their bodyguards. They are found centered near Rathkeale.

Some of them changed their name to Joy, and of that family was the Irish judge, Baron Joy. His line was considered to be "originally the same" as the Joyces of Connemara, "a race of men of Tall and manly stature".

McSheehy is given as a principal name of Limerick in 1659, and the name is generally found without the "O" prefix by 1890. This remains true into modern times.

Originally most of the gallowglass served in the north of Ireland. The name however remains one of the Kerry, Limerick and Cork areas today, with 55 births of the name of Sheehy recorded in 1890.

The family can be found mentioned as warriors in several battles, and are often found with the MacSweeney clan in war as well.

240

Sheppard

The Irish Book of Arms plate 68

The Sheppard family of Kilcunahanbeg, (formerly called Clifton), in Co. Tipperary is given in the Irish Book of Arms. Two brothers of this are said to have come to Ireland. One of those two came over in Cromwells army and was the Governor of New Ross, Co. Wexford in 1659.

Sheares

Sheeres, Sheare

Said to be originally of English extraction, the name of Sheares is relatively rare in Irish records. Two of the name (John and Henry Sheares) are found executed in the revolt of 1798. Families of the name are found early settled in Cork and Wexford.

The name has been given as well as among the adventurers for land in Cromwellian times in Ireland.

Sheeran

Shearan, Sheerin, O'Sherin, Shearing,

O'Sheerin was a principal name of Co. Fermanagh in the census of 1659. O'Shearing was given as a principal name of Co. Donegal in that same census. Some have equated these two families as one, but we have no evidence of the same. Moving into the 19th century we find several families of the name in Leix (Queens Co.).

The noted Edward MacLysaght reports finding a now extinct line of the name in Co. Cork.

O'Sheridan

Irish Book of Arms plates 169, 202

O Sirideain

Sherden, Sherdon, Sherdan, Sherodan,

The O'Sheridans, an ancient clan in Co. Cavan, and numerous at the time cited in Keatings History, were centered in the barony of Clanmahon there.

Several are cited as brilliant literary talents, such as Rev. Dr. Thomas Sheridan, president of the great school of Cavan and his son Thomas a celebrated actor and author of an English dictionary. This family was noted for a line of talented artists as such. General Philip Henry Sheridan (d. 1888) was the famous commander during the American civil war, and he was of Co. Cavan origins as well.

The Cavan family served under the ruling O'Reillys of Breffny in the early days.

The family name is also found anciently in Granard barony in Co. Longford, where they are found as Erenaghs.

The 1890 birth index gives the family in Cavan, Dublin and Mayo with 145 births around that time. The family name was a principal one of Co. Louth in 1659 as well.

Two old books may be of interest here. "The Lives of the Sheridans", a 2 vol. set, by Percy Fitzgerald published in 1886 and "The Sheridan Family" 1687-1867, by Harold Nicolson, published in London in 1937.

Sherwin

Sharvin

Those of the Sherwin name in Ireland are said by Woulfe to be of the same line as the O'Sharvan family of Co. Roscommon. Most of the name in our records hail from Dublin, and many are of English extraction here.

Sherlock

Irish Book of Arms plate 91

According to "Keatings History" the name is among the chief families of English descent settling in Waterford and Tipperary. These English families primarily possessed the territory called from them Gal-tir, signifying the country of the foreigners," now the barony of Gaultiere."

Note the place names of Sherlockstown and Sherlocks Castle in Co. Kildare where the family has been on records for 6 centuries, found traditionally linked with the barony of North Nass there.

The family is also found in Meath in our records.

The Sherlock family of Rahan Lodge, King's Co., descend from Christopher Sherlock, of Littlerath and Derrindarragh, Co. Kildare.

The birth index of 1890 finds the family centered in Dublin.

Sherry

Sharry, O'Sherry, Mac Sherry, McShery,

The 1890 birth index finds the family of Sherry centered in Monaghan, Dublin and Meath, and McSherry centered in Co. Armagh at that time. The census of 1659 gives McSherry and McShery as principal names of Co. Armagh, and O'Sherry as a principal name of Monaghan. The name is found with both the Mac and O' prefix at times in older records. Some of the name are also found in Co. Cork, but these are of completely separate origins from the above.

O' Shiel, Sheilds

Irish Book of Arms plates 170, 220

O Siadhail

Sheilds, Shield, Shiel, Sheil, Shiell

The O'Shiel or O'Sheil family of Ireland is most often found in Dublin, Donegal and Londonderry in the 1890 birth index of Ireland. It is found, as it almost always is, without the "O" prefix before the name there. The family is also noted in Down and Antrim. It is obviously a name of Ulster based on a search of existing records.

Most of the name likely descend from O'Siadhail when of true gaelic origins. This family is found serving as physicians to the chiefs of Ireland, and they claim ancient descent from Niall of the Nine Hostages.

Note the place name of Ballysheil, in the parish of Gillen, Co. Offaly. One branch of the family is found centered here, and they served as physician to the MacCoughlan in centuries past.

Many of the name are found settling in France, and one attained high rank there in 1775.

The name of Shields or Sheilds is found in the 1890 birth index in counties Antrim and Down, and no doubt represents Shiel families under a variant spelling in many instances.

The spelling of Shiell is found used as a principal name in Queens Co. (Leix) in the census of 1659. The "O" before the name had been largely dropped throughout the country at that time as well.

Barry Fitzgerald, the American actor, was actually William Shiels at birth. More anciently Murtagh O'Shiel served as hereditary physician to Mac Coughlan, who died in 1548. Connach O'Shiel became bishop of Elphin in 1545.

Shuldham

The Irish Book of Arms plate 52

The Shuldham family of Balymulvey, and Ballymahon, Co. Longford , are originally given as coming from Norfolk before settling in Ireland.

Sheenan

Shannon, Shenan, Synan, Sheanan

O'Sheanan was a principal name of Co. Fermanagh in the 17th century, and the name of Sheenan is also found in the 1890 birth index of Ireland. Being a not too common name, it has been changed to similar sounding names such as Shannon on occasion. We find the family often linked to Co. Tyrone in our records.

Shelly

Shelley, Shelloe, Shallowe, Shalloo

Some of the name of Shelly will be of English heritage for the name is one of England at times. The 19th century birth index records indicate that the family of Shelly was centered in Tipperary and Dublin at that time. Spelled as Shally the family name is found centered around Galway in that same index. In earlier times the family name was most often associated with Co. Cork.

Mac Shere

According to "Keatings History" the name is given as an Irish name which was also adopted by Anglo-Norman or English families in lieu of their original surnames.

The Poers of Kilkenny and Waterford changed their name to Mac Shere.

Singleton

The Irish Book of Arms plate 59

The Singleton family of Aclare, Co. Meath is found in the Irish Book of Arms. The birth index of 1890 finds the family centered in Cork and Down.

Shevlin

The 19th century birth index find the name of Shevlin centered in the province of Ulster. Anciently a family name of Offaly and Mayo, the O' prefix found in early records before the name was dropped. Presumably the Mayo family spread into Co. Donegal, where many of the name were found.

Shine

Irish Book of Arms plate 201

O'Seighin or Seigene (small)

Shine, O'Shine

Shine is traditionally considered to be a name of the province of Munster in Ireland. Historically the family is found as a sept of Counties Cork and Kerry. The 1890 birth index places the name in County Cork, and Milesian families gives the name as Dal Cassian sept, settled in Cork, Kerry and Limerick. Some mention of the name has been made in county Clare, but reference to the family should always center on Cork and Kerry to begin with. Several of the name are found in the Kenmare estate manuscripts, and in deeds and wills from the 1700's onwards in that area.

The name is considered to be an ancient Irish one, although the Welsh name of Shinn or Shine has been said to have arrived in Ireland at some date in the past, as well.

242

Slacke

The Irish Book of Arms plate 106

Slack

The Slacke family of Ashleigh, are descended from William Slacke, of Annadale, Co. Leitrim, which was the seat of power for the family in Ireland.

Skahan, Skehan

Mac Skeaghan or O'Sceachain

Skehan, Thornton

The family name of Skehan and its variant Skahan are considered to be names of Louth and Monaghan originally. In the census of 1659 Skehan is found listed as a principal name of County Louth. The name can also be found in northern Co. Tipperary, where Fr. Woulfe says the name originally had the 'O' prefix, not the 'Mac'.

The name may be taken from the gaelic 'sceach' which means briar, hence the translation of the name on occasion to Thornton.

Skerrett

of English origins

Scared, Scaret, Huscared, Skeret, Skerrit

The Skerrett, Scaret..etc.. family name is a rare one in Ireland. It has not been found in the 1890 birth index listings nor in the 'census' of 1659 at first glance.

One of the 14 tribes of Galway, they are of English origins and held lands under De Burgo in Connaught. Several of the name can be found as important officials in Galway city, i.e. as mayor etc.. One of the name is found serving as Archbishop of Tuam.

They held sizable estates in the Galway and Clare areas of the country, but the name is relatively rare there now. They are cited specifically in Finvarra in Co. Clare and in Ballinduff, Co. Galway, in earlier times.

Smith, Smyth

Irish Book of Arms plates 43, 47, 104

of various origins, MacGowen etc..

Smythe, Smithe, Mac Gorhain, Going,

Smith is one of the most numerous names in England, Scotland and America. In Ireland the name ranks among the 10 most numerous surnames. In America Smith is the #1 name. The spellings of Smyth and Smythe are found commonly in Ireland as well.

"Smith" is found in the 1659 census as a principal name of Donegal. The birth index of 1890 gives "Smith" as the most common spelling of the name with 471 births concentrated in Antrim, Cavan, Dublin and Kerry. Smyth, had some 277 births were recorded then.

Smyth is found as a principal name in various locations in 1659. McSmythe was then in Antrim.

Families of the name have arrived here from several countries, and it can be difficult to determine origins. One Irish family of the name can be found originally as MacGowan, not Smith. In Co. Cavan, many of the name are really Mac Gowans, their names being translated into Smith. Keating finds the them as Mac Gorhains or Mac Gowans, driven into Donegal by the English, found in Leitrim in Rossinver and Cavan. A part of the Clanna Rory. . . Keating also gives Mac Gobhains or O'Gobhains, in the parishes of Lovey, Laragh, and Killinkere. They were originally of Down, and served as 'chiefs of gallowglasses' under the O'Reillys.

Smyth is a principal name of several areas in Ireland as well. That spelling is traditionally given in Co. Antrim, Antrim Union in the Templepatr district. Arms for Smythe of Barbavilla, Westmeath and Smith of Annesbrook, Meath, are given in the Irish Book of Arms with others. Estate papers on the Smith family in Ireland are at the National Library of Ireland in Dublin.

Smyly

The Irish Book of Arms plate 107

Smiley, Smily

The Smyly family of Camus and Castlederg, Co. Tyrone, descend from John Smyly who came from Scotland and settled at Carrygullion near Camus in 1628, this family is given in the Irish Book of Arms. The birth index of 1890 finds the family centered in Antrim.

Slone

Sloan, Sloane, Slones, Slowan, Slowey

The names of Sloan and Sloan are found mainly in Co. Antrim in the 19th century. Two centuries earlier we find Sloane given in Co. Down as well. The apparently unrelated name of Slones is found in Tipperary, and Slowan is found in Down, in the census of 1659. Some of the name are of Scottish origin when found in Ireland, particularly when found in the province of Ulster.

The Irish family name of Sloan is traditionally linked to counties Antrim and Down in the province of Ulster.

The name of Slowey is thought to be of older Irish origins in Ulster.

Smithwick

Smithick, Smythwick

Families of the name are given to be of English origins when found in Ireland, and the census of 1659 finds some of the name in counties Louth and Carlow. The problem of the shortened form of the name as Smith, or Smyth is evident, for that has likely happened in isolated cases. Another family of the name of Smithwick is on record in Co. Cork from the 17th century there.

243

Somerville

Irish Book of Arms plate 102

Somers

Families of the name of Somerville may have arrived from Scotland or England upon settling in Ireland. As expected most of the name are found in the province of Ulster, and one family of the name is found in Co. Cork, coming from Scotland in the 17th century.

The Somerville family of Drishane, Co. Cork, descend from a Church of England minister in Scotland who fled from persecution there in 1692.

The birth index of 1890 finds the family name of Somers centered in Wexford and Dublin.

Snee

Snee

The name of an old Irish family found centered near Swinford in Co. Mayo, remaining there at the time of the 1890 birth index of Ireland.

Snow

One family of the name is found in Co. Kilkenny, and of this line was one of the name who served as R.M. of Co. Tyrone.

Soden

Sodan, Sodin, Soudan

The name of a family found centered in Co. Sligo and Cavan in the 19th century. The family is generally given to be of fairly recent introduction into Ireland, settling from England in the 17th century.

Sorahan

Soraghan, Soran, O'Soraghan

The name of a family traditionally associated with counties Monaghan and Cavan in Ireland.

Spaight

Irish Book of Arms plate 59

Speight, Spate

Families of the name of Spaight are scarce in Ireland. We find reference to some families of the name arriving in Limerick and Tipperary in the mid 17th century, and these were of English origins.

It is given to be the name of a family traditionally associated with counties Limerick, Clare and Tipperary. The family is often given to be of English origins, found settling early in Co. Derry, and branching into Clare, where one of the name is found as high sheriff at the end of the 17th century.

Mc Sorley

Mc Sorely,

The name of a family found centered in Tyrone and Fermanagh in the 1890 birth index of Ireland, also said to have settled in Antrim, coming from Scotland in the 17th century. The name also serves as one of the Clan McDonald and the Clan Cameron, of Scottish origins.

Speer

Speers

One family of the name is found of Balnasaggart and Tullybryan in Co. Tyrone. The same family is also found in Stewartstown in the 17th and 18th century.

The 1890 birth index finds the family most numerous in Co. Antrim, under the name of Speers.

Spence

The name of Spence is given to be one of a Scottish family of the Clan MacDuff, found numerous in Co. Antrim and Co. Down into modern times.

St. Lawrence

Irish Book of Arms plate 92

Lawrence

According to "Keatings History" the name is that of a principal family of Dublin city or county, and of Anglo-Norman descent.

The Gaisford - St. Lawrence family of Howth Castle, Co. Dublin are given in the Irish Book of Arms. The birth index of 1890 finds the family centered in Dublin and Tipperary.

Spring

Springham, Springe

Families of the name of Spring are found in counties Dublin and Kerry in the 17th century, and families of the name of Springham are found in Dublin and Londonderry at that time. Spring, of course, could in isolated instances be an abbreviated form of other "Spring" names such as Springham. It is interesting to note that the name is not found in Ulster in the 1890 birth index of Ireland. Co. Kerry is the county most often associated with the name.

Sproule

Sproul, Sprool, Sprowle, Spruell

Families of the name of Sproule are given as centered in Co. Tyrone in the 1890 birth index, and in the census of 1659 we find the name in Co. Donegal spelled as Spruell.

Spinks

De Spynk

One family of the name obtained a grant of lands in Munster in the reign of Queen Elizabeth, and earlier we find the name of De Spynk as that of a friar at St. Augustines Monastery at Warrington. The name is also found centered at Mount Nugent in Co. Cavan in the 18th and 19th centuries.

244

de Stackpole

Irish Book of Arms plate 22

Stackpoole, De Stacpoole

According to "Keatings History" the name belonged to a Norman settler family in Co. Cork, which was of some note. The family of de Stacpoole of Mount Hazel, Co. Galway and Tobertynan Co. Meath, is given in the Irish Book of Arms.

Stapleton

Gaul

The name of a Norman family settling in Ireland with the coming of the 12th century invasions. The name is found as a principal one of Co. Tipperary in the 17th century, and remained centered in Tipperary and Kilkenny some two centuries later. Dublin and Limerick are also given as early areas of settlement by the family. Several of the name are found subsequently in France and Spain as a result of the troubles in Ireland.

The 1890 birth index finds the family most numerous in Tipperary and Kilkenny.

Stanihurt

According to "Keatings History" the name is that of a principal family of Dublin city or county, and of Anglo-Norman descent.

Stokes

Stoke

An English settler family found in Ireland quite early. Several noted individuals of the name can be found in the annals of Irish history. The name appears to be most often associated with counties Kerry and Limerick.

The family name is as well cited in Co. Dublin and Co. Down in the 15th century or prior, in the works of O'Hart.

Stafford

Irish Book of Arms plate 71

Staford

According to "Keatings History" the name is given as that of an old English family which settled in Wexford. The 1890 birth index finds the family most numerous in Wexford and Dublin.

Stone

According to "Keatings History" the name of Stone can come originally from the name of O'Mulclohy, a family of the barony of Cairbre, in Co. Sligo. Others find one family of the name of Huguenot descent. The 1890 birth index finds the family most numerous in the province of Leinster.

Sherrard

Sherard, Sherrerd

The name of a family found centered in counties Londonderry and Antrim in the 19th century. Co. Derry remains the county with which is is most often associated. The name is of English origins.

Strahan

Strain, Straghan, Strachan

Given to be a family of the province of Ulster in Ireland, the spelling of Strain is found centered in Co. Down in the 19th century, and Strahan was a spelling of both Ulster and Leinster at that time. Only 9 births were recorded under the latter spelling.

Skinnion

Skinnan, Skinnon

The name of a family found in more recent times in Leitrim and Cavan, they are said to have hailed anciently from Roscommon, and some of the name subsequently served under the O'Donnells as historians, in the province of Ulster.

Stannus

Irish Book of Arms plate 44

Stanehouse

The Stannus family of Carlingford Co. Louth, and of Portarlington in Queens Co., descend from one William Stanehouse of Carbolzie, Scotland. Found in the year 1618, as settling during the plantation of Ulster.

Stritch

Strich, Stretch, Striche

Families of the name of Stritch and Strich are found mainly in Co. Clare and Co. Limerick according to our records. Both Stritch and Strich are found in Clare in the census of 1659, where Strich was given as a principal name at that time. The family is usually given to be of English origins. In Limerick several of the name are found as public officials

Skelton

of English origin

Skelten

Skelton is a name which we have found in Dublin in the 15th century and in Leix (Queens) in the following century. Of English origins, the name has also been found in Ulster. The census of 1659 finds the name in the city of Dublin. At the end of the last century the name had only 8 recorded births in Ireland, and only in the provinces of Leinster and Ulster.

Skillen

Skilling

O'Hart gives this family name as a variant spelling of O'Scallan, but others say the name arrived from England, or after the Norman invasions. The birth index of 1890 finds the name centered in Down and Antrim, and the former is the county where the family often found.

245

Staunton, Stanton

Irish Book of Arms plate 88 (Staunton)

Stanton, McEvilly

According to "Keatings History" the name is given among the chief Anglo-Norman and English settlers in Ulidia, under DeCourcey and his successors.

Being found in Ireland in the wake of the 12th century Norman invasions the family is found settled often in Co. Mayo, and also in Co. Galway subsequently. Some of the name are said to have taken on the surname of McEvilly as well.

The 1890 birth index finds the family most numerous in Mayo and Galway when spelled as Staunton, and in Mayo and Cork when spelled as Stanton.

Skurlock

Sherlock

According to "Keatings History" the name is one of a noted family in Meath. The name is found commonly as both Skurlock and Sherlock.

Slaine

Slain, Slane, Slaney

The name of a family found in Co. Meath and Co. Tyrone in our records. The similar sounding name of Slaney is found in Co. Kilkenny in the 17th century.

Shipsey

Shipsea, Shippy, Shipward, Shipton,

Shipsey families are traditionally located in county Cork, with some of the name being found in Co. Waterford as well in our records. The name is of likely English origins. A similar name, that of Shippy, is found in the census of 1659 in Co. Kildare, Shipward and Shipton are found in Co. Cork, and Shipcott is found in Dublin city in that census.

Stawell

The Irish Book of Arms plate 61

The Stawell family of Crobeg, Co. Cork has been in that area for over 300 years.

Steele

of likely English origin

Steel, Steill, O'Steille, O'Steill

The surname of Steele is another of the many names in Ireland which are of probable English origin. The name can be found in Northern Ireland, and is indeed of English heritage there. In the birth index of Ireland for the last century, we find both the Steele and Steel spellings. Both are grouped together by Mattheson. Steele is found 37 times in this report, while the less popular Steel is found only 17 times. The main location of the name at this time was in counties Antrim and Londonderry.

Looking exclusively at the Steele spelling, we find the name listed in Dublin city on the census of 1659. Milesian families gives the name as an English one, arriving in 1640 and settling in Kildare at that time. Other possible spellings include Steill and O'Steill principal names of Antrim in 1659. O'Steille is also given as a minor spelling in Antrim. These spellings are not likely of the same family, but it might prove worth knowing in your future family research.

The Steele family of Ballyclough, Co. Antrim, is one which has been documented in the book entitled 'Families of Ballyrashane', by Mullin. Two listings are found in this book, including William, Sarah, John, Samuel, Jane and Mary Steele of Ballyclough. (incidental mention only)

Stewart

Irish Book of Arms plates 24, 28, 48

Of Scottish origins

Stuart, Steuart, Steward

Families of the name of Stewart, etc.. in Ireland are assumed to be of Scottish origins unless known otherwise. It is among the top 10 names of Scotland, and is therefore a settler name in the north of Ireland in the province of Ulster. Stewart ranks as among the top 60 surnames of Ireland as well.

The 1890 birth index gives 255 births of the name in counties Antrim, Down, Londonderry, Donegal and Tyrone.

The Irish Book of Arms gives the family of Stewart of Ards, Co. Donegal, as earlier coming from Co. Down. Families are given as well in Summerhill, Co. Dublin and in Horn Head, Co. Donegal, in that work.

A book of interest here is "Genealogical and Historical Sketch of the Stuarts of Castle Stuart in Ireland", by Andrew G. Stuart, Edinburgh, 1954.

Stevenson

Stephenson, Stephens

Families of the name of Stevenson and Stephenson are said to be of both Scottish and English extraction when found in Ireland. They are found in Ireland no later than the 17th century settlements of Ulster. The 1890 birth index finds the family most numerous in Antrim, Armagh and Down.

246

Stoney

Irish Book of Arms plate 27

Stony

The Stoney family of the Downs, Delgany, Co. Wicklow, are found in the Irish Book of Arms.

Stephens

Mac Giolla Stiofain

Stephen, Stephenson, Fitzstephen.

In more modern times Stephens is listed in the 1890 birth index in County Mayo. It is today considered a name of Dublin and County Mayo. In 1659 however, we find the name in both Cork city and county, as well as in Kilkenny and Limerick.

'Stephenson', a name which can be shortened to Stephens on occasion, is found in 1659 as a name of Dublin city. It is also listed as a name of Ulster in the 1890 index being found in Antrim, Armagh and Down.

The name may have originally come from the Norman name of Fitzstephen or FitsStephen, or from English plantations. Woulfe refers to Mac Giolla Stiofain, as a family of County Leix (Queens County today).

Without the final 's', Milesian families refers to 'Stephen' as a name of Donegal and Derry settled in 1683 from Wales.

Slavin

Irish Book of Arms plate 253 (Slevin)

Slevin, Sleevin

The name of a family most often associated with the province of Ulster in Ireland. Slevin was a principal name of Westmeath in the 17th century, and 11 births of the name of Slavin were recorded in 1890, mostly in Ulster.

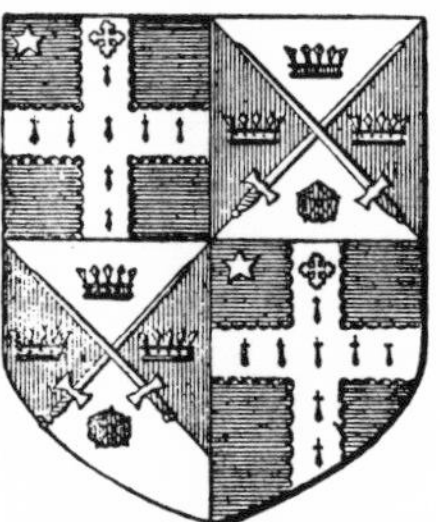

Stoughton

The Irish Book of Arms plate 103

The Stoughton family of Owlpen, co. Gloucester, and of Ballyhorgan in Co. Kerry Ireland, are given in the Irish Book of Arms.

Sinnot

Synott, Synot, Synnott, Sinnott

Sinnot families in Ireland are generally assumed to have settled in Ireland from abroad at some point in time. Spelled as Sinnott, the family is found centered in Co. Wexford in the 1890 birth index. Spelled as Synnott the name is one of Dublin at that time, with a total of 12 recorded births.

It is believed that this family arrived in Ireland after the Norman invasions of the 12th century, and they are traditionally cited as one of the "old English families" that settled in Co. Wexford.

Sinon

Synan, Sinane, Shynane

A rare name today, the family is found early in Co. Cork and subsequently in Co. Clare in Ireland. Most records show the name spelled with a "y" in earlier times.

Slattery

Irish Book of Arms plate 234

Slattary, Slatery

Note the place name of Ballyslattery in the barony of Tulla Upper in Co. Clare. The family is traditionally linked to Co. Clare but it is found fairly widespread in surrounding counties, as far south as Co. Cork, as well. The 1890 birth index finds the family most numerous in Tipperary, Kerry, Cork, Clare and Limerick.

Studdert

The Irish Book of Arms plate 102

Studdert family Bunratty Castle, Co. Clare descend from the Chancellor of the Diocese of Limerick in the year 1669 and this family is given in the Irish Book of Arms. The birth index of 1890 finds the family centered in Clare with 5 births and in Kerry with 1 birth in that index.

Sutton

not of Gaelic origin

de Sutun

The Sutton name is recorded in Keatings history as that of an old English family who settled in Wexford. Indeed the family has been in the Wexford and Kildare areas since the 13th century. The census of 1659 records the name in Wexford, and the 1890 birth index gives the name in Dublin, Wexford and Cork.

The presumed earlier form of the name would have been 'de Sutun'.

The family of Sutton of Ballykeerogue, Co. Wexford, are said to have originally arrived in England with William the Conqueror. Another family of the name is found seated at Tipper, Co. Kildare.

Shorten

Shorten is considered to be a variant spelling of Shortall, and is found numerous in Cork city and county. The 1890 birth index finds the family most numerous in Co. Cork, with 5 of 7 births of the name located in that county.

247

O'Sullivan

Irish Book of Arms plates 170, 201

Suillabhain

Sulliban, Sulivan, Soolivan

The O'Sullivan name is the third most numerous name in all of Ireland, following only Kelly and Murphy in prominence. The main branches of the Sullivan clan are as follows. First, O'Sullivan Beara, of Co. Cork and known as "princes of Beara" in earlier days. Secondly, O'Sullivan Mor, who were lords of Dunkerron, and thirdly, O'Sullivan of Conc Raffan, chiefs of Knockgraffen in Co. Tipperary.

The O'Sullivan population today remains concentrated in Counties Cork and Kerry, but the name can be found throughout the land. Sullivan was the preferred spelling of the name in 1890, with 839 recorded births in those counties and in Dublin, Antrim and Galway. O'Sullivan had 139 registered births of that spelling, mainly in Kerry, Cork and Limerick.

O'Sullivan Beara held lands south of the Kenmare River and were seated at Dunboy, with castles at Bantry and Carriganass. O'Sullivan Mor castles include those at Dunkerron and Dunloe, the latter of which guards the gap of Dunloe.

There are several unrelated families of the name in Ireland, and they are seen as coming to the fore after the Anglo Norman invasions, in contrast to others who fell from power at that time.

The O'Sullivan surname is said to be most often taken from the personal name of "Suillabhain", which meant the one-eyed or hawk eyed. They descend from Milesius, the great king of the Celts or Milesians, through the Eugenian line.
(Speaking of the most noted family).

Many works have been published on the families of the name, and they are worthy of review for the researcher.

Mac Sweeney

Irish Book of Arms plates 170, 258

MacSuibhne

Sweeny, Sweany, Sweaney, Swiney

Keatings History gives, "Mac Suibni or the Mac Sweenys", a branch of the O'Neills which settled in Donegal, and formed three great families, namely , Mac Sweeny of Fanaid, whose extensive territory lay west of Lough Swilley, and whose castle was at Rathmullin; Mac Sweeny Boghamach , or of Tir Beghani, now the barony of Banagh, who had his castle at Rathain, an in which territory was situated Reachrain Muintiri Birn, now Rathlin-O'Beirne Islands; and Mac Sweeny Na d-Tuath, signifying Mac Sweeny of the Battle Axes. His districts were also called...the districts of the Tory Island. His possessions lay in the barony of Kilmakrenan.

These were called Mac Sweeny Na d-Tuagh, or Mac Sweeny of the Battle axes, a title derived from being standard bearers and marshals to the O'Donnells, and chiefs of Galloglasses.

A branch of these MacSweenys, noted military leaders, settled in Munster in Co. Cork, in the 13th century as commanders under MacCarthy, prince of Desmond. They were brought from Tirconnell or Donegal to Desmond. They had the parish of Kilmurry, in the barony of Muskerry, Co. Cork, and their chief castle at Clodagh, by Macroom, and Castlemore in the parish of Movidy. Keatings' notes that many of the name were settled in Sligo and Mayo.

The gallowglass or galloglas were paid soldiers who fought for the Irish chieftains of the day. Most of them were recruited from Scotland.

By the time of the 1890 birth index, the "Mac" before the name had largely been dropped. Regardless of spelling, most of the name were found in Cork and Donegal at that time. Most also spelled the name with an "ey" ending.

Swift

Irish Book of Arms plate 76

Swifte, Tappy, Fodey, O'Tapa

As a settler name from England the name of Swift has only been found relatively late in our records. One such family is recorded in Dublin, and subsequently in Kilkenny. Note the place name of Swiftstown in Kilkenny, where the name has traditionally been found located.

One old Irish family of the name is on record as having used the name of Swift, in Co. Mayo, and they are considered native Irish.

The families of Fodey, O'Tapa or Tappy have been cited as changing their name into Swift on occasion, in the areas of Co. Mayo and Co. Sligo.

The Irish Book of Arms gives the family of Swift of Foulksrath Castle, Co. Kilkenny.

The birth index of 1890 finds the family centered in Mayo.

Sweetman

Sweteman

Families of the name in Ireland are given to be of Norse origins, arriving as early as the 12th century Norman invasions. The name is traditionally tied to Co. Kilkenny throughout its history in Ireland, into modern times.

They are given in the county and city of Dublin as among the principle families of foreign descent from the 12th to the 18th centuries according to O'Hart. Sweteman is as well listed as a principal family of Kilkenny from the 12th to the 15th century, and two of the name are found in the Irish Brigades in Spain in the Hibernia Regiment in the 18th century.

Both the census of 1659 and the 1890 birth index find the name in Cork and Dublin. Other questionable records show the name arriving in Dublin and Clare in the year 1572 from England.

248

Synge

Irish Book of Arms plate 51

A settler family in Ireland, several Bishops and clerics of the name are found in the Protestant church in Ireland. John M. Synge (1871 - 1909) was the noted author and playwright of the name, of Dublin roots.

The Irish Book of Arms gives the family of Synge of Glanmore Castle.

Short

Shortall

The name of Short is generally assumed to be that of settler families in Ireland, coming from both Scotland and England where the name is also found in some numbers. As would be expected many of the name are found in the province of Ulster and in Dublin.

Skiddy

Skidy

The Skiddy family is traditionally associated with the town and county of Cork, where they are found at an early date, subsequent to the 12th century invasions of Ireland. Here, they were numerous in former days along with the Coppinger, Gould, Galway, and Terry families.

Given to be originally of Norse background, they are noted as having adopted to the Irish way of life most thoroughly.

One Nicholas Skiddy cited as from Dingleicoush and from Cork in the first half of the 1600's is found. In 1703 a.d., J. Skiddy was in the Irish Brigades of the French army, in the Regt. de Clare.

Stubbs

The Irish Book of Arms plate 85

The Stubbs family from the area of Danby, Co. Donegal are given in the Irish Book of Arms as published by the Irish Genealogical Foundation.

Supple

Suipeal, de la Chapelle

Suppels, Suppel, Soople

Supple is another family name which arrived in Ireland along with the invasion by Strongbow around 1171. This family name is traditionally associated with Cork and Limerick. The original individual of the name was 'de la Chapelle' who came with Strongbow. The family maintained power and lands until the troubles of the 16th century.

One family of the name, centered in Castletown, Co. Limerick, were transplanted as papists under Cromwellian orders.

Spelled as Soople, the name is found in Roscommon. 'Suppels' is given in Milesian families as an English name which arrived in Dublin in 1270. The census of 1659 finds the Supple name in Limerick and Cork. The province of Munster remained the center for the name at the turn of the century, with only 5 recorded births of the name.

Shortall

Short

Note the place name of Shortalls town in counties Kilkenny and Wexford. The former county is the one where the name is traditionally linked to. An English family of the name is found settling there in the wake of the Norman invasions. The 1890 birth index finds the family most numerous in Dublin and Kilkenny.

Synnott

Irish Book of Arms plate 49

Synott, Sinnott

Note the place name of Sinnottstown in Co. Wexford. Families of the name are found settled in the baronies of Bargy and Forth in that county in the wake of the 12th century Norman invasions. The name is, as well, found in early records of Dublin city.

Sugrue

Sughrue, Sugrew, Shagrue

Most often linked with Co. Kerry in Ireland, the Sugrue family is also found in Co. Cork in the 1890 birth index of Ireland.

Swanton

of English origins

Swan

Swanton families are assumed to be of English settler origins. The family is found in Co. Cork in the 17th century. Cork is traditionally considered the home for the name. The 1890 birth index and Griffiths survey give the name centered in Cork as well. The 1890 index finds 5 of the name in Cork and 2 of the name in Dublin. "Swan" is found in Dublin and Antrim then.

Several are found in the works of O'Hart, and some are found as 'wild geese', in the ranks of foreign armies on the continent, as was one James Swanton of the Irish Brigades in France, 1760 - 1828.

Several of the name held estates in Cork in the last century. At least one of the name is found as a sheriff in Co. Kildare in the latter half 17th century.

Passengers From Ireland:
JAMES, AGE 24, ABOARD 'COLONIST' APRIL 8,1850.
WM. AGE 24, ABOARD 'METOKA' MAY 19,1848.

249

Sigerson

Mac Siogair

Segerson, Seagerson

While Sigerson is a rare name in Ireland in more modern times, it has been on record in Ireland since at least the 16th century. It is considered a Norse surname coming from Sigfrid or Sigrid. As to early appearances of the name in Ireland 'Seagerson' appears on the Hearth Money Rolls for Co. Armagh in the 17th century, and Sigerson of Halveston is found as a constable of Co. Kildare in 1608.

Today it is most often considered a name of Co. Kerry and as such has been found at Ballinskelligs in the 1700's.

Simms

Simpson, Sims, Sime, Simes.

The name of a family centered in Co. Antrim in the 19th century. Most of the name likely arrived from Great Britain in the 17th century. Simms may also be connected to the name of Simpson, which was centered in Antrim as well, in the 1890 birth index. Simpson however, was found in Roscommon in the census of 1659.

The similar sounding names of Simes was found in Kilkenny, and Sime was found in Donegal in the 17th century.

Simpson

Simson, Sim, Simon

The name of Simpson is given to be that of several settler families arriving in Ireland from both Scotland and England. The name ranks among the top 50 most numerous in Scotland alone. The name is often found in Ulster as would be expected, but is dispersed throughout the country as well. The 1890 birth index finds the family most numerous in Antrim.

Spillane

Spillan, Splaine, Mac Spillane, O'Spillane, Spalane, Spallon, Spellman

The 1890 index of Ireland finds the Spillane family most numerous in Cork with 23 births, and in Kerry with 11 births. The name is found under various spellings, and has even been changed to Spellman or Spelman in parts of Sligo. In the 17th century O'Spillane is found as a principal name of Cork, as well as being found in Kerry at that time.

There are at least two apparent origins of the name in Ireland. One family is anciently found as Mac Spillane, today more often found as Spalane or Spalon in Co. Offaly. O'Spealain, on the other hand, is found centered in the barony of Eliogarty in Tipperary, where they held sway until the rise of the O'Dwyers in that region. Subsequently we find these Spillanes in Cork and Kerry, as cited previously. Those of the name in Co. Sligo may well be of the same descent as the Spillanes of Co. Kerry and Cork today.

Keatings History gives two separate entries on the name of Spillane. First, he gives the name as that of a clan still numerous in counties Mayo and Sligo. Secondly he gives us "O'Spelain, or O'Spillan, chief of Ui Luighdeach", as mentioned by O'Heerin:

"The chief of Ui Luighdeach of slender spears,
Is O'Spillan of the bright spurs,
Mighty is the march of the warrior's battalions,
Increasing as they proceed along the plains of Macha"

The territory of the O'Spillans given above appears to have been on the borders of Tipperary and Kilkenny, as given in that work.

Note the place names of Ballyspellane in Kilkenny and Tipperary, and of Ballyspillane in Co. Cork and Co. Kerry.

Stack

of English origins

Stac, de Stack, Stackpoll, Stackpoole.

Stack is the name of a well known English family which settled in Ireland in the 13th century. They soon 'became Irish', and several of the name fought against British rule (Elizabethan wars..) in later days.

Traditionally considered a name of County Kerry in Ireland, several of the name intermarried with notable families of the area in Kerry. 'Stack's Country' as it was called was known earlier as 'Pobble Stack. 'STACK'S COUNTRY', is to be found near the Stack Mountains between Tralee and Abbeyfeale in County Kerry.

In Keatings History the Stack family was listed as a principal English family of County Kerry, along with the Browns, Godfreys and Rices.

Names such as Stackpoll and Stackpoole may have been shortened into the name of Stack, as well.

Both John and Phillip Stack were Bishops of Ardfert in the 16th century. General Edward Stack (d. 1833) was of the Irish Brigades in the service of France.

In the census of 1659 the name of Stack is given as a principal one of Co. Kerry. By the time of the 1890 birth index of Ireland the name was still mainly located in Co. Kerry, with some of the name in counties Cork and Limerick at that time as well.

Individuals of the name :

MAURICE, OF KINGS COUNTY.

EDMUND, OF KING JAMES OFFICERS.

ROBERT, CAPTAIN IN 1745 OF THE IRISH BRIGADES IN FRANCE.

LIEUT. STACK-WOUNDED AT FONTENOY, OF THE IRISH BRIGADES IN FRANCE, Lallys' Regt.

250

Taaffe

Irish Book of Arms plates 9,83,170

Tath

Taa, Taff, Taafe, Taffe

Those of the Taafee family name in Ireland are given to be of Welsh descent. They are found in Ireland around the time of the Norman invasions of the 12th century. They can subsequently be found in Dublin and Louth. They served as Sheriffs in Louth for several generations, and as Earls of Carlingford, they are found settled in Sligo as well. One center for the name in that county was at Ballybragan. Ballybragan was lost however with the coming of the confiscations of 1641.

In Sligo they are found also as "Viscount Taaffe", and in Ballymote, Co. Sligo, Sir William Taaffe served as sheriff in 1588. A family castle was found in that town as well.

Another family castle can be found at Carlingford, Co. Sligo. In Louth you will find Smarmore Castle near Ardee, site of another Taaffe castle. O'Creans castle, in Co. Sligo marks the birthplace of Nicholas Taaffe (d. 1752), the 6th Viscount Taaffe.

In the 17th century Taaffe was a principal name of Louth, and Taaff was found in Meath in the 1659 census. With fewer than 20 recorded births of the name in the 1890 index, the name remained scattered at that time.

The Irish Book of Arms gives one Taafe of Smarmore Castle, and Glenkieran, Co. Louth. The pedigree of one family found was of Louth and Sligo, said to have been settled in Ireland since the time of Edward I.

The "Memoirs of the Family of Taafe" was published by Count E.F.J. Taaffe in Vienna in the year 1856.

The name is anciently taken from the Welsh "Tath", meaning David.

Talbot

Irish Book of Arms plate 28, 64

One family of the name was of old Norman ancestry, having arrived in England with William the Conqueror. Two of this line are said to have settled in Ireland, Richard Talbot settled at Malahide, Co. Dublin and the name is of long standing there.

Sir William Talbot, of Carton, Co. Kildare is found in the early 17th century. The Talbot family of Talbot Castle, Co. Wexford is given in the Irish Book of Arms. The Talbot family of Mt. Talbot, Co. Roscommon, descends from Richard Talbot of Templeoge, Co. Dublin in the 16th century.

Tallon

The Tallon family is given as settling early in areas around Dublin, and they are found bearing one of the principal names of Co. Louth in the 17th century. Our 19th century records show the family centered in Dublin. Found in several counties, they were also prominent in Meath.

Talty

The name of a family traditionally linked to Co. Clare in Ireland, it remained centered there at the time of the 1890 birth index of Ireland.

Tannian

Tannion

A rare name in Ireland, some are found in Co. Galway in relatively recent times.

Tally

Irish Book of Arms plates 171, 221

Mac an Tuile, O Maoltuile, Taithligh

MacTully, Mac Atilla, O'Tully, Flood

Families of the name of Tally in Ireland may spring from one of several unrelated families. Some of the name may even find that they are of original English stock.

One family of the name served as hereditary physicians to the O'Connors of Connaught and the O'Reillys of Breffny. O'Dugan gives the "Muintir Taithligh, or Mac Tullys" as chiefs of Lough Lir, near the barony of Lurg, close to Lough Erne. The family has also been cited in the Cavan/Longford area by other sources.

The Tally name has also been interchanged with the name Flood. Keatings History says that "Tuile", which signifies a "flood", gave some MacTullys reason to change the name to Flood. This source gives both O'Maoltuili and MacTully as names which were changed as such. Note as well that the Tullys of Galway and the Floods of Kilkenny claim usage of similar coats-of-arms.

Note also near the Cavan/Longford border the place name of Tullystown in the barony of Fore, in Co. Westmeath.

The MacTullys have also been cited as chiefs in the barony of Tullygarvey, in the parish of Drung.

In 1659 Tally was a principal name of Co. Roscommon, and a century ago the name was most common in Galway, Dublin and Cavan, with a total of 45 recorded births of the name.

Other variant spellings of the name include Mac Atilla and O'Tully. Of the latter we have no explanation but that it may have been added onto the name in error, long after the "Mac" prefix had been dropped.

Tarleton

The Irish Book of Arms plate 91

The Tarleton family of Killeigh and Fenter in Kings County, descend from Gilbert Tarleton of Hazlewood, near Liverpool in England.

Tangney

O TEANGANA

TANGLEY ?, TANGNY.

Families of the name of Tangney are traditionally linked with Co. Kerry in Ireland. A relatively rare surname, only 8 births of the name were found recorded in 1890, and all but one of those were recorded in Co. Kerry. The remaining birth was in Co. Cork. So it has been for centuries, with the name constantly found in Co. Kerry, if no where else.

In Co. Kerry we also find the surname of "Tangley". Some of the name say that their name was originally Tangney.

Tanner

le Tanner(e)

Tannere

The Tanner name in Ireland has been found throughout the country and does not seem to have centered in any one location. It may be of interest however to note that of the 7 births recorded in the 1890 index, none were from the province of Connaught. We do have a location for the name in 1659 for Tanner is found in Queens County in the 'census' for that year. It is a name also found in the Poll Money Ordinance survey near that time.

An Anglo-Norman name which was originally spelled as 'le Tanner' or 'le Tannere', it is on record in Ireland from Medieval times.

Taylor

Irish Book of Arms plate 69

Tailor, Tayler, Tailer

The name of Taylor, and it variant spellings, is traditionally linked with the province of Ulster in Ireland. The name is found settled here quite in advance of the 17th century plantations. Families of the name generally are given as of English and Scottish extraction, for the name is among the top 5 most numerous names in England and the top 30 most numerous names in Scotland.

One family of the name came from Yorkshire in England and subsequently settled at Swords, in Co. Dublin. Another English family of the name is found centered at Ballyhaise, in Co. Cavan. Other families of the name of note are those of Taylor of Ballyphilop, Co. Cork, Taylor of Old Court, Harolds Cross in Dublin, Taylor of Cranbrook, Co. Fermanagh, Taylor of Athboy, Co. Meath, Taylour of Dublin City, Taylour of Carrickfergus, and Taylour , Earl of Bective.

The Taylor family of Ardgillan Castle, Co. Dublin, is given in the Irish Book of Arms.

Tansey

Mac an Tanaiste?

Tansy, Mac Tansey

Although some say that the name is of Norman origins, arriving near the time of the 12th century Norman invasions of Ireland, the name of " Mac Tansey", can be found in Sligo and Roscommon of likely old Irish origins.

The 1890 birth index recorded only 13 births of the name, all in the province of Connaught.

Temple

Irish Book of Arms plate 60

Templeton

A Huguenot family of Ireland as given in some older records. The Temple family of Waterston, Co. Westmeath is found in the Irish Book of Arms.

The birth index of 1890 finds the family name of Templeton centered in Co. Antrim. There were 6 births of the name of Temple in that index as well.

Tempest

The Tempest family is given in Co. Louth in the census of 1659. Most of the name are of likely English origins, but Woulfe gave the name as an old Irish one as well. Sir Thomas Tempest served as Attorney General in Ireland in 1640.

Tenison

NOT OF LIKELY GAELIC ORIGIN

TENNISON

Families of the name of Tenison, Tennison etc.. are assumed to be of settler origin in Ireland. The name is quite rare here, and is of likely English origins.

Individuals of the name found:
RICHARD TENISON OF THOMASTOWN, CO. LOUTH, AND HIS DAUGHTER ELIZABETH.

THOMAS TENISON OF THE IRISH HOUSE OF COMMONS OF 1797.

Passengers From Ireland:

JAMES,MICHAEL AND ROSE TENISON, ABOARD 'NIAGRA' FEB. 12, 1849. FROM LIVERPOOL TO NEW YORK.

JAMES TENNISON AGE 20, MALE, ABOARD 'NEW HAMPSHIRE' APRIL 25, 1850.FROM LIVERPOOL.

252

Thackwell

The Irish Book of Arms plate 81

The Thackwell family of Aghada Hall, Co. Cork, and also of Coneragh, Co. Waterford, are given in the Irish Book of Arms.

Telford

When looking for the Telford family in Ireland it is wise to consider it a name of northern Ireland (Ulster). There it has been found for several hundred years, since the 1600's at least, and is considered to be a name of English or Scottish heritage originally. The name has remained in that area into modern times, as evidenced by the 1890 birth index which gives County Antrim as the main location for the name.

Terry

Mac Toirdealbhaigh

Tyrry, Tirry, Therry, O'Terry, Terri

The family name of Terry in Ireland is traditionally tied to the city and county of Cork. Here it is listed as a principal name of Cork city in 1659 and County Cork remains the main location for the name in the 1890 index. Scores of the name have served as Mayors in the city of Cork, and it is on record there from the 1200's onward. In 1641 you may find the name given as freeholders in the barony of Barretts and barony of Barrymore in the 13th century. O'Terry has as well been found in the 16th century in Tipperary.

The name of course, may come from the French 'Terri' or on a more isolated occasion from the Irish MacToirdealbhaigh.

In Keatings History they are given to be of Danish descent along with the Coppingers, Goulds, Gallways and Skiddys.

Thompson

Irish Book of Arms plate 100

McAvish, McTavish, Tomson, Thomson,

The numerous family name of Thompson ranks among the top 50 names in Ireland, Scotland and England. It is actually the 4th most common in Scotland and the 15th most common surname of England. Thus, those of the name in Ireland often have Scottish or English backgrounds.

Several other families now using the name of Thompson etc.. in Ireland were originally of another surname entirely.

McTavish and McAvish are two such instances. People of these names have changed their names into Thompson on occasion, as documented by the Registrar-General in relatively recent times.

Most of the name are likely of settler origins in Ireland, found mainly in the province of Ulster. Note that the name of Thomson has been said more often to denote a Scottish origin when found in Ireland. When spelled as Thompson it origins are more likely English according to sources in the past.

The Thompson family of Rathnally and Ross, Co. Meath, descend from John Thompson of Muckamore.

The Thompson family of Clonfin, Co. Longford, descend from the first of that family to settle in Ireland, one Capt. William Thompson, b. 1655, who came here with King William II in 1688.

The 1890 birth index finds 317 births of the name, mainly in Antrim, Down, Armagh, Londonderry, Dublin, Fermanagh and Longford.

The census of 1659 finds Thompson in Wexford, Meath, Armagh and Clare. The spelling of Thomsone at that time is found in County Donegal.

Thornton

Irish Book of Arms plate 101

Of English Origin

Thorton

Thornton is considered to be a name of English origin, which arrived in Ireland on numerous occasions. One family settled in Co. Limerick under the Elizabethan plantations. The name is also said to have settled in Waterford and Cork being of Welsh origin. In Derry, the name is said to be of English origin.

The census of 1659 finds the name in Dublin city and Kildare.

The birth index of 1890 finds the family centered in Galway, Dublin and Mayo.

Teahan

Tehan, Tegan, Teaghan, Teehan

The Tehan family name is given as a principal name of Queens County in the census of 1659. Woulfe gives the family as anciently from Roscommon, but we find most of the name in Co. Kerry.

Teeling

Telyng

The Teeling family is most often associated with Co. Meath in Ireland, and several notables of the name are found there. We find the name in Co. Westmeath in the census of 1659, and centered in Dublin in the 19th century. Given to be a family of foreign origins in Ireland, they are on record here not too long after the Norman invasions of Ireland.

Teevan

The Teevan family is found centered in Ulster, primarily in Co. Cavan and adjoining areas. One landed family of the name held estates in Donegal and Fermanagh in the 19th century.

253

Thunder

The Irish Book of Arms plate 63

The Thunder family of Lagore, Co. Meath and Ballaly of Dublin is found in the Irish Book of Arms. The birth index of 1890 finds the family centered in Dublin, where all of the name were found at that time.

Tesky

The name of a Palatinate family, settling in Limerick at the turn of the 18th century, coming from Germany.

Tevlin

Tefelin

The name of a family primarily found in counties Cavan and Meath in Ireland. One center of location for the name is in and around Kells, in Meath.

Mac Thomas

Thomas

According to "Keatings History" the name is given as an Irish name which was also adopted by Anglo-Norman or English families in lieu of their original surnames.

The Fitzgeralds changed their name to MacThomas and MacMaurace.

The 1890 birth index finds the family most numerous in Antrim, under the spelling of Thomas.

Mac Timlin

Tomilin, Timilin, Timlen

The name of a family long associated with Co. Mayo, and who according to the works of Woulfe were of Welsh or Anglo-Norman descent. In the 19th century we find the name centered in counties Mayo and Sligo.

Tickell

The Irish Book of Arms plate 73

The Tickell family of Carmolway, Co. Kildare is found in the Irish Book of Arms.

Timmins

Timmons, Timon, Timmin, Tomin,

The Timmins family is found centered in counties Dublin, Kildare and Wicklow in the 19th century. Often identified with Co. Carlow, many of the name spring from that county. The spelling of Tomin is found in Cavan in 1659. The spelling of Toman is found in Down and Antrim in 1890.

Timony

Timpany, O'Timony

Only nine births of the Timony name are recorded in the 1890 index of Ireland. Here the name is found mainly in the province of Connaught. Several are found earlier in counties Donegal and Tyrone in our records. The name of Timpany is of likely completely separate origins, found earlier in Down.

Mc Tire

According to Keatings History this family is given as chiefs in the barony of Imokilly, in Co. Cork, alongside O'Bregan and O'Glaisin.

Twigg

The Irish Book of Arms plate 81

The Twigg family, formerly of Thorndale, are found in the 17th century in Cavan on the Muster Rolls of Ulster.

O'Tierney

Irish Book of Arms plates 170, 251

O Tighearnaigh

Teirney, Tierny, Tiernan

Families of the O'Tierney name in Ireland have been traditionally identified with Co. Mayo there. Here they are found in older records as the Lords of the barony of Carra. In O'Harts work, which is not always reliable, O'Tierney and O'Kieran are identified as chiefs of Fermanagh in Tir Owen, in the 12th century.

The "O" prefix before the name was generally dropped fairly early in Irish history. One can even find the name of MacTierney, which could be the result of family members adding the wrong prefix to the name, or that spelling could actually come from the original name of Mac Tiernon, a separate family altogether.

O'Dugan found the O'Tierneys as chiefs of Moy Ith anciently, and their territory included the baronies of Raphoe and Tirkeeran in Co. Derry. The name has also been found in older records in Donegal and Westmeath.

In the census of 1659 "Tierny" was a principal name of Tipperary, and "Tierney" was given in Dublin, Tipperary and Galway in the 1890 birth index.

Taggart

McTagart, Tegart, Teggart

Families of the name of Taggart, etc.. are traditionally linked to the province of Ulster in Ireland, and specifically with Co. Antrim of that province.

Mac Tighe, McTeague

Irish Book of Arms plate 48

Taidgh

Teige, Tiege, Tighe, McTeague, McTague

Families going by the name of Tighe or McTighe etc.. in Ireland have taken their name from an ancestor whose name was Teige. Teige was a first name or personal name in olden times, thus the son of Teige took on the name of "MacTeigue". The name can be spelled in several different ways as given above.

It is difficult to trace this name back very far, for often it appears to have been adopted at random by people whose father may have been named Teige. Thus you may have an ancestor with an altogether different surname.

Of the different spellings of the name in 1890, Tighe was the most common with 33 births recorded in Co. Mayo. McTighe ranked second with 12 births in Mayo, while McTague was given in Cavan with 4 births and McTeague in Donegal with 3 births.

The name is said by some to stem from "Taidgh" meaning poet or philosopher in gaelic.

The Tighe family of Woodstock, Co. Kilkenny, settled in Ireland, where one of the family became Mayor of Dublin in 1651.

O'Tapa

According to "Keatings History" the name is cited as that of a clan of Mayo and/or Sligo. The name of O'Tapa was also said to have been 'translated' into the name of 'Swift' for many of the family.

Tarsnane

The name of a family given in the works of Woulfe, and some can be found in Co. Clare in modern times.

Tisdall

The Irish Book of Arms plate 95

Tisdall, Teesdale

The Tisdale family of Charlesfort, Co. Meath, descend from Michael Tisdall who is first found at Castle Blaney in Co. Monaghan. The birth index of 1890 finds the family centered in Dublin.

O'Toler

Irish Book of Arms plate 259 (Tolar)

O'Tolairg

According to "Keatings History" the name is that of the chief of Quirene, now the barony of Kilkenny West, in Westmeath.
The name is taken from the old Irish family of O'Tolairg.

Tone

The Tone family name is a rare one in Ireland. The most noted of the name was Theobald Wolfe Tone (1763 - 1798) of noted historical importance. Of his line were some coachbuilders in Dublin by trade.

Toner

O'Toner

O'Toner is found as a principal name of Co. Armagh in the census of 1659, and Toner is given as mainly found in Armagh, Londonderry and Antrim in the 19th century. The family is generally given as one of the province of Ulster in Ireland, and is traditionally linked with Co. Donegal anciently.

Tobin

Irish Book of Arms plate 170

de St. Aubyn (French)

Tobyn, Tobbine, Tobynn, Tobine, Tobynn

Originally the Tobin or Tobyn family was found in Ireland under the spelling of de Saint Aubyn, and then the "t" in the word "Saint" was taken to form the name of Taubyn or Tobin. (The "Sain" was dropped from the word Saint). They are found in Ireland around the time of the 12th century Norman invasions.

The family is found early in Tipperary and Kilkenny, and note the place name of Ballytobin or Ballaghtobin near Callan in the barony of Kells in the latter. In Tipperary the family is found noted as "Barons of Coursey". Keatings history gives the name as numerous in Waterford and Tipperary.

In the census of 1659 various spellings of the name are found. It was a principal name of Co. Tipperary under the spellings of Tobbine, Tobine, and Ttobyyn. Found simply as Tobin, it was a principal name of Limerick at that time.

In modern time the name is found simply as Tobin, and in the 1890 birth index 98 births of the name were recorded in Waterford, Cork, Tipperary, Limerick, Dublin and Kilkenny.

The Irish Book of Arms gives the family of Tobin of Tipperary and Kilkenny, centered at Kelaghy, Co. Tipperary. The family name is also found centered at Ballytobin, Co. Kilkenny, at Ballincollig, Co. Cork, and at Nantes in France.

Towey

A name traditionally linked to Co. Roscommon in Ireland. The 1890 birth index centers the family in Mayo and Roscommon.

Todd

Irish Book of Arms plate 101

Tod

As given in the Irish Book of Arms, this family of Todd was seated for a considerable time in the north of Ireland, and was of ancient Scottish descent.

William Thornton Todd, of Buncrana Castle, Co. Donegal, son of Daniel Todd, is cited as well.

Todd has been given as both of Scottish and English origins when found in Ireland. In 1659 Todd is found in Kilkenny, and in the 1890 index the family is found in Antrim and Down, in the north of Ireland.

The Irish Book of Arms gives the family of Todd of Buncrana Castle, Co. Donegal. This family is said to be of Scottish heritage originally.

Tohill

Toohil, Toohill, Tohill, Tohull, Tohall,

Tohill, and its variant spellings such as Toghill etc..represent a family anciently of Co. Down. Note the name of the parish of Deserttoghill in that county. In Co. Cork and surrounds, some of the O'Toole family is said to have adopted the Tohill spellings.

Tolan

Toolan, Toland, Twolan

Tolan families are found centered in Co. Mayo in the 19th century, and Toland families are found centered in Co. Antrim at that time. It is also thought that the spelling as O'Toolan, which was a principal name of Donegal in the 17th century, represents the same family. In the 1890 birth index Toolan was centered in Co. Roscommon. O'Donovan gives many of the Tolan family leaving Donegal for Mayo in the company of the O'Donnells in the 17th century.

O'Toole

Irish Book of Arms plates 170, 261

O Tuathail

Toal, Tuhill, O'Tool

The most noted O'Toole family is found in Wicklow, in the baronies of Talbotstown and Shilelagh. According to Aryan they held lands from there to the hill of Allen in Kildare, including lands in the baronies of Naas, Kilcullen, Kilkea, Moone and Connell.

Their chief castle and center of power was found at the Glen of Imalie in Co. Wicklow, and they held other castles at Carnew, Castledermot and Castlekevin. The O'Toole name is probably taken from the 10th century chief, "Tuathail".

Family power was maintained to the coming of Cromwell, when their lands were confiscated. Many are subsequently found among the ranks of the "wild geese" in armies of France and Spain.

Aryan speaks of the family thusly: "O'Toole of the fortress famed for mead, is chief of the valiant tribe of UiMurray"

Their lands, well suited for defense, was around the diocese of Glendalough.

In the province of Connaught, according to Hardiman, the O'Tooles of Inisturk may actually be a branch of the O'Malley family that adopted the name. The family has been found at early dates in Counties Galway and Mayo as well.

In the province of Ulster we also find a likely unrelated family of the O'Toole name, also taken anciently from "Tuathail". Here the name is believed changed to Toal, and 20 births of that name are found in Armagh and Antrim in the 1890. It is as well an older spelling found in Co. Monaghan.

Estates of the O'Tooles in Wicklow, and of O'Toole of Castledermot in Kildare were given to Walter de Riddlesford in the reign of King John.

Toole was the most common spelling in 1890, found located in Dublin, Galway, Mayo and Wicklow etc..

Tottenham

Irish Book of Arms plate 24

Tottonham, Totten, Totton

The Tottenham family of Tottenham Green Co. Wexford and of Woodstock, Co. Wicklow, are given in the Irish Book of Arms.

The birth index of 1890 finds the family name of Totten centered in Antrim, and the name of Totton centered in Armagh.

Torpey, Tarpey

O'TARPAIGH (TARPACH=STURDY)

TORPY,TARPEY

Dealing with the family names of Tarpey and Torpey, one must remember that they have been used interchangeably on occasion, and that they may also represent two distinct and separate families. The name of Tarpey is most often found in Sligo, and subsequently in Co. Galway. In Sligo, the parish of Skreen marks the homeland for one older family of the name. Families of the name remained in Galway into modern times.

We also find a family of the name, presumably of completely separate and distinct origins in Co. Cork. Here in Cork, the name was most often found spelled as Torpey. The spelling of Torpey is also found in Tipperary several centuries ago.

Spelled as Tarpey, 12 births of the name were given in the 1890 birth index of Ireland. 8 of the name were in Mayo, 3 of the name in Roscommon, and 1 of the name in Galway.

Individuals of the name:

MICHL. TORPEY, AGE 30, ABOARD 'WATERLOO' MARCH 4, 1851.

PAT TORPEY, AGE 24, MALE, ABOARD 'NEW WORLD'. SEPT. 27,1850.

256

Townshend

Irish Book of Arms plate 35

Townsend, Townesende

The Townshend family of Castle Townshend, Co. Cork was founded by a soldier whose regiment arrived in Ireland in 1647, and hence he commanded forces in battle near Mallow, Co. Cork.

Torrens

Torrance, Torrans, Torrens, Torrins,

Families of the name of Torrens are given to be of the province of Ulster in Ireland, centered in Co. Antrim. Torrance is given to be a sometimes variant spelling of Torrens. Furthermore, Thornton is an English form of the name adopted by some families of the name of Torrens in Ulster, and of the name of Tarrant of Co. Cork.

Some find that the name of Tarrant is English and that the name of Torrance is Scottish, but over time some confusion has taken place. Torrens is often given to be a family of Co. Derry, and some sources give that family, or at least some of it, Swedish origins.

Tougher

Tooher, Toher, Togher

Families of the Tougher name are found centered in Co. Mayo in the 19th century. In the 17th century however the family name was a principal one of Kings Co. (Offaly). In the former source, the name of Tooher was also recorded with some 5 births.

Families of the name may spring from two possible sources according to the works of Woulfe. In the province of Connaught the name is often found with the 'g' in it, as Togher, Tougher etc.. Elsewhere we often find the 'g' removed. These spellings have been used interchangeably by many however, making origins hard to trace.

O'Tracy

Irish Book of Arms plates 9, 257

O Treasaigh

Treacy, Tressy, Tracey, Trasey, O'Trassy,

There are several likely unrelated families of the name of Tracey, Treacy..etc.. found in Ireland. In 1890 the Treacy spelling was most popular with 37 births recorded in Tipperary and Galway. Tracey had 31 births in Dublin, and Tracy had 16 births in Dublin. The "O" prefix before the name had largely been dropped by that time.

The Treacy family of Galway/Limerick seems to have favored that spelling at the time of the index, but today in America the name may have changed its form to one of the other variant spellings of the name.

Another family of the name hailed in older times from Co. Cork, where the name is not common today. Some of this line are said to have settled in Limerick as well. This makes things difficult when tracing family lineage at first, for an Anglo-Irish family of the name is on record as having settled there too, becoming baronets in Limerick.

In Co. Leix (Queens Co.) we find mention of another family that served as Lords of Slievemargy, and note in nearby Wexford the place names of Ballytracy and Tracystown.

Although the name was found mainly in Dublin, Tipperary and Galway under three spellings in 1890, older records show a wider scope for the name. In 1659 (O)Tressy was a principal name of Kildare and Fermanagh, Tracey was the same in Louth, Trassey in Kings, and (O)Trassy was so in Tipperary and Limerick. Trasy was a spelling of Kildare at that time.

John Tracey was found in the 2nd Regt. of Corcorans Irish Legion of American fame, and a Tracey also achieved status as a Viscount around 1797, entering the Peerage of Ireland.

O'Trehy

Irish Book of Arms plate 170

O Troighthigh

Troy, Trohy, Trehy, Trahey

In ancient records the O'Trehy family is found in Co. Clare earliest, but they are found centered near Clogheen, in Co. Tipperary subsequently. Note the place name of Ballytrehy in the barony of Iffa and Offa West in Tipperary. Here in Tipperary the name is found as Trohy in the census of 1659, in the baronies of Ikerrin and Eliogarty.

The name is found in Limerick early on as well. The name is a prominent one in the city of Limerick, with several assuming official positions there. Note the place name of Castletroy in that area. They are found here roughly from the time of the 12th century Norman invasions of Ireland.

In the 17th century "Trahey" was a principal name of Kings County (Offaly), and Trohy was the same in Tipperary. By the time of the 1890 birth index the preferred spelling of the name was Troy, with 31 births recorded in Kings, Cork and Tipperary.

Tonge

Tong, Tongue

The family of the name in Ireland is most often found in connection with Co. Wexford and the city of Dublin in our records. The family is generally given to be of English origins when found in Ireland.

Tosh

Despite the relative scarcity of the name, the 1890 birth records give the family still extant in Ireland at that time. Found in the province of Ulster, it is believed to be a simple shortened form of MacIntosh, which is of Scottish origins.

257

Trench

The Irish Book of Arms plate 100

The Trench family of Sopwell Hall, co. Tipperary are given in the Irish Book of Arms.

Trant

According to "Keatings History" the name is that of a principal family of Dublin city or county, and of Anglo-Norman descent. The 1890 birth index finds the family most numerous in Kerry.

Travers

Traverse

The family of Travers may be of English or Irish origins most anciently. A settler family of the name is found in Co. Cork as early as the 16th century. Of the possible Irish origins for the family name, Travers may also have been taken from the older form of O'Treabhair in and around Co. Leitrim.

The 1890 birth index finds the family most numerous in Donegal, Dublin and Leitrim.

Tormey

Torney, Tormy

Families of the name of Tormey are found with nine recorded births in the 1890 index, and most of these were in the province of Leinster. O'Torney is given as a principal name of Co. Fermanagh in the 17th century.
The name is most often linked with county Longford and surrounds in Ireland.

Truell

Irish Book of Arms plate 26

Truel

The Truell family of Clonmannon, Co. Wicklow is found in the Irish Book of Arms.

Mac Traynor, Trainor

Mac Threinfhir

Treanor, Trainor, Trainer, Mc Trenor

Traynor, Treanor, or Trainor families may take their name from the original "Mac Threinfhir" in gaelic. The Mac prefix had generally been dropped by the time of the 1890 birth index.

At that time "Traynor" was the preferred spelling with 35 births listed in Dublin. Treanor had 28 births in Antrim, Armagh and Monaghan, and Trainor had 12 births in Tyrone.

Anciently the family is found on the old lands of Oriel, and the name is predominantly one of Ulster today.

In Gaelic the name of Mac Traynor is said to mean "son of the strong ", hence some adopted the English name of Armstrong. Mac Lysaght gives the spelling of Mac Crainor as a variant of the name, as the "t" at the beginning of the root name is aspirated in gaelic, we have no reports of this however.

In Dublin, the spelling of Traynor was favored. McTrenor, a spelling used in the census of 1659, was given as a principal name of Co. Monaghan.

Tuohy

Traditionally linked to Galway, Clare and Tipperary, 10 variant spellings of the name are on record, including those of Towey, Touhy, Touhey etc.. In 1890 the family is most numerous in Clare and Galway spelled as Tuohy. The spelling of Towey is centered in Roscommon and Mayo at that time.

Tuite

Irish Book of Arms plate 61

de Tiuit

Tuit, Tuitte, de Tiuit

Several spellings of this name are on record in Ireland. In its original form it was spelled as de Tiuit, being of Norman extraction. In the census of 1659 we find it spelled three ways. First, as Tuit in County Roscommon. Secondly as Tuitte, as a principal name of Westmeath. Thirdly, as Tuite, as a name of County Longford. Tuite is also given as a name of the province of Leinster in the 1890 index, and as a Norman name settling in Westmeath in 1172 as found in Milesian families.

Keatings history confirms the Westmeath location for in his words, 'The Tuites received the title of barons of Moyashell in Westmeath'. Additional lineage may be found in Burkes Peerage. The arms cited above are for the family of Westmeath. The Irish Book of Arms gives the family of Tuite, of Sonna, Co. Westmeath, and of Tuite of Sonnagh, Co. Westmeath. Of this line it was said that Richard Le Tuite arrived in Ireland in 1172, obtaining possessions in Co. Westmeath.

Tubrit

Tubridy

A fairly scarce name in Ireland, spelled both as Tubridy and Tubrit, sometimes found in Co. Clare and surrounds.

258

Turnly

The Irish Book of Arms plate 84

Turnley

The Turnly family of Drumnasole, Co. Antrim descend from Francis Turnly of Downpatrick, Co. Down as given in the Irish Book of Arms.

Tumelty

Tumalti, Tumiltey, Tumelty, Tumilty,

Only five births of the name were recorded in the 1890 birth index of Ireland, under the heading of Tumelty, and these were all in the provinces of Leinster and Ulster. Found in fairly widespread locations, i.e. Galway, Monaghan etc.., the name may represent more than one original family in Ireland.

Tunney

Tunny

Anciently found in Sligo and Donegal, the name has been most often linked to Co. Mayo subsequently.

Tuthill

Irish Book of Arms plate 48

The Tuttle family of Kilmore is given in the Irish Book of Arms.

Tweedy

Irish Book of Arms plate 48

Tweedie

Those of the Tweedy name may be of Scottish origins when found in Ireland, for there is a Scottish family of the name, most often spelled Tweedie. A name of the province of Ulster, ten births of the name were recorded in 1890.

The Tweedy family of Cloonamahon, Co. Sligo is found in the Irish Book of Arms.

Turkington

Turkinton

The Turkington family is found centered in Co. Armagh in the 1890 birth index, and this English family is on record there for several centuries.

Turner

The name of Turner may be of English, Scottish or Welsh origins when found in Ireland. It ranks among the top 30 most numerous names in England and Wales. As expected, many of the name are found in the province of Ulster, but the name is scattered throughout the countryside as well. The 1890 birth index finds the family most numerous in Dublin, Antrim, and Cork.

Tutty

Tutthil, Tuttil, Tuttle

Most often the name of an English family or families settling in Ireland from the 17th century onward. They are found with holdings in several counties, including lands in Limerick.

Twamley

Twamly

The name of an English family found to have settled in Co. Wicklow several centuries ago.

O'Twomey

Irish Book of Arms plate 201

O Tuama

Toomey, Toomy, Twomy

O'Twomey and its various spellings belong to a family traditionally associated with Co. Cork. The name is found there in the census of 1659 in some numbers, and it remains so to this day.

In that same census we find that O'Twomy was a principal name of Cork City. In 1890 Twomey is found in Cork and Kerry, while Toomey was found in Dublin and Limerick, in much lesser numbers. The "O" prefix before the name had generally been dropped by that time.

John Toomey of Limerick has been cited as a miscellaneous poet who died in 1775.

Tynte

Irish Book of Arms plate 47

Tynt

The Tynte family of Tynte Park and Saunders Grove, Co. Wicklow and Tynte Lodge Co. Leitrim, descend from a family originally of Somerset before settling in Ireland.

Tynan

Tynane

The family of Tynan has traditionally been linked to Co. Leix (Queens Co.), down into modern times.

259

Tyrell

Irish Book of Arms plate 267, 268

Tyrrell

Tyrell is an Anglo-Norman family arriving in Ireland with the 12th century invasions. They are noted for settling in areas around Dublin, Kildare and in Westmeath. Note the place names of Tyrells pass and Tyrellstown in the barony of Fertullagh in Westmeath. Older maps will show several locations in different counties bearing the name. In more modern times the family is often found in Co. Wicklow.

Several branches of the name are found on record in Ireland, including Tirrell of Westmeath and Dublin, Tyrell, Mayor of Dublin, and Tyrrell of Dublin. Mentioned are those of Athboy, Symonstown, Kilbride, Caverstown and Fertulagh in Co. Westmeath.

In 1890 the family is most numerous in Dublin, Kildare and Wicklow.

...

Uniacke

Irish Book of Arms plate 39

Unack, Uniack

The name of a family closely identified with Co. Cork. In 1659 we find the spelling of Unack there, townlands of the name of Mount Uniacke are found.

The Uniacke family of Mt. Uniacke, Co. Cork, is found in the 16th century near Youghal. The Uniacke family of Castletown, Co. Cork is as well given in the Irish Book of Arms.

Upton

The Irish Book of Arms plate 80

The Upton family of Coolatore, Moate, Co. Westmeath descend from Arthur Upton of L'Upton, as given in the Irish Book of Arms.

...

Ussher

Irish Book of Arms plate 73

Usher

A settler family in Ireland of Norman origins, one line of the name was said to have taken on the name of Ussher, as a result of their occupation held at that time in service to the king. Their original name before the change was that of Nevill.

The family is found most prominent in the county and city of Dublin in early records and they are also found in Armagh, Waterford and Galway. The Ussher family of Eastwell, Co. Galway descend from Arland Ussher, Bailiff of Dublin in 1460.

Christopher Ussher was twice the Mayor of Dublin city. Henry Ussher is cited as the Archbishop of Armagh, and in Waterford one of the name served as M.P.. The family is given in O'Harts work as one of the chief families settling in Waterford and Dublin.

Some Irish families of the name of Hession, took on the surname of Ussher on occasion.

Vandeleur

The Irish Book of Arms plate 91

Van Deleur, Deleur

The Vandeleur family of Kilrush, and Cahiracon, Co. Clare descend from Giles Van Deleur, who settled at Rathlahine, Co. Clare around 1660.

Mac Vaddock

Wadeck, Bhaday

One old family of the name in Ireland is said to be found in and about the town of Gorey in Co. Wexford. It was said that the name was sometimes rendered as Bhaday in English.

de Valences

According to "Keatings History" the name is that of an ancient titled family in Co. Wexford. They are given as lords of Wexford.

Vallely

Vallily, Vally

Vallely is given as a name centered in Co. Armagh in the 19th century birth index. The name of Varrilly is given as a variant of Vallely on occasion, but Varrilly is a separate name unto itself also.

Vance

One family of the name is said to be found centered in and around Coagh, Co. Tyrone, with a branch in Co. Antrim as well. The family is found in Dublin as well, said to be of English extraction, found at Rutlandsquare in Dublin. The family is also mentioned in Dungannon.

The 1890 birth index finds the family most numerous in Antrim.

260

Mc Veagh

Irish Book of Arms plate 33

Mac an Bheatha

Mc Vey, Mc Bay, Mc Veigh

The McVeagh family of Drewtown, Co. Meath is found in the Irish Book of Arms.

The is the name of an Irish family traditionally linked to the province of Ulster in Ireland.

Veale

Veal, le Veel

The Veale family is found centered in Co. Waterford (in the barony of Decies), from the time of the census of 1659 and prior. The original name has also been said to have been translated as "Calf" as well as Veale. The 1890 birth index finds the family most numerous in Waterford.

Verdon

Verdun, de Verdun

The Verdon family is on record in Ireland roughly from the time of the Norman invasions of the 12th century. They became a family of some note, with considerable holdings in Co. Louth. Note the place name of Verdonstown there. One branch of the family is known to have settled in Limerick in the 16th century where they were also of some note. Originally from Verdun in France by most accounts, the family is said to have settled in England, and thus moved into Ireland with the Norman invasions. The 17th century also finds the name a principal one of Co. Roscommon.

Vernon

Irish Book of Arms plate 38, 101

We find one family of the name coming from England and settling near Clontarf, Co. Dublin and at Ballyhugh Co. Cavan. Another family is found, that of John Vernon, of Clonmore, in the barony of Ardee, Co. Louth, who lost lands in the Cromwellian settlement.

The Vernon family of Erne Hill, Co. Cavan descends from a family found earliest at Clontarf Castle in Co. Dublin.

The Vernon family of Clontarf Castle are given in the Irish Book of Arms.

Verschoyle

Irish Book of Arms plate 38

The Verschoyle family of Cashelshanaghan, and of Ballybodonnel, and of Dunkineely in Co. Donegal, are found in the Irish Book of Arms. The family of Verschoyle of Kilberry, Co. Kildare came from Holland in the 16th century as a result of religious persecution, settling in Dublin in the 17th century.

Vigors

Irish Book of Arms plate 36

The Vigors family of Burgage, Co. Carlow, stems from a family of foreign origins of North Devon, the first of the name said to have settled in Ireland was born in 1578.

Mc Vitty

MacViety, Mac Veety, Mavity, Mac Vitty,

A family found in Co. Longford in our records.

Vaughan

Irish Book of Arms plate 70

Vaughn, Vaughan, Vaughen

Families of the name of Vaughan in Ireland may spring from any of several different origins. Some of the name are of Welsh extraction, other of old Irish heritage and others still are of unknown settler origins.

Note the place name of Ballyvaughan in Co. Clare, and several Irish families of the name hail from that county and its surrounds. Most of the name are found in the province of Munster in official records on file.

The Vaughan family of Quilly, Co. Down descend from the first of that family in Ireland which was Rev. George Vaughan b. 1634, who stayed at Ardee for some period of time.

261

Wakely

Irish Book of Arms plate 78

Wakeley

One family of the name is found at Ballyburly, Kings County (Co. Offaly), in Ireland in the early 17th century, and that family is given in the Irish Book of Arms.

Wadding

According to "Keatings History" the name is among the chief families of English descent settling in Waterford and Tipperary. These English families primarily possessed the territory called from them Gal-tir, signifying the country of the foreigners," now the barony of Gaultiere."

Wade

Quade, McQuade

Families of the name of Wade in Ireland are generally considered to be of English extraction. The name is found concentrated in Dublin for several centuries. Due to similarity in sound, the names of Wade and McQuaid are said to have been confused at times.

Waldron

Waldren

Most of the name of Waldron in Ireland are of English extraction. Several families of the name are found settled in the midlands of Ireland however, and one branch of the Costelloe family of Mayo is said to have assumed the name of Waldron in the past. The 1890 birth index finds the family most numerous in Mayo, Roscommon and Dublin.

Wall

Irish Book of Arms plate 171

de Valle

Walls, Wale

The earliest records of the Wall family are as "de Valle" "du val" or "De Vale", and it is also found early spelled as Wale and Faltagh. O'Donovan gives Faltagh as the common form of the name. It is also be noted that Wall is a name found in England, and this accounts for some of the name in Ireland as well.

The Wall family believed to be of Norman origins first spelled the name as "de Valle" etc.., said to originally mean "of the valley". Some of the name are found in 12th century Dublin records.

The family name is also found in the barony of Rathvilly, in Ardristan, Co. Carlow, and in the barony of Forth. In Kilkenny the family is found in the barony of Shillelogher. Note the place name of Wallstown in Co. Cork, commemorating the family name there.

In 1659 Wall was a principal name of Co. Clare, and found in Limerick and Kilkenny as well. The spelling of Wale was found in Tipperary and Waterford at that time, but O'Wale was given as a completely separate name in Co. Roscommon.

"Walls", likely a completely separate name for most, had some 11 births recorded in 1890, in scattered locations mainly in the province of Ulster.

Wall, with 58 births of the name recorded at that time was found in Dublin, Waterford, Cork, Limerick and Tipperary etc.. Keatings History also found the name in Waterford, Tipperary and Dublin more anciently.

The Irish Book of Arms gives the family of West Muskerry, Co. Cork, centered in Dunmoylen and also in Coolnamuck and Kilrush Castle.

"The Wall Family in Ireland 1170 - 1970" by Hubert Gallwey was published in Dublin in 1970.

Waller

The Irish Book of Arms plate 87, 107, 109

The Waller family of Allenstown Co. Meath, and the Waller family of Castletown and Castle Grey, Co. Limerick are of the same line and are given in the Irish Book of Arms.

The Waller family of Prior Park, Co. Tipperary is also found in the Irish Book of Arms, as is the Waller family of Rockvale, Co. Tipperary. The family is given to descend from one William Warren, alias Waller. All of the above families are given in the Irish Book of Arms.

Walker

The family name of 'Walker' when found in Ireland is considered to be an English name. The name is found most commonly in Dublin and in Ulster in Ireland. In America the name ranks as the 20th most popular of all surnames.

The census of 1659 records the family name in Counties Tipperary, Kings, and Fermanagh. Milesian families gives the name as English and settling in Wexford in 1580. The 1890 index gives the name in Counties Antrim and Dublin, much the same as it remains today.

Wallace

Wallis, Walis, Walsh

Most of the name of Wallace in Ireland are given to be of Scottish extraction, settling in the province of Ulster in the 17th century. The name of Walsh has been interchanged with Wallace at times, notably in Co. Galway, as given by the registrar of Ireland circa 1890.

One Wallis family is found centered at Killeny, in Queens Co., in the late 17th century. Subsequently the family is also found at Portrane, Co. Dublin.

262

Walsh, Welsh

Irish Book of Arms plates 49, 133, 171

Welshman

Welch, Walshe

Walsh is the 4th most popular name in Ireland, following only Murphy, Kelly and Sullivan. Today it is recognized as an "Irish" name, even though the origins of the name are from Wales.

The reason for the great number of the name here is that anyone from Wales could have become Walsh or Welsh, because it denoted a Welshman. Hence, other Welsh names were put aside for the name of Walsh. In Ulster the name of Mac Bratney has been taken on by some, meaning the "son of the Welshman". (from Breathnach)

Several adopted the name with the coming of the 12th century Norman invasions in Ireland. Phillip the Welshman, (i.e. Phillip Walsh) did so. His line is found settled in Kilkenny at Castlehowel, in Waterford at Ballyrichmore, in Leix at Ballykileavan and in Dublin around Bray and Carrickmines.

Place names commemorating the family name are numerous. Note the names of Walshtown, and the name of Walsh Mountains in Kilkenny.

Another family of the name in Mayo is believed to have descended from another Welshman who arrived at the time of the Norman invasions. This is but one example of such.

In the 1890 index "Walsh" was the most popular spelling of the name with 887 recorded births in Cork, Mayo and Waterford. Walshe was of Galway, Dublin and Wexford, and Welsh was of Antrim at that time.

Maurice Walsh (d. 1964), wrote the book "The Quiet Man", upon which the well known movie is based.

The Irish Book of Arms finds Walsh of Fanningstown, Co. Kilkenny, & Walsh of Mul Hussey, Co. Roscommon.

Wandesforde

The Irish Book of Arms plate 108

The Wandesforde family of Castlecomer, Co. Kilkenny Ireland, and of Kirklington, Hipswell, and Hudswell abroad in Co. York, is given in the Irish Book of Arms.

Mac Walter

Qualter, Walters, Walter

The name of MacWalter was used by a branch of the Burke family of Connaught and other Norman families.

In the census of 1659 the family of Walter is given in Tipperary and Cork. McWalter was given as a principal name of Co. Carlow. "Walters" was a name of Co. Clare then, and some of them may descend from the Burkes originally.

In the 1890 index 5 births are found under the spelling of Walters, centered in Ulster. Some of the name are doubtless of foreign origins when found in Ireland.

Warke

Warick

The name of an English family said to have settled in Ireland primarily found in the province of Ulster. The name of Warick, sometimes found in Fermanagh, bears no known relationship to this.

Mc Vicker

Vicar, Mac Vickar, Vickers

The name of Scottish families who settled in Ulster, where the name is most numerous today. In the 1890 birth index the family was centered in counties Antrim and Londonderry. The name of Vickers also represents a completely separate family in other parts of Ireland.

Warburton

The Irish Book of Arms plate 70

The family of Warburton of Garryhinch, Kings Co. is given in the Irish Book of Arms.

Waters,

Mac Watters, Watters, de Auters

Waters may be of English or Irish origin when found in Ireland. There are settler families from England of the name as well as older Irish families. The origin of the English name seems to stem from 'water' and also from the personal name of Walter.

When spelled as Watters or MacWatters the name is often found in the province of Ulster.

It has also been stated that the 'Waters' of County Cork is derived from 'de Auters', a Norman name established there in the end of the 12th century.

There are several Gaelic names from which the form 'Waters' was developed. O huisce, from the province of Connaught and was probably also translated into Hiskey, Heskin, and Hoskins. Mac Uaitear, which can be found in the older Fiants, usually in the province of Leinster where MacWatters and MacQuatters are found as well. Mac Con Uisce, (from cu = hound and uisce = water?), a minor family near Farney, County Monaghan. They were associated with the Mac Mahon family in earlier times.

McWatters is found in Antrim in 1890, and Watters is given in Tyrone, Antrim and Louth at that time. Waters however, was a name of Cork in 1659, and of Sligo, Wexford and Monaghan in the 1890 index.

263

Mac Ward

Irish Book of Arms plates 70, 237

Mac an Ward

Ward, Macanward, Mac Award

Families of the 'Ward' name in Ireland may spring from either English or older Irish origins. In fact, the "Ward" surname can be found in England and Wales, thus some of the name in Ireland are of that extraction originally.

The Irish families of the name can descend from "Mac an Bhaird" in Donegal. This family served as bards to the O'Donnells, and they were 'very learned men' according to Keatings History. They were of some repute in those times, for they as well served the O'Kellys of Galway in that capacity. Note the place names of Ballymacward in Galway and Lettermacaward in Donegal standing in tribute to the family name.

In Galway the family is found in the barony of Tiaquin, where they served as one of the 6 chiefs of Sodhan, according to O'Dugan. The main chief of the area was O'Manning or O'Mannin, the other chiefs were O'Scurry, O'Lennan, O'Cashin, O'Giallain and O'Maginn.

Those of the name seeking to find some coat of arms for the same will find that the English family of Co. Down, (viscounts Bangor), carry the most well known and displayed heraldry today.

The variant spellings of Mac an ward and Mac Award are closer to the original gaelic spelling of the name used.

A century ago the name was most common in Donegal and Galway, a traditional homeland for the family. The name was also concentrated in Dublin at that time, as so many Irish family names are as a result of the attraction of that large city.

The Irish Book of Arms gives Ward of Bangor Castle, Co. Down.

Warren

Irish Book of Arms plate 91

Note the place name of Warrens Court in Co. Cork, marking the territory of the family in Co. Cork, where they are found centered in the barony of Carbery in earlier times. Most of the name are given to be of English extraction when found in Ireland, and families of the name are on record in Monaghan and Wicklow as such.

One English family of the name is found in Co. Down in the 17th century, centered in Waringtown, Co. Down, and also in Lurgan, Co. Armagh.

The Warren family of Rathfarnham Park, Co. Dublin and of Ballydonarea, Co. Wicklow, descend from Robert Warren, of Carson, Co. Monaghan.

The birth index of 1890 finds the family centered in Kerry, Cork and Dublin.

Mac Warnock

Warnock is the name of a family found centered in counties Tyrone and Down in the 1890 birth index of Ireland. Of Scottish origins, the family is a branch of the clan Graham. Primarily a name of the province of Ulster.

Watson

Most of the name in Ireland are assumed to be of Scottish heritage, but since the name ranks among the top 30 most numerous in Scotland, Wales and England, it is often difficult to determine origins in Ireland. Families of the name have settled over time in Ireland, and are found settling in Ulster in the 17th century along with many others. The name is given to mean "Son of Wat" or son of Walter.

The 1890 birth index finds the family most numerous in Antrim, Armagh and Down.

Webb

Irish Book of Arms plate 78

Webber

Families of the name of Webb in Ireland are given to be of settler origin when found here. They are among the families found settling in Ulster in the 17th century, centered in Co. Antrim at that time. Not unexpectedly the family is also found in Dublin records, and the name is often found outside these areas as well.

The Webb family of Kilmore, Nenagh, Co. Tipperary, and of Knocktoran, Knocklong, Co. Limerick is given in the Irish Book of Arms.

The birth index of 1890 finds the family centered in Dublin and Antrim.

Mac Wattin

According to "Keatings History" the name is given as an Irish name which was also adopted by Anglo-Norman or English families in lieu of their original surnames.

The Barrett family of Co. Mayo is said to have adopted the name of MacWattin.

Waugh

Waughe

The name of a family of the province of Ulster in Ireland, they are also found in Scotland and northern England, where the family earlier hailed from. Some times the name of Mac Veigh etc..has been confused with Waugh, and the name of Mac Waugh is also extant. Five births under the heading of Waugh are recorded in 1890, all in the province of Ulster.

264

Webber

Irish Book of Arms plate 41

The Webber family of Leekfield and Kellavil, Co. Sligo, and of Kellavil, Queens Co., and of Mitchelstown Castle Co. Cork, are given to be of the same origins, and are given as such in the Irish Book of Arms.

Mc Way

Mac Aodha (son of Hugh)

Mac Wey, MacQuey, MacQuay, Mackey...

MacWay is said to be a form of Mackay or Mac Aodha of more ancient origin. It is most likely of Scottish derivation when found in Ireland. The name of 'Way', without the Mc prefix, is found in the Census of 1659 in the county of Cork.

Other possible related spellings may include: Mac Waughe found in the Co. Donegal Hearth Money Rolls, and the name of MacVeagh.

A fairly rare name in Irish records, you must consider variant spellings when looking for your family name.

Weaver

Weever, Weafer, Wafer

Most likely an English name when found in Ireland. Some give the Weaver family as English, settling in 1640 in Dublin and Limerick. In the census of 1659 the name is found in Kings County (Offaly).

The name of Weafer is that of a family most often linked to Co. Wexford from the 17th century onwards, with earlier origins in Co. Meath.

Mc Weeney

Mc Weeny, Mc Wynee

Families of the name of McWeeney are found centered in Co. Leitrim in the 19th century. More anciently they hailed from Co. Roscommon.

West

Irish Book of Arms plate 133

One noted family of the name is traced back to Rock, Co. Wexford, no later that the 17th century.

Weir

Wier, MacWeir

Most families of the name of Weir are considered to be of Scottish extraction, and the name is traditionally found in the province of Ulster in Ireland. Some of the name may be of older Irish origins in that area, but research remains unclear on that.

The 1890 birth index finds the family most numerous in Antrim and Armagh.

Weldon

de Weldon, Veldon

Families of the name are found centered in Co. Meath in the census of 1659. Two centuries later we find the name most often in the province of Leinster, with 14 recorded births of the name in 1890. Several of the name are found settling in Ireland quite early, presumably from England. One landed family of the name is found in Co. Leix (Queens) and Co. Kildare.

Wellesley

de Wellesley

One noted family of the name is said to have been in Ireland since the 13th century, and settled notably at Dangan, in Co. Meath. Of this line was the Baron Mornington (created in 1746).

...

Westby

The Irish Book of Arms plate 56

The Westby family of Roebuck Castle, Co. Dublin and Kilballyowen and Rosroe in Co. Clare are given to be of the same line, as found in the Irish Book of Arms.

Westropp

Irish Book of Arms plate s 28, 60, 123, 128.

Westrop, Westhrop

Families of the name of Westropp are traditionally linked to counties Limerick and Clare in Ireland, on record as having settled in Limerick in the 16th century.

Ralph Westropp of Maryfort is listed in O'Harts pedigree of O'Moroney of Clare and America pedigree.

The Irish Book of Arms gives the family of Westropp of Att Flin, Co. Clare, and the Westropp family of Mellon, Co. Limerick.

Some 26 births of the name are found in the 1890 birth index, in scattered locations.

265

Whelen, Phelan

Irish Book of Arms plates 167, 214

O Faolain

Felan, Whalan, Phellane, Phalen, Whelan,

The family names of Whelan and Phelan stem from the same Irish name of O'Faolain. Together, they form one of the top 50 most numerous surnames in all of Ireland, with Whelan being the most popular spelling of the two forms, by a 2 to 1 margin.

Phelan is found mainly in Waterford, Kilkenny, Queens (Leix), and Tipperary. Whelan is mainly found in Dublin, Wexford, Waterford, Tipperary and Carlow in the 1890 birth index. Anciently the name is often found in the province of Ulster.

Anciently, before the 12th century Norman invasions of Ireland, the O'Phelans were known as the princes of Desi. Subsequently they lost their lands and titles in Co. Waterford. Their holdings were taken by the Le Poers and other settler families in the wake of the aforementioned invasions. They are given in Keatings History as numerous in the same counties as given in the 1890 birth index, that is, in Waterford, Tipperary, Kilkenny and Queens counties.

Of the same descent at O'Bric, the other chief of the Decies, they are thus cited by Aryan;

"Two gentle chiefs whose names I tell,
Rulle the Desi, I affirm it,
O'Bric the exactor of tributes,
With him the wise and fair O'Felan.
In Moylacha of the fertile slopes,
Rules O'Felan for the benefit of his tribe,
Great is the allotted territory,
Of which O'Felan holds possession."

A branch of this Decies family of Waterford was settled in the barony of Iverk in Co. Kilkenny.

White

Irish Book of Arms plates 34, 67, 73,85

Bannon

Whyte, Whight, Bane, Bawn

White is among the 100 most numerous names in Ireland. The name is found throughout the country, and most are of original English stock. These English families have likely settled in Ireland ever since the 12th century Norman invasions.

The family is found located in Clare, Galway, Limerick, Waterford and Kilkenny early. Many are found as owners of large tracts of land and as local officials in early Irish records.

The Norman families are cited as settling in Co. Cork early, and as obtaining some prominence there. They are also cited as a family of English descent in Tipperary and Waterford in Keatings History. The name is further cited as a chief Anglo-Norman or English family to settle in Ulster.

The name of White is also cited by some as being of Welsh extraction.

Old Irish families may bear the name, several surnames were translated into White in earlier times. The Irish word for white is "ban". Hence, names such as Bane or Bawn, had their surnames translated into "White".

Note the place name of Whyteshall, Co. Kilkenny.

The preferred spelling is "White", which had 269 births recorded mainly in Antrim, Cork, Dublin and Wexford, in the 1890. When spelled as Whyte, 22 births of the name were found.

Several locations have been noted concerning this family, including the families of White at Loughbricland, Co. Down, those of Clongell, Co Meath, those of Limerick, those of Whytes Hall, Co. Kilkenny, of Gracefield in Queens Co. and those of Clonmel.

White is also found as a Huguenot family of Ireland/Great Britain.

Whitney

Irish Book of Arms plate 83

Whitny, Whittny, de Whitney, Whiteney

The Whittny family is given in Queens county in the 17th century, and the 1890 birth index finds the family centered in counties Longford and Wexford under the spelling of Whitney. Some undocumented sources give at least one family of the name Welsh origins.

The Whitney family of Brayfort, Bray, Co. Wicklow, are found in the Irish Book of Arms.

Whitaker

Whitacre, Whiteacre, Whytacre, Whitegar,

Several variant spellings of the name exist as shown in part above. Considered in more modern times to be a name of the province of Ulster, early records find the name more scattered, and today several of the name are found in Co. Cork as well. The family name is considered to be of foreign extraction when found in Ireland.

Whitty

Mc Whitty, Whittey

The census of 1659 and the 1890 birth index of Ireland both place the Whitty family in Co. Wexford, where the family is of long standing, and it may be of Norman origins there. The family is also found in some numbers in Co. Waterford.

Wilkinson

Most of the name of Wilkinson in Ireland are given to be originally of English extraction, settling in Ireland over time. The 1890 birth index finds the family most numerous in Antrim and Armagh.

266

Wilson

Irish Book of Arms plates 26, 42, 90, 102, 125

Willison, Willson

Wilson is one of the most popular names in the regions surrounding Ireland. It is the 8th most numerous name in Scotland, the 11th most numerous name of England, and the 26th most common name in Ireland itself.

Hence, most of the name likely arrived in Ireland over time as settler families. Early records find the name in Antrim, and the province of Ulster remains the concentrated area of the name.

The Wilson family of Daramona House, Co. Westmeath, is supposed to have descended from the family of the name found in Co. Antrim in the 17th century.

The Wilson family of Maryville and Cranmore, Co. Antrim, are said to descend from an old established family of Dumfriesshire and are given in the Irish Book of Arms.

The 1890 birth index finds 366 births of the name recorded mainly in Antrim, Armagh, Down, Tyrone, Dublin, Londonderry and Fermanagh.

Willis

Willis is a name given to be that of English families who settled in Ireland. The name can be found in several areas in Ireland. The 1890 birth index finds the family most numerous in Antrim and Down.

Willmore

Willmer, Wellmore

A scarce name in Ireland, we find some of the family in Dublin, and in scattered locations earlier in history. The name is likely of English origins.

Winter

The Irish Book of Arms plate 54

Winters

The Winter family of Agher, Co. Meath and of Lisnabin, Co. Westmeath are of the same line, and are given in the Irish Book of Arms.

...

Wogan

Irish Book of Arms plate 59

Wogane

According to "Keatings History" the name is that of a principal family of Dublin city or county, and of Anglo-Norman descent.

We find a family of the name centered one time at New-Hall, Co. Kildare

Woodside

A fairly rare name in Irish records, the birth index of 1890 finds the family in the counties of Antrim and Dublin. The name like so many others, is one of the many settler names in Ireland. A search of the city records in Dublin and Belfast would likely prove most fruitful.

Woods

Irish Book of Arms Wood plate 86

various origins

Wood, Quill, Quilly

One Woods family is given as an English one, settling in Dublin in 1640. It is also found in Cork, Limerick, Meath and Dublin. In modern times the name is found in Antrim and Armagh.

The name of Wood (without the 's'), is found in Milesian families as English, arriving in Co. Sligo in 1649. In the census of 1659 the name is found in Sligo, Leitrim, Cork and Dublin.

Concerning variant spellings, names such as Woodsy and Woodside could have been shortened to form Woods or Wood. Some are English when found in Ireland, others are of ancient Irish heritage. The name has been used as a variant spelling of MacIlhoyle, Quilty, and MacEnhill to name just three examples. (some variants are based on the word for 'wood' in gaelic.)

The name is found most often spelled as "Woods" rather than "Wood", the latter of which is one of the top 20 names in England and Wales.

The Wood-Martin family of Cleveragh, Sligo are found in the Book of Arms.

Wolverston

One family of the name is found buried in the churchyard of Kiladreney according to O'Hart, one mile from Newtown - Mountkennedy near the main road from Dublin and Wexford. This was the family of Captain William Wolverston (d.1731).

Woodlock

According to "Keatings History" the name is that of a principal family of Dublin city or county, and of Anglo-Norman descent.

267

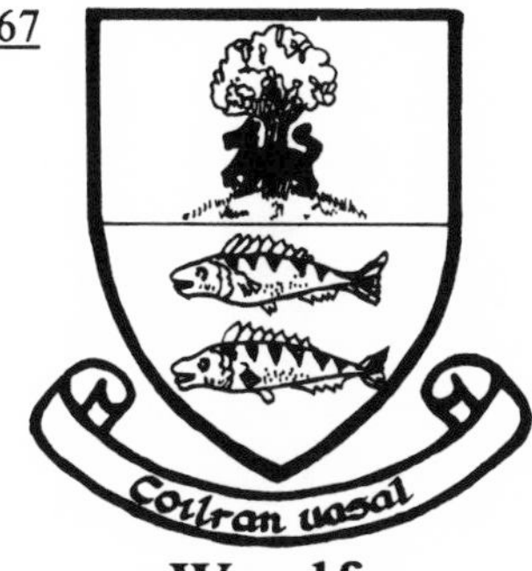

Woulfe

Irish Book of Arms plates 77, 171

de Bhulbh (le Woulf)

Wolf, Wolfe, Woolfe, Wulf, Ulf

The Woulfe families arrived in Ireland mainly as a result of the early Norman invasions of Ireland in the 12th century. In County Kildare 'Woulfe's Country' bore the name of the family and were located near Athy.

The family also held a great amount of land in Cork and Limerick. The Wolfes of Forenaughts (of Kildare) held lands in Limerick well into the 19th century. Records in the city of Limerick often bear the name of Woulfe as well.

Ancient records also show a gaelic sept of O'Mactire of eastern Co. Cork. Since the Gaelic for Mactire means wolf, it could have easily been translated into English as such.

Fr. Patrick Woulfe was the noted author of "Sloinnte Gaedeal is Gall", or Irish Names and Surnames. We owe him a debt of gratitude for his research on Irish family names.

Although in more modern times the name has been concentrated in county Limerick, Wolfe and Woolfe are both listed in County Clare in the 1659 census.

The Irish Book of Arms gives the family of Woulfe of Tiermaclane Co. Clare. That family originally came from Limerick.

Published works of possible interest:
1) The Wolfe Family of Co. Kildare. George Wolfe. 1899 - 1902. Journal of Co. Kildare Arch. Society.
2) Wolfes of Forenaghts, Blackhall, Baronrath, Co. Kildare and Tipperary. R.T. Wolfe. 1893.

Wright

Irish Book of Arms plate 68, 134

Right

This name is given to be that of settler families arriving from England and Wales, for the name ranks among the top 50 most numerous in both of those countries. As expected, most of the name are found settled in Ulster, with a fair number found in the records of the city of Dublin.

The 1890 birth index finds the family most numerous in Antrim, Down, Dublin and Armagh.

Wybrants

One family of the name is found originally as a merchant from Antwerp, settling in Ireland in the city of Dublin in the early 17th century.

Wyer

Weir, Wyre

The name of a family, under the Wyer spelling, associated in the past with Co. Westmeath. The names of Wyer and Weir have been used as synonyms for some time in Ireland. The census of 1659 records the name of Wyre as a principal one of Co. Westmeath as well.

Wylder

Wyld, Wilde, Wylie, Wilders, de Wylde

Wilder is found in the Poll Money Ordinance Surveys around 1660, and the name of Wilders is found in County Longford in the census of 1659.

"de Wylde" is given to be in Ireland subsequent to the Norman invasions and has been found quite early in Dublin and Limerick.

Wyse

Irish Book of Arms plate 62

Wise

According to "Keatings History" the name is among the chief families of English descent settling in Waterford and Tipperary. These English families primarily possessed the territory called from them Gal-tir, signifying the country of the foreigners," now the barony of Gaultiere."

The Wyse family of the Manor of St. John's, Co. Waterford originally hailed from Greston in Cornwall.

Wylie

Wily, Wiley, Wily

The name of several settler families in Ireland, arriving in Ulster no later than the 17th century. The family is found centered in Co. Antrim at that time, represented by both Scottish and English families of the name. The 1890 birth index finds the family most numerous in Antrim.

Wynn

Wynne

The name of a family from Wales found settling in Co. Sligo in the 17th century on one occasion. The name is found most often across the mid-section of Ireland. The 1890 birth index finds the family most numerous in Dublin and Sligo.

268

Williams

Irish Book of Arms plate 268

Mac Uilliam

William, McWilliam, Mac Quillan,

There are several possible origins of the name of Williams in Ireland. In Keatings History the story of two branches of the name will prove interesting. In the beginning of the 14th century two principal families of the name of Burke became "MacWilliam", and in doing so became completely Irish. They held large possessions in Mayo (Edmund Burke). Ulick Burke, of the Earls of Clanrickare, held lands in Galway and Roscommon.

In addition to the possible Norman origins cited above, MacWilliams may also be a branch of the Scottish clan Mac Farlane. MacWilliam has also been used as a synonym of MacQuillan in Co. Down.

According to "Keatings History" the name of Mac William is given as an Irish name which was also adopted by Anglo-Norman or English families in lieu of their original surnames. This is the name adopted by one branch of the Burke or De Burgo family of Connaught as cited above. The name is as well among the top 3 most numerous surnames in England and Wales, hence many of the name are originally of those origins when found in Ireland.

In modern times the name is found mainly in Antrim and Londonderry, as evidenced by the 1890 birth index of Ireland. MacWilliam is found as a principal name of Limerick in 1659. McWilliam was a principal name of Co. Clare as well as being found in Cork at that time.

The birth index of 1890 finds the family name of Williamson centered in Antrim, Armagh, Londonderry and Tyrone. It is estimated that there are over 20,000 people of the name today in America.

Young

Irish Book of Arms plate 23, 95

Most of the name of Young are of Scottish heritage when found in Ireland, for the name ranks among the top 20 most numerous in Scotland itself. Found mostly concentrated in the province of Ulster as would be expected, families of the name are also on record in Roscommon and Donegal.

One family of the name is found centered at Annahilla, Co. Tyrone, no later than the year 1700. One of that line settled in San Francisco (USA), and was an official in that city.

The Young family of Harristown, Co. Roscommon is given in the Irish Book of Arms. This family is said to have arrived in Ireland in the persons of the brothers who settled in Castlerea, Co. Roscommon in the year 1706.

The Young family of Brockley Park, Stradbally, Queens Co., are of Scottish descent, and most of the name of Young are said to have settled in Co. Londonderry and subsequently in Co. Antrim in the 17th century. This family is said to descend from Samuel Young, of Portglenone, Co. Antrim in the early part of the 18th century.

The Young family of Galgorm Castle, Co. Antrim, appears to be of the same line as the foregoing Young family and both of them are given in the Irish Book of Arms.

...

Vesey

The Irish Book of Arms plate 88

The Vesey family of Derrabard, Co. Tyrone, descend from George Vesey of Hollymount, Co. Mayo and are given in the Irish Book of Arms.

Yourell

Uriel, Iriel, Eurell, de Urielle, Urrell

The name of a Norman family most often linked to Co. Westmeath, where the family was of some note in the past.

Yeats

Yeates, Yeats, Yates

The Yeats or Yates..etc.. family is traditionally linked to Dublin when found in Ireland. A settler name in Ireland, the family is also a noted one of Co. Sligo in past times. William Butler Yeats (1865-1957) was the noted poet of the name in modern times.

The Yeats family is as well, listed among the adventurers for land in Ireland in the 16th century.

The 1890 birth index finds the family most numerous in Antrim and Dublin when spelled as Yeates, and in Co. Cork when spelled as Yates.

Locations

Part II

17th - 19th Century Locations

Locations

Extracts from the 'Master Book of Irish Surnames'

Partial listings taken from the 'Master Book of Irish Surnames' which contains over 80,000 Irish Surname / Source / Location listings from the IGF Library. Space does not permit a full listing of surnames or information here.
For more information consult the original work which contains 50,000 listings not shown here.

Key

PN = Principal name in 1659.
PMO= Poll Money Ordnance.
*** = Special location, see page 295-296.**
Irish Counties Sometimes Abbreviated.

(Names are listed as if the O' or Mac before the name were removed, hence O'Connor is found with Connor, etc..)

Location Index

Locations of Irish families from the 17th to the 19th centuries. These entries are part of fuller listings as found in "The Complete Book of Irish Family Names." Names are listed alphabetically - ignoring the Mac or O prefix. i.e. O'Conner = Connor. An * denotes special location as given at the end of this index.

Key: PN = Principal Name in 1659 in county -------.
PMO= Poll Money Ordnance @ 1660.
Wat= county Waterford. Ker = Co. Kerry..etc...
Lond = Co. Londonderry Long = Co. Longford
* = special location given on page 295 - 296.

ABBOT PMO
ABBOTT FER,CORK / DUI
ABDY PMO
Abercrumber LEITRIM.
ABOTT TIP.
ABRAHAM CORK/ ARMA(
ABSOM LIM
ACHESON ANTRIM,ARMA
ACHMOOTY AUGHMUT
ACHYSON ARMAGH.
ACKLAND KILKENNY.
ACTERY WESTMEATH.
ADAIR LEIX,1170 A.D., SA
ADAIRE LONG, ANTRIM.
MC ADAM P.N. DUB.CIT
ADAMS CORK,KILK,LNDE
ADAMSON ARMAGH, DO
ADARE PMO
Mac ADARRA ALSO LOU
MC ADARRAH *450
ADAYRE PMO
ADDERLY CORK.
ADDERTON KILKENNY.
ADGER *433,*503.
ADHBENSON KINGS
ADHOW KILKENNY.
ADIRE ANTRIM
ADLUM *74, ALSO ODLUN
ADORIAN *411/ DOWN.
ADRIAN PMO
ADRYAN DUBLIN
MC AFEE ANTRIM.
AFFLACK *429
AFFLECK *429
AGAR *303, ALSO SEE EAC
AGGAS WESTMEATH.
AGHARNE CORK.
AGHERIN CLARE.
O AGHERNS CORK
AGHMONTY PMO
AGHMOOTY LONGFORD.
AGHWELL DUBLIN CITY.
M' AGHY ANTRIM
AGNEW ANTRIM 1659 / AN
AHEARN CORK, LIM, 9 BI
AHEARNE *77
AHERLY LIMERICK
AHERN CORK, LIM,92 BIR
AHERNE CORK , LIM, *77 /
AHMONTY PMO
AICKEN *55
AIDY *310, ALSO ADAMS.
AIKEN ANTRIM

AIKENS *410
AILDWOOD PN OF KILKE
AILMER KILDARE
AKMOOTH PMO
MC ALARY *19
M' ALASHER *319
MC ALASHER *276
MC ALAY *60
ALBONAGH PN SLIGO
ALCOCK CORK,PMO / 5 B
ALCORN LIM,CLARE,1690
ALDERDICE ANTRIM, AR
ALDERSEE WESTMEATH
MC ALDIN *429
ALDING DUBLIN CITY
ALDRICH MONAGHAN
ALDRIDGE *249, ALSO AL
ALDWARTH CORK CITY
ALDWOOD KILKENNY
ALDWORTH PMO/ DUBLI
ALE WATERFORD
MC ALEAVEY DOWN, AF
MC ALEENAN VAR.
MC ALEER 13 OF 17 BIRT
MC ALEESE ANTRIM,LON
MC ALESHER *238,*276
MC ALESTER PN ANTRIN
ALEWARD WATERFORD
ALEXANDER ANTRIM,161
ALGOE DONEGAL
ALIN TIPPERARY
MC ALINDEN ARMAGH,
ALINER TIPPERARY
MC ALINGEN *201
ALINION *238
MC ALINON *217
MC ALISTER ANTRIM,M
MC ALIVERY *216
M' ALL *279
ALLAND WATERFORD
MC ALLEN PN DUBLIN CI
ALLEN WEX.,1640 SAXON/
ALLERDICE *249, ALSO A
MC ALLESTER PN LOND
ALLEXANDER DUBLIN C
MC ALLIN DONEGAL
ALLINE LEITRIM
ALLINGHAM 4 OF 5 BIRT
ALLISON DUBLIN,LIMERI
MC ALLISTER DON, DER
ALMER MEATH
ALMES KERRY
MC ALONEY 4 BIRTHS IN

MC ALOONE PN Donegal
MC ALPIN MEATH,WESTM
ALPIN *241
Mac ALSHENDER *112
Mac ALSHINDER *44,*33
ALTIMES *287, ALSO ALTC
Alwoodhouse DUBLIN CIT
AMANSHAM DUBLIN CIT
AMBERSON *358
AMBROSE CORK,LIMERIC
AMERY DUBLIN,LIMERICK
AMOOTY *215,ALSO ACHI
MC ANALLY ANTRIM,AR
MC ANARE *48B.
M' ANAUL *364
ANCTHILL PMO
ANDERSON WATER,1690 .
ANDERSONE DONEGAL
MC ANDLESS *358
MC ANDREW FERM 1640
ANDREW MEATH
ANDREWES FERM, LIME,
ANDREWS CORK 1650, SC
MC ANENY ALL OF TYRC
ANESLEY KILDARE
ANGER DUBLIN CITY
ANGIER PMO, ALSO AUNG
ANGLIN CORK.
ANGUS DOWN, ANTRIM
ANKETTILL MONAGHAN
ANKETTLE TIPPERARY
ANKLE *199, ALSO ANKLA
ANNESLEY CORK, 1625 A
ANNETT DOWN, ANTRIM
Mac ANREE *40
ANSLA *73, ALSO ANNESL
ANTHONY DUBLIN,WATE
MC ANTIRE *155
ANTRIM ANTRIM
MC ANULLA *367
MC ANULLY PN OF KILD
MC ANULTY PN DON.165
APPELLWHITE ANTRIM
MC ARAGH *275
ARBERRY CITY OF CORK
ARCHBALD LONGFORD
ARCHBOLD KILDARE,164
ARCHBOULD PN DUBLIN
ARCHDALE PMO/ ALSO FI
ARCHDALL FERMANAGH
ARCHDEACON CORK / *1
ARCHDEAKIN PN Tip.
ARCHDEKIN WATERFORI

ARCHER WAT,KER,FER,11
ARCHFIELD *224
ARCHIBALD LONDONDE
MC ARDELL PN ARMAGI
ARDENTON LOUTH AND/(
ARDGLASSE DOWN
MC ARDLE LOUTH,MEAT
ARDOUGH DUBLIN CITY
ARDWAHER KILKENNY
M' AREADY *254
MC AREE ANTRIM,MONA
Mac ARHA *397
ARKLEY *435
ARLAND PN Waterford
ARLANT PN Waterford
ARMESTRONG KINGS
ARMIN WESTMEATH
ARMITAGE LOUTH,1570 I
ARMOUR ANTRIM
ARMSTRONG CLA,OFF,A
ARMSTRONGE TIPPERAR
ARNALDS KERRY
ARNOLD ANTRIM, DUBLI
ARNOLD PMO
ARNOLT FERMANAGH
ARNOP DUBLIN CITY
ARNOT FERM H/ALSO AN
ARNOTT CORK. 5 BIRTHS
ARRALL ARMAGH
ARRUNDEL PMO
ARTHOP KINGS
ARTHUR PN CLARE,LIM.
ARTHURE WEXFORD
ARTHURS ANTRIM,TYRO
M' ARTIE *199
ARUNDALL DUBLIN CITY
ARUNDELL DUB,WAT,LIN
ASH LIM. CITY,LOND,KILD
ASHE KERRY,ANTRIM
ASHENHURST LOUTH OR
MC ASHINAH *165
ASHLY DUBLIN CITY
ASHTON DUBLIN,KERRY,
ASHWORTH CARLOW
ASKE TIPPERARY, ROSCOM
ASKIN LIMERICK / HESKIN
ASKINS *410
ASPEL WEXFORD, *436
ASPELL *435
ASPILL *72,*364
ASSIN DUBLIN CITY
ASTEN LOUTH AND DROG
ASTIN *8, ALSO AUSTIN

MC ASTOCKER *433
ASTON DUBLIN COUNTY,P
MC ATAMNEY LOND, 6
ATCHESON PMO
MC ATEE *13
MC ATEER ARMAGH,ANT
MC ATEGGART VAR.
MC ATILLA *314
MC ATIRE PN Donegal
ATKINS CORK, 1678 ENGL
ATKINSON Mayo,Offaly,Tip
ATMOTY CARLOW
AUCKETIL PMO
AUHER *135
MC AULA PN Antrim
Mac AULAY *300,*480.
AULD 6 BIRTHS, 3 IN ANTR
MC AULEY ANTRIM, DON
MC AULIFE PN CORK
AULIFE PN CORK
MC AULIFFE 29 BIRTHS
MC AULLY PN Antrim
AURACHAUN *488
AUSTIN DUBLIN,CORK,137
AUSTINE DOWN
AUWLL *93, ALSO AUL
MC AVADDY *486
MC AVADY *119
AVERY DUBLIN CITY
MC AVEY *477
MC AVINCHY *385
M' AVINUE *308
MC AVISH *191,*138
AVORY DUBLIN
M' AVOY *195
MC AVYNNY PN Ferm.
MC AWARD PN DONEGA
Mac AWLY P.M.O. OF 166
Mac awly PN Ferm.
MC AWLY SLIGO
AYLEMER TIPPERARY
AYLEWARD PN Waterford
AYLMER KILD,FERM,TYR
AYLWARD KILKENNY,11
AYNGER MEATH
O B DUBLIN CITY
BAAL WESTMEATH
BABBITT DUBLIN,DERRY,
BABER TIPPERARY
BABINGTON CORK,LONC
BACCON TIPPERARY
BACK LIMERICK CITY
BACKER DONEGAL

BACON DUBLIN,LIM, 1570
BADLEY PMO
BAGG WATERFORD
BAGLEY CORK
BAGNALL DOWN,CORK,P
BAGOTT LIMERICK
BAGWORTH DUBLIN
BAILEY DUBLIN,WAT,LIM
BAILIE DOWN,ROSCOMMO
BAILLY DOWN
BAILY *145
BAINLETT WATERFORD
BAIRD DUBLIN, LIM, 1692
BAITH *72, ALSO BATES
BAKER DUBLIN,CORK,TIP,
BALDIN PN WATERFORD/
BALDON PN Waterford
BALDOON *262, ALSO BA
BALDWIN DUB,CORK, 117
BALE DUBLIN CITY
BALFE ROSC 1640 NORMA
BALFOUR LOUTH,FERM,
BALFREMON KILKENNY
BALL DUB,CORK,LIM, 1642
BALLANTINE ANTRIM
BALLENTINE ANTRIM
BALLY LIMERICK
BALMER DOWN, 8 BIRTH
BALTEZAR WATERFORD
BALTON *390
BALY WESTMEATH
BAMBRICK QUEENS
BAMFORD ANTRIM, 9 BI
BAMPTON FERMANAGH
BANAN PN Tip.
O BANAN PN Ferm.
BANANE KINGS, *142,*50
BANCKS KILKENNY
BANDY TIPPERARY
BANE PN CORK, LIM,TIP,C
BANFELL *131, ALSO BAN
BANGFIELD WESTMEATH
BANISTOR CARLOW
BANKS DUBLIN CITY/ 8 BI
BANNAN PN Kings
BANNANE KINGS
BANNISTER 5 BIRTHS
BANNON TIPP, 21 BIRTHS
BANTING LIM CITY,PMO.
BARBER DUB,LIM, 1640 E
BARCLAY CORK,LIM,157(
BARCROFT QUEENS
BARDON PN LONG,WESTM

BARETT DOWN
BARINGTON QUEENS
BARKELL LIMERICK CITY
BARKER MEATH 1625 NOI
BARKLEY CORK,LIM 1570
BARKLIMORE *86, ALSC
BARLEY *519, ALSO BARI
BARLOW LIMERICK 1603 I
BARLOWE DUBLIN CITY,
BARNACLE *28, *250
BARNANE *227
BARNARD CORK
BARNAWELL ROSCOMM
BARNES DUB CITY,ARMA
BARNETT CARLOW/CORK
BARNEWALL MEATH 16
BARNEWELL PN MEATH,
BARNIDGE *488, ALSO B
BARNWALL DUBLIN CIT
BARNWELL ROSCOMMON
BARON PN Kilkenny
BAROY CORK
BARR CORK,LIM 1646 SCO
O BARR PN Donegal
BARRABY LIMERICK
BARRAN PN Louth
BARRET PN CORK CITY,D
BARRETT LIM, 1170 NORM
BARRETT DUB,COR,KER,I
BARRIMORRE PMO
BARRINGTON DUB,LIM,
BARROE CORK
MC BARRON FERMANA
BARRON WAT, 1690 NOR/
BARRON Pn KILK,LIM,WE
BARROW DUBLIN CITY, P
BARRY CORK 1171 NOR/P
BARRYMORE CORK
BARRYTT DUBLIN CITY
BARTLESS LIMERICK CIT
BARTLEY 8 BIRTHS
BARTNETT *488, ALSO B
BARTON TIP,FER,1560 EN
BARY DUBLIN
BASE CORK
BASIL PMO
BASILL DUBLIN
BASKET QUEENS
BASSETT CORK CITY / 6 B
BATEMAN KERRY,DOWN
BATES DUBLIN, 22 BIRTH
BATH DUBLIN 1560 NORMA
BATHER DUBLIN
BATHRIPP DUBLIN CITY
BATHURST CORK,DUBLI
BATTEN LOUTH
BATTER *431, ALSO BATT
BATTERSBY WIC,KILD,T
BATTLE SLIGO, 6 BIRTHS
BATTY WESTMEATH, 900 I

BAUCROFT KINGS
BAUKLEY TIPPERARY
BAULDWINE KINGS
BAULMAN DUBLIN
BAUN *488
BAUNISTER CORK
BAWN *76,*146,*210.
BAXTER DONEGAL,DUBL
MC BAY CAVAN,FERMAN
BAYGOTT KILKENNY
BAYLEY CORK CITY/ TIP
BAYLY WICKLOW,TIP,169
BEACON WATERFORD
BEADLE PMO
BEAGHAM PN Kings
BEAGHAN PN KILD,QUE,I
BEALE CORK
BEALING DUBLIN CITY, W
BEALL KILKENNY
BEAME DUBLIN
BEAMISH CORK,1690 ENC
BEAR PMO
O BEARA LIMERICK
BEARD MONAGHAN, QUE
BEARE CORK CITY,CORK
BEARES DOWN
BEARKIN CLARE
BEARY PMO
BEASLEY PMO
BEATAGH *329, ALSO BE
BEATS CORK
BEATTIE ANTRIM,DOWN,
BEATTY DUBLIN,ARMAG
BEAUCHAMP PMO
BEAUMONT *7
BECK ANTRIM, DOWN
BECKET DUBLIN CITY
BECKETT ANTRIM
BEDBOROUGH KILKENN
BEDBORROUG QUEENS
BEDLOW PN Louth
BEECHAM *162
BEECHER *488
BEECHER CORK
BEERS ANTRIM
BEGANE *508
BEGETT TIPPERARY
BEGG ROSCOMMON,ANTR
O BEGGAN PN Mon.
BEGGAN PN WEXFORD/ M
BEGGE WESTMEATH
BEGGS ANTRIM,DUBLIN
BEGHANE PN Kings
BEGLAN *274, ALSO BAG
BEGLEY 36 BIRTHS, *238,*
BEGNEY *495,ALSO BAGN
BEHAN DUBLIN, KILDARE
BEHANE *47, *51, *352.
BEIRN ROSCOMMON,PMO.
O BEIRNE 9 BIRTHS

BEIRNE ROSCOMMON,LEI
BELFORE PN Ferm.
BELFOUR FERMANAGH
BELL WAT,CORK,LIM 1640
BELLEN MEATH
BELLENY WATERFORD
BELLEW PN LOUTH,CORK
BELLINGHAM DUBLIN C
BELLOW CLARE
BELLOWE CORK
BELLUE CORK
BELTON LONGFORD, LOU
O BENAGHAN PN SLIGO
BENATHY *89, ALSO ABE
BENBO *464
BENDEN LIMERICK
BENDON PMO
BENGER CORK CITY
BENIOR WATERFORD
BENISON *35
BENNELL DUBLIN CITY
BENNES PMO
BENNET KILKENNY
BENNETT CORK,OFFALY I
BENNIS LIMERICK CITY,C
BENNISH CLARE
BENSON DUB CITY,LIM,L
BENSON DUB CTY,LIM,LO
BENSONE DONEGAL
BENT CORK CITY
BENTHAM LIMERICK
BENTLEY LIMERICK CITY
BEOLAN PN KINGS, SLIG
BEOLANE PN CLARE, KIN
BERA *154
BERESFORD LONDONDE
BERFORD DUBLIN CITY
BERGAN *68
BERGIN PN KILKENNY,QU
BERGMAN *410
BERISFORD PMO
BERKERY TIPPERARY,LIN
BERKLEY LIMERICK
BERMAGH PN Waterford
BERMINGHAM PN KILDA
O BERN PN Down.
BERNARD KILDARE,CAR,
O BERNE PN Rosc.
BERRANE *138,ALSO BAR
BERRELL PN Louth
BERRESFORD LONDOND
BERRIGAN *384
BERRISFORD PMO
BERRY CORK,LIM,MEA, 11
BERSTOW DUBLIN CITY
BERY KINGS
BESSWORTH CORK
BEST LEITRIM,DON,1642 E
BESTWILL WESTMEATH
BETAGH ROSCOMMON

Mac BETH *141
BETSWORTH LIMERICK
BETSWORTHY CORK
BETTIN DUBLIN CITY
BETTS ANTRIM, TIPPERAR
BETTY WESTMEATH,LONG
BEUCHAMP DUBLIN CIT
BEVANS MEATH,PMO
BEVINS PMO
BEVRIDGE CORK
BEWAR KILKENNY
BEXWICK LOUTH
MC BEY *480
BICKER *429
BICKERS *429
BICKERSTAFF DOWN,A
Bickerstaffe ANTRIM, LO
BICKERSTAY *197
BICKERTON ARMAGH
BIERAST SLIGO
O BIERNE PN Rosc.
BIG TIPPERARY,CLARE
BIGGANE MONAGHAN,W
BIGGEDON QUEENS
BIGGER KILKENNY
BIGGERSTAFF *195
BIGGINS MAYO, 6 BIRTHS
BIGLEAN PN Long.
BIGO PMO
BIGOE KINGS
BILLIGAM *59
BILLINGSLEY PMO
BILLINSLEY DUBLIN
BILLKINTON CORK
M' BIN *429
BINANE *142
BINDON PMO
BINGHAM MAYO, 1560 SA
BINGLEY PMO
BIRCH 9 BIRTHS
BIRD LIM,GAL,1560 SAX/C
BIRFORD DUBLIN
BIRKETT KILDARE
BIRKEY *494
BIRMINGHAM DUB,LIM.
BIRN PN West.
O BIRNE PN DON,MON,R
BIRNE PN,(VARIOUS)
MC BIRNEY DOWN, ANT
BIRNEY 6 BIRTHS
BIRRIN PN Leitrim
BIRTLES PMO
BISHOP PMO / DUBLIN
BISHOPP KILK, DUBLIN C
BISSE DUBLIN CITY
BISSETT *364
BLACAGH *40
BLACER ARMAGH
BLACHFORD PMO
BLACK DUB,MEA, 1570 EN

BLACKAND DUBLIN CITY
BLACKBURN DUBLIN,M
BLACKEN LOUTH
BLACKENDER *86
BLACKER WEX,ARMAGH
BLACKHALL LIMERICK
BLACKHAM *409
BLACKMORE PMO
BLACKNELL KILKENNY
BLACKSTOCK ANTRIM,
BLACKWELL CLARE, DU
BLACKWOOD ANTRIM
BLADEN DUBLIN CITY, P
BLAIN ANTRIM, DOWN
BLAIR PN ANTRIM,PMO/ A
BLAIRE LONDONDERRY
BLAKE GAL,MAY,1172 NO
BLAKES *254
BLAKNEY LIMERICK
BLAKSTON CORK
BLANCH WATERFORD /
BLANCHETT CORK
BLANCHFIELD PN KILK,
BLANCHVILL PN Kilkenn
BLANEY COR,LIM,1172 N
BLANFORD CORK CITY
blannerhaset PMO (BLAN
BLANY PMO
BLARE LONDONDERRY, P
BLATCHFORD CORK
BLEACH *469
BLEAK *131
BLEAKLEY ANTRIM
BLEEKS *478
BLEHEEN *330
BLEHEIN *36
BLEHEINE *298
Blenerhasset PMO
blenerhassett KERRY
blennerhaset PMO (BLEN
Bleuer Hasset FERMANAG
Bleuer Hasset
bleverhassett LIMERICK,
BLIGH DUBLIN CITY,PMO
BLIGH PMO, DUBLIN CITY
BLOMEFIELD LOUTH
BLOMFIELD LOUTH
BLONG KINGS
BLOOMER ANTRIM, TYR
BLOUD PMO
BLOUK # 136
BLOUNT KILDARE
BLOWICK *136
BLUETT LIMERICK, ANTR
BLUNDEL PMO
BLUNDELL PMO, KINGS,
BLUNDEN KILKENNY
BLUNT PMO, LOUTH,KILK
BOAGE TIPPERARY
BOAGHAN PN Kildare

BOAL ANTRIM, DOWN, *83
BOALE PN Antrim
BOAR *124
BOCKOCAN *401
BOCULLY PN Kings
BODEL *238
BODELEY PMO
BODELL *450
BODELY CARLOW
BODGE KILKENNY
BODING PN Louth
BODINGTON LOUTH
BODKIN CLARE / GALWA
BODLE *238, *247
BODLEY DUBLIN,WAT, 16
O BOE P.N. KILKENNY,WE
BOE PN TIPPERARY, KILK
BOEMAN LIMERICK CITY.
BOG *107
BOGAN WEXFORD
BOGHAN PN Kildare
O BOGHELLY PN CORK
BOGUE FERMANAGH
BOHAN LEITRIM,GALWAY
BOHANAN TIPPERARY
BOHANE P.N. LEITRIM/ A
BOHANNA *397,*92
BOHANNON *55,*233
BOHELLY PN Kings
BOHUNNAN *432
BOIDE DOWN
O BOIGD PN CORK
BOIL *225
BOLAN *454B
BOLAND KILDARE ROSCO
BOLE *59, *91
BOLES 7 BIRTHS OF THIS
BOLGER KILK,1640 AD,E
BOLLARD DUBLIN CITY/
BOLLES PMO
BOLTON WEX,WAT,MEA,
BOMUS ROSCOMMON & A
BONAR DONEGAL, *479,*4
BOND LONGFORD 1563 AD
BONER *271
BONES 7 BIRTHS IN 1890
BONISON *503
BONNER *340,*479
BONNY *497
BONOLE DUBLIN CITY
BONORLY DUBLIN CITY
BOOHIER CORK CITY
BOOKBY PMO
BOOKELEY KILKENNY
BOOKER PMO
BOORE LIMERICK
BOORKE TIPPERARY,DUB
BOOTH ANTRIM,DOWN,16
BORDEN DUBLIN CITY
BORELAND *19

BORNE KILKENNY
BORR DUBLIN
BORSTON PMO
BOSWEL PMO
BOSWELL LIMERICK, GAI
BOTHWELL 7 BIRTHS IN I
BOUCHER 5 BIRTHS OF T
BOUDLER DUBLIN CITY
BOUGHANE PN CORK
BOUGHLA *249
BOUHILLY PN Tip.
BOULD DUBLIN CITY
BOULSFELD ARMAGH
BOULTON TIPPERARY,CA
BOUND LIMERICK
BOURDEN KILKENNY
BOURK PN LIMERICK,CLA
BOURKE LIMERICK,1171,I
BOUSTER TIPPERARY
BOWDEN 8 BIRTHS IN 189
BOWDRAN PN Waterford
BOWE PN QUEENS/ KILKE
O BOWE PN Queens.
BOWEN CORK,1642 WELCI
BOWER WEXFORD IN 1659
BOWERS LIMERICK, 1646
BOWES DUBLIN. 10 BIRTH
BOWLER PN KERRY/ ALL
BOWLES CORK/ 5 BIRTHS
BOWLS PMO
BOWMAN DUBLIN,MAYO
BOWNES *229
BOWREMAN CORK.
BOXTER KILKENNY
BOY PN OF DOWN,CLARE,
BOYCE DONEGAL,DOWN,I
BOYD WEX,DON,1646 SCO
O BOYD PN Antrim
BOYDE DOWN
BOYER ROSCOMMON AND
BOYES *175.
MC BOYHEEN LEITRIM
BOYL PMO/SEE *471
BOYLAN P.N. OF DUBLIN,
O BOYLAN PN Mon.
BOYLE P.N. MON,TIP,DUB
O BOYLE P.N. ANT,DON, M
BOYLES LIMERICK
BOYNE DUBLIN
O BOYNS ARMAGH
BOYSE WEXFORD,1670 EN
BOYTON ROSCOMMON &
BRABANT CORK
BRABAZON MAYO,LOU,
BRABSON ROSCOMMON &
BRABZON DUBLIN CITY
BRACKANE PN Kings
BRACKEN PN KINGS/DUE
BRADBURN P.M.O.
BRADDEN *12

BRADFORD DERRY,LOUT
BRADHURST WESTMEAT
BRADIGAN PN, LOUTH &
BRADLE P.M.O.
BRADLEY P.M.O. / LON,A
BRADLY ROSCOMMON &
BRADSHAW DUBLIN,DUI
BRADSTON CORK
BRADY P.N. LONG,L & D, I
O BRADY PN Ferm.
BRAEDIN DONEGAL
BRAFIELD WESTMEATH
BRAGG DUBLIN CITY
BRAGHALL KILDARE
BRAILY CORK
O BRALLAGHAN *254
BRAMBLE CORK
BRAMHALL PMO
BRAMLEY LIMERICK
BRAMPTON DUBLIN CITY
BRAMSTON MONAGHAN
BRANAGAN DUBLIN
BRANAGH PN KILDARE, (
BRANAN PN KINGS,WEST
BRANDON DUBLIN, 1640
BRANGAN *72,*137
BRANHAM DUBLIN CITY
BRANIFF *268
BRANKIN *197
BRANNAGH WEXFORD,1
BRANNAN DONEGAL// *1
BRANNICK *506
BRANNIE *267
BRANNIGAN ARMAGH, M
BRANNOCK *51
BRANNON DONEGAL
BRANSFIELD ALL IN COI
Branthwaite WESTMEATH
BRASIER LONDONDERRY
BRASSELL PN WATERFOI
BRASSIL *47
BRATHWAIT PMO
MC BRATNEY ANTRIM,
BRATTY *372
BRAUDERS *109, *117
BRAWNICK *179
BRAY LOUTH & DROGHED
BRAYLY CORK
BRAYNE PN Dublin
BRAZIER PMO
BRAZIL CORK,LIMERICK,(
BREACKAN PN Kildare
BREADBEARD CORK
BREADON FERMANAGH,T
BREARELY DOWN
MC BREARTY TYRONE,I
BRECKAN PN KILDARE,K
BREDAN PN Queens.
BREEDETH WESTMEATH
BREEDING PMO

BREEN PN QUEENS/ WEXF
O BREENAN PN Donegal
O BREENE Pn KERRY,WE
BREERS ANTRIM
BREERTON ANTRIM
BREHAN PN ROSCOMMON
BREHENY ROSCOMMON,S
BREHONY *105,*339,*454
MC BREHUNY PN SLIGO
O BREIN PN Ferm.
BREMEGHAM PN LOUTH
BREMIGAM *45
BREN PN Kilkenny
BRENAGH PN CITY OF CO
O BRENAN PN CARLOW,F
BRENAN PN TIPPERARY,C
BRENANE PN TIPPERARY
O BRENANE PN KERRY,S
BRENNAGH CITY OF COR
BRENNAN P.N. ROSCOMM
BRENNIGAN *174
BRENOGH PN Kilkenny
BRENON PN Kilkenny
BRENT PMO
BRERETON CORK,QUEEN
BRERTON DUBLIN
BRESLAND *12
BRESLANE *375
BRESLAUN *16
BRESLAWN *243
BRESLIN DONEGAL, 42 RE
BRETLERIDGE CORK
BRETRAGE PMO
BRETT CLARE,DUBLIN C
BREW CLARE
BREWSTER *421
BRIAN PN LIMERICK/SEE *
O BRIAN PN LIM. CITY,LI
MC BRIAN PN Lim.
BRIANE PN Kings
BRICE LONDONDERRY,DU
BRICK KERRY, 9 BIRTHS I
BRICKAIN WATERFORD
BRICKARDICK PMO
BRICKDALL CLARE
BRICKELSBY KINGS
BRICKLEY ALL COUNTY
MC BRIDE DONEGAL,160
Mac BRIDE *40
BRIDGAL PMO
BRIDGEMAN CLARE
BRIDGES WAT,COR,1643,E
BRIDGET 5 BIRTHS IN 189
BRIDGIN KILKENNY
O BRIEN PN CORK,LIM/DU
MC BRIEN FERMANAGH,
M' BRIEN *82,*308
BRIEN COR,DUB,WEX,TIP,
BRIENE *146
BRIGDALL CLARE

BRIGG TIPPERARY
BRIGGS ANTRIM,DOWN
BRIGHNESS DUBLIN CITY
BRIGHT ROS & ATHLONE
O BRILLAGHAN DONEG,
BRIMAGE *424
BRIMAGUM *386
BRIMINGHAM PN DUBL
BRIMLEY *428
BRIMMAGEM *72,378
BRIMMIGAN
MC BRIN PN Down.
BRIN PN,DUB CITY,KILD,K
BRINAGH PN Kerry
BRINAN ROSCOMMON AN
BRINANE *227
O BRINE P.N. LIMERICK,K
M' BRINE PN LIMERICK/S
BRINE PN MEATH,LEITRIM
BRINEGAN PN LOUTH & I
BRINF DOWN
BRINGHURST MEATH,PM
MC BRINN PN Down.
BRINNE PN Kildare
BRINSMEADE WATERFO
BRIODY LONGFORD,CAV
BRISCOE TIP,WEST, 1560 I
O BRISLAN PN Ferm.
O BRISLANE PN Donegal
MC BRITANY PN Antrim
BRITT PN TIP,KILK / TIP,W
BRITTAINE PMO
BRITTON WESTMEATH/ 9
BRIVER WATERFORD, PM
`BROADBEAR P M O .
BROCK DONEGAL,ANTRIM
BROCKE LIMERICK
BROCKET PMO
BROCKLESBY CORK CIT
BRODBEAR PMO
BRODDERS *109
BRODER KERRY,LIMERIC
BRODERICK CORK,PMO/
BRODIE Pn WEXFORD/ *50
BRODIER PN Kilkenny
O BRODIR PN CORK
BRODRIDGE KILKENNY
BRODSTON KILKENNY
BRODY CLARE, 6 BIRTHS
BROE 8 BIRTHS
BROGAN PN WESTMEATH
BROGHANE PN Kings
BROGHIL PMO
BROGHILL CORK CITY, PI
BROHY PN TIP,KILK,QUE.
BROKETT CORK
BROLLY LONDONDERRY,
BROMAGEN DUBLIN,ROS
BROMFIELD KINGS
BROMLOE ARMAGH

BROMWEL PMO
BROMWELL WESTMEATH
BRONTHROPT ROSCOMM
BROODER *117
BROOK DONEGAL
BROOKE DUBLIN, 1690 EN
BROOKES TIP,CORK,DUB
BROOKIN CORK
BROOKING DUBLIN CITY
BROOKS CORK,PMO/ COR
BROOTHERS *316
BROPHY DUBLIN,KILK,QU
BROSNAN KERRY, *8, *37
BROTHERS *78
BROUGHALL DUBLIN
BROUGHILL *435
BROUN DUBLIN CITY
BROUNE PN KILKENNY,W
BROWDER *65
BROWN COR,LIM,GAL,MA
BROWNE CORK,MAYO,WE
BROWNE PN ANTRIM,DON
BROWNING FERM,WAT/ (
BROWNLEE ANTRIM,ARM
BROWNLOW *154
BROWSTER *41
BRUCE CORK,LIM, 1650 SC
BRUDER *134,349
BRUDHER *378
BRUEN CARLOW, 1640 NOI
BRUERTON LOUTH & DRO
MC BRUINE PN Down.
BRUISTER DUBLIN CITY
BRUMIGEM *401
BRUMIGER *40
BRUMLEY LIMERICK
BRUMMAGEN *72
BRUMMAGEN *473
BRUNTY *359
BRUODY PN CLARE
BRUTON DUBLIN, *121,42
BRUTTNELL LIMERICK
BRYAN WEX. 1640 SCOTS/
O BRYAN PN FERM,CORK
Mac BRYAN PN Long.
MC BRYAN PN FERM,LIN
BRYANE PN KINGS.
BRYANS ANTRIM, DOWN
MC BRYD PN Antrim
MC BRYDE PN Down.
BRYDE PN Meath
MC BRYEN PN CLARE,KE
O BRYEN PN CLARE,COR
BRYEN PN CLARE,LIM,TIP
BRYN PN Mon.
O BRYN PN Mon.
O BRYNAN PN Mon.
BRYNAN PN LOUTH & D,V
MC BRYNE PN DOWN,LII
O BRYNE PN ARM,LIM,WA

BRYNE PN WATERFORD,M
BRYNER WATERFORD
BRYNNE KILDARE
O BRYON PN Tip.
BRYON PN TIPPERARY,KI
BRYSCOE DUBLIN
BRYSON DON,MEA, 1632 S
BRYTTANIE PN Tip.
BRYTTEN PN Tip.
BUCHANAN DON,DOW/DI
BUCHNAN LOUTH & DRO
BUCK DUBLIN,1646 ENGLI
BUCKARTON DUBLIN CI
BUCKLES *257, ALSO ARE
BUCKLEY COR,LIM,TIP, 1
BUCKLY QUEENS
BUCKS PMO
BUDGENS WEXFORD, 169
BUEG *227
BUHILLY *420
BUICK ANTRIM, 7 BIRTHS
BUIE WATERFORD
BULGER CLARE. *263
BULINER LOUTH & D.
BULKELEY *373
BULKELH LOUTH & D.
BULKELY LOUTH & D.
BULKLEY DUBLIN, P.M.O.
BULL CORK
BULLA *358
BULLENBROO PMO
BULLIN LOUTH
BULLION *19,*482
BULLMAN CORK, 5 BIRTI
BULLOCKE CITY OF CORI
BULWORTHY ANTRIM
BUNBURY CARLOW 1690
BUNTING ANTRIM,ARMA(
BUO PN Waterford
O BUOIGE PN CORK
BUOIGE PN CORK
O BUOY PN CORK
BURCELL CARLOW
BURCHALL KILKENNY
BURCHAM CORK
BURCHILL CORK, 6 BIRT
BURDET PMO
BURDIT PMO
BURGES LIMERICK,MEAT
BURGESS DUBLIN, 19 BIR
BURGOYNE DUBLIN,LIM
BURK PN Kings
BURKE GAL,LIM,CLA,TIP
BURKER LIMERICK
BURLY DOWN
BURNE PN DUBLIN,KILDAI
BURNEHAM CORK
BURNELL CORK
BURNES PN Antrim
BURNETT DUBLIN/ 7 BIRT

MC BURNEY DOWN,ANT
BURNEY *86
BURNISTON PMO
BURNS ANT,DOWN,ARM,C
BURNSIDE LONDONDERR
BURRAGE CORK
BURREL PMO
BURRELL QUEENS,PMO /
BURREN PN Tip.
BURRIL PMO
BURRILL KILKENNY,PMO
BURROUGHES CORK
BURROUGHS PMO
BURROWES DUBLIN CIT
BURROWS DOWN, 15 BIR
BURSTED PMO
BURT DUBLIN CITY,WATE
BURTEN DONEGAL
BURTON CLA,WIC, 1610 N
BURTSIDES LOUTH
BURWELL CORK
BURY CORK,LIMERICK,16
BURYE KILDARE
BUSBRIDG PMO
BUSBRIDGE KINGS,PMO
BUSH WATERFORD,1670, N
BUSHELL DUBLIN CITY,*
BUSTARD DONEGAL, 7 BI
BUSTEAD CORK
BUSTEED CITY OF CORK
BUSTON DUBLIN CITY
BUTHELLS ANTRIM
BUTLER CLA, 1170 N/ DUB
BUTTERFIELD DUBLIN,1
BUTTERLY PN DUBLIN.
BUTTLER PN TIPPERARY,
BUTTON *86, ALSO ARBU
BWEE *341,*459,*381
BYERS CAVAN, 10 BIRTHS
BYRCE *259,*260
BYRINE CARLOW
BYRNE DUBLIN,WICKLOW
M' BYRNE *163
O BYRNE PN CARLOW/ DU
BYRNE PN CARLOW,LOUT
BYRON DUBLIN, ANTRIM,
BYRT ANTRIM
BYSSE PMO
MC CABA PN Leitrim
MC CABE PN FER,MON,L
CADDELL DUB,GAL, 1172
CADDEN 5 BIRTHS
CADIE MONAGHAN
CADMORE DUBLIN CITY
CADOGAN PMO/ 6 BIRTH
CADWELL DUBLIN CITY
MC CAE CLARE
CAFFERKY 19 BIRTHS, M
CAFFERTY 6 BIRTHS, CA
MC CAFFERTY DONEGA

MC CAFFERY *460
CAFFERY LEITRIM/ *82
MC CAFFERY PN FERM
CAFFREY DUBLIN,MEATH
MC CAFFREY FERMANA
MC CAFFRY *238,247
M' CAGHERTY *210
CAHALANE CORK, KERR
MC CAHAN PN Antrim
O CAHAN PN LOND,ROSC
CAHAN PN WATERFORD/ *
CAHANE P. N. CLARE,KE
O CAHANE P.N. CORK,K
CAHASSY PN KERRY
CAHASY PN TIPPERARY
CAHELL PN TIPPERARY,K
O CAHELL PN LIMERICK,
O CAHESEY PN KERRY
CAHESSY PN TIPPERARY
O CAHESY PN Lim.
O CAHILL PN CLARE
CAHILL PN CLARE,TIP,LO
MC CAHON 6 BIRTHS, A
CAHOON PMO/ *91
MC CAHUGH
CAHY *429
M' CAHY *429
CAIN MAYO. / *22.*40,*420
CAINAN *284
CAIRDIE *191
CAIRNS SLIGO,DON, 1603
O CALAGHANE CLARE
CALDERWOOD ANTRIM
CALDWELL MEATH, 1706
CALENE PN CLARE
CALFE CORK
CALHOUNE DONEGAL
MC CALL ARMAGH, CAV
MC CALLA *372, *411.
O CALLAGHAN PN DON
CALLAGHAN CORK,KER
O CALLAGHAN CORK, *
Callaghanan *373
O Callaghane PN CLARE,
CALLAGHANE PN CLAR
MC CALLAGHANE PN
CALLAGHER *279
O CALLAHANE PN COR
O CALLAN PN Mon.
CALLAN PN DUBLIN,LOU
MC CALLAN PN FER,MO
CALLANAN GALWAY,CO
CALLANANE CORK
O CALLANE PN Donegal
CALLCATT ANTRIM
MC CALLELY PN Rosc.
CALLEN PN DUBLIN
MC CALLIN PN ANTRIM,
CALLIN PN DUBLIN CITY,
CALLINA *38

CALLINAN CLARE
CALLINANE PN CLARE
MC CALLION ANTRIM,D
M' CALLISTER *358
MC CALLNON *97
MC CALLY *348
O CALLY PN Donegal
MC CALMONT PN Antrim
CALMY PN Kildare
CALNAN *77,*397
MC CALSHENDER *58,
MC CALSHINDER *75,*
CALTHORPE WATERFOR
CALVERT DONEGAL,DER
CALVEY SLIGO
CALVILL PMO
CALWELL *58
CAMBBELL DOWN
CAMBIER TIPPERARY
CAMBRIDGE CORK/ COR
MC CAMBRIDGE ANTR
CAMBY PMO
CAMERON ANTRIM,1642,
CAMINE PMO
MC CAMLEY DOWN, 161
CAMP *185
CAMPBELL DON,DER,ME
MC CAMPBELL PN Antri
CAMPEL PMO
CAMPELL DONEGAL, PM
CAMPIAN PN Queens.
CAMPION CORK/ KILKE
CAMPSIE LONDONDERRY
Mac CAN PN DUBLIN
MC CAN PN Lond.
CANAAN *27,*72
CANALLY *312
O CANAN PN Donegal
MC CANAN PN Meath
CANAVAN 22 BIRTHS, *4
CANDIT DUBLIN CITY
CANDLER KILKENNY,164
MC CANDLESS DOWN,1
MC CANE PN Armagh,
CANFIELD ARMAGH
MC CANN PN ARMAGH,
MC CANNA PN FERMAN
O CANNAN PN Donegal
CANNAN *72
MC CANNE PN Antrim
CANNIFF CORK, 5 BIRTH
O CANNIFFE PN CORK
CANNING LOND,PMO/ LO
CANNON ANTRIM/ DONE
O CANNON PN Leitrim
CANNY CLARE, MAYO
CANON MEATH
CANOVANE CLARE
CANTIE CORK
CANTRELL QUEENS

CANTWELL LIM,CLA,GAL
CANTY PN CORK/ CORK,L
CANUGHAN SLIGO
CAORISH *393
CAPLE CORK CITY
CAPLEMAN CLARE
CAPPACKE CORK CITY.
CAPPLES *65
CAPPOCKE PN LOUTH
CARAHER *414
CARBERRY ANTRIM
CARBERY PN WAT,KILD,
O CARBRY PN Armagh,
CARBY CORK CITY
CARD TIPPERARY
MC CARDELL PN ARMA
CARDIFF 5 BIRTHS
CARDLE *210
MC CARDLE *392
CARDWELL ANTRIM, *21
CARDYFF DUBLIN CITY
CAREW WATERFORD,1172
CAREY CORK,DON,1666,G
MC CAREY PN West.
CARFELOTT LOUTH
CARGAN PN Meath
CARGY PN Long.
CARHA KILDARE.
CARIE LONDONDERRY
CARLAN *432
CARLAND *64,*141
CARLETON CORK,TIP,FE
CARLEY DUBLIN,1642,EN
CARLIN TYRONE,LOND, *
CARLISLE ANTRIM,DOW
CARMICHAEL ANTRIM
CARMICK PN MEATH,WE
CARMODY PN CLARE/ C
CARNAHAN *175
CARNE PN West.
CARNEY PN TIPPERARY,L
MC CARNEY *185
O CARNEY PN Donegal
CARNS *155
CARNY CORK
O CARNY PN Donegal
CAROLAN MAYO,CAVAN
CAROLL PN KILKENNY,K
CARPENTER DUBLIN,LIM
CARR CORK,LIM,1603 SCO
O CARR PN ARMAGH,DO
CARRAHER *414
O CARRAN PN Donegal
CARRAN TIPPERARY
MC CARRAN PN ARMA
O CARRANE PN Tip.
CARRANE PN TIPPERARY
CARRE DUBLIN CITY
CARRELL PN MEATH,WES
CARREN PN TIPPERARY,

MC CARREY PN West.
CARRICK KERRY/ 7 BIRT
CARRICKE DUBLIN CITY
CARRIGAN FERMANAGH
CARROLAN PN Queens.
O CARROLL PN LIM. CIT
MC CARROLL PN QUEE
CARROLL PN TIPPERARY
MC CARROLY PN Rosc.
MC CARRON DONEGAL,
CARRON PN Kildare
O CARRULL PN CLARE, I
CARRUTHERS 7 BIRTHS
CARRY LOUTH
MC CARRY DONEGAL
CARSON DUBLIN, LIM,15
CART DUBLIN
MC CART ANTRIM
MC CARTAN DOWN/ DO
CARTAN PN KILDARE, LO
CARTEN PN LEITRIM
MC CARTEN *381
CARTER LIM. CITY, PMO,I
MC CARTER PN DONEG
MC CARTEY ANTRIM
CARTHER KERRY
CARTHEY CORK
MC CARTHEY PN CORK
O CARTHY PN CORK/ *52
CARTHY PN CLARE ETC...
MC CARTHY PN CLARE,
CARTHY OGE PN CORK
MC CARTIE *288
CARTIN *159
CARTMILL 5 BIRTHS, AL
MC CARTNEY TYRONE,I
MC CARTON *175
CARTON PN LOUTH/DUBL
CARTWRIGHT CORK CIT
CARTY PN LIM,WAT / ROS
MC CARTY PN CORK
MC CARVEY PN FERMA
CARVILL ARMAGH,DOWN
CARVILLE ROSCOMMON
CARVIN *495
CARWAY *124
CARWELL PN LOUTH.
MC CARWELL PN MON
CARY PN KINGS,MEATH
CASEY PN CLARE, DUBLI
CASH TIPPERARY, WEXFO
O CASHEDY PN Ferm.
CASHIN PN QUEENS/ 11 B
CASHMAN LIMERICK,GA
CASIE PN LIMERICK,LON
CASKEY ANTRIM
MC CASLAN *18
CASLEY *410
CASSADIE PN KINGS
O CASSADY PN DONEGA

CASSEDY PN LOUTH
CASSELLS ARMAGH
CASSERLY ROSCOMMON
CASSEY PN LIMERICK,WA
CASSIDY DONEGAL,DUBL
O CASSIDY FERMANAGH
CASSIN PN TIPPERARY/5 E
CASSY PN CLARE,DUBLIN
O CASSYDY PN FERMAN
MC CASSYE PN MONAG
CASTELLO ROSCOMMON
Mac CASTGUILE PMO
Mac CASTLAN PMO
CASTLE PMO
CASY PN LIMERICK,DUBL
O CASY PN LIMERICK
CATCHCART FERMANA
CATCHCARTT PN FERM.
CATHCART FERMANAGH
CATHER DONEGAL
CATHERWOOD ANTRIM,
O CATO PN Lim.
MC CATO PN LIMERICK
CATTLE CORK
O CAUGHAN *19
MC CAUGHAN ANTRIM,
MC CAUGHERTY *267
CAUGHEY DOWN, ANTRI
MC CAUGHEY ANTRIM,
MC CAUGHIN *202
MC CAUGHLEY *197
CAUGHY *429
MC CAUL ARMAGH, CAV.
M' CAULAY *71
CAULDRON WEXFORD
MC CAULEY ANTRIM, D
M' CAULFIELD *480
CAULFIELD DUBLIN CITY
CAULIN *178A
CAUNAGH PN ROSCOMM
MC CAUSLAND DERRY,
CAVAN DUBLIN, PMO. / *1
CAVANAGH PN DUBLIN/
MC CAVANAGH *461
CAVENAGH PN DUBLIN C
CAVENAH PN DUBLIN
MC CAVILL *216
MC CAVISH *60,*138
CAVISH *301
MC CAW PN ANTRIM/ AN
MC CAWEL *417
MC CAWELL PN ARMAG
CAWELL PN LOUTH.
CAWFIELD PMO
MC CAWLE PN Armagh,
M' CAWLEY *340
CAWLEY MAYO, SLIGO, *
CAWLIN *495
MC CAWLY PN Ferm.
CAWSY PN LOUTH

MC CAY PN ANTRIM, *19
CEARNES *218
CEREIGHTON FERMANA
CERTAINE LONGFORD
CHABNER DUBLIN
CHADWICK LIMERICK,M.
CHAFE PMO
CHAFINE PMO
CHALLENOR LOUTH
CHALMERS *254
CHAMBERLIN PN LOUTI
CHAMBERLIN LEITRIM,
CHAMBERLYN WEXFORI
CHAMBERS DUBLIN CIT'
CHAMBRE LOUTH
CHAMPINES DUBLIN CIT
CHANDLER DUBLIN CITY
CHANEY CORK CITY
CHAPMAN PN WEX,WESI
CHAPPELL ARMAGH, KEI
CHARLES 7 BIRTHS
CHARLETON TYRONE, A
CHARLTON DUBLIN CITY
CHARTERS 8 BIRTHS
CHARTHY *525
CHARTRES CORK
CHEARNELEY TIPPERAR
CHEEVERS LOUTH
CHELLING PMO
CHENEING LOUTH
CHERRY LIMERICK,TIP. 1
CHESIRE KILKENNY
CHESLIN PMO
CHESTERMAN LIMERICI
CHETTLE CORK
CHEURS PN WEXFORD
CHEVERS PN LOUTH
CHEYNE *429
MC CHEYNE *429
CHICESTER ROSCOMMON
CHICHESTER DUB, 1466
CHICHISTER PMO
CHIDLEIGH CORK
chillingworth PMO
chilngsworth PMO
CHILTON KILKENNY, PM(
CHISEL *249
CHISM *418
CHISOM *86
CHISSELL QUEENS
CHOISEUL *249
CHOUN *240
CHRISMAS WATERFORD
CHRISTIAN PN ANTRIM, I
CHRISTIE ANTRIM
CHRISTMAS WESTMEAT
CHRISTOPHER WATERF(
CHRISTOPHER PN WATE
CHRISTY ANTRIM
CHURCH LONDONDERRY,

CHUTE KERRY, 1570 ENG./
CHYTTWOOD WEXFORD
`MC CILTRY KINGS
CINGEN *117
MC CLAFFERTY DONEC
CLAFFEY 7 BIRTHS
CLAHANE *131
MC CLAMON *254
MC CLANCHIE CLARE
CLANCHY PN CLARE,TIPI
CLANCY PN LIMERICK/ CI
CLANHY PN TIPPERARY
CLANSY WATERFORD
CLAPHAM DUBLIN CITY,
CLARE DUBLIN
CLARK DERRY,1703 ENG/ I
CLARKE PN DUB CITY, ET
CLARKINS *380
CLARKSON 5 BIRTHS
MC CLARNON ANTRIM
CLARY KINGS
CLASKEY PN MEATH
MC CLATCHEY ANTRIM
MC CLATTY *478, ALEX/
MC CLAUE PN Mon.
MC CLAVE *460
CLAVEEN *179
CLAY CORK,1642 ENG/ DUI
MC CLAY ANTRIM/ LOND
CLAYBROOK PMO
CLAYBROOKE WATERF(
CLAYPOOLE DUBLIN CIT
CLAYTON DUB,WEX,1172
CLEA CORK
CLEABEAR DUBLIN CITY
MC CLEALAND PN Antri
MC CLEAN DERRY,1605 S
CLEAR QUEENS,WEXFORD
CLEARE PN TIPPERARY
CLEARK MEATH,PMO
CLEARKE PN Lond.
CLEARY PN TIP,WAT,KILI
CLEBURNE DUBLIN,CORI
CLEENE PN LONGFORD
CLEERE PN KILKENNY,QU
O CLEERY PN Donegal
MC CLEERY ANTRIM, LC
CLEGG DOWN, ANTRIM
CLELAND DOWN,1706 SC(
MC CLELAND PN LONDC
MC CLELLAN ANTRIM,1(
MC CLELLAND ANTRIM
CLEMENS DUBLIN CITY
CLEMENT PMO
MC CLEMENT *254
CLEMENTS CAVAN,1640 I
CLENAGHAN 5 BIRTHS A
MC CLENAGHAN ANTR
CLENDINNING ANTRIM
O CLENICAN PN FERMA

CLERE KILKENNY,DUBLIN
O CLEREGAN PN MONA(
O CLERIAN PN MONAGH/
O CLERICAN PN FERMA]
O CLERIGAN PN FERMA]
O CLERIKAN PN FERMA]
CLERK PN DOWN,PMO.
O CLERKAN PN MONAGH
CLERKE CORK,WEST,KIN
CLERKIN 11 BIRTHS, NON
MC CLERNON ANTRIM,I
CLERY PN KINGS, *317
O CLERY PN LIMERICK
CLERYAN LOUTH
CLIBURNE WESTMEATH
CLIFF DUBLIN CITY,PMO
CLIFFE WEXFORD, 1646 EN
CLIFFORD CORK,TIP, 117
CLIFTON PMO
M' CLIMOND *175
CLINCH DUBLIN
CLINE *54
CLINT WEXFORD
MC CLINTOCK DONEGA
CLINTON DUBLIN,LIM,117
CLITTERDY *503
CLOFFY PN WESTMEATH
CLOHERTY ALL IN GALW
CLOHESSY CLARE,LIMER
CLONE KILKENNY
O CLONINE PN LONGFOR
CLONY PN KILKENNY
CLOONAN GALWAY
CLOPPAM ROSCOMMON
MC CLORY DOWN
CLOSE ANTRIM/ARMAGH,
MC CLOSKER PN LONDC
MC CLOSKEY PN LONDC
CLOTWORTHY DUBLIN (
MC CLOUGHRY *57
CLOUNY PN WEXFORD
O CLOVAN PN CARLOW,
CLOVANE PN CLARE
CLOVEN *468
CLOWNEY *155
CLOWNY *155,*429
MC CLOY DONEGAL,DER
MC CLUGHAN ANTRIM,
CLUGSTON ANTRIM
CLULLEN PN QUEENS
CLUNE CLARE, *109
MC CLUNG DONEGAL, 16
MC CLURE DOWN,1706 S(
MC CLURG ANTRIM, DOV
CLUSBY *214
CLUSKER *72,*364
CLUSKEY *364
MC CLUSKEY ANTRIM, I
clutterbooke LONDONDER
CLUVANE *8, *377

O CLUVANE PN LIMERIC
CLYDE ANTRIM, LONDONI
CLYNE LEITRIM, LONGFOI
CLYNS *38
CNOGHER PN KILKENNY
MC CNOGHOR PN CORK
cnoghor oge PN CORK
MC CNOHOR PN CORK.
O CNOHOR PN CORK
CNOHOR OGE PN CORK
MC CNOUGHER PN COR
MC CNOUGHOR PN COI
COACH PMO
COADY DONEGAL,DERRY,
COAKLEY CORK
COATE KINGS
COATES FERMANAGH,AN
COBAYNE LOUTH
COBB LIMERICK
COBLEIGH WATERFORD
COBOURN *450
COBRAM *450
COBURN DOWN,ARMAGH
COCHRANE *72,*410
COCHRANE ANTRIM,LON
COCKAIN PMO
COD PMO
CODD PN WEXFORD/ WEXI
CODDINGTON DUBLIN
CODDY PN TIPPERARY
CODE DONEGAL,DERRY,14
CODON KILKENNY
CODY DERRY,ANT, 1462 S/
COEN GALWAY, ROSCOMN
COEY ANTRIM, DOWN, 6 B
COFFEY WESTMEATH/ KE
COFFIE PN ROSCOMMON
COFFY PN WESTMEATH,R(
COGAN WICKLOW,KIL,169
COGANE PN CORK
COGELY PN Wexford
COGHAN PN Waterford
COGHELL PN Kilkenny
COGHILL PN Kilkenny
COGHLAN PN KINGS,ROS
COGHLANE PN CORK , KI
COGHRAN DOWN
O COGLEY PN Ferm.
COGLEY *243,*245
COGLY PN Louth
COHANE PN Rosc.
COHEN *71
COHOLANE *397
COHOUN *399
COID *91
COILES *60
COIN *40,*312
COINYN KERRY
COKAIN PMO
COKELY *15

COLAVIN *154
COLBERT CORK, WATERF
COLCLOUGH WEX,1642,
COLCLOUGHA *155
COLDRICK *52
COLE KILD,MON,1646 ENG/
MC COLE DONEGAL,*259
COLELOUGH ROSCOMM(
COLEMAN PN WAT,DUB,I
COLGAN DUBLIN,KINGS,/
MC COLGAN DONEGAL,]
COLHOON *399
COLHOUN LOND, TYRONI
COLHOUNE DONEGAL
O COLHOUNE PN Donegal
COLHOWN PMO
COLIGAN *454B
COLIN *498
COLINS *489
COLL DONEGAL
MC COLL *91
O COLLAGHANE PN Keri
O COLLANE PN Lim.
COLLEN *17,*410,*489
COLLENS WESTMEATH,LI
MC COLLENY FERMANA
COLLERAN MAYO, GALW
COLLERY *485
COLLEY PMO
MC COLLGAN PN Donega
COLLIER WEXFORD/ PN M
COLLIGAN 5 BIRTHS, NO]
MC COLLIN PN DONEGAI
COLLINS COR,LIM,CLA,11
COLLIS SLIGO, KERRY,PM
COLLISSON LIMERICK CI
MC COLLO ANTRIM
MC COLLOGH PN Down.
COLLOM *65
O COLLOUNE PN Donegal
MC COLLUM PN ARMAG
COLLUN PMO
COLLVILL ANTRIM
COLLY PN ROSCOMMON,K
M' COLLYUMS *503
COLMAN *72
MC COLMAN *429
COLNAN *103
COLOTHAN *173
COLOVIN *154
COLPOISE PMO
COLPOYSE PMO
COLQUHOUN *399,*244
COLQUOHOUN *91
COLREAVY *132,*215,*46
COLUER PN Wexford
COLVILL PMO
COLVIN WAT, CORK,LIM,
COLWELL *58,*92
COLWILL ANTRIM

COMAN PN TIPPERARY,W
COMANE PN CLARE, TIPP
O COMANE PN Lim.
MC COMB DERRY, 1686 S
COMBA *445
COMBE PMO
COMBEL CORK CITY
COMBER MAYO, *329
COMBES PMO, DUBLIN CI
MC COME PN Down.
COMER *329
COMERFORD LEIX,1172
COMERTON *526
COMFORD *120
COMFORT *135
MC COMICK *410
COMIN PN QUEENS,LIMER
COMINE CLARE
COMISKEY *153,*154
COMJEAN *107
COMJEENS *109
MC COMLEY *197
COMMAN PN Kildare
COMMANE *45,*39,*509,
COMMASKEY *246
COMMEFORT *72
COMMERFOR *246
MC COMMINGS *358
COMMINS MAYO,WATER
COMMON *109
COMMONS KILK, GAL,M
COMMUNE ARMAGH
COMPTON DUBLIN,WEX,
COMYN CORK,CLA,GAL, 1
COMYNE PN TIPPERARY,(
M' CONA *271
CONAGHAN DONEGAL, L
O CONAGHAN PN Donega
MC CONAGHY ANTRIM,
O CONAGILL PN Donegal
CONALLONE PN KINGS
CONALLY PN WESTMEAT
MC CONAMY *181
O CONAN PN Leitrim
CONATY CAVAN, *211
M' CONAUGHTY *367
CONBOY ROSCOMMON,SI
CONCANNON GALWAY,I
CONDERICK *162
CONDON CORK,LIM,1172
CONDRICK *162
CONDRON CORK,LIM,158
CONDY TYRONE, FERMAN
CONE CORK
CONEFRY LEITRIM
CONELAN PN Kildare
CONELLAN PN SLIGO
O CONELLANE PN CLAR
CONELLANE PN CLARE,S
CONELLY PN WESTMEATI

CONERAN PN KILDARE
CONGREIFE LIMERICK
CONHEENY *386
CONICK PN Wexford
O CONIGAN PN Donegal
O CONIGHAN PN Donegal
CONIHY PN Long.
CONILLAN PN SLIGO
CONIN TIPPERARY
CONINGHAM PMO
MC CONKEY ANTRIM
CONLA *429
CONLAN PN KILD/ ROS,M
CONLAND *321
CONLIN *372
CONLOGUE *447
CONLON ROSCOMMON,M.
CONLY DUBLIN CITY
CONMEE *209
CONN DOWN, ARMAGH
MC CONN PN Tip.
CONNALAN PN West.
O CONNALLY PN Donegal
CONNARD CORK
Connaughton GALWAY, I
CONNEALLY *307
CONNEALY *463
CONNEELY GALWAY,*46
CONNEL PMO
CONNEL PMO
CONNELAN PN LOUTH,W
CONNELL PN CLA,TIP,WA
O CONNELL PN CLA,COR
MC CONNELL PN ANT,D
CONNELLAN PN LOUTH/
O CONNELLANE PN ARN
O CONNELLY PN DON,FI
CONNELLY PN TIP, LEITR
CONNER PN TIPPERARY,I
MC CONNER PN QUEEN:
CONNERNEY *21
CONNERTON *255
M' CONNERTY *367
CONNERY CLARE/ *431
CONNEY LOUTH/ 5 BIRTH
CONNIERS PMO
CONNIFF *447
CONNILLAN PN LONGFO
CONNINGHAM PMO
CONNOHOR PN WATERF
O CONNOHOR PN WATE
CONNOLA PN WATERFOR
CONNOLAN PN LOUTH
CONNOLAY PN WATERFC
CONNOLLY CORK,MON,G
CONNOLY PN LOUTH
O CONNOLY PN MONAGI
MC CONNON LOUTH, *2
O CONNOR PN DON, ETC
MC CONNOR PN LOND,

CONNOR PN CLA, TIP, WA
CONNORS PN WEXFORD/
O CONNORS PN WEXFOR
CONNORTON *3,*255
CONNORY PN WATERFOR
O CONNORY PN WATERF
CONNY PN CLARE
CONNYN QUEENS
O CONOGHER PN ANTRI
CONOGHYE PN ANTRIM
MC CONOHY *265
CONOLAN PN KILDARE
MC CONOLY PN MONAG
MC CONOMY *159,*418.
CONOO *249
CONOR PN CARLOW, KILI
O CONOR PN SLIGO
MC CONOR PN CARLOW
CONOW PN CORK
CONRAGHY PN KINGS,Q
CONRAHY PN QUEENS,*(
CONRAN PN KINGS, QUE
M' CONREADY *254
CONROY GALWAY,QUEE
CONRY PN ROSCOMMON/
CONSDIN PN CLARE
MC CONSIDAN CLARE
CONSIDIN PN CLARE
MC CONSIDIN PN CLARI
CONSIDINE CLARE, LIME
MC CONSIDN PN CLARE
CONSTABLE LOUTH
O CONTY PN LIMERICK
CONVERY LONDONDERR
CONVEY MAYO, DOWN
MC CONVILLE ARMAGH
CONVOY PN KILKENNY
CONWAY PN KILK,KINGS
MC CONWAY PN DONEG
CONWELL *58
CONY KERRY
CONYEEN *3
CONYER PMO
CONYERS KERRY, *456
MC COO ARMAGH, ANTR
COOCH PMO
COODY PN KILKENNY
MC COODY PN QUEENS
O COOGAN PN MONAGH
COOGAN DUBLIN,KILK, N
COOGANE CLARE
COOK PMO
MC COOK *254
MC COOKE PN ANTRIM, I
COOKE CORK,WEST, 1640
COOKE ANTRIM,DUB,COR
MC COOL DONEGAL, TYR
COOLE FERMANAGH,TIP./
COOLEY PMO/ ANTRIM, G
COOLMAN TIPPERARY

COON *96
COONAGHAN *347
COONEY MAYO, DUBLIN
COONIHAN *224
COONOON *488
COONY PN CLARE
COOPER LIM,MAY,TIP 164
COOPER ANTRIM, DUBLI
COOT PMO
COOTE LIM,1690 NOR/ROS,
COPE ARMAGH, 1640 NOR/
COPELAND DUBLIN,DOW
COPELTON *414
COPELY LIMERICK
COPINGER CORK CITY
COPLETON *55,*89,*489
COPLEY CORK/ CORK
COPPINGER CORK, 1172 I
COPPLEN LIMERICK
CORATHERS *181
CORBALLY PN DUBLIN,/
CORBAN PN WATERFORD
CORBANE PN CLARE, WA
O CORBANE PN LIMERIC
CORBET PMO
CORBETT LIM,TIP,1172 W
CORBIN CORK,LIMERICK
CORCKRON PN KILKENN
CORCORAN MAYO,CORK
MC CORD DOWN 1686 SC
CORDAN *47
CORDNER ARMAGH
O CORE PN LONDONDERR
COREGAN PN KINGS
COREY WAT,CORK,LIM 11
CORIBEEN *174
CORISH 5 BIRTHS,*28
CORK PMO
CORKAN PN SLIGO
CORKCRANE PN KINGS
CORKDYALE WESTMEAT
CORKE CORK
CORKEN *257
CORKERAN PN WATERFC
CORKERANE PN KINGS
O CORKERANE PN COR
CORKERIN PN WATERFOI
CORKERRY *51
CORKERY CORK,LIM,KEI
MC CORKILL LEITRIM,D
CORKIN DOWN
CORKRON KILKENNY
CORLESS GALWAY
CORLEY 6 BIRTHS
CORLEY *435
CORMAC *448
CORMACK PN KILD, LON
O CORMACK PN CORK,L
MC CORMACK PN DOW
CORMICAN GALWAY, *6

MC CORMICK PN ANT, I
CORMICK PN LONGFORD
O CORMICK PN FERMAN
CORMICKE KILKENNY
MC CORMILLA *319
CORMOCKE PN TIPPERAI
MC CORMUCK PN LONI
CORMUCKE PN TIPPERA
CORN *289,*481
CORNEWELL LONDONDE
CORR PN MEATH, ALSO TI
O CORR PN ARMAGH , LO
CORR DUBLIN, TYRONE
CORRAN *374
CORREN PN CARLOW, KII
CORREY KILKENNY
O CORRICAN PN FERMA
O CORRIGAN PN FERMA
CORRIGAN PN LONG/ DU
CORROLL TIPPERARY
O CORRONEY PN FERM/
O CORRONY PN FERMAN
CORRY DOWN, 1709 ENG/
MC CORRY PN FERMANA
O CORRYGAN PN FERM.
CORSTELLOW CORK
CORTHORP PMO
CORTON KINGS
CORY PMO/ 48B
COSBY LEIX 1550 ENG./ Q
COSCOR *183
COSGRAVE DUBLIN, WE
COSGROVE MAYO,GALW
O COSHEDY PN FERMAN
COSHMAN *304A
COSKER *412
MC COSKER PN FERMAN
COSKERRY *111
COSS *149
COSSENS MONAGHAN, LI
COSTELL DOWN
COSTELLO PN TIPPERARY
COSTELLOE LIMERICK, G
COSTELLY PN TIPPERARY
COSTIGAN PN KINGS, QU
COSTIGIN PN KILKENNY,
COSTILY *316
COSTLE KILKENNY
COSTLELOE DUBLIN CITY
COSTLEY *197,*381
COSTOLOE *309.
MC COTTAR *343
O COTTER PN CORK
COTTER CORK/ CORK
MC COTTER *397
COTTERELL WEXFORD
MC COTTIER *53
COTTLE DUBLIN
COTTON DUB CTY, WEX,I
MC COUBREY DOWN, A

COUE WESTMEATH
COUGHLAN LIMERICK CI
COUGHLANE PN CORK, \
COUGHLIN *61
O COUGLANE PN CORK
COULPYS CLARE
COULTER DUBLIN,CORK,
COULTHURST CORK
COUMEY *224
COUN PN DOWN
COUNE PN ARMAGH
COUNIHAN KERRY, *42,*
COUNTY *47
COURCY CORK
COURIGAN *3
COURN *420
COURNANE ALL KERRY,
COURNEEN *390
COURSEY PN CORK
MC COURT PN LOUTH/ L
COURTAYNE *303
COURTENAY LIMERICK
COURTES FERMANAGH
COURTESS PMO
COURTHOP CORK CITY
COURTNEY KERRY,ANTR
COURTNEY ANTRIM,TIPP
MC COURTNEY *494
COUSINE *109
COUSINS 18 BIRTHS,NONI
COUVANE *47
COUZEENS *109
COVENEY CORK
COVER PMO
COVET PMO
COVETT CORK CITY
COWAN PN ANTRIM/ ANTI
MC COWAN PN ANTRIM
COWAY PN KILKENNY
COWDIE *210
MC COWELL *163,*418
COWEN *397
COWLEY MAYO
COWLEY *231
COWMAN *244,*408
MC COWMAN PN WATEI
MC COWNLEY *69
COWSE DUBLIN
COX WEX,LIM 1642 ENG/DU
COXE *294
COY 5 BIRTHS
MC COY TYRONE,1710 SC
COYD *91
COYLE PN ROSCOMMON/ I
COYN PMO
COYNE GALWAY, MAYO, *
COYSH WESTMEATH
COZENE CORK
CRA *67
CRAAN *72

CRABB LIMERICK CITY, PI
MC CRACKEN FERMAN/
CRAFFORD SLIGO, DONE
CRAFORD PN ANTRIM, L
CRAG PMO
CRAGE *259
CRAGH PN WATERFORD, :
MC CRAGH CORK,LIM CI
CRAHAN *72
CRAIG DOWN,LOU,MEA, 1
CRAIGE PN ANTRIM,ALSO
CRAIGH *97
CRAINE CORK CITY
Mac CRAITH PN LIMERIC
MC CRAITH LIMERICK,*:
CRAMBY DUBLIN CITY
CRAMPSEY *271
CRAMPSIE *479,*482
CRAMPSY DONEGAL, *36
CRAMPTON 7 BIRTHS, AI
CRANE PMO/ 8 BIRTHS, *3:
MC CRANN *128
CRANNY 6 BIRTHS, NONE
Cransborogh WATERFORI
Cransborrow CLARE
CRANSTON ARMAGH, AN
CRANWELL PMO
CRANWELL DUBLIN CITY
CRASTON SLIGO
MC CRATH PN TIPPERAR
CRAUEN LIMERICK CITY
CRAVEN WATERFORD, KI
CRAWFORD DON,DER,MI
CRAWFURD DOWN
CRAWLEY LOUTH, ROSC
MC CREA ANTRIM, TYRO
MC CREADY DOWN,ANT
CREAGH PN CLARE, LIME
CREAMER DUBLIN CITY,:
CREAN KERRY, CORK,WE
O CREAN DONEGAL
CREANE *72
CREANEY ARMAGH,DOW
MC CREARY 5 BIRTHS
CREATON 8 BIRTHS
M' CREECH *248
CREED LIMERICK,1173 NOI
CREEDON CORK
CREEGAN LEITRIM, SLIGC
CREELAND *381
MC CREERY PN ANTRIM
MC CREESH MONAGHAN
CREGAN LIMERICK, MEAT
CREGG ROSCOMMON, *34
CREHAN GALWAY
CREIGHTON ANTRIM, DU
CRELLY *429
CREMEEN *79
CREMIN CORK, KERRY, *
CREORY PN QUEENS

MC CRERIE PN DOWN
MC CRERY PN FERMANA
CRERY PN FERMANAGH
CRESANS DOWN
CRESKITT KILKENNY
CREVY PN WESTMEATH
CREWSE PMO
CRIBBON •435
CRICKARD •175
Crickenham •274
CRICKET •175
CRIGHLEY •98
CRIGHTONE DONEGAL
CRILLY ANTRIM, LOND,L
CRIMBLE MONAGHAN
CRIMMEEN •79
CRIPPS LIMERICK CITY, P
CRISPE CORK CITY
CRISPP WESTMEATH
CROAKER PMO
CROFFTON ROSCOMMON
CROFTON LEITRIM, 1642
CROFTS CORK CITY, PMO
CROGHAN PN ROSCOMM
CROGHEN CLARE
MC CROHAN ALL IN KE
CROKE TIPPERARY, WATE
CROKER LIMERICK, 1640
MC CROLEY PN LOUTH
CROLLY PN LOUTH
MC CROLY PN LOUTH
O CROMEENE PN LIMER
CROMEWELL DOWN
CROMIE ARMAGH, DOWN
CROMWELL CLARE,GAL
O CROMY PN ARMAGH
CRONE CORK/ CORK, ANT
O CRONEENE PN KERRY
CRONIN CORK, KERRY, L
O CRONINE PN CORK
CRONOUGE •128
CRONVY •185
O CRONYNE PN CORK
CROOKE TIPPERARY, KIL
CROOKER PMO
CROOKS ANTRIM, LONDO
Crooksshanks •429
CROOOTHER LOUTH
CROPLEY WESTMEATH
MC CRORY TYRONE,AN
CROSBIE DUBLIN
CROSBY PN KERRY
CROSS ARMAGH 1610 ENG
CROSSAN LONDONDERR
MC CROSSAN TYRONE
CROSSE CORK
CROSSEY WESTMEATH
CROSTENTON DUBLIN C
CROSTON SLIGO
CROTHERS ANTRIM, DO
CROTTY LOUTH,1590 SCO
CROUGH •510
CROWE CLARE, 1172 NOR
O CROWLE CLARE
CROWLEY CORK/CORK,
O CROWLEY PN CORK
CROWLEY PN CORK
O CROWLY PN CORK
CROWLY PN CORK.
CROWTHER PMO
CROZIER PN FERMANAG
M' CRUB •60
CRUCE LIMERICK, 1172 E
MC CRUDDEN ANTRIM,
CRUIHLY QUEENS
CRUISE LIMERICK,1172,E
CRULLY •489
MC CRUM 8 BIRTHS
CRUMLISH •260
CRUMMY •185
CRUSE PMO
CRYAN ROSCOMMON
CRYMBLE DOWN/ ANTRI
MC CUDDEN •492
CUDDIHY KILKENNY, •15
CUDDY 8 BIRTHS, •15,•45
MC CUE •259,•341
CUE •397
CUELL KILKENNY
CUFF CLARE,DUB CTY, PN
CUFFE TIPPERARY,PMO/ N
CUHY •15
O CUILLEN PN LEITRIM
CUINANE •138
CULANE PN CLARE
CULBERT ANTRIM, •19,•8
O CULENANE PN CLARE
CULHANE LIMERICK
CULHOUN •244
CULINANE PN CLARE
CULL 10 BIRTHS.
MC CULL •16
MC CULLAGH PN ANTRI
CULLAN PN DUBLIN
O CULLAN PN DONEGAL
CULLANE PN CORK, LIME
O CULLANE PN DON,COR
CULLE •318
O CULLEANE PN LIMERI
CULLEEN PN CLARE
CULLEENY •189
CULLEGANE PN CLARE
CULLEN PN CARLOW, KIL
O CULLEN PN ARMAGH,
MC CULLEN •495,•515
CULLENANE PN CORK
O CULLENANE PN CORK
CULLETON WEXFORD
CULLIAN •447
CULLIGAN CLARE, •308,•
CULLILANE PN CORK
CULLIN PN DONEGAL, DU
MC CULLIN PN MONAGH
O CULLIN PN MONAGHA
CULLINAN CLARE
CULLINANE CORK, WAT
CULLION •356,•459
MC CULLION •351
CULLIVAN •49
CULLNANE CORK
MC CULLOCH •159
MC CULLOGH PN ANTRI
CULLOON •245
CULLOTY ALL IN KERRY
MC CULLOUGH PN ANT
MC CULLOW •423
O CULLUN PN WEXFORD
CULLY PN WESTMEATH/ A
MC CULLY MEATH, 1610
MC CULLYAM •55
CULME PMO
CULREAVY •33,•153,•357
CULWELL ARMAGH
CUMBERFORD•289
CUMISKEY CAVAN, LON
CUMMANE PN CORK CIT
CUMMING DUBLIN, ANT
CUMMINGS ANTRIM,•43
CUMMINS DUBLIN,CORK
CUNAGUM •386
O CUNANE PN SLIGO
MC CUNE ANTRIM, ARM
CUNEEN PN CLARE, •136,
CUNEGAN ROSCOMMON
CUNIGAM PN CLARE
CUNIGANE LEITRIM
O CUNIGANE PN CLARE
CUNIGHAM DOWN
CUNIHAN •406
CUNINGHAM PN DONEG
O CUNINGHAM PN DON
CUNINGHAME DONEGA
CUNION •172
CUNNAGHER •50
CUNNAHAN •61
CUNNAIN •105
CUNNANE MAYO, ROSCO
CUNNEA •126,•259
CUNNEEN •237,•297
CUNNEENY •386
CUNNIAM •207,•332.
CUNNIFFE GALWAY,MAY
CUNNIGAN •329
MC CUNNIGAN •260
CUNNIGHAN •216
CUNNINGHAM TYRONE,
CUNNION •132
CUNNOO •249
CUNNY PN CLARE/ •5
CUNNYER •240
CUNREE •419
CUNREEN •485
CUNYNGHAM PN DONE
CUNYNGHAM DONEGAL
CUOLOHAN •420
CUPPAGE PMO, WEXFOR
CUPPLES ANTRIM, ARMA
CURAN PN KERRY
CURANE PN WATERFORD
CURD CLARE,PMO
MC CURDY DOWN,LOUT
CURLEY CORK/ ROSCOMM
O CURMINE PN LEITRIM
CURNANE •511,•512
O CURNANE PN KERRY
CURNEEN •370
CURNIN •370
CURRAN PN KERRY/ DON
O CURRANE PN KERRY,
CURRANE ALL KERRY, •
CURREEN •224,•235
CURREENE PN WATERFO
CURREN PN CARLOW,KIL
CURRID SLIGO, WEXFOR
CURRIE ANTRIM, •91,•250
CURRIGAN ROSCOMMON
CURRIN PN WATERFORD,
O CURRIN PN DONEGAL
CURRINE PN LEITRIM
O CURROBEEN •40
O CURRY •189
CURRY PMO/ ANTRIM, •2
MC CURRY PN ANTRIM/
O CURTAINE PN CORK,K
MC CURTAINE PN KERR
MC CURTANE PN LIMER
CURTEOIS LIMERICK
CURTIN CORK,LIMERICK,
CURTIS CLARE, ROSCOMM
CUSACK DUB,LIM,TIP 117
CUSACKE PN CLARE
CUSAKE KINGS
CUSCO •33
CUSHANAN •91
CUSHEN •468
CUSHIN WESTMEATH
CUSHING •468
CUSHLEY •385
CUSKER •274
MC CUSKER ANTRIM, 16
MC CUSKERN •429
CUSKERN •367
CUSKERY •372
CUSKOR •104
CUSSACK PN KINGS
CUSSACKE KINGS
CUSSANE •157B,•229,•52
CUSSEN CORK,LIMERICK,
CUSSIN PN WEXFORD
CUSSOCK KILKENNY
CUSSOCKE PN CLARE
MC CUSSOCKE PN CLA
CUSSOK WESTMEATH
MC CUTCHEON TYRON
CUTHBERT LIMERICK, D
CYRCH DUBLIN CITY
D.L. •450
D'ELL •267,•279
D'EVELYN •257,•429
DACEY PN CORK
MC DACKER •401
DACY PN CORK
O DACY PN SLIGO
MC DAE PN CLARE
O DAE PN CLARE
DAGG 7 BIRTHS-LEINSTER
DAHILL ALL TIPPERARY
MC DAID LIM,GAL,DON,1
DAILY •223
DALE MEATH,1646 ENG./C
DALEY PN KINGS
DALHOUSE •254
DALIE PN/KILDARE,WEST
DALLAS ANTRIM
DALLI PN KILDARE
DALLWAY ANTRIM
DALLY PN CLARE, KERRY,
O DALLY PN ARMAGH, M
DALTON DUB,LIM,CLA,W,
DALWAY ANTRIM 1573 E
DALY PN CORK,DUB, LON
O DALY PN CORK, KERRY
DALYELL DOWN
DALZELL DOWN
DANAHER LIMERICK,DU
DANCER WATERFORD,DU
DANDRIDGE DUBLIN,DE
DANE PN ROSCOMMON, F
DANGER •121
DANIEL DUBLIN,TIPPERA
MC DANIEL 8 BIRTHS,•2
DANIELL PN VARIOUS
MC DANIELL PN CLARE
O DANIELL PN LIMERICK
DANIHY •100
DANLEY •72
MC DANLL PN CARLOW
O DANNELL PN LIMERIC
DANNELLY •487
DANT PMO
M' DARA •450
DARBY OFFALY,1640 ENG
DARCEY PN WESTMEATH
DARCY GAL,MAY,WEST 1
DARDIS DUBLIN 1171 N/W
DARGAN DUBLIN/
O DARIAN •411
DARLEY CORK, •172
DARLING DUBLIN CITY/5
DARLY KINGS
DARMODY TIPPERARY, •
DARRAGH ANTRIM
MC DARRAGH PN ANTR
DARSON TIPPERARY
DARSY KILDARE,KINGS
DARWELL WATERFORD
DASHWOOD CORK
DASON KILKENNY, DUBLI
DATON DUBLIN, 1172 N/P
DAUENPORT LONDONDE
MC DAUID PN CORK, KE
DAUIES LIMERICK CITY
DAUIS KILDARE, ROSCOM
DAUNT CORK,1640 NORM
DAUSON DUBLIN CITY
DAVANE PN TIPPERARY
DAVENPORT CORK
DAVERN TIPPERARY
DAVEY SLIGO,ANTRIM
MC DAVID LIMERICK,GA
DAVIDSON ANTRIM,DOW
DAVIE LEITRIM,DONEGAL
DAVIES PN ANTRIM
DAVIN TIPPERARY,GALW
DAVIS WEX,WAT,1172 W/
DAVISON ANTRIM,•177,•
DAVISS PN ANTRIM
DAVITT 8 BIRTHS,•486
MC DAVITT KERRY,COR,
O DAVOREN PN CLARE
O DAVORIN PN TIPPERA
DAVY DONEGAL 1684 SCO
DAVYS •72
DAWKINS DUBLIN
DAWLEY CORK,•69,•382
DAWLY PMO,•397,•431
DAWNEY •429
DAWSON DERRY 1680 EN
DAWTIN •117
DAY TIPPERARY/13 BIRTH
DAYLEY •224
DAYLY CORK CITY
O DAYLY PN CORK, KERR
DE ERMOT •177
De'AP •58,•238,•352
DEA 10 BIRTHS,•280
O DEA PN LIMERICK/ CLA
DEACON LIMERICK 1570
DEADY KERRY
DEAKE ANTRIM
DEALY •397
DEAN LIMERICK 1790 SCO
DEANE PN TIP, LIM, DUB,
DEARE WATERFORD
DEASY CORK,MAYO
DEATICK KERRY
DEBART DUBLIN CITY
DEBOIS •204
DEE DUBLIN CITY/WATERF
O DEE LIMERICK

DEEGAN DUBLIN,KINGS,(

DEEHAN LONDONDERRY,

DEELY GALWAY,*360

DEEN *290

DEENEY DONEGAL,LOND(

DEENY DONEGAL,LONDON

DEERING MONAGHAN

DEERMOTT *343,*482

DEERY TYRONE,MONAGH,

DEEVEY *249

DEEVY KILKENNY

DEEY PMO

DEFFELY *454B

DEHORTY *529

DEIGHAN *59

O DEL PMO

DELACHERIOS *318

DELACOURT CORK

DELAFYELD MEATH

DELAHIDE CORK CITY

DELAHOYD DUBLIN

DELAHUNT KILDARE

DELAHUNTY 10 BIRTHS,I

DELAMAR ROSCOMMON/

DELAMARE PN WESTME/

DELANE *50

DELANEY DUBLIN,QUEEN

DELANY DUBLIN,QUEENS

DELAPP DONEGAL

DELARAHE KILKENNY

DELASALE DUBLIN CITY

DELAY *397

DELEA *134

O DELL WATERFORD,LIM,

DELLAHOIDE LOUTH

DELLANY PN KINGS

DELOOHERY *99,*318

DELOOREY *99

DELOUGHRY *47

DEMPSEY PN KILDARE, K

DEMPSTER ANTRIM,DOW

DEMPSY PN KINGS, QUEE

O DEMSIE PN LONDONDE

DEMSY PN WEXFORD

DENEHER *232

O DENELIN PN ARMAGH

DENISON WEXFORD,*179

DENN PN KILKENNY

DENNEHY CORK,KERRY,*

DENNING *370

DENNIS WICKLOW 1680 FI

DENNISH ROSCOMMON

DENNISON ARMAGH,ALL

DENNY KERRY 1172 ENGL

DENT DUBLIN CITY

DENY PMO

O DEORAN PN WEXFORD

DERBON DUBLIN CITY

DERBY ANTRIM

DERBY KINGS

MC DERBY PN TIPPERAR

DERHAM LOUTH

MC DERMOD PN CORK,

DERMOD OGE PN CORK

DERMODY 9 BIRTHS,NON

DERMODY PN CLARE, TI

MC DERMODY PN CORK

DERMOND PN LOUTH,*1(

O DERMOND PN DONEG/

MC DERMOT PN KILDAR

DERMOTT PN DUBLIN, L(

MC DERMOTT PN FER, (

DERRMOTT PN LONGFOR

O DERROGAN PN LEITRI

DERRY DUBLIN CITY

DESMINEER PMO,DUBLI

DESMINEERS DUBLIN CI

DESMOND LIMERICK,117

MC DESMOND PN CORK

DESMONEER PMO

DESNEY TIPPERARY

O DETT PMO

DEUENISHE KILDARE

O DEUER PN DONEGAL

DEUERAX CARLOW

DEUEREUX PN WEXFORD

DEVANE PN TIPPERARY/K

DEVANEY MAYO,GALWA

DEVANY MAYO,GALWAY

MC DEVE PN DONEGAL

DEVEN PN WATERFORD,*4

DEVENNY MAYO,GALWA

O DEVENY PN DONEGAL

DEVER MAYO

DEVEREUX WEXFORD

DEVEREUX WEXFORD,11

DEVERILL *249

DEVERS MAYO,WEXFORD

DEVERY WATERFORD,117

MC DEVET PN DONEGAL

DEVIN *159

DEVINE TYRONE,DUBLIN,

DEVITT CLARE,DUBLIN,*4

MC DEVITT CORK,LIMER

DEVLIN ANTRIM,TYRONE,

DEVON *416

DEVOROUX KILKENNY

DEVOY PN QUEENS

MC DEWETT PN LONDON

DEY PMO,LOUTH

DEYER CORK

DEYERMOND *344

DEYERMOTT *271,*356,*

DEYS CORK

O DHEERQ *378

DIAMOND CORK CITY,LO

DIARMID *341,*381,*423

DIARMOD *271

DIARMOND *344

DICK KILDARE,CARLOW 1

DICKEY ANTRIM

DICKINSON CORK

DICKSON LIM,LEIT,1780 E

MC DIER PN SLIGO

DIERMOTT *240,*260

O DIFF *40

DIFFEN *18

DIGAN KINGS,*249,*420

DIGBY KINGS

DIGGIN KERRY

DIGGS DUBLIN CITY

DIGNAN WESTMEATH

DILLAN PN CARLOW

DILLANE LIMERICK,GALV

O DILLANE PN LIMERICK

O DILLENE PN LIMERICK

DILLON PN KINGS, LONG,

O DILLON PN ROSCOMMC

DILLONE KINGS

DILLOUGHERY *431

DILWORTH *99

DIMMETT *325

DIMOCK PMO

DINAN CORK

DINANE PN CORK

O DINE PN WATERFORD

DINEEN CORK,*142

DINGAVAN *431

DINGLE TIPPERARY,PMO

DINHAM PMO

DINNEEN CORK

DINNEGAN *3

DINSMORE LONDONDERI

M' DIRE *259

DIRRANE GALWAY

DISBROW KINGS

DISKIN ALL GALWAY

DISNEY WESTMEATH,LOU

DIUEN PN ARMAGH

O DIUIN PN ARMAGH

DIURMAGH *391

DIVANE *382

DIVELIN ANTRIM

DIVER DONEGAL

DIVER *271

O DIVER PN DONEGAL

O DIVET PN DONEGAL

DIVIN *240,*480

MC DIVITT *271

DIVOY PN QUEENS

DIXEY PN LOUTH

DIXON LIM,DON,1642 ENG

DIXSON DUBLIN CITY

DIXY PMO

DOAVE CORK

DOB ANTRIM,PMO

DOBBIN CAVAN,ARMAGH

DOBBINS PMO

DOBBS ANTRIM 1596 ENGI

DOBIN *115

DOBSON WEXFORD,DUBL

DOCKERY ROSCOMMON

DOCKRELL DUBLIN,ALL

DODD LIM,ROS,1646 ENG/(

DODDS DOWN,ARMAGH,1(

DODGIN CORK

DODLESTON KILDARE

DODS *71

DODSON DUBLIN CITY

DOELANE PN Kings

DOEY *76

DOGGAN PN Waterford

DOGHERTY PN SLIGO, PM

O DOGHERTY PN DONEC

O DOGHERTYE PN DONE

DOGHON PN Tip.

O DOGHON PN Tip.

DOHENY *189

DOHERTY LONDONDERR

O DOHERTY 7 BIRTHS,*3

DOLAN PN LEIT, ROS/FER,

O DOLAN PN Ferm.

DOLANE PN Rosc.

MC DOLE *95

DOLLANE PN Rosc.

DOLLARD 5 BIRTHS

DOLLOGHANE PN KINGS

DOLLOWAY PMO

DOLOGHAN *59

DOLWAY PMO

DOLY PN DUBLIN CITY

DOMEGAN *175

DOMVIL PMO

DOMVILE PMO

DONAGH *332

MC DONAGH PN CORK,

DONAGHEY *159

MC DONAGHEY PN Ferm

O DONAGHOW PN Lim.

DONAGHY ANTRIM,TYRC

O DONAGHY PN Lond.

DONAHY *447

DONALD ANTRIM,ALL UL

MC DONALD DON,DER 1

DONALDSON PMO/ANTR

DONCHO PN Long.

DONDEN LIMERICK

DONE PMO

DONEGAN PN WESTMEAT

DONELAN PN KINGS, ROS

O DONELAN ROSCOMMO

DONELL PN ANT, DUB, KI

MC DONELL PN ANT, AR

O DONELL PN DONEGAL,

DONELLAN PN Queens.

DONELLEE PN Long.

O DONELLY PN ARMAGH

DONELSON PN ANTRIM

O DONELY PN Armagh,

O DONEVAN PN LIMERIC

DONGAN KILDARE/*72

DONGARVAN CORK

MC DONIELL PN LIM. CI

O DONILY PN Long.

DONLAN GALWAY,*274,*

O DONLEN PN Kildare

DONLON LONGFORD,*274

DONLY *448

DONN PN DUBLIN

DONNAN DOWN

DONNEGAL ANTRIM

DONNELAN PMO

DONNELL PN ANT,WAT,K

MC DONNELL DUB,MAY

MC DONNELL PN ARMA(

O DONNELL PN ANT, DO

DONNELLAN DUBLIN/CL

DONNELLY ANT,TYR,AR

DONNELON PMO

MC DONNOGH PN CLA,(

DONNOGHER ROSCOMM

DONNOLDSON ANTRIM

MC DONNOUGH PN Tip.

DONNOVANE CORK

DONOCHO *211

DONOGH PN Tip.

MC DONOGH PN CLARE,

DONOGH OGE PN CORK

DONOGHOE PN Waterford

DONOGHOW PN CLARE,

O DONOGHOW PN CLAR

DONOGHUE KERRY,CORI

O DONOGHUE KERRY,C(

MC DONOGHY PN Lond.

DONOHOE DUBLIN,LONG

DONOHUE *109

DONOLDSON ANTRIM

DONORTY PN Waterford

MC DONOUGH PN KING

DONOVAN CORK

O DONOVAN CORK,LIME

DONOVANE PN CORK

MC DONOVANE PN COR

O DONOVANE PN CORK

DOOAL *113

DOODY PN TIPPERARY/ LI

O DOODY PN Tip.

DOOEY *314,*432,*113

DOOGAN DONEGAL,*109,

O DOOGAN *189

O DOOGHANY *189

DOOGIN PN CLARE,TIPPEI

DOOHAN DONEGAL,CLAR

DOOLADY *132

DOOLADY *132

DOOLAN DUB,LOUTH,COI

O DOOLAN *189

DOOLEY PN TIPPERARY/

DOOLIN PN CARLOW, KIL

DOOLING PN QUEENS/ *2(

DOOLY PN KILKENNY, *12

DOONA *309

DOONAN LEITRIM,ROSCO

DOONER PN Long.

DOONEY ROSCOMMON

DOONICAN *420

DOORLY *54

DORAN PN KILD,MEATH,

O DORAN PN Down.

DORANE PN WEXFORD,L(

DORCEY *472

DORE DUBLIN 1686 FRENC

DORGAN CORK

DORMAN DOWN

DORNAN ANTRIM,DOWN,

O DORNAN *112

DORNEY CORK,TIPPERAR

O DORNEY PN CORK

DORRAN *411

DORRIAN 7 BIRTHS,ALL I

DOUD *307

DOUDS *347

DOUGAN ANTRIM,ARMAC

DOUGHENY *189

DOUGHERTY *355

O DOUGHERTY FERMAN

O DOUGHERTYE PN Lon

DOUGLAS ANTRIM,LOND

DOUGLE *461

DOUGS *461

O DOVOREN CLARE

DOWD ROS,DUB,KER,GAL

O DOWD SLIGO,*307,*361

DOWDALL DUBLIN,LIM,1

DOWDS *381,*433

MC DOWELL PN ARMAG

O DOWER PN Waterford

O DOWEY PN LONDONDEI

MC DOWGALL PN Antrim

DOWLAN *30

MC DOWLE PN Long.

DOWLEY *129

DOWLIN *91

DOWLING DUBLIN,KILK,(

DOWNES CLARE,LIMERIC

DOWNEY LIMERICK,TIP 1

MC DOWNEY *429

DOWNING LIMERICK,DER

O DOWY PN Donegal

O DOY PN Donegal

DOYLE DUB,WEX,WIC,CAI

MC DOYLE PN West.

O DOYLE PN CARLOW,WE

DRAIN ALL ANTRIM,*450.

DRAKE WEXFORD,DERRY,

DRAPER LIMERICK,TIPPEI

O DREA PN Kilkenny

DREILING PN Kilkenny

DREINAN *40

DRENNAN ANTRIM,TIPPE

DREW CORK,LIM 1598 ENG
DRIBSON LIMERICK
DRINAN *506
DRINANE *419
DRISCOLL PN CORK/COR
O DRISCOLL PN CORK,A
DRISKELL *107
DROCHAN PN Waterford
DROGHAN PN WATERFOR
DROHAN WATERFORD,CC
DROMGOLD OFFALY 117
MC DROMMA PN Ferm.
O DROMMA PN FERMAN
DROOPE PMO
DROPE PMO
DROPS FERMANAGH
DROUGH *63
DROUGHT OFFALY,LEIX,I
DRUE WEXFORD
DRUERY ROSCOMMON
DRUM FERMANAGH
O DRUM PN FERMANAGH
DRUMM *154
DRUMMOND ANTRIM
DRUMMY CORK,SLIGO,*
DRURY DON,DER,1586 SCC
DUANE GALWAY
DUBLACK *30
DUCKENFIELD WESTME
DUCKETT KILDARE,CARL
DUCKINGFIEL QUEENS
880 DUCKLOW
DUDDY LONDONDERRY
DUDERAN PN LONGFORD
DUDGEON 6 BIRTHS
DUDLEY CORK,1646 ENG/
DUDLY DUBLIN CITY
DUFF LIM,1586 SCOT/PN T
DUFFE PN CAR, KILD,MEA
DUFFEY PN LOUTH
DUFFIE PN LOUTH, WESTM
O DUFFIE PN MONAGHAN
DUFFIN PN LOUTH/ ANTRI
DUFFY PN LONG,WEST/MA
DUGAN PN WATERFORD/
DUGEN PN KINGS
DUGGAN COR,DUB,TIP,W
DUGIN PN TIPPERARY
DUGINE KINGS
DUHIG CORK,KERRY
DUHY PN SLIGO,*235
DUIGAN *420
DUIGEN PN KINGS
O DUIGENAN PN LEITRIM
DUIGNAN LEITRIM,ROSCO
DUIN PN KILDARE,KILKEN
DUINE PN KILDARE
DUING PN KILKENNY
DUKE KILKENNY,SLIGO/AI
O DULANE PN KINGS

DULANTY *493
DULANY PN KILKENNY
O DULE PN LIMERICK CIT
DULEY PN KINGS
O DULINGE PN KERRY
DULINTY *104
DULLAGHAN LOUTH
DULLAHUNTY PN KILKE
DULLANIE PN KILDARE
DULLANY PN TIP,QUEENS
DULLARD PN KILKENNY/
DULLCHANTY KINGS
DULLEA *397
O DULLEGHAN PN LOUT
DULLENTY *249
DULLES ALL IN CORK
DULLY KINGS
O DULLY PN WESTMEATH
DULLYNE PN QUEENS
DUMEGAN *175
DUN PN KING,QUEENS,*18
MC DUNAGAN PN FERM
DUNBAR LOUTH 1620 SCC
DUNBARE DONEGAL
DUNBARR FERMANAGH
DUNCAN DONEGAL,DERR
DUNCHOWE PN QUEENS
DUNDASSE DOWN
DUNDON LIMERICK,TIP,1
DUNE PN ROSCOMMON
DUNEGAN PN WESTMEAT
DUNFY PN KILKENNY
DUNGAN DUBLIN 1646 EN
DUNICAN *420
DUNILY PN ROSCOMMON
DUNION *161
DUNKIN CORK
DUNLAPE ANTRIM
DUNLEA CORK
DUNLEAVY MAYO,SLIGO
DUNLOP DONEGAL 1600 S
DUNN PN DUBLIN,KILDAR
MC DUNN PN FERMANAG
DUNNE PN DUB,KILD/DUB
DUNPHY WATERFORD,DU
DUNSANY MEATH
DUNSCOMBE CORK CITY
DUNSHEE *58
Dunsterfield DONEGAL
DUNWOODY ANTRIM
DUOGIN PN WATERFORD
DURCAN *5
DURELY PN KINGS
O DURINGG PN FERMAN
DURKAN MAYO,SLIGO
DURKIN *5
DURLY PN KINGS
DURMODY *295
DURNIAN *482
DURNIN LOUTH

DURNION *313
DURRIAN *60
DUTTON DUBLIN,DONEGA
DUVAL *179
DUVALLEY *179
DUVICK *312
DUVIN PN WATERFORD
DUYGIN PN WESTMEATH
O DUYNE PN ARMAGH
DWAINE PN TIPPERARY,K
DWANE TIPPERARY,CORK
DWAYNE PN TIPPERARY
O DWAYNE PN TIPPERAR
DWIER LIMERICK
O DWIER PN LIMERICK
DWIGIN PN QUEENS
DWIGINE PN KINGS
DWIRE PN KINGS
DWYER PN LIM,TIP/TIP, C
O DWYER PN TIPPERARY/
DWYRE PN TIPPERARY,AL
O DWYRE PN CLARE,TIPP
DYAS DUBLIN
DYER CORK,ROSCOMMON
O DYER PN LIMERICK
DYERMOTT *374
O DYEYNEENE CORK
DYINS WATERFORD
DYLE *485
O DYMAN PN LONDONDE
DYMNOCK TIPPERARY
DYNAN *325
O DYODDAN PN FERMAN
DYVOY PN QUEENS
EADIE *210,ALSO ADAMS
EAGAN PN TIPPERARY
EAGAR 4 BIRTHS,NONE IN
EAGER PMO/3 BIRTHS,*42,
EAGERTON *399
EAKIN 5 BIRTHS,*159,*374
EAKINS 6 BIRTHS,*91,ALS
EAMES LIMERICK
EARL 5 BIRTHS,LEINSTER
EARLE CORK 1642 ENGLIS
EARLSMAN CORK,KILKE
EARLY DUBLIN CITY/LEITI
EARPH ARMAGH
EASTWOOD DUBLIN CITY
EATON LIMERICK,PMO/LO
EATTON CORK,ALSO ETON
EBERCRUMBE LEITRIM,
MC EBOY PN KILDARE
EBZURY WESTMEATH
ECCLES TYRONE 1602 SCC
ECKLES FERMANAGH
ECLSTON LOUTH
MC EDD LIMERICK
EDERY *431
EDGAR ANTRIM,DOWN
EDGWORTH LONGFORD,I

EDIMSON *76,ALSO ADAM
EDKINS DUBLIN CITY
EDMOND KERRY,ALSO FI
MC EDMOND PN CLARE,
EDMONDS DUBLIN,LIMEI
EDMONDSON QUEENS
EDMONSTON ANTRIM
MC EDMUND PN LIMERI
EDMUNDSTON PMO
EDWARDS DUBLIN,WEXF
EDWARDS WICKLOW 164
EDWORTH KILDARE
EGAN PN KINGS/GAL, DUB
MC EGAN PN ROSCOMMC
EGANE PN TIPPERARY,KIN
MC EGANE PN TIPPERAR
EGGART ANTRIM
EGGLINGTON *333
EGGLINTON *333
EIRONS *91
EIVERS *333
EKIN DUBLIN CITY,ALSO A
ELCHINDER *59,ALSO AL
ELDER ANTRIM,LONDOND
MC ELDOWNEY ALL LO
MC ELDUFF *417
ELFRED *40
MC ELGUN *167
MC ELGUNN *350
MC ELHAR *206
MC ELHILL *216
MC ELHINNEY DONEGA
ELIOTT CARLOW
ELLARD DUBLIN,TIPPERA
ELLET FERMANAGH
ELLICE ROSCOMMON
ELLIES *421
MC ELLIGOTT KERRY
ELLIOT FERMANAGH,ANT
ELLIOTT ANTRIM,FERMAI
ELLIS LIMERICK 1172 WEL
ELLISH ARMAGH
ELLISON KILKENNY 1230
Mac ELLISTRAM *47
ELLOT PN FERMANAGH
ELLOTT DUBLIN
ELLWOOD LOUTH/*381
ELLY TIPPERARY
MC ELLYGOTT KERRY
ELLYOTT PN FERMANAGH
MC ELMEEL MONAGHAN
ELMER TIPPERARY
MC ELMURRAY *238,*4
ELOTT MONAGHAN
MC ELROY LOUTH 1682 S
ELSHANDER *55,ALSO AI
MC ELSHENDER *204,AI
ELSHINDER *347,ALSO AI
ELSHNER *488,ALSO ALEX
MC ELSHUNDER *60,AL

ELTON CARLOW
ELUIN LONDONDERRY
MC ELVEAINE PN LEITR
ELWARD DUBLIN CITY
MC ELWEE DONEGAL 168
ELWELL CORK
ELWOOD PMO/MAYO,*381
EMERSON CLARE,KILDAI
EMO. *94,*153
EMPSON KILKENNY
MC ENAW PN LEITRIM
MC ENCROE PN CLARE
END CORK
MC ENEANEY 8 BIRTHS,
MC ENEANY 5 BIRTHS M
Mac ENERNEY *235
MC ENERY *429,*445,*11
ENGLAND CLARE/5 BIRTH
ENGLISH DERRY 1642 EN
ENGLISHBY *13,*214
MC ENIRY LIMERICK
ENITH WATERFORD
ENNIS PN DUBLIN, KINGS/
ENNOS PN DUBLIN
ENOCKE CORK CITY
MC ENOLLY PN LOUTH
ENOS PN KILDARE
ENOSE PN KILDARE
ENRIGHT LIMERICK,KERR
MC ENROE CAVAN,*417
MC ENTEE PN MONAGHA
M' ENTEER *26
M' ENTEGART *42
MC ENTIRE *246
MC ENTYRE *223
Mac EOIN *512
Mac EOWN *40
MC ERLAIN ANTRIM,DER
MC ERLEAN ANTRIM,DE
EROUGHT *143
ERSKIN DONEGAL,PMO/*5
ERSKINE ANTRIM
ERVINE ANTRIM,DOWN,*
ERVING SLIGO
ERVINGE ROSCOMMON,A
ERWIN DONEGAL 1586 SCC
ESBAL *428,ALSO ARCHIB
ESBALD *234,*254,ALSO A
ESBALL *254,ALSO ARCHI
ESBEL *19,*343,ALSO ARC
ESBIL *177,ALSO ARCHIBA
ESBLE *59,ALSO ARCHIBA
ESCOTT CORK
ESDALE *254,ALSO ARCHI
ESLENAN PN LONGFORD
ESLER ALL ANTRIM
ESMOND KILKENNY 1172
ESMONDE *109
ESNOR *112,ALSO ALEXAN
MC ETEGGART PN LOUT

ETON DUBLIN CITY
EUANSON ROSCOMMON
MC EUCHAE PN SLIGO
Mac EUCHROE *189
EUSTACE DUB,WIC,COR,C
MC EVADDY *119,*486
EVANS DUB,COR,LIM,TYR
EVANSON ROSCOMMON
EVANTON PMO
EVARALD CLARE
EVASTER KINGS
EVEERS PMO
EVELIN LOUTH
MC EVELY *501
EVENS CORK CITY,CORK
EVERAID TIPPERARY
EVERARD WESTMEATH 1
EVERS CLARE,CAR,KILD,
EVERSON CORK CITY
MC EVINIE *92
M' EVINIOGH *137
EVORARD TIPPERARY
EVOY PN KINGS,QUEENS
Mac EVOY KINGS
MC EVOY PN QUEENS/ DU
Mac EWAN *91
EWART ANTRIM
MC EWEN *210,*429,*91
EWERS CARLOW,PMO
EWING DONEGAL 1685 SCC
EXHAM LIMERICK,PMO
EXTEN PMO
EXTON WATERFORD
EYRES WATERFORD
MC FADDEN ANTRIM 16
MC FADEN PN DONEGAL
Mac FADIN PMO
M' FADZEN *13
FAGAN PN MEATH, WEST
FAGGY *139,*206
FAGON DUBLIN
FAHERTY ALL GALWAY
FAHEY GALWAY,TIPPERAI
FAHY PN TIPPERARY/ GAL
O FAHY PN SLIGO
FAIR *350,6 BIRTHS,NONE
FAIRFAX DONEGAL
FAIRIS *381
FAIRLEY DOWN
FAIRY *381
FAITH ANTRIM
MC FALL ANTRIM 1650 SC
FALLAHER *509
FALLAN ROSCOMMON
FALLARD DUBLIN CITY
FALLON PN ROSCOMMON
FALLOON ARMAGH
FALLOONE CLARE
FALUEY PN KERRY
FALUY PN KERRY

FALVEY CORK,CLARE,KE
FANING CLARE
FANINGE PN TIPPERARY
FANNER PMO
FANNIN WEXFORD,TIPPER
FANNING PN KILKENNY/
FANNINGE PN TIPPERARY
FANNYING TIPPERARY
FANNYNG TIPPERARY
FANNYNGE TIPPERARY
FARADAY *364
FARAGHER *307
FARAHER *307
FARDYE PN WEXFORD
FARELY CORK
FARGUSON PN ANTRIM
FARHAN PN WATERFORD
FARIHY PN SLIGO
FARIS *410
MC FARLAND DUBLIN 1
MC FARLANE DUBLIN 1
FARLEY CORK,KERRY 164
FARMER WEXFORD 1660
FARMOR MONAGHAN
FARNAN 10 BIRTHS,LEINS
FARNAND *417
FARNEHAM WATERFORD
FARNHAM *18
FARNON *91
FARR ANTRIM,ALL ULSTE
FARRAGHER MAYO,GAL
FARRAHILL *361
FARRALL PN DUBLIN, RO
O FARRAN PN DONEGAL
FARRAR WICKLOW,ALL I
FARRELL PN VARIOUS/DU
O FARRELL 19 BIRTHS,*
FARRELLY CAVAN,MEAT
FARREN CORK CITY/DONI
FARRER KILKENNY,PMO
FARRINGTON 5 BIRTHS
FARRY 5 BIRTHS
FARSFEELD ROSCOMMO
FARSHIN *227
FARTHING PMO,CORK
O FARY PN DONEGAL
FAUGHNAN LEITRIM
FAUGHTON *303B
FAULKNER DUBLIN,KILK
FAULKNEY *136
FAY DONEGAL,1586 SCOT/I
O FEA PN WATERFORD
FEAGON *461
FEAKE KILKENNY
FEALAN *443
FEALY *491
FEARNELY DUBLIN
FEARON ARMAGH,DOWN
FEDEGAN PN LOUTH
FEE ANTRIM,CAVAN,FERM

FEE *38
O FEE PN FERMANAGH
FEEHAN LOUTH
FEEHARRY *305
FEEHELY *454B
FEELEY *329
FEELY DONEGAL,ROSCOM
FEENEY SLIGO,MAYO,GAL
FEENY GALWAY,ROSCOM
O FEENY PN LONDONDER
FEERICK MAYO,GALWAY
Mac FEERISH *189
MC FEETERS LONDONDI
FEGAN PN LOUTH/ARMAG
O FEGAN PN DOWN
O FEGGAN PN DOWN
FEGHANY *124
FEHILLY 6 BIRTHS,NONE
FEHILY *454B,*329
FEHONEY *125
FEIGHAN *17
FEIGHERY *249
FEIGHNEY *476,*501
FEILD LIMERICK
FELAN PN QUEENS, KILDA
FELEY *371
FELLANE PN LEITRIM
FELTHAM TIPPERARY
FENAGHTY *382
FENAUGHTY *47
FENDLON *468
FENEGAN PN LOUTH
FENELL LIMERICK
FENELLY PN KINGS
FENELON *468
O FENIGHAN PN ARMAG
FENLEY *68
FENLON CARLOW,DUBLIN
FENNELL DUB,KILK,QUE,
FENNELLY KILKENNY *6
FENNESSY WATERFORD
FENOSY PN TIPPERARY
FENOUGHTY *309
FENTERELL LOUTH
FENTON CORK 1646 ENG/
FENWICK PMO
FENWICKE ROSCOMMON
FEOGHNEY *378
FEOLANE PN CLARE
FEPPS CORK
FERALL PN SLIGO
O FERALLY PN LIMERICK
FERBERNE ARMAGH
FERBISHY PN SLIGO
FERELL PN WESTMEATH
FERGIE *267
FERGUS MAYO,*267
FERGUSON DUBLIN,LIME
O FERGUSSA PN LEITRIM
FERGUSSON SLIGO

O FERILL PN DONEGAL
FERILLY CLARE
FERILRY PN CLARE
FERINSHAUGH LIMERICK
FERIS KERRY
FERLY *401
FERN *91
FERNELEY PMO
FERNELY PMO
FERRALL PN LONGFORD,
O FERRALL PN ARMAGH
FERRALLY PN LIMERICK
FERRAN *91
MC FERRAN ANTRIM
FERRELL PN WATERFORD
FERRILLA PN CLARE
FERRIS WICK,WEX 1172 N
FERRY DUBLIN,CORK 164
O FERRY PN DONEGAL
FERTERN PN WEXFORD
FETHERSTON ARMAGH/I
MC FETRIDGE ANTRIM,I
FIDGEON *205
FIE *167
FIELD CORK 1660 ENGLAN
O FIHILY PN MONAGHAN
FILAN PN KILDARE,ALIAS
FILBIN *40
O FILBIN *40
O FINAGAN PN MONAGH
O FINAGHAN PN ARMAG
FINALAY *409
FINAN PN ROSCOMMON/ R
O FINAN PN ARMAGH
FINANE PN ROSCOMMON
FINCH LIMERICK,TIPPERA
MC FINEEN CLARE
MC FINEENE PN CLARE
FINEGAN PN LOUTH/MON
O FINEGANE PN SLIGO
FINERTY GALWAY
FINES WESTMEATH
O FININE PN CORK
FINLAY ANTRIM,DOWN *6
FINN CORK,MAYO,DUBLIN
O FINN PN CORK
FINNALLY *68
MC FINNE PN CORK
FINNEGAN ARMAGH,CAV
FINNELLY *332
FINNERAN GALWAY
FINNERTY GALWAY
FINNEY 7 BIRTHS,NONE I
FINNY PN ROSCOMMON,*
FINUCANE 10 BIRTHS,AL
FINY PN ROSCOMMON, SLI
O FINY PN ROSCOMMON
MC FINYNE PN CORK
FIRMAN *249
FISE CORK

FISHER CORK,LIM 1648 E
FITCH *71,*276,*441,*429
FITTS WEXFORD
FITZ KILKENNY 1171 NOR
FITZ-HENRY KERRY,LIM
FITZDAVID PN KILKENN
FITZEDMD. PN KERRY
FITZEDMOND PN WATER
FITZGERALD CORK,LIM
FITZGERALD WAT,COR,
FITZGERGALD LIMERICK
FITZGEROLD WATERFOR
FITZGERRALD PM LIM,C
FITZGERROLD PN CLAR
FITZGIBBON KERRY 117
FITZHARRIS KERRY,LIM
FITZHERBORE LOUTH
FITZIMONS *436
FITZJAMES PN CLARE,CC
FITZJOHN PN TIPPERARY,
Fitzmaurice KERRY 1171
FITZMERIE CLARE
FITZMORISH PN WATER
FITZMORRICE PN KERR
FITZMORRIS KERRY 117
FITZMORRISH PN KERR
FITZNICHAS PN WATERF
FITZNICHOLA PN WATE
FITZPATRICK PN QUEEN
FITZPHILLIP PN TIPPERA
FITZRICHARD PN WATE
FITZSIMONS DUBLIN,DO
FITZSUMMON *410
FITZSUMONS *246
FITZSYMONDS ROSCOM
FITZSYMONS PMO
FITZTHOMAS FERMANA
FITZWALTER CORK,KER
FITZWILLIAM ARMAGH,
FITZWILLIAM DUBLIN C
FIXER PMO
FLACK 8 BIRTHS
FLADGER *503
FLAGETTER CORK
FLAGETTOR CORK
FLAGHERTY *307
FLAHAVAN CORK,WATE
FLAHERTY GALWAY,KER
O FLAHERTY 16 BIRTHS
FLAHY *189
FLANAGAN PN MON,KIN
O FLANAGAN PN FERMA
FLANAGANE PN KINGS
FLANEGAN PN LOUTH
FLANERGAN PN KINGS
FLANG *37
FLANIGAN PN ROSCOMM
FLANIGANE PN CLARE
O FLANIGANE CLARE
O FLANNAGAN PN FER

FLANNERY MAYO,TIPPE
FLANORA PN TIPPERARY
FLANORY TIPPERARY
FLANURY PN TIPPERARY
FLARERGAN PN KINGS
MC FLARTY PN DONEGA
FLATTERY PN KINGS/KI
FLATTLEY MAYO
FLAVELL 5 BIRTHS,ALL I
FLAVIN *452
FLEEMING DONEGAL
FLEENS *72
FLEETWOOD CORK,WES
FLEMING PN CORK CITY,
FLEMMING PN LIMERICK
FLEMMINGE KILDARE
FLEMON *427
FLEMYNE PN TIPPERARY
FLEMYNG PN WATERFOR
FLENTEN CARLOW
FLENTER CARLOW
FLETCHER DUBLIN,CORK
FLETTHERY LOUTH
FLEURY *3,*420
FLIN PN WATERFORD, ROS
O FLIN PN ROSCOMMON
O FLINE PN CORK,LEITRI
FLING PN WATERFORD
O FLING PN WATERFORD
FLINGE PN TIPPERARY
FLINGE PN Tip.
O FLINGE PN TIPPERARY
M' FLINN *385
FLINNE CORK CITY
FLINT CORK CITY
FLOOD KILKENNY 1646 W
FLOODY *72,*515
FLOWER DUBLIN CITY,DU
FLOWRE PMO
FLOYD KILKENNY 1646 W
FLOYNE PN WATERFORD
O FLUEN PN SLIGO
FLYN PN LOUTH, MEATH,
FLYNE PN WATERFORD
O FLYNE PN CORK CITY,
FLYNG PN CORK,WATERF
FLYNN CORK,DUBLIN,WA
FLYNN PN KINGS
O FLYNN 5 BIRTHS,ULSTE
FLYNNE PN KINGS
O FLYNNE PN CORK CITY
FOALY PN KILDARE
FOARD *40
FODAGHAN *413
FODHA *488
FOESTER DUBLIN
FOG PMO
FOGARTY TIPPERARY,DU
FOGATON *185
FOGG KILKENNY,LOUTH

FOGURTY PN TIPPERARY
FOLAN GALWAY,MAYO
FOLEY LIM,CLA,TIP 1171
FOLLIARD MAYO,ROSCO
FOLLIOT DONEGAL,PMO
FOLLIOTT ROSCOMMON
FOLLON PN WATERFORD
FOLY PN CARLOW
FONTAINE WEXFORD
O FOODHY *40
FOODY *138,*528
FOOKES DUBLIN CITY
FOOLEY *453
FOOLUIAH *47
FOORD PMO
FOORDE *16
FOOTE CLARE
FOOTS *381
FORAN PN WAT,KINGS, Q
FORANE PN WATERFORD
FORBES DON,DOW 1673 S
FORBESS LONGFORD
FORBISH *228
FORD PMO,DUBLIN CITY/C
FORDE WEX,DOW 1642 EN
FOREHAN *382
FOREHANE *199,*303B
FOREMAN 5 BIRTHS,4 IN
FORESTALL PN QUEENS
FORGAY *60
FORGEY *428,*524
FORGIE *267
FORGY *71
FORHAN *303A
FORHANE *199
FORKER *429,*489
FORKIN ALL IN MAYO,*50
FORREST DUBLIN CITY/C
FORSTALL PN KILKENNY
FORSTER DUBLIN,MONA
FORSYTHE ANTRIM,DOW
FORT PMO
FORTESCEW ANTRIM
FORTESCUE PMO
FORTH MEATH,DUBLIN,DU
FORTUNE WEXFORD,*227
FOSSY QUEENS
FOSTER LOUTH 1646 ENG/
FOTTERELL KILDARE
FOULES DUBLIN CITY
FOULK PMO
FOULKARD *181
FOULKE CORK CITY,WAT
FOULKS PMO
FOULY PN WEXFORD
FOUNBAINE DUBLIN CIT
FOUNTAIN PMO
FOUNTAINE PMO,DUBLIN
FOURBES PMO
FOURHANE *303B

FOURKER *429
FOURSIDES *429
FOWKE CORK,PMO
FOWKES TIPPERARY
FOWLER MEATH 1771 ENG
FOWLOW PN WATERFORD
O FOWLOW PN CORK CIT
O FOWLOWE PN CORK
FOWLUE PN CORK
O FOWLUE PN KERRY
O FOWLY PN WEXFORD
FOX PN CLARE,KINGS,WES
FOXALL DUBLIN CITY
FOXEN LIMERICK CITY
FOXON PMO
FOXWICH DUBLIN CITY
FOY DUBLIN/MAYO,CAVAN
FOYE DUBLIN
FRAHER WATERFORD,LIM
FRAIN MAYO,ROSCOMMO
FRANCEY ANTRIM
FRANCIS 13 BIRTHS,NONE
FRANCIS WEXFORD 1446
FRANCK PMO
FRANKE WEXFORD
FRANKLIN DUB,CORK 15
FRASER DUBLIN,ANTRIM,
FRAWLEY LIM,CLARE,TI
FRAYNE WESTMEATH
FRAZER MEATH 1585 SCO
FREBORNE WEXFORD
FREE GALWAY,MAYO 1586
FREEBURN ANTRIM,ALL
FREEKE CORK
FREEMAN LIMERICK 1646
FREIND CARLOW
FRENCH GALWAY 1171 IS
FREND LIMERICK 1000 D. &
FRENIER PMO
FRESTONE LIMERICK CO
FRIARY *470
FRIEL DONEGAL,TYRONE,
O FRIELL PN DONEGAL
FRIEND LIMERICK,PMO
FRINKE CORK
FRISPE KILKENNY
FRIZELL 6 BIRTHS,IN ULS
FRIZZLE *6,*197,*257,*19
FROMPTON WEXFORD
FROST MEATH/7 BIRTHS,5
FRY GALWAY,DONEGAL 15
FRYARR *523
FRYER DUBLIN CITY
FRYPE KILKENNY
FRYTH WATERFORD
FUGE *488
FUGILL MEATH
FULHAM PN DUBLIN,DUE
FULLAM PN DUBLIN CITY
FULLER KINGS,CORK/COF
FULLERTON DUBLIN,DO
FULTON WESTMEATH 164
FUOLY PN WEXFORD.FOL
FUREY CORK 1690 FRENC
FURLONG LIMERICK 1642
FURY PN WESTMEATH/GA
FYE *482
FYFEE *350
FYINN PN QUEENS
MC FYINN PN QUEENS
FYLAND *511
MC FYNYNE CORK
FYNYNE OGE PN CORK
FYTZ LOUTH & DRO
GABBERD LIMERICK
GABBEY DOWN,ANTRIM
GABBRYTH FERMANAGH
GAFF *249
GAFFENY PN KILDARE
GAFFEY PN ROSCOMMON,
M' GAFFIGAN *169
GAFFNEY CAVAN,DUBLIN
GAFFNY PN LONGFORD/*
GAGAN *122,*435
GAGE DUBLIN,CLARE 1646
MC GAGGY *222
GAHAGAN *137,*170,*217
GAHAN WEXFORD,*206
MC GAHAN LOUTH
MC GAHEY ANTRIM,MON
GAIGE KILDARE
GAINER *167
GAITENS *206
GALAGHER DONEGAL,M
GALAVIN *100
GALBELLY DUBLIN CITY
GALBRAITH LONGFORD,
GALBREATH FERMANAG
GALBRITH PMO
GALCOR PN WESTMEATH
GALE PN KILKENNY,.WES
O GALLAGHER PN LEIT
GALLAGHUR PN SLIGO
GALLAND ANTRIM
GALLATURE PMO
GALLAUGHER *159,*340
GALLE PN TIPPERARY
GALLEGHOR KERRY
GALLEN DONEGAL,TYRON
GALLIGAN CAVAN,*92,*2
GALLIVAN PN KERRY/KE
O GALLOGHER PN DONE
GALLOGLY *214
GALLOWAY ANTRIM
GALLWAY PN KERRY,.CC
GALLWEY PN CORK CITY
GALT LONDONDERRY
GALVAN PN ROSCOMMO
GALVIN CORK,CLARE,KE
GALWAY CORK 1171 NOR
GALWEY PN CORK
GAMBLE CORK CITY,LON
GAMEL *397
GANAN MEATH
GANLEY 7 BIRTHS,NONE
MC GANLEY PN WESTMI
MC GANN PN LOUTH/18
MC GANNA PN LEITRIM
GANNON KILDARE 1690 F
GANTLY *40
GARA DONEGAL,ROSCOM
MC GARA PN SLIGO
O GARA PN SLIGO/ROSCO
GARAHAN *54
GARAHY *249
GARBLANY PN LOUTH
GARDINER DUBLIN,CORK
GARDNER ANTRIM
GARDNER LONDONDERR
GARGAN 7 BIRTHS,LEINS
MC GARGILL PN DONEG
GARLAND LIMERICK,TIP
GARNER DUBLIN CITY/*9
GARNET LIMERICK CITY,
MC GARR PN WESTMEAT
GARRE PN KINGS,WESTM
GARRETT CARLOW 1666
MC GARRETT PN LIMER
O GARRIGA *450
GARRIGAN *26,*72,*332
GARRON *18
GARRY 14 BIRTHS,*323
MC GARRY PN LEITRIM/
MC GARTLAN *72
GARVANE CLARE
GARVEN *456,*489
GARVEY MEATH 1171 ENG
MC GARVEY DONEGAL,
GARVIN 5 BIRTHS,ULSTE
GARVY PN DOWN
GARWIN *69
GASH CORK
GASKIN LOUTH/DUBLIN
GASSON *72
GASTIN LOUTH
GASTON ANTRIM
GATELY ROSCOMMON
GATER KILDARE
MC GATTELY PN ROSCO
GATTERY DONEGAL
GATTINS *314
GAUAN PN WESTMEATH
GAUEN PN WESTMEATH
GAUGHAN MAYO,SLIGO,
MC GAUGHEY ANTRIM,
GAUGHNEY *234
GAUGHRAN MEATH,LOU
MC GAUGHY *163,*256
MC GAUGIE LISTED
GAUL WEXFORD,WATERF
GAULE 5 BIRTHS,WEXFOR
GAULT ANTRIM
GAUNA PN SLIGO
MC GAURAN *82,*238,*
MC GAURN *264
GAUT *494
GAVAGHAN 13 BIRTHS,M
GAVAN 19 BIRTHS,MAYO,
GAVIGAN *429
GAVIN MAYO,GALWAY,*2
GAW DOWN,ANTRIM
GAWEN LONDONDERRY,P
GAWLE KILKENNY
GAWLEY SLIGO,ULSTER
MC GAWLEY *410
GAY CORK CITY,DUBLIN C
GAYLE QUEENS
GAYNARD MAYO,*179
GAYNOR PN WESTMEATH
GAYSON CARLOW
MC GEADY DOWN,LOUTH
GEAGH CORK
GEALE QUEENS,SLIGO
GEALES WESTMEATH
GEANEY CORK
GEANY CORK
GEARN *260
GEARNS *259
GEARTY *454B
GEARY CORK
MC GEARY TYRONE,*38
GEASE LIMERICK
GEBARD LIMERICK
GEDDIS ANTRIM,DOWN
GEE WATERFORD
MC GEE PN ANT,FER,LEIT
GEEHAN *526
MC GEEHAN DONEGAL
GEELAN 6 BIRTHS,NONE I
GEFFERYES CORK CITY
GEGAN *189,*262
GEHINN PN CARLOW
GELLEGAN PN KINGS
GENELLY PMO
MC GENIS PN LOUTH,RO
GENNAGH *352
GENNEN PN KINGS
GENNERY CORK
GENNETT MEATH
MC GENNIS *370
GEOGAN CORK/*152
GEOGH PN MEATH
GEOGHAN *337
GEOGHEGAN PN KINGS,
GEORGE DUBLIN,ROS 117
MC GEOUGH PN ARMAG
MC GEOWN ARMAGH,*5
GERAGHTY PN SLIGO/GA
GERALD PN WATERFORD,
GERALDIN PN KILKENNY
GERANE PN CLARE
GERARTY *124
GERITY *249
GERMAN CORK
GERNON WESTMEATH 11
GEROLD PN KINGS
MC GERR *18,*97
MC GERR *18,*97
GERRALD PN CORK CITY
O GERRANE PN LIMERIC
GERRET *401
GERROLD PN TIPPERARY
GERRY DUBLIN CITY
MC GERRY *429
GERVIS *17
GERY *429
GETHING PMO
MC GETTIGAN ALL DON
GETTY ANTRIM,LONDOND
GEYLES QUEENS
GHEGAN *348
MC GHIE *481
MC GHOON *49
GIBB 5 BIRTHS,SCATTERE
GIBBINS LIMERICK
GIBBON PN LIMERICK,WA
MC GIBBON LIMERICK,C
GIBBONES DOWN
GIBBONS MAYO 1171 WEL
GIBBS DUBLIN,DERRY 172
GIBLIN LIMERICK,LEITRIM
GIBNEY WATERFORD,KIL
GIBSEY *179
GIBSON ANTRIM,CARLOW
GIBULAWN *179
GIFFEN ANTRIM
GIFFORD WEXFORD 1640
MC GILASPIE PN ANTRI
GILBERT DUBLIN,LEIX 11
GILCHRIST ANTRIM,DOW
GILCRIST ANTRIM
GILDEA DONEGAL,MAYO
GILDOWNY *429
GILEARD PMO
GILES CORK,LIMERICK,PM
MC GILFOYLE PN QUEE
GILGAN SLIGO
GILGUNN *238
GILHOOL *475
GILHOOLY LEITRIM
GILKIE *53
GILL PN LONGFORD/DUB,G
MC GILL WESTMEATH 164
GILLACYNNY PN LEITRI
GILLAGHER PN SLIGO
MC GILLAGHLEN PN SL
MC GILLAHOLY PN LEI
GILLAN ANTRIM,SLIGO
GILLAN PN SLIGO/*112
MC GILLASPICK PN DO
MC GILLBRIDE *429
GILLCONNELL PN SLIGO
MC GILLCUSKELL PN
MC GILLDOWIE *429
M' GILLDOWNEY *429
MC GILLDOWNY *429
GILLDUFF PN KINGS
GILLEANE PN KINGS
GILLECLIN ROSCOMMON
GILLEECE 6 BIRTHS,IN M
GILLELORIN PN SLIGO
GILLEN ANTRIM,DONEGA
GILLENANE CLARE
MC GILLEROY PN LEITR
GILLESBY *214
GILLESPIE ANTRIM,DOW
GILLETT CORK
GILLFOYLE PN KINGS
GILLGAM PN SLIGO
GILLGON PN FERMANAG
GILLGUN PN FERMANAG
GILLIARD *409
GILLICK CAVAN
MC GILLICUDDY ALL I
GILLIGAN *92,*246
GILLIGAN DUBLIN
MC GILLIKELLY CLARE
GILLILAND ANTRIM
GILLIN PN SLIGO
MC GILLIREADIE CLAR
GILLMAN CORK CITY
GILLMARTIN PN KILDAR
MC GILLMARTIN PN F
GILLMARTINE PN KING
MC GILLMARTYN PN D
MC GILLNESKE PN DON
MC GILLON PN ANTRIM
MC GILLOWAY LONDO
M' GILLOWY *161
GILLPATRICK *429
MC GILLPATRICK *429
MC GILLREAVY *429
MC GILLROY *429
MC GILLSHENAN *429
MC GILLTRICH PN SLIG
MC GILLY *460
GILMAN CORK
GILMARTIN SLIGO,LEITR
O GILMOR PN DOWN
GILMORE 54 BIRTHS,ANT
GILMOUR 18 BIRTHS,ANT
MC GILOSKER PN FERM
GILPIN ARMAGH,CAVAN,A
GILROY LEITRIM,MAYO
MC GILROY PN FERMAN
GILSENAN 6 BIRTHS,LEIN
GILSHENAN *214
GILTENANE *318,*323
GILTINANE *299,*318,*32
M' GILWAY *161

MC GIMPSEY DOWN ANI
MC GIN PN ARMAGH/*119
GINATY *220
M' GINDLE *154
MC GING MAYO,LEITRIM
MC GINIS DOWN
MC GINITY *167,*319
MC GINLEY DONEGAL
GINN 6 BIRTHS,NONE IN C
MC GINN ULSTER,*434
GINNA *309
GINNAW *51,*144
MC GINNE PN ARMAGH
GINNEL *92
MC GINNELLY PN DONE
MC GINNIS PN MONAGH.
GINTY MAYO
MC GINTY DONEGAL,*13
GIRAGHTY PN KILDARE,
MC GIRAGHTY PN ROSC
GIRANE PN CLARE
MC GIRR TYRONE,*163,*
MC GIRR PN ARMAGH
GIRVAN ANTRIM,ALL IN U
GIRVIN ANTRIM
GITTONS *101
GIVEEN *356
GIVEN *489
MC GIVENA *332
MC GIVERN ARMAGH,D
Mac GIVIR *40
MC GIVNEY ALL CAVAN
MC GIVNEY *212
MC GLADE DOWN 1660 S
GLADSTON PMO
MC GLAGHLIN PN DONE
GLAN *63,*447
GLANAN PN WESTMEATH
MC GLANCHY PN LEITR
GLANCY 5 BIRTHS,*515
GLANDERS *120
GLANFLEID *63
GLANNY *429
GLANVILL KERRY
GLASCOCK PN KILDARE
GLASCORD DUBLIN CITY
GLASCOTT WEXFORD, 16
GLASGOW TYRONE,ANTR
MC GLASHAN *114,*314
GLASHBY *13
MC GLASHIN *114,*314
GLASPY *407
GLASS ROSCOMMON/ANTI
O GLASSANE PN LIMERI
M' GLAUGHLIN *358
GLAVIN CORK,KERRY
GLAZIER *51
O GLE WESTMEATH,LIMEF
O GLEASANE PN LIMERI
GLEAZER *51

GLEESON TIPPERARY,LIM
GLENAN PN WESTMEATH
GLENN ANTRIM,LONDOND
GLENNON 22 BIRTHS,NON
MC GLEOINE PN LEITRIN
MC GLEVINE PN LEITRIN
GLINAN PN WESTMEATH
MC GLINCHEY TYRONE
MC GLINN PN ROSCOMM
GLISANE PN TIPPERARY
GLISON PN KILKENNY
O GLISSAN CLARE
GLISSANE PN CLARE ANI
O GLISSANE PN CLARE,I
GLOBER PMO
GLOGHLEN PN LEITRIM
MC GLOIN DONEGAL,SLI
MC GLONE TYRONE,*124
GLOUER ROSCOMMON,LI
MC GLOUGHLEN PN AN
GLOVER DUBLIN CITY/AN
GLOWER LOUTH
MC GLOYRE PN DUBLIN
GLYNN PN WESTMEATH/G
MC GLYNN 26 BIRTHS,*4
O GLYNN PN WESTMEATH
GLYSANE PN TIPPERARY
GLYSSANE PN TIPPERAR
GNA *8
GOAN *97,*238
GOBIN *156
GOBLE CORK CITY
GODBOLD LONDONDERR
GODBOLT PMO
GODDART CORK
GODFREY KERRY 1660 EN
GODKIN WEXFORD
GODSON *199
GODSUFFE CORK
GODWIN TIPPERARY/*40,*
GODWINE TIPPERARY
MC GOEY 5 BIRTHS,NONE
GOFF WEXFORD,ROS 1643
GOFFE WEXFORD
GOGAN PN CORK
GOGARTY MEATH,LOUTH
GOGE KILKENNY
GOGGIN CORK,KERRY,*3
MC GOGGY *222
GOHARY *420
GOINE PN KILDARE
GOLAGLEY *81
GOLBORNE ROSCOMMON
GOLBOURN PMO
GOLBURN PMO
GOLD CORK 1172 ENGLAN
GOLDEN LIMERICK,ANCIE
GOLDIE *89
GOLDING GALWAY,*89,*9
GOLDRICK *106,*128

MC GOLDRICK ROSCOM
GOLE CORK
GOLIGHER *159
GOLLIHER *178A
O GOLLOGHER PN DONE
GOLOGY *312
GOLOHER *137
MC GOLRICK *417
GONELL PN LOUTH
MC GONIGLE DONEGAL,
MC GONNELL PN MONA
GONOUDE *249
GOOD CORK
GOODBODY 5 BIRTHS,AL
GOODFELLOW FERMAN
GOODMAN ARMAGH,MO
GOODWIN CORK,KILK,WI
MC GOOGAN *254
GOOKIN CORK
MC GOOKIN ANTRIM,AR
GOOLD CORK,1172 ENG/PN
GOOLDEN *199
GOOLEY *381
GOOLY *55,*381
GOONAN *107,*390,*509
GOONERY *274
GOONEY *509
GOONRY *505
MC GOOREGAN PN ARM
GORAGH DUBLIN CITY
GORDON LIM,ANT,DOWN
GORDWIN PMO
GORE CLARE,LEITRIM 1642
GOREY *435
GORG MEATH
GORGE PMO
GORGE PMO
GORGES LONDONDERRY
GORHAM GALWAY,ALL C
GORINOUGE PN QUEENS
MC GORISH *319
MC GORISK *127B
GORMAN PN CLARE,DUB
MC GORMAN *319
O GORMAN PN ARMAGH
GORMELY PN WESTMEAT
O GORMELY PN ARMAGI
GORMLEY ANTRIM,TYRC
GORMLY PN DUBLIN,ROS
MC GORMLY PN ARMAC
GORMOCKE PN TIPPERA
GORMOGE PN TIPPERARY
GORMOGUE PN QUEENS
GORMON PN CLARE,TIPPI
MC GORMON PN MONA
GORRY *435
MC GORRY *515
GOSNOLD CORK
GOTER LOUTH
GOUGE DUBLIN CITY

GOUGH WEX,ROS 1643 EN
MC GOUGH PN MONAGH
GOULBORNE DUBLIN CIT
GOULD CORK 1172 ENG/DU
GOULDING CORK,DUBLIN
MC GOULDRICK *175
GOULDSMITH KILDARE
GOULDY *381
MC GOUNE PN ANTRIM
GOURLEY ANTRIM
MC GOURNOSON *175
MC GOURTY LEITRIM
MC GOVERN FERMANAC
GOW *416,*515
GOWAN PN LEITRIM,*319
MC GOWAN PN DONEGA
O GOWAN PN MONAGHA
GOWEN PN SLIGO/CORK,*
MC GOWEN PN FERMAN
O GOWEN PN FERMANAG
GOWER WEXFORD
GOWNE PN DOWN,.DOWN
GOWRAN PN LEITRIM
MC GOWREN PN LEITRIN
GOYNOR PN WESTMEATH
MC GRA PN FERMANAGH
GRACE WEX,LEIX,TIP,ROS
GRACEY DOWN,ARMAGH
GRADDY PN TIPPERARY/*
GRADY PN CLARE,PMO,LI
MC GRADY ANTRIM,DOV
O GRADY PN CLARE,LIMI
GRAEME *415
O GRAFFAN PN LONDON
MC GRAGH PN DONEGAI
MC GRAGHTY PN ROSC
GRAHAM WAT,GAL,ANT
GRAHAMS PN QUEENS
GRAHINE DOWN
GRAINGER WATERFORD
GRANDFIELD *203
MC GRANE DUBLIN
GRANEER PMO
MC GRANELL PN LEITRI
GRANFILL *203
GRANGE DUBLIN,ANTRIM
GRANIER CLARE
GRANIERS PMO
GRANNY *113,*271
O GRANNY PN DONEGAL
GRANT CORK,WAT 1672 S
MC GRATH PN TIPPERAR
GRATRIX WEXFORD
GRATTAN 5 BIRTHS,ALL I
GRATTIN *435
GRAUES MEATH
GRAUNT ANTRIM
GRAVELL *274
GRAVENOR CORK CITY
GRAVES DUBLIN CITY,LO

MC GRAW 5 BIRTHS,ALL
GRAY DUBLIN,OFF 1570 SC
GRAYDON DUBLIN/6 BIR
GREADY TIPPERARY
MC GREAL MAYO,LEITRI
GREALISH ALL IN GALWA
GREALLY GALWAY,MAYO
MC GREAN PN DONEGAL
GREANY KERRY,GALWAY
GREATRAKES WATERFO
GREAVES *333
GREDY PN TIPPERARY
GREEG DONEGAL
GREEHY WATERFORD,COI
GREEN DUB,WAT,LIM,MA
GREENAN *464
GREENAN CAVAN
GREENAWAY *409
GREENAWAY DOWN,AN
GREENE CORK,KILD,KILK
MC GREENE PN LONGFO
GREENHAIGH *429
GREENHAY *429
GREENWAY PMO/*429
GREER TYRONE 1608 SCOT
MC GREEVY DOWN,ANT
GREGAN 5 BIRTHS,4 IN LI
GREGG ANTRIM,DOWN
MC GREGOR DONEGAL,I
GREGORY GALWAY 1642
GREHAN MAYO,GALWAY,
GREIA ARMAGH
GREIG LEITRIM,DONEGAL
GRENE *333
GRENHAM KINGS
GRENNAN MAYO,DUBLIN
GRESSAM *254
GREWALL KILKENNY
GRIBBEN ANTRIM,ARMA
GRIBBLE CORK
GRICE KINGS,LIMERICK
GRIER *301,*333
O GRIFFEN PN CORK,KE
GRIFFIN KER,GAL,1636 W
O GRIFFIN PN CORK
GRIFFITH SLIGO 1172 WE
GRIGGE CORK
GRIGGES PMO
MC GRILLISH *166
GRIMASON ARMAGH,ALI
GRIMES TYRONE,MAYO,*
GRIMLEY ARMAGH
GRIPHA PN CLARE
O GRIPHA PN CLARE
O GRIPHAE PN LIMERICK
GRIPHEEN CLARE
GRISM *254
GRISSOM *197
GROARKE MAYO
GROCE ANTRIM

GROGAN PN WESTMEATH
GROGANE PN KINGS,ALS
GROLLIAX DUBLIN CITY
M' GRONAN *18,*97
GRONEL *40
GROOM PMO
MC GRORKE PN ROSCOM
MC GRORY PN ARMAGH
GROSVENOR WATERFOR
GROUES KILKENNY
GROVE DONEGAL 1640 EN
GROVES CORK,DONEGAL
GROWDER PN LOUTH
MC GROYRE PN LOUTH
GROZET *414
GRUMLEY *72,*364
GRUMMELL *521
GRUNDLE ARMAGH
GRYFFITH DUBLIN,SLIGO
GRYMBALL TIPPERARY
GRYPHA PN CLARE
O GRYPHA PN CLARE
GUAN PN SLIGO
MC GUAN PN SLIGO
MC GUANE ALL CLARE
GUARE *318
GUBBINS LIMERICK 1642
GUBBY *97
GUCKIAN *128
MC GUCKIN LONDONDE
O GUE PN QUEENS
GUERIN LIMERICK,*329
MC GUFFIN *410
GUICKEN *106
GUIDER *457
GUIDON ROSCOMMON
GUIDRA *457
MC GUIEHAN *212
MC GUIGAN ANTRIM,TY
MC GUIGGAN *222
GUIHEEN *128
GUIHEN ALL ROSCOMMON
GUILAVAN *397
GUILFOYLE DUBLIN,*509
MC GUILLAN *319
GUILLIM PMO
GUILMARTIN *457
GUINA *303
GUINAN KINGS
GUINANE TIPPERARY,*49
GUINEVAN *488
GUINEY CORK
MC GUINN SLIGO
GUINNA *303
GUINNATY *220
MC GUINNESS DUBLIN,
MC GUIR LIMERICK
Mac GUIRE PM FERMANA
MC GUIRE PN FERMANA
MC GUIRK DUBLIN

GUIRY LIMERICK,*437,*48
GUIST WATERFORD
GUITHERS PMO
GUIY DUBLIN CITY
GULLAMS CORK
MC GULLIAN *357
GULLION *19
MC GULLION *215
GULLIVANT CORK CITY
GULLYNANE LIMERICK
GUNN KERRY 1641 SCOTL/
GUNNER *381
GUNNING WESTMEATH/A
GUNSHINAN *215
GUPPY CORK CITY
GURD KINGS
GURDAN *485
MC GURK DERRY 1680 SC
GURKMAN KINGS
M' GURN *238
GURRY ARMAGH/5 BIRTH:
GUTCH DUBLIN CITY
GUTHRIE DUBLIN,CORK 1
GUTTERY *410
GUY DUBLIN,LIMERICK 14
GUYN CORK CITY
O GUYRY PN WATERFORI
MC GWILL PN ARMAGH
GWILLIAMS ANTRIM
GWINN PMO
GWITHER PMO
GWYNN TIPPERARY
GWYRE PN LONGFORD
MC GWYRE PN LOND,LO
GYDAGH PN TIPPERARY
GYLES DUBLIN
O GYRIE PN CORK
HABBAGAN *3
HABBERT *142
HACKER KILKENNY
HACKET PMO
HACKETT TIP,1596 SAXON
HADDEN 6 BIRTHS,MAINL
HADDER CORK
HADDOCK ARMAGH
HADDON 8 BIRTHS,MAINL
HADDONE CORK
HADIAN *329
HADOCK PMO
HADRACH KILKENNY
HADSKEATH *381
HAELLY PN TIPPERARY
HAFFEY *279
HAFFORD *63
HAFORD PMO
HAGAN ARMAGH,TYRONE
O HAGAN PN ARMAGH,L(
O HAGANE PN LIMERICK
HAGANS *267
O HAGGAN PN ARMAGH
HAGGENS *267
HAGHEN *185
HAGHERIN PN WATERFOI
O HAGHERINE PN CORK
HAGNES CORK
HAGNES CORK
HAHASIE PN WATERFORD
HAIR *342,*348
HAIRE ANTRIM
MC HALE DUBLIN,LIM,DC
HALEFEILD KILDARE
HALEY PN TIPPERARY
O HALEY PN LIMERICK
HALFEPENNY PN LOUTH
HALFPENNY LOUTH,*72,
HALGAN PN LOUTH
HALIGHAN PN KILKENNY
O HALIHANANE PN COR
HALL DUB,DON,GAL,DOWI
O HALLAGHANE PN WA
HALLAHAN CORK
HALLAM PMO
HALLENANE PN WATERF
HALLEY *519
HALLEY PN TIPPERARY
HALLIDAY ANTRIM
HALLIGAN ROSCOMMON,
HALLINAN CLARE,*510
HALLINAN *134
Hallingworth WESTMEAT
HALLISSEY *227
HALLISSY CORK,KERRY
HALLOM PMO
HALLORAN CLARE,GALW
O HALLORAN LIMERICK
HALLSEY WATERFORD
HALLURANE PN CLARE
O HALLURANE PN CLAR
HALLY PN CLARE/TIPPERA
O HALLY PN CLARE,LIME
HALPIN DUB,MEATH 1562
HALSEY PMO
HALTON WEXFORD 1641 E
HALY PN CORK CITY,TIPP
HAM *397
HAMBERY KERRY
HAMBILTON FERMANAC
HAMBLETON FERMANA(
O HAMELL PN MONAGH/
HAMELTON ARMAGH,PM
HAMERTON PMO
HAMILL ANTRIM,ARMAGI
O HAMILL *112
HAMILTON DUB,DON,DO
HAMILTONE DOWN
HAMLYN CORK CITY
HAMMILTON ANTRIM,D(
HAMMON TIPPERARY
HAMMOND DONEGAL 15(
HAMON QUEENS
HAMOND KILDARE
HAMPTON ARMAGH 1590
O HAMSON PN LONDOND
HAMTIN LOUTH
O HANAFANE PN KERRY
HANAFIN KERRY
HANAGAN PN WATERFOR
HANATY *432
HAND DUBLIN
HANDCOCK CORK,PMO
HANDCOCKE ROSCOMM
HANDRAHAN *130,*442
HANDY DUB,TIP 1760 ENG/
HANEEN *509
O HANEEN PN CLARE
HANELY TIPPERARY
HANFORD LONDONDERR
HANGLY MEATH
HANIFIN KERRY
Mac HANIFRY *267
HANIN PN ROSCOMMON
HANKSHAW DUBLIN CIT
Hankswoorth LIMERICK
HANLAN *236
O HANLEN PN ARMAGH
HANLEY KILDARE/CORK
HANLON *134
HANLON PN KILD,LOUTH
O HANLON PN ARMAGH/
HANLY PN ROSCOMMON/R
O HANLY PN ROSCOMMOI
HANNA ANTRIM,DOWN,AI
HANNAN GALWAY,ROSC(
HANNIGAN DUBLIN,WAT
HANNON GALWAY,ROSC(
HANNY ARMAGH
HANON PN ARMAGH
HANRAGHAN PN SLIGO
HANRAGHANE LIMERICI
O HANRAGHANE PN CL
HANRAHAN CLARE,LIME
O HANRAHANE PN LIMI
HANRATTY LOUTH,ARM/
HANRICK *468
HANSBURY *386
HANSON *97
HANTON *526
HANVEY 5 BIRTHS,4 IN UI
HANWAY DUBLIN CITY
HANY PN TIPPERARY
HARA PN SLIGO/ALL GALW
O HARA PN ANTRIM,LON(
HARAGHAN PN QUEENS
HARAN MAYO,*239
HARBERT CORK,*121
HARBINSON *410
HARBISON ANTRIM
HARBORNE DUBLIN CITY
HARDICK LOUTH
HARDIMAN GALWAY
HARDING KERRY,LIM 159
HARDINGE CORK
HARDLYE LONDONDERRY
HARDY DUBLIN 1646 ENG/
HARE ANTRIM
O HARE ARMAGH,LOUTH,
HAREN CLARE,*238,*390
HARFORD PN DUBLIN/DU
HARGADEN *251
HARGADON SLIGO,LEI,R
HARGAN 5 BIRTHS,MAINI
HARHAN *239,*469
HARIES KILDARE
HARINGTON DUBLIN CIT
HARINGTONN KILDARE
HARIS DONEGAL
O HARKAN PN DONEGAL
HARKER *410
HARKIN DONEGAL,LOND(
HARKNESS ANTRIM
HARLEY 7 BIRTHS,NONE
HARMAN CARLOW,KILDA
HARMER PMO
HARMON WICKLOW
HARNET DUBLIN CITY
HARNETT LIMERICK,KERI
HARNEY TIPPERARY,GAL
HARNY PN WATERFORD,R
HAROLD CORK
O HARON PN LONDONDEI
HAROUGHTEN *143
HAROUGHTON *47
HARPER ANTRIM 1640 NO
HARPUR WEXFORD
HARRAWAY ANTRIM
HARRELL 4 BIRTHS,MAIN
HARREN *201,*238,*270
HARRETT *92
HARRIGAN *47
HARRIHY *141
HARRINGTON DUBLIN 1(
HARRIS LIM,TIP 1642 ENG
HARRISON COR,LIM,DOW
HARRISONE DONEGAL
HARRISSON PMO
HARRITY *3
HARROLD PN CLARE/LIM
O HARRON PN FERMAN/
HARROT *20
Harroughton *142
HARRY DONEGAL
HARSON DUBLIN CITY
HART DONEGAL 1640 NOR/
O HART PN CLARE,CORK,
HARTE SLIGO,LEITRIM,RO
O HARTE PN CORK
HARTFORD MONAGHAN
HARTIGAN LIMERICK
O HARTIGAN PN CLARE
HARTIN ANTRIM,LONGFO
HARTNANE *144
HARTNETT KERRY 1171 N
HARTNEY DUBLIN CITY/L
HARTOP CARLOW
HARTRY *488
HARTSHORN PMO
HARTSTRONG PMO
HARTT ARMAGH,CLARE
HARTWELL PMO,LIMERI(
HARTY TIPPERARY,CORK,
HARVEY WEX,DON,DER 1
HARVIE ANTRIM
HARVY DUBLIN CITY,PMC
HARVYE WEXFORD
HARWOOD *523
O HARY PN ARMAGH
HARYSON TIPPERARY
HASELDEN *429
O HASHEA PN CLARE
HASLAM DUBLIN
HASLETT ANTRIM,LONDO
HASSARD FERMANAGH 1
HASSART FERMANAGH
HASSELHAM DUBLIN CI
HASSELLS PMO
HASSELS PMO
HASSET PMO
Hassett FERMANAGH(BLEU
HASSETT KERRY/CLARE,T
HAST DUBLIN CITY
HASTIE *97
HASTINGS CORK, 1170 SA
HATCH MEATH,PMO
HATFIELD DUBLIN CITY,I
HATHORNE LONDONDERI
HATTER DUBLIN CITY
HATTON *367
HATTON LONDONDERRY,I
MC HATTON *367
HAUGH CLARE
HAUGHEAN *248
HAUGHEY ARMAGH,DON
HAUGHIAN *381
HAUGHRAN *511
HAUGHTON DUBLIN,COR
HAUGLIN CORK
HAVARIN PN KINGS
HAVERIM KINGS
HAVERINE PN KINGS
HAVERN *429
HAVEY *435
O HAVIN PN ROSCOMMON
HAVY *435
HAWARD LONDONDERRY
HAWE 7 BIRTHS,NONE IN
HAWES 5 BIRTHS,NONE IN
HAWFORD KILKENNY
HAWKES CORK
HAWKINS DUB,WAT 1172
HAWNEY *488
HAWTHORNE ANTRIM,D
HAY PN WEXFORD/5 BIRTH
HAYDEN DUBLIN,LIMERI(
HAYDOCK PMO
HAYDON DUBLIN CITY
HAYES CORK/CORK,LIMEF
HAYNE PN CLARE
O HAYNE PN CLARE
HAYNES PMO,*134
HAYSLIP *410
HAYTEN *305
HAZARD CORK
HAZLETON *356
HAZLETT ANTRIM,LONDO
HAZLEY *381
HEA PN CLARE,CORK,LIME
O HEA PN CLARE,CORK,KI
HEAD WATERFORD,DERRY
HEADE PN TIPPERARY
HEADEN PN TIPPERARY,C
O HEADEN PN CARLOW
HEADON PN CARLOW
HEAGAN PN WATERFORD
O HEAGERTY PN CORK
HEALANE PN TIPPERARY
HEALLY PMO
HEALY PN CORK,TIP,KILD
O HEALY PN CORK,KERR
HEANEN *175
HEANEY ANTRIM,ARMAG
HEANUE GALWAY,DONEG
HEANY PN TIPPERARY,WA
O HEANY PN LONDONDER
HEAPHY CORK
O HEAR *76
HEARD CORK 1590 ENGLIS
HEARIN PN KILDARE
HEARN WATERFORD,*155,
HEARNE LOUTH/WATERF(
HEARTY LOUTH,MONAGH
HEASLETT *256
HEASLEY *381
HEASTER MEATH
HEATHER TIPPERARY
HEAVANE PN TIPPERARY
HEAVEN PMO
HEAVENS WATERFORD
HEAVEY 6 BIRTHS,NONE I
HEAVY 5 BIRTHS,NONE IN
HEAZLEY *381
HEBAN PN KILKENNY
HEBBS TIPPERARY
HECKER PMO
HEDERY *431
HEDGES CORK 1642 ENGL
HEDIEN PN KILDARE
HEDIVAN *63
HEDUVAN *63
O HEEFIE PN WATERFORD
HEEKY PN LIMERICK

HEEL *154
HEELAN WATERFORD,*12(
HEENAN TIPPERARY
HEERD KERRY
HEFFERNAN TIPPERARY
HEFFERNANE LIMERICK
MC HEFFEY *279
HEFFRON ALL IN MAYO,*
HEGAN PN TIPPERARY,KI
HEGARTY CORK,DONEGA
O HEGERTIE PN CORK
O HEGERTY PN DONEGAL
O HEGGERTYE PN LOND
O HEHERTY PN ARMAGH
O HEHIIR PN CLARE
HEHIR CLARE,LIMERICK,*
O HEHIR PN CLARE
HEIDEN PN KILKENNY
HEIFY *51
HEILSHON KILKENNY
HEILY PN MEATH
O HEINE CLARE
O HEIRE PN DOWN
HEIREN PN KILDARE
O HEIVER PN SLIGO
HELAN PN KILDARE,QUEE
HELING KILDARE
HELLY PN SLIGO
HELY PN LIMERICK,KILDA
O HELY PN SLIGO
O HELYHY PN LIMERICK
HELYOTT FERMANAGH
HEMP *405,*439
HEMPE *333
HEMPHILL TIPPERARY 17
HEMPSTALL *333
HENAN PN KINGS
HENDERSON DUBLIN,DO
HENDRICK DUBLIN
MC HENDRIE *429
HENDRON *6,*409
HENDRY *347
HENEBERY *422
HENEBRY *427
HENEGHAN MAYO
HENEHAN MAYO,*119,*26
HENEKAN *506
HENELAN PN CARLOW
HENERY *429
HENESSY PN CLARE,TIPP
O HENESSY PN CLARE
HENESY PN LIMERICK
HENEY PN LOUTH
HENLEY KINGS
HENLOWE FERMANAGH
HENNAN *175
HENNEBERRY WATERFC
HENNESSY CLARE/CORK
HENNY PN TIPPERARY
HENRY PN LOND,LOUTH,M
MC HENRY PN ANT,LONI
O HENRY PN LONDONDER
HENSBRY *422
HENSEY KINGS
HENSIE KINGS
HENSY *420,*511
HENTHORN *383
HENZY *249
HEOGAN PN TIPPERARY
HEPBURNE LONDONDER
HERAGHTY MAYO,DONE(
HERALD *71
HERBERT KERRY,TIP 165(
HERBERTT KERRY
HERDMAN ANTRIM
O HERERIN PN KILDARE
HERGUSSON *364
HERLEY *100
HERLIHY CORK,KERRY
O HERLYHY PN LIMERIC
HERNE PMO
O HERNE CORK CITY
HERNON GALWAY,*249
HERON LOUTH/ANTRIM,D(
O HERRALL PN DONEGAL
HERRICK CORK
HERRON ANTRIM,DONEG
HERTNAN *249
HESLIN LEITRIM
HESSION GALWAY,MAYO
HESTER MAYO,ROSCOMM
HESTIN *361
HESTION *361
Hetherington MEATH,QUI
Hethrington PMO
O HEVERAN PN ANTRIM
O HEVIN PN ROSCOMMON
HEWARD LIMERICK CITY
HEWES CLARE
HEWET PMO
HEWETSON KILKENNY 1(
HEWETT DUBLIN,WEXFOF
HEWITT ANTRIM,ARMAGH
HEWSON *279,*238,*506
HEYDON CORK CITY,PMO
HEYFRON *384
HEYNE LIMERICK
O HEYNE PN CLARE,LIME
HEYNHAM DUBLIN CITY
HEYNS PN KINGS
HIBBARD PN WATERFORI
HIBBART WATERFORD
HICKES WATERFORD
HICKEY PN CORK,.KILDAI
HICKIE PN CLARE,LIMERI(
O HICKIE PN LIMERICK
HICKMAN CLARE 1640 N(
HICKS DUB,WIC 1642 ENG.
HICKSON KERRY 1646 SA:
HICKY PN CLARE,LIMERI(
O HICKY PN LIMERICK
HIDE CORK,MEATH,PMO
HIERLY CLARE
HIERNANE PN CLARE
HIFFERNANE PN CLARE,
O HIGGAN PN FERMANA(
HIGGIN PN KINGS,QUEEN:
O HIGGIN PN ROSCOMMO
HIGGINS MAYO,GALWAY
HIGGINSON ANTRIM
HIGHGATE PMO
HIGHMORE CARLOW,PM(
HIGIN PN ROSCOMMON
O HIGIN PN ROSCOMMON
HIGNES PMO
HIGNET PMO
HIGNETT LIMERICK CITY
HIKY PN TIPPERARY
HIKYE PN TIPPERARY
HILAN PN KILDARE
HILBERT *121
HILL CORK 1646 ENG/PN AI
HILLAND ANTRIM,DOWN
HILLIARD DUBLIN
HILLIGAN *410
HILLIS ANTRIM
HILLMAN ANTRIM,LOND(
HILLMON LONDONDERRY
HILMON PMO
HILO *487
HILTON DUBLIN,DONEGAI
HINCHY LIMERICK,CLARE
HINDE ROSCOMMON
HINDS DOWN,ROSCOMMO
HINEGAN PN KILDARE
HINES *333
HINKS LOUTH
HINSY *420,*511
HINTON *523
HIPPS *436
HIRL *123
HIRLY PN QUEENS
HITCHMONGH CORK
HOARE CORK 1640 ENG/KI
HOBAN DUBLIN,LIMERICK
HOBART *47
HOBBIKIN *40
HOBBS WEXFORD,CORK,T
HOBIGAN PN LONGFORD
HOBSON LOND,CLARE,PM
HODDEN CORK
HODDER CORK 1620 ENGI
HODEN KINGS
HODGE 6 BIRTHS,NONE IN
HODGEN DOWN
HODGER *364
HODGES CORK,DUBLIN CI
HODGIN *76
HODGINS TIPPERARY
HODGKINS DUBLIN CITY
HODNETT CORK,TIPPERAI
HODSER DUBLIN CITY
O HOEN PN FERMANAGH
HOEY PMO/LOUTH,DUBLIN
HOG *487
HOGAN PN CLARE,TIP,WA
O HOGAN PN LIMERICK C
HOGANE PN CLARE,CORK
O HOGANE PN CLARE,CO
HOGART *59
HOGARTY *179
HOGG ANTRIM,LONDONDE
HOINS *165,*71,*216
HOLAGHAN PN QUEENS
HOLAN PN KILDARE
HOLCOMBE CORK
HOLCROFT CORK
HOLDCOMB PMO
HOLDEN DUBLIN,WATERF
HOLDER KINGS
HOLFORD DUBLIN CITY
HOLIAN *40
O HOLLAHAN PN FERMA
HOLLAN KINGS
HOLLAND KERRY,PMO/C(
HOLLANDE MONAGHAN
HOLLAWAY DUBLIN
HOLLERAN GALWAY,MA
HOLLINS KILDARE
HOLLOWWOO FERMANA
HOLLY LONDONDERRY,CC
HOLLYDAY CORK
HOLLYWOOD DUBLIN,LI
HOLMAN 5 BIRTHS,NONE
HOLMES KERRY,LIM 1596
HOLMS PMO
HOLOGHANE PN KILKEN
HOLOGHON PN KILKENN
HOLOHAN KILKENNY,*18
HOLT DUBLIN,CORK 1572 I
HOLTON CORK
HOMAN QUEENS,WESTME
HONE PMO
O HONE PN FERMANAGH
HONETT KILKENNY
HONWER KILKENNY
HOOD DUBLIN,WAT,CORK
HOOK DUBLIN 1642 ENGLI
HOOKE DUBLIN CITY
HOOKER DUBLIN CITY,KI
HOOKES DUBLIN CITY
HOOLIHAN *54
O HOONE PN FERMANAGI
HOOPER LIMERICK CITY
HOORST LIMERICK CITY
HOP *439
HOPE PN WESTMEATH/6 BI
HOPKINS CLARE,GAL 171
HOPPER TYRONE
HOPPS *274
HOPSON CORK CITY
HOPTON LOUTH,PMO
O HORA ALL IN MAYO
HORAHO *294
HORAN PN KILDARE/MAY(
HORANE PN KINGS
O HORCHOY PN SLIGO
HORD CORK,KERRY 1571 I
HORE WEXFORD 1170 NOR
HORGAN PN CORK/CORK
HORISH DUBLIN/*48B
HORN PMO
HORNE 4 BIRTHS,NONE IN
HORNER ANTRIM
HORNETT *318
HORNIBROOK ALL IN C(
HOROGHON PN KILKENN
HOROHO *486
HOROHOE *454B
HORRIBON KILDARE
HORRIGAN CORK,*283,*
HORRIGON *431
HORSDENEL PMO
HORSEY KILKENNY,CORK
HORSMAN ANTRIM
HOSFORD CORK,9 OF 10 I
HOSKINS KERRY,WESTME
HOSSY KILKENNY
HOSTY MAYO,GALWAY
HOUEDEN CORK
HOUGH TIPPERARY,LIMER
HOUGHEGAN *262,*419
HOUGHTON WATERFORD
HOULAHAN *485
HOULBERT LIMERICK CI
HOULDEN CORK
HOULDER SLIGO
HOULDON *485
HOULIHAN KERRY,LIMEI
HOULT DUBLIN CITY
HOUNEEN *318,*323
HOUREGAN CLARE
HOURICAN *264
HOURIGAN LIMERICK,TI
HOURIHANE CORK,ALL I
HOUSE *397
HOUSTAN ANTRIM
HOUSTON LIM,DON,DER 1
HOUTSONE DONEGAL
HOVEDEN CORK
HOVELL CORK
HOW CORK
HOWARD CORK,KER,LIM
O HOWAY TIPPERARY
HOWE LOUTH,TIPPERARY,
HOWELL KILKENNY 1172
O HOWEN PN FERMANAG
HOWENDON CLARE
HOWES SLIGO,PMO
HOWK PMO
HOWKE PMO
HOWLETT WEXFORD,DUE
HOWLEY CLARE,MAYO,SI
HOWLIN WEXFORD 1640 N
HOWLING PN KILKENNY
O HOWRANE PN KERRY
O HOWREGANE PN LIM
O HOWRIGANE PN LIME
O HOWROGANE PN LIM
HOWTH DUBLIN,PMO
HOY PN LOUTH,PMO/ANTR
O HOY PN LOUTH
HOYE KILDARE
HOYLE LOUTH
HOYNE KILKENNY
HOYNES *101,*238,*517
HOYSE WESTMEATH
HUBBARD PN WATERFOR
HUBBART PMO
HUDDLE WEXFORD
HUDSON KERRY 1460 S/C
HUEGHS PN WESTMEATH
O HUER PN CLARE
HUES PN WESTMEATH
HUESON *506
HUET *410
HUETSON PMO
HUGES CARLOW
HUGGARD 8 BIRTHS,SCAT
HUGGINS CORK 1640 WEL
HUGH KILKENNY
MC HUGH PN FERMANAG
O HUGH PN ARMAGH,MO
HUGHES DUBLIN 1650 WE
HUGHESTON *279
HUGHEY TYRONE,ALL IN
HUGHS PN DUBLIN CITY,W
HUGHSON PMO
MC HUGO *330
MC HUIGH PN KILDARE
HULAHUN *82
HULEATT CLARE
HULL WEX,WAT,CORK 164
HULME KILDARE/*91
HULNANE *77
HULSON FERMANAGH
HULTAGHAN *238,*247,*
HULTAHAN *154
O HULTIGAN PN FERMA
HUME FERMANAGH/ANTR
HUMES FERMANAGH,KIL
HUMFREYS PMO
HUMPHERY FERMANAGH
HUMPHREYS PMO
HUMPHRIES ARMAGH,D
HUMPHRY WESTMEATH
HUMPHRYS *398
HUNEEN *299
HUNGERFORD CORK 164
HUNT CORK,LIM 1172 NOR

HUNTER DONEGAL,ANT 1.
HUNTINGTON DUBLIN,LI
HUOTT CLARE
HURAGHAN PN QUEENS
HURD CORK,KERRY 1570 1
O HURE *189
HURLEY PN CORK/CORK,'
HURLY PN CLARE,CORK,L
HURSON LONGFORD,TYR
HURST CORK,10 BIRTHS
HURT WATERFORD
HUSNELL FERMANAGH
HUSSEY DUBLIN,MEATH
HUSSY PMO
HUSTON CORK,KER,LIM 1
HUTCHENS CORK
HUTCHIN CORK
HUTCHINS CORK 1641 SA
HUTCHINSON DOWN 159
HUTCHISON LONDONDEI
HUTCHONE ANTRIM
HUTHINGS LIMERICK
HUTSON *274
HUTTON WEXFORD/*76
HUTTON WEXFORD,CORK
HYATT DOWN
HYDE CORK 1566 ENG/WES
HYEGATE WEXFORD
HYLAN PN KILDARE
HYLAND MAYO,DUBLIN,(
HYLANE PN TIPPERARY
HYLLA SLIGO
HYND PMO
HYNDMAN ANTRIM,LONI
HYNDS DOWN,ROSCOMM(
HYNES GALWAY,CLARE,M
IAGO *40
IGOE LONGFORD, MAYO, R
MC IHONE *60
MC ILAN PN Antrim
MC ILBOY *55, *293
MC ILBREED PN Donegal
MC ILBREEDY PN Doneg
M' ILBWEE *381
MC ILCHOLE PN Donegal
MC ILCHON *175
MC ILCHRIST PN Antrim
MC ILCREVE PN Armagh,
MC ILCRIVY PN Armagh,
M' ILDOWNEY *429
ILDOWNEY *429
M' ILEBOY *175
MC ILEBOY PN Down.
MC ILEPATRICKE PN D
MC ILFATRICK *59
MC ILFEDERICK *43
MC ILHAIR *459
MC ILHONE *60, *97
MC ILHONEY *59
MC ILHOSE *254

MC ILHOYLE *59
MC ILHUN *59
MC ILIMCHELL PN Antri.
MC ILLEAVY PN Long.
Mac ILLESHER
MC ILLOY PN Louth
MC ILMORRY PN Armagl
MC ILMURRY PN Armagl
MC ILRAVY *19
MC ILROILL PN Antrim
ILROY *137
MC ILROY PN ANTRIM, A
MC ILTERNY PN Armagh,
MC ILTRAINE DONEGAL
MC ILVALLULY PN Arm
MC ILVEEN ANTRIM, DO
MC ILWAINE ANTRIM, D
MC ILWEE DONEGAL / *5
MC INCARGY PN CLARE
MC INCARIGIE PN CLAF
INDERME CLARE
MC INEELY *119
MC INERHIDNY CLARE
MC INERHNY PN CLARE
MC INERNEY CLARE, LI
MC INERNY PN CLARE
INGOLDESBY CLARE
INGOLDSBY PMO
INGOULDESBY LIMERICI
INGOWEN PN Tip.
INGRAM DONEGAL,DERR
INGRAME LIMERICK
INGRY CORK CITY, PMO
INMON KILKENNY
INNIS *433
MC INRILLY PN Louth
INSGELBY *402
M' INTEE *246
MC INTEER *309
MC INTOSH ANTRIM 166(
MC INTYRE LONDONDER
INWOOD KILKENNY
IPSLIE CLARE
IRELAND LOUTH, PMO / A
IRVINE FERMANAGH 1686
IRVING SLIGO
IRWIN *91
IRWIN PN FERMANAGH, PI
IRWING ROSCOMMON
MC IVER CAVAN 1603 SC(
IVERS LIMERICK, TIPPERA
IVERY WEXFORD
MC IVOR TYRONE, LOND
IVORY DUBLIN
IZOD ANCIENT IRISH / ROS
JACK 8 BIRTHS, 5 IN ULSTI
JACKSON LIMERICK 1750
JACKSON ANTRIM, ARMA
JACOB WEXFORD, PMO/ D
JACSON LIMERICK

JAGIUES WESTMEATH
JAGOE CORK
JAMES CORK 1560 ENG/ C(
MC JAMES PN CLARE, C(
JAMESON GALWAY 1756 ;
JAMIESON LIMERICK, GA
JAMISON ANTRIM, DOWN
JAMISONE DONEGAL
JANNES PMO
JARDINE *210, *429
JAUNCY WEXFORD
JEANES PMO
JEENES LOUTH
JEFFERS 12 BIRTHS
JEFFERY DUBLIN CITY
MC JEFFEY PN Long.
JEFFORD DUBLIN CITY, PI
JEGNYS TIPPERARY
JELLIS *274
JENKINS CORK, CLARE 16
JENKINSON DUBLIN
JENNINGS DUB, LIM, TIP
JEONAR PMO
JEONER PMO
JEONOR KILKENNY
JEPHSON PMO, WESTMEA
JEPSON PMO
JERETY *152
JERMIN CORK, PMO
JERVICE DUBLIN CITY
JERVIS *17
JERVOIS CORK
JESS LIMERICK CITY/ ALL I
JEWELL KILKENNY
JOAKES DUBLIN CITY
JOANES DUBLIN, ARMAGI
JOHN DUBLIN CITY
MC JOHN PN CORK, LIME
ST. JOHN DUB, LIMERICK
JOHNES WESTMEATH
JOHNSON CORK, LIM 165(
JOHNSTON LEIT,DOW,FEI
JOHNSTONE CAVAN, LON
JOHNSTOUNE DOWN
JOINT PMO
JOLLY DUBLIN, CORK 168(
JONE KILKENNY
JONES COR,ANT,KILK,CA\
JORDAN MAYO 1172 NORM
JORDAN PN WATERFORD,
JORDANE TIPPERARY
JOUE PN Kilkenny
JOUIE PN Kilkenny
JOURDAN *300
JOURDON PN Wexford
JOY CLARE/ WATERFORD
JOYCE GALWAY 1735 WAL
JUBBS LIMERICK
JUDGE MAYO, DUBLIN, TY
JULLY CLARE

JUMPHREY *489
JUNKIN *66
JURDAN *138
JURIN LIMERICK
JUSSEY ROSCOMMON
JUSTICE CORK, KERRY
JUYCE WESTMEATH
M' KAIN *358
O KALLY PN Lim.
KALSHANDER *9, *210, /
KANAVAGHAN *181
KANE ANTRIM, LOND, DUI
MC KANE 8 BIRTHS, 5 IN
O KANE ANTRIM/ LONDON
KANGLEY *211
Mac KANRY WESTMEATH
KARR *175
O KARRAN PN Donegal
KAUANAGH PN CARLOW
KAUENAGH PN CARLOW
KAVANAGH CARLOW, R(
KAVANANAGH KILKENN
KAY DUBLIN CITY
Mac KAY *189
M' KAY *383, *410, *19
MC KAY PN DONEGAL/ A
Mac KAY PMO
KEA PN Queens.
KEADAGANE PN CORK
KEADY GALWAY
MC KEAG DOWN, 1642 SC
KEAGANE PN Kings
KEAGHERY *307
KEAGHO PN Kildare
KEAGHOE PN Kildare
KEAHANE PN Waterford
O KEALLOGHAN PN Arm
KEALY PN TIPPERARY, CA
O KEALY PN Lim.
KEAN *72, *381
MC KEANAN PN Kerry
KEANE GALWAY, CLARE, I
KEANEY *370
KEANY LEITRIM, GALWAY
KEARAN *72
KEARIN *382
KEARN *319
KEARNAN PN West.
KEARNE PN West.
KEARNEY PN TIPPERARY,
KEARNS DUBLIN, MAYO,
KEARNY PN KILKENNY,..
KEAROGAN PN DUBLIN
KEARON 7 BIRTHS, ALL IN
KEAROVAN PN DUBLIN
KEARSEY *249
KEARY CORK/ *167, *517
MC KEARY *319
KEATING LIMERICK 1586 I
KEATINGE PN Tip.

KEATLEY *348
KEATY *189, *302
KEAVANAGH PN DUBLIN
KEAVENY GALWAY, SLIG
KEE 6 BIRTHS, ALL IN ULST
MC KEE PN ANTRIM, ARM
KEEFE PN Kilkenny
O KEEFE PN CORK, LIMEI
KEEFFE CORK, WATERFOI
O KEEFFE PN CORK CITY/
KEEGAN PN LONGFORD, V
KEELER WESTMEATH, PM(
KEELEY DUBLIN, WICKLO
KEELING *409
KEELTAGH *175
KEELY PN KILDARE, KING
KEENA 7 BIRTHS, 4 IN LEII
KEENAN ANTRIM, MONAC
KEENE CORK
MC KEENE PN Armagh,
O KEENEEN *40
KEENOY *38
KEERAWIN *427
KEERN *58
KEERNAN PN Long.
KEERVAN ROSCOMMON
KEERY *63
KEEVANE *142, *144
MC KEEVER LONDONDEI
KEEVERS *214
M' KEEVOR *410
KEGAN PN KILDARE, LEITI
KEGHAN
MC KEGHAN PN Antrim
KEGIN PN Queens.
KEGLEY *383
KEGRY PN West.
KEHAN KINGS
KEHELLY *397
KEHILLY *227
KEHOE PN KILKENNY/WE)
KEICHE TIPPERARY
O KEIFE PN Lim.
KEIGHRON *370
O KEILE PN Lond.
O KEILLY PN Lim.
KEILTOGH *175
KEILY CORK, LIMERICK, W
KEIRAN *319
KEIRANS *72, *319
KEISH DOWN
KEITH CORK, KERRY, LIM
Mac KEL *429
KELAGHAN *374
KELAN PN Kings
O KELEY PN Ferm.
KELL ANTRIM, *112
KELLAGHAN *374
M' KELLAN *418
KELLARD *277

KELLEHER CORK, KERRY
KELLER *100, *199, *376
KELLETT CAVAN, DUBLIN
KELLEY PN Louth
KELLIE PN Kildare
KELLIHER CORK, KERRY
O KELLOGHANE PN Arm
KELLOHER CLARE
KELLS 10 BIRTHS, LEINSTI
KELLSALL WATERFORD
KELLY PN SCATTERED / DI
O KELLY PN ARM,DON, E
MC KELLY PN ARMAGH,
KELLYE PN Kildare
MC KELSHENTER *489,
KELSO ANTRIM
MC KELVEY ULSTER
MC KEMMIN *429
KEMP 6 BIRTHS, MUNSTER
KEMPTON KILKENNY/ AN
KEN PMO
Mac KEN MAYO, LOUTH, I
KENADY PN Donegal
O KENADY PN Donegal
KENAGHT PN Wexford
O KENAN PN ARMAGH, D(
MC KENAN LEITRIM
KENANE PN Kings
MC KENDRY ANTRIM, *:
KENE PN Long.
KENEDIE PN West.
KENEDY PN SCATTERED
O KENEDY PN Lond.
MC KENEDY PN Lim.
KENELLY *530, *119
KENESHANE PN Kings
KENESLON KILKENNY
KENN LIMERICK CITY
KENNA PN KILDARE, QUEI
MC KENNA PN MONAGH/
KENNAH *431
O KENNAN PN Lond.
KENNEALLY CORK, WAT
KENNEDAY PMO
KENNEDY PN MEATH / TII
O KENNEDY PN Lim.
MC KENNEDY PN Lim.
KENNELLY CORK, WATEI
KENNEY PMO
KENNING *197
KENNINGTON *422
KENNON PN LOUTH, *388
KENNY DUB, GAL 1556 NO
O KENNY PN ARMAGH, D(
MC KENNY PN FERMANA
KENRICK 5 BIRTHS, 4 IN I
KENSELLAGH WEXFORD
KENSLY PN Wexford
KENT DERRY, ANTRIM 170:
KENTLY *358

KENY PN KILDARE, LOUTH
O KENY PN Armagh,
MC KENY PN Rosc.
MC KENZIE DONEGAL, A
KEOGAN •20
KEOGH PN CLARE/ DUBLIN
MC KEOGH PN LIMERICK
MC KEOGHE PN CARLOW
KEOGHOE •472
KEOGHY •246
KEOHANE ALL CORK, •39
MC KEOINE PN Leitrim
KEON DONEGAL, DOWN, F
MC KEON LEITRIM, LOUT
M' KEON •332
MC KEONE PN LEITRIM/ I
KEONEEN •506
KEONEEN •506
KEOUGH •435
KEOWN DERRY 1768 SCO
MC KEOWN ANT, DOWN,
Mac keown •512
O KEOYNE PN SLIGO
KER •175
KERBIN •413
KERBY •413
KEREEN •403
O KEREGAN PN Leitrim
KERELLY PN Rosc.
KEREVAN •295, •316
O KERGAN PN Armagh,
KERIN KERRY, CLARE
O KERIN PN SLIGO
O KERINE CLARE
KERISK •111, •143
KERIVIN •130,•442
KERKE DUBLIN CITY
KERLEY LOUTH
KERLY •249
KERNAGHAN ARMAGH,
KERNAN PN DUBLIN CITY
O KERNAN PN Ferm.
MC KERNAN PN FERMAN
KERNOHAN ALL ANTRIM
KERNON •153
KERNY PN ROSCOMMON..
KERR LOUTH, MEATH 1556
MC KERRAN PN Donegal
KERRANE MAYO , GALWA
KERRIGAN MAYO, DONE
O KERRIN CLARE
KERRINS •448
KERRIS DUBLIN
KERRISH •377
KERRISK ALL KERRY, •30
KERRYN PN Waterford
O KERRYN PN Waterford
O KERVALLAN PN Doneg
KERWICK KILKENNY
KERWICKE PN Waterford
KERWIN •427
KESSIDY •72
KET PMO
KETCHEN •429
MC KETIAN •481
KETIN ROSCOMMON
KETING MEATH
KETT DUBLIN CITY
MC KETTRICK •97
KEVAN TIPPERARY
KEVANAGH PN Kilkenny
KEVANE KERRY, •8, •203
KEVERNY •469
MC KEVITT LOUTH
MC KEVOR •42
MC KEW •332
KEY KINGS
Mac key PN LON, LOUTH/•
M' KEY •358
Mac KEY DUBLIN, CORK,
KEYES DONEGAL 1640 NO
KEYGIN PN Queens.
MC KEYNE PN Armagh,
KEYS PMO / FERMANAGH,
MC KIBBIN DUBLIN, DER
O KIBBON •40
KICKHAM DUBLIN CITY
KIDD DONEGAL 1586 SCOT
KIDDER QUEENS, PMO
KIDNEY ALL IN COUNTY
MC KIE PN DOWN/ •69
O KIEFE CLARE
KIELT •254
O KIELT •254
KIELTY GALWAY, ROSCOM
KIELY CORK, LIMERICK, W
KIERAN •319
O KIERAN •319
KIEREVAN •498
KIERNAN PN ROSCOMMO
MC KIERNAN 9 BIRTHS,
KIERUSSY PN Waterford
KIERVAN •102
KIERVANE CLARE
KIFFIN QUEENS
KIGAN PN West.
MC KIGAN PN Rosc.
KILBANE ALL IN COUNTY
KILBRIDE 7 BIRTHS, LEIN
KILCOYNE MAYO, SLIGO,
KILCULLEN SLIGO, •475
KILDARE
KILDEA •206
KILDUFF 5 BIRTHS, LEINS
KILDUNN •5, •501
KILGALLON ALL IN COUN
KILGANNON GALWAY, S
KILKELLY GALWAY, ROS
KILKENNY LEITRIM, MAY
KILKENNY •72
KILKEY •234
KILLBY •429
MC KILLEAGHER PN Le
KILLEEN PN WESTMEATH
KILLELEA GALWAY, ROS
KILLEN PN WESTMEATH /
MC KILLEN ALL IN ANTR
KILLEN PN WESTMEATH/
KILLFOYLE PN Tip.
KILLIAN ROSCOMMON, W
KILLIMITH •152
KILLIN PN Rosc.
O KILLIN PN Down.
KILLION •24, •329
M' KILLION •417
MC KILLKER PN Donegal
KILLMALLOC CLARE
KILLOGH LOUTH
MC KILLOP PN Antrim
KILLORAN ROSCOMMON,
KILLPATRICK PN ANTRI
KILLUM •421
KILLY ROSCOMMON
KILMARTIN ROSCOMMO
MC KILMARTIN PN Fern
KILMARY •344
KILMET •152
KILMURRAY •238
KILNER LONDONDERRY
KILPATRICK ANTRIM, •4
KILROY MAYO, ROSCOMM
MC KILROY PN Ferm.
KILWELL •279
KIMINS •42
KIMMINGS •137
KIMMINS •347, •498
Mac KIN MONAGHAN, •41
KINAGHAN •214
KINAHAN DUBLIN, LOUT
KINAN PN Long.
KINANE TIPPERARY, •498
KINASTON CORK CITY
Mac KINAUL •72
KINAVAN •36
KINCAIRT •374
KINCART •301, •432
KINCHELLA •3
KINCHLEY •3
KINDER QUEENS
KINE •40, •329
KINERNEY •389
KING PN WESTMEATH/ GAL
KINGHAM MEATH
KINGHAN DOWN, MAYO,
Kingshellogh PN Queens.
KINGSMELL CORK
KINGSMILL DONEGAL, T
KINGSTON DONEGAL, DE
KINIGAM •346, •372
KINIGHAN •42
KINIRY •431
KINLAR DONEGAL
MC KINLAY PN ANTRIM,
MC KINLEY ANTRIM, DO
KINNA •458, •249
KINNANE TIPPERARY, •72
KINNEALY •530
KINNEAR 5 BIRTHS, 3 IN U
KINNEARY •249
KINNEEN •360
KINNEGAN •137
MC KINNEY ANTRIM, TY
KINNIAN •205
MC KINNIE •86
KINNIGHAM •279
M' KINNY •19, •429
KINSALAGH PN Wexford
KINSELAGH PN CARLOW
KINSELAGH PN CARLOW,
KINSELLA DUBLIN, WEXF
KINSLAGH •429
KINSTONE CORK
MC KINSTRY DONEGAL
KINUCANE •302
KINVETON KERRY
KIRAGHTY PN West.
KIRBERRY •413
KIRBY ROSCOMMON, CAV
KIRK ANTRIM, LOUTH, •43
KIRKLAND 6 BIRTHS, 5 IN
KIRKPATRICK ANTRIM,
KIRKWOOD ANTRIM, LIM
KIRLE CORK, PMO
KIRLEY •249
KIRLIN •159
KIRRANE ALL IN MAYO, •
KIRWAN DUBLIN, WEXFO
KISSANE KERRY
O KISSANE PN CORK
KISSICK •204
KITCHEN •238, •429
Kitchingman PMO
Kithinyman DUBLIN CITY
KITSON •238, •429
KITTAGH FERMANAGH
KITTERICK ALL IN MAYO
MC KITTERICK 5 BIRTH
MC KITTRICK •97
MC KIVIRKING •524
KIVNAHAN •271
KIVNEEN •329
Mac KLE ARMAGH
KLISHAM •189
MC KNABB LOUTH
KNACK PN Kilkenny
KNALLY PN West.
Knarisborogh KILKENNY
knarisboroug' KILKENNY
KNAVEN PN Waterford
O KNAWSIE PN Donegal
KNIGHT DUBLIN, WATERF
MC KNIGHT ANTRIM, DO
KNOCK PN Kilkenny
MC KNOGHER PN Lond.
KNOLAN PN LONGFORD, \
KNOLAND PN Long.
Knorisborogh KILKENNY
KNOT DUBLIN CITY
KNOWLAN PN LONGFORD
KNOWLAND PN Long.
KNOWLE CORK
KNOWLES CORK/ DUBLIN
KNOX MAYO, DERRY 1610 :
MC KONE •137
KORISH •104
KORTON CARLOW
KOUGH •295
KROWLEY •150
KUNE ANTRIM
O KURGAN PN Armagh,
MC KWEY PN Long.
MC KYE PN Antrim
KYERTY •142
KYERY KERRY
KYES PMO
KYLE ANTRIM, LONDONDE
KYNE PN KINGS/ GALWAY,
KYNIN PN Queens.
KYNYN PN Queens.
KYR(.)E PMO, KYRLE, KIF
KZONEEN •330
L'ESTRANGE 8 BIRTHS, A
LACARY CARLOW
LACEY DONEGAL, DERRY
LACIE LIMERICK
LACKWORTH ARMAGH
LACY WEXFORD, DUBLIN,
O LACY PN Lim.
LACYE PN LIMERICK, WEX
LADRIGAN •170
LAFFAN LIMERICK, TIPPE
LAFFANE PN Tip.
LAFFERTY DONEGAL, LO
LAFFEY GALWAY, MAYO
LAGAN LONDONDERRY, •4
LAGHLEN CLARE
LAHEY 7 BIRTHS, NONE IN
LAHIFF DUBLIN, CLARE •1
LAHIVE •131
LAHY PN TIPPERARY/ •117,
LAIRD DUBLIN, ANTRIM 1
LALLOR PN Kilkenny
LALLY MAYO, GALWAY
LALOR PN KILDARE, KILK
LALY ROSCOMMON
LAMB DONEGAL 1686 ENG
LAMBART DUBLIN CITY ,
LAMBE WEXFORD/ DUBLI
LAMBERT CORK CITY, LC
M' LAMOND •19
LAMOND •254
LAMONT ANTRIM, •178B
LAMOR PMO
LAMOT PMO
LAMPORT WEXFORD, 117
LANALLYN CORK CITY
LANAN PN Kildare
LANCE LONDONDERRY
LANDER PN WATERFORD,
LANDERS WATERFORD, K
LANDON CORK
LANDY TIPPERARY, GALW
LANE CORK, LOND, LIM, P
LANEGAN PN Kilkenny
LANEY •305, •324, •432
LANG ANTRIM 1586 SCOTL
LANGAN PN LIMERICK, KI
LANGARIDGE PMO
LANGDALE DUBLIN CITY
LANGDEN PMO
LANGFORD ANTRIM, FER
LANGHAM LOUTH
LANGLEY TIPPERARY, WA
LANGOR CORK
LANGRISS LOUTH
LANGSTONE KINGS
LANGTON KILKENNY 179(
LANIGAN KILKENNY
LANNAN •67
LANNON PN KILDARE/ KI
O LAPAN PN Armagh,
LAPP WATERFORD, PMO
LAPPIN ARMAGH, TYRONE
LAPSTY QUEENS
LARAGH PN West.
LARCAN PN Wexford
LARISSY PN Queens.
LARKAN PN LOUTH,...DU
LARKIN KINGS/ DUBLIN, /
LARMOUR ANTRIM, DOW
LARNEY •282
MC LARNON ANTRIM
MC LARY •19
LARY PN MEATH, WEXFOR
O LARY PN Wexford
LASLEY ANTRIM
LASTLY •396
LATHAM LONDONDERRY,
LATHOM TIPPERARY
LATIMER DUBLIN, KERRY
LATSFORD CORK
LAUDER CORK/ 3 BIRTHS,
Mac LAUGHLIN •355
LAUGHLIN PN WESTMEA
MC LAUGHLIN PN DON,
LAULES PN Kilkenny
LAUNDY PN DUBLIN
LAURENCE PMO/ DUBLIN
LAUSON KILKENNY
LAVAN MAYO, ROSCOMMO

MC LAVE *460
LAVELLE DUBLIN, GALW/
O LAVERTY *348
LAVERTY ANTRIM, ALL II
LAVERY ARMAGH, ANTRI
MC LAVIN *152
LAVIN MAYO, ROSCOMMO
LAW KILDARE / ANTRIM
LAWCES PN DUBLIN
LAWDER 3 BIRTHS, NONE
LAWELL *40
LAWFORE ARMAGH
LAWLER PN CAR, DUB, K
LAWLES PN LOUTH, MEAT
LAWLESS CORK 1640 ENG
LAWLIS PN DUBLIN
LAWLISS CLARE
LAWLOR PN KILKENNY,..
LAWN DONEGAL, TYRONE
ST LAWRANCE DUBLIN
LAWRENCE GALWAY 158
ST LAWRENCE DUBLIN,
O LAWRY PN Down.
LAWS *409
LAWSON LONDONDERRY,
LAWTEN KINGS
LAWTON CORK
LAYNE *54
Le Strange PN WESTMEAT
Le Strange PN West.
LEA LOUTH, QUEENS, CAR
LEACY WEXFORD, DUBLIN
LEADAM *429
LEAGH PN CORK
LEAGHY PN CORK, KERRY
O LEAGHY PN CORK CITY
LEAH PN CORK
LEAHY CORK, KERRY, LIM
LEAKE DUBLIN
MC LEAN DONEGAL, ANT
O LEANAGHANE PN COI
LEANE KERRY, LIMERICK,
LEANY PN Tip.
LEARY PN CORK,..KERRY,
O LEARY PN CORK CITY,
LEASE WESTMEATH
LEATHEM ARMAGH
LEATHES ANTRIM
LEAUE PN CORK
LEAVY PN LONGFORD/ LO
LECCH DUBLIN CITY
LECCHFIELD DUBLIN CI
LECKY CARLOW 1792 SCOT
LECORA DUBLIN CITY
LEDDY WESTMEATH 1610
LEDWICH ROSCOMMON
LEDWIDGE MEATH 1506 E
LEDWITH DUBLIN, *63
LEE TIPPERARY 1601 ENG/ I
MC LEE *72
LEECH MAYO 1664 ENG/DC
LEEHY PN CORK CITY
LEES 6 BIRTHS, NONE IN U
LEESON DUBLIN, *249
ST LEGER DUBLIN, CORK
LEGERSTONE CORK
LEGG PMO
LEGGE ANTRIM, 1690 NOR
LEGLAND WESTMEATH
LEGROND KILKENNY
LEHANE CORK, 1 IN KERR
LEHUNT PMO
LEICESTER *429
ST LEIGER PMO
LEIGH WESTMEATH, PMO,
O LEIN PN Lim.
LEITCHFIELD DONEGAL
MC LELLAN ANTRIM 164
LEMON DUBLIN 1640 ENGI
LEMOND DUBLIN CITY
LENAGH PN West.
LENAGHAN SLIGO/ ANTRI
MC LENAGHAN ANTRIM
LENAHAN *420
LENAN PN CARLOW, KILD.
LENANE *352, *375
MC LENANY PN SLIGO
LENCHY PN CLARE
O LENCHY PN Lim.
LENCY PN KERRY, WESTM
O LENCY PN KERRY, LIMI
LENDSIE PN Waterford
LENESAY WEXFORD
LENGLY WESTMEATH
LENIHAN LIMERICK
LENING DONEGAL, PMO
O LENNAGHAN PN Rosc.
LENNAN PN DUBLIN, LOU
O LENNAN PN Louth
O LENNANE PN CORK
LENNARD LIMERICK CITY
LENNON DUBLIN, ARMAG
LENNOX DONEGAL/ ANTR
LENORD *516
LENOX LONDONDERRY
LENY PN West.
LEO CLARE/ ALL LIMERICK
LEONARD KERRY, LIMER
MC LERNEY *137
MC LERNON 8 BIRTHS, A
LERYE MONAGHAN
LESAW DUBLIN CITY
LESBY PMO
LESLEY LIMERICK, ANTRI
LESLIE DONEGAL, ANT, DC
LESLY PMO
LESQUIRE ARMAGH, DOV
M' LESTER *410
LESTER 5 BIRTHS, NONE I
LESTRANGE KINGS, PMC
LETSOME *104
LEUETT DUBLIN CITY
LEVERAN *449
LEVESEY PMO
LEVESON *503
LEVINGSTON ARMAGH, .
LEVINS 7 BIRTHS, ALL IN
LEVISTON *417
LEVITT TIPPERARY
LEWERS *137, *175
LEWIS DUB, KILD, MON 16
LEWLING WEXFORD
LEY MONAGHAN
LEYDEN SLIGO, CLARE
LEYEN KILDARE
LEYHANE *325
LEYNAGH PN Kildare
LEYNE *8
O LEYNE PN CORK, LIMEI
LEYNES ROSCOMMON
MC LICE *363
LIDDANE CLARE, *131, *4
O LIDDEENE LIMERICK
LIDDEL *429
LIDDY CARLOW 1610 SCOT
LIE CORK
LIFFE *152
LIGGET *358
LIGGETT ARMAGH, ANTRI
LIGHTBODY ALL IN COUI
LILL PMO
LILLEY ANTRIM, DOWN
LILLIS 5 BIRTHS, 4 IN MUN
LILLY ANTRIM, DOWN
LIMRY PMO
LIN PN Antrim
LINAHAN *420, *249
LINAN PN Meath
LINANE LIMERICK, KERRY
LINCHEY *175
LINCHY PN CORK, LIMERI
O LINCHY PN Lim.
LINCOLN WATERFORD
LINCY PN Long.
LIND *87
MC LINDEN *478, *429
LINDEN *289, *429, *478
LINDON PMO
LINDSAY LIM, TYR 1610 S
LINDSEY PMO
LINE PN Antrim
O LINE PN CORK CITY
LINEHAN CORK
LINGANE PN Lim.
LINN *350
LINNANE LIMERICK, KERI
LINNEN *120
LINNINGTON WEXFORD
LINSEY PMO
LINSY PN Long.
O LINSY PN Long.
M' LINTOCK *321
LINTON DUBLIN 1560 SCOT
LION *259
LIPSETT 6 BIRTHS, MAINL
LISAUGHT CORK
LISLE WESTMEATH
LISTER ROSCOMMON / *42
LISTON LIMERICK
LITCHFIELD KILDARE
LITTERELL MEATH
LITTLE WIC, WEX 1650 EN
LITTLETON *409
O LIUER CORK CITY, LIMI
LIVING PN Louth
LIVINGSTON DUBLIN, DC
LIVINGSTONE ARMAGH,
LLOYD WAT, LIM, WEST 1
LOBB WESTMEATH
LOCK CORK, PMO / *523
LOCKARD DUBLIN CITY
LOCKE DUBLIN CITY AND
LOCKHART ARMAGH, AN
LOCKINGTON QUEENS
LODG PMO
LODGE KILKENNY, PMO
LODLOWE DUBLIN
LOFFAN QUEENS
LOFFTUS QUEENS
LOFTUS DUBLIN, CLARE 1
LOGAN ANTRIM, DOWN, T
LOGGAN PN ANTRIM
LOGHLEN PN Tip.
O LOGHLEN PN CLARE
MC LOGHLEN PN CLARE
LOGHLIN PN DUBLIN, SLI
MC LOGHLIN PN CLARE,
LOGHMAN PN Kilkenny
LOGHNAN *517
O LOGHNAN PN Rosc.
LOGHNANE PN Tip.
LOGUE LONDONDERRY, D
LOHAN GALWAY
LOHAN *307, *386
LOMBARD DUBLIN, LIME
LOND WATERFORD
LONDAY PN Waterford
LONDRIGAN TIPPERARY,
LONDY *429
LONE WATERFORD
LONELL WATERFORD
LONERGAN PN TIPPERAR
LONERGANE PN Tip.
LONG DONEGAL, DERRY 1
LONGFORD PMO
LONGLEY DUBLIN, WATE
LONNERGANE PN Tip.
LOOBY PN TIPPERARY/ TII
LOOGUE *329
MC LOONE DONEGAL
LOONEY CORK, CLARE
MC LOONIE *429
LORD DUBLIN, CORK 1680
LORDAN ALL IN COUNTY
LORDE WESTMEATH
LORENAN PN Antrim
LORIMER ANTRIM
LORIMOUR *197
MC LORINAN *433
LORKAN PN Kilkenny
LOSKE PN Antrim
M' LOSKY *209, *240
LOUE WESTMEATH, CORK
LOUELACE ROSCOMMON
LOUGHAN *307, *6, *76
LOUGHBEE DOWN
LOUGHEED 5 BIRTHS, SC
LOUGHLAN *116
O LOUGHLIN CLARE, DU
LOUGHLIN KINGS/ LEITRI
MC LOUGHLIN PN ROSC
LOUGHMAN PN QUEENS/
LOUGHNAN PN WEXFORI
LOUGHNANE 10 BIRTHS,
LOUGHRAN TYRONE, AN
LOUGHREY 12 BIRTHS, S
LOUGHRY *189
LOUTON WESTMEATH
LOVAT *329
LOVE PMO / LONDONDERR
LOVELACE PMO
LOVELLIS QUEENS
O LOVERTIE PN Antrim
LOVETT DONEGAL, DERR
LOW WESTMEATH, WEXFO
O LOWAN PN Mon.
LOWE LIMERICK 1750 SCO
LOWERS *411
LOWERY *174
LOWNEY ALL IN COUNTY
LOWNSDALE *381
LOWNSEL *381
LOWROO *189
LOWRY PN ANTRIM,....FEI
O LOWRY PN DONEGAL, I
LOWTHER PMO, DUBLIN (
LOY 5 BIRTHS, ULSTER
LOYDE LIMERICK
M' LROY *358
LUBY KILDARE / TIPPERAR
LUCAS CORK, CLARE, OFF
LUCEY CORK, KERRY
LUCKNAWNE *190
LUDDEN *119
LUDERDALE FERMANAG
LUDINGTON TIPPERARY
LUDLO KILKENNY
LUDLOW DERRY 1174 WEI
LUGG CORK
LUKE LONDONDERRY / AN
LUMMACKS
LUNDY 12 BIRTHS, ULSTE
LUNN ARMAGH
LUNNEEN *24, *329
LUNNEY FERMANAGH
O LUNNIN PN Ferm.
LUNNY FERMANAGH
O LUNSHAGHAN PN Dor
O LUOG PN Donegal
LUOGUE *329
M' LURE *432
LURKANE PN Kings
O LURKANE PN Armagh,
LURKEN PN Kings
LUSSY *396
LUTE CORK / *7
LUTHER KINGS, CORK
LUTTERELL GALWAY, 11
LUTTRELL DUBLIN 1171 N
LYACH ROSCOMMON
LYDON GALWAY, MAYO
LYEDIE PN CLARE
LYEE KILDARE
LYHAN *228
LYHANE *365
LYLE ANTRIM, ALL ULSTEF
LYNACAR DUBLIN CITY
LYNAGH 6 BIRTHS, CONN
LYNAM DUBLIN, KINGS, *
LYNAN PN West.
LYNANE *45
LYNAP *30
LYNAS ANTRIM, DOWN
LYNCH LIMERICK, GALWA
LYNCHAHAN *113
LYNCHY PN CLARE, DUBI
LYNDAN WEXFORD
LYNE PN CLARE / KERRY,
O LYNE PN KERRY, ROSC
LYNESS ANTRIM, DOWN,
LYNHAM KILDARE
LYNN WATERFORD, PMO/
LYNNAN PN Louth
O LYNNAN PN Ferm.
MC LYNNAN PN Ferm.
LYNON KINGS
LYNSEY DUBLIN
LYNSHY PN Meath
LYNSIE PN Antrim
LYNSKEY GALWAY, MAY
LYNSY PN Tip.
LYON PN Kildare
LYONS ANTRIM, WEST 160
LYSAGERT LIMERICK
LYSAGH PMO
LYSAGHT CLARE / LIMER
LYSAT PMO
LYSTER *273
LYTLE *321
LYTTLE ANTRIM, DUBLIN,

M' MA •344
MC MA •106
MA-JURY •494
MACK LIMERICK, TIPPER/
O MADAGANE PN Lim.
MADDEN PN KINGS / GAL
MADDIGAN •367
MADDIN PN Tip.
MADDOCK WEXFORD
MADESLON FERMANAGH
MADIGAN LIMERICK, CL/
MADIGANE PN CLARE
O MADIGANE PN Lim.
MADILL 5 BIRTHS, 4 IN UI
MADISON KILKENNY
MADOCKS WESTMEATH
MADOLE •381
MADOWELL •461
MADOX CORK
MAGAHARAN •308
MAGAHERN •46
MAGAN PN WESTMEATH/
MAGANN •54
MAGAURAN CAVAN, •82
MAGAURN •264
MAGAWRAN •246
MAGEE PN ANTRIM, ARM/
MAGENIS PMO
MAGG DUBLIN CITY
MC MAGH •19
MAGHAN PN West.
MAGHER PN CARLOW/ •1(
MAGHER PN WEXFORD
MAGHERY •97
MC MAGHONE PN Mon.
MAGILL PMO / ANTRIM, A
MAGILLOWY •432
MAGILLY •460
MAGINES DOWN
MAGINLEY •259
MAGINN ULSTER
MAGINNIS •409
MAGIVERIN •358
MAGLAMERY •18
MAGLAMMER •429
MAGNER PN CORK / CORK
MAGOMERIE LONDONDI
MAGON •59
MAGONE •524
MAGORISK •137
MAGORLICK •201
MAGOUGH •40
Magournahan •175
MAGOVERN •35, •505
MAGOWAN DONEGAL, LI
MAGRANE DUBLIN
MAGRATH PN TIPPERARY
MAGRAUE PN Meath
MAGRAW •481
MAGREECE •276

MAGRGH PN CLARE
MAGROGAN PN Antrim
MAGRORY •153
MAGUIGAN •137
MAGUIL •429
MAGUIR LIMERICK
MAGUIRE PN FERMANAG
MAGULLION •215
MAGURN •201
MAGUYRE PN Louth
MAGWIRE FERMANAGH
MAGWYRE FERMANAGH
MAHEIR •409
MAHER TIPPERARY, DUBI
MAHIER •410
MAHOLLUM •381
MAHOLM •18, •429, •461
MAHON PN CLARE, DUBLI
MC MAHON PN FER,CLA
MC MAHONE PN CORK
MAHONEY •158, •291
MAHONY PN CLARE, KER
O MAHONY PN CORK,...C
MC MAHONY PN CLARE
MAHOOD ANTRIM, DOWN
MAHOONE PN Long.
MAHOWN PMO
MAHOWNE PN DUBLIN
O MAHOWNE PN CORK
MAHOWNY PN CORK, KE
O MAHOWNY PN CORK
MC MAHOWNY PN COR
MAHOWY PN Tip.
MAHUR PN Kings
MAID •410
MAIKIM •340
MAILEY ANTRIM, ALL IN I
MAINES FERMANAGH
MAIRS ANTRIM
MAISTERSON WEXFORD
MAITLAND 7 BIRTHS, AL
MAJOR LONDONDERRY / /
MAKATYE PN Armagh,
MAKELLCREE PN Armagl
MAKEON •40
MAKEPEACE KILKENNY
MAKINS KILKENNY
MALADY •332
MALCOLM DONEGAL 168
MALCOLMSO ARMAGH
MALCOMSON ARMAGH
MALEY •370
MALIA •174, •342, •179
MALIE •40
MALLAGH •210
MALLAVIN •152
MALLEW •137
O MALLEY MAYO, •72, •
MALLEY MAYO, GALWAY
MALLON ARMAGH, ANTR

MALLONE PN DUBLIN CI
MALLOONE PN CLARE, K
MALLOWNEY •231
MALMONA •276
MALONE PN DUBLIN, KIL
O MALOWNE PN CORK
MALOY •19
MALSEED DONEGAL, LON
MALY PN Kildare
MALYAN ROSCOMMON
MANAGHAN PN Leitrim
O MANAGHAN PN Ferm.
MANALLY •17
MC MANAMON ALL IN M
MANBY PMO
MANDEVILE TIPPERARY
MANDOWELL CLARE
MANEILLY •66
MANELIS •12, •259
MANGAN DUBLIN, LIMER
MANION •63
MANLY CORK, TIPPERARY
MANN TYRONE 1600 ENGL
MANNARING KILKENNY
MANNERINGE CORK
MANNEY DUBLIN CITY
MANNING CORK, DUBLIN
MANNION GALWAY, ROS
MANNIX WATERFORD, CC
MANNORING KILKENNY
MANRON •73
MANSEL PMO / •393
MANSELL PN Tip.
MANSERY CORK
MANSERYHE CORK
MANSFIELD DONEGAL 1(
MANSON DOWN, TIPPERA
MANSWER PMO
MANTELL KILKENNY
MANUS •140, •457
Mac MANUS PN FERMAN
MC MANUS PN FERMAN/
MANWARING KILKENNY
MANWERING PMO
MANYHYNE LIMERICK
MANYNE ROSCOMMON
MAPES DUBLIN CITY
MAPOTHER ROSCOMMON
MARA PN TIPPERARY/ TIPI
MARCAGHAN CLARE
MARK •409
MARKAM DUBLIN CITY
MARKES QUEENS
MARKEY PN LOUTH/ DUB
MARKHAM DUBLIN CITY
MARKHAME TIPPERARY
MARKS PMO / ANTRIM
MARLEY WESTMEATH/ D(
MARLOW DUBLIN, TYRON
O MARLY PN Armagh,

MARNANE •283
MARNELL CLARE
MARREN SLIGO
MARRILLY •259
MARRINANE •80
MARRON MONAGHAN
MC MARROWE PN Tip.
MARSH LEIX 1626 ENGLAN
MARSHALL DUBLIN, LIM
MARSHALL ANTRIM, LO
MARTEN DOWN, LOUTH I
MC MARTEN PN Ferm.
MARTIN PN ANTRIM, ARM
MARTIN GALWAY, 1170 S(
MARTINE PN DOWN, COR
MARTYN GALWAY 1171 N
O MARY PN Lim.
MC MARYNE PN Ferm.
MASIE CORK
MASON DUBLIN, WATERF
MASSA •17
MASSEY LIMERICK, CLAR
MASSON KINGS
MASSY CORK, KERRY, LIN
MC MASTER CAVAN 158
MASTERS CORK, 1703 EN(
MASTERSON DUBLIN, D(
MASTINE LOUTH
MASTRON ROSCOMMON
MATCHETT CORK, GALW
MATEER ANTRIM
MATHERS ARMAGH, •410
MATHEWES PN Louth
MATHEWS LOUTH, DUBL
MATHEWS ROSCOMMON,
MATTHEWS CORK, KERR
MAUFFIELD DONEGAL
MAUGHAN MAYO, •269, •
MC MAUGHON PN Louth
MAUL PMO
MAULE DUBLIN CITY
MAUNSELL LIMERICK, KI
MAURICE •515
MAWE •488
MAWHANNON •55
MAWHINNEY ANTRIM, •
MAWHINNY ANTRIM
MAXEL •210
MAXWEL PMO
MAXWELL LIM 1592 SCOT
MAY DUB, WAT, CORK 147
MAYBERRY ANTRIM
MAYBIN •112
MAYBURY KERRY, LIME
MAYDUCK •429
MAYES ANTRIM, ARMAGH
MAYLARD WATERFORD
MAYNARD CORK, PMO
MAYNE MONAGHAN 1576
MAYPOWDER •72

MEA ALL IN MAYO, •40, •1(
MEAD PMO
MEADE CLARE, LOUTH, C(
MEAGH PN CORK CITY, LI
MEAGHAN PN Tip.
O MEAGHAN PN Tip.
MEAGHER PN CLARE, TIF
O MEAGHER PN Tip.
MEAGHIR PN Waterford
MEAHOHAN PN Tip.
MEALIA •72, •128
MEALLEY •342
O MEALUE •128
MEALY •128
O MEALY PNDONEGAL, •
MEANE PN Antrim
MEANY MONAGHAN 1576
MEARA PN TIPPERARY / T
O MEARA PN TIPPERARY/
MEARINGE PN Waterford
MEARN •425
M' MEARTY •432
MEARY PN Tip.
O MEARY PN LIMERICK,
MEASE LIMERICK
MEATH DUBLIN CITY, PM(
MC MECHAN •411
MEDOLE ANTRIM, 1710 GI
MEE DUBLIN CITY/ ROSCOI
MEEGAN MONAGHAN, •1:
O MEEGHANE CLARE
MEEHAN GALWAY, SLIGC
O MEEHAN PN Ferm.
O MEEHON •237
MEEK ANTRIM, •381
MEEKE ANTRIM
MC MEEKIN ANTRIM
MEEKIN •87
MC MEEL •256
MEENAGH •40
MEENAN DONEGAL, TYR(
MEENHAN •322
MEERE •509
MEGARRY •38, •347
MEGHAN PN Louth
MEGHER PN Kings
MEGLAMRY •429
MEGLAUGHLI •223
MEGRAW •175, •267
MEHANE PN Kings
MEHARG ALL ANTRIM
MEIGHAN •117, •316, •41(
MEIRS PMO
MEKILL •429
O MELAGHLIN PN Rosc.
MELAGHLINE KINGS
MELAY •316
MELDON •19, •249
MELIA GALWAY, •72, •128
O MELLAN PN Louth

MC MELLEN PN Down.
MELLET •40
MELLIFONT PMO
MELLON TYRONE, •180
MELLOTT •40
MELLY •208
MELODY 5 BIRTHS, MUNS
MELOGHLEN PN Tip.
MELROY •119
MELVILLE DUBLIN, LIME
MELVIN MAYO, •175
MENAGHT •267
MC MENAMIN DONEGA
MENAUTT •347
MC MENDA CLARE
MENDAN QUEENS
MENEESE •411
MC MENIM •418
MENOCHER •367
MENTAN PN Queens.
MEOGAND PN Tip.
MEOLAN PN Queens.
O MEOLANE PN CLARE
MERCER DUBLIN CITY / A
MERDIFF •401
MERDY •411
MEREDETH DUBLIN CITY
MEREDITH MAYO 1657 W
MERIDETH PMO
MERIDITH KILDARE, PMC
MERIMAN DOWN
MERMONT •310
MERNA •440
O MERRAN PN Antrim
MERRICK 6 BIRTHS, SCA
MERRICKE DUBLIN CITY
MERRIGAN DUBLIN
MERRIMAN •274
MERRYMAN •98, •305, •
MC MERTY •314
MERVIN DUBLIN CITY, PN
MESKELL CORK CITY
MESLVYNE DOWN
MESSICK CORK CITY
METCALF ARMAGH
METHAM CLARE
MEVERALL PMO
MEVERELL WESTMEATH
MEWHANAN •347
MEWHIRTER •281
MEYLER PN WEXFORD/ W
MEYLOR PN Wexford
MIAGH CORK
MC MICHAEL ROSCOMM
MICHAEL PMO
MICHAELBUR PMO
MICHEL PMO
MICHELBURN PMO, WES
MICHELL DUBLIN CITY
MC MICHELL PN Antrim

MICKLE WATERFORD
MIDCALFE LOUTH
MIDDLESEX ARMAGH
MIDDLETON LIMERICK, .
MIDLETON LIMERICK
MIGHANE CLARE
O MIGHANE PN CLARE
MIHIL PMO
MIHILL CARLOW
MILBORN KILDARE
MILDRUM ROSCOMMON
MILEGAN PN SLIGO
MILES DONEGAL 1648 SCO
MC MILLAN ANTRIM, DC
MILLAN PN ANTRIM/ *429
MILLANE *253
MILLAR DON, DERRY 170:
MILLCOD KILKENNY
MILLEA PN KILKENNY/ *1
MC MILLEN ANTRIM, DC
MILLEN ANTRIM
MILLER MAYO 1646 ENG/P
MILLES KILDARE
MILLICAN *254
MILLIGAN ANTRIM, DOW
MILLIGEN *18
MILLIKEN ANTRIM, DOW:
MC MILLIN *466
MILLIN *267
MILLINTON DUBLIN CITY
MILLS DERRY 1706 SCOT/R
MILNE *429
MILNER CORK
MIMNAGH *215
MINAGH *132
MINCHIN OFFALY, TIPPEF
MINES LONDONDERRY
MINETT *310
MINFORD *494, *112
MINGANE *303
MINIECE *429
MINIGHANE PN CLARE
MINIHANE CORK
MC MINN ANTRIM
MINNIS ANTRIM, ALL IN U
MINNISH *429
MINNITT TIPPERARY 1643
MINNOCK KINGS
MINOCHOR *60
MINOGHER *53
MINOGUE CLARE, *330, *
MINOHER *53
MINTEER *175
MISKELLY ALL IN ANTRII
MISSKIMMINS *19
MITCHELL LIM, ROS 1642
MITTEN 7 BIRTHS, 5 IN LE
MITTY *109
MC MLAGHLEN PN COR
MOAN MONAGHAN, *42, *

MOANY *410
MOCKLER PN TIPPERARY
MODRELL PMO
MOEN *42
MOENY PN Waterford
MOFFAT DUBLIN, DONEG
MOFFATT ANTRIM, SLIGC
MOFFET ANTRIM, SLIGO,
MOFFETT ANTRIM, SLIGC
MOFFIT ANTRIM, SLIGO,
MOFFITT DUBLIN, DONEG
MOGHAN PN QUEENS/ *31
MOGHER PN WATERFORD
MOHAN MONAGHAN, *26
O MOHIR PN CORK
MOIR *91
MOLINEUX LONGFORD, I
O MOLLAN *410
O MOLLANE CLARE
MOLLANY PN SLIGO
O MOLLEANY PN SLIGO
MOLLENEX DUBLIN CITY
MOLLEY PN Kings
MOLLINENX ROSCOMMC
MOLLONE PN Waterford
MOLLOWNY PN LIMERIC
MOLLOY PN KINGS,...ROS
MOLONEY LIMERICK, CL
MOLONY LIMERICK, CLAI
MOLOY PN Kings
MOLPHY *484
MOLUMBY *354
MOLYNEAUX 6 BIRTHS,
MONABOE *154
MONAGHAN PN DONEGA
O MONAGHEN PN Ferm.
MC MONAGLE DONEGA
MONAHAN GALWAY, MA
MONARTO CLARE
MONCKLONE PMO
MONCREIFE LONDONDE
MONCRIEFE PMO
MONDY *82, *350, *460
O MONE PN Armagh,
MONEGAN PN Long.
MONEHAN *186
MONELL PMO
MONEY *76
O MONEY PN Antrim
MONEYPEANY DOWN
MONGAN 6 BIRTHS, 5 IN
O MONGANE PN CORK
MONGNEY *467
MONGOMERIE LIMERICK
MONGON *38
MONIPENNY DOWN
MONKE CORK
MONKS DUBLIN, *364
MONLEY *301
MONNELLY MAYO

MONOHAN *304A
MONRO DOWN
MONROE *269
MONSELL LIMERICK 1633
MONTAGUE ANTRIM 117
MONTANE *488
MONTANG *488
MONTANGUE *488
MONTGOMERI DOWN
MONTGOMER DOWN
MONTGOMER DON, LOU
MONTRAY DONEGAL
O MONY PN Antrim
MOODY ANTRIM, DOWN
MOON 6 BIRTHS, SCATTER
O MOONE PN Armagh,
MOONEY PN KILDARE, K
MOONY PN KINGS, MEATI
MOOR PN Kings
MOORE LOUTH, OFFALY 1
MOOREHEAD DONEGAL
MOORHEAD PMO
MOORY DUBLIN CITY
MORA CARLOW
MORAHAN LEITRIM
MORAN PN KILD,KINGS, M
O MORAN PN DONEGAL,
MORANE PN Tip.
MC MORCHEY PN Ferm.
MORDUCK CORK
MORE CORK
MOREEN *304B
MOREGHY PN Waterford
MOREHEY PN Waterford
MORELAND ANTRIM, DO
MOREN PN Kildare
MORESSY PN Waterford
MORETON *104
MOREY KILKENNY/ 7 BIRT
MC MOREY PN SLIGO
O MOREY PN Rosc.
MORGAN WAT, KILK, 117
O MORGAN PN Down.
MORIARTO PN CLARE
MORIARTY KERRY, *125
MORIN PN KILDARE/ *380
MC MORIS PN Lim.
MORISEY PN Tip.
MORISH PN WATERFORD,
MC MORISH PN LIMERIC
MORISON LONDONDERRY
MORISS *91
MORISSY PN TIPPERARY,
MORLEY CORK CITY AND
MORNELL KILKENNY
MC MOROGH PN TIPPER
O MOROGHOE PN Waterf
O MOROHOW PN CORK
MOROLY DUBLIN CITY
MORONEY CLARE, LIMEF

MC MOROUGH PN TIPP
MORPHEU PN Lim.
MORPHEY PN TIPPERARY
MC MORPHEY PN Ferm.
MORPHY PN LIMERICK, T
MORRAN PN DUBLIN, WE
MORRANE PN Tip.
O MORRANE PN TIPPER
MORREN PN Kildare
MORRES CLARE 1764 WEI
MORRESSE TIPPERARY
MC MORREY PN Leitrim
MORRICE GALWAY, MON
Mac MORRICE PN Kerry
MC MORRICE PN KERRY
MORRIN PN KINGS / 6 BIR
MORRIS WAT, COR 1625 V
MC MORRIS PN CORK CI
O MORRIS PN Ferm.
MORRISH PN Tip.
MC MORRISH PN CORK,
O MORRISH PN Ferm.
MORRISON LIM, TIP 1610
MORRISROE ROSCOMMC
MORRISSEY WATERFORI
O MORROE PN Wexford
MORROGH PN WEXFORD.
MC MORROGH PN CLAF
O MORROGHOW PN CO
MORROLLY *50
MORROSSEY *91
MORROUGH *72
MC MORROW LEITRIM,
MORROW ANTRIM, DONE
O MORROW PN Wexford
MORRY PN West.
O MORRY PN Armagh,
MORSH ROSCOMMON
MORTAGH PN WESTMEA
MC MORTAGH PN Queen
MC MORTATH PN CLAR
MC MORTAUGH PN CO
MORTIMER DONEGAL, PI
MORTIMOR SLIGO
MORTOMER DUBLIN CIT
MORTON DUBLIN, LIMERI
MORYERGH KILKENNY
MOSS TYRONE
MOSSE CORK CITY, KING
MOTER *104
MOTHERWAY ALL IN CC
MOTLEY CARLOW
MOTLY CARLOW
MOTON *457
MOUCKTON LIMERICK
MOUGHAN *117
MOUGHTY *63
MOULD DUBLIN CITY
MOULTON ROSCOMMON
MOUNGOMER PN Antrim

MOUNRAG WESTMEATH
MOUNTFORD CORK, PM
MOUNTGOME PN ANTRI
MOUNY PN Meath
MOWHANNAN *410
MOYLAN CLARE, CORK, T
MOYLES *31
MOYNAN *249
MOYNES DUBLIN CITY
MOYNEY *249
MOYNIHAN KERRY, COR
MOYRANE PN *210
O MRISANE PN Donegal
MUCKAREE *71
MUCKEDAN *63
MUCKEEN *38
MUCKIAN *127A
MUCKILBOUY *71
MUCKLEBORN DUBLIN C
MUCKLEBREE *97
MUCKLER *108
MUCLAHY PN Lim.
MUINAGH *132
MUIR DUBLIN, LIMERICK
MUIRLAND *267
MUISE *91
O MULAN PN Armagh,
MULAVILL *262
MULCAGHY PN Waterford
O MULCAHA PN CORK
MULCAHY CORK, LIMERI
MULCHAELL PN Queens.
MULCKAMP DOWN
O MULCLAHY PN LIM. C
MULCLYFF PN Kings
MULCONRY ROSCOMMO
O MULCREVE PN Armagh
MULCREVY PN Louth
MULDERG *259, *260
MULDERRIG *300
MULDON *72
MULDONY PN Queens.
MULDOON FERMANAGH,
O MULDOWNE PN Ferm.
MULDOWNEY 5 BIRTHS,
MULDOWNY PN KILKEN
O MULGOHERY PN Leitri
MULGREW TYRONE
MULGRIEVEY *267
MULGROO *279
MULHAELL QUEENS
MULHALL DUBLIN, KILKI
MULHALLAM MONAGH
MULHALLOM MONAGH
MULHARTAGH *41, *70,
MULHERIN 7 BIRTHS, UL
MULHERN 8 BIRTHS
MULHOLLAND CORK, DC
O MULHOLLAND LOND
MULHOLLUM *429

MULHOLM *83
MULKEEN MAYO, ROSCOI
O MULKERANE PN Arma
MULKERRIN GALWAY
O MULKIRAN PN Rosc.
MULLALY 8 BIRTHS
MULLAN PN ANTRIM / TY
MC MULLAN PN DOWN/
O MULLAN PN ARMAGH,
MULLANE CORK / CORK,
O MULLANE *189
MULLANY PN WATERFOR
O MULLANY PN Rosc.
MULLARKEY MAYO, GA
MULLARKY PN SLIGO
MULLCLAHY PN Lim.
MULLEDY PN Long.
MULLEE *157A
MULLEGAN PN ANTRIM,
MULLEN PN LOUTH / TYR
MC MULLEN DONEGAL,
MULLEPLATE KINGS
MULLER LONDONDERRY
MULLERANE PN Kings
O MULLFOYLE PN Lond.
MULLGAN PN WESTMEA
O MULLGHILL PN Doneg
MULLHOLLAN PN Lond.
MULLICAN PN West.
O MULLICAN PN Ferm.
MULLIGAN PN WESTMEA
O MULLIGAN PN Ferm.
O MULLIGAN PN Ferm.
MULLIN PN ANTRIM/ TYR
MULLINENX ROSCOMMC
O MULLINIHILL PN SLI
MULLINS CORK, CLARE
O MULLMOGHE PN Don
MULLOCK *249
MC MULLOGHRY PN Le
MULLON *159
MULLONY PN CLARE, TIP
MULLOWNEY PN TIPPER
MULLOWNY PN CLARE, I
O MULLOWNY PN CLAR
MULLOY PN Leitrim
O MULLOY PN Donegal
O MULLPATRIC PN Fern
MULLRAYN PN Tip.
MULLREANE PN Kings
MULLRONIFIN PN SLIGC
MULMONA *421
MULOLY PN Meath
MULONE PN Queens.
O MULPATRICK PN Long
MULQUEEN LIMERICK, C
MULREANY *154
MULRENNAN 5 BIRTHS,
MULRIAN PN LIM. CITY
MULRIAN PN LIM. CITY

O MULRIAN PN Lim.
O MULRIANE PN Lim.
MULROE MAYO, GALWAY
MULRONEY CLARE
MC MULRONIFIN PN SI
MULRONY PN Kilkenny
MULROONEY 9 BIRTHS,
MULROW *174
MULROY MAYO, *119
MULRY PN ROSCOMMON /
MULRYAN PN TIPPERARY
MULSHENOGE CORK
MULVANERTY *35, *380,
MULVANNY 4 BIRTHS, N
MULVANY 4 BIRTHS, NO
O MULVENA PN Antrim
MULVENNA ALL IN ANTR
MULVEY LEITRIM, *221
MULVIGHILL PN Long.
MULVIHILL PN LONGFOR
O MULVOG PN Donegal
MUNCKE DUBLIN CITY
MUNCKTEN PMO
MUNDAY *247, *350, *259,
MUNEY PN Kings
O MUNEY PN Donegal
MUNGAN WESTMEATH
MUNIGHANE PN CORK
MUNNELLY MAYO, CONN
MUNNYHANE PN CORK
MUNS PMO
O MURACHA *40
MURAN *400
MURCAN PN Kings
MC MURCHEY PN Ferm.
O MURCHEY PN Ferm.
MURCHOE PN Wexford
O MURCHOE PN Wexford
O MURCHY PN Antrim
MURDOCH ANTRIM, *210
MURDOCK DONEGAL, DE
MURDOUGH *91
MC MURDY *210
MURDY *210
MURESIE PN Waterford
O MURESIE PN Waterford
MC MUREY PN SLIGO
MURFAY PN Kings
MURFIE PN Waterford
MURFY PN Queens.
MURHILLA *397
M' MURLAN *71
MURLAND *175, *267
MURNANE LIMERICK, CC
MURPHEY PN KILDARE, I
MC MURPHEY PN Ferm.
MURPHY PN VARIOUS/ CC
MC MURPHY PN Down.
O MURPHY PN ANTRIM, .
MURRAY DONEGAL, PMO

MC MURRAY LIMERICK
O MURRAY PN Donegal
MURREANE PN CORK
MURREY PN DUBLIN, KIL
MC MURREY PN Lond.
MURRICOHU *65
MURRICOHU *65
MURRIHY *291
MURRIHY *291
MURRIN 6 BIRTHS, LEINS
O MURROGHOW PN COI
MURRONY CLARE
MURROUGH CORK
MURRY PN ANTRIM, CARI
MC MURRY PN Down.
O MURRY PN ARMAGH, I
MURT *429
MURTAGH PN LONG, LOU
MC MURTAGH PN CORK
MURTIN ANTRIM
MC MURTRY ALL ANTRI
MURY PN Kings
O MURY ARMAGH, LOUTI
MUSCHAM CORK
MUSCHAMP PMO
MUSTIAN DUBLIN
MYERS WEXFORD, ANTRI
MYHAN *117
O MYHAN PN Leitrim
MYLES 7 BIRTHS, NONE II
MYLOTT *174, *179
MYLOTTE *40
MYNOGE PN Tip.
MYTHEN *109
MC NABB 8 BIRTHS, ULS
MC NABO *26, *153, *275
MC NABOE *154, *265, *4
NAGHTEN PN ROSCOMMC
MC NAGHTEN *358, *23
NAGHTENN ROSCOMMON
NAGLE LIMERICK 1171 NOI
NAIL *381
MC NAIR ANTRIM
NAISH LIMERICK 1171 NOF
NALLY MAYO, ROSCOMMC
MC NALLY PN ARMAGH/
MC NAMA *128, *380
MC NAMARA PN LIMERI
MC NAMAROW PN LIM.
MC NAMEE LONDONDER
MC NAMORROW *267
NANANY *454B
NANGLE LIMERICK, KILD.
NAPER MEATH 1590 ENGL.
NAPIER DUBLIN 1598 SCOT
NAPPER DOWN, PMO
NARBETT TIPPERARY
NARY *485
NASH CORK, LIMERICK 11
NAUGHER *113

M' NAUGHT *432
NAUGHTEN PN WESTMEA
MC NAUGHTEN PN Antri
NAUGHTON GALWAY, M.
NAVILL DUBLIN CITY
NAVIN MAYO
NAY LIMERICK
NAYLOR DUBLIN
O NEA PN Lim.
NEAL 6 BIRTHS, LEINSTER
NEALAN CLARE
NEALANE PN CLARE
O NEALANE PN CLARE
NEALE PN TIP,WAT, CAR,
O NEALE PN ARM, DOW, I
MC NEALE PN Lond.
NEALL PN Kings
O NEALL PN ANTRIM, CL
MC NEALL ANTRIM
O NEALLE DOWN
NEAPHSEY *501
NEARY MAYO, ROSCOMM
NEAVE PMO
NEE GALWAY
MC NEECE *359
NEEDHAM WESTMEATH /
NEEF *497
NEEHAN *134
NEELY 9 BIRTHS, ULSTER
MC NEELY PN Antrim
NEENAN CLARE, *283
NEEPER *175, *381, *429
NEESON ANTRIM, ALL IN
MC NEICE ANTRIM
MC NEIGHT *494
NEILAN GALWAY, ROSCO
NEILE PN Kilkenny
O NEILE PN ARMAGH, LO
NEILL ANTRIM, CORK, KE
O NEILL PN ANTRIM / DUE
MC NEILL ANTRIM 1706 S
MC NEILLY ANTRIM, DO
NEIPER *76
NEISBETT ARMAGH
NELIS LONDONDERRY, MA
MC NELIS ALL IN DONEG.
MC NELLUS PN Donegal
NELSON DUBLIN 1646 ENC
MC NELUS PN Donegal
MC NEMARA PN CLARE,
MC NEMARRA PN CLAR
MC NEMEE PN Leitrim
MC NENDA CLARE
MC NENY PN Mon.
O NEO PN Waterford
NEPER *429, *489
M' NERLIN *19
NESBIT DONEGAL
NESBITT CAVAN 1640 ENC
NESMITH LONDONDERRY

NEST KILDARE, PMO
NESTOR GALWAY, CLARE
NETERVILL ROSCOMMON
NETREUILE MEATH
NETTLE WATERFORD
NEUILL PN CORK CITY, WI
NEUNHAN LIMERICK
NEUPORT PN Wexford
NEVEREL PMO
NEVILL KILKENNY
NEVILLE KILKENNY 1649
NEVIN DOWN / 22 BIRTHS,
NEWBOLT QUEENS
NEWBOROUG PMO
NEWBURGH PMO
NEWCE CORK
NEWCOMB DUBLIN, 1630
NEWCOME *72
NEWCOMEN DUBLIN, KI
NEWCOMENT DUBLIN
NEWELL CORK, LIMERICK
NEWENHAM CORK, 1680
NEWGENT PN LONGFORD
NEWMAN CORK 1640 ENG
NEWTON TYRONE 1596 EN
NEWTOWNE DONEGAL
NEYLON CLARE, *455
NIBLOCK ANTRIM, ALL IN
NICHOL KILDARE 1610 SC
NICHOLAS WATERFORD,
MC NICHOLAS DOWN 16
NICHOLL ANTRIM, LOND
NICHOLLS DUBLIN CITY,
NICHOLS *409
NICHOLSON SLIGO, CORI
NICHOLSON LEITRIM, DC
NICKLE *421
MC NICKLE TYRONE
NICKOLDS WESTMEATH
NICKOLLS LOUTH, QUEE
NICOL *91
NICOLSON PMO
MC NIECE ANTRIM
MC NIFF DONEGAL, DERR
MC NIGHT *358, *433
NIGHTINGALE PMO
NIGHTINGALL CLARE
NIGHTON DONEGAL
NIHILL CLARE
O NIHILL PN CLARE
NILAN GALWAY, ROSCOM
MC NINCH ALL IN ANTRI
NISBIT DONEGAL, PMO
NISBITT DONEGAL
NIX *11, *404
NIXON CAVAN, FER 1610 E
NIXSON PN Ferm.
NOBLE DUBLIN, LIMERICK
NOCHER *175
NOCKER *17

NOCTER *261
NOCTON *307, *419
MC NOGER *59
NOGHAR *59
MC NOGHER *60
NOGHER *71, *137
NOHER *71
MC NOHOR *343
NOLAN PN CARLOW, KILK
NOLAND PN CARLOW
NOLLANE PN Tip.
O NONANE PN LIMERICK
NOONAN CORK, CLARE, L
NOONE GALWAY, ROSCOM
NORMAN DONEGAL, DER
NORMILE LIMERICK, CLA
NORRICE DOWN, MONAG
NORRIS CORK, CARLOW,
NORRIS KILKENNY, 1213
NORRIT *55, *411
NORSE PMO
NORTH CARLOW, DUBLIN
NORTH DUBLIN 1646 ENGL
NORTHRIDGE *164
NORTHRIDGE ALL IN CO
NORTON DONEGAL 1710 S
NORTON DUBLIN
NORWICK WESTMEATH
NOSS KILKENNY
NOTLEY FERMANAGH
NOUGHTON *23
NOURY *19
NOVIS CORK
NOWLAN PN KILDARE, WI
NOWLAND PN DUBLIN, K
NOWLANE PN DUBLIN
NUGENT GALWAY, DOW,
NUGENT ARMAGH, DUBLI
MC NULTY DONEGAL, M.
NULTY DUBLIN CITY / ME.
NUNAN *303
NUNANE PN Lim.
NUNN WEXFORD, 1649 ENC
NUNUN *469
NURSE *142
MC NUSKE PN Down.
OAKELEY CORK
OAKLEY DUBLIN, CORK 1
OATS *36, *386
OB DUBLIN CITY
ODWAY WATERFORD
OFFLING P N WATERFOR
OGAN PN WEXFORD, ALSC
OGE PN CLARE, WATERFO
OGILVIE ANTRIM
OGLE 6 BIRTHS, ALL ULSTI
OINS *429
OLDFIELD WATERFORD, I
OLIVER WICKLOW, CORK,
OLLIFFE CORK

OLLIGAN *446
OOGAN *364, *495
ORGAN *135
ORMESBY ROSCOMMON
ORMOND 6 BIRTHS, LEINS
ORMONDE KILKENNY
ORMSBEY LIMERICK
ORMSBY KER, MAYO, SLI
ORPHYE WEXFORD
ORPIN ANTRIM, PMO
ORR DUB, CORK, DON 1626
ORRSLEY WEXFORD
ORSON DUBLIN CITY, LOU
OSBALDES ROSCOMMON
OSBERNE WATERFORD
OSBORNE WATERFORD, T
OSBOURN PMO
OSBOURNE PMO
OSBURN PMO
OSBURNE WATERFORD
M' OSCAR *367, *429
OSWALD ALL IN ULSTER
OTWAY TIPPERARY 1640 E
OUGAN *72, *178A, ALSO I
OUGLE QUEENS
OULAHAN *63
OULDIS CORK
OUNIHAN *73
OUSLEY PMO
OUZZELL LIMERICK CITY
OVINGTON TIPPERARY
OVINTON DOWN
OWEN WAT, KILK 1713 WE
MC OWEN PN CLARE, CO
MC OWEN BWY CORK
OWEN OGE P N CORK
OWENS DUBLIN, KILD, ME
OWGAN P N WEXFORD,..A
OWNYAN DUBLIN
OWTTON KILDARE
OXBRIDGE KINGS
OXBRUGH KINGS
OZENBROOKE FERMANA
PACKEHAM PMO
PACKENHAM MEATH, PN
PADDEN MAYO
MC PADEN MAYO
PADGETT QUEENS
MC PADIN PN Donegal
PADLE PN TIPPERARY
PADMORE DUBLIN CITY
PAGE DUBLIN, CORK 1646
PAGENHAM WESTMEATH
PAGET DUBLIN, LIMERICK
PAGETT FERMANAGH
PAGNAM *217
PAINE LIMERICK 1586 ENG
PAINTER CORK
PAISLEY DUBLIN, ANTRIN
PAKER KINGS

PALFERY DUBLIN CITY
PALFREY PMO
PALLIS KILDARE
PALMER WAT, MAY, OFF,
PALMES PMO
PALMS PMO
PALUIS LIMERICK
PAPPING CLARE
PAPWORTH CARLOW
PARAGON *364
PARDON WESTMEATH
PAREFOY MEATH
PARIELL ROSCOMMON
PARILL *245
PARIS CORK, LIMERICK 16
PARISH LIMERICK, TIPPER
PARK SLIGO 1646 ENGLANI
PARKE SLIGO 1646 ENGLA
PARKER LIM, TIP 1642 EN
PARKHILL LONDONDERR
PARKINS FERMANAGH
PARKINSON ARMAGH, PI
PARKS PMO / ANTRIM, ARI
MC PARLAN PN ARMAGI
MC PARLAND ARMAGH
PARLE ALL IN WEXFORD
PARLON *458
PARLONE PN Leitrim
PARNALL DUBLIN CITY
PARR CORK / 5 BIRTHS, SC
PARRICAN *72
PARRIS TIPPERARY
PARROTT QUEENS
PARSONS DOWN / 12 BIR
MC PARTLAN LEITRIM,
M' PARTLAND *238
MC PARTLIN LEITRIM
PARTRIDGE QUEENS
PATCHET *155
PATCHY *292, *293
PATERSON FERMANAGH/
PATIENCE WESTMEATH
PATISON *429
PATON DONEGAL, LONDO
PATRICAN *449
PATRICK ANTRIM 1710 SC
PATRICKESON WESTME
O PATTAN PN DONEGAL
PATTEN MAYO
PATTERSON DONEGAL, I
PATTON DUBLIN, MAYO 1
PATTY *381
PAUL QUEENS / LONDONDI
PAULE CARLOW
PAUSY LIMERICK CITY
PAYN PMO
PAYNE DUBLIN, LIMERICK
PAYTON PMO
PEACHEN DUBLIN CITY
PEACOCK LIMERICK CITY
PEACOCKE LIMERICK
PEACOKE LIMERICK
PEAK PMO
PEAKE DUBLIN CITY, MEA
MC PEAKE PN Lond.
PEARCE CORK, LIMERICK
PEARCELL CORK
PEARD CORK
PEARLE PN WEXFORD
PEARSANE DONEGAL
PEARSON WESTMEATH /
PEARTREE MEATH
PEASLEY KILDARE 1646 E
PEASLIE KILDARE
PEASLY PMO
PECK PMO
PECKE TIPPERARY
PEEL ANTRIM
PEEPES DUBLIN CITY
PEERCY CORK CITY
PEG *523
PEGNIM *247
PEIRCE LOUTH, PMO
PEIRSON QUEENS
PEISLEY KILDARE 1646 EN
PELAN *306
PENDER WEXFORD, *32, *
PENDERGAST CORK, LIM
PENDERGRAS PN CARLC
PENDERGRAS CORK, LI
PENDERS *373
PENDY *151, *352, *65, *51
PENEFAITHER KILKENN
PENFORD CORK
PENNEFATHER WICKLOV
PENNFATHER TIPPERAR
Pennifeather PMO
PENNIGTON CORK CITY
PENNINGTON CORK, DU
PENNY ANTRIM, DUBLIN,
PENNYFETHER TIPPERAI
PENOYX DUBLIN
PENTENY DUBLIN CITY, D
PENTLAND DOWN, ARMA
PENTONY PN MEATH
PEOPLES DONEGAL, ALL
PEPARD MEATH
PEPPARD LIMERICK, LOU
PEPPER MEATH, TIP 1646 I
PEPPERD LOUTH, MEATH
PEPYS PMO
PERCE PN Wexford
PERCHY SLIGO
PERCIVAL SLIGO 1556 EN
PERCIVALE CORK
PERCIVALL CORK
PERCY CORK CITY / *249
PERKINS DUBLIN, LIMERI
PERRIMAN *249
PERROT PMO
PERROTT CORK, MUNSTE
PERRY DUB, LIM, TYR 164
PERSON KILDARE
PERSONS KINGS
PERT KILKENNY
PETDITD QUEENS
PETER KILKENNY
PETERS TIPPERARY
PETERSON LIMERICK, GA
PETFORD LIMERICK
PETHERICK *250
PETIT *109
PETSWORTH PMO
PETTICREW ANTRIM
PETTIGREW ANTRIM
PETTIT DUB, WEXFORD 16
PETTITT WESTMEATH
PEYTON MAYO, LEITRIM 1
MC PHAIL *422
MC PHATRICKS ANTRI
PHEALAN TIPPERARY, KI
PHELAN PN WAT, KILK, Q
PHELAND PN Kilkenny
PHELANE PN Waterford
PHELLANE PN Tip.
PHERMAN *249
MC PHETRISH ANTRIM
PHIBBS SLIGO
PHILAN *511
PHILBIN MAYO, GALWAY
PHILIPIN *276
PHILIPS LIMERICK, TIPPEI
MC PHILLIP PN MONAGH
PHILLIPIN *223
MC PHILLIPP PN TIPPER.
PHILLIPPS TIPPERARY, D
MC PHILLIPS CAVAN, M
PHILLIPS PN CORK CITY /
PHILLPOT DUBLIN CITY
PHILLPS LOUTH
PHILOMY *55
PHILPOT PMO
PHILPOTT CORK
PICKEN FERMANAGH, PMO
PICKNALL DUBLIN CITY
PICTON CARLOW
PIDGEON 5 BIRTHS, ALL I
PIERCE PMO, LOUTH, CLA
PIERCEFIELD MEATH
PIERS PN KERRY, ...WEST
PIERSE *47
PIERSON PMO / *333
PIGETT QUEENS
PIGGOT PMO
PIGGOTT PN QUEENS
PIGOTT WEXFORD, CORK,
PIGOTT CORK
PIKE KILKENNY, PMO
PILKINGTON WESTMEAT
PILLSWORTH LONGFORI
PIN DUBLIN CITY
PINDARS *249
PINDER *120, *274
PINDERS *249
PINDY *304A, *142
PINE CORK
PINKERTON ANTRIM
PINKEY *524
PINKLE WEXFORD
PINKY *55
PINSEN PMO
PINSENT PMO
PINSON DUBLIN CITY, PM
PIPER *243
PIPPIN TIPPERARY
PIRIE *91
PIRRIE *91, *356
PITT LONDONDERRY
PITTS DUBLIN CITY
PLATT LONDONDERRY
PLAYFORD DUBLIN CITY
PLELLPS LIMERICK CITY
PLOVER CORK
PLUKENET ANTRIM
PLUMER CORK
PLUNCKET PMO
PLUNKET DUBLIN, TYRON
PLUNKETT PN DUBLIN, L
POAG *9, *411
POAKRICH MONAGHAN
POCHER KILKENNY
POCKERIDG PMO
POCKERISH PMO
POCKRICH MONAGHAN
POE TIPPERARY 1646 PALA
POEKRICH MONAGHAN
POER PN WATERFORD/ *10
POGUE *10, *175, *383
POINTS ARMAGH, CORK
POINTZ PMO
POKE *234, *482
POLAND 5 BIRTHS, LEINS
POLE SLIGO/ *253
POLEWHEELE ANTRIM
POLEXFIELD DUBLIN CIT
M' POLIN *410
MC POLIN ALL IN COUNT
POLIN *410
POLK *254
POLLARD WESTMEATH 1
POLLOCK GALWAY, MEA
PONNTNEY WESTMEATH
PONSONBY CORK 1170 N
PONTIN KILDARE
PONTONEY DUBLIN CITY
PONY DUBLIN CITY
POOER CARLOW
POOL PMO
POOLE CORK 1628 ENGLA
POOLEY PMO
POOLY DUBLIN CITY
POOPE DUBLIN CITY
POOR *316
POORDOM QUEENS
POORE PN WATERFORD, C
POOTS DOWN, ANTRIM, A
POPE LIMERICK CITY, PMC
PORSONBY KILKENNY
PORTER TYRONE 1640 EN
PORTIS KILKENNY
POTT DUBLIN
POTTER KERRY, DUBLIN (
POUDYHARD DUBLIN CI
POUEY ROSCOMMON
POULDEN CORK
POUNTNEY PMO
POURDON PMO
POVEY PMO
POWEL PMO
POWELL LIMERICK 1649 W
POWER WATERFORD 1171
POWRE PN TIPPERARY, KI
PRATER CORK, PMO
PRATT CAVAN 1641 ENG/ I
PREIST CORK
PRENCH WESTMEATH
PRENDER *67, *229, *242
PRENDERGAS PN Wexfor
PRENDERGAS CORK, LI
PRENDIBLE *443
PRENDY *249, *352
PRENTICE 8 BIRTHS, 7 IN
PRESCOTT 5 BIRTHS, LEI
PRESSICK PMO
PRESSLY FERMANAGH, *
PRESTON DUBLIN, MEATI
PRESTWITCH CLARE
PREY *523
PRIALL *301
PRICE DOWN 1640 WELCH/
PRICHARD *6, *381
PRIDDIN CORK CITY
PRIGGE CORK
PRIGGET DUBLIN CITY
PRINN DUBLIN
PRIOR QUEENS, PMO / CA
PRITCHARD WATERFORI
PRITCHET DUBLIN CITY
PRITTY CARLOW
PROCTOR ARMAGH / ANT
PROTHEROE LOUTH
PROUD WEXFORD
PROUT TIPPERARY
PRUNTY LONGFORD
PUE WEXFORD
PUNCH PN CORK CITY / C
PURCELL CORK 1171 NOR
PURDON CLARE, LOUTH I
PURDY DUBLIN, LIMERICI
PUREFAY PMO
PUREFOY DUBLIN 1170 N
PURFOY CLARE, ALSO PA
PURSELL CORK 1171 NOR
PURSHELL ROSCOMMON
PURTILL LIMERICK, ALL I
PURTLE *72
PURVIS 8 BIRTHS, 4 IN UL
PYLLE TIPPERARY
PYNE PMO / CORK, CLARE
QUADE *91
MC QUADE PN MONAGH
MC QUAID MONAGHAN,
QUAIL ANTRIM, DOWN
QUALTER *506, *507
MC QUAN PN Leitrim
MC QUAY *185
QUEE ALL IN COUNTY ANT
QUEEN *383
QUEENAN *147
QUELCH WESTMEATH
QUELLY PN CLARE
O QUELLY PN CLARE
QUELSH PMO
QUENAN *106
QUENN *17
QUICK *325
QUIDDIHY PN TIPPERAR
QUIDDILY PN Kilkenny
O QUIG PN Lond.
QUIGG 6 BIRTHS, ALL IN U
QUIGGLY PN Queens.
QUIGLEY LONDONDERRY,
O QUIGLEY PN DONEGAL
QUILIGAN *318
MC QUILKAN *43
MC QUILKIN *44
QUILL CORK
QUILLAN *154, *194, *246,
MC QUILLAN ANTRIM, M
QUILLEN *92
M' QUILLEN *351
QUILLENANE PN Waterfor
MC QUILLIAMS *385
QUILLIGAN LIMERICK, C
QUILLINAN TIPPERARY, *
QUILTY LIMERICK, WATE
QUIME PN Kings
QUIN PN MON, TIP, KILK, L
O QUIN PN ANTRIM, LOND
QUINANE *498
QUINE PN CLARE, WATERI
O QUINE PN ARMAGH, CL
QUING PN Kilkenny
QUINLAN TIPPERARY, KE
QUINLIN PN Tip.
QUINLIVAN CLARE, ULST
QUINN PN WAT, DUB/ DUB
MC QUINN KERRY
QUINNE PN DUBLIN, KINC
O QUINNE PN DOWN, TIP

QUIRK *36, *386, *500
QUIRKE PN TIPPERARY/ T
O QUIRKE PN Tip.
MC QUISTON ANTRIM, 1
MC QUOD PN Armagh,
QUOID *91
MC QUOID PN ARMAGH/
QUYNALL CORK CITY
QUYNN PN Kildare
O RAAVERTY PN Armagh
RABBIT 10 BIRTHS, LEINS
RACARDS *526
RACTIGAN ALL IN COUN
RADFORD WEXFORD / 7 I
RADWILL *468
RAFFERTY ANTRIM, TYR
RAFTER PN QUEENS / DUE
RAFTERY GALWAY, ROSC
RAFTISS *117
RAGETT TIPPERARY
RAGGETT TIPPERARY, KI
RAGGOTT KILKENNY
RAGHTER PN Kildare
RAHILLY KERRY, CORK
RAINALDS DOWN
RAINE PN Waterford
RAINEY ANTRIM, DOWN
RAINLLOW DUBLIN CITY
RALAGH LIMERICK
RALEIGH WATERFORD, C
RALL *154
RALLY *394
RALPH 12 BIRTHS, LEINST
RAM CLARE, GALWAY, KI
RAMSAY ANTRIM
RAMSBOTTOM *249
RAMSEY DONEGAL, DERI
RANAGHAN *196
M' RANALD *254
RANDALL DUBLIN, CORK
RANDALSON *185
RANDELL WEXFORD
RANKIN WATERFORD, CO
MC RANN *443
M' RANNAL *429
RANNELAGH PMO
RANSOM WESTMEATH
RASHFORD *133, *526
RASHLEIGH CORK
RATH *254
RATHERAM LIMERICK
RATHWELL *468
RATIGAN MAYO, ROSCOM
RATSFORE ARMAGH
RATTIGAN MAYO, ROSCC
RATTY *72, *368
RAUTH PN Louth
RAVERTY *348
RAVY *485
RAWDEN ANTRIM, PMO

RAWDON PMO
O RAWE ALL IN COUNTY
RAWKINES WEXFORD
RAWLEY PN Lim.
RAWLINGSON DUBLIN C
RAWLINS QUEENS, PMO
RAWLINSON DUBLIN CIT
RAWSON QUEENS, PMO
RAY 7 BIRTHS, NONE IN C
RAYMOND KERRY, LIME
RAYNALDS DOWN
RAYNE PN LIMERICK, TIPI
O RAYNN PN Lim.
RAYNOR DUBLIN
REA KILDARE/ ANTRIM, DC
O REA PN Lim.
READ CLARE, GALWAY 11
READE PN Lond.
READEINGE DUBLIN
READER PMO
READY *518
REAGANE PN CORK
O REAGANE PN CORK
REAGH PN CORK
O REALLY PN Ferm.
REALY PN DUBLIN, MEATI
O REALY PN CORK
REAMON KILKENNY
REAMS *249
REAN PN Kings
REANEY 5 BIRTHS, CONN.
REARDON *303
RECROFT MEATH
RECUBIE KINGS
REDDAN 7 BIRTHS, NONE
REDDIN 6 BIRTHS, NONE I
REDDINGTON MAYO, GA
REDDY DUBLIN, KILKENN
REDFERN 5 BIRTHS, SCAT
REDINGTON GALWAY 12
REDMAN KILKENNY, PMC
REDMOND WEXFORD 117
MC REDMOND PN KING
REDPATH ANTRIM
REDWORTH ANTRIM
REED CLARE, GALWAY 117
REEDE TIPPERARY
REEL 5 BIRTHS, LEINSTER
REEMES ARMAGH
REEN CORK, KERRY, *100,
REENES KILDARE
REEUES CLARE, DUBLIN C
REEVES CLARE 1646 WELC
REGAN PN KINGS/ CORK, I
O REGAN PN LIMERICK, F
REGANE PN CORK
O REGANE PN CORK, LIN
REID ANTRIM, DUBLIN, DO
REIDY KERRY, CLARE
O REIGAN PN Rosc.

REIGH *109
REIGNE PN Lim.
REILIGH KILKENNY
O REILLY DUBLIN, *17, *4
REILLY CAVAN, LONG, DU
REILY PN Long.
REIUES LONDONDERRY, W
REKLE *351
O RELEY PN Ferm.
RELICK DUBLIN CITY
RELIHAN CORK, KERRY
O RELLY PN Rosc.
RELY PN Kilkenny
O RELY PN Ferm.
RELYE PN West.
REMNANT CORK
RENAL PMO
RENAN *429
RENDER KILKENNY
RENEHAN *96
RENNIE *410
RENOLDS ANTRIM/ *91
RENOLLS DOWN
RENSHAW PMO
REPPET *429
O RERGANE PN Lim.
REVELL PN Wexford
REVEN *498
REVILLE WEXFORD
REYLIE PN Rosc.
REYLY PN WATERFORD, D
REYNER MEATH
REYNEY PN SLIGO
M' REYNOLD *429
MC REYNOLDS ANTRIM
REYNOLDS PN LEITRIM /
REYNOLDSON *185
RHOADES PMO
RICE WAT, LIMERICK, 1647
RICH DUBLIN CITY, CORK
RICHARD DUBLIN CITY, I
RICHARD 6 BIRTHS, LEIN
MC RICHARD PN CORK,
RICHARDS WEXFORD 164
RICHARDSON CORK,DOI
RICHESIES KILDARE
RICHEY *348
RICHMOND ALL IN COUN
RICHT DUBLIN CITY
RIDD *58
RIDDAGHAN PN Leitrim
RIDDELL ANTRIM, ULSTE
RIDDINGE KINGS
O RIDEENE CLARE
RIDEOUT CARLOW
RIDER DUBLIN CITY
RIDGBY ANTRIM
RIDGE GALWAY
RIDGELEY WEXFORD
O RIEDY PN KERRY, LIM.

RIELLY CAVAN, LONGFOR
RIENARD CORK
RIERDAN CLARE
O RIERDAN PN Lim.
RIERDANE PN CORK, KEI
O RIERDANE PN CORK, I
RIERGANE PN CORK
RIEVE PMO
RIEVES PMO
RIGDEWAY KILKENNY
RIGG DUBLIN CITY
RIGGS CORK, 1640 ENGLA
RIGNEY 9 BIRTHS, KINGS
RIGNY PN Kings
RILEY PN WESTMEATH / *
RING CORK, *186
RINGLAND DOWN, ANTRI
O RIORDAN CORK, ALL I
RIORDAN CORK, KERRY,
O RIORDANE PN CORK C
RIPPET *76, *429, *489
RIPPIT *75
RISE PMO
RITCHIE ANTRIM
RITKABY ANTRIM
ROADES QUEENS
ROANE *30
ROARKE *61
ROARTY DONEGAL, TYRC
MC ROARY *95
ROAYNE WATERFORD
ROBB ANTRIM
ROBBINS CORK, MEATH 1
ROBERT DUBLIN CITY
MC ROBERT PN Waterford
Mac ROBERTS *338
MC ROBERTS CAVAN 16
ROBERTS CORK, LIMERIC
ROBERTSON ANTRIM, D
ROBINS KILKENNY/ *409
ROBINSON DONEGAL, DE
ROBINSONE DOWN
ROBOTHAM DUBLIN CIT
ROBSON DOWN, ALL IN U
ROCH WATERFORD 1507 N
ROCHE LIMERICK ?, 1507 I
ROCHFORD DUBLIN
ROCHFORT CORK, CARL
ROCHNEEN *327
ROCHWELL PN Waterford
ROCK PN KILKENNY / DUB
RODAGHAN PN Leitrim
O RODAN PN Donegal
RODAUGHAN *484
RODDEN DONEGAL
RODDY MAYO, ROSCOMM
RODEN *46
RODGERS DUBLIN, CORK
RODMAN *177, *433
RODMONT *177

ROE WEXFORD 1666 ENG/ P
ROGAN ANTRIM, DOWN, L
O ROGAN PN Down.
O ROGANE PN CORK
ROGERS CORK 1640 ENG/\
ROHAN DUBLIN 1180 NOR
ROICE *109
ROKEBY WESTMEATH
ROLEDGE KILKENNY
ROLLESTON OFFALY, AR
ROLLINS ANTRIM, DOWN
ROLLS KINGS
ROLSTON TYRONE, ANTR
ROMA ANTRIM
RONAGHAN *196
O RONAGHAN PN Armagh
RONALDSON *185
RONAN DONEGAL, 1646 SC
RONANE PN Waterford
RONAYNE CORK
RONEY PN LOUTH, SLIGO.
ROOKSBY PMO
ROONEEN *371
ROONEY DUBLIN, LEITRI
ROONOO *189
ROONYE MONAGHAN
ROOTH KILKENNY
ROPER CORK
RORAGH *383
ROREY PN Kings
RORISON *59
MC RORKAN PN Ferm.
RORKE PN LOUTH, WESTM
O RORKE PN LOUTH /*61
RORQUE PN Kildare
Mac RORY *153
RORY PN Rosc.
MC RORY PN FERMANAG
O RORY PN Rosc.
ROSDELL CLARE
ROSE LIMERICK, TIP 1640 I
ROSEBERY *254
ROSEBROUGH *240
ROSENGRANE DUBLIN C
ROSEVILL SLIGO
ROSEY *262
ROSMOND *128
ROSS CLARE 1625 SCOTLA
ROSSBORO *91
ROSSE FERMANAGH
ROSSETOR PN WEXFORD
ROSSINGTON CORK
ROSSITER WEXFORD, WI
ROTH KILKENNY
ROTHERAM WEXFORD, P
ROTHERHAM MEATH 16
ROTHWELL MEATH 1720
ROUANE *502
ROUGHAN 5 BIRTHS
ROUGHANE PN CORK

O ROUGHNANE PN CLA
ROUGHNEEN *486
ROULSTON TYRONE, AN
ROUNDTREE *332
ROUNEY PN Louth
ROUNTREE ARMAGH
ROURKE PN KERRY, WAT
O ROURKE PN LEITRIM /
O ROVERTY PN Armagh,
O ROVERTY PN Armagh,
ROW WEXFORD, PMO
ROWAN LEITRIM, 1548 SC
ROWE WEXFORD 1666 ENG
ROWELL CORK
ROWLAND MEATH 1660 E
ROWLES DUBLIN, KILDAR
ROWLEY MEATH, 1666 EN
ROWLS PMO
ROWLSTON PMO
ROWLY LONDONDERRY, F
ROWNEY *410
ROWNYN KILDARE
ROWTH LONDONDERRY
ROXBERY *254
ROXBOROUGH *254
ROY ANTRIM, DOWN, *154
ROYALL LIMERICK CITY
ROYAN *147
ROYCROFT CORK
ROYDY PN Kerry
ROYSTON WATERFORD
RUAN *3
RUANE MAYO, GALWAY, *
RUARE ARMAGH
RUARKE *61
RUBEY CORK CITY
Mac RUBS *338
RUDAN CLARE
RUDANE PN CLARE
RUDD WEXFORD
RUDDELL LIMERICK, AR
RUDDEN CAVAN, *46
M' RUDDERY *483
RUDDLE LIMERICK, ARM
RUDDOCK PMO / DOWN,
RUDDON *429
RUDDY MAYO, DONEGAL,
RUDICAN *484
RUINEEN *370
M' RUM *489
RUMBALL TIPPERARY
RUMNEY CORK
RUMNY KERRY
RUMSEY CLARE, PMO
RUNIAN *41
RUOE PN CORK
RUORK LEITRIM
RURK *189
RUSEL CARLOW
RUSELL LIMERICK

RUSH MAYO
RUSHFORD *173
RUSSELL DUBLIN, DOWN
RUST LONDONDERRY
RUTH KINGS / 6 BIRTHS, 5
RUTHERFORD ANTRIM,
RUTLEDGE CLARE, GALW
RUTLIDG KILDARE
RUTLIDGE KILDARE
RUTTER CORK, LOUTH, PI
RUTTLE 6 BIRTHS, 5 IN LE
RUXTON LOUTH 1640 ENC
RYAL PMO
RYAN PN LIMERICK, TIP, V
O RYAN PN LIMERICK, WI
RYANCE CLARE
RYANE PN CLARE, LIMERI
O RYANE PN CLARE, LIM
RYARDANE PN Tip.
RYDER MAYO, *495
RYE CORK 1640 ENGLISH /
RYELY *1
RYEN PN Tip.
RYERDANE PN KERRY, T
O RYERDANE PN Lim.
RYLE KERRY
RYND MEATH, FERMANAC
RYNN *48A
RYVES PMO
SADLER TIPPERARY
SADLIER GALWAY, TIP 16
SAGE *94, *219, *474
SALISBURY PMO
SALL WATERFORD
SALLANGER *508
SALLENGER *273
SALLI TIPPERARY
SALLINGER *472, *497, *5
SALLSIBERY WESTMEAT
SALMON 21 BIRTHS, SCA
SALMON DUBLIN CITY
SALT KILDARE, PMO
SALTERS *91
SALTERSON PMO
SALTFEELD LIMERICK CI
SALTFIELD PMO
SALTINSBALL DUBLIN C
SALTONSTALL PMO
SAMBAGE KILDARE
SAMFORD KILKENNY
SAMMING LOUTH
SAMON PN Kildare
SAMPSON LIMERICK
SANCKEY PMO
SANCKY DUBLIN CITY
SANDERS CORK 1642 ENG
SANDERSON CAVAN 164
SANDFORD DUBLIN CITY
SANDS KERRY 1640 ENGLI
SANDYS LONGFORD

SANFORD KERRY 1170 NC
SANKEY TIPPERARY, FER
SANTRY ALL IN COUNTY
SARGENT CORK, LIMERIC
SARJEANT PMO
SARSEIL *40
SARSFIELD CORK 1172 EN
SAUADGE DOWN, KILDAR
SAUAGE DOWN, CORK CI
SAUCE TIPPERARY
SAUNDERS WICKLOW, K
SAURIN *281
SAUSE PN Tip.
SAUSHEIL *40
SAVADGE KILKENNY, DU
SAVAGE DOWN 1170 NOR/
SAVELL CORK CITY
SAVIDGE PN Antrim
SCAFEELD ROSCOMMON
SCALLAN PN WEXFORD/
SCALLY PN LONGFORD / F
SCANLAN KILKENNY / KI
O SCANLAN PN Kerry
SCANLANE PN CLARE
O SCANLANE PN SLIGO
SCANLON KERRY, CLARE
SCANNELL PN KERRY / C
O SCANNELL PN CORK
Scarborough DUBLIN
Scarborrough DUBLIN
SCHUMACKER *287
MC SCOLLOG *319
SCONE PMO
SCOT PN Kings
SCOTNEY CORK
SCOTT DERRY 1688 SCOT/
SCRIMPTON TIPPERARY
SCRIMSHAW KILKENNY
SCUDAMORE CORK CIT
SCUDMORE PMO
O SCULLEN PN Lond.
O SCULLIN PN Lond.
SCULLION ANTRIM, LONI
MC SCULLOGE PN Ferm.
SCURLOCK *474
SCURLOG ROSCOMMON
SCUSE CORK
SEAGRAVE DUBLIN, WIC
SEAMAN DUBLIN CITY
SEAMOR WATERFORD
SEARGEANT WATERFORI
SEATON PMO, LONGFORD
SEAVER *184
SEAWARD CORK
SEAX KILDARE
SEDEN DUBLIN CITY
SEDGRAUE DUBLIN, WES
SEDGWICK *410
SEEDS ANTRIM, DOWN
SEERY WESTMEATH, DUB

SEGNOCK CARLOW
SEGRAVE CORK
SEGRAY KINGS
SEGRE *332
SEIX CARLOW, KILKENNY
SELBY CORK
SELENGER *473
SELLING WEXFORD
SEMPHILL DONEGAL
SEMPLE DUBLIN, DONEG
SERGEANT DUBLIN CITY,
SERGENT DUBLIN CITY
SERLE PMO
SEVERS ARMAGH
O SEVNAGH *40
SEWARD DUBLIN
SEWELL 6 BIRTHS, NONE
SEXTEN PN CLARE
SEXTON PMO, CLARE / CO
SEYMOUR GALWAY 1710
MC SHAEN WESTMEATH
SHAGINS PN Lim.
SHAGROE PN Kerry
SHAILS *59
SHAKELTON KERRY
SHALLCROSS TIPPERAR
SHALLOWE PN Tip.
SHALLY GALWAY
MC SHAN *216
MC SHANAGHY *82
SHANAGHY *92, *132, *47
SHANAHAN CORK, KERR
SHANAHANE PN TIPPER
SHANAHY *153
SHANAN *408
SHANE ANTRIM, DUBLIN (
MC SHANE DONEGAL, LC
MC SHANE PN ARMAGH,
SHANE OGE PN CORK
SHANEGHANE PN Waterfc
SHANEHAN PN Waterford
SHANKS ANTRIM, DOWN
SHANLEY LEITRIM
MC SHANLY PN Leitrim
SHANNAHANE PN Tip.
SHANNOHAN PN Lim.
SHANNON CORK/ ANTRIM
SHANOGHAN PN Lim.
SHAPCOT PMO
SHARKEY DONEGAL, DER
SHARPE CORK CITY, KILK
MC SHARRY LEITRIM, D
O SHARRY PN ARMAGH,
SHARVIN *72
SHAUGHINISY PN Lim.
SHAUGHNESS *232, *435
O SHAUGHNESS LIMERI
SHAUGHNESS GALWAY
SHAW DUBLIN, ANTRIM 15
SHAWE ANTRIM, TIPPERAI

SHEA PN CLARE, CORK, E
MC SHEA KILKENNY
O SHEA PN CORK, KERRY,
MC SHEAGHAN *319
O SHEAGHANE PN Lim.
SHEAGHINSY PN Lim.
SHEAHAN CORK, KERRY,
O SHEALE PN DONEGAL,
SHEALL WESTMEATH
O SHEALL PN ARMAGH, I
SHEALS *358
O SHEANAN PN Ferm.
MC SHEANE PN Lim.
SHEAPHEARD DUBLIN C
SHEAPHERD TIPPERARY,
SHEARER 5 BIRTHS, ULST
SHEARES WEXFORD
SHEARHOON *144
SHEARHY PN Waterford
O SHEARING PN Donegal
SHEE PN KILKENNY, *393
O SHEE PN Queens.
SHEEDY CLARE, *509
SHEEHAN CORK, KERRY,
O SHEEHANE PN CORK C
SHEEHY KERRY, LIMERIC
MC SHEEHY PN Lim.
SHEENAN *168
SHEEPHERD WESTMEATH
SHEERAN 18 BIRTHS, LEI
O SHEERIN PN Ferm.
SHEERY PN West.
SHEFFIELD PMO
SHEGHANE PN CORK
O SHEGHANE PN CLARE
SHEHANE PN CORK
SHEILD MEATH
SHEILDS ANTRIM, DOWN
SHEILE KILDARE
SHEILL WESTMEATH
O SHEILL ANTRIM
SHEILS DUBLIN, DONEGAL
SHELDON TIPPERARY
SHELLOE *438
SHELLY DUBLIN, TIPPERA
SHELTON DONEGAL, DER
SHEPARD DONEGAL, ANT
SHEPHEARD PMO, LOUT
SHEPHERD CARLOW/ *33
SHEPPARD 12 BIRTHS, N
SHERBROKE WESTMEAT
SHERDIAN *35
SHERDING DUBLIN CITY
O SHEREDON PN Louth
SHERIDAN CAVAN, DUBL
SHERIGLEY MONAGHAN
SHERLOCK PN MEATH / I
SHERLOCKE WATERFORI
SHERMAN 5 BIRTHS, LEI
SHERRA *343

SHERRAR *343
SHERRARD LONDONDER
SHERRY MONAGHAN, DU
MC SHERRY PN ARMAG
O SHERRY PN Mon.
SHERTLIFF PMO
SHERWOOD 8 BIRTHS, N
MC SHERY PN Armagh,
SHEVLIN 8 BIRTHS, MAIN
SHEWEL PMO
SHEWELL KERRY, PMO
MC SHIDA PN CLARE
SHIEL *420
SHIELDS ANTRIM, DOWN
SHIELL PN Queens.
SHIELS DUBLIN, DONEGAL
O SHIGHANE PN CORK
MC SHIHY PN Lim.
SHILLADY *71
SHILLIADY *279
SHILLIDAY ANTRIM, DO
SHINAGH *179
SHINE CORK, *329
SHINER CARLOW
SHINGLY PMO
SHINNAGH *40
SHINNAHAN *191
SHINNOCK *393
SHIPCOTT DUBLIN CITY
SHIPPY KILDARE
SHIPTON CORK
SHIPWARD CORK
SHIRLEY 7 BIRTHS, LEINS
SHONAHAN *512
SHONOGH *174
SHORE DUBLIN
SHORELAHAN *480
SHORT DUBLIN CITY, QUE
SHORTALL PN KILKENN
SHORTEN CORK, *397
SHORTLE *526
SHORTT 8 BIRTHS, LEINS
SHORTTLIFFE KERRY
SHOYE *40
SHRELD PMO
SHREWBRIDG ANTRIM
SHRIMPTON PMO
SHUNAGH *262
SHUNNY *393
SHURDEN *319
SHURLOG DUBLIN CITY
SHUTE CORK, PMO, LIMER
Shuttleworth WESTMEATH
SHYDY LIMERICK
O SHYGHANE PN Lim.
SHYHANE LIMERICK
MC SHYHY PN Lim.
SHYRIN PN Queens.
SHYRYDAN PN Leitrim
SIBBAULDS QUEENS

SIBTHORPE LOUTH
Sichsheuerall ARMAGH
SIE *71
SILK GALWAY, *262
SILVER CORK, WATERFOR
SIME DONEGAL
SIMES KILKENNY
SIMMONS KILKENNY, 131
SIMMS ANTRIM, *409
SIMON *54
SIMONS *54
SIMPSON LEITRIM, 1689 S
SIMVIL *233
SINACK KILKENNY
SINACKE KILKENNY
SINANE CLARE
SINCLAIR TYRONE 1646 S
SINES KILKENNY
SINGEN *315, *393, *498
SINGIN *25
SINGLETON CLARE, LOU
SINHOUSE CORK CITY
SINJUN *316
SINNOTT WEXFORD, 22 B
SIREY PN West.
SISNANE PN CORK
SIZE *436
SKALLAN PN Wexford
SKALLY PN West.
O SKANLANE PN Lim.
O SKANNELL PN CORK C
MC SKEAN *383
SKEEPER WESTMEATH
SKEFFINGTON ANTRIM /
SKEHAN PN LOUTH / 7 BIR
SKELLY PN WESTMEATH /
SKELSON WESTMEATH
SKELTON DUBLIN CITY/ 8
SKEVINGTON MEATH, PN
SKIDDY DUBLIN, WEXFOR
O SKIDDY PN Ferm.
SKILLEN DOWN, ANTRIM
MC SKIMMINS *344
SKINNER CLARE, WEXFOR
SKINNION *153
SKIPTON DERRY 1617 ENG
SKOLY MEATH
SKOOLIN *58
SKULLY PN TIP, KILDARE
SKYDDY CORK CITY
SLACK FERMANAGH
SLADE PMO, ROSCOMMON
SLAMON *249
SLANE *483
SLANEY KILKENNY
SLATIER LOUTH
SLATOR DUBLIN
SLATTERY PN CLARE, TII
O SLATTERY PN CLARE
SLAVIN 11 BIRTHS, MAINL

SLEVIN PN WESTMEATH /
SLOAN ANTRIM
SLOANE DOWN / ANTRIM
SLOEY *167
SLONES TIPPERARY
SLOSE KILDARE
SLOUGHTER TIPPERARY
SLOWAN PN Down.
SLOWEY *167
SLOY WESTMEATH / *211
SMALL CORK, TIPPERARY
SMALLBONE TIPPERARY
SMALLWOOD LOUTH, PN
SMALLWOODS *53
SMART CORK
SMARTE ROSCOMMON
SMARTH CORK
SMILEY ANTRIM
SMIMS CORK
SMITH MEATH 1640 ENG/P
SMITHICK PMO
SMITHWICK LIMERICK
SMULLEN DUBLIN
SMYLIE ANTRIM
SMYTH WAT, CORK, LEIX
MC SMYTH PN Antrim
SMYTHE *494
SNEDDEN ANTRIM
SNEE MAYO, ALL IN LEINS
SNELL CORK CITY
SNODDY ALL ANTRIM
SNOW WESTMEATH
SNOWDEN *9
SOARE KILDARE
SODEN SLIGO / *281
SODIN *281
SOGH PN West.
SOLOVART PN CORK
SOMERS DONEGAL, DERR
SOMERSETT CORK
SOMERVILLE 18 BIRTHS
SONAHAUN
SOOKER TIPPERARY
SOOLIVAN *109
SORAGHAN *92, *383
MC SORLEY ANTRIM 168
SORSON MEATH
SOUTH ANTRIM
SOUTHCOTT LIMERICK
SOUTHWELL LIMERICK,
SOUTHY DUBLIN CITY
SOY *71
SPAIN 7 BIRTHS, NONE IN
SPARKE ANTRIM
SPARKS WATERFORD 164
SPARLING WATERFORD
SPEARE ARMAGH
MC SPEDDIN *358
SPEED *50
SPEERS ANTRIM

SPELESSY *8
SPELLANE PN Waterford
O SPELLANE PN CORK
SPELMAN GALWAY, ROS
SPEMER CORK
SPENCE DUBLIN CITY / AN
SPENCER DUBLIN, DONE
SPENSUR MEATH
SPIERMS WESTMEATH
SPIKE WESTMEATH
SPILLANE CORK, KERRY
O SPILLANE PN CORK, K
SPILLESSY *142
SPILLMAN TIPPERARY, K
SPLAINE *77
SPOLLAN PN Kings
SPOLLEN *455
SPONEOWES CARLOW
SPOONE KILKENNY
SPRANGER LIMERICK, DI
SPRATT CORK 1640 ENGL
SPRING DUBLIN, KERRY /
SPRINGHAM DUBLIN, LC
SPROOL *91
SPROULE TYRONE
SPRUELL DONEGAL
SQUIBB TIPPERARY
SQUIBBE KINGS
SQUIRE DONEGAL, LONDC
STACEY 5 BIRTHS, MAINL
STACK PN KERRY / KERR
STACKPOLL CLARE
STACKPOOL PN CLARE
STACKPOOLE CLARE 164
STACKPOOLL CLARE
STAFFORD CLARE 1640 E
STAMERS CLARE
STAMP PMO, KILKENNY,
STAMPE KILKENNY
STANBRIDE LOUTH
STANBRIDGE PMO
STANDISH LIMERICK 164
STANFORD DUBLIN CITY
STANLEY DUBLIN, CORK
STANLY WATERFORD, DU
STANTON GALWAY 1634 E
STAPERS TIPPERARY
STAPLEHIL PMO
STAPLEHILL PMO
STAPLES PMO, LONDOND
STAPLETON DUBLIN, LIM
STARKERS WATERFORD
STARKEY CLARE, WESTM
STARKIE CLARE
STARLING PMO
STARRETT ANTRIM, LON
STAUGHTON DUBLIN CIT
STAUNTON GALWAY 163
STAWELL CORK, 1640 EN
MC STAY ARMAGH

STAYLEHILL ROSCOMMC
MC STAYNE PN SLIGO
STEEL ANTRIM, LONDOND
STEELE KILDARE 1640 ENC
STEEN 6 BIRTHS, ALL IN U
STEENSON ANTRIM, ARM
STEERS PMO
STEEVENSON FERMANA
STEILL PN Antrim
O STEILL PN Antrim
O STEILLE ANTRIM
STEINSON *58
STENSON SLIGO, *63, *515
STEPHENS CORK CITY, KI
STEPHENS *185
STEPHENSON DUBLIN CI
STEPNEY CORK, PMO
STERLING DUBLIN, LOUT
STERN PMO / *91
STERNE WESTMEATH
STEUART *374
STEUENS CORK CITY
STEVEN PMO
STEVENS DONEGAL 1683
STEVENSON ANTRIM, AR
STEWARD DUBLIN CITY,
STEWART LIM, DON, DOW
STEYLES CORK
STIFFE CORK CITY
STILES DUBLIN CITY
STINCHMAN CORK
STINSON 12 BIRTHS, ULS
STIRLING ANTRIM, *91
STIRRATT
STIRRETT *91
STITT ANTRIM
STOAKES TIPPERARY, DU
STOCKDEN CLARE
STOCKMAN 7 BIRTHS, 6
STODDARD CLARE 1171 E
STODDART *410
STODHARD PMO
STOKER LOUTH
STOKES KERRY 1582 ENGL
STONE TIPPERARY 1640 EN
STOOKER LOUTH
STOPFORD DUBLIN CITY
STOREY CAVAN 1740 ENG
STORMONT DONEGAL
STORTON DUBLIN CITY
STOTHERG *410
STOTNARD WEXFORD
STOUGHTON DUBLIN CIT
STOUT PMO
STOUTE CORK, WATERFO
STRABANE DUBLIN
STRADFORD PMO
STRAFFORD KILDARE
STRAHAN 9 BIRTHS, LEIN
STRAIN DOWN, *429

STRANGE DUBLIN, WICKI
STRATFORD CORK
STRATON FERMANAGH,
STRAUGHTON DUBLIN
MC STRAVICK ARMAGH
STREATTON *429
STRECKLAN KILDARE
STREELLE MEATH
STREETEN *429
STRICH PN CLARE
STRINGER KILKENNY / 9
STRITCH CLARE
STROAKER KINGS
STROND DOWN
STRONG DUBLIN, LIMERI
STRONGMAN TIPPERAR
STROWD PMO
STRYNY DUBLIN CITY
STUARD TIPPERARY
STUART PN ANTRIM, PMO
MC STUART PN Antrim
STUARTT ANTRIM
STUCKLEY ANTRIM
STUDDERT CLARE 1171 E
STUMBLES TIPPERARY
STURGEON 8 BIRTHS, AL
STURGIS TIPPERARY
STURT CORK
STYLES KERRY
SUGARS CORK
SUGHERNE KERRY
SUGRUE KERRY, CORK
MC SUILE *43
SULEVAN PN Waterford
SULEVANE PN CLARE, C
O SULEVANE PN CORK
SULIUANE CORK
SULLEUAN PN Kerry
O SULLEUANE PN Ferm.
SULLEVAN PN Lim.
SULLEVANE PN CORK
O SULLEVANE PN CLARI
SULLIUAN PN Kerry
SULLIUANE PN CORK
O SULLIVAN KERRY, CO
SULLIVAN KERRY / CORK
SULLIVANE PN CORK, KE
SULLIVANE PN CORK, KE
SUMAHEAN *329
SUMERIL *489
SUMERLY *174
SUMERWELL FERMANA
O SUMMACHAN *40
SUMMARS DUBLIN CITY
SUMMER DUBLIN CITY
SUMMERS *72
SUMMERS CLARE
SUMNER PMO
SUNBERY CORK
SUNDERLAND WEXFORD

SUNIET WATERFORD
SUPPLE LIMERICK, CORK,
SURGENOR ANTRIM
SURGEONER ANTRIM
SURLEY *197
SUSSERS TIPPERARY
SUTHERLAND 6 BIRTHS,
SUTHERN *311
SUTTON WEXFORD / DUBI
SUVANE PN Kerry
SUXBURIE PMO
SUXBURY PMO
SWABBY CORK CITY
SWADLING PMO
SWALLOW CORK CITY
SWAN WEXFORD 1572 ENC
SWANN WATERFORD
SWANTON CORK, DUBLIN
SWANWICK PMO
SWARBRICKE ARMAGH
SWAYNE LIMERICK
MC SWEENEY CORK
SWEENEY CORK, DONEG
SWEENY CORK / CORK, D
MC SWEENY CORK / *18
SWEET PMO
SWEETE CORK
SWEETMAN DUBLIN, CL
SWETENHAM DONEGAL
SWIFT WESTMEATH 1710 E
MC SWINE *114, *374
SWINE *349
MC SWINEY *283, *77, *
SWINEY *314, *374
SWINFEILD DUBLIN
Swinglehurst KINGS
SWITZER 7 BIRTHS, LEINS
SWORDS 8 BIRTHS, DUBL
MC SWYNE PN DONEGAL
MC SWYNIE CLARE
SWYNY PN CLARE, TIPPE
MC SWYNY PN CLARE, C
SYBALLS PMO
SYBHALS PMO
SYCAMORE WATERFORD
SYMERELL FERMANAGH
SYMKINS LONDONDERRY
SYMNER MEATH
SYMONS PN West.
SYMS PMO, LIMERICK
SYNNOTT PN WEXFORD /
SYNOTT PN Wexford
SYNYRES DUBLIN CITY
SYRIDAN PN Long.
TAAFF MEATH
TAAFFE LOUTH 1171 NOR
TACKER DUBLIN CITY
TACKNEY *515
TAGAN PN Kildare
MC TAGART PN Down.

TAGGARD PN Antrim
MC TAGGART *201
TAGGART ANTRIM
MC TAGHLAN?
MC TAGHLIN *482
MC TAGUE CAVAN, *46,
TAGUE *97, *423, *350
` TAIT LONDONDERRY
TALANT DUBLIN CITY
TALBOT WEXFORD, ROSC
TALBOTT ROSCOMMON, V
TALLANT PMO
TALLBOTT LOUTH, KILKI
TALLON DUBLIN, LIMERIC
TALLY *215
TALTY CLARE
TANGNEY KERRY, CORK
TANIST PN SLIGO
TANNER QUEENS, PMO / 7
TANSEY ALL IN CONNAU
TARLETON OFFALY 1642
TARPEY MAYO, ROSCOMN
TARRANT CORK, *100, *1
TATE DUBLIN, LIMERICK 1
TATH PN Louth
TATTE KILDARE
TAVEY *137
MC TAVISH *60
MC TAYER PN Antrim
MC TAYLER PN Antrim
TAYLOR DUB, GAL, DON,
MC TEAGUE ALL IN DON
TEAGUE 6 BIRTHS, ALL IN
TEAHAN KERRY
TEAPE CORK
TEE *183
TEELING WESTMEATH / D
TEERRY *254
TEG *413
TEGGART *201
MC TEGGART PN Ferm.
TEGGARTY *42
TEHAN PN Queens.
Mac TEIGE PN Lim.
MC TEIGE PN CLARE, CO
O TEIGE PN Rosc.
TEIGE (OGE) PN CORK
TEIGH PMO
TEIGUE *165
MC TEIGUE PN QUEENS,
MC TEIRE PN SLIGO
TELFORD ANTRIM
TEMPEST LOUTH
TEMPLE ANTRIM 1642 ENC
TEMPLETON DONEGAL, I
TEMPSON KILKENNY
TENANE PN Kilkenny
TENCH WEXFORD 1171 NO
TENCK WEXFORD
TENNANT 5 BIRTHS, NON

TENTCH PMO
MC TERLAGH PN Lim.
TERNAN •72
MC TERNAN PN LEITRIM
TERNY PN Leitrim
TERRELL DUBLIN, DONEG
TERRILL ROSCOMMON
TERRY DUBLIN, LIMERICK
TERTY PN Louth
TETHRINGTON CORK
THEAKER ARMAGH
THEOBALLS LIMERICK C
MC THERLAGH LIMERI(
THERLAGHLE CLARE
THESWELL DUBLIN CITY
O THINA •179
THIRRY CORK
THOBBIN CLARE
THOBIN CLARE
THOHY PN Tip.
THOMAS DUBLIN, LIM, TI
MC THOMAS PN CLARE,
THOMKINS LONDONDERI
THOMLINSON LOUTH, L
THOMOMOND PMO
THOMOND PMO
THOMPSON LONG 1688 EI
THOMSON ANTRIM 1608 S
THOMSONE DONEGAL
Thorenbor'ogh LIMERICK
THORLOE OGE LIMERICI
THORN •72
THORNBURG •511
THORNE LIMERICK
THORNETON CLARE, CAI
THORNHILL WEXFORD, P
THORNTON DERRY 1740 I
THORNTON DUBLIN CITY
THORPE 5 BIRTHS, LEINST
THRENCHARD LIMERICI
THRESHER WEXFORD
Throgmorton KILKENNY
THUNDER MEATH 1647 EN
THURLUS TIPPERARY
THWAITS DUBLIN CITY
TIBB SLIGO
TIBBS WESTMEATH
TICHBORNE DUBLIN CIT
TICHBOURN PMO
TICHBURNE LEITRIM
TIERNAN LOUTH
MC TIERNAN PN LEITRIN
TIERNEY •390, DUBLIN, T
TIERNY PN Tip.
TIFFORD SLIGO, PMO
TIGER •305
TIGH PMO
TIGHE PMO / MAYO / •46, •
MC TIGUE MAYO
TILLY LIMERICK

TILSON CORK
TIMLIN MAYO, SLIGO
TIMMIN •397
TIMMINS DUBLIN, KILDA
TIMONY 9 BIRTHS, CONN
TIMOTHY •528
TINAN PN Kilkenny
TINANE PN Kilkenny
TININ •211
TINKLER •435
TINOHIT TIPPERARY
TINSLEY 5 BIRTHS, LEIN
TINT PMO
TIPPING LEITRIM / •58
TIRRELL KILDARE, LIMEF
TISDALL 6 BIRTHS, ALL II
TITCHBORNE PMO
TITCHBOURN PMO
TITTERTON •381
TOAL ARMAGH, ANTRIM, •
TOBBINE PN Lim.
TOBIN DUB, LIM, TIP 1272
TOBINE TIPPERARY
TOBYN PN Tip.
TOBYNN TIPPERARY
TOD SLIGO
TODD DONEGAL 1642 SCOT
TOHALL •97
TOHER PN Kings
TOHULL •97
TOHY PN Tip.
TOLAN MAYO
TOLAND ANTRIM, •432
TOLLER PMO
TOMAN DOWN, ANTRIM
TOMIN PN CARLOW
TOMKINS 7 BIRTHS, LEIN
TOMLIN CORK CITY
TOMLINS DUBLIN CITY, I
TOMLINSON PMO, WATE
TOMPKINS CLARE
TOMPSON TIPPERARY, PI
TOMSON PMO
TOMSSON TIPPERARY
TONER ARMAGH, LONDON
O TONER PN Armagh,
TONSON •65
TONSTALL DUBLIN CITY
TOOGOOD TIPPERARY, DI
TOOHER 5 BIRTHS, ALL II
TOOKE LOUTH
TOOLAN ROSCOMMON
O TOOLAN PN Donegal
TOOLE PN DUBLIN, KILDA
O TOOLE PN ARMAGH / DI
TOOLEY ANTRIM / DUBLIN
TOOMEY DUBLIN, LIMER
TOOMPANE •131
TOORISH •482
TOPPING ANTRIM, ARMA(

TORKINGTON •333
TORLTONE DONEGAL
TORMEY 9 BIRTHS, MAIN
O TORNEY PN Ferm.
TORRENS ANTRIM, ALL II
TORRY •254
TOSH •175, •197
TOTTEN DUBLIN 1640 ENG
TOTTERICKE DUBLIN CI
TOTTIE WEXFORD
TOTTON ARMAGH
TOTTY PMO
TOUCHSTONE LIMERICK
TOUGHER PN KINGS / ALL
TOUGHIE PN Tip.
TOULSON DUBLIN CITY
TOURISK •419
TOUSON CORK
TOVEY CORK CITY
TOVOMY CORK CITY
TOWERS PMO, LOUTH, DI
TOWES LIMERICK
TOWEY ROSCOMMON, MA
TOWGOOD PMO
O TOWLAN PN Donegal
TOWLER PMO
O TOWLOW CLARE
TOWNER LIMERICK
TOWNLEY CORK, 1680 EN
TOWNSEND CORK, 1660 E
TOWNSLEY •89
TOWNSLY LOUTH
TOWSE CORK
TOXTETH PMO
TOXTITH LOUTH
TOYE DUBLIN
TRACEY PN LOUTH/ DUBL
TRACY DUBLIN
TRAGHNE LIMERICK
TRAHEY PN Kings
TRAINOR •256
TRAINOR ANTRIM, ARMA
TRANT PN KERRY / KERRY
TRAPNELL PN Waterford
TRASSEY PN Kings
TRASSY PN Tip.
O TRASSY PN Lim.
TRASY PN Kildare
TRAUERS CORK CITY
TRAVERS CORK, DUBLIN,
TRAYL PMO
TRAYNOR DUBLIN
TREACY TIPPERARY, GAL
TREANOR ANTRIM, ARM/
TREASLEY WATERFORD
TREHERNE ANTRIM
TREHY •457
TRENNWITH CORK
TRENOR •429
MC TRENOR PN Mon.

TRESILLEAN CORK
TRESSY PN KILDARE, KIL
O TRESSY PN Ferm.
TREUERS PN Kildare
TREUOR DOWN
TREVILL WEXFORD
TREVOR PMO
TREVORS PMO
TREVORS PMO
TRIALL PMO
TRIAR DUBLIN
TRIM-LAVERY •197
TRIMBLE 12 BIRTHS, MAI
TRINLAVERY •6, •257, •
TRODY PN Kildare
TROHY PN Tip.
TROLAND •367
TROLEN •367
TROLLY PMO
TROLY LOUTH
TROTTER 12 BIRTHS, 11 IN
TROWER •370
O TROWER PN Leitrim
TROY KINGS, CORK, TIPPE
TRUEMAN 5 BIRTHS, 4 IN
TRUMAN LONDONDERRY
TRUMBLE PN SLIGO
TRURK PMO
M' TRUSTRY •85
TRYN-LAVERY •6
TUBBERND PN Waterford
TUBBS TIPPERARY
TUBMAN PMO
TUBRIT •509
TUCKE QUEENS
TUCKER CORK CITY / 10 E
TUCKEY CORK CITY
TUHILL •189
TUINON DUBLIN CITY
TUIT ROSCOMMON
TUITE WESTMEATH 1172 N
TUITTE PN West.
TULLY PN ROSCOMMON / (
TUMBLETON •526
TUMBLINSON •59
TUMELTY 5 BIRTHS, LEIN
TUMMON •413
TUNBRIDGE WATERFORI
TUNDALL LOUTH
TUOHY CLARE, GALWAY,
TURBETT WESTMEATH/ •3
TURBRIDGE LOUTH
TURISH •161, •483
TURK •83, •204
TURKINGTON ARMAGH
MC TURLAGH PN Lim.
TURLEY 7 BIRTHS, NONE
TURNBALL TIPPERARY
TURNBULL 5 BIRTHS, LE
TURNEBOWLE TIPPERAF

TURNER ROSCOMMON, C(
TUTTY 5 BIRTHS, LEINSTE
TWADELL LONDONDERRY
TWAMLEY 6 BIRTHS, LEI
TWAYTS LIMERICK CITY
TWEEDIE 10 BIRTHS, ULS
TWIGG ANTRIM
TWIGLEY •87, •433
TWISDEN CORK
TWOHIG ALL IN CORK
TWOMEY CORK, KERRY
O TWOMY PN CORK CITY
TYERNY PN Tip.
TYGHE •183
TYLER TIPPERARY, KINGS
TYLY KINGS
TYNAN PN QUEENS / QUEI
TYNDALL CARLOW
TYNE PMO
TYNER 6 BIRTHS, LEINSTE
TYNNAN •32
TYNT PMO
TYRRELL KILDARE 1171 E
TYRRELL PN West.
TYRRILL WESTMEATH
TYTH DUBLIN CITY
UISKE •40
ULTAGH DONEGAL / •312
UMPHREY FERMANAGH
UNACK CORK
UNEHAN •73
UNETT CORK
UNGERDELL PN CORK
UNGLY KILKENNY
UNILL WESTMEATH
UPCOLE CORK
UPRICHARD ARMAGH, A
UPTON LOUTH, 1750 ENGL
URRELL •152
USHART •254
USHER DUBLIN CITY AND
USHER 6 BIRTHS, LEINSTE
USSHER DUBLIN, WEXFOI
USTACE DUBLIN CITY
UUSTICE DUBLIN CITY
MC VAGH PN ARMAGH, I
VAGHAN QUEENS
VAHEY •38
VAHY •28
VALE CLARE
VALENTINE DUBLIN
VALLANNE LIMERICK
VALLELY ARMAGH, •160
VALLILY •362
VALLY •344
MC VANAMY •48A
VanBOGARDE PMO
VANCE DONEGAL, DERRY
VANDELEW PMO
VANDELURE CLARE, PM(

VANDERLEW PMO
VANDERLURE CORK CIT
VANDERPUER DUBLIN
VanHOGARDE CLARE, PI
VanHUGARDE LIMERICK
VARGIS •78
VARGUS •109, •527
VARILY •160
VARLEY •39, •160, •174
VARRILLY •160
VAS DONEGAL
VAUGH
VAUGHAN CORK, DUBLIN
MC VEAGH PN Antrim
VEAKINS •335
VEALE PN WATERFORD / V
MC VEIGH ANTRIM, DOW
VELDON ROSCOMMON / •
VENNER PMO
VENNOR WESTMEATH
VENTON •128
VERDON LOUTH 1172 NOR
VERKERS CORK CITY
VERNER DOWN
VERSCOYLE DUBLIN CIT
MC VICKER ANTRIM, LO
VICKERS 5 BIRTHS, ALL I
VICTORY •154, •265, •470
VILLERS LEITRIM
VINCENT LIMERICK, CLAI
VIVERS QUEENS
VIZARD CORK, DUBLIN CI
VOGAN 5 BIRTHS, ALL IN
VOICE KILKENNY
VULCOUGHA •488
WADDELL DOWN / 12 BIR
WADDEY WEXFORD
WADDING •526, •527
WADDINGTON PMO
WADDOCK •16
WADDY WEXFORD 1640 SA
MC WADE •175A
WADE MEATH 1640 SAXON
WADKINS WEXFORD
WADMAN ANTRIM
WADOCK •16
WAGGONER CORK
WAGH FERMANAGH
WAIGHT DUBLIN CITY
WAILE DOWN
WAILSE PN Tip.
WAILSH PN LIMERICK, KI
WAINMAN DUBLIN CITY
WAITS CORK
WAKEFIELD DUBLIN, WI
WAKEHAM PMO, CORK C
WAKELY KINGS, PMO
WAKHAM CORK
WALCHOTT LIMERICK
WALCOT PMO

WALCOTT ANTRIM
WALDING WESTMEATH
WALDO WESTMEATH
WALDRON PMO / MAYO, :
WALDRONN ARMAGH
WALDRUM LEITRIM
WALE PN TIPPERARY, WA'
O WALE ROSCOMMON
WALKAM CORK
WALKER WEXFORD 1580
1 WALKES TIPPERARY
WALL LIM, TIP 1640 ENG/ P
WALLACE LIMERICK, CL/
WALLE PN Tip.
WALLER MEATH 1641 ENC
WALLIS CORK, LIM, CLAR
WALLS 11 BIRTHS, MAINL'
WALNNE KINGS
WALSH CORK, LIM, KILK I
WALSHE CORK, MAYO, W
WALSHMAN DUBLIN
WALTER TIPPERARY, COF
MC WALTER PN CARLOV
WALTERS CLARE / 5 BIRT
WALTON WEXFORD, COR
WAMOUGHT DUBLIN CIT
WANDRICH WATERFORD
WANDWICK CORK
WANSANTON KILDARE
WANSBURGH TIPPERAR'
WAPLES LIMERICK CITY
WARBURTON OFFALY 1
WARD PN MEATH, WESTM
MC WARD PN ARMAGH,
WARDEN PMO
WARDINGE LIMERICK
WARDLAW DOWN
WARDLOW ANTRIM, ARM
WARE CORK 1588 SAXON /
WAREN KILDARE
WARICK FERMANAGH
WARING DOWN 1600 ENG
WARINGE ANTRIM
WARMAND KILKENNY
WARNEFORD PMO
WARNER CORK / CORK, N
WARNFORD QUEENS, PM
WARNOCK TYRONE, DOV
WARR LIMERICK CITY
WARRAN DONEGAL
WARRECK *429
WARREING ANTRIM
WARREN TIPPERARY 1649
WARRICK *429
WARRING ANTRIM, KILK
WARRIS PMO
WARTER TIPPERARY
WARWICK ALL IN ANTRI
WASBERY DUBLIN CITY
WASH PN Waterford
WASLEY WESTMEATH
WASSHER KILKENNY
WASSON 5 BIRTHS, ALL I
WATCH *329
WATER PMO
WATERHOUSE DUBLIN C
WATERS KILKENNY, WES
WATERSON *52, *522
WATKINS WATERFORD, K
WATSON CARLOW 1641 E
WATT ANTRIM
MC WATTERS ANTRIM
WATTERS TYRONE, ANTR
WATTERSON ANTRIM
WATTKINS QUEENS
WATTS DUBLIN CITY, CLA
WAUGH 5 BIRTHS ALL IN I
WAY CORK
WAYBRENT DUBLIN CITY
WAYMAN DUBLIN CITY
WEABB KILDARE
WEADOCK *16
WEAMAN KINGS
WEATHERBY KILKENNY
WEATHERS CARLOW
WEATHERUP ALL IN ANT
WEAVER DUBLIN, LIMER
WEBB TIPPERARY 1586 EN
WEBBER SLIGO, LEIX 164
WEBSTER DONEGAL, DER
WEDGWOOD KILDARE
WEEDIN CLARE
WEEKE CORK
WEEKES CORK
WEEKS LIMERICK 1642 EN
MC WEENEY LEITRIM
WEILSH LIMERICK
WEIR ANTRIM, ARMAGH
WEIRE FERMANAGH
WELBY ALL IN GALWAY
WELCH WATERFORD, KILI
WELDON PN MEATH / 14 I
WELLAHANE PN Kings
WELLS DUBLIN, LIMERICK
WELSH KILKENNY 1170 WI
WEMYS LIMERICK, GALW
WENDLE LIMERICK
WENMAN KILDARE
WENTWORTH PMO
WENWELL DUBLIN CITY
WESBY DUBLIN CITY
WESH PN WATERFORD, LC
WESSBIE KILDARE
WEST WATERFORD, CORK
WESTBROOKE ANTRIM
WESTENRA DUBLIN CITY
WESTINRA DUBLIN CITY
WESTLY KILDARE
WESTON DUBLIN 1710 EN
WETHERALL DUBLIN CIT
WETHEREL PMO
WETHERELL LOUTH, COI
WEYMES KILKENNY, PMC
WEYMS PMO
WHALEY KILKENNY, PMC
WHALLEY PMO
WHALLOP WESTMEATH
WHALLY PMO
WHALY DUBLIN CITY
MC WHANNON *429
WHAPLES PMO
WHARRY ALL IN ANTRIM
WHARTON WESTMEATH/
WHATOPE DOWN
WHEELER DONEGAL 1586
WHEITE PN CORK
WHELAHAN *172, *249, *
WHELAN PN WEXFORD / I
WHELANE PN TIPPERARY
WHELANN PN Waterford
WHELEGHAN *312
WHELEHAN *136, 5 BIRTH
WHELPLY CORK
WHELTON CORK, KERRY
WHETCOMB CORK
WHETCOME WESTMEATH
WHETCRAFT CORK
WHETLOCK DUBLIN CITY
WHIALON KILKENNY
WHIFFLE *249
WHIN *292
WHINE PMO
WHINN *461
MC WHINNEY DOWN, AI
WHIRLOE PMO
MC WHIRTER ANTRIM 1
WHISLADE CORK CITY
WHISSED WESTMEATH
WHITAKER *333
WHITCHURCH LIMERICK
WHITCRAFT CORK
WHITE PN ANTRIM, DONE
WHITECHAN PN West.
WHITEFIELD DUBLIN
WHITEHEAD ANTRIM, M
WHITERE LIMERICK
WHITESIDE DUBLIN 1710
WHITFIELD QUEENS
WHITGROVE DUBLIN CIT
WHITIHELL DUBLIN CITY
WHITLA ANTRIM 1646 ENC
WHITLEY ANTRIM 1646 EN
WHITLOCK WESTMEATH
WHITMAN WESTMEATH
WHITMORE DUBLIN CITY
WHITNEY WEXFORD 1171
WHITNY PMO
WHITSITT *429
WHITT LOUTH
WHITTBY WATERFORD
WHITTELL KINGS
WHITTINGHA CORK
WHITTINGTON PMO
WHITTLE PN WATERFORD
WHITTNY QUEENS
WHITTON 5 BIRTHS, NON
WHITTY PN WEXFORD / W
WHITWELL CORK CITY
WHOLIHANE *325
WHOOLEY *164
WHORLLOE LOUTH
WHORRISKEY *504
WHYTE PN LOND, LIM CIT
WIAY LIMERICK
WIBRANT PMO
WICKEN KILKENNY
WICKHAM WEXFORD
WICKOMBE DUBLIN
WIDMAN PMO
WIDMAY WESTMEATH
WIDOWES WESTMEATH
WIERS TIPPERARY
WIGFIELD PMO
WIGGINS 6 BIRTHS, NONE
WIGHTMAN DOWN, ALL
WIGTONE DONEGAL
WILBORE WEXFORD, PMC
WILBY *102
WILCOX DUBLIN CITY
WILDBOAR PMO
WILDER PMO
WILDERS LONGFORD
WILEMAN MONAGHAN
WILEY *95, *250, *494
WILHAIR *459
WILKES FERMANAGH
WILKIE *55
WILKINS LONDONDERRY
WILKINSON WATERFORD
WILLIAM PN Tip.
Mac WILLIAM PN Lim.
MC WILLIAM DUBLIN, D
MC WILLIAMS ANTRIM,
WILLIAMS DUBLIN, WAT
WILLIAMSON PMO, CORI
WILLIAMSONE DOWN
WILLINGHAM CORK, PM
WILLIS DUBLIN 1646 ENGL
WILLISBIE KILDARE
WILLOUGHBY ANTRIM,
WILLS ROSCOMMON 1586
WILLSON CORK, LIMERIC
WILLY CORK, LIMERICK
WILMONT *177
WILSBY KILKENNY
WILSHIER LOUTH
WILSON PN ANTRIM / ANT
WILTON WESTMEATH, PM
WIMBS *125
WINCKFIELD PMO
WINDOWES WEXFORD
WINDSOR LONDONDERRY
WINGFIELD SLIGO
WINKFIELD PMO
WINKWORTH WEXFORD
WINNE LOUTH
WINSPEARE CORK
WINTERS 15 BIRTHS, SCA
WIRE *146
WISE CORK 1646 SCOT/ PN
WISHERT FERMANAGH
WITHAMS DUBLIN CITY
WITHER *254
WITHERILL TIPPERARY
WITHERS CORK, PMO / 5 I
WITHERSTON PMO
WITTER LOUTH
WIXSTEAD KINGS
WIZARD DUBLIN CITY
WLTAGH PN Donegal
MC WM. PN CORK, LIME
WOLFE KILDARE 1171 NOR
WOLVERSTON DUBLIN
WOOD SLIGO 1649 ENGLIS
WOODCOCK PMO
WOODCOCKE KILKENNY
WOODHOUSE LOUTH 15
WOODLIF PMO
WOODLIFF PMO
WOODLIFFE CORK CITY
WOODLOCKE PN Tip.
WOODLY CORK, PMO
WOODROFFE CORK
WOODRUFFE CORK
WOODS *381
WOODSIDE ANTRIM, DUI
WOODSY PN Antrim
WOODWARD MEATH 164
WOOGON KILKENNY
WOOLE DOWN
WOOLFE CLARE
WORDON KILKENNY
WORKEMAN TIPPERARY
WORKMAN DUBLIN CITY
WORRELL CORK
WORSELY WESTMEATH
WORSHIP DUBLIN CITY, F
WORSLY QUEENS
WORSOP PMO
WOTON MEATH
WOULFE LIMERICK
WOULFE-NIX *405
WRAY DONEGAL, PMO / *4
WREN PMO / 12 BIRTHS, 1
WRENN *128, *186
WRENNE CORK CITY
WRIGHT DONEGAL 1586 E
WROTHAM CLARE
WRYNN *465
WYATT MONAGHAN
WYBER *249
WYBRANT DUBLIN CITY,
WYBRUNE DONEGAL
WYBURNE DUBLIN
WYE ANTRIM, PMO
WYER
WYKE DOWN
WYLIE ANTRIM
WYNN LEITRIM, PMO / *82
WYNNE SLIGO 1640 WELC
MC WYNNY PN Ferm.
WYOTT CLARE
WYRE PN West.
WYSE CORK 1646 SCOTLA
WYTHERS WEXFORD
YARDO CORK
YARNER PMO
YARWELL LIMERICK CITY
YATES DUBLIN CITY / COF
YEADON ROSCOMMON
YEARD TIPPERARY
YEATES ANTRIM, DUBLIN
YEO ANTRIM
YEOMANS CORK
YOUNG DUB,CORK, DON, I
YOUNGE DONEGAL
ZORKIN *40

*** Key to numbered Location Index.** The location of entries with a *35 etc.. in the preceeding index. Gives #, Registrars District, & Union, in Ireland. N.=North Mt.=Mount New.=Newtown '=missing letter. +=more info.

295

\# . Registrars' District / Union

1- Abbey / Tuam
2- Abbeyfeale / Newcastle
3- Abbeyshrule / Ballymahon
4- Achill / Westport
5- Aclare / Tobercurry
6- Aghalee / Lurgan
7- Ahoghill / Ballymena
8- Anascall / Dingle
9- Annahilt / Lisburn
10- .... / Antrim
11- Ardagh / Newcastle
12- Ardara / Glenties
13- .... / Ardee
14- Ardee / Ardee
15- Ardmore / Youghal
16- Arklow / Rathdrum
17- Armagh / Armagh
18- .... / Armagh
19- Articlave / Coleraine
20- Arvagh / Cavan
21- Athenry / Loughrea
22- Athleague / Roscommon
23- Athlone, No.2 / Athlone
24- .... / Athlone
25- .... / Athy
26- .... / Bailieborough
27- Balbriggan / Balrothery
28- Balla / Castlebar
29- Bal'aghader'e'n / Castlerea
30- Balickmoylr & / Carlow
31- Ballina / Ballina
32- Ballinakill / Abbeyleix
33- Ballinalee / Granard
34- Ballinameen / Boyle
35- Ballinamore / Bawnboy
36- .... / Ballinasloe
37- Ballincollig / Cork
38- Ballindine / Claremorris
39- .... / Ballinrobe
40- Ballinrobe / Ballinrobe
41- Ballintra / Ballyshannon
42- Ballybay / Castleblayney
43- .... / Ballycastle
44- Ballycastle / Killala
45- Ballyclough / Mallow
46- Ballyconnell / Bawnboy
47- Ballyduff / Listowel
48a- Ballyfarnon, / Boyle
48b- Ballygawley / Clogher
49- Ballyhaise / Cavan
50- Ballyhaunis / Claremorris
51- Ballyhorgan / Listowel
52- Ballyjamesduff / Oldcastle
53- Ballykelly / Limavady
54- Ballyleague / Roscommon
55- Ballylesson / Lisburn
56- .... / Ballymahon
57- Ballymahon / Ballymahon
58- .... / Ballymena
59- Ballymoney / same
60- .... / Ballymoney
61- Ballymore / Ballymahon
62- Ballymote / Sligo
63- Ballynacargy / Mullingar
64- balyn'hinch / downpatrick
65- Ballynoe / Fermoy
66- Ballynure / Larne
67- Ballyragget / Castlecomer
68- Ballyroan / Abbeyleix
69- .... / Ballyshannon
70- Ballyshannon /
71- Ballyward / Banbridge
72- Banbridge / Banbridge
73- .... / Baltinglass
74- Banagher / Birr
75- .... / Banbridge
76- Banbridge / Banbridge
77- Bandon / Bandon
78- Bannow / Wexford
79- .... / Bantry
80- Bantry / Bantry
81- Barronstown / Dundalk
82- .... / Bawnboy
83- Belfast #1 / Belfast
84- Belfast #2 / Belfast
85- Belfast #3 / Belfast
86- Belfast rural #4 / Belfast
87- Belfast #6 / Belfast
88- Belfast #7 / Belfast
89- Belfast #9 / Belfast
90- Belfast #11 / Belfast
91- .... / Belfast
92- Baellananagh / Cavan
93- Bellarena / Limavady
94- Belturbet / Cavan
95- Benburb / Dungannon
96- Birr / Birr
97- Blackwatertown / Armagh
98- blanch'rdstown+ / Dub. n.
99- Blarney / Cork
100- Boherboy / Kanturk
101- Borris / Carlow
102- Bor'isinOssory / Roscrea
103- .... / Borrisokane
104- Bourney / Roscrea
105- .... / Boyle
106- Boyle / Boyle
107- Bridgetown / Wexford
108- Broadford / Newcastle
109- Broadway / Wexford
110- Brookeboro / Lisnaskea
111- Brosna, #2 / Tralee
112- broughshan' / bal'ymena
113- Buncrana / Inishowen
114- Burt / Londonderry
115- Bushmills / Ballymoney
116- Caher / Clogheen
117- .... / Callan
118- Callan / Callan
119- cap'aghduff / ballinrobe
120- Cappoquin / Lismore
121- Carberry / Edenderry
122- Carlow / Carlow
123- Carndonagh / Inishowen
124- Carney #1 / Sligo
125- Carney #2 / Sligo
126- Carrick / Glenties
127a- .... / Carrickmacross
127b- Carrickmacross / same
128- ... / Car'ick-on-Shan
129- Carrick-on-Suir / same
130- .... / Carrick-on-Suir
131- Carrigaholt / Kilrush
132- Carrigallen / Mohill
133- Carrigbyrne / New Ross
134- Carrignavar, #1 / Cork
135- .... / Cashel
136- .... / Castlebar
137- Castleblayney / same
138- castleconor / dromoreW.
139- .... / Castlederg
140- Castlederg & / same
141- Castlefin / Strabane
142- Castlegregory / Dingle
143- Castleisland / Tralee
144- Castlemaine / Tralee
145- Castlemartyr / Midleton
146- Castlepollard / Delvin
147- Castlerea / Castlerea
148- Castlereagh#2 / Belfast
149- Castletown / Abbeyleix
150- Castletown / Castletown
151- Castletown / Croom
152- Castletown / Mullingar
153- .... / Cavan
154- Cavan / Cavan
155- .... / Celbridge
156- churchhill / bal'yshan'on
157a- .... / Claremorris
157b- Claremorris / same
158- Clarina / Limerick
159- Claudy / Londonderry
160- .... / Clifden
161- Cloghan / Stranolar
162- .... / Clogheen
163- Clogher / Clogher
164- Clonakilty / Clonakilty
165- clonavad'y / dungan'on
166- Clonelly / Irvinestown
167- .... / Clones
168- Clones / Clones
169- Clonmany / Inishowen
170- .... / Clonmel
171- Clonmel / Clonmel
172- Clonmellon / Delvin
173- Clonroche / Enniscorthy
174- cloonbur#1 / oughterard
175- Clough / Downpatrick
176- .... / Coleraine
177- Coleraine / Coleraine
178a- Collon #1 / Ardee
178b- Comber / Newtownards
179- Cong / Ballinrobe
180- .... / Cookstown
181- cookstown / cookstown
182- Coolacasey / Limeick
183- Coolgreany / Gorey
184- coolrain / mountmellick
185- .... / Cootehill
186- Coom / Killarney
187- Cork, Urban #2 / Cork
188- Cork, Urban #7 / Cork
189- Corrofin / Corrifin
190- Creagh / Ballinasloe
191- Croagh / Ballycastle
192- Croom / Croom
193- .... / Croom
194- Crossakeel / Oldcastle
195- Crossgar / Banbridge
196- cros'magl'n / castleblany
197- Crumlin / Antrim
198- Crusheen / Ennis
199- Cullen / Millstreet
200- Delvin / Delvin
201- Derrylin / Lisnaskea
202- Dervock / Ballymoney
203- Dingle / Dingle
204- Doagh / Antrim
205- dona'm'yn' / caric'm'cros'
206- Donegal / Donegal
207- Donnybrook / Dublin S.
208- Doocharry / Glenties
209- draperst'wn / magheraf'lt
210- Dromore / Banbridge
211- Drum / Cootehill
212- drum'ha're / man'rhamilt'i
213- Drumbeg / Lisburn
214- Drumconrath / Ardee
215- Drumlish / Longford
216- Drumquin / Castlederg
217- dr'msh'mbo / caricshan'n
218- dublin n. #1W / dublin n.
219- Dublin N. #3 / Dublin N.
220- .... / Dundalk
221- dundr'm+ / rathdown
222- .... / Dungannon
223- Dungannon / same
224- .... / Dungarvan
225- Dungloe #1 / Glenties
226- Dunkineely / Donegal
227- .... / Dunmanway
228- Dunmanway / same
229- Dunmore / Glenamaddy
230- Dunnamanagh / Strabane
231- Easky / Dromore West
232- Edenderry / Edenderry
233- Ederney / Irvinestown
234- Eglinton / Londonderry
235- Emly / Tipperary
236- Ennis #1 / Ennis
237- .... / Ennis
238- .... / Enniskillen
239- Feakle / Scarriff
240- Feeny / Limavady
241- Fenagh and / Carlow
242- .... / Fermoy
243- Ferns / Enniscorthy
244- Fethard #1 / New Ross
245- Fethard #2 / New Ross
246- Finnea / Granard
247- flor'nc'court / enniskilen
248- Forkhill / Newry
249- Frankford / Parsonstown
250- Galgorm / Ballymena
251- .... / Galway
252- Galway #1 / Galway
253- Galway #3 / Galway
254- Garvagh / Coleraine
255- Glassan / Athlone
256- Glasslough / Monaghan
257- Glenavy / Lisburn
258- Glennamaddy / same
259- .... / Glenties
260- Glenties / Glenties
261- Gorey / Gorey
262- .... / Gort
263- Gowran / Kilkenny
264- .... / Granard
265- Granard / Granard
266- Grean / Tipperary

. Registrars' District / Union

267. grey abbey / newtownard
268. Gurteen / Boyle
269. Hollymount / Ballinrobe
270. Holywell / Enniskillen
271. .... / Inishowen
272. Inishbofin / Clifden
273. Inistioge / Thomastown
274. Innfield / Trim
275. Irvinestown / same
276. .... / Irvinestown
277. Kanturk / Kanturk
278. Keadue / Boyle
279. Keady / Armagh
280. Kealkill / Bantry
281. .... / Kells
282. Kells / Kells
283. .... / Kenmare
284. Kilbeggan / Tullamore
285. kilcatherin' / castletown
286. Kilcock / Celbridge
287. Kilfinane / Kilmallock
288. Kilgarvan / Kenmare
289. .... / Kilkeel
290. Kilgobban / Tralee
291. Kilkee / Kilrush
292. Kilkeel #1 / Kilkeel
293. Kilkeel #2 / Kilkeel
294. Kilkelly / Swineford
295. .... / Kilkenny
296. Kilkenny #2 / Kilkenny
297. Kilkishen / Tulla
298. Killaan / Ballinasloe
299. .... / Killadysert
300. Killala / Killala
301. .... / Killala
302. Killanniv / Ennis
303a. .... / Killarney
303b. killarney #1 / killarney
304. Killeagh / Youghal
305. Killeen / Dunshaughlin
306. Killenagh and / Gorey
307. killeroran / mountbellew
308. Killeshandra / Cavan
309. Killorglin / Killarney
310. Killough / Downpatrick
311. Killoughy / Tullamore
312. Killucan / Mullingar
313. Killygordon / Stranorlar
314. Kilmacrenan & / Milford
315. .... / Kilmacthomas
316. Kilmaganny / Callan
317. Kilmallock / Kilmallock
318. Kilmihil / Kilrush
319. Kilmore / Monaghan
320. Kilpatrick / Cashel
321. Kilrea / Coleraine
322. Kilrush / Kilrush
323. .... / Kilrush
324. kilsal'aghan / balrothery
325. Kilshannig / Mallow
326. Kilsheelan / Clonmel
327. Kiltimagh / Swineford
328. Kiltinan / Clonmel
329. Kiltoom / Athlone
330. Kiltormer / Ballinasloe
331. Kilworth / Fermoy
332. kingscourt / baili'boroug
333. kingstown#2 / rathdown
334. Kinlough / ballyshan'on
335. Kinsale / Kinsale
336. Kinvarra / Gort
337. knocknalow'r / belmul'et
338. Larne / Larne
339. Leitrim / Car.on Shan'on
340. .... / Letterkenny
341. Letterkenny / same
342. Lettermore / Oughterard
343. .... / Limavady
344. Limavady / Limavady
345. Limerick #2 / Limerick
346. Lisbellaw / Enniskillen
347. .... / Lisburn
348. Lisburn / Lisburn
349. Lismore / Lismore
350. .... / Lisnaskea
351. Lisnaskea / Lisnaskea
352. .... / Listowel
353. Listowel / Listowel
354. Littleton / Thurles
355. Lond.Urban #2 / Lond.
356. .... / Londonderry
357. .... / Longford
358. lo'ghbri'kl'nd / banbridg
359. Loughgall / Armagh
360. .... / Loughrea
361. louisburgh #1 / westport
362. louisb'rgh #2 / westport
363. Lurgan #2 / Lurgan
364. Lusk / Balrothery
365. Macroom / Macroom
366. .... / Macroom
367. Maghera / Magherafelt
368. Malahide / Balrothery
369. Malin / Inishowen
370. manorhamilton / same
371. .... / Manorhamilton
372. Markethill / Armagh
373. Maryborou / Mt. Mellick
374. .... / Milford
375. Milford / Kanturk
376. .... / Millstreet
377. Milltown / Killarney
378. .... / Mitchelstown
379. .... / Mohill
380. Mohill / Mohill
381. Moira / Lurgan
382. Molahiffe / Killarney
383. .... / Monaghan
384. Monasterevan / Athy
385. mon'ym're / magherafelt
386. .... / Mountbellew
387. Mountmellick / same
388. Mountnorris / Newry
389. Mountrath / Mt.mellick
390. Mountshannon / Scarrif
391. Moville / Inishowen
392. Mullaghglass / Newry
393. Mullinahone / Callan
394. Mullingar / Mullingar
395. .... / Mullingar
396. multyfarnh'm / mullingar
397. Murragh / Bandon
398. Murroe / Limerick
399. Naas and Carragh / Naas
400. .... / Naas
401. .... / Navan
402. Navan / Navan
403. Nenagh / Nenagh
404. .... / Newcastle
405. Newcastle / Rathdrum
406. Newport / Nenagh
407. Newport / Nenagh
408. New Ross / New Ross
409. Newry #1 / Newry
410. Newry #2 / Newry
411. Newtownards / same
412. newt.bar'y / en'iscorthy
413. Newtownbutler / Clones
414. new.ham'lt'n / castl'bl'ny
415. newt.stew'rt / strabane
416. Oldcastle / Oldcastle
417. .... / Omagh
418. Omagh #2 / Omagh
419. .... / Oughterard
420. .... / Parsonstown
421. Pettigoe / Donegal
422. Pilltown / CarrickonSuir
423. Plumb Bridge / Strabane
424. Pomeroy / Cookstown
425. Portaferry / Downpatrick
426. Portglenone / Ballymena
427. Portlaw / Carrick-on-Suir
428. Portrush / Coleraine
429. Poyntzpass / Newry
430. Quin / Tulla
431. Rahan / Mallow
432. Ramelton / Milford
433. Randalstown / Antrim
434. Raphoe / Strabane
435. Rathangan / Edenderry
436. Rathcoole / Celbridge
437. Rathcormach / Fermoy
438. Rathdowney / Abbeyleix
439. .... / Rathdrum
440. Rathdrum / Rathdrum
441. Rathfriland / Newry
442. rathgorm'ck / car'ic-Suir
443. .... / Rathkeale
444. Rathkeale #1 / Rathkeale
445. Rathkeale #2 / Rathkeale
446. Rathmore / Naas
447. Rathmullan / Milford
448. Rathvilly / Baltinglass
449. Ratoath / Dunshaughlin
450. Ravensdale / Dundalk
451. Rhode / Edenderry
452. Ringville / Dungarvan
453. riverst'wn / parsonst'wn
454a. Riverstown / Sligo
454b. Roosky / Strokestown
455. Roscommon / same
456. .... / Roscommon
457. Roscrea #1 / Roscrea
458. Roscrea #2 / Roscrea
459. Rosguill / Milford
460. Rosslea / Clones
461. Rostrevor / Kilkeel
462. Roundstone #1 / Clifden
463. Roundstone #2 / Clifden
464. Rowan / Mohill
465. Rynn / Mohill
466. Saintfield / Lisburn
467. St. Mary's / Drogheda
468. St. Mullin's / New Ross
469. .... / Scarriff
470. Scrabby / Granard
471. shercock / bailieboro'gh
472. .... / Shillelagh
473. Shinrone / Roscrea
474. Silvermines / Nenagh
475. Skreen / Dromore West
476. .... / Sligo
477. Sligo #2 / Sligo
478. stew'rtst'wn / cookstown
479. .... / Strabane
480. Strabane / Strabane
481. strangford / downpatrick
482. .... / Stranorlar
483. Stranorlar / Stranorlar
484. Street, #1 / Granard
485. .... / Strokestown
486. .... / Swineford
487. Swords / Balrothery
488. Tallow / Lismore
489. Tanderagee / Bandbridge
490. Tarbert #1 / Listowel
491. Tarbert #2 / Listowel
492. Tartaraghan / Lurgan
493. Templemore / Thurles
494. Templepatrick / Antrim
495. termonfeckin / drogheda
496. Terryglass / Borrisokane
497. .... / Thomastown
498. .... / Thurles
499. Thurles / Thurles
500. Timoleague / Clonakilty
501. .... / Tobercurry
502. Tobercurry / Tobercurry
503. Toome / Ballymena
504. Tory Island / dunfanaghy
505. Trim / Trim
506. Tuam #1 / Tuam
507. Tuam #2 / Tuam
508. Tulla / Tulla
509. .... / Tulla
510. Tullamain / Cashel
511. .... / Tullamore
512. Tullamore / Tullamore
513. Tullaroan / Kilkenny
514. Tullow / Carlow
515. Tullyvin / Cootehill
516. Turloughmore / Galway
517. .... / Urlingford
518. Ullid / Waterford
519. Urlingford / Urlingford
520. Valencia / Caherciveen
521. Ventry / Dingle
522. Virginia / Oldcastle
523. Waringstown / Lurgan
524. Warrenpoint / Newry
525. .... / Waterford
526. .... / Wexford
527. Wexford / Wexford
528. Wil'iamstown / Glen'ama
529. Woodstown / Waterford
530. Youghal / Youghal

Index

Part III

This book is the first volume of a 32 volume set now in progress. The index covers this volume, and volumes 2, 3, 4 & 5 .

Page numbers appear only for this volume.

Only volume numbers **(V)** appear for names found in other volumes to the set, as follows:
v 2 = Families of Co. Kerry, Ireland*
v 3 = Families of Co. Clare, Ireland*
v 4 = Families of Co. Cork, Ireland*
v 5 = Families of Co. Limerick, Ireland*

√ Page '269...' indicates that the surame is found in the section which begins on page 269.

√ Names are listed as if the O' or Mac before the name were removed, hence O'Connor is found with Connor, etc..

* Published volumes to the set as of April 1977.

Illustration taken from "Families of Co. Kerry',
volume 2 of the Irish Families series.

Abberton 1
Abbot **V3**
Abbot 269...
Abbot(t) 1
Abbott **V3**
Abbott **V4**
Abbott **V5**
Abbott 269...
Abdy 269...
Abell Able **V5**
Abercombie **V3**
Abercomby **V3**
Abercrombie 69
Abercromby **V3**
Abercrumber 1
Abercrumber 269...
Abernathy **V4**
Aberneathy **V4**
Abernethy **V4**
Aberton 1
Abot(t) 1
Abott **V3**
Abott **V4**
Abott 269...
Abraham **V4**
Abraham 269...
Mac Abraham **V4**
(mac Abraham 1
Mac Abram 1
Abrehan 1
Mac Abrehon 1
Abrill 96
Absom **V5**
Absom 1
Absom 269...
Acard **V2**
Achard **V2**
Acheson 269...
Acheson 34
Achmootie 34
Achmooty 269...
Achmouty 34
Achmuty 2
Achyson 269...
Ackland 1
Ackland 269...
Actery 1
Actery 269...
Mac Adaim **V2**
Adair 269...
Adair(e) 1
Adaire 269...
Adam **V4**
Mac Adam **V2**
Mac Adam **V3**
Mac Adam **V4**
Mac Adam 1,29
Mc Adam **V3**
Mc Adam 269...
Mac/ Adam(s) 1,29
Adames **V2**
Adams **V2**
Adams **V3**
Adams **V4**
Adams 269...
Mac Adams **V3**
Mc Adams **V2**
Mc Adams **V4**
Mc Adams 1
Adamson 1,2
Adamson 269...
Adare 1
Adare 269...
Mac Adarra 269...
Mac Adarra 76
Mc Adarrah 269...
Adayre 1
Adayre 269...
Adderley **V4**
Adderly **V4**
Adderly 1
Adderly 269...
Adderton 1
Adderton 269...
Addis **V4**
Addis 2
Aderly **V4**
Adger 269...
Adhbenson 269...
Adhow 269...
Adire 269...
Adlam 213
Adlum 213
Adlum 269...
Mac Adorey 2
Adorian 269...
Mac Adory 2
Adrain 2
Adreane 2
Adrian 2
Adrian 269...
Adrien 2
Adryan 2
Adryan 269...
D' Aethy 5
Mc Afee 269...
Afflack 269...
Affleck 269...
De Affoun **V3**
Agar **V2**
Agar 269...
Agard **V2**
Agard **V3**
Agard **V4**
Agarde **V4**
Agas **V2**
Agaurd **V3**
Agaurd **V4**
Ager **V2**
Aggas 2
Aggas 269...
Agharne **V4**
Agharne 2
Agharne 269...
Aghearn 2
Agherin **V3**
Agherin 269...
Agherns **V4**
Agherns 2
O Agherns **V4**
O' Agherns 269...
De Aghirnily **V4**
Aghmonty 269...
Aghmooty 2
Aghmooty 269...
Aghwell 2
Aghwell 269...
M' Aghy 269...
Mac Aghy 44
Aglin 90
Agnew 269...
Agnew 3
Ahearn **V3**
Ahearn **V4**
Ahearn 269...
Ahearn(e) 2,145
Ahearne **V3**
Ahearne 269...
O Aher **V4**
Aheran 2
Aherin 2
Aherly **V5**
Aherly 269...
Ahern **V2**
Ahern **V3**
Ahern **V4**
Ahern 269...
O' Ahern **V3**
O Ahern **V4**
O Ahern(e) 2
Aherne **V3**
Aherne **V4**
Aherne 269...
O' Aherne **V3**
O' Aherne **V5**
Aheron 2
Ahmonty 269...
Aicken 269...
Aicken 3
Aidy 269...
Aiken 269...
Aiken(s) 3,135
Aikens 269...
Aikins 3
Aildwood 269...
Aildwood 4
Oh Ailee **V2**
Aileward 7
Mac Ailin **V2**
Ailmer **V3**
Ailmer 269...
Ailmer 6
Mac Aindrui **V2**
Oh Ainlige **V2**
Ainsworth **V2**
Air **V4**
Air(e)y 4
Airachdan **V2**
Aire **V4**
Ais **V2**
Aitken 3
Akin 3
Akmooth 269...
Mc Alary 269...
M' Alasher 269...
Mc Alasher 269...
Mc Alay 269...
Albonagh 269...
Albonagh 4
Albro **V4**
Albro **V5**
Alcher **V2**
Alcock **V4**
Alcock 269...
Alcock(e) 2
Alcocke **V4**
Alcorn **V3**
Alcorn **V5**
Alcorn 269...
Alcorn 5
Alcorne **V3**
Alder **V4**
Alderdice 269...
Alderdice 5
Alderdise 5
Aldersee 269...
Aldersee 5
Mc Aldin 269...
(mc) Aldin 5
Alding 269...
Alding 5
Aldrich 269...
Aldrich 5
Aldridge 269...
Aldwarth **V4**
Aldwarth 269...
Aldwarth 3
Aldwell **V2**
Aldwood 269...
Aldwood 5
Aldworth **V2**
Aldworth **V4**
Aldworth 269...
Aldworth 3
Aldworth, Sir **V2**
Ale 269...
Ale 6
Mac Alea 175
Mac Aleary 6
Mac Aleavey 6
Mc Aleavey 269...
Mc Aleenan 269...
Mac Aleenen 7
Mac Aleenon 7
Mc Aleer 269...
Mc Aleer 7
Mc Aleese 269...
Mc Aleese 7
Mac Alenden 7
Mc Alesher 269...
Mc Alester 269...
Mc Alester 7
Aleward 269...
Alex. 3
Alexandar 3
Alexander **V3**
Alexander 269...
Alexander 3
Alexandre 3
Algoe 269...
Mac Alily 179
Alin 269...
Alin 3
Mc Alinden 269...
Mc Alinden 7
Aliner 269...
Mc Alingen 269...
Alinion 269...
Mc Alinon 269...
Alison 7
Mc Alister 269...
Mc Alivery 269...
M' All 269...
Allan **V2**
Allan **V5**
Mac Allan 3
Alland 269...
Allcorn **V3**
Allen **V2**
Allen 269...
Mac Allen **V2**
Mac Allen 3
Mc Allen 269...
Allerdice 269...
Alleson 7
Mc Allester 269...
Allexander 269...
Alley 7
Alleyn 3
Mc Alliffe **V4**
Mc Allin 269...
Alline 269...
Allingham 269...
Mc Allion 36
Allison **V5**
Allison 269...
Allison 7
Allisson 7
Mac Allister **V2**
Mc Allister 269...
Mc Allister 7
Allman **V2**
Allman 8
Allmen 8
Allon 3
Alltraighe **V2**
Alltraighe **V3**
Ally 7
Allyn 3
Alman 8
Almer 269...
Almes **V2**
Almes 269...
Mc Aloney 269...
Mc Aloone 269...
Alpin 269...
Mac Alpin **V2**
Mc Alpin 269...
Mac Alshender 269.
Mac Alshinder 269.
Altimas 8
Altimes 269...
Altmas 8
Alton **V2**
Alton 73
Altry, **V2**
Mac Alustruim **V2**
Alwoodhouse 269..
Mac Amalgada **V2**
Amansham 269...
Amberson 269...
Ambros **V2**
Ambrose **V2**
Ambrose **V4**
Ambrose **V5**
Ambrose 269...
America **V2**
America **V4**
Amery **V2**
Amery **V5**
Ames **V2**
Ames **V4**
Ames **V5**
Amooty 2
Amooty 269...
Amory **V2**
Mac An Coilib **V2**
Mac An Leagha 176
Mac Anally 206
Mc Anally 269...
Mac Anany 8
Mc Anare 269...
M' Anaul 269...
Mac Ancarrigg **V3**
Ancient **V4**
Ancient **V2**
Ancient **V3**
Ancthill 269...
Andersen 8
Anderson **V2**
Anderson 269...
Anderson 8
Andersone 269...
Mac Andless 38
Mc Andless 269...
Andrew 269...
Mac Andrew **V2**
Mc Andrew 269...
(mac Andrew(s) 4
Andrewes **V5**
Andrewes 269...

Andrews **V2**
Andrews **V3**
Andrews **V4**
Andrews269...
Mc Anelly206
Mc Anen(e)y8
Mc Aneny269...
Anesley269...
Anesley8
Anger269...
Anger8
Angier269...
Angier8,13
Angland8
Anglesey **V2**
L' Angleys99
Anglican **V2**
Anglim **V4**
Anglin **V4**
Anglin269...
Anglin(d)8
Mac Angoill **V2**
Angove **V2**
(de) Angulo, **V2**
Angus269...
Angus8
Mac Aniascaire **V2**
Anketel **V4**
Ankettill269...
Ankettill8
Ankettle269...
Ankettle8
Ankle269...
Mac Anliss38
Mac Anna35
O Annachain **V4**
Oh Annain **V2**
Annals Of **V3**
Annesley **V2**
Annesley **V4**
Annett269...
Oh Anracain **V2**
Mac Anree269...
Mac Anscoloige **V2**
Ansla269...
Anthony **V2**
Anthony9
Mc Antire269...
Antrim269...
Mc Anulla269...
Mc Anully269...
Mac Anulty210
Mc Anulty269...
Mac Any9
Anyas **V4**
Mac Aoda **V2**
Mac Aodagain **V2**
Ap Rees' **V2**
Appellwhite269...
Appendix **V4**
Appleyard **V2**
Appleyard **V3**
Aprice220
Mc Aragh269...
Arberry **V4**
Arberry269...
Arbuthnot **V3**
Arbuthnut **V3**
Archbald269...
Archbold269...
Archbould269...
Archdale10,34
Archdale269...
Archdall10
Archdall269...
Archdeacon **V4**
Archdeacon10
Archdeacon269...
Archdeakin10
Archdeakin269...
Archdekin10
Archer **V2**
Archer **V4**
Archer269...
(le) Archer11
Archfield235
Archfield269...
Archibald269...
De Arci, Dearcy74
Ardagh10
Ardea **V2**
Ardell11
Mc Ardell269...
Ardenton10
Ardenton269...
Ardfert **V2**
O Ardghala **V4**
Ardglasse11
Ardglasse269...
Ardhill11
Ardif(f)11
Ardilaun, L. **V2**
(mc) Ardill11
Mc Ardle11
Mc Ardle269...
Ardogh10
Ardonton10
Ardough10
Ardough269...
Ardwaher269...
M' Aready269...
Mc Aree11,164
Mc Aree269...
Arendall **V4**
Argue11
Mac Arha269...
Arinon **V5**
Arkens12
Arkins **V3**
Arkins12
Arkley269...
Arlan(d)12
Arland269...
Arlant269...
Arlend12
Arm(e)strong4
Armada, **V3**
Armestrong269...
Armin269...
Armitage **V4**
Armor **V4**
Armorica **V2**
Armour **V4**
Armour269...
Arms -cork **V4**
Arms-munster **V4**
Armstrong **V2**
Armstrong **V3**
Armstrong269...
Armstrong4
Armstronge269...
Arnalds **V2**
Arnalds269...
Arnes **V2**
Arnold **V2**
Arnold269...
Arnold269...
Arnolt269...
Arnop269...
Arnot **V4**
Arnot269...
Arnott **V4**
Arnott269...
M' Arory68
Oh Arractain **V2**
Arragan139
Arrall269...
O Arrny **V3**
Arrundel269...
Arrundell **V4**
Oh Artagain **V2**
Artagh, Co. **V2**
Mac Artan38
Mac Arte **V4**
Oh Artgaile **V2**
Arther **V3**
Arthop269...
Arthur **V2**
Arthur **V3**
Arthur **V4**
Arthur **V5**
Arthur269...
Mac Arthur **V2**
Mac Arthur **V3**
Mc Arthur **V4**
(mac Arthur(e)4,39
Arthure **V4**
Arthure269...
Arthurs269...
Arthurs4
Mc Arthy39
M' Artie269...
Mc Artney39
De Artobridmore V4
Mac Artuir **V2**
Arundall **V4**
Arundall269...
Arundell **V4**
Arundell **V5**
Arundell12
Asbury **V5**
Ash **V2**
Ash **V3**
Ash269...
Ash(e)5,207
Ashbrook **V4**
Ashbrook **V5**
Ashby **V4**
Ashe **V2**
Ashe **V3**
Ashe269...
Ashe, Ash **V5**
Ashebrook **V4**
Ashebrook5
Ashenhurst269...
Mac Ashinah109
Mc Ashinah269...
Ashly269...
Ashton **V2**
Ashton **V4**
Ashwood **V2**
Ashworth269...
Aske269...
Mac Askie61
Askin **V5**
Askin269...
Askin45
Askins269...
Aspel269...
Aspell269...
Aspill269...
Asplen, G. **V2**
Assin269...
Mac Assy **V2**
Asten269...
Astin269...
Mc Astocker269...
Aston269...
Mc Atamney269...
Mac Atarsny12
Atasac **V2**
Mac Atasney12
Mac Atav(e)y12
Atcheson269...
Mac Atee100
Mc Atee269...
Mc Ateer12,156
Mc Ateer269...
Mc Ateggart269...
(de) Athy5
M' Atilla107,250
Mc Atilla269...
Mc Atire269...
Atkins **V2**
Atkins **V4**
Atkins269...
Atkins5
Atkinson **V2**
Atkinson **V5**
Atkinson269...
Atkinson5
Atkinson, J. **V2**
Atmoty269...
Att(e)ridge12
Attridge **V4**
Aucher **V2**
Auchmuty2
Aucketil269...
Audley **V5**
Audley12,34
Auger **V2**
Aughmuty2
Auher269...
Mc Aula269...
Mc Aula34
Mac Aulay269...
Mac Aulay6
Auld269...
Mac Auley **V2**
Mac Auley6,63
Mc Auley **V4**
Mc Auley269...
(mc) Aulif(f)e6
Aulife269...
Mc Aulife **V4**
Mc Aulife269...
Aulife Auliffe **V4**
Mc Auliff **V4**
Mac Auliffe **V2**
Mac Auliffe **V5**
Mc Auliffe **V4**
Mc Auliffe269...
Mc Aulliffe **V4**
Mc Aully269...
D' Aungier(s)8,13
Aurachaun269...
(mac Aurthur4
Mc Auslan(d)41
Austan13
Austen13
Austin **V2**
Austin **V3**
Austin **V4**
Austin269...
Austin(e)13
Austin, Eliz. **V2**
Austine269...
Auston13
Australia **V3**
Australia **V4**
Australia, In **V2**
Austrian **V2**
De Auters262
Auwll269...
Mac Avaddy186
Mc Avaddy269...
Mc Avady269...
Mc Avealy13
M' Aveely13,171
Averill **V2**
Avery **V2**
Avery269...
Mc Avey269...
Mac Avin133
Mc Avinchy269...
Mac Avinna129
M' Avinue269...
Mac Avinue129
Mc Avish252
Mc Avish269...
Avory269...
M' Avoy269...
Mc Avynny269...
Mac Award263
Mc Award269...
Awley **V4**
(mac Awley6,63
Awlif6
Mac Awly269...
Mac Awly269...
Mc Awly269...
Aylemer269...
Aylemer6
Ayleward269...
Ayleward7
Aylmer **V3**
Aylmer **V5**
(d') Aylmer6
Aylward **V2**
Aylward269...
Aylward7
Aylworth **V2**
Aynger269...
Ayre(s)98
O' B269...
B'hassett **V2**
Baal269...
Babbage **V2**
Babbington **V4**
Babbitt269...
Babe13
Baber269...
Babington **V2**
Babington **V4**
Babington269...
Baccon269...
Bachelor155
Back **V5**
Back269...
Backas13
Backer269...
Backus13
Bacon **V3**
Bacon **V5**
Bacon269...
Bacstar18
Badham **V4**
Badley269...
Bagally **V3**
Bagby **V4**
Bagby **V5**

Surname Index

 Names Listed as if the O' or Mac before the name were removed. Only page #'s for this volume are shown

Bagenal 7
Bagg 269...
Baggott **V3**
Bagley **V4**
Bagley 19
Bagley 269...
Bagly **V3**
Bagly **V4**
Bagnall **V4**
Bagnall 269...
Bagnall 7
Bagnel **V5**
Bagnell **V4**
Bagot **V3**
Bagot(t) 7
Bagott **V3**
Bagott **V5**
Bagott 269...
Bagster 18
Bagworth 269...
Baicer **V2**
Bailey **V2**
Bailey **V3**
Bailey **V4**
Bailey **V5**
Bailey 269...
Bailey Bayly **V4**
Bailie 269...
Baille **V2**
Baillie 34
Bailly 269...
Baily **V2**
Baily **V3**
Baily **V4**
Baily 269...
Bain(e) 18
Baine **V3**
Baines **V3**
Bainlett 269...
Bainley **V2**
Baird **V5**
Baird 269...
Baireid **V2**
O' Baiskind **V3**
O Baiskind 13
O Baiskinn 13
Baith 269...
Baker **V2**
Baker **V3**
Baker **V4**
Baker 205
Baker 269...
(le) Baker(e) 14
Bakey **V3**
Bakey **V4**
Bakey 18
Balbirnie **V4**
Balbirnie 13
Balburney 13
Balburnie 13
Baldin 269...
Baldon 269...
Baldoon 269...
Baldrick 14
Baldwin **V2**
Baldwin **V4**
Baldwin 15
Baldwin 269...
Bale 269...
Balfe 269...
Balfe, Balffe 15,19
Balfour 269...
Balfour(e) 15,19,34
Balfremon 269...
Baliste 16
Ball **V2**
Ball **V3**
Ball **V4**
Ball **V5**
Ball 269...
Ball 8
Ballagh 15
Ballanger **V3**
Ballantine 269...
Ballard **V2**
Ballenger **V3**
Ballenger 16
Ballentine 269...
Ballester 16
Ballesty 16
Ballicar **V3**
Ballinger **V3**
Ballinger 16
Ballough 15
Ballue **V4**
Balluntyne **V2**
Bally **V5**
Bally 269...
Ballybeggan **V2**
Ballycarbery **V2**
Ballyclogh **V3**
Ballyheigue **V2**
Ballykealy **V2**
Ballykit **V3**
Ballymalis **V2**
Ballymalus **V2**
Ballyneanig **V2**
Balmer 269...
Balrick 14
Baltezar 269...
Balton 269...
Baly 269...
Bamberry 16
Bambrick 16
Bambrick 269...
Bambury **V2**
Bambury **V5**
Bambury 16
Bamford 269...
Bampton 269...
Ban(e) 18
Banan 269...
O' Banan 269...
Banane 269...
Banane 8
Banard **V3**
Banastre **V4**
Banbo 213
Bancks 269...
Bandon, Co. **V4**
Bandon Medal **V4**
Bandy 269...
Bane **V3**
Bane **V4**
Bane **V5**
Bane 269...
Bane 8,16,265
Banfell 269...
Banfield **V4**
Bangfield 269...
Banigan 16
Banin 8
Banion 8
Banistor 269...
Banks 16
Banks 269...
O Bann(i)on 8
Bannan 269...
Bannan 8
Bannane 269...
Bannatyne **V3**
Bannegan 16
Banning **V4**
Bannion **V2**
Bannister **V4**
Bannister 269...
Bannon 269...
Banting **V5**
Banting 269...
Banyon 8
Barbador 16
Barber **V3**
Barber **V5**
Barber 16
Barber 269...
Barbier 16
Barbodoes **V2**
(le) Barbour 16
Barclay **V3**
Barclay **V4**
Barclay **V5**
Barclay 269...
Barcroft 269...
Barcroft 8
Bardane 16
Barden **V2**
Bardon 269...
Bardsley **V5**
Barett **V3**
Barett 269...
Barett 9
Barham **V2**
Bari **V4**
O Bari **V4**
Barington 269...
Barington 9
Bariod **V2**
Barkeley 34
Barkell **V5**
Barkell 269...
Barker 269...
Barkey **V2**
Barkley **V4**
Barkley **V5**
Barkley 269...
Barklimore 269...
Barkman 205
Barley 269...
Barlow **V5**
Barlow 269...
Barlowe 269...
Barnabas **V3**
Barnacle 269...
Barnacle 65
Barnane 269...
Barnard **V2**
Barnard **V3**
Barnard **V4**
Barnard 269...
Barnawell 269...
Barnes **V2**
Barnes **V4**
Barnes 269...
Barnes 34
Barnett **V5**
Barnett 269...
Barnett 9
Barnewall **V4**
Barnewall 9
Barnewell **V4**
Barnewell 269...
Barney **V5**
Barnidge 269...
Barns **V4**
Barnstable 17
Barnstaple 17
Barnwall **V4**
Barnwall 269...
De Barnwall **V4**
De Barnwall 9
Barnwell **V3**
Barnwell 269...
Barnwell 9
Baroid **V3**
Baron 17
Baron 269...
Barony Map Viii
Baroy **V4**
Baroy 269...
Barr **V4**
Barr **V5**
O' Barr 269...
Barr(e) 10
(de) Barra **V2**
Barraby **V5**
Barraby 269...
Barran 269...
Barrat 9
Barret **V3**
Barret **V4**
Barret 269...
Barret(t) 9
Barrett **V2**
Barrett **V3**
Barrett **V4**
Barrett **V5**
Barrett 269...
Barretts **V2**
Barretts **V3**
Barretts **V4**
Barrey 10
Barri(e) 10
Barrie **V3**
Barrie **V4**
Barrimorre 269...
Barrington **V4**
Barrington **V5**
Barrington 269...
Barrington 9
Barroe **V4**
Barroe 269...
Barron **V2**
Barron **V5**
Barron 17
Barron 269...
Barron 269...
Mc Barron 269...
Barrow **V2**
Barrow **V4**
Barrow 269...
Barrowbier 205
Barry **V2**
Barry **V3**
Barry **V4**
Barry **V5**
Barry 269...
Barry, Col. J. **V2**
Barry(e) 10
Barry, John **V2**
Barry Oge **V4**
Barry, Rich. **V4**
De Barry Tomb **V4**
Barrye **V4**
Barrymore **V4**
Barrymore 269...
Barrymore, Earl **V4**
Barrytt 269...
Barter **V4**
Barter 17
Bartholomew **V2**
Bartless **V5**
Bartless 269...
Bartlett **V2**
Bartley **V2**
Bartley 214
Bartley 269...
Bartnett 269...
Bartnett 9
Barton **V2**
Barton 10,34
Barton 269...
Barton, Rv. **V2**
De Bartun **V2**
(de) Bartun 10
Bary **V4**
Bary 269...
Base **V4**
Base 269...
Basford **V4**
Basil 269...
Basill 269...
Basket 269...
Baskin **V3**
Basnett 17
Basquill 17
Bass **V2**
Bassett **V4**
Bassett 269...
De Bastabla **V2**
Bastable **V2**
Bastable **V4**
Bastable 17
Bastard **V3**
Bastick 17
Bat(t) 11
Bataille 18
Batchelier 155
Batchelor **V2**
Bate **V3**
Batell 18
Bateman **V2**
Bateman **V4**
Bateman 10
Bateman 269...
Bateman, **V2**
Bates 269...
Batey 18
De Bath 17
Bather 269...
Bathripp 269...
Bathurst **V4**
Bathurst 269...
Battell 18
Batten 269...
Batter 269...
Battersby 11
Battersby 269...
Battle 18
Battle 269...
Baucroft 269...
Baudair 155
Baudkin 26
Baudry 155
Baudwin 15
Baukley 269...
Bauldwine 269...
Baulman 269...
Baun 269...
Baunister **V4**
Baunister 269...
Bawn 265

V2 = Families of Co. Kerry **V3** = Families of Co. Clare **V4** = Families of Co. Cork **V5** = Families of Co. Limerick

Surname Index

Bawn269...
Baxter269...
(mac Baxter18
Mc Bay260
Mc Bay269...
Bayes V4
Baygott269...
Bayl(e)y11
Baylee V3
Bayley V2
Bayley V3
Bayley V4
Bayley269...
Bayly V3
Bayly V4
Bayne(s)16,18
O' Beacain V2
Beacon269...
Beadle269...
Beagham269...
Beaghan269...
Beak(e)y18
Beakey V3
Beakey V4
Beaky V3
Beale V4
Beale269...
Beale Castle V2
Beale, T. V2
Bealing269...
Beall269...
Beame269...
Beamish V2
Beamish V4
Beamish12
Beamish269...
Bean V2
O Bean18
Bear V2
Bear269...
O' Beara V5
O' Beara269...
Beard18
Beard269...
Beare V4
Beare V4
Beare269...
Beares269...
Bearken V3
Bearkin V3
Bearkin269...
Bearsford13
Beary269...
Beary27
Beasl(e)y18
Beaslai V2
Beasley V2
Beasley269...
Beasly V2
Beasty18
Beat(t)y18
Beatagh269...
Beats V4
Beats269...
Beattie18
Beattie269...
Beatty269...
Beauchamp269...
Beaufoy155
Beaumont269...
Becher V4
Becher18
Beci V4
O Beci18
O Beci Bantry V4
Beck V4
Beck18
Beck269...
Becket269...
Beckett269...
Beckford V2
Bedborough269...
Bedborrough269...
Bedlow269...
Beecham269...
Beecher V4
Beecher18
Beecher269...
Beecher269...
Beemish12
Beers269...
Beery27
Beets V4
Beg(g)18
Begally V3
Begane269...
Begett269...
Begg269...
Beggan269...
O' Beggan269...
Beggan(e)18,22
Begge18
Begge269...
Beggs18
Beggs269...
Beghane269...
Beginners V4
Beglan269...
Begley V2
Begley V3
Begley V4
Begley269...
O Begley V2
O Begley V4
O' Begley V5
O Begley19
Begly V2
Begly V3
Begney269...
Behan V2
Behan19
Behan269...
Behane269...
O' Beirgin V2
Beirn269...
Beirne V2
Beirne269...
O' Beirne V2
(o) Beirne12,25,34
O' Beirne269...
Belfore19
Belfore269...
Belfour19
Belfour269...
Bell V2
Bell V4
Bell V5
Bell20
Bell269...
Bellen269...
Belleny269...
Bellew V3
Bellew V4
Bellew12
Bellew269...
Bellinger V3
Bellingham19
Bellingham269...
Bellow V3
Bellow V4
Bellow269...
Bellowe V3
Bellowe V4
Bellowe269...
Bellue V3
Bellue V4
Bellue269...
Belton20
Belton269...
O' Benaghan269...
Benathy269...
Benbo213
Benbo269...
Benchy22
Benden V5
Benden269...
Bendon269...
Benes V3
Benfield V3
Benger V4
Benger269...
Benior269...
Benison269...
Benn V2
Bennell269...
Benner V2
Benner205
Bennes V3
Bennes269...
Bennet269...
Bennett V2
Bennett V3
Bennett V4
Bennett V5
Bennett20
Bennett269...
Bennis V5
Bennis269...
Bennis, V3
Bennish269...
Benson V2
Benson V5
Benson269...
Bensone269...
Bent V4
Bent269...
Bentham V5
Bentham269...
Bentley V3
Bentley V5
Bentley269...
Bently V2
Bently V3
O' Beoilain V2
Beolan269...
Beolan(e)17
Beolane V3
Beolane269...
O Beolane V3
Bera269...
Beresford13
Beresford269...
Beretcheart' V4
Bereton V3
Bereton V4
Bereton V5
De Berewa32
Berford269...
O' Berga V5
O Berga20
Bergan269...
Bergen20
Bergin V2
Bergin269...
(o) Bergin20
Bergman269...
Beridge13
Berisford269...
Berkeley, V4
Berkery V5
Berkery269...
Berkley V5
Berkley269...
Bermagh269...
Bermingham V4
Bermingham14
Bermingham269...
Berminghan14
O' Bern269...
Bernard V2
Bernard V3
Bernard V4
Bernard269...
Bernard, V2
O' Berne269...
Berrane269...
Berrell269...
Berresford269...
Berridge13
Berrigan269...
Berrill23
Berrisford269...
Berry V2
Berry V4
Berry V5
Berry10
Berry269...
Berstow269...
Bery269...
Bessworth V4
Bessworth269...
Best V2
Best V4
Best269...
Best(on)21
Beston V5
Bestwill21
Bestwill269...
Betagh18,21
Betagh269...
Mac Beth269...
Bethel V5
Bethel21,205
Betsworth V5
Betsworth269...
Betsworthy V4
Betsworthy269...
Bettin269...
Betts269...
Bettsworthy V4
Bettworthy V4
Betty269...
Beuchamp269...
Bevan V5
Bevans269...
Bevins269...
Bevridge V4
Bevridge269...
Bewar269...
Bexwick269...
Mc Bey269...
Bhaday259
Bibliogr'phy V2
Bicker269...
Bickers269...
Bickerstaff22
Bickerstaff269...
Bickerstaffe269...
Bickerstay269...
Bickerton269...
Bierast269...
Bierne V3
(o) Bierne12,25,28
O' Bierne269...
(o) Bierne28
Big269...
Big Bigg V3
Big(g)18
Biger22
Bigg V2
Biggane269...
Biggar22,133
Bigge18
Biggedon269...
Bigger22
Bigger269...
Biggerstaff269...
Biggins269...
(o) Biggins18,22
Biggs V3
Biglean269...
Bigly19
Bigo269...
De Bigods22
Bigoe V3
Bigoe269...
Bilder V5
Biles V4
Bill V4
Bill23
Billery23
Billigam269...
Billings V5
Billingsley269...
Billinsley269...
Billkinton V4
Billkinton269...
O' Billraidhe V3
O' Billry V3
O Billry23
O' Billry Bilrey V5
M' Bin269...
Binane V2
Binane269...
Binch(e)y22
Binchy V4
Binden V3
Bindon V3
Bindon V5
Bindon23
Bindon269...
Bingham V2
Bingham V3
Bingham13
Bingham269...
Bingley269...
Birch V3
Birch269...
Bird V4
Bird V5
Bird155,209
Bird269...
Birel23
Birford269...
Birkett269...
Birkey269...
Birmingham V4
Birmingham V5
Birmingham14
Birmingham269...
Birmingham V2

V2 = Families of Co. Kerry **V3** = Families of Co. Clare **V4** = Families of Co. Cork **V5** = Families of Co. Limerick

Birn 269...
Birne 269...
O' Birne 269...
Birney 269...
Mac Birney **V2**
Mc Birney 269...
Birnie 13
Birrell 23
Birrin 269...
Birth Index **V3**
Birtles 269...
Bishop 269...
Bishopp 269...
Bisse 269...
Bissett 23
Bissett 269...
Blacagh 15
Blacagh 269...
Blacer 269...
Blachford 269...
Black **V4**
Black 14,155
Black 269...
Black(h)all 23
Black Irish **V2**
Black & Tans **V2**
Blackall **V3**
Blackand 269...
Blackburn 269...
Blacken 269...
Blackender 269...
Blacker **V2**
Blacker 14
Blacker, St. **V2**
Blackhall **V3**
Blackhall **V5**
Blackhall 269...
Blackham 269...
Blackmore 269...
Blacknell 269...
Blackney 23
Blackstock 269...
Blackwell **V3**
Blackwell **V4**
Blackwell 24
Blackwell 269...
Blackwood **V2**
Blackwood 24
Blackwood 269...
Bladen 269...
(de) Blagd **V2**
Blagrafe **V3**
Blagrave **V3**
Blagrofe **V3**
Blagrove **V3**
Blain 269...
Blair 269...
Blair(e) 24
Blaire 269...
Blak(e)ney 15,23
Blake **V2**
Blake **V3**
Blake **V4**
Blake 14,15
Blake 269...
Blakeney **V5**
Blaker 14
Blakes 15
Blakes 269...
Blakney 269...
Blakston **V4**
Blakston 269...
Blan(e)y 16
Blanch 24
Blanch 269...
Blanchett **V4**
Blanchett 269...
De Blancheville 24
Blanchfield 24
Blanchfield 269...
Blanchvill 269...
Bland **V2**
Bland **V5**
Bland 15
Bland Arms **V2**
Bland, Eliz. **V2**
Blaney **V4**
Blaney **V5**
Blaney 269...
Blanford **V4**
Blanford 269...
Blankenship **V3**
Blankinshop **V3**
Blannerhaset 269..
Blany 269...
Blare 24
Blare 269...
Blarney **V4**
Blatchford **V4**
Blatchford 269...
Blayney 16
Bleach 15
Bleach 269...
Bleahan 24
Bleak 269...
Bleakley 269...
Bleeheen 24
Bleeks 269...
Bleheen 269...
Blehein 269...
Blehein(e) 24
Bleheine 269...
Blen'erhas'et **V2**
Blend 15
Blenerhaset 16,34
Blenerhasset 269...
Blenerhassett 269..
Blenkinsop **V3**
Blenner 145
Blennerhaset 269..
Blennerhasse **V5**
Bleuer Hasset 269..
Bleuer Hasset 269..
Bleverhassett 269..
Blewitt 24
Bligh 16
Bligh 269...
Bligh 269...
Bloet, P. **V2**
Blomefield 269...
Blomfield 269...
Blond **V5**
Blondell **V5**
Blong 269...
Blood **V3**
Blood 17
Blood Arms **V3**
Bloomer **V2**
Bloomer 123
Bloomer 269...
Bloud 17
Bloud 269...
Blouk 15
Blouk 269...
Blount **V2**
Blount 269...
Blowick 15
Blowick 269...
Bluet(t) 24
Bluett **V4**
Bluett **V5**
Bluett 269...
Blundel 269...
Blundel(l) 24
Blundell **V2**
Blundell 269...
Blunden 24
Blunden 269...
Blundon 24
Blunt 269...
Blunte 34
Blythe **V2**
Boage 269...
Boaghan 269...
Boake **V2**
Boal 269...
Boal(e) 19,24
Boale 269...
Boar 269...
Bobanizer 205
Bobington **V4**
Bochier 155
Bockocan 269...
Bocully 269...
Bod(e)kin 26
Bodel 269...
Bodeley 269...
Bodell 269...
Bodely 269...
(o) Boden 25
Bodge 269...
Boding 269...
Bodington 269...
Bodkin **V3**
Bodkin 269...
Bodle 269...
Bodley **V4**
Boe 269...
Boe 27
O' Boe 269...
Boeman **V5**
Boeman 269...
Boffy 155
Bog 19
Bog 269...
Bogan 269...
(o) Bogan 24
Bogas 34
Boggan 24
Boggin 24
Boghan 24
Boghan 269...
Boghelly **V4**
O Boghelly **V4**
O' Boghelly 269...
Boghley **V4**
Bogue **V4**
Bogue **V4**
Bogue 269...
Bogue(s) 26
Bohan **V4**
Bohan 269...
Bohan(e) 27
Bohanan 269...
Bohane **V4**
Bohane 269...
Bohanna 269...
Bohannon 269...
Bohelly 23
Bohelly 269...
Bohilly **V4**
Bohunnan 269...
Boice 31
Boid 19
Boide 269...
Boigd **V4**
O Boigd **V4**
O' Boigd 269...
Boil **V4**
Boil 19
Boil 269...
Bois 155
Boisrond **V4**
Bolan **V3**
Bolan 269...
O Bolan(d) 17
Boland **V2**
Boland **V3**
Boland 269...
O Bolchan 29
Boldrick 14
Bole 269...
Bole(s) 19,24
Boler 27
Boles 269...
Bolger **V2**
Bolger **V3**
Bolger 269...
(o) Bolger 26
Bolgier **V3**
Bollard 24
Bollard 269...
Bolles 269...
(de) Bolltun **V2**
Bolmer **V5**
Bolster **V2**
Bolster **V4**
Bolster 26
Bolten **V3**
Bolten 17
Bolton **V2**
Bolton **V3**
Bolton 17
Bomford 18
Bomus 269...
Bon(n)ar 26,57,17
Bon(n)er 26
Bona **V2**
Bonar **V5**
Bonar 269...
Bonas(s) 26
Bonbounous **V4**
Bond 269...
Bonefield 26
Boner 269...
Bones 269...
Bonfield **V3**
Bonfield **V5**
Bonfield 26
Bonguelimi **V2**
Bonham **V2**
Bonison 269...
Bonnaire 26
Bonner 269...
De Bonneville 26
Bonney **V2**
Bonnfield 26
Bonny 269...
Bonole 269...
Bonorly 269...
Bonynge 18
Boohier **V4**
Boohier 269...
Bookby 269...
Bookeley 269...
Booker 269...
Boon **V3**
Boone **V3**
Boore **V5**
Boore 269...
Boorke 269...
Booth 269...
Bor 26
Bor(r)owes 26
Bordell **V2**
Bordell **V2**
Borden 269...
Boreham **V2**
Boreland 19
Boreland 269...
Boreman **V2**
Borne 269...
Boroimhe, **V3**
Borough **V3**
Borr 269...
Borston 269...
Boru **V3**
Boru, Brian **V2**
Boru, Brian **V4**
Bostick 17
Bostock 17
Boston, Ma. **V2**
Boswel 269...
Boswell **V5**
Bothwell 25
Bothwell 269...
Bothwick **V2**
Boucher 26
Boucher 269...
Bouchier **V3**
Boudakyn 26
Bouden 25
Boudler 269...
Boudon 25
Boudran 27
O' Bough 27
Boughane **V4**
Boughane 269...
Boughilie **V4**
Boughill **V4**
Boughla **V4**
Boughla 23
Boughla 269...
Bouhilly 269...
Bould 269...
Bouldger **V2**
Boulsfeld 269...
Boulton 269...
Bounce **V2**
Bound **V5**
Bound 269...
Boundes **V2**
Bourchier **V5**
Bourchier 26
Bourden 269...
Bourgeais 155
Bourgh **V2**
Bourk **V3**
Bourk **V4**
Bourk 269...
Bourke **V2**
Bourke **V3**
Bourke **V4**
Bourke **V5**
Bourke 25
Bourke 269...
Bourke Burke **V3**
Bourke, Maj. **V2**
Bourne **V3**
Boursin **V2**
Bouster 269...

Bovenizer **V2**
Bovinger205
Bowden25
Bowden269...
Bowdern27
Bowdran **V4**
Bowdran269...
Bowdran27
Bowdren27
Bowe **V4**
Bowe269...
O Bowe **V4**
O' Bowe269...
(o) Bowe(s)27
Bowen **V2**
Bowen **V4**
Bowen18,205
Bowen269...
Bowen, **V2**
Bower **V2**
Bower155
Bower269...
Bowerman **V4**
Bowers **V5**
Bowers269...
Bowes269...
Bowland17
Bowler **V2**
Bowler269...
Bowler27
Bowles **V2**
Bowles **V4**
Bowles24
Bowles269...
Bowls269...
Bowman205
Bowman269...
Bownes269...
Bowreman **V4**
Bowreman269...
Bowy(e)r30
Boxer155
Boxter269...
Boy **V2**
Boy **V3**
Boy269...
Boy31
Boyce269...
Boyce31
Boycot(t)33
Boycott **V4**
Boyd **V2**
Boyd **V4**
Boyd19,34
Boyd269...
O' Boyd269...
Boyde269...
Boye **V2**
Boyer155
Boyer269...
Boyes269...
Mc Boyheen269...
Boyl19
Boyl269...
Boylan **V2**
Boylan269...
O' Boylan269...
Boylan(d)19
Boyle **V2**
Boyle **V4**
Boyle269...
(o) Boyle19,24
O' Boyle269...
Boyle, Henry **V4**
Boyle, R. **V2**
Boyle, Sir R. **V4**
Boyles **V5**
Boyles269...
Boyn(e)20
Boyne269...
O' Boyns269...
(de) Boys(e)31,15
Boyse31
Boyton269...
(de) Boyton33
Brabant **V4**
Brabant269...
Brabazon20
Brabazon269...
Brabson269...
Brabzon269...
Brackane269...
Bracken269...
O Bracken29
Brackleyer **V2**
De Brackleyer **V2**
O' Bradain **V2**
Bradburn269...
Bradbury **V5**
Bradbury, J. **V2**
Bradden269...
(mac Bradey20
Bradford **V2**
Bradford **V5**
Bradhurst269...
Bradigan269...
(o) Bradl(e)y29
Bradle269...
Bradley **V2**
Bradley **V4**
Bradley269...
O Bradley **V4**
Bradly **V2**
Bradly **V4**
Bradly269...
Bradner22
Bradshaw **V2**
Bradshaw269...
Bradshaw29
Bradston **V4**
Bradston269...
Brady **V2**
Brady **V3**
Brady269...
Mac Brady **V5**
(mac Brady124
(mac Brady20,32
O' Brady269...
Brady, Wm. **V2**
Braedin269...
O Braein30
Brafield269...
Bragg269...
Braghall269...
Brahan **V5**
Brailey **V4**
Braily **V4**
Braily269...
Mac Brairty30
Brak(e)y34
Braken29
O' Brallaghan269...
Bramble **V4**
Bramble269...
Bramhall269...
Bramley **V5**
Bramley269...
Brampton269...
Bramston269...
Bramston34
Bramstone **V2**
Branach **V4**
Branagan269...
Branagh269...
Branan269...
Brandon **V2**
Brandon269...
Mac Brandon **V2**
Brandon, L. **V2**
Brangan269...
Branham269...
Braniff21
Braniff269...
Branigan34
Brankin269...
Branl(e)y34
Branley **V3**
Branly **V3**
Brannagh **V2**
Brannagh **V4**
Brannagh269...
Brannan21
Brannan269...
Brannelly34
Brannick269...
Brannie21
Brannie269...
Brannigan269...
O Brannigan34
Brannigin34
Brannock269...
Brannon269...
Bransfield **V4**
Bransfield269...
Branthwaite269...
Mac Braoin **V2**
O' Braoin **V2**
Brasier **V4**
Brasier21
Brasier269...
Brassel **V2**
Brassell269...
Brassell30
Brasseur155
Brassil269...
Brassil30
Brassill **V2**
Brassy155
Brathwait269...
Mc Bratney269...
Brattach **V4**
Brattach **V4**
Brattach **V5**
Bratty269...
Brauders269...
Brawne30
Brawnick269...
Bray269...
Bray30
Brayly **V4**
Brayly269...
Brayne269...
Braz(i)er21
O Braz(z)il30
Brazel30
Brazier **V4**
Brazier269...
Brazil **V3**
Brazil **V4**
Brazil **V5**
Brazil269...
Di Bre30
Breackan269...
Breadbeard **V4**
Breadbeard269...
Breadon269...
Break(e)y34
Mac Breandain **V2**
Brearely269...
Mac Brearty30
Mc Brearty269...
O' Breasail **V2**
Breatnach **V4**
Breckan269...
Bredan269...
(o) Bree30
Breedeth269...
Breeding269...
Breen **V2**
Breen **V4**
Breen269...
Breen30
O Breen **V4**
O' Breenan269...
O Breene **V2**
O' Breene269...
Breers269...
Breerton269...
Breerton31
Bregan **V4**
O Bregan **V4**
O Bregan30
O Bregan Imokilly **V4**
O Breghain **V4**
Brehan269...
Brehaney30
M' Breheney1,30
Breheny **V4**
Breheny269...
Brehony **V4**
Brehony269...
Brehony30
Mc Brehuny269...
Mc Brehuny30
O Brein21
O' Brein269...
Breislen31
Bremegham269...
Bremigam269...
Bremigan14
Bremmer **V2**
Bren269...
Brenagh **V2**
Brenagh **V4**
Brenagh269...
Brenan269...
Mc Brenan **V2**
O' Brenan **V2**
O' Brenan269...
Brenane269...
O Brenane **V2**
O' Brenane269...
Brendan, St. **V2**
Brennagh **V4**
Brennagh269...
Brennagh **V5**
Brennan **V2**
Brennan269...
O' Brennan **V2**
(o) Brennan21
Brennan, **V2**
Brennigan269...
Brenogh269...
Brenon21
Brenon269...
Brent269...
Brereton **V4**
Brereton **V4**
Brereton269...
Brereton31
Brerton269...
Bresland269...
Bresland31
Breslane269...
Breslane31
Breslaun269...
Breslaun31
Breslawn269...
Breslawn31
Breslen31
Breslin269...
O Breslin31
Bresnahan33
O Bressyl30
Brethower205
Bretleridge **V4**
Bretleridge269...
Breton155
Bretrage269...
Brett **V2**
Brett **V3**
Brett269...
Brett31
Brett, De **V2**
Brew **V2**
Brew **V3**
Brew269...
Brew32
Brewer **V2**
Brewster **V2**
Brewster **V4**
Brewster269...
Brewster, Sir **V2**
De Bri30
O' Briain **V2**
Brian **V3**
Brian **V5**
Brian269...
Mac Brian **V3**
Mc Brian **V5**
Mc Brian269...
O' Brian **V2**
O' Brian **V3**
O' Brian **V5**
O Brian21
O' Brian269...
Briane21
Briane269...
Bric **V4**
O' Bric **V2**
O Bric **V4**
O Bric30
Brice269...
Briceson33
Brick **V2**
Brick **V4**
Brick269...
Brick30
Brickain269...
Brickardick269...
Brickdall **V3**
Brickdall269...
Brickelsby269...
Bricklea **V4**
Brickley **V4**
Brickley269...
Brickley30
Mac Bride **V2**
Mac Bride269...
(mac Bride31
Mc Bride269...

Bridgal 269...
Bridgeman **V3**
Bridgeman 269...
Bridges **V2**
Bridges **V4**
Bridges **V5**
Bridget 269...
Bridgin 269...
Brien **V2**
Brien **V4**
Brien 269...
M' Brien 269...
Mc Brien 269...
O' Brien **V2**
O' Brien **V3**
O Brien **V4**
O Brien **V5**
O Brien 21
O' Brien 269...
O' Brien Arms **V3**
O' Brien Births **V3**
O Brien Clare **V4**
O' Brien, Donal **V2**
Brien(e) 30
O' Brien In **V3**
O' Brien, Kings **V3**
O' Brien Of **V3**
Briene 269...
O' Briens **V3**
O Brigan **V4**
Brigdale **V3**
Brigdall 269...
Brigg 269...
Briggs 269...
Brighness 269...
Bright **V2**
Bright 269...
O' Brillaghan 269..
Brimage 14
Brimage 269...
Brimagum 14
Brimagum 269...
Brimingham 269...
Brimley 269...
Brimmagem 269...
Brimmigan 269...
Brin 269...
Mc Brin 269...
Brinagh **V2**
Brinagh 269...
Brinan 269...
Brinane 269...
Brine **V3**

Brine 269...
M' Brine **V5**
M' Brine 269...
O' Brine **V5**
O' Brine 269...
Brinegan 269...
Brinf 269...
Bringhurst 269...
Brinkl(e)y 22
Mac Brinn 34
Mc Brinn 269...
Brinne 269...
Brinsmeade 269...
Briody **V3**
Briody 269...
(o) Briody 20,32
(de) Briotun **V2**
Briscoe **V4**
Briscoe 32
O' Brislan 269...
O' Brislane 269...
Britain **V4**
Britain 31
O Britain **V4**
Mc Britany 269...
Briton 31
Britt 269...
(de) Britt **V2**
Brittaine 269...
Brittaine 31
Brittan 31
Brittas **V3**
Britton 269...
Britton 31,155
Briver 269...
Broadbeare 269...
Broadford **V3**
Broadhurst **V2**
Brocain **V4**
O Brocain **V4**
Brocas 32
Brock 129
Brock 269...
Brocke **V5**
Brocke 269...
Brocket 269...
Brocklesby **V4**
Brocklesby 269...
Brodbear 269...
Brodders 22
Brodders 269...
Broder **V2**
Broder **V4**

Broder **V5**
Broder 269...
Broder Arms **V2**
Broder(ick) **V4**
O Broder(ick) **V2**
O Broder(ick) **V4**
O Broder(ick) **V5**
O Broder(ick) 22
Broderick **V2**
Broderick **V4**
Broderick 22
Broderick 269...
Brodie 269...
Mac Brodie **V3**
Brodier 269...
Brodin **V3**
M' Brodin, Mac **V3**
O Brodir **V4**
O' Brodir 269...
Brodrick **V4**
Brodridge 269...
Brodston 269...
Brody **V3**
Brody 269...
Mac Brody **V3**
(mac Brody 32
Broe 269...
Broe 32
Brogan **V4**
Brogan 269...
O Brogan 32
Broghall 33
Broghane 269...
Broghe 32
Broghil 269...
Broghill **V4**
Broghill 269...
Brohale 33
Brohel 33
Brohy 269...
O' Broin **V2**
Brokas 32
Brokett **V4**
Brokett 269...
O Brolchain 29
Brolly 269...
Bromagen 269...
Bromfield 269...
Bromley **V5**
Bromloe 269...
Bromwel 269...
Bromwell 269...
Broncar **V2**

Bronig **V4**
Bronte 217
Bronthropt 269...
Broo 32
Brooder 22
Brooder 269...
Brook **V4**
Brook 269...
Brook(e)(s) 32
Brooke **V2**
Brooke **V4**
Brookes **V2**
Brookes **V4**
Brookes 269...
Brookin **V4**
Brookin 269...
Brooking 269...
Brooks **V4**
Brooks 269...
Broothers 269...
Brophy 269...
Brophy 33
Brosnahan 33
O' Brosnahan **V2**
Brosnan **V2**
Brosnan 269...
Brosnan **V5**
Brosnan(e) 33
Brothel 33
Brothers 22
Brothers 269...
M' Broudin **V3**
Mac Broudin 33
Brough **V4**
Broughall 269...
Broughall 33
Broughill 269...
Broughill 33
Broun 269...
Broune 22
Broune 269...
Browder 269...
Brown **V2**
Brown **V3**
Brown **V4**
Brown 155
Brown 269...
Brown(e) 22,34
Browne **V2**
Browne **V3**
Browne **V4**
Browne **V5**
Browne 269...

Browne 269...
Browne, A. **V2**
Browne Arms **V3**
Browne, J. **V2**
Browne, N. **V2**
Browne, V. **V2**
Brownes **V2**
Browning **V3**
Browning **V4**
Browning **V5**
Browning 269...
Brownlee 269...
Brownlee 32
Brownlow 269...
Brownlowe 32,34
Brownrigg **V5**
Browns **V3**
Browster 269...
O' Bruadair **V2**
Bruce, **V2**
Bruce **V4**
Bruce **V5**
Bruce 23
Bruce 269...
Bruder 269...
Brudher 269...
Bruen 269...
Mc Bruen **V4**
(o) Bruen 30,33
Bruerton 269...
Mc Bruine 269...
Bruister 269...
Brumigem 269...
Brumiger 269...
Brumley **V5**
Brumley 269...
Brummagen 269...
Brummagen 269...
Brunig. **V4**
Brunkar **V2**
Brunnocks 33
Brunty 269...
Bruodin **V3**
Mac Bruodin **V3**
Bruody **V3**
Bruody 269...
(de) Brus **V2**
De Bruth 32
Bruton **V2**
Bruton 269...
Bruttnell **V5**
Bruttnell 269...
De Bruys 23

Bryan **V2**
Bryan **V4**
Bryan 269...
Mac Bryan **V3**
Mac Bryan 269...
Mc Bryan **V5**
Mc Bryan 269...
O' Bryan **V2**
O' Bryan **V3**
O Bryan **V4**
O' Bryan **V5**
(o) Bryan 21,23
O' Bryan 269...
Bryan Brian **V4**
Bryane 269...
Bryans 269...
Bryant **V2**
Mc Bryd 269...
Bryde 269...
Mc Bryde 269...
Bryen **V5**
Bryen 269...
Mc Bryen **V2**
Mc Bryen **V5**
Mc Bryen 269...
O Bryen **V2**
O' Bryen **V3**
O Bryen **V4**
O' Bryen **V5**
O' Bryen 269...
Bryen Mc, O' **V3**
O Bryen, **V4**
Bryn 269...
O' Bryn 269...
Brynan 269...
O' Brynan 269...
Bryne 269...
Mc Bryne **V5**
Mc Bryne 269...
O' Bryne **V5**
O' Bryne 269...
Bryner 269...
Brynne 269...
Bryon 269...
O' Bryon 269...
Bryscoe 269...
Bryson 269...
Bryson 33
Bryttanie 269...
Brytten 269...
O' Buacalla **V2**
Buchanan 269...
Buchnan 269...

Buck 269...
Buck(e)ley 23
Buckarton 269...
Buckford **V2**
Buckingham **V5**
Buckles 269...
Buckley **V2**
Buckley **V4**
Buckley **V4**
Buckley **V5**
Buckley 269...
O Buckley **V4**
Buckly 269...
Bucks 269...
Budden **V3**
Budgens 269...
Budkin 26
Budran 27
Bueg 269...
Buey **V2**
Buggle(r) 33
Buggler **V3**
Buggy **V2**
O Buggy 33
Bugle(r) 33
Bugler **V3**
Buhilly **V4**
Buhilly 269...
O Buhilly 23
Buick 269...
Buie 269...
Buie 31
(de) Buitileir **V2**
Bulfin 33
Bulger **V3**
Bulger 269...
Buliner 269...
Bulkeley 23,24
Bulkeley 269...
Bulkelh 269...
Bulkely 269...
Bulkley 269...
Bull **V2**
Bull **V4**
Bull 269...
Bulla 269...
Bullard 24
Bullen **V4**
Bullenbrook 269...
Bullfin 33
Bullin 269...
Bullion 17,19
Bullion 269...

Bullman **V4**
Bullman269...
Bullock **V4**
Bullocke **V4**
Bullocke269...
Bulworthy269...
Bunberry24
Bunbury **V2**
Bunbury24
Bunbury269...
Bunce **V2**
Bunnion **V2**
Bunratty **V3**
Buntin(e)33
Bunting269...
Bunting33
Bunton33
Bunworth **V2**
Bunworth **V4**
Bunworth(e)33
Bunyan **V2**
Buo269...
Buo27
Buoige **V4**
Buoige269...
O Buoige **V4**
(o) Buoige26
O' Buoige269...
O Buoy **V4**
O' Buoy269...
(de) Burc **V2**
Burcell269...
Burchall269...
Burcham **V4**
Burcham **V4**
Burcham269...
Burchill **V2**
Burchill **V4**
Burchill269...
Burden **V2**
Burdet269...
Burdett **V3**
Burdett24
Burdit269...
Burdon **V4**
Burges **V5**
Burges269...
Burges(s)25,155
Burgess **V3**
Burgess269...
(de) Burgh25
Burghleys **V2**
(de) Burgos **V2**
Burgoyne **V5**
Burk **V3**
Burk **V4**
Burk269...
Burk(e)25
Burke **V2**
Burke **V3**
Burke **V4**
Burke269...
Burke Bourke **V5**
Burke, **V2**
Burke In **V3**
Burke, Sir **V2**
Burke's **V2**
Burker **V5**
Burker269...
Burkes **V3**
Burkett **V2**
Burly269...
Burn **V3**
Burn12,28,34
Burne269...
Burneham **V4**
Burneham269...
Burnell **V3**
Burnell **V4**
Burnell269...
Burnes269...
Burnet(t)32
Burnett269...
Burney269...
(mac Burney13,33
Mc Burney269...
Burnham **V2**
Burnham **V4**
Mac Burnie33
Burniston269...
Burns **V2**
Burns **V3**
Burns **V4**
Burns269...
(o) Burns12,25
Burns Of **V3**
Burnside269...
Burnside33
Burrage **V4**
Burrage269...
Burrel269...
Burrell269...
Burren269...
Burren **V2**
Burren, The **V3**
Burridge13
Burril269...
Burrill269...
Burroughes **V4**
Burroughes269...
Burroughs269...
Burrow(e)s26
Burrowes **V4**
Burrowes269...
Burrows **V4**
Burrows269...
Burscough **V2**
Bursted269...
Burt269...
Burtchael(l)26
Burten269...
Burton **V3**
Burton **V5**
Burton26
Burton269...
Burtsides269...
Burwell **V4**
Burwell269...
Bury **V3**
Bury **V4**
Bury **V5**
(de) Bury(e)27
Burye269...
Busbridg269...
Busbridge269...
Bushe27
Bushell269...
Busher34
Bustard269...
Buste(a)d34
Bustead **V2**
Bustead **V4**
Bustead269...
Busteed **V4**
Busteed269...
Busteed34
Busteed, **V2**
Buston269...
Butcher **V2**
Butcher155
Butcher Arms **V2**
Buthells269...
Butler **V2**
Butler **V3**
Butler **V4**
Butler269...
Butler27,34
Butler In **V3**
Butler, James **V2**
Butler-creagh **V3**
Buttamore34
Butter Port **V4**
Butterfield269...
Butterl(e)y34
Butterly **V2**
Butterly269...
Butterly, Lau. **V2**
Buttevant **V4**
Buttimer **V4**
Buttimer34
Buttivant, **V4**
Buttler **V5**
Buttler269...
Buttler27
Button269...
Buyllbreacki **V4**
Bwee269...
Bwee31
O Bwoeghele **V4**
Byers269...
Bynane **V2**
Byrce269...
Byrine269...
Byrne **V2**
Byrne **V4**
Byrne269...
Byrne269...
M' Byrne269...
Mc Byrne34
O' Byrne269...
Byrne, M.j. **V2**
O Byrne(s)12,34
O Byrne(s)25,28
Byron269...
Byron28,34
Byrt269...
Bysse269...
Mac Caba28
Mc Caba269...
Caball **V2**
Mac Cabe **V2**
Mac Cabe28
Mc Cabe269...
Mac Caddan29
Caddell15
Caddell269...
Cadden269...
(mac Cadden29
Cade **V2**
Cades **V2**
Cadgan **V2**
O' Cadhla **V3**
Cadie269...
Cadigan **V4**
Cadigan35
O' Cadla **V2**
Cadmore269...
Cadogan **V2**
Cadogan **V4**
Cadogan269...
Cadogan35
Cadogane **V4**
Cadwell269...
Cady **V5**
Mc Cae **V3**
Mc Cae269...
O Caelidh **V4**
Cafferky269...
Mc Cafferky36
Cafferty269...
Mac Cafferty **V2**
Mac Cafferty36
Mc Cafferty269...
Caffery269...
Mc Caffery269...
Mc Caffery269...
Caffrey269...
Mc Caffrey269...
M' Caffrey(s)36,41
Mc Caffry269...
Cagherty36
M' Cagherty269...
Mac Caghey44
Cagn(e)y35
Cagney **V2**
Cagney **V4**
O Cagney **V4**
Cagny **V4**
Cahalan **V4**
Cahalan(e)35
Cahalane **V2**
Cahalane **V4**
Cahalane269...
Cahan **V2**
Cahan **V3**
Cahan **V4**
Cahan269...
Mc Cahan **V3**
Mc Cahan269...
O' Cahan **V3**
O' Cahan269...
O Cahan(e)37,160
Cahane **V2**
Cahane **V3**
Cahane **V4**
Cahane269...
O Cahane **V2**
O' Cahane **V3**
O Cahane **V4**
O' Cahane **V5**
O' Cahane269...
Cahassy **V2**
Cahassy269...
O Cahassy44
Cahasy269...
Mac Cahee44
Cahell269...
O Cahell **V4**
O' Cahell **V5**
O' Cahell269...
O Caheny35
Mac Caherty36
O Cahesey **V2**
O' Cahesey269...
Cahessy269...
O' Cahesy **V5**
O' Cahesy269...
(mac Cahey44
(mc) Cahil28
Cahill **V2**
Cahill **V3**
Cahill **V4**
Cahill269...
O' Cahill **V2**
O' Cahill **V3**
O' Cahill269...
(o) Cahill28
Cahill Loch **V4**
Cahillane35
Mc Cahon269...
Mc Cahon36
Cahoon269...
Mc Cahugh269...
Cahy203
Cahy269...
M' Cahy269...
Mac Cail146
Cain160
Cain269...
O' Cain **V2**
Cainan269...
Caine **V3**
Caine **V4**
Cairach **V2**
Cairdie269...
Mac Cairill172
Cairle172
Cairns269...
Cairns36,168
Calaghan35
O Calaghan **V4**
O' Calaghane269...
Calahan35
Calan36
O Calannains **V4**
Calcut **V3**
Calderwood269...
Calderwood36
Caldwell269...
Caldwell29
Calene **V3**
Calene269...
Calfe **V4**
Calfe269...
Calfer57
Calfhill41
Calhoun(e)48
Calhoune269...
California **V3**
Mc Call269...
Mc Call28,41
Mc Calla269...
Callaghan **V2**
Callaghan **V3**
Callaghan **V4**
Callaghan269...
O Callaghan **V4**
O' Callaghan269...
O' Callaghan269...
O Callaghan35
O' Callaghan **V3**
O' Callaghan, **V2**
O' Callaghan, **V2**
O Callaghan **V4**
Callaghanan269...
Callaghane **V3**
Callaghane **V4**
Callaghane269...
Mc Callaghane **V4**
Mc Callaghane269
O' Callaghane **V3**
O Callaghane **V4**
O' Callaghane269..
Callagher269...
Callahan **V3**
Callahan **V4**
Callahan35
O Callahane **V4**
O' Callahane269...
O' Callahane **V5**
Callan269...

V2 = Families of Co. Kerry **V3** = Families of Co. Clare **V4** = Families of Co. Cork **V5** = Families of Co. Limerick

Mc Callan 269...
(mc) Callan 36,48
O' Callan 269...
Callan, Battle **V4**
O' Callanain **V2**
Callanan **V4**
Callanan 269...
Callanan 37
O Callanan **V4**
Callanane **V4**
Callanane 269...
O' Callane 269...
Callcatt 269...
Mc Callely 269...
Callen 269...
Callen 36
Callen Glen **V2**
Mac Callenan 37
Callenen 37
Mac Callery 36
Callihan 35
Callin 269...
Callin 36
Mc Callin 269...
Callina 269...
Callinan **V3**
Callinan **V4**
Callinan 269...
O Callinan **V4**
O Callinan(e) 37
Callinane **V2**
Callinane **V3**
Callinane 269...
Mc Callion 269...
Mc Callion 36
M' Callister 269...
Mac Callister 7
Mc Callnon 269...
Mc Callon 36
Callopy 58
Callues **V2**
Mc Cally 269...
O' Cally 269...
Mac Calmont 35
Mc Calmont 269...
Calmy 269...
Calnan 269...
Calnan 37
Mac Calshender 3
Mc Calshender 269.
Mc Calshinder 269.
Calthorpe 269...
Calthorpe 36
Calthrop 36
Calverly **V2**
Calvert 269...
Calvert 34
Calvey 269...
Mc Calvey 171
Calvill 269...
Calwell 269...
Calwell 29
Cambbell 269...
Cambell 39
Cambier 269...
Cambrensis **V2**
Cambridge **V2**
Cambridge **V4**
Cambridge 269...
M' Cambridge 38
Mac Cambridge **V4**
Mc Cambridge 269.
Camby 269...
Camden **V3**
Cameron **V2**
Cameron 269...
Camine 269...
Mc Camley 269...
Camp **V2**
Camp 269...
Camp 39
Campbell **V2**
Campbell 269...
Campbell 39
Mc Campbell 269..
Campe **V2**
Campel 269...
Campell 269...
Campian 269...
Campian 40
Campion **V4**
Campion 269...
Campion 40
Cample 39
Campsie 269...
Campyon 40
Mac Can 269...
Mc Can 269...
Canaan 269...
Canada **V3**
Canada **V4**
Canada **V3**
Canada **V2**
Canally 269...
Mc Canan 269...
O' Canan 269...
Canavan 269...
Canavan 38
Canaven 38
Canavon 38
Candit 269...
Mac Candless 38
Mc Candless 269...
Mc Candlish 38
Cane **V4**
Cane 160
Mc Cane 269...
Canfield 269...
Canlon **V2**
Mac Cann **V2**
Mac Cann **V5**
Mc Cann **V3**
Mc Cann 269...
(mc) Cann 35,117
Mac Canna **V2**
Mac Canna 35
Cannady **V4**
Cannan 269...
Cannan 40,118
O' Cannan 269...
Mc Canne 269...
Cannell **V2**
Canniff **V4**
Canniff 269...
O Canniff **V4**
Canniffe **V4**
O Canniffe **V4**
O' Canniffe 269...
Canning 269...
Canning 39
Cannon 269...
Mac Cannon 40,11
O' Cannon 269...
O Cannon 40
Cannovan **V3**
Cannovane **V3**
(de) Canntual **V2**
Canny **V3**
Canny **V5**
Canny 269...
(mac Canny 35,45
(o) Canny 45
Canon 269...
Canovane **V3**
Canovane 269...
(de) Cantelowe **V2**
(de) Cantelupe **V2**
Cantey **V4**
Cantey 46
Cantie **V4**
Cantie **V4**
Cantie 269...
Cantillon **V2**
Cantillon **V3**
Cantillon **V5**
Cantillon 45
(de) Cantillon **V2**
Cantillon **V2**
Cantillons **V2**
Cantlin 45
Cantlon **V2**
Cantlon 45
(de) Cantlon's **V2**
Canton **V4**
Cantrel **V5**
Cantrell 269...
Cantrell 39
Cantuncon **V4**
Cantwell **V2**
Cantwell **V3**
Cantwell **V5**
Cantwell 269...
Cantwell 41
Canty **V2**
Canty **V4**
Canty **V5**
Canty 269...
Canty 46
Canty Cantie **V4**
Canughan 269...
Canvery 70
O' Caoimh **V2**
O Caoimh **V4**
O' Caomain **V2**
Caorish 269...
Cap'an'cushy **V2**
Cap'anacos' **V2**
Capel **V3**
Capell **V3**
(de) Capella **V2**
Capelman **V3**
Capels 46
Caple **V3**
Caple **V4**
Caple 269...
Capleman **V3**
Capleman 269...
Caplice 46
Caplise 46
Cappa Castle **V3**
Cappacke **V4**
Cappacke **V4**
Cappacke 269...
Cappel **V3**
Cappelman **V3**
Capple **V4**
Capples 269...
Capples 46
Capplis **V4**
Capplis 46
Cappocke 269...
Car 170
Caraher 269...
Caraher 43
Carberry 269...
Carberry 36
Carbery 269...
Carbry **V4**
Carbry 36
O Carbry **V4**
O' Carbry 269...
Carby **V4**
Carby 269...
Card 269...
Mc Cardell 269...
Carden 36
Cardiff 269...
Cardle 269...
Mac Cardle 11
Mc Cardle 269...
Cardwell 269...
Cardwell 46
Cardyff 269...
Care 42
Mac Carehir 43
Carew **V2**
Carew **V4**
Carew **V5**
Carew 269...
Carew 41
(de) Carew, Wm. **V2**
Carewe **V4**
Carews **V2**
Carey **V2**
Carey **V4**
Carey 269...
Mc Carey 269...
Mc Carey 37
O Carey 37
Carfelott 269...
Cargan 269...
Cargy 269...
Carha 269...
Carhoo **V2**
Carie 269...
Carie 37
Carish **V2**
Carlan 269...
Carlan(d) 41
Carland 269...
Carleton **V3**
Carleton **V4**
Carleton 269...
Carleton 38,42
Carley 269...
Carlin 269...
(o) Carlin 41
Carlisle 269...
Carlton **V3**
Carlton 38
Carmedy 41
Carmichael 269...
Carmick 269...
Carmody **V2**
Carmody **V3**
Carmody **V5**
Carmody 269...
Carmody 41
O' Carmody **V3**
(m') Carn(e)y 46,16
Carnahan 269...
Carne 269...
Carnellisson **V3**
Carnett **V4**
Carney **V2**
Carney **V3**
Carney 269...
Mc Carney 269...
O' Carney 269...
Carns 269...
Carny **V4**
Carny 269...
O' Carny 269...
(o) Carol 38,42
Carolan 269...
Carolan 41
Caroll 269...
Caroll 38,46
Mac Caron 46
Carpenter **V2**
Carpenter **V5**
Carpenter 269...
Carr **V2**
Carr **V3**
Carr **V4**
Carr **V5**
Carr 269...
O' Carr 269...
(o) Carr 42,170
O' Carra **V2**
Carragher 43
Carraher 269...
(m') Carraher 43
Carran 269...
Mc Carran 269...
O' Carran 269...
Carrane 269...
O' Carrane 269...
Carre 269...
Carrell 269...
Carren 269...
Mc Carren 46
Mc Carrey 269...
Carrick **V2**
Carrick 269...
Carrick 46
Carricke 269...
Carrig **V2**
Mc Carrig 46
Carrig-a- **V2**
Carrigaholt **V3**
Carrigan **V2**
Carrigan 269...
Carrigan 54,171
Carrigg **V3**
Carrique **V2**
Carrol 38,46
O Carrol, **V3**
Carrolan 269...
Carrolan 42
Carroll **V3**
Carroll **V4**
Carroll **V5**
Carroll 269...
(m') Carroll 38,46
Mc Carroll 269...
O' Carroll **V2**
O Carroll **V4**
O' Carroll **V5**
O' Carroll 269...
O Carroll 38
O Carroll Ely **V4**
O' Carroll **V2**
Carroll Of **V3**
Carrollan 42
Carrolly 38
Mc Carroly 269...
Carron 269...
Mc Carron 269...
Mc Carron 46
Carrothers 47

O' Carrull **V3**
O' Carrull **V5**
O' Carrull269...
(de) Carrun **V2**
Carruthers269...
Carruthers47
Carry269...
Carry42
Mc Carry269...
Carson **V2**
Carson **V5**
Carson269...
Carson42
Cart269...
Mc Cart269...
Cartan269...
(mac Cartan38
Mc Cartan269...
Carten269...
Mc Carten269...
Carter **V2**
Carter **V3**
Carter **V5**
Carter269...
Carter39
Mc Carter269...
Carterett **V2**
Cartey **V4**
Mc Cartey269...
Carther **V2**
Carther269...
Carthey **V4**
Carthey269...
Mc Carthey **V4**
Mc Carthey269...
Mc Carthie **V4**
Carthy **V2**
Carthy **V3**
Carthy **V4**
Carthy269...
Mac Carthy **V2**
Mac Carthy **V4**
Mc Carthy **V2**
Mc Carthy **V3**
Mc Carthy **V4**
Mc Carthy **V5**
Mc Carthy269...
(mc) Carthy39,43
O' Carthy **V3**
O Carthy **V4**
O' Carthy269...
Mac Carthy & **V2**
Mac Carthy Mor **V4**
Mc Carthy Mor **V2**
Carthy Oge **V4**
Carthy Oge269...
Mac Carthys **V2**
Cartie **V4**
Mc Cartie **V4**
Mc Cartie269...
Mac Cartie **V2**
Mac Cartie Of **V2**
Mc Cartie **V4**
Mac Carties **V2**
Cartin269...
Cartmell47
Cartmill269...
Cartmill47
Mc Cartn(e)y39
Cartney **V4**
Mc Cartney **V3**
Mc Cartney **V4**
Mc Cartney **V5**
Mc Cartney269...
Carton269...
Mac Carton38
Mc Carton269...
Cartright **V4**
Cartwright **V4**
Cartwright269...
Carty **V4**
Carty **V5**
Carty269...
Mc Carty **V4**
Mc Carty269...
Mc Carty43
O Carty **V4**
(o) Carty39,43
Carty Of **V3**
Mac Carty Of **V2**
Cartye **V4**
Mc Cartye **V4**
Caruth47
Mc Carvey269...
Carvill269...
Mac Carvill38
Carville269...
Carvin269...
Carway269...
Carwell269...
Mc Carwell269...
Cary **V2**
Cary269...
Cary37
Casaday40
Casement **V5**
Casement40
Casey **V2**
Casey **V3**
Casey **V4**
Casey **V5**
Casey269...
Mac Casey44
O' Casey **V2**
O' Casey **V3**
O Casey **V4**
O Casey **V5**
(o) Casey44
Casey & **V3**
O Casey Mitchelstown **V4**
Cash269...
O Cashea, **V3**
O' Cashedy269...
Casheen **V4**
Cashel **V3**
Cashel **V4**
Cashen42
Casheran **V4**
Cashin269...
Cashin(e)42
Cashman **V4**
Cashman **V5**
Cashman269...
Cashman43
Casidy40
Casie **V5**
Casie269...
Caskey269...
(mc) Caskey61
M' Caskie61
Caskin45
Casky61
Mc Caslan269...
Casley269...
Casley40
Mac Casmond(e)40
Cassadie269...
O' Cassady269...
Cassan40
Cassedy269...
Cassedy40
Cassells269...
Casserl(e)y44
Casserly269...
Cassey **V3**
Cassey **V5**
Cassey269...
O Cassid(a)y40
Cassidy269...
O' Cassidy **V3**
O' Cassidy269...
Cassilly **V4**
Cassin269...
Cassy **V3**
Cassy269...
O' Cassydy269...
Mc Cassye **V3**
Mc Cassye269...
Castello269...
Mac Castguile269.
Mac Castlan269...
Castle269...
Castle **V2**
Castle Cor **V2**
Castle Drum **V2**
Castle Forbes **V2**
Castle **V2**
Castle Lyons **V2**
Castle Mac- **V2**
Castle **V2**
Castle Maine **V2**
Castle Mayne **V2**
Castlemore **V4**
Castlequin **V2**
Castles40
Castles In **V4**
Castles **V3**
Casy **V3**
Casy **V5**
Casy269...
O' Casy **V5**
O' Casy269...
O' Catain **V2**
O' Catasaig **V2**
Catchcart269...
Catchcartt269...
Catelline52
Catelyn52
O' Cathaill **V3**
Cathal **V3**
Cathcart269...
Cather269...
Catherwood269...
Catherwood36
Mac Catigan46
Catlin52
Mc Cato **V5**
Mc Cato269...
O' Cato269...
O Cattely119
Cattigan46
Cattle **V4**
Cattle269...
Caufield41
Mc Caughan269...
Mc Caughan46
O' Caughan269...
M' Caugherty36,43
Mc Caugherty269..
Caughey269...
Mac Caughey44
Mc Caughey269...
Mc Caughin269...
Mc Caughley269...
Caughy203
Caughy269...
Mac Caul135
Mc Caul269...
M' Caulay269...
Cauldfield41
Cauldron269...
Cauley6,63
Mac Cauley **V2**
Mc Cauley269...
Caulfield269...
M' Caulfield269...
(m') Caulfield41
Caulfield, Dr. **V4**
Caulin269...
Caunagh269...
De Caunteton49
De Cauntincton **V4**
Caunton **V4**
Causabon **V4**
Causgrove48
Mc Causland269...
Mc Causland41
Cavan **V2**
Cavan269...
Mac Cavana47
Cavanagh **V2**
Cavanagh160
Cavanagh269...
Mc Cavanagh269..
Cavenagh269...
Cavenah269...
Caveny47
Mc Cavill269...
Mac Cavina47
Cavish148
Cavish269...
Mc Cavish269...
Mac Cavock77
Mc Caw269...
Mc Cawel269...
Cawell269...
Mac Cawell41
Mc Cawell269...
Cawfield269...
Cawfield41
Cawldwell29
Mc Cawle269...
Cawley269...
M' Cawley269...
Mac Cawley63
O Cawley63
Cawlin269...
Mc Cawly269...
Cawsy269...
Caxon **V2**
Mc Cay **V3**
Mc Cay269...
O' Ceadagain **V2**
O' Ceadfadha **V3**
O' Cearnaig **V2**
Cearnes269...
Cecil **V2**
Ceileachair **V2**
Ceilor **V2**
O' Cein **V2**
O' Ceirise **V2**
O' Ceitearnaig **V2**
O Cennagain **V4**
Cereighton269...
Certaine269...
Chabner269...
Chadwick **V5**
Chadwick269...
Chaf(f)y47
Chafe269...
Chaffee47
Chafine269...
Chaigneau **V4**
Chainey48
Challenor269...
Chalmers269...
Chamberlain **V3**
Chamberlain45
Chamberlayn45
Chamberlin269...
Chamberline **V5**
Chamberline269...
Chamberlyn269...
Chambers **V2**
Chambers **V3**
Chambers **V4**
Chambers **V4**
Chambers269...
Chambers42
Chambre269...
Chambres42
Chamney42
Champ **V2**
Champines269...
Champion **V2**
Champion40
Chandler269...
Chandley **V2**
Chaney **V4**
Chaney269...
Chant **V2**
Chaoilli **V4**
Chaplin **V3**
Chapling **V3**
Chapman **V2**
Chapman **V5**
Chapman269...
Chappell **V2**
Chappell269...
Chapuis155
Charles269...
Charleton269...
Charley42
Charlie42
Charlton269...
Charly42
Charters269...
Charthy269...
Chartres **V4**
Chartres269...
Mc Charty **V4**
Chase **V4**
Chase **V5**
Chatterton **V4**
Chearneley269...
Cheasty48
Cheevers269...
Cheevers43,48
Cheke **V2**
Chelling269...
Cheneing269...
Chenevix **V3**
Cheney **V4**
Cheney48,49
Cherry **V5**
Cherry269...
Cherry47
Chesire269...
Cheslin269...
Chesnaye49
M' Chesney48,49

V2 = Families of Co. Kerry **V3** = Families of Co. Clare **V4** = Families of Co. Cork **V5** = Families of Co. Limerick

Chesterfield, **V2**
Chesterman **V5**
Chesterman269...
Chesters **V2**
Chestnut **V2**
Cheston **V2**
Chettle **V4**
Chettle269...
Chetwood **V2**
Cheurs269...
Chevers269...
Chevers43
Cheyne269...
Mc Cheyne269...
Cheyney48
Chianaig **V4**
Chicago, Il. **V2**
Chicester269...
Chichester43
Chichister269...
Chidleigh **V4**
Chidleigh269...
Chidley **V4**
Chifl(e)y49
Chillingwort 269..
Chilngswort 269...
Chilton269...
Chinnery **V3**
Chinnery **V4**
Chinnery **V5**
Chinnery52
Chisel269...
Chism269...
Chisom269...
Chissell269...
Choiseul269...
Cholmain **V4**
Cholmondele **V4**
Cholmondele **V5**
Choun269...
Chrisholm **V2**
Chrismas269...
Christal69
Christian **V2**
Christian269...
Christie269...
Christie49
Christison **V2**
Christmas269...
Christopher **V4**
Christopher **V4**
Christopher269...
Christopher269...
Christopher49
Christy269...
Christy49
Church **V2**
Church **V3**
Church **V4**
Church269...
Church51
Church Rep. **V2**
Chuse **V2**
Chute **V2**
Chute, Capt. **V2**
Chute, Dan'l **V2**
Chute, Rev. **V2**
Chute, Wm. **V2**
Chyttwood269...
O Ciaran Imokilly **V4**
O' Ciarda **V2**
Ciarraige, **V2**
Cicill **V2**
Cicill, John **V2**
Mc Ciltry269...
O Cindergain **V3**
Mac Cineait **V2**
Cineal **V3**
Cinel **V2**
Cingen269...
Civerac, **V2**
Claff(e)y49
Mc Clafferty269...
Claffey269...
Clahane269...
Claiborne53
Clairborne53
Clairke44
Mc Clamon269...
Clan An **V3**
Clan Cashel **V2**
Clan Cian **V4**
Clan Conaire **V2**
Clan Cuilean **V3**
Clan Culein **V3**
Clan Dermot **V3**
Clan Fergail **V2**
Clan Lorcain **V3**
Clan- **V2**
Clan Turlogh **V3**
Clanawley **V4**
Clancarthie **V4**
Clancartie **V4**
Clanchie **V3**
Mc Clanchie **V3**
Mc Clanchie269...
Clanchy **V3**
Clanchy **V4**
Clanchy269...
Clanchy43
O' Clanchy **V3**
O Clanchy **V4**
O' Clanchy **V5**
Clancy **V2**
Clancy **V3**
Clancy **V4**
Clancy **V5**
Clancy269...
Mac Clancy **V2**
Mac Clancy **V3**
Mac Clancy **V5**
Mac Clancy43
Clancy **V3**
Mac Clancys **V3**
Clandeboys **V2**
Clandenan **V2**
Clangibbon **V2**
Clanhy269...
Clanmaurice **V2**
Clansy269...
Clansy43
Clapen34
Clapham269...
Claphame34
Clapman **V2**
Claras **V3**
Clare **V3**
Clare269...
De Clare **V3**
De Clare **V5**
(de) Clare34,44
Clare Castle **V3**
Clare Town **V3**
Clare-surname **V3**
Clarey **V3**
Claridge **V2**
Clark **V3**
Clark **V4**
Clark269...
Clark(e)44,45
Clarke **V2**
Clarke **V3**
Clarke **V4**
Clarke269...
Clarkins269...
Clarkins44
Clarkson269...
Mac Clarnon176
Mc Clarnon269...
Clary **V3**
Clary269...
Claskey269...
Mc Clatchey269...
Mc Clatty269...
Mc Claue269...
Mc Clave269...
Claveen269...
Claveen52
Clavin52
Clay **V4**
Clay269...
Mc Clay269...
Claybrook269...
Claybrooke269...
Claypoole269...
Clayton **V2**
Clayton **V4**
Clayton269...
Clayton52
Clea **V4**
Clea269...
Cleabear269...
Cleaburne **V4**
Mc Clealand269...
Mc Clean269...
Mc Clean52
Clear269...
Cleare269...
Cleark269...
Clearke269...
Cleary **V2**
Cleary **V3**
Cleary **V4**
Cleary **V5**
Cleary269...
(mac Cleary44,45
Mc Cleary **V3**
(de) Cleatun **V2**
Cleborne 53
Cleburne **V4**
Cleburne **V5**
Mc Cleen52
Cleene269...
Cleere269...
Cleery45
Mc Cleery269...
O' Cleery269...
Clegg **V2**
Clegg269...
Clein **V5**
O' Cleirig **V2**
Cleland269...
Mc Cleland269...
Mac Clelland53
Mc Clelland269...
Clemens269...
Clemens44
Clement269...
Mc Clement269...
Mac Clement(s)44
Clements **V4**
Clements269...
Clenaghan269...
Mc Clenaghan269.
Clench(e)53
Clendinning269...
Clenesha **V2**
Clenett **V3**
O' Clenican269...
Clere269...
O' Cleregan269...
Clerian52
O' Clerian269...
O' Clerican269...
O' Clerigan269...
O' Clerikan269...
Clerk269...
Clerk Clarke **V4**
O' Clerkan269...
Clerke **V4**
Clerke269...
Clerke44
Clerken45
Clerkin269...
Clerkin44
O' Clerkin **V3**
Mc Clernon269...
Clery **V4**
Clery269...
O Clery **V4**
O Clery **V5**
O' Clery269...
O Clery45
Cleryan269...
O Cleryxx **V4**
Clibborn53
Cliborne53
Cliburne **V4**
Cliburne269...
Cliff269...
Cliff(e)45,53
Mac Clifferty52
Clifford **V2**
Clifford **V3**
Clifford **V4**
Clifford269...
Clifford53
Clifton **V2**
Clifton269...
Clignett **V3**
M' Climond269...
Clin54
Clinch269...
Clinche(y)53
Cline269...
Cline54
Clint269...
Mac Clintock **V2**
Mc Clintock269...
Mc Clintock45
Clinton **V5**
Clinton269...
Clinton52
Clisham53
Clitterdy269...
Cloffy269...
O Cloghessy54
Cloghessy, **V3**
De Cloghinagh **V4**
Cloherty269...
Cloherty53
Clohessy269...
O' Clohessy **V3**
O' Clohessy **V5**
O Clohessy54
(de) Clohuile **V2**
Clohulle **V2**
Clonderlaw **V3**
Clone269...
O' Clonine269...
Clonroad **V3**
Clontarf, **V2**
Clony269...
Cloon **V3**
Cloonan269...
Cloonan53
Cloonherna **V3**
Cloppam269...
(mc) Clor(e)y53,13
Mc Clory269...
Close269...
Close46
Mc Closker269...
Mc Closkey269...
Mc Closky55
O Clossey54
Clossick53
Clotherty **V2**
Clotworthy269...
Mc Cloud54
Mc Cloughry269...
Clouny269...
Clouon **V4**
Clovan62
O' Clovan269...
Clovane **V3**
Clovane269...
Cloven269...
Cloven62
Clowney269...
Clowny269...
Mc Cloy269...
Cloyne **V4**
Mc Clughan269...
Clugston269...
Clullen269...
O' Clumain **V2**
Clune269...
Clune53
Clune, **V3**
Mc Clung269...
Mac Clure **V2**
Mc Clure269...
Mc Clure54
M'c Clure House **V2**
Mc Clurg269...
Clusby125
Clusby269...
Clusker269...
Cluskey269...
Mac Cluskey **V2**
Mc Cluskey269...
Mc Cluskey55
M'c Cluskey **V2**
O Clussey54
Clutterbooke269..
Cluvane269...
Cluvane62
O' Cluvane **V5**
O' Cluvane269...
Clyde269...
Clyn(e)54
Clyne269...
Clynes54
Clyns269...
Mc Cnocgor **V2**
Cnogher269...
Mc Cnoghor **V4**
Mc Cnoghor269...
Cnoghor Oge **V4**
Cnoghor Oge269..

V2 = Families of Co. Kerry **V3** = Families of Co. Clare **V4** = Families of Co. Cork **V5** = Families of Co. Limerick

Mc Cnohor **V4**
Mc Cnohor 269...
O Cnohor **V4**
O' Cnohor 269...
Cnohor Oge **V4**
Cnohor Oge 269...
Mc Cnohorxx **V4**
Mc Cnougher **V4**
Mc Cnougher 269..
Mc Cnoughor **V4**
Mc Cnoughor 269..
Coach 269...
Coach 34,205
Coady **V4**
Coady 269...
Coady 56
Coak(e)ley 54
Coakley **V2**
Coakley **V4**
Coakley 269...
Coal 47
Coalman 62
Coalpis **V3**
Coat(e)s 56
Coate 269...
Coates 269...
Cobayne 269...
Cobb **V3**
Cobb **V5**
Cobb 269...
Cobb(e) 46
Cobh, Co. **V4**
O' Cobhthaigh **V2**
Cobleigh 269...
Cobourn 269...
Cobram 269...
Coburn 269...
Coch 130
Cocherane **V4**
O Cochlainn **V4**
Cochlayn **V4**
Cochraine 63
Cochran(e) 63
Cochrane 269...
Cochrane 269...
Cochren 63
Cock **V2**
Cockain 269...
Cockerill 155
Cockrane 63
Cocks **V3**
Cocks **V4**
Cocks 67
Cockson **V3**
Mac Coclain **V2**
Cocoran **V4**
O Cocoran **V4**
Cod 269...
Cod(d) 10,56
Codd 269...
Coddington 269...
Coddington 46
Coddy 269...
Coddy 56
Code 269...
Codey **V4**
Codon 269...
Cody **V4**
Cody 10,56
Cody 269...
Mc Cody **V4**
Coen 269...
Coen 56,65,169
Coey 269...
Cof(f)ee 47
Coffe **V2**
Coffee **V3**
Coffee **V4**
Coffey **V2**
Coffey **V4**
Coffey 269...
O Coffey **V3**
O Coffey **V4**
O Coffey 47
Coffey, **V2**
O' Coffey Of **V3**
Coffie **V2**
Coffie **V3**
Coffie 269...
Coffy 269...
Cogan **V4**
Cogan 269...
De Cogan **V2**
Cogan(e) 56,71
Cogan, **V2**
Cogane **V3**
Cogane **V4**
Cogane 269...
Cogely 269...
Coghan 269...
Coghell 269...
Coghill 269...
Coghill 55
Coghlan **V2**
Coghlan **V4**
Coghlan 269...
Mc Coghlan **V4**
Coghlan(e) 56
Coghlane **V4**
Coghlane 269...
Coghlin 56
Coghran 269...
Cogley 222
Cogley 269...
O' Cogley 269...
Coglin **V4**
Cogly 269...
Cohalan **V4**
Cohalan 56
O Cohan **V4**
Cohane **V4**
Cohane 269...
Cohen 269...
Cohen 56
Cohey **V2**
Coholane 269...
Cohoun 269...
Coid 269...
Coilens **V2**
Coiles 269...
Coin 269...
Coin 65,169
O' Coinin **V2**
Coinyn **V2**
Coinyn 269...
Cokain 269...
Coke **V2**
Cokely 269...
O Colahan **V2**
O Colahan 57
Colavan 72
Colavin 269...
Colavin 29,72
Colbert **V4**
Colbert 269...
Colbert 56
Colclough **V2**
Colclough 269...
Colclough 54
Colcloughan 269...
Coldrick 269...
Coldwell 29
Cole 269...
Cole 47,57,205
Mc Cole 269...
Colelough 269...
Coleman **V2**
Coleman **V4**
Coleman 269...
O Coleman **V4**
O Coleman **V5**
O Coleman 62
Coley 58
Colfer 57
Colgan 269...
Mac Colgan 47
Mc Colgan 269...
O' Colgan **V2**
Colgen 47
Colgun 47
Colhoon 269...
Colhoun 269...
Colhoun 48
Colhoune 269...
O' Colhoune 269...
Colhown 269...
Coligan 269...
Coligan 47
Colin 269...
Colins 269...
Colivan 72
Colkly 54
Coll **V2**
Coll **V5**
Coll 269...
Coll 57,58
Mc Coll 269...
O' Colla **V2**
O Collag(h)ane 57
O Collaghane **V2**
O' Collaghane 269.
O' Collane **V5**
O' Collane 269...
Mac Colleghan 57
Colleman **V4**
Collen, **V4**
Collen 269...
Collen 48
Collens **V3**
Collens **V5**
Collens 269...
Mc Colleny 269...
Colleran 269...
Collery 269...
Colletan 70
Collett **V5**
Colley 269...
Colley, 58
Mc Collgan 269...
Collie 58
Collier **V2**
Collier 269...
(le) Collier 48
Colligan **V2**
Colligan 269...
Colligan 47,57
Colliher 116
Collin **V4**
Mc Collin 269...
Collingwood **V2**
Collins **V2**
Collins **V3**
Collins **V4**
Collins **V5**
Collins 269...
Collins 48,59,60
O Collins **V4**
Collins **V2**
Collis **V2**
Collis **V4**
Collis 269...
Collis 49
Collis Of **V2**
Collis Of **V2**
Collis, S. E. **V2**
Collis-sande **V2**
Collisson **V5**
Collisson 269...
Mc Collo 269...
Mc Collogh 269...
Collom 269...
Collom 62
Collopy **V4**
Collopy **V5**
Collopy 58
O' Colloune 269...
Collum **V2**
Mc Collum 269...
(mc) Collum 62
Collun 269...
Collvill 269...
Colly 269...
(mac Colly 58
Collyn **V4**
Collyne **V4**
M' Collyums 269...
Colmain **V2**
Colman **V2**
Colman **V4**
Colman 269...
Colman 62
Mc Colman 269...
Colnan 269...
Colohan **V2**
Colohan 57
Colomb 62
Colothan 269...
Colovin 269...
Colovin 72
Colpois **V3**
Colpoise 269...
Colpoy **V3**
Colpoys **V3**
Colpoyse 269...
Colquhoun 269...
Colquhoun 48
Colquohoun 269...
Colreavy 269...
Colthurst **V2**
Colthurst **V4**
Colthursts **V2**
Coltsman **V4**
Coltsman, **V2**
Coltsmann **V2**
Coluer 269...
Mac Coluim **V2**
Mac Coluim, F. **V2**
Colum(b) 62
Columb **V2**
Columby 58
Colvan 62
Colven 62
Colvil(le) 62
Colvill 269...
Colvin **V2**
Colvin **V4**
Colvin **V5**
Colvin 269...
Colvin 62
Colwell 269...
Colwell 29
Colwill 269...
Colyer 48
O' Comain **V2**
Coman 269...
Comane **V3**
Comane 269...
O' Comane **V5**
O' Comane 269...
Comasky 72
Mc Comb 269...
M' Comb(s) 58,148
Comba 269...
Combe 269...
Combel **V4**
Combel 269...
Comber 269...
Combes 269...
Mac Comdain **V2**
Mc Come 269...
Comer 269...
Comerford **V2**
Comerford 269...
Comerford 59
Comerton 269...
Comesk'y 59,72
Comford 269...
Comfort 269...
Mc Comick 269...
Comin **V3**
Comin **V5**
Comin 269...
Comine **V3**
Comine 269...
Mac Comish 148
M' Comisk'y 59,72
Comiskey 269...
Comjean 269...
Comjeens 269...
Mc Comley 269...
Comman 269...
Commane **V2**
Commane **V3**
Commane 269...
Commaskey 269...
Commefort 269...
Commerford 269...
Commerford 59
Comminge **V5**
Mc Commings 269.
Commins 269...
Commins 65
Commiskey 59
Common 269...
Commons 269...
Commons 65
Commune 269...
Commyns **V2**
Compton **V2**
Compton 269...
Comyn **V2**
Comyn **V4**
Comyn **V5**
Comyn 65
Comyn, **V3**
Comyne **V3**
Comyne 269...
M' Cona 269...
Conaghan 269...
O' Conaghan 269...
Conaghty 58,62

Mc Conaghy269...
O' Conagill269...
O' Conaing **V2**
O Conaing **V3**
Conall50
Conallone269...
Conally269...
Mc Conamy269...
O' Conan269...
O Conan58
Mac Conarchy **V2**
Conary51
Conary, Race **V2**
Conaty269...
Conaty58
M' Conaughty269..
Conaway52
O Conbaidhe **V4**
Conboy269...
Conboy52,59
O Concanain49
Concannon269...
O Concannon49
Concanon49
Condan49
Conde155
Conderick269...
Condon **V2**
Condon **V4**
Condon **V5**
Condon269...
Condon49
Condran60,70
Condrick269...
Condron **V4**
Condron **V5**
Condron269...
Condron49,60,70
Mac Conduib **V2**
Condun **V2**
Condy269...
Cone **V4**
Cone269...
Mac Conefrey61
Conefry269...
Conel **V4**
Conel50
Conelan269...
Conellan269...
Conellane **V3**
Conellane269...
O' Conellane **V3**
O' Conellane269...
Conelly **V4**
Conelly269...
Coner **V4**
Coner51
Coneran269...
Coneran70
Coners **V4**
Conery **V3**
Conery51,61
Confiscated **V2**
Confree61
Confrey61
O' Conghaile **V2**
Congreife **V5**
Congreife269...
Conheeny269...
Conick269...
Conier51
O' Conigan269...
O' Conighan269...
Conihy269...
Conillan269...
Conin269...
Coningham269...
Mc Conkey269...
O' Conklin **V3**
O' Conklin **V5**
Conla269...
Conlan269...
Conlan50,62
Conland269...
Conlen62
Mac Conley60,61
Conlin269...
Conliss221
Conlogue269...
Conlon269...
Conlon50,62
Conly269...
(mac Conly60,61
Mac Conmara206
Mac Conmara Bk. V
Mac Conmaras **V3**
Conmee269...
Conn269...
Mc Conn269...
Conn Of 100 **V4**
O' Connaghain **V2**
Connalan269...
Connalan50
Connally50
O' Connally269...
O Connanen49
Connard **V4**
Connard **V4**
Connard269...
Connaughton269..
O Connaughton62
Conneally269...
Connealy269...
Conneely269...
Conneely50,61
Conneff **V2**
Connel269...
Connel269...
Connel50
Connelan269...
Connell **V2**
Connell **V3**
Connell **V4**
Connell **V5**
Connell269...
Mac Connell **V2**
Mc Connell **V5**
Mc Connell269...
(mc) Connell50,61
O' Connell **V2**
O Connell **V3**
O Connell **V4**
O' Connell **V5**
O' Connell269...
(o) Connell50
O' Connell, C. **V2**
O' Connell, D. **V2**
Connell **V2**
O' Connell, J. **V2**
O' Connell, M. **V2**
Connellan **V3**
Connellan269...
O' Connellan **V3**
O' Connellan **V5**
(o) Connellan222
(o) Connellan(e)50
Connellane **V3**
O' Connellane269.
O' Connells **V2**
Connelly **V2**
Connelly **V4**
Connelly269...
Connelly50
O' Connelly269...
Connelly **V2**
Conner **V2**
Conner **V3**
Conner **V4**
Conner269...
Conner51
Mc Conner269...
O' Conner **V3**
O' Conner **V2**
Connerney269...
Conners **V4**
Connerton269...
M' Connerty269...
Connery **V3**
Connery **V5**
Connery269...
Connery61
Conney269...
Mac Connick70
Conniers269...
Conniff269...
Connillan269...
Conningham269..
Connington62
Connohor269...
O' Connohor269...
Connol **V3**
Connola269...
Connolan269...
Connolay269...
Connole70
Connolly **V2**
Connolly **V3**
Connolly **V4**
Connolly269...
O Connolly50,61
Connoly269...
Connoly50
O' Connoly269...
Mc Connon269...
Connor **V2**
Connor **V3**
Connor **V4**
Connor269...
Mc Connor **V3**
Mc Connor **V4**
Mc Connor **V5**
Mc Connor269...
O' Connor **V2**
O Connor **V3**
O Connor **V4**
O' Connor **V5**
O' Connor269...
O Connor51
O' Connor Arms **V2**
O' Connor Arms **V3**
O' Connor, **V2**
O Connor Fermoy **V4**
O' Connor In **V3**
O' Connor, J. **V2**
O' Connor, **V2**
Connor **V2**
O' Connor, M. **V2**
Connor Of **V2**
Connor, Rev **V2**
Connors **V4**
Connors269...
O' Connors **V2**
O' Connors **V3**
O' Connors269...
Connorton269...
Connorton62
Connory269...
O' Connory **V3**
O' Connory269...
Mac Connulty210
Conny **V3**
Conny269...
Connyn269...
O' Connyn **V2**
O' Conogher269...
Conoghye269...
Mc Conohy269...
Conol(l)y50
Conolan269...
O' Conole **V3**
O Conole70
Mc Conoly269...
Mc Conomy269...
Conoo269...
Conor **V3**
Conor269...
Mc Conor269...
O' Conor **V3**
O' Conor269...
O Conor51
O' Conor, C. **V2**
Conor Of **V3**
Conory **V3**
Conow **V4**
Conow269...
Conoyle70
Conraghy269...
Conrahy269...
Conrahy51
Conran269...
(o) Conran60,70
M' Conready269...
Conree51
Conroi **V2**
Mac Conroi **V2**
Mac Conroi **V2**
Conroy **V2**
Conroy **V3**
Conroy **V4**
Conroy **V5**
Conroy269...
O Conroy51,61,16
Conry **V3**
Conry269...
Conry61,164
Mc Conry **V5**
Consadine51
Consdin269...
Mc Consdin, **V3**
Mac Considan51
Mc Considan269...
Mc Considan **V3**
Considin **V3**
Considin269...
Mc Considin269...
O' Considin **V3**
M' Considin(e)51
Considine **V5**
Considine269...
Mac Considine **V3**
Mac Considine **V5**
Considine In **V3**
Mc Considn269...
Mc Considn51
Constable269...
Contents, **V2**
O' Conty **V5**
O' Conty269...
O' Conuing **V3**
O Convally70
Convery269...
Convery70
Convey269...
Convey52
Convict Poet **V3**
Mc Conville269...
Mc Conville70
Convoy269...
Conway **V2**
Conway269...
Mc Conway269...
O Conway **V3**
Conway Of **V2**
Conwaye **V4**
Conways **V3**
Conwell269...
Cony **V2**
Cony269...
Conyeen269...
Conyer269...
Conyer(s)51,70
Conyers **V2**
Conyers269...
Conyn **V2**
Conyngham52,60
O' Conyns **V2**
Mc Coo269...
Cooch269...
Coody269...
Mc Coody269...
Mac Cooey64,71
Coogan269...
Coogan56,71
O' Coogan269...
Coogane **V3**
Coogane269...
Cooihan66
Cook **V3**
Cook **V4**
Cook269...
Mc Cook269...
Cook, Capt. **V4**
Cook(e)52
Cooke **V2**
Cooke **V3**
Cooke **V4**
Cooke **V5**
Cooke269...
Mc Cooke269...
Cooke, **V2**
Cool **V3**
Mc Cool269...
(mc) Cool72
Coola(g)han57,71
Coole **V3**
Coole269...
Cooley269...
Cooley66
Coolican57
Cooling66
Coolman269...
Cooly58,66
Coom **V3**
Coomy **V4**
Coon269...
Coonaghan269...
Coonahan64,66
Coonan58,66
Cooney **V2**
Cooney **V4**
Cooney269...

V2 = Families of Co. Kerry **V3** = Families of Co. Clare **V4** = Families of Co. Cork **V5** = Families of Co. Limerick

O Cooney **V3**
O Cooney 66
Coonihan 269...
Coonihan 64
Coonoon 269...
Coonor **V4**
Coony **V3**
Coony 269...
Coony 66
Cooper **V2**
Cooper **V3**
Cooper **V4**
Cooper **V5**
Cooper 269...
Cooper 269...
Cooper 53,155
Coot 269...
Coot(e) 53
Coote **V2**
Coote **V4**
Coote **V5**
Coote 269...
Cope 34,53
Copeland 269...
Copeland 53,71
Copelton 269...
Copely **V5**
Copely 269...
Copinger **V4**
Copinger 269...
Copinger 71
Copinger, **V4**
Copleton 269...
Copley **V3**
Copley **V4**
Copley 269...
Copley, **V2**
Coppenger **V3**
Coppenger 71
Coppinger **V3**
Coppinger 71
Coppinger, **V4**
Coppingers **V4**
Copplen **V5**
Copplen 269...
Coquerel 155
Corathers 269...
Corballis 71
Corbally 269...
Corbally 71
Corban **V4**
Corban 269...
Corban 71
Corbane **V3**
Corbane 269...
Corbane 71
O' Corbane **V5**
O' Corbane 269...
Corbet **V2**
Corbet 269...
Corbett **V3**
Corbett **V4**
Corbett **V5**
Corbett 269...
Corbett 71
Corbin **V4**
Corbin **V5**
Corbin 269...
Corbitt **V4**
Corca **V3**
Corca **V2**
Corca **V3**
Corcabaskin **V3**
O' Corcain **V2**
O Corcaran 64
Corckron 269...
Corckron 64
Corcomroe **V3**
Corcoran **V2**
Corcoran **V4**
Corcoran 269...
M' Corcoran 63,71
M' Corcoran 64
O Corcoran **V4**
O' Corcra **V2**
Corcu **V3**
Corcu **V2**
Mc Cord 269...
(mc) Cord 71
Cordan 269...
Cordan 67
Cordew 71
Cordner 269...
Cordue **V3**
Cordue 71
Corduff 71
Core **V4**
O' Core 269...
Coregan 269...
Corey **V4**
Corey **V5**
Corey 269...
Coribeen 269...
Corigan 54
Corish 269...
Cork 269...
Cork, Earl Of **V2**
Corkan 269...
Corkcrane 269...
Corkdyale 269...
Corke **V4**
Corke 269...
Corken 269...
Corker **V4**
Corker(r)y 71
Corkeran 269...
Corkerane **V4**
Corkerane 269...
O Corkerane **V4**
O' Corkerane 269...
O Corkerane 64
Corkerin 269...
Corkerry **V2**
Corkerry 269...
Corkery **V2**
Corkery **V4**
Corkery **V5**
Corkery 269...
Corkery, D. **V2**
Mc Corkill 269...
Corkin 269...
Corkron 269...
Corkry 71
Corless 269...
Corley 269...
Corley 269...
Cormac 269...
Mc Cormac 64
O' Cormac **V5**
Cormac Cas **V4**
Cormac Chapel **V4**
Mac Cormac(k) **V2**
Cormacan 66
Cormacin 66
Cormack **V3**
Cormack **V4**
Cormack 269...
Mac Cormack **V4**
Mac Cormack **V5**
Mac Cormack 64
Mc Cormack **V2**
Mc Cormack **V4**
Mc Cormack 269...
O Cormack **V4**
O' Cormack **V5**
O' Cormack 269...
Mac Cormack **V2**
Mac Cormacke **V2**
Mc Cormacke **V2**
Cormacs **V4**
Mac Cormaic **V2**
Cormican **V3**
Cormican 269...
Cormican 66
Cormick **V3**
Cormick 269...
Mc Cormick **V2**
Mc Cormick **V4**
Mc Cormick 269...
Mc Cormick 64
O' Cormick **V3**
O' Cormick 269...
Cormicke 269...
O' Cormicks **V3**
Mc Cormilla 269...
Cormocke 269...
Mc Cormocke **V4**
Mc Cormuck 269...
Cormucke 269...
Corn 269...
Corneil 205
Corner 66
Cornewall 34
Cornewell 269...
Cornewell 54
Cornock 54
Cornwall **V2**
Cornwall 54
Cornwell 54
(o) Cornyn 66
Corofin **V3**
Corr **V3**
Corr 269...
Corr 269...
O' Corr 269...
Corr, Corry 66
Corra 65,66
O' Corra **V2**
Corradain **V2**
O' Corragain **V2**
O' Corrain **V2**
Corran 269...
Corregan 54
Corren 269...
Correy 269...
Corrican 54
O' Corrican 269...
Corridan **V2**
Corridan 67
Corridon **V2**
Corridon **V3**
Corrie 65,66
Corrigan **V2**
Corrigan **V4**
Corrigan 269...
O' Corrigan 269...
O Corrigan 54
Corrigen 54
Corrodan **V2**
Corrodan **V3**
Corrodan 67
Corroll 269...
O' Corroney 269...
O' Corrony 269...
Corry **V3**
Corry **V4**
Corry 269...
Mc Corry 269...
O' Corry **V3**
O Corry **V4**
(o) Corry 65,66
O' Corrygan 269...
Corscadden 67
Corstellowe **V4**
Corstellowe 269...
Corthorp 269...
Corton 269...
Cory 269...
Cory 65
Cosby 55
Coscor 269...
Coscraigh **V4**
Coscrain **V4**
O Coscrain **V4**
O Coseraigh **V4**
Cosgrave **V2**
Cosgrave **V4**
Cosgrave 269...
Mac Cosgrave 48
O Cosgrave **V4**
(o) Cosgrave 48
(o) Cosgrave 66,67
Cosgro(o)ve 48,67
Cosgrove **V2**
Cosgrove **V4**
Cosgrove 269...
O Cosgry 66
O' Coshedy 269...
Coshman 269...
Cosker 269...
Cosker 70
Mc Cosker 269...
Coskeran **V4**
Coskerry 269...
Mac Coskley 66
Coss 269...
Cossens **V5**
Cossens 269...
Costell 269...
Costello **V3**
Costello 269...
Mac Costello **V5**
Mac Costello 55
Costelloe **V2**
Costelloe **V3**
Costelloe **V4**
Costelloe **V5**
Costelloe 269...
Mc Costelloe **V3**
Mc Costelloe **V5**
Costellow 55
Costelly 269...
Mac Costey 142
Costigan **V2**
Costigan 269...
Mac Costigan 66
Costigin 269...
Costigin 66
Costillo 55
Costily 269...
Costily 55
Costle 269...
Costleloe 269...
Costley 269...
Costolloe 55
Costoloe 269...
Mac Costy 142
Cotes 56
Mac Cotir **V4**
Cott **V4**
Mc Cottar 269...
Cotte **V4**
Cottel 66
Cotter. **V2**
Cotter **V3**
Cotter **V4**
Cotter 269...
Mac Cotter **V4**
Mac Cotter 55
Mc Cotter 269...
O Cotter **V4**
O' Cotter 269...
(o) Cotter 55
Cotterell 269...
Cotters **V4**
Mc Cottier 269...
Cottingham 56
Cottir **V4**
Mc Cottir 55
Cottle 269...
Cottle 66
Cotton 269...
Cottor 55
Mac Cottyr 55
Mc Coubrey 269...
Coue 269...
Coughlan **V4**
Coughlan **V5**
Coughlan 269...
Mac Coughlan **V4**
(mac Coughlan 56
Coughlane **V4**
Coughlane 269...
Coughlen 56
Coughlin 269...
Couglan **V4**
Couglane **V4**
O Couglane **V4**
O' Couglane 269...
Coul **V3**
Coule **V3**
Coulpys **V3**
Coulpys 269...
Coulter **V4**
Coulter 269...
Coulter 67
Coulthurst **V2**
Coulthurst **V4**
Coulthurst 269...
Coultry **V5**
Coumey 269...
Coumey 64,66
Coun 269...
Counahan 64
Coune 269...
Counihan **V2**
Counihan 269...
(o) Counihan **V2**
(o) Counihan 60,64
(o) Counihan 66
County **V2**
County 269...
County 46
De Courcey 77
Courcie 77
Courcy **V4**
Courcy 269...
Courcy 77
Courigan 269...
Courn 269...
Cournane **V2**

Cournane269...
(o) Cournane V2
(o) Cournane71
Courneen269...
Coursey V2
Coursey V4
Coursey269...
Coursie V4
Coursy V4
Mc Court269...
(mc) Court71
Courtayne269...
Courtenay269...
Courtes269...
Courtess269...
Courthop V4
Courthop269...
Courtney V2
Courtney V4
Courtney V5
Courtney269...
Courtney269...
Courtney71
Mc Courtney269...
Courtny V4
Cousine269...
Cousins V2
Cousins269...
Couvane269...
Couzeens269...
Mac Covelin222
Coveney V4
Coveney269...
Cover269...
Covert V2
Covet269...
Covett V4
Covett269...
Cowan269...
Cowan71
Mc Cowan269...
Coway269...
Cowdie269...
Cowell71
Mc Cowell269...
Cowen269...
Cowen71
Mac Cowen V2
Mac Cowen's V2
Cowhey47
Cowhig47
O Cowhig V4
O Cowhys V4
O Cowig V4
Cowley269...
Cowley269...
Cowley58
O Cowley V4
Cowman269...
Cowman67
Mc Cowman269...
Mc Cownley269...
Cowse269...
Cox V2
Cox V3
Cox V4
Cox269...
Cox67,155
Cox, Mac V5
Cox, Sir R. V4
Coxe269...
Coxon V2
Coy269...
Mac Coy V2
Mc Coy V5
Mc Coy269...
(mc) Coy64,151
Coyd269...
Coyle V2
Coyle269...
Coyle72
Coyn269...
Coyn(e)65
Coyne169,171
Coyne269...
Coysh269...
Cozene V4
Cozene269...
Cra269...
Craan269...
Crabb V5
Crabb269...
Mc Cracken269...
(mc) Cracken67
Mc Crackin67
Craddock V2
Craddock67
Crafford269...
Craffy68
Craford V5
Craford269...
Crag269...
Crage269...
Cragg V3
Cragh V4
Cragh269...
Mc Cragh V4
Mc Cragh V5
Mc Cragh269...
(mc) Cragh57
Cragmore V3
Mac Crah V2
Crahan269...
Craig V3
Craig269...
Craig34,57
Craige269...
Craigh269...
Craine V4
Craine269...
Craith V4
Mac Craith V5
Mac Craith269...
Mc Craith V4
Mc Craith269...
Cramby269...
Cramer V4
Cramer56,68
Cramps(e)y26,57
Crampsey269...
Crampsie269...
Crampsie57,171
Crampsy269...
Crampton269...
Cramsey171
Cramsie57
Crane269...
Crane, C.p. V2
Cranfield V2
Crangle67
Cranitch V2
Mc Crann269...
Cranny269...
Cransborogh269..
Cransboroug V3
Cransborrow V3
Cransborrow269...
Cranston269...
Cranwell V4
Cranwell269...
Cranwell269...
Craobac V2
Crassus V2
Craston269...
Mac Crath V2
Mc Crath269...
Cratloe V3
Crauen V5
Crauen269...
Craughwell67
Craven V3
Craven132
Craven269...
Crawford V2
Crawford269...
Crawford34,57
Crawfurd269...
Crawley269...
Crayford34
Mac Crea232
Mc Crea269...
Mc Cready269...
Creagan V3
Creagh V2
Creagh V3
Creagh V4
Creagh V5
Creagh269...
Mc Creagh V2
Mc Creagh V4
(mc) Creagh57
O' Creagh V2
O' Creagh V3
Creagh Arms V3
Creagh, V2
Creagh Mc V4
Creagh, V2
Creaghe V4
O' Creain V2
Creamer269...
Creamer68
Creamor68
Crean V2
Crean V4
Crean269...
Mac Crean58
O' Crean269...
O Crean58
Creane269...
Creaney269...
Mc Creary269...
Mc Creary68
Creaton269...
Creaton68
Credan V4
O Credan V4
O Credan68
M' Creech269...
Creed V2
Creed V4
Creed V5
Creed269...
Creedan V4
Creedon V4
Creedon269...
Creedon68
Creegan V2
Creegan V3
Creegan269...
Creegan58,68
O' Creehan V5
O Creehan68
Creeland269...
Creemer68
Creemins V4
Creen58
Mc Creery269...
Mc Creery68
Mac Creesh68
Mc Creesh269...
Creevy134
Cregan V2
Cregan V3
Cregan V5
Cregan269...
Cregan58
Cregg V3
Cregg269...
Crehan V2
Crehan269...
Crehan58,68
Mac Crehan V2
Mac Crehans V2
Creighton269...
Crelly269...
Creman68
Cremeen269...
Cremen68
Cremin V2
Cremin V4
Cremin269...
Cremin68
Cremins V2
Creory269...
Mc Crerie269...
Crery269...
Mc Crery269...
Cresans269...
Creskitt269...
Crevy269...
Crewly, J. V2
Crews V3
Crewse269...
O' Criagain V2
Cribben134
Cribbon269...
Crichad An V4
Crickard269...
Crickenham269...
Cricket269...
Crifferty68
Crighley269...
Crightone269...
Crilly269...
Crilly68
Crimble269...
Crimeen68
Crimmeen269...
Crimmins V2
Cripps V5
Cripps269...
Crispe V4
Crispe269...
Crispp269...
Critchley V2
Croaker V4
Croaker269...
Croc68
Crocker V5
Croffton269...
Croffy68
Croft V4
Crofton58
Crofts V3
Crofts V4
Crofts269...
Croghan V3
Croghan269...
Mac Croghan68
Croghane69
Croghen V3
Croghen269...
Crohan68
Mac Crohan V2
Mc Crohan V2
Mc Crohan269...
Mac Crohan V2
Mc Crohon68
O' Croidain V2
O' Croideain V2
O' Croinin V2
Crok(e)68,155
Crok, Maine V4
Croke269...
Croke Of V2
Croker V2
Croker V3
Croker V4
Croker V5
Croker58
Croker, T. V2
Crol(l)y59
Crole59
Mc Croley269...
Crolly269...
Mc Croly269...
Crom(m)ie69
O' Cromeene V5
O' Cromeene269...
Cromewell269...
Cromewell69
Cromie269...
Crommy69
Cromwell V2
Cromwell V3
Cromwell V5
Cromwell69
Cromwellian V3
O' Cromy269...
O Cromy69
O Cromyne V4
O' Cronain V2
Cronan V4
Crone V4
Crone269...
Crone69
Croneen V4
O Croneene V2
O' Croneene V5
O' Croneene269...
O Croneene69
Cronekan V4
Cronekan69
Cronen69
Cronin V2
Cronin V4
Cronin269...
O Cronin V2
O Cronin V4
O Cronin V5
O Cronin(e)69
O Cronine V4
O' Cronine269...
Cronnelly, V2
Cronouge269...
Cronsberry205
Cronvy269...
Cronyn69
Cronyne V4
O Cronyne V4
O' Cronyne269...

V2 = Families of Co. Kerry **V3** = Families of Co. Clare **V4** = Families of Co. Cork **V5** = Families of Co. Limerick

Cronyng **V4**
Crook **V4**
Crooke **V4**
Crooke 269...
Crooke 68
Crooker 269...
Crooks 269...
Crooksshank 269..
Croroother 269...
Cropley 269...
Cropman **V5**
Mc Crory 129
Mc Crory 269...
Crosberry **V2**
Crosbie **V2**
Crosbie 269...
Crosbie 59
Crosbie, B. **V2**
Crosbie **V2**
Crosby **V2**
Crosby 269...
Crosby 59
Cross **V4**
Cross 155
Cross 269...
Crossan **V2**
Crossan 269...
Crossan 69
Mc Crossan 269...
Crosse **V4**
Crosse 269...
Crossen 69
Crossey 269...
Crostenton 269...
Croston 269...
Crothers 269...
Crottie **V4**
O Crottie 69
O Crottie, **V4**
Crotty 269...
O Crotty 69
Crotty, **V3**
Crough 269...
Crough 97
Crow **V3**
Crow **V4**
Crow 97
Crowane 69
Crowe **V2**
Crowe **V3**
Crowe **V4**
Crowe 269...
Mac Crowe 97
O Crowelie **V4**
O Crowl(e)y 59
O' Crowle 269...
O Crowle O' **V3**
Crowley **V2**
Crowley **V4**
Crowley 269...
O Crowley **V4**
O' Crowley 269...
Crowley Oge **V4**
Crowley Oge 269...
Crowly 269...
O Crowly **V4**
O' Crowly 269...
Crowlye **V4**
O Crowlye **V4**
(m') Crown(e) 69
Crowther 269...
Crozier 269...
M' Crub 269...
Cruce **V5**
Mc Crudden 269...
Cruden **V2**
Cruice **V3**
Cruihly 269...
Cruise **V3**
Cruise **V5**
Cruise 269...
Cruise 69
Mac Cruitin 61
O' Cruitin **V2**
Crully 269...
Mc Crum 269...
Crumlish 269...
Crummy 269...
Crumpe Of **V2**
Cruse 269...
Crutchley **V3**
Cruys 69
Cryan 269...
Crymble 269...
O Crymyne **V4**
Mac Crystal 69
O Cuan **V4**
O' Cuanacain **V2**
O' Cuarthain **V2**
Cudah(e)y 70
Cudahy **V4**
Cuddahy 70
Cuddehy 70
Mc Cudden 269...
Cuddihy 269...
Cuddihy 70
Cuddy 269...
Cudmore **V4**
Cudmore 70
Cue 269...
Mc Cue 269...
Cuell 269...
Cuff **V4**
Cuff 269...
Cuff, Cuffe **V3**
Cuffe **V3**
Cuffe **V4**
Cuffe 269...
Cuggeran **V3**
Cuggeran 63,70
Cuhy 269...
O' Cuil **V2**
O' Cuileannain **V2**
Mac Cuill **V2**
O' Cuillein **V3**
O' Cuillen 269...
Cuin **V3**
O' Cuin **V3**
Cuinane 269...
O' Cuinin **V3**
Mac Cuinn **V2**
O' Cuinn **V2**
O Cuinn **V4**
O Cuinn 223
Cuinneagain **V2**
Cuirc **V4**
Mac Cuirc **V4**
O' Cuirc **V2**
(de) Cuirteis **V2**
Mac Cuirtin **V2**
Mac Cuirtin 61
Cuisin **V2**
(de) Cuitleir **V2**
Culane **V3**
Culane 269...
Culane 59
Culbert 269...
Culclough **V2**
Culein **V3**
Culenain 60
O' Culenane **V3**
O' Culenane 269...
Culhane **V2**
Culhane **V5**
Culhane 269...
Culhane 48,59
Culhoun 269...
Culhoun 60
Culigan 70
Culinane **V3**
Culinane 269...
Cull 269...
Mc Cull 269...
Mac Cullagh **V2**
Mc Cullagh 269...
Mc Cullagh 72
Cullan **V3**
Cullan 269...
O' Cullan 269...
Cullane **V3**
Cullane **V4**
Cullane 269...
O' Cullane **V3**
O Cullane **V4**
O Cullane **V5**
O' Cullane 269...
(o) Cullane 48,59
Cullaton 70
Culle 269...
O' Culleane **V5**
O' Culleane 269...
Culleen **V3**
Culleen 269...
Culleeny 269...
Cullegane **V3**
Cullegane 269...
Cullen **V2**
Cullen **V3**
Cullen **V4**
Cullen 269...
Mac Cullen **V2**
Mac Cullen 60
Mc Cullen 269...
O Cullen **V4**
O' Cullen 269...
(o) Cullen 48,60,72
O Cullenan **V4**
Cullenane **V4**
Cullenane 269...
O Cullenane **V4**
O' Cullenane 269...
O Cullenane 60
Cullenen 37
Cullens 60
Culleton 269...
Culleton 70
Cullian 269...
Culligan **V3**
Culligan **V5**
Culligan 269...
Culligan 47,70,21
Culligan Of **V3**
Cullilane **V4**
Cullilane 269...
Cullin 269...
Mc Cullin 269...
(mc) Cullin 60
O' Cullin 269...
Cullinan **V3**
Cullinan **V4**
Cullinan 269...
O' Cullinan **V3**
O Cullinan **V4**
O Cullinan(e) 60
O Cullinan, **V4**
Cullinane **V2**
Cullinane **V4**
Cullinane 269...
Cullinane Of **V3**
Cullington 70
Cullion 269...
Mc Cullion 269...
Culliton 70
Cullivan 269...
Cullivan 72
Culliver **V3**
Cullnane **V4**
Cullnane 269...
Mc Culloch 269...
Culloe **V3**
Mc Cullogh 269...
Mc Cullogh 72
Culloo **V3**
Culloon 269...
Culloon 60
Culloty **V2**
Culloty 269...
Culloty 72
Mc Cullough **V3**
Mc Cullough 269...
(mc) Cullough 72
Cullow **V3**
Mc Cullow 269...
(mc) Cullow 72
Cullum **V2**
O' Cullun 269...
Cully **V2**
Cully 269...
Mc Cully 269...
(mc) Cully 72
Mc Cullyam 269...
Culme 269...
Culoty 72
Culreavy 269...
Culwell 269...
Cumberford 269...
Cumiskey 269...
Mac Cumiskey 72
Cummane **V2**
Cummane **V4**
Cummane 269...
Cumming 269...
Cumming(s) 65
Cummings 269...
Cummins **V2**
Cummins **V4**
Cummins **V5**
Cummins 269...
Cummins 65
Cun'ingham **V2**
Cunagum 269...
O' Cunane 269...
Cundane **V4**
Cundun **V4**
Cundy 155
Mc Cune 269...
Cuneen **V3**
Cuneen 269...
Cunegan 269...
Cunigam **V3**
Cunigam 269...
Cunigan **V3**
Mac Cunigan 60
Cunigane **V3**
Cunigane 269...
O' Cunigane **V3**
O' Cunigane 269...
Cunigham 269...
Cunihan 269...
O' Cuning **V5**
O Cuning 72
Cuningham 269...
Cuningham 34
O' Cuningham 269.
Cuninghame 269...
Cuninghame, **V2**
Cunion 269...
Cunlis 221
Cunnagher 269...
Cunnahan 269...
Cunnain 269...
Cunnane 269...
Cunnane 72
Cunnard **V4**
Cunnea 269...
Cunneen 269...
Mac Cunneen 72
Cunneeny 269...
Cunniam 269...
Cunniffe 269...
Cunnigan 269...
Mc Cunnigan 269..
Cunnighan 269...
Cunningham **V2**
Cunningham **V3**
Cunningham **V4**
Cunningham 269...
Cunningham 52,60
Cunnion 269...
Cunnoo 269...
Cunny **V3**
Cunny 269...
Cunnyer 269...
Cunree 269...
Cunree 51
Cunreen 269...
Cunyngham 269...
Cunyngham 34
Cunynghame 269..
Cuolaghan 57
(o) Cuolahan 57
Cuolohan 269...
Cuppage 269...
Cupples 269...
Curan **V2**
Curan 269...
Curane 269...
O' Curathain **V2**
Curbstone **V2**
Curcy 77
Curd **V3**
Curd 269...
Mac Curdy 72
Mc Curdy 269...
Curinys **V2**
Curle **V4**
Curlestone **V2**
Curlew **V2**
Curley **V4**
Curley 269...
Mac Curley **V4**
Mac Curley **V5**
Mac Curley 72
Curling 72
Curly **V4**
O' Curmine 269...
O' Curnain **V2**
Curnane **V3**
Curnane 269...
O Curnane **V2**
O' Curnane 269...

V2 = Families of Co. Kerry **V3** = Families of Co. Clare **V4** = Families of Co. Cork **V5** = Families of Co. Limerick

Curneen 269...
Curneen 66
Curnin 269...
Curphy 63
Curr 66
Curra(u)gh 63
Curran **V2**
Curran **V3**
Curran 269...
O' Curran **V2**
O' Curran **V3**
Currane **V2**
Currane **V3**
Currane 269...
O Currane **V2**
O' Currane **V5**
O' Currane 269...
Currans **V2**
Curreen 269...
(o) Curreen 66
Curreene 269...
Curren **V3**
Curren 269...
Currens **V2**
Currid 269...
Currid 65
Currie 269...
Currie 65
Currigan 269...
Currin 269...
Currin 66
O' Currin 269...
Currine 269...
O' Currobeen 269...
Curry **V2**
Curry **V3**
Curry 269...
Mc Curry 269...
O' Curry **V3**
O' Curry 269...
(o) Curry 65,66
O Curry Clan **V4**
O Curry, Corry **V4**
Mac Curtain **V4**
Curtaine 61
Mc Curtaine **V2**
Mc Curtaine 269...
O Curtaine **V2**
O Curtaine **V4**
O' Curtaine **V5**
O' Curtaine 269...
Curtais **V2**
Mc Curtane **V4**
Mc Curtane **V5**
Mc Curtane 269...
Curtayne, J. **V2**
Mc Curten **V3**
Mc Curten **V4**
Mc Curten **V5**
Curteois **V5**
Curteois 269...
Curtesse **V2**
Curtin **V2**
Curtin **V3**
Curtin **V4**
Curtin **V5**
Curtin 269...
Mac Curtin **V3**
Mac Curtin **V4**
Mac Curtin **V5**
(mac Curtin 61
Curtin, J. **V2**
Curtis **V2**
Curtis **V3**
Curtis 269...
Cusack **V2**
Cusack **V3**
Cusack **V5**
Cusack 269...
Cusack(e) 61
Cusack In **V3**
Cusack, M. **V2**
Cusack Of **V3**
Cusack Of **V3**
Cusacke 269...
Cusake 269...
Cusake 61
Cusco 269...
Cushanan 269...
Cushen 269...
Cushin 269...
Cushine **V4**
Cushing **V4**
Cushing 269...
Mac Cushion **V2**
Cushley 269...
Cushley 55
Cushyne **V4**
Cusker 269...
Mc Cusker 269...
(mc) Cusker 70
Cuskern 269...
Mc Cuskern 269...
Cuskery 269...
Cuskor 269...
Cussack 269...
Cussack(e) 61
Cussacke 269...
Cussane 269...
Cussen **V2**
Cussen **V4**
Cussen **V5**
Cussen 269...
Cussen 69
Cussen, E. **V2**
Cussin 269...
Cussock 269...
Cussocke **V3**
Cussocke 269...
Mc Cussocke **V3**
Mc Cussocke 269...
Cussok 269...
Mac Cutcheon **V2**
Mc Cutcheon 269...
Mc Cutcheon 70
Cuthbert **V5**
Cuthbert 269...
Cuthbert, **V2**
Cuthbertson **V2**
Cyrch 269...
D' Aeth 155
D.l. 269...
D'altera **V4**
D'alton **V2**
D'alton **V3**
D'anvers **V4**
D'arcy **V3**
D'ell 269...
D'esterre **V3**
D'evelyn 269...
D'oilier 155
Mac Daboe **V2**
Dacey **V4**
Dacey 269...
Mc Dacker 269...
Dackham **V2**
Dackson **V3**
Dacy **V4**
Dacy 269...
O' Dacy 269...
Mc Dade **V5**
Mc Dade 73
Dae **V3**
Mc Dae **V3**
Mc Dae 269...
O' Dae **V3**
O' Dae 269...
Mc Dae, O'dae **V3**
Daffy **V3**
Daffy 73
O' Daffy **V3**
Dag(g) 74
Dagg **V2**
Dagg 269...
Dahill **V4**
Dahill 269...
Dahill 74
O Dahill **V4**
Mac Daibid **V2**
Daibis **V2**
Mc Daid **V4**
Mc Daid 269...
(mc) Daid 73,85
Dailey **V3**
Dailey **V4**
Daily **V2**
Daily **V3**
Daily **V4**
Daily 269...
Daily 73
Daintrey **V4**
Dairsig **V2**
Dal Gcas **V3**
O' Dalaig **V2**
Dalcassion **V3**
Dalcassions **V4**
Dale **V4**
Daley **V2**
Daley **V3**
Daley 269...
O Daley **V4**
Dalhouse 269...
Dalie 269...
O' Dallagher **V5**
Dallaher **V5**
Dallaher 74
Dallas 269...
Dalley **V3**
Dalli 269...
O Dallie **V4**
Dallis **V3**
Dallway 269...
Dally **V2**
Dally **V3**
Dally 269...
O' Dally **V3**
O Dally **V4**
O' Dally **V5**
O' Dally 269...
Daltin 73
Dalton **V2**
Dalton **V3**
Dalton **V4**
Dalton **V5**
Dalton 269...
Dalton 73
Daltons Of **V2**
Daly **V2**
Daly **V3**
Daly **V4**
Daly 269...
O' Daly **V2**
O' Daly **V3**
O Daly **V4**
O' Daly **V5**
O' Daly 269...
O Daly 73
O' Daly, A. **V2**
Daly In 1659 **V3**
Daly In **V3**
O Daly Of **V4**
O Daly Poets **V4**
O' Daly, Rev. **V2**
Daly's Lane **V2**
Dalyell 269...
Dalzell 269...
Dalziel **V2**
Damer **V2**
Danaher **V2**
Danaher **V5**
Danaher 269...
Danaher 75
Dancer 269...
Dancey 74
Dandridge 269...
Dane 269...
Dane 75
Danesfort, L. **V2**
Danger 269...
Daniel **V2**
Daniel **V5**
Daniel 269...
Mc Daniel **V2**
Mc Daniel **V3**
Mc Daniel **V4**
Mc Daniel **V5**
Mc Daniel 269...
(mc) Daniel 73,91
Daniell **V4**
Daniell 269...
Mc Daniell **V2**
Mc Daniell **V3**
Mc Daniell **V4**
Mc Daniell 269...
(mc) Daniell 73,83
O' Daniell **V5**
O' Daniell 269...
Daniels **V2**
Daniels **V3**
Daniels **V4**
Danihy 269...
Danley 269...
Mc Danll 269...
Dannaher **V5**
Dannaher 75
O' Dannell **V5**
O' Dannell 269...
Dannelly 269...
Dannelly 84
Dant 269...
Danter **V3**
Danter **V4**
Danville, Il. **V2**
M' Dara 269...
Mac Darac **V2**
Darby **V2**
Darby **V5**
Darby 269...
(mac Darby 74
Darcey **V3**
Darcey 269...
O Darcey 74
Darcy **V2**
Darcy **V3**
Darcy 269...
(mac Darcy 74
Darcys **V2**
Dardis 269...
Dardis 75
Darditz 75
Dargan **V4**
Dargan 269...
Dargan 76,155
O Dargan **V4**
Dargent 155
O' Darian 269...
Darl(e)y 76
Darley **V2**
Darley **V4**
Darley 269...
Darley, **V2**
Darling 155
Darling 269...
Darly **V4**
Darly 269...
Darmody 269...
Darmody 81
Darra 76
Mac Darra(g)h 76
Darrach 76
Darrack **V2**
Darragh 269...
Darragh 76
Mc Darragh 269...
Darren 76
Darrynane, **V2**
Darson 269...
Darsy 269...
Dartnell **V3**
Darwell 269...
Dashwood **V2**
Dashwood **V4**
Dashwood 269...
Dason 269...
Datun **V2**
Dauenport 269...
Daugherty **V3**
Daugherty **V4**
Daughton **V2**
Dauid **V4**
Mc Dauid **V2**
Mc Dauid **V4**
Mc Dauid **V5**
Mc Dauid 269...
Dauies **V5**
Dauies 269...
Dauis 269...
Daunt **V4**
Daunt 74
Daunte **V4**
Dauntre **V4**
Dauson 269...
Davane 269...
Davenport **V3**
Davenport **V4**
Davenport 269...
Davern 269...
Davern 75
Davey 269...
Mac David 76
Mc David **V4**
Mc David **V5**
Davidson **V2**
Davidson 269...
Davies **V2**
Davies 269...
Davies 76
Davies, Eliz. **V2**
Davin 269...
Davine 82
Davis **V2**

V2 = Families of Co. Kerry **V3** = Families of Co. Clare **V4** = Families of Co. Cork **V5** = Families of Co. Limerick

Davis **V3**
Davis269...
Davis76,200
Davison269...
Davison85
Daviss269...
Davit **V3**
Mc Davit **V4**
(mc) Davit(t)73,85
Davitt269...
Mc Davitt **V2**
Mc Davitt **V4**
Davock77
Davoran75
O' Davoran **V3**
Davoren **V3**
O' Davoren **V3**
O' Davoren269...
O Davoren75
Davorin75
O' Davorin269...
Davy **V4**
Davy269...
Davy Davie **V4**
Davys269...
Davys34
Daw75
Dawes **V3**
Daweson75
Dawkins269...
Dawl(e)y73
Dawley **V4**
Dawley269...
Dawly **V4**
Dawly269...
Dawney269...
Dawson **V2**
Dawson **V3**
Dawson **V4**
Dawson269...
Dawson75,94
Dawtin269...
Dawton **V2**
Daxon **V3**
Day **V2**
Day **V3**
Day269...
O' Day **V3**
(o) Day75
Day, Francis **V2**
Day, Isabella **V2**
O' Day, O'dea **V2**
O' Day, O'dea **V5**
Day, Rev. **V2**
Day-stokes **V2**
Dayhill74
Dayley269...
Dayley73
O Dayley **V4**
Dayly **V4**
Dayly269...
O Dayly **V2**
O Dayly **V4**
O' Dayly **V5**
O' Dayly269...
O Dayly75
Days **V4**
De Angulo **V2**
De Angulo **V4**
De Auliffe **V4**
De Baroid **V4**
De Barra **V2**
De Barrie **V4**
De Blagd **V2**
De Bolltun **V2**
De **V2**
De Braose **V3**
De Briotun **V2**
De Britt **V2**
De Brus **V2**
De Buitileir **V2**
De Burc **V2**
De Burgh76
De Burgo **V3**
De Burgos **V2**
De Canntual **V2**
De Canntun **V4**
De Cantelowe **V2**
De Cantelupe **V2**
De Cantillon **V2**
De Cantlon's **V2**
De Capella **V2**
De Cappell **V4**
De Carew **V2**
De Carrun **V2**
De Caunteton **V4**
De Clahull **V2**
De Clare **V3**
De Cleatun **V2**
De Clohuile **V2**
De Clohulle **V2**
De Cogan **V2**
De Cogan **V3**
De Cogan **V4**
De Courcey **V4**
De Courcey, **V2**
De Courcy **V2**
De Courcy **V4**
De Courcys **V4**
De Coursy **V4**
De Cuirteis **V2**
De Cuitleir **V2**
De Dannan **V2**
De Ermot269...
De Foy155
De Freins **V2**
De Gaillide **V2**
De Grandison **V2**
De Grote129
De Guines **V4**
De Hal **V2**
De Hore **V2**
De Keting **V2**
De **V4**
De La Cousa **V2**
De La Huse **V2**
De La Roche **V2**
De La Roche **V4**
De Lacies **V3**
De Lacy **V2**
De Lap78
De Lappe **V4**
De Laundre **V2**
De Lench **V4**
De Long **V3**
De Long79
De Marascal **V2**
De Marisco **V2**
De Moleyns **V2**
De Nagle **V4**
De Nais **V2**
De Nogla **V2**
De Pierce **V2**
De Pionbroc **V2**
De Poer **V2**
De Portuil **V2**
De Roche **V4**
De Roiste **V4**
De Rupe **V4**
De Ruthyen **V2**
De Stacabul **V2**
De Stack **V2**
De Stokke **V2**
De Thick **V2**
De Wilton **V2**
De Wyk **V2**
De'ap269...
Dea **V2**
Dea269...
O' Dea **V2**
O' Dea **V3**
O' Dea269...
O Dea75
O' Dea In 1850s **V3**
O Dea, O' Day **V3**
O' Dea, Story Of **V3**
Deacon **V4**
Deacon **V5**
Deacon269...
O' Deadig **V2**
Deady **V2**
Deady269...
O' Deagaid **V2**
O' Deagain **V2**
Deagan76
Deake269...
Dealy269...
Dealy73
Dean **V3**
Dean269...
Deane **V2**
Deane **V3**
Deane **V4**
Deane **V5**
Deane269...
Deane76
Deane, Jas. **V2**
Deane, Sir M. **V4**
Deare269...
Deargan **V4**
Mc Deargan **V4**
Mc Deargan **V5**
Dearing79
O' Deas **V3**
Dease **V2**
Dease **V4**
Dease77
Deasey **V4**
Deasey77
O Deasey **V4**
Deasy **V4**
Deasy269...
Deasy77
Deasy, Dease **V4**
Death155
Deathy5
Deatick **V2**
Deatick269...
Debart269...
Debois269...
Decourcy **V4**
Decourcy77
Dee **V2**
Dee **V4**
Dee269...
O' Dee **V5**
O' Dee269...
O Dee75
Deece77
Deegan **V2**
Deegan269...
Deegan76,89
Deegin **V2**
Deehan269...
Deeley77
Deelie77
Deely269...
Deely73,77
Deen **V2**
Deen269...
Deeney269...
Deeney77,215
Deenihan **V2**
Deenihan87
Deeny269...
Deeny77
Deering **V2**
Deering269...
Deering79
Deermott269...
Deery269...
Deery77
Deevey269...
Deevey80,83
Deevoy83
Deevy269...
Deevy80,83
Deey269...
Deffely269...
Deffely82
Defoe155
Defoix155
Degane76
Dehorty269...
Deighan269...
O Deighan77
Del **V2**
O' Del **V2**
O' Del269...
Dela Touche76
Delacherios269...
Delacherois76
Delacourt **V4**
Delacourt269...
Delafeld112
Delafield79,112
Delafyeld269...
Delahanty **V3**
Delahide **V3**
Delahide **V4**
Delahide269...
Delahoid79
Delahoyd269...
Delahoyde **V3**
Delahoyde79
Delahunt269...
Delahunt79
Delahunty **V3**
Delahunty269...
Delahunty79
Delahyde **V3**
Delahyde79
Delamar269...
Delamare269...
Delamere79
Delane269...
Delane77
Delaney **V2**
Delaney **V3**
Delaney269...
O Delaney77
Delanty79
Delany269...
O' Delany **V3**
Delap **V2**
Delapp269...
Delarahe269...
Delargy79
Delasale269...
Delay269...
Delea269...
Delea95
(van) Deleur259
O Dell **V4**
O Dell **V5**
O Dell77
Dellahoide269...
Dellany269...
Dellany77
Delmage **V3**
Delmege **V2**
Delmege **V3**
Delmege82
Delmore79
Deloohery269...
Deloorey269...
Deloughry **V2**
Deloughry269...
Demcy78
Dempsey **V2**
Dempsey **V4**
Dempsey269...
O Dempsey78
Dempsie78
Dempster269...
Dempsy269...
Dempsy78
Demsey78
O' Demsie269...
Demsy269...
Demsy78
Den79
Deneher269...
Denehy **V4**
Denehy79
O Denehy **V4**
O' Denelin269...
Denison269...
Denn **V3**
Denn **V4**
Denn269...
Dennan **V4**
Dennehey79
Dennehy **V2**
Dennehy **V4**
Dennehy269...
Dennehy78,79
Dennehy, **V2**
Denning269...
Dennis **V2**
Dennis **V4**
Dennis94
Dennis, M. **V2**
Dennish269...
Dennison269...
Denny **V2**
Denny **V4**
Denny269...
Denny78,94
Denny, **V2**
Denny, Col. **V2**
Denny Of **V2**
Denny **V2**
Denny's **V2**
Dennys **V2**
Dent269...
Denver80
Denvir80
Deny269...
O' Deorain **V2**
O' Deoran269...

Deprendevill **V2**
Depri'ndargas **V2**
Derane 85
Derbon 269...
Derby **V3**
Derby 269...
Derby 269...
Mac Derby 74
Mc Derby 269...
Derenzy 80
Derham 269...
Derivin 80
Mc Dermitt **V4**
(mc) Dermitt 78
Dermod **V4**
Mc Dermod **V2**
Mc Dermod **V4**
Mc Dermod **V5**
Mc Dermod 269...
Dermod Oge **V4**
Dermod Oge 269...
Mc Dermodii **V4**
Dermody **V3**
Dermody **V4**
Dermody 269...
Dermody 269...
Dermody 78,81
Mc Dermody **V4**
Mc Dermody **V5**
Mc Dermody 269...
Dermond 269...
O' Dermond 269...
Dermoody 81
Mac Dermot **V5**
Mac Dermot 78,81
Mc Dermot **V3**
Mc Dermot 269...
Dermott 269...
Dermott 78
Mac Dermott **V2**
Mc Dermott **V3**
Mc Dermott **V4**
Mc Dermott **V5**
Mc Dermott 269...
Derrane 85
Derrick, S. **V2**
Derriquin **V2**
Derrmott 269...
O' Derrogan 269...
Derry 269...
Dervan 80
Derwin 80
Des Autiers **V4**
Desmineer 269...
Desmineers 269...
Desmond **V2**
Desmond **V4**
Desmond **V5**
Desmond 269...
Desmond 79
Mc Desmond **V4**
Mc Desmond 269...
Desmond **V2**
Desmoneer 269...
Desmonie **V4**
Desney 269...
Despair 155
Despard 155
Dester **V3**
Dethick **V2**
O' Dett 269...
Dettrick **V2**
Deuenishe 269...
O' Deuer 269...
Deuerax 269...
Deuereux 269...
Devally 82
Devan(e)y 81
Devane **V2**
Devane 269...
Devane 80,82
Devaney **V2**
Devaney 269...
Devany 269...
Mc Deve 269...
Develin 88
Deven 269...
Devenney 81
Devenny 269...
O' Deveny 269...
Dever 269...
(mac Dever 82,88
Deveraux 79
Devere 82,155
Devereaux **V2**
Deverell 79
Devereux 269...
Devereux 269...
Devereux 79,82
Deverill 269...
Devers 269...
Devery 269...
Devery 79
Mc Devet 269...
Devey 80
Devilley 82
Devilly 82
Devily 77
Devin 269...
Devin 82
Devine **V2**
Devine **V4**
Devine 269...
O Devine 82
Devitt **V3**
Devitt **V4**
Devitt 269...
Mc Devitt **V4**
Mc Devitt **V5**
Mc Devitt 269...
(mc) Devitt 73,85
Devlin **V2**
Devlin 269...
O Devlin 88
Devon 269...
Devoroux 269...
Devoy 269...
O' Devoy **V2**
O Devoy 83
Dew **V2**
Mc Dewett 269...
Dey 269...
Deyer **V4**
Deyer 269...
Deyermond 269...
Deyermott 269...
Deys **V4**
Deys 269...
Dezieres **V4**
O' Dheerq 269...
Diamond **V4**
Diamond 269...
Diamond 86
Mac Diarmada **V2**
Diarmid 269...
Diarmod 269...
Diarmond 269...
O' Dicholla **V3**
Dick 269...
Dick 79,80
Dickey 269...
Dickinson **V4**
Dickinson 269...
Dickson **V3**
Dickson **V4**
Dickson **V5**
Dickson 269...
Dickson 80
Mc Dier 269...
Diermott 269...
Dieudonne 155
O' Diff 269...
Diffen 269...
Diffly 82
Digan 269...
Digby **V2**
Digby 269...
Diggin **V2**
Diggin 269...
Diggin 86
Diggins **V4**
Diggs 269...
Digin 86
Dignam 94
Dignan **V2**
Dignan 269...
Dignan 94
Dillan **V4**
Dillan 269...
Dillane **V2**
Dillane **V3**
Dillane **V4**
Dillane 269...
O Dillane **V2**
O Dillane **V4**
O Dillane **V5**
O' Dillane 269...
(o) Dillane 77,80
(o) Dillane 87
O' Dilleen **V3**
O' Dilleen **V5**
O Dilleen 87
O' Dillene **V5**
O' Dillene 269...
Dillion 80
Dillon **V2**
Dillon **V3**
Dillon 269...
Dillon 34,155
Dillon 80,87
(le) Dillon **V2**
O' Dillon 269...
Dillon, **V5**
Dillon Of **V3**
Dillon Of **V2**
Dillone 269...
Dilloughery 269...
Dilworth 269...
Dimmett 269...
Dimock 269...
Dinaghane 87
Dinahan 87
Dinahine 87
Dinan **V4**
Dinan 269...
O' Dinan **V2**
O' Dinan **V3**
O Dinan **V4**
(o) Dinan 80,87
Dinan Of **V3**
Dinane **V4**
Dinane 269...
Dinane 80
O' Dinane **V3**
O Dinane **V4**
O' Dine 269...
Dineen **V2**
Dineen **V4**
Dineen 269...
Dineen 80
Dinehan 87
O' Dinehan **V5**
Dineley **V3**
O Dinerty 86
Dingavan 269...
Dingavan 85
Dingle 269...
Dinham 269...
Dinighan 87
O' Dinnahan **V3**
Dinnahane **V2**
Dinnahane **V5**
Dinnahane 87
Dinneen **V4**
Dinneen 269...
O Dinneen **V4**
O' Dinneen **V5**
O Dinneen 80
Dinneen, **V2**
Dinnegan 269...
Dinnerty 86
Dinsmore 269...
O' Diomasaig **V2**
Diprose 155
Dirane 85
M' Dire 269...
Directories **V3**
Dirrane 269...
Dirrane 85
Dirvan 80
Disbrow 269...
Disken **V4**
Disken 88
Diskin 269...
Diskin 88
Disney 269...
Disney 90
Disny 90
Dispard 155
Diuen 269...
O' Diuin 269...
Diurmagh 269...
Divane 269...
Divelin 269...
Divelin 88
Diver 269...
Diver 269...
Diver 82,88
O' Diver 269...
Divers 88
O' Divet 269...
Divey 83
Divin 269...
Divine **V4**
Divine 82
Diviney 81
Mc Divitt 269...
Divoy 269...
Dixey 269...
Dixon **V3**
Dixon **V4**
Dixon **V5**
Dixon 269...
Dixon 80
Dixson 269...
Dixy 269...
Doave **V4**
Doave 269...
Dob 269...
O' Dobailein **V2**
Dobbin 269...
Dobbin 81
Dobbins 269...
Dobbs 269...
Dobbs 89
Dobbs, Dob **V2**
Dobbyn 81
Dobe 205
Dobin 269...
Dobson 269...
Dobyn 81
Docartaig **V2**
Dockery 269...
Dockery 89
Dockory 89
Dockrell 269...
Dockry 89
Doda **V2**
Dodd **V2**
Dodd **V5**
Dodd 269...
Dodd 86
Dodd, W. H. **V2**
Dodds 269...
Dodgin **V4**
Dodgin 269...
Dodleston 269...
Dods 269...
Dodson 269...
O Doelan 90
Doelane 269...
Doey 269...
O' Dogair **V2**
Doggan 269...
Dogherty **V2**
Dogherty **V3**
Dogherty 269...
O' Dogherty 269...
Dogherty(e) 81
O' Doghertye 269...
Doghon 269...
O' Doghon 269...
O Doghwyn 92
Dogood 129
Doheny **V4**
Doheny 269...
Doheny 89
Doherty **V2**
Doherty **V4**
Doherty 269...
O' Doherty 269...
O Doherty 81
Dohorty 81
Doil 87
Dolan **V4**
Dolan 269...
O' Dolan 269...
(o) Dolan 90
Dolane 269...
Dolane 90
Mc Dole 269...
Dolin **V2**
Dollagher 74
Dollaher 74
Dollane 269...
Dollard 269...
Dolling 81
Dolloghane 269...
Dolloway 269...
Dolmage **V3**
Dolmage **V5**

Dolmage 82
Dologhan 269...
Dologhan 80
Dolphin 90
Dolway 269...
Doly 269...
Domegan 269...
Domnaill **V2**
Mac Domnaill **V2**
O' Domnaill **V2**
Domvil 269...
Domvile 269...
Domvile 82
Domville 82
Mac Donagan **V3**
Donagh **V4**
Donagh 269...
Mac Donagh **V2**
Mac Donagh **V4**
Mac Donagh **V5**
Mac Donagh 82
Mc Donagh **V4**
Mc Donagh 269...
Donaghey 269...
Mc Donaghey 269..
O' Donaghoe **V2**
O' Donaghow **V5**
O' Donaghow 269..
Donaghue **V2**
Donaghue **V3**
Donaghue **V4**
Donaghue 84
O' Donaghue **V2**
Donaghy 269...
O' Donaghy 269...
Donahoe 84
Donahoo **V2**
Donahue **V2**
Donahue **V3**
Donahue 84
Donahy 269...
Donal **V3**
Donal **V4**
Donal 83
Donald 269...
Mac Donald **V2**
Mc Donald 269...
Mc Donald 83,91
Donaldson 269...
Donaldson 84
Donaugh 94
Donavan 85
Doncho 269...

Donden **V5**
Donden 269...
Dondon **V5**
Done 269...
Donegan **V2**
Donegan **V3**
Donegan **V4**
Donegan 269...
Donegan 91
O Donegan **V4**
Donegan **V2**
Donel **V3**
Donel **V4**
Donel 83
Donelan 269...
Donelan 84
O' Donelan 269...
Donell 269...
Mc Donell **V4**
Mc Donell **V5**
Mc Donell 269...
O' Donell 269...
O Donell 83
Donellan 269...
Donellee 269...
Donelly 84
O' Donelly 269...
Donelson 269...
Donely **V4**
Donely 84
O' Donely 269...
O' Donevan **V5**
O' Donevan 269...
Dongan 269...
Dongarvan **V4**
Dongarvan 269...
Mc Doniell **V5**
Mc Doniell 269...
O' Donily 269...
Donion 84
O Donivan **V4**
Donlan 269...
Donlan 84
Donlea 95
Donleavy 83
O' Donlen 269...
Mac Donlevy 83
Donlon 269...
Donlon 84
Donly 269...
Donly 8 4
Donn 269...
O' Donnabain **V2**

Donnagain **V4**
O' Donnagain **V2**
O Donnagain **V4**
Donnal 83
Donnan 269...
Mac Donncadha **V4**
Donnegal 269...
Donnegan **V3**
Donnegan **V4**
Donnegan 91
Donnegan Ogorm... **V4**
Mc Donnel **V3**
Donnelan 269...
Donnell **V3**
Donnell **V4**
Donnell 269...
Donnell 83
Mac Donnell **V2**
Mac Donnell **V3**
Mac Donnell **V5**
Mac Donnell 83
Mc Donnell **V3**
Mc Donnell **V4**
Mc Donnell 269...
Mc Donnell 269...
Mc Donnell 91
O' Donnell **V2**
O Donnell **V3**
O Donnell **V4**
O' Donnell **V5**
O' Donnell 269...
O Donnell 83
O' Donnell **V2**
Donnell **V2**
O' Donnell Of **V3**
Donnellan **V3**
Donnellan 269...
O Donnellan 84
Donnellen 84
O' Donnells Of **V2**
Donnelly **V2**
Donnelly **V4**
Donnelly 269...
O Donnelly **V4**
O Donnelly 84
Donnelly **V2**
Donnelon 269...
O' Donngaile **V2**
Mc Donnogh **V2**
Mc Donnogh **V3**
Mc Donnogh **V4**
Mc Donnogh **V5**
Mc Donnogh 269...

Donnogher 269...
O' Donnoghue, **V2**
Donnoldson 269...
Mac Donnough **V3**
Mc Donnough 269.
Mc Donnough 82
Donnovane **V4**
Donnovane 269...
Donocho 269...
O Donogan **V4**
Donogh 269...
Mac Donogh **V3**
Mac Donogh 82
Mc Donogh **V2**
Mc Donogh **V3**
Mc Donogh **V4**
Mc Donogh **V5**
Mc Donogh 269...
Mac Donogh Duhallow **V4**
Mac Donogh Of **V2**
Donogh Oge **V4**
Donogh Oge 269...
Mc Donoghe **V4**
Donoghoe 269...
O' Donoghoe **V2**
O Donoghoe **V4**
Donoghow **V3**
Donoghow **V4**
Donoghow 269...
O' Donoghow **V3**
O Donoghow **V4**
O' Donoghow 269..
Donoghue **V2**
Donoghue **V4**
Donoghue 269...
O' Donoghue **V2**
O Donoghue **V3**
O Donoghue **V4**
O' Donoghue 269...
O Donoghue 84
O' Donoghue **V2**
O Donoghue **V4**
O' Donoghue **V2**
Donoghue **V2**
O' Donoghue Of **V2**
Mc Donoghy 269...
Donogoroge **V3**
Donohoe **V3**
Donohoe **V4**
Donohoe 269...
Donohoe 84
Donohue 269...
O' Donohue In **V3**

Donojo 84
Mc Donold 91
Donoldson 269...
Donorty 269...
Donough **V3**
(m') Donough 82
(m') Donough 94
Mac Donough **V2**
Mac Donough **V4**
Mc Donough 269...
Donoughoe 84
Donovan **V2**
Donovan **V4**
Donovan 269...
O' Donovan **V3**
O Donovan **V4**
O' Donovan **V5**
O' Donovan 269...
O Donovan 85
O Donovan Castle **V4**
O' Donovan **V2**
Donovan - **V4**
O' Donovan Of **V2**
Donovane **V4**
Donovane 269...
Donovane 85
Mc Donovane **V4**
Mc Donovane 269..
O Donovane **V4**
O' Donovane 269...
O Donyvane **V4**
Dooal 269...
Dooal 87
Doocey 95
Doocy 95
Doody **V2**
Doody **V4**
Doody **V5**
Doody 269...
Doody 86
O Doody **V4**
O' Doody 269...
Dooey 269...
Doogan **V3**
Doogan 269...
Doogan 89
O' Doogan **V3**
O' Doogan 269...
Dooghan 90
O' Dooghany 269...
Doogin **V3**
Doogin 269...
Doohan **V3**

Doohan 269...
O' Doohan **V3**
O Doohan 90
Doohey 93
Doohig **V2**
Doolady 269...
Doolady 269...
Doolan **V2**
Doolan **V4**
Doolan 269...
Doolan 90
O' Doolan **V2**
O' Doolan 269...
Doolen 86
Dooley **V2**
Dooley **V3**
Dooley **V4**
Dooley 269...
O Dooley **V4**
O Dooley 91
Doolin **V4**
Doolin 269...
Doolin(g) 86
Dooling **V2**
Dooling 269...
Dooly **V4**
Dooly 269...
Dooly 86,91
Doona **V2**
Doona 269...
Doonan 269...
Doonan(e) 94
Dooner 269...
Dooney 269...
Doonican 269...
Door **V2**
O Doorie 91
Doorley 90
Doorly 269...
Doorly 90
Doorty 81
O Dooyiorma 92
Doran **V2**
Doran **V4**
Doran 269...
O' Doran 269...
(o) Doran 85
Doran Arms **V2**
Doran **V2**
Dorane **V4**
Dorane 269...
Dorane 85
O' Dorcain **V2**

Dorcan 93
Dorcey 269...
Dore **V2**
Dore **V5**
Dore 269...
Doren 85
Dorgan **V2**
Dorgan **V4**
Dorgan 269...
Dorgan 76
Dorian 85
Dorling **V4**
Dorling 155
Dorman 269...
Dormer 94
Dornan 269...
Dornan 94
O' Dornan 269...
Dorney **V4**
Dorney 269...
Dorney 95
O' Dorney **V2**
O Dorney **V4**
O' Dorney 269...
O' Dorney **V2**
Dorny 95
Dorohey 95
Dorohy **V2**
O' Dorohy **V2**
O Dorohy 95
Dorran 269...
Dorrance 92
Dorrell **V4**
Dorrian 269...
Dorrity 81
Doud 269...
Doud 86
Douds 269...
Dougan 269...
Dougan 89
Doughan 90
Dougheny 269...
Doughertie **V2**
Dougherty **V3**
Dougherty **V4**
Dougherty 269...
O' Dougherty 269...
O' Doughertye 269.
Douglas **V2**
Douglas 269...
Douglas(s) 85
Douglasse 34
Dougle 269...

Dougles 85
Dougs 269...
Dount 74
Dounter **V3**
Dousse 95
Dovany 81
O' Dovoren **V3**
O' Dovoren 269...
Dow 95
Dowd **V2**
Dowd 269...
O' Dowd **V2**
O' Dowd 269...
O Dowd 86
Dowdal **V2**
Dowdales **V2**
Dowdall **V2**
Dowdall **V5**
Dowdall 269...
Dowdall 86
Dowdall **V2**
Dowden **V4**
O Dowdican 95
Dowds 269...
Dowds 86
Dowdy **V4**
Mc Dowell 269...
Mc Dowell 94
Dower **V2**
O' Dower 269...
Dowey 93
O' Dowey 269...
Mc Dowgall 269...
Dowgane **V4**
Dowlan 269...
Dowlan 86
Dowlapp 78
Mc Dowle 269...
Dowley **V3**
Dowley 269...
Dowley 86
Dowlin 269...
O' Dowlin **V2**
Dowlin Of **V2**
Dowling **V2**
Dowling **V3**
Dowling 269...
O Dowling 86
Dowling Of **V2**
Dowlins **V2**
Mc Dowll 94
Dowly **V4**
Dowly 91
O Dowly **V4**
Dowman **V2**
Downan **V4**
Downbarr 34
Downdaniel **V4**
Downes **V2**
Downes **V3**
Downes **V5**
Downes 269...
Downes 92
Downey **V2**
Downey **V3**
Downey **V4**
Downey 269...
Mc Downey 269...
O' Downey **V2**
O Downey **V4**
O' Downey **V5**
O Downey 92
Downing **V2**
Downing **V4**
Downing **V5**
Downing 269...
Downing 80
Downs **V5**
Downs 92
Downy **V4**
Downy 92
Dowse 95
Dowty **V4**
O' Dowy 269...
O' Doy 269...
Doyle **V2**
Doyle **V3**
Doyle **V4**
Doyle 269...
Mc Doyle 269...
(mc) Doyle 87
O' Doyle **V2**
O Doyle **V3**
O Doyle **V4**
O' Doyle 269...
O Doyle 87
(o) Doyne 87,89
Doynes 87
Dracot 94
Draddy **V4**
Draddy 95
Drahan 94
Drain 2
Drain 269...
Drake **V2**
Drake **V4**
Drake 269...
Drake 87
Draper **V4**
Draper **V5**
Draper 269...
Draughan 94
O' Drea **V2**
O' Drea 269...
O Drea 95
Drean 2
Dreiling 269...
Dreinan 269...
Dreng 95
Drennan 269...
O' Drennan **V3**
O Drennan 92
Drew **V2**
Drew **V3**
Drew **V4**
Drew **V5**
Drew 269...
Drew 88,95
Drew, Rev. **V2**
Drewery 88
Drewitt 155
Drewry 88
Dribson **V5**
Dribson 269...
De Drinagh **V4**
Drinan **V3**
Drinan **V4**
Drinan 269...
Drinan 92
O Drinan **V4**
Drinane **V4**
Drinane 269...
Dring **V4**
Dring 95
Driscall 88
Drischolle **V4**
Driscol **V4**
O Driscol **V4**
Driscoll **V2**
Driscoll **V4**
Driscoll 269...
O' Driscoll **V2**
O Driscoll **V3**
O Driscoll **V4**
O' Driscoll 269...
O Driscoll 88
O Driscoll Clan **V4**
O Driskeill **V4**
Driskell 269...
Driskill 88
O Driskoill **V4**
Driskol **V4**
Driskol 88
Drislane **V4**
Drislane 95
Drochan 269...
Droghan 269...
Drohan **V4**
Drohan 269...
Drohan 94
Drohane **V4**
O' Droighneain **V3**
O' Droma **V2**
Dromgoole 95
Mc Dromma 269...
O' Dromma 269...
Dromond 34
Droope 269...
Drope 269...
Drops 269...
Drouet 155
Drough 269...
Droughan 94
Droughon 94
Drought 269...
Drought 88,155
O' Druaid **V2**
Drue 269...
Druery 269...
Druery 88
Drum, **V2**
Drum 269...
Drum 94
O' Drum 269...
Drumgold 95
Drumgool(d) 95
Drumgoole 95
Drumm 269...
Drumm 94
Drummond **V2**
Drummond 269...
Drummond 34,94
Drummy **V4**
Drummy 269...
Drummy 94
Drury **V2**
Drury **V3**
Drury 269...
Drury 88
Drury, Drew **V4**
Dryden **V4**
Du Cane 155
Du Quesne 155
Duane **V4**
Duane 269...
Duane 80
O' Duane **V2**
O' Duane **V3**
O' Duane **V5**
Duant 74
O' Dubagain **V2**
O' Dubain **V2**
O' Dubda **V2**
O' Duben **V2**
O Dubhduin **V3**
O' Dubhghuill **V2**
Dublack 269...
O' Dublainn **V2**
O' Dublavic **V2**
O' Dubtaig **V2**
O' Dubuidir **V2**
Ducey **V2**
O Ducey 95
Ducie 95
Duckenfield 269...
Duckett **V2**
Duckett 92
Duckingfield 269...
880 Ducklow 269...
Duclos **V4**
Ducy 95
Duddy 269...
Duddy 86
Duderan 269...
Dudgeon **V2**
Dudgeon 269...
Dudican(e) 95
Dudley **V2**
Dudley **V4**
Dudley 269...
Dudly 269...
Dudney 155
Duff **V5**
Duff 269...
(o) Duff 89,92
Duffay 93
Duffe **V4**
Duffe 269...
Duffesy **V2**
Duffey **V4**
Duffey 269...
Duffey 93
Duffie 269...
Duffie 93
O' Duffie 269...
Duffield **V2**
Duffin 269...
Duffin 92
Duffy **V3**
Duffy **V4**
Duffy 269...
O Duffy **V4**
O Duffy 93
Duffyne 92
Mac Dugall 94
Dugan **V3**
Dugan **V4**
Dugan 269...
Dugan 76,89
Mc Dugan **V4**
O' Dugan **V3**
O Dugan **V4**
O Dugan Fermoy **V4**
Dugen 269...
Duggan **V2**
Duggan **V4**
Duggan 269...
O Duggan **V4**
O Duggan 89
Duggen 89
Dugin 269...
Dugine 269...
Duheny 89
Duhig **V2**
Duhig **V4**
Duhig 269...
Duhig 93
Duhy 269...
O' Duibginn **V2**
O' Duibluacra **V2**
Duigan 269...
Duigen 269...
Duigenan 94
O' Duigenan 269...
Duigin **V3**
O' Duigin **V3**
Duignan 269...
Duignan 94
O' Duilleain **V2**
Duin 269...
Duine 269...
O' Duineacair **V2**
O' Duineacda **V2**
Duing 269...
O' Duinin **V2**
O Duinin Poets **V4**
O' Duinn **V2**
Duke **V2**
Duke 269...
O' Dulane 269...
Dulanty 269...
Dulany 269...
Dulany 77
Dulapp 78
Dulau 155
O' Dule **V5**
O' Dule 269...
Duley 269...
O Dulinge **V2**
O' Dulinge 269...
Dulinty 269...
Dullaghan 269...
O Dullaghan 93
Dullahunty 269...
Dullaney 77
Dullanie 269...
Dullanty **V5**
Dullanty 79
Dullany 269...
Dullard 269...
Dullchanty 269...
Dullea 269...
Dullea 95
O' Dulleghan 269...
Dullenty 269...
Dulles **V4**
Dulles **V4**
Dulles 269...
Dully 269...
O' Dully 269...
Dullyne 269...
Dulmage 205
Dumas **V2**
Dumegan 269...
Dun 269...
Dun 89
O' Dunadaig **V2**
O' Dunady **V2**
O' Dunady **V5**
O Dunady 93
Mc Dunagan 269...
Dunagin 91
Dunahoo **V2**
Dunasy **V4**
Dunbar 269...
Dunbare 269...
Dunbarr 269...
Dunbarr 34
Duncan 269...
Dunchowe 269...
Dundan **V4**

V2 = Families of Co. Kerry **V3** = Families of Co. Clare **V4** = Families of Co. Cork **V5** = Families of Co. Limerick

Dundasse269...
Dundon V3
Dundon V5
Dundon269...
Dune269...
Dunegan269...
Dunford V2
Dunfy269...
Dungan269...
Dungan91
Dungarvan V4
O Dunghasa V4
Dunican269...
Dunican91
Dunigan91
Dunily269...
Dunion269...
Dunkerron V2
Dunkin V4
Dunkin269...
Dunlape269...
Dunlapp78
Dunlavy83
Dunlea V2
Dunlea V4
Dunlea269...
Dunlea95
Dunleavy V2
Dunleavy269...
Dunleavy83,95
Dunlevy V2
Dunloe V2
Dunlop V2
Dunlop269...
Dunn V3
Dunn V4
Dunn269...
Dunn89
Mc Dunn269...
Dunnady93
O' Dunnady V2
Dunnagin V4
Dunne V2
Dunne V3
Dunne V4
Dunne269...
(o) Dunne89
Dunnigan91
Dunning95
Dunphy269...
Dunphy94
Dunraven, V2
Dunsany269...
Dunscomb V4
Dunscombe V4
Dunscombe269...
Dunseath95
Dunseeth95
Dunseith95
Dunsheath95
Dunshee269...
Dunshee95
Dunsterfield269...
Dunwoody269...
Duogin269...
Durack95
O' Durack V3
O' Durack Of V3
Durcan269...
Durcan93
Durely269...
O' Duringg269...
Durkan269...
(mac Durkan93
Durkin269...
Durly269...
Durmody269...
Durnan94
(o) Durnane94
Durnian269...
Durnian94
Durnin269...
Durnin94
Durnion269...
Durnion94
Durrian269...
Durrian94
Dustin V4
Dutchman V2
Dutton269...
Duval269...
Duvalley269...
(m') Duvany81,94
Duvick269...
Duvin269...
Duwhig V4
Duygin269...
O' Duyne269...
Dwaine269...
Dwane V2
Dwane V4
Dwane269...
Dwane80
O Dwane V4
Dwayne269...
O' Dwayne269...
Dwier V5
Dwier269...
Dwier90
O' Dwier V5
O' Dwier269...
Dwigin269...
Dwigine269...
Dwire V3
Dwire269...
Dwire90
Mc Dwire V3
Dwyar90
Dwyer V2
Dwyer V3
Dwyer V4
Dwyer269...
O Dwyer V3
O' Dwyer V5
O' Dwyer269...
O Dwyer90
O' Dwyer In V3
O' Dwyer, Rev. V2
O' Dwyers Of V3
Dwyre V3
Dwyre269...
Dwyre90
Mc Dwyre V3
O' Dwyre V3
O' Dwyre269...
Dyas269...
Dyche V2
Dyer V2
Dyer V3
Dyer V4
Dyer269...
Mac Dyer V4
Mac Dyer V5
Mac Dyer95
O' Dyer V5
O' Dyer269...
Dyermott269...
O Dyeyneene V4
O' Dyeyneene269..
Dyins269...
Dyle269...
Dyle87
O' Dyman269...
Dymnock269...
Dynan269...
Dynan80
O' Dyoddan269...
Mac Dyre95
Dysert O'dea V3
Dysert O'dea V3
Dyvoy269...
Eachard V2
Eadie V2
Eadie269...
Eagan269...
Eagan96,165
Eagar269...
Eagar96
Eagar, Alex. V2
Eagar V2
Eagar, Rev. V2
Eagen165
Eager V2
Eager269...
Eager(s)96
Eagerton142
Eagerton269...
Eakin269...
Eakins269...
Ealcher V2
Eames V5
Eames269...
Oh Eamtaig V2
Oh Eanna V2
Earl269...
Earl, Errill96
Earl Of Cork - V4
Earl Of V2
Earle V4
Earle269...
Earley98
Earls Of V2
Earlsman V4
Earlsman V4
Earlsman269...
Early269...
Early98
Earph269...
Eastwood269...
Eaton V2
Eaton V3
Eaton V5
Eaton269...
Eatton V4
Eatton269...
Eber V2
Ebercrumber269...
Mc Eboy269...
Ebril(l)96
Ebrill V5
Ebzury269...
Ecclen90
Eccles269...
Ecclin90
Echard V2
Echlin(e)90
Echling90
Eckles269...
Eclston269...
Edalicke V2
Edalicke V2
Mc Edd V5
Mc Edd269...
Edery269...
Edgar269...
Edge90
Edgeworth V2
Edgeworth96
Edgewurth96
Edgworth269...
Edgworth96
Edimson269...
Edkins269...
Edmond V2
Edmond V3
Edmond V4
Edmond269...
Mc Edmond V2
Mc Edmond V3
Mc Edmond V4
Mc Edmond V5
Mc Edmond269...
Edmonds V5
Edmonds269...
Edmondson269...
Edmonston269...
Edmund V3
Mc Edmund V5
Mc Edmund269...
Edmundson97
Edmundston269...
Edney34
Edwards V2
Edwards V3
Edwards269...
Edworth269...
Egan V2
Egan V4
Egan269...
Mac Egan V2
Mac Egan V4
(mac Egan96,165
Mc Egan269...
O Egan V3
Mac Egan As V4
Egane269...
Mc Egane269...
(mc) Egane96
Egar V2
Egar96
Egelton V2
Egerton V4
Eggart269...
Egglington269...
Egglinton269...
Egmont, Earl V4
Egyr V2
Oh Eilide V2
Einey V2
Eirons269...
Eivers269...
Ekin269...
Ekin3
M'c El'istum V2
Elchinder269...
Elder269...
Mac Elderry96
Mac Eldowney92
Mc Eldowney269..
Mc Elduff269...
Elfred269...
Mc Elgun269...
Mc Elgunn269...
Mac Elhar42
Mc Elhar269...
Mac Elheran97
Mac Elheron97
Mc Elhill269...
Mc Elhinney269...
Mc Eligod V2
Eligot V2
Eligot97
Eliott269...
Eliott98
Elison96
Elizabeth V4
Ellard V4
Ellard269...
Ellaw V4
Ellet269...
Ellice269...
Ellies269...
Mac Elligots & V2
Mac Elligott V2
Mac Elligott V5
Mac Elligott97
Mc Elligott269...
Mac Elligott, M. V2
Mc Elligott, V2
Elliot269...
Mc Elliot97
Elliot(t)98
Elliott V2
Elliott V3
Elliott269...
Elliott, Alex. V2
Ellis V3
Ellis V4
Ellis V5
Ellis269...
Ellis96
Ellis, Maj. V2
Ellish269...
Ellison269...
Ellison7,96
Mac Ellistram269..
Mac Ellistrum V2
Ellot269...
Ellott269...
Ellsworth V4
Ellwood269...
Elly269...
Mc Ellygott V2
Mc Ellygott269...
Ellyott V2
Ellyott269...
Mac Elmeel100
Mc Elmeel269...
Elmer269...
Mc Elmurray269...
Elott269...
Elrington V2
Elroi99
Mac Elroy99
Mc Elroy269...
Elshander269...
Mc Elshender269..
Elshinder269...
Elshinder3
Elshner269...
Mc Elshunder269..
Elsworth V4
Elton269...
Eluin269...
Mc Elveaine269...
Mc Elvee171
Mc Elveen156
Mac Elvogue98
Elward269...
Elward7
Mc Elwee269...

V2 = Families of Co. Kerry V3 = Families of Co. Clare V4 = Families of Co. Cork V5 = Families of Co. Limerick

(mc) Elwee 98,171
Elwell **V4**
Elwell **V4**
Elwell 269...
Elwood 269...
Ely **V3**
Em(m)et 99
Embury 205
Emerson **V3**
Emerson 269...
Emigrants **V2**
Emmet **V2**
Emmet **V4**
Emmett **V2**
Emmett **V4**
Emo. 269...
Empson 269...
Mc Enaw 269...
Mc Encarriga **V3**
Mac Enchroe **V3**
Mac Enchroe 97
Mac Enchroe Of **V3**
Mc Encroe **V3**
Mc Encroe 269...
Mac Encroe Mac **V3**
End **V4**
End 269...
Endean **V2**
Mac Endoo **V2**
Mc Eneaney 269...
Mc Eneany 269...
Mac Eneiry **V3**
Mc Eneiry **V4**
Mc Eneiry **V5**
Enernay **V4**
Mac Enerney 269...
Mac Enery **V2**
Mc Enery 269...
Mac Enerys Ln. **V2**
Mc Enestis **V4**
L' Enfaunt 101
England **V3**
England 269...
England 99
English **V2**
English **V4**
English **V5**
English 269...
English 99
English **V3**
English **V2**
Englishby 269...
Englonde 99
L' Englys 99
Mac Eninry 144
(m) Eniry 144
(m) Eniry 156
Mc Eniry **V5**
Mc Eniry 269...
Enith 269...
Mac Ennery **V2**
Ennes 100
Ennis **V3**
Ennis 269...
Ennis Illus. **V3**
Ennis(s) 100
Ennistymon **V3**
Ennos 269...
Ennoss 100
Enocke **V4**
Enocke 269...
Mc Enolly 269...
Enos 100
Enos 269...
Enose 269...
Enra(u)ght 98
Enright **V2**
Enright **V3**
Enright **V4**
Enright **V5**
Enright 269...
Enright 98
Enrite 98
Mac Enroe 229
Mac Enroe 9,97
Mc Enroe 269...
Ensor 100
Mac Entaggert 100
Mac Entasny 12
Mac Entee 100
Mc Entee 269...
M' Enteer 269...
M' Entegart 269...
Mc Entire 269...
Entivistle **V2**
Mc Entyre 269...
Eogan Mor **V4**
Eoganacht **V2**
Eoganacht **V2**
Eoganacht **V2**
Eoghan Mor **V4**
Eoghanacht **V4**
Mac Eoin 269...
Mac Eotac **V2**
Mac Eown 269...
O Erc 100
Ercke 100
Mc Erlain 100
Mc Erlain 269...
Erle Early **V4**
Mac Erlean 100
Mc Erlean 269...
Mc Erleen 100
Mac Erlen 100
(d') Erley 98
Mac Erlyn 100
Erought 269...
Erraught **V2**
Erskin 269...
Erskin(e) 100
Erskine 269...
Ervine 156
Ervine 269...
Erving 269...
Ervinge 269...
Erwin 156,157
Erwin 269...
Esbal 269...
Esbald 269...
Esball 269...
Esbel 269...
Esbil 269...
Esble 269...
Escott **V4**
Escott 269...
Esdale 269...
Eslenan 269...
Esler 269...
Esmond(e) 79,99
Esmonde **V5**
Esmonde 269...
Esnor 269...
D' Espard 155
Estmound 99
(l') Estrange 97
Etchingham 156
Mac Etegart 100
Mc Eteggart 269...
O Etigan 147
Eton 269...
Ettigan 121
Mac Etye 100
Euanson 269...
Mc Euchae 269...
Mac Euchroe 269...
Eugenian **V2**
Eugenian **V4**
Euleston 100
Eurell 268
Eustace **V3**
Eustace **V4**
Eustace 269...
Eustace 97
Eustice 97
Eustis **V4**
Eustis 97
Mc Evaddy 269...
Evans **V2**
Evans **V3**
Evans **V4**
Evans **V5**
Evans 269...
Evans 98
Evans Evens **V4**
Evanson 269...
Evanton 269...
Evarald **V3**
Evarald 269...
Evaster 269...
Eve, Dorothy **V2**
Eveers **V3**
Eveers 269...
Eveleigh **V2**
Evelin 269...
Mc Evely 269...
Evens **V4**
Evens 269...
Everaid 269...
Everard **V3**
Everard 269...
Everard 99
Everatt **V2**
Everhard 99
Evers **V3**
Evers 269...
Everson **V4**
Everson 269...
Mc Evilly 245
Mc Evinie 269...
M' Eviniogh 269...
Mac Evinney 129
D' Evivex 79
Evorard 269...
Evoy 269...
Mac Evoy **V2**
Mac Evoy 269...
Mac Evoy 98
Mc Evoy 269...
Mac Ewan 269...
Ewart 269...
Ewen 100
Mc Ewen 269...
Ewers 269...
Ewin 100
Ewing 269...
Ewing(s) 100
Exham **V2**
Exham **V5**
Exham 269...
Exten 269...
Exton 269...
Eyles **V2**
Eyre(s) 98
Eyres **V3**
Eyres 269...
D' Ezmondiis 99
Mc Fadden 101
Mc Fadden 269...
Faddin 101
Mc Faden 269...
Fadian 101
Mac Fadin 269...
Fadyen 101
M' Fadzen 269...
De Fae 103
O Faelain **V4**
Fagan **V2**
Fagan 101,108
Fagan 135
Fagan 269...
Faggy 269...
Fagherty **V3**
Faghy 101
Fagin 101
Fagon 269...
Faherty 269...
O' Faherty **V3**
O Faherty **V4**
O Faherty 101,106
Fahey 101
Fahey 269...
Fahie 101
Fahy **V2**
Fahy **V3**
Fahy 269...
O Fahy 101
O' Fahy 269...
O' Failbe **V2**
O' Failbhe **V2**
Fair 269...
Fairfax 269...
Fairfield **V2**
Fairis 269...
Fairley 269...
Fairy 269...
Faith 269...
Falhan **V2**
Falkiner 101
Mac Fall 101
Mc Fall 269...
Fallaher 103
Fallaher 269...
Fallan 102
Fallan 269...
Fallard 269...
Fallen 102
Fallin 102
Fallon **V3**
Fallon **V4**
Fallon 269...
O' Fallon **V2**
O Fallon **V4**
(o) Fallon 102
Falloon **V3**
Falloon 102
Falloon 269...
Falloone **V3**
Falloone 269...
(mc) Falls 101
Falquiere **V4**
Faluey **V2**
Faluey 269...
Faluy **V2**
Faluy 269...
Falvey **V2**
Falvey **V3**
Falvey **V4**
Falvey 269...
O' Falvey **V2**
O' Falvey **V3**
O Falvey **V4**
O Falvey 103
O' Falvey **V2**
O' Falveys **V2**
Families Cork **V4**
Famine, The **V2**
Fanan 104
Fanin(g) 104
Faning 269...
Faning **V3**
Faninge 269...
Fanner 269...
Fannesy **V4**
Fannin 104
Fannin 269...
Fanning **V3**
Fanning **V4**
Fanning **V5**
Fanning 104
Fanning 269...
Fanninge 269...
Fannon **V5**
Fannon 104
Fannying 269...
Fannyng 269...
Fannynge 269...
Fant **V5**
(la) Fant 101
Fanyng **V3**
O' Faolain **V2**
Faraday 269...
Faragher 269...
Faraher 269...
Farding **V2**
Fardye 269...
Farel 102
Farelly 102
Farely **V4**
Farely 102
Farely 269...
Faressy **V4**
Farguson 269...
Farhan 269...
Farihy 269...
De Farindon 105
Faris 269...
(mc) Farlan 105
Mac Farland **V2**
Mc Farland 105
Mc Farland 269...
Mc Farlane 269...
Farley **V2**
Farley **V4**
Farley 102
Farley 269...
Farmer **V2**
Farmer 269...
Farmor 269...
Farnan 269...
Farnand 269...
Farneham 269...
Farnham 269...
Farnon 269...
Farr 269...
Farragher 105,115
Farragher 269...
Farraher 115
Farrahill 269...
Farral 102
Farrall 269...
O' Farran 269...

Surname Index

Farrar 269...
Farrell **V2**
Farrell **V4**
Farrell 269...
O Farrell **V4**
O Farrell 102
O' Farrell 269...
Farrelly **V3**
Farrelly **V4**
Farrelly 269...
O' Farrelly **V5**
O Farrelly 102
Farren **V4**
Farren 103
Farren 269...
Farrer 269...
Farressy **V2**
Farressy **V4**
Farrington **V4**
Farrington 105
Farrington 269...
Farris **V2**
Farrissey 105
Farrissy 105
Farron 103
Farry 269...
De Farrynecotter V
Farsfeeld 269...
Farshin 114
Farshin 269...
Farthing **V2**
Farthing **V4**
Farthing 269...
O' Fary 269...
De Faryngton 105
Faucett **V4**
Faugherty **V3**
Faughnan 269...
O Faughnan 105
Faughton 269...
Faulkner 269...
Faulkney 269...
Fawsitt **V4**
Fay 269...
De Fay 103
(du) Fay 101,103
(du) Fay 114
(o) Fay 106
Fay, O'feic **V2**
Faye 103
O' Fea 269...
Feagan 101
Feaghan 106
Feagon 101
Feagon 269...
Feahan **V4**
Feake 269...
Fealan 269...
Fealy **V2**
Fealy 103
Fealy 269...
O' Feargail **V2**
O' Fearguis **V2**
Fearnely 269...
Fearon 103
Fearon 269...
Fearris-beal **V2**
Mac Fearriss **V2**
Feddis 106
Fedegan 269...
O Fedegan 106
Fee 269...
Fee 269...
(mc) Fee 103,106
(mc) Fee 114
O Fee 106
O' Fee 269...
Feehan **V4**
Feehan 101,106
Feehan 269...
O Feehan **V4**
Feeharry 269...
Feehely 269...
Feeheny 152
Feehily 107
Feel(e)y 107
Feeley 269...
Feely **V4**
Feely 269...
Feemu **V4**
O Feenaghty 108
Feeney **V2**
Feeney 269...
O Feeney 108
Feeny 108
Feeny 269...
O' Feeny 269...
Feerick 107
Feerick 269...
Mac Feerish 269...
Mc Feeters 269...
Fegan 101,108
Fegan 269...
O' Fegan 269...
O' Feggan 269...
Feghan 108
Feghany 269...
Feghin 101
Feheely 107
Fehilly 269...
Fehily 269...
Fehoney 269...
O' Feibeannaig **V2**
O' Feic **V2**
Feighan 106,111
Feighan 269...
Feighery 269...
Feighney 269...
Feild **V5**
Feild 112
Feild 269...
Felan 265
Felan 269...
Feley 237
Feley 269...
Fell **V2**
Fellane 269...
Feltham 269...
Fenaghty **V2**
Fenaghty 107,113
Fenaghty 269...
Fenaughty 269...
Fendlon 269...
Fenegan 269...
Fenell **V5**
Fenell 109
Fenell 269...
Fenelly 269...
Fenelon 109
Fenelon 269...
Fenessy 109
O' Fenighan 269...
Fenix **V2**
Fenley 269...
Fenlon 109
Fenlon 269...
Fennar **V3**
Fennell **V2**
Fennell **V3**
Fennell **V4**
Fennell 109
Fennell 269...
Fennelly 109
Fennelly 269...
Fenness(e)y 109
Fennessy **V5**
Fennessy 269...
Fennesy **V4**
Fenosy 269...
Fenoughty 269...
Fenterell 269...
Fenton **V2**
Fenton **V4**
Fenton **V4**
Fenton 107
Fenton 269...
Fenwick 269...
Fenwicke 269...
Feoghney 269...
Feolane **V3**
Feolane 269...
Mac Feorais 109
Fepps **V4**
Fepps 269...
Ferall 269...
O' Ferally **V5**
O' Ferally 269...
Ferberne 269...
Ferbishy 269...
Feregan 111
Ferell 269...
Fergesun 113
Fergie 269...
Fergus 269...
Mc Fergus **V2**
Fergusen 113
Ferguson **V2**
Ferguson **V5**
Ferguson 113
Ferguson 269...
Ferguson's **V2**
O' Fergussa 269...
Fergusson 269...
Ferick 107
O' Ferill 269...
Ferilly **V3**
Ferilly 269...
Ferilry **V3**
Ferilry 269...
De Feringdon 105
Ferinshaugh **V5**
Ferinshaugh 269...
Feris **V2**
Feris **V3**
Feris 269...
Feritter 111
Ferly 102
Ferly 269...
Fermoy **V4**
Fermoy, **V4**
Fermoy Map **V4**
Fern 269...
Ferneley 269...
Fernely 269...
Ferrall 102
Ferrall 269...
O' Ferrall 269...
Ferrally **V5**
Ferrally 269...
Ferran 269...
Mc Ferran 110
Mc Ferran 269...
Ferrell 269...
Ferrely 102
Ferren 110
Ferreter **V2**
Ferreter 111
(o) Ferrigan 111
Ferrilla **V3**
Ferrilla 269...
Ferrilla **V3**
Ferrilly **V3**
Mc Ferrin 110
Ferris **V2**
Ferris **V3**
Ferris **V4**
Ferris 269...
Ferriss **V4**
Ferriter **V2**
Ferriter 111
Mc Ferron 110
Ferry **V4**
Ferry 111
Ferry 269...
O' Ferry 269...
Fertern 269...
Fetherston 269...
Fetrick 111
Mc Fetridge 111
Mc Fetridge 269...
Fetrish 111
Fettridge 111
Fewer 111
Fey **V4**
Fey 103,114
Fey 152
Ffenton **V4**
Ffrench 110
Mac Fheorais **V2**
Mac Fhinn 112
Mac Fhloinn **V4**
O ' Fiaca **V2**
O Fiachain **V4**
O' Fiaie **V2**
Mac Fian'adhuigh V
Fians 111
Mac Fiarais **V2**
O' Fidgeallaig **V2**
Fidgeon 269...
Fie 269...
Field **V2**
Field **V4**
Field **V5**
Field 112
Field 269...
De Field 79
Field Barryroe **V4**
Figgis **V2**
Figgis 111
Figgle 205
O Fihelly **V4**
O' Fihily 269...
Filan 269...
Filbin 269...
O' Filbin 269...
Filgate 111
O' Finagan 269...
O' Finaghan 269...
Finaghty **V2**
Finalay 269...
Finan 111
Finan 269...
O' Finan 269...
Finane 269...
Finch **V2**
Finch **V3**
Finch **V4**
Finch **V5**
Mac Fineen **V2**
Mc Fineen **V3**
Mc Fineen 269...
Fineene **V4**
Mc Fineene **V3**
Mc Fineene 269...
Finegan 269...
Finegan(e) 103
O' Finegane 269...
Fineran 110
Finerty 113
Finerty 269...
Fines 269...
Fing **V4**
Finglas 108
Finigan 103
Finine **V4**
O Finine **V4**
O' Finine 269...
Finlay 269...
Finn **V2**
Finn **V4**
Finn 269...
Mac Finn **V2**
Mac Finn 112
O' Finn **V2**
O Finn **V4**
O Finn 112
O' Finn 269...
Finnally 269...
Finne **V4**
Mc Finne **V4**
Mc Finne 269...
Mac Finneen **V2**
Mac Finneen 112
Mc Finneen **V2**
Finnegan, **V2**
Finnegan 269...
O Finnegan 103
Finnellan 109
Finnelly 269...
Finneran 269...
O Finneran 110
Finnerrell **V3**
Finnerrell 111
Finnerty **V2**
Finnerty 113
Finnerty 269...
O' Finnerty **V2**
Finnevar 112
Finney **V4**
Finney 104,108
Finney 269...
Finnigan 103
Mac Finnin Of **V2**
Finnucane **V2**
Finnucane 103
M' Finnucane 114
Mac Finnucane **V2**
Mac Finnucane **V3**
Mac Finnucane **V5**
Finny 104,108
Finny 269...
Fintan **V2**
Finucane **V2**
Finucane 114
Finucane 269...
Finy 269...
O' Finy 269...
Mc Finyne **V4**
Mc Finyne 269...
O' Fionnacta **V2**
O' Fionnagain **V2**

V2 = Families of Co. Kerry **V3** = Families of Co. Clare **V4** = Families of Co. Cork **V5** = Families of Co. Limerick

Fiontain V2
Mac Firbis V3
Firman 269...
Fise V4
Fise 269...
Fish V4
Fishe 34
Fisher V2
Fisher V4
Fisher V5
Fisher 269...
Fisher, V2
Fisher, V2
O' Fitceallaig V2
Fitch 105
Fitch 269...
Fitchpatrick 105
Fitgerald, J. V2
Fits 198
Fitton V3
Fitts 269...
Fitz 105,112
Fitz 198
Fitz 269...
Fitz.edmond V4
Fitz.gerrald V4
Fitz Gibbon V3
Fitz.gibbon V4
Mc Fitz James V3
Fitz V2
Fitz.richard V4
Fitz.robert V4
Fitz (see Fz.) V4
Fitz-henry V5
Fitz-henry 269...
Fitz-stephen V4
Fitzandrew 4
Fitzanthony V2
Fitzaucher V2
Fitzauger V2
Fitzaunger V2
Fitzdavid 269...
Fitzedmd. V2
Fitzedmd. 269...
Fitzedmond V3
Fitzedmond 269...
Fitzedmund V2
Fitzell V2
Fitzelle V2
Fitzelle 115
Fitzerald 104
Fitzerin V2
Fitzgarrett Donegal V4
Fitzgerald V2
Fitzgerald V3
Fitzgerald V4
Fitzgerald V5
Fitzgerald 104
Fitzgerald 269...
Fitzgerald V3
Fitzgerald V2
Fitzgerald In V3
Fitzgerald In V3
Fitzgerald Of V2
Fitzgerald, Rev. Richard V2
Fitzgeralds V2
Fitzgeralds V3
Fitzgeralds V4
Fitzgeralds - V2
Fitzgergald 269...
Fitzgerold V4
Fitzgerold 104
Fitzgerold 269...
Fitzgerrald V3
Fitzgerrald V4
Fitzgerrald 104
Fitzgerrald 269...
Fitzgerrold V3
Fitzgerrold 104
Fitzgerrold 269...
Fitzgibbon V2
Fitzgibbon V3
Fitzgibbon V4
Fitzgibbon 104
Fitzgibbon 269...
Fitzgibbon(s V5
Fitzgibbons V4
Fitzgibbons 104
Fitzgibbons 122
Fitzgriffin V2
Fitzharris V2
Fitzharris V3
Fitzharris V5
Fitzharris 112
Fitzharris 269...
Fitzharry 112
Fitzhenry V2
Fitzhenry 112,144
Fitzhenry, V2
Fitzherbert V2
Fitzherbert 105
Fitzherbore 269...
Fitzhubert 105
Fitzhugh V5
Fitzimmons V2
Fitzimons 269...
Fitzjames V2
Fitzjames V3
Fitzjames V4
Fitzjames 269...
Fitzjohn V2
Fitzjohn V3
Fitzjohn 269...
Fitzmaurice V2
Fitzmaurice V3
Fitzmaurice V4
Fitzmaurice 105
Fitzmaurice 269...
Fitzmeiler 201
Fitzmerie V3
Fitzmerie 269...
Fitzmorice 105
Fitzmorish 105
Fitzmorish 269...
Fitzmorrice V2
Fitzmorrice V3
Fitzmorrice 269...
Fitzmorris V4
Fitzmorris 269...
Fitzmorrish V2
Fitzmorrish V3
Fitzmorrish 269...
Fitzmorriss V2
Fitznichas 269...
Fitznicholas V2
Fitznicholas V3
Fitznicholas 269...
Fitzotho V2
Fitzpatrick V2
Fitzpatrick V3
Fitzpatrick V4
Fitzpatrick 105
Fitzpatrick 168
Fitzpatrick 215
Fitzpatrick 269...
Fitzpatrick, V2
Fitzphillip 269...
Fitzpierce V2
Fitzrhys V2
Fitzrichard 269...
Fitzrobert V4
Fitzrobert V4
Fitzsimmon 112
Fitzsimmons V2
Fitzsimmons V5
Fitzsimmons 112
Fitzsimon V2
Fitzsimon V4
Fitzsimon(s) 112
Fitzsimon(s) 171
Fitzsimons 269...
Fitzstephen V2
Fitzstephen 246
Fitzsummons 269...
Fitzsumons 269...
Fitzsymon V2
Fitzsymon 112
Fitzsymonds 112
Fitzsymonds 269...
Fitzsymons V2
Fitzsymons 269...
Fitzthomas V2
Fitzwalter V2
Fitzwalter V3
Fitzwalter V4
Fitzwilliam V2
Fitzwilliam V3
Fitzwilliam 106
Fitzwilliams V2
Fitzwilliams 269...
Fivey 115
Fixer 269...
Fizzell V2
Fizzell 115
Flack 269...
Fladger 269...
Flagetter V4
Flagetter 269...
Flagettor V4
Flagettor 269...
Flagherty 106
Flagherty 269...
O' Flagherty V3
Flahavan V4
Flahavan 269...
Flahaven V4
Flahaven 114
Flahavin V2
Flaherty V2
Flaherty V3
Flaherty 101
Flaherty 269...
O' Flaherty V3
O Flaherty 106
O' Flaherty 269...
Flahive V2
Flahy 269...
O' Flaiteamain V2
O' Flaithri V3
Flaitim V2
Flanagan, V2
Flanagan V3
Flanagan V4
Flanagan 269...
O Flanagan V4
(o) Flanagan 106
O' Flanagan 269...
Flanagane V4
Flanagane 269...
Flanaghan V3
Flanegan 269...
Flaneley 115
Flanergan 269...
Flanery 113
Flang 106
Flang 269...
Flanigan V3
Flanigan V4
Flanigan 106
Flanigan 269...
Flanigane V3
Flanigane V4
Flanigane 269...
O' Flanigane V3
O' Flanigane 269...
Flanly 115
O' Flannabra V2
O' Flannagain V2
Flannagan 106
O' Flannagan 269...
O Flannell 115
Flannelley 115
O Flannelly 115
Flannery V2
Flannery V3
Flannery 269...
O' Flannery V3
O' Flannery V5
O Flannery 113
O' Flanngaile V2
Flannigin 106
Flanora 269...
Flanory 113
Flanory 269...
Flanury 113
Flanury 269...
Flarergan 269...
Mc Flarty 269...
Flatery 114
Flathery V4
O Flathery V4
O' Flathery V5
Flatley 114
Flatly 114
Flattelly 114
Flattery V4
Flattery 114
Flattery 269...
O' Flattery V3
Flattley 269...
Flavell 269...
Flaven 114
O' Flavey V2
Flavin V2
Flavin V4
Flavin 114
Flavin 269...
O Flavin V4
Fleeming 269...
Fleens 107,113
Fleens 269...
Fleete V2
Fleetwood V4
Fleetwood 269...
Fleetwoode V4
Fleetwoods V2
Fleming V2
Fleming V3
Fleming V4
Fleming V5
Fleming 107
Fleming 269...
(le) Fleming V2
Fleminge V4
Flemish N. 129
Flemming V4
Flemming 269...
Flemming(e) 107
Flemminge 269...
Flemmyng 107
Flemon 107
Flemon 269...
Flemyne 269...
Flemyng V2
Flemyng 107
Flemyng 269...
Flemyng V3
Flenten 269...
Flenter 269...
Fletcher V2
Fletcher V4
Fletcher 269...
Fletcher V2
Fletthery 269...
Fleury 269...
Flin 269...
O Flin V4
O' Flin 269...
O Fline V4
O' Fline 269...
Fling V4
Fling 113
Fling 269...
O' Fling 269...
Flinge 269...
Flinge 269...
O' Flinge 269...
Flinn V2
Flinn 107,113
M' Flinn 269...
Flinne V4
Flinne 269...
O Flinne V4
Flint V4
Flint 269...
Flinter 111
O' Floin V2
Mag Floinn V2
O Floinn V4
Flood 107,115
Flood 250
Flood 269...
Floody 269...
Florette V2
Flow'rdewe 34
Flower V2
Flower V3
Flower 269...
Flowre 269...
Floyd V2
Floyd V3
Floyd 107,115
Floyd 269...
Floyne 269...
O' Fluen 269...
Flyming V2
Flyming V4
Flymynge V3
Flyn 269...
Flyn(e) 107,113
Flyne 269...
O Flyne V2
O Flyne V4
O' Flyne V5
O' Flyne 269...
Flyng V4
Flyng 107,113
Flyng 269...
Flynn V2
Flynn V4
Flynn 269...

Flynn269...
O Flynn **V3**
O Flynn **V4**
(o) Flynn113
O' Flynn269...
O Flynn Carberry **V4**
O Flynn(e)107
O' Flynn, Fr. **V2**
Flynn Loch **V4**
Flynn Of **V2**
Flynne269...
O Flynne **V4**
O' Flynne269...
Foaly269...
Foard114
Foard269...
Fodaghan269...
Fodey247
Fodha269...
Ne Fody **V4**
De Foe155
Foester269...
Fog269...
O' Fogartaig **V2**
Fogarty **V2**
Fogarty **V4**
Fogarty269...
O Fogarty **V4**
(o) Fogarty108
(o) Fogarty118
Fogaton269...
Fogerty108
Fogg269...
Fogurty269...
O' Foillide **V2**
Folan115
Folan269...
Foley **V2**
Foley **V3**
Foley **V4**
Foley **V5**
Foley269...
O' Foley **V2**
O Foley **V4**
(o) Foley113,237
(o) Foley 240
Foley Family **V2**
Foli113
Folkiner101
Folliard269...
Folliot269...
Folliott269...
Follon269...
Foly269...
La Font101
Fontaine269...
O' Foodhy269...
Foody269...
Fookes269...
Fooley113
Fooley269...
Fooluiah113
Fooluiah269...
Foord **V3**
Foord269...
Foord(e)114
Foorde269...
Foot **V3**
Foot **V4**
Foot108
Foote **V3**
Foote **V4**
Foote269...
Foots269...
Foran **V2**
Foran **V5**
Foran269...
(o) Foran114
Foran Ford **V4**
Forane114
Forane269...
Forbes108
Forbes269...
Forbes Castle **V2**
Forbess269...
Forbish269...
Forbs108
Ford **V3**
Ford **V4**
Ford269...
Forde **V2**
Forde **V3**
Forde **V4**
Forde114
Forde269...
Forehan269...
Forehane269...
Foreman269...
Forest **V2**
Forest, Sir **V2**
Forestall **V3**
Forestall115
Forestall269...
Forester **V5**
Forgay269...
Forgey269...
Forgie269...
Forgy269...
Forhan114
Forhan269...
Forhane269...
O Forhane **V4**
O Forhane114
Foristel115
Forker269...
Forkin269...
Format **V4**
Format Of **V3**
Fornan **V2**
Forrest **V4**
Forrest115
Forrest269...
Forrestal **V3**
Forrestal(l)115
Forrester **V3**
Forstal **V3**
Forstall **V3**
Forstall115
Forstall269...
Forster **V3**
Forster115
Forster269...
Forsythe269...
Fort269...
Fort Wayne **V2**
Fortescew269...
Fortescue109
Fortescue269...
Forth269...
Fortune114
Fortune269...
Fosberry **V2**
Fosbery **V5**
Fosbery, Mr. **V2**
Fossy269...
Foster **V3**
Foster269...
Fotterell269...
Fouey **V4**
Foules269...
Foulk **V3**
Foulk269...
Foulkard269...
Foulke **V4**
Foulke269...
Foulkes **V2**
Foulks269...
Fouly269...
Founbaine269...
Foundes **V2**
Fountain269...
Fountaine269...
Fourbes269...
Fourhane269...
Fourker269...
Foursides269...
Fowke **V4**
Fowke269...
Fowkes269...
Fowler269...
Fowler34,109
Fowley **V4**
Fowlke **V4**
Fowlkiner101
Fowloo113
Fowlow **V4**
Fowlow269...
O Fowlow **V4**
O' Fowlow269...
O Fowlowe **V4**
O Fowlowe113
O' Fowlowe269...
Fowlue **V4**
Fowlue113
Fowlue269...
O Fowlue **V2**
O' Fowlue269...
Fowly113
O' Fowly269...
Fox **V2**
Fox **V3**
Fox **V5**
Fox109
Fox269...
Fox Of **V3**
Foxall269...
Foxen **V5**
Foxen269...
Foxon269...
Foxwich269...
Foy269...
De Foy155
Foy(e)101,103
Foy(e)114
Foy, O'fiaie **V2**
Foye269...
Foyle115
Foyll115
Foynes111
Fr. Mathews **V4**
Fraher **V5**
Fraher115
Fraher269...
Frahill115
Frain115
Frain269...
Frame **V4**
Frame108
France, To **V2**
Frances110
Francey269...
Francis **V2**
Francis110
Francis269...
Francis, **V5**
Franciscan **V2**
Franck110
Franck269...
Frane115
Frank(e)110
Franke **V4**
Franke269...
Franklin **V4**
Franklin **V5**
Franklin269...
Franks110
Franks Of **V2**
Fraser **V4**
Fraser114
Fraser269...
Fraser, J. **V2**
Fraser, S. **V2**
Frasier **V2**
Frawley **V2**
Frawley **V3**
Frawley **V5**
Frawley114
Frawley269...
Frayne269...
Frazer **V2**
Frazer114
Frazer269...
Frazier **V4**
Frazier114
O' Freagaile **V2**
Freak **V4**
Freal110
Freborne269...
Free269...
Free Passage **V3**
Freeburn269...
Freek **V4**
Freeke **V4**
Freeke269...
Freel110
O Freely110
Freeman **V2**
Freeman **V3**
Freeman **V5**
Freeman113
Freeman269...
Freena **V3**
(o) Frehill110,115
Freil110
Freily110
Frein115
Freind269...
(de) Freins **V2**
Freisel115
Freke **V4**
French **V2**
French **V3**
French **V4**
French110
French269...
French Army **V2**
French 155
Frend **V3**
Frend **V5**
Frenier269...
Fresel115
Frestone **V5**
Frestone269...
Frew112
Frewan **V2**
Frewen **V4**
Frewen112
(de) Freyn(e)115
Friary269...
Friel269...
O Friel(l)110
O' Friell269...
Friely110
Friend **V2**
Friend **V3**
Friend **V5**
Friend269...
Frinke **V4**
Frinke269...
Friseal **V2**
Frispe269...
Friuin **V2**
Frizell **V4**
Frizell269...
Frizell(e)115
Frizelle **V2**
Frizil115
Frizzle115
Frizzle269...
Frompton269...
Frost **V3**
Frost269...
Froude, J. A. **V2**
Fry **V2**
Fry269...
Fryarr269...
Fryer269...
Frype269...
Fryth269...
Fs.gerrold **V4**
O Fuada153
O' Fuartain **V2**
Fuedal **V2**
Fuge269...
Fugill269...
Fulford **V5**
Fulham115
Fulham269...
Fullam269...
(de) Fullam115
Fullarton111
Fuller **V2**
Fuller **V4**
Fuller111
Fuller269...
Fuller Arms **V2**
Fullerton **V2**
Fullerton111
Fullerton269...
Fulton111
Fulton269...
Fuoly269...
Furey **V4**
Furey111
Furey269...
Furlong **V5**
Furlong106
Furlong269...
Furnell **V4**
Furnell **V5**
Furnell111
Furphy115
Fury111
Fury269...
Fyan(s)108,111
Fye114
Fye269...
Fyenell109
Fyfe **V2**
Fyfee269...
Fyinn269...

Mc Fyinn 269...
Fyland 269...
O Fynne **V4**
Mc Fynnin **V4**
Mc Fynyne **V4**
Mc Fynyne 269...
Fynyne Oge **V4**
Fynyne Oge 269...
Fytz Herbert 269...
Fz.adam **V4**
Fz.andrew **V4**
Fz.christoph **V4**
Fz.david **V4**
Fz.edd.gerald **V4**
Fz.edmond **V4**
Fz.garrett **V4**
Fz.gerald **V4**
Fz.gerrald **V4**
Fz.gerrold **V4**
Fz.james **V4**
Fz.john **V4**
Fz.morris **V4**
Fz.oliver **V4**
Fz.patrick **V4**
Fz.phillip **V4**
Fz.phillipp **V4**
Fz.pierce **V4**
Fz.redmonde **V4**
Fz.richard **V4**
Fz.robert **V4**
Fz=(see Fitz) **V4**
Fz.stephen **V4**
Fz.thom.gerr **V4**
Fz.ulicke **V4**
Fz.walters **V4**
Fz.willmi **V4**
Fzitz.gerrald **V4**
Gabberd **V5**
Gabberd 269...
Gabbett **V3**
Gabbett **V5**
Gabbey 269...
Gabbryth 269...
Gabriel **V2**
O' Gadra **V2**
Gaff 269...
Gaffeny 269...
Gaffey 118
Gaffey 269...
M' Gaffigan 269...
Gaffney **V2**
Gaffney 269...
(o) Gaffney 41,118
Gaffny 269...
Gafiney 118
Gafney 118
Gagan 269...
Gage **V2**
Gage **V3**
Mc Gaggy 269...
Gahagan 119
Gahagan 269...
Gahan 269...
(m') Gahan 120,190
Mc Gahan 269...
Mc Gahey 269...
Gaige 269...
Mac Gailey **V2**
(de) Gaillide **V2**
Gaine **V2**
Gaine 120
Gainer 269...
Gaines **V5**
Gainor **V2**
Gainor 119
O' Gairbit **V2**
Gaitens 269...
Galagher 269...
O' Galain **V2**
Galavan **V4**
Galavin **V4**
Galavin 269...
Galbelly 269...
Galbraith 269...
Galbreath 269...
Galbrith 269...
Galcor 269...
Gale 269...
(mac Gale 116
Gallagher **V2**
(o) Gallagher 116
O' Gallagher 269...
Gallaghur 269...
Gallaher 116
Galland 269...
Gallature 269...
Gallaugher 269...
Gallavan **V4**
O Gallavan **V4**
O' Gallcobair **V2**
Galle 269...
Galleghor **V2**
Galleghor 269...
Gallen **V2**
Gallen 269...
Gallerus **V2**
Gallery **V3**
Galligan **V4**
Galligan 269...
(o) Galligan 116
(o) Galligan 127
Gallivan **V2**
Gallivan 269...
Gallivan(e) 117
O' Gallogher 269...
Gallogly 269...
Gallougher 116
Galloway **V4**
Galloway 116
Galloway 269...
Galloway, **V5**
Gallowey **V4**
Gallway **V2**
Gallway **V2**
Gallway **V4**
Gallway 116
Gallway 269...
Gallways **V4**
Gallwey **V2**
Gallwey **V4**
Gallwey 116
Gallwey 269...
Gallwey, **V2**
Gallwey, T. **V2**
Galt 116
Galt 269...
Galvan **V4**
Galvan 117
Galvan 269...
Galvin **V2**
Galvin **V3**
Galvin **V4**
Galvin 269...
O' Galvin **V2**
O Galvin **V3**
O Galvin 117
Galvin Of **V3**
Galway **V2**
Galway **V3**
Galway **V4**
Galway 269...
Galway **V3**
Galwaye **V4**
Galwey **V2**
Galwey **V3**
Galwey **V4**
Galwey 116
Galwey 269...
Galwey, M. **V2**
Gam(m)el 116
Gambell 116
Gamble **V4**
Gamble 116
Gamble 269...
Gamel 269...
O' Gamna **V2**
M' Gan 117
Mc Gan **V3**
Ganan 269...
Gander **V2**
Gandsey **V2**
Gandsey 116
Ganley 117
Ganley 269...
Mc Ganley 269...
Ganly 117
(m') Gann 116,117
(m') Gann 118
Mc Gann **V3**
Mc Gann 269...
Mc Ganna 117
Mc Ganna 269...
Gannessy 116
Gannon **V2**
Gannon **V4**
Gannon 269...
(m') Gannon 118
M' Gannon 40,117
O Gannon **V3**
Gannon, N. **V2**
Gansey 116
Gantly 269...
O' Gaoitin **V2**
Gara 269...
Mc Gara 269...
O' Gara **V5**
(o) Gara 117
O' Gara 269...
Garaghan 117
Garahan 117
Garahan 269...
Garahy 269...
O' Garbain **V2**
Garblany 269...
Gardiner **V4**
Gardiner 269...
Gardner **V4**
Gardner 269...
Gardner 269...
Gargan 269...
Mc Gargill 269...
Garlan(d) 117
Garland **V5**
Garland 119
Garland 269...
(mc) Garland 117
Garner 269...
Garnet **V5**
Garnet 269...
Garney **V4**
Garnon 119
Mc Garr 269...
Garrahan 117
Garre 269...
Garrett 117
Garrett 269...
Mc Garrett **V3**
Mc Garrett **V5**
Mc Garrett 269...
Garrett, T. **V2**
Garrey 119
Garrie 119
O' Garriga 269...
Garrigan 269...
Garrihy 119
Garron 269...
Garry 269...
(m') Garry 11,119
Mc Garry 269...
Garstan 118
Garsten 118
Garstin 118
Garston **V5**
Mc Gartlan 269...
Gartland 117
Garvan **V3**
Garvan **V4**
O Garvan **V2**
O Garvan **V4**
(o) Garvan 118,120
(o) Garvan 127
Garvane **V3**
Garvane 120
Garvane 269...
Garven 120
Garven 269...
Garvey **V2**
Garvey **V4**
Garvey 120
Garvey 269...
Mac Garvey **V2**
Mac Garvey **V4**
Mac Garvey 118
Mc Garvey 269...
Garvin **V4**
Garvin 118,120
Garvin 269...
Garvy 118
Garvy 269...
Garwin 269...
Gascoigne **V5**
Gascoigne 45
Gash **V4**
Gash 269...
Gaskin 269...
Gaskin 45
Gason 130
Gasson 269...
Gastin 269...
Gaston 269...
Gately 269...
(o) Gately 119
Gater 269...
Mac Gatteley 119
Mc Gattely 269...
Gattery 269...
Gattins 121
Gattins 269...
Gauan 120
Gauan 269...
Gauen 269...
Gaughan 269...
O Gaughan 120
Mc Gaughey 269...
Gaughney 118
Gaughney 269...
Gaughran 124
Gaughran 269...
Mc Gaughy 269...
Mc Gaugie 269...
Gaul 269...
Gaul(e) 116, 244
Gaule 269...
Gault 269...
Gauna 269...
Mac Gauran 120
Mc Gauran 269...
Mc Gaurn 269...
Gaussen 130
Gaut 269...
Gavaghan 120
Gavaghan 269...
Gavan **V2**
Gavan 120
Gavan 269...
Gaven 120
Gavey **V2**
Gavigan 269...
Gavin **V4**
Gavin 120
Gavin 269...
Mc Gavin **V4**
Gaw 269...
Gawen 269...
Gawle 269...
Gawley 269...
Mac Gawley 6
Mc Gawley 269...
Gay **V4**
Gay 269...
Gayle 269...
Gaynard 269...
Gayner 119
Gaynor **V2**
Gaynor 119
Gaynor 269...
Gayson 269...
Mc Geady 269...
Geagh 269...
Geahan **V2**
O' Gealbain **V2**
Geale 269...
Geales 269...
Geane 120
Geaney **V2**
Geaney **V4**
Geaney 269...
(mac Geaney 120
O Geaney 120
Geany **V2**
Geany **V4**
Geany 120
Geany 269...
O' Gearain **V2**
Gearn 269...
Gearns 269...
Gearty 269...
Geary **V2**
Geary **V4**
Geary 117
Geary 269...
Mc Geary 269...
O Geary **V4**
Gease **V5**
Gease 269...
Geaveney 167
Gebard **V5**
Gebard 269...
Gebon 155
Geddis 269...
Gee 269...

V2 = Families of Co. Kerry **V3** = Families of Co. Clare **V4** = Families of Co. Cork **V5** = Families of Co. Limerick

Surname Index

Mac Gee **V2**
Mc Gee **V3**
(mc) Gee 129,165
Mc Gee 269...
Geehan **V2**
Geehan 269...
Mc Geehan 269...
Geelan 269...
Geeleher **V4**
Geery **V4**
Gefferyes **V4**
Gefferyes 269...
Gegan 119
Gegan 269...
Gegynn **V3**
Gehegan 119
Gehinn 269...
O' Geibinn **V2**
O Gelbroin 121
Gellegan 269...
Genealogi'l **V4**
Genealogy Vii
Genelly 269...
Mac Genis 128
Mc Genis 269...
Gennagh 269...
Gennen 269...
Gennery **V4**
Gennery 269...
Gennett 269...
Genney **V2**
Gennis **V2**
Gennis 187
Mc Gennis 269...
Gennys **V2**
Gentleman **V3**
Gentleman 118
Gentleman **V2**
Geogan **V4**
Geogan **V4**
Geogan 269...
Geogh 269...
Mac Geogh 130
Geoghan 119
Geoghan 269...
Geoghegan 269...
M' Geoghegan 119
Mac Geoghegan **V2**
Geography Ix
Geography **V3**
Geohagen **V3**
George 269...
George, St. 128
Mc Geough 269...
Mc Geown 269...
Geraghty 269...
Mac Geraghty 119
Gerald **V3**
Gerald **V4**
Gerald 269...
Geraldin 269...
Geraldine **V2**
Geraldines **V2**
Geraldino **V2**
Geran **V2**
Geran **V4**
O' Geran **V3**
O Geran, **V3**
Gerane 269...
Gerane & **V3**
Gerarty 269...
Gerity 119
Gerity 269...
German **V4**
German 269...
Gernan 119
Gernon **V4**
Gernon 117,119
Gerold **V4**
Gerold 269...
Mac Gerr 127
Mc Gerr 269...
Mc Gerr 269...
Gerrald **V2**
Gerrald **V4**
Gerrald **V5**
Gerrald 269...
O' Gerrane **V5**
O' Gerrane 269...
Gerret 269...
Gerrold **V4**
Gerrold 269...
Gerry 269...
Mc Gerry 269...
Gerty 119
Gervais **V4**
Gervais 128
Gervis 269...
Gery 269...
Gethin **V4**
Gething 269...
Getigan 121
(mc) Gettigan 121
Mc Gettigan 269...
Getty 120
Getty 269...
Geyles 269...
Mac Ghee **V3**
(mc) Ghee 129
Ghegan 269...
Mc Ghie 269...
Mac Ghir 127
Mc Ghoon 269...
Mac Gib **V2**
Gibb 269...
Gibb 34
Gibbes **V4**
Gibbings **V3**
Gibbings **V4**
Gibbings **V5**
Gibbings 120
Gibbins **V5**
Gibbins 269...
Gibbon **V3**
Gibbon **V4**
Gibbon **V5**
Gibbon 155
Gibbon 269...
(m') Gibbon 122
Mac Gibbon **V2**
Mac Gibbon 104
Mc Gibbon **V3**
Mc Gibbon **V4**
Mc Gibbon **V5**
Gibbones 269...
Gibbons **V3**
Gibbons **V4**
Gibbons **V5**
Gibbons 104,122
Gibbons 269...
O' Gibealla **V2**
Giblin **V5**
Giblin 121,122
Giblin 269...
Gibney 119
Gibney 269...
Gibny 119
Gibsen 122
Gibsey 269...
Gibson **V2**
Gibson **V3**
Gibson 122
Gibson 269...
Gibulawn 269...
Giffen 269...
Gifford **V4**
Gifford 269...
Mc Gil'ycud'y **V2**
Mac Gil'ycud'y **V2**
Mc Gilaspie 269...
Gilbeart **V2**
Gilbee 122
Gilbert **V2**
Gilbert 155
Gilbert 269...
Gilbey 122
O Gilbie 122
Gilboy 122
Mc Gilbride 31
Gilchreest 122
Gilchrist 269...
(m') Gilchrist 122
Gilcrest 122
Gilcriest 122
Gilcrist 269...
Gilday 120
Gildea 269...
Mc Gildea **V5**
Mc Gildea 120
Gildowney 92
Gildowny 269...
(m') Gilduff 89,123
Gileard 269...
Giles **V2**
Giles **V4**
Giles **V4**
Giles **V5**
Giles 269...
Gilespy 125
Gilfoil 121
Mac Gilfoyle 121
Mc Gilfoyle 269...
Gilgan 124
Gilgan 269...
Mac Gilgoddy **V2**
Gilgunn 124
Gilgunn 269...
Gilhool 269...
Gilhool(y) 123
M' Gilhooley 123
Mac Gilhooley **V5**
Gilhooly 269...
Gilkelly **V3**
Gilkie 269...
Gilkinson 121
Gill **V2**
Gill 269...
Mac Gill **V2**
(mc) Gill 127,189
Mc Gill 269...
Gillacoddy **V2**
Mac Gillacoddy **V2**
M' Gillacuddy 121
Gillacynny 269...
Gillagher 269...
Mc Gillaghlen 269.
Mc Gillaholy 269..
Gillan 124
Gillan 269...
Gillan 269...
M' Gillanders 124
Mac Gillapatrick V
Mac Gillareigh **V3**
Mac Gillariabhach '
Mc Gillaspick 269.
Mc Gillbride 269...
Gillconnell 269...
Mc Gillcuskell 269.
Mc Gilldowie 269..
M' Gilldowney 269.
Mc Gilldowny 269.
Gillduff 269...
Gilleane 269...
Gilleclin 269...
Gilleece 124
Gilleece 269...
Gilleese 124
M' Gillehanna **V3**
Gillelorin 269...
Gillen 124,127
Gillen 269...
Gillenane 269...
Gillenane **V3**
Mac Gillereage **V3**
Mac Gilleroy 99
Mc Gilleroy 269...
Gillery **V3**
Gillesby 125
Gillesby 269...
Gillespie 125
Gillespie 269...
Gillett **V4**
Gillett 269...
Gillfoyle 269...
Gillgam 269...
Gillgon 269...
Gillgun 269...
Gilliard 269...
Mac Gillicd'y **V2**
Gillice 124
Gillick 269...
M' Gillicuddy 121
Mac Gillicuddy **V2**
Mc Gillicuddy **V2**
Mc Gillicuddy 269..
Mac Gillicutty **V2**
Gilliesaght **V2**
Gilligan **V3**
Gilligan 116
Gilligan 269...
Gilligan 269...
Mac Gilligan 127
Gilligin 116
Mc Gillikelly **V3**
Mc Gillikelly 269..
Gilliland 269...
Gillilea 170
Gillin 124
Gillin 269...
Mc Gillireadie **V3**
Mc Gillireadie 269.
Gillman **V4**
Gillman 121
Gillman 269...
Gillmartin 269...
Mc Gillmartin 269.
Gillmartine 269...
Mc Gillmartyn 269.
Gillmore 126
Mc Gillneske 269..
Mc Gillon 269...
Gilloran 170
Mac Gilloway 98
Mc Gilloway 269...
M' Gillowy 269...
Gillpatrick 269...
Mc Gillpatrick 269.
Mc Gillreavy 269...
Mc Gillroy 269...
Mc Gillshenan 269.
Mc Gilltrich 269...
Mc Gilly 269...
M' Gillycuddy 121
Mac Gillycuddy **V2**
M' Gillycuddy, **V2**
Mac Gillycuddy's **V**
Mac Gillycuddy's **V**
Gilman **V4**
Gilman 121
Gilman 269...
Gilmarten 170
Gilmartin 170,192
Gilmartin 269...
Gilmer 126
O' Gilmor 269...
Gilmore 126
Gilmore 269...
Gilmour **V2**
Gilmour 126
Gilmour 269...
Mc Gilosker 269...
Gilpatrick **V3**
Gilpatrick 168
M' Gilpatrick 105
Gilpin 125
Gilpin 269...
Mac Gilprior 220
Gilroy 269...
(m') Gilroy 169
(m') Gilroy 99,164
Mc Gilroy 269...
Mc Gilsacoddys **V2**
Gilsenan 269...
Mac Gilsenan **V3**
Gilshenan 238
Gilshenan 269...
Gilstrap 125
Giltenane 269...
Gilthorpe 125
Giltinan Of **V3**
Giltinane 269...
Giltrap 125
M' Gilway 269...
(mc) Gimpsey 127
Mc Gimpsey 269...
Mc Gimpsy 127
Mc Gimsey 127
Mc Gin 269...
Mc Gin(g) 123
Ginaty 269...
M' Gindle 269...
Giney **V2**
Mc Ging 269...
Mc Ginis 269...
Mc Ginity 269...
Mac Ginley **V2**
Mc Ginley 128,169
Mc Ginley 269...
Mc Ginly 128
Ginn 269...
Mac Ginn **V2**
Mc Ginn 123
Mc Ginn 269...
Ginna 269...
Ginnane 169
Ginnaw **V2**
Ginnaw 162
Ginnaw 269...
Mc Ginne 269...
Ginnel 269...
Mc Ginnelly 269...

Ginney **V2**
Ginnis **V2**
Mc Ginnis 269...
Ginnis's **V2**
Ginty 269...
(mac Ginty 120
Mc Ginty 269...
Mac Giobuin **V2**
Mac Giolla **V2**
Mac Giolla Eain **V2**
Mac Giolladuinn **V2**
O' Gionnain **V2**
Gipsey 122
Giraghty 269...
Mc Giraghty 269...
Giran **V3**
Girane **V3**
Girane 269...
Mac Girr 127
Mc Girr 269...
Mc Girr 269...
M' Girrigine **V3**
Girvan **V2**
Girvan 127
Girvan 269...
Girvin 127
Girvin 269...
Gissane 169
Gittons 269...
Giunings **V2**
Giveen 133
Giveen 269...
Given 133
Given 269...
Mc Givena 269...
Mc Giverin 133
Mc Givern 133
Mc Givern 269...
Mac Givir 269...
Mc Givir 133
Givney 119
Mc Givney 129
Mc Givney 269...
Mc Givney 269...
Mc Glad 133
(mc) Gladdery 133
Mc Glade 133
Mc Glade 269...
Mc Gladery 133
Mc Gladon 133
Gladston 269...
Mc Glaghlin 269...
O' Glaimin **V2**
Glaisin **V4**
O Glaisin **V4**
O Glaisin 129
O Glaisin Imokilly **V4**
O' Glaisne **V2**
Glan 269...
Glanan 269...
Glanbehy **V2**
Glanchy 43
Mc Glanchy 269...
Glancy 269...
Glancy 43
Glandenning 134
Glanders 124
Glanders 269...
Glandore, **V2**
Glanfleid 269...
Glanny 269...
Glanvill **V2**
Glanvill 269...
O' Glasain **V2**
Glascock 133
Glascock 269...
Glascord 269...
Glascott **V4**
Glasgow 133
Glasgow 269...
Mc Glashan 269...
Glashby 125
Glashby 269...
Mc Glashin 269...
Glaspy 125
Glaspy 269...
Glass **V3**
Glass 269...
Glassane 130
O' Glassane **V5**
O' Glassane 269...
Glasscock 133
M' Glaughlin 269...
Glavin **V2**
Glavin **V4**
Glavin 269...
O' Glavin **V2**
Glazier **V2**
Glazier 269...
O' Gle **V5**
O' Gle 269...
O' Gleasain **V2**
O' Gleasane **V5**
O' Gleasane 269...
Gleason **V2**
Gleason **V3**
Gleason **V4**
Gleason 130
O' Gleason **V2**
Gleasur **V2**
Gleasure **V2**
Gleazer 269...
Gledstanes 122
Gleeson **V2**
Gleeson **V3**
Gleeson **V4**
Gleeson 269...
O Gleeson **V4**
O' Gleeson **V5**
O Gleeson 130
Glegge 34
Glen(n) 130
Glenan 269...
Glendening 134
Glenn **V4**
Glenn 269...
Glennon 130
Glennon 269...
Glenny 130
Mc Gleoine 269...
Mc Glevine 269...
Glinan 269...
Mc Glinchey 133
Mc Glinchey 269...
Mc Glinchy 133
Mc Glinn 269...
Glisane **V3**
Glisane 130
Glisane 269...
Glison 269...
O' Glissan 269...
Glissane **V2**
Glissane **V3**
Glissane 269...
O' Glissane **V3**
O' Glissane **V5**
(o) Glissane 130
O' Glissane 269...
Glober 269...
Gloghlen 269...
Mac Gloin **V3**
Mc Gloin 269...
Gloinn **V3**
Mc Glone 269...
Mac Gloran, 130
Glorney 133
Glory 133
Gloster **V2**
Gloster **V3**
Gloster **V5**
Gloster 134
Glouer **V5**
Glouer 269...
Mc Gloughlen 269.
M' Gloughlin 181
Glouster 134
Glover **V2**
Glover 269...
Glower 269...
Mc Gloyre 133
Mc Gloyre 269...
Glozier 205
Mac Gluin Glynn **V**
Gluinn **V3**
Glynn **V2**
Glynn **V3**
Glynn **V4**
Glynn 269...
Mac Glynn **V2**
Mac Glynn **V4**
(mc) Glynn 130
Mc Glynn 269...
O Glynn 130
O' Glynn 269...
Glysane 269...
Glyssane 130
Glyssane 269...
Gna 269...
O Gneeves 117
Gnew 3
(o) Gnive(s) 3,117
Goan 269...
Gobin 269...
Goble **V4**
Goble 269...
Goch 130
Godbold 269...
Godbolt 269...
Goddard **V2**
Goddart **V4**
Goddart 269...
Godding **V2**
Godfr(e)y 134
Godfrey **V2**
Godfrey **V4**
Godfrey 269...
Godfrey **V2**
Godfrey Of **V2**
Godkin 269...
Godley **V2**
Godolphin **V2**
Godson **V2**
Godson 269...
Godsuffe **V4**
Godsuffe 269...
Godwin 269...
Godwine 269...
Mc Goey 269...
Goff **V2**
Goff 122,130
Goff 269...
Goff, Jos. **V2**
Goffe 269...
Mac Goffrey 36
Gofton **V2**
Gogaine **V4**
Gogame **V4**
Gogan **V4**
Gogan 269...
Gogane **V4**
Gogarty 108,118
Gogarty 269...
Goge 269...
Goggan **V4**
Goggin **V2**
Goggin **V4**
Goggin 269...
Mc Goggy 269...
Gohary 269...
Gohery 134
O' Goidin **V2**
O' Goillide **V2**
Goin(e) 134
Goine 269...
Going **V3**
Going 134,242
Golagley 269...
Golborne **V4**
Golborne 269...
Golbourn 269...
Golburn 269...
Gold **V2**
Gold **V4**
Gold 134
Gold, Golden **V4**
Goldborne **V4**
Golden **V2**
Golden **V4**
Golden **V5**
Golden 134
Golden 269...
Goldie 269...
Golding **V4**
Golding 134
Golding 269...
Goldrick 134
Goldrick 269...
Mac Goldrick **V2**
Mc Goldrick 133
Mc Goldrick 269...
Goldsmith 134
Gole **V4**
Gole 269...
Goligher 269...
Golliher 269...
O' Gollogher 269...
Golloher 116
Gology 269...
Goloher 269...
Mc Golrick 269...
Gonell 269...
Mc Gonigal 133
Mc Gonigle 133
Mc Gonigle 269...
Mc Gonnegal 133
Mc Gonnell 269...
Gonoude 269...
Good **V4**
Good 269...
Goodbody 269...
Goode **V2**
Goode **V4**
Goodfellow 269...
Goodin **V4**
Gooding **V2**
Goodlake **V2**
Goodman **V2**
Goodman 269...
Goodrich **V5**
Goodwin **V2**
Goodwin **V3**
Goodwin **V4**
Goodwin **V4**
Goodwin 269...
Mc Googan 269...
Gookin **V4**
Gookin 269...
Mc Gookin 133
Mc Gookin 269...
Goold **V2**
Goold **V3**
Goold **V4**
Goold 123
Goold 269...
Goolden 269...
Gooley 269...
Gooly 269...
Goonan 269...
Goonery 269...
Gooney 269...
Goonry 269...
Mc Gooregan 269..
Gor. 122
Goragh 269...
Gorden 133
Gordon **V2**
Gordon **V5**
Gordon 133
Gordon 269...
Gordwin 269...
Gore **V3**
Gore 122
Gorevan 134
Gorey 121
Gorey 269...
Gorg 269...
Gorge 269...
Gorge 269...
Gorges 269...
Gorges, Mary **V2**
Mac Gorhain 242
Gorham **V2**
Gorham 269...
Gorings **V2**
Gorinouge 269...
Mc Gorish 269...
Mc Gorisk 269...
(o) Gorley 134
Mc Gorly 134
O' Gormain **V3**
Gormaly 123
Gorman **V2**
Gorman **V3**
Gorman **V4**
Gorman 269...
Mac Gorman **V3**
(mac Gorman 123
Mc Gorman 269...
O' Gorman **V3**
O Gorman **V4**
O' Gorman **V5**
O Gorman 123
O' Gorman 269...
Mac Gorman Arms **V**
O' Gorman In **V3**
Gormely 269...
O' Gormely 269...
Gormley 269...
O Gormley 123
Gormly 269...
Mc Gormly 269...

Gormocke 269...
O Gormog 130
Gormoge 269...
Gormogue 269...
Gormon **V3**
Gormon 123
Gormon 269...
Mc Gormon 269...
Gormooly 123
Gorr(e)y 121
Gorry 269...
Mc Gorry 269...
Goslin 130
Gosnel(l) 130,134
Gosnell **V4**
Gosnold **V4**
Gosnold 130
Gosnold 269...
Goss **V2**
Goss 130
Gossan 130
Goter 269...
Mac Gotraid **V2**
Gouge 269...
Gough **V3**
Gough 130
Gough 269...
Mac Gough **V2**
Mc Gough 269...
Gough, Jos. **V2**
Goulborne 269...
Gould **V2**
Gould **V3**
Gould **V4**
Gould **V5**
Gould 123
Gould 269...
Gouldborne **V4**
Goulde **V4**
Goulding **V2**
Goulding **V4**
Goulding 134
Goulding 269...
Mc Gouldrick 269..
Gouldsmith 269...
Gouldy 269...
Goule 123
Mc Goune 190
Mc Goune 269...
Goupe 129
Gouran **V2**
Gourley 269...
(mac Gourley 134
Mc Gournoson 269.
Mc Gourty 269...
Gouvernet 122
Gouverney 122
Mc Goverin 124
Mac Govern **V2**
Mac Govern 124
Mac Govern 134
Mc Govern 269...
Governey 122
M' Govran 124
Gow 269...
Gowan **V4**
Gowan 269...
M' Gowan 131,242
Mc Gowan 269...
O Gowan **V4**
O Gowan 131
O' Gowan 269...
Gowen 269...
Mac Gowen **V2**
Mc Gowen 269...
O' Gowen 269...
Gower 269...
Gowing 134
Gowla **V3**
Gowne 269...
Gowran 269...
Mc Gowren 269...
Goynor 269...
Mac Gra 125
Mc Gra 269...
Grace **V3**
Grace 131
Grace 269...
Grace, Gras **V2**
Gracey 269...
O' Grada **V2**
O' Grada **V3**
Graddy 124
Graddy 269...
Gradwell 124
Grady **V2**
Grady **V3**
Grady 269...
Mc Grady 269...
O' Grady **V2**
O Grady **V3**
O' Grady **V5**
O Grady 124
O' Grady 269...
O' Grady Arms **V3**
O' Grady & **V3**
O' Grady In **V3**
O' Gradys **V3**
Graeme 269...
Graff **V5**
O' Graffan 269...
Mc Gragh 269...
Mc Graghty 269...
Graham **V2**
Graham 269...
Graham(s) 125
Grahams 269...
Grahine 269...
Mc Grail 131
Grainger 131
Grainger 269...
O' Grainne **V2**
Grainseir **V2**
Mc Graith **V4**
Grandfield 269...
(de) Grandison **V2**
Mc Grane 269...
Graneer 269...
Mc Granell 269...
Granfield **V2**
Granfill 269...
Grange 269...
Granger **V2**
Granger 131
Granier **V3**
Granier 269...
Graniere **V3**
Graniers 269...
Grannell 233
Granny 269...
O' Granny 269...
Grant **V2**
Grant **V4**
Grant 132
Grant 269...
Granville **V2**
Gras **V2**
(le) Gras 131
Gratan 132
Grath **V4**
M' Grath **V3**
Mac Grath **V2**
Mac Grath 125
Mc Grath **V4**
Mc Grath 269...
Mc Grath In **V3**
Gratrakes **V4**
Gratrix 269...
Grattan 132
Grattan 269...
Gratten 132
Grattin 269...
Graues 269...
Graunt 269...
Gravell 269...
Graven 132
Gravenor **V4**
Gravenor 132
Gravenor 269...
Graves **V2**
Graves **V5**
Graves 132
Graves 269...
Graves, A.p. **V2**
Mac Graw 125
Mc Graw **V3**
Mc Graw **V4**
Mc Graw 269...
Gray **V2**
Gray **V3**
Gray 269...
Gray, Dan. **V2**
Gray(e) 125
Graydon 269...
O' Greacain **V2**
Gready 124
Gready 269...
Greahy **V4**
Mc Greal 269...
Mc Greal(e) 131
Grealish 269...
Greally 269...
Mc Grean 269...
Greaney **V2**
Greaney **V5**
Greaney 133
Greany **V2**
Greany 269...
Grear **V5**
Grear 126
Greatrakes **V4**
Greatrakes 269...
Greatrax **V4**
Greaves 269...
Gredy 269...
O' Greefa **V2**
Greeg 269...
Greehan 133
Greehey 133
Greehy **V4**
Greehy 133
Greehy 269...
Green **V2**
Green **V3**
Green **V4**
Green 269...
Green(e) 126
Green, **V5**
Green & Tans **V2**
Green, Tom - **V4**
Greenan 134
Greenan 269...
Greenan 269...
Greenaway 269...
Greenaway 269...
Greene **V3**
Greene **V4**
Greene 269...
Mc Greene 269...
Greenfield **V5**
Greenhaigh 269...
Greenhay 269...
Greenway **V3**
Greenway 269...
Greer 126
Greer 269...
Mc Greev(e)y 134
Mc Greevy 269...
Gregan 269...
Gregg **V3**
Gregg 269...
Gregg Of **V3**
Mac Gregor **V2**
Mc Gregor 269...
Gregorie 132
Gregory **V2**
Gregory 132
Gregory 269...
Gregory **V2**
Gregry 132
Grehan 133
Grehan 269...
Greia 269...
Greig 269...
De Grenan 134
Grene **V3**
Grene 269...
Grenham 269...
Grennan 269...
(o) Grennan 134
Grenville **V4**
Gressam 269...
Mac Gretten 132
Greville **V2**
Mac Grevy **V2**
Grew 202
Grewall 269...
Grey **V2**
Grey 125
Grey(s) **V2**
Gribben 269...
(mac Gribben 134
O Gribben 134
Gribbin 134
Gribble **V4**
Gribble 269...
Grice **V2**
Grice **V5**
Grice 269...
Grier 126
Grier 269...
Grifee 126
Griffa **V3**
Griffen **V3**
Griffen **V4**
Griffen 126
O Griffen **V2**
O Griffen **V4**
O' Griffen 269...
Griffen **V3**
Griffey **V3**
O' Griffey **V3**
Griffey In **V3**
Griffin **V2**
Griffin **V3**
Griffin **V4**
Griffin **V5**
Griffin 269...
O' Griffin **V2**
O Griffin **V4**
O' Griffin 269...
Griffin In **V3**
Griffin(s) 126
Griffith 269...
Griffiths **V2**
Griffiths **V3**
Griffy **V3**
Griffy **V4**
O Griffy **V3**
(o) Griffy 126
Grifith 126
O Grigg **V4**
Grigge **V4**
Grigge 269...
Grigges 269...
O Griggin **V4**
Mc Grillish 269...
Grimason 269...
Grimes 123,221
Grimes 269...
Grimley 269...
Grinson **V2**
O' Griobta **V2**
O' Griobtain **V2**
O' Griobtha **V2**
O' Griobtha **V3**
Gripha **V3**
Gripha 269...
O' Gripha **V3**
O' Gripha 269...
O' Griphae **V5**
O' Griphae 269...
Gripheen **V3**
Gripheen 269...
Grisken 134
Mac Griskin 134
Grism 269...
Grissom 269...
Groarke 269...
Groce 269...
Grogan **V2**
Grogan **V3**
Grogan **V5**
Grogan 269...
Grogan(e) 127
Grogane 269...
Groggan 127
Grolliax 269...
Gromail **V2**
Gromwell 69
M' Gronan 269...
Gronel 269...
Groogan 127
Groom 269...
Groome **V2**
Groot 129
Mc Grorke 269...
Mac Grory 68,129
Mc Grory 269...
Mac Grory, **V5**
Le Gros 131
(le) Gros, R. **V2**
(le) Grosse **V2**
Grosse Isle **V3**
Grosvenor 269...
Mac Grotty 134
Groues 269...
Grove(s) 127
Grover **V2**
Groves **V2**
Groves **V4**

Groves **V5**
Groves 269...
Growder 269...
Mc Groyre 269...
Grozet 269...
O' Gruagain **V2**
Grub(b) 127
Gruer 205
Grugan(e) 127
Grumley 269...
Grummell **V2**
Grummell 269...
Grummell 69
Grundle 269...
Grunse 205
Gryffith 269...
Grymball 269...
Grypha **V3**
Grypha 269...
O' Grypha **V3**
O' Grypha 269...
Guaine **V2**
Guan 269...
Mc Guan 269...
Mc Guane **V3**
Mc Guane 269...
Guare **V2**
Guare 269...
Gubbins **V5**
Gubbins 134
Gubbins 269...
Gubby 269...
Mac Gucarrick **V3**
Mc Guckia 133
Guckian 269...
Mc Guckin 133
Mc Guckin 269...
O' Gue 269...
Guerin **V2**
Guerin **V5**
Guerin 269...
Guest 133
Mc Guffin 269...
Guicken 269...
Guider 269...
Guidon 269...
Guidra 269...
Mc Guiehan 269...
Mc Guigan 133
Mc Guigan 269...
Mc Guiggan 269...
Guihan **V2**
Guiheen **V2**
Guiheen 269...
Guihen 269...
Guilavan 269...
Guilbert 155
Guilfoyle 121
Guilfoyle 269...
Mc Guillan 269...
O' Guillernane **V3**
Guilligan **V3**
Guillim 269...
Guilmartin 269...
Guin **V4**
Guina 269...
Guinan 269...
Guinane 169
Guinane 269...
Guinaw **V2**
Guinell **V2**
Guines **V4**
Guinevan 269...
Guiney **V4**
Guiney 167
Guiney 269...
O' Guinide **V2**
Guinies **V2**
Guinis **V2**
Mc Guinn 269...
Guinna 269...
Guinnaty 269...
Guinness **V2**
(mc) Guinness 128
Mc Guinness 269...
Mc Guir **V5**
Mc Guir 269...
Mac Guire **V2**
Mac Guire 128,186
Mac Guire 269...
Mc Guire 269...
Mc Guirk 132
Mc Guirk 269...
Guiry **V5**
Guiry 117
Guiry 269...
Guist 133
Guist 269...
Guithers 269...
Guiy 269...
Gul **V2**
Gullams **V4**
Gullams 269...
Mc Gullian 269...
Gullion 269...
Mc Gullion 269...
Gullivant **V4**
Gullivant 269...
Gullynane **V5**
Gullynane 269...
Gumbleton **V4**
Gun **V2**
Gun **V4**
Gun Family **V2**
Gun Of **V2**
Gun, Town. **V2**
Gun, W. **V2**
Gunn **V2**
Gunn 269...
Gunner 269...
Gunning **V2**
Gunning **V3**
Gunning **V5**
Gunning 132
Gunning 269...
O Gunning **V3**
Gunshinan 269...
Guppy **V4**
Guppy 129
Guppy 269...
Guppy's **V2**
Gurd 269...
Gurdan 269...
Gurk 132
Mc Gurk 269...
Mc Gurke 132
Gurkman 269...
M' Gurn 269...
Gurnett **V2**
Gurry 121
Gurry 269...
Gutch 269...
Guthrey **V4**
Guthrie **V3**
Guthrie **V4**
Guthrie 269...
Guttery 269...
Guy **V5**
Guy 269...
Guyn **V4**
Guyn 269...
O' Guyry 269...
Gware 118
Mc Gwill 269...
Gwilliams 269...
Gwinn 133
Gwinn 269...
Gwinnett 133
Gwither 269...
Mac Gwyer 186
Mc Gwyer 128
Gwyn **V4**
Gwyn(n) 133
Gwynn 269...
Gwyre 269...
Mc Gwyre 269...
Gydagh 269...
M' Gyl'ysaghta 184
Gyles 269...
Gynes **V2**
Gyrie **V4**
O Gyrie **V4**
O' Gyrie 269...
O H Uaitne **V2**
Habbagan 151
Habbagan 269...
Habbart **V2**
Habbert **V2**
Habbert 269...
Hacker 269...
Hacket 269...
Hackett **V2**
Hackett **V4**
Hackett 269...
(mac Hackett 135
Hackins **V3**
Hadden 269...
Hadder **V4**
Hadder 269...
Haddock 269...
Haddon 269...
Haddone **V4**
Haddone **V4**
Haddone 269...
Hadian 269...
Hadl(e)y 135
Hadley **V5**
Hadock 269...
Hadrach 269...
Hadskeath 269...
Haelly 269...
Haestricht 129
Haffey 269...
Hafford 269...
Haford 269...
O Hagain 135
Hagan 269...
O' Hagan **V3**
O' Hagan **V5**
O' Hagan 269...
O Hagan(e) 135
Hagan(s) 101,147
O' Hagane 269...
Hagans 269...
Hagarty **V3**
Hagarty **V4**
O' Hagarty **V2**
O Hagarty **V4**
Hagerine **V4**
Hagerty **V4**
Hagerty 142
O' Haggan 269...
Haggarty **V3**
Haggarty 142
Haggens 269...
Haghan 145
Haghen 141
Haghen 269...
Hagherin 269...
Hagherine **V4**
O Hagherine **V4**
O' Hagherine 269...
O Hagirtie **V4**
Hagnes **V4**
Hagnes 269...
Hagnes 269...
Hahasie 269...
Haherney 139
Hahn 141
Mac Haiceid **V2**
Haig 34
Haines **V4**
Hair 269...
Haire **V3**
Haire 140
Haire 269...
O Hairnin 135
Hairt 139
Haket(t) 135
(de) Hal **V2**
Hale **V2**
Mac Hale **V5**
(mac Hale 146
Mc Hale 269...
Halefeild 269...
Hales **V4**
Haley **V4**
Haley **V5**
Haley 269...
(o) Haley 151
O' Haley 269...
O' Haley(s) **V3**
Halfepenny 269...
Halfpenny 135
Halfpenny 269...
Halgan 269...
Halighan 269...
Halihanane **V4**
O Halihanane **V4**
O' Halihanane 269..
Halinan 139
Hall **V3**
Hall 269...
(m') Hall 135
Hall, De Hal **V2**
Hall, S.c. **V2**
Hallagan 148
Hallaghan **V4**
Hallaghan 143,148
O' Hallaghane 269..
Hallahan **V4**
Hallahan 148
Hallahan 269...
Hallam 269...
Hallaran **V2**
O' Hallaran **V2**
Hallaron 136
Hallenane 269...
Hallett **V2**
Halley **V2**
Halley **V3**
Halley 269...
Halley 269...
O Halley 151
Hallidan **V2**
Halliday 269...
Halliden **V2**
Halligan 143,148
Halligan 269...
Hallighan 143
Hallinan **V2**
Hallinan **V3**
Hallinan **V4**
Hallinan **V5**
Hallinan 269...
Hallinan 269...
O' Hallinan **V3**
Hallinan(e) 3,139
Hallinane **V3**
O Hallinane **V4**
Hallingworth 269..
Hallion 3
Hallisey **V2**
Hallissey **V2**
Hallissey **V4**
Hallissey 135
Hallissey 269...
Hallissy **V2**
Hallissy **V4**
Hallissy 269...
Hallisy 135
Hallom 269...
Halloran **V3**
Halloran **V4**
Halloran 152
Halloran 269...
O' Halloran **V2**
O' Halloran **V3**
O' Halloran **V5**
O Halloran 136
O' Halloran 269...
Halloran **V3**
O' Halloran In **V3**
Hallorin 136
Halloron **V2**
Halloron 136
Hallsey 269...
Halluran **V2**
Hallurane **V3**
Hallurane 136
Hallurane 269...
O' Hallurane **V3**
O' Hallurane 269...
Hally **V3**
Hally **V4**
Hally 269...
O' Hally **V3**
O' Hally **V5**
(o) Hally 151,154
O' Hally 269...
Halpen 135
Halpenny 135
Halpin **V2**
Halpin **V3**
Halpin **V5**
Halpin 135
Halpin 269...
Halsey **V2**
Halsey 269...
Halton 269...
Haly **V4**
Haly 269...
(o) Haly 151,154
Ham **V3**
Ham 269...
O' Hamailltin **V2**
Hambery **V2**
Hambery 269...
Hambilton 269...
Hambleton 269...
O' Hamell 269...

V2 = Families of Co. Kerry **V3** = Families of Co. Clare **V4** = Families of Co. Cork **V5** = Families of Co. Limerick

Surname Index

Hamelton 269...
Hamerton 269...
O Hamery 136
Hamil(l) 136
Hamill 269...
O Hamill 136
O' Hamill 269...
Hamilton V2
Hamilton V3
Hamilton 269...
Hamilton 34
Hamilton(e) 136
Hamiltone 269...
Hamlin V4
Hamlyn V4
Hamlyn 269...
Hammilton 269...
Hammon 269...
Hammond V2
Hammond 137
Hammond 269...
O Hammoyle 136
Hamon 269...
Hamon(d) 137
Hamond 269...
Hampson 138
Hampston 138
Hampton V2
Hampton 138
Hampton 269...
Hamptson V2
O Hamson 138
O' Hamson 269...
Hamtin 269...
O Hanafane V2
O' Hanafane 269...
Hanafin V2
Hanafin 269...
Hanagan 269...
Hanahoe 137
Hanaty 269...
Hancock V2
Hancock V4
Hancock 136
Hand V2
Hand 136
Hand 269...
Handcock V3
Handcock V4
Handcock 136
Handcock 269...
Handcocke 269...
Handion 137
Handley V4
Handly 137
Handrahan 138
Handrahan 269...
Hands'mb'dy 155
Handy 269...
Hanebry 148
Haneen V4
Haneen 269...
O' Haneen 269...
O' Haneen, V3
Hanely 269...
Hanen V3
Hanford 269...
Hangly 269...
Hanifin V2
Hanifin 269...
Haniford V2
Mac Hanifry 269...
Hanily 137
Hanin 269...
Hankshaw 269...
Hankswoorth V5
Hankswoorth 269...
Hanlan 137
Hanlan 269...
Hanlen 137
O' Hanlen 269...
Hanley V2
Hanley V3
Hanley V4
Hanley 137
Hanley 269...
Hanley(s) V3
Hanlin 137
Hanlon V2
Hanlon V4
Hanlon 269...
Hanlon 269...
O Hanlon 137
O' Hanlon 269...
Hanly 269...
O' Hanly V5
(o) Hanly 137
O' Hanly 269...
Hanna 269...
Hanna(h) 137
Hannafin V2
Hannagan 141
Hannan V4
Hannan 269...
Hanneen 137
Hannen 137
Hannigan V4
Hannigan 141
Hannigan 269...
Hannin 137
Hannon V2
Hannon V4
Hannon 269...
O' Hannon V5
(o) Hannon 137
Mac Hannraoi V2
Hanny 269...
Hanon V3
Hanon 269...
Hanover V2
Hanraghan 269...
Hanraghane 138
Hanraghane 269...
O Hanraghane V3
O' Hanraghane 269.
O Hanraghty 138
Hanrahan V2
Hanrahan V3
Hanrahan V4
Hanrahan 269...
O Hanrahan V4
O' Hanrahan V5
O Hanrahan 138
O' Hanrahane 269...
Hanratty 138
Hanratty 269...
Hanrick 269...
Hansard V2
Hansbury 269...
Hanson 269...
O Hanson 138
Hanswell V2
Hanton 269...
Hanv(e)y 142
Hanvey V4
Hanvey 269...
O Hanvey V4
Hanway 269...
Hany 269...
O Haodha V4
Hara V2
Hara V4
Hara 269...
O Hara V4
O Hara 138,155
O' Hara 269...
O' Hara, Cath. V2
Haraghan 269...
Harah 138
Haran 149
Haran 269...
Harbert V4
Harbert 269...
Harbeson 141
Harbinson 141
Harbinson 269...
Harbison 141
Harbison 269...
Harbord V2
Harborne 269...
Harbourne V2
Harcan 139
Harcourt V4
Harcourt V5
Hard 141
Hardick 269...
Hardier V2
Hardiman V2
Hardiman 141
Hardiman 269...
Harding V2
Harding V4
Harding V5
Harding 269...
Harding, Rd. V2
Hardinge V4
Hardinge 269...
Hardlye 269...
Hardy V2
Hardy 141
Hardy 269...
Hare V2
Hare 269...
O' Hare V3
(o) Hare 140,147
O' Hare 269...
Haren V3
Haren 149
Haren 269...
Harenc(?), V2
Harford 140
Harford 269...
Hargaden 269...
Hargadenm 140
Hargadon 140
Hargadon 269...
Hargan V4
Hargan 269...
O Hargan V4
(o) Hargan 139
Hargedon 140
Hargon V4
Hargon V5
Hargon 139
Hargrave V2
Harhan 149
Harhan 269...
Haries 269...
Harington 143
Harington 269...
Haringtonn 269...
Haris 269...
Harisson 143
O' Harkan 269...
Harker 269...
Harkin 269...
Harkin(s) 12,139
Harkins V3
Harkins V4
Harkness V5
Harkness 138
Harkness 269...
Harknett 143
Harley V2
Harley 269...
Harman V2
Harman 139
Harman 269...
Harman, V2
Harmer 269...
Harmon 139
Harmon 269...
Harms V2
Harnet 269...
Harnett V2
Harnett V5
Harnett 143
Harnett 269...
Harnett Of V2
Harnett, Wm. V2
Harney 269...
O Harney 139
Harny 139
Harny 269...
Haroid 139
Harold V2
Harold V3
Harold V4
Harold V5
Harold 139
Harold 269...
O' Haron 269...
Haroughten 269...
Haroughton 269...
Harp 154
Harper V4
Harper 154
Harper 269...
Harpor 154
Harpur 154
Harpur 269...
Harraghton V2
Harran V2
Harraway 269...
Harrell 269...
Harren 269...
Harrengton V4
Harrett 269...
Harricks V4
Harrigan 269...
Harrihy 143
Harrihy 269...
Harrington V2
Harrington V4
Harrington 143
Harrington V2
Harris V2
Harris V3
Harris V4
Harris V5
Harris 143
Harris 269...
Harrisen 143
Harrison V2
Harrison V3
Harrison V4
Harrison V5
Harrison 143
Harrison 269...
Harrisone 269...
Harrisson 269...
Harrity 269...
O Harroghue 155
Harrold V3
Harrold V4
Harrold V5
Harrold 139
Harrold 269...
O' Harron 269...
Harrot 269...
Harroughten 143
Harroughton 269...
Harrowe V2
Harry 269...
Harson 269...
Hart V3
Hart V4
Hart 269...
O' Hart V3
O Hart V4
(o) Hart 139,140
(o) Hart 144
O' Hart 269...
Hart(e) V2
Hart Families V2
Hart Harte V2
Hart Of V3
Hartagan 140
Harte 139
Harte 269...
O Harte V4
O' Harte 269...
Harte, L. V2
Harte, V2
Hartford 269...
Hartican 140
Hartigan V2
Hartigan V4
Hartigan 269...
O' Hartigan V3
O Hartigan V4
O' Hartigan V5
O Hartigan 140
O' Hartigan 269...
Hartigan Of V3
Hartigans V3
Hartin 269...
Hartley V2
(o) Hartley 140
Hartly 140
Hartnane 269...
(o) Hartnet(t) 143
Hartnett V2
Hartnett V4
Hartnett 269...
O Hartnett V2
O Hartnett V4
O Hartnett V5
Hartnett, V2
Hartnetty 143
Hartney V2
Hartney V3
Hartney V5
Hartney 269...
Hartop V2
Hartop 269...
Hartopp, E. V2
Hartr(a)y 144
Hartry 269...
Hartshorn 269...
Hartstrong 269...

Surname Index

Hartt **V3**
Hartt 269...
Hartwell **V4**
Hartwell **V5**
Hartwell 269...
Harty **V2**
Harty **V4**
Harty 141,142
Harty 144,145
Harty 269...
Harvey **V2**
Harvey **V4**
Harvey 140
Harvey 269...
Harvie 269...
Harvison 141
Harvy 140
Harvy 269...
Harvye 269...
Harwell **V3**
Harwood 269...
O' Hary 269...
Haryson 269...
Haselden 269...
Haselope 146
Haset(t) 145
Hasett **V3**
O' Hashea **V3**
O' Hashea 269...
Haslam 269...
Haslett 269...
Hasley **V3**
Haslopp **V3**
Hassan 142
Hassard 269...
Hassart 269...
Hasselham 269...
Hassells 269...
Hassels 269...
Hassen 142
Hasset **V3**
Hasset 269...
Hasset(t) 16,145
Hassett **V2**
Hassett 269...
Hassett 269...
Hassett, Col. **V2**
Hassetts **V3**
O Hassey 145
Hast 269...
Hastie 155
Hastie 269...
Hastings **V2**
Hastings **V3**
Hastings **V4**
Hastings 143,155
Hastings 269...
Hasty 142
Hatch 269...
Hatfield 269...
Hatherne **V4**
Hatheron **V2**
Hathorne 269...
Hatter 269...
Hattery **V2**
Hatton **V5**
Hatton 141
Hatton 269...
Hatton 269...
Mc Hatton 269...
Haugh **V3**
Haugh 269...
Haughan 141
Haughean 269...
Haugherne **V4**
Haughey 145,152
Haughey 269...
Haughian 269...
Haughran 149
Haughran 269...
Haughton **V4**
Haughton 145
Haughton 269...
Haughy 152
Hauglin **V4**
Hauglin **V4**
Hauglin 269...
Havarin 269...
Haverim 269...
Haverin 146
Haverine 269...
Havern 269...
Haveron 146
O Haverty 144
Havey 269...
O' Havin 269...
Havron 146
Havy 269...
Haward 269...
Hawe 269...
Hawes 269...
Hawford 269...
Hawkes **V4**
Hawkes 269...
Hawkin **V2**
Hawkins **V3**
Hawkins **V4**
Hawkins 141
Hawkins 269...
Hawney **V2**
Hawney 269...
O Hawrde 152
Hawthorne 269...
Hay 146,152
Hay 269...
Hayden **V2**
Hayden **V4**
Hayden **V5**
Hayden 145
Hayden 269...
Haydock 269...
Haydon 269...
Haye(s) 141,146
Hayes **V2**
Hayes **V3**
Hayes **V4**
Hayes 269...
Hayes, Hays **V5**
Hayes In **V3**
Hayne **V3**
Hayne 269...
O' Hayne **V3**
O' Hayne 269...
Haynes **V4**
Haynes 154
Haynes 269...
Hays 141
Hays, Dehays **V4**
Hayslip **V2**
Hayslip 146
Hayslip 269...
Hayten 269...
Haywood **V2**
Hazard **V4**
Hazard 269...
Hazleton 269...
Hazlett 269...
Hazley 269...
Hazlip 146
Hea **V3**
Hea **V4**
Hea **V5**
Hea 269...
O' Hea **V2**
O Hea **V4**
O' Hea **V5**
O Hea 141,146
O' Hea 269...
O' Hea, Hea **V3**
O Hea Pobble **V4**
Head **V4**
Heade 269...
Headen 269...
O' Headen 269...
Headley **V2**
Headley **V2**
Headon 269...
Heafy **V4**
Heagan 269...
O Heagerty **V4**
O' Heagerty 269...
Healane 269...
O Healathaigh **V4**
O Healehie **V4**
O Healiey **V4**
O Healihy 154
O Healihye **V4**
Heally 269...
O Healuighthe **V4**
Healy **V2**
Healy **V3**
Healy **V4**
Healy 269...
O Healy **V2**
O Healy **V4**
O' Healy **V5**
O Healy 154
O' Healy 269...
Healy, J.n. **V4**
Healy Of **V3**
O Healy Of **V4**
Hean(e)y 146
Heanen 269...
Heaney 269...
Heanne **V2**
Heanue 269...
Heany 269...
O' Heany 269...
Heaphy **V2**
Heaphy **V4**
Heaphy **V4**
Heaphy 146
Heaphy 269...
O' Hear 269...
Heard **V2**
Heard **V4**
Heard 142
Heardinman **V2**
Hearin 269...
O Hearlihy **V4**
Hearn **V4**
Hearn 269...
O' Hearn **V3**
O Hearn **V4**
O' Hearn **V5**
Hearn(e) 2,145
Hearnden **V2**
Hearne **V3**
Hearne **V4**
Hearne 269...
Hearst **V4**
Hearty 145
Hearty 269...
Heas 141
Heaslett 269...
Heasley 269...
Heaslip 146
Heaster 269...
Heathcott **V3**
Heather 269...
Heav(e)y 146
Heavane 269...
Heaven 269...
Heavener 205
Heavens 269...
Heavey 269...
Heavy 269...
Heazley 269...
Heban 269...
Hebbs 269...
Hecker 269...
Hedderman **V4**
Hederman **V3**
Hederman 146
O' Hederman **V3**
Hedery 269...
Hedges **V4**
Hedien 269...
Hedivan 269...
(o) Hedroman 146
Heduvan 269...
O' Heefie 269...
Heek 205
Heeky **V5**
Heeky 269...
Heel 269...
Heelan 269...
Heenan 269...
Heerd **V2**
Heerd 269...
O' Heerin **V2**
O' Heerin **V3**
O Heerin **V4**
O Heffernain 142
Heffernan **V2**
Heffernan **V4**
Heffernan 269...
O' Heffernan **V3**
O Heffernan **V4**
O' Heffernan **V5**
O Heffernan 142
Heffernane **V3**
Heffernane 142
Heffernane 269...
Mc Heffey 269...
Heffron 146
Heffron 269...
Hegan 269...
Hegan 96,135
Hegarty **V2**
Hegarty **V3**
Hegarty **V4**
Hegarty 269...
O Hegarty **V4**
O Hegarty 142
O Hegertie **V4**
O Hegertie 142
O' Hegertie 269...
Hegerty 142
O' Hegerty 269...
O' Heggertye 269...
Hegher 147,149
O' Heherty 269...
O' Hehiir 269...
Hehir **V2**
Hehir **V3**
Hehir 269...
O' Hehir **V3**
O' Hehir **V5**
(o) Hehir 147,149
O' Hehir 269...
O' Hehir In **V3**
Hehir In **V3**
Heiden 269...
Heify 269...
Heilshon 269...
Heily **V2**
Heily 269...
O' Heine 269...
Heines **V3**
O' Heire 269...
Heiren 269...
O Heitigein 147
O' Heiver 269...
Helan 269...
Heling 269...
Hell Or **V3**
Helliwell **V2**
Helly 269...
Helm(e) 147
Hely **V5**
Hely 269...
O Hely **V4**
O Hely 154
O' Hely 269...
O' Helyhy **V5**
O' Helyhy 269...
Helyott 269...
Hemp 269...
Hempe 269...
Hempenstal 145
Hempenstall **V2**
Hemphill 143
Hemphill 269...
Hempstall 145
Hempstall 269...
Hen **V3**
Henan 269...
Henchy **V2**
Henchy 143,144
Henchy, **V3**
Hendericken **V2**
Henderson **V2**
Henderson 147
Henderson 269...
Hendley **V4**
Hendrick 269...
(mc) Hendrick 143
Mc Hendrie 269...
Hendron 147
Hendron 269...
Hendry 144,147
Hendry 269...
Henebery 269...
Henebry 148
Henebry 269...
Henegane **V4**
Heneghan 148
Heneghan 269...
Henehan 148
Henehan 269...
Henekan 269...
Henelan 269...
Henery 269...
Henesey **V4**
Henessy **V3**
Henessy 144
Henessy 269...
O' Henessy 269...
O' Henessy, **V3**
Henesy **V5**

V2 = Families of Co. Kerry **V3** = Families of Co. Clare **V4** = Families of Co. Cork **V5** = Families of Co. Limerick

Henesy 144
Henesy 269...
Heney 269...
O Heney **V3**
Henigan **V2**
Henihan 148
Henikan 148
Henley **V4**
Henley 137
Henley 269...
Henlowe 269...
Henly **V5**
Henn **V3**
Henn 144
Henn Arms **V3**
Hennan 269...
Henneberry 148
Henneberry 269...
Hennessey **V3**
Hennessey **V4**
Hennessey 144
Hennessy **V2**
Hennessy **V3**
Hennessy **V4**
Hennessy 143
Hennessy 269...
O Hennessy **V3**
O Hennessy **V4**
O' Hennessy **V5**
O Hennessy 144
Hennesy **V4**
Hennesy 144
Hennigan **V2**
Hennigan **V4**
Hennigan 141
O Hennigan **V4**
Hennings 34
Henny 269...
Henrick 143
Henry **V2**
Henry 269...
(mc) Henry 144
Mc Henry 269...
O Henry 144
O' Henry 269...
Henry I I **V2**
Mc Henry, **V5**
Hensbry 269...
Hensey 144
Hensey 269...
Hensie 269...
Hensy 269...
Henthorn 269...
Henzy 269...
Heogan 269...
O Heoghy 150
Hepburne 269...
Hepburne 34
Hepenstal 145
Heraghty **V2**
Heraghty 143,147
Heraghty 269...
Herald 269...
Herald's **V2**
Heraty 147
Heraughty 147
Herbert **V2**
Herbert **V5**
Herbert 145
Herbert 269...
Herbert, A. **V2**
Herbert Arms **V2**
Herberts **V2**
Herberts Of **V2**
Herbertt **V2**
Herbertt 269...
Herbeson 141
Hercules **V2**
Herdman 269...
Hereford 140
O' Hererin 269...
Hergusson 269...
Herley 269...
O Herley **V4**
Herlihey 149
Herlihy **V2**
Herlihy **V4**
Herlihy **V5**
Herlihy 149,153
Herlihy 269...
O' Herlihy **V2**
O Herlihy **V4**
O Herlyhy 149
O' Herlyhy 269...
Hern **V4**
Hernan 149
O Hernane **V3**
Herne **V4**
Herne 269...
O Herne **V4**
O' Herne 269...
Hernon **V3**
Hernon 149
Hernon 269...
Heron 269...
Heron 34
Herr **V3**
Herr **V5**
Herr 149
O' Herrall 269...
Herrick **V4**
Herrick 269...
Herron 269...
Hertford 140
Hertnan 269...
Hervey 140
Hervie 140
O' Hery **V2**
Heskin **V4**
Heslen 149
Heslin 149
Heslin 269...
Heslip 146
Heslop 146
Hession 149
Hession 269...
Hester 149
Hester 269...
Hestin 143,155
Hestin 269...
Hestings 143
Hestion 143,155
Hestion 269...
Hestor 149
Hetherington 269...
Hethrington 269...
Hetigan 147
Hetreed **V2**
Hettromain 146
Hettroman 146
O' Heveran 269...
O' Hevin 269...
Hevron 146
Heward **V5**
Heward 269...
Hewes **V3**
Hewes **V4**
Hewes 269...
Hewet 269...
Hewet(t) 145
Hewetson 145
Hewett **V3**
Hewett **V4**
Hewison 145
Hewitt **V3**
Hewitt **V4**
Hewitt 145
Hewitt 269...
Hewson **V2**
Hewson 145,151
Hewson 269...
Hewson, **V2**
Hewsons **V2**
Heydon **V4**
Heydon 269...
Heyfron 269...
Heyne **V5**
Heyne 154
Heyne 269...
O' Heyne **V3**
O' Heyne 269...
O Heyne Heine **V3**
Heynes **V3**
Heynes **V4**
O Heynes **V4**
Heynham 269...
Heyns 269...
Heys 141
Heyslip 146
Hibart **V3**
Hibbard 269...
Hibbart 269...
Hickes 269...
Hickey **V2**
Hickey **V3**
Hickey **V4**
Hickey 269...
O' Hickey **V3**
O Hickey **V4**
O' Hickey **V5**
O Hickey 146
Hickey In **V3**
Hickie **V2**
Hickie **V3**
Hickie 146
Hickie 269...
O' Hickie 269...
Hickie, Wm. **V2**
Hickman **V2**
Hickman **V3**
Hickman **V4**
Hickman 146
Hickman **V3**
Hicks **V2**
Hicks **V3**
Hicks 269...
Hickson **V2**
Hickson 146
Hickson **V2**
Hicky **V3**
Hicky 146
Hicky 269...
O' Hicky **V2**
O' Hicky 269...
Hide **V3**
Hide **V4**
Hide 269...
O Hierlihie **V4**
O Hierlihy **V4**
Hierly **V3**
Hierly 269...
Hierlyhy **V4**
Hiernane **V3**
Hiernane 269...
Hiffernan 142
Hiffernane **V3**
Hiffernane **V5**
Hiffernane 269...
Hifle **V2**
Hifle 205
Higby **V5**
Higens 147
O' Higgan 269...
Higgens 147
Higgin 269...
Mac Higgin 147
O Higgin 147
O' Higgin 269...
Higgins **V2**
Higgins **V4**
Higgins 147,155
Higgins 269...
Higginson 147
Higginson 269...
Highgate 269...
Highmore 269...
Higin 269...
O' Higin 269...
Higins 147
Hignes 269...
Hignet 269...
Hignett **V5**
Hignett 269...
Higstone 147
Hiky 269...
Hikye 269...
Hil(l)yard 149
Hilan 269...
Hilan(d) 142
Hilbert 269...
Hill **V2**
Hill **V3**
Hill **V4**
Hill 149,150
Hill 269...
Hilland 269...
Hillard 149
Hillary 149
Hillee **V2**
Hillery **V3**
Hillery **V4**
Hillery 149
Hilliard **V2**
Hilliard **V3**
Hilliard 149
Hilliard 269...
Hilliard, B. **V2**
Hilliard Of **V2**
Hilligan 269...
Hillis 269...
Hillman 269...
Hillmon 269...
Hilly **V2**
Hilmon 269...
Hilo 269...
Hilton 269...
Hinchy **V2**
Hinchy **V5**
Hinchy 269...
Hinchy, **V3**
Hinde 269...
Hinds 269...
Hine **V3**
Hinegan 269...
Hines **V3**
Hines **V4**
Hines 154
Hines 269...
Hingerdell **V4**
Hingerty 149
Hingey **V2**
Hingston **V4**
Hingston 147
Hinks 269...
O Hinmh'nein **V4**
Hinsy 269...
Hinton 269...
Hipps 269...
Hipwell **V2**
Hipwell 149
Hirl 269...
Hirly 269...
Histon **V2**
Histon **V5**
Histon 143,155
Hitchcock **V2**
Hitchmongh **V4**
Hitchmongh 269...
Hiwys **V3**
Hoadly **V4**
Hoadly **V5**
Hoar **V2**
Hoar Hoare **V2**
Hoard **V2**
Hoard **V4**
Hoard **V5**
Hoare **V2**
Hoare **V4**
Hoare 269...
Hoban **V5**
Hoban 269...
Hoban(e) 144
Hobart 269...
Hobb 151
Hobbikin 269...
Hobbins **V2**
Hobbs **V4**
Hobbs 269...
Hobigan 269...
Hobkine 151
Hobson **V3**
Hobson 269...
Hodden **V4**
Hodden 269...
Hodder **V4**
Hodder 148
Hoden 269...
Hodge 269...
Hodgen 269...
Hodger 269...
Hodges **V3**
Hodges **V4**
Hodges 269...
Hodgin 269...
Hodgins 269...
Hodgins, **V2**
Hodgkins 269...
Hodnet **V4**
Hodnet 151
Hodnett **V4**
Hodnett 269...
Hodser 269...
Hodson, **V2**
Hoek 129
O' Hoen 269...
Hoey 150
Hoey 269...
Hoff **V3**
Hoffman **V2**
Hoffman 205
Hog 269...

Surname Index

Hogain 148
Hogan **V2**
Hogan **V3**
Hogan **V4**
Hogan 269...
O Hogan **V3**
O Hogan **V4**
O' Hogan **V5**
O Hogan 148
O' Hogan 269...
Hogan In **V3**
Hogan In **V3**
O' Hogan Of Ara **V3**
Hogan Of **V3**
Hogane **V3**
Hogane **V4**
Hogane 148
Hogane 269...
O Hogane **V4**
O' Hogane 269...
O' Hogane, **V3**
Hogart 152
Hogart 269...
Hogarty 269...
Hogen 148
Hogg 269...
Hogin 148
Hoibeard **V2**
Hoins 269...
Holaghan 269...
Holan 269...
Holbrow **V2**
Holcombe **V4**
Holcombe 269...
Holcroft **V4**
Holcroft 269...
Holdcomb 269...
Holden 152
Holden 269...
Holder 269...
Holehan **V4**
Holford 269...
Holian 150
Holian 269...
O' Hollahan 269...
Hollan 269...
Holland **V2**
Holland **V3**
Holland **V4**
Holland **V5**
Holland 269...
Holland(e) 150
Hollande 269...

Hollaway 269...
Holleran 269...
O Holleran 152
Holley **V2**
Holley **V4**
Holley 152
Holliday **V4**
Hollins 269...
Holloran **V2**
Holloran **V3**
Holloran **V4**
Hollowwood 269...
Holly **V2**
Holly **V4**
Holly 152
Holly 269...
Holly, **V4**
Hollyday **V4**
Hollyday **V4**
Hollyday 269...
Hollywood 140
Hollywood 269...
Holman 269...
Holme(s) 148
Holmes **V2**
Holmes **V4**
Holmes **V5**
Holmes 269...
Holms 148
Holms 269...
Hologhane 269...
Hologhon 269...
Holohan 150
Holohan 269...
Holt **V2**
Holt **V4**
Holt 269...
Holton **V4**
Holton 269...
Holyoake **V2**
Holywood **V5**
Homan 269...
Home 34
Homes 148
Honan 149
Hone 269...
(o) Hone 149
O' Hone 269...
Honeen **V3**
Honeen **V4**
O' Honeen **V3**
O Honeen 126,149
Honett 269...

Honwer 269...
O' Honyn **V3**
Honynge 34
Hood **V4**
Hood 269...
(mac Hood 151
Hooke 269...
Hooker 269...
Hookes 269...
Hooks **V2**
Hoolahan **V4**
O Hoolahan **V4**
Hoolihan 150
Hoolihan 269...
O' Hoone 269...
Hooper **V2**
Hooper **V5**
Hooper 269...
Hooregan **V3**
Hoorst **V5**
Hoorst 269...
Hop 269...
Hopditch **V3**
Hope 269...
Hopgood **V2**
Hopkins **V3**
Hopkins 151
Hopkins 269...
Hopper 269...
Hopps 269...
Hopson **V4**
Hopson 269...
Hopton 269...
O Hora 155
O' Hora 269...
Horaho 269...
Horan **V2**
Horan **V4**
Horan 269...
O Horan **V4**
O' Horan **V5**
O Horan 149
Horane 269...
O' Horchoy 269...
Hord **V2**
Hord **V4**
Hore 150
(de) Hore **V2**
(le) Hore **V2**
Horen 149
Horgan **V2**
Horgan **V4**
Horgan 139,155

Horgan 269...
Horgen 155
Horish 269...
Horn 269...
Horne 269...
Horner 269...
Hornett 269...
Hornibrook **V4**
Hornibrook 269...
Horoghon 269...
Horoho 269...
Horoho(e) 155
Horohoe 269...
Horribon 269...
Horrigan **V4**
Horrigan 155
Horrigan 269...
Horrigon 269...
Hors(e)ford 145
Horsdenel 269...
Horsey **V4**
Horsey 269...
Horsford 145
Horsman 269...
Horten 155
Horton 155
Horwick **V2**
De Hose 153
O' Hosey **V2**
O Hosey 153
Hosford **V4**
Hosford 145
Hosford 269...
Hoskin **V4**
Hoskins **V2**
Hoskins 269...
Hossy 269...
Mac Hoste 142
Mac Hostie 142
Hosty 142
Hosty 269...
Hotten 145
Houeden **V4**
Houeden 269...
Hough **V5**
Hough 269...
Houghegan 269...
Houghton 145
Houghton 269...
Houlahan 269...
Houlbert **V5**
Houlbert 269...
Houlden **V4**

Houlden 269...
Houlder 269...
Houldon 269...
Houlihan **V2**
Houlihan **V3**
Houlihan **V4**
Houlihan 269...
O' Houlihan **V3**
O' Houlihan **V5**
(o) Houlihan 150
Hoult 269...
Houneen 269...
O Houneen 126
Houregan **V3**
Houregan 269...
Hourican 269...
Hourigan **V3**
Hourigan **V5**
Hourigan 139
Hourigan 269...
Hourighan **V2**
Hourihan 137, 149
Hourihan(e) 138
Hourihane **V4**
Hourihane **V4**
Hourihane 269...
Housaye **V2**
House 269...
De Houssaye 153
Houstan 269...
Houston **V5**
Houston 269...
Houston 70,150
Houtsone 269...
Hoveden **V4**
Hoveden **V4**
Hoveden 269...
Hovell **V4**
Hovell 269...
Hovenden **V3**
Hovenden **V4**
Hovenden 150
Hovendon 150
How **V4**
How 269...
Howard **V2**
Howard **V4**
Howard **V5**
Howard 152
Howard 269...
O' Howard **V3**
Howatson **V2**
O' Howay 269...

Howe **V2**
Howe **V4**
Howe 269...
Howell 269...
(ap) Howell 146,21
Howen 149
O' Howen 269...
Howenden **V3**
Howendon 269...
Howes **V3**
Howes 269...
Howk 269...
Howke 269...
Howland **V4**
Howlett 269...
Howley **V3**
Howley 269...
O' Howley **V3**
(o) Howley 155
Howlin 269...
Howlin(g) 152
Howling 269...
Howly 155
O Howrane **V2**
O' Howrane 269...
O' Howregane 269..
O' Howrigane **V5**
O' Howrigane 269..
O' Howrogane 269..
Howth 151
Howth 269...
Hoy 141,145
Hoy 152
Hoy 269...
O' Hoy 269...
Hoye 269...
Hoyle 269...
Hoyle, C. **V2**
Hoyne 140
Hoyne 269...
Hoynes 269...
Hoyse 269...
O Huada 153
Huban(e) 144
Hubbard **V4**
Hubbard 155
Hubbard 269...
Hubbart 269...
Hubberd 155
Hubbort **V2**
Hudde 151
Huddle 269...
Huddlestone **V2**

Hudleston, I. **V2**
Hudson **V2**
Hudson **V4**
Hudson 153
Hudson 269...
Hudson, E. **V2**
Hueghs 269...
O' Huer **V3**
O' Huer 269...
Hues 269...
Hueson 145
Hueson 269...
Huet 269...
Huetson 269...
Huges 269...
Huggard **V2**
Huggard 269...
Huggins **V4**
Huggins **V4**
Huggins 155
Huggins 269...
Hugh 269...
Mac Hugh **V2**
Mac Hugh 151
Mc Hugh 269...
O Hugh 141,151
O' Hugh 269...
Hughe(s) 151
Hughes **V2**
Hughes **V3**
Hughes **V4**
Hughes 269...
Hugheston 269...
Hughey 269...
Hughs **V5**
Hughs 269...
Hughson 269...
Mc Hugo 269...
Mc Huigh 269...
Huihir **V2**
Huir **V3**
O' Huir **V3**
Hulahun 269...
Huleatt **V3**
Huleatt 269...
Huleattz **V3**
Hulihan 150
Hull **V4**
Hull 135,150
Hull 269...
Hulme 147
Hulme 269...
Hulnane 269...

V2 = Families of Co. Kerry **V3** = Families of Co. Clare **V4** = Families of Co. Cork **V5** = Families of Co. Limerick

Surname Index

Hulott **V3**
Hulson 269...
Hultaghan 269...
Hultahan 269...
O' Hultigan 269...
Hume 269...
Hume 34,151
Humes 269...
Humfrey 152
Humfreys 269...
Humphery 269...
Humphrey 152
Humphreys **V2**
Humphreys 269...
Humphries 152
Humphries 269...
Humphry 269...
Humphry(s) 152
Humphrys 269...
Humpton **V2**
Huneen **V3**
Huneen 126
Huneen 269...
Hungerdell **V4**
Hungerford **V4**
Hungerford 152
Hunt **V2**
Hunt **V3**
Hunt **V4**
Hunt **V5**
Hunt 269...
(le) Hunt **V2**
Le Hunt 152
(le) Hunt, Col. **V2**
Hunt(e) 114,152
(le) Hunte **V2**
Hunter **V2**
Hunter 152
Hunter 269...
Huntington **V5**
Huntley **V3**
Huntly **V3**
Huolahan **V2**
Huolyn 152
Huoneen **V3**
Huonyne **V3**
Huott **V3**
Huott 269...
Huraghan 269...
Hurd **V2**
Hurd **V3**
Hurd **V4**
Hure **V3**
O Hure 152
O' Hure 269...
Hurihane 137
Hurl(e)y 149,153
De Hurle 153
Hurley **V2**
Hurley **V4**
Hurley 269...
O' Hurley **V3**
O Hurley **V4**
O' Hurley **V5**
O Hurley 153
Hurley, **V2**
Hurley Of **V2**
O' Hurley, T. **V2**
Hurly **V2**
Hurly **V3**
Hurly **V4**
Hurly 269...
Hurly Arms **V2**
Hurrell **V2**
Hurson 269...
Hurst **V4**
Hurst 269...
Hurt 269...
Huscared **V3**
Huscared 242
Huscarett **V3**
Huscarred **V3**
Huscarredd **V3**
Huscarrett **V3**
Husnell 269...
Huss(e)y 153
Hussey **V2**
Hussey 269...
Hussey **V2**
Hussey Of **V2**
Husseys' **V2**
Hussy 269...
Huston **V2**
Huston **V4**
Huston **V5**
Huston 150
Huston 269...
Hutchens **V4**
Hutchens 269...
Hutchin **V4**
Hutchin 269...
Hutchins **V4**
Hutchinson **V2**
Hutchinson **V4**
Hutchinson 269...
Hutchison 269...
Hutchone 269...
Huthings **V5**
Huthings 269...
Hutson 269...
Hutton **V4**
Hutton 269...
Hutton 269...
Huyghens 155
Hy Cormac **V3**
Hy Garman **V3**
Hyatt 269...
Hyde **V2**
Hyde **V3**
Hyde **V4**
Hyde **V4**
Hyde 153
Hyde 269...
Hyde, In **V2**
Hyegate 269...
O Hyerlyhy **V4**
Hylan 269...
Hylan(d) 142
Hyland 269...
Hylane 269...
Hylla 269...
Hyman **V5**
Hynd 269...
Hyndman 269...
Hynds 269...
Hynebry 148
Hynes **V2**
Hynes **V3**
Hynes **V4**
Hynes 269...
O Hynes **V4**
O' Hynes **V5**
(o) Hynes 154
Hynton **V2**
Iago 269...
Ibrickan Map **V3**
Ievers **V3**
Ievers 157
Igoe 269...
Mc Ihone 269...
Il. Auto. **V2**
Mc Ilan 269...
Mc Ilboy 269...
Mc Ilbreed 269...
Mc Ilbreedy 269...
M' Ilbwee 269...
Mc Ilchole 269...
Mc Ilchon 269...
Mac Ilchrist 122
Mc Ilchrist 269...
Mc Ilcreve 156
Mc Ilcreve 269...
Mc Ilcrivy 156
Mc Ilcrivy 269...
Mac Ilderry 96
Ildowney 269...
M' Ildowney 269...
M' Ileboy 269...
Mc Ileboy 269...
Mc Ilepatricke 269.
Mc Ilfatrick 269...
Mc Ilfederick 269...
Mc Ilhair 269...
Mac Ilhaney **V2**
Mac Ilharry 11
Mc Ilhone 269...
Mc Ilhoney 269...
Mc Ilhose 269...
Mc Ilhoyle 269...
Mc Ilhun 269...
Mc Ilimchell 269...
Mc Illeavy 269...
Mac Illesher 269...
Mc Illoy 269...
Mc Ilmorry 269...
Mc Ilmurry 269...
Mc Ilravy 269...
Mac Ilrea 125
Mc Ilroill 269...
Ilroy 269...
Mc Ilroy 269...
Mc Ilterny 269...
Mc Iltraine 269...
Mc Ilvaine 156
Mc Ilvalluly 269...
Mc Ilveen 156
Mc Ilveen 269...
Mc Ilwaine 156
Mc Ilwaine 269...
Mc Ilwee 269...
Inaugurat'n Of Chiefs **V4**
Mc Incargy **V3**
Mc Incargy 269...
Mc Incarigie **V3**
Mc Incarigie 269...
Mac Incarrick **V3**
Mac Incarrigg **V3**
Mac Incarrigg(a), **V**
Inchiquin, **V2**
Inchiquin, Earl **V4**
Inderme **V3**
Inderme 269...
Mc Ineely 269...
Mac Ineiridhe **V3**
Mc Inerhidny **V3**
Mc Inerhidny 269..
Mc Inerhny **V3**
Mc Inerhny 269...
Mac Inerney **V2**
Mac Inerney **V5**
Mac Inerney 156
Mc Inerney **V3**
Mc Inerney 269...
Mc Inerney **V3**
Mac Inerneys **V3**
Mc Inerny 269...
Inglis 99
Ingoldesby 269...
Ingoldsby 269...
Ingoldsby, **V3**
Ingoldsby's **V2**
Ingouldesby **V5**
Ingouldesby 269...
Ingowen 269...
Ingram **V5**
Ingram 269...
Ingrame 269...
Ingry **V4**
Ingry 269...
Inmon 269...
Mc Innerney 156
Innis 269...
Mac Innis 128
Innisfallen **V2**
Mac Inprior 220
Mc Inrilly 269...
Insgelby 269...
M' Intee 269...
Mc Inteer 269...
De Interberg **V3**
Mc Intire 156
Mac Intosh **V2**
Mc Intosh 269...
(mc) Intyre 12,156
Mc Intyre 269...
Inwood 269...
Ui Ionmhainein **V4**
Mac Ionnractaig **V2**
Ipslie **V3**
Ipslie 269...
Ireland 156
Ireland 269...
Ireland, To **V2**
Ireton **V2**
Iriel 268
Irish 156
Irish Brigade **V2**
Irish Family **V4**
Irish Forces **V2**
Irish In **V2**
Irish **V2**
Irish **V3**
(mc) Irvin 156,157
Irvine 156,157
Irvine 269...
Irving 156
Irving 269...
Irwin **V2**
Irwin 269...
Irwin 269...
Irwin(g) 156,157
Irwing 269...
Isham **V2**
Islands In **V3**
Itchingham 156
(mc) Iver 157,172
Mc Iver 269...
Ivers **V2**
Ivers 157
Ivers 269...
Ivers Castle **V3**
Ivers Ievers **V3**
Ivers Ivars **V5**
Ivery 269...
Mc Ivor 157,172
Mc Ivor 269...
Ivors 157
Ivory 157
Ivory 269...
Jack 269...
Jackson **V2**
Jackson **V3**
Jackson **V4**
Jackson **V5**
Jackson 157
Jackson 269...
Jackson 269...
Jacob 157
Jacob 269...
Jacobite **V2**
Jacobus **V4**
Jacson 269...
Jaffe **V5**
Jagiues 269...
Jagoe **V4**
Jagoe **V4**
Jagoe 269...
Jakeman **V2**
James **V2**
James **V3**
James **V4**
James **V5**
James 129
James 269...
Mc James **V3**
Mc James **V4**
Mc James 269...
James I I **V2**
Jameson **V2**
Jameson 157
Jameson 269...
Jamieson 157
Jamieson 269...
Jamison **V5**
Jamison 269...
Jamison(e) 157
Jamisone 269...
Jannes 269...
Jardine 269...
Jarlath, Fr. **V2**
Jarvis **V5**
Jauncy 269...
Jeanes 269...
Jeenes 269...
Jeffcott **V2**
Jeffers **V2**
Jeffers **V4**
Jeffers 269...
Jeffery 269...
Jefferys **V4**
Mc Jeffey 269...
Jefford 269...
Jeffrey **V4**
Jeffreys **V2**
Jeffreys **V4**
Jegnys 269...
Jellis 269...
Jenings 158
Jenkins **V3**
Jenkins **V4**
Jenkins **V5**
Jenkins 269...
Jenkinson 269...
Jennings **V2**
Jennings **V4**
Jennings **V5**
Jennings 158
Jennings 269...
Jennison **V4**
Jenynges **V2**
Jeonar 269...

Jeoner 269...
Jeonor 269...
Jephson **V4**
Jephson 269...
Jepson 269...
Jerety 119
Jerety 269...
Jerm **V2**
Jermin **V4**
Jermin 269...
Jermyn **V4**
Jerome **V5**
Jervice 269...
Jervis **V4**
Jervis 269...
Jervois **V4**
Jervois 269...
Jess **V2**
Jess **V5**
Jess 269...
Jewell 269...
Joakes 269...
Joanes 269...
John **V3**
John 269...
Mc John **V4**
Mc John **V5**
Mc John 269...
St. John **V5**
St. John 269...
Johnes 269...
Johns **V5**
Johnson **V2**
Johnson **V4**
Johnson **V5**
Johnson 158
Johnson 269...
Johnston **V2**
Johnston **V3**
Johnston 269...
Johnston(e) 158
Johnstone **V3**
Johnstone 269...
Johnstoune 269...
Joint 159
Joint 269...
Joley 158
Jolifemme 155
Jolley **V3**
Jolley **V4**
Jolley 158
Jolliff **V4**
Jolliff **V5**
Jolliff 158
Jolly **V3**
Jolly **V4**
Jolly 269...
Joly 158
Jone 269...
Jones **V2**
Jones **V3**
Jones **V4**
Jones 159
Jones 269...
Jones Of **V2**
Jordan **V2**
Jordan 269...
Jordan 269...
Mac Jordan 159
Mc Jordan **V5**
Jordane 269...
De Jorse 159
Joue 269...
Jouie 269...
Jourdan 269...
Jourdon 269...
Journal -irish **V3**
Joy **V2**
Joy **V3**
Joy 157, 239
Joy 269...
Joyce **V2**
Joyce **V4**
Joyce 159
Joyce 269...
Joynt **V3**
Joynt **V5**
Joynt 159
Jubbs **V5**
Jubbs 269...
Judge 1,157
Judge 269...
Julian **V2**
Julley **V3**
Jully **V3**
Jully 269...
July 158
Jumphrey 269...
Junkin 269...
Jurdan 269...
Jurin **V5**
Jurin 269...
Jussey 269...
Justice **V2**
Justice **V4**
Justice 157
Justice 269...
Juyce 269...
Kain **V4**
M' Kain 269...
Kain(e) 160
O Kalannain **V4**
O Kalehan **V4**
O' Kally **V5**
O' Kally 269...
Kalshander 269...
Kanavaghan 269...
Kane **V4**
Kane 269...
Mc Kane 160
Mc Kane 269...
O' Kane 269...
(o) Kane 37,160
Kane Keane **V3**
Kangley 269...
Mac Kanry 269...
Kantinton **V4**
Kanturk **V2**
Kar 170
Kari **V4**
Karney 46
Karr 269...
O' Karran 269...
Kary 37
Kasey 44
Kauanagh 269...
Kauenagh 269...
Kavanagh **V2**
Kavanagh 160,200
Kavanagh 269...
Kavananagh 269...
Kavanaugh **V2**
Kavanaugh 160
Kay **V2**
Kay 269...
M' Kay 165,170
M' Kay 189
M' Kay 269...
M' Kay 64,151
Mac Kay **V2**
Mac Kay **V3**
Mac Kay 269...
Mac Kay 269...
Mc Kay **V3**
Mc Kay 269...
Kea 269...
Keadagane **V4**
Keadagane 269...
Keady 269...
(mc) Keady 168
Mac Keag 169
Mc Keag 269...
Keagane 269...
Keaghery 269...
Keagho 269...
Keaghoe 269...
Mac Keague 169
Keahane 269...
Mac Keal 146
Keal(e)y 168
Kealiher **V2**
O' Kealloghane 269
Kealy 269...
O' Kealy **V5**
O' Kealy 269...
Kean **V3**
Kean 269...
Kean 37,160
Mac Kean 160, 201
Mc Keanan **V2**
Mc Keanan 269...
Keane **V2**
Keane **V3**
Keane **V4**
Keane 269...
O Keane **V3**
(o) Keane 37,160
Keane Births **V3**
Keaney 163,166
Keaney 269...
Keany 163
Keany 269...
Kearan 269...
Kearin 269...
Kearn 269...
Kearnan 269...
Kearne 269...
Kearney **V2**
Kearney **V4**
Kearney 269...
O' Kearney **V3**
O Kearney **V4**
O' Kearney **V5**
(o) Kearney 46,161
O' Kearney, **V3**
O Kearney **V4**
Kearns **V4**
Kearns 269...
Kearns 36,164,168
Kearny **V2**
Kearny **V4**
Kearny 269...
Kearogan 269...
Kearon 164
Kearon 269...
Kearovan 269...
Kearsey 269...
Keary **V3**
Keary **V4**
Keary 269...
Keary 37,166
Mc Keary 269...
Keasit **V2**
Keating **V2**
Keating **V3**
Keating **V4**
Keating **V5**
Keating 269...
Mac Keating 161
(o) Keating 161
Keatinge 269...
Keatings **V3**
Keatings **V4**
Keatley 269...
Keaton **V3**
Keaty 168
Keaty 269...
Keavanagh 269...
Keaven(e)y 167
Keaveney **V4**
Keaveny 269...
Keay **V2**
Kedihan **V2**
Kee 269...
Mac Kee **V2**
Mc Kee 165, 189
Mc Kee 269...
Kee(s) 172
Mc Keedy 168
Keefe **V3**
Keefe **V4**
Keefe 269...
O' Keefe **V2**
O' Keefe **V3**
O Keefe **V4**
O' Keefe **V5**
(o) Keefe 161
O' Keefe 269...
O Keefe **V4**
O Keefes **V4**
Keeffe, **V2**
Keeffe **V3**
Keeffe **V4**
Keeffe 269...
O Keeffe 161
O' Keeffe 269...
O Keeffe **V4**
Keegan **V3**
Keegan **V4**
Keegan 269...
(m') Keegan 96,165
Keeleher **V4**
Keeler 269...
Keeley 269...
Keeling 269...
Keeltagh 269...
Keely **V2**
Keely 162,168
Keely 269...
Muc Keen 201
Keena 269...
Keenan 269...
Mac Keenan 165
O Keenan 165
Keene **V4**
Keene 269...
Mc Keene 269...
O' Keeneen 269...
Keenoy 269...
Keerawin 269...
Keern 269...
Keernan 269...
Keervan 269...
Keery 269...
O' Keeshan **V2**
Keeting 161
O Keevan 160,169
Keevane 169,172
Keevane 269...
Keeveny 167
Mc Keever 172
Mc Keever 269...
Keevers 269...
M' Keevor 269...
Kegan 269...
Keghan 269...
Mc Keghan 269...
Kegin 269...
Kegley 222
Kegley 269...
Kegry 269...
Kehan 269...
Kehelly 269...
Keherney 161
Kehilly 269...
Kehily 162
Kehoe 163
Kehoe 269...
Keiche 269...
Keife 161
O' Keife **V3**
O Keife **V4**
O' Keife 269...
O Keiffe **V4**
Keighron 269...
O' Keile 269...
O' Keilly **V5**
O' Keilly 269...
Keiltogh 269...
Keily **V4**
Keily 162,168
Keily 269...
Keiran 269...
Keirans 269...
Keish 269...
Keith **V2**
Keith **V4**
Keith **V5**
Keith 269...
Mac Kel 269...
Kelaghan 269...
Kelan 269...
Keley 162
O' Keley 269...
Keliher **V2**
Keliher **V4**
Kell 269...
Mac Kell 189
Kellaghan 269...
M' Kellan 269...
Kellard 269...
Kelleher **V2**
Kelleher **V4**
Kelleher 269...
O' Kelleher **V2**
O Kelleher **V4**
O Kelleher 165
O' Kelleher **V3**
Keller 165
Keller 269...
Kellett 269...
Kelley 162
Kelley 269...
Kellie 162
Kellie 269...
Kelliher **V2**
Kelliher **V4**
Kelliher 165
Kelliher 269...
O' Kelliher **V3**
(mac Kelloch 170

V2 = Families of Co. Kerry **V3** = Families of Co. Clare **V4** = Families of Co. Cork **V5** = Families of Co. Limerick

O' Kelloghane 269.
Kelloher V3
Kelloher 269...
Kellops 170
Kellough 170
Kells 269...
Kellsall 269...
Kelly V2
Kelly V3
Kelly V4
Kelly 269...
Mc Kelly V5
Mc Kelly 269...
(o) Kelly 162,168
O' Kelly 269...
Kelly Births V3
Kelly, Dan. V2
Kelly, H. V2
O Kelly Imokilly V4
O' Kelly Of V3
Kelly Of V3
O' Kelly, P. V2
Kelly-kenny V3
Kellye 162
Kellye 269...
Kellys V2
Mc Kelshenter 269.
Kelso 269...
Kelter V2
Mc Kelv(e)y 171
Mc Kelvey 269...
Mac Kemmie V2
Mc Kemmin 269...
Kemp 269...
Kemp 39
Kempton 269...
Ken 269...
Mac Ken 269...
Ken'ebeck V4
Kenady 269...
O' Kenady 269...
Kenaght 269...
Kenah 162
Mc Kenan 269...
O' Kenan 269...
Kenane 269...
Kendall 167
Mc Kendree 167
(mc) Kendrick 172
Mc Kendry 167
Mc Kendry 269...
Kene 269...
O' Kenealy V2
Kenedie 162
Kenedie 269...
Kenedy V3
Kenedy V4
Kenedy 162
Kenedy 269...
Mc Kenedy V5
Mc Kenedy 269...
O' Kenedy 269...
Kenefick V4
Kenefick 172
Kenelly 269...
Keneshane 269...
Keneslon 269...
Kenmare, V2
Kenmare, V2
Kenmare, V2
Kenn V5
Kenn 269...
Kenna V2
Kenna V4
Kenna 269...
Mac Kenna V2
Mac Kenna V4
Mac Kenna 162
Mc Kenna V2
Mc Kenna 269...
O Kenna V4
Kennagh 162
Kennah 269...
Kennan 165
O' Kennan 269...
Kenneally V4
Kenneally 172
Kenneally 269...
Kenneday 162
Kenneday 269...
Kennedy V2
Kennedy V3
Kennedy V4
Kennedy 269...
Mc Kennedy V5
Mc Kennedy 269...
O' Kennedy V2
O Kennedy V4
O' Kennedy V5
O Kennedy 162
O' Kennedy 269...
O' Kennedy Of V3
Kennedy, V2
O' Kennedys V3
Kennefick(e) 172
Kennelly V2
Kennelly V4
Kennelly V5
Kennelly 166,172
Kennelly 269...
Kenney V2
Kenney 163,166
Kenney 269...
Kenning 269...
Kenning 72
Kennington V2
Kennington 269...
Kennon 269...
Kennon 40,118
Kenny V2
Kenny V3
Kenny V4
Kenny 269...
Mc Kenny 269...
O' Kenny V5
(o) Kenny 163,166
O' Kenny 269...
Kenrick V4
Kenrick 269...
(mc) Kenrick 172
Kensellagh 269...
Kensly 269...
Kent V3
Kent V4
Kent 172
Kent 269...
Kently 269...
Keny 269...
Mc Keny 269...
O' Keny 269...
Kenyon 72
Mc Kenzie 269...
M' Keo 163
Keogan 269...
Keogh V2
Keogh V3
Keogh 269...
Mac Keogh V5
(mac Keogh 163
Mc Keogh 269...
Keoghe 163
Mc Keoghe 269...
Keoghoe 269...
Keoghy 269...
Keohane V4
Keohane 269...
Mc Keoine 163
Mc Keoine 269...
Keon 165
Keon 269...
M' Keon 269...
Mc Keon 269...
Mac Keon(e) 163
Mc Keone 269...
Keoneen 269...
Keoneen 269...
Keough V2
Keough V3
Keough 269...
Keown 269...
(m') Keown 41,163
Mac Keown 269...
Mc Keown 269...
O' Keoyne 269...
Ker 269...
Ker 42
Kerbin 269...
Kerby 269...
Kereen 269...
O' Keregan 269...
Kerelly 269...
Kerevan 269...
O' Kergan 269...
Kerin V2
Kerin V3
Kerin 269...
O' Kerin V3
O' Kerin 269...
Kerin(s) 164
(o) Kerin(s) 172
O' Kerine V3
O' Kerine 269...
Kerins V4
O Kerins V2
O' Kerins V3
O Kerins V4
Kerisk 269...
Kerivin 269...
Kerke 269...
Kerley 269...
Kerley 72
Mc Kerlie 172
Kerlin 42
Kerly 269...
Mc Kern 170
Kernaghan 269...
Kernahan 170
Kernan 269...
Mc Kernan 170
Mc Kernan 269...
O' Kernan 269...
Kernohan 269...
Kernon 269...
Kerns 168
Kerny 269...
Kerovan 167
Kerr 269...
Kerr 42,170
Mc Kerran 269...
Kerrane 269...
Kerrane 42,164
Kerribly 169
Kerrigan V2
Kerrigan 171
Kerrigan 269...
O' Kerrin V3
O' Kerrin 269...
Kerrins 269...
Kerris 269...
Kerrish 269...
Kerrisk V2
Kerrisk 269...
Kerry Castle V2
Kerry V3
Kerry Eagle V2
Kerry V2
Kerry V2
Kerryn 269...
O' Kerryn 269...
Kerrys Army V2
(de) Kertmel 47
O' Kervallan 269...
Kerwan 167
Kerwick 169
Kerwick 269...
O' Kerwick V5
Kerwicke 269...
Kerwin V3
Kerwin 269...
Kessidy 269...
Mac Kessy V2
Ket 269...
Ketchen 269...
Mc Ketian 269...
Ketin 269...
Keting 269...
(de) Keting V2
Ketrick 171
Kett V3
Kett 172
Kett 269...
O' Kett V3
Kettel 129
Ketterick 171
Kettle 129,172
Mc Kettrick 269...
Kettyle 172
Kevan 269...
Kevan(e) 169,172
Kevanagh 269...
Kevane V2
Kevane V4
Kevane 269...
Keveny 118
Keverny 269...
Mac Kevin 133
Mc Kevit(t) 172
Mc Kevitt 269...
Kevlihan 171
Kevney 167
Mc Kevor 269...
Mc Kew 269...
Key V4
Key 269...
M' Key 269...
Mac Key V4
Mac Key 269...
Mac Key 269...
(mc) Key 189
(mc) Key(e) 165
Key(e)s 172
Keyes 269...
Keygin 269...
Mc Keyne 269...
Keys 269...
Kian Clann V4
Kiarraide V2
Mc Kibben 168
Mc Kibbin 168
Mc Kibbin 269...
Mac Kibbon V2
O Kibbon 168
O' Kibbon 269...
Mc Kibbons 168
Kickham 168
Kickham 269...
Kid(d) 168
Kidd V2
Kidd 269...
Kidder 269...
Kidney V4
Kidney 269...
Mc Kie 269...
Kiefe 161
O Kiefe V3
O' Kiefe 269...
Kieffe V4
O Kieffe V4
Kieley 168
Kielt 269...
O' Kielt 269...
Kielty 218
Kielty 269...
Kiely V2
Kiely V4
Kiely V5
Kiely 168
Kiely 269...
Kieran 269...
Mac Kieran 172
O Kieran 164
O' Kieran 269...
Kierevan 269...
Kiernan 170
Kiernan 269...
(mc) Kiernan 164
Mc Kiernan 269...
Kierussy 269...
Kiervan 269...
Kiervane V3
Kiervane 269...
Kifee V2
Kiffin 269...
Kigan 269...
Mc Kigan 269...
Kilbane 156
Kilbane 269...
Kilbehenny V4
Kilbride 269...
Kilbride 31
Kilchrist 122
Kilclyne 54
Kilcoman V4
Kilcoyne 269...
Kilcoyne 65,169
Kilcullen 169
Kilcullen 269...
Kildare V4
Kildare 269...
Kildea 269...
Kilduff 269...
Kilduff 89,123
Kildunn 269...
Kildysert V3
Kilfarboy V3
Kilfenora, V3
Kilgallen 169,170
Kilgallon 169,170
Kilgallon 269...
Kilgannon 269...
Mac Kililea 170

Kilkee **V3**
Kilkelley 170
Kilkelly 269...
(m') Kilkelly 170
Kilkenny 170
Kilkenny 269...
Kilkenny 269...
Kilkey 269...
Killaha **V2**
Killaloe **V3**
Killaloe **V3**
Killaloe **V3**
Killarney **V2**
Killby 122
Killby 269...
Mc Killeagher 269.
Killeen **V3**
Killeen 269...
O' Killeen **V3**
(o) Killeen 170
Killelea 170
Killelea 269...
Killen 170
Killen 269...
Killen 269...
Mc Killen 269...
Killfoyle 269...
Killian **V2**
Killian **V3**
Killian 170
Killian 269...
O' Killian **V2**
Killien 170
Killikelly 170
Killilea 170
Killimith 269...
Killin 269...
O' Killin 269...
Killion 170
Killion 269...
M' Killion 269...
Mc Killip 170
Killips 170
Mc Killker 269...
Killmallock **V3**
Killmallock 269...
De Killmallock **V4**
Killmore 126
Killogh 170
Killogh 269...
Mac Killop 170
Mc Killop 269...
Killoran 170
Killoran 269...
Killorglin **V2**
Killough 170
Killoughry 167
Killoury 167
Killpatrick 269...
Killum 269...
Killy 269...
Kilmacduagh **V3**
Kilmartin 170,192
Kilmartin 269...
Mc Kilmartin 269..
Kilmary 269...
Kilmet 269...
Kilmurray **V5**
Kilmurray 204
Kilmurray 269...
Kilner 269...
Kiloughery **V3**
Kiloughery 167
Kilpatrick **V3**
Kilpatrick 168
Kilpatrick 269...
Kilroy **V3**
Kilroy 269...
Kilroy 99,169
Mc Kilroy 269...
Kilrush **V3**
Kiltartan, **V4**
O Kilte 218
Kilty **V4**
O Kilty **V4**
Mc Kilveen 156
Mc Kilvie 171
Kilwell 269...
Kimins 269...
Kimmings 269...
Kimmins 269...
Mac Kin 269...
Kinaghan 169
Kinaghan 269...
Kinahan 169
Kinahan 269...
Kinan 269...
Kinane 165,169
Kinane 269...
Kinaston **V4**
Kinaston 269...
Mac Kinaul 269...
Kinavan 269...
Kincade 169
Kincaide 169
Kincairt 269...
Kincart 269...
(mc) Kinch(e) 169
Kinchella 166
Kinchella 269...
Kinchley 269...
Kindellan 222
Kinder 269...
Kine 269...
Kine 65,171
Kineally 172
Kinealy 166
O' Kinealy **V3**
Kinegam 169
Kinelea, Co. **V4**
Kinerney 269...
King **V2**
King **V3**
King **V4**
King **V5**
King 155,164
King 269...
King, Edward **V4**
King From **V2**
King, Giles **V2**
King, Henry **V2**
King Henry **V3**
King Henry **V2**
King Henry **V2**
King, J. **V2**
King John **V2**
Kingan 165
Kingham 269...
Kinghan 165
Kinghan 269...
Kingsat **V3**
Kingshellog 269...
Kingsmell **V4**
Kingsmell 269...
Kingsmill **V3**
Kingsmill 165
Kingsmill 269...
Kingston **V2**
Kingston **V4**
Kingston 269...
Kingston(e) 165
Kingstone **V4**
Kingstoun **V4**
Kinigam 269...
Kinigan 169
Kinighan 269...
Kiniry 269...
Kinkaid 169
Kinlar 269...
Mc Kinlay 269...
Mc Kinley 128,169
Mc Kinley 269...
Mc Kinly 169
Kinna 269...
Kinnane 169
Kinnane 269...
Mac Kinnawe 114
O' Kinneally **V5**
(o') Kinneally 166
Kinnealy **V2**
Kinnealy 269...
Kinnealy 61
Kinnear 269...
Kinneary 269...
Kinneen 269...
Kinnegan 169
Kinnegan 269...
Kinnerk **V3**
Kinney 163
Mc Kinney 166
Mc Kinney 269...
O Kinney 163, 166
Kinnian 269...
Kinnie 163,166
Mc Kinnie 269...
Kinnigham 269...
Kinny **V3**
M' Kinny 269...
Kinsalagh 269...
Kinsale **V4**
De Kinsale **V4**
Kinsel(l)a 166,200
Kinselagh 269...
Kinselagh 269...
Kinsella 269...
Kinsellagh 166
Kinselow 166
Kinslagh 166
Kinslagh 269...
Kinstone **V4**
Kinstone 269...
Mc Kinstry 269...
Mac Kintosh **V2**
Kinucane 269...
Kinveton **V2**
Kinveton 269...
Kiraghty 269...
Kirberry 269...
Kirby **V2**
Kirby **V3**
Kirby **V4**
Kirby **V5**
Kirby 269...
O Kirby **V4**
(o) Kirby 169
Kirk 167,169
Kirk 269...
Kirkland 269...
Kirkpatrick 167
Kirkpatrick 168
Kirkpatrick 269...
Kirkwood **V5**
Kirkwood 167
Kirkwood 269...
Kirle **V4**
Kirle 269...
Kirley 269...
Kirlin 269...
Kirrane 269...
Kirwan **V2**
Kirwan **V3**
Kirwan 269...
O Kirwan 167
O' Kirwick **V3**
O Kirwick **V5**
O Kirwick 169
Kirwin 167
Kisane 169
Mc Kissack 171
Kissane **V2**
Kissane **V4**
Kissane 169
Kissane 269...
O Kissane **V4**
O' Kissane 269...
Kissick 269...
Mc Kissick 171
Mc Kissock 171
Kitchen 269...
Kitchen 70
Kitchener **V2**
Kitchingman 269..
Kithinyman 269...
Kitson 269...
Kitson, G. L. **V2**
Kittagh 269...
Kitterick 269...
Mac Kitterick 171
Mc Kitterick 269...
Kittrick 171
Mc Kittrick 269...
Mc Kivirking 269..
O Kivlehan 171
Kivnahan 269...
Kivneen 269...
Mac Kle 269...
Klincke **V2**
Klisham 269...
Mc Knabb 269...
Knack 269...
Knally 206
Knally 269...
Knarisborog 269...
Knarisborou 269...
Knatchbull 171
Knaven 269...
Knavin 207
O Knawsie 171
O' Knawsie 269...
Kneafsey 171
Mc Kneight 171
Knight **V2**
Knight 269...
Mc Knight 171
Mc Knight 269...
Knight Of **V2**
Knightley **V2**
Knights Of **V2**
Knights **V2**
Knock **V3**
Knock 269...
Knockalappa **V3**
Knockdrum **V4**
Knockdrum **V4**
Knockton 207
Mc Knogher 269...
Knolan 269...
Knoland 269...
Knopoge **V3**
Knorisborog 269..
Knot 269...
Knot(t) 171
Knowels 171
Knowlan 269...
Knowlan(d) 210
Knowland 269...
Knowle **V4**
Knowle 269...
Knowle(s) 171,208
Knowles **V4**
Knowles 269...
Knowley 59
Knowls 171
Knox **V3**
Knox 168
Knox 269...
Koch 67,155
Mc Kone 269...
Korish 269...
Korton 269...
Kotter 55
Kough 269...
Kramer **V4**
Kramer 56,68
Krowley 269...
Kune 269...
O' Kurgan 269...
Mc Kwey 269...
Mc Kye 269...
O Kyeff **V4**
Kyerty 269...
Kyery **V2**
Kyery 269...
Kyes 269...
Kyle 171
Kyle 269...
Kyllayn **V4**
Kyne 269...
Kyne 65,171
Kynin 269...
Kynyn 269...
Kyr(.)e 269...
Kyrvan 167
Kzoneen 269...
L'estrange 269...
(de) La Cousa **V2**
La Croix 155
(de) La Huse **V2**
(de) La Roche **V2**
Labatte **V4**
Labhles 174
Lacary 269...
Lacey **V2**
Lacey 269...
Lacey, De **V3**
Lacey, De **V5**
Lacey, De 173
Lachtnain **V4**
O Lachtnain **V4**
Lacie **V5**
Lacie 173
Lacie 269...
Lackworth 269...
O' Lactnain **V2**
Lacy **V2**
Lacy 269...
(de) Lacy **V2**
O' Lacy **V5**
(o) Lacy 173
O' Lacy 269...
Lacy, T.h. **V2**

Lacye 269...
Ladden **V2**
Ladrigan 180
Ladrigan 269...
Laferty 177
Laffan **V5**
Laffan 177,185
Laffan 269...
Laffane 269...
Lafferty 106
Lafferty 269...
Laffey 269...
Lagan 269...
Laghlen **V3**
Laghlen **V4**
Laghlen 269...
Lahey 269...
Lahiff **V3**
Lahiff 269...
Lahive 269...
Lahy 176
Lahy 269...
Laid **V2**
Laide **V2**
O' Laidig **V2**
O' Laidin **V2**
O' Laigin **V2**
Laird 177
Laird 269...
Lairy 175
Lake **V2**
Lallor 269...
Lally **V2**
Lally 173,199
Lally 269...
Lalor 269...
O' Lalor **V2**
(o) Lalor 173
Lalours **V2**
Laly 173
Laly 269...
De Lamare 79
Lamb **V2**
Lamb 176
Lamb 269...
Lambart 174
Lambart 269...
Lambe 269...
Lambert **V2**
Lambert **V4**
Lambert 174
Lambert 269...
Lamberton 174
De Lamere 79
Lamond 269...
M' Lamond 269...
Lamont 269...
Lamont 44,176
Lamor 269...
Lamot 269...
Lampriere **V4**
Lanagan 177
Lanallyn **V4**
Lanallyn 269...
Lanan 269...
Lance 269...
Land **V4**
Landa 177
Lande **V4**
Lander **V2**
Lander 269...
Landers **V2**
Landers 174,177
Landers 269...
Landers Of **V2**
Landon **V2**
Landon **V4**
Landon 269...
Landsdown **V2**
Landy 177
Landy 269...
Lane **V2**
Lane **V3**
Lane **V4**
Lane **V5**
Lane 269...
(mc) Lane 174,184
Lanegan 269...
Laney 269...
Lang 269...
Langan **V2**
Langan **V5**
Langan 175
Langan 269...
Langaridge 269...
Langdale 269...
Langden 269...
Langen 175
Langford **V2**
Langford 269...
Langford Of **V2**
Langham 269...
Langl(e)y 174
Langley 269...
Langor **V4**
Langor 269...
Langriss 269...
Langstone 269...
Langton **V4**
Langton 269...
Lanigan 177
Lanigan 269...
Lannan 269...
Lannder **V4**
Mc Lannin **V4**
Lannon 269...
Lansdowne, **V2**
O' Laoghain **V2**
O Laoidhigh **V4**
Lap **V4**
(de) Lap **V2**
O' Lapain **V2**
O' Lapan 269...
Lapin 177
Lapp 177
Lapp 269...
Lappe **V4**
De Lappe 78
Lappin 269...
(o) Lappin 78,177
Lapsty 269...
Laragh 269...
Larcan 269...
Larcher 11
Larcom, T. **V2**
Lardner 177
Mc Larinon 176
Lariss(e)y 176
Larissy 269...
Larkan 269...
Larkin **V2**
Larkin 185
Larkin 269...
Larmer **V2**
Larminie 176
Larmour 269...
Le Larndiner 177
Larney 269...
Mc Larnon 176
Mc Larnon 269...
Larriss(e)y 176
Larrissy 176
Lary 269...
Mc Lary 269...
O' Lary 269...
Lasley 269...
Lastly 178
Lastly 269...
Lasty 178
Latchford **V2**
Latham 269...
Lathom 269...
Latimer **V2**
Latimer **V5**
Latimer 269...
Latsford **V4**
Latsford 269...
Lauder **V2**
Lauder **V4**
Lauder 269...
Laughlin **V4**
Laughlin 269...
(m') Laughlin 181
Mac Laughlin 269...
Mc Laughlin **V4**
Mc Laughlin 269...
O' Laughlin **V3**
O Laughlin 181
Laughnane **V4**
O Laughran 176
Laules 269...
Laulors **V2**
De Launde 177
(de) Laundre **V2**
Laundy 177
Laundy 269...
Laurence 269...
Lauson 269...
Lavallin **V4**
Lavallyn **V4**
Lavan 185
Lavan 269...
Lavarty 177
Mc Lave 269...
Lavell(e) 176
Lavelle 269...
Laverty 106,177
Laverty 269...
O' Laverty 269...
Lavery **V2**
Lavery 269...
Lavery 4,177,182
O' Lavery, Capt. **V2**
Lavin **V2**
Lavin 269...
Mc Lavin 185
Mc Lavin 269...
(o) Lavin 185
Lavins 185
Law 177
Law 269...
Lawces 269...
Lawder 269...
Lawder 34
Laweles 174
Laweless **V2**
Lawell 269...
Lawfore 269...
Lawlee **V2**
Lawler **V2**
Lawler 173
Lawler 269...
Lawles 269...
Lawles(s) 174,177
Lawles(s) 179
Lawless **V2**
Lawless **V3**
Lawless **V4**
Lawless **V5**
Lawless 269...
Lawlis 269...
Lawliss **V3**
Lawliss 269...
Lawlor **V2**
Lawlor **V3**
Lawlor 173
Lawlor 269...
Lawlor In **V2**
Lawn 269...
Lawndy 177
St Lawrance 269...
Lawrence **V4**
Lawrence 174,243
Lawrence 205
Lawrence 269...
St Lawrence 269...
Lawrence-st. 174
Lawrence-st. 243
O' Lawry 269...
Laws 269...
Lawson **V4**
Lawson 179
Lawson 269...
Lawten 269...
Lawton **V4**
Lawton 269...
Laycock 155
Layne 269...
O' Layne **V2**
Le Blanc 155
Le Blount 155
Le Cog 155
Le Dillon **V2**
Le Fevre 155
Le Fleming **V2**
(de) (le)gray 125
Le Gros, **V2**
Le Grosse **V2**
Le Hore **V2**
Le Hunt **V2**
Le Hunt, Col. **V2**
Le Hunte **V2**
Le Jeune 155
Le Maitre 155
Le Marshall **V2**
Le Maur 155
Le Monnier 155
Le Noir 155
Le Palmer, **V2**
Le Roy 155
Le Strange 269...
Le Strange 269...
Le Waleys **V4**
Le Walies **V4**
Lea **V4**
Lea 175
Lea 269...
Leach **V5**
Leach 176
Leacy 269...
Leadam 269...
Leade **V2**
Leader **V2**
Leader **V4**
Leader 175
O Leadon **V3**
Leagh **V4**
Leagh 269...
Leaghie **V4**
O Leaghie **V4**
Leaghy **V2**
Leaghy **V4**
Leaghy 269...
O Leaghy **V4**
O' Leaghy 269...
Leah **V4**
Leah 269...
Leahey **V4**
Leahey 176
Leahy **V2**
Leahy **V4**
Leahy **V5**
Leahy 269...
O' Leahy **V2**
O Leahy 176
Leahy Arms **V2**
Leahy, Col. **V2**
Leahy, John **V2**
Leahy, Mary **V2**
Leahy- **V2**
Leake **V2**
Leake 269...
Leamy 178
Mac Lean **V2**
Mc Lean 269...
Mc Lean 52
Leanaghane **V4**
O Leanaghane **V4**
O' Leanaghane 269.
Leane **V2**
Leane **V5**
Leane 176
Leane 269...
O' Leannain **V2**
Leany 178
Leany 269...
O Learie **V4**
Leary **V2**
Leary **V4**
Leary 269...
O' Leary **V2**
O' Leary **V3**
O Leary **V4**
O' Leary **V5**
O Leary 175
O' Leary 269...
O' Leary, A., **V2**
O Leary Clan **V4**
O Leary Iveleary **V4**
O' Leary, **V2**
O Learye **V4**
Lease 269...
Leash 173
Leason 176
Leathem 269...
Leathes 269...
De Leau 155
Leaue **V4**
Leaue 269...
Leavy 269...
Leavy 83,178
Lecch 269...
Lecchfield 269...
Lecky 269...
Lecora 269...
Leddy 269...
Ledman **V2**
Ledmon **V2**
Ledwell 179
Ledwich 175
Ledwich 269...

V2 = Families of Co. Kerry **V3** = Families of Co. Clare **V4** = Families of Co. Cork **V5** = Families of Co. Limerick

Ledwick 205
Ledwidge 175
Ledwill 179
Ledwith 175
Ledwith 269...
Lee **V2**
Lee **V3**
Lee **V4**
Lee 269...
(mc) Lee 175,183
Mc Lee 269...
O Lee **V4**
O Lee 175
O' Lee, Lea **V5**
Leech **V2**
Leech **V3**
Leech 176,183
Leech 269...
Leeh(e)y 176
Leehey **V2**
Leehey **V4**
Leehey **V5**
Leehy **V4**
Leehy 269...
Leeke 129
Leen **V2**
Leen 176
Leery 175
O Leery **V4**
Lees 269...
De Lees 173
Leeser **V2**
Leeser, J. **V2**
Leeson **V2**
Leeson 176
Leeson 269...
Lefroy **V3**
Lefroy 177
Legardere **V4**
Legends **V4**
St. Leger **V4**
St Leger 269...
Legerstone **V4**
Legerstone 269...
Legg 269...
Legge 269...
Legland 269...
Legrond 269...
Lehan **V4**
O Lehan **V4**
O Lehan, **V4**
O Lehan 178,184
Lehane **V2**
Lehane **V4**
Lehane 174,184
Lehane 269...
Lehe **V4**
Lehunt 269...
Lehy 176
Leicester 269...
St Leiger 269...
Leigh 269...
Leigh 34
(m') Leigh 175,177
Leighie **V4**
O Leighin **V4**
O Lein **V4**
O' Lein **V5**
O' Lein 269...
O Leine **V4**
Mac Leish **V2**
Leitchfield 269...
Mac Lellan 53
Mc Lellan 269...
Lemass 178
Lemon 269...
Lemond 269...
Mac Lemont 44
Lenagh 269...
Lenaghan 269...
Mc Lenaghan 174
Mc Lenaghan 269...
O' Lenaghan **V5**
O Lenaghan 174
Lenahan 269...
Lenan 269...
Lenane 269...
Mc Lenany 269...
Lenard 177
Lench **V3**
Lenchy **V3**
Lenchy 269...
O' Lenchy **V5**
O' Lenchy 269...
Lency **V2**
Lency 269...
O Lency **V2**
O' Lency 269...
Lendrum 177
Lendsie 269...
Lenegane **V4**
Lenesay 269...
Lenglas 99
Lengly 269...
Lenighan **V4**
Lenighan 174
Lenighane **V4**
Lenihan **V2**
Lenihan **V4**
Lenihan **V5**
Lenihan 174
Lenihan 269...
Lening 269...
O' Lennaghan 269...
Lennan 269...
O Lennan 185
O' Lennan 269...
Lennane **V2**
O Lennane **V4**
O' Lennane 269...
Lennard **V5**
Lennard 155
Lennard 269...
Lennon **V3**
Lennon 269...
Mc Lennon **V4**
O' Lennon **V2**
O' Lennon **V3**
O Lennon **V4**
O' Lennon **V5**
O Lennon 185
Lennox 269...
Lenoir 155
Lenord 269...
Lenox 269...
Lentaigne 178
Lentall **V2**
Leny 269...
Leo **V3**
Leo **V5**
Leo 269...
Mac Leod **V2**
Mc Leod Of **V2**
Leoge 183
Mac Leoid **V2**
Leonard **V2**
Leonard **V3**
Leonard **V4**
Leonard **V5**
Leonard 177
Leonard 269...
Leonard, Dan **V2**
Leonard, **V2**
Lerhihan 177
Mc Lerney 269...
Lernighan **V3**
Lernighan 177
Lernihan **V3**
Lernihan 177
Mc Lernon 176
Mc Lernon 269...
Lerye 269...
Lesaw 269...
Lesby 269...
Lesley **V5**
Lesley 178
Leslie **V2**
Leslie **V2**
Leslie **V3**
Leslie 178
Leslie 269...
Lesly 269...
Lesquire 269...
Lester 269...
M' Lester 269...
(mac Lester 7,184
Lestrange 178
Lestrange 269...
Letellier 155
Letsome 269...
Lett, Anne **V2**
(de) Lett(e) 178
Letters **V2**
Leuett 269...
Levallen **V4**
Levallen 178
Levallin **V4**
Leventhal **V2**
Lever 155
Leveran 269...
Levereau 155
Levesey 269...
Leveson 269...
Levi 178
Levin **V5**
Levingston 180
Levingston 269...
Levins 185
Levins 269...
Levison **V2**
Leviston 269...
Levitt 269...
Levy 178
Lewers 269...
Lewin **V2**
Lewis **V2**
Lewis **V4**
Lewis **V5**
Lewis 178
Lewis 269...
Lewling 269...
Ley 269...
Leyden **V3**
Leyden 179,183
Leyden 269...
Leydon **V3**
Leyen 269...
Leyhane 269...
O Leyn **V4**
Leynagh 183
Leynagh 269...
Leyne **V2**
Leyne **V4**
Leyne **V5**
Leyne 269...
O' Leyne **V2**
O Leyne **V4**
(o) Leyne 176,184
O' Leyne 269...
Leyne, Jerh. **V2**
Leynes 269...
Leyns 183
De Leyte 178
De Leyudperun **V3**
O' Liatain **V2**
O' Liathan **V2**
O Liathan **V4**
Mc Lice 269...
Lick Castle **V2**
Liddane **V2**
Liddane **V3**
Liddane 179,183
Liddane 269...
O' Liddeene **V5**
O' Liddeene 269...
Liddel 269...
Liddy **V3**
Liddy 269...
(o) Liddy 179
O' Liddys **V3**
Lidwell 179
Lidwill 179
Lie **V4**
Lie 269...
Liegh 177
Liffe 269...
Ligget 269...
Liggett 269...
Lightbody 269...
Lill 179
Lill 269...
Lilley 179
Lilley 269...
Lillie 179
Lillis **V3**
Lillis **V4**
Lillis **V5**
Lillis 179
Lillis 269...
Lilly 179
Lilly 269...
Limbrick 179
Limerick 179
Limerick, **V2**
Limry 269...
Lin 269...
Linahan **V4**
Linahan 269...
Linan 269...
Linane **V2**
Linane **V3**
Linane **V5**
Linane 269...
Linche **V4**
O Linchehan **V4**
Linchey 269...
Linchy **V4**
Linchy **V5**
Linchy 269...
O' Linchy **V2**
O' Linchy **V5**
O' Linchy 269...
Lincoln 269...
Lincy 269...
Lind 269...
Lind(e)say 179
Linden 269...
Mc Linden 269...
Lindesay **V2**
Lindon **V2**
Lindon 269...
Lindsay **V2**
Lindsay **V3**
Lindsay **V5**
Lindsay 179
Lindsay 269...
Lindsey 269...
Lindsey 34
Lindsey 34
Line **V3**
Line **V4**
Line 269...
O Line **V4**
O' Line 269...
Linehan **V4**
Linehan 174
Linehan 269...
Lingane **V5**
Lingane 269...
Linn 269...
Linnane **V2**
Linnane **V3**
Linnane **V5**
Linnane 185
Linnane 269...
Linnegar **V2**
Linnen 269...
Linnington 269...
Linsey 269...
Linshie **V4**
O Linshie **V4**
Linsy 269...
O Linsy **V4**
O' Linsy 269...
M' Lintock 269...
Linton 269...
Lion 269...
Lions **V4**
Lipsett 269...
Lisack **V2**
Lisaght **V4**
Lisaught **V4**
Lisaught 269...
Liscahane **V2**
Liscannor **V3**
Mac Lise, Daniel- **V4**
Lisle 269...
Lister 184
Lister 269...
Liston **V5**
Liston 269...
Listowel **V2**
Listowel, **V2**
Litchfield 269...
Litten 179
Litterell 269...
Little 180
Little 269...
Littleton 269...
Litton **V4**
Litton 179
Liuer **V4**
O Liuer **V4**
O' Liuer **V5**
O' Liuer 269...
Living 269...
Livingston 180
Livingston 269...
Livingstone 180
Livingstone 269...
Lloyd **V2**

V2 = Families of Co. Kerry **V3** = Families of Co. Clare **V4** = Families of Co. Cork **V5** = Families of Co. Limerick

Surname Index

Lloyd **V3**
Lloyd **V5**
Lloyd 179
Lloyd 269...
Lobb 269...
O Lochlinn 181
Lochrane 176
Lock **V2**
Lock **V4**
Lock 269...
Lockard 269...
Lockart 180
Locke **V2**
Locke **V4**
Locke 269...
Lockhart 180
Lockhart 269...
Lockheart 180
Lockington 269...
Mac Loclainn **V2**
O' Loclainn **V2**
Lodg 269...
Lodge **V5**
Lodge 180
Lodge 269...
Lodge **V2**
Lodlowe 269...
Loffan 269...
Lofftus 269...
Loftie, Rev. **V2**
Loftis 180
Loftus **V3**
Loftus 180
Loftus 269...
Logan 181
Logan 269...
Loggan 269...
Loghan 181
Loghlen 269...
Mc Loghlen **V3**
Mc Loghlen **V5**
Mc Loghlen 269...
O' Loghlen **V3**
O Loghlen 181
O' Loghlen 269...
Loghlin 269...
Mc Loghlin **V3**
Mc Loghlin 269...
Loghman 269...
Loghnan 269...
O' Loghnan 269...
Loghnane 269...
Loglin 181

Logue **V2**
Logue 269...
O Logue **V3**
O Logue 183
Lohan 269...
Lohan 269...
O' Loideain **V2**
O Loingsigh **V4**
O' Loinn **V2**
Lombard **V2**
Lombard **V2**
Lombard **V4**
Lombard **V5**
Lombard 269...
Lombard(e) 180
O Lomley **V4**
Lond 269...
Londay 269...
Londer **V4**
Londers 174
Londregan **V4**
Londrigan **V4**
Londrigan 180
Londrigan 269...
Londy 269...
Lone **V3**
Lone 269...
Lonell 269...
Lonergan **V4**
Lonergan 269...
O' Lonergan **V3**
O Lonergan **V4**
O Lonergan 180
Lonergane 269...
Long **V2**
Long **V3**
Long **V4**
Long 205
Long 269...
Long 79, 181
Long, J. **V2**
Long, **V5**
M' Longahan 181
O' Longaig **V2**
O Longaigh **V4**
O' Longain **V2**
Longan 181
Longe **V4**
O Longe **V4**
Longfield **V3**
Longfield **V4**
Longfield 181
Longford 269...

Longley 269...
O Longy **V4**
Lonnergane 269...
Lcob(e)y 182
Looby 269...
Loogue 183
Loogue 269...
Mc Loone 269...
Looney **V2**
Looney **V3**
Looney **V4**
Looney 269...
O' Looney **V5**
O Looney 182
Mc Loonie 269...
Loony 182
Lopdell **V3**
O Lorcain 185
(o) Lorcan 185
Lord **V2**
Lord **V4**
Lord 269...
O' Lordain **V2**
Lordan **V2**
Lordan **V4**
Lordan 269...
Lorde 269...
Lorenan 269...
Lorimer 269...
Lorimour 269...
Mc Lorinan 269...
Mc Lorinon 176
Lorkan 185
Lorkan 269...
Los Angeles **V3**
Loske 269...
Mc Loskey 55
M' Losky 269...
Losse 180
Losty 178
Loue **V2**
Loue **V4**
Loue 269...
Louelace 269...
Lough Gur - **V4**
Loughan 269...
Loughbee 269...
Lougheed 269...
O Lougheran 176
Loughery **V4**
Loughlan 269...
O' Loughlen **V3**
Loughlin **V2**

Loughlin **V3**
Loughlin 269...
Mac Loughlin **V2**
Mac Loughlin 181
Mc Loughlin **V3**
Mc Loughlin 269...
O' Loughlin **V2**
O' Loughlin **V3**
(o) Loughlin 181
O' Loughlin 269...
Mac Loughlin, **V2**
O' Loughlin In **V3**
Loughman **V4**
Loughman 269...
Loughnan **V4**
Loughnan 269...
Loughnan(e) 182
Loughnane **V2**
Loughnane **V4**
Loughnane 180
Loughnane 269...
Loughnane **V3**
Loughran 184
Loughran 269...
O Loughran 176
Loughrey 269...
Loughry 182
Loughry 269...
Louton 269...
Lovat 269...
Love **V4**
Love 177
Love 269...
Lovelace 269...
Lovellis 269...
Lover, S. **V2**
O' Lovertie 269...
Lovett **V2**
Lovett 269...
Low 269...
Low(e) 182
O' Lowan 269...
Lowden **V2**
Lowe **V2**
Lowe **V5**
Lowe 269...
Lowers 269...
Lowery 269...
Lowery 4, 182
O Lowery **V4**
Lowes 205
Lowney **V4**
Lowney 269...

Lownsdale 269...
Lownsel 269...
Lowroo 269...
Lowry 269...
O Lowry **V4**
O Lowry 182
O' Lowry 269...
Lowther 182
Lowther 269...
Loy 269...
Loyd **V3**
Loyd 179
Loyde **V5**
Loyde 269...
M' Lroy 269...
O' Luain **V2**
O' Luasaig **V2**
Lub(e)y 182
O' Lubaig **V2**
Lube 182
Luby **V2**
Luby 269...
Luby, Cath. **V2**
Luc(e)y 184
Lucas **V3**
Lucas **V4**
Lucas 182
Lucas 269...
Lucey **V2**
Lucey **V4**
Lucey 269...
Lucid **V2**
Lucknawne 269...
Lucy **V2**
Lucy **V4**
Lucye 184
Ludden 269...
Luderdale 269...
Ludington 269...
Ludlo 269...
Ludlow **V2**
Ludlow(e) 183
Mac Lugada **V2**
Lugg **V4**
Lugg **V4**
Lugg 269...
Luiseid **V2**
Luke 269...
Lumbard(e) 180
O Lumley **V4**
Lummacks 269...
Lumsden **V2**
(de) Lunde 183

Lundergan 180
Lundy 183
Lundy 269...
Lunergan 180
Luney 184
Lunham **V2**
Lunn 183
Lunn 269...
Lunn(e)y 182, 184
Lunneen 269...
Lunney **V2**
Lunney 269...
O' Lunnin 269...
Lunny **V2**
Lunny 269...
O' Lunshaghan 269.
O' Luog 269...
Luogue 269...
Lupton **V2**
M' Lure 269...
Mc Lure 54
O' Lurkan **V3**
Lurkane 269...
O' Lurkane 269...
Lurken 269...
Lusher 34
Lussy 269...
Lusty 178
Lute **V4**
Lute 269...
Luther **V4**
Luther 269...
Lutheran 176
Lutrell 184
Lyach 269...
Mac Lychy 183
Lydden 183
Lyden **V2**
Lyden 183
Lydon **V3**
Lydon 269...
(o) Lydon 179, 183
(mac Lye 177
Lyedie **V3**
Lyedie 269...
Lyee 269...
Lyhan 269...
Lyhane 269...
Lyle 269...
Lyn **V2**
Lyn(n)ott 181
Lynacar 269...
Lynagh 183

Lynagh 269...
Lynam 183
Lynam 269...
Lynan 183
Lynan 269...
Lynane 269...
Lynap 269...
Lynas 269...
Lynass 177
Lynch **V2**
Lynch **V3**
Lynch **V4**
Lynch **V5**
Lynch 269...
O' Lynch **V3**
(o) Lynch 182, 183
Lynch Births **V3**
Lynch **V2**
Lynchahan 269...
O' Lynche **V3**
Lynchy **V3**
Lynchy **V4**
Lynchy 183
Lynchy 269...
Lyndan 269...
Lyndon **V2**
Lyndsay **V3**
Lyne **V2**
Lyne **V3**
Lyne **V4**
Lyne 174, 176
Lyne 269...
O Lyne **V2**
O Lyne 184
O' Lyne 269...
Lyness 177
Lyness 269...
Lynham 269...
Lynis 177
Lynn 269...
O Lynn 107
Lynnan 269...
Mc Lynnan 269...
O' Lynnan 269...
Lynne **V2**
Lynnes Of **V2**
Lynon 269...
Lynsey 269...
Lynshy 269...
Lynsie 269...
Lynskey 269...
(o) Lynskey 182
Lynsy 269...

V2 = Families of Co. Kerry **V3** = Families of Co. Clare **V4** = Families of Co. Cork **V5** = Families of Co. Limerick

Lyon269...
Lyon(s)184
Lyons **V2**
Lyons **V3**
Lyons **V4**
Lyons **V5**
Lyons174, 176
Lyons269...
O Lyons **V4**
Lyons Castle **V2**
Lysagert **V5**
Lysagert269...
Lysagh269...
Lysaght **V3**
Lysaght **V4**
Lysaght269...
(m') Lysaght184
Mac Lysaght **V3**
Mac Lysaght **V5**
Mac Lysaght **V3**
Lysaght, **V4**
Lysat184
Lysat269...
Lyster184
Lyster269...
Lytle269...
Lyttle180
Lyttle269...
M' Ma269...
Mc Ma269...
Ma-jury269...
Mac91
Macabe28
Macadams1
Macaddon29
Macain190
Macanerny156
Macanward263
Macarth(e)y39
Macassy **V2**
Macauley **V2**
Macauley6
Macintosh **V2**
Mack **V2**
Mack **V3**
Mack **V5**
Mack269...
Mack91
Mackassy **V2**
Mackell189
Macken **V4**
Macken190
Mackessy **V2**
Mackessy **V5**
Mackessy190
O' Mackessy **V3**
Mackesy **V4**
Mackey **V2**
Mackey **V4**
Mackey170,189
Mackey264
Mackie **V4**
Mackin190
Mackintosh **V2**
Mackle189
Mackler201
Macky189
Macnamara **V3**
Maconchy186
Macreavy134
Macrehan **V2**
O' Madagain **V2**
O' Madagan **V3**
Madagane186
O' Madagane **V5**
O' Madagane269...
Madden **V2**
Madden **V3**
Madden **V4**
Madden269...
O' Madden **V5**
(o) Madden186
Madden **V2**
Maddigan186
Maddigan269...
Maddin269...
Maddock269...
Maddock(s)189
Maddox **V4**
Maddox189
Madegan186
Madeslon269...
Madget **V2**
Madigan **V2**
Madigan **V3**
Madigan269...
O Madigan **V5**
(o) Madigan(e)186
Madigane **V3**
Madigane269...
O' Madigane269...
Madill269...
Madison269...
Madocks269...
Madole269...
Madowell269...
Madox **V4**
Madox269...
O Maelbleoghaid **V4**
O Maelbleoghaig **V4**
O' Maelchalloin **V3**
O' Maeleithigh **V3**
O Maelfabhail **V4**
O' Maelmacasa **V3**
Maelor201
Mag Guyn **V2**
Magahan190
Magaharan269...
Magahern269...
Magan186
Magan269...
Magane **V2**
Magann269...
Magarthy, D. **V2**
Magauran124
Magauran269...
Magaurn269...
Magawley63
Magawran269...
Magee **V2**
Magee **V3**
Magee129
Magee269...
Magenis187
Magenis269...
Magennis128,187
Mageown131
Magg269...
Mc Magh269...
Maghan187
Maghan269...
Magher187
Magher269...
Magher269...
Magherie **V4**
Maghery269...
Maghlin **V3**
Mc Maghone269...
Magill269...
Magill, **V2**
Magilligan127
Magillowy269...
Magilly269...
Magines269...
Maginley269...
Maginn **V2**
Maginn112,123
Maginn269...
Maginnis269...
Maginty120
Magiverin269...
Maglamery269...
Maglammery269..
Maglin130
Maglynn **V3**
Magner **V4**
Magner **V5**
Magner190
Magner269...
Magnier190
Magnir190
Magnor190
Magomerie269...
Magon269...
Magon(e)190
Magone269...
Magoon190
Magorisk269...
Magorlick269...
Magough269...
Magournahan269..
Magovern269...
Magowan131
Magowan269...
Magown131
Magrane269...
Magrath **V2**
Magrath **V3**
Magrath **V4**
Magrath **V4**
Magrath125
Magrath269...
Magraue269...
Magraw125
Magraw269...
Magreece269...
Magreevy134
Magrgh **V3**
Magrgh269...
Magrogan127
Magrogan269...
Magrory269...
Maguigan133
Maguigan269...
Maguil269...
Maguir **V5**
Maguir269...
Maguire128,186
Maguire269...
Maguirke132
Magullion269...
Magurn269...
Maguyre269...
Magwire269...
Magwyre269...
Mahaffy186
Maheir187
Maheir269...
Maher **V2**
Maher **V3**
Maher187
Maher269...
Maher **V2**
Mahier269...
Mahieu155
Mahollum269...
Maholm269...
Mahon **V2**
Mahon **V3**
Mahon269...
Mac Mahon **V2**
Mac Mahon **V3**
Mac Mahon **V5**
(mac Mahon187
Mc Mahon **V3**
Mc Mahon269...
Mc Mahon Arms **V3**
Mc Mahon **V3**
Mc Mahon In **V3**
Mc Mahon Of **V3**
Mc Mahone **V4**
Mc Mahone269...
Mahoney **V2**
Mahoney **V3**
Mahoney **V4**
Mahoney269...
Mc Mahoney188
O' Mahoney **V2**
O' Mahoney **V3**
O Mahoney **V4**
O' Mahoney **V5**
(o) Mahoney188
Mahoney, **V2**
O Mahoney **V4**
Mahoney, D. **V2**
Mahoney **V2**
Mahoney **V2**
Mahoney In **V3**
O Mahoney **V4**
Mahoney Of **V2**
Mahony **V2**
Mahony **V3**
Mahony **V4**
Mahony269...
Mc Mahony **V2**
Mc Mahony **V3**
Mc Mahony **V5**
Mc Mahony269...
O' Mahony **V2**
O Mahony **V4**
O' Mahony269...
Mahony, **V2**
Mahony Of **V2**
Mahony Of **V2**
Mahood151
Mahood269...
Mahoone269...
Mahoune **V4**
Mahown269...
Mahowna **V3**
Mahowne269...
O Mahowne **V4**
O' Mahowne269...
Mahowney **V4**
Mahowney188
Mahowny **V2**
Mahowny **V4**
Mahowny269...
Mc Mahowny **V4**
Mc Mahowny269..
O Mahowny **V4**
O' Mahowny269...
Mahowy269...
Mahur269...
Maid269...
Mac Maige **V2**
Maikim269...
Mailey188
Mailey269...
O' Maille **V2**
O' Maille **V3**
Mailor **V3**
Mailor201
Main **V2**
Mac Maine **V2**
O Maine **V3**
Maine River **V2**
Maine. U S A **V4**
Maines269...
Mainey197
Mainin187
O' Mainin **V2**
O' Mainnin **V2**
Mainwaring **V3**
Mair **V2**
Mairs269...
Maisterson269...
Maitland269...
Majhery **V4**
Major191
Major269...
Majur191
Makatye269...
Makellcree269...
Makeon269...
Makepeace269...
Makins269...
Malachy **V2**
Malady269...
Malboeuf **V4**
Malcolm269...
Malcolmson269...
Malcomson269...
Maledy198
Maley188
Maley269...
Malia188
Malia269...
Malie269...
Mallagh269...
Mallarky202
Mallavin269...
Mallefont **V4**
Mallew269...
Malley **V2**
Malley269...
O' Malley **V3**
O' Malley **V5**
(o) Malley188
O' Malley269...
Malley **V2**
O' Malleys **V3**
Mallon **V3**
Mallon269...
O Mallon191
Mallone188
Mallone269...
Malloon **V3**
Malloone **V3**
Malloone188,191
Malloone269...
Mallow **V4**
Mallow, Co. **V4**
Mallowney **V4**
Mallowney189
Mallowney269...
Malmona269...
Malone **V2**
Malone **V3**
Malone **V4**
Malone269...

O' Malone **V3**
O Malone **V4**
O Malone 188
Malone **V2**
Malone In **V3**
Maloney **V2**
Maloney **V3**
O' Maloney **V5**
O Maloney 189
Maloney **V3**
Maloughney 189
Malown **V4**
O Malowne **V4**
O Malowne 191
O' Malowne 269...
Malowny 189
Maloy 269...
Malseed 269...
Malvey **V2**
Malvey **V2**
Maly 188
Maly 269...
Malyan 269...
Manaanan **V2**
O' Manacain **V2**
Managhan 269...
O' Managhan 269...
Manahan 191
Manaher **V2**
Manaher **V2**
Manally 269...
Mc Manamon 269..
Manby 269...
Mandevile 269...
Mandeville **V5**
Mandeville 191
Mandowel **V3**
Mandowell 269...
Maneilly 269...
Manelis 269...
Mangan **V2**
Mangan **V4**
Mangan 269...
O' Mangan **V2**
O Mangan **V4**
O' Mangan **V5**
O Mangan 189
Manghan 189
Mangin 189
Manice 190
Manihan 191
Maninains **V3**
Maning 192

Manion 189
Manion 269...
Manis 190
Manix **V4**
Manix **V5**
Manley **V4**
Manley 191
Manly **V4**
Mann 187
Mann 269...
Mannaring 269...
Mannering **V2**
Mannering **V4**
Manneringe **V4**
Manneringe 269...
Manney 269...
Mannihan 191
Mannin(g) 187
Mannin(g) 192
Manning **V2**
Manning **V4**
Manning 269...
Mannion **V2**
Mannion 269...
(o) Mannion 187
Mannions **V3**
Mannix **V2**
Mannix **V4**
Mannix 191
Mannix 269...
O Mannog **V4**
Mannoring 269...
Manron 269...
Mansal **V3**
Mansel 192
Mansel 269...
Mansell **V2**
Mansell 269...
Mansergh **V4**
Mansergh 189
Mansery **V4**
Mansery 269...
Manseryhe **V4**
Manseryhe 269...
Mansfield **V2**
Mansfield **V4**
Mansfield 190
Mansfield 269...
Mansfield 34
Mansill 192
Manson 269...
Manswer 269...
Mant **V3**

Mantell 269...
Manus 269...
Mac Manus **V2**
(mac Manus 190
Mac Manus 269...
Mc Manus **V5**
Mc Manus 269...
Manwaring 269...
Manwering 269...
Manyhyne **V5**
Manyhyne 269...
Manyne 269...
O Maoelconery **V3**
O' Maoilmeda **V3**
Maolain **V3**
O' Maolalaid **V2**
Maolconnery **V3**
Map Cork 1576 **V4**
Map Families **V4**
Map Of Clare **V3**
Map Of Cork **V4**
Mapes 269...
Mapother 193
Mapother 269...
Mara **V3**
Mara 187
Mara 269...
O' Mara **V3**
O' Mara Of **V2**
(o) Marah 194
Marcaghane **V3**
Marcaghane 269...
March **V3**
Mareschall **V2**
Margetson **V3**
Marisco **V2**
Marisco 191
Mark 269...
O Mark(e)y 192
Markam 269...
Markes 269...
Markey 269...
Markham **V3**
Markham 269...
Markhame 269...
Marks 269...
Marl(e)y 190
Marlay 190
Marley 269...
Marlow 269...
O' Marly 269...
Marmion 191
Marnane 204

Marnane 269...
Marnell **V3**
Marnell 192
Marnell 269...
Maron(e)y 198
Maroney **V2**
Marra 194
Marran 193
Marren 193
Marren 269...
Marrilly 269...
Marriman 191
Marrinane 269...
Marron 193
Marron 269...
Mc Marrowe 269...
Marsh **V4**
Marsh **V4**
Marsh 191
Marsh 269...
Marshal(l) 191
Marshall **V2**
Marshall **V5**
Marshall 269...
(le) Marshall **V2**
Marsham 191
Marshell 191
O' Martain **V2**
Martel **V2**
Martell **V4**
Martell 193
Martelli **V2**
Marten 192
Mc Marten 269...
Martenn **V4**
Martin **V2**
Martin **V3**
Martin **V4**
Martin 192
Martin 269...
Martin 269...
Martine **V4**
Martine 269...
Martyn **V3**
Martyn **V4**
Martyn 192
Marvault **V4**
Marwards 193
O' Mary **V5**
O' Mary 269...
Mc Maryne 269...
Mashanaglas **V4**
Masie **V4**

Masie 269...
Mason **V2**
Mason 269...
Mass(e)y 192
Massa 269...
Massereene **V2**
Massey **V3**
Massey **V4**
Massey 269...
Masson 269...
Massy **V2**
Massy **V4**
Massy **V5**
Mc Master 193
Mc Master 269...
Masters **V4**
Masters 155
Masterson 193
Masterson 269...
Mastine 269...
Mastron 269...
Masurier 155
Matchett **V4**
Matchett 269...
Matchett 34
Mateer 269...
Mathers 269...
Matheson **V3**
Mathew(e)s 192
Mathewes 269...
Mathews **V2**
Mathews **V4**
Mathews **V5**
Mathews 269...
Mathews 269...
Matson **V2**
Matthews **V2**
Matthews **V4**
Matthews 192
Matthews 269...
Mattimore 193
Mauffield 269...
Maughan 187
Maughan 269...
Mc Maughon 269...
Maul 269...
Maule 269...
Maunsal **V3**
Maunsall **V3**
Maunsel **V5**
Maunsel 190
Maunsel(l) 192
Maunsell **V2**

Maunsell **V3**
Maunsell 269...
Mac Maurace 193
Maurice **V3**
Maurice **V4**
Maurice 193, 198
Maurice 269...
Fitz Maurice **V3**
Mac Maurice **V2**
Mavity 260
Mawe **V2**
Mawe 269...
Mawe, Dr. **V2**
Mawhannon 269...
Mawhinney 269...
Mawhinny 269...
Maxel 269...
Maxwel 269...
Maxwell **V2**
Maxwell **V5**
Maxwell 193
Maxwell 269...
May **V2**
May **V4**
May 269...
(de) May 195
Mayberry 195
Mayberry 269...
Maybin 269...
Maybury **V2**
Maybury **V5**
Maybury 269...
Mayduck 269...
Mayes 195
Mayes 269...
Mayhew 155
Mayhugh **V4**
Mayhugh **V5**
Maylard 269...
Maynard **V2**
Maynard **V4**
Maynard 269...
Maynarde **V4**
Mayne **V3**
Mayne 269...
Mayner **V4**
Mayo **V4**
Mayo **V5**
Mayo 195
Maypother 193
Maypowder 193
Maypowder 269...
Mayrick 194

Maziere **V4**
Mc Inerny **V4**
Mc Robiston **V4**
Mcloghlen **V3**
Mea 269...
O' Meacair **V2**
O Meachair 187
Mead **V3**
Mead **V4**
Mead 269...
Mead(e) 193
Meade **V2**
Meade **V3**
Meade **V4**
Meade 269...
Meadows 194
O' Meadra **V2**
Meagh **V4**
Meagh **V5**
Meagh 269...
Meaghan 269...
O' Meaghan 269...
Meaghane **V3**
Meagher **V2**
Meagher **V3**
Meagher 187
Meagher 269...
O' Meagher 269...
Meaghir 269...
Meahan **V2**
Meahohan 269...
Meale **V3**
Mealia 269...
Mealley 269...
O' Mealue 269...
Mealy 269...
O' Mealy 269...
Mean(e)y 197
Meane 269...
Meaney **V3**
Meaniman **V3**
Meanman **V3**
Meany **V3**
Meany 269...
Meara **V2**
Meara **V3**
Meara 269...
O' Meara **V2**
O Meara **V4**
O Meara 194, 195
O' Meara 269...
O' Meara, **V5**
Meare **V3**

V2 = Families of Co. Kerry **V3** = Families of Co. Clare **V4** = Families of Co. Cork **V5** = Families of Co. Limerick

Meares **V3**
Mearinge269...
Mearn269...
Mears195
M' Mearty269...
Meary269...
O' Meary **V5**
O' Meary269...
Mease **V5**
Mease269...
Measure155
Mc Meater **V4**
Meath269...
Meath, Co. **V4**
Mc Mechan269...
Meddows194
Mee269...
Meed193
Meegan194
Meegan269...
Meeghan **V4**
Meeghane194
O' Meeghane **V3**
O' Meeghane269...
Meehan **V2**
Meehan **V3**
Meehan **V4**
Meehan269...
O' Meehan **V3**
O Meehan **V4**
O' Meehan **V5**
O Meehan194
O' Meehan269...
Meehan, C.p. **V2**
Meehan Of **V3**
O' Meehans **V3**
O' Meehon269...
Meek **V2**
Meek269...
Meek(e)195
Mc Meekan195
Meeke269...
Mc Meeken195
Meekin195
Meekin269...
Mc Meekin194
Mc Meekin269...
Mac Meel100
Mc Meel269...
Meenagh269...
Meenan195
Meenan269...
Meenhan195
Meenhan269...
Meeny197
O Meera194
Meere **V3**
Meere195
Meere269...
Meers Of **V3**
Megarry269...
Meghan269...
Megher269...
Meglamry269...
Meglaughlin269...
Megraw269...
Mehane269...
Meharg269...
Mehegan194
O Mehegane **V4**
Mehigan **V2**
Meighan194
Meighan269...
O Meighan **V4**
O' Meighan **V5**
Meirs269...
Mekill269...
Melaghlin181
O' Melaghlin269...
Melaghline269...
Melay269...
Melbourne, **V2**
Melden195
Meldon195
Meldon269...
Meledy198
Melia188
Melia269...
Mellan201
O' Mellan269...
Mellefont **V4**
Mellen201
Mc Mellen269...
Mellet269...
Mellifont269...
Mellon269...
(o) Mellon191,201
Mellot204
Mellott269...
Melly269...
Melod(e)y198
Melody **V3**
Melody269...
Meloghlen269...
Melroy269...
Melville **V2**
Melville **V4**
Melville **V5**
Melville269...
Melvin269...
Menaght269...
Mc Menamen198
Menamin **V3**
Mc Menamin198
Mc Menamin269...
Menarry211
Menautt269...
Mac Menda **V3**
Mc Menda **V3**
Mc Menda269...
Mendan269...
Meneese269...
Mc Menemen198
Mc Menim269...
Menocher269...
Mentan269...
Meogand269...
Meolan269...
Meolane **V3**
O Meolane **V3**
O' Meolane269...
Mercer **V2**
Mercer269...
Merdiff269...
Merdy269...
De Mere195
Meredeth269...
Meredith **V2**
Meredith269...
Meredith Of **V2**
O Mergain201
Merideth269...
Meridith269...
Merie **V3**
Meriman269...
Merineau155
Mermont269...
Merna193
Merna269...
Mernagh **V2**
Mernagh193
O' Merran269...
Merrick269...
Merrick(e)194
Merricke269...
Merrigan269...
Merriman269...
Merryman **V3**
Merryman191
Merryman269...
Mertell **V4**
Mc Merty269...
Mervin269...
Meryon155
Mescal198
Mescall **V3**
Meskell **V3**
Meskell **V4**
Meskell198
Meskell269...
Meskill **V2**
Meslvyne269...
Messick **V4**
Messick269...
Metcalf269...
Metcalfe **V5**
Metham **V3**
Metham269...
Meverall269...
Meverell269...
Mewhanan269...
Mewhirter269...
Mexican **V3**
Mey195
Meyer, K. **V2**
Meyer(s)201
Meyler201
Meyler269...
Meylor269...
Meyrick194
Miagh **V4**
Miagh **V4**
Miagh269...
Mich205
Michael269...
Mac Michael **V2**
Mac Michael100
Mc Michael269...
Michaelburn269...
Michel269...
Michelburn269...
Michell205
Michell269...
Mc Michell269...
Mickle269...
O Mictire **V4**
O Mictire **V4**
Midcalfe269...
Middlesex269...
Middleton **V5**
Middleton269...
O' Midir **V2**
Midleton269...
Midleton, **V4**
Midleton, **V2**
Mighane **V3**
Mighane269...
O Mighane **V3**
O' Mighane269...
Mihigan **V2**
Mihil269...
Mihill269...
Mil **V4**
Milan Of **V3**
Milborn269...
Mildmays **V2**
Mildrum269...
Milegan269...
Miler195
Miles **V2**
Miles **V4**
Miles269...
Mac Miles **V2**
Milet(te)204
Milford202
Miligan205
Millan269...
Mc Millan203
Mc Millan269...
Millane269...
Millar195,205
Millar269...
Millcod269...
Millea195
Millea269...
Millen269...
Mc Millen203
Mc Millen269...
Miller **V3**
Miller **V4**
Miller155,195
Miller269...
Millerick202
Milles269...
Millet(t)204
Millican205
Millican269...
Milligan205
Milligan269...
Milligen203
Milligen269...
Millikan205
Milliken203
Milliken269...
Millikin205
Millin269...
Mc Millin269...
Millinton269...
Mills **V4**
Mills205
Mills269...
Milmoy **V3**
Milne269...
Milner **V2**
Milner **V4**
Milner269...
Miltown **V3**
Milward **V2**
Mimnagh269...
Minagh269...
Minard **V2**
Minch195
Minchin **V2**
Minchin195
Mines269...
Minett269...
Minford269...
Mingane **V2**
Mingane269...
Miniece269...
Minighane **V3**
Minighane205
Minighane269...
Minihan **V4**
Minihan(e)205
Minihane **V3**
Minihane **V4**
Minihane269...
Mc Minn269...
Minnis269...
Minnish269...
Minnitt269...
Minnock269...
Minochor269...
Minog(u)e201
Minogher269...
Minogue **V2**
Minogue269...
Minogue **V3**
Minoher269...
Minorgan209
Minteer269...
Miscall198
Miskelly198
Miskelly269...
Missett **V4**
Misskimmin269..
Mitchel(l)200,205
Mitchell **V2**
Mitchell **V4**
Mitchell **V5**
Mitchell269...
Mitten269...
Mitty269...
Mc Mlaghlen **V4**
Mc Mlaghlen269..
Moan269...
Moany269...
Moarn197
Mochlehayn **V2**
Mockler201
Mockler269...
Modler205
Modrell269...
Mody202
Moen269...
Moeny269...
Moeran197
Mofett201
Moffat269...
Moffat(t)201
Moffatt269...
Moffet269...
Moffett201
Moffett269...
Moffit269...
Moffitt269...
Mofitt201
Moghan269...
Mogher199
Mogher269...
Mohan269...
Moher **V4**
Moher199
O Mohir **V4**
O Mohir199
O' Mohir269...
O Mohowny **V4**
Moir197,199
Moir269...
Moizel **V5**
Molahiffe **V2**
Molan **V3**
Molan(d)199
Moland **V3**
Moleyns **V2**
(de) Moleyns **V2**
Molineux203
Molineux269...
Mollahan **V3**
O' Mollan269...

Mollane **V3**
O' Mollane **V3**
O Mollane 199
O' Mollane 269...
Mollany 269...
Mollarky 202
O' Molleany 269...
Mollenex 269...
Molley 195
Molley 269...
Mollinenx 269...
Mollohan **V3**
Mollone 269...
Mollowny **V5**
Mollowny 269...
Molloy **V2**
Molloy 269...
(o) Molloy 195
Moloney **V2**
Moloney **V3**
Moloney **V4**
Moloney **V5**
Moloney 269...
O' Moloney **V3**
Moloney **V3**
Moloney In **V3**
Molony **V2**
Molony **V3**
Molony 269...
Moloy 269...
Molphy 269...
Molumby 269...
Molyneaux **V2**
Molyneaux 269...
Momerie 155
Monaboe 212
Monaboe 269...
Monaghan 269...
(o) Monaghan 196
O' Monaghen 269..
Mc Monagle 199
Mc Monagle 269...
Monahan **V2**
Monahan 269...
Monanimy **V4**
Monarto **V3**
Monarto 269...
Moncklone 269...
Moncreife 269...
Moncriefe 269...
Mondy 269...
O' Mone 269...
Mc Monegal 199
Monegan 269...
Monehan 269...
Monell 269...
Money 269...
O' Money 269...
Moneypeany 269..
Moneypeny 34
O' Mongain **V2**
Mongan **V4**
Mongan 269...
O Mongan **V4**
Mongan(e) 189
O Mongane **V4**
O' Mongane 269...
Mongney 269...
Mongomerie **V5**
Mongomerie 269...
Mongon 269...
Mc Monigal 199
Monighan **V2**
Mc Monigle 199
Monihan **V3**
Monipenny 269...
Monk **V4**
Monke **V4**
Monke 269...
Monks 269...
Monley **V4**
Monley 191
Monley 269...
Monnaughan 196
Monnelly 269...
Monohan 196
Monohan 269...
Monro 269...
Monroe 204
Monroe 269...
Monsell **V3**
Monsell **V5**
Monsell 192
Monsell 269...
Monsfield 190
Monson **V2**
Montague 269...
Montane 269...
Montang 269...
Montangue 269...
Montch'nsey 202
Monteagle **V2**
Montgomerie 269..
Montgomerre 269..
Montgomery **V2**
Montgomery **V4**
Montgomery 133
Montgomery 196
Montgomery 269..
Montgomery **V2**
Montgomry 196
Montm'rency 196
Montray 269...
O' Mony 269...
Moode 202
Moodie 202
Moody 202
Moody 269...
Moon 269...
O' Moone 269...
Mooney **V2**
Mooney 269...
O Mooney **V4**
O Mooney 197
Moony 269...
Moor **V2**
Moor **V3**
Moor 269...
(o) Moor(e) 197
Moore **V2**
Moore **V3**
Moore **V4**
Moore 269...
O' Moore **V2**
Moore **V2**
Moore, S. **V4**
Moorehead 269...
Moores **V2**
Moorhead **V2**
Moorhead 201
Moorhead 269...
O' Moors **V2**
Moory 269...
Mora 269...
Morahain **V2**
Morahan 196
Morahan 269...
Moran **V2**
Moran **V3**
Moran 269...
O' Moran **V2**
O Moran 197
O' Moran 269...
Moran **V2**
Morane 269...
Mc Morchey 269...
O' Morda **V2**
Morduck **V4**
Morduck 269...
More **V2**
More **V3**
More **V4**
More 269...
O' More **V2**
(o) More 197
Moreen 269...
Moreghy 269...
Morehead 201
Morehey 269...
Moreland 269...
Moren 197
Moren 269...
Mores 198
Moressy 269...
Moreton 269...
Morey 197
Morey 269...
Mc Morey 269...
O' Morey 269...
Morgan **V2**
Morgan **V3**
Morgan 269...
O Morgan **V4**
O Morgan 196
O' Morgan 269...
Morgan **V2**
Morgell **V2**
Morgen 196
O Morghow **V4**
Morgin 196
Moriarto **V3**
Moriarto 269...
Moriarty **V2**
Moriarty **V3**
Moriarty 269...
Mac Moriarty 198
O' Moriarty **V2**
O Moriarty **V4**
O Moriarty 198
Moriarty **V2**
Moriarty, **V2**
Moriarty **V2**
Mac Moriarty **V2**
Moriarty Loch Lein **V4**
Moriartys **V2**
Morice **V3**
Mc Morihirtagh **V4**
Morin 197
Morin 269...
Moris **V4**
Moris 196
Mc Moris **V5**
Mc Moris 269...
Morisey 196
Morisey 269...
Morish 105
Morish 269...
Mc Morish **V5**
Mc Morish 269...
Morison 269...
Moriss 269...
Morissey **V3**
Morissy 269...
Morl(e)y 196
Morley **V2**
Morley **V4**
Morley 269...
Morley **V2**
Morly **V2**
Mornell 192
Mornell 269...
O' Morny **V3**
O Morny 201
Mc Morogh 269...
Moroghe **V4**
O' Moroghoe 269...
O Morohow **V4**
O' Morohow 269...
Moroly 269...
Moroney **V2**
Moroney **V3**
Moroney 269...
O' Moroney **V3**
O' Moroney **V5**
O Moroney 198
Moroney **V2**
Morony **V2**
Morony Of **V3**
Mc Morough 269...
Morpheu **V5**
Morpheu 269...
Morphey 269...
Mc Morphey 269...
Morphy **V2**
Morphy **V5**
Morphy 269...
Morphy, **V2**
Morphy **V2**
Morrally 196
Morran 269...
Morrane 269...
O' Morrane 269...
Morrelly 196
Morren 269...
Morres **V3**
Morres 198
Morresse 269...
Mc Morrey 269...
Morrice **V2**
Morrice **V3**
Morrice 105
Mac Morrice **V2**
Mac Morrice 269...
Mc Morrice **V2**
Mc Morrice 269...
Morrin 269...
Morris **V2**
Morris **V3**
Morris **V4**
Morris 193,196
Morris 198
Morris 269...
Mac Morris **V2**
Mc Morris **V4**
Mc Morris **V5**
Mc Morris 269...
O' Morris 269...
Morrisen 199
Morrish **V3**
Morrish **V4**
Morrish 105
Morrish 269...
Fitz Morrish **V3**
Mc Morrish **V2**
Mc Morrish **V4**
Mc Morrish 269...
O' Morrish 269...
Morrison **V2**
Morrison **V5**
Morrison 196,198
Morrison 199
Morrison 269...
Morrisroe 269...
Morrissey **V2**
Morrissey **V4**
Morrissey **V5**
Morrissey 196
Morrissey 269...
Morrisson 199
Morrissy **V3**
O' Morroe 269...
Morrogh **V2**
Morrogh 269...
Mc Morrogh **V3**
Mc Morrogh **V5**
Mc Morrogh 269...
Morrogh, W. **V2**
Morrogh-ber **V2**
O Morroghow **V4**
O' Morroghow 269.
Morrolly 269...
Morrossey 269...
Morrough 269...
Mac Morrough **V3**
Morrow **V3**
Morrow **V4**
Morrow 269...
(m') Morrow 202
Mc Morrow **V3**
Mc Morrow 269...
O Morrow **V4**
O' Morrow 269...
Morry 269...
O' Morry 269...
Morse **V5**
Morsh 269...
Mortagh **V3**
Mortagh 269...
Mc Mortagh 269...
Mc Mortath **V3**
Mc Mortath 269...
Mc Mortaugh **V4**
Mc Mortaugh 269..
Mortimer 269...
Mortimor 269...
Mortomer 269...
Morton **V3**
Morton **V5**
Morton 269...
Moryergh 269...
Moryson **V2**
Moseley **V3**
Mosley **V2**
Moss **V4**
Moss 269...
Mosse **V4**
Mosse 269...
Moter 269...
Motherway **V4**
Motherway 269...
Motley 269...
Motly 269...
Moton 269...
Mou **V3**
Mouckton **V5**
Mouckton 269...
Moughan 269...
Moughty 269...
Mould 269...
De Moulins 155
Moulton 269...

V2 = Families of Co. Kerry **V3** = Families of Co. Clare **V4** = Families of Co. Cork **V5** = Families of Co. Limerick

Moungomery 269..
Mounrag 269...
Mounsal V3
Mountford V4
Mountford 269...
Mountfort V4
Mountgomer 269..
Mouny 269...
Mourn 197
Mouroghu V4
Mowbray 202
Mowhannan 269...
Moy(e) 201
Moylan V2
Moylan V3
Moylan V4
Moylan 201
Moylan 269...
Moylane V3
Moyle(s) 201
Moylen 201
Moyles 269...
Moynan 269...
Moynes 269...
Moyney 269...
Moynihan V2
Moynihan V3
Moynihan V4
Moynihan 196
Moynihan 269...
Moyrane 269...
O' Mrisane 269...
Mubrell V3
De Mucegros V3
Muckaree 269...
Muckedan 269...
Muckeen 201
Muckeen 269...
Muckeyin 201
Muckian 201
Muckian 269...
Muckilbouy 269...
Muckleborne 269..
Mucklebreed 269...
Muckler 269...
Muckley 203
Muckross V2
Muclahy V5
Muclahy 269...
Mudy 202
Mug V2
Muinagh 269...
Muintear V3
Muir V5
Muir 269...
O' Muiray V2
Muirhead 201
Muirland 269...
Muirlihy V2
O Muirthile V4
Muise 269...
Mulally V2
Mulally 199
O' Mulan 269...
Mulaney 202
Mulavill 269...
Mulbrennan 203
Mulbride 31
Mulcaghy 269...
O Mulcaha V4
O' Mulcaha 269...
Mulcahey V4
Mulcahy V2
Mulcahy V4
Mulcahy 269...
O Mulcahy V4
O' Mulcahy V5
O Mulcahy 203
Mulcair 42
Mulcare V2
Mulchaell 269...
Mulchay 203
Mulchinock V2
Mulchinock V2
Mulchinock V4
Mulchinock 201
Mulchinock, V2
Mulckamp 269...
O' Mulclahy V5
O' Mulclahy 269...
Mulclohy 203
O Mulclohy 201
Mulclyff 269...
Mulconery V3
Mulconnery V3
Mulconry V3
Mulconry 269...
O Mulconry 51
Mulcreevy 202
O' Mulcreve 269...
Mulcrevy 269...
Mulcrew 202
O Mulcrian V4
Mulderg 269...
Mulderrig 202,232
Mulderrig 269...
Muldon 269...
Muldony 269...
Muldoon 269...
O' Muldoon V3
O Muldoon 201
Muldoone 201
O' Muldowne 269...
Muldowney 269...
Muldowney 92
Muldowny 269...
Mulgan 203
O' Mulgohery 269..
Mulgrew 202
Mulgrew 269...
Mulgrievey 269...
Mulgroo 269...
O Mulgrue 202
Mulhaell 269...
Mulhal(l) 202
Mulhall 269...
Mulhallam 269...
Mulhallom 269...
Mulhartagh 269...
Mulherin 269...
Mulhern 269...
Mulholland V3
Mulholland V4
Mulholland 150
Mulholland 199
Mulholland 202
Mulholland 269...
O' Mulholland 269.
Mulhollum 269...
Mulholm 269...
Mulkeen V4
Mulkeen 269...
O Mulkerane 202
O' Mulkerane 269...
(o) Mulkerin 202
Mulkern 202
Mulkerrin 202
Mulkerrin 269...
Mulkin V4
O' Mulkiran 269...
Mullagen 203
Mullally V2
O Mullally V4
O Mullally 173
O Mullally 199
Mullaly 173,199
Mullaly 269...
Mullan V3
Mullan V4
Mullan 269...
Mc Mullan 269...
O' Mullan 269...
(m') Mullan(e) 199
(m') Mullan(e) 203
Mullane V2
Mullane V3
Mullane V4
Mullane V5
Mullane 269...
O Mullane V4
O' Mullane 269...
O Mullaney 202
Mullany 202
Mullany 269...
O' Mullany 269...
Mullarkey 202
Mullarkey 269...
Mullarky 269...
Mullclahy V5
Mullclahy 269...
Mulledy 269...
O Mulledy 203
Mullee 195
Mullee 269...
Mulleeny 202
Mullegan 269...
Mullen V3
Mullen 199
Mullen 269...
Mac Mullen V2
Mc Mullen 203
Mullens V2
Mullens V3
Mullens V4
Mullens V2
Mullens Of V2
Mulleplate 269...
Muller 269...
Mullerane 269...
Mullerick V4
Mullerick 202
Mullery 205
O' Mullfoyle 269...
Mullgan 269...
O' Mullghill 269...
Mullholland 269...
Mullican 203
Mullican 269...
O' Mullican 269...
Mulligan V2
Mulligan 269...
O Mulligan 203
O' Mulligan 269...
O' Mulligan 269...
Mullin 269...
Mullin(s) 199
Mullinenx 269...
Mullineux V2
O' Mullinihilly 269
Mullins V2
Mullins V3
Mullins V4
Mullins 155
Mullins 269...
Mullins Of V2
Mullis V2
O' Mullmoghery 26
Mullock 269...
Mc Mulloghry 269.
Mullon 269...
Mullony V3
Mullony 269...
Mulloon V3
Mullowney V3
Mullowney V4
Mullowney 269...
Mullowny V3
Mullowny 269...
O' Mullowny V3
O' Mullowny V5
O' Mullowny 269...
Mulloy 195
Mulloy 269...
O Mulloy V4
O' Mulloy 269...
O' Mullpatrick 269.
Mullrayn 269...
Mullreane 269...
Mullronifin 269...
Mullvihill 200
O' Mulmea V3
Mulmona 269...
Mulmory 205
Mulmoy V3
Muloly 269...
Mulone 269...
O' Mulpatrick 269..
Mulqeen V4
Mulqeeny V4
Mulqueany V3
Mulqueen V3
Mulqueen V5
Mulqueen 202
Mulqueen 269...
O Mulqueen V3
Mulquinn V2
Mulrains 231
Mulready 232
Mulreany 269...
O Mulrenan 203
Mulrennan 269...
Mulrian 269...
Mulrian 269...
O' Mulrian V5
O' Mulrian 269...
O' Mulriane V5
O' Mulriane 269...
Mulroe 269...
Mulroney V3
Mulroney 269...
Mc Mulronifin 269.
Mulrony 269...
Mulroon(e)y 203
Mulroone 198
Mulrooney V3
Mulrooney 198
Mulrooney 233
Mulrooney 269...
Mulrow 269...
Mulroy 203
Mulroy 269...
Mulry 203,205
Mulry 269...
Mulryan 269...
O Mulryan 231
Mulshenagh 201
Mulshenoge V4
Mulshenoge 269...
Mulshinock 201
Mulshinoge 201
Multon V4
Mulvan(n)y 204
Mulvanerty 269...
Mulvaney 204
Mulvanny 269...
Mulvany 269...
Mulvehill V2
Mulvehill V3
O' Mulvena 269...
Mulvenna 204
Mulvenna 269...
Mulvey 204
Mulvey 269...
Mulvighill 269...
Mulvihill V2
Mulvihill 269...
O' Mulvihill V2
O' Mulvihill V3
O' Mulvihill V5
O Mulvihill 200
Mulville V3
Mulville 200
O' Mulvog 269...
Mulvogue 183
Mulvy 204
Mummery 155
Munchas V2
Muncke 269...
Munckten 269...
Munday 269...
Mundy, Maj. V2
Muney 269...
O' Muney 269...
Mungan 269...
Munighane V4
Munighane 269...
Munnelly 269...
Munnihane 205
Munnyhane V4
Munnyhane 269...
Munro V2
Munroe 204
Munrow 204
Muns 269...
Munster V4
O' Muracha 269...
Muran 269...
O' Murcada V2
O Murcain 204
Murcan 269...
O Murcan 204
O Murchadha V4
Mc Murchey 269...
O' Murchey 269...
Murchoe 200
Murchoe 269...
O' Murchoe 269...
O' Murchy 269...
Murdoch V2
Murdoch 204,205
Murdoch 269...
Murdock V2
Murdock 204,205
Murdock 269...
Murdough 269...
Murdy 269...
Mc Murdy 269...
Mac Muregain 204
Muresie 269...
O' Muresie 269...
Mc Murey 269...

V2 = Families of Co. Kerry V3 = Families of Co. Clare V4 = Families of Co. Cork V5 = Families of Co. Limerick

Murfay 269...
Murfhy 200
Murfie **V4**
Murfie 269...
Mc Murfie **V4**
Murfy 269...
Murhila 153
Murhill **V2**
Murhilla 269...
Murily 153
M' Murlan 269...
Murland 269...
Murley **V4**
Murnaghan 204
Murnahan 204
Murnain 204
O' Murnain As **V2**
Murnan(e) 204
Murnane **V2**
Murnane **V4**
Murnane **V5**
Murnane 269...
Murnayne **V4**
Murney 204
Murphey 269...
Mc Murphey 269...
Murphy **V2**
Murphy **V3**
Murphy **V4**
Murphy **V5**
Murphy 200
Murphy 269...
Mc Murphy 269...
O Murphy **V2**
O Murphy **V4**
O' Murphy 269...
Murphy **V3**
Murphy In **V3**
O Murphy **V4**
Murray **V2**
Murray **V4**
Murray 204
Murray 269...
Mc Murray **V5**
Mc Murray 269...
O' Murray 269...
Murray Of **V3**
Murreane **V4**
Murreane 269...
Murrey 269...
Mc Murrey 269...
Murricohu 269...
Murricohu 269...
Murrie, **V2**
Murrigan 196
O Murrigan 203
Murrihy 204
Murrihy 269...
Murrihy 269...
Murrin 269...
Murrogh **V4**
Mc Murrogh **V3**
O Murroghow **V4**
O' Murroghow 269.
Murrony **V3**
Murrony 269...
Murrough **V4**
Murrough 269...
Mac Murrough **V3**
Mac Murrough 200
Mac Murrough 202
O Murrough **V4**
Murry 269...
(mc) Murry 204
Mc Murry 269...
O Murry **V4**
O' Murry 269...
Murt 269...
Murta 205
Murta(u)gh 205
Murtagh **V5**
Murtagh 198
Murtagh 269...
Mc Murtagh **V4**
Mc Murtagh 269...
Murtaugh **V3**
Murtaugh **V4**
O Murthuile **V4**
Murtin 269...
Mc Murtry 269...
Mury 269...
O' Mury 269...
Muscham **V4**
Muscham 269...
Muschamp **V2**
Muschamp 269...
Musgrave **V2**
Music, Sheet. **V4**
Muskerie **V4**
Muskry **V4**
Muster Roll **V2**
Mustian 269...
Myaghe **V2**
Myer(s) 195,201
Myers **V2**
Myers 269...
Myhan 269...
O' Myhan 269...
Myles **V2**
Myles **V4**
Myles 269...
Mylott 269...
Mylotte 269...
Mynoge 269...
Mythen 269...
Mc Nabb 209
Mc Nabb 269...
Mc Nabo 269...
Mc Nabo(e) 212
Mc Naboe 269...
Mc Nabola 213
Mc Naboola 213
Mc Nabow 212
Mc Nabully 213
Nagell **V4**
Naghten **V3**
Naghten 269...
Mc Naghten 269...
O' Naghten 207
Naghtenn 269...
Nagle **V2**
Nagle **V3**
Nagle **V4**
Nagle 206
Nagle 269...
Nagle, **V4**
Nagle, **V5**
Nail 269...
Mc Nair 269...
(de) Nais **V2**
Naish **V5**
Naish 207
Naish 269...
Nally **V2**
Nally 269...
Mac Nally **V2**
Mac Nally 206,207
Mc Nally 269...
Mc Nama 269...
Mac Namara **V2**
Mac Namara **V3**
Mc Namara **V5**
Mc Namara 206
Mc Namara 269...
M' Namara Arms **V3**
Mc Namara **V3**
Mac Namara **V2**
Mc Namarow **V5**
Mc Namarow 269...
Mc Namarra **V4**
Mc Namee 206
Mc Namee 269...
Names,family **V4**
Nammock **V2**
Mc Namorrow 269..
Nanany 269...
Nangle **V2**
Nangle **V4**
Nangle **V5**
Nangle 206
Naper 269...
(le) Naper 207
Napier 207
Napier 269...
Napper 207
Napper 269...
Narbett 269...
Mc Nari 211
Nary 269...
(mac Nary 211
Nash **V2**
Nash **V3**
Nash **V4**
Nash **V5**
Nash 269...
Nash, C. F. **V2**
Nash(e) 5,207
Nason 213
Nasse 207
Natt **V2**
Naugher 269...
M' Naught 269...
Naughten 269...
Mc Naughten 269...
Naughton **V2**
Naughton 269...
Naughton 62
(m') Naughton 207
Naughton, **V3**
Mc Naul 207
Naungle **V4**
Navill 269...
Navin 207,209
Navin 269...
Nay **V5**
Nay 269...
Naylor **V2**
Naylor 269...
O' Nea **V5**
O' Nea 269...
O Neachtain **V3**
O' Neaghtain **V5**
Neagle **V3**
Neagle **V4**
Neagle 206
Neal 269...
O' Neal **V2**
O Neal **V4**
Nealan 269...
Nealane **V3**
Nealane 269...
O' Nealane **V3**
O' Nealane 269...
Neale 269...
Mc Neale 269...
O' Neale **V2**
O Neale **V4**
O' Neale **V5**
O' Neale 269...
Neales Views **V2**
Neall 269...
Mc Neall 269...
O' Neall **V3**
O' Neall 269...
O' Nealle 269...
Nealon **V2**
Neaphsey 269...
Neary 269...
(mac Neary 211
Neave 269...
O' Nedi **V2**
O Nedi 207
Nee 269...
Mac Nee 213
Mac Neece 213
Mc Neece 269...
Needham 269...
Neef 269...
Neehan 269...
Neehane 211
Neel(e) 208
Mc Neela 207
Neely 269...
Mc Neely 207
Mc Neely 269...
Neenan **V2**
Neenan **V3**
Neenan 211,212
Neenan 269...
Neeper 269...
Neeson 213
Neeson 269...
Mc Neice 269...
Mc Neight 269...
O' Neigill **V2**
Neil 208
O' Neil Family **V2**
O' Neil Rebells **V2**
Neilan **V2**
Neilan 269...
O Neilan 208
O' Neilan Arms **V3**
Neiland **V3**
Neile 269...
O' Neile 269...
Neill **V2**
Neill **V4**
Neill 269...
Mac Neill **V2**
Mc Neill 208
Mc Neill 269...
O' Neill **V2**
O' Neill **V3**
O Neill **V4**
O Neill 208
O' Neill 269...
O' Neill In **V3**
Neillan **V3**
O' Neillan **V3**
O' Neills Defeat **V2**
Mac Neilly 209
Mc Neilly 269...
Neilon **V3**
Neilson **V2**
Neilson 208
Neiper 269...
Neisbett 269...
Neish 207
Neizer 205
Nelan 208
Mc Neley 209
Neligan **V2**
O' Neligan **V2**
O Neligan **V4**
O Neligan 212
Neligan, J. **V2**
Neligan, W. **V2**
Nelis 269...
Mc Nelis 269...
Nellie 209
Nelligan **V2**
Nelligan **V4**
Nelligan 212
Nelligon 212
Nellson **V2**
Mc Nellus 269...
Mc Nelly **V3**
(mc) Nelly 206,209
Nelson **V2**
Nelson 208
Nelson 269...
Mc Nelus 269...
Mc Nemara **V3**
Mc Nemara 269...
Mc Nemarra **V3**
Mc Nemarra 269...
Mc Nemee 269...
O Nena 209
Mc Nenda **V3**
Mc Nenda 269...
Mc Neny 269...
O Neny 209
O' Neo 269...
Neper 269...
M' Nerlin 269...
Nerney 156
Nesbit 269...
Nesbitt 269...
Nesmith 269...
Nest 269...
Nestor **V3**
Nestor 269...
Mc Nestor **V3**
Netervill 269...
Netreuile 269...
Nettervill(e) 208
Nettle 269...
Nettles **V4**
Neuill **V4**
Neuill 269...
Neunhan **V5**
Neunhan 269...
Neuport 269...
Mc Neven 209
Neverel 269...
Nevill **V4**
Nevill 269...
Nevill(e) 209
Neville **V2**
Neville **V4**
Neville **V5**
Neville 269...
Nevin **V2**
Nevin 269...
(m') Nevin 207,209
New Haven **V2**
New York **V2**
New York **V4**
New York, **V2**
New Zealand **V2**
New Zealand **V3**

Newbolt 269...
Newborough 269...
Newburgh 269...
Newby 209
Newce **V4**
Newce 269...
Newcom(b) 209
Newcomb 269...
Newcome 209
Newcome 269...
Newcomen 269...
Newcoment 269...
Newel(l) 171,208
Newell **V4**
Newell **V5**
Newell 269...
Newenham **V4**
Newfoundlan **V4**
Newgent 269...
Newland 208
Newlin **V2**
Newlin **V3**
Newlin **V5**
Newman **V3**
Newman **V4**
Newman 209
Newman 269...
Newmarket **V3**
Newmen 209
Newport **V4**
Newspapers **V3**
Newspapers **V2**
Newton **V2**
Newton **V4**
Newton 209
Newtowne 269...
Neylan **V3**
Neylan 208,213
Neyland 213
Neylon 269...
O' Neylon **V3**
Neylon In **V3**
Neylon In **V3**
O' Niallain **V2**
Niblock 269...
Nichlas **V4**
Nichol 269...
Nicholas **V2**
Nicholas **V3**
Nicholas **V4**
Nicholas 269...
Mc Nicholas 210
Mc Nicholas 269...
Nicholl 212
Nicholl 269...
Nicholls 269...
Nicholls, M, **V2**
Nichols **V2**
Nichols **V3**
Nichols **V4**
Nichols 269...
(mc) Nichols 210
Nicholson **V4**
Nicholson 210,212
Nicholson 269...
Nicholson 269...
Nickle 269...
Mc Nickle 269...
Nickolds 269...
Nickolls 269...
Nicol 269...
Nicoll 212
Nicolsen 210
Nicolson 269...
Mc Niece 269...
Niel 208
Nielson 208
Mc Niff 269...
Mc Night 269...
Nightengale **V3**
Nightingale 269...
Nightingall **V3**
Nightingall 269...
Nighton 269...
Nihan(e) 211
Nihane **V4**
Nihell **V2**
O' Nihell **V3**
Nihill **V2**
Nihill **V3**
Nihill 208
Nihill 269...
O' Nihill **V3**
O' Nihill 269...
Nihilly **V2**
O' Nihilly, Rory **V2**
Nilan **V3**
Nilan 269...
Nilan(d) 208,213
Mc Ninch 269...
Mac Niocoil **V2**
Nisbit 269...
Nisbitt 269...
Nix **V5**
Nix 269...
Nixon **V2**
Nixon 211
Nixon 269...
Nixson 269...
Nobel 210
Noble **V2**
Noble **V5**
Noble 210
Noble 269...
Nocher 269...
Nochtin 207
Nocker 269...
Nocter 269...
Nocton 269...
Nogent 211
Mc Noger 269...
Noghar 269...
Nogher 269...
Mc Nogher 269...
(de) Nogla **V2**
Noher 269...
Mc Nohor 269...
Nolan **V2**
Nolan **V3**
Nolan 269...
O Nolan **V4**
O Nolan 210
Nolan Of **V2**
Noland 269...
Nollane 269...
Nolte 210
Nolty 210
O' Nonane **V5**
O' Nonane 269...
Noonan **V2**
Noonan **V3**
Noonan **V4**
Noonan **V5**
Noonan 212
Noonan 269...
O Noonan **V4**
Noone 212
Noone 269...
Norcott **V4**
(mac Norgan 209
Norman **V3**
Norman **V2**
Norman Map Iv
Norman **V3**
Normans **V4**
Normile **V3**
Normile **V5**
Normile 211
Normile 269...
Normoyle **V3**
Normoyle 211
Norreys **V2**
Norrice 211
Norrice 269...
Norris **V2**
Norris **V4**
Norris 211
Norris 269...
Norris 269...
Norrit 269...
Le Norrys 211
Norse 269...
Norten **V3**
North 269...
North 269...
Northcott **V2**
Northridge **V4**
Northridge 269...
Northridge 269...
Norton **V2**
Norton **V3**
Norton **V4**
Norton 207
Norton 269...
Norton 269...
Norval **V2**
Norwick 269...
Noss 269...
Notley 269...
Nott **V2**
Nott 171
Noughane **V2**
Noughton **V2**
Noughton 269...
Nourse 211
Noury 269...
Novis **V4**
Novis 269...
Nowlan 269...
O Nowlan 210
Nowland 269...
Nowlane 269...
Nownane **V4**
Nowry 211
O' Nuallain **V2**
O Nuanain **V4**
Nuane 212
Nugent **V2**
Nugent **V3**
Nugent **V4**
Nugent **V5**
Nugent 269...
Nugent 269...
(de) Nugent 211
Nughent 211
Nulty 269...
(mc) Nulty 207,210
Mc Nulty 269...
Numan **V4**
Nunan 269...
O Nunan **V4**
O' Nunan **V5**
(o) Nunan 212
O Nunan **V4**
Nunane 269...
Nunun 269...
Nurse **V2**
Nurse 211
Nurse 269...
Mc Nuske 269...
Nutterville 208
Nye **V2**
Nyhan 211
Nylan **V3**
Nyland 213
Nyland, **V3**
Nyle **V2**
(de) (o)broy 33
(mc) (o)conway 52
O'callaghan **V3**
Oakeley **V4**
Oakeley **V4**
Oakeley 269...
Oakley **V4**
Oakley **V4**
Oakley 269...
Oaks **V2**
Oats 269...
Oatts **V2**
Ob 269...
Odell **V4**
Odle 77
Odlum 213
Odway 269...
Mc Oeven **V4**
Offerba **V2**
Offington 150
Offling 269...
Ogam **V2**
Ogan 148
Ogan 269...
Oge **V3**
Oge 269...
Ogg **V2**
Ogilby 213
Ogilvie 269...
Ogle 269...
Oil Mills **V3**
Oiler 175
Oins 269...
L' Oiseau 155
Mac Oisin **V2**
Mac Oistin 70
Mac Oitir **V2**
Oitter **V4**
Oldfield 269...
Oldwood 5
Olier 155
Oliver **V2**
Oliver **V4**
Oliver **V5**
Oliver 212
Oliver 269...
Oliver, Maj. **V2**
Oliver, R. S. **V2**
Olliffe **V4**
Olliffe 269...
Olligan 269...
Oloynsig **V2**
Onaght **V2**
Oogan 269...
Orange Party **V2**
Organ 269...
Origins Of **V4**
Orkney, Earl **V2**
D' Orleans 155
Orm'thwaite **V2**
Orme 213
Ormesby 269...
Ormond **V4**
Ormond 269...
Ormonde 269...
Ormsbey 269...
Ormsby **V2**
Ormsby **V5**
Ormsby 213
Ormsby 269...
Ormsby, A., **V2**
Orpen **V2**
Orpen 212
Orpen, R. H. **V2**
Orpen, Sir **V2**
Orphye 269...
Orpin 269...
Orr **V4**
Orr 213
Orr 269...
Orrsley 269...
Orson 269...
Ortelius Map **V2**
Ortelius Map **V3**
Ortelius Map **V4**
Osbaldes 269...
Osbaldiston **V2**
Osberne 269...
Osborne 269...
Osbourn 269...
Osbourne 269...
Osburn 269...
Osburne 269...
M' Oscar 269...
Mac Oscar 70
D' Ossone 75
Mac Osticin **V2**
Ostmen **V4**
Oswald 269...
Otnonia **V2**
Otway, C. **V2**
Ougan 269...
Ougle 269...
Oulahan 269...
Ouldis **V4**
Ouldis **V4**
Ouldis 269...
Oulihan 150
Ounihan 269...
Ous(e)ley 213
Ousley 269...
Outlaw(e) 174,177
Ouzzell **V5**
Ouzzell 269...
Ovens **V2**
Ovington 150
Ovington 269...
Ovinton 269...
Owen **V5**
Owen 269...
Mc Owen **V2**
Mc Owen **V3**
Mc Owen **V4**
Mc Owen **V5**
Mc Owen 269...
Mc Owen Bwy **V4**
Mc Owen Bwy 269.
Owen Oge **V4**
Owen Oge 269...
Owen(s) **V5**
(mc) Owen(s) 213
Owens **V2**
Owens **V3**
Owens **V4**

V2 = Families of Co. Kerry **V3** = Families of Co. Clare **V4** = Families of Co. Cork **V5** = Families of Co. Limerick

Surname Index

Owens 163
Owens 269...
Owenson 213
Owgan **V4**
Owgan 269...
Owlsly, 213
Ownyan 269...
Owtton 269...
Oxbridge 269...
Oxbrugh 269...
Oylear 175
Oyler 155
Ozenbrooke 269...
Ozzard **V2**
Packeham 269...
Packenham 214
Packenham 269...
Padden 269...
Mac Padden 9
Mc Paden 269...
Padgett 269...
Mc Padin 269...
Padle 269...
Padmore 269...
Page **V2**
Page **V4**
Page 269...
Pagenham 269...
Paget **V5**
Paget(t) 214
Pagett 269...
Pagit 214
Pagnam 269...
Pails **V2**
Pain 155
Paine **V2**
Paine **V5**
Paine 155
Painter **V4**
Painter 269...
Paisley 269...
Pakenham 214
Paker 269...
Palatine **V2**
Palfery 269...
Palfrey 269...
Pallis 269...
Palliser **V3**
Palliser 214
Palmer **V2**
Palmer **V5**
Palmer 214
Palmer 269...
Palmer Arms **V2**
Palmer, **V2**
Palmer Of **V2**
Palmes 269...
Palms 269...
Paluis **V5**
Paluis 269...
Panorma **V2**
Panskore **V3**
Papists List **V2**
Papping **V3**
Papping 269...
Papworth 269...
Paradine **V2**
Paragon 269...
Pardon 269...
Parefoy 269...
Pariell 269...
Parill 269...
Paris **V4**
Paris **V5**
Paris, France **V2**
Parish **V5**
Park **V2**
Park 269...
Park(s) 215
Parker **V2**
Parker **V3**
Parker **V4**
Parker **V5**
Parker 215
Parker 269...
Parkes **V2**
Parkhill 269...
Parkins 269...
Parkinson **V2**
Parkinson **V5**
Parkinson 269...
Parks 269...
Parl(e) 214
Parlan 214
Mc Parlan 269...
Mc Parland 269...
Parle 269...
Parlon 269...
Parlone 269...
Parnall 269...
Parnell **V4**
Parnell **V5**
Parnell 214
Parr **V2**
Parr **V4**
Parr 269...
Parrell 214
Parrican 269...
Parris 269...
Parrott 269...
Parry **V3**
Mac Parson 214
Parsons **V2**
Parsons **V3**
Parsons **V4**
Parsons 269...
Parsons 34,214
Mc Partlan 269...
(mc) Partlan(d) 105,
M' Partland 269...
Partlin 214
Mc Partlin 269...
Partridge **V2**
Partridge 269...
Passengers **V3**
Patchet 269...
Patchy 269...
Patersen **V3**
Paterson 215
Paterson 269...
Patience 269...
Patison 269...
Paton 269...
Patrican 105
Patrican 269...
Patrick **V3**
Patrick 105
Patrick 167
Patrick 269...
Mac Patrick 215
Patrickeson 269...
Patt **V2**
O' Pattan 269...
Patten 214,217
Patten 269...
Pattersen 215
Patterson **V2**
Patterson **V3**
Patterson 215,216
Patterson 269...
Pattin 214
Pattison **V2**
Patton 214
Patton 269...
Patty 269...
Patwell **V2**
Paul 155
Paul 269...
Paul, Sir R. **V2**
Paule 269...
Paulin **V2**
Paull 155
Pausy **V5**
Pausy 269...
Pawlett 214
Payn 269...
Payne **V2**
Payne **V5**
Payne 155
Payne 269...
Payne Paine **V2**
Payton 217
Payton 269...
Peables 215
Peachen 269...
Peacock **V2**
Peacock 269...
Peacocke **V2**
Peacocke **V4**
Peacocke **V5**
Peacocke 215
Peacocke 269...
Peacoke 269...
Peak 269...
(mac Peak(e) 215
Peake 269...
Mc Peake 269...
Pearce **V3**
Pearce **V4**
Pearce **V5**
Pearce 216
Pearce Piers **V4**
Pearcell **V4**
Pearcell **V4**
Pearcell 269...
Peard **V4**
Peard 269...
Pearl 214
Pearle 269...
Pearsane 269...
Pearse 216
Pearson **V2**
Pearson 269...
Peartree 269...
Pease **V3**
Pease Of **V3**
Peaslie 269...
Peasly 269...
Pebbles 215
Peck **V4**
Peck 269...
Pecke 269...
Pedestrian **V2**
Peebles 215
Peel 269...
Peepes 269...
Peercy **V4**
Peercy 269...
Peers **V3**
Peerse **V4**
Peet **V2**
Peet **V5**
Peet, Francis **V2**
Peevers **V2**
Peg 269...
Pegnim 269...
Pegum **V2**
Peile 215
Peirce **V3**
Peirce 216
Peirce 269...
Peirson 269...
Pelan 269...
Le Pele 215
Pelham **V2**
Pelican **V2**
(de) Pelle 215
Pelletier 155
Pellican **V2**
Pelly **V3**
Pelly 215
Pelter 155
Pembroke **V2**
Pen'efeather 216
Pen'yfeather 216
Penal Laws **V2**
Pender **V3**
Pender 220
Pender 269...
Pendergas **V4**
Pendergas(t) 220
Pendergass **V4**
Pendergast **V2**
Pendergast **V3**
Pendergast **V4**
Pendergast **V5**
Pendergras 269...
Pendergrass **V3**
Pendergrass **V4**
Pendergrass **V5**
Pendergrass 269...
Penders 269...
Pendeville **V2**
Pendred **V2**
Pendy 220
Pendy 269...
Penefaither 269...
Penford **V4**
Penford 269...
Penn **V4**
Pennefather **V4**
Pennefather 216
Pennefeather **V4**
Pennfather 269...
Pennifeather 269...
Pennigton **V4**
Pennigton 269...
Pennington 269...
Penny 216
Penny 269...
Pennyfather 216
Pennyfether 269...
Penoyx 269...
Penrose **V4**
Penrose **V4**
Penteny 269...
Pentland 269...
Pentony 269...
Peoples 269...
Peoples 77,215
Peorais 109
Pepard 269...
Peppard **V2**
Peppard **V3**
Peppard **V5**
Peppard 216
Peppard 269...
Peppards At **V2**
Pepper 216
Pepper 269...
Pepperd 269...
Pepys **V2**
Pepys 269...
Pepys Lands **V2**
Perce 269...
Perceval 216
Perchy 269...
Percival **V4**
Percivale **V4**
Percivale 269...
Percivall **V4**
Percivall 269...
Percy **V4**
Percy 269...
Perdu **V4**
Periman **V2**
Perkens 216
Perkins **V5**
Perkins 216
Perott **V4**
Perrier **V4**
Perrill 214
Perriman 269...
Perrot 269...
Perrott **V4**
Perrott 269...
Perry **V2**
Perry **V5**
Perry 269...
Perryman **V2**
Pers 216
Perse **V3**
Person 269...
Persons 269...
Persse **V4**
Persse **V5**
Persse Perse **V3**
Pert 269...
Pery **V2**
Pery Perry **V3**
Pet(t)it 216
Petditd 269...
Peter 269...
Peters 216
Peters 269...
Peterson **V5**
Peterson 216
Petford **V5**
Petford 269...
Petherick 269...
Petit 155
Petit 269...
Petsworth 269...
Pettane 217
Petticrew 269...
Pettigrew 269...
Pettitt 155
Pettitt 269...
Petty **V2**
Petty **V3**
Petty, Sir W. **V2**
Peyton 217
Peyton 269...
Mc Phail 269...
Phaire **V2**
Phalen 265
Phalon **V4**
Pharlon 214
Mc Phatricks 269...
Phealan 269...
Pheasant **V3**

Phelan **V2**
Phelan **V3**
Phelan 265
Phelan 269...
Pheland 269...
Phelane 269...
Phelips **V2**
Phellane 265
Phellane 269...
Phelps **V3**
Phepoes 216
Pherman 269...
Mac Pherson 214
Phetiplas **V5**
Mc Phetrish 269...
Phibbs 216
Phibbs 269...
Philan 269...
Philbin 269...
Mac Philbin 216
Philip **V2**
Philipin 269...
Philippot 155
Philips **V2**
Philips **V5**
Philips 217
Phillip **V4**
Mc Phillip **V4**
Mc Phillip **V5**
Mc Phillip 269...
(m') Phillip/s 216
(m') Phillip/s 217
Phillipin 269...
Mc Phillipp **V4**
Mc Phillipp 269...
Phillipps 269...
Phillips **V2**
Phillips **V4**
Phillips 269...
Mc Phillips **V4**
Mc Phillips 269...
Phillpot 269...
Phillps 269...
Philomy 269...
Philpot 155
Philpot 269...
Philpott **V4**
Philpott 269...
Mag Phinn 112
Phipps 216
Pholey **V3**
Picken 269...
Pickford **V2**
Picknall 269...
Picton 269...
Pidgeon 269...
Pierce **V2**
Pierce **V3**
Pierce **V4**
Pierce 269...
(de) Pierce **V2**
Mac Pierce **V2**
Mac Pierce 216
Piercefield 269...
Piercie **V5**
Piers **V2**
Piers **V3**
Piers **V4**
Piers 216
Piers 269...
Pierse **V2**
Pierse **V4**
Pierse 269...
Piersey, Miss **V2**
Pierson **V2**
Pierson 269...
Pig(g)ott 217
Pigett 269...
Piggot 269...
Piggott **V2**
Piggott **V4**
Piggott 269...
Pigot 155
Pigott **V2**
Pigott **V4**
Pigott 269...
Pigott 269...
Pigou 155
Pike **V4**
Pike 218
Pike 269...
Pilcher **V2**
Pilkington **V3**
Pilkington 269...
Pillar Stone **V4**
Pillar Stones- **V4**
Pillsworth 269...
Pin 269...
Pinchin **V2**
Pindars 269...
Pinder 269...
Pinders 269...
Pindy 269...
Pine **V3**
Pine **V4**
Pine 218
Pine 269...
Pinkerton 269...
Pinkey 269...
Pinkle 269...
Pinky 269...
Pinsen 269...
Pinsent 269...
Pinson 269...
(de) Pionbroc **V2**
Piper 205
Piper 269...
Pippin 269...
Pirie 269...
Pirrie 269...
Pitch **V3**
Pitt 269...
Pitts 269...
Placenames **V3**
Plaince **V4**
Planche 155
Plank 155
Platt 269...
Playford 269...
Plellps **V5**
Plellps 269...
Plover **V4**
Plover 269...
Plowman **V2**
Pluinceid **V2**
Plukenet 269...
Plum(m)er 219
Plumer **V4**
Plumer 269...
Plummer **V2**
Plummer **V4**
Plummer **V5**
Pluncket 269...
Plunket(t) 218
Plunkett **V2**
Plunkett **V4**
Plunkett 269...
Plunkitt 218
Poag 269...
Poakrich 269...
Pocher 269...
Pockeridg 269...
Pockerish 269...
Pockrich 269...
Poekrich 269...
Poer 269...
(de) Poer **V2**
Poff **V2**
Pogue 269...
De Poher 219
Points **V4**
Points 269...
Pointz 269...
Poke 269...
(mc) Polan(d) 217
Poland 269...
Polard **V2**
Pole 269...
Polewheele 269...
Polexfield 269...
Polin 269...
M' Polin 269...
(mc) Polin 217
Mc Polin 269...
Polk 269...
Pollard **V2**
Pollard 269...
Pollock 216
Pollock 269...
Ponce 217
Ponntney 269...
Ponsonby **V2**
Ponsonby **V4**
Pontin 269...
Pontoney 269...
Pony 269...
Ponz 217
Pooer 269...
Pool 269...
Poole **V3**
Poole **V4**
Poole 269...
Pooler 218
Pooley 269...
Pooly 269...
Poope 269...
Poor 269...
Poor Law **V3**
Poor(s) 219
Poordom 269...
Poore 269...
Poots 269...
Pope **V5**
Pope 269...
Pope, W. **V2**
Population **V3**
Population **V4**
Porsonby 269...
Port **V2**
Porter 269...
(le) Porter 219
Portis 269...
(de) Portuil **V2**
Potar **V2**
(le) Poter 217
Pott 269...
Potter **V2**
Potter 217
Potter 269...
Pottinger **V2**
Poudyhard 269...
Pouey 269...
Poulden **V4**
Poulden **V4**
Poulden 269...
Pountney 269...
Pourdon 269...
Povey 269...
Powel 269...
Powell **V2**
Powell **V4**
Powell **V5**
Powell 121,217
Powell 269...
Powell 34
Power **V2**
Power **V3**
Power **V4**
Power 269...
Power, H. **V2**
Power(s) 219
Powers **V5**
Powerscourt **V3**
Powre 219
Powre 269...
Prater **V4**
Prater 269...
Pratt **V4**
Pratt 219
Pratt 269...
Pray 215
Preist **V4**
Preist 269...
Prench 269...
Prender 269...
Prendergass **V3**
Prendergass 269...
Prendergast **V2**
Prendergast **V3**
Prendergast **V4**
Prendergast **V5**
Prendergast 220
Prendergast 269...
Prendeville **V2**
(de) Prendeville **V2**
Prendible 269...
Prendy 269...
Prentice 269...
Prescott 269...
Pressick 269...
Pressly 269...
Preste **V2**
Preston **V3**
Preston 269...
(de) Preston 220
Prestwich **V3**
Prestwitch **V3**
Prestwitch 269...
Pretyman 155
Prey 269...
(o) Prey 215
Priall 269...
Price **V2**
Price **V4**
Price **V5**
Price 220
Price 269...
Price, Dr. **V2**
Prichard 269...
Priddin **V4**
Priddin 269...
Prigge **V4**
Prigge 269...
Prigget 269...
Prim 129
Prince **V2**
Princely 217
Prindeville **V4**
Prindeville **V5**
Prinn 269...
De Priondargas **V2**
Prionnbiol **V2**
Prior 269...
(mac Prior 220
Pris **V2**
Prise **V2**
Pritchard 269...
Pritchet 269...
Pritty 269...
Procter **V2**
Proctor **V2**
Proctor 269...
Proinseis **V2**
Pronte 217
Pronty 217
Prosser **V2**
Prossor **V2**
Protestant **V2**
Protheroe 269...
Proud 269...
Prout 269...
De Proux 155
Providence Gazette **V4**
Province Ii
Prunty 217
Prunty 269...
Pryme 129
Ptolemy **V3**
Ptolemy **V4**
Public **V2**
Pucksly 220
Pue 269...
Punch **V4**
Punch **V5**
Punch 217
Punch 269...
Purcell **V2**
Purcell **V3**
Purcell **V4**
Purcell 221
Purcell 269...
Purcell, **V2**
Purcell **V3**
Purcells **V3**
Purcill 221
Purcy **V4**
Purdon **V2**
Purdon **V3**
Purdon **V4**
Purdon **V5**
Purdon 221
Purdon Arms **V3**
Purdon, **V2**
Purdy **V5**
Purdy 269...
Purefay 269...
Purefoy 221
Purefoy, **V3**
Purfoy 269...
Purland **V4**
Pursell **V2**
Pursell **V4**
Pursell 217,221
Purshell 217,221
Purshell 269...
Purtel 217
Purtell **V3**
Purthill 217
Purtill **V2**
Purtill **V3**
Purtill **V5**

Purtill 217,221
Purtill 269...
Purtle **V3**
Purtle 217
Purtle 269...
Purvis 269...
Puxl(e)y 220
Puxley **V4**
Pyke 218
Pylle 269...
Pyn Pine **V4**
Pyne **V3**
Pyne **V4**
Pyne **V4**
Pyne 218
Pyne 269...
Quade 269...
Mac Quade **V2**
(mc) Quade 218,261
Mc Quade 269...
Mc Quaid 269...
Mc Quaid(e) 218
Mac Quaide **V2**
Mc Quaide **V5**
Quail 221
Quail 269...
O Quain **V4**
Quaine **V4**
Quaine 221
Qualey **V3**
Qualter 218,262
Qualter 269...
Qualy **V3**
(mac Quan 221
Mc Quan 269...
Quane **V2**
Quane **V4**
Quane **V4**
(o) Quane 221
Mac Quay 264
Mc Quay 269...
Quayle 221
(mac Queale 221
Quealey **V3**
Queally 162
O' Quealy **V3**
Quealy, **V3**
Quee 269...
Queen 223
Queen 269...
Queen Anne **V2**
Queen Eliz. **V2**
Queenan 269...
Queenstown **V4**
Quelch 269...
Quelly **V3**
Quelly 269...
O' Quelly **V3**
O' Quelly 269...
Quelsh 269...
Quen 223
Quenan 269...
Quenedy **V3**
Quenedy 162
Quenn 269...
Quesnay 49
Mac Question 70
Mac Quey 264
Quick 269...
O Quicke **V4**
Quiddihy 269...
Quiddihy 70
Quiddily 269...
O' Quig 269...
Quigg 269...
Quiggly 269...
Quigley 269...
O Quigley 222
O' Quigley 269...
Quilan 222
Quiligan 269...
Mc Quilkan 269...
Quilkin 221
Mc Quilkin 269...
Quill **V2**
Quill **V4**
Quill 269...
O' Quill **V2**
O Quill **V4**
(o) Quill 222,266
(o) Quill 67,221
Quill, Eliz. **V2**
Quillan 152,221
Quillan 269...
M' Quillan 222
M' Quillan 268
Mc Quillan 269...
Quillane 48
Quillen 269...
M' Quillen 269...
Quillenane 269...
Mc Quilliams 269..
Mac Quillians 222
Quilligan **V3**
Quilligan **V4**
Quilligan **V5**
Quilligan 269...
Quilligan 70,219
Quillinan **V2**
Quillinan 269...
Quilly 266
M' Quilly 67
Quilter **V2**
Quilty **V5**
Quilty 269...
(mac Quilty 218
O Quilty **V4**
O Quilty 218
Quime 269...
Quin **V2**
Quin **V4**
Quin 221
Quin 269...
O' Quin **V3**
O' Quin 269...
Quin Abbey **V3**
(o) Quin(n) 223
Quinan 72
Quinane 269...
Quine **V3**
Quine 269...
O' Quine **V3**
O' Quine 269...
Quing 269...
Quinlan **V2**
Quinlan **V4**
Quinlan 269...
O' Quinlan **V2**
O' Quinlan **V5**
O Quinlan 222
Quinlevan 222
Quinlevin 221
Quinlin 269...
Quinlish 221
Quinlisk 221
Quinlivan **V3**
Quinlivan **V5**
Quinlivan 221
Quinlivan 269...
Quinliven **V2**
Quinn **V2**
Quinn **V3**
Quinn **V4**
Quinn 269...
Mac Quinn **V2**
Mc Quinn **V2**
Mc Quinn 269...
O' Quinn **V5**
Quinn In **V3**
Quinne 223
Quinne 269...
O' Quinne 269...
Quinnell **V2**
Quinnelly 166
Quinty **V2**
Mac Quirc **V4**
Mc Quircke **V4**
Quirk **V2**
Quirk **V4**
Quirk 269...
(m') Quirk(e) 132
(m') Quirk(e) 169
(m') Quirk(e) 221
Quirke **V2**
Quirke 269...
O' Quirke 269...
Mc Quiston 269...
Quit Rent **V2**
Mac Quoad 218
Mc Quod 269...
Quoid 269...
Mc Quoid 269...
Quynall **V4**
Quynall 269...
Quynn 269...
O' Raaverty 269...
Rabbit 269...
Rabbitt **V3**
Rabbitt 72
Racard(s) 223
Racards 269...
Rackard 223
Ractigan 224
Ractigan 269...
Radford 269...
Radman 224
Radwill 269...
Rae **V2**
Mac Rae **V2**
Rae, Edw. **V2**
Rael **V2**
Rafferty 269...
O Rafferty 223
Rafter 223,224
Rafter 269...
Raftery 269...
O' Raftery 223,224
Raftiss 269...
Ragan 225
Ragett 269...
Raggett 269...
Raggott 269...
O Ragher 223
Raghter 269...
O Raghter 224
Mac Ragnaill **V2**
Rahilly **V2**
Rahilly **V4**
Rahilly 269...
O' Rahilly **V2**
O' Rahilly Dies **V2**
O' Rahilly Of **V2**
O' Raigue **V2**
Railway, G. **V2**
Rainalds 269...
Raine 223
Raine 269...
Rainey 223
Rainey 269...
Rainllow 269...
Mac Rait **V2**
Mac Raith **V2**
Ralagh 223
Ralagh 269...
Raleigh **V2**
Raleigh **V4**
Raleigh **V5**
Raleigh 223
Raleigh 269...
Raleston 34
Rall 269...
De Ralleye 223
Rally 223
Rally 269...
Ralph 269...
Ram **V3**
Ram 224
Ramage **V2**
Ramsay 228
Ramsay 269...
Ramsbottom 269...
Ramsey **V3**
Ramsey 269...
Ramsey(e) 228
Ramsy 228
Ranaghan 269...
M' Ranald 269...
Randal **V2**
Randall **V2**
Randall **V4**
Randalson 269...
Randell **V4**
Randell 269...
Randle **V2**
Randles **V2**
Randolph **V5**
Raney 223
Ranken 228
Rankin **V4**
Rankin **V4**
Rankin 228
Rankin 269...
Mc Rann 269...
M' Rannal 269...
Mac Rannall 233
Mc Rannall 224
Rannelagh 269...
Mc Rannell 224
Ransom 269...
Rape 225
Rashford 269...
Rashleigh **V4**
Rashleigh 269...
Rath 269...
Rathborne 224
Ratheram **V5**
Ratheram 269...
Rathfoclane **V3**
Rathlahine **V3**
Rathwell 269...
Ratican 224
Ratigan 224
Ratigan 269...
Ratoo Castle **V2**
Ratsfore 269...
Rattigan 269...
Rattray **V2**
Ratty 269...
Rauth 269...
Raverty 269...
Ravy 269...
Raw 232
Rawden 269...
Rawdon 269...
O' Rawe 269...
Rawkines 269...
Rawleigh **V2**
Rawley **V5**
Rawley 223
Rawley 269...
Rawlings **V5**
Rawlingson 269...
Rawlins **V2**
Rawlins 269...
Rawlinson 269...
Rawson **V3**
Rawson 269...
Ray, **V2**
Ray 269...
Mac Ray **V2**
Raycroft **V2**
Raygan 225
Raymond **V2**
Raymond **V4**
Raymond **V5**
Raymond 129
Raymond 269...
Raymond, **V2**
Raynalds 269...
Rayne **V5**
Rayne 269...
O' Raynn **V5**
O' Raynn 269...
Raynor 269...
Rea **V4**
Rea **V5**
Rea 232
Rea 269...
O' Rea 269...
Rea Reagh **V4**
Read **V2**
Read **V4**
Read, Reid, **V3**
Reade **V3**
Reade 232
Reade 269...
Readeinge 269...
Reader 269...
Readie **V3**
Reading **V2**
Ready **V2**
Ready **V3**
Ready 225
Ready 269...
Reagan **V2**
Reagan **V3**
Reagan **V4**
Reagan 225
Reagane **V4**
Reagane 269...
O Reagane **V4**
O' Reagane 269...
Reagh **V4**
Reagh 232
Reagh 269...
Real 224
(o) Really 224,225
O' Really 269...
Realy 269...
O Realy **V4**
O Realy 224

O' Realy 269...
Reamon 269...
Reams 269...
Rean 269...
Reaney 223
Reaney 269...
Reany **V2**
Reap 225
Reapy 225
Reardon **V2**
Reardon **V3**
Reardon **V4**
Reardon 227
Reardon 269...
Reave **V3**
Reaves **V2**
Reaves **V3**
Reavy 232
Records On **V2**
Recroft 269...
Recubie 269...
Reddan **V3**
Reddan 269...
O' Reddan **V3**
O Reddan 225
Reddane **V3**
Reddin **V2**
Reddin 225
Reddin 269...
Reddington 225
Reddington 269...
Reddy **V3**
Reddy 225,229
Reddy 269...
Redfern 269...
Redin **V2**
Redington 269...
Redman 269...
Redmon **V2**
Redmon(d) 224
Redmond **V2**
Redmond 269...
Mc Redmond 269...
Redmont 224
Redmun 224
Redpath 269...
Redworth 269...
Reed **V2**
Reed **V3**
Reed(e) 232
Reede 269...
Reedy **V3**
Reedy 229
Mc Reedy **V4**
Mc Reedy **V5**
Reegan **V3**
Reegan 225
Reel 224
Reel 269...
Reemes 269...
Reen **V2**
Reen **V4**
Reen 226
Reen 269...
Reenes 269...
(ap) Rees' **V2**
Reese **V4**
Reeues 269...
Reeve **V3**
Reeves, **V2**
Reeves **V3**
Reeves 225
Reeves Arms **V3**
Regan, **V2**
Regan **V3**
Regan **V4**
Regan 269...
Mac Regan **V3**
O' Regan **V3**
O Regan **V4**
O' Regan **V5**
O Regan 225
O' Regan 269...
Regane **V4**
Regane 269...
O Regane **V4**
O' Regane 269...
Mac Regnie 229
Mac Rehan **V2**
Reid **V2**
Reid **V3**
Reid 232
Reid 269...
Reid(e)y 229
Reidy **V2**
Reidy **V3**
Reidy **V4**
Reidy 269...
Reidy In **V3**
O Reigan **V4**
O' Reigan 269...
Reigh 269...
Reigne **V5**
Reigne 269...
Reiligh 269...
Reilly, **V2**
Reilly **V4**
Reilly 269...
O' Reilly **V2**
O Reilly **V4**
O Reilly 225
O' Reilly 269...
O' Reilly's **V2**
Reily 225
Reily 269...
Reiues 269...
Rekle 269...
O' Reley 269...
Relf **V2**
Relick 269...
Relihan **V2**
Relihan **V4**
Relihan 269...
O Relly 225
O' Relly 269...
Rely 269...
O' Rely 269...
Relye 269...
Remnant **V4**
Remnant 269...
Remyngton 34
Renaghan **V4**
Renaghan 226
Renal 269...
Renalls 155
Renan 269...
Render 269...
Renders **V3**
Reneghan 226
Renehan **V4**
Renehan 226
Renehan 269...
Renighan 226
Rennie 269...
Renolds 269...
Renolls 269...
Renshaw 269...
Reoghe **V4**
Reordon 227
Reppet 269...
Reqaettus **V4**
O' Rergane **V5**
O' Rergane 269...
Research **V2**
Restrick **V2**
Reve **V3**
Reveil 155
Revell 226
Revell 269...
Reven 269...
Revill 155
Revill(e) 226
Reville 269...
Revington **V2**
Mac Revy 226
Rex **V4**
Reyeane **V4**
Reyley 225
Reylie 269...
Reyly 269...
Reynell 226
Reyner 269...
Reyney 269...
M' Reynold 269...
Reynolds, **V2**
Reynolds **V3**
Reynolds 155
Reynolds 233
Reynolds 269...
Mc Reynolds 269...
Reynoldson 269...
Rezin **V2**
Rhattican 224
Rhineheart 205
Rhoades 269...
Rhodes **V4**
Rhys **V2**
Rhys **V3**
Rhys **V4**
Rhys 220,233
Mac Riabaig **V2**
O' Riabaig **V2**
O Riady **V4**
O' Riady **V5**
O' Riagan **V2**
Rial **V4**
Riall 226
Rian **V3**
Ricard **V4**
Rice **V2**
Rice **V3**
Rice **V4**
Rice **V5**
Rice 220,233
Rice 269...
Rice, Edw. **V2**
Rice Family **V2**
Rice, Justice **V2**
Rice Of Paris **V2**
Rice, Steph. **V2**
Rich **V4**
Rich 269...
Richard **V5**
Richard 269...
Richard 269...
Mac Richard 223
Mc Richard **V2**
Mc Richard **V4**
Mc Richard **V5**
Mc Richard 269...
Richards **V2**
Richards **V3**
Richards 223
Richards 269...
Richardsen 226
Richardson **V2**
Richardson **V4**
Richardson 226
Richardson 269...
Richesies 269...
Richey 269...
Richmond 269...
Richt 269...
Mac Rickard 223
Ridd 269...
Riddaghan 269...
Riddell 229
Riddell 269...
Riddinge 269...
Riddle **V5**
Riddles 229
Rideene **V3**
O Rideene **V3**
O' Rideene 269...
Rideout 269...
Rider **V3**
Rider 269...
Ridg(e)way 223
Ridgby 269...
Ridge 229
Ridge 269...
Ridgeley 229
Ridgeley 269...
Ridgewale 34
Ridgeway 229
Ridgeway 34
Ridson **V3**
Riedy **V3**
Riedy 229
O Riedy **V2**
O' Riedy **V5**
O' Riedy 269...
Rielly **V4**
Rielly 269...
O' Rielly **V2**
Rienard **V4**
Rienard 269...
Rierdan **V3**
Rierdan 227
Rierdan 269...
O' Rierdan **V5**
O' Rierdan 269...
Rierdane **V2**
Rierdane **V4**
Rierdane 269...
O Rierdane **V4**
O' Rierdane 269...
Rierdon 227
Riergane **V4**
Riergane 269...
Rieve 269...
Rieves 269...
Rigdeway 269...
Rigg 269...
Riggs **V4**
Right 267
Rign(e)y 229
Rigney 269...
Rigny 269...
Riley **V2**
Riley **V4**
Riley 225
Riley 269...
O Riley **V4**
Riney **V2**
Ring **V2**
Ring **V4**
Ring 226,232
Ring 269...
Ringland 269...
Ringrose **V3**
Ringrose 226
Rinn **V2**
O' Rinn **V2**
(o) Rinn 226,232
Rinuccini **V2**
Riordan **V2**
Riordan **V3**
Riordan **V4**
Riordan 269...
O' Riordan **V2**
O Riordan **V4**
O Riordan 227
O' Riordan 269...
O Riordan **V4**
O' Riordan, **V5**
O Riordane **V4**
O' Riordane 269...
Rippet 269...
Rippit 269...
Rise 269...
Ritchie 269...
Ritkaby 269...
River Maine **V2**
Rly., G.s.w. **V2**
Roach **V3**
Roach **V4**
Roach 228
Roache **V4**
Roaches **V3**
Roachford **V2**
Roachford **V3**
Roachforde 228
Roades 269...
Roan, Roane **V3**
Roane 269...
Roark(e) 230
Roarke 269...
Roarty 223
Roarty 269...
M' Roary 68
Mc Roary 269...
Roayne 269...
Robb 269...
Robbins **V4**
Robenson 228
Robert **V3**
Robert 269...
Mac Robert **V2**
Mc Robert 269...
Robert(s) 227
Roberts **V2**
Roberts **V4**
Roberts **V5**
Roberts 269...
Mac Roberts 269...
Mc Roberts 269...
Robertson 227
Robertson 269...
Robins 269...
Robinsen 228
Robinson **V2**
Robinson **V4**
Robinson 228
Robinson 269...
Robinsone 269...
Mc Robinston **V4**
Mc Robistan **V4**
Robiston **V4**
Robotham 269...
Robson 269...

V2 = Families of Co. Kerry **V3** = Families of Co. Clare **V4** = Families of Co. Cork **V5** = Families of Co. Limerick

Surname Index

Roch V2
Roch V3
Roch V4
Roch(e)228
Roch Roache V3
Roche, V2
Roche V3
Roche V4
Roche269...
Roche, V2
Roche, V4
Roche, V5
Roche, V2
Rocheford228
Roches V3
Roches V4
Rochett129
Rochford V3
Rochford V4
Rochford228
Rochford269...
Rochfort V3
Rochfort V4
Rochfort228
Rochfort, C. V2
Rochneen269...
Rochwell269...
Rock269...
Rod'nbucher205
Rodaghan269...
Rodan225
O Rodan V3
O' Rodan269...
Rodaughan269...
Rodd V2
Rodden269...
Roddy230
Roddy269...
Roden269...
Rodger68
Rodgers V2
Rodgers V4
Rodgers V5
Rodgers129,231
Rodgers269...
Rodk. Dan. V2
Rodman227
Rodman269...
Rodmont269...
Rody230
Roe V2
Roe V3
Roe V4
Roe V5
Roe229
Roe269...
Roe, Miss. V2
Rogan V4
Rogan269...
O' Rogan269...
(o) Rogan(e)229
Rogane V4
O Rogane V4
O' Rogane269...
Rogers V2
Rogers V3
Rogers V4
Rogers V5
Rogers129,231
Rogers269...
Rogers68
Rohan V2
Rohan269...
Roice233
Roice269...
Rokeby269...
Rokes, V2
Roland226
Rolandson226
Roledge269...
Roleston229
De Roley231
Rolleston229
Rolleston34
Rollins269...
Rolls269...
Rolston269...
Roma269...
Ronaghan269...
O' Ronaghan269...
Ronaine V4
Ronaldson269...
Ronan V2
Ronan V4
Ronan269...
O Ronan V4
Ronan(e)227
Ronan, V4
O' Ronan, Wm. V2
Ronane V4
Ronane269...
Ronayne V2
Ronayne V3
Ronayne V4
Ronayne227
Ronayne269...
O Ronayne V4
Roney233
Roney269...
Rook V2
Rooke V2
Rookes V2
Rooksby269...
Roome V2
Rooneen269...
Rooney V2
Rooney203
Rooney269...
O Rooney233
Roonoo269...
Roony203,233
Roonye269...
Rooth230
Rooth269...
Roper V2
Roper V4
Roper269...
Roragh269...
Rorey269...
Rorison269...
Mc Rorkan269...
Rorke230
Rorke269...
O' Rorke269...
O' Rorke, C. D. V2
Rorque230
Rorque269...
Rory269...
Mac Rory129
Mac Rory269...
Mc Rory V3
Mc Rory V4
Mc Rory V5
Mc Rory269...
O' Rory269...
Rosdell V3
Rosdell269...
Rose V2
Rose V5
Rose205,226
Rose269...
Rosebery269...
Rosebrough269...
Rosengrane269...
Rosevill269...
Rosey269...
Rositer228
Rosmond269...
Rosney V2
Ross V2
Ross V3
Ross V4
Ross230
Ross269...
Ross Castle V2
Ross Diocese V4
Rossboro269...
Rosse269...
Rossetor228
Rossetor269...
Rossington V4
Rossington V4
Rossington269...
Rossiter228,230
Rossiter269...
Rossitor228
Rossroe V3
Rosster228
Rosswell230
Roth269...
Roth(e)230
Rothe V4
Rothe V4
Rotheram269...
Rothes V3
Rothwell230
Rothwell269...
Rouane231
Rouane269...
Roughan V3
Roughan230
Roughan269...
O Roughan V3
Roughane V4
Roughane269...
O' Roughane V3
O Roughnane V3
O' Roughnane269..
Roughnayne V3
Roughneen227
Roughneen269...
Roulston269...
Roulstone229
Round Tower - V4
Round V2
Roundtree V3
Roundtree269...
Rouney269...
Rountree269...
Rourke V2
Rourke269...
Mc Rourke230
O' Rourke V2
O Rourke230
O' Rourke269...
O Rourke V4
O' Roverty269...
O' Roverty269...
Roviere V4
Row269...
Rowan V2
Rowan230
Rowan269...
O' Rowan V2
Rowe V2
Rowe V3
Rowe229
Rowe269...
Rowell V4
Rowell269...
Rowland V2
Rowland226
Rowland269...
Rowlendson226
Rowles269...
Rowley269...
(o) Rowley231
Rowls269...
Rowlston229
Rowlston269...
Rowly231
Rowly269...
Rowney269...
Rownyn269...
Rowth269...
Roxbery269...
Roxborough269...
Roy V5
Roy228
Roy269...
Royall V5
Royall269...
Royan231
Royan269...
Roycroft V4
Roycroft269...
Roydy V2
Roydy269...
Roynane V4
Roynane's V2
Royston269...
Ruachtain V2
Ruairc V2
Ruan269...
Ruan(e)231
Ruane269...
Ruare269...
Ruarke269...
Ruayne231
Rubey V4
Rubey269...
Rubin V2
Mac Rubs269...
Ruckee205
Rudan V3
Rudan269...
Rudane V3
Rudane269...
Rudd V2
Rudd269...
Ruddan225
Ruddane V3
O Ruddane V3
Ruddanes225
Ruddell V5
Ruddell269...
Rudden269...
Ruddery171
M' Ruddery269...
Mac Ruddery230
Ruddle V2
Ruddle V5
Ruddle269...
Ruddock V4
Ruddock269...
Ruddon269...
Ruddy230
Ruddy269...
Rudican269...
Rudy230
Ruineen269...
Ruish(e)227
M' Rum269...
Rumball269...
Rumney V2
Rumney V4
Rumney269...
Rumny V2
Rumny269...
Rumsby V2
Rumsey V3
Rumsey269...
Runey233
Runian269...
Mac Runnell224
Ruoe V4
Ruoe269...
Ruork269...
De Rupe228
Rurk269...
Rusel269...
Rusell231
Rusell269...
Rush269...
Rush(e)227
Rushford227
Rushford269...
Rusk V2
Russel(l)231
Russell V2
Russell V3
Russell V4
Russell V5
Russell269...
Russell34
Russels V3
Russia V2
Rust269...
Rut(t)ledge231
Ruth269...
Ruth(e)230
Rutherford269...
(de) Ruthyen V2
Rutledge V3
Rutledge269...
Rutlidg269...
Rutlidge269...
Rutter V4
Rutter269...
Ruttle V2
Ruttle269...
Ruxton226
Rvoes, K. V2
Ryal269...
Ryall V4
Ryan V2
Ryan V3
Ryan V4
Ryan269...
O' Ryan V3
O Ryan V4
O Ryan231
O' Ryan269...
Ryan Births V3
Ryan, Jas., V2
O' Ryan, V5
Ryan Of V3
Ryance269...
Ryane269...
O' Ryane V3
O' Ryane269...

V2 = Families of Co. Kerry **V3** = Families of Co. Clare **V4** = Families of Co. Cork **V5** = Families of Co. Limerick

Ryardane269...
Rycroft **V2**
Ryder **V2**
Ryder **V3**
Ryder269...
Rye **V4**
Rye232
Ryeeves **V2**
Ryely269...
Ryen269...
Ryerdane **V2**
Ryerdane269...
O' Ryerdane **V5**
O' Ryerdane269...
Ryeves **V2**
Ryeves, W. **V2**
Ryland **V4**
Ryland232
Ryle **V2**
Ryle269...
Rynd **V3**
Rynd232
Rynd, W. R. **V2**
Rynn **V3**
Rynn226,232
Rynn269...
Rynne **V3**
Ryves269...
Sacheverell34
Sadleir234
Sadler **V2**
Sadler234
Sadler269...
Sadlier **V2**
Sadlier269...
Sage269...
Sal(l)mon234
Salaman234
Sale234
Salisbury269...
Sall234
Sall269...
Sallanger269...
De Salle234
Sallenger269...
Salli269...
Sallinger269...
Sallsibery269...
Salmon **V3**
Salmon **V4**
Salmon269...
Salmon269...
Salt269...
Salters269...
Salterson269...
Saltfeeld **V5**
Saltfeeld269...
Saltfield269...
Saltinsball269...
Saltonstall269...
Sambage269...
Samford269...
Samming269...
Sammon **V3**
Sammon234
Samon269...
Sampson, **V2**
Sampson **V3**
Sampson **V5**
Sampson269...
Samson **V2**
Samson **V3**
Samsun **V2**
San **V2**
Sanborn **V4**
Sanckey269...
Sancky269...
Sand235
Sand(e)s235
Sanders **V2**
Sanders **V4**
Sanders **V5**
Sanders234
Sanders, Dr. **V2**
Sanders, **V4**
Sanderson234
Sandes **V2**
Sandes **V3**
Sandes Arms **V2**
Sandes Of **V2**
Sandford **V2**
Sandford269...
Sands **V2**
Sands **V3**
Sands269...
Sandys235
Sandys269...
Sandys, D. **V2**
Sanford **V2**
Sankey **V2**
Sankey235
Santry **V4**
Santry269...
O' Saoraide **V2**
Sargent **V4**
Sargent **V5**
Sargent269...
Sarjeant269...
Sarsefeld235
Sarseil269...
Sarsfield **V3**
Sarsfield **V4**
Sarsfield **V5**
Sarsfield235
Sarsfield269...
Sarsfield, **V4**
Sarsfields **V3**
Sauadge269...
Sauage **V4**
Sauage269...
Sauce269...
Saul234
Saunders **V2**
Saunders **V4**
Saunders234
Saunders269...
Saunders, A. **V2**
Saurin269...
Sause269...
Sausheil269...
Sauvage155
Savadge **V2**
Savadge234
Savadge269...
Savage **V2**
Savage **V4**
Savage155
Savage234
Savage269...
Savell **V4**
Savell269...
Saveroy155
Savery155
Savidge269...
Savin **V2**
Sawers **V2**
Sawters **V4**
Sawyer **V2**
Say155,235
Sayers **V2**
Sayers235
Scad(d)en235
Scadan235
Scafeeld269...
Mac Scahill235
(o) Scahill235
Scaife **V2**
Scales **V3**
Scallan235
Scallan269...
Scallon235
Scally236
Scally269...
Scanlan **V2**
Scanlan **V3**
Scanlan **V4**
Scanlan269...
O' Scanlan **V2**
O' Scanlan **V3**
O' Scanlan269...
Scanlan(e)236
Scanlan, **V2**
O' Scanlan Of **V2**
Scanlane **V3**
Scanlane269...
O' Scanlane269...
Scanlon **V2**
Scanlon **V3**
Scanlon **V4**
Scanlon269...
O' Scanlon **V2**
O Scanlon **V4**
O' Scanlon **V5**
O Scanlon236
O' Scannail **V2**
Scannell **V2**
Scannell **V4**
Scannell269...
O Scannell **V4**
O Scannell236
O' Scannell269...
Scannlain **V2**
O' Scannlain **V2**
Scarborough269...
Scarborrough269..
Scardeville155
Scared242
Scaret242
Scargill **V2**
Scariff **V3**
Scarred **V3**
Scarrett **V3**
Scarritt **V3**
Scarry235
Schifley49
Schumacker269...
Scofield **V4**
Scollard **V2**
Mc Scollog269...
Scone269...
Scot269...
Scotney **V4**
Scotney269...
Scott **V2**
Scott **V3**
Scott236
Scott269...
Scott Of **V2**
Scrimpton269...
Scrimshaw269...
Scriven **V4**
Scudamore **V4**
Scudamore269...
Scudmore **V4**
Scudmore269...
O' Scullen269...
Sculles **V2**
Scullin236
O' Scullin269...
Scullion236
Scullion269...
Mc Sculloge269...
Scully **V2**
O' Scully **V3**
O Scully **V4**
O' Scully **V5**
(o) Scully236
Scurlock269...
Scurlog269...
Scurry235
Scuse **V4**
Scuse269...
Sea'lbach Clan **V4**
O' Seadha **V2**
Mac Seafraid **V2**
Seaganstown **V2**
Seagerson249
Seagrave **V4**
Seagrave237
Mac Seain **V2**
Sealy **V2**
Sealy **V4**
Sealy, **V2**
Seaman269...
Seambar **V2**
Seamor269...
Seargeant269...
Sears **V2**
Sears235
Seary **V2**
Seaton269...
Seaver269...
Seaward **V2**
Seaward **V4**
Seaward269...
Seax269...
Sedborough34
Seden269...
Sedgewick **V2**
Sedgraue269...
Sedgwick269...
Seeds269...
Seekins **V2**
Seery269...
Seever **V2**
Segerson **V2**
Segerson249
Seghrue **V2**
Segnock269...
Segrave **V4**
Segrave237
Segrave269...
Segray269...
Segre269...
Segrue **V2**
Seix269...
Selby **V4**
Selby269...
Selenger269...
Selick **V2**
Sellers **V2**
Selles **V2**
Selling269...
Semphill269...
Sempill237
Semple237
Semple269...
Sennott **V4**
Mac Seoin **V2**
Sergeant269...
Sergent269...
O Serky237
Serle269...
Settler **V3**
Settler Fams. V
Settlers **V2**
Severs269...
O' Sevnagh269...
Seward **V4**
Seward269...
Sewell **V2**
Sewell269...
O' Sexon **V2**
O Sexon **V4**
O' Sexon **V5**
Sextan237
Sexten **V3**
Sexten237
Sexten269...
Sexton **V2**
Sexton **V3**
Sexton **V4**
Sexton **V5**
Sexton237
Sexton269...
O Sexton **V4**
Seymour **V5**
Seymour237
Seymour269...
Shackl'ton/e237
Shade **V2**
Mc Shaen269...
Shagins **V5**
Shagins269...
Shagroe **V2**
Shagroe269...
Shagrue248
Shails269...
Shakelton **V2**
Shakelton269...
Shakleton237
Shallcross269...
Shalloo241
Shallowe241
Shallowe269...
Shally269...
Shamrock **V4**
Mc Shan269...
Shanaghan **V2**
Shanaghan **V3**
Shanaghy269...
Mc Shanaghy269..
Shanahan **V2**
Shanahan **V4**
Shanahan **V5**
Shanahan269...
O' Shanahan **V2**
O' Shanahan **V3**
(o) Shanahan238
Shanahan **V2**
Shanahan Of **V3**
Shanahane269...
Shanahy109
Shanahy269...
Shanan269...
O Shanassy238
Shane269...
(m') Shane237,239
Mc Shane **V3**
Mc Shane **V4**
Mc Shane269...

Surname Index

Mc Shane 269...
Shane Oge **V4**
Shane Oge 269...
Shaneghane 238
Shaneghane 269...
Shanehan 269...
Shanessy 238
Shanks 269...
Shanley 269...
(mac Shanley 238
Shanly 238
Mc Shanly 269...
Shanna **V3**
O Shanna, **V3**
Shannahane 269...
Shannen 238
Shannohan 269...
Shannon **V2**
Shannon **V3**
Shannon **V4**
Shannon 269...
O' Shannon **V3**
(o) Shannon 238
(o) Shannon 241
Shannon, B. **V2**
O' Shannon,sha **V5**
Shanny **V3**
O' Shanny **V3**
Shanoghan 269...
Shapcot 269...
Sharket 237
Sharkey **V2**
Sharkey **V2**
Sharkey 269...
O Sharkey 237
Sharp **V4**
Sharpe **V4**
Sharpe 269...
(mc) Sharry 237
(mc) Sharry 240
Mc Sharry 269...
O' Sharry 269...
Sharvin 240
Sharvin 269...
Sharwell 155
Shaughinisy 238
Shaughinisy 269...
O Shaughlin 238
O Shaughnes'y 238
Shaughness 269...
Shaughnessy **V2**
Shaughnessy 269..
O' Shaughnessy **V2**
O Shaughnessy **V3**
O' Shaughnessy **V5**
O' Shaughnessy 269
Shaughnessy **V2**
Shaw **V2**
Shaw 269...
Shaw(e) 238
Shawe 269...
Shay 239
Shea **V2**
Shea **V3**
Shea **V4**
Shea 269...
Mc Shea 239
Mc Shea 269...
O' Shea **V2**
O Shea **V4**
O' Shea **V5**
(o) Shea 239
O' Shea 269...
O' Shea **V2**
O' Shea, Chief **V2**
Shea House- **V2**
O' Shea, Poem **V2**
Sheady **V3**
Mc Sheaghan 269..
O' Sheaghane 269..
Sheaghinsy **V5**
Sheaghinsy 269...
Sheahan **V2**
Sheahan **V4**
Sheahan 239
Sheahan 269...
O Sheahan **V3**
Sheahy **V3**
Sheahy 239
O' Sheale 269...
Sheall 269...
O' Sheall 269...
Sheals 269...
Sheanan 241
O' Sheanan 269...
Mc Sheane **V5**
Mc Sheane 269...
Sheapallh **V2**
Sheapheard 269...
Sheapherd 269...
Shearan 240
Sheare(s) 240
Shearer 269...
Sheares **V4**
Sheares 269...
Shearhoon 269...
Shearhy 269...
Shearing 240
O' Shearing 269...
Shee **V3**
Shee **V4**
Shee 269...
Mac Shee 239
(o) Shee 239
O' Shee 269...
Sheean 239
Sheedy **V3**
Sheedy 269...
Sheehan **V2**
Sheehan **V3**
Sheehan **V4**
Sheehan 269...
O' Sheehan **V2**
O' Sheehan **V3**
O Sheehan **V4**
O' Sheehan **V5**
O Sheehan 239
Sheehan **V2**
O Sheehane **V4**
O' Sheehane 269...
Sheehey **V4**
Mc Sheehey **V3**
O' Sheehey **V3**
Sheehie **V4**
Mac Sheehies **V4**
Sheehy **V2**
Sheehy **V4**
Sheehy 269...
Mac Sheehy **V2**
Mac Sheehy **V3**
Mac Sheehy **V4**
Mac Sheehy **V5**
(mac Sheehy 239
Mc Sheehy 269...
Sheehy **V2**
Sheen 239
Sheenan 241
Sheenan 269...
Sheepherd 269...
Sheeran **V4**
Sheeran 240
Sheeran 269...
Sheeres **V2**
Sheeres 240
Sheerin 240
O' Sheerin 269...
Sheery 269...
Sheffield 269...
Sheghane **V4**
Sheghane 239
Sheghane 269...
O' Sheghane **V3**
O Sheghane **V4**
O' Sheghane **V5**
O' Sheghane 269...
Shehane **V4**
Shehane 269...
Sheil 241
Sheild 269...
Sheilds 241
Sheilds 269...
Sheile 269...
Sheill 269...
O' Sheill 269...
Sheils 269...
Sheldon **V2**
Sheldon 269...
Shell(e)y 241
Shelloe 241
Shelloe 269...
Shelly **V4**
Shelly 269...
Shenan 241
Shepard 269...
Shepheard 269...
Shepherd **V2**
Shepherd 269...
Sheppard 240
Sheppard 269...
Sherard 244
Sherbroke 269...
Sherdan 240
Sherden 240
Sherdian 269...
Sherding 269...
Sherdon 240
Mac Shere 241
O' Sheredon 269...
Sheridan **V2**
Sheridan 269...
O Sheridan 240
Sherigley 269...
O Sherin 240
O Sherkott 237
Sherlock **V4**
Sherlock 240,245
Sherlock 269...
Sherlocke 269...
Sherman 269...
Sherodan 240
Sherra 269...
Sherrar 269...
Sherrard 244
Sherrard 269...
Sherrerd 244
Sherry **V4**
Sherry 269...
Sherry 47,240
Mac Sherry 237
Mac Sherry 240
Mc Sherry 269...
O Sherry 240
O' Sherry 269...
Shertliff 269...
Sherwin 240
Sherwood 269...
Mc Shery 240
Mc Shery 269...
Shevlin 241
Shevlin 269...
Shewel 269...
Shewell **V2**
Shewell 269...
Mc Shida **V3**
Mc Shida 269...
Shiel 269...
(o) Shiel 241
Shield(s) 241
Shieldham **V4**
Shields 269...
Shiell **V2**
Shiell 241
Shiell 269...
Shiels 269...
Shier 205
Shiercliffe **V2**
Shiers **V4**
Shifley 49
Shighane **V4**
O Shighane **V4**
O' Shighane 269...
Mc Shihy 269...
Shillady 269...
Shilliady 269...
Shilliday 269...
Shinagh 269...
Shinane **V3**
Shine **V2**
Shine **V3**
Shine **V4**
Shine **V5**
Shine 269...
O' Shine **V2**
O Shine **V4**
(o) Shine 241
Shiner 269...
Shingly 269...
Shinnagh 269...
Shinnahan 269...
Shinnock 109
Shinnock 269...
Ship Sirius. **V4**
Shipcott 245
Shipcott 269...
Shippool Castle **V4**
Shippy 245
Shippy 269...
Shipsea 245
Shipsey **V4**
Shipsey 245
Shipton **V4**
Shipton 245
Shipton 269...
Shipward **V4**
Shipward 245
Shipward 269...
Shirley **V2**
Shirley 269...
Mc Shitterye **V4**
Shochett **V5**
Shoemaker 205
Shonahan 269...
Shonogh 109
Shonogh 269...
Shoppee 155
Shore 269...
Shorelahan 269...
Short 248
Short 269...
Short Castle **V2**
Shortal **V2**
Shortall **V2**
Shortall 248
Shortall 269...
Shortcliffe **V2**
Shortell **V5**
Shorten **V4**
Shorten 246
Shorten 269...
Shortis **V2**
Shortle 269...
Shortt 269...
Shorttliffe 269...
Shorttliffe **V2**
Shoughnes'y 238
Shoultare 205
Shoye 159
Shoye 269...
Shreld 269...
Shrewbridge 269...
Shrimpton 269...
Shuel **V2**
Shuell **V2**
Shuldham **V3**
Shuldham 241
Shunagh 269...
Shunewire 205
Shunny 109
Shunny 269...
Mac Shurdan 159
Shurden 269...
Shurlog 269...
Mac Shurton 159
Shute **V2**
Shute **V3**
Shute **V4**
Shute **V5**
Shute 269...
Shuttleworth 269...
Shydy **V5**
Shydy 269...
O' Shyghane **V5**
O' Shyghane 269...
Shyhane 269...
Mc Shyhy **V5**
Mc Shyhy 269...
Shynane 246
Shyne, Denis **V2**
Shyrin 269...
Shyrydan 269...
Sibbaulds 269...
Sibthorpe 269...
Sichsheuerall 269..
Sidney **V4**
Sie 269...
Sigen 234
Sigerson **V2**
Sigerson 249
Siggens 234
Siggins 234
Sigurd **V2**
Silies **V2**
Silk 269...
Silles **V3**
Sills **V3**
Silver **V4**
Silver 269...
Sim(s) 249
Sime 269...
Sime(s) 249
Simes 269...

V2 = Families of Co. Kerry **V3** = Families of Co. Clare **V4** = Families of Co. Cork **V5** = Families of Co. Limerick

Simmons269...
Simms **V2**
Simms249
Simms269...
Simon **V2**
Simon **V4**
Simon249
Simon269...
Simons **V2**
Simons269...
Simple237
Simpson **V3**
Simpson **V4**
Simpson249
Simpson269...
Simpson, R. **V2**
Simson **V3**
Simson **V4**
Simson249
Simvil269...
Sinack269...
Sinacke269...
Sinan **V3**
Sinan **V4**
Sinane **V3**
Sinane246
Sinane269...
Sinclair269...
Sinclair, St. 63
Sincox **V2**
Sines269...
Singen269...
Singin269...
Singleton **V2**
Singleton **V3**
Singleton **V4**
Singleton241
Singleton269...
Sinhouse **V4**
Sinhouse269...
Sinjun269...
Sinnette **V2**
Sinnot(t)246,248
Sinnott **V4**
Sinnott269...
Sinon **V3**
Sinon **V4**
Sinon246
Sinone **V3**
O Siochain **V4**
O Siodhchain **V4**
O' Sionan **V2**
O' Sionnaig **V2**
Sirey269...
Sisk **V4**
Sisk **V5**
Sisnane **V4**
Sisnane269...
Mac Siurtan159
Sixmilebridg **V3**
Size269...
Skahan242
Skallan235
Skallan269...
Skally269...
(mac Skally236
Skanlane236
O' Skanlane **V5**
O' Skanlane269...
O Skannell **V4**
O' Skannell269...
Mc Skean269...
Skeeper269...
Skeffington269...
Skehan **V3**
Skehan241,242
Skehan269...
Skelly269...
(o) Skelly236
Skelson269...
Skelten244
Skelton244
Skelton269...
Skeret242
Skeritt **V3**
Skerrett **V3**
Skerrett242
Skerrit242
Skevington269...
Skiddy **V2**
Skiddy **V4**
Skiddy248
O' Skiddy269...
Skiddys **V4**
Skidy248
Skillen244
Skillen269...
Skilling244
Mc Skimmins269..
Skinger **V2**
Skinnan244
Skinner **V2**
Skinner **V3**
Skinner269...
Skinnion244
Skinnion269...
Skinnon244
Skipworth **V2**
Skoly269...
Skoolin269...
Skully **V4**
Skully236
Skully269...
Skurlock245
Skyddy **V4**
Skyddy269...
Slack269...
Slack(e)242
Slade269...
Slain(e)245
Slamon269...
Slane245
Slane269...
Slaney **V4**
Slaney245
Slaney269...
Slatery246
Slatier269...
Slator269...
Slattary246
Slattery **V2**
Slattery **V3**
Slattery **V4**
Slattery **V5**
Slattery246
Slattery269...
O' Slattery **V3**
O Slattery **V4**
O' Slattery269...
Slavin246
Slavin269...
Sleath **V2**
Sleator **V2**
Sleeper205
Sleevin246
Slevin246
Slevin269...
Sliney **V4**
Sloan269...
Sloan(e)242
Sloan, Slone **V2**
Sloane269...
Sloey269...
Slone(s)242
Slones269...
Slose269...
Sloughter269...
Slowan242
Slowan269...
Slowey242
Slowey269...
Sloy269...
Smailholme34
Small **V4**
Small269...
Smallbone269...
Smallwood269...
Smallwoods269...
Smart **V4**
Smart269...
Smarte269...
Smarth **V4**
Smarth269...
Smelhome34
Smiley242
Smiley269...
Smily242
Smims **V4**
Smims269...
Smith **V2**
Smith **V3**
Smith **V4**
Smith155
Smith269...
Smith, Alias **V2**
Smith, C. **V2**
Smith(e)131,242
Smith, Ed., **V2**
Smith, G.n. **V2**
Smith Of **V3**
Smith, **V2**
Smith Smyth **V3**
Smithick242
Smithick269...
Smithwick **V4**
Smithwick **V5**
Smithwick242
Smithworthe **V2**
Smullen269...
Smylie269...
Smyly242
Smyth **V2**
Smyth **V4**
Smyth242
Smyth269...
Mc Smyth269...
Smythe **V3**
Smythe242
Smythe269...
Smythwick242
Snares **V3**
Snedden269...
Snee243
Snee269...
Snell **V4**
Snell269...
Snoddy269...
Snow243
Snow269...
Snowden269...
Soare269...
Sodan243
Soden243
Soden269...
Sodin243
Sodin269...
Sogh269...
O Solivan **V4**
Soloman234
Solovart **V4**
Solovart **V4**
Solovart269...
Somers **V2**
Somers **V3**
Somers120,124
Somers243
Somers269...
Somersett **V4**
Somersett269...
Somerville **V4**
Somerville243
Somerville269...
Sommers **V3**
Sonahaun269...
Sooker269...
Soolivan247
Soolivan269...
Soople248
Soraghan269...
(o) Soraghan243
Sorahan243
Soran243
Mc Sorely243
Mc Sorley243
Mc Sorley269...
Sorson269...
Soudan243
Sources **V2**
Sources **V3**
Sources Vi
Sources For **V2**
South269...
Southcott **V5**
Southcott269...
Southwell **V3**
Southwell **V4**
Southwell **V5**
Southwell269...
Southwell, **V2**
Southworth **V2**
Southy269...
Soy155
Soy269...
Spaight **V3**
Spaight **V5**
Spaight243
Spain269...
Spain, To **V2**
Spalane **V4**
Spalane249
Spanish **V2**
Sparke269...
Sparks **V2**
Sparks269...
Sparling205
Sparling269...
Spate **V3**
Spate243
Speare269...
Speart **V2**
Mc Speddin269...
Speed269...
Speer(s)243
Speers269...
Speight243
Spelessy269...
O' Spellan **V2**
Spellane269...
O Spellane **V4**
O' Spellane269...
Spellissy **V3**
Spelman269...
Spemer **V4**
Spemer269...
Spence243
Spence269...
Spencer **V2**
Spencer **V4**
Spencer269...
Spenser **V2**
Spensur269...
Spicer **V2**
Spierms269...
Spike269...
Spillan(e)249
Spillane **V2**
Spillane **V4**
Spillane269...
Mac Spillane249
O Spillane **V2**
O Spillane **V4**
O' Spillane **V5**
O Spillane249
O' Spillane269...
Spillane, D. **V2**
Spiller129
Spillessy269...
Spillman269...
Spinks243
Splaine249
Splaine269...
Spollan269...
Spollen269...
Sponeowes269...
Spoone269...
Spotswood **V2**
Spotswood, **V2**
Spranger **V5**
Spranger269...
Spratt **V2**
Spratt **V4**
Spratt269...
Spread, C. **V2**
Spring **V2**
Spring **V3**
Spring269...
Spring(e)243
Springham243
Springham269...
Sproo1243
Sproo1269...
Sproul(e)243
Sproule269...
Sprowle243
Spruell243
Spruell269...
De Spynk243
Squibb269...
Squibbe269...
Squiddy **V4**
Squire269...
O Ssulluayn **V2**
St. Alban **V3**
St. George128
St. John205
St. Lawrence174
St. Lawrence243
St. Ledger205
St. Leger **V2**
Stac(k)249
(de) Stacabul **V2**

V2 = Families of Co. Kerry **V3** = Families of Co. Clare **V4** = Families of Co. Cork **V5** = Families of Co. Limerick

Stacey269...
Stack **V2**
Stack **V4**
Stack **V5**
Stack269...
(de) Stack **V2**
De Stack249
De Stackpole **V4**
De Stackpole244
Stackpoll **V3**
Stackpoll249
Stackpoll269...
Stackpool **V3**
Stackpool269...
Stackpoole **V2**
Stackpoole244
Stackpoole249
Stackpoole **V3**
Stackpooll **V3**
Stackpooll269...
Stackstown **V2**
Stacpoole **V3**
De Stacpoole244
Stafford **V3**
Stafford **V4**
Stafford244
Stafford269...
Staford244
Staigue Fort **V2**
Stainstreet **V2**
Stak **V2**
Stake **V2**
Stamer **V3**
Stamers **V3**
Stamers269...
Stammer **V3**
Stammers **V3**
Stamp269...
Stampe269...
Stanbride269...
Stanbridge269...
Standish **V5**
Stanehouse244
Stanford269...
Stanhowe34
Stanihurt244
Stanley **V2**
Stanley **V4**
Stanley269...
Stanly269...
Stannard **V4**
Stannus244
Stanton **V4**
Stanton245
Stanton269...
Stapers269...
Staplehil269...
Staplehill269...
Staples269...
Stapleton **V3**
Stapleton **V4**
Stapleton **V5**
Stapleton244
Stapleton269...
Stark205
Starkers269...
Starkey **V3**
Starkey269...
Starkie **V3**
Starkie269...
Starky **V3**
Starling269...
Starrett269...
Staughton **V2**
Staughton269...
Staunton245
Staunton269...
Stawell **V4**
Stawell245
Mc Stay269...
Staylehill269...
Mc Stayne269...
Steel269...
Steel(e)245
Steele **V2**
Steele **V3**
Steele269...
Steen269...
Steenson269...
Steere **V2**
Steers269...
Steevenson269...
Steill269...
(o) Steill245
O' Steill269...
O Steille245
O' Steille269...
Steinson269...
Stenson269...
Stephen(s)245
Stephen(s)246
Stephens **V2**
Stephens **V3**
Stephens **V4**
Stephens **V5**
Stephens269...
Stephens269...
Stephens, **V2**
Stephenson **V2**
Stephenson **V3**
Stephenson245
Stephenson246
Stephenson269...
Stephenton **V4**
Stepney **V4**
Stepney269...
Sterling269...
Stern269...
Sterne **V2**
Sterne269...
Steuart245
Steuart269...
Steuens **V4**
Steuens269...
Steven269...
Stevens **V3**
Stevens **V4**
Stevens269...
Stevenson **V2**
Stevenson **V3**
Stevenson245
Stevenson269...
Steventon **V4**
Steward245
Steward269...
Stewart **V2**
Stewart **V5**
Stewart269...
Stewart34,245
Stewart, Rev. **V2**
Steyles **V4**
Steyles269...
Stiffe **V4**
Stiffe269...
Stiles **V2**
Stiles **V4**
Stiles269...
Stiles, J. **V2**
Stinchman **V4**
Stinchman269...
Stinson269...
Stirling269...
Stirratt269...
Stirrett269...
Stitt269...
Stoakes **V3**
Stoakes269...
Stock **V2**
Stockden **V3**
Stockden269...
Stocker129
Stockman269...
Stoddard **V3**
Stoddart **V3**
Stoddart269...
Stodhard269...
Stoke(s)244
Stoker269...
Stokes **V2**
Stokes **V3**
Stokes **V5**
Stokes269...
Stokes, **V2**
Stokesfield **V2**
(de) Stokke **V2**
Stokys **V2**
Stone **V2**
Stone244
Stone269...
Stone Circle - **V4**
Stoney246
Stony246
Stooker269...
Stopford269...
Storey **V3**
Storey269...
Stormont269...
Storton269...
Stotherg269...
Stotnard269...
Stoughton **V2**
Stoughton246
Stoughton269...
Stout269...
Stoute **V4**
Stoute269...
Strabane269...
Strachan244
Stradford269...
Strafford269...
Straghan244
Strahan244
Strahan269...
Strain244
Strain269...
Strange **V2**
Strange **V3**
Strange269...
(le) Strange178
Stratford **V3**
Stratford **V4**
Stratford269...
Straton269...
Straugh205
Straughton269...
Mc Stravick269...
Streatton269...
Strecklan269...
Streelle269...
Street **V2**
Streeten269...
Stretch244
Stretton **V2**
Strich **V3**
Strich244
Strich269...
Stringer **V2**
Stringer269...
Stritch **V2**
Stritch **V3**
Stritch **V5**
Stritch269...
Stritch(e)244
Stritches **V3**
Stroaker269...
Strond269...
Strong **V4**
Strong **V5**
Strong269...
Strongbow **V2**
Strongman269...
Strowd269...
Stryny269...
Stuard269...
Stuart **V2**
Stuart **V4**
Stuart269...
Stuart34,245
Mc Stuart269...
Stuartt269...
Stubbs248
Stuckley269...
Studdart **V3**
Studdert **V2**
Studdert **V3**
Studdert **V5**
Studdert246
Studdert269...
Studdert Arms **V3**
Studdert, T. **V2**
Stumbles269...
Stundon **V2**
Sturgeon269...
Sturgis269...
Sturt **V4**
Sturt269...
Styles **V2**
Styles **V4**
Styles269...
Suffren155
Sugars **V4**
Sugars269...
Sugherne **V2**
Sugherne269...
Sughrue248
Sugrena Sept **V2**
Sugrew248
Sugrue **V2**
Sugrue **V4**
Sugrue248
Sugrue269...
Sugrue **V2**
Mac Suibhne **V4**
Mc Suile269...
Suipeil **V2**
Sulevan269...
Sulevane **V3**
Sulevane **V4**
Sulevane269...
O Sulevane **V4**
O' Sulevane269...
Suliuane **V4**
Suliuane269...
Sulivan247
Sullavane **V4**
Sulleuan **V2**
Sulleuan269...
O' Sulleuane269...
Sullevan269...
Sullevane **V3**
Sullevane **V4**
Sullevane269...
O' Sullevane **V3**
O Sullevane **V4**
O' Sullevane269...
Sulliban247
Sulliuan **V2**
Sulliuan269...
Sulliuane **V4**
Sulliuane269...
Sullivan **V2**
Sullivan **V3**
Sullivan **V4**
Sullivan269...
O' Sullivan **V2**
O Sullivan **V4**
O' Sullivan **V5**
O Sullivan247
O' Sullivan269...
Sullivan **V2**
O Sullivan **V4**
Sullivan **V2**
Sullivan **V2**
O' Sullivan In **V3**
O' Sullivan **V2**
Sullivan **V4**
Sullivane **V2**
Sullivane **V4**
Sullivane269...
Sullivane269...
O Sullivane **V4**
O' Sullivans **V2**
O' Sullivanx **V2**
O Sullyvane **V4**
Sumahean269...
Sumeril269...
Sumerly269...
Sumers **V3**
Sumerwell269...
O' Summachan269.
Summars269...
Summer269...
Summers **V3**
Summers269...
Summers269...
Sumner269...
Sunbery **V4**
Sunbery269...
Sunderland **V2**
Sunderland269...
Suniet269...
Suppel(s)248
Supple **V2**
Supple **V3**
Supple **V4**
Supple **V5**
Supple248
Supple269...
Supple, E. K. **V2**
Surgenor269...
Surgeoner269...
Surley269...
Surname **V2**
Sussers269...
Sutcliffe **V2**
Sutherland269...
Suthern269...
Sutton **V2**
Sutton **V4**
Sutton246
Sutton269...

V2 = Families of Co. Kerry **V3** = Families of Co. Clare **V4** = Families of Co. Cork **V5** = Families of Co. Limerick

De Sutun 246
Suvane **V2**
Suvane 269...
Suxburie 269...
Suxbury 269...
O Suylivane **V4**
Swabby **V4**
Swabby 269...
Swadling 269...
Swaine **V4**
Swallow **V4**
Swallow 269...
Swan 248
Swan 269...
Swann 269...
Swanton **V4**
Swanton 248
Swanton 269...
Swanwick 269...
Swanzy **V2**
Swarbricke 269...
Swayn **V4**
Swayne **V2**
Swayne **V4**
Swayne **V5**
Swayne 269...
Sweaney **V2**
Sweaney **V3**
Sweaney 247
Sweany **V3**
Sweany 247
Sweatman **V2**
Sweeney **V2**
Sweeney **V3**
Sweeney **V4**
Sweeney 269...
Mac Sweeney **V2**
Mac Sweeney **V3**
Mac Sweeney **V4**
Mac Sweeney 247
Mc Sweeney **V2**
Mc Sweeney **V4**
Mc Sweeney 269...
O Sweeney **V4**
Mc Sweeney **V2**
Mac Sweeney **V4**
Sweeny **V2**
Sweeny **V4**
Sweeny 247
Sweeny 269...
Mc Sweeny **V4**
Mc Sweeny 269...
Mac Sweeny Kilm... **V4**
Sweet **V4**
Sweet 269...
Sweete **V4**
Sweete **V4**
Sweete 269...
Sweetman **V2**
Sweetman **V3**
Sweetman **V4**
Sweetman 247
Sweetman 269...
Sweltzer 205
Sweteman 247
Swetenham 269...
Swift **V2**
Swift **V3**
Swift 269...
Swift(e) 247
O Swillevane **V4**
O Swillyvane **V4**
Swindel **V2**
Swine 269...
Mc Swine 269...
Swiney 247
Swiney 269...
Mac Swiney **V2**
Mac Swiney **V4**
Mc Swiney 269...
Swinfeild 269...
Swinglehurst 269..
Switzer **V2**
Switzer 205
Switzer 269...
Swords **V2**
Swords 269...
Mc Swyine **V4**
O Swylevane **V4**
O Swylivane **V4**
O Swylyvane **V4**
Mc Swyne 269...
Mc Swynie **V3**
Mc Swynie 269...
Swyny **V3**
Swyny 269...
Mc Swyny **V3**
Mc Swyny **V4**
Mc Swyny 269...
O Swyny **V4**
Syballs 269...
Sybhals 269...
Sycamore 269...
Sydney, Sir **V3**
Symerell 269...
Symkins 269...
Symner 269...
Symons **V2**
Symons 269...
Syms **V5**
Syms 269...
Synan **V2**
Synan **V4**
Synan 241,246
Synge **V2**
Synge **V3**
Synge 248
Synnott 246,248
Synnott 269...
Synot(t) 246,248
Synott **V4**
Synott 269...
Synyres 269...
Syridan 269...
Syvrac **V2**
Taa 250
Taafe 250
Taaff 269...
Taaffe **V2**
Taaffe **V3**
Taaffe 250
Taaffe 269...
Tackaberry **V2**
Tacker 269...
Tackney 269...
Taff(e) 250
Taffe **V3**
Tagan 269...
Mc Tagart 253
Mc Tagart 269...
Tagert 100
Taggard 269...
Taggart 253
Taggart 269...
Mc Taggart 269...
Taggert 100
Mc Taghlan? 269...
Mc Taghlin 269...
Tague 269...
Mc Tague 254
Mc Tague 269...
Tailer 251
Taillebois 155
Tailor **V3**
Tailor 34,251
` Tait 269...
Taite **V2**
Talant 269...
Talbot **V2**
Talbot **V3**
Talbot 250
Talbot 269...
Talbot- **V2**
Talbott 269...
Talboys 155
Tallant 269...
Tallbott 269...
Tallon **V5**
Tallon 250
Tallon 269...
Tally 250
Tally 269...
Talty **V3**
Talty 250
Talty 269...
Tangley 251
Tangney **V2**
Tangney **V4**
Tangney 251
Tangney 269...
Tangny 251
Tanist 269...
Tanner 269...
Tanner(e) 251
Tannian 250
Tannion 250
Tansey 269...
(mac Tansey 251
Tansley **V2**
Tansy **V4**
Tansy 251
O Tapa 247,254
Tapper **V2**
Tappy 247
Tara, Four **V2**
Tarleton 251
Tarpey **V4**
Tarpey 255
Tarpey 269...
Tarrant **V2**
Tarrant **V4**
Tarrant 269...
Tarsnane **V3**
Tarsnane 254
Tarsney 12
Tate **V5**
Tate 269...
Tath 269...
Tatlow **V3**
Tatte 269...
Tavey 12
Tavey 269...
Mc Tavish 252
Mc Tavish 269...
Mc Tayer 269...
Tayler **V3**
Tayler 251
Mc Tayler 269...
Taylor **V2**
Taylor **V3**
Taylor **V4**
Taylor 251
Taylor 269...
Taylor, Eliza **V2**
Taylour 155
Teaghan 252
Teague 269...
Mc Teague 254
Mc Teague 269...
Teahan **V2**
Teahan 252
Teahan 269...
Teape **V4**
Teape 269...
O Tedgamna **V4**
Tedmarsh **V2**
Tee 269...
Teehan 252
Teeling 252
Teeling 269...
Teer **V2**
Teerry 269...
Teesdale 254
Teevan 252
Tefelin 253
Teg 269...
Tegan 252
Tegart 253
Teggart 100,253
Teggart 269...
Mc Teggart 269...
Teggarty 100
Teggarty 269...
Tehan 252
Tehan 269...
Mc Teig **V4**
Teige **V4**
Teige 254
Mac Teige **V5**
Mac Teige 269...
Mc Teige **V2**
Mc Teige **V3**
Mc Teige **V4**
Mc Teige 269...
O' Teige 269...
Teige (oge) **V4**
Teige (oge) 269...
Teigh 269...
Mc Teighe **V4**
Teigue 269...
Mc Teigue 269...
Mc Teire 269...
Teirney 253
Telford 252
Telford 269...
Telyng 252
Tempest 251
Tempest 269...
Temple **V4**
Temple 251
Temple 269...
Templeton 251
Templeton 269...
Tempson 269...
Tenane 269...
Tench **V4**
Tenck 269...
Tenison 251
Tennant 269...
Tennison 251
Tentch 269...
Mc Terlagh **V5**
Mc Terlagh 269...
Terms Used Iii
Ternan 269...
Mac Ternan 164
Mc Ternan 269...
Terny 269...
Terri 252
Terrill 269...
Terry **V4**
Terry **V5**
Terry 269...
Terry 72,252
O Terry 252
Terty 269...
Tesky **V5**
Tesky 205
Tesky 253
Tesley 205
Test Oath **V2**
Tethrington **V4**
Tethrington 269...
Tettler 205
Tevlin 253
Thackwell **V4**
Thackwell 252
The Lough **V3**
Theaker 269...
Theoballs **V5**
Theoballs 269...
Mc Therlagh **V5**
Mc Therlagh 269...
Therlaghlen **V3**
Therlaghlen 269...
Therry **V4**
Therry 252
Theswell 269...
(de) Thick **V2**
O' Thina 269...
Thirry **V4**
Thirry 269...
Thistall **V2**
Thobbin 269...
Thobin 269...
Thohy 269...
Thomand **V3**
Thomand **V4**
Thomand **V3**
Thomand **V3**
Thomas **V2**
Thomas **V4**
Thomas **V5**
Thomas 269...
(mac Thomas 253
Mc Thomas **V2**
Mc Thomas **V3**
Mc Thomas **V4**
Mc Thomas **V5**
Mc Thomas 269...
Thomas, **V3**
Mac Thomas, **V2**
Thomkins 269...
Thomlinson **V5**
Thomlinson 269...
Thomomond 269...
Thomond **V3**
Thomond 269...
Thompkins **V3**
Thompson **V2**
Thompson **V3**
Thompson 252
Thompson 269...
Thomson **V2**
Thomson **V3**
Thomson 252
Thomson 269...
Thomsone 269...
Thorenbor'o **V5**
Thorenbor'o 269...
Thorloe Oge **V5**

Thorloe Oge 269...
Thorn 269...
Thornburg 269...
Thorne **V5**
Thorne 269...
Thorneton **V3**
Thorneton 269...
Thornhill **V2**
Thornhill **V4**
Thornhill 269...
Thornton **V2**
Thornton **V3**
Thornton **V4**
Thornton **V5**
Thornton 242,252
Thornton 269...
Thornton 269...
Thorpe 269...
Thorton 252
Threnchard **V5**
Threnchard 269...
Thresher 269...
Throgmorton 269..
O Thuama **V4**
Thunder 253
Thunder 269...
Thungut 129
Thurlus 269...
Thurston **V2**
Thwaits 269...
Thwantes **V2**
Thynne **V3**
Tibb 269...
Tibbs 269...
Tichborne 269...
Tichbourn 269...
Tichburne 269...
Tickell 253
Tidings **V2**
Mc Tieg **V4**
Tiege **V3**
Tiege 254
Mc Tiege **V4**
O' Tiegrnach **V2**
Tiegue **V3**
Tiernan 164,253
Tiernan 269...
Mc Tiernan 269...
Tierney **V2**
Tierney 269...
O Tierney 253
Tierny 253
Tierny 269...
Tifford 269...
Tiger 100
Tiger 269...
Tigh 269...
Tighe 269...
(mac Tighe 254
Mc Tigue 269...
Tilly **V5**
Tilly 269...
Tilson **V4**
Tilson 269...
Timilin 253
Timlen 253
Timlin 269...
Mac Timlin 253
Timmin 269...
Timmin(s) 253
Timmins **V2**
Timmins 269...
Timmons **V3**
Timmons 253
Timon 253
Timony **V2**
Timony 269...
(o) Timony 253
Timothy 269...
Timpany 253
Tinan 269...
Tinane 269...
Tinin 269...
Tinkler 269...
Tinohit 269...
Tinsley 269...
Tint 269...
Tinte **V4**
Tipperary **V3**
Tipping 269...
Mc Tire **V4**
Mc Tire 253
Tirrell **V5**
Tirrell 269...
Tirrey **V4**
Tirry **V4**
Tirry 252
Tisdall **V2**
Tisdall 254
Tisdall 269...
Titchborne 269...
Titchbourn 269...
Titterton 269...
De Tiuit 257
Toal 255
Toal 269...
Tobbine **V5**
Tobbine 254
Tobbine 269...
Tobin **V2**
Tobin **V4**
Tobin **V5**
Tobin 269...
Tobin(e) 254
Tobin **V3**
Tobine 269...
Tobyn **V2**
Tobyn **V3**
Tobyn **V4**
Tobyn 269...
Tobyn(n) 254
Tobynn 269...
Tod 269...
Tod(d) 255
Todd 269...
Togher 256
Togher **V2**
Tohall 255
Tohall 269...
Toher 256
Toher 269...
Tohill **V4**
Tohill 255
Tohull 255
Tohull 269...
Tohy 269...
Ui Toird'lb'aigh **V3**
Tolan 269...
Tolan(d) 255
Toland 269...
O Toler 254
Toller 269...
Toman 269...
O Tomey **V4**
Tomfinlough **V3**
Tomilin 253
Tomin 253
Tomin 269...
Tomkins 269...
Tomlin **V4**
Tomlin 269...
Tomlins 269...
Tomlinson 269...
Tomo **V4**
Tompkins **V3**
Tompkins 269...
Tompson 269...
Tomson **V3**
Tomson 252
Tomson 269...
Tomsson 269...
Tone 254
Toner 269...
(o) Toner 254
O' Toner 269...
Tong **V2**
Tong **V3**
Tong(e) 256
Tongue 256
Tonnelier 155
Tonson **V3**
Tonson 269...
Tonstall 269...
Toogood 129
Toogood 269...
Tooher **V2**
Tooher 256
Tooher 269...
Toohil(l) 255
Toohill **V4**
Tooke 269...
O Tool(e) 255
Toolan 255
Toolan 269...
O' Toolan 269...
Toole 269...
O' Toole **V5**
O' Toole 269...
Tooley **V5**
Tooley 269...
Toomey **V4**
Toomey **V5**
Toomey 258
Toomey 269...
Toompane 269...
Toomy 258
Toorish 269...
Topham **V2**
Topping **V2**
Topping 269...
Torkington 269...
Torltone 269...
Tormey 257
Tormey 269...
Tormy 257
Tornain **V4**
O Tornain **V4**
Torney 257
O' Torney 269...
Torpey 255
Torpey, **V4**
Torpy 255
Torrance 256
Torrans 256
Torrens 256
Torrens 269...
Torrins 256
Torry 269...
Tosh 256
Tosh 269...
Totten 255
Totten 269...
Tottenham **V4**
Tottenham 255
Totterick 269...
Tottie 269...
Totton 255
Totton 269...
Tottonham 255
Totty 269...
(la) Touche 76
Touchstone **V5**
Touchstone 269...
Touey **V4**
Tough **V2**
Tougher 256
Tougher 269...
Toughie 269...
Toulson 269...
Touomy **V4**
Tourisk 269...
Touson **V4**
Touson 269...
Tovey **V4**
Tovey 269...
Tovomy **V4**
Tovomy 269...
Towell **V2**
Towers 269...
Towes **V5**
Towes 269...
Towey 254
Towey 269...
Towgood 269...
O' Towlan 269...
Towler 269...
O Towlow **V3**
O' Towlow 269...
Towner **V5**
Towner 269...
Townes **V2**
Townesende 256
Townley **V4**
Townsend **V2**
Townsend **V4**
Townsend 256
Townsend 269...
Townshend **V4**
Townshend 256
Townsley 269...
Townsly 269...
Towse **V4**
Towse 269...
Toxteth 269...
Toxtith 269...
Toye 269...
Tracey **V2**
Tracey **V3**
Tracey **V4**
Tracey 256
Tracey 269...
Tracy **V4**
Tracy 269...
O' Tracy **V3**
O' Tracy **V5**
O Tracy 256
Tradraighe **V3**
Traghne **V5**
Traghne 269...
Trahey 256
Trahey 269...
Train To Cork **V4**
Trainer 257
Trainor 257
Trainor 269...
Trainor 269...
Tralee **V2**
Dela Tranche 155
Tranfield **V2**
Trant **V2**
Trant 257
Trant 269...
Trant Arms **V2**
Trant Castle **V2**
Trant Of **V2**
Trante **V2**
Trapnell 269...
Trasey 256
Trassey 269...
Trassy **V2**
Trassy 269...
O' Trassy **V5**
O Trassy 256
O' Trassy 269...
Trasy 269...
Trauers **V4**
Trauers 269...
Traunte **V2**
Travers **V4**
Travers **V4**
Travers 269...
Travers(e) 257
Traverse **V4**
Trawdsome **V2**
Trayl 269...
Trayle 34
Traynor 269...
(m') Traynor 4,257
Treacey **V3**
Treacy **V3**
Treacy **V4**
Treacy 256
Treacy 269...
Treanor 257
Treanor 269...
Treasley 269...
Treawant **V2**
Treddle **V2**
Treherne 269...
Trehy 269...
O' Trehy **V3**
O' Trehy **V5**
(o) Trehy 256
Trench **V2**
Trench 155
Trench 257
Trennwith **V4**
Trennwith 269...
Trenor 269...
Mc Trenor 257
Mc Trenor 269...
Tresillean **V4**
Tresillean 269...
Tressy 256
Tressy 269...
O' Tressy 269...
Tretton **V2**
Treuers 269...
Treuor 269...
Trevill 269...
Trevor 269...
Trevors 269...
Trevors 269...
Triall 269...
Triar 269...
Triggs **V4**
Trim-lavery 269...
Trimble 269...
Trimlet **V2**
Trinlavery 269...
Trinlavery 4

Tristam **V2**
Trodden **V2**
Trody 269...
Trohy **V3**
Trohy 256
Trohy 269...
Troland 269...
Trolen 269...
Trolly 269...
Troly 269...
Trotter 269...
Trotter, Capt **V4**
Trousdell **V3**
Trowent **V2**
Trower 269...
O' Trower 269...
Troy **V4**
Troy 256
Troy 269...
Truel(l) 257
Trueman 269...
Truman **V2**
Truman 269...
Trumble 269...
Trurk 269...
M' Trustry 269...
Tryn-lavery 269...
O Tuama **V4**
Tuath Mumha **V3**
Tuath Sen **V2**
Tubbernd 269...
Tubbs **V3**
Tubbs 269...
Tubman 269...
Tubrid **V3**
Tubriddy **V2**
Tubridy 257
Tubrit 257
Tubrit 269...
Tubrit **V3**
Tubrity **V3**
Tuchet 34
Tucke 269...
Tucker **V2**
Tucker **V4**
Tucker 269...
Tuckey **V4**
Tuckey 269...
Tuff **V2**
Tuhill 255
Tuhill 269...
Tuinon 269...
Tuit 269...
Tuit(e) 257
Tuite **V2**
Tuite 269...
Tuitte 257
Tuitte 269...
Tuke **V3**
Tully 269...
Mac Tully 107,250
O Tully 250
Tumalti 258
Tumbleton 269...
Tumblinson 269...
Tumelty 258
Tumelty 269...
Tumherlach **V3**
Tumilt(e)y 258
Tummon 269...
Tunbridge 269...
Tundall 269...
Tunn(e)y 258
Tunstead **V3**
Tuohill **V2**
Tuohill, R., **V2**
Tuohy **V2**
Tuohy **V3**
Tuohy **V4**
Tuohy 257
Tuohy 269...
O Tuohy **V4**
Tuomey **V2**
Tuomy **V4**
O Tuomy **V4**
O' Tuomy **V5**
Turbett 269...
Turbridge 269...
Turish 269...
Turk 269...
Turkington 258
Turkington 269...
Turkinton 258
Turl(e)y 72
Mc Turlagh **V5**
Mc Turlagh 269...
Turley 269...
Turnball 269...
Turnbull 269...
Turnebowle 269...
Turner **V2**
Turner **V4**
Turner **V5**
Turner 258
Turner 269...
Turnl(e)y 258
Turvin 34
Tuthill **V3**
Tuthill 258
Tutthil 258
Tuttil 258
Tuttle 258
Tutty **V5**
Tutty 258
Tutty 269...
Twadell 269...
Twaml(e)y 258
Twamley 269...
Twayts **V5**
Twayts 269...
Tweedie 258
Tweedie 269...
Tweedy 258
Twembrock **V3**
Twigg 253
Twigg 269...
Twigley 222
Twigley 269...
Twimbroch **V3**
Twimbrock **V3**
Twinbrock **V3**
Twisden **V3**
Twisden **V4**
Twisden 269...
Twiss **V2**
Twiss Of **V2**
Twiss Of **V2**
Twiss Of **V2**
Twohig **V2**
Twohig **V4**
Twohig 269...
Twolan 255
Twomey **V2**
Twomey **V4**
Twomey 269...
O' Twomey **V2**
O Twomey **V4**
O' Twomey **V5**
O Twomey 258
Twomy 258
O Twomy **V4**
O' Twomy 269...
Tyerny 269...
Tyghe 269...
Tyler **V2**
Tyler 269...
Tyly 269...
Tymons **V3**
Tynan 269...
Tynan(e) 258
Tyndall **V2**
Tyndall 269...
Tyne 269...
Tyner 269...
Tynnan 269...
Tynt **V4**
Tynt 269...
Tynt(e) 258
Tynte **V4**
Tynte **V5**
Tyrell 259
Tyrrell 259
Tyrrell 269...
Tyrrell 269...
Tyrrey **V4**
Tyrrill 269...
Tyrry 252
Tyter **V2**
Tyth 269...
U. S. Civil **V2**
Ua Ciardha **V2**
Mac Uaid **V2**
Ufford **V2**
Ui Bloid **V3**
Ui Caisin **V3**
Ui Cearnaigh **V3**
Ui Cormaic **V3**
Ui Dtorna **V2**
Ui Fearba **V2**
Ui Ferba **V2**
Ui Floinn **V3**
Ui Ifernain **V3**
Ui Ronghaile **V3**
Oh Uiginn **V2**
Uiske 269...
Ulf 267
Ulster Plant. 34
Ultagh 269...
Umphrey 269...
Unack **V4**
Unack 259
Unack 269...
Undertakers **V2**
Underwood **V2**
Unehan 269...
Unett **V4**
Unett 269...
Ungerdell **V4**
Ungerdell 269...
Ungly 269...
Uniack(e) 259
Uniacke **V4**
Unill 269...
Upcole **V4**
Upcole 269...
Uppington **V2**
Uprichard 269...
Upton **V3**
Upton 259
Upton 269...
Uriel 268
De Urielle 268
Urrell 268
Urrell 269...
Ursb'lba'gh 205
Usburne, T. **V2**
Ushart 269...
Usher **V2**
Usher **V3**
Usher 259
Usher 269...
Usher 269...
Usher, Henry **V2**
Ussher 259
Ussher 269...
Ustace 269...
Ustace 97
Uustice 269...
Mac Vaddock 259
Mc Vagh 269...
Vaghan 269...
Vahey 101
Vahey 269...
Vahy 269...
Vale **V2**
Vale **V3**
Vale 269...
De Valences 259
Valentine 269...
Vallanne **V5**
Vallanne 269...
Valle **V2**
Vallely 259
Vallely 269...
Vallily 259
Vallily 269...
Vally 259
Vally 269...
Van Leuwen **V4**
Mc Vanamy 269...
Vanbogarden 269..
Vance 259
Vance 269...
Vancouver, **V2**
Vandeleur 259
Vandeleur **V3**
Vandelew 269...
Vandelure **V3**
Vandelure **V4**
Vandelure 269...
Vanderlew 269...
Vanderlure **V4**
Vanderlure 269...
Vanderpuer 269...
Vandervorte **V3**
Vanhogarden 269..
Vanhogarden **V3**
Vanhugarden **V5**
Vanhugarden 269...
Vargis 269...
Vargus 269...
Varian **V4**
Varily 269...
Varley 269...
Varrilly 269...
Vas 269...
Vauckler **V2**
Vaucleere **V2**
Vauclier **V2**
Vaugh 269...
Vaughan **V2**
Vaughan **V3**
Vaughan **V4**
Vaughan **V5**
Vaughan 260
Vaughan 269...
Vaughen 260
Vaughn 260
Mc Veagh 269...
(mc) Veagh 98,260
Veakins 269...
Veal(e) 260
Veale **V4**
Veale 269...
Le Veel 260
Mac Veety 260
Mc Veigh 269...
(mc) Veigh 98,260
Veldon 264
Veldon 269...
La Velle 176
Venner 269...
Vennor 269...
Venton 269...
Ventry, Lord **V2**
Verdon **V4**
Verdon **V5**
Verdon 260
(de) Verdun 260
De Vere 155
Verecker **V3**
Vereker **V3**
Verkers **V4**
Verkers 269...
Verlin **V4**
Verner 269...
Vernon 260
Verschoyle 260
Verscoyle 269...
Vesey **V2**
Vesey **V3**
Vesey 268
Mc Vey 260
Vicar 262
Vicars **V2**
Mac Vickar 262
Mc Vicker 262
Mc Vicker 269...
Vickers 262
Vickers 269...
Vickery **V2**
Victory 212
Victory 269...
Mac Viety 260
Vigors **V2**
Vigors 260
Viking MapIv
Viking Raids **V3**
Vikings **V4**
Villebois 155
Villers 269...
Vincent **V2**
Vincent **V3**
Vincent **V5**
Vincent 269...
Vine **V2**
Virginia **V2**
Virginia, To **V2**
(mc) Vitty 260
Vivers 269...
Vizard **V4**
Vizard 269...
Voakley **V2**
Vogan 269...
Voice 269...
Vulcougha 269...
Vynes **V2**
Vynes, Vine **V2**
Waddell 269...
Waddey 269...
Wadding 261

V2 = Families of Co. Kerry **V3** = Families of Co. Clare **V4** = Families of Co. Cork **V5** = Families of Co. Limerick

Wadding 269...
Waddington 269...
Waddock 269...
Wade **V2**
Wade **V4**
Wade 261
Wade 269...
Mc Wade 269...
Wadeck 259
Wadkins 269...
Wadman 269...
Wadock 269...
Wafer 264
Waggoner **V4**
Waggoner 269...
Wagh 269...
Waight 269...
Waile 269...
Wailse 269...
Wailsh **V5**
Wailsh 269...
Wainman 269...
Waits **V4**
Waits 269...
Wakefield 269...
Wakeham **V4**
Wakeham 269...
Wakel(e)y 261
Wakely 269...
Wakham **V4**
Wakham 269...
Walche **V4**
Walchott **V5**
Walchott 269...
Walcot **V3**
Walcot 269...
Walcott 269...
Walding 269...
Waldo 269...
Waldren 261
Waldron 261
Waldron 269...
Waldron 34
Waldronn 269...
Waldrum 269...
Wale **V4**
Wale 261
Wale 269...
O' Wale 269...
Walies **V4**
Walis 261
Walkam **V4**
Walkam 269...
Walker **V2**
Walker **V3**
Walker 261
Walker 269...
1 Walkes 269...
Wall **V2**
Wall **V3**
Wall **V4**
Wall **V5**
Wall 269...
Wall(s) 261
Wallace **V2**
Wallace **V3**
Wallace **V4**
Wallace **V5**
Wallace 261
Wallace 269...
Wallcott **V3**
Walle 269...
Waller **V2**
Waller **V3**
Waller **V5**
Waller 261
Waller 269...
Waller, Sir **V2**
Wallis **V3**
Wallis **V4**
Wallis **V5**
Wallis 261
Wallis 269...
Wallplate **V3**
Walls **V4**
Walls 269...
Walnne 269...
Walpole **V2**
Walsche **V2**
Walsh **V3**
Walsh **V4**
Walsh **V5**
Walsh 269...
Walsh Con- **V2**
Walsh(e) 261,262
Walsh In **V3**
Walsh Of **V2**
Walsh, **V4**
Walshe **V4**
Walshe 269...
Walshman 269...
Walter **V3**
Walter **V4**
Walter 269...
Mac Walter **V3**
Mac Walter 262
Mc Walter 269...
Walter(s) 262
Walter, **V2**
Walters **V3**
Walters **V4**
Walters 269...
Walton **V3**
Walton **V4**
Walton 269...
Wamought 269...
Wandesforde 262
Wandrich 269...
Wandwick **V4**
Wandwick 269...
Wansanton 269...
Wansburgh 269...
Waples **V5**
Waples 269...
Warburton **V2**
Warburton 262
Ward **V2**
Ward **V3**
Ward 269...
(mac Ward 263
Mc Ward 269...
Warde 34
Wardell **V2**
Warden **V2**
Warden 269...
Warden, Col. **V2**
Wardinge **V5**
Wardinge 269...
Wardlaw 269...
Wardlow 269...
Ware **V2**
Ware **V3**
Ware **V4**
Waren 269...
Warham **V2**
Warick 262
Warick 269...
Waring 269...
Waringe 269...
Warke 262
Warmand 269...
Warneford 269...
Warner **V2**
Warner **V4**
Warner 269...
Warnford 269...
Warnock 269...
Mac Warnock 263
Warr **V5**
Warr 269...
Warrall **V3**
Warran 269...
Warreck 269...
Warreing 269...
Warrell **V3**
Warren **V2**
Warren **V3**
Warren **V4**
Warren 263
Warren 269...
Warrick 269...
Warring 269...
Warris 269...
Warter 269...
Warwick **V2**
Warwick 269...
Wasbery 269...
Wash 269...
Washington **V3**
Wasley 269...
Wassher 269...
Wasson 269...
Watch 269...
Water 269...
Waterhouse 269...
Waters **V3**
Waters **V4**
Waters 155
Waters 269...
Mc Waters **V4**
(mc) Waters 262
Waterson **V2**
Waterson 269...
Watkins **V2**
Watkins **V4**
Watkins 269...
Watson **V2**
Watson **V3**
Watson **V4**
Watson 263
Watson 269...
Watt 269...
Watters **V2**
Watters **V3**
Watters 269...
(mac Watters 262
Mc Watters 269...
Watterson 269...
Mac Wattin 263
Wattkins 269...
Watts **V2**
Watts **V3**
Watts **V4**
Watts **V5**
Watts 269...
Wattson **V3**
Waugh **V3**
Waugh 269...
Waugh(e) 263
Way **V4**
Way 269...
Mc Way **V4**
Mc Way 264
Waybrent 269...
Wayman 269...
Weabb 269...
Weadock 269...
Weafer 264
Weakley **V3**
Weakly **V3**
Weaman 269...
Weatherby 269...
Weatherhead **V4**
Weatherhead **V5**
Weathers 269...
Weatherup **V2**
Weatherup 269...
Weaver **V5**
Weaver 264
Webb **V2**
Webb **V5**
Webb 263
Webb 269...
Webber **V4**
Webber 263,264
Webster **V3**
Webster 269...
Wedgwood 269...
Weedin **V3**
Weedin 269...
Week **V4**
Weeke **V4**
Weeke 269...
Weekes **V2**
Weekes **V4**
Weekes 269...
Weekly **V3**
Weeks **V2**
Weeks **V5**
Mc Weeney 264
Mc Weeney 269...
Mc Weeny 264
Weever 264
Weilsh **V5**
Weilsh 269...
Weir **V2**
Weir 155
Weir 269...
(mac Weir 264,267
Weire 269...
Welby 269...
Welch 262
Welch 269...
Weldon **V2**
Weldon 269...
(de) Weldon 20,264
Weldon, **V2**
Weldun 20
Wellahane 269...
Welland **V2**
(de) Wellesley 264
Wellings **V2**
Wellmore 266
Wells **V5**
Wells 269...
Welsh **V3**
Welsh **V4**
Welsh 262
Welsh 269...
Welshmen **V2**
Welstead **V2**
Welstead **V4**
Welsted **V2**
Welsted **V4**
Welton **V2**
Wemys **V5**
Wendle **V5**
Wendle 269...
Wenman 269...
Wentworth 269...
Wenwell 269...
Wesby 269...
Wesh 269...
Wessbie 269...
West **V2**
West **V4**
West 264
West 269...
West Indies **V2**
Westbrook **V2**
Westbrooke 269...
Westby **V3**
Westby 264
Westcombe **V2**
Westenra 269...
Westhrop 264
Westinra 269...
Westly 269...
Weston 269...
Westrop(p) 264
Westropp **V3**
Westropp **V5**
Westropp **V3**
Wetcraft **V4**
Wetherall 269...
Wetherel 269...
Wetherell **V4**
Wetherell 269...
Mac Wey 264
Weymes 269...
Weyms 269...
Whalan 265
Whaley 269...
Whalley 269...
Whallop 269...
Whally 269...
Whaly 269...
Mc Whannon 269..
Whaples 269...
Wharry 269...
Wharton **V2**
Wharton 269...
Whately **V3**
Whatope 269...
Wheeler **V3**
Wheeler 269...
Wheite **V4**
Wheite 269...
Whelahan 269...
Whelan **V2**
Whelan **V4**
Whelan 269...
Whelane 269...
Whelann 269...
Wheleghan 269...
Whelehan 269...
Whelen 265
Whelply **V4**
Whelply 269...
Whelton **V2**
Whelton **V4**
Whelton 269...
Whetcomb **V4**
Whetcomb 269...
Whetcome 269...
Whetcraft **V4**
Whetcraft 269...
Whetlock 269...
Whetstone **V3**
Whetwell **V4**
Whialon 269...

Whidingham **V4**
Whiffle269...
Whight265
Whin269...
Whine269...
Whinn269...
Mc Whinney269...
Whirloe269...
Mc Whirter269...
Whislade **V4**
Whislade269...
Whissed269...
Whiston **V2**
Mac Whiston70
Whitacre265
Whitaker **V4**
Whitaker265
Whitaker269...
Whitchurch **V5**
Whitchurch269...
Whitcom **V3**
Whitcomb **V3**
Whitcraft **V4**
Whitcraft269...
White **V2**
White **V3**
White **V4**
White **V5**
White155
White16,18
White265
White269...
White, Geo. **V2**
White Of **V3**
Whiteacre265
Whitechan269...
Whitefield269...
Whitegar265
Whitehead269...
Whiteney265
Whitere **V5**
Whitere269...
Whiteside269...
Whitewood **V4**
Whitfield269...
Whitgrove269...
Whitihell269...
Whitla269...
Whitley269...
Whitlock269...
Whitman269...
Whitmore269...
Whitney269...
(de) Whitney265
Whitny265
Whitny269...
Whitsitt269...
Whitson **V2**
Whitstone **V3**
Whitt269...
Whittaker **V2**
Whittby269...
Whittell269...
Whittey265
Whittingham **V4**
Whittingham269..
Whittington269...
Whittle269...
Whittny265
Whittny269...
Whitton269...
Whitty **V3**
Whitty269...
(mc) Whitty265
Whitwell **V4**
Whitwell269...
Wholey155
Wholihane269...
Wholly **V2**
Whooley269...
Whorlloe269...
Whorriskey269...
Whytacre265
Whyte **V3**
Whyte **V4**
Whyte **V5**
Whyte265
Whyte269...
Wiay **V5**
Wiay269...
Wibrant269...
Wicken269...
Wickham269...
Wickombe269...
Widenham **V4**
Widman269...
Widmay269...
Widowes269...
Wier264
Wiers269...
Wigfield269...
Wiggins269...
Wightman269...
Wigtone269...
Wilbore269...
Wilby269...
Wilcox269...
Wild(e)155
Wild(e)234,267
Wild Geese **V2**
Wildboar269...
Wilde **V2**
Wilder269...
Wilders267
Wilders269...
Wileman269...
Wiley **V3**
Wiley267
Wiley269...
Wilhair269...
Wilkes269...
Wilkie **V2**
Wilkie269...
Wilkins269...
Wilkinson **V3**
Wilkinson **V4**
Wilkinson **V5**
Wilkinson265
Wilkinson269...
Willet **V4**
Willey **V3**
William **V3**
William269...
Mac William **V3**
Mac William **V5**
Mac William269...
Mc William **V3**
Mc William **V4**
Mc William268
William I I I **V2**
William Of **V3**
William(s)268
Williamis155
Williams **V2**
Williams **V3**
Williams **V4**
Williams **V5**
Williams155
Williams205
Williams269...
Mc Williams269...
Williams, F. **V2**
Williamson **V4**
Williamson268
Williamson269...
Williamsone269...
Willingham **V4**
Willingham269...
Willis **V2**
Willis266
Willis269...
Willisbie269...
Willison266
Willmer266
Willmore **V2**
Willmore266
Willmot **V4**
Willoe **V2**
Willoughby **V3**
Willoughby269...
Willove **V2**
Wills **V4**
Wills269...
Willson **V3**
Willson **V4**
Willson **V5**
Willson266
Willson34
Willy **V4**
Willy **V5**
Willy269...
Wilmont269...
Wilmot **V2**
Wilsby269...
Wilshier269...
Wilson **V2**
Wilson **V3**
Wilson266
Wilson269...
Wilton269...
(de) Wilton **V2**
Wily267
Wimbs269...
Wimpris **V2**
Winckfield269...
Windele **V2**
Windele **V4**
Windele, J. **V2**
Windle **V2**
Windowes269...
Windsor269...
Wingfield **V3**
Wingfield269...
Winkfield269...
Winkworth269...
Winn **V2**
Winne269...
Winnington **V3**
Winspeare **V4**
Winspeare269...
Winter(s)266
Winters **V2**
Winters269...
Winthorpe **V4**
Wire269...
Wirrall34
Wise **V2**
Wise **V4**
Wise267
Wise269...
Wiseman **V4**
Wishart34
Wishert269...
Withams269...
Wither269...
Witherall **V2**
Witherill269...
Withers **V4**
Withers269...
Witherston269...
Witter **V3**
Witter269...
Wittingham **V4**
Wixstead269...
Wizard269...
Wltagh269...
Wm. **V4**
Mc Wm. **V4**
Mc Wm. **V5**
Mc Wm.269...
Wodell77
Wogan(e)266
Wolf(e)267
Wolfe **V3**
Wolfe **V4**
Wolverston266
Wolverston269...
Wood **V3**
Wood **V4**
Wood269...
Wood(s)221,266
Woodcock269...
Woodcocke269...
Woodfin **V3**
Woodhouse **V2**
Woodhouse269...
Woodlif269...
Woodliff269...
Woodliffe **V4**
Woodliffe269...
Woodlock266
Woodlocke269...
Woodly **V4**
Woodly269...
Woodroffe **V4**
Woodroffe269...
Woodruff **V4**
Woodruffe **V4**
Woodruffe269...
Woods **V2**
Woods **V4**
Woods **V5**
Woods269...
Woodside266
Woodside269...
Woodsy269...
Woogon269...
Woole269...
Woolf **V3**
Woolf, B.s. **V2**
Woolfe **V3**
Woolfe267
Woolfe269...
Wooster **V3**
Wooster Of **V3**
Wooten **V4**
Wooton **V3**
Wootton **V4**
Wootton **V5**
Wordon269...
Wordspin **V3**
Workeman269...
Workman269...
Worrell **V3**
Worrell **V4**
Worrell269...
Worsely269...
Worship269...
Worsly269...
Worsop269...
Worth **V3**
Worthington **V2**
Woton269...
Woulf **V4**
Woulfe **V2**
Woulfe **V3**
Woulfe **V4**
Woulfe **V5**
Woulfe267
Woulfe269...
Woulfe Arms **V3**
Woulfe-nix269...
Wray232
Wray269...
Wreil **V2**
Wren **V2**
Wren **V3**
Wren **V4**
Wren269...
Wren Family **V2**
Wrenn226,232
Wrenn269...
Wrenne **V4**
Wrenne269...
Wright **V2**
Wright **V3**
Wright **V4**
Wright267
Wright269...
Wright, G. **V2**
Wrixon **V2**
Wrixon **V3**
Wrixon **V4**
Wrotham **V3**
Wrotham269...
Wrynn269...
Wulf267
Wyatt269...
Wyber269...
Wybrant269...
Wybrants267
Wybrune269...
Wyburne269...
Wye269...
Wyer267
Wyer269...
Wyk **V2**
(de) Wyk **V2**
Wyke269...
Wykehamist **V2**
Wyld267
De Wylde267
Wylder **V5**
Wylder267
Wylie267
Wylie269...
Wyllie **V2**
Wynch **V3**
Wyndham **V3**
Mc Wynee264
Wynn **V3**
Wynn269...
Wynn(e)267
Wynne **V2**
Wynne269...
Mc Wynny269...
Wyott **V3**
Wyott269...
Wyrall34
Wyre267
Wyre269...

V2 = Families of Co. Kerry **V3** = Families of Co. Clare **V4** = Families of Co. Cork **V5** = Families of Co. Limerick

Wyrenn **V4**
Wyse **V4**
Wyse 267
Wyse 269...
Wyseman **V4**
Wysse **V4**
Wythers 269...
Yardo **V4**
Yardo 269...
Yarner 269...
Yarwell **V5**
Yarwell 269...
Yates **V4**
Yates 268
Yates 269...
Yeadon 269...
Yeard 269...
Yeates 268
Yeates 269...
Yeats **V4**
Yeats 268
Yeeden **V2**
Yeo 269...
Yeoman **V3**
Yeomans **V4**
Yeomans 269...
Yielding **V2**
Ykeleachair **V2**
Yorke **V3**
Young **V2**
Young **V3**
Young **V4**
Young 155
Young 205
Young 268
Young 269...
Younge **V4**
Younge 269...
Yourell 268
Zorkin 269...
Zouche **V2**

Appendix

√ Barony Map of Ireland

√ Administrative Divisions

√ Guide to Member Services

√ Irish Families (journal) content

√ Map of Ireland

BARONIES OF IRELAND

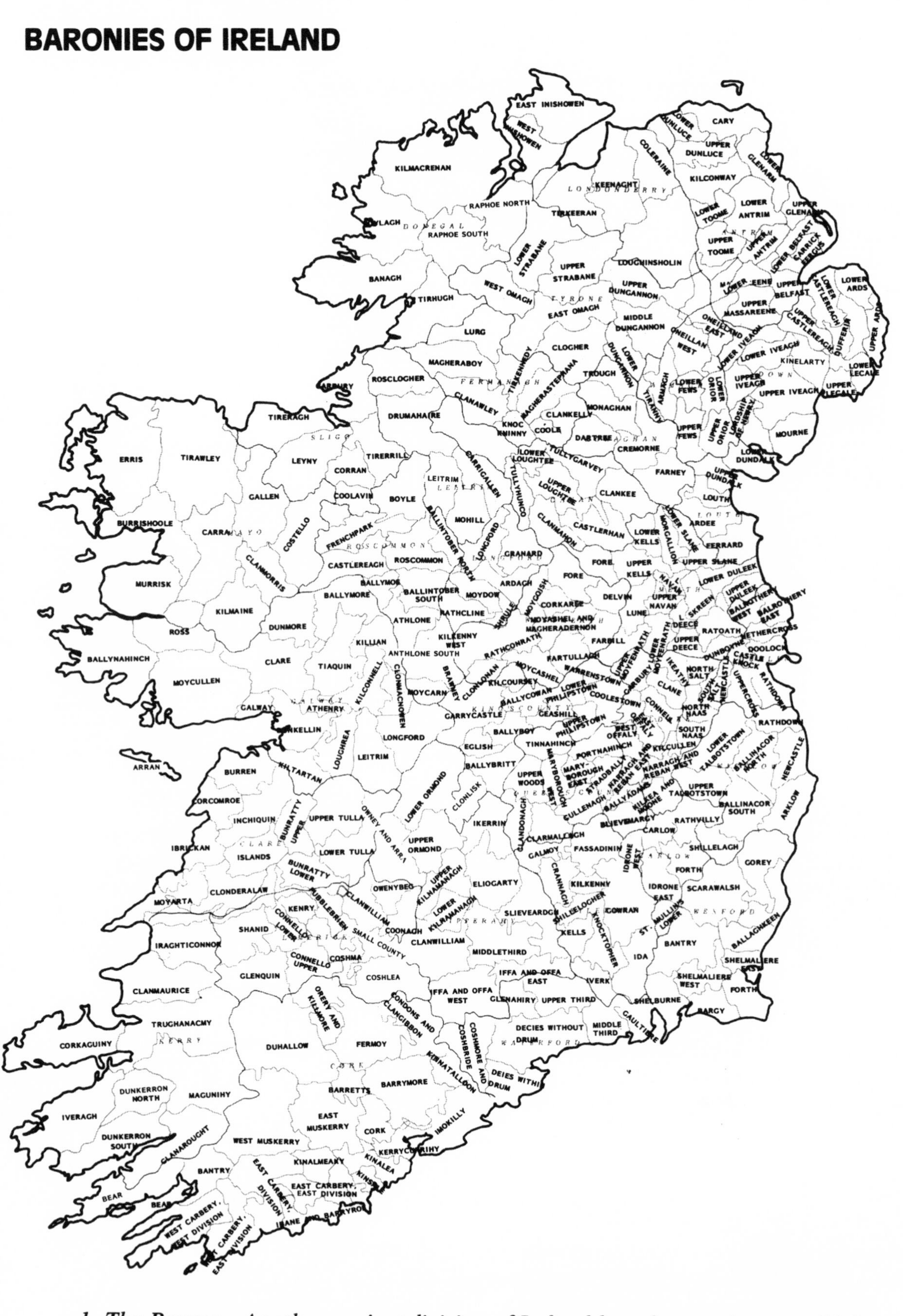

1. The Barony - Another ancient division of Ireland based upon the great Irish families territorial holdings. A total of 325 baronies exist. They were used as an unit in the 19th Century Land Valuations. Normally composed of several parishes

ADMINISTRATIVE DIVISIONS

The Province

Ancient Kingdoms of Ireland. The four provinces were: (1) Ulster in the north; (2) Leinster in the east; (3) Connaught in the west; and (4) Munster in the south. The old province of Meath became incorporated into Leinster. The kingdoms of Oriel and Aileach merged with Ulster in the 17th century.

The County

The largest local administrative division of more modern times. The first 12 counties came into existence in the year 1210, and the last county (Wicklow) was formed in 1605.

The Barony

Another ancient division of Ireland based upon the great Irish families territorial holdings. A total of 325 baronies exist. They were used as a unit in the 19th Century Land Valuations. Normally composed of several parishes.

The Parish

Existing as both civil and ecclesiastical districts. The parish was the smallest administrative unit of the Catholic Church. This religious parish was a subdivision of the diocese (which were 28 in number in 1883). The civil parish was used for census and taxation purposes. Civil and religious parishes were often of different names entirely.

The Townland

The smallest civil district of Ireland. The words, "towne," "hamlet," and "vil" were also used to describe this 17th century geographic division. A rural subdivision of the civil parish.

Poor Law Unions

Usually comprised several townlands and came into begin as a result of the Poor Law Relief Act of 1838. Formed for taxation purposes to support the poor and destitute of the area. The "Poor House" itself was normally situated in a local market town of the area.

The I.G.F. is dedicated to the discovery and promotion of the Irish culture worldwide. Our member programs include a lending library by mail, free surname registration and publication of a monthly journal.

Our rare book program is quite unique, salvaging works from centuries past. We also publish new works on a yearly basis.

All titles selected for publication are based upon member requests. For more information contact the IGF at Box 7575, Kansas City, MO. 64116 U.S.A.

Special Reports

√ **Birth Index** of Ireland. All Surnames and Co. locations. (19th century). Gives the locations for all surnames in Ireland with 5 or more recorded births in the year the index was recorded.

√ **1659 Irish Census.** All Surnames & county locations., indexed by county, by original spelling as recorded in 1659.

√ **Master Index Search** of 60,000 records and Print Out of source books that contain your surname or placename Pick any surname, place, or subject.

√ **Full 12 year index** to the Irish Family Journal. The complete index of names, places and subjects .

√ **5,000 family searches** listed by members. The full list of family searches on file here at the Journal. Over 5,000 in all. Updated yearly.

√ **Address list** of others Researching your family name(s). Up to three surnames or spellings allowed . Updated Daily. As available.

√ **Irish Coat of Arms.** Initial search and copy of a coat of arms in Ireland, as found in our library. Specify name.

√ **Detailed Map** of Your County and search for your Irish placename. From the *Master Book of Irish Placenames...* Specify County or placename.

√ **Rare Irish Book** & lending Library Catalog. The Listing of Used Books for Sale, and lending library selections.

√ **History of your name** In Ireland. from our files. Rare names may not be available, (we may substitute the Master Index Print out in that event)

√ **Beginners Guide to Irish Family Research.** The common sense guide for the beginner. First steps. Easy for anyone to Understand. illus.

√ **Current Phone # and address** of any parish in Ireland.

Hardbound Books

The Book of Irish Families great & small (v 1)

The Families of Co. Kerry. (v 2)
The history/location of over 1,000 specific Kerry families. 12,000 listings. 272 p. maps, illus.

Families of Co. Clare (v3)
Families of Co. Cork (v4)
Families of Co. Limerick(v5)

The Master Book of Irish Surnames.
THE Master index of Irish Family names, denoting Locations, Origins, Spelling Groups and Sources. Includes the surname index to all IGF works, the 1890 birth index, the 1659 census.

The Master Atlas & Book of Irish Placenames
Placename Locator for all of Ireland. 60 Maps indexed to find your placename . 17th & 19th century placenames. Spellings. History. 250 p.

Sloinnte Gaedeal is Gall
'Irish Names and Surnames'. the original, classic dictionary of Irish surnames by Woulfe, (1923) with notes on Gaelic origins. All New index. Includes Irish Names for Children.

Tribes & Customs of Hy Many The Classic by O'Donovan on families of Roscommon & Galway.

Tribes/Customs/Genealogies of Hy Fiachrach
The Classic by John O'Donovan on the families of Co. Mayo and Sligo.

Keatings History of Ireland.
Complete 3 v. set. New index with genealogies. Nowhere else in print! O'Mahoney trans.. ISBN 940134440. Priceless footnotes & folk history.

The Poetry and Song of Ireland.
The historic collection by John Boyle O'Reilly, with historical footnotes.

Irish Settlers on the American Frontier. #1 work on the Irish in Missouri westward 1770-1900.

Ortelius Map of Ireland.
Orig. pub. 1572 a.d., location of Families, Old English/Latin. Suitable for framing.

The Irish Book of Arms The largest Illustrated collection of Irish Coats-of- Arms in print. Includes Irish and settler families. 1,000 + arms.

King James's Irish Army List 1690. The classic by D'Arcy, over 1,000 pages, family histories tracing family origins in Ireland.

A Social History of Ancient Ireland. Classic by P.W. Joyce, 2 v. set, 350 encyclopedic illustrations .

Our International Journal

OLochlainns Journal of Irish Families. ISSN 10560378. Finding your family heritage worldwide! (see next page for content sample).

A Sampling of topics found in *Irish Families* , the monthly membership journal of the Irish Genealogical Foundation:

Volume 2 (1986-87)

#1.The Black Irish-The Celtic High Cross - 'Donaghue of Kerry - Music - Keatings History - Mollys Soda Bread - Starting Your Search #2. Brigids Cross - Prolific Murphy Clan - 'O' and 'Mac' - Bagpipes - Families of Clare. #3. Fitz names - Families of Co. Kerry - The Irish Harp -1890 Birth Index - Fitzgerald, Fitzpatrick, Fitzsimmons. #4. The Real St. Patrick - P.R.O. Dublin - Viking Irish? -Irish Eyes are smiling. #5. The Molly Maguires - Brian Boru, last High King - Ft. Wayne, Indiana - Murray, Duffy and Boyle - family histories in our library - N. Y. note. #6. **Irish heraldry** - California Irish - Irish News- papers - Used Books - O'Neil, Neil, etc..Confusing Byrne, Burns, & Beirne - Minnesota - Shannon Searchers

Volume 3 (1987-88)

#1. Boston Strong Boy, John L. Sullivan - Fogartys Castle - **Hiring Research** - Irish Wilderness - Molly Malone - King, Thornton and Martin. #2, Ports of Departure - Hebrew names - Scully, McCoy, Laughran, McWay, Histon, McNulty, Ratican, Sharkey, Dorrance, Mattimore . #3. - Sheehan vs. Sullivan - Irish Arms - Parish Histories - The Potatoe - Dorrance, Lee, Lacey, Cudahy, Falvey #4 Irish names in America - McNamara's Band - Texas - O'Hare, Hargon, O'Kerins, McKillip, McKissick, Larkin, Hahn, McGivney, Hadley . #5 'de la' Irish names - German names - family lands - Great O'Neill - Great Hunger - Foy, Freeman, Gale, McGimsey, Elliott, Farrington, Fians. #6 Civil War-Wild Geese- Mulligans Brigade-Keenan- Ball Game

Volume 4 (1988-89)

#1. Irish From England - Spalpeen - Clark - Kennelly - Family Historian. #2 (12 pgs.) Welsh names - Wrong Way Corrigan - Leinster . #3 (12 pgs) Kennedy - Researching N. Ireland & District Map (illus) - Heritage Centers - Lynch - Conley. #4 (12pgs) Addresses in Ireland - Guinivan - De danaan - The Claddagh - McPartland - Concannon - Duggan - Kinney - Fitzmaurice - Connaughton - Mahoney - Graven - Meara - Condon. #5 (12 p) Shillelagh - Brady - McMahon - Conley - Woodside - Casey - **Ordinance Survey Maps** - Mayo Bed & Breakfast - Skully . #6 (12 p.) The art of Blarney - Phone Home - O'Connor - Lynskey - Gandsey - Roche - Dublin Ancestors - LDS -

Volume 5 (1989-90)

#1. Ancient Family Colors - Heritage Centers - Phone Numbers in Ireland - Dance Master - Blarney Stone - Dillon, Driscoll, Norton - #2 Florida - Gore, O'Rourke, Moor(e) - Kennelly, Farrell - Gaelic Titles - Ulster Folk Park - #3 Irish Newspapers - Dillon, Sweetman, O'Shaughnessy #4. Beginners Guide - Kendall, McDonald, Brown, Galloway, O'Donnells Castle. #5. Shame(rock) - O'Malley, MacSweeney, Barrett - **Irish vs. Scots Irish** - Foley News - Daugherty reunion - Irish Fests - Periodical Index - Books in Review #6. St. Louis Irish - Top 50 Scots-Irish names - Irish Chiefs and Gaelic......

Volume 6 (1990-91)

Friel, Nyland, Devitt, Doherty international, letters from Ireland, Clan Reunions, Heritage Centers, Arkansas Irish, Todd- Lincoln, Brooks, Myers, McWatters, Walker, Flight of the Earls, Colors of Ireland. 1,000 searches, Lee, Ireland, Donegan, Porter, Ignew, Driskill, Phelan, O'Donnell-Casey, **Penpals**, Nevada Irish, Chalk Sunday, Costello, Caughey, The Spanish Connection, Irish Newspapers, Saving old Photo's, Falls, O'Brien, MacRae, Sullivan, Killoran...

Volume 7 (1991-92)

Pen pals - Alcorn - Armagh Records - Australia - Barry - Best - Brady, Brennan, Brown researchers - California -Chicago Irish - O'Connell Soc. - Cork Archives - O'Dea Castle - Falls Pedigree - Finding Fitzgeralds - Florida Irish - Heritage Centers - **Huguenot Families** - Jews in Ire.-Larkin Pedigree - Limerick center - Mayo heritage - Neal -Offaly Hist. Soc.- Ortelius Map-Spain - Queenstown project - Roscommon Center - San Francisco Irish - Scots Families in Ireland - Tipperary Research - Viking Names -Walsh researchers - White surname - Wisconsin Irish..

Volume 8 (1992-93)

Armagh Records - Barbadoes Journal - Barry - Blake Seat - O'Brien Castle - Burrell pedigree - Coleman news - O'Connor Kerry - Cuban Irish - Derry Genealogy - Donahue -Donegal Ancestry - Dublin Her. Group - Irish Famines -Galway Heritage Center - Grace Family - Irish Brigade - Kerry Co. Library - **Lending Library** - O'Maley spellings - Murphy of Taiwan - MacNamara Book - Nova Scotia Irish -Offaly Hist. Soc. - Prodigy - Shamerock Awards -Sullivan Brothers - Sweeney of Clare - Tipperary Heritage Center - Westmeath - Translations - Travel Tips.

Volume 9 (1993-94)

Name Changes: Polish & German. Tipperary research stopped- California Irish (p-2) -Denied Access in Ireland -Why? Prodigy decline? - New York Archives - Emigrant Letter - Sullivan in Baseball - Hy-Fiachrach book - O'Dowd and Mac Egan clan info - O'Connell Clan Rally - Milwaukee Fest - Mac vs. Mc - Babe Ruth & Graney - Quebec Roots - Australian Roots - Galway Journal - New Clare Centre - Dead End Research - Tipperary Estate List - Kerry Sources - Scuffle of Boffin - 1,000 family searches listed - Claddagh Village - Rhode Island Irish - Co. Westmeath tips - Newsletters - Cork Librarian - Co. **Donegal** Heritage Center Report - Heraldry.

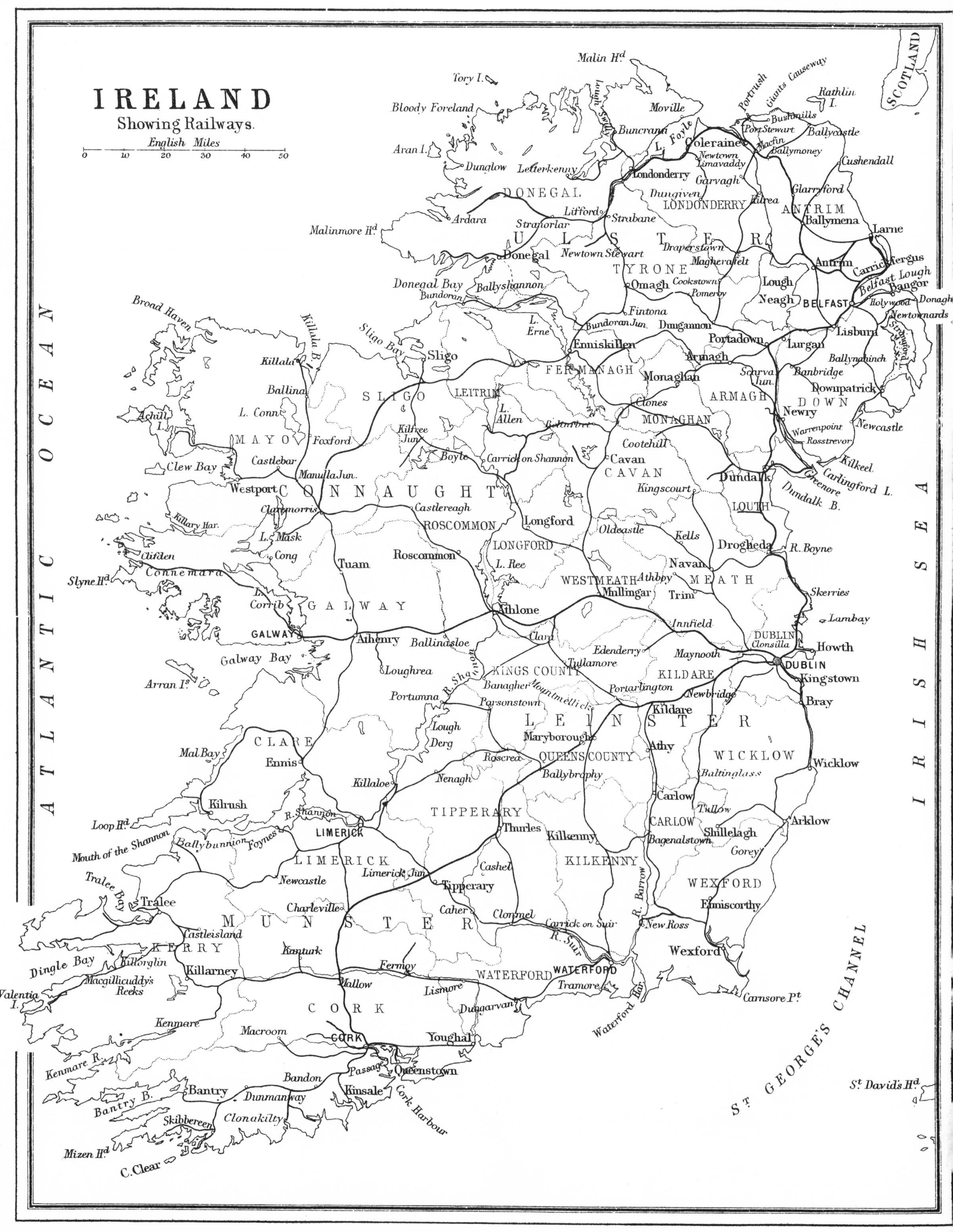
IRELAND
Showing Railways.
English Miles
0 10 20 30 40 50
ATLANTIC OCEAN
IRISH SEA
ST GEORGE'S CHANNEL
SCOTLAND
ULSTER
CONNAUGHT
LEINSTER
MUNSTER
DONEGAL
LONDONDERRY
ANTRIM
TYRONE
FERMANAGH
ARMAGH
DOWN
MONAGHAN
CAVAN
LOUTH
SLIGO
LEITRIM
MAYO
ROSCOMMON
LONGFORD
WESTMEATH
MEATH
DUBLIN
GALWAY
KINGS COUNTY
KILDARE
QUEENS COUNTY
WICKLOW
CLARE
TIPPERARY
CARLOW
KILKENNY
WEXFORD
LIMERICK
KERRY
CORK
WATERFORD
Malin Hd
Tory I.
Bloody Foreland
Aran I.
Lough Swilly
Moville
Buncrana
L. Foyle
Portrush
Giants Causeway
Rathlin I.
Bushmills
Port Stewart
Ballycastle
Coleraine
Macfin
Ballymoney
Newtown Limavaddy
Cushendall
Dunglow
Letterkenny
Londonderry
Garvagh
Glarryford
Dungiven
Kilrea
Ardara
Lifford
Strabane
Ballymena
Larne
Malinmore Hd
Stranorlar
Draperstown
Newtown Stewart
Magherafelt
Donegal
Antrim
Carrickfergus
Belfast Lough
Bangor
Donegal Bay
Bundoran
Ballyshannon
Omagh
Cookstown
Pomeroy
Lough Neagh
BELFAST
Holywood
Donaghadee
Newtownards
Fintona
Strangford
Broad Haven
Killala B.
Sligo Bay
L. Erne
Bundoran Jun.
Dungannon
Portadown
Lisburn
Lurgan
Enniskillen
Sligo
Armagh
Killala
Scarva Jun.
Banbridge
Ballynahinch
Monaghan
Ballina
Downpatrick
L. Conn
Clones
Achill I.
Newry
L. Allen
Kilfree Jun.
Foxford
Warrenpoint
Rosstrevor
Newcastle
Kilkeel
Cootehill
Boyle
Carrick on Shannon
Castlebar
Cavan
Clew Bay
Manulla Jun.
Dundalk
Carlingford L.
Greenore
Dundalk B.
Westport
Kingscourt
Claremorris
Castlereagh
Killary Har.
Longford
L. Mask
Oldcastle
Kells
Drogheda
R. Boyne
Cong
Clifden
Roscommon
Tuam
Navan
Connemara
L. Ree
Slyne Hd
Athboy
Trim
Mullingar
L. Corrib
Skerries
Athlone
Innfield
Lambay
GALWAY
Athenry
Clara
Howth
Clonsilla
Ballinasloe
Edenderry
Maynooth
Tullamore
Galway Bay
Loughrea
Kingstown
R. Shannon
Arran Is.
Banagher
Mountmellick
Portarlington
Newbridge
Portumna
Parsonstown
Kildare
Bray
Lough Derg
Maryborough
Athy
Mal Bay
Roscrea
Ennis
Ballybrophy
Wicklow
Killaloe
Nenagh
Baltinglass
Kilrush
Carlow
Loop Hd
Tullow
Arklow
LIMERICK
Thurles
Kilkenny
Shillelagh
Mouth of the Shannon
Foynes
Ballybunnion
Bagenalstown
Gorey
Cashel
Limerick Jun.
Tralee Bay
Newcastle
Tipperary
R. Barrow
Enniscorthy
Charleville
Tralee
Caher
Clonmel
Carrick on Suir
New Ross
Castleisland
R. Suir
Kanturk
Wexford
Dingle Bay
Killorglin
Fermoy
WATERFORD
Killarney
Tramore
Macgillicuddy's Reeks
Mallow
Lismore
Valentia I.
Carnsore Pt.
Dungarvan
Waterford Har.
Kenmare
Macroom
CORK
Youghal
Kenmare R.
Passage
Queenstown
Bandon
Bantry
Kinsale
Bantry B.
Dunmanway
Cork Harbour
Skibbereen
Clonakilty
St. David's Hd.
Mizen Hd
C. Clear